Wine be the labeı

2005 edition

Philip Williamson & David Moore

'An incredibly in-depth and addictively readable survey of wines of quality from around the world with intelligent tasting notes and informative background to the producers, plus stockists and UK prices. For me, by far the best of the wine guides'
Steven Spurrier, Decanter Magazine

'This is Robert Parker territory but succinct and cheaper'
Joanna Simon, Sunday Times

'I heartily recommend this book as a thorough independent overview of the world's best wine estates'
Tom Cannavan, wine-pages.com

'As essential to the sommelier as their corkscrew'
Paul Dwyer, BBC Radio 5 Live and BBC Radio Scotland

'If you are passionate about your wine and pay serious attention to sampling the world's finest bottles then this book should be on your shelf... I would strongly recommend this excellent guide'
Dr Edward Fitzgerald, Oxford University Wine Society

'...a tremendously useful and comprehensive reference work...(it) is bang up to date. Any wine nut will have a lot of fun with this book'
Jamie Goode, wineanorak.com

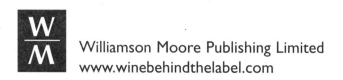

Williamson Moore Publishing Limited
www.winebehindthelabel.com

First published in 2003 by Williamson Moore
This edition published in 2004
34 Ivy Close Winchester Hampshire SO22 4QR United Kingdom
Tel/Fax +44 (0)1962 865 693
E-mail: info@williamson-moore.co.uk

A catalogue record for this book is available from the British Library.

ISBN 0-9544097-4-4

Editorial assistance from Bill Evans and Ed Francis

Printed and bound in Great Britain by Biddles Limited King's Lynn

Whilst every care has been taken in the preparation of this guide,
the publishers and authors cannot accept responsibility of any kind for
consequences arising from reliance upon information contained in it.

Contents

Contents/continued

Our concept

When we finalised the concept of this guide nearly two years prior to releasing the 2003 edition, we were aware of the frustration of wine drinkers at the lack of a single authoritative guide that could provide both depth and criticism about quality wines whatever their provenance. In an age of 'dumbing down' we opted instead for 'wising up' yet endeavoured to produce a reference that is accessible to the novice and learned alike. Even more important than providing a critical assessment of a producer's wine we are trying to provide more pertinent information about as many quality wine producers as possible. It is a guide for enthusiasts or would-be enthusiasts, not for those who can't detect any differences or don't care too. Those producers profiled with their own entry are a selection of the best established producers and some of the new and upcoming stars. In this, the 2005 edition, we have added a significant number of new producers of quality wine yet it is still far from exhaustive. The very best of those listed at the end of each section and those we have in our work in progress will be profiled in future editions.

Our philosophy

The industrial mentality which has given us brilliant cars and computers doesn't have a place in high quality wine (or food) production. An essential difference between a high production brand and one produced on a more human scale is the personal effort and commitment that the family or individuals who make it have put into it. We have tried to bring the producer a little closer to whoever is drinking their wine so that some inkling of their philosophy and effort might enrich the enjoyment the wine brings. It is our intention to give strong support both to small producers and talented winemakers but every quality wine is considered on it merits. A small producer, no matter how earnest or sincere, will not make good wine if he or she doesn't manage their vineyards well and employ sound winemaking practice. Equally, spending exorbitant sums on PR and marketing doesn't always mean the wine in the bottle is poor – though it is likely given the money spent that it could be better value. More and more of the world's finest wines are hard to get hold of but in many instances there is a first point of contact that will sell direct by mail-order or over the Internet. (see also Buying Guide under Agent codes). Browsing a section will also highlight alternatives.

Winemaking ethics

Specifically bringing to account those involved in bad or unethical production is not within the scope of this book. However we do want to encourage producers to be open in providing as much information as possible about what they are producing and what techniques are employed in the winemaking. Rather than making judgements about new technologies we'd simply like to give the reader a clearer idea of to what extent their wine has been processed (including the use of additives and the extent of fining and/or filtration). We want, too, to pass on information about whether the wines are produced according to organic or biodynamic principles. The current trend to giving more detail about a wine's provenance we'd also like to encourage. Even if a wine is sourced from numerous small parcels and these change from year to year, any single vintage of a wine has to be sourced from a definable area or areas. It is not an argument about the quality of single vineyard wines versus blends as the latter may often be superior. It is a case of providing more information and allowing the consumer to learn something of the individual parcel or parcels that play a part in the wine's character. It is also of course a way of keeping tabs on the biggest premium brands. Some famous names have for instance, lost some of the finest vineyard sources which contributed to their early quality and fame. It is also our hope that more producers will also provide information concerning the total production of a given vintage, yield per ha, density of vines per hectare and most importantly average yield per vine.

Help

This guide does contain a lot of information about producers and their wines. This year we have added three new features we hope will help you find the information you need more quickly. The lists of producers by appellation or region at the end of each section's introduction now have the page number where you can find their entries. This should also make it clearer as to who is covered, and from where. We have also for the first time added single page map inserts as a quick reference which you can use with the lists of producers by appellation or region. Exciting new producers are emerging all the time and we now have a 'work in progress' in many sections listing producers who we will be assessing for the next edition. We continue to appreciate that most readers probably only have the time to dip in and out of the book. To this end we added an 'Author's choice' at the end of each section in the 2004 edition. These contain a selection of some of the best and most interesting wines though are necessarily more limited in their usefulness in the regions with the most extensive coverage. We hope that they will continue to serve as an alternative starting point to discovering new wines. They will continue to be overhauled in future editions.

The response to our first two editions has been fantastic and for the 2006 we want to do still more. We'd like as much input as possible and will encourage this through our website as we develop it further. Alternatively please write to, or email, us with your constructive criticisms.

Tasting, ratings, and assessing producers

Our ratings as explained in the How to Use section more fully reflect a wine's true quality as they are almost always based on a minimum of two vintages. These are recent vintages as we give short shrift to the one vintage wonders or those where the quality has fallen away. Wine shows and competitions encourage the production of wines of flattering first impressions but don't always reward those that show at their best with age. Nor do they address the implications of the vintage characteristics. Rather than a snapshot, consensual tasting mentality we believe in tasting wines again and again (both blind and non-blind) in order to gain a better understanding of a wine's style and when it should be drunk. This we have endeavoured to pass on in individual producer entries. A rating combined with an understanding of the style is the key to discovering the best wines. A higher rating doesn't necessarily reflect a better wine but one that may develop more complexity, have the structure for greater longevity or simply show greater intensity or persistence in the mouth.

We have focussed less on whether a wine tastes of this or that and more on whether it brings enjoyment. The question should always be which wine works best now, reflects my mood, personality or whatever? What flavours do I want? How much flavour? Whether the wine is drunk immediately or cellared. If it is kept the character of different vintages of the same wine can be contrasted. Alternatively from a case of the same wine the gradual development and increasing maturity of a specific vintage can be assessed over a decade or more.

Conclusion

Think of this book as a catalogue to a vast array of vinous riches. Choose with the certainty of trying wines of dependable quality that our labours and experience provide through our rating system. If you haven't tasted Austrian Grüner Veltliner or Californian Syrah then try a three star example from at least two or three profiled producers. Buy the best new reds from the Languedoc-Roussillon or Portugal's Douro, try old-vine Barossa Shiraz or a Barolo of certifiable class. Alternatively seek out new names from Burgundy, Bordeaux or the Rhône. Most of all we implore you to sample more widely.

About the authors

Philip Williamson

I only took a serious interest in wine in my mid-twenties having rarely drunk it before then, well save a nasty bottle or two at University. After entering the wine trade in 1987 I have spent more than half the subsequent 17 years devoted solely to assessing wine quality and writing about it. My greatest inspiration has been great bottles of wine and some of the wonderful individuals who have created them; propelled on by special moments whether a sip of Domaine Leflaive whites or tasting with Aldo Conterno in Piedmont.

I've also enjoyed working with Oz Clarke and share his enthusiasm for every new bottle opened that represents human effort and skill. I feel fortunate to have immersed myself in wine during an era of its production that continually provides ever more stimulating and exciting finds. My taste is eclectic and extends from the old classics of Port, Sherry and Madeira, to relatively modern styles such as Barossa Shiraz, Priorat reds or Wachau Riesling even if I'm most passionate about Burgundy and Italy. My considerable experience as both an editor and specialist contributor to leading wine books I believe formed an important part of my apprenticeship prior to undertaking this joint collaboration with my friend, colleague and expert wine taster, David Moore.

Despite a perception of glamour, tasting professionally is often arduous, requiring a disciplined and analytical approach to wine assessment. Yet for me, the most exciting wines continue to provoke an emotional response. Writing about wine also means taking a more detached, considered view – understanding the global picture while being uncompromising in the support of local traditions and diversity. The integrity and honesty I see in the best producers I want to reflect in taking a serious approach to writing about their wines. I want to convey quality and style in such a way as to encourage its wider appreciation including by those normally intimidated by the complexity of the subject. I care most that wine is drunk and enjoyed, a magic drink that should be accessible to all, yet not trivialised or abused; rather a source of pleasure, fun and stimulation – both sensuous and cerebral.

Philip Williamson

David Moore

Like many people I became interested in wine quite by chance. In my case it was a trip to the Loire Valley in 1988 and the lure of the trade quickly followed. Since then I've sold and bought wine before teaching, lecturing and for over six years writing about and tasting wine critically. In between I've managed to fit in six months getting my hands dirty in wineries in Australia. This as much as anything has taught me what is involved in producing wines of real quality. I've had the good fortune to witness first hand that wine at its best, is about both the land and people. I'm at my happiest listening to a winemaker in their cellar enthusing about what they do. What I hope we achieve in this book is to guide you to those characters and give a real indication of what they do in making their wines and how they seek to achieve it. Sometimes the results are great and sometimes not.

In the seven or eight years that we spent throwing ideas about and researching this guide what continues to intrigue and fascinate me is the sheer diversity that wine has to offer. I'm always at a loss when someone asks me what my favourite wine or region is. Its almost impossible to say. The most important thing is individuality. Really pleasurable drinking can be had when you find wine that truly displays its character and it doesn't have to be expensive. Philip and I have both been judges for a series of themed tastings for the New York Times for wine regions right across the globe. What never ceases to amaze me, even tasting through 120 wines in a day from the same region, is the sheer range of flavours, styles and quality differences often within a single appellation.

What are my dislikes in wine? I feel it should always be enjoyed and not speculated on, the thought of cases of fine claret tucked away in bonded warehouses never likely to see the light of day is a thoroughly depressing one. I also dislike the intellectualising of wine, there is no good reason why people should be made to feel intimidated by the subject. I hope we will go some way in these pages to telling you how it is but lending some interest and understanding to what you're drinking and buying. My greatest hobby is riding a motorcycle at weekends for fun. Not the most conformist of activities but I always feel the greatest wines are made by characters who don't conform either and their wines always excite me most. Hopefully you'll get some inspiration from these pages and discover some of these gems as well.

David S. Moor

How to use this guide

Within each section you will find an introduction including, where possible, vintage information. In this edition we have also added a list of the producers, either by region or appellation, that have been profiled within the A-Z that makes up the bulk of the section. At the end of the A-Z of producers, is a list of other wines of note from that region. Many are of high quality or produce at least one good wine. The best of these are likely to be added to the guide in future editions after further assessment. Some in these lists also produce more quality wines than are indicated as we have included only those we have tasted at least once. For the 2005 edition we have also added a 'Work in progress' list of producers we will be assessing over the next twelve months. At the very end of each section under Author's Choice we have added lists of wines that are a personal selection but are also often themed by a shared style or grape variety and so should aid navigation. For individual A-Z entries we have provided the winery addresses and wherever possible we have also provided website addresses. In some instances we have provided email addresses where there is no website. The use of CAPS (eg Louis JADOT) indicates the existence of a cross-referenced entry that can be found from the Index.

Vintages Charts:

In those sections where vintages have the greatest significance, Vintage Charts are also provided (as is text on individual years for the classic wines of Bordeaux, Burgundy, Piedmont, Tuscany and Port). Specific styles of wine are given an overall vintage rating between one and five stars for individual years. In some instances it is not possible to provide a balanced judgement on the vintage until nearer the wines' release (with Brunello di Montalcino for example). These have been designated NYR (not yet rated). When to drink the wines of a given vintage is a largely subjective, personal judgement and can depend as much on mood or context but the letter (A-D) following the ratings gives a general indication of their likely development:

A - wines to Anticipate, not ready for drinking

B - wines that can be Broached, but with much more to give

C - wines to Consume, at or near their best

D - wines likely to be in Decline, past their best

A-Z Order:

The order of the A-Z entries is based on the name they are most commonly referred to and they appear as they are written but with priority to surnames. 'Domaine' is ignored but 'Château', 'Castello', 'Quinta' etc are respected as is the definite article when implicitly part of the name (eg Il Poggione appears under 'I'). The only exception to these principles is in Bordeaux where the name of the château or estate takes precedent.

A: (Agent code)

For readers based in the UK, 'A' in A-Z producer entries indicates the existence of a UK agent or stockists of a producer's wines. An exclusive agent appears in **bold**. Details of these codes can be found in the Agent Codes section. Also given here is general information on buying wine. Though not all agents can sell direct to consumers they will at least be able to give details of where the wines can be bought. In future editions we plan to provide details of agents and stockists in other markets.

Ownership:

Ownership is also given throughout and wherever this appears in **bold** it refers to a corporate owner rather than an individual or individuals. Obviously contact with a corporate owner shouldn't be assumed to be possible via the winery's address that follows it.

The entries follow this simple 'all you need to know' format

	Producer	wine region	website	Agent or stockist (UK only)

Owner's name and address

CH. HAUT-BRION | Pessac-Léognan 1er CC | www.haut-brion.com | A:AAA

Owner: Domaine Clarence Dillon 33608 Pessac Cedex

Individually researched entry

One of the four original properties classified as a First Growth in the 1855 Classification of the red Bordeaux wines. The vineyards are planted in superbly drained gravel soils that provide an almost ideal supply of moisture to optimise fruit ripening. Reds grapes occupy 43 ha, while less than 3 ha provides a tiny amount of exquisite, subtly barrel-fermented white from Sémillon and Sauvignon Blanc. The property, now surrounded by the ever-encroaching suburbs of Bordeaux, is small in comparison to the other First Growths, producing a total of some 12,500 cases a year. Both red and white have been magnificent through the late 1990s, only the 1997 and 91 red dipping a little. Great older vintages include 1990, 89, 86, 82, 75 and the astonishing 61. The second wine, Le Bahans, can also be very impressive. (DM)

Red, white or rosé

● Château Haut-Brion Pessac-Léognan ✪✪✪✪✪ £H ● Le Bahans Haut Brion★★★ £E

O Château Haut-Brion Pessac-Léognan ✪✪✪✪✪ £G

Quality rating indicator

Estimated price bracket

Symbols:

● red wine   O white wine   ◉ rosé wine

Ratings:

★   *a wine of good quality, not just sound but of good fruit and with some character.*

★★   *a wine with more depth, interest and concentration, usually with some aging potential.*

★★★   *a very good, even fine, wine. In the case of many reds repaying lengthy cellaring.*

★★★★   *a wine of very high quality, among the very best even in a top appellation or region.*

★★★★★ *outstanding quality, potentially a classic.*

✪✪✪✪✪ *super 5 stars, restricted to the true classics, out-and-out world class.*

We have rated as many of a producer's wines as possible, but in some instances the wines are too new or, too scarce to have yet received a rating. Such wines are covered in the text only.

Tasting notes and scores:

It is not in the style of this guide to provide tasting notes for individual vintages along with their scores. However this information will be provided through our website over the coming year and we intend to give readers the opportunity to receive the scores for currently available vintages by electronic means. Given that scores are vintage specific, they sometimes exceed or fall short of the rating that is based on repeated tastings. (also see 'Tasting, Ratings, and assessing producers' in the Introduction)

Prices:

A code is provided which represents an estimated retail price bracket and is based on a standard 75cl bottle size. Price codes for those produced only in 1.5 litre (magnums), 50 cl (half litre) or 37.5 cl (half bottle) formats have been given 75cl equivalents. A half bottle costing £8.95/$16.00 for instance will have a price code of £D.

£A: *less than £5:00 ($9.00)*	£E: *£20 - 30 ($36 - 54)*
£B: *£5 - 10 ($9 - 18)*	£F: *£30 - 50 ($54 - 90)*
£C: *£10 - 15 ($18 - 27)*	£G: *£50 - 75 ($90 - 135)*
£D: *£15 - 20 ($27 - 36)*	£H: *£75 or more ($135 or more)*

In order to make sense of France as a whole we have devoted a section to each of its major wine regions. As an aid to orientation, the major appellations are listed under their respective regions. More detail of each, as well as on other exciting smaller appelations, can be found at the start of the individual chapters that follow this Overview.

Bordeaux

For both quality and quantity this is France's most important wine region. Wines vary from simple everyday reds to some of the worlds most expensive classic crus.

Médoc, Graves & Sauternes

The **Médoc** provides all but one of the great Cabernet based Classed-Growths of the Right Bank, the best sites at **Margaux**, **Saint-Julien**, **Pauillac** and **Saint-Estèphe** are found on superbly drained gravel soils. Good wines can also be found in the **Haut-Médoc**, **Listrac** and **Moulis** ACs but the *terroir* is less propitious. **Pessac-Léognan** is a source of not only some great reds but whites which at their best rival the great wines of the Côte de Beaune. **Graves** to the south produces some good wines without the depth or class of Pessac-Léognan. Some of the worlds greatest botryitised sweet wines are produced at **Sauternes** and **Barsac**.

St Emilion, Pomerol & other Bordeaux

Almost all the new wave of Bordeaux reds have emerged from the Right Bank. Many top Châteaux have been isolating special crus and bottling them separately and other small volume garage style wines have also emerged. Some are exceptional, some decidedly less so. This revolution has largely occurred in **Saint-Emilion**, rather than the much smaller **Pomerol** AC. Some of the best value has begun to emerge from the lesser and satellite appellations. The vast track of the **Entre-Deux-Mers** to the south of Saint Emilion continues to offer good value whites.

Burgundy

This most famous wine region makes some of the finest examples of both Chardonnay and Pinot Noir. Chardonnay can achieve success almost anywhere but the tricky Pinot Noir achieves rare greatness here.

Chablis & Yonne

One of the wine world's most famous names. Located halfway between Beaune and Paris, these are distinctly cool climate Chardonnays. The white ACs include **Petit Chablis**, **Chablis**, **Chablis Premier Cru** and **Chablis Grand Cru**. The best wines have both a piercing minerality as well as a complex citrus and cheesy lees character. Some red is also made as **Bourgogne Irancy**.

Côte d'Or & Côte Chalonnaise

The Côte d'Or is synonymous with Burgundy and includes all its great red wines. It is comprised of two parts. The more northerly Côte de Nuits (mostly red) includes the famous villages of **Gevrey-Chambertin**, **Morey Saint-Denis** and **Vosne-Romanee**. In its southern continuation, the Côte de Beaune, some of the worlds greatest dry whites are produced from **Meursault**, **Chassagne-Montrachet** and **Puligny-Montrachet** as well as some very fine reds, from the likes of **Volnay** and **Pommard**. The Cote Chalonnaise offers some wines of character and depth both red and white. With a few exceptions the better examples from the Cote d'Or's lesser ACs tend to offer more excitement.

Mâconnais

Perhaps the most exciting of Burgundies regions, certainly in terms of the number of emerging top quality small producers.. Big, full and rich Chardonnay is produced from a number of appellations, pre-eminent among them being **Pouilly-Fuissé**. **Saint-Véran** the various **Macon-Villages, Pouilly-Loché** and **Pouilly-Vinzelles** are also important.

Beaujolais

The vast majority of Beaujolais is red and produced from Gamay. Generic examples come mainly from the south of the region. However it is the superior granite soils of the northern sector where the better **Beaujolais-Villages**, the *crus* **Brouilly, Chénas, Chiroubles, Côte de Brouilly, Juliénas, Régnié, Saint-Amour** together with the structured more ageworthy **Fleurie, Morgon** and **Moulin-à-Vent** offer wines of sometimes heady strawberry-scented intensity.

Alsace

One of the most northerly of France's regions in the north-east of the country. The warm, dry, sunny climate of the area, enabled through protection by the Vosges Mountains, provides uniquely rich and strikingly aromatic wines which are labelled by grape variety and classified as **Alsace** AC or **Alsace Grand Cru** AC. There is also a spakling wine classification **Crémant d'Alsace**.

Champagne

The world's greatest sparkling wine comes from this exposed marginal climate in northern France. Much of the wine is of potentially very high quality. All is produced from Chardonnay, Pinot Noir and Pinot Meunier and made by the classic Champagne method, emulated almost everywhere else for fine sparkling wines, with a secondary fermentation almost always in bottle.

Loire Valley

An extensive region which stretches from the Atlantic coast at Nantes and follows the Loire River to its source in central France. The Pays Nantais is dominated by just one wine, Muscadet, from a number of ACs. Anjou-Saumur is a source of the great sweet wines of the **Coteaux du Layon, Bonnezeaux** and **Quarts de Chaume** as well as some fine dry white from **Savennières**. Good, structured red and white are provided by **Saumur** and Cabernet based reds emanate from **Saumur-Champigny**. Touraine is home to the diverse, ageworthy Chenin Blancs of **Vouvray** and **Montlouis** as well as some fine red based on Cabernet Franc from **Bourgeuil, Chinon** and **Saint-Nicolas-de-Bourgeuil**. To the east are the vineyards of **Sancerre** and **Pouilly-Fumé**. Some of finest minerally, gooseberry scented Sauvignon Blanc is made here. The region also stretches south to the Auverne, where some soft easy-drinking red is made.

Rhône Valley

This huge sprawling area stretches down the narrow river valley of the Rhône towards Provence. The bulk of the regions output is generic **Côtes du Rhône**, almost exclusively from the south. There are also many high quality wines red and white produced throughout the region.

Northern Rhône

Some of the worlds finest red and white wine is produced here. Syrah is the mainstay of the reds including the great wines of **Hermitage, Côte-Rôtie** and **Cornas. Saint-Joseph** and **Crozes-Hermitage** are increasingly important. A small amount of very ageworthy white is made at Hermitage and elsewhere from mainly Marsanne and some Roussanne. The exotically peachy **Condrieu** is the ultimate expression of the aromatic Viognier.

Southern Rhône

As well as the sea of generic red produced here there are some striking and classic reds from the large AC of **Châteauneuf-du-Pape.** As elsewhere in the southern Rhône the wines are based on Grenache, and some of the finest expressions of the variety emanate from here. Its also well worth considering the reds of **Gigondas** and **Vacqueyras** as well as the reds and whites from many of the emerging **Côtes du Rhône Villages.** These are wines that currently offer exciting quality and often great value.

Languedoc-Roussillon

This vast geographical area, still the purveyor of a vast lake of bulk produced vin de table and vin de pays, is also the source of some of the most exciting, newly-emerging wines in France.

Languedoc

Of the two sub-regions, this is much the larger. Key to quality in all the appellations are the isolation of excellent hillside *terroirs* and the planting of Rhône varieties both red and white. The Carignan variety is also proving a valueable resource old bush vines. The **Coteaux du Languedoc** is by far the largest of the appellations with the smaller ACs **Faugeres** and **Saint-Chinian** also providing wines of real substance. The appellations round the coast towards the Roussillon, including **Minervois** and **Corbières** tend to produce softer, lighter wines.

Roussillon

Perhaps the greatest potential in the Midi comes from the vineyards of the Roussillon. The region was best known for the quality of its splendid fortified reds, **Maury, Rivesaltes** and **Banyuls.** However many old vine plantings are now providing exceptional raw material for a growing number of high quality light dry reds and a few very impressive whites also. Old Grenache and Carignan are of great importance and increasing amounts of Syrah and Mourvèdre are also being planted. Some wines are classified as vin de pays others are **Côtes du Roussillon** and **Côtes du Roussillon-Villages.**

Provence & Eastern France

Provence is becoming justifiably better known for the quality of its reds. Rhône varieties are widely planted in the key appellations. Cabernet Sauvignon is also becoming increasingly important. The top red AC, **Bandol** provides striking, long-lived reds largely based on Mourvèdre. Corsica offers some sound reds from interesting idigenous varieties and fine sweet Muscat. The Alpine vineyards of Jura and Savoie provide some of the most unusual and strikingly flavoured whites and the rare Jura speciality *vin jaune.*

South-West France

A wide and diverse range of wines are produced in this large area. To the north **Bergerac** produces reds and whites from the Bordeaux varieties. Big structured reds are produced to the south at **Cahors,** largely from Auxerrois (Malbec) and at **Madiran** mainly from Tannat. Some exceptional white is produced at **Jurançon**, including great moelleux, and good whites also emerge from **Pacherenc du Vic-Bilh.** Some of the most unusual and diverse styles come from **Gaillac** to the north-east of Toulouse.

1   Bordeaux
2   Chablis
3   Burgundy
4   Beaujolais
5   Alsace
6   Champagne
7   Loire Valley
8   Northern Rhône
9   Southern Rhône
10 Languedoc & Roussillon
11 Provence
12 South-West France
13 Jura
14 Savoie

To most people Bordeaux is probably the most well-known of France's great wine regions. In recent years it has enjoyed bountiful harvests, the maintenance of quality – and many improvements too – and until the last couple of years a remarkably buoyant market for its premium wines. The last few years have also seen dynamic changes on the Right Bank of the Gironde in Saint-Émilion, with major investment in established properties and the creation of a number of exciting new labels. The development of the so-called garagiste wines, produced in tiny quantities all over the Saint-Émilion appellation, has been welcome in instances where exotic and fine and ageworthy blends have been produced from isolated first-class terroirs. However, where these wines are sourced from lesser sites, they are often over-extracted, lacking in class but nevertheless still marketed and sold at high prices. Perhaps if the current trend towards more realistic pricing in general continues there may be a much-needed reality check. The lesser areas like Fronsac and particularly the Côtes de Castillon continue to forge ahead with exciting developments at prices that mere mortals can afford. It is also important not to lose sight of the fact that there are properties, particularly on the Left Bank in the Médoc, which have consistently been producing some of the world's greatest wines for decades and continue to do so.

Geography

The Bordeaux region can effectively be looked at in three parts. There are the appellations surrounding Bordeaux itself and stretching to both the north and south. These vineyards are all located on the western side of the Gironde estuary and further south the river Garonne. This is often referred to as the Left Bank. The Right Bank comprises the vineyard areas east of the Gironde and the river Dordogne, particularly the appellations of Saint-Émilion and Pomerol near Libourne. There is another vast tract of vineyard land between the Dordogne and the Garonne. This is neither Left nor Right Bank and is largely dry white wine territory, including the large Entre-Deux-Mers AC. The vast bulk of Bordeaux's commercial wine trade emanates from the city itself. Libourne, though, is also important commercially, with a number of its own *négociants*.

Generic Bordeaux

AC **Bordeaux**, the bottle you're most likely to come across, can be sourced anywhere within the large Bordeaux region, which includes the areas mentioned above and other outlying appellations. The total production is mind-boggling. Some 5.5 to 6 million hectolitres of red and nearly another million of white are produced every year. Around two-thirds of this is generic Bordeaux. This would not be such a huge problem in itself but most of the red is vinified from Merlot, the workhorse grape of the region and often grown in heavy and productive soils. This allied to over-ambitious yields is always going to present a challenge to fully ripening the crop. So much generic Bordeaux not only tastes dilute but can also have a green, vegetal component. Ripening the white grapes here tends to be less of a problem and these wines can often be better bets.

Médoc, Graves and Sauternes

Some of the world's greatest and noblest red wines are produced here as well as benchmark sweet whites and a very small amount of immensely stylish dry white. The **Médoc** AC itself, rather than the area of the Médoc which runs from Bordeaux north to Soulac at the mouth of the Gironde, is centred around the small town of Lesparre-Médoc and is the northernmost of the Left Bank ACs. There is a higher proportion of clay in the soil rather than the fabled gravel and the wines are generally soft and forward, with a few better examples. The **Haut-Médoc** encompasses all four of the great communal appellations close to the Gironde (Saint-Estèphe, Pauillac, Saint-Julien and Margaux) as well as Listrac and Moulis. There can be a wide variation in quality in the Haut-Medoc AC but a few properties are very serious indeed, producing classic, long-lived cedary reds. Both **Listrac-Médoc** and **Moulis** are located just to the north-west of Margaux. Listrac seems to offer less potential but there are attempts here to fashion some modern *garagiste*-style wines and make the best of the fruit available. Moulis has greater potential, with a number of very good properties.

The northernmost of the great red wine appellations of the Médoc is **Saint-Estèphe**. There are five Classed Growths and the wines are generally the densest, sturdiest examples of the area. Modern winemaking has gone some way to address those firm youthful tannins and the wines are more approachable than they were even a decade ago and are very impressive at their best. **Pauillac** is synonymous with some of the greatest wines of the region. Châteaux Latour, Lafite-Rothschild and Mouton-Rothschild are all here. The deep gravel vineyards provide an ideal base for these strikingly rich styles laden with cassis and spice. The top wines need considerable age. To the south, the wines of **Saint-Julien** are less opulent than Pauillac, more perfumed and with intense cigar box and cedar notes. There are eleven Classed Growths and the extraordinarily refined Léoville-Las-Cases should be a First Growth in many people's books. **Margaux** is just to the north of Bordeaux and contains 21 Classed Growths. At their best these are are the most elegant and refined wines of the Médoc. For a long time Margaux has been an underperforming appellation but change is happening aplenty – new investment, a renewed commitment to quality and, in Marojallia and Clos du Jaugueyron, the first serious *garagiste* wines on the Left Bank. Marojallia is vinified by Jean-Luc Thunevin, owner of Valandraud, one of the first *garagiste* wines in Saint-Émilion.

Immediately south of Bordeaux, indeed part of the AC is in the outer suburbs of the city, are the vineyards of **Pessac-Léognan**. Originally part of the larger **Graves** appellation it was granted its own appellation status in 1987 in recognition of the superior quality of its sites. The soil is finely drained deep gravel and all of the properties in the 1959 Classification of the Graves are to be found here. Only Haut-Brion, with its First Growth status in the 1855 Classification, was absent from the list. Some splendid reds are produced here as well as a small number of dry whites. At their best these are rich, complex and very ageworthy and rival the great whites of the Côte de Beaune (see Burgundy). White winemaking in general throughout the Graves has improved immeasurably in recent years. The rest of the region stretches to the east and some way south of the Garonne. It is never as good as Pessac-Léognan but some good red and dry white are regularly produced. There are also a few sweet wines under the **Graves Supérieures** AC, but these are largely pretty dull.

Just north-west of the town of Langon are the great sweet wine appellations of Sauternes and Barsac. A third sweet wine appellation, **Cérons**, is immediately to the north but does not benefit to the same degree as the other two AC's from the remarkable geographical influence of the tiny Ciron river, which creates the conditions for the development of noble rot. Cérons and also the sweet wines from immediately across the Garonne in **Sainte-Croix-du-Mont** and **Loupiac** can be impressive but they never achieve the same intense botrytis quality as **Sauternes**. **Barsac** is one of the five communes of Sauternes and properties here may chose to label their wines Sauternes or Barsac. After a run of very successful vintages in the 1980s these wines are now fetching the kinds of prices that make their production economic and indeed profitable. Fifteen to 20 years ago it was nigh-on impossible for producers to achieve a commercial return. Harvesting is incredibly labour-intensive, with multiple *tris* (passes through the vineyard), and the yield is necessarily tiny. However, major investment has dramatically changed the area. Many wines of truly magnificent concentration and intensity are now being made. In the lesser years cryo-extraction has been used by a number of châteaux to improve quality.

Saint-Émilion, Pomerol and the Rest of Bordeaux

Saint-Émilion and Pomerol are the two great names associated with the Right Bank but there are an increasing number of well-priced, exciting wines emerging from the other ACs. It is also interesting to note that these are all red wine appellations. **Saint-Émilion** itself is the driving force in terms of volume and accounts for some 40 per cent of all wines produced here. As a result it's not surprising that there is a wide variation in quality and very diverse *terroirs*, some exceptional and some, particularly in the southern plains of the AC, distinctly ordinary, with heavy productive soils. Many of Bordeaux's major developments in vinification techniques and the influence of consultant winemakers have their origins in Saint-Émilion. Pre-fermentation cold soaking (or maceration), malolactic fermentation in barrel and micro-oxygenation are now practised all over the world.

Saint-Émilion's Classification was last revised in 1996 and will be again in 2006. There are 14 Premiers Grands Crus Classés with two A-rated properties, Ausone and Cheval-Blanc, as well as 51 properties rated Grand Cru Classé. There have been major investments in recent years in both vineyards and cellars, resulting in some highly priced wines made in very limited quantities. The most notable of these has been La Mondotte, produced at Canon-La-Gaffelière. Many other tiny-production wines or *vins des garagistes* have also emerged. Some have been very impressive, but many are over-extracted and all are expensive.

Pomerol, in contrast, continues to provide some impressive and startlingly opulent wines, full of dark and spicy fruit, generally supple and more approachable than many of the other top wines in Bordeaux. Inevitably there are exceptions to the rule and these tend to occur where there is a higher proportion of Cabernet Franc or Cabernet Sauvignon planted or the soil has more gravel. Pomerol's clay soils suit Merlot very well and provide this uniquely exotic style. Pomerol's wines can also be some of the priciest anywhere on the globe. There has been investment and development here but not on the scale of Saint-Émilion's. The lower tier of the appellation, though, can disappoint. The odd wine of distinction is also beginning to emerge from the lesser Saint-Émilion satellite ACs, **Lussac-Saint-Émilion, Montagne-Saint-Émilion, Puisseguin-Saint-Émilion** and **Saint-Georges-Saint-Émilion,** as well as **Lalande-de-Pomerol.**

To the north-west of Libourne are the areas of **Côtes de Bourg** and **Côtes de Blaye.** The former produces reds, some decent and some very impressive while dry whites are produced in the latter. To the immediate west of Libourne are **Fronsac** and **Canon-Fronsac.** Good, stylish, well-made dark-fruited styles have been produced here for a decade or so. To the east of Saint-Émilion are the **Côtes de Castillon** and **Bordeaux-Côtes de Francs.** Again these are areas of great potential and the best wines are still well-priced, if becoming less so.

Between the Dordogne and Garonne rivers is a substantial vineyard area comprising some nine appellations. Geographically and physically by far the most important is the **Entre-Deux-Mers,** an appellation devoted to dry whites. A number of properties here are also producing good AC Bordeaux red. The appellation is all about maximising modern white winemaking with some good results, using pre-fermentation skin contact, ageing on lees and, in the more expensive wines, limited barrel-fermentation and ageing with new wood as well. Some well-priced wines have been available for some time now. Vibrant red and rosé is made in the **Premières Côtes de Bordeaux,** just to the east across the Garonne from the city of Bordeaux, and there are good sweet wines on the eastern bank of the river at **Cadillac, Loupiac** and **Sainte-Croix-du-Mont.** In the far east is **Saint-Foy-de-Bordeaux,** where there are reds as well as dry and sweet whites.

A-Z of producers by appellation/region

Médoc, Graves & Sauternes

Barsac
CH. CLIMENS	29
CH. COUTET	30
CH. DOISY-DAËNE	31
CH. DOISY-VÉDRINES	31
CH. NAIRAC	41

Graves
CH. DE CHANTEGRIVE	27
CLOS FLORIDÈNE	29
VIEUX-CHÂTEAU-GAUBERT	46
CH. VILLA BEL AIR	47

Haut-Médoc
CH. D'AGASSAC	24
CH. BELGRAVE	25
CH. CAMENSAC	26
CH. CANTEMERLE	27
CH. CHARMAIL	28
CH. CISSAC	28
CH. LA LAGUNE	35
CH. LANESSAN	36
MA VÉRITÉ	40
CH. PEYRABON	42
CH. SOCIANDO-MALLET	45
CH. LA TOUR CARNET	37

Listrac-Médoc
CH. CLARKE	29
CH. MAYNE-LALANDE	40

Margaux
CH. D'ANGLUDET	24
CH. BEL AIR MARQUIS D'ALIGRE	25
CH. BOYD-CANTENAC	25
CH. BRANE-CANTENAC	26
CH. CANTENAC-BROWN	27
CH. DAUZAC	30
CH. FERRIÈRE	31
CH. GISCOURS	32
CH. D'ISSAN	34
CH. KIRWAN	34
CH. MALESCOT-SAINT-EXUPÉRY	39
CH. MARGAUX	39
CH. PALMER	41
CH. PRIEURÉ-LICHINE	43
CH. RAUZAN-SÉGLA	43
CH. DU TERTRE	46

Médoc
CH. POTENSAC	42
CH. ROLLAN-DE-BY	44

Moulis
CH. CHASSE-SPLEEN	28
CH. POUJEAUX	43

Pauillac
CH. D'ARMAILLAC	24
CH. BATAILLEY	25
CH. CLERC-MILON	29
CH. DUHART-MILON	31
CH. GRAND-PUY-LACOSTE	33
CH. HAUT-BATAILLEY	33
CH. LAFITE-ROTHSCHILD	35
CH. LATOUR	37
CH. LYNCH-BAGES	38
CH. MOUTON-ROTHSCHILD	41
CH. PICHON-LONGUEVILLE	42
CH. PICHON-LONGUEVILLE-LALANDE	42
CH. PONTET-CANET	42

Pessac-Léognan
CH. CARBONNIEUX	27
CH. LES CARMES HAUT-BRION	27
DOM. DE CHEVALIER	28
CH. COUHINS-LURTON	30
CH. DE FIEUZAL	32
CH. DE FRANCE	32
CH. HAUT-BAILLY	33
CH. HAUT-BRION	34
CH. LARRIVET HAUT-BRION	36
LA SERÉNITÉ	36
CH. LATOUR MARTILLAC	37
CH LAVILLE HAUT-BRION	37
CH. LA LOUVIÈRE	38
CH. MALARTIC-LAGRAVIÈRE	39
CH LA MISSION HAUT-BRION	40
CH. PAPE-CLÉMENT	41
CH. SMITH-HAUT-LAFITTE	45
CH. LA TOUR HAUT-BRION	46

Saint-Estèphe
CH. CALON-SÉGUR	26
CH. COS D'ESTOURNEL	30
CH. COS LABORY	30
CH. HAUT-MARBUZET	34
CH. LAFON-ROCHET	35
CH. MONTROSE	40

Saint-Julien
CH. BEYCHEVELLE	25
CH. BRANAIRE	26
CH. DUCRU-BEAUCAILLOU	31
CH. GLORIA	32
CH. GRUAUD-LAROSE	33
CH. LAGRANGE	35
CH. LANGOA-BARTON	36
CH LÉOVILLE-BARTON	37
CH. LÉOVILLE-LAS-CASES	38
CH. LÉOVILLE-POYFERRÉ	38
CH. SAINT-PIERRE	44
CH. TALBOT	45

Sauternes
CH. D'ARCHE	24
CH. BASTOR-LAMONTAGNE	24

Saint-Emilion, Pomerol & other Bordeaux

1   Médoc
2   Haut-Médoc
3   Saint-Estèphe
4   Pauillac
5   Saint-Julien
6   Listrac-Médoc
7   Moulis
8   Margaux
9   Pessac-Léognan
10   Graves
11   Cérons
12   Barsac
13   Sauternes
14   Premières Côtes de Bordeaux
15   Loupiac
16   Sainte-Croix-du-Mont
17   Entre-Deux-Mers
18   Ste-Foy-Bordeaux
19   Côtes de Castillon
20   Côtes de Franc
21   Saint-Émilion satellites
22   Saint-Émilion
23   Pomerol
24   Lalande-de-Pomerol
25   Fronsac & Canon-Fronsac
26   Côtes de Bourg
27   Côtes de Blaye / Premières Côtes de Blaye

Bordeaux vintages

As in other parts of France Bordeaux has been generally fairly lucky with vintages during the last six or seven years, particularly at the turn of the millenium. There haven't been the number of great years as the Rhône Valley from 1998 but after the disappointments of the early 1990s things have been decidedly better. Winemaking has evolved here and generally for the better. With the top reds, particularly, it is worth bearing in mind if you are purchasing from a fine current vintage that the approach in the cellar is different to that of 20 years ago. The wines are suppler and more approachable but it remains to be seen whether they will be as long-lived as some of their predecessors.

2003: Marked by a very hot summer this is likely to be a year of very good Left Bank reds, in particular to the north of the Medoc. To the south Graves was more uneven. There are likely to be some exceptional examples from the Right Bank from sites with good moisture retention. Those who picked at optimum ripeness will be very fine. Many though are either under or overipe.. A small amount of very rich Sauternes is likely to emerge.

2002: This looks likely to be a good rather than a great year for reds. The year has turned out to be more successful in the Medoc, particularly Saint-Julien and to the north. It is predominantly a Cabernet Sauvignon year. Earlier-ripening Merlot was most hit by late September rains. Some very good whites were produced and this will be a good year too for Sauternes.

2001: After the magnificent 2000 red vintage this is a good, sometimes very good year for reds with once again an abundant crop. The style is sturdy, dense and with firm tannins and notable but not excessive acidity. These are classically structured wines rather than particularly ripe or opulent ones. Look for good wines on both the Left and Right Banks, including some fine examples from the lesser appellations. Sauternes and sweet wines in general look to be very impressive indeed. This could be the best vintage for botrytised wines since 1990. The dry whites were also close to exceptional.

2000: Quite simply a magnificent year for red Bordeaux. The crop was bountiful and the quality exceptional. The combination of a hot dry August followed by a long even and balmy ripening period throughout September provided the châteaux with perfect late-harvesting conditions. Grapes were picked full of deep colour, super-ripe, fine, supple tannins and intense and heady flavour. This is the best vintage since 1990 for reds throughout Bordeaux. While dry whites enjoyed conditions nearly as good, this was a disappointing year for Sauternes, with minimal quantities and low levels of botrytis, the warm weather paradoxically having a negative effect.

1999: A generally impressive year throughout the region for all wine styles with an impressively large crop, indeed the largest overall during the late 1990s. The summer was good, with warm consistent weather, however early rains in September meant that there was some variation. Those châteaux who went for maximum ripeness and harvested late did well. Whites have generally been good and were harvested before the rain, whereas Sauternes had a successful late harvest and some splendid wines have been produced.

1998: There was a lot of late September rain in the Médoc and quality is variable. To the south Graves fared a little better but it was mainly earlier-ripening Merlot on the Right Bank that did best, producing wines with suppler and riper tannins. Dry whites were good and generally harvested in ideal weather. Sauternes was also very good although the crop was tiny.

1997: A generally trying year, the one exception being Sauternes, which produced its best vintage since 1990. Quantities, though, were small, which kept upward pressure on prices. Indeed, considering the overall quality of the vintage it was surprising that the Bordelais managed to get away with hyping prices as much as they did. The top châteaux, who were rigorous in their selection, produced the best results. The dry whites were generally average to good but some properties harvested grapes lacking in full flavour development and many of these wines should now be drunk.

1996: This was another year when the Bordeaux money men should have been singing the praises of the gods. It was the second very large harvest in a row, a trend that was to continue through to the millennium. It was also a year of great wines in the Médoc, particularly in the northern appellations. The Right Bank fared less well, being hit by rain just as the Merlot ripened. Late-harvested Cabernet Sauvignon was consistently more successful. Very good dry whites were produced and the best wines are drinking well now. Sauternes had its best year since 1990. The wines are rich, heady and very intense.

1995: A good, indeed very good year for both Left and Right Bank. The harvest was reasonably consistent and although there was some rain during Setember it was not heavy enough to cause real problems with ripening. The results were very good in Pauillac and Saint-Julien and the wines are not only classically structured but have rich ripe fruit as well. The lesser reds are now beginning to drink well, the top wines need more time. There were some good dry whites and these are now drinking well. However Sauternes was generally disappointing.

1994: After a warm and at times hot, dry summer had promised much, September turned out to be a great disappointment, with persistent rain. Careful control during selection and throughout vinification produced generally agreeable reds on both Right and Left Banks. Many top wines are now beginning to drink well. It was a good year for dry whites and the top wines will still be showing well. Lesser white Pessac-Léognan should now be drunk. This was a dismal year in Sauternes.

1993: This was a disappointing vintage throughout the region with a wet harvest for all styles. The odd decent result emerged on both Banks and these wines should now be drunk. Sauternes was disastrous.

1992: A very disappointing year in the Médoc, while slightly better on the Right Bank.

1991: Much of France was hit by severe spring frosts and Bordeaux was no exception. The yield was poor and the resulting wines lacked substance.

1990: The finest red wine vintage since 1982. Also impressively good for dry whites, some of the very best are still drinking well now. It was exceptional for Sauternes. The weather was remarkably even up to and throughout the harvest and the wines consequently had exceptional balance. Most reds, apart from the very top growths, are drinking now but will continue to develop.

1989: This was generally a very good year, producing excellent reds on both banks, the only question mark being excessive ripeness. The wines turned out to have considerable extract and fruit but not entirely perfect balance. Sweet wines were very good and many are now drinking well.

1988: A good rather than great year. The top wines turned out well. The reds are classically structured and restrained and in general will continue to drink well for at least another decade. Excellent Sauternes, which is drinking and will continue to develop harmoniously.

1986: A great vintage in the Médoc with many harmonious long-lived wines. More patchy on the Right Bank though. A very fine year for Sauternes as well.

1985: Good for both Left and Right Banks but exceeded by the quality of the 1986s.

1983:-Dependable for both Banks. Some exceptional Margaux's. Very top wines will keep.

1982: This was a classic year with many superb reds being made. The Médocs look to have turned out better than those from the Right Bank.

For older vintages great Médocs from 1978 and 1970 are superb, the best will evolve further. A handful of 1975s have turned out very well. 1966 was good in the Médoc. 1964 might be worth a look for top Saint-Émilion or Pomerol. 1961 was a classic and many wines are still excellent. You could also consider 1959, 55, 49, 47, 45 and if you're exceptionally adventurous 35 or 28. Bear in mind that the provenance of the wine is as important as anything if you are acquiring very old vintages.

Bordeaux vintage chart

	Northern Médoc inc Saint-Èstephe, Paulliac, Saint-Julien	Southern Médoc inc Margaux	Red Graves	White Graves
2003	★★★★/★★★★★ A	★★★★ A	★★★★ A	★★★★ A
2002	★★★★ A	★★★/★★★★ A	★★★★ A	★★★★ A
2001	★★★/★★★★ A	★★★/★★★★ A	★★★/★★★★ A	★★★★/★★★★★ A
2000	★★★★★ A	★★★★★ A	★★★★★ A	★★★★ A
1999	★★★/★★★★ A	★★★/★★★★ A	★★★/★★★★ A	★★★★ B
1998	★★★/★★★★ A	★★★/★★★★ A	★★★★ A	★★★★/★★★★★ B
1997	★★★ B	★★★ B	★★★ B	★★★★ C
1996	★★★★/★★★★★ A	★★★★ A	★★★★ B	★★★★ C
1995	★★★★ A	★★★★ B	★★★★ B	★★★/★★★★ C
1990	★★★★★ B	★★★★★ B	★★★★ C	★★★★/★★★★★ C
1989	★★★★ C	★★★★ C	★★★★ C	★★★/★★★★ C
1988	★★★★ B	★★★/★★★★ C	★★★★ C	★★★★ D
1986	★★★★/★★★★★ C	★★★★ C	★★★★ C	★★★ D
1985	★★★★ C	★★★★ C	★★★★ C	-
1982	★★★★★ C	★★★★/★★★★★ C	★★★★★ C	-

	Saint-Émilion	Pomerol	Sauternes
2003	★★★★ A	★★★★ A	★★★★/★★★★★ A
2002	★★★/★★★★ A	★★★/★★★★ A	★★★★/★★★★★ A
2001	★★★★ A	★★★★ A	★★★★/★★★★★ A
2000	★★★★★ A	★★★★★ A	★★ A
1999	★★★/★★★★ A	★★★/★★★★ A	★★★★ A
1998	★★★★ A	★★★★/★★★★★ A	★★★★ A
1997	★★★ B	★★★ B	★★★★ A
1996	★★★/★★★★ B	★★★/★★★★ B	★★★★/★★★★★ B
1995	★★★★ B	★★★★ B	★★★/★★★★ B
1990	★★★★★ B	★★★★★ B	★★★★ C
1989	★★★★/★★★★★ C	★★★★/★★★★★ C	★★★★ C
1988	★★★★ C	★★★★ C	★★★★★ C
1986	★★★/★★★★ C	★★★/★★★★ C	★★★★/★★★★★ C
1985	★★★★ C	★★★★ C	★★★★ C
1982	★★★★★ C	★★★★★ C	★★★ D

Médoc, Graves & Sauternes

CH. D'AGASSAC Haut-Médoc www.agassac.com   A:AAA

Owner: Groupama 33290 Ludon-Médoc
Things are taking a turn for better at this medium-sized operation based in the southern part of the
Haut-Médoc and owned by the insurance company Groupama. The wine is now showing good depth and
some attractive dark fruit notes and harmonious tannins. A medium-weight style, better with five or six
years' ageing. Good in 2000 and 99, a little less impressive in 98. (DM)
● **Château d'Agassac** Haut-Médoc★★ £C

CH. D'ANGLUDET Margaux www.chateau-dangludet.fr   A:AAA

Owner: Sichel family 33460 Cantenac
Well-established Cru Bourgeois with 25-year-old vineyards planted to Cabernet Sauvignon, Merlot and
Petit Verdot, which comes from the oldest parcel of vines and adds extra character. The emphasis at the
property is to achieve a natural balance in the vineyard and this shows through in the quality of the wine
which is medium-weight with refinement and finesse. There is a second label, La Ferme d'Angludet, and a
rosé, Clairet d'Angludet. Impressive in 2001 and 00 but the wines have generally shown more class in the
late 90s. (DM)
● **Château d'Angludet** Margaux★★★ £D

CH. D'ARCHE Sauternes 2ème CC

Owner: Pierre Perromat 33210 Sauternes
Only around 5,000 cases a year are produced here from 29 ha. This is reasonably impressive, full and
concentrated Sauternes with a generally good performance in the most favourable vintages over the two
decades since Pierre Perromat became involved. Harvesting is as selective as necessary, and a portion of new
oak is used to age the wine. Good in 2001 and 00; 98 and 97 are also worth seeking out. (DM)
O **Château d'Arche** Sauternes★★★ £E

CH. D'ARMAILHAC Pauillac 5ème CC www.bpdr.com   A:AAA

Owner: Baron Philippe de Rothschild SA 33250 Pauillac
Like its prestigious neighbour MOUTON ROTHSCHILD this château is also owned by Baronne Philippine
de Rothschild. At its best, in years like 2000, 99, 98 and 95, this medium-sized property is undoubtedly
producing three-star Pauillac. When conditions are less favourable, though, the wine struggles a little.
Grown in relatively light soils the wine is structured but not overly so, retaining some of the marked cassis
and cedar notes of its big brother, and will provide good drinking at six or seven years. (DM)
● **Château d'Armailhac** Pauillac★★★ £D

CH. BASTOR-LAMONTAGNE Sauternes www.bastor-lamontagne.com

Owner: Michel Garat 33210 Preignac
A consistently fine, small to medium-sized operation which has performed admirably over a long period,
providing the essence of Sauternes at an affordable price. As well as Sémillon and Sauvignon Blanc, Michel
Garat has just a small amount of Muscadelle to add aroma. The wine is barrel-fermented for an extended
three to four weeks with around 15 per cent new oak to lend structure and shows classic honeyed, peachy
botrytis character even in lesser years. Look out for 1998, 97 and 96. 2001 also looks very promising. The
second wine produced from young vines is Les Remparts de Bastor. (DM)
● **Château Bastor-Lamontagne** Sauternes★★★ £E

CH. BATAILLEY Pauillac 5ème CC   A: AAA

Owner: Héritiers Castéja 33250 Pauillac
A consistently reasonably priced Fifth Growth, Batailly is a wine that has performed reliably throughout the 1990s but never more than that. Good classic blackcurrant and cedar notes can be found, and the wine has sufficient oak with creamy vanilla notes and a supple texture aided by malolactic in barrel. Good without great depth or real complexity. (DM)

● **Château Batailley** Pauillac★★ £D

CH. BEL AIR MARQUIS D'ALIGRE Margaux   A: AAA

Owner: Jean-Pierre Boyer 33460 Soussans
Cru Bourgeois property that has been performing impressively in recent years. This small château consists of just 13 ha with a surprisingly high (35 per cent) proportion of Merlot. Production is low at less than 3,000 cases a year. Low volume, a careful control of yields and meticulously tended vineyards all contribute to the consistently excellent results achieved here. The wine is a refined medium-weight, rather than blockbuster style, a proper Margaux with a real fruit intensity and stylish perfume. Very good in 1998, 96, 95 and in the great 1990 vintage. (DM)

● **Château Bel Air Marquis d'Aligre** Margaux★★★ £D

CH. BELGRAVE Haut-Médoc 5ème CC   A: **Dou**,AAA

*Owner: **Vignobles Dourthe** 33112 Saint-Laurent-de-Médoc*
Purchased by Vignobles Dourthe in 1980, it was only with the 1998 vintage that this property really began to forge ahead. During the past two decades the vineyard has been replanted. Cabernet Sauvignon dominates the blend, with a tiny amount of Petit Verdot. Now that the vines are maturing, the wine is evolving from the straightforward, essentially fruit-driven style of the early to mid-1990s to one where there is real depth and refinement. It represents particularly good value for money. (DM)

● **Château Belgrave** Haut-Médoc★★★ £D

CH. BEYCHEVELLE Saint-Julien 4ème CC www.beychevelle.com   A: AAA

*Owner: **SC Grands Millésimes de France** 33250 Saint-Julien-Beychevelle*
Beychevelle is a sizeable property with 90 ha of vineyards planted to Cabernet Sauvignon, Merlot, Cabernet Franc and a little Petit Verdot. It is a Classed Growth with a reasonable, rather than spectacular track record over recent years. At its best the wine shows real finesse, splendid purity of fruit and very subtle oak, not full and powerful but more refined and elegant. Choose your vintage with a bit of caution and avoid lesser years. Amiral de Beychevelle, the second wine, is entitled to the Saint-Julien AC, while Les Brulières-de-Beychevelle is from vineyards in the Haut-Médoc. (DM)

● **Château Beychevelle** Saint-Julien★★★ £E

CH. BOYD-CANTENAC Margaux 3ème CC www.boyd-cantenac.fr   A: AAA

Owner: Lucien Guillemet 33460 Margaux
This Third Growth property is turning out very good elegant Margaux. This was not always so. Boyd-Cantenac spent decades in the doldrums and would not have been on anyone's shopping list until the vintages of the late 1990s, which have shown a marked turn for the better. An increasing use of new oak – up to 60 per cent – and, since 1997, no filtration has contributed to this improvement. The wine is fragrant and supple with attractive dark berry fruit and an increasing richness. The rating applies to vintages from 1998 on. (DM)

● **Château Boyd-Cantenac** Margaux★★★ £E

CH. BRANAIRE Saint-Julien 4ème CC www.branaire.com A: AAA

Owner: Patrick Maroteaux 33250 Saint-Julien

For a long time this was a seriously underachieving property. However there has been a significant turnaround here during the last six or seven years. Investment in the cellar, along with a commitment to quality that avoids filtration and employs only limited egg-white fining and racking by gravity, is undoubtedly paying off. The style has moved from light to much fuller and richer. The Cabernet Sauvignon component now really shows and the wines are sturdier and denser with much greater depth and power. Almost all the vintages since 1994 have impressed. 1995, 96, 98 and 99 are all on the cusp of four stars. (DM)

● **Château Branaire** Saint-Julien★★★ £F

CH. BRANE-CANTENAC Margaux 2ème CC www.lucienlurton.com A: AAA

Owner: Domaines Lucien Lurton & Fils 33460 Margaux

Since the late 1990s Brane-Cantenac has been showing real evidence of its status as a Second Growth. After 1996 the only vintage which has disappointed has been the 97. The wine is a classic blend of Cabernet Sauvignon, Merlot and Cabernet Franc with intense, cedary Margaux perfume, subtle oak and sheer class and intensity. Domaines Lucien Lurton also own a number of other important châteaux, among them CLIMENS in Barsac, DURFORT-VIVENS in Margaux and BOUSCAUT in Pessac-Léognan. 1999 is particularly fine. The second wine, Baron de Brane, is of decent quality. (DM)

● **Château Branaire** Margaux★★★★ £F ● **Baron de Brane**★★ £D

CH. CAILLOU Sauternes 2ème CC www.chateaucaillou.fr A: AAA

Owner: Michel & Marie-Josée Pierre 33720 Barsac

This is one of those confusingly labelled properties which takes the Sauternes AC although it is located in Barsac. There are two *cuvées* of the principal wine, the regular Caillou and a barrel selection, La Private Cuvée, produced in top years such as 1995, 97 and 99. Fermentation is in a mix of new oak and *inox* and ageing is between 18 and 24 months with a marked new oak component. This is an intense and heady sweet white but inevitably the regular Caillou suffers in those vintages when La Private Cuvée is released. A second wine, Château Haut-Mayne, is also produced. (DM)

O **Château Caillou** Sauternes★★★ £E

CH. CALON-SÉGUR Saint-Estèphe 2ème CC A: AAA

Owner: Denise Capbern-Gasqueton 33180 Saint-Estèphe

Like many Bordeaux properties Calon-Ségur has shown a marked upturn in quality during the late 1990s. As well as a more meticulous approach in the vineyard, which has resulted in a reduced crop, the objective in the winemaking has been to produce an altogether suppler, more harmonious style. The wine achieves this and is both opulent and modern with weight, concentration and power. It has a much more velvety texture than of old. Very good since 1996 and seemingly improving with the vintages since 2000. Only below par in 97 and 99. (DM)

● **Château Calon-Ségur** Saint-Estèphe★★★★ £F

CH. CAMENSAC Haut-Médoc 5ème CC www.chateaucamensac.com A: AAA

Owner: Forner family Route de Saint-Julien, 33112 Saint-Laurent-de-Médoc

The quality of this property has gradually improved since it was acquired in 1964 by the Forner family. Much of the vineyard has been replanted and there is now a relatively high proportion of Merlot (25 per cent) contributing to the style, which is round, forward and accessible. The wine drinks well at five years or so. Just a notch up in 1999 and 00. (DM)

● **Château Camensac** Haut-Médoc★★ £D

CH. CANTEMERLE Haut-Médoc 5ème CC www.chateau-cantemerle.com A: AAA

Owner: Philippe Dambrine 33460 Macau
The 87 ha at Cantemerle are planted to a mix of 50 per cent Cabernet Sauvignon and, unusually for the Left Bank, a whopping 40 per cent Merlot, with the remaining 10 per cent divided evenly between Cabernet Franc and Petit Verdot. Production is sizeable, with 50,000 cases produced annually. After significant replanting two decades ago the vine age is beginning to show and this together with the high proportion of Merlot provides a rich, vibrantly dark-fruited Médoc at its best. The very latest vintages are promising and 1998 and 96 are good. It has to be said, though, that the wine has not performed well in lesser years, particularly in the early 1990s. (DM)
● **Château Cantemerle** Haut-Médoc★★ £E

CH. CANTENAC-BROWN Margaux 5ème CC www.cantenacbrown.com A: AAA

Owner: AXA Millésimes 33460 Cantenac
Purchased in 1987 by AXA Millésimes, which also owns a number of other prestigious Bordeaux properties including PICHON-LONGUEVILLE and SUDUIRAUT in Sauternes. Quality has been disappointing throughout the 1970s, 80s and, with the exception of 1990, the 90s prior to 96. The rating is for its current performance rather than earlier vintages and, given the performance of other châteaux within the AXA group, one would expect things here to continue to improve. (DM)
● **Château Cantenac-Brown** Margaux★★★ £E

CH. CARBONNIEUX Pessac-Léognan CC A: F&R,N&P,Tur

Owner: Antony Perrin 33850 Léognan
Good rather than memorable red and white Pessac-Léognans. Production is substantial for the appellation at over 30,000 cases a year. The white is good and has performed well throughout the 1990s. Some skin contact is allowed before fermentation in barrel, around half of which is new, and ageing is on lees. The red doesn't quite reach the same level but has also been consistent over recent vintages. Sound, well-crafted and approachable, it is lighter than other Pessac-Léognan reds but displays attractive berry fruit and a fine mineral undercurrent. Both white and red will benefit from five years' bottle-ageing. Château Haut-Vigneau is another solid property producing decent red under the AC and there is a second wine, La Tour Léognan, produced in both red and white. The latter can often impress. (DM)
● **Château Carbonnieux** Pessac-Léognan★★ £E ● **Château Haut-Vigneau** Pessac-Léognan★ £D
O **Château Carbonnieux** Pessac-Léognan★★★ £E

CH. LES CARMES HAUT-BRION Pessac-Léognan A:AAA

Owner: Chantecaille-Furt family 197 Avenue Jean Cordier33600 Pessac
This a tiny property and, like HAUT-BRION, located amongst the suburbs of Bordeaux. Just 4.5 ha are under vine, with an unusually high proportion of 50 per cent Merlot, along with 40 per cent Cabernet Sauvignon amd 10 per cent Cabernet Franc. Dedication to quality has delivered impressive results in the late 1990s. Vinification in small vats enables plots within the vineyard to be fermented separately. Malolactic takes place in barrel and around one-third new wood is used. The wine is supple and rich, with firm but nicely rounded tannins. (DM)
● **Château les Carmes Haut-Brion** Pessac-Léognan★★★ £E

CH. DE CHANTEGRIVE Graves www.chateau-chantegrive.com

Owner: Henri Lévèque 33720 Podensac
This property consists of 50 ha of red varieties and 38 ha of white, with production now quite substantial at over 40,000 cases a year. Four wines are produced. A good red with a fine balance of dark fruit, cedar and subtle oak is joined by a regular white Graves, an easy, fruit-driven style fermented at low temperatures.

There is also the limited production Cuvée Caroline, barrel-fermented in a portion of new oak with regular use of *bâtonnage* to add weight and a rich, creamy texture. The sweet Cérons is a full, fat style with good depth and some honeyed complexity. (DM)

● **Château de Chantegrive** Graves★★ £C
O **Château de Chantegrive** Graves★ £B Cuvée Caroline★★★ £C
O **Château de Chantegrive** Cérons★★ £C

CH. CHARMAIL   Haut-Médoc   A:AAA

Owner: Olivier Seze   33180 Saint-Seurin-de-Cadourne
A consistent performer during the last five or six vintages, located just to the north of Saint-Estèphe. The wine, which has a high proportion of Merlot (55 per cent of the vineyard) is modern and stylish. Neither fined nor filtered, it is marked by supple tannin and attractive, forward, dark berry fruit and hints of cassis, not least as a result of a touch of pre-fermentation maceration. There are none of the often green and herbaceous notes found in some lesser Bordeaux reds dominated by the variety. (DM)

● **Château Charmail** Haut-Médoc★★★ £D

CH. CHASSE-SPLEEN   Moulis   www.chasse-spleen.com   A:AAA

Owner: Céline Villars-Foubet   33480 Moulis-en-Médoc
Chasse-Spleen, along with POUJEAUX and MAUCAILLOU, is one of the only wines in the Moulis AC really to perform with any consistent class. The property is sizeable, with just under 85 ha under vine. The wine is a blend of Cabernet Sauvignon, Merlot and Petit Verdot. With the odd exceptions (1997, 94 and 91) this property has fashioned a rich, concentrated and harmonious red. The 2001, 00 and 99 are noteworthy. It's a shame there aren't more properties turning out wines of this class in the appellation. The second wine, L'Ermitage de Chasse-Spleen, can be better than most. (DM)

● **Château Chasse-Spleen** Moulis★★★ £E

DOM. DE CHEVALIER   Pessac-Léognan CC   www.domainedechevalier.com   A: AAA

Owner: Olivier Bernard   102 Chemin de Mignoy, 33850 Léognan
An important and sizeable producer, noted particularly for its splendid white. The production of this is very low, with just 4.5 of the 37.5 ha vineyard planted to Sauvignon Blanc and Sémillon. There is a high proportion of Sauvignon (70 per cent) in the blend. Barrel-fermented and aged, it is a remarkably fine and elegant white capable of considerable age. The red has been less impressive than the white in recent years but since 1996 there has been a fair step up in quality and the wine has regularly been of four-star quality. In short, solid and ageworthy and reasonable value. (DM)

● **Domaine de Chevalier** Pessac-Léognan★★★★ £E
O **Domaine de Chevalier** Pessac-Léognan✪✪✪✪✪ £F

CH. CISSAC   Haut-Médoc   www.chateau-cissac.com   A:AAA

Owner: Danielle Viallard   33250 Cissac-Médoc
Cissac is still made in a traditional, firm Médoc style but it is very fairly priced and generally well-crafted. But, although structured and austere when very young, it is increasingly rounder and suppler than of old with a little age. Wooden as well as stainless steel vats are used for fermentation and an increasing amount of new wood (30 to 40 per cent) is used to age the wine. From the best vintages the wine is undoubtedly complex and harmonious but really needs cellaring for eight to ten years to show at its best. (DM)

● **Château Cissac** Haut-Médoc★★★ £C

CH. CLARKE   Listrac-Médoc   chateau.clarke@wanadoo.fr

Owner: Baron Benjamin de Rothschild   33480 Listrac
Listrac, like Moulis, is quite a long way inland from the Gironde and the soil here has even less gravel than it does nearer the estuary, which will always hinder the admirable efforts made here. This property with increasingly old vines outclasses almost all of its neighbours but there remains a slightly coarse note. However, since 1995 the wine is more concentrated and harmonious, while retaining its soft and supple, earthy, dark fruit character. (DM)

● **Château Clarke** Listrac-Médoc★★ £C

CH. CLERC-MILON   Pauillac 5ème CC   www.bpdr.com   A: AAA

*Owner: **Baron Philippe de Rothschild SA**   33250 Pauillac*
Moderate-sized property, with some 30 ha of vineyards and production running at just under 15,000 cases a year. The Cabernet Sauvignon component is quite low at less than 50 per cent and 35 per cent of the vineyard is planted to Merlot. As a result the style is very rounded and surprisingly approachable for Pauillac. While overshadowed by its sister château and neighbour MOUTON-ROTHSCHILD, Clerc-Milon is nevertheless an excellent, stylish source of the appellation, with a harmonious mix of dark fruits and cedar, all of which is nicely underpinned by its ripe and plummy Merlot component. At its current level since 1995. (DM)

● **Château Clerc-Milon** Pauillac★★★★ £F

CH. CLIMENS   Barsac 1er CC   www.chateau-climens.fr   A: AAA

Owner: Bérénice Lurton   33720 Barsac
Climens is an exceptional sweet wine and the leading property in the Barsac commune. It is outclassed only by Château d'YQUEM amongst the great botrytised wines of the Sauternes. Production is low at just over 3,000 cases a year and the vineyard, which is just 29 ha, is planted solely to Sémillon. Despite the absence of Sauvignon Blanc the wine possesses not only intense and very concentrated honeyed fruit but a marvellously fresh acid balance as well. Best to age it for at least five years and it will be better with twice that time in the cellar. The wine was truly great in 1998, 96, 90, 88 and 86. A few hundred cases are also produced under the Doisy-Dubroca label. (DM)

● **Château Climens** Barsac✪✪✪✪✪ £G

CLOS FLORIDÈNE   Graves   www.denisdubourdieu.com   A: F&R,Dec

Owner: Denis & Florence Dubourdieu   21 Route de Cardan, 33410 Beguey
The main focus is on white wine, with 13 ha planted as opposed to 5.5 ha for red varieties. The white is a particularly impressive example and puts many more exalted Pessac-Léognans to shame. It is barrel-fermented and aged with *bâtonnage* to add richness but it is the citrus and mineral quality of the fruit that really marks it out. It will evolve nicely over the short to medium term. The red is sound and well-crafted but lacks the same excitement. Denis Dubourdieu also produces the wines of Château REYNON. (DM)

● **Clos Floridène** Graves★ £C
O **Clos Floridène** Graves★★★ £C

CH. CLOS HAUT-PEYRAGUEY   Sauternes 1er CC   A: AAA

Owner: J & J. Pauly   33210 Bommes
Very small Sauternes property. There are just 12 ha of vineyards, 90 per cent of which are Sémillon, the balance Sauvignon Blanc. Quality is good to very good but the wine just lacks the depth and intensity of the best of the other First Growths of the appellation. The style is more one of finesse and elegance than sheer weight and concentration. Very good in 2001, 98, 97, 90 and 88, while other years are not quite of

the same order. The second wine is Château Haut Bommes. (DM)

● **Château Clos Haut-Peyraguey** Sauternes★★★ £E

CH. COS D'ESTOURNEL Saint-Estèphe 2ème CC www.estournel.com A: AAA

Owner: Taillan group 33180 Saint-Estèphe

One of the greatest wines of the Médoc and the premier château in Saint-Estèphe. Purchased from Bruno Prats by the Taillan Group, who also own GRUAUD-LAROSE, in 1998. Jean-Guillaume Prats remains in charge of the property and it is to be hoped that the Prats family's exceptional standards here throughout the 1970s, 80s and 90s will be maintained. However, the vintages of the late 1990s and 2000 have not reached the usual exemplary standards. Using sophisticated vinification including must concentration, malolactic in barrel and new oak for ageing, the wine is very powerful as well as opulent. It should, however, show remarkable depth and harmony with a decade or more in the cellar. The second wine was originally called MARBUZET, which is itself a Cru Bourgeois, but is now labelled Les Pagodes de Cos. The former has regularly been at one to two stars throughout the 1990s. (DM)

● **Château Cos d'Estournel** Saint-Estèphe❂❂❂❂❂ £G

CH. COS LABORY Saint-Estèphe 5ème CC cos-labory@wanadoo.fr A: THt,AAA

Owner: Bernard Audoy 33180 Saint-Estèphe

Although overshadowed by its famous neighbour COS D'ESTOURNEL, this property improved greatly in the late 1980s and some of the vintages since have been impressive. 1996, 95, 90 and 88 were all a notch up on what has generally been achieved here over the last 12 to 15 years. The late 1990s have somewhat disappointingly not maintained this level but the wine looks promising once more in the 2002 and 03 vintages. At its best the wine is full, marked by impressive blackcurrant fruit and underpinned by a firm, rounded, tannic structure. (DM)

● **Château Cos Labory** Saint-Estèphe★★★ £E

CH. COUHINS-LURTON Pessac-Léognan CC ww.andrelurton.com A: AAA

Owner: Les Vignobles André Lurton 33420 Grézillac

André Lurton is now a major proprietor in the Graves, Entre-Deux-Mers and Margaux. At this tiny 5.5-ha Pessac property he produces less than 2,000 cases of very stylish white a year from Sauvignon Blanc. No Sémillon is planted here but the wine is barrel-fermented in 50 per cent new wood and aged with *bâtonnage* and has the structure and density to age well in bottle. Both 1999 and 2000 were particularly good examples. (DM)

O **Château Couhins-Lurton** Pessac-Léognan★★★ £E

CH. COUTET Barsac 1er CC A: AAA

Owner: Baly family 33720 Barsac

Very good property and near neighbour of CLIMENS, although the wine here doesn't quite reach the same heights. As well as Sémillon, which accounts for 75 per cent of the blend, and Sauvignon Blanc, there is a little Muscadelle, just 3 per cent. There is no doubt that there is a marked aromatic character in the wine in addition to its classic rich vanilla and peach notes. In exceptional years a special super-concentrated Cuvée Madame is released. This is certainly of super-five quality. (DM)

O **Château Coutet** Barsac★★★★ £F

CH. DAUZAC Margaux 5ème CC www.andrelurton.com A: CRs

Owner: Les Vignobles André Lurton 33460 Labarde

Another André Lurton-controlled property. There are 46 ha under vine here and production is just shy of 25,000 cases, so it is a sizeable operation. The style is supple and rich with an emphasis on approachable dark fruit and well-judged oak. The wine is only kept in barrel for 12 months but 50 to 80 per cent is new. Quality has improved dramatically since the 1990s. (DM)

● **Château Dauzac** Margaux★★★ £E

CH. DOISY-DAËNE   Barsac 2ème CC   www.denisdubourdieu.com   A: AAA

Owner: Pierre & Denis Dubourdieu   33720 Barsac

This is a Barsac marked by its elegance rather than its sheer weight or richness. It can be piercingly aromatic, though, and very intense. Of a completely different order – richer and fuller – is an occasional very limited *cuvée* called L'Extravagance. It is only produced in exceptional vintages, including 2001, 97 and 96. As well as the sweet wines a good dry Bordeaux Blanc is rich and fruity. (DM)

O **Château Doisy-Daëne** Barsac★★★ £E   O **Bordeaux**★★ £C

CH. DOISY-VÉDRINES   Barsac 2ème CC   A: AAA

Owner: Pierre Castéja   1 Rue Védrines, 33720 Barsac

This is the biggest of the three Doisy properties with 27 ha. In contrast to DOISY-DAENE and most other fine Barsacs, this property tends to produce wine with more overt luscious honeyed fruit. It is very impressive, retaining an elegant finesse in lighter years when the wine carries less sheer weight. There is 5 per cent Muscadelle planted here, which provides an aromatic undercurrent to the wine. (DM)

● **Château Doisy-Védrines** Sauternes★★★★ £E

CH. DUCRU-BEAUCAILLOU   Saint-Julien 2ème CC   A: AAA

Owner: Borie family   33250 Saint-Julien-Beychevelle

One of the greatest wines of Saint-Julien. The 50 ha of Ducru based in the south of the appellation are planted to a mix of Cabernet Sauvignon (65 per cent), Merlot (25 per cent), and an equal portion of Cabernet Franc and Petit Verdot. It is a very impressive, classically structured example of the appellation: always elegant, very intense, with subtle cedar and dark fruit underpinned by finely integrated oak. It requires patience and cellaring. From the current crop of excellent vintages 2000, 1998, 96 and 95 were exemplary but 97 was something of a disappointment. (DM)

● **Château Ducru-Beaucaillou** Saint-Julien✪✪✪✪✪ £H

CH. DUHART-MILON   Pauillac 4ème CC   www.lafite.com   A: AAA

*Owner: **Domaines Barons de Rothschild/Chalone Wine Group**   33250 Pauillac*

Intriguingly, this Rothschild property is also part-owned by the Chalone Wine Group from the USA, which established its reputation with the CHALONE winery in Monterey, California. There is no doubt that the 50 ha of vineyards have benefited greatly from the Lafite input since the property was purchased in 1962. Fermentation is modern in stainless steel and ageing taking place in barrels, 50 per cent new, that are coopered at Lafite-Rothschild. 1999, 98 and 96 were all nudging four-star quality. (DM)

● **Château Duhart-Milon** Pauillac★★★ £E

CH. FERRIÈRE   Margaux 3ème CC   www.ferriere.com

Owner: Merlaut family   33460 Margaux

Small Classed Growth which has improved dramatically during the 1990s. Production is barely more than 4,000 cases a year and the dedicated commitment to quality here by Claire Villars (aided by the Merlaut family who run the Taillan group, owners of COS D'ESTOURNEL and GRUAUD-LAROSE) has ensured that this is one of the best properties in the Margaux appellation. The wine is rich, intense and concentrated and now shows great harmony and refinement. There is minimal processing with egg-white fining and malolactic in barrel. The wine comfortably absorbs the impact of 60 per cent new oak. (DM)

● **Château Ferrière** Margaux★★★★ £E

CH. DE FIEUZAL Pessac-Léognan CC www.fieuzal.com   A: THt, AAA

Owner: Lachlann Quinn   124 Avenue de Mont-de-Marsan, 33850 Léognan
The style here, particularly with the red, is to produce opulent, richly textured, forward, modern and approachable wines, accessible very shortly after release. The white, which unlike the red is not in fact a Cru Classé, also shows rich, forward, honeyed fruit with a solid dose of new oak but with a depth and structure that ensures good, medium-term cellaring and is the more impressive of the two. These wines, particularly the whites, offer very good value. (DM)

● **Château de Fieuzal** Pessac-Léognan★★★ £E
O **Château de Fieuzal** Pessac-Léognan★★★★ £E

CH. DE FRANCE Pessac-Léognan

Owner: Bernard Thomassin   33850 Léognan
Inproving medium-sized Pessac property of some 35 ha. Just 3 ha of the vineyard is so far planted to white varieties, with Sauvignon accounting for 70 per cent and the balance Sémillon. Red grapes are 60 per cent Cabernet Sauvignon and 40 per cent Merlot. The quality of the wines has greatly improved since the late 1990s, particularly the red. In part this is due to the involvement of Michel Rolland who advises on the winemaking. Vinification is traditional with a fermentation temperature in the low 30s celsius and malolactic is conducted in *cuve*. Ageing is for 14 to 18 months in *barrique*. Medium-weight, with lightly cedary fruit the wine will add flesh with four or five years' age. The white, which is barrel-fermented with *bâtonnage* and bottled with a light filtration, doesn't have quite the depth of the red. (DM)

● **Château de France** Pessac-Léognan★★ £D
O **Château de France** Pessac-Léognan★ £C

CH. GISCOURS Margaux 2ème CC www.chateau-giscours.com   A: AAA

Owner: Eric Albada Jedgersma   10 Route de Giscours, 33460 Margaux
Giscours like du TERTRE is now in the ownership of Eric Albada Jedgersma and similarly has been performing at a much improved level in recent vintages. Investment in the vineyard and cellars with reduced yields and careful vinification has produced some impressive examples. The property is sizeable and covers 85 ha of vineyards planted to Cabernet Sauvignon (55 per cent), Merlot (40 per cent) and Cabernet Franc. Despite the high proportion of Merlot the wine, at its recent best, is richly textured, powerful and less obviously perfumed than other examples of the appellation. Two secondary wines are produced which both offer some of the character of the Grand Vin. Sirene de Giscours takes the Margaux appellation and there is a budget label, Haut-Médoc de Giscours. The top wine will add increasing richness with 8 to 10 years' age. (DM)

● **Château Giscours** Margaux★★★★ £E

CH. GLORIA Saint-Julien   A: AAA

Owner: Triaud family   33250 Saint-Julien-Beychevelle
This has been a consistently sound Cru Bourgeois over the years. Gloria has performed admirably throughout the 1970s, 80s and 90s. It is a sizeable property, with widely scattered plots, with some 47 ha under vine producing around 25,000 cases a year. The wine is not immensely complex or long-lived but is full of vibrant, dark, brambly blackcurrant fruit, nicely judged oak and an elegant hint of cedar in the background. (DM)

● **Château Gloria** Saint-Julien★★ £D

CH. GRAND-PUY-LACOSTE Pauillac 5ème CC   A: AAA

Owner: Borie family 33250 Pauillac
Under the same ownership as DUCRU-BEAUCAILLOU, this has been an admirable and classic red Bordeaux for the past three decades and there have been many admirable vintages since World War II. This is the quintessential example of what you expect from fine Pauillac, a wine loaded with cassis and cedar, refined and elegant but with real power and density. 1990, and more recently 95 and 96, are wines of significant class and 2000 looks very much of the same order. (DM)
● **Château Grand-Puy-Lacoste** Pauillac★★★★ £F

CH. GRUAUD-LAROSE Saint-Julien 2ème CC   A: AAA

Owner: Taillan group 33250 Saint-Julien-Beychevelle
Large Saint-Julien property with production approaching 40,000 cases a year, responsible for some formidable and massively structured wines during the 1980s. 1982 and 86 were without a doubt of super-five star quality, with a number of others on the cusp. Quality generally has remained impressive throughout the 1990s but not at quite the same level. These are powerful, dense and tannic reds in need of at least 8 to 10 years' cellaring. The second wine, Sarget de Gruaud-Larose, can be good, particularly in better years. (DM)
● **Château Gruaud-Larose** Saint-Julien★★★★ £F

CH. GUIRAUD Sauternes 1er CC www.chateauguiraud.fr   A: AAA

Owner: Narby family 33210 Sauternes
Xavier Planty, in charge of production here, turned out impressive Sauternes in the top vintages of the 1990s. A consistent replanting process has much improved the ratio of Sémillon to Sauvignon Blanc and plantings of the former now account for 70 per cent of the vineyard. The result is wines of sometimes blockbuster proportions, rich, very honeyed and peachy, with spice and vanilla from new oak. It is not to all tastes, and on occasion more refinement would help. (DM)
O **Château Guiraud** Sauternes★★★★ £F

CH. HAUT-BAILLY Pessac-Léognan CC www.chateau-haut-bailly.com   A: RsW, AAA

Owner: Robert J Wilmers Route de Cadaujac, 33850 Léognan
A supple, elegant and consistently well-crafted red which is both approachable and refined. In contrast with most neighbouring properties, no white is made here. Haut-Bailly was purchased by Robert Wilmers, an American banker, in 1998 but the original proprietors, the Sanders family, are still involved in the direction and management. Consistent throughout the mid- to late 1990s. The wine ages very well indeed. (DM)
● **Château Haut-Bailly** Pessac-Léognan★★★★ £E

CH. HAUT-BATAILLEY Pauillac 5ème CC je-borie@je-borie-sa.com   A: AAA

Owner: Borie family 33250 Saint-Julien-Beychevelle
Under the same ownership as DUCRU-BEAUCAILLOU and GRAND-PUY-LACOSTE. Quality here used to be somewhat variable and lesser vintages were light and lacking in substance as well as possessing a hard, at times austerely firm edge. This was surprising given the quality of the other properties owned by the Borie family but the mid-1990s saw an improvement and change in style. The wine is now less aggressive and raw and possesses a fine, more supple and even texture. It is altogether more accessible and harmonious. Significantly more impressive in 1995 and 96 and 00 also looks very promising. (DM)
● **Château Haut-Batailley** Pauillac★★ £E

CH. HAUT-BRION Pessac-Léognan 1er CC www.haut-brion.com A: AAA

Owner: Domaine Clarence Dillon 33608 Pessac Cedex
One of the four original properties classified as a First Growth in the 1855 Classification of the red Bordeaux wines. The vineyards are planted in superbly drained gravel soils that provide an almost ideal supply of moisture to optimise fruit ripening. Reds grapes occupy 43 ha, while less than 3 ha provides a tiny amount of exquisite, subtly barrel-fermented white from Sémillon and Sauvignon Blanc. The property, now surrounded by the ever-encroaching suburbs of Bordeaux, is small in comparison to the other First Growths, producing a total of some 12,500 cases a year. Both red and white have been magnificent through the late 1990s, only the 1997 and 91 red dipping a little. Great older vintages include 1990, 89, 86, 82, 75 and the astonishing 61. The second wine, Le Bahans, can also be very impressive. (DM)

● **Château Haut-Brion** Pessac-Léognan❂❂❂❂❂ £H ● **Le Bahans Haut Brion**★★★ £E
O **Château Haut-Brion** Pessac-Léognan❂❂❂❂❂ £G

CH. HAUT-MARBUZET Saint-Estèphe A: PBW,Col

Owner: Henri Duboscq 33180 Saint-Estèphe
Henri Duboscq produces a fleshy, powerful, very rich Saint-Estèphe marked by well-integrated spicy new oak. Not only is this an outstanding Cru Bourgeois but it is only surpassed within the appellation by COS D'ESTOURNEL and MONTROSE. Production is not inconsiderable at close to 30,000 cases a year. The wine has been impressive in recent years, particularly from 2000 to the difficult 2002 vintage and has been performing comfortably out of its class. It offers very good value and there is a decent soft and forward second label, Chambert-Marbuzet. (DM)

● **Château Haut-Marbuzet** Saint-Estèphe★★★★ £E

CH. D'ISSAN Margaux 3ème CC www.chateau-issan.com A: AAA

Owner: Cruse family 33460 Cantenac
This property was often disappointing in the late 1980s and early 90s. However since 1995 things have been looking decidedly better and the wine is once more in the elegant, cedary and perfumed style that represents fine Margaux. Major investment in both vineyard and cellars and input on the winemaking from Jacques Boissenet (one of a number of high-profile Bordeaux consultants, who also advises André Lurton as well as the Napa Valley QUINTESSA operation) are clearly having a positive effect. (DM)

● **Château d'Issan** Margaux★★★ £E

CH. KIRWAN Margaux 3ème CC www.chateau-kirwan.com A: AAA

Owner: Schÿler family 33460 Cantenac
The Schÿler family, who also run the Schroder and Schÿler *négociant* operation in Bordeaux, had sold their interest in this small to medium-sized property in the early 1990s but promptly bought it back again a couple of years later. The result has been a real boost for the fortunes of the property and in particular the quality of the wine. Michel Rolland has provided guidance on the winemaking front and quality has been consistently good since 1996, if a touch overextracted in 98. (DM)

● **Château Kirwan** Margaux★★★ £E

CH. LAFAURIE-PEYRAGUEY Sauternes 1er CC A: AAA

Owner: Domaines Cordier 33210 Bommes
From 40 ha under vine in the commune of Bommes, with a grape mix of Sémillon (90 per cent), Sauvignon Blanc (8 per cent) and Muscadelle (just 2 per cent), some of the finest Sauternes is now being made at this property. This has only been the case for the last 15 years or so. The 1970s were a disappointment but the wines are now quite exemplary. They combine the intense richness and honeyed concentration of the finest

Sauternes with something of the elegance found in CLIMENS. The wines are very stylish and long-lived. The 1999, 98 and 97 are all extraordinarily fine super-fives and 2001 may have the potential to be exquisite. (DM)

● **Château Lafaurie-Peyraguey** Sauternes★★★★★ £F

CH. LAFITE-ROTHSCHILD   Pauillac 1er CC   www.lafite.com   A:AAA

*Owner: **Domaines Barons de Rothschild**   33250 Pauillac*

One of the world's great wines and a consistent and superlative performer throughout the mid- to late 1990s. The 2000, 98 and 96 are exceptional wines and 2003 shows similar promise, which is not surprising considering the quality of the vintage. However, all has not always been rosy here and 20 or so years ago the quality was much more uneven. The vineyard is planted to some 100 ha of Cabernet Sauvignon (75 per cent), Merlot (20 per cent), Cabernet Franc (4 per cent) and Petit Verdot (a mere 1 per cent). A minimum of 15 to 20 years is required to achieve a harmony between the formidable, powerful tannins and the intense and fragrantly rich cedar and cassis fruit. 1982 marked a real turning point in the quality of the wine and other years of particular note are 1986, 88 and 90. The 53 and 59 were both superb but surprisingly 61 failed to achieve the high quality of that year. The second wine, Les Carruades de Lafite-Rothschild, is very impressive for a second label. (DM)

● **Château Lafite-Rothschild** Pauillac✪✪✪✪✪ £H ● **Les Carruades de Lafite-Rothschild**★★★★ £F

CH. LAFON-ROCHET   Saint-Estèphe 4ème CC   A:AAA

Owner: Tesseron family   33180 Saint-Estèphe

Under the same ownership as PONTET-CANET, Lafon-Rochet has performed well, sometimes very well throughout the mid- to late 1990s. The vintages of the early 1990s did not achieve the same level but that is unsurprising given the difficult conditions of those years. The wine is a great deal more supple and approachable than it used to be and much of the reason has been a progressive replanting of the vineyard with a higher proportion of Merlot, now some 40 per cent. 2001, 00, 98, 96 and 95 stand out. (DM)

● **Château Lafon-Rochet** Saint-Estèphe★★★ £E

CH. LAGRANGE   Saint-Julien 3ème CC   www.chateau-lagrange.com   A:Eno,SsG

*Owner: **Suntory**   33250 Saint-Julien-Beychevelle*

The Japanese-owned Suntory company has pushed wine quality at this property forward dramatically since its purchase in the early 1980s and Lagrange is now very well run by Marcel Ducasse. Lagrange is very large, even by the standards of the Médoc, with over 110 ha under vine. The wine is rich and concentrated, but in an approachable style, with supple, well-rounded tannin. Consistently good over the last five or six years, it just needs that extra dimension to take it into the top division. (DM)

● **Château Lagrange** Saint-Julien★★★ £F

CH. LA LAGUNE   Haut-Médoc 3ème CC   A:AAA

Owner: Ducellier Family   33290 Ludon-Médoc

Some great reds were made at this property during the 1970s and 80s but more recently this sizeable 77-ha estate has produced some less exciting wines. The vineyard is mainly Cabernet Sauvignon (60 per cent), Merlot (20 per cent) and the balance Cabernet Franc and Petit Verdot. Under the current ownership things appear to be taking a turn for the better. Some medium-weight, elegant and cedary claret is being made using stainless steel temperature-controlled tanks for vinification, with ageing in an increasing amount of new oak. (DM)

● **Château La Lagune** Haut-Médoc★★ £F

CH. LAMOTHE-GUIGNARD Sauternes 2ème CC

A: AAA

Owner: Philippe & Jacques Guignard 33210 Sauternes
This is the larger of the two Lamothe properties in Sauternes. The other Lamothe, owned by Guy Despujols, does not quite reach the same heights. 90 per cent of the vineyard is planted to Sémillon along with 5 per cent Muscadelle and 5 per cent Sauvignon Blanc. The style is increasingly elegant with luscious botrytis character showing through in the best years. (DM)

O **Château Lamothe-Guignard** Sauternes★★★ £E

CH. LANESSAN Haut-Médoc

A: AAA

Owner: SCEA Delbos Bouteiller 33460 Cussac-Fort-Médoc
This is a somewhat old-fashioned style of Médoc located close to Saint-Julien. Medium- rather than full-bodied or super-rich, the wine can be long-lived, elegant and intense, particularly in the best vintages when it can really ripen its at times angular tannins. With time, complex cedar and elegant, evolved tertiary characters emerge. It was particularly good in 1996 and 2000 shows real promise also. (DM)

● **Château Lanessan** Haut-Médoc★★ £D

CH. LANGOA-BARTON Saint-Julien 3ème CC

A: AAA

Owner: Anthony Barton 33250 Saint-Julien-Beychevelle
Sister property to LÉOVILLE-BARTON and in the Barton family for nearly two centuries. This has always been a consistent performer, producing elegant Saint-Julien with attractive dark fruit and some cedary complexity, but inevitably it is overshadowed by its sibling château, being a mere Third Growth. Both wines are in fact vinified at Langoa, as Léoville has no winery, and are renowned for their fair prices. Both also share the same label for the second wine, Réserve de Léoville-Barton, which can be good. 2001, 00 and 98 stand out among recent vintages. (DM)

● **Château Langoa-Barton** Saint-Julien★★★ £E

CH. LARRIVET HAUT-BRION Pessac-Léognan

A: BBR,F&R,N&P,Sec

Owner: Société Andros 84 Route de Cadaujac, 33850 Léognan
There are 52 ha of vines planted here, 43 ha of which account for an even split of Cabernet Sauvignon and Merlot. The white varieties are also evenly split, between Sémillon and Sauvignon Blanc. Both wines are impressive and consultancy input on the winemaking is provided by Michel Rolland. The property is worthy of being upgraded to Cru Classé status. Both 1998 and 99 are very good and the potential for 2000 and 01 looks very good also. The red, particularly, is nudging four-star quality. It is stylish, refined and approachable at a few years, while the white is an elegant and notably piercing barrel-fermented style with a harmonious mix of fresh green and citrus fruits and subtle oak. (DM)

● **Château Larrivet Haut-Brion** Pessac-Léognan★★★ £E
O **Château Larrivet Haut-Brion** Pessac-Léognan★★★ £E

LA SERÉNITÉ Pessac-Léognan

Owner: Bernard Magrez 7. Rue du Professeur-Bernard, 33170 Gradignan
This is a special *garagiste*-style label produced at Château POUMEY. Proprietor Bernard Magrez has also released a number of other similarly styled wines from small, low-yielding properties throughout the region. The wines are marketed as Terroirs d'Exception and have been sourced from a number high quality vineyard sites owned by both Bernard Magrez and film actors Gérard Depardieu and Carole Bouquet; not only in Bordeaux but also in the Midi, Italy, Morocco and Algeria. La Serénité is a very full, rich and extracted style. Produced from an almost equal blend of Merlot and Cabernet Sauvignon, it is vinified and aged in wood and everything in the cellars is handled by gravity. (DM)

● **La Serénité** Pessac-Léognan★★★ £E

CH. LATOUR Pauillac 1er CC www.chateau-latour.com A: AAA

Owner: François Pinault Saint-Lambert, 33250 Pauillac
To many this is the greatest of all the great wines of the Médoc and to some the greatest in the entire region. There is no doubt that it is one of the world's most remarkable reds, which at its magnificent best is both massive and concentrated but at the same time harmonious and very refined. It requires cellaring and you should allow one or preferably two decades. While the wine performs consistently at a very high level now, a number of vintages in the early to mid-1980s were less impressive, nowhere near its current super-five ranking. Fortunately, with a production of over 30,000 cases a year, the wine is not impossible to find – unlike a number of new 'super' wines being made elsewhere around the world. Recent vintages of particular note include 1999, 96, 95 and 90. Among the great earlier years 82, 71, 66, 61, 59 and 49 are all legendary. Les Forts de Latour is a very impressive second wine. (DM)
● **Château Latour** Pauillac✪✪✪✪✪ £H ● **Les Forts de Latour**★★★★ £F

CH. LA TOUR CARNET Haut-Médoc A: L&W,BBR,N&P,Tur

Owner: Bernard Magrez 33112 Saint-Laurent-Médoc
A rich, fleshy style of Médoc which is produced from Cabernet Sauvignon (52 per cent), Merlot (42 per cent) and a little Cabernet Franc and Petit Verdot. Michel Rolland consults over the winemaking for which fermentation is carried out in wooden vats with malolactic typically in *barrique*. Around 70 per cent new oak is used and all operations are now carried out by gravity. the wine is ripe and reasonably forward; four to five years are required to integrate the fruit and initially dominant oak. (DM)
● **Château La Tour Carnet** Haut-Médoc★★★ £C

CH. LATOUR-MARTILLAC Pessac-Léognan CC www.latour-martillac.com A: AAA

Owner: Kressmann family 33650 Martillac
Good to very good white and red Pessac is produced at this property, with around three-quarters of the output red. Increasing vine age is one of the reasons why quality has surged forward during the 1990s. The red varieties now average 30 years and the whites a full 40 years. The red is an approachable, supple wine with refined tannins and nicely judged oak that varies between 30 and 50 per cent depending on the year. The white is rich and honeyed, with a real toasty, creamy character from barrel-fermentation and *bâttonage* underpinned by loads of character and style. Both offer good value for money. (DM)
● **Château Latour-Martillac** Pessac-Léognan★★★ £D
O **Château Latour-Martillac** Pessac-Léognan★★★ £D

CH. LAVILLE HAUT-BRION Pessac-Léognan CC A: F&R,C&R

Owner: Domaine Clarence Dillon 33608 Pessac
Like HAUT-BRION this property is owned by the Domaine Clarence Dillon. The wine, a blend of Sémillon (70 per cent), Sauvignon Blanc (27 per cent) and just a hint of Muscadelle (at 3 per cent), is produced at LA MISSION HAUT-BRION, as is LA TOUR HAUT-BRION, although all three are from separate and distinct vineyard plots. Laville is one of the great Pessac whites, powerfully structured and developing intense honeyed, mineral notes with age. It is barrel-fermented and aged mostly in new oak and requires considerable cellaring to show all its magic – at least seven or eight years. (DM)
O **Château Laville Haut-Brion** Pessac-Léognan✪✪✪✪✪ £G

CH. LÉOVILLE-BARTON Saint-Julien 2ème CC A: AAA

Owner: Anthony Barton 33250 Saint-Julien-Beychevelle
This marvellously consistent red has long been one of Bordeaux's great-value wines. It is produced from 48 ha of vineyards planted to a mix of Cabernet Sauvignon (70 per cent), Merlot (22 per cent) and Cabernet

Franc (8 per cent). It is vinified at its sister property LANGOA-BARTON as there is no winemaking facility on the Léoville property. The wine is a stylish, cedary, medium-full claret with well-judged oak and a supple but youthfully firm texture that requires time to achieve balance and harmony. It is no blockbuster but very good and long-lived nonetheless. It was seriously nudging super-five in 1996 and potentially 2000 as well. The 89, 86 and 82 were also very fine. (DM)

● **Château Léoville-Barton** Saint-Julien★★★★★ £F

CH. LÉOVILLE-LAS-CASES   Saint-Julien 2ème CC   A: AAA

Owner: Delon family   33250 Saint-Julien-Beychevelle

Almost universally regarded now as the finest of the super-seconds, on many occasions this magnificent property outclasses the First Growths. Not surprisingly the wine carries a price to match this performance and has in a number of vintages held up extraordinarily well on auction markets. This is also a fairly significant château, with 97 ha under vine. The high standards in place here ensure that a significant amount of the Grand Vin is declassified as Clos du Marquis, which is one of the very best of the Médoc's second labels. The quality was top-notch throughout the 1990s – only 1992 and 91 saw some ground lost, and the wine was a testament to the trying conditions of those years. Recent benchmarks are 2000, 96, 95 and 90, while 86 and 82 are also legendary. (DM)

● **Château Léoville-las-Cases** Saint-Julien✪✪✪✪✪ £H   ● **Clos du Marquis**★★★ £E

CH. LÉOVILLE-POYFERRÉ   Saint-Julien 2ème CC   www.leoville-poyferre.fr   A: AAA

Owner: Cuvelier family   33250 Saint-Julien-Beychevelle

The third among the great Léoville super-seconds. This was originally regarded as the first among equals and today, after a period of relative decline in the 1960s and 70s, it is once more challenging the other two Léoville properties. Poyferré, while a serious, dense and powerfully structured wine, is more approachable than the other two. It has a more vibrant, upfront, dark blackcurrant and mulberry fruit character and is an altogether more opulent style, partly achieved through a portion of the wine being put through malolactic in barrel. Nevertheless it remains very refined and elegant, an excellent expression of its *terroir*. 2000, 96 and 90 were all extremely fine examples of five-star quality. The second wine, Moulin Riche, is good to very good on occasion. (DM)

● **Château Léoville-Poyferré** Saint-Julien★★★★ £F

CH. LA LOUVIÈRE   Pessac-Léognan   www.andrelurton.com   A: AAA

Owner: Les Vignobles André Lurton   33890 Léognan

This is one of several property in the André Lurton Graves empire. As well as the wines of La Louvière, two other labels are vinified here: Château de CRUZEAU and Château ROCHEMORIN. The La Louvière vineyard comprises some 48 ha, of which 33 ha are planted to Cabernet Sauvignon and Merlot. The smaller white vineyard holding is dominated by Sauvignon Blanc, which accounts for around 85 per cent, the balance being Sémillon. Both wines are approachable and forward in style but will also age well in the medium term. The red is supple, with refined, nicely rounded tannin and the white ripe and full of citrus and subtle toasted oak. (DM)

● **Château la Louvière** Pessac-Léognan★★★ £E
○ **Château la Louvière** Pessac-Léognan★★★ £E

CH. LYNCH-BAGES   Pauillac 5ème CC   www.lynchbages.com   A: AAA

Owner: Jean-Michel Cazes   33250 Pauillac

Regarded rightly during the 1980s as one of the great super-seconds despite its lower official classification. Talented Jean-Michel Cazes unquestionably had a vast influence on quality here during that period. During the late 1990s he has lost just a touch of the sheen. The wine at its best is still very fine, full of dark cassis and ripe stylish tannin, and is surprisingly approachable. A good straightforward lightly oaked Bordeaux Blanc is also produced, along with the second wine, Haut-Bages-Avérous. Among recent vintages the 2000, 96 and 95 Grand Vin were all very impressive. Among earlier years the trio of 88, 89 and 90 were very fine, as were 85, 82 and 70. (DM)

● **Château Lynch-Bages** Pauillac★★★★★ £F
O **Château Lynch-Bages** Bordeaux★★ £D

CH. MALARTIC-LAGRAVIÈRE Pessac-Léognan CC   A: F&R,N&P

Owner: Alfred-Alexandre Bonnie 43 Avenue de Mont-de-Marsan, 33850 Léognan
This property was sold by Champagne house LAURENT-PERRIER to the Bonnie family in 1997 and since then there has been significant investment with a dramatic raising of standards. Quality since the 1997 vintage has been very good. Prior to this the whites had shown class on occasion but the red was generally a disappointment. The vineyard is now tended organically with reduced yields and a massive renovation of the cellars now means that winery operations are handled where possible by gravity. Denis Dubourdieu consults for the whites and Michel Rolland for the reds. With 20 per cent Sémillon added to the white it offers a ripe and opulent, lightly oaked style with none of the sulphur of old, while the red is rich, ripe and approachable. Both will develop well over the medium term. The second label for both red and white, Le Sillage de Malartic, now offers reliable drinking. (DM)

● **Château Malartic-Lagravière** Pessac-Léognan★★★ £E
O **Château Malartic-Lagravière** Pessac-Léognan★★★★ £E

CH. MALESCOT-SAINT-EXUPÉRY Margaux 3ème CC   A:AAA

Owner: Zuger family 33460 Margaux
During the 1980s and early 90s this was a reliable if somewhat unexciting Margaux, but reasonably priced. Quality has taken a significant step up in recent vintages and the price has risen but not excessively so. As is so often the case, a new generation has meant progressive moves forward. The wine is now riper and fuller but not at all extracted, retaining a typically elegant, perfumed Margaux character. With the exception of 1997, which was a touch below par, every recent vintage looks pretty good. (DM)

● **Château Malescot-Saint-Exupéry** Margaux★★★★ £F

CH. DE MALLE Sauternes 2ème CC   A:AAA

Owner: Comtesse de Bournazel 33210 Preignac
The Comtesse de Bournazel has been producing consistently fine and elegant Sauternes since the late 1980s. The château itself is registered as a national monument and is open to the public. The wine increasingly shows a rich opulent character as well as an intense fragrance. It perfectly balances weight and finesse. It was very good in 1997 and 98 was of very good four-star quality. 2001 looks equally promising. A decent white Graves, M de Malle, is also made as well as a red, Château de Cardaillan. (DM)

● **Château de Malle** Sauternes★★★★ £E

CH. MARGAUX Margaux 1er CC www.chateau-margaux.com   A:AAA

Owner: Agnelli & Mentzelopoulos families 33460 Margaux
Corinne Mentzelopoulos and general manager Paul Pontallier have crafted truly great red Bordeaux now for upwards of two decades. The wine is not only remarkably elegant, with the unmistakably intense perfume of the appellation, but also enormously rich. Loaded with dense but supple tannins, Margaux is remarkably powerful and needs a minimum of 10–12 years' ageing to begin to reveal itself. Meticulous care in the vineyard and at harvest, along with traditional vinification in wooden fermenters, defines the style and quality. The second label, Pavillon Rouge, ensures the integrity of the Grand Vin but is itself regularly very impressive. As well as the 78 ha of red varieties planted there are some 12 ha of Sauvignon Blanc, which

produce an intense floral, grassy and complex white sold under the humble Bordeaux AC. Among the great years are 2000, 99, 96, 95, 90, 86, 83, 82, 79 and 78. It was very uneven prior to this and the Mentzelopoulos family involvement. 1961, good for most other top Bordeaux châteaux, was disappointing. (DM)

● **Château Margaux** Margaux✪✪✪✪✪ £H ● **Pavillon Rouge de Château Margaux**★★★★ £F
O **Pavillon Blanc de Château Margaux** Bordeaux★★★★★ £F

CH. MAYNE LALANDE   Listrac-Médoc   A: F&R

Owner: Bernard Lartigue 33480 Listrac-Médoc
Small 17 he Listrac property producing increasingly impressive and structured examples of this lesser appellation. The vineyards are planted to a combination of Cabernet Sauvignon (45 per cent), Merlot a whopping 45 per cent also and five per cent each of Petit Verdot and Cabernet Franc. Despite this the wine is firm, sturdy and marked by an intense cedary rather than plummy character. The 2000 here was particularly good, clearly three stars, expect recent vintages to develop well in bottle for five to seven years. There is also a special limited cuvée Alice-Jeanne. (DM)

● **Château Mayne Lalande** Saint-Estèphe★★ £C

MA VÉRITÉ   Haut-Médoc

Owner: Gérard Depardieu c/o Terroirs d'Exception, 33330 Saint-Christophe des Bardes
Produced from a tiny 2-ha vineyard, this is marketed along with a number of other properties throughout the region including LA SERÉNITÉ, PASSION DU PRIEURÉ MALESAN and LA CROIX DE PEYROLIE as part of the Terroirs d'Exception range by Bernard Magrez. The clay and limestone soils are planted to a mix of 55 per cent Cabernet Sauvignon, 40 per cent Merlot and the balance Cabernet Franc and Petit Verdot. Yields are kept very low at less than 20 hl/ha and leaf plucking and *vendange vert* are practised in the vineyard. Richly textured with considerable extract, the wine nevertheless possesses an elegant cedary character as well as offering copious quantities of ripe cassis and spicy new oak. It will benefit from five or six years' ageing. (DM)

● **Ma Vérité** Haut-Médoc★★★★ £F

CH. LA MISSION HAUT-BRION   Pessac-Léognan CC   www.haut-brion.com   A: AAA

Owner: Domaine Clarence Dillon 33608 Pessac
Like HAUT-BRION, LAVILLE HAUT-BRION and LA TOUR-HAUT-BRION this property is owned by the Domaine Clarence Dillon. La Tour-Haut-Brion used to be the second wine at La Mission but is now handled as its own separate vineyard and property. La Mission is only surpassed among Graves reds by Haut-Brion itself. This is a massive, dense and powerful red. Dark, mineral and black fruits are underpinned by cedar and oak. While the wine perhaps lacks the absolute refinement of its illustrious stablemate, it hasn't fallen far short and is on occasion the more impressive of the two. 2000, 98 and 95 are recent benchmarks and 90, 89, 82, 78 and 75 were all of legendary quality. The second wine, La Chapelle de la Mission Haut-Brion, is a four-star wine in the ripest years. (DM)

● **Château la Mission Haut-Brion** Pessac-Léognan✪✪✪✪✪ £H

CH. MONTROSE   Saint-Estèphe 2ème CC   A: AAA

Owner: Charmolüe family 33180 Saint-Estèphe
This 68-ha property produces around 28,000 cases of exceptional Saint-Estèphe a year. The property is second only behind fellow Second Growth COS D'ESTOURNEL in the appellation hierarchy. These are massive, powerful, brooding wines – dense, tannic and long-lived. Sometimes the fruit struggles to emerge through the iron fist in which it is enveloped. Generally though, in the last decade the wine has become suppler and possesses greater harmony and it was consistently good through the 1990s. 1990 and 95 suggest

super-five quality and 2000 may well turn out the same. La Dame de Montrose is an impressive second wine. (DM)

● **Château Montrose** Saint-Estèphe★★★★★ £F La Dame de Montrose★★★ £E

CH. MOUTON-ROTHSCHILD   Pauillac 1er CC   www.bpdr.com   A:AAA

Owner: Baron Philippe de Rothschild SA   33250 Pauillac

Unique among the First Growths of Bordeaux in that the wine was elevated to its current classification only in 1973, after the successful lobbying of Baron Philippe de Rothschild. The wine is the most opulent and approachable of the top growths, full of dark cassis and cigar box aromas, supported by powerful, supple tannin. Stunning wine was produced in 1982 and 86 but there was some loss of form in the late 80s and early 90s. However, 1996, 98, 99 and 00 have all been back among the very best. The second wine is Le Petit Mouton, and a small amount of a premium white Aile d'Argent is also produced. There is a sizeable merchant business owned by Baronne Philippine de Rothschild, producing a range of pretty ordinary generic AC labels along with the dreary Mouton Cadet. Of greater interest are the two premium partnerships of OPUS ONE with ROBERT MONDAVI in California and ALMAVIVA with CONCHA Y TORO in Chile. (DM)

● **Château Mouton-Rothschild** Pauillac❂❂❂❂❂ £H

CH. NAIRAC   Barsac 2ème CC   A:AAA

Owner: Nicolas Tari-Heeter   33720 Barsac

A small property of just some 17 ha with annual production of barely more than 1,000 cases. The wine often outperforms its Second Growth status. Always picked very ripe, it gains real structure from a high proportion of new oak used for ageing. At times this can seem almost overpowering in its youth but given patience the wine can show a marvellous balance of intense, peachy botrytised fruit and almost sweet vanilla oak. Definitely cellar for six or seven years. (DM)

● **Château Nairac** Barsac★★★★ £E

CH. PALMER   Margaux 3ème CC   www.chateau-palmer.com   A:AAA

Owner: Mahler Besse/Sichel Families   Cantenac, 33460 Margaux

This marvellous property is often thought of as a Second Growth and for a period before the Mentzelopoulos years at Château MARGAUX it was also the benchmark for the AC. At its best the wine displays not only the perfume of the appellation but ripe, powerful, almost sumptuous dark fruit. In part this must be down to the very high proportion of Merlot planted, at 47 per cent the same as Cabernet Sauvignon. The second wine, Alter Ego de Palmer, tends to have an even higher proportion of Merlot in the final blend. 2000, 99, 98, 96 and 95 Palmer were of a very high standard and the most recent vintages have similar promise. Of the great years here, 89 and 83 also stand out as do the earlier years of 70, 66 and 61. (DM)

● **Château Palmer** Margaux★★★★★ £G

CH. PAPE-CLÉMENT   Pessac-Léognan CC   www.pape-clement .com   A:AAA

Owner: Léo Montagne/Bernard Magrez   216 Avenue du Docteur-Nancel-Pénard, 33650 Martillac

Excellent 32.5-ha property dominated by red vine plantings and like Haut-Brion engulfed by the suburbs of Bordeaux. The white varieties account for a mere 2.5 ha with 10 per cent of this being Muscadelle. Both wines are rich and powerful and the red has real density and grip but remains approachable and harmonious. The tiny production of white has an elegant, intense mineral and citrus streak adding to its complexity and all nicely supported by sufficient creamy new oak. Generally very good throughout the 1990s and particularly after 1995. The red in 98 and 99 was worth a five-star rating. (DM)

● **Château Pape-Clément** Pessac-Léognan★★★★ £E
O **Château Pape-Clément** Pessac-Léognan★★★★ £E

CH. PEYRABON Haut-Médoc   A: BBR,F&R

Owner: Jacques Babeau 33250 Saint-Sauveur-en-Médoc

Sizeable Cru Bourgeois Haut-Médoc property producing close to 30,000 cases a year. Most comes from close to 30 ha in the Haut-Médoc but there is also a limited volume of Pauillac. Both represent excellent-value modern, stylish, cedary claret. The Haut-Médoc typically blends Cabernet Sauvignon, Merlot and Cabernet Franc, while the Pauillac often has a hint of Petit Verdot also. The Fleur Peyrabon just has that added dimension with hints of cassis and spice adding a little extra complexity. Both wines are likely to add further complexity with five or six years' cellaring. (DM)

● **Château Peyrabon** La Fleur Peyrabon Pauillac★★★ £D
● **Château Peyrabon** Haut Médoc★★ £C

CH. PICHON-LONGUEVILLE Pauillac 2ème CC   A: AAA

Owner: AXA Millésimes 33250 Pauillac

Sizeable Second Growth with some 73 ha under vine, bought in 1987 by AXA Millésimes – the fine-wine arm of the AXA insurance company. Jean-Michel Cazes, who owns Château LYNCH-BAGES, took over the management of the Bordeaux AXA operation and quality quickly improved with very successful vintages in 1989 and 90. These are world-class, super-five wines: deep, dark, powerful Pauillac but very finely balanced. Quality in the late 90s has not been at quite the same heady heights; although the most recent vintages look to be back on form. (DM)

● **Château Pichon-Longueville** Pauillac★★★★ £F

CH. PICHON-LONGUEVILLE-LALANDE Pauillac 2ème CC   A: AAA

Owner: Lencquesaing family 33250 Pauillac

A property marked by its rich, elegant, almost sumptuous style of wine. It is no surprise that there are considerable plantings of Merlot (35 per cent). The balance is Cabernet Sauvignon (45 per cent), Cabernet Franc (12 per cent) and a relatively whopping 8 per cent of very old Petit Verdot. The vineyards border Saint-Julien and this also helps contribute to the wine's intense, fragrant and complex style. However, there have been some strange variations in quality over the last couple of decades. Vintages of the late 1990s have been disappointing, whereas 1995 and 96 were magnificent, clear super-five wines. 2000 and 2001 look to be back in the top division. Other exceptional years have included 86, 83 and, of course, the legendary 82. Réserve de la Comtesse is the second wine. (DM)

● **Château Pichon-Longueville-Lalande** Pauillac★★★★★ £G ● **Réserve de la Comtesse**★★ £E

CH. PONTET-CANET Pauillac 5ème CC www.pontet-canet.com   A: AAA

Owner: Tesseron Family 33250 Pauillac

This property has been in the ownership of the Tesseron Family, who also own Château LAFON-ROCHET, for over two decades. They have been responsible for bringing it up to its current level, where it has generally justified its Fifth Growth status. Produced from vineyards planted on some of the best gravel soils of the appellation, at its peak it is exactly what you think of as quintessential Pauillac – big, powerful and dense with supple, well-rounded tannin and an intense fragrance of cassis and cedar. 1989 saw a significant upturn in quality. After the generally poor years between 1991 and 93, really only 97 has been lighter and less impressive, indeed 00 and 99 clearly rated four stars. (DM)

● **Château Pontet-Canet** Pauillac★★★ £F

CH. POTENSAC Médoc www.chateau-potensac.com   A: AAA

Owner: Delon family 33340 Ordonnac

Under the same ownership as LÉOVILLE-LAS-CASES, this is without doubt the finest property sold as

Médoc AC. The now very old vines are planted on a mix of alluvial gravel and clay soils. The wine is consistently excellent: ripe but sufficiently firm, with a hint of new wood (about 20 per cent) providing additional depth. Bottled without filtration it is better with five years' cellaring. Both 2000 and 96 are particularly impressive. All in all this is a very good-value claret. (DM)

● **Château Potensac** Médoc★★★ £D

CH. POUJEAUX Moulis www.chateaupoujeaux.com A:AAA

Owner: Theil family 33480 Moulis-en-Médoc

Along with CHASSE-SPLEEN, this is one of the two best wines in the Moulis AC. It has performed with an impressive consistency throughout the last 10 years and more. There are 53 ha under vine here, with Cabernet Sauvignon accounting for slightly more of the vineyard than Merlot. As with most quality-conscious wine producers, there is a dedication in the vineyard and cellar which contributes to the final wine. The style is rich and sumptuous with a hint of vanilla from its 12 months of oak-ageing. Handling is kept to a minimum, with just egg-white fining and no filtration. A further notch up from 1996, including 97. (DM)

● **Château Poujeaux** Moulis★★★ £E

CH. PRIEURÉ-LICHINE Margaux 4ème CC prieure.lichine@wanadoo.fr A:AAA

Owner: Ballande family 34 Avenue de la Cinquième République, 33460 Cantenac

The Ballandes, who run the *négociant* operation the Ballande group, purchased this property from the Lichine family in 1999. Unusually there are parcels of vineyard spread throughout the appellation. There has been consultancy input from Michel Rolland as well as the talented young enologist Stéphane Derenoncourt. The wine is increasingly sumptuous and supple. This is an ambitious operation and it will be interesting to see how quality develops over the next five years or so. The wine showed good potential in 1996, 98 and 00 and this standard looks likely to be maintained. (DM)

● **Château Prieuré-Lichine** Margaux★★★ £E

CH. RABAUD-PROMIS Sauternes 1er CC A:AAA

Owner: Philippe Dejean 33210 Bommes

After a long period in the doldrums, this 33-ha property has now been making impressive Sauternes for well more than a decade. This is a full, rich and honeyed wine with not only impressive depth, concentration and the structure to age very well but also real balance and harmony. It can be very intense and stylish, particularly in top years. Very impressive since 1994 and prior to that 90, 89 and 88 are very good indeed. (DM)

○ **Château Rabaud-Promis** Sauternes★★★★ £F

CH. RAUZAN-SÉGLA Margaux 2ème CC A:AAA

Owner: Wertheimer family 33460 Margaux

This château was acquired by the Wertheimers, who own the Chanel perfume business, in 1994 and a large amount of investment has been put into the property since then. They also now own Château CANON in Saint-Émilion. Prior to the change of ownership the property performed remarkably well in the run of vintages from 1988 to 90 but this wasn't always so. Vinification is now very modern, using temperature-controlled stainless steel, and ageing is in 60 per cent new oak for 18 months. The wine has a fine, elegant texture and displays a complex array of dark fruits and cedar. There is surprising tannin here, though, and the wine will improve with at least five or six years' cellaring. It has been very consistent since 1995, with the exception of 97 which was a disappointment. (DM)

● **Château Rauzan-Ségla** Margaux ★★★★ £F

CH. RAYMOND-LAFON Sauternes www.chateau-raymond-lafon.fr A: AAA

Owner: Meslier family 33210 Sauternes
The production is tiny at just over 1,600 cases a year from the 18 ha of vineyard. The blend is 80 per cent Sémillon with the balance Sauvignon Blanc and no Muscadelle. Not a Classed Growth, Raymond-Lafon is located right next to Yquem and has consistently produced wines in the great years of the last two decades which rival all but the absolute best in Sauternes. This has been achieved through a dedicated approach in the vineyard, tiny yields of just 8.5 hl/ha, careful and repeated selective harvesting (*tris*) and extensive use of new oak in the cellar. The wine is barrel-fermented and aged for up to three years in wood. (DM)
O **Château Raymond-Lafon** Sauternes★★★★★ £F

CH. DE RAYNE-VIGNEAU Sauternes 1er CC A: VOC

Owner: SC Ch. de Rayne-Vigneau La Croix Bacalan, 109. Rue Achard, BP 154, 33042 Bordeaux
This relatively sizeable property has some 80 ha of vineyards. It is under the same ownership as Château GRAND-PUY-DUCASSE in Pauillac. The gravel soils here suggest a real potential to the *terroir* that has not yet fully been realised. However, like so many Sauternes châteaux, its reputation has improved over the last two decades. The wine is characterised by its elegant and complex botrytised fruit, with a tight, restrained structure. These are not overfull, super-weighty wines but at their best are impressively refined and intense. (DM)
O **Château de Rayne-Vigneau** Sauternes★★★ £E

CH. RIEUSSEC Sauternes 1er CC www.lafite.com A: AAA

Owner: Domaines Baron de Rothschild 33210 Fargues-de-Langon
Under the same ownership as LAFITE-ROTHSCHILD, this Sauternes is generally regarded as being second only in weight and power to YQUEM. It has generally performed at that level since 1995 and particularly during the trio of great Sauternes years from 88 to 90. Aged in a high proportion of new oak it is almost always a powerful, very rich, opulent but classically structured wine in need of 8 to 10 years' ageing, often longer in truly great vintages. (DM)
O **Château Rieussec** Sauternes✪✪✪✪✪ £F

CH. ROLLAN-DE-BY Médoc www.rollandeby.com

Owner: Jean Guyon 7 Route Rollan-de-By, 33340 Bégadan
This 37-ha property has performed with distinction throughout the past decade and is a shining light for other producers in the outlying areas of the Médoc. The vineyard is planted with a sizeable 70 per cent Merlot and this, allied to the judicious use of new oak, accounts for the ripe, almost lush, plump and approachable fruit style. Haut-Condissas is a premium label with more Cabernet Sauvignon in the blend. (DM)
● **Château Rollan-de-By** Médoc★★ £D Haut-Condissas ★★★ £E

CH. SAINT-PIERRE Saint-Julien 2ème CC A: N&P,F&R

Owner: Triaud family 33250 Saint-Julien-Beychevelle
This property was purchased in 1981 by the late Henri Martin (the former owner of GLORIA) and is now run by his daughter, Françoise Triaud. Although the wine has been consistently good throughout the last 10 years, it has never quite achieved the potential that its classification suggests. The approach to vinification is always meticulous, with a rigorous selection pre-fermentation and judicious use of new oak. The wine was certainly above average in 1990 and should achieve similar heights again with the fine 2000 vintage. (DM)
● **Château Saint-Pierre** Saint-Julien★★★ £E

CH. SIGALAS-RABAUD Sauternes 1er CC A: AAA

Owner: Lambert des Granges family 33210 Bommes
This is the smaller part of the original Château Rabaud, which was divided nearly a century ago. The other half is RABAUD-PROMIS and both are Sauternes First Growths. The wine is very rich and gloriously honeyed and can show very marked botrytis but it is still refined and very elegant. Indeed the wine has been impressive for years and was one of the few properties to perform well in the 1960s and 70s, a period of recession in the appellation. The great vintages in these decades can at least be approached with some optimism. More recently 2001, 99, 98, 97and 96 were all on top form and are nudging five stars, as are the great trio of 88, 89 and 90. (DM)
O **Château Sigalas-Rabaud** Sauternes★★★★ £F

CH. SMITH HAUT LAFITTE Pessac-Léognan CC A: AAA

Owner: Daniel & Florence Cathiard 33650 Martillac
The wines here under the current ownership are now very good. Around 80 per cent of the production is red, with a mix of 55 per cent Cabernet Sauvignon, 35 per cent Merlot and the balance Cabernet Franc. The white is dominated by Sauvignon Blanc but there is a sprinkling of Sémillon and more unusually Sauvignon Gris (similar in flavour to Sauvignon Blanc but with a slight pink tinge to its skin). The red is lighter in style than some of its neighbours but now possesses impressive depth. The white is fermented relatively cool to retain a marked floral, herbal core and is aged in 50 per cent new oak. Neither wine is filtered and both have performed admirably since 1995, 97 being a touch weak for the red, but 2000 was on the cusp of five stars for both red and white. (DM)
● **Château Smith Haut Lafitte** Pessac-Léognan★★★★ £F
O **Château Smith Haut Lafitte** Pessac-Léognan★★★★ £F

CH. SOCIANDO-MALLET Haut-Médoc A: AAA

Owner: Jean Gautreau 33180 Saint-Seurin-de-Cadourne
This is now undoubtedly the most impressive estate in the Haut-Médoc, a title that at one stage would almost invariably have been given to La LAGUNE. Quality here since 1995 has been good to very good. Perhaps in 97 and 98 it did not quite rate four stars but the wines are impressive dark, powerful and very ageworthy all the same. The style is of a true *vin de garde*, in part due to the well-drained gravel soils, which produce supple but youthfully firm, powerful tannins. Impressive earlier vintages include 1990, 89 and the classic 82. The second wine is Demoiselle, which can be good. (DM)
● **Château Sociando-Mallet** Haut-Médoc★★★★ £E

CH. SUDUIRAUT Sauternes 1er CC www.suduiraut.com A: AAA

Owner: AXA Millésimes 33210 Preignac
More care has been taken with harvesting at this property which neighbours YQUEM since its purchase by AXA in 1992. The fruit is now picked more selectively and late enough to maximise the effect of noble rot. As a result the wine has become increasingly full and rich. It is aged for 18 to 24 months in barrel, further adding to its impressive depth and concentration. It was very good in 1989 and 90 as well as more recently in 95, 96 and 97. 2001 also looks extremely promising. The second wine, Castelnau de Suduiraut, can be of sound quality and ensures the integrity of the Grand Vin. (DM)
O **Château Suduiraut** Sauternes★★★★★ £F

CH. TALBOT Saint-Julien 2ème CC www.chateau-talbot.com A: AAA

Owner: Lorraine Rustmann & Nancy Bignon 33250 Saint-Julien-Beychevelle
Originally a Cordier *négociant* property, Talbot has been retained by members of the family and the quality of the Grand Vin has remained reasonably consistent, particularly after 1995. It is now very international

in styled and quite different to some of the very firm earlier examples under Cordier ownership. 1998 and 00 were both very good and 01 looks to be similarly promising. The second wine, Connetable Talbot, has been good in the better years and there is a small amount of a white, Caillou Blanc, produced under the Bordeaux AC. This used to be variable with marked sulphur but a more modern approach to its vinification is now undertaken with better results. (DM)

● **Château Talbot** Saint-Julien★★★ £F

CH. DU TERTRE Margaux 5ème CC   A:AAA

Owner: Eric Albada Jedgersma   Chemin de Ligondras, 33460 Arsac
Eric Albada Jedgersma and his wife also own the revitalised Château GISCOURS, another Classed Growth Margaux property. While not the size of its sister château, du Tertre is by no means small with 50 ha under vine, planted in sandy gravel soils in the commune of Arsac. Cabernet Sauvignon accounts for a mere 40 per cent of the vineyard, with 35 per cent Merlot, 20 per cent Cabernet Franc and the balance a small amount of Petit Verdot. Its only since the 1999 vintage that the property has begun to show its true worth but du Tertre is one of the most beguiling and perfumed of all Margaux reds. Cellaring for six or more years will result in further complexity. (DM)

● **Château du Tertre** Margaux★★★★ £F

CH. LA TOUR BLANCHE Sauternes 1er CC   A: **Col**

*Owner: **Ministère de l'Agriculture** 33210 Bommes*
There are a total of some 40 ha under vine at this property run by the Ministry of Agriculture and although this is also an agricultural school very high standards are maintained. The vineyards are particularly well sited and result in a big, full-bodied Sauternes produced with marked botrytis and well-judged new oak. The wines have real intensity and power. 1998, 97 and 96 have all been good and the trio of 88, 89 and 90 were also excellent. (DM)

O **Château la Tour Blanche** Sauternes★★★★ £F

CH. LA TOUR HAUT-BRION Pessac-Léognan CC   A: BBR,N&P,Sec,Tur

*Owner: **Domaine Clarence Dillon** 33608 Pessac*
Originally the second wine at LA MISSION HAUT-BRION, this property stands alone with its own identity now that the vineyard is ageing. It neighbours its former big brother and although the wines are still overshadowed by the powerful dense style of La Mission they are becoming increasingly impressive in their own right. Eighty per cent of the vineyard is planted to Cabernet Sauvignon and Cabernet Franc, resulting in a very sturdy style in the wine's youth. 1995 and 98 were both very impressive and 00 looks to have equal potential. (DM)

● **Château la Tour Haut-Brion** Pessac-Léognan★★★★ £F

VIEUX CHÂTEAU GAUBERT Graves   A: BBR,CTy

Owner: Dominique Haverlan 33640 Portets
One of the best properties in the Graves AC and a model for many less than perfect performers in the supposedly superior Pessac-Léognan. Both red and white are produced. The red is a 50/50 blend of Cabernet Sauvignon and Merlot and this is emphasised in its vibrant dark plummy fruit character. Structure and depth are lent by an extended fermentation and maceration of 15 to 20 days and 12 months in 40 per cent new wood. The white, from a roughly equal blend of Sémillon and Sauvignon Blanc, is barrel-fermented in 60 per cent new oak and aged on lees with *bâtonnage*. Nonetheless it is remarkably restrained with intense citrus and lightly grassy aromas subtly supported by sophisticated oak. It will be all the better for two or three years' ageing in bottle. (DM)

● **Vieux Château Gaubert** Graves★★★ £C
O **Vieux Château Gaubert** Graves★★★ £C

CH. VILLA BEL AIR   Graves   www.villabelair.com

A: **PFx**,BBR,Far,Sec,F&R

Owner: Jean-Michel Cazes   33650 Saint-Morillon

Reliable Graves property producing around 12,000 cases each of red and white Graves. The property was taken over by Jean-Michel Cazes in 1990 and the cellars were modernised and the winemaking brought up to speed. Barrel-fermentation for the white and a red which emphasises attractive dark, black fruit in a supple, approachable style are the keys here. Generally good in 2000, 99 and 98 although prices do seem to be creeping up as well. (DM)

● **Château Villa Bel Air** Graves★★ £C
O **Château Villa Bel Air** Graves★★ £C

CH. D'YQUEM   Sauternes 1er GCC

A: AAA

Owner: LVMH   33210 Sauternes

Arguably the greatest sweet wine in the world. Owned by the Lur Saluces family for more than two centuries, it was purchased by LVMH in 1999. Alexandre de Lur Saluces continues to make the wine. There are 103 ha under vine but the vineyards have a superb exposure in the centre of the appellation and enjoy an ideal mix of morning mist and warm sunshine. With a sizeable production of around 8,000 cases a year it is certain that, while occasional TBAs from Germany or SGNs from Alsace might rival it for sheer depth, dimension and fruit intensity, they never will match the volume produced at Yquem. The same remarkable level of attention is spent producing the wine, with harvesting not so much by *tris* but more berry by berry and at a microscopic yield. New oak is used throughout and the wine is bottled without filtration after spending more than three years in cask. These are wines of supreme quality that will last for half a century or more, always outstanding in top years. (DM)

O **Château d'Yquem** Sauternes❂❂❂❂❂ £H

MÉDOC, GRAVES & SAUTERNES/OTHER WINES OF NOTE

CH. BEL-AIR ● **Saint-Estèphe** £C
CH. BELLE VUE ● **Haut-Médoc** £C
CH. BISTON-BRILLETTE ● **Moulis** £C
CH. BROWN ● **Pessac-Léognan** £D
CH. BERNADOTTE ● **Haut-Médoc** £C
CH. BOURNAC ● **Médoc** £C
CH. BOUSCAUT O **Pessac-Léognan** £E   O **Pessac-Léognan** £D
CH. CANTELYS ● **Pessac-Léognan** £D
CH. CAMBON LA PELOUSE ● **Haut-Médoc** £C
CH. CITRAN ● **Haut-Médoc** £C
CH. CLAUZET ● **Saint-Estèphe** £D
CH. CRABITEY ● **Graves** £C
CLOS DU JAUGEYRON ● **Haut-Médoc** £C   ● **Margaux** £F
CH. COUFRAN ● **Haut-Médoc** £C
CRU BARRÉJATS O **Sauternes** £F
CH. DE CRUZEAU ● **Pessac-Léognan** £D   O **Pessac-Léognan** £D
CH. DESMIRAIL ● **Margaux** £E
CH. DURFORT-VIVENS ● **Margaux** £E
CH. DES EYRINS ● **Margaux** £C
CH. DE FARGUES O **Sauternes** £F
CH. FILHOT O **Sauternes** £E
CH. FONBADET ● **Pauillac** £D
CH. FOURCAS-DUPRÉ ● **Listrac** £C
CH. LA GARDE ● **Pessac-Léognan** £D
CH. GILETTE O **Sauternes** £G

CH. GRAND-PUY-DUCASSE ● Pauillac £E

CH. LES GRANDS CHÊNES ● Médoc £D Prestige £D

CH. GREYSAC ● Médoc £C

CH. HAUT-BAGES-LIBÉRAL ● Pauillac £D

CH. HAUT BEASÉJOUR ● Médoc £D

CH. HAUT-BERGERON O Sauternes £E

CH. HAUT-BERGEY ● Pessac-Léognan £E O Pessac-Léognan £E

CH. HAUT-GARDÈRE ● Pessac-Léognan £D

CH. LES JUSTICES O Sauternes £E

CH. LABÉGORCE-ZÉDÉ ● Margaux £E

CH. LACOMBE NOAILLAC ● Médoc £C

CH. LAFON ● Médoc £C

CH. LALANDE DE GRAVELONGUE ● Médoc £D

LA PATACHE ● Médoc £C

CH. LASCOMBES ● Margaux £E

CH. LA TOUR DE BY ● Médoc £C

CH. LILIAN-LADOUYS ● Saint-Estèphe £D

CH. LIOT O Barsac £D

CH. LIVERSAN ● Haut-Médoc £C

CH. LYNCH-MOUSSAS ● Pauillac £E

MAGREZ TIVOLI ● Haut-Médoc £F

CH. MARBUZET ● Saint-Estèphe £C

CH. MARQUIS-DE-TERME ● Margaux £D

CH. MAUCAILLOU ● Moulis £C

CH. MEYNEY ● Saint-Estèphe £D

CH. MILLE-ROSES ● Haut-Médoc £C

CH. MONBRISON ● Margaux £D

CH. DU MOULIN ROUGE ● Haut-Médoc £C

CH. NOAILLAC ● Médoc £C

CH. OLIVIER ● Pessac-Léognan £D O Pessac-Léognan £D

CH. LES ORMES-DE-PEZ ● Saint-Estèphe £D

CH. LES ORMES-SORBET ● Médoc £D

CH. PATACHE D'AUX ● Médoc £D

CH PETIT-BOCQ ● Saint-Estèphe £D

CH. DE PEZ ● Saint-Estèphe £D

CH. PHÉLAN-SÉGUR ● Saint-Estephe £D

CH. PIBRAN ● Pauillac £E

CH. POUMEY ● Pessac-Léognan £D

CH. RAHOUL ● Graves £C O Graves £C

CH. RAMAGE-LA-BATISSE ● Haut-Médoc £C

CH. RAUZAN-GASSIES ● Margaux £E

CH. RESPIDE ● Graves £C O Graves £C

CH. RESPIDE-MÉDEVILLE ● Graves £D O Graves £D

CH. DE ROCHEMORIN O Pessac-Léognan £E

CH. ROMER-DU-HAYOT O Sauternes £D

CH. DE ROUILLAC ● Pessac-Léognan £D

CH. SÉNÉJAC ● Haut-Médoc £C Cuvée Karolus £D

CH. SIRAN ● Margaux £E

CH. SOUDARS ● Haut-Médoc £C

CH. SUAU O Barsac £E

CH. TOUR-HAUT-CAUSSAN ● Médoc £C

CH. TOUR DU HAUT-MOULIN ● Haut-Médoc £C

CH. VERDIGNAN ● Haut-Médoc £C

VIEUX CHÂTEAU-LANDON ● Médoc £C

CH. VIEUX ROBIN ● Médoc £C

Work in progress!!

Wines from the following producers under consideration for the next edition

CH. DES EYRINS (MARGAUX)
CH. LES GRANDS CHÊNES (MÉDOC)
CH. LAMOTHE (SAUTERNES)
CH. LIEUJEAN (MÉDOC)
CH. LOUSTEAUNEUF (MÉDOC)
MAROJALLIA (MARGAUX)
CH. MOULIN DE LA ROSE (SAINT-JULIEN)
CH. SÉGUR DE CABANAC (SAINT-ÈSTEPHE)

Author's choice (DM)

MÉDOC, GRAVES & SAUTERNES

Great cellarworthy Left Bank reds

CH. COS D'ESTOURNEL ● Saint-Estèphe 2ème CC
CH. DUCRU-BEAUCAILLOU ● Saint-Julien 2ème CC
CH. HAUT-BRION ● Pessac-Léognan I er CC
CH. LAFITE-ROTHSCHILD ● Pauillac I er CC
CH. LATOUR ● Pauillac I er CC
CH. LÉOVILLE-LAS-CASES ● Saint-Julien 2ème CC
CH. MARGAUX ● Margaux I er CC
CH. LA MISSION-HAUT-BRION ● Pessac-Léognan CC
CH. MOUTON-ROTHSCHILD ● Pauillac I er CC
CH. PICHON-LONGUEVILLE-LALANDE ● Pauillac 2ème CC

The best of Sauternes and Barsac

CH. CLIMENS O Barsac I er CC
CH. COUTET O Barsac I er CC
CH. GUIRAUD O Sauternes I er CC
CH. LAFAURIE-PEYRAGUEY O Sauternes I er CC
CH. RABAUD-PROMIS O Sauternes I er CC
CH. RAYMOND-LAFON O Sauternes
CH. RIEUSSEC O Sauternes I er CC
CH. SIGALAS-RABAUD O Sauternes I er CC
CH. SUDUIRAUT O Sauternes I er CC
CH. D'YQUEM O Sauternes I er GCC

Classic dry whites

CH. CARBONNIEUX O Pessac-Léognan CC
DOM. DE CHEVALIER O Pessac-Léognan CC
CLOS FLORIDÈNE O Graves
CH. DE FIEUZAL O Pessac-Léognan
CH. HAUT-BRION O Pessac-Léognan
CH. LAVILLE-HAUT-BRION O Pessac-Léognan CC
CH. LA LOUVIÈRE O Pessac-Léognan
CH. PAPE-CLÉMENT O Pessac-Léognan
PAVILLON BLANC DE MARGAUX O Bordeaux
CH. SMITH-HAUT-LAFITTE O Pessac-Léognan

Saint-Emilion, Pomerol & other Bordeaux

DOM. DE L'A   Côtes de Castillon   A: N&P

Owner: Stéphane Derenoncourt   Pavie Nord, 33330 Saint-Émilion
This is the tiny 4-ha home property of winemaking guru Stéphane Derenoncourt. It is planted to old-vine Merlot, Cabernet Franc and a little Cabernet Sauvignon and is farmed biodynamically. The result is remarkably dense and powerful wine from this outlying Bordeaux appellation. The wine is fermented in wood, aged on lees to add weight and texture and afterwards bottled without fining or filtration. Along with a number of other small impressive properties, this is a model for producers from the region's lesser ACs. (DM)
● **Domaine de l'A** Côtes de Castillon★★★ £E

CH. D'AIGUILHE   Côtes de Castillon   www.neipperg.com   A: BBR,N&P,Tur

Owner: Comte Stephan von Neipperg   33350 Saint-Philippe-d'Aiguilhe
This very fine Castillon property is under of the same ownership as CANON LA GAFFELIÈRE and LA MONDOTTE. The property consists of 65 ha of which 42 are planted to vines on the upper slopes which not only have an excellent southerly exposure but also very well-drained clay/limestone soils. The wine is blended from Merlot (80 per cent) and Cabernet Franc. Fermentation is in oak vats but with temperature control and the wine is aged in a very high proportion (80 per cent) of new oak on its lees. It is neither fined nor filtered. Lushly textured, concentrated and impressively complex, it has a fine tannic structure, firm in its youth, which needs a good five or six years' ageing. (DM)
● **Château d'Aiguilhe** Cotes de Castillon★★★★ £E

CH. ANGÉLUS   Saint-Émilion 1er GCC   www.angelus.com   A: AAA

Owner: Boüard de Laforest et Fils   33330 Saint-Émilion
This has consistently been one of the top-performing Saint-Émilion Grands Crus Classés over the last 10 to 15 years. In 1996 the property was upgraded to Premier Grand Cru Classé. These are deeply coloured, concentrated and extracted wines with deep, and dark blackcurrant and plum fruit. They are always produced with well-judged oak treatment but very finely balanced as well. 1995 and 2000 have both been outstanding vintages. Hubert de Boüard de Laforest is also one of the partners in the recently established MASSAYA winery in Lebanon's Bekaa Valley. (DM)
● **Château Angélus** Saint-Émilion Grand Cru Classé★★★★★ £H

CH. L'ARROSÉE   Saint-Émilion GCC   A: AAA

Owner: François Rodhain   33330 Saint-Émilion
Solid and consistent Grand Cru Classé producing ripe, moderately dense and powerful wines. They tend to be marked by their lush and velvety texture and can be broached at around five years or so, despite having around 40 per cent Cabernet Sauvignon in the blend. At present this is a good, rather than great property. 2000 was a step up, clearly three stars, and both 02 and 03 may well turn out the same. (DM)
● **Château l'Arrosée** Saint-Émilion Grand Cru Classé★★ £F

CH. AUSONE   Saint Émilion 1er GCC   A: AAA

Owner: Alain Vauthier   33330 Saint-Émilion
One of the great wines of the Right Bank. Ausone, along with CHEVAL-BLANC, has always been considered to stand out and the two are classified Premiers Grands Crus Classés A-grade properties. The wine has been consistently impressive since the late 1980s and in the last half a dozen years has been produced in a rich, supple and immensely velvety style. Very fine and complex, it is now increasingly rich and oaky. Alain Vauthier has gained valuable input on the winemaking approach from Michel Rolland. The blend comprises a roughly equal proportion of Merlot and Cabernet Franc. It has been absolutely top-flight

since 1995 with the exception of 97. Approachable at five or six years, the wine benefits from twice that time. (DM)

● **Château Ausone** Saint Émilion Grand Cru Classé✪✪✪✪✪ £H

CH. BEAU-SÉJOUR BÉCOT   Saint-Émilion 1er GCC   A: AAA

Owner: Gérard & Dominique Bécot   33330, Saint-Émilion

This 16.5-ha property was reintroduced to the ranks of the Premiers Grands Crus Classés in 1996. The style is one of considerable extraction and the Bécot brothers seek to produce an opulent, rich, heavily oaked red with sumptuous, plummy fruit. In general they succeed very well. They also make a *garagiste*-style *cuvée* called La Gomerie. Less than a thousand cases are produced of this Merlot aged in 100 per cent new oak. It is sourced from a tiny 2.5-ha plot which is itself unclassified. Both wines need five or six years to shed the hard edge of their tannins. (DM)

● **Château Beau-Séjour Bécot** Saint-Émilion Grand Cru Classé★★★★ £G
● **La Gomerie** Saint-Émilion Grand Cru★★★★★ £H

CH. BEAUREGARD   Pomerol   A: AAA

Owner: Vincent Priou   33500 Pomerol

One of Pomerol's lesser-known châteaux, this 17.5-ha property has an unusually high proportion of Cabernet Franc planted, around 30 per cent. This is in part because of a high gravel component in the soil. The wine is ripe and forward, with attractively brambly fruit and a hint of oak spice, but with less overtly fleshy, plummy Merlot fruit than some others in the appellation. Very good in 1998 and particularly 2000, which was of clear four-star quality, tight, intense and composed. It is approachable and supple at four or five years. (DM)

● **Château Beauregard** Pomerol★★★ £E

CH. BEAUSÉJOUR   Saint-Émilion 1er GCC   www.premiers-saint-emilion.com   A: AAA

*Owner: **Héritiers Duffau-Lagarrosse**   33330 Saint-Émilion*

Prior to 1985 this property was a notable underperformer among the Premier Grands Crus Classés. Since then the wine has been altogether more impressive. The style is medium to full with a marked black fruit opulence but sufficiently firm tannins to provide the structure needed for real cellaring. 1990 was truly impressive and the property has been consistent throughout the 90s with 2000 again looking like it will provide that additional dimension. (DM)

● **Château Beauséjour** Saint-Émilion Grand Cru Classé★★★★ £E

CH. LA BIENFAISANCE   Saint-Émilion GC   www.labienfaisance.com   A: F&R

Owner: Duval-Fleury family   33330 Saint-Christophe-des-Bardes

Good small property located on the northern plateau of Saint-Émilion with a total of 16 ha planted in limestone, sand and clay/limestone soils across three parcels. Merlot dominates plantings at around 80 per cent with 15 per cent Cabernet Franc and a smattering of Cabernet Sauvignon. Vinification for La Bienfaisance is traditional with fermentation in cement and ageing in a small proportion of new oak. A richer and more opulent garage-style wine, Sanctus, is aged in 100 per cent new oak. Produced with consultation from Stéphane Derenoncourt, it is less extracted and better balanced than many of its peers. Consistently good in recent vintages it is a very marked step up on the regular label. (DM)

● **Château La Bienfaisance** Saint-Émilion Grand Cru ★★ £D
● **Sanctus** Saint-Émilion Grand Cru ★★★★ £E

CH. LE BON PASTEUR Pomerol   A: AAA

Owner: Michel Rolland 33500 Pomerol
Small Pomerol property of less than 7 ha owned by roving wine consultant Michel Rolland. The vineyards, planted to a combination of 80 per cent Merlot plus Cabernet Franc, are rigorously maintained and yields tightly harnessed. The wine is inevitably fleshy, rich and characteristic of the Rolland style with malolactic fermentation instigated in barrel. While structured and ageworthy the wine is supple, rounded and approachable with just a few years' cellaring. (DM)
● **Château le Bon Pasteur** Pomerol★★★★ £F

CH. BONNET Entre-Deux-Mers www.andrelurton.com   A: **For**, AAA

Owner: André Lurton 33420 Grézillac
This now very substantial operation is owned by André Lurton who achieves first-class results with a number of Châteaux in the Graves and Pessac-Léognan appellations, including Château La LOUVIÈRE. Output is around 125,000 cases a year and the property has some 122 ha of red and 103 ha of white varieties under vine. Red, white and a Bordeaux *clairet* – a lightly coloured style of rosé – are all produced. The reds take the Bordeaux appellation and include a Réserve aged partly in new wood. The dry whites, a tank-fermented Classique and barrel-fermented Réserve, are sold as Entre-Deux-Mers. A new prestige red *cuvée,* Divinus, has been added to the range as well as a Lussac Saint-Émilion Barbe-Blanche. (DM)
● **Château Bonnet** Bordeaux Réserve★★ £B

CH. CANON Saint-Émilion 1er GCC contact@chateau-canon.com   A: AAA

Owner: Wertheimer family 33330 Saint-Émilion
Now under the same ownership as Château RAUZAN-SEGLA. Historically a very significant property and one that is now making a welcome return to the top division of Saint-Émilion estates. The vineyard has recently been extended with the purchase of Château Curé-Bon, which has been incorporated into Canon. The cellars have also been cleaned up and modernised after taint problems. The 1998 was a clear step-up in quality and 2000 and 01 were both four-star wines. The latest vintages look like maintaining this trend. Prior to this you should tread with caution. At its best this is a taut, restrained style with finely structured tannin. It is elegant, medium in weight and once more very ageworthy. (DM)
● **Château Canon** Saint-Émilion Grand Cru Classé★★★ £F

CH. CANON-DE-BREM Canon-Fronsac   A: C&B, Far

Owner: Carrefour 33500 Libourne
Impressive property formerly owned by the Moueix family's *négociant* arm and now by Carrefour. Performance here was somewhat erratic during the early 1990s but has shown a significant improvement of late. The style is purposefully structured and the tannin can be almost austere when the wine is young. Additional refinement is achieved through limited use of new oak and from 1998 the wine has shown an impressive level of ripe, dark plummy fruit and a fleshy if gripping texture. Better with five years' ageing. (DM)
● **Château Canon-de-Brem** Canon-Fronsac★★★ £C

CH. CANON-LA-GAFFELIÈRE Saint Émilion GCC www.neipperg.com   A: AAA

Owner: Vignobles von Neipperg 33330 Saint-Émilion
Canon-la-Gaffelière is now one of a number of striking labels and properties run by Stéphan von Neipperg, who owns the CLOS DE L'ORATOIRE, also in Saint-Émilion, and the outperforming Château D'AIGUILHE in the Côtes de Castillon. The style here, as with all the von Neipperg wines, is opulent, rich and supple, with finely integrated oak and soft, velvety tannin. Canon-la-Gaffelière is itself surprisingly approachable at three or four years. The property is located on the lower-lying limestone slopes below the town of Saint-Émilion. Dominated by old-vine Cabernet Franc, it has been consistently good over the last six or seven

vintages. The *super-cuvée* La MONDOTTE is also now made here. (DM)

● **Château Canon-la-Gaffelière** Saint Émilion Grand Cru Classé★★★★ £F

CH. CARIGNAN   Premières Côtes de Bordeaux   A: C&B

Owner: Philippe Pieraerts 33360 Carignan de Bordeaux

This 25-ha property is producing very good well-priced Bordeaux from one of the outlying appellations. The vineyards are planted on well-sited south-facing slopes in clay-limestone soils covered with stony gravel, which provides excellent drainage. Unlike at CARSIN, only reds are produced from a combination of Merlot (65 per cent), Cabernet Sauvignon (25 per cent) and Cabernet Franc. The splendid château here was originally built in 1452 and the origins of the property date back to the 11th century. Roughly one-third of the vineyard is now over 40 years old and where replanting takes place vine density is being increased. Consultancy advice comes from Louis Mitjaville, whose father owns TERTRE-ROTEBOEUF. The richly textured, dark plum and spice Prima is one of the best examples from the lesser appellations and is aged in 100 per cent new wood for 18 months. An additional premium label, Quator gets 14 to 18 months in four different types of oak. The regular wine is rich, berry-scented and displays very good fruit and the second wine, L'Orangerie de Carignan, ensures the integrity of the top labels. (DM)

● **Château Carignan** Premières Côtes de Bordeaux Prima★★★ £C
● **Château Carignan** Premières Côtes de Bordeaux★★ £B

CH. CARSIN   Premières Côtes de Bordeaux   www.carsin.com

Owner: Julia Berglund 33410 Rions

A good example of what many properties are now beginning to achieve in the less fashionable outlying appellations of Bordeaux. It is based in the Premières Côtes de Bordeaux and the reds are labelled as such, the whites as Bordeaux AC. The regular bottlings are sound and attractive enough, with nicely developed forward fruit, but it is the white Cuvée Prestige and red Cuvée Noire that particularly stand out here. The white has a touch of barrel-fermentation and is ripe and lightly tropical, with well-judged oak. The red is supple, soft and approachable, with just a hint of vanilla oak underpinning it. Signature l'Etiquette Gris is a limited-production white from Sauvignon Gris and there is also a sweet, moderately intense Cadillac. (DM)

● **Château Carsin** Premières Côtes de Bordeaux Cuvée Noire★★ £C
O **Château Carsin** Bordeaux Cuvée Prestige★★ £B

CH. CERTAN-DE-MAY   Pomerol   A: AAA

Owner: Mme Barreau-Badar 33500 Pomerol

Very good, stylish and elegant Pomerol from a tiny holding of vineyards close to PÉTRUS. This is more classically structured than many of its peers and is tight and almost austere when young. Cabernet Franc accounts for 25 per cent of the vineyard, along with a little Cabernet Sauvignon that lends tannin and grip. The wine becomes very harmonious with up to a decade's age. (DM)

● **Château Certan-de-May** Pomerol★★★★ £H

CH. CHAUVIN   Saint-Émilion GCC   www.chateauchauvin.com   A: BBR,F&R,Tur

Owner: Marie-France Février et Beatrice Ondet   1 Cabanne Nord, 33330 Saint-Émilion

This property has been a consistent performer through most of the mid- to late 1990s and continues to be so. Consultancy input comes from Michel Rolland and the style is full, rich and fleshy, with supple, well-rounded tannins and real complexity in 2001, 00, 99 and 98. A special bottling, Vieux Château Chauvin, has so far only been produced in 1998. (DM)

● **Château Chauvin Saint-Émilion** Grand Cru Classé★★★★ £E

CH. CHEVAL BLANC   Saint-Émilion 1er GCC   www.chateau-cheval-blanc.com   A: AAA

Owner: Bernard Arnault & Albert Frère 33330 Saint-Émilion

One of the two great wines of Saint-Émilion and produced in much greater quantity than AUSONE – some 12,500 cases a year as against barely 2,000. It has also regularly performed at the very highest level throughout the last two decades. Cheval Blanc is located close to the appellation boundary with Pomerol. There is a high proportion of Cabernet Franc in the vineyard (over 50 per cent), which makes the wine quite different to those of its near neighbours. Bernault Arnault and Albert Frère purchased the property in the late 1990s and no expense will be spared in attempting to establish Cheval Blanc as the greatest property on Bordeaux's Right Bank. The style is rich, concentrated and opulent, with intensely complex, dark berry fruit and spice all underpinned by a structured velvety texture. To fully appreciate it in all its glory, 10 years or more of ageing is required. A wine of truly legendary proportions in 1990, 83 and 82 and 2000 may yet reach similar heights. (DM)

● **Château Cheval Blanc** Saint-Émilion Grand Cru Classé❀❀❀❀❀ £H

CH. CLINET   Pomerol   www.wines-uponatime.com   A: AAA

Owner: Jean-Louis Laborde 3 Rue Fénelon, 33000 Bordeaux

Michel Rolland has provided consultancy input at this property for over 10 years, first to the late Jean-Michel Arcaute and now to Jean-Louis Laborde. The style has remained consistent throughout the period. Ripe to very ripe, full, rich and almost opulent with a supple silky texture, the wine is always bottled with neither fining nor filtration and is aged in 100 per cent new oak. Don't be fooled, though, as there is both depth and a firm tannic structure to the young wine. Best with at least five years' ageing. (DM)

● **Château Clinet** Pomerol★★★★ £G

CLOS L'ÉGLISE   Pomerol   A: J&B,AAA

Owner: Sylvain Garcin-Cathiard 33500 Pomerol

There are just 6 ha of vines producing this fine and impressively dense and powerful Pomerol. The wine is lent considerable structure by the inclusion of up to 40 per cent Cabernet Franc. Very rich and fleshy, it is loaded with dark plum and spicy vanilla oak. It was very stylish in 2001, 00, 99 and 98 and will cellar well for up to a decade. There is also a good second wine, L'Esprit de l'Église. (DM)

● **Clos l'Église** Pomerol★★★★ £H

CH. LA CLOTTE   Saint-Émilion GCC   A: F&R

Owner: SCEA du Château la Clotte 33330 Saint-Émilion

The quality at this 4-ha property planted to mainly Merlot with a little Cabernet Franc and less Cabernet Sauvignon was good prior to 1997 but really no more. with vineyards on sand and gravel soils close to PAVIE-MACQUIN there should be real potential here. Things are taking a turn for the better, though. Consultancy is provided by Stéphane Derenoncourt and the style is now more opulent and concentrated with harmonious, well-judged oak and sufficient depth and firm, structured tannin to develop well in bottle over five years or so. A property to watch. (DM)

● **Château La Clotte** Saint-Émilion Grand Cru Classé★★★ £E

CH. LA CONSEILLANTE   Pomerol   chateau.la.conseillante@wanadoo.fr

Owner: Nicolas family 33500 Pomerol

One of the great Pomerol names, La Conseillante has an excellent vineyard aspect and is located close to L'ÉVANGILE and CHEVAL BLANC across the appellation boundary. With some Cabernet Franc (20 per cent) as well as Merlot (80 per cent) planted in gravel soils, the wine is both rich, fleshy and full of dark fruit but also firmly structured. The best years show a remarkably complex array of dark fruits and oriental spices.

The wine benefits from six to seven years' ageing at least. 2000 could well be exceptional and of a similar order to the great 89 and 90. Earlier classics were 85 and 82. (DM)

● **Château La Conseillante** Pomerol★★★★★ £G

CH. LA COUSPAUDE St-Émilion GCC   www.la-couspaude.fr   A: AAA

Owner: Vignobles Aubert   33330 Saint-Émilion
This is now a very impressive property located to the east of the appellation and planted with Merlot and 15 per cent each of Cabernet Sauvignon and Cabernet Franc in limestone soils. The property is another of many benefiting from Michel Rolland's consultancy and the style is characteristically sumptuous and fleshy, with supple, velvety tannin and a complex, dark fruit character with abundant oak spice. Half a decade or so of ageing is needed to throw off the initially firm tannic grip. (DM)

● **Château La Couspaude** Saint-Émilion Grand Cru Classé★★★ £F

CH. LA CROIX-DE-GAY Pomerol   A: AAA

Owner: Chantal Lebreton & Alain Raynaud   33500 Pomerol
This is a good middle-ranking Pomerol with an attractive plump, plummy Merlot character after three or fours years of bottle-age but without any great depth or complexity. There are 10 ha planted, 90 per cent to Merlot. What marks the property out is the quality of a superior selection called la Fleur-de-Gay. Produced from 100 per cent Merlot, this is dense, opulent, rich and oaky. Not surprisingly it is fairly pricey. (DM)

● **Château La Croix-de-Gay** Pomerol★★ £E
● **La Fleur-de-Gay** Pomerol★★★★ £H

CH. LA DOMINIQUE Saint-Émilion GCC   A: AAA

Owner: Clément Fayat   33330 Saint-Émilion
This property, with an ideal location in very close proximity to CHEVAL BLANC, has been a reasonably consistent performer since the late 1980s. The wine is vinified with consultancy input from Michel Rolland. The style is not only opulent and fleshy with marked new oak and rich, concentrated, spicy, dark fruit but there is an underlying finesse and quality here. The wine is supple but well-structured and very ageworthy. 1998 was very good and 2000 looks set to be in the same mould. A small-volume garage wine, Saint Dominique, is made from an parcel adjacent to the property. (DM)

● **Château La Dominique** Saint-Émilion Grand Cru Classé★★★★ £G

CH. L'ÉGLISE-CLINET Pomerol   A: AA

Owner: Denis Durantou   33500 Pomerol
Magnificent small Pomerol property with a holding of just 5.5 ha of Merlot and Cabernet Franc. The vineyard is very old, with some of the vines nearing 100 years. The style bears little comparison with those neighbours who opt for modern extracted wines and dollops of new oak. L'Église-Clinet is structured, dense and backward when young. Given six or seven years the result is an elegant, velvety and classically proportioned example of the appellation. Very impressive in 2000, 98, 97, 96 and 95. 2001 should be every bit as good. (DM)

● **Château L'Église-Clinet** Pomerol✪✪✪✪✪ £H

CH. L'ÉVANGILE Pomerol   www.lafite.com   A: AAA

*Owner: **Domaines Barons de Rothschild**   33500 Pomerol*
This is an impressively deep, structured and powerful example of Pomerol. Like L'ÉGLISE-CLINET, it is markedly different from many of its supple, rounded, softly structured contemporaries. Owned since 1990 by the Rothschilds, the wine is traditionally vinified and possesses sturdy, dense, firm tannin when young,

along with formidably concentrated levels of complex, dark, spicy fruit. There is oak evident here but its very harmoniously integrated. It has been remarkably good in the best years of the last decade or so; 1990 was of legendary quality – super-five stars – and 2000 may well end up of a similar stature. (DM)

● **Château l'Évangile** Pomerol★★★★★ £H

EXCELLENCE DE BOIS PERTUIS   Bordeaux

Owner: Bernard Magrez   c/o Terroirs d'Exception, 33330 Saint-Christophe des Bardes
Although merely a humble AC Bordeaux this is one of a number of wines released by Bernard Magrez under his Terroirs d'Exception label. Others include LA SERÉNITÉ in Pessac-Léognan and Gérard Depardieu's property MA VERITÉ in the Haut-Médoc. The 2 ha vineyard is planted solely to Merlot which is now 25 years old. Yields are kept very low at just over 20 hl/ha and crop thinning is practised. The wine is fermented in wooden vats and ageing is in new wood. It is rich, dense and opulently plummy with marked extract. The initially firm tannins need three or four years to subside. (DM)

● **Excellence de Bois Pertuis** Bordeaux★★★ £D

CH. FALFAS   Côtes de Bourg   A: **GWW**,Adm

Owner: Cochran family   33740 Bayon-sur-Gironde
Decent Bourg property run on biodynamic lines by John Cochran. The winemaking origins of the property go back to 1612. There are 22 ha of vines planted, 55 per cent Merlot, 30 per cent Cabernet Sauvignon and unusually 10 per cent of Malbec. The balance is Cabernet Franc. There is a cold soak for 48 hours, traditional fermentation and malolactic in *cuve*, followed by ageing in 30 per cent new wood. The wines are richly textured and full of dark plummy fruit and a marked spicy, tobacco character no doubt emphasised by the inclusion of Malbec. The top label, Le Chevalier, has an added dimension and was on the edge of three stars in 2000. (DM)

● **Château Falfas** Côtes de Bourg★★ £B   Côtes de Bourg Le Chevalier★★ £B

CH. FAUGÈRES   Saint-Émilion GC   www.chateau-faugeres.com   A: AAA

Owner: Corinne Guisez   Saint-Étienne-de-Lisse, 33330 Saint-Émilion
Major investment in both the vineyard and cellars under the current ownership has wrought major change and delivered increasingly impressive wines. The Château Faugères regular Saint-Émilion is a dense, richly concentrated and spicy Grand Cru which is aged in 100 per cent new oak and has the depth and structure to develop well over a decade or more. Since 1998 a super-rich special *cuvée*, Château Péby Faugères, has been produced which is both sumptuously fleshy and very powerful. The Cap de Faugères is a supple, rounded and forward style produced from vineyards owned in the Côtes de Castillon. (DM)

● **Château Faugères** Saint-Émilion Grand Cru★★★ £E

CH. FIGEAC   Saint-Émilion 1er GCC   www.chateau-figeac.com   A: AAA

Owner: Thierry Manoncourt & Eric d'Aramon   Saint-Etienne-de-Lisse, 33330 Saint-Émilion
The traditional qualities of this Premier Grand Cru Classé – namely refinement, elegance and a harmonious balance of subtle, dark, spicy fruit and lightly smoky oak – have been apparent in a number of recent vintages but strangely absent in others when one would expect the property to have performed well. The vineyard has an unusually high proportion of Cabernet Sauvignon and Cabernet Franc for Saint-Émilion, mainly because of the marked gravel component of the soil, with just one-third planted to Merlot. The resulting wines are inevitably powerful and structured when at their best and long-lived. Recent vintages look very good, four stars at least, but 1996 and 97 were disappointing. (DM)

● **Château Figeac** Saint-Émilion Grand Cru Classé★★★ £G

CH. FLEUR-CARDINALE   Saint-Émilion GC   A: THt

Owner: Dominique Decoster   33330 Saint-Émilion

Well-priced and improving Saint-Émilion Grand Cru which has shown a consistent upturn in quality since the late 1990s. Both the 1999 and 2000 were full of rich, fleshy fruit and well-balanced new oak. The 2003 looks certain to be of at least a similar order. The property is situated in the north-east of the appellation and planted to 70 per cent Merlot, the balance equal proportions of Cabernet Sauvignon and Cabernet Franc, in *argilo-calcaire* soils. The average age of the vines is now 35 years and under the insistence of consultant Jean-Luc Thunevin yields are being reduced in a consistent drive for quality. Richly textured, approachable reds are likely to be a regular occurence here. The wine will nonetheless benefit from three or four years age. (DM)

● **Château Fleur-Cardinale** Saint-Émilion Grand Cru★★★ £D

CH. LA FLEUR-PÉTRUS   Pomerol   A: AAA

Owner: Moueix family   33500 Pomerol

Like PÉTRUS itself this property is owned by the Moueix family. The vineyards have a higher proportion of gravel than is commonly found here and the wine is less opulent and rich than many of its neighbours. It is refined, medium- rather than full-bodied and tightly structured and restrained in its youth. With age it will become very fine and complex and is extraordinarily long-lived. 1975 still seems youthful. Somewhat erratic in the 1980s, the wine has been a model of consistency since the mid- to late 90s. (DM)

● **Château la Fleur-Pétrus** Pomerol★★★★ £G

CH. FOMBRAUGE   St-Émilion GC   www.fombrauge.com   A: AAA

Owner: Bernard Magrez   33330 Saint-Christophe des Bardes

Bernard Magrez, owner of PAPE-CLEMENT in Pessac-Léognan, purchased Fombrauge in 1999. While Fombrauge has been going from strength to strength, particularly throughout the late 1990s, it has achieved new heights under the current ownership. With over 50 ha of vineyards and located to the north-east of the appellation, away from the established grandee properties, Fombrauge is proving as elsewhere that the less-fancied plots in this sizeable appellation can provide impressive wines. A limited-production, highly priced special *cuvée*, Magrez-Fombrauge, has also now been released. Massively powerful and extracted, it remains to be seen how this wine will develop, as with other *super-cuvées* from lesser plots, but it has considerable promise. Bernard Magrez has also produced a number of small-scale *garagiste*-style wines of great potential from a number of properties throughout the region and has provided input to actor Gérard Depardieu and actress Carole Bouquet in similar properties in both Bordeaux and the Midi and most excitingly Morocco and Algeria. (DM)

● **Château Fombrauge** Saint-Émilion Grand Cru★★★ £D
● **Magrez-Fombrauge** Saint-Émilion Grand Cru★★★★★ £G

CH. FONTENIL   Fronsac   A: THp

Owner: Michel & Dany Rolland   33141 Saillans

This small Fronsac property is owned by Michel and Dany Rolland. The 9 ha are planted to 90 per cent Merlot, the balance Cabernet Sauvignon. The wine is lushly textured, rich, supple and full of opulence, with just a hint of cassis adding depth and weight to the bramble and dark berry fruit. The new oak so apparent when the wine is young will become more balanced and harmonious with time. One of the better examples of this lesser appellation. A tiny-production *super-cuvée*, Défi de Fontenil, is also now produced. (DM)

● **Château Fontenil** Fronsac★★★★ £D

CH. FOUGAS   Côtes de Bourg   A: F&R,Sec,N&P,Tur

Owner: Jean-Yves & Michèle Béchet   33710 Lansac

This is the larger of the two properties of the Béchets, who also own the tiny Saint-Émilion property RIOU DE THAILLAS. There are just 11 ha under vine here, planted to Merlot (50 per cent) and equal proportions of Cabernet Sauvignon and Cabernet Franc. The site is surrounded by two streams which provide excellent natural drainage from its alluvial soils. Each parcel of vines is vinified separately after cold maceration, and the wines spend a small period on their gross lees. The special *cuvée* Maldoror is sourced from the best individual plots on the property and is aged in 100 per cent new oak. Both wines will stand a litle age and the richly textured, dark plum and spice Maldoror demands two to three years to integrate the not inconsderable high-toast oak. (DM)

● **Château Fougas** Côtes de Bourg★★ £B   Côtes de Bourg Maldoror★★★ £C

CLOS FOURTET   Saint-Émilion 1er GCC   www.premiers-saint-emilion.com   A: THt

Owner: Philippe Cuvelier   3330 Saint-Émilion

Under new ownership since 2001. There are 20 ha of vineyards planted to a mix of Merlot (80 per cent), Cabernet Sauvignon (12 per cent) and Cabernet Franc. The resulting wines have generally been big, full and sturdy, particularly during the last decade, which has seen a consistent raising of standards. The wine is densely extracted and sees a high proportion of new oak. Recent vintages have been refined and classy with great intensity. The 2003 has splendid potential, and may turn out to be worthy of five stars so this trend is likely to continue and the property should move towards greater things. (DM)

● **Clos Fourtet St-Émilion** Grand Cru Classé★★★★ £F

CH. FRANC-MAYNE   Saint-Émilion GCC   www.chateau-francmayne.com   A: N&P,F&R

Owner: Georgy Fourcroy   33330 Saint-Émilion

Relatively tiny Grand Cru Classé property of just 7 ha which has produced increasingly good wine in recent vintages. The vineyards are planted in limestone soils to the west of the town of Saint-Émilion, close to neighbouring GRAND-MAYNE. The limited *cuvée* La Gomerie from BEAU-SÉJOUR BÉCOT is also sourced from these slopes. Merlot dominates plantings at 90 per cent; the balance is Cabernet Sauvignon. The wine is richly textured and impressively concentrated with dark spicy fruit and sufficiently supple tannin to drink well with three or four years' ageing. Michel Rolland provides the winemaking direction and the style of the wine reflects his input. Malolactic is in barrel and copious new oak is used for ageing. Total output is barely 3,000 cases and around a third of this is earmarked for the very decent second label, Les Cèdres de Franc-Mayne. (DM)

● **Château Franc-Mayne** Saint-Émilion Grand Cru Classé★★★ £E

CH. LA GAFFELIÈRE   Saint-Émilion 1er GCC   www.chateau-la-gaffeliere.com   A: AAA

Owner: Comte de Malet Roquefort   33330 Saint-Émilion

After a period when this 22 ha property was relatively disappointing in the early to mid-1990s the wines appear to be consistently improving. There has been no new ownership or marked change in the style, just, it would appear, a general sharpening of the act. This is very much a classically structured Saint-Émilion: stylish,, medium- rather than full-bodied with a restrained mineral character as well as subtle, smoky, dark fruit. It will add weight with five years' cellaring. (DM)

● **Château la Gaffelière** Saint-Émilion Grand Cru Classé★★★ £G

CH. GAZIN   Pomerol   www.gazin.com   A: AAA

Owner: Balliencourt family   Le Gazin, 33500 Pomerol

This is among Pomerol's larger properties, with 23 ha under vine, the vast majority being Merlot, with small amounts of Cabernet Sauvignon and Cabernet Franc also planted. The vineyards consist of gravel/clay soils and are sited next to PETRUS and L'EVANGILE. 10,000 cases a year are produced, 8,000 of which are the Grand Vin, the balance being the second wine L'Hospitalet de Gazin. The wines have been cosistently good now for a decade. The 1990s have seen a transformation, with improved management and control in both vineyard and cellar. The trio of vintages 1998, 99 and 00 were particularly good here. The style is rich, forward and opulent with ripe and plummy dark fruit and an increasing amount of new oak used. (DM)

● **Château Gazin** Pomerol★★★★ £G

CH. GRAND CORBIN-DESPAGNE   Saint-Émilion GC   A: **Col**,BBR,F&R,Tur

Owner: Despagne family 33330 Saint-Émilion
Moderate-sized Grand Cru property with just over 26 ha under vine. The Despagne family have been producing good well-priced examples of the appellation since the 1998 vintage. As well as their Grand Vin they also produce a decent second label, Petit Corbin-Despagne. The vineyard, which is a mix of Merlot (75 per cent), Cabernet Franc (24 per cent) and a tiny amount of Cabernet Sauvignon, is planted in sandy-clay soils. The harvest is carefully sorted and with an average vine age of nearly 40 years the wine has no problem handling the 20 to 30 days of vatting and ageing in 50 per cent new wood for up to 18 months. Rich and fleshy in style, it requires four to five years' cellaring to throw the aggressive character of its youthful tannin. (DM)

● **Château Grand Corbin-Despagne** Saint-Émilion Grand Cru★★★ £D
● **Château Grand Corbin-Despagne** Saint-Émilion Petit Corbin-Despagne★ £C

CH. GRAND-MAYNE   Saint-Émilion GCC   www.grand-mayne.com   A: AAA

Owner: Nony family 33330 Saint-Émilion
Grand-Mayne produces impressively dark, dense and well-structured Saint-Émilions. There are some 17 ha under vine and the estate is located towards the western side of the appellation. Quality has much improved in recent vintages and the wine is suppler and has better fruit quality than of old. An increasing use of new oak is helping to underpin the character of the château. While firmly structured when young, the wine avoids austerity. (DM)

● **Château Grand-Mayne** Saint-Émilion Grand Cru Classé★★★★ £F

CH. GRAND-PONTET   Saint-Émilion GCC   A: N&P,Tur

Owner: Pourquet-Bécot family 33330 Saint-Émilion
There are 14 ha of vines here, mainly Merlot with a reasonably high proportion of Cabernet Franc (15 per cent) and Cabernet Sauvignon (10 per cent). The clay-rich soils provide a subtle and elegant style. The wine has been at least good throughout the mid- to late 1990s, with greater fruit ripeness and suppler tannins. (DM)

● **Château Grand-Pontet** Saint-Émilion Grand Cru Classé★★★ £D

CH. GREE LAROQUE   Bordeaux Supérieur

Owner: Benoit de Nyvenheim Arnaud Laroque, 33910 Saint-Ciers-d'Abzac
This tiny-volume wine sourced from 1.6 ha of vineyards to the north of Libourne and Fronsac is a testament to the commitment of Benoit de Nyvenheim and the winemaking skills of consultant Stéphane Derenoncourt. The vines, a mix of Merlot (75 per cent) and Cabernet Franc (20 per cent) as well as a sprinkling of Cabernet Sauvignon, are planted in well-drained gravel, clay and clay/limestone soils. Of equal importance is the age of the vineyard at over 40 years, virtually unheard of in this lesser appellation. Vinification is modern and precise. The harvest is carefully sorted and malolactic takes place in barrel with the wine aged on lees for 12 to 18 months in one-third new oak. Bottled unfiltered, the wine is impressively deep and concentrated with dark, spicy fruit, opulent oak and just a hint of dark pepper in the background. Give it three to four years. (DM)

● **Château Gree Laroque** Bordeaux Supérieur★★★ £D

LA CROIX DE PEYROLIE   Lussac-Saint-Émilion

Owner: Carole Bouquet   c/o Terroirs d'Exception, 33330 Saint-Christophe des Bardes
Owned by French film actress Carole Bouquet, a former Bond girl, La Croix de Peyrolie is marketed under the Terroirs d'Exception label by Bernard Magrez, owner of FOMBRAUGE. The vineyard is tiny at just 1.3 hectares and yields a mere 12.5 hl/ha, so this is very much a garage-style operation. Vinification is in wooden barrels with manual *pigeage* and malolactic is instigated in new oak, where the wine spends 20 months. Rich and very concentrated, with a fine and firmly tannic structure in its youth it will benefit from five or six years' ageing. I feel, as with a number of Magrez wines, that there can be just a touch too much extract in a lesser year like 2002. Very impressive nonetheless. (DM)
● **La Croix de Peyrolie** Lussac-Saint-Émilion★★★★ £F

CH. LAFLEUR   Pomerol   A: AAA

Owner: Marie Robin   Grand Village, 33240 Mouillac
Tiny Pomerol property consisting of a mere 4.5 ha of vines, half surprisingly planted to Cabernet Franc. This component helps provide the considerable structure which enables the wine to age gracefully for two decades and more. In recent vintages an increasing amount of new oak has been used and the wine possesses not just a finely structured, almost mineral core but a rich, concentrated, black-fruited opulence also. It was remarkably consistent throughout the 1990s and outperformed in the difficult years early in the decade. (DM)
● **Château Lafleur** Pomerol❁❁❁❁❁ £H

CH. LAROZE   Saint-Émilion GC   www.ch-laroze.com

Owner: Meslin family   33330 Saint-Émilion
This is another Saint-Émilion property much improved in the late 1990s. The wine is crafted in a lush, fleshy and opulent style with supple tannins and a very appealing youthful character. Dark, spicy plummy fruit is very apparent. Part malolactic in barrel helps to underpin the style. The 27 ha of vineyards are located on the western plateau of the appellation and are planted in sandy soils with a chalky/clay bedrock offering good drainage. The estate has been farmed biodynamically since 1991 and the vine age is gradually creeping up although it is still relatively young at 20 years. Certainly it would appear that the best is yet to emerge here. The wine is bottled unfiltered. (DM)
● **Château Laroze** Saint-Émilion Grand Cru★★★ £D

LA MONDOTTE   Saint-Émilion   www.neipperg.com   A: AAA

Owner: Comte Stephan von Neipperg   33330 Saint-Émilion
Along with Le DÔME, this is one of the two great garage wines to emerge in the last half decade. Produced at CANON-LA-GAFFELIÈRE, the vineyard consists of 4.5 ha planted on clay/silt soils over a rocky subsoil. It is superbly drained with an unusually steep south-facing aspect. It is this low-yielding *terroir* that is responsible for a wine of remarkable depth and concentration. Blended from 80 per cent Merlot and 20 per cent Cabernet Franc, it offers a truly opulent and exotic array of dark fruits and oriental spices. It is produced in the classic Derenoncourt style with ageing on lees in new oak for a year and a half and is bottled unfiltered. (DM)
● **La Mondotte** Saint-Émilion Grand Cru★★★★★ £H

CH. LATOUR-À-POMEROL   Pomerol   A: AAA

Owner: Mme Lacoste-Loubat/Moueix Family   33500 Pomerol
This is another property under the Moueix family umbrella. These are supple, ripe and at their best richly plummy examples of Pomerol, produced to showcase the more opulent character of the appellation. The wine has generally performed well during the period from 1994 onwards, with just the odd hint of

aggressive tannin sometimes marring the style. It develops well with six or seven years' age. (DM)

● **Château Latour-à-Pomerol**★★★ £H

LE DÔME Saint-Émilion info@teyssier.fr A: AAA

Owner: Jonathan Maltus 33330 Vignonnet

This vies with LA MONDOTTE to be first among the garage wines of Saint-Émilion. It is produced by Jonathan Malthus at his property Château TEYSSIER, from a single parcel of 2.85 ha which neighbours Château ANGELUS. Cabernet Franc is the main component at 70 per cent, with the balance Merlot. The wine is modern in style with a pre-fermentation maceration and both *pigeage* and pumping over are employed during fermentation. Malolactic is conducted in barrel and then 50 per cent is drawn off and aged in a second series of brand new oak barrels. Yet while it is deep and very concentrated, the wine's fine mineral structure provides exemplary balance. It will require seven or eight years' patience to show at its peak. (DM)

● **Le Dôme** Saint-Émilion Grand Cru★★★★★ £G

CH. LUCIE Saint-Émilion GC

Owner: Bortolussi family 316 Grands-Champs, 33330 Saint-Sulpice-de-Faleyrens

A recently established tiny property with less than 2 ha under vine. The wines are made with consultancy advice from Stéphane Derenoncourt. The first wines were vinified here in the 1995 vintage although a sizeable proportion of the vines date back over 100 years, which contributes a great deal to the style and quality achieved. The vineyard is planted to Merlot and Cabernet Franc on a mix of sand and clay with a part on clay/limestone. L'ANGÉLUS is a neighbouring property. This is a true garage wine: the vinification takes place in the town of Saint-Émilion but in excellent underground cellar conditions with good ventilation. Malolactic in barrel and ageing in new oak for 12 to 15 months help create the rich, opulent style. The wine is loaded with dense, dark fruit but there is a real purity and depth often missing in other wines made in a similar style from the region. Accessible from a young age, the wine will nevertheless add further complexity with cellaring. (DM)

● **Lucia** Saint-Émilion Grand Cru★★★★ £E

CH. MAGDELAINE Saint-Émilion 1er GCC www.premiers-saint-emilion.com A: AAA

Owner: Moueix family 33330 Saint-Émilion

Another Moueix family property. This is an opulent, richly plummy, Merlot-dominated wine crafted from older vines than is usual for the region. Supple and approachable but nevertheless possessing a fine, well-structured mineral backbone, the wine can be enjoyable with as little as five years' cellaring and will keep for much longer. (DM)

● **Château Magdelaine** Saint-Émilion Grand Cru Classé★★★★ £D

CH. MONBOUSQUET Saint-Émilion GC www.chateaupavie.com A: AAA

Owner: Vignobles Perse 33330 Saint-Émilion

A typically modern extractive style of winemaking produces a ripe and bold style of Saint-Émilion here. Michel Rolland is the consultant and his techniques of ripe, late-harvested fruit, deep colour and malolactic in barrel are all on show. The driving force behind the renaissance of this once-mediocre property is Gérard Perse, who also owns PAVIE and PAVIE-DECESSE. Expect the wines to develop well in the medium term. (DM)

● **Château Monbousquet** Saint-Émilion Grand Cru★★★★ £F

CH. MOULIN HAUT-LAROQUE Fronsac www.moulinhautlaroque.fr.st   A: N&P

Owner: Jean-Noël Hervé Le Moulin, 33141 Saillans
This is one of the more impressive properties in the increasingly fashionable Fronsac appellation. The 15 ha are mainly Merlot but there is a significant amount of old-vine Cabernet Franc, along with Cabernet Sauvignon and Malbec. The style is ripe and full with an element of new oak showing through and a supple, velvety structure. Better with four to five years' age. (DM)
● **Château Moulin Haut-Laroque** Fronsac★★ £C

CH. MOULIN PEY-LABRIE Canon-Fronsac   A: C&B

Owner: Bénédicte & Gregoire Hubau 33126 Fronsac
Small property of some 6.5 ha producing modern, stylish and ripe reds with a high proportion of Merlot and increasing use of new oak. The approach mirrors that of other quality-minded properties from lesser Bordeaux appellations in emphasising forward, dark and richly plummy fruit in a soft, fleshy, textured style. The rounded, velvety tannin is assisted by completion of the malolactic fermentation in barrel. (DM)
● **Château Moulin Pey-Labrie** Canon-Fronsac★★★ £D

CH. MOULIN SAINT-GEORGES Saint-Émilion GC   A: AAA

Owner: Vauthier Family 33330 Saint-Émilion
Located in close proximity to AUSONE and in fact owned by the same family. Quality here has been consistently improving in recent vintages, and has rated four stars since 1998. The 8-ha, Merlot-dominated vineyard is meticulously managed and careful vinification produces richly fruity and fleshy wines often high in alcohol with marked new oak. They will be all the better for four or five years' ageing. (DM)
● **Château Moulin Saint-Georges Saint-Émilion** Grand Cru★★★★ £F

CLOS DE L'ORATOIRE Saint-Émilion GCC info@neipperg.com   A: AAA

Owner: Vignobles von Neipperg 33330 Saint-Émilion
Under the same ownership as CANON-LA-GAFFELIÈRE and the *super-cuvée* LA MONDOTTE. As at Stéphan von Neipperg's other properties, the style here is modern and approachable but the wine is neither overripe nor excessively extracted. There is a hallmark of underlying refinement and elegance. The finely crafted tannins need five or six years to achieve real harmony. Classy and ageworthy. (DM)
● **Clos de l'Oratoire Saint-Émilion** Grand Cru Classé★★★★ £G

PASSION DU PRIEURÉ MALESAN Premières Côtes de Blaye

Owner: Bernard Magrez c/o Terroirs d'Exception, 33330 Saint-Christophe des Bardes
This is one of a number of wines that Bernard Magrez is now marketing as Terroirs d'Exception. It is a tiny-production garage-style wine from one of Bordeaux's humbler appellations produced from mainly Merlot but also a little Cabernet Franc. The vineyard yields a miserly 20 hl/ha or less. The result is a wine which is deeply extracted, rich and concentrated with very evident new oak. It will benefit from three or four years' ageing. Magrez also works with French film actor and vineyard owner Gérard Depardieu in this project. Similarly impressive reds have been made in the Roussillon along with Depardieu's North African Domaine SAINT AUGUSTIN and LUMIÈRE wines. (DM)
● **Passion du Prieuré Malesan** Premières Côtes de Blaye★★★ £D

CH. PAVIE Saint-Émilion 1er GCC www.chateaupavie.com   A: AAA

Owner: Vignobles Perse 33330 Saint-Émilion
This property was purchased in 1998 by Gérard Perse who also owns PAVIE-DECESSE, MONBOUSQUET and PETIT-VILLAGE. Quality was formerly variable but substantial investment in the cellars should bring

greater consistency. However, the Perse wines and particularly Pavie have become the most controversial of the new wave of late-harvested and highly extracted reds which focus on opulence and concentration perhaps more than elegance or purity. Achieving a balance of the two is what marks the greatest of the new wave. Pavie is increasingly very late-harvested and more akin to a full-blown Napa red than a classical Saint-Émilion of the old school. If you are a fan of rich and concentrated reds with massive extract and not inconsiderable alcohol then this will appeal, otherwise you may prefer to look elsewhere. There is no doubting the commitment to quality, with a modern and sophisticated approach to vinification and minimal handling in the cellars. How well the current generation of vintages will age remains to be seen. Prior to 1998 the wines were adequate at best with only the earlier vintages of 1990, 89, 86 and 82 being of real note. (DM)

● **Château Pavie** Saint-Émilion Grand Cru Classé★★★★ £H

CH. PAVIE-DECESSE   Saint-Émilion GCC   www.chateaupavie.com   A: AAA

Owner: Vignobles Perse   33330 Saint-Émilion
Like PAVIE, owned by Gérard Perse and now producing wines of greater density and power than a few years back. The style, as at Pavie, is for rich and opulent reds but there has always been a tighter, leaner edge to Decesse when compared with its larger, more illustrious neighbour. The wine is reasonably harmonious with copious quantities of sweet, dark fruit and lots of spicy, vanilla-scented oak. Since 1997 it is of a much richer style than of old. It should age reasonably well but is reasonably approachable young. (DM)

● **Château Pavie-Decesse** Saint-Émilion Grand Cru Classé★★★★ £G

CH. PAVIE-MACQUIN   Saint-Émilion GCC   pavie.macquin@wanadoo.fr   A: AAA

Owner: Corre-Macquin family   33330 Saint-Émilion
Consultancy input here comes from Stéphane Derenoncourt and the property is farmed biodynamically. It shares the same limestone plateau as PAVIE-DECESSE and has an elegant hard, tight and structured mineral edge to its character. In the cellar minimal handling is the order of the day and the results are enormously impressive. The wines are dense, powerful and structured, with seamlessly integrated dark, spicy fruit and oak as well as displaying marvellous purity. They age very well. Only 1992 looks really disappointing. The wines of the late 1990s show a serious hike in quality. (DM)

● **Château Pavie-Macquin** Saint-Émilion Grand Cru Classé★★★★★ £F

CH. PETIT-VILLAGE   Pomerol   A: AAA

Owner: Vignobles Perse   33500 Pomerol
Once part of AXA Millésimes, this property used to be under the same ownership as PICHON-LONGUEVILLE in Pauillac. It has now been purchased by Gérard Perse, who owns the revitalised PAVIE and PAVIE-DECESSE. The style here has been for fairly sturdy, structured wines without necessarily the refinement and depth one might wish for. There has, however, been a step up here since the property changed hands in 1998 and the Perse influence will no doubt ensure this continues. (DM)

● **Château Petit-Village** Pomerol★★★ £G

CH. PÉTRUS   Pomerol   A: AAA

Owner: Moueix family   1 Rue Petrus-Arnaud, 33500 Pomerol
One of the most expensive wines in the world, it used to be the most expensive by a long way but has been challenged in recent years not only by near neighbours but also by limited-production special *cuvées* in California. Much depends on the vagaries of the international auction markets. There is no doubt, though, that Pétrus is one of Bordeaux's truly great reds. A very high proportion of Merlot (95 per cent), with the balance Cabernet Franc, is planted in vineyards that sit upon a plateau of remarkably well-drained clay soils and provide a unique *terroir*. Extraordinary care is taken in both the vineyard and cellars in producing a

wine that is immensely rich and concentrated with a bewildering array of dark fruits, oriental spices and seamlessly integrated oak, all supported by very fine supple tannins. It is consistently great and perhaps only struggles very slightly in lesser years, but then so does every other property in the region. (DM)

● **Château Pétrus** Pomerol✪✪✪✪✪ £H

CH. LE PIN Pomerol

A: AAA

Owner: Jacques Thienpont Les Grands Champs, 33500 Pomerol
Production here is tiny at only around 700 cases a year and two decades ago the wine was just a hobby of owner Jacques Thienpont. However, it has become an auction favourite and, partly because of its scarcity, has on occasion fetched higher prices than PÉTRUS. The style is for ripe, opulent and approachable wines rather than ones that are overstructured and austere and the vinification reflects this approach. Malolactic is carried out in barrel and the wine sees 100 per cent new oak which is seamlessly integrated. Undoubtedly a very fine and richly opulent example of Pomerol. (DM)

● **Château le Pin** Pomerol✪✪✪✪✪ £H

CH. LE PIN BEAUSOLEIL Bordeaux-Supérieur arno.pauchet@wanadoo.fr A: Cam,F&R

Owner: Elizabeth Leriche & Arnaud Pauchet Le Pin, 33420 Saint-Vincent-de-Pertignas
Small-production, top-quality red from one of the region's humbler appellations. The property is located just the other side of the Dordogne from the Côtes de Castillon and is producing similarly impressive results to some of the better examples of that AC. Less than 2,000 cases a year are made from the 5 ha here. The vineyards are planted to Merlot (60 per cent), Cabernet Franc (20 per cent), Cabernet Sauvignon (17 per cent) and a tiny amount of Malbec. Initially backward and firm in structure, it displays an array of dark, spicy almost exotic flavours. Give it four or five years to round out. (DM)

● **Château Le Pin Beausoleil** Bordeaux Supérieur★★★ £C

CLOS PUY ARNAUD Côtes de Castillon

A: F&R

Owner: Thierry Valette 7 Puy Arnaud, 33350 Belvès de Castillon
This is one of a handful of really impressive properties from this now excellent satellite appellation. Unlike neighbouring Château d'AIGUILHE, the vineyard area here is small at a mere 7 ha. Planted to a mix of 70 per cent Merlot, 20 per cent Cabernet Franc and the balance Cabernet Sauvignon, its aspect is excellent with south facing slopes and the limestone-based soils provide excellent drainage. The vines are also now farmed biodynamically. Clos Puy Arnaud is dense and richly concentrated with dark berry fruit, spicy oak and supple, firmly structured tannin all in evidence. Consultant Stéphane Derenoncourt uses all his techniques during vinification: pre-fermentation maceration, malolactic in barrel and ageing on lees in 50 per cent new oak. The wine is consistently right on the cusp of four stars; 2000 was undoubtedly so. Pervenche Puy Arnaud is a very decent second wine. (DM)

● **Clos Puy Arnaud** Côtes de Castillon★★★★ £D
● **Château Pervenche Puy Arnaud** Côtes de Castillon★ £B

CH. PUYGUERAUD Bordeaux-Côtes de Francs

A: Sec,F&R

Owner: Nicolas Thienpont 33570 Saint-Cibard
There are a number of impressive producers in this small appellation north-east of Saint-Émilion but Puygueraud particularly stands out. The wine is both refined and surprisingly structured for a lesser appellation and displays an impressive array of cedar, dark fruit and oriental spices, all tightly gripped by firm youthful tannin. The wine will benefit from a few years in the cellar. A special limited production wine, Cuvée Georges, was produced in 2000. (DM)

● **Château Puygueraud** Bordeaux-Côtes de Francs★★★ £C

CH. QUINAULT Saint-Émilion GC   www.chateau-quinault.com   A: CTy,BBR,Sec,N&P,F&R

Owner: Alain Raynaud   30 Chemin Videlot, 33500 Libourne

Alain Raynaud produces around 5,000 cases a year, mainly from some very old Merlot and Cabernet Franc. There are a total of 15 ha; Merlot accounts for 65 per cent and Cabernet Sauvignon and Malbec just 15 per cent between them, with the balance Cabernet Franc. Despite being only a regular Saint-Émilion Grand Cru, this is a serious enterprise and the wine bears little resemblance to many of the *garagiste* operations that produce barely more than a few hundred cases a year. Quality is certainly helped by a vineyard with an average age of around 50 years. The style is rich, supple and opulent and is best with 8 to 10 years' age. A limited-production special bottling has been produced in 2003, Oriel l'Absolu. (DM)

● **Château Quinault L'Enclos** Saint-Émilion Grand Cru★★★★ £F
● **Château Quinault L'Enclos** Saint-Émilion Grand Cru Lafleur de Quinault★★ £D

CH. REIGNAC Bordeaux-Supérieur   chateau.reignac@wanadoo.fr   A: CTy,Tur,F&R

Owner: Vatelot family   33450 Saint-Loubès

Stéphanie and Yves Vatelot produce one of the very best examples of this lesser appellation and it should be a benchmark for others. They have a sizeable holding of some 76 ha of which just 2 ha are devoted to whites, producing a good but pricey white Reignac. The red blend has a slightly higher proportion of Merlot than Cabernet Sauvignon and the wine is dense, dark and structured. It should develop very well in the medium term. There is also a special limited-release Reignac, again with a high proportion of Merlot (75 per cent). Modern and fleshy, the wine is cold-macerated before fermentation, with malolactic on lees in barrel. (DM)

● **Château Reignac** Bordeaux Supérieur★★ £C Bordeaux Supérieur Reignac★★★★ £D

CH. REYNON Premières Côtes de Bordeaux   www.denisdubourdieu.com   A:Han

Owner: Denis & Florence Dubourdieu   21 Route de Cardan, 33410 Beguey

Denis Dubourdieu, the owner of CLOS FLORIDÈNE in the Graves, is an extremely well-known and respected professor of enology in the region. At Château Reynon, he makes some very good dry white and red, along with a little sweet Cadillac from a total of some 57 ha of vineyards. The red is good and stylish in a medium-weight style; the regular white is crisp and fresh; and the Vieilles Vignes is classier and subtly barrel-fermented. Both the Vieilles Vignes white and the red will evolve nicely in the short term. (DM)

● **Château Reynon** Premières Côtes de Bordeaux★★ £C
O **Bordeaux** Vieilles Vignes★★ £B

CH. RIOU DE THAILLAS Saint-Émilion GC   A:Jas

Owner: Jean-Yves Béchet   33330, Saint-Émilion

The Béchets also own the impressive Château FOUGAS in the Côtes de Bourg. This property is smaller and they make just one wine, a dense, powerful and initially tannic Saint-Émilion. There are a total of just 3 ha of Merlot set on a hilltop with an aspect facing directly south. At present the vines are just over 20 years old, so more is yet to come. The sandy-clay subsoil and gravelly topsoil provides good drainage. Vinification is partly traditional with fermentation in small wooden vats with manual punching down of the cap. Formidably extracted, the wine is rounded out by malolactic in barrel and maturation in new oak for 18 months. The oak is well integrated although the ferocious nature of the wine in its youth could do with a little taming. Given six or seven years' patience the wine will offer increasing richness and complexity. (DM)

● **Château Riou deThaillas** Saint-Émilion Grand Cru★★★★ £F

CH. DE LA RIVIÈRE Fronsac   www.chateau-de-la-riviere.com   A: Cam

Owner: Jean & Jeanne Le Prince   33126 La Rivière

A decade ago this substantial Fronsac property was producing wines of somewhat variable quality. There are 59 ha under vine, mainly Merlot with Cabernet Sauvignon, Cabernet Franc and a few hectares of Malbec.

During the late 1990s some of the quality achieved during the mid-1980s has been replicated, although the wines are now modern and produced in an attractively ripe, dark berry fruit style with soft velvety tannins. A special bottling, Aria, is very good but pricey and a *clairet* is also made. The reds will benefit from four or five years' aging. (DM)

● **Château la Rivière** Fronsac★★ £D

CH. ROC DE CAMBES   Côtes de Bourg   A: C&B,Sav

Owner: François Mitjaville   33330 Saint-Laurent-des-Combes
This property is not only a serious benchmark for the Côtes de Bourg but also for all the lesser Right Bank appellations. The property is relatively small at 10 ha and Merlot dominates the plantings, accounting for 60 per cent of the vineyard. Always harvested as late as possible and from very low yields, the wine is typically rich and ripe, always displaying dense, dark, spicy berry fruit and a hefty dollop of well-integrated oak. It is long, complex, powerful and ageworthy. Minimal cellar handling helps to ensure consistently impressive results. 2000, 99 and 98 were all very impressive. (DM)

● **Château Roc de Cambes** Côtes de Bourg★★★★ £F

CH. LA ROUSSELLE   Fronsac

Owner: Jacques & Viviane Davau   33126 La Rivière
The Davau's tiny property with just 3.5 ha under vine is one of the emerging lights of Fronsac. Wine consultant Stéphane Derenoncourt also helps by weaving his own elegant magic on the wine. The vineyard is planted to a mix of Merlot (65 per cent), Cabernet Franc (25 per cent) and the balance Cabernet Sauvignon on finely drained argilo-calcareous soils. Traditionally vinified and aged for around a year in oak, the wine shows marked Merlot character when young as well as impressive purity and depth. Rich, dark plum aromas are underpinned by a subtle leafy character and firm youthful tannin. Four or five years' ageing will provide greater richness and weight. (DM)

● **Château La Rousselle** Fronsac★★★ £C

CH. TERTRE-RÔTEBOEUF   Saint-Émilion GC   A: AAA

Owner: François Mitjaville   33330, Saint-Laurent-des-Combes
Although this remarkable Saint-Émilion has not been elevated to Grand Cru Classé status, the property enjoys a highly propitious site for producing fine wine. Low yields, meticulous care in the vineyard and ageing in new oak for a year and a half all contribute to the very high quality of the wine, which has been exemplary for the last 15 years. It is immensely complex with a myriad of dark and spicy fruits and stylish oak. It will age gracefully and requires six or seven years' patience. (DM)

● **Château Tertre-Rôteboeuf** Saint-Émilion Grand Cru★★★★★ £H

CH. TEYSSIER   Saint-Émilion GC   A: AAA

Owner: Maltus family   33330 Saint-Émilion
Englishman Jonathan Maltus purchased this property in 1994 and since then has added a number of other more impressively sited vineyard holdings. Teyssier itself is a soft and attractive, relatively forward, spicy Saint-Émilion full of fleshy, dark, plummy fruit. It is sourced from the low-lying vineyards in the south of the appellation and is a testament to what can be achieved from these lesser sites. Vinification is modern, as with all the wines here, with pre-fermentation maceration, malolactic in barrel and ageing on lees for added richness. Château Laforge is produced from a number of superior Grand Cru sites, including the Le Chatelot vineyard purchased from Château CANON in 2000. The wine is rich and supple, finely structured and with impressive depth and concentration. The high Merlot content (92 per cent) of the blend accounts for its opulent, exotic style. Le DÔME is the top red label and comes from a single parcel neighbouring Château ANGELUS. There is also an excellent barrel-fermented white, Clos Nardian, which blends all three

white Bordeaux varieties. The Muscadelle comes from vines planted in the mid-1930s. Sourced from three tiny, ideally exposed parcels in limestone soils just across the river Dordogne south of the Saint-Émilion AC, this is a rich and complex, subtly oaked white. Maltus also produces a good red and white Bordeaux, Château LACROIX, both of which are vinified at Teyssier. (DM)

● **Château Teyssier** Saint-Émilion Grand Cru★★★ £D
● **Château Laforge** Saint-Émilion Grand Cru★★★★ £F
O **Clos Nardian** Bordeaux★★★★ £F

CH. THIEULEY   Bordeaux   A: **CTy**

Owner: Francis Courselle   La Sauve, 33670 Créon
This is an excellent example of what can be achieved under the humble Bordeaux AC but so very rarely is. Francis Courselle now has some 80 ha of vineyard, 45 ha of which are planted to red varieties. These go towards the crafting of stylish, straightforward, berry-fruited AC Bordeaux, impressively dense, structured Supérieur Réserve and attractively fruity *clairet*. A Premières Côtes de Bordeaux, Clos Sainte-Anne, is also now produced. The regular white is crisp and fresh and full of grassy green apple fruit, whereas the Cuvée Francis Courselle, which is barrel-fermented and aged with *bâtonnage,* is elegantly toasty and oaky. (DM)

● **Château Thieuley** Bordeaux★ £B   Bordeaux Supérieur Francis Courselle Réserve★★ £C
O **Château Thieuley** Bordeaux★ £B   Bordeaux Cuvée Francis Courselle★★ £C

CH. TROPLONG-MONDOT   Saint-Émilion GCC   A: AAA

Owner: Valette family   33330 Saint-Émilion
This has been a consistently excellent source of top Saint-Émilion over the past decade and longer and is unquestionably a serious candidate for elevation to Premier Grand Cru Classé status. There are some 30 ha of vines, the bulk of which are Merlot. This high percentage is reflected in the wine, which is full, rich, plump and fleshy with marked new oak and considerable refinement. The initial firm tannic structure means the wine needs six or seven years' cellaring. Very long and impressive and top-notch in recent vintages. The 2000 was of five-star quality. (DM)

● **Château Troplong-Mondot** Saint-Émilion Grand Cru Classé★★★★ £G

CH. TROTANOY   Pomerol   A: AAA

Owner: Moueix family   33500 Pomerol
Typically small Pomerol property of 7 ha, which, like PÉTRUS, is owned by the Moueix family. The wine is dense and very seriously structured, with considerable grip and tannin when young. Seven or eight years' cellaring will see the evolution of all sorts of opulent black fruit characters and oriental spices all effortlessly wrapped up in very classy new wood. On top form since 1997, although there were a number of disappointing vintages in the 1980s. (DM)

● **Château Trotanoy** Pomerol★★★★★ £H

CH. DE VALANDRAUD   Saint-Émilion GC   www.thunevin.com   A: **Far**,AAA

Owner: Jean-Luc Thunevin   6 Rue Guadet, 33330 Saint-Émilion
This is really the original *garagiste* wine, first made in 1991. Like most of its kind it was originally produced in limited volume, although that is increasing following vineyard acquisitions. The property consists of various plots, some of them on the low-lying plain below the town of Saint-Émilion. New plots have been added in 1998 and 99 and there are now two second labels, Clos Badon and Belair, which will help in ensuring the integrity of Valandraud. Yields are resticted and the harvest is carefully sorted prior to vinification. The winemaking is modern, with a pre-fermentation cold soak and malolactic in barrel. The wine is neither fined nor filtered and, while dense, fleshy and extracted, tends to lack the outright refinement of the best of the appellation. Although the style is forward and accessible, there is impressive grip and structure. Jean-Luc Thunevin is involved with the production of a number of other small-scale

projects, among them GRACIA and Andréas in Saint-Emilion, Griffe de Cap d'Or in Saint-Georges-Saint-Émilion and the micro-vinification MAROJALLIA in Margaux. (DM)

● **Château de Valandraud** Saint-Émilion Grand Cru★★★★ £F

CH. LA VIEILLE CURE Fronsac www.expressions-de-fronsac.com A: N&P,F&R

Owner: Colin Ferenbach Coutreau, 33141 Saillans

This is yet another of a number of outperformers in Bordeaux's lesser appellations and money has been pumped into the property to improve quality over the last 15 years. There are 18 ha under vine, 75 per cent planted to Merlot. Michel Rolland has provided consultancy input and the wine is typically extracted, ripe and seductive in style. Only the slightest hard edge can occasionally drift into the equation. The wine is a good medium-term ageing prospect. It has been good to very good since the late 1990s. There is also now an impressive second wine, Sacristie de La Vieille Cure, which other more esteemed properties from grander appellations would struggle to emulate. (DM)

● **Château La Vieille Cure** Fronsac★★★ £D

VIEUX-CHÂTEAU-CERTAN Pomerol www.vieuxchateaucertan.com A: AAA

Owner: Thienpont family 33500 Pomerol

Cabernet Franc and Cabernet Sauvignon account for 40 per cent of the 14 ha of vineyard here and this is in part the reason for the surprisingly dense and powerful structure of the wine. The tannin can be very firm in the wine's youth and it really needs a decade to begin to show its true class, when it becomes very refined and harmonious. Excellent from 1998 on – five stars. 1995 and 90 were also very good here. (DM)

● **Vieux-Château-Certan** Pomerol★★★★★ £H

SAINT-ÉMILION, POMEROL & OTHER BORDEAUX/OTHER WINES OF NOTE

CH. BALESTARD-LA-TONNELLE ● **Saint-Émilion** Grand Cru Classé £E

CH. BARDE-HAUT ● **Saint-Émilion** Grand Cru £E

CH. BARRABAQUE ● **Canon-Fronsac** Cuvée Prestige £C

CH. BAUDUC O **Bordeaux** Les Trois Hectares £C

CH. BEAULIEU ● **Bordeaux** £C

CH. BEAU-SOLEIL ● **Pomerol** £E

CH. BEL AIR LA ROYÈRE ● **Premières Côtes de Blaye** £D

CH. BELLEFONT-BELCIER ● **Saint-Émilion** Grand Cru £D

CH. BELLEVUE ● **Saint-Émilion** Grand Cru £D

CH. BERLIQUET ● **Saint-Émilion** Grand Cru Classé £E

CH. BONALGUE ● **Pomerol** £E

CH. BOURNEUF-VAYRON ● **Pomerol** £F

CH. BRANDA ● **Puisseguin-Saint-Émilion** £C

CH. BRÛLESÉCAILLE ● **Côtes de Bourg** £B

CH. BRUN DESPAGNE ● **Bordeaux Supérieur** £B

CH. CADET BON ● **Saint-Émilion** Grand Cru Classé £E

CH. CANON ● **Canon-Fronsac** £C

CH. CANTELAUZE ● **Pomerol** £F

CH. CAP DE MOURLIN ● **Saint Émilion** Grand Cru Classé £D

CH. CASSAGNE HAUT-CANON ● **Canon-Fronsac** £B Truffière £C

CH. DE CÉRONS O **Cérons** £B

CH. DU CHAMP DES TREILLES ● **Bordeaux Supérieur** La Chapelle d'Aliénor £C

CH. CHAUVIN ● **Saint-Émilion** Grand Cru Classé £E

CLOS DU CLOCHER ● **Pomerol** £E

CH. CLOS DAVIAUD ● **Montage-Saint-Émilion** Les Cimes £B

CH. CLOS DES JACOBINS ● **Saint-Émilion** Grand Cru Classé £E

CONFIANCE ● **Premières Côtes de Blaye** £E

CH. CORBIN MICHOTTE ● Saint-Émilion Grand Cru Classé £F
CH. CÔTE DE BALEAU ● Saint-Émilion Grand Cru £D
CH. CÔTE MONPEZAT ● Côtes de Castillon £C
CH. DU COURLAT ● Lussac-Saint-Émilion £C
DOMAINE DE COURTEILLAC ● Bordeaux Supérieur £B ○ Bordeaux Supérieur £B
LA CROIX CANON ● Canon-Fronsac £C
CROIX DE LABRIE ● Saint Émilion £G
CH. DU CROS ○ Loupiac £C
CH. DALEM ● Fronsac £D
CH. DASSAULT ● Saint-Émilion Grand Cru Classé £E
CH. DE LA DAUPHINE ● Fronsac £B
CH. DESTIEUX ● Saint-Émilion Grand Cru £E
CH. L'ENCLOS ● Pomerol £E
CH. FAIZEAU ● Montagne Saint-Émilion £C
CH. FEYTIT-CLINET ● Pomerol £F
CH. FONROQUE ● Saint-Émilion Grand Cru Classé £E
CH. DE FRANCS ● Bordeaux-Côtes de Francs £B
CH. LE GAY ● Pomerol £E
GRACIA ● Saint-Émilion Grand Cru £F
CH. GRAND PONTET ● Saint-Émilion Grand Cru Classé £E
CH. GRAND RENOUIL ● Canon-Fronsac £C
CH. HAUT-BALLET ● Fronsac £C
CH. HAUT-BERTINERIE ○ Premières Côtes de Blaye £C ● Premières Côtes de Blaye £C
CH. HAUT-CARLES ● Fronsac £D
CH. HAUT-CHAIGNEAU ● Lalande-de-Pomerol £B
CH. HAUT-CORBIN ● Saint-Émilion Grand Cru Classé £E
CH. HAUT-MACO ● Côtes de Bourg Cuvée Jean £C
CH. HAUT-SEGOTTES ● Saint-Émilion Grand Cru £D
CH. HAUT-TROPCHAUD ● Pomerol £E
HOMMAGE DE MALESAN ● Bordeaux £D
CH. HOSANNA ● Pomerol £F
CH. LES JONQUEYRES ● Premières Côtes de Blaye £B
CH. LABADIE ● Côtes de Bourg Vieilli en Fûts de Chêne £C
CH LA CROIX DU CASSE ● Pomerol £C
LA FLEUR DU BOÙARD ● Lalande-de-Pomerol £E
CH. LAFLEUR-GAZIN ● Pomerol £E
CH. LAGRANGE ● Pomerol £E
CH. LA GRANGERE ● Saint-Émilion Grand Cru £D
CH. LA GRAVE ● Fronsac £B
CH. LA GRAVE ● Pomerol £E
CH. LARMANDE ● Saint-Émilion Grand Cru Classé £E
CH. LARCIS-DUCASSE ● Saint-Émilion Grand Cru Classé £E
CH. LA SERGUE ● Lalande-de-Pomerol £E
CH. LA TOUR FIGEAC ● Saint-Émilion Grand Cru Classé £E
CH. LA TOUR-DU-PIN-FIGEAC ● Saint-Émilion Grand Cru Classé £E
CH. DES LAUDES ● Saint-Émilion Grand Cru £C
CH. LA VIOLETTE MANOIR DU GRAVOUX ● Côtes de Castillon £B
CH. LOUBENS ○ Sainte-Croix-du-Mont £C
CH. DU LYONNAT ● Lussac-Saint-Émilion £C
CH. MARSAU ● Bordeaux-Côtes de Francs £C
CH. MERCIER ● Côtes de Bourg Cuvée Prestige £C
CH. MONGIRON ● Bordeaux La Fleur Mongiron £C
CH. MONTVIEL ● Pomerol £F
CH. MOULIN SAINT-GEORGES ● Saint-Émilion Grand Cru £F
CH. NÉNIN ● Pomerol £F
CH. NODOZ ● Côtes de Bourg £B

CH. PENIN ● Bordeaux Supérieur Grande Sélection £B
CH. PEYROUTAS ● Saint-Émilion Grand Cru £C
CH. PLAISANCE ● Saint-Émilion Grand Cru £D
CH. LA POINTE ● Pomerol £D
CH. PRESSAC ● Saint-Émilion Grand Cru £D
CH. LA RAME ○ Sainte-Croix-du-Mont Tradition £C Réserve £E
CH. RAUZAN DESPAGNE ○ Bordeaux Blanc Cuvée Passion £C
CH. REMPIMPLET ● Côtes de Bourg £B
CH. ROCHER BELLEVUE FIGEAC ● Saint-Émilion Grand Cru £D
CH. ROL VALENTIN ● Saint-Émilion £F
CH. ROUGET ● Pomerol £E
CH. SAINTE-COLOMBE ● Côtes de Castillon £C
CH. DE SALES ● Pomerol £D
CH. SANSONNET ● Saint-Émilion Grand Cru £F
CH. SEGONZAC ● Premières Côtes de Blaye £B
CH DE SEGUIN ● Bordeaux Supérieur £B Prestige £C
CH. TAILLEFER ● Pomerol £E
CH. TAYAC ● Côtes de Bourg Cuvée Prestige £C Cuvée Reservée £C
CH. TERTRE-DAUGAY ● Saint-Émilion Grand Cru Classé £E
CH. TEYSSIER ● Montagne-Saint-Émilion £C
CH. TOUR DE MIRAMBEAU ● Bordeaux Cuvée Passion £C
CH. TROTTEVIEILLE ● Saint-Émilion 1er Grand Cru Classé £F
CH. VILLARS ● Fronsac £B
CH. VILLEMAURINE ● Saint-Émilion Grand Cru Classé £D
CH. YON FIGEAC ● Saint-Émilion Grand Cru Classé £E

Work in progress!!

Wines from the following producers under consideration for the next edition

AMAVINUM (BORDEAUX)
CH. AMPÉLIA (CÔTES DE CASTILLON)
BALTHUS (BORDEAUX SUPÉRIEUR)
CH. DU CHAMP DES TREILLES (SAINTE-FOY BORDEAUX)
CH. CHAPELLE MARACAN (BORDEAUX SUPÉRIEUR)
CH. CHARRON (PREMIÈRES CÔTES DE BLAYE)
CH. DE CHELIVETTE (PREMIÈRES CÔTES DE BORDEAUX)
CH. CROS FIGEAC (SAINT-ÉMILION GRAND CRU)
ESSENCE DES VIGNOBLES DOURTHE (BORDEAUX)
CH. FRANC-MAILLET (POMEROL)
CH. DU GABY (CANON-FRONSAC)
CH. GARRAUD (LALANDE-DE-POMEROL)
GIROLATE (BORDEAUX)
CH. GRAND-ORMEAU (LALANDE-DE-POMEROL)
CH. HOSTENS-PICANT (SAINTE-FOY BORDEAUX)
CH. JEAN DE GUÉ (POMEROL)
CH. JOANIN BÉCOT (CÔTES DE CASTILLON)
CH. LA CLÉMENCE (POMEROL)
CH. LA COUSPAUDE (SAINT-ÉMILION GRAND CRU CLASSÉ)
CH. LA COMMANDERIE DE MAZEYRES (POMEROL)
CH. LA CROIX (POMEROL)
CH LA CROIX BELLEVUE (LALANDE-DE-POMEROL)
CH. LA CROIX SAINT-GEORGES (POMEROL)
CH. LA GRAVIÈRE (LALANDE-DE-POMEROL)
CH. LA MAURIANE (PUISSEGUIN-SAINT-ÉMILION)
CH. LA SERRE (SAINT-ÉMILION GRAND CRU CLASSÉ)

CH. DE LAUSSAC (CÔTES DE CASTILLON)
LE DOYENNÉ (PREMIÈRES CÔTES DE BORDEAUX)
CH LE MOULIN (POMEROL)
CH. LES TROIS CROIX (FRONSAC)
CH. MÉMOIRES (PREMIÈRES CÔTES DE BORDEAUX)
DOM. MONDÉSIR-GAZIN (PREMIÈRES CÔTES DE BLAYE)
CH. MONT-PÉRAT (PREMIÈRES CÔTES DE BORDEAUX)
CH. PLAISANCE (PREMIÈRES CÔTES DE BORDEAUX)
CH. POMMEAUX (POMEROL)
CH. ROCHEBELLE (SAINT-ÉMILION GRAND CRU)
CH. ROLAND LA GARDE (PREMIÈRES CÔTES DE BLAYE)
CLOS SAINTE-ANNE (PREMIÈRES CÔTES DE BORDEAUX)
CH. TIRE-PÉ (BORDEAUX SUPÉRIEUR)
CH. TOURNEFEUILLE (LALANDE DE POMEROL)
CH. TRIANON (SAINT-ÉMILION GRAND CRU)
CH. VEYRY (CÔTES DE CASTILLON)
VIEUX CH. CHAMPS DE MARS (CÔTES DE CASTILLON)
CH. VIEUX MAILLET

Author's choice (DM)

SAINT-ÉMILION, POMEROL & OTHER BORDEAUX

Great cellarworthy Right Bank reds
CH. AUSONE ● Saint-Émilion 1 er Grand Cru Classé
CH. CHEVAL-BLANC ● Saint-Émilion 1 er Grand Cru Classé
CH. LA CONSEILLANT ● Pomerol
CH. L'ÉVANGILE ● Pomerol
CH. LAFLEUR ● Pomerol
CH. PAVIE-MACQUIN ● Saint-Émilion Grand Cru Classé
CH. PÉTRUS ● Pomerol
CH. LE PIN ● Pomerol
CH. TERTRE-RÔTEBOEUF ● Saint-Émilion Grand Cru
CH. TROPLONG-MONDOT ● Saint-Émilion Grand Cru Classé

New Right Bank classics
CH. BEAU-SÉJOUR BÉCOT ● Saint-Émilion La Gomerie Grand Cru
CH. LA BIENFAISANCE ● Saint-Émilion Sanctus Grand Cru
LE DÔME ● Saint-Émilion Grand Cru
CH. FAUGÈRES ● Saint-Émilion Péby-Faugères Grand Cru
LA FLEUR DU BOÙARD ● Lalande-de-Pomerol
CH. FOMBRAUGE ● Saint-Émilion Magrez-Fombrauge Grand Cru
LA MONDOTTE ● Saint-Émilion Grand Cru
CH. PAVIE ● Saint-Émilion Grand Cru Classé
CH. QUINAULT ● Saint-Émilion Quinault l'Enclos Grand Cru
CH. DE VALANDRAUD ● Saint-Émilion Grand Cru

Emerging reds from the satellites
DOM. DE L'A ● Côtes de Castillon
CH. D'AIGUIHE ● Côtes de Castillon
LA CROIX DE PEYROLIE ● Lussac-Saint-Émilion
CH. FONTENIL ● Fronsac

Bordeaux

CH. MOULIN PEY-LABRIE ● Canon-Fronsac

CLOS PUY ARNAUD ● Côtes de Castillon

CH. PUYGUERAUD ● Bordeaux-Côtes des Francs

CH. DE LA RIVIÈRE ● Fronsac

CH. ROC DE CAMBES ● Côtes de Bourg

CH. LA VIEILLE CURE ● Fronsac

An overview

Burgundy can be considered as four distinct entities. In the north lies Chablis, at its heart is the Côte d'Or, next comes the Côte Chalonnaise then, still further south, the Mâconnais. The main appellations for each are given below, with more detail in the individual sections that follow.

Chablis & Yonne

Chablis and the surrounding vineyards are isolated from the heart of Burgundy, being almost halfway to Paris from the Côte d'Or. All Chablis is produced from the Chardonnay grape and is classified by vineyard site as either **Petit Chablis, Chablis, Chablis Premier Cru** or **Chablis Grand Cru**. Other than Chablis there's Sauvignon under the **Saint-Bris** AC and occasional pure cherryish Pinot Noir from **Irancy** AC. Pinot Noir or Chardonnay from other villages in the Yonne is suffixed **Bourgogne**.

Côte d'Or & Côte Chalonnaise

The Côte d'Or is synonymous with Burgundy and includes all its great red wines. The two parts are the more northerly Côte de Nuits (mostly red) and extending southwards, the Côte de Beaune (white and red). The CÔTE DE NUITS is Burgundy's most classic red wine district and based primarily on just one grape variety, Pinot Noir. It runs from **Marsannay** and **Fixin** through the leading communes of **Gevrey-Chambertin** (including leading *grands crus* **Chambertin** and **Clos de Bèze**), **Morey-Saint-Denis** (with *grands crus* **Clos de la Roche, Clos Saint-Denis, Clos des Lambrays** and **Clos de Tart**), **Chambolle Musigny** (with **Bonnes Mares** and **Le Musigny**) and **Vougeot** (for **Clos Vougeot**), Flagey-Echezeaux (for **Echezeaux** and **Grands Echezeaux**), **Vosne-Romanée** (*grands crus* **La Romanée, Romanée-Conti, Richebourg, Romanée-Saint-Vivant, La Grande Rue**, and **La Tâche**) to **Nuits-Saint-Georges**. The CÔTE DE BEAUNE is famous for great white Burgundy made from Chardonnay, although more Pinot Noir is planted. Much of both is at least potentially very high quality. In a confusion of appellations in the north, **Aloxe-Corton** with the famous *grands crus* of **Corton** (mostly red) and **Corton-Charlemagne** (white) stands out. **Beaune, Pernand-Vergelesses** and **Savigny-lès-Beaune** produce fine reds but some good whites too, while the celebrated **Pommard** and **Volnay** are restricted to red. **Monthélie**, and **Auxey-Duresses** provide more affordable red and a little white, while **Saint-Romain** and the often excellent **Saint-Aubin** do better with white. The big three white Burgundy appellations are **Meursault, Puligny-Montrachet** (including *grands crus* **Chevalier-Montrachet, Le Montrachet** and part of **Bâtard-Montrachet**) and **Chassagne-Montrachet**. The latter also produces red as do **Santenay** and **Maranges** in the tail of the Côte d'Or.

The CÔTE CHALONNAISE begins close to this tail. Both the wines and the countryside are distinctly different but the village appellations are again classified for wines from Chardonnay and/or Pinot Noir – with the exception the first village, **Bouzeron**, which is classified for Aligoté. **Rully** makes more white than red, while **Mercurey** and **Givry** produce mostly red. The southernmost appellation, **Montagny**, is for Chardonnay alone. **Crémant de Bourgogne** is for the region's sparkling wine.

Mâconnais

As in the Côte de Beaune here too there is greatness in white wine (from Chardonnay), with a new wave of excellent producers beginning to emerge. Quality wine production is focused on **Pouilly-Fuissé** (with its four communes of Chaintré, Fuissé, Solutré and Vergisson), adjoined at its eastern end by the small **Pouilly-Loché** and **Pouilly-Vinzelles** ACs. Many other vineyards north and south of Pouilly-Fuissé qualify as **Saint-Véran**. There is fine quality too from **Viré-Clessé** and increasingly from several of some 43 villages that can be suffixed to Mâcon (eg **Mâcon-Bussières**).

SEREIN

2

1

2

Chablis

Auxerre

2

•Dijon

3

•Marsannay

•Fixin

•Gevrey-Chambertin

•Morey-Saint-Denis

•Chambolle-Musigny

•Vougeot

4 •Vosne-Romanée

•Nuits-Saint-Georges

•Pernand-Vergelesses

Savigny-lès-Beaune• *5* •Aloxe-Corton

6

•Beaune

•Pommard

Volnay•

•Auxey-Duresses

•Meursault

6

•Puligny-Montrachet

Chassagne-Montrachet•

•Chagny

Santenay

Bouzeron•

•Rully

•Mercurey

7

Givry• •Chalon-sur-Saône

•Montagny

SAÔNE

8

•Viré

9

•Clessé

Milly-Lamartine• •La Roche Vineuse

Vergisson• *12*

10

12 •Pouilly •Mâcon

Fuissé *11*

10 •Chaintré

1   Chablis
2   Yonne (other vineyards)
3   Côte de Nuits
4   Hautes Côtes de Nuits
5   Côtes de Beaune
6   Hautes Côtes de Beaune
7   Côte Chalonnaise
8   Mâcon, Mâcon-Villages
9   Viré-Clessé
10 Pouilly-Fuissé
11 Pouilly-Loché, Pouilly-Vinzelles
12 Saint-Véran

Chablis is one of the great white wines of the world, and partly because the cultivation of the Chardonnay grape in these cool hills is so close to the limit of where obtaining full ripeness is possible. Success rarely comes easily, fraught with an annual battle against frost and rain, demanding constant diligence. The importance of fully ripe fruit cannot be understated. The wines should be vigorous, fresh, suffused with minerality but also with generosity and length of flavour without the greeness, harshness or indeed sulphur that some disciples have been duped into believing was authentic Chablis character.

Chablis

Style

So what defines that unique Chablis character? A fine, subtle gun-flint, smoke or stony mineral character and greengage plum aromas are typical – but these must be ripe plums. Some wines are more floral or appley, citrusy or peachy but there should still be an unmistakable minerally, steely aspect and marvellous depth, with a toasty, nutty (or honeyed) complexity with age. The vintage matters greatly; while the longevity of Chablis should never be underestimated, most wines from a weaker vintage will evolve quite quickly and the leaness, often greeness on the palate will never disappear.

Controversy

Two major areas of debate in the past two decades have been the extension of the *premier cru* vineyard area and the use of new oak but as important to quality are the issues of yield (often too high) and mechanical harvesting, which is widespread. The Union des Grands Crus in Chablis recently banned mechanical harvesting but many *premiers crus* are harvested in this way, in part due to the greater ease of using this method here in contrast to the Côte d'Or, where difficulties are posed by the more fragmented ownership of vineyards. Much of the argument over expansion of the *vignoble* concerns soil types and whether Portlandian and other limestones are capable of the same quality as fossilised Kimmeridgian limestone found in the established *grands* and *premiers crus*. The second area of debate is whether to oak or not to oak. There are now many good exponents of both schools of thought, though the style of each varies significantly. A *grand cru* from Domaine François Raveneau (aged in used oak) is a benchmark but most of the new oak versions from Drouhin or Verget are also of very high quality and have as much validity as those from the unoaked camp. Quality is the key, the question of style is more subjective and unless the oak overwhelms the wine it is down to personal choice. That said, Chablis should always taste of its origins and not be mistaken for something from the Côte de Beaune or further afield.

Classification

Understanding the Chablis classification is straightforward. There are four levels: **Chablis Grand Cru**, **Chablis Premier Cru**, **Chablis** and **Petit Chablis.** The seven *grands crus* that total 106 ha of vineyards (the total Chablis vineyard area is now 4,500 ha) are Blanchot, Bougros, Les Clos, Grenouilles, Preuses, Valmur and Vaudésir. Arguably the most consistent class comes from Les Clos, Valmur and Vaudésir but the producer is more important and a good producer's best *premiers crus* easily outperform weaker *grand cru* efforts. Seven times the area is designated Chablis Premier Cru, encompassing forty names. Less than half of these are in common usage as the main *premier cru* name is usually taken. This unfortunately causes confusion and better definition of these large vineyard areas might make for easier quality identification. Those *premiers crus* with the greatest potential to be fine are Fourchaume, Montée de Tonnerre and Mont de Milieu, all lying on the same side (northern, right bank) of the river Serein as the *grand crus* and with similar exposures. But poorer examples of these will be surpassed easily by the best versions of *premiers crus* from the other side of the Serein (left bank), especially Montmains, Vaillons and Vau de Vey. The quality of regular Chablis is very much dependent on the producer whilst Petit Chablis is, for the most part, best avoided.

Yonne - life beyond Chablis

Most of the wines made in the area surrounding Chablis are made from Chardonnay, Pinot Noir or Aligoté. If conditions are generally less favoured in terms of soil and climate than in much of Chablis, it is possible to produce wines of reasonable concentration and sufficient ripeness in both colours from villages such as Coulanges-la-Vineuse and Irancy providing there is a fastidious approach to viticulture – the wines of Anita & Jean-Pierre Colinot are proof enough. **Irancy** is an AC for red in its own right; other villages are suffixed Bourgogne (**Bourgogne Coulanges-la-Vineuse, Bourgogne Chitry**) for red and white. **Bourgogne Côtes d'Auxerre** covers other villages in the vicinity of Auxerre (including Pinot Noir and Chardonnay from Saint-Bris-le-Vineux) while those from around Tonnerre, to the east of Chablis, are labelled **Bourgogne Épineuil**. Some growers are at least as successful with rosé as red. If the cultivation of Sauvignon in the Yonne seems unusual, consider that it's a relatively short hop to the Central Vineyards of the Loire Valley from here. However, few examples of **Saint-Bris** (Sauvignon from around Saint-Bris, Irancy and Chitry) are better than green and edgy, despite its promotion in 2003 to appellation status. Goisot is an exception. Further afield, some Chablis-like white is made some 50 km to the south of Chablis and Auxerre at Vézelay (**Bourgogne Vézelay**).

A-Z of producers by appellation/region

Chablis & Yonne

Chablis

JEAN-CLAUDE BESSIN	78
BILLAUD-SIMON	78
DOM. DE BOIS D'YVER	78
JEAN-MARC BROCARD	79
LA CHABLISIENNE	79
DOM. DE CHANTEMERLE	79
DANIEL DAMPT	80
RENÉ ET VINCENT DAUVISSAT	80
DANIEL-ÉTIENNE DEFAIX	81
JEAN-PAUL DROIN	81
JOSEPH DROUHIN	81
GÉRARD DUPLESSIS	82
JEAN DURUP ET FILS	82
WILLIAM FÈVRE	82
JEAN-PIERRE GROSSOT/C. PERCHAUD	83
DOM. LAROCHE	83
BERNARD LEGLAND/DES MARRONNIERS	84
LONG-DEPAQUIT	84
DOM. DES MALANDES	84
DOM. LOUIS MICHEL ET FILS	84
DOM. LOUIS MOREAU	85
MOREAU-NAUDET	85
DIDIER & PASCAL PICQ	85
DOM. LOUIS PINSON	86
DENIS POMMIER	86
DENIS RACE	86
DOM. FRANÇOIS RAVENEAU	86
GÉRARD TREMBLAY	87
DOM. DE VAUROUX	87
DOM. VOCORET	87

Irancy

ANITA ET JEAN-PIERRE COLINOT	80

Saint-Bris

GHISLAINE ET JEAN-HUGUES GOISOT	83

Chablis vintages

No two vintages in Chablis are quite alike and even from a good producer the choice of vintage can make a significant difference to the quality in your glass. Given the problems of frost, the not uncommon struggle for ripeness in cooler years, the incidence of mildew and rot in wetter years, and, too often, lack of a rigorous grape selection, short of being able to afford Raveneau from every vintage it is important to choose a vintage carefully especially if the wines are intended for cellaring.

The last five vintages in Chablis have been by no means bad though conditions have been highly variable, necessitating a flexible response from producers in their approach to vinification and ageing. 2003★★/★★★★: A hitherto almost inconceivable vintage in Chablis, which suffered the same extreme heat as much of Europe, the like of which had never before been experienced here. With temperatures over 40C, conditions resulted in a small, extremely early harvest (late August!). Expect rich, powerful, probably short-lived wines from the best producers but not a classic expression of Chablis minerality and structure. 2002★★★★/★★★★★: This was a much more complete vintage than 2003 (and a bit closer to normality), despite some swings in the weather. The wines are ripe and concentrated, although just occasionally a little broad and diffuse. From the top echelon of producers there are many outstanding, balanced and ageworthy examples. 2001★★/★★★★: A difficult vintage: the wet and cold conditions of July and September resulted in rot and under-ripeness for many, and even where ripeness was achieved some wines lack balance. Nonetheless where there was a diligent grape selection the wines can be very good and very expressive of terroir (Fèvre for instance). 2000★★★/★★★★: Overall quality was higher than in 2001 with a warm sunny run-in to another early vintage in late September. However yields were generally high (a few producers excepted) and some wines are evolving quite quickly. The best, though, are concentrated, structured and balanced. 1999★★★★: Like 2000, 1999 was also fine. Despite some growers being affected by the late rains there are some excellent wines for drinking now while the best *grands crus* should be kept another 5 to 10 years.

Of early vintages, there were several other good vintages in the 1990s but (1990 apart) all come from the latter half of the decade. **1995**, **1996** and **1997** all produced good wines, particular the latter despite a very hot August. Due to an adverse growing season (frost, hail, mildew) **1998** Chablis is generally better avoided now as are the vast majority of wines from 1994, 1993, 1992, and 1991. However for a taste of how well Chablis can age consider the best from 1990 (an exceptional vintage), 1988 or even 1986.

JEAN-CLAUDE BESSIN
A: **M&V**, NYg

Owner: Jean-Claude Bessin 3 Rue de la Planchotte, 89800 Chablis

One of Chablis' best small domaines. Former architects Jean-Claude Bessin and his wife had the good fortune to inherit (from her family) prime Chablis vineyards. Seven of their 12 ha are located in three leading *crus*, the *premiers crus* Montmains and Fourchaume, and *grand cru* Valmur; the Fourchaume in particular contains a wealth of fine old vines. Bessin has only been bottling his own wine since 1992 but has already produced plenty of rich, fruit-intense, unoaked Chablis notable for its ripeness. Oak is now employed for the Valmur but doesn't overwhelm its concentrated fruit, instead adding structure that should enhance its longevity. The regular Chablis can be drunk quite young, but the *crus* are better with three years' age or more. (PW)

O **Chablis Grand Cru** Valmur★★★ £D
O **Chablis Premier Cru** Montmains★★ £C   Fourchaume★★★ £C   O **Chablis**★★ £B

BILLAUD-SIMON
A: BBR, CTy, L&W, HHB, IGH, WSc, NYg, Sel

Owner: Billaud-Simon family   Quai de Reugny, BP 46, 89800 Chablis

A family domaine dating from 1815 making brilliant, predominantly unoaked Chablis under the winemaking direction of Samuel Billaud. Together with his uncle Bernard Billaud, they have considerably advanced the quality level over the past decade. The estate's 20 ha include a little of three *grands crus* (Les Clos, Preuses and Vaudésir) and a tiny bit of Blanchots, as well as significant vineyards in the *premiers crus* of Mont de Milieu, Montée de Tonnerre and Vaillons, and a little Fourchaume. Except for Fourchaume, there is a high proportion of old vines – the Mont de Milieu is also made in a Vieilles Vignes bottling. This contributes to the depth and concentration of the wines, which have a distinctive minerally, occasionally smoky, ripe fruit character and great definition and structure. A carefully temperature-controlled vinification in stainless steel is followed by a lengthy low-temperature *débourbage*. Barrel-fermentation and ageing are only employed exceptionally, as in the case of the Les Clos (from 55-year-old vines), where it enhances the structure but takes nothing from the wine's purity. In short, these are quite delicious, graceful, stylish Chablis with extra distinction and depth at the *premier cru* level and wonderful dimension and complexity at the *grand cru* level. If the prices are edging upwards they still represent marvellous value vis-à-vis similar quality from the Côte de Beaune. Even the Petit Chablis is worth considering here. (PW)

O **Chablis Grand Cru** Preuses★★★★ £E   Vaudésir★★★★★ £E   Les Clos★★★★★ £E
O **Chablis Grand Cru** Blanchots Vieilles Vignes★★★★★ £F
O **Chablis Premier Cru** Vaillons★★★★ £C   Mont de Milieu★★★★ £C   Montée de Tonnerre★★★★ £C
O **Chablis Premier Cru** Fourchaume★★★ £D
O **Chablis**★★ £B   Tête d'Or★★★ £C   O **Petit Chablis**★ £B

DOMAINE DE BOIS D'YVER
A: JNi, CPp, Hrd

Owner: Georges Pico & Eleana Puentes   Grande Rue Nicolas Droin, Courgis, 89800 Chablis

This 22-ha estate at Courgis makes a sound range of Chablis both from its own vineyards and from grapes bought in from another grower. The wines show something of a leesy influence, though this is more pronounced at the lower levels, with added minerality and fruit depth in the Vaillons and Montmains *premiers crus*. Though for the most part machine-harvested, they usually show good ripeness, a certain elegance and good balance. Used oak is employed for ageing the Blanchots, which shows a *grand cru*-like complexity, though wants for greater fruit intensity on the finish for a higher rating. Those from bought-in grapes, which includes the Blanchots, are labelled only as 'mis en bouteille par Domaine de Bois d'Yver'. (PW)

O **Chablis Grand Cru** Blanchots★★★ £E
O **Chablis Premier Cru** Beauregard★★ £C   Vaillons★★★ £C   Montmains★★★ £C
O **Chablis**★★ £B

A & F BOUDIN/DOM. DE CHANTEMERLE
A: **L&S**, Rae, IGH, Maj

Owner: Adhémar & Francis Boudin   27 Rue de Serein, La Chapelle Vaupelteigne, 89800 Chablis
The Domaine de Chantemerle is an exciting small domaine based in the village of La Chapelle Vaupelteigne, producing ripe, characterful Chablis from 15 ha of vineyards close by. Low yields, manual harvesting and vinification in inert vats contribute to a rich, ripe, almost buttery style (yet minerally too) but without any oak influence. Particularly worth seeking out is L'Homme Mort, bottled separately from the rest of Fourchaume – not perhaps an inspiring choice of name but the wine has great vitality and individuality. All the wines can be drunk quite young but if you think their immediacy suggests they won't keep, you are wrong. The depth, structure and concentration of fruit means they'll keep for a decade and that often includes the regular Chablis. (PW)
O **Chablis Premier Cru** Fourchaume★★★ £C L'Homme Mort★★★ £D   O **Chablis**★★ £B

JEAN-MARC BROCARD   www.domaine-brocard.fr
A: **JBa**, Adm, BWC, J&B, Odd

Owner: Jean-Marc Brocard   3 Route de Chablis, Préhy, 89800 Chablis
Thirty years ago Jean-Marc Brocard had a single hectare of vines, now he has 96 ha and climbing (though not all of it in the Chablis AC). Based at Préhy, on the edge of the Chablis region, he has turned out reasonably consistent, lively, assertive Chablis since the early 1980s. The emphasis is on producing 'typical' Chablis that is minerally and elegant. Though for the most part from mechanically harvested grapes, these stainless steel-vinified Chablis usually deliver adequate fruit and structure, particularly with a couple of years' bottle-age, but they can sometimes be a bit lean and underripe. The most interest and character is to be found among the *premiers* and *grands crus*, which if not first rate can offer decent value for money. They should, however, not be drunk too young (four years is a minimum). A series of Bourgogne Blancs produced to differentiate between different soil types in the Chablis region are of good Petit Chablis quality, while newer is a series of blended Premier Cru Chablis that go some way to live up to their names: Minéral, Extrème, Sensuel and Paradoxe (the last sees some new oak). Chablis Domaine de la Boisseneuse is a biodynamically produced example. Other Yonne wines include an Irancy from Domaine Sainte Claire. Also produced in 2002 was a refined, intense example of *grand cru* Valmur. All in all, the wines are a good bet in a fine vintage but more variable from lesser years. (PW)
O **Chablis Grand Cru** Bougros★★ £E Vaudésir★★★ £E
O **Chablis Premier Cru** Montmains Le Manant★★★ £C Beauregard★★ £C Vaucoupin★★ £C
O **Chablis Premier Cru** Montée de Tonnerre★★ £C Côte de Jouan★ £C
O **Chablis**★ £B Vieilles Vignes★ £B
O **Bourgogne Blanc** Jurassique★ £B Kimméridgien★ £B Portlandien★ £B
O **Bourgogne Aligoté**★ £B

LA CHABLISIENNE   www.chablisienne.com
A: **SsG, Cib**, E&T, Maj, WSc

Owner: 'Cooperative'   8 Boulevard Pasteur, BP 14, 89800 Chablis
With 1,100 ha of vineyards the La Chablisienne co-op draws on a massive chunk of the Chablis *vignoble*, producing a quarter of all Chablis made. Much of what appears under the labels of the large Beaune *négociants* is sourced from here. The operation is very competently run by Hervé Tucki and considerable sums are spent on renewing a battery of oak barrels. At the village level or lower (Petit Chablis) the wines can be lean and dilute, while some of the *premiers crus* and *grands crus* are excessively oaked despite the intention to bring out the *terroir*. Certainly in weaker vintages there just doesn't seem to be fruit of sufficient quality to achieve this. That said, and while a bad bottle can put you off, *premiers crus* like Vaulorent, Montmains and Montée de Tonnerre can be really good and the Vieilles Vignes with some oak influence is typically concentrated with good balance. The most prized wine is that bottled from the best part of 6 ha of Grenouilles as Château Grenouilles, though sadly the oak can be a bit overdone. Most significantly, quality and style depend to a large degree on the requirements of the customer, be it a *négociant* or supermarket chain. If its standards are high then expect a decent Chablis. While a Chablis from a good small grower is

still likely to be a better bet, nonetheless there are some fine bottles that may be encountered in top restaurants and elsewhere. Unfortunately, while a co-op can mean great value, prices for Chablisienne-labelled wines are near the top of the hierarchy for their respective appellations. Listed below are the most consistent of the leading *crus*. (PW)

O **Chablis Grand Cru** Blanchots★★★ £E Grenouilles★★★ £E Preuses★★★ £E Château Grenouilles★★ £F
O **Chablis Premier Cru** Montmains★★ £D Montée de Tonnerre★★ £D Vaulorent★★ £D
O **Chablis** Vieilles Vignes★★ £C

ANITA ET JEAN-PIERRE COLINOT   Irancy

Owner: Anita et Jean-Pierre Colinot   1 Rue des Chariats, 89290 Irancy
If the pure, pristine, cherry-scented character of very cool-climate Pinot drives you to distraction then this is the place to come. One or two others in Irancy can also make enticing red but their wines are let down more often by a lack of complete ripeness. From 10 ha (which, typically for this Auxerrois region, includes a little César), Jean-Pierre Colinot and his wife make light but very elegant wines with a gentle charm and good intensity of flavour and length. Of the various *cuvées*, the Côte du Moutier has perhaps the most structure, Palotte slightly more obvious fruit. As well as those below, wines come from other parcels of vines, including Les Mazelots. Unfortunately the wines have a certain following in France and can be difficult to find but it's worth the effort, particularly from a good vintage. Though light in body, the wines are not fragile and will keep well for five years. For another intriguing Auxerrois red see Ghislaine et Jean-Hugues GOISOT. (PW)

● **Irancy** Vieilles Vignes★★ £B Palotte★★ £B Côte du Moutier★★ £B

DANIEL DAMPT   www.dampt-defaix.com   A: Bal, HHC, NYg

Owner: Dampt family   1 Rue des Violettes, Milly, 89800 Chablis
Daniel Dampt married the daughter of Jean Defaix, a respected *vigneron* who little by little reclaimed vineyards abandoned following phylloxera in the late 19th century. The Dampts now make very good Chablis from 26 ha of vineyards, including 13 ha of *premiers crus* (predominantly Côte de Léchet and Vaillons). The wines are vinified in stainless steel, with the emphasis on a ripe fruit and floral character but retaining firm acidity and a minerally influence. The pride of the domaine are the Côte de Léchet vineyards, which lie close to the winery and produce arguably the most classic, minerally wine, but there is good quality in all the *premiers crus*. If not amongst the top names this is nonetheless a good inexpensive source of Chablis that drinks well with three or four years' age but will keep for longer in the case of the *premiers crus*. (PW)

O **Chablis Premier Cru** Beauroy★★★ £C Vaillons★★ £C Fourchaume★★★ £C Côte de Léchet★★★ £C
O **Chablis**★★ £B

RENÉ ET VINCENT DAUVISSAT   A: DDr, HHB, J&B, L&S, Tan, IGH, F&M

Owner: René & Vincent Dauvissat   8 Rue Émile Zola, 89800 Chablis
The Dauvissats have deep roots in the region going back centuries. Vincent's grandfather started domaine bottling in the 1930s and his father René built up and maintains a rich viticultural resource; almost all of the 11.5 ha are either *premier* or *grand cru*. In the vineyard, a uniform high average vine age is maintained as old or weak vines are replaced individually, grafted from the best existing vines (*sélection massale*). In addition, all the grapes are manually picked, not just the leading *crus* – a relatively rare occurrence in Chablis. Vincent uses oak, used not new, to ferment and age most of the wines. The resulting Chablis are simply marvellous, characterised by their depth, breadth and body, filled with a gently honeyed ripeness and stylish minerality. All are fine, even the Petit Chablis, but the distinctive minerally yet contrasting *premiers crus* Vaillons and Forest are surpassed by the bigger, more concentrated *grands crus* Preuses and Les Clos. The latter need six or seven years' ageing, *premiers crus* four or five, and even the regular Chablis three or four. The wines can be in short supply, having long been favoured by top Parisian restaurants. (PW)

O **Chablis Grand Cru** Preuses★★★★★ £F Les Clos❂❂❂❂❂ £F

O **Chablis Premier Cru** Séchet★★★★ £E Forest★★★★ £E Vaillons★★★★ £E
O **Chablis**★★★ £C O **Petit Chablis**★★ £B

DANIEL-ÉTIENNE DEFAIX www.chablisdefaix.com A: **GFy**, BBR, Con, Tan, Han, IGH

Owner: Daniel Defaix & family 23 Rue de Champlain, Milly, 89800 Chablis
The Defaix lineage goes back centuries in the Chablis region. Even recent history relating to the domaine goes back to the 18th century. The domaine's reputation rests with three *premiers crus* of 4 ha each, almost half the estate's total of 25 ha. Viticulture is effectively organic, though not certified as such, vine age is high and grape selection rigorous. A sustained fermentation and long lees contact also contribute to the character of these wines. There is less of the floral, mineral and pure fruit character of other good producers but there is depth, intensity and complexity. The Les Lys has more mineral, citrus character plus honey with age; in Côte de Léchet and Vaillons there is more of a leesy influence but a little more structure too, particularly in the latter. Rarely seen is a little Bourgogne Rouge from very old vines, successful in the best vintages. A tiny amount of Grand Cru Blanchots is also made. Most of the wines can be drunk soon after their delayed release but will keep for longer. (PW)
O **Chablis Premier Cru** Côte de Léchet★★★ £D Les Lys★★★ £D Vaillons★★★ £D
O **Chablis** Vieilles Vignes★★ £C

JEAN-PAUL DROIN www.jeanpaul-droin.fr A: **RsW, DDr**, BBR, Bib, A&B, IGH, UnC

Owner: Jean-Paul Droin 14 bis Rue Jean Jaurès, 89800 Chablis
Jean-Paul Droin and his son Benoît draw from 20 ha of vines spread over five *grands crus* (with around 1 ha each of Vaudésir, Valmur and Les Clos) and seven *premiers crus*. The range is generally of high quality. At the *premiers* and *grands crus* levels the wines are (to a greater or lesser degree) fermented and aged in oak of varying age and provenance, resulting in rich, ripe (occasionally too ripe), full wines. The use of oak has become gradually more refined over the past decade and, though there are still some oak flavours, these now rarely overwhelm the ripe, minerally fruit. Nearly all the wines can be drunk with just three or four years' ageing, but will improve for as long again. Try the *crus*, particularly the Montée de Tonnerre, Vaudésir and Les Clos; the regular Chablis and Petit Chablis are more variable. In addition to those below, a little *grand cru* Blanchots and *premiers crus* Côte de Lechet and Vaucoupin are also made. The 2001s are of variable quality, the best being Montée de Tonnerre, Grenouilles and Les Clos. (PW)
O **Chablis Grand Cru** Valmur★★★ £E Grenouilles★★★★ £E Vaudésir★★★★ £E Les Clos★★★★ £E
O **Chablis Premier Cru** Vaillons★★★ £C Montmains★★★ £C Montée de Tonnerre★★★★ £C
O **Chablis Premier Cru** Fourchaume★★★ £C Vosgros★★★ £C

JOSEPH DROUHIN (CHABLIS) www.drouhin.com A: **DAy**, Add, MCW, WsB

Owner: Drouhin family Moulin de Vaudon, Chichée, 89800 Chablis
Under Robert Drouhin, the house of Joseph DROUHIN, an important high-quality Beaune *négociant*, added Chablis vineyards to its holdings in the Côte d'Or in the late 1960s. Though the wines are vinified at the company's headquarters in Beaune, the grapes from more than 40 ha are pressed locally. The estate includes 3 ha of *grand cru* vineyards spread over four *climats*, mostly Vaudésir and Les Clos but a little Bougros and Preuses too. Low yields contribute to ripe, concentrated fruit and, though oak is important to the style, it is only used in the top wines and there is usually a good minerally aspect to their character. As well as *premiers crus* Vaillons and Sécher, some Montmains and a regular Chablis Premier Cru from a blend of other sites are bottled separately. (PW)
O **Chablis Grand Cru** Preuses★★★ £F Vaudésir★★★★ £F Les Clos★★★★★ £F
O **Chablis Premier Cru** Sécher★★★ £E Vaillons★★★ £E
O **Chablis**★ £B Domaine de Vaudon★★ £C

GÉRARD DUPLESSIS

A: **RsW**, A&B, Rae, Maj

Owner: Gérard Duplessis 5 Quai de Reugny, 89800 Chablis
This excellent small grower's 7 ha of vineyards are mostly in four of the very best *premiers crus*. Gérard Duplessis vinifies in stainless steel and matures in old wood for classic Chablis flavours. The wines can start out a little austere but there is that wonderful Chablis combination of underlying richness and a steely, minerally character that can provide wonderful drinking with five years' ageing, and is even better with another 5 or 10 in a top vintage. (PW)

O **Chablis Grand Cru** Les Clos★★★★ £E
O **Chablis Premier Cru** Fourchaume★★★ £D Montée de Tonnerre★★★ £D Montmains★★★ £D
O **Chablis Premier Cru** Vaillons★★ £D O **Chablis**★★ £C

JEAN DURUP ET FILS www.durup-chablis.com

A: ABy, DDr, THt, HRp, Tan, Hrd

Owner: Jean Durup 4 Grande Rue, Maligny, 89800 Chablis
Jean Durup led the movement for expansion of the Chablis *vignoble* in direct opposition to WILLIAM FÈVRE in the 1970s and 80s. His estate, partly as a consequence of the authorised expansion, is the largest in the region (much of it regular Chablis but there are also substantial holdings of *premiers crus*). It is very competently run and is increasingly directed by Jean Durup's son, Jean-Paul. While derided by some at the time, Jean has gradually earned greater respect for the quality of his wines. He has also been a leading advocate of unoaked Chablis. The wines are generally well-balanced, with adequate richness if sometimes lacking a little character and extra flair. Most of the wines drink well with two to five years' ageing but *premiers crus* can age for up to a decade. The 2001s were rather weak after some good 2000s. While the most important labels are Jean Durup, Domaine de l'Eglantière and Château de Maligny, the same wines are also bottled under Domaine de la Paulière and Domaine des Valéry labels for some importers. Some *grand cru* Vaudésir has been made in the most recent vintages. (PW)

O **Chablis Premier Cru** Fourchaume★★ £C Montée de Tonnerre★★ £C L'Homme Mort★★★ £C
O **Chablis Premier Cru** Vau-de-Vey★★ £C
O **Chablis**★ £B Vieilles Vignes★★ £B Vigne de la Reine★★ £C Carré de César★★ £C

WILLIAM FÈVRE www.williamfevre.com

A: **JEF, HBJ**, BBR, WSc, F&M

Owner: Joseph Henriot (Champagne) 21 Avenue d'Oberwesel, 89800 Chablis
Over the last five to six years, the William Fèvre domaine has reassumed the leadership of Chablis – combining both outstanding quality and significant quantity. Its revival followed the takeover by Joseph Henriot (also see HENRIOT Champagne and BOUCHARD PÈRE in the Côte d'Or). The Domaine de la Maladière comprises 47 ha and includes an unrivalled collection of *premiers* and *grands crus*. Almost 16 ha are *grand cru* and include six of the seven *climats*. In the late 80s and early 90s William Fèvre was the staunchest and most vocal of those opposed to the expansion of the Chablis vineyards. The use of new oak became an increasing theme too, to the point of compromising the inherent fruit character of Chablis. Now, under the direction of Didier Séguier, there has been a return to manual harvesting and much more rigorous grape selection. New oak is still used but the wines are bottled later and there is better concentration and something more of each wine's origin is captured and enhanced by the oak. Though most of the wines are domaine-sourced, some also are made from bought-in grapes. Wines appear also under the Domaine de la Maladière label and the names Ancien Domaine Auffray and Jeanne-Paule Filippi have also been used. Vintages since 1998 and older vintages are highly recommended, but those from the mid-1990s are more variable. (PW)

O **Chablis Grand Cru** Les Clos🟠🟠🟠🟠🟠 £F Vaudésir🟠🟠🟠🟠🟠 £F Preuses★★★★★ £F Valmur★★★★★ £F
O **Chablis Grand Cru** Bougros Côte de Bougerots★★★★★ £F Bougros★★★★ £E Grenouilles★★★★ £F
O **Chablis Premier Cru** Fourchaume★★★★ £E Mont de Milieu★★★★ £D Montée de Tonnerre★★★★ £D
O **Chablis Premier Cru** Vaillons★★★★ £D Montmains★★★ £D Butteaux★★★ £D
O **Chablis Premier Cru** Les Lys★★★ £D Forêts★★ £D Beauroy★★ £D O **Chablis**★★ £C

GHISLAINE ET JEAN-HUGUES GOISOT   Saint-Bris   A: **DDr**, HHB, Rae

Owner: Ghislaine & Jean-Hugues Goisot 30 Rue Bienvenu Martin, 89530 Saint-Bris-le-Vineux
The Goisots' vineyards lie outside the Chablis appellation in the less than glamorous Saint-Bris, which promotes Sauvignon rather than Chardonnay. But both Sauvignon and Chardonnay are produced here (an extremely rare occurrence in France, in contrast to much of the New World) along with Aligoté and Pinot Noir from a total of 27 ha of vineyards. Through meticulous and dedicated work in the vineyards and cellars, all the wines are of extremely high quality yet don't command high prices thanks to their lowly appellations. The pure-fruited Chardonnay and perfumed Pinot Noir are sold as Bourgogne Côtes d'Auxerre, the pungent green-pepper Sauvignon now as newly promoted Saint-Bris AC, while the Aligoté appears as humble Bourgogne. The wines are ripe, concentrated and aromatic, with lovely definition and length, and under the Corps de Garde label are worth keeping for two or three years. Also made but not tasted are prestige *cuvées* from Côtes d'Auxerre whites, Biaumont and Gondonne, and an Irancy, Mazelots. (PW)

O **Bourgogne Côtes d'Auxerre**★★ £B Corps de Garde★★★ £C
O **Saint-Bris**★★ £B Corps de Garde Gourmand★★ £B
O **Bourgogne Aligoté**★ £B ● **Bourgogne** Rouge★ £B Corps de Garde★★ £C

JEAN-PIERRE GROSSOT & CORINNE PERCHAUD   A: **L&W**, Lib, Eno, IGH

Owner: Jean-Pierre Grossot & Corinne Perchaud 4 Route de Mont de Milieu, Fleys, 89800 Chablis
This is a great source for Chablis whether labelled Grossot or sold under the label established by his wife, Corinne Perchaud. If initially a little austere, the wines are intensely fruity, with excellent definition, weight and fine perfumes. Though there are no *grands crus*, the 18 ha includes some excellent *premiers crus*. Stainless steel dominates their production but some oak is used for the Fourneaux and Mont de Milieu *premiers crus* and the village *cuvée*, 'Grossot' or Fûts de Chênes. Only the latter is obviously oaky, the others properly racy and minerally. While the wines are delicious with three or four years' ageing, they will keep. Solid quality and reasonable prices too. (PW)

O **Chablis Premier Cru** Fourneaux★★ £C Vaucoupin★★ £C Fourchaume★★★ £C Mont de Milieu★★★ £C
O **Chablis**★ £B Fûts de Chênes★ £B La Part des Anges★★ £C

DOM. LAROCHE   www.michellaroche.com   A: **Bib**, NYg

Owner: Michel Laroche L'Obédiencerie, 22 Rue Louis Bro, 89800 Chablis
Michel Laroche is one of Chablis' major players and has recently become almost as well-known for wines made in the South of France (he also has a joint venture with Jorge Coderch in Chile) as for his many prestigious Chablis *crus*. The estate's offices are based in the Obédiencerie in the heart of Chablis, originally a monastery dating back to the ninth century. The Saint-Martin monks here established Chablis' first vines. Though the Laroche domaine dates from the mid-19th century, its major expansion has been only recently, under Michel and his father Henri, and it now covers 100 ha of vines. Most of the the wine is exported around the globe. There are 6 ha of *grands crus*, mostly Blanchots but also some Les Clos and a little Bouguerots (Bougros), and 29 ha of *premiers crus* centred on Fourchaume, Vaillons and Vau de Vey. Lesser wines can be a bit light, but can show typical minerally fruit. In the top wines the style is more unusual, with marked oak influence and sometimes a discernible lactic character in the top *crus*. The wines are supple and gently creamy, without the austerity more characteristic of young Chablis but still retaining a mineral stamp. *Grands crus* can be very good; a small portion of the Blanchots is set apart for the top wine, Réserve de l'Obédience, while the Fourchaumes and Vaillons are labelled Vieilles Vignes for their old vine fruit. Good as the wines can be, the price-for-quality ratio is less convincing. (PW)

O **Chablis Grand Cru** Les Clos★★★★ £F Blanchots★★★ £E Blanchots Réserve de l'Obédience★★★★ £F
O **Chablis Premier Cru** Vaillons Vieilles Vignes★★★ £D Fourchaumes Vieilles Vignes★★★ £D
O **Chablis Premier Cru** Beauroy★★ £D Montmains★★ £D Vau de Vey★★★ £C
O **Chablis** Saint-Martin★ £B

BERNARD LEGLAND/DOM. DES MARRONNIERS
A: **Bib**, GWW

Owner: Bernard Legland   Rue de Chablis, Préhy, 89800 Chablis

This is a good source of attractive, well-made and relatively inexpensive Chablis. Bernard Legland's 18 ha doesn't include much in the way of prime vineyards; 2.5 ha of Montmains is the most prized possession. The domaine was established in 1976 and has adhered to a principle of unoaked Chablis. Previously the *premiers crus* (there is also a little Côte de Jouan) were made from relatively young vines but these are now more than 20 years old, giving the wines added richness and depth. (PW)

O **Chablis Premier Cru** Côte de Jouan★★ £C   Montmains★★★ £C
O **Chablis**★ £B

LONG-DEPAQUIT
A: **Bal**, BBR

*Owner: **Maison Albert Bichot**   45 Rue Auxerroise, 89800 Chablis*

This historic estate dates from the time of the French Revolution. There are now 65 ha but much of it has been acquired in the last 30 years or so. As well as a sprinkling of wines from *premier* and *grand cru* vineyards, the wine of the famous La Moutonne vineyard is made here. Acquired in 1791 by Simon Depaquy, it is a *monopole* of 2.35 ha that straddles part of *grands crus* Vaudésir and Preuses that belonged originally to the monks of the Abbey of Pontigny. Though most of the wines are both vinified and aged in stainless steel in order not to compromise the classic, flinty, minerally Chablis style, the *grands crus* see varying percentages of oak. Quality can be a bit uneven but at their best they have intensity, style and finesse; the top wines, especially La Moutonne, develop a gentle honeyed richness with age. The selected *crus* below are the most consistently fine and ageworthy, lesser wines are more of a gamble but can also be good. Prices are on the high side for the quality level. (PW)

O **Chablis Grand Cru** Blanchots★★★ £E Vaudésir★★★ £E Les Clos★★★ £E La Moutonne★★★★ £E
O **Chablis Premier Cru** Vaucoupin★★ £C Vaillons★★ £C Montée de Tonnerre★★★ £D

DOM. DES MALANDES   www.domainedesmalandes.com
A: **CHk**, H&B, Evg, WSc

Owner: Jean-Bernard et Lyne Marchive   63 Rue Auxerroise, 89800 Chablis

Established in 1986 from the family inheritance of Lyne Marchive (*née* Tremblay), this 26-ha estate has a good following for unoaked Chablis. The reputation has been built on producing wines from low yields and fully ripe fruit and a non-interventionist winemaking philosophy. The wines are ripe, more floral and fruit-driven in the lesser *cuvées* but with more minerally intensity and complexity, as well as concentration, in the *grands crus*. Fourchaume and Montmains are perhaps the pick of the *premiers crus* but a fruit-emphasized Vau de Vey and very mineral, more classically austere Côte de Lechet are also very good. Both the *grands crus* are very classy, reflecting their respective terroir but with similar breadth, depth and length. Though all can be drunk fairly young, these are the wines to keep. (PW)

O **Chablis Grand Cru** Vaudésir★★★★★ £E Les Clos★★★★ £E
O **Chablis Premier Cru** Côte de Léchet★★★ £C Montmains★★★ £C Fourchaume★★★ £C
O **Chablis Premier Cru** Vau de Vey★★★ £C
O **Chablis**★★ £B Vieilles Vignes Tour du Roy★★ £C   O **Petit Chablis**★ £B

DOM. LOUIS MICHEL ET FILS
A: **OWL, DAy**, BBR, Eno, IGH, Odd, WSc

Owner: Jean-Loup Michel   9-11 Boulevard de Ferrières, 89800 Chablis

Fifth-generation Jean-Loup Michel has made the wines here in recent years but the 23-ha estate's international reputation was established by his father, Louis Michel, who died in 1999. Much of the production is now exported and widely available but remarkably without the high prices and compromised quality of some exporters. For its unoaked style of Chablis this is perhaps the most lauded producer in the English-speaking press. The wines spend an extended period of time in stainless steel before a relatively late bottling. Austere but with an underlying minerally fruit richness when young, the *premiers crus* are always better with three to five years' ageing, the *grands crus* with five or more. At their best these are excellent Chablis with fine *terroir* definition and real elegance and length on the palate if not the texture or dimension of the very best. That said these are wines to buy from the better vintages only; a cool or wet or generally more difficult vintage (such as 2001) can reveal a lack of full ripeness as well as a tendency to age more rapidly than usual. (PW)

○ **Chablis Grand Cru** Grenouilles★★★★ £E Vaudésir★★★★ £E Les Clos★★★★★ £E
○ **Chablis Premier Cru** Montée de Tonnerre★★★★ £D Vaillons★★★ £C
○ **Chablis Premier Cru** Fourchaume★★★ £C Montmains★★★ £C
○ **Chablis**★★ £B ○ **Petit Chablis**★ £B

DOM. LOUIS MOREAU   www.domaine-louismoreau.com   A: **PBW**,ACh

Owner: Louis Moreau   10 Grande Rue, Beines, 89800 Chablis

Louis and Anne Moreau control 120 ha comprising mostly village Chablis and including the separate estates of Domaine de Biéville and Domaine du Cèdre Doré. The wines should not be confused with those of the *négociant* house, Moreau. Vinified in stainless steel, without recourse to any wood, the wines are quite racy and austere when young but have great reserves of fruit underneath, particularly in the two *premiers crus*, Vaulignot (Vau Ligneau) and Fourneaux. Some top *grands crus,* previously leased out, have been produced since the 2002 vintage. These see a little new oak and though only moderately concentrated should add richness with age. Led by a classy Vaudésir, they also include Valmur, Les Clos and, from a plot of vines within Les Clos, Clos des Hospices. (PW)

○ **Chablis Grand Cru** Valmur★★★★ £E Vaudésir★★★★ £E Les Clos Clos des Hospices★★★★ £E
○ **Chablis Premier Cru** Fourneaux★★★ £C Vaulignot★★ £C
○ **Chablis**★ £B Domaine du Cèdre Doré★★ £B Domaine de Biéville★★ £B

MOREAU-NAUDET   A:OWL, L&S, SVS, Tan, WSc, Hrd

Owner: Roger et Stéphane Moreau   5 Rue des Fossés, 89800 Chablis

Stéphane Moreau, not related to the Moreaus of Domaine Louis Moreau, has been running this 21-ha estate since 1999 and the wines are now very good indeed. Machine harvesting is only used for the regular wines yet even at this level, both Petit Chablis and Chablis as well as some special *cuvées*, the fruit is ripe and intense with a mineral aspect. Several excellent *premiers crus*, including a Montée de Tonnerre imbued with smoke, mineral and citrus, give good expression to their origins. Deep, minerally Valmur is long and classy, an excellent and affordable example of this often pricey *grand cru*. Cuvée Les Pargues and an old-vine Charactère will be added with further tastings. (PW)

○ **Chablis Grand Cru** Valmur★★★★ £D
○ **Chablis Premier Cru** Vaillons★★★ £C Montée de Tonnerre★★★ £C Montmains★★★ £C
○ **Chablis**★★ £B

DIDIER & PASCAL PICQ   A: **M&V**, NYg

Owner: Didier & Pascal Picq   3 Route de Chablis, Chichée, 89800 Chablis

The small village of Chichée lies some 3km south-east of the town of Chablis. Here the Picqs have 13 ha, including a little of Chichée's two *premiers crus*. Didier Picq is responsible for the winemaking, while his brother, Pascal, maximises grape quality. The grapes are picked as late as possible and both fermentation and ageing are in stainless steel. The wines are crisp and fresh, quite floral and fruity in style but with good intensity in the Vieilles Vignes and extra character and concentration in the *premiers crus*. From most vintages the Vieilles Vignes should be drunk with at least three years' ageing, the *premiers crus* with five or more. The wines are also labelled Gilbert Picq et Fils. (PW)

○ **Chablis Premier Cru** Vaucoupin★★★ £C Vosgros★★★ £C
○ **Chablis**★★ £B Vieilles Vignes★★ £B

DOM. PINSON FRÈRES www.domaine-pinson.com

A: A&B, CPp, L&W, NYg

Owner: Laurent & Christophe Pinson 5 Quai Voltaire, 89800 Chablis

Perpetually rustic would perhaps best describe the atmosphere *chez* Pinson as almost anyone who has visited the estate over the past couple of decades I'm sure would agree. But brothers Laurent and Christophe, the current generation in charge of this small 11.5-ha estate, seem set on a new image while continuing to make Chablis of real depth and character. The parcels of vines are all of the first order, including 2.5 ha of Les Clos and nearly 5 ha of Mont de Milieu. Used oak is employed in their ageing (only the regular Chablis is unoaked), which contributes to their excellent texture and breadth but only subtly influences flavour, though it is sometimes more apparent on the Montmains. The wines have been a little uneven in terms of their ability to age but quality is often remarkably high. All the wines are better with five years' ageing or more, the Les Clos often with 10 or more. A little of the *premiers crus* Vaillons and Vaugiraut are also made. (PW)

O **Chablis Grand Cru** Les Clos★★★★ £D
O **Chablis Premier Cru** La Forêt★★★ £C Mont de Milieu★★★ £C Montmains★★★ £C
O **Chablis**★★ £B

DENIS POMMIER www.denis-pommier.com

A: L&S, Han

Owner: Denis Pommier 31 Rue de Poinchy, Poinchy, 89800 Chablis

Denis Pommier started out with just 2.5 ha in 1990 but now has 11 ha. He is already forging a reputation as a young *vigneron* of some talent. Though he has started fermenting and ageing his *premiers crus* in barrel, apart from the Beauroy, only part of the wine gets this treatment and then only a small percentage of the oak is new. Certainly the quality of the grapes is very good and the wines show concentrated ripe fruit; the mineral and citrus intensity is set against a spicy oak character and a gently buttery texture in the most recent vintages of the Côte de Léchet. The overall balance and oak integration in the Beauroy has been less convincing but it will be interesting to see how the style evolves here. At present the small production quickly sells out. The Vieilles Vignes also shows some oak influence but the regular version sees no oak whatsoever. A very small amount of Fourchaume is also made from relatively young vines. (PW)

O **Chablis Premier Cru** Côte de Léchet★★★ £C Beauroy★★ £C
O **Chablis**★★ £B Croix aux Moines★★ £B Vieilles Vignes★★ £B

DENIS RACE www.chablisrace.com

A: **M&V**, All, Mar, PWa

Owner: Laurence & Denis Race 5a Rue de Chichée, 89800 Chablis

Denis Race is an exponent of unoaked Chablis. He and his wife have 15 ha of vines including 5.5 ha of *premier cru* Montmains. There is careful attention to the grapes prior to harvesting (and what is left ready for picking) – the key to quality when the grapes are machine-harvested as so much in Chablis now is. The Montmains appears in two bottlings, the Vieilles Vignes version from vines that are 65 years old. Sometimes in Chablis this designation is applied even though there isn't that much really old-vine fruit either in the blend or apparent in the resulting wine, but there is a marked difference in depth and concentration in the Race wines. All the wines show good *terroir* definition. A steely, minerally Mont de Milieu contrasts with a softer, more elegant Vaillon. A little *grand cru* Blanchots is also made. (PW)

O **Chablis Premier Cru** Montmains Vieilles Vignes★★★ £D Montmains★★ £C
O **Chablis Premier Cru** Mont de Milieu★★ £C Vaillon★★
O **Chablis**★ £B

DOM. RAVENEAU

A: JAr, HHC, Sec, Blx

Owner: Jean-Marie & Bernard Raveneau 9 Rue de Chichée, 89800 Chablis

If I had to chose one source of Chablis above all others this would be it. Continuing the work of their father, François Raveneau, brothers Jean-Marie and Bernard Raveneau make superb Chablis from just 7.5 ha of *premier* and *grand cru* sites. Unquestionably the grape quality is paramount – all are hand-picked and from low-yielding vines – but if anyone makes the case for the use of oak and how it should be used, surely this is the model to emulate. The wines have fabulous structure yet never taste as if they have seen the inside of a barrel. Typically pure minerally, citrusy, greengage notes prevail on the nose, if occasionally more floral or with a hint of smoke, while the palate is taut, intense and steely when young but with wonderful dimension, underlying concentration and depth that builds in richness and complexity over a decade or longer. No two wines are quite the same but there is fine quality here even in weaker vintages. The domaine also has small plots in Chapelot, Forest (Forêt) and Montmains. Prices are surprisingly reasonable unless you buy them second- or third-hand. (PW)

O **Chablis Grand Cru** Blanchots★★★★★ £E Valmur★★★★★ £E Les Clos❍❍❍❍❍ £E
O **Chablis Premier Cru** Butteaux★★★★ £E Vaillons★★★★ £E Montée de Tonnerre★★★★ £E

GÉRARD TREMBLAY   www.chablis-tremblay.com   A: Anl, Eno, Cav

Owner: Tremblay family   12 Rue de Poinchy, 89800 Chablis
This is a well-established family domaine with a good record of producing classic minerally Chablis. Around 20,000 cases are produced from 33 ha of vineyards. There is some use of oak, around 20 per cent for the *premiers crus* and 40 per cent for *grands crus*, but it is rarely obvious and as a result of intelligent vinification and ageing the wines impress most for their structure. They open out with some bottle age, the mineral, floral aspects apparent when young becoming allied to a rich, ripe fruit depth, especially with four to five years' age from a good vintage. *Premiers crus* Côte de Lechet, Fourchaume and Montmains all illustrate the style handsomely. Vaudésir from 0.62 ha shows the classic stone-spice-floral quality of this *grand cru* though was less good than usual in 2001. Some *grand cru* Valmur is also made. (PW)

O **Chablis Grand Cru** Vaudésir★★★★ £E
O **Chablis Premier Cru** Fourchaume★★★ £C Montmains★★★ £C
O **Chablis Premier Cru** Côte de Léchet★★★ £C   O **Chablis**★★ £B

DOM. DE VAUROUX   www.domaine-de-vauroux.com   A: Cav, L&W, Con, Eno

Owner: Claude & Olivier Tricon   Route d'Avallon, 89800 Chablis
Oliver Tricon has taken over full responsibility for the running of this estate from his uncle only since 1999 but is already a very experienced winemaker and *négociant*. A thoroughly modern operation, the domaine has 30 ha of vines, mostly village Chablis but with a little *grand cru* Bougros and a reasonable quantity of *premiers crus* Montmains and Montée de Tonnerre. The style is for stainless steel-vinified and aged Chablis and the resulting wines are clean and flinty, with good concentration and fruit. The wines are given some bottle-ageing before release. As well as the Vauroux wines, estate wines have also been made under the Domaine Olivier Tricon label, while *négociant* wines appear as Maison Olivier Tricon. Prices are reasonable for the quality. (PW)

Domaine de Vauroux:
O **Chablis Grand Cru** Bougros★★★ £E
O **Chablis Premier Cru** Montmains★★ £C Montée de Tonnerre★★★ £C
O **Chablis**★ £B Vieilles Vignes★★ £C

DOM. VOCORET   www.vocoret.com   A: HHB, IGH, Maj

Owner: Patrice & Jérôme Vocoret   40 Route d'Auxerre, 89800 Chablis
This family domaine of 40 ha includes around 4 ha of *grands crus* (mostly Blanchots and Les Clos) and more than 15 ha of *premiers crus* (especially Vaillons and La Forêt). Third-generation Jérôme makes the wines while his uncle Patrice manages the vineyards. Though much of the fruit is mechanically harvested, the fruit is generally ripe and concentrated. Vinification is in stainless steel but the *crus* are aged in large used oak. Quality is generally very good with an intense, vibrant fruit character and reasonable depth, though the wines can miss a little extra concentration in more difficult vintages. In addition to those below, small quantities of the *grands crus* Valmur and Vaudésir and *premier cru* Mont de Milieu are also made. (PW)

O **Chablis Grand Cru** Blanchot★★★ £D   Les Clos★★★ £D
O **Chablis Premier Cru** Côte de Léchet★★ £C   La Forêt★★ £C   Montmains★★ £C
O **Chablis Premier Cru** Montée de Tonnerre★★ £C   Vaillons★★ £C
O **Chablis★** £B

Also see the following Burgundy *négociants* with an entry in the section *Côte D'Or & Côte Chalonnaise:*
OLIVIER LEFLAIVE FRÈRES
VERGET

CHABLIS & YONNE/OTHER WINES OF NOTE

CHRISTAN ADINE/DOM. DE LA CONCIÈRGERIE O **Chablis Premier Cru** Montmains £C
DOM. BARAT O **Chablis Premier Cru** Côte de Léchet £C   Fourneaux £C   Vaillons £C
DOM. BERSAN O **Chablis Premier Cru** Montmains £C
PASCAL BOUCHARD O **Chablis Grand Cru** Les Clos £E   Vaudésir £E
O **Chablis Premier Cru** Fourchaumes Vieilles Vignes £D
DOM. DU CHARDONNAY O **Chablis Premier Cru** Montée de Tonnerre £C   Montmains £C
O **Chablis Premier Cru** Vaillons £C
DOM. JEAN COLLET ET FILS O **Chablis Grand Cru** Valmur £E
O **Chablis Premier Cru** Vaillons £C   Montmains £C   O **Chablis** £B
DOM. DU COLOMBIER O **Chablis Premier Cru** Fourchaume £C   Vaucoupin £C   O **Chablis** £B
DOM. D'ÉLISE O **Chablis** £B
DOM. ALAIN GAUTHERON & FILS O **Chablis Premier Cru** Les Fourneaux Vieilles Vignes £D
DOM. ALAIN GEOFFROY O **Chablis Grand Cru** Les Clos £F
O **Chablis Premier Cru** Beauroy £C   Fourchaume £C   O **Chablis** Vieilles Vignes £B
THIERRY HAMELIN O **Chablis Premier Cru** Beauroy £C   Vau Ligneau £C   O **Chablis** Vieilles Vignes £B
SYLVAIN MOSNIER O **Chablis Premier Cru** Beauroy £C   Côte de Léchet £C
O **Chablis** £B   Vieilles Vignes £B
DOM. OUDIN O **Chablis Premier Cru** Vaugiraut £C   Vaucoupin £C
FRANCINE ET OLIVIER SAVARY O **Chablis Premier Cru** Fourchaume £D
O **Chablis** Vieilles Vignes £C   O **Chablis** £C
DOM. SERVIN O **Chablis Premier Cru** Montée de Tonnerre £C   Vaillons £C
PHILIPPE TESTUT O **Chablis Premier Cru** Montée de Tonnerre £D   O **Chablis** £B
DOM. LAURENT TRIBUT O **Chablis Premier Cru** Beauroy £C   Côte de Léchet £C   O **Chablis** £B

Author's Choice for Chablis & Yonne (PW)

15 'true' Chablis
JEAN-CLAUDE BESSIN O **Chablis**
BILLAUD-SIMON O **Chablis** Premier Cru Vaillons
ADHÉMAR & FRANCIS BOUDIN O **Chablis** Premier Cru L'Homme Mort
DANIEL DAMPT O **Chablis** Premier Cru Côte de Léchet
RENÉ ET VINCENT DAUVISSAT O **Chablis**
JEAN-PAUL DROIN O **Chablis** Premier Cru Montée de Tonnerre
JOSEPH DROUHIN O **Chablis** Grand Cru Les Clos
WILLIAM FEVRE O **Chablis** Grand Cru Valmur
JEAN-PIERRE GROSSOT O **Chablis** Premier Cru Mont de Milieu
DOM. LAROCHE O **Chablis** Grand Cru Blanchots Réserve de l'Obédience
DOM. DES MALANDES O **Chablis** Premier Cru Fourchaume
DOM. LOUIS MICHEL O **Chablis**
DIDIER & PASCAL PICQ O **Chablis** Vieilles Vignes
DOM. PINSON O **Chablis** Premier Cru Mont de Milieu
DOM. RAVENEAU O **Chablis** Grand Cru Blanchots

Burgundy/Côte d'Or & Côte Chalonnaise

What a difference a new generation and a responsive market can make. Younger, highly-trained and talented winemakers have played their part in transforming quality in this the most complex and magical of France's wine regions. No stronger argument can be made for the validity of terroir than in Burgundy, where subtle differences of climate, soil composition and aspect identified over the course of centuries and expressed in individual climats make this region so complex and fascinating. Red Burgundy should enthrall with its perfume, complexity, finesse and textural qualities rather than power, oak and out-and-out concentration. White Burgundy should express complexity in both aroma and flavour, be it more minerally or buttery and nutty, and have a depth, structure and balance proportionate to its origins. Both should be more than just the most noble expression of two grapes, now familiar the world over, Pinot Noir and Chardonnay.

A change of direction

In the Côte d'Or, Burgundy's heart, the fragmentation of the vineyard area is extreme, and a complete contrast to Bordeaux's more coherent, larger patchwork. With a few rows here and a few there and the difficulties of vinifying such small quantities of grapes, it made sense to sell to a *négociant* as almost all growers did in the early 20th century. The cost in terms of quality has been well documented but through buying, trading and marriage a host of new independent growers have formed an important part of the new desire for quality.

Yet as recently as 20 years ago Burgundy was in dire straits. Excessive use of potassium and other chemicals on the soils (especially in the Côte de Nuits) led to reduced natural acidity levels and the dependence on pesticides, in turn leading to generally debilitated vineyard health. The resulting grapes were low in both sugar and acidity. Many producers considered it necessary to both over-chaptalize and acidify, a dual-pronged desperation made illegal in 1987. Whilst one practice or the other may be employed within strict limits there is little doubt that some producers still continue to do both despite some high-profile prosecutions by the authorities. Others, though, have sought to restore the health of their vineyards and obtain grapes of high quality and a new order of producers has emerged, better qualified but more often than not getting back to basics. They have improved the soil and plant health and consequently that of the grapes and wines. A movement towards organic and biodynamic viticulture has been stronger here than probably anywhere else in the wine-producing world. Currently many top estates take the advice of soil scientist Claude Bourguignon to enhance further the quality of their soils. Another consequence of the Burgundy's weak constitution was a tendency towards excessive fining and filtration in order to ensure the wine's stability. Better fruit quality as well as widely expressed criticism of heavy reliance on these practices, mean this trend has been reversed. Much too is made of lower yields, but there is still plenty of argument about how this is best achieved – whether through winter pruning, increasing vine densities, the use of different rootstocks or the use of green harvesting.

The best wines are now cleaner, riper and much more consistent even in more difficult years – though in the 1990s nature seems to have rewarded the many varied efforts – yet the wines are far from standardised. And even though there has been a general trend to ever bigger, oakier and more concentrated wines, at least some succeed admirably in retaining balance without losing the stamp of *terroir*. Where there were pockets of quality and occasional bright spots in some of the larger appellations now there are many producers turning out consistently high-quality wines. Yet from too many of the big merchants or *négociants* the wines continue to be very mediocre and it is why so many of them are missing from the following producer profiles. The ones included are the exception and in some instances are very good indeed. Much of the best wine comes from the smaller growers but an increasing number now also buy in some grapes.

Côte d'Or:

The basic hierarchy in the Côte d'Or is of *grands crus* at the top, followed by *premier crus* – always associated with one of 25 villages (*premiers crus* are often blended together due to fragmentation, so labelled simply Premier Cru) – then the level of the village itself (e.g. Gevrey-Chambertin) before the sub-regional appellations (such as Côte de Nuits-Villages) and finally the regional generics: **Bourgogne Rouge** (Pinot Noir), **Bourgogne Blanc** (Chardonnay) and **Bourgogne Aligoté**. The lowest level is not necessarily the humblest, however, as wine from any level may be sold as a generic (for instance, recently replanted vines that have only just come into production or vines that lie just outside a classified area). It is also worth noting that *premier cru* wine may also be included in part of a village-level bottling. This may be due to insufficient quantities for a separate bottling or a grower's decision not to compromise the integrity of his *premier cru* when faced with unsatisfactory quality in a difficult vintage. Also important to understanding the appellation system in Burgundy is the concept of *climat* or individual vineyard areas. Occasionally only part of a named area may be designated *premier cru* (e.g Chambolle-Musigny la Combe d'Orveaux) while within the unclassified village areas (which may be large, as in Meursault) the named vineyards (*lieux-dits*) may be added to the label (e.g. Meursault Tillets). The best of these will be close to *premier cru* level, just as several *premiers crus* are comparable to some of the less well-defined *grands crus*. Note too that the spelling of a particular vineyard can vary slightly from one producer to another. What follows is a brief breakdown of the most important villages and their most important *crus*.

Côte de Nuits

Production from the more northerly Côte de Nuits is almost exclusively red. **Marsannay** and **Fixin** at the north end of the Côte de Nuits, begin the band of mostly east-facing hills that stretches, with twists and breaks, until Santenay and Maranges in the tail of the Côte de Beaune. Marsannay tends to be light but scented and produces, unusually for the Côte de Nuits, a significant amount of rosé and white. Fixin in contrast, produces quite forceful, earthy Burgundy, including some powerful reds from *premiers crus* on slopes above the village. The wine, like that from the southern end of the Côte de Nuits, can be sold as **Côte de Nuits-Villages**. After the briefest of interludes (around Brochon) begins Burgundy's great rich seam of red.

Gevrey-Chambertin has 26 *premiers crus* including the outstanding Clos Saint-Jacques (*grand cru* in all but name) and Les Cazetiers at the centre of an arc of *premiers crus* on slopes to the east of the town. South of the village itself begins the great chain of *grands crus* that run almost to the southern edge of Vosne-Romanée. Of the nine in Gevrey, the 12.9-ha **Chambertin** and 15-ha **Clos-de-Bèze** are easily the most important. Seven others all append the name Chambertin: **Mazis-Chambertin** and **Ruchottes-Chambertin** are arguably the next best in potential; **Griottes-Chambertin**, **Charmes-Chambertin** (under which much of **Mazoyères-Chambertin** is sold) and **Chapelle-Chambertin** are also capable of greatness; the last, **Latricières-Chambertin**, rarely reaches the quality of the best *premiers crus*. Gevrey at any level should be distinguished by its greater power, concentration and structure than its neighbouring communes. Despite a radical improvement, too much of it remains pretty poor. **Morey-Saint-Denis** undeservedly lacks the lustre of Gevrey and Chambolle, but can combine the muscle of the former with the elegance of the latter, though which prevails to the greater degree depends as much on the grower as the on vineyard site. A tiny amount of white is made here too. While significantly smaller than Gevrey, it still boasts 20 *premiers crus* and four *grands crus* – **Clos de la Roche** (17 ha), **Clos Saint-Denis** (6.6 ha), **Clos des Lambrays** (8.8 ha) and **Clos de Tart** (7.5 ha) – as well as a thin slice of the 15 ha **Bonnes Mares** which falls mostly in **Chambolle-Musigny**. Bonnes Mares, with its mixed soils, is of variable style but is usually sturdier when sourced from the Morey end of the vineyards. Then the chain of *grands crus* is broken, before continuing with **Le Musigny** (10.7 ha) at the southern end of the commune. Some fine *premier cru* vineyards lie between the two, including Cras, Fuées and Baudes, but closest in style and proximity to Musigny are the often superb Amoureuses and Charmes. Musigny, like no other *cru*, can express the sumptuous elegant beauty of red Burgundy.

The commune of **Vougeot** is dominated by the massive 50-ha *grand cru* of **Clos Vougeot**. Though continuous and walled-in, in its lower, flatter reaches it juts deep into what corresponds to only village-quality land in neighbouring Vosne-Romanée. Arguably it ought to be partitioned into three different levels. Without due care you may find you have paid a *grand cru* price for what is, in effect, only village-level wine, although your choice of grower among the 80 owners of the vineyard counts for as much as the position of the vines. At its highest it adjoins both Musigny and Grands Echezeaux and at its best it is full, rich and complex if less aristocratic than the former. Both of the *grands crus* **Echezeaux** and **Grands Echezeaux** (with 32 ha and 9 ha respectively in production) fall in the commune of Flagey-Echezeaux. At their best both produce sturdy, characterful Burgundy, though much of Echezeaux lacks the class expected in a *grand cru*. Neighbouring **Vosne-Romanée** is a commune like no other in the Côte de Nuits. Behind the village lie the great vineyards that produce Burgundy's most expensive and sought-after wines. At the heart of 27 ha of *grands crus* are **La Romanée** (0.85 ha) and **Romanée-Conti** (1.8 ha) with **Richebourg** (8 ha) to the north, **Romanée-Saint-Vivant** (9.4 ha) closer to the village, and **La Grande Rue** (1.65 ha) and **La Tache** (6.1 ha) to the south. These in turn are flanked by some marvellous *premiers crus* including Malconsorts, Chaumes and Clos des Réas on the southern edge of the commune with Nuits-Saint-Georges; with Brûlées, Suchots and Beaux Monts on the northern side, the latter two pressing up against Echezeaux. The best of these are rich, intense and concentrated but with varying degrees of finesse, opulence or silkiness, dependent as much on producer as location. Village-level Vosne comes from east of the village.

The last major village in the Côtes de Nuits is **Nuits-Saint-Georges** though vineyards continue on south to Comblanchien. Here, the best wines offer power and intensity as well as a degree of finesse in the best of 38 *premiers crus* (which extend into the more southerly commune of Prémeaux). Damodes, Boudots and Murgers are some of the best between Nuits-Saint-Georges (the town) and Vosne-Romanée; Vaucrains, Pruliers and Les Saint-Georges are the most notable to the south of Nuits. There are no *grand crus*. Lesser wine can be flavoursome if chunky but the worst is rough and dilute. The cooler hinterland of the Côte de Nuits contains pockets of vineyards in favourable sites which constitute the **Hautes-Côtes de Nuits**. South of the town of Beaune is the equivalent **Hautes-Côtes de Beaune**. A significant amount of the wine is made by the co-op Les Caves des Hautes-Côtes; these wines or an example from a top grower can be good in an exceptional vintage.

Côte de Beaune

The Côte de Beaune's reputation is more for white than red yet the majority of wines are in fact red. From here south the gradients are lower and the swathe of vineyards wider, occasionally receding into the hills behind the main slopes. It begins in a cluster of villages around the famous hill of Corton. The humble AC of **Ladoix** (with seven *premiers crus*) is not widely seen and some of the wine is sold under the sub-regional appellation of **Côte de Beaune-Villages**. Wine for the latter can also come from another 15 villages, making it much more important than the Nuits equivalent. **Aloxe-Corton** at the foot of the Corton hill includes the famous appellations of Corton and Corton-Charlemagne, though vineyards spill into adjoining Ladoix and Pernand-Vergelesses. Most of the white from Burgundy's largest *grand cru* is sold as **Corton-Charlemagne** (51 ha) and most of the red as **Corton** (98 ha), though there is a little white Corton too (2.5 ha). The trend to planting Chardonnay begun in the mid-19th century continues, the paler soils at the top of the hill being the best site. Great Corton-Charlemagne is full-bodied but slow-developing due to a powerful structure and requires patience. Red Corton (which oftens attaches one of several *lieu-dit* names) can be similarly austere when young but develops a richness and a distinctive minerally elegance with age. Aloxe-Corton AC, almost entirely red, includes 13 *premiers crus* which lie directly below the red Corton vineyards. To the west of the Aloxe-Corton commune lies **Pernand-Vergelesses**, some of it tucked into the folds in the hills. Increasingly good red and white is made under the AC. The best *premier cru*, Ile de Vergelesses, favours reds of finesse rather than power but they add weight with age. To the south, it adjoins **Savigny-lès-Beaune**, which extends east up a little valley to the village itself. The best vineyards lie on both sides, the more northern band of *premiers crus* (including Guettes, Serpentières and Lavières) are more elegant than those from the southern band (including Dominodes, Marconnets, Narbantons and Peuillets), which tend to be fuller and firmer. Importantly, this is a reasonably plentiful source of good-value Burgundy. Rarely exciting is wine from **Chorey-lès-Beaune**, from flat land to the east of the Savigny AC.

Beaune, historically and commercially, is the heart of Burgundy but it is also one of the three leading Côte de Beaune red wine villages and includes some excellent *premiers crus* from the gentle slopes west of the town. Due to diverse soil types, leading *premiers crus* vary from the full and firm to softer, more elegant wines.

Marconnets, Fèves and Bressandes are of the first category, Grèves and Teurons are richer and softer, Clos des Mouches full but elegant too. Important vineyard owners such as Jadot, Albert Morot, Bouchard Père and Drouhin all provide the opportunity to compare and contrast some of the best *crus* from a single source. Another major vineyard owner, and one of the most important in the Côte de Beaune, is the Hospices de Beaune, their many (often oaky) *cuvées* (unique blends of predominantly *premiers crus* named for their benefactor) are sold at the famous auction in November. The wines are then 'finished' by the purchasing *négociant*, a factor that has a further bearing on their (variable) quality. The rarely seen **Côte de Beaune** AC is for a few vineyards in the hills behind Beaune AC. **Pommard** is a continuation of Beaune and its reputation for sturdy, full-bodied reds is in part due to more clayey, often iron-rich, soils than its neighbours. Grands Epenots and Rugiens Bas are the finest *premiers crus*. In **Volnay** the soils are lighter and poorer, contributing to the wine's refinement and elegance. Most of the best *premiers crus* come from south of the village, including Taillepieds, Clos des Chênes, Caillerets Dessus and Santenots. Santenots actually lies within the adjacent Meursault but is generally sold as Volnay when made from Pinot Noir, and as Meursault if from Chardonnay. South and west of Volnay an ascending flank of vineyards extends into the hills and includes the villages of **Monthelie, Auxey-Duresses** and **Saint-Romain**. The first two can provide excellent reds from several *premiers crus* but also a little good village white, especially in Auxey-Duresses. Good Saint-Romain white can be better than its position in the Hautes-Côtes de Beaune hills might suggest.

Meursault is one of the three biggest communes in the Côte d'Or and is the most important white wine village. But as with Beaune or Gevrey-Chambertin, with size comes variability. At its worst it is heavy and characterless but good examples are full, ripe and fruit-rich. The finest are intense, stylish and in the case of the would-be *grand cru*, Perrières, minerally and refined. There are no *grands crus* but other fine *premiers crus* include the best examples of Genevrières, Charmes, Poruzots and Goutte d'Or. Village *lieux-dits* names of note include Chevalières, Grands Charrons, Narvaux, Tessons and Tillets. **Blagny** is a small red wine outpost nestled against Meursault and **Puligny-Montrachet**. 'Puligny' and 'world's best' often share the same sentence and with good reason. The village includes the *grands crus* **Chevalier-Montrachet** (7.36 ha), **Bienvenues-Bâtard-Montrachet** (3.69 ha) and half of the 8 ha **Le Montrachet** and 6 ha of the 11.87 ha **Bâtard-Montrachet**. Le Montrachet is the greatest, and most expensive, of all but is a wine capable of marvellous concentration, sublime proportions and exquisite complexity. Chevalier-Montrachet, from thinner soils above, is potentially the closest in quality but Bâtard-Montrachet, from flatter vineyards, can offer superb richness and intensity too. There are many outstanding *premiers crus* which also command high prices. Caillerets (including Les Demoiselles) and Pucelles, adjoining the *grands crus*, will surpass any *grand cru* not at its full potential. Clavoillon and Folatières and the more elevated Champ Gain and La Garenne can highlight the Puligny finesse and intensity as can Champ-Canet, Combettes and Referts which extend as far as Meursault's Perrières and Charmes. As well as the continuation of *grands crus* Le Montrachet and Bâtard-Montrachet, the village of **Chassagne-Montrachet** adds the tiny 1.57-ha *grand cru* of Criots-Bâtard-Montrachet. The wines sold under the Chassagne AC were once predominantly red but its reputation is now emphatically white. Leading *premiers crus* include Caillerets, Champs Gains, Embrazées, Morgeots, La Romanée and Ruchottes – mostly confined to lighter-coloured soils on the higher slopes. Reds vary from the thin and unripe to full and fleshy and can be a source of good value (they only command around half the price of a white from the same vineyard, thus the trend to white continues). La Boudriotte, Clos Saint-Jean, La Maltroie, Morgeots and Chenevottes are the most noted red *premiers crus*. Behind Chassagne and Puligny lies the commune of **Saint-Aubin**. Some remarkably good white is produced by the best growers from the most worthy *premier cru* vineyards: La Chatenière and those that adjoin Chassagne (Le Charmois) and Puligny (En Remilly and Murgers des Dents de Chien – backing on to the Mont Rachet hill). Reds tend to be relatively light and slightly earthy.

Santenay is the Côte de Beaune's last significant commune for quality as the tail of the vineyard area swings west. From south-facing vineyards red wines dominate, the best of these are both full and stylish. These are likely to come from the *premiers crus* Gravières, La Comme and Clos des Tavannes that extend to the edge of Chassagne. One or two excellent whites are also being produced. While a fast improving AC with some excellent-value wines, Santenay is not so good from a weaker vintage or from a mediocre producer when the wine may be lean and stalky. To the west the vineyards adjoin **Maranges**, more earthy and robust than the best Santenay, though exceptions exist.

Côte Chalonnaise:

As a source of quality and value the best Côte Chalonnaise growers provide a real alternative to the lesser villages of the Côte d'Or. To the east of the Santenay and Maranges vineyards, and south of the town of Chagny, lie those of **Bouzeron**, the first of five separate appellations within the Côte Chalonnaise region. This is not a continuation of the Côte d'Or but an area of less sheltered rolling hills where the grapes ripen later and the wines are lighter. Bouzeron is classified for Aligoté only, its Pinot Noir and Chardonnay sold as **Bourgogne Côte Chalonnaise**. **Rully** lies east and south of Bouzeron and makes more white than red – both of which can reveal ripe, attractive fruit in a top example. Less ripe Chardonnay is likely to be made into **Crémant de Bourgogne**. South of Rully is **Mercurey**, the most important Chalonnaise appellation. Most of the wine is a quite structured red, surprisingly rich and intense from a combination of a top year and producer, but often hard and lean when not. A little good white is also produced. Slightly more supple yet stylish reds are produced in **Givry**, where the balance of red and white is similar to that of Mercurey. The southernmost appellation is **Montagny**, where exclusively white wine is made. The wines can be fuller if sometimes less distinguished than those from Rully. The reputable Buxy co-op, La Cave des Vignerons de Buxy, is based here.

A-Z of producers by appellation/region

Côte d'Or *(from north to south)*

Marsannay
BRUNO CLAIR	109

Gevrey-Chambertin
DENIS BACHELET	100
LUCIEN BOILLOT ET FILS	103
RENÉ BOUVIER	104
ALAIN BURGUET	105
PHILIPPE CHARLOPIN	107
DOM. PIERRE DAMOY	112
CLAUDE DUGAT	114
BERNARD DUGAT-PY	114
FRÉDÉRIC ESMONIN	116
SYLVIE ESMONIN	116
DOM. FOURRIER	117
GEANTET-PANSIOT	118
DENIS MORTET	133
DOM. ARMAND ROUSSEAU	140
CHRISTIAN SÉRAFIN	141
DOM. TRAPET PÈRE ET FILS	142

Morey-Saint-Denis
CLOS DE TART	110
DOM. DUJAC	114
ROBERT GROFFIER	120
DOM. DES LAMBRAYS	126
HUBERT LIGNIER	129
DOM. MICHEL MAGNIEN ET FILS	129
PERROT-MINOT	135
DOM. PONSOT	136

Chambolle-Musigny
AMIOT-SERVELLE	98
GHISLAINE BARTHOD	101
HUDELOT-NOËLLAT	122
JACQUES-FRÉDÉRIC MUGNIER	133
DOM. ROUMIER	140
DOM. COMTES GEORGES DE VOGÜE	143

Vosne-Romanée
DOM. ROBERT ARNOUX	100
SYLVAIN CATHIARD	106
BRUNO CLAVELIER	109
DOM. CONFURON-COTÉTIDOT	111
DOM. RENÉ ENGEL	115
DOM. JEAN GRIVOT	120
ANNE GROS	121
MICHEL GROS	121
FRANÇOIS LAMARCHE	125
MÉO-CAMUZET	130
MUGNERET-GIBOURG/G. MUGNERET	133
DOM. DE LA ROMANÉE-CONTI	139
EMMANUEL ROUGET	139

Nuits-Saint-Georges
BERTRAND AMBROISE	98
DOM. DE L'ARLOT	99
ROBERT CHEVILLON	108
DOM. JEAN-JACQUES CONFURON	111
DOM. FAIVELEY	116
DOM. HENRI GOUGES	119
DOMINIQUE LAURENT	127
NICOLAS POTEL	136
DOM. DANIEL RION ET FILS	138

Côte d'Or & Côte Chalonnaise vintages

In general terms red Burgundy doesn't offer the same potential longevity as do Bordeaux or other great Cabernet-based wines. Exceptional wines can, however, be very long-lived, and it is not unusual for the top whites to outlast the best reds. Ageing potential also depends as much on the style favoured by the particular producer or on the origin of the wines. Therefore comments about the character of the vintage made here should be considered against remarks made in the individual producer profiles. The very best estates, aided by a generally fine run of vintages in the past decade or so, now produce consistently high quality. Yet away from the top names and most famous sites the choice of vintage remains crucial, especially at a lower level, given the struggle for ripeness in Burgundy's many more marginal vineyard sites.

2003: An extraordinarily hot year that required both intelligence and speed from growers. There will undoubtedly be some overblown reds due to the extreme heat but some exceptional quality seems likely too. The prospects for whites seem less good – if balanced, their expected richness and power is likely to appeal most if drunk fairly young but the best wines will not be assessed until 2005.

2002: This is certainly an exciting red wine vintage in Burgundy despite a spell of warm but wet weather in early September. Yields were low, the grapes small but high in sugar, with good colour and acidity that has ensured intense, ripe and ageworthy wines throughout the Côte d'Or. Some of the most exceptional young reds have come from Volnay and Nuits-Saint-Georges. Whites are promising too, including those from the Côte Chalonnaise - the best with concentration, structure, perfectly ripe fruit and good balance that should match the high quality from 99 and 2000.

2001: A repeat of 2000 in the sense that the more northerly Côte de Nuits looks better than the Côte de Beaune (with reduced quantities in Volnay and Pommard due to hail). A wet year but with a mostly fine finish, one where only the best-managed vineyards produce ripe, concentrated grapes with good acidities.A good producer is essential but the wines have improved considerably in the bottle and show good terroir expression. The difficult weather also made for variable white wines; some have both good acidity and concentration but others lack ripeness.

2000: In red this was a much better vintage in the Côte de Nuits than the Côte de Beaune. Santenay was particularly badly affected by rain. Not one to cellar but fine quality further up the hierarchy. Generally a very good vintage for whites if slightly less consistent than 1999. Opinions are divided amongst growers as to the better of the two years for white; some have better ripeness, concentration and acidity in the latter, some in the former. Decent quality in the Côte Chalonnaise.

1999: A generally excellent large vintage for reds with remarkable colour, good acidity and ripe tannins. The size of the crop encouraged growers to be more rigorous in removing the less promising bunches. These reds, particularly good in the Côte de Beaune, are vigorous and intense and only the generic or more humble village appellations be should be drunk now. Whites were plentiful too, and, though more variable than the reds, are also fine with some outstanding examples from the top estates. An excellent vintage in the Côte Chalonnaise in both colours.

1998: A problematic growing season lowered expectations but this has turned out to be a vintage with more potential than 1997 thanks to better acidity and more stuffing. Quantities were down due to severe Easter frosts. Though generally very good, quality is much more irregular at a lower level, with a lack of full ripeness in the tannins due in part to some very hot August days. Isolated hail hit the volume of whites, especially in Meursault, and quality is variable; some wines lack concentration and others will evolve quite quickly. The best, though, will not disappoint.

1997: A much smaller vintage of more forward reds than 1996 but very attractive and one that has already given much pleasure. The wines have lowish acidities but it is a good vintage for drinking now if not for keeping. Whites can have lowish acidities too but there is no lack of richness or intensity in the top wines. The best in both colours will still keep.

1996: One of the finest red wine vintages of the 1990s, with both quantity and quality at the top level. There is excellent fruit intensity and ripeness in the tannins allied to good acidity that will repay further keeping. The best have closed up but more humble appellations from a good grower can be drunk now. Also a vintage in which exceptional reds and whites from the Côte Chalonnaise might still be drinking.

1995: Not a vintage of great richness in the reds but fine nonetheless. The best have added weight with age, are ripe and structured and will still improve. An excellent vintage for whites; good examples can be drunk now but will continue to improve.

1994: Arguably the weakest red wine vintage in the last 15 years but there is not much between this and 1992 in quality. A better bet in the Côte de Nuits than the Côte de Beaune. Whites are merely attractive when from a good producer, others are best left for the unwary.

1993: A very fine red wine vintage with great vigour, structure and intensity. Good village-level examples or those from lesser *climats* should be drunk now but the best will still improve. Much weaker in the whites, though some have both concentration and structure and provide rich, mature drinking now. Only the very best will still improve.

1992: A large red harvest, though not as much as 1990, and some of it full and charming though missing the extra concentration or structure of a really good vintage. Producers noted for their low yields are a safer bet though generally there is a lack of intensity and definition. Whites showed some delicious fruit but only in the top examples can this still be enjoyed.

1991: Many rich, concentrated and structured reds. The best still have plenty of life but some lack harmony and fully ripe tannins. Find a good bottle, though, and it's likely to be much cheaper than the 1990 of the same wine. Good drinking now, though a handful might keep a bit longer. Whites were mostly ordinary at best and should only be bought with extreme care.

1990: A superlative vintage for red wines and unequalled in recent decades for the overall quality of the vintage, though due to vinicultural improvements many individual producers have made wines of higher quality since. A very good vintage for whites too. Many fine bottles, including those from some of the lesser *climats*, and these will last for many years to come.

1989: A warm, plentiful vintage with relatively low acidity in the reds, though it is still good at top level. Whites had particularly good structure and have proved more long-lived than 1988, 90 or 92.

1988: A rather firm, austere vintage with high acidity and tannins in the reds. It has taken a long time to come into its own but the best examples are only now revealing the underlying refinement. Whites are less good though some have aged well.

Earlier years

At the top level 1985 can still provide good drinking, though whites are a safer bet as the once rich, ripe reds are mostly past their best due to low acidity levels. A few of the structured reds from the 1983 vintage can still be vigorous where rot was avoided. Even older vintages might only be considered for an outstanding *cru* from an impeccable source. Vintages from the 1970s include 78, 76 and 71 while the more successful 1960s include 69, 66, 64, 62 and 61. For these and wines from any older vintages, however, consider the advice of a trusted merchant or friend who still has other bottles of the same wine, or consult Michael Broadbent's *Vintage Wine*.

Côte d'Or & Côte Chalonnaise vintage chart

	Côte de Nuits Red	Côte de Beaune Red	Côte Chalonnaise Red	Côte de Beaune White
2003	★★/★★★★★ A	★★/★★★★★ A	★★/★★★★★ A	★/★★★★ A
2002	★★★★/★★★★★ A	★★★★/★★★★★ A	★★★★A	★★★★/★★★★★ A
2001	★★/★★★ A	★★/★★★ B	★★/★★★ B	★★★ B
2000	★★★ B	★★ B	★★ C	★★★★/★★★★★ B
1999	★★★★ B	★★★★/★★★★★ A	★★★★/★★★★★ B	★★★★/★★★★★ B
1998	★★★/★★★★ B	★★★ B	★★★ C	★★/★★★ C
1997	★★★ C	★★/★★★ C	★★/★★★ C	★★★/★★★★ B
1996	★★★★/★★★★★ B	★★★★/★★★★★ B	★★★★ C	★★★★/★★★★★ B
1995	★★★★ C	★★★★ C	★★★/★★★★ D	★★★★/★★★★★ B
1994	★/★★ C	★/★★ C	★★ D	★★★ C
1993	★★★★ B	★★★★ C	★★★ D	★★ D
1992	★★ C	★★ C	★★ D	★★★★ C
1991	★★★/★★★★ C	★★★/★★★★ C	★★★/★★★★ D	★★/★★★ D
1990	★★★★★ C	★★★★★ C	★★★★/★★★★★ C	★★★/★★★★ C
1989	★★★★ C	★★★★ C	★★★★ D	★★★★/★★★★★ C
1988	★★★★ C	★★★★ C	★★★ D	★★★/★★★★ D

Côte d'Or & Côte Chalonnaise/A-Z of producers

BERTRAND AMBROISE Nuits-Saint-Georges www.ambroise.com A: CTy, Bal, BBR, Win

Owner: Bertrand Ambroise Rue de l'Église, Prémeaux-Prissey, 21700 Nuits-Saint-Georges

Ambroise's red Burgundies are at one extreme of the Burgundian spectrum of wine styles. Their colour and strength are virtually unmatched in the Côte d'Or. The biggest reds are bold, oaky and tannic when young but the depth and concentration ensure that both something of the wine's origin and a certain finesse come with age. Of some 20 ha of vineyards spread over several communes in the centre of the Côte d'Or, around a quarter is for whites, with some notable Saint-Aubin and Corton-Charlemagne. Whites are rich and not excessively oaky and show a structure and depth worthy of their appellations, often with a real succulence that encourages early drinking. If not to everyone's taste, the wines are consistent and well-priced. Lesser reds (Bourgogne Rouge and Bourgogne Rouge Vieilles Vignes) and whites (Bourgogne Chardonnay and Hautes-Côtes de Nuits) can seem a little coarse but don't lack for fruit or flavour. 2002 Nuits-Saint-Georges *premiers crus* though deep and characterful are over-extracted, even in the context of the style here. (PW)

● **Corton Le Rognet★★★** £F ● **Clos de Vougeot★★★** £F
● **Nuits-Saint-Georges★★** £D Vieilles Vignes★★★ £D 1er Cru Rue de Chaux★★★ £E
● **Nuits-Saint-Georges** 1er Cru Clos des Argillières★★★ £E 1er Cru Les Vaucrains★★★ £E
● **Côte de Nuits-Villages★** £C ● **Vougeot** 1er Cru Les Cras★★ £D
O **Chassagne-Montrachet** 1er Cru Maltroie★★★ £E O **Corton-Charlemagne★★★★** £F
O **Saint-Romain★** £C O **Saint-Aubin** 1er Cru Murgers Dents de Chien★★ £C

DOM. GUY AMIOT ET FILS Chassagne-Montrachet A: Bal, Bib, HHB, HRp, L&S, F&R

Owner: Guy & Thierry Amiot 13 Rue de Grand-Puits, 21190 Chassagne-Montrachet

Guy Amiot and his son Thierry make a string of white Chassagne-Montrachet *crus*, which have shown increasing refinement and complexity in the most recent vintages. The wines are now bottled later than previously but perhaps more importantly Thierry has made changes in the vineyard resulting in richer, riper fruit from vines with an increasingly high average age (especially Vergers and Caillerets). At least as interesting if not at the same quality level are the red wines, which have very good richness for southern Côte de Beaune reds, with added length and style in the Clos Saint-Jean bottling. All the better reds deserve at least three or four years' age. Only a very little Puligny-Montrachet Premier Cru Les Demoiselles and Montrachet are made. Lesser whites can be drunk young but the best need at least three or four years' ageing. (PW)

O **Chassagne-Montrachet** 1er Cru Les Caillerets★★★★ £E 1er Cru Les Vergers★★★ £E
O **Chassagne-Montrachet★★★** £D 1er Cru Les Baudines★★★ £E 1er Cru Les Macharelles★★★★ £E
O **Chassagne-Montrachet** 1er Cru Clos Saint-Jean★★★ £E 1er Cru Champgains★★★ £E
O **Puligny-Montrachet** 1er Cru Les Demoiselles★★★★★ £E O **Saint-Aubin** 1er Cru En Remilly★★★ £E
● **Chassagne-Montrachet** 1er Cru Clos Saint-Jean★★★ £E 1er Cru La Maltroie★★★ £E
● **Chassagne-Montrachet★** £C Les Chaumes★★ £C ● **Santenay** La Comme Dessus★ £C

AMIOT-SERVELLE Chambolle-Musigny www.amiot-servelle.com A: CTy, Add, Jas

Owner: Christian & Elizabeth Amiot 21220 Chambolle-Musigny

Christian and Elizabeth Amiot farm almost 7 ha of vines. The wines are sturdy, and can at times be a little too structured to let the fruit sing through. However, when it does, the wines are rich and plump as in 1995, 96 and 97. The 98s and 99s are firmer, more robust and in their youth seemed rather hard, extracted and lacking in generosity. Nevertheless these are fine, often from old vines and as always are beginning to offer more with a few years' bottle-age. As well as a concentrated Chambolle-Musigny Amoureuses, the little known *premier cru* Derrière la Grange (which lies below Les Fuées) can show lots of style and there's some well-sited Clos de Vougeot. After some very good 2001s, some superb 02s have been produced. Bourgogne Rouge and a little Aligoté and Chardonnay are also made. (PW)

● **Clos de Vougeot★★★★** £F
● **Chambolle-Musigny** 1er Cru Les Amoureuses★★★★★ £F 1er Cru Les Charmes★★★★ £F
● **Chambolle-Musigny★★★** £D 1er Cru Derrière la Grange★★★★ £E

MARQUIS D'ANGERVILLE Volnay

A: C&B, CTy, JAr, OWL, Res, Maj

Owner: D'Angerville family Volnay, 21190 Meursault

The greatly respected Jacques d'Angerville died in 2003 but the legacy of his estate and wines seems certain to continue. These marvellous expressions of Volnay are taut and structured when tasted very young but are classy and refined with concentrated, intense fruit underneath. Production from 13 ha is dominated by four *premiers crus*, including the prize 2.4 ha *monopole* Clos des Ducs. Low yields, with rigorous selection and full destemming are part of the formula and the red-fruits intensity is always well integrated with subdued oak. The wines have been on very good form since the late 1980s. Through a string of very different vintages in the late 90s and early in the new century (the 2002s are superb) the wines are wonderfully consistent but in every vintage deserve to be drunk with at least five or six years' age. All *crus* show the elegance and refinement of Volnay. Of the four most important *crus*, the elegant, stylish Frémiets is complemented by a medium-full, fragrant yet quite powerful Champans. Taillepieds combines great refinement and fullness while Clos des Ducs reveals a marvellous structure and superb length and class. There is no Caillerets from current vintages due to replanting. A powerful Meursault-Santenots white has lots of substance and fruit richness. (PW)

● **Volnay** 1er Cru Clos des Ducs★★★★★ £F 1er Cru Taillepieds★★★★★ £F
● **Volnay** 1er Cru Caillerets★★★★ £E 1er Cru Frémiets★★★★ £E 1er Cru Champans★★★★ £E
○ **Meursault-Santenots** 1er Cru★★★★ £E

DOM. DE L'ARLOT Nuits-Saint-Georges

A: ABy, Goe, JAr, L&W, HRp, WSc

Owner: Jean-Pierre de Smet RN74 Prémeaux-Prissey, 21700 Nuits-Saint-Georges

This worthy estate, created in 1987 after the purchase of an existing domain by French insurance giant AXA Millésimes, has now had 15 years of steady direction under Jean-Pierre de Smet. Some 14 ha includes 2 ha of white grapes and two substantial Nuits-Saint-Georges *monopoles*, the 7-ha Clos des Fôrets-Saint-Georges and 3-ha Clos de l'Arlot. Great care is taken in the vineyards and there is minimal interference in the vinification and only a moderate use of new oak. The whites are more consistent than the reds as they do not tend to show the leanness encountered in lighter vintages for reds. Due at least partly to a policy of not destemming, there can be a lack of both flesh and depth to the reds and at times a stemmy quality (as some of the stalks included must still retain a green aspect, despite careful selection). However, in the ripest vintages this is rarely a problem and elegance and class shine through. The wines will always put on weight with age too, losing any sturdiness of youth to become very refined and harmonious. Recent vintages have been better, though even the best 1997s and 00s do not compare with the superior 98s and 99s. Nuits-Saint-Georges was particularly favoured in 2002 and generally this is reflected here though the Clos du Chapeau is poor. A regular Nuits-Saint-Georges made from young vines in the Clos des Fôrets has been redesignated *premier cru* from 2000. (PW)

● **Romanée-Saint-Vivant**★★★★ £G ● **Vosne-Romanée** 1er Cru Les Suchots★★★ £E
● **Nuits-Saint-Georges** 1er Cru★★ £D 1er Cru Clos de l'Arlot★★★ £E
● **Nuits-Saint-Georges** 1er Cru Clos des Fôrets-Saint-Georges★★★ £E
● **Côtes de Nuits-Villages** Clos du Chapeau★ £C
○ **Nuits-Saint-Georges** Cuvée Jeunes Vignes★★ £E 1er Cru Clos de l'Arlot★★★ £F

COMTE ARMAND www.domaine-des-epeneaux.com

A: HRp, GFy, L&S, L&W, M&V, Gau

Owner: Comte Armand Place de l'Église, 21630 Pommard

The Comte Armand's Domaine des Epeneaux for long produced just one wine, the famous Pommard Clos des Epeneaux from a 5-ha vineyard that forms part of the *premier cru* Les Grands Epenots. Since 1995 red and white Auxey-Duresses have been added, as has a very good Volnay Frémiets. Yields are low and the reds are notable for their colour, structure and depth. In 1999 Benjamin Leroux took over making the wines from Pascal Marchand, who had firmly established a quality regime here from the mid-1980s. Pascal's minimal use of chemicals has been taken a stage further with biodynamic practices now in place. The Clos continues to be made from three separately vinified parcels of vines differentiated by their age. The wine is always full-bodied and powerful but balanced and complex. Village Pommard is produced from some of the younger-vine fruit not used in the Clos. A little Meursault, Meix-Chavaux has also been produced. Very good 2001s, even better 02s. (PW)

● **Pommard**★★★ £E 1er Cru Clos des Epeneaux★★★★★ £F
● **Volnay** Frémiets★★★★ £E ● **Auxey Duresses** 1er Cru★★★ £D O **Auxey-Duresses**★★ £C

DOM. ROBERT ARNOUX Vosne-Romanée A: A&B, BWC, Eno, CTy, HRp, Res, JAr, Gau

Owner: Arnoux family RN3 21700 Vosne-Romanée
Pascal Lachaux is the son-in-law of the late Robert Arnoux and he has been making better and better wines here over the past decade. The top wines, of which there are several, receive 100 per cent new oak treatment but rarely is this obvious. The wines are sturdy, structured with at times almost overwhelming intensity and power. In vintages like 1996, 99 and 02 *premiers crus* such as Corvées Pagets and Suchots show their inherent class to best effect while the *grands crus* reveal great depth and texture but all are also very good in other recent vintages too. (PW)

● **Romanée-Saint-Vivant**❂❂❂❂❂ £H ● **Clos de Vougeot**★★★★★ £F ● **Echezeaux**★★★★★ £F
● **Vosne-Romanée**★★★ £D Les Hautes-Maizières★★★ £E 1er Cru Les Chaumes★★★★ £E
● **Vosne-Romanée** 1er Cru Aux Reignots★★★★ £F 1er Cru Les Suchots★★★★ £F
● **Nuits-Saint-Georges**★★★ £D Les Poisets★★★ £E 1er Cru Les Procès★★★ £E
● **Nuits-Saint-Georges** 1er Cru Les Corvées Pagets★★★★ £E

DOM. D'AUVENAY Saint-Romain A: Far, J&B, HRp, F&R

Owner: Lalou Bize-Leroy Domaine d'Auvenay, 21190 Meursault
This is the private estate of Madame Lalou Bize and is quite distinct from both the considerably larger Domaine LEROY and the Leroy *négociant* business. Though there are just 3.9 ha (farmed biodynamically) there are several exquisite small *crus* which are made to the same exacting standards as Domaine Leroy. While reds dominate the production of Domaine Leroy, apart from a little *grand cru* Bonnes-Mares and Mazis-Chambertin, here it is white magic that prevails. The wines are rich, pure and concentrated – even at the level of Auxey-Duresses or Bourgogne Aligoté. Prices are astoundingly high and though the same general ratings apply (five stars for the *grands crus*, four for the *premier crus* and three for the other wines), I'd find the individuality and grandeur of the Domaine Leroy reds a greater temptation if I had the money to spend. The wines to look out for are: Chevalier-Montrachet, Criots-Bâtard-Montrachet, Puligny-Montrachet (La Richarde, Premier Cru Folatières), Meursault (Narvaux, Premier Cru Goutte d'Or), Auxey-Duresses (Boutonniers, Les Clous) and some Bourgogne Aligoté. A straight village Meursault is sometimes bottled separately as Chaumes de Perrières and Pré de Manche. (PW)

DENIS BACHELET Gevrey-Chambertin A: HRp, M&V

Owner: Denis Bachelet 54 Route de Beaune, 21220 Gevrey-Chambertin
Denis Bachelet's wines are not that widely seen, such are the small quantities he produces, but they are wines of great finesse and class with lovely fruit intensity and harmony. In fact they might almost be considered atypical for an appellation that delivers up powerful, meaty, sometimes tannic, examples of Pinot. If the rich, intense Premier Cru Les Corbeaux and complex and classy *grand cru* Charmes-Chambertin are hard to find, the village Gevrey-Chambertin Vieilles Vignes is a super example at this level; all three are made from old vines. There's also reasonable quantities of a Côte de Nuits-Villages and a Bourgogne Rouge that make delicious red Burgundy seem almost affordable. (PW)

● **Charmes-Chambertin**★★★★★ £F
● **Gevrey-Chambertin** Vieilles Vignes★★★★ £D 1er Cru Les Corbeaux★★★★ £E
● **Côte de Nuits-Villages**★★ £C ● **Bourgogne Rouge**★★ £B

GHISLAINE BARTHOD   Chambolle-Musigny   A: RsW, BBR, Rae, Tan, Sec

Owner: Barthod-Noëllat family   Rue du Lavoir, 21220 Chambolle-Musigny
This small family domaine has just 6.5 ha of vineyards but all lie within this pretty commune that epitomises finesse in the Côte de Nuits. Seven small plots of *premiers crus* can all be measured in ares rather than hectares, such is their size. Ghislaine Barthod's wines have grace, finesse and succulence, there is nothing brash or harsh yet they have very good structure and personality. Cras and Charmes are the top two wines though the Véroilles (only the family's holding is of *premier cru* status) is also consistently fine. Cras is the most structured and profound, Charmes is concentrated and classy but there are no weak wines here, as even the village Chambolle-Musigny is always an excellent example and the Bourgogne Rouge is attractive, fruity and delicious. (PW)

- **Chambolle-Musigny** 1er Cru Les Cras★★★★★ £E 1er Cru Les Charmes★★★★★ £E
- **Chambolle-Musigny** 1er Cru Les Chatelots★★★★ £E 1er Cru Les Véroilles★★★★ £E
- **Chambolle-Musigny** 1er Cru Les Beaux Bruns★★★ £E 1er Cru Les Fuées★★★★ £E
- **Chambolle-Musigny**★★★ £D 1er Cru Les Baudes★★★ £E ● **Bourgogne Rouge**★★ £B

ROGER BELLAND   Santenay   www.domaine-belland-roger.com   A: Lib, BBR, BSh, B&T

Owner: Roger Belland   3 Rue de la Chapelle, B P 13, 21590 Santenay
This is now an excellent source of top white Burgundy. Roger Belland is based in Santenay but a little over 4 ha of a total of 23 ha of vineyards include fine Chassagne-Montrachet (Morgeot Clos Pitois, a *monopole*), some Puligny and even some of the tiny Criots-Bâtard-Montrachet *grand cru*. In common with many of the great domaines, Belland is a dedicated viticulturalist and goes to great lengths in the vineyard to maximise the quality of the fruit. Whites see new oak – 100 per cent for the *grand cru* Criots – but the intensity and depth of the fruit are only enhanced by it. Red Santenay includes the leading *premiers crus* at the northern end of this sizeable appellation; these are very good examples, full of ripe berry fruits but with good structure and length too. A source of great value Burgundy too. (PW)

- O **Criots-Bâtard-Montrachet**✪✪✪✪✪ £H
- O **Chassagne-Montrachet** 1er Cru Morgeot Clos Pitois★★★★ £E
- O **Puligny-Montrachet** 1er Cru Les Champs Gains★★★★ £F
- O **Santenay**★★ £C 1er Cru Beauregard★★★ £C
- ● **Pommard** Les Cras★★★ £E ● **Volnay** 1er Cru Santenots★★★ £E
- ● **Chassagne-Montrachet** 1er Cru Morgeot Clos Pitois★★★ £D
- ● **Santenay** 1er Cru Commes★★★ £C 1er Cru Beauregard★★★ £C 1er Cru Gravières★★★ £C
- ● **Santenay** Charmes★★ £C ● **Maranges**★ £B 1er Cru La Fussière★★ £C

DOM. SIMON BIZE ET FILS   Savigny-lès-Beaune   A: ABy, HRp, JAr, L&W, OWL

Owner: Patrick Bize   12 Rue du Chanoine-Donin, 21420 Savigny-lès-Beaune
This serious and expanding operation, now with 22 ha, is one of the leading exponents of Savigny-lès-Beaune. The wines have greatly improved since 1999 after some rather flat and slightly over-extracted wines in the mid- to late 1990s contrasted starkly with the refinement and class of the likes of Jean-Marc PAVELOT. Long *cuvaison* times and only partial destemming contribute to a bold, sturdy and sometimes gamy style. Yet despite a tendency to rusticity at the bottom of the range, the best wines show increasing refinement and composure with bottle-age and there is enough fruit and structure for them to improve well beyond five years. Best are the *premiers crus*, with good weight and richness in the Marconnets (an extension of Beaune Marconnets) and real intensity in Aux Vergelesses, if not the elegance others achieve here. Whites are good, with plenty of fruit and good structure in both versions of Savigny and additional style in Corton-Charlemagne. Basic Bourgogne Rouge and Blanc made from Les Perrières vineyards and can be every bit as good as the 'lesser' Savignys. A little Latricières-Chambertin is also made. (PW)

- ● **Savigny-lès-Beaune** 1er Cru Aux Vergelesses★★★ £D 1er Cru Marconnets★★ £D
- ● **Savigny-lès-Beaune** 1er Cru Aux Serpentières★★ £D 1er Cru Aux Guettes★★ £D

● **Savigny-lès-Beaune** 1er Cru Les Fourneaux★★ £D Aux Grands Liards★★ £C Les Bourgeots★★ £C
● **Aloxe-Corton** Le Suchot★ £D ● **Bourgogne Rouge** Les Perrières★★ £B
○ **Corton-Charlemagne**★★★ £F ○ **Savigny-lès-Beaune**★★ £C Aux Vergelesses★★★ £D
○ **Bourgogne Blanc** Les Perrières★★ £B

BLAIN-GAGNARD Chassagne-Montrachet   A: JAr, HHC, Maj, F&R

Owner: Jean-Marc et Claudine Blain-Gagnard 15 Route de Santenay, 21190 Chassagne-Montrachet
Jean-Marc and his wife Claudine (whose father is Jacques Gagnard) have a small selection of precious sites, thanks largely to her family. The wines are handled carefully with restrained oak and not overworked, resulting in wines of good richness and structure that remain true to their origins. A ripe, minerally and well-structured regular Chassagne develops nicely with three to four years' age. The *premiers crus* add more depth and richness and, although they can be drunk fairly young, deserve four or five years' age. Considerably more expensive but a big step up in quality is a Bâtard-Montrachet made in reasonable quantities. This has the characteristic Bâtard power and terrific dimension on the palate, becoming marvellously complex with even a little age. A little Criots-Bâtard-Montrachet is also made and a tiny amount of Le Montrachet (from Jacques Gagnard) has also recently been added. *Premier cru* Chassagne red is reasonably elegant if sometimes lean, while Clos Saint-Jean adds a little more depth. Both, as with all the whites, are reasonably priced. Gagnard-Delagrange is Jacques Gagnard's label, which includes three-star La Boudriotte and Morgeots and outstanding, super-five Bâtard-Montrachet and Montrachet. Though the vineyards have been gradually relinquished to the next generation some of the wines have continued to be made in recent vintages. (PW)

○ **Bâtard-Montrachet**★★★★★ £F ○ **Puligny-Montrachet**★★★ £E
○ **Chassagne-Montrachet** 1er Cru Caillerets★★★★ £E 1er Cru Morgeots★★★★ £E
○ **Chassagne-Montrachet**★★★ £D 1er Cru Clos Saint-Jean★★★ £E 1er Cru La Boudriotte★★★ £E
● **Chassagne-Montrachet** 1er Cru Clos Saint-Jean★ £C ● **Volnay** 1er Cru Champans★★★ £D
● **Pommard**★★ £D

DOM. JEAN BOILLOT ET FILS Volnay   A: Anl, Eno, CCC, CTy, L&S, F&M, F&R

Owner: Jean Boillot Rue des Angles, 21190 Volnay
Henri Boillot, brother of Jean-Marc BOILLOT, is now making the wines on his father's domaine as well as running an expanding *négociant* business, Maison Henri Boillot. Though the domaine is based in Volnay, there's a decent parcel of Puligny vines, including a substantial wholly owned *lieu-dit* within Perrières, Clos de la Mouchère, as well as one or two other choice *crus*. The fruit is picked very late, the reds 100 per cent destemmed and both reds and whites see a lot of new oak. The wines are rich, even opulent and consequently can be drunk quite young, though the Volnays, particularly the excellent Caillerets, deserve at least four or five years' aging. The pick of the whites, Les Pucelles, which reflects the class and finesse of that wonderful site, also demands a little patience. The *négociant* Henri Boillot wines includes some top-notch *crus*, and can be very good indeed if slightly less consistent. (PW)

Domaine Jean Boillot:
● **Volnay** 1er Cru Frémiets★★★★ £E 1er Cru Chevrets★★★★ £E 1er Cru Caillerets★★★★ £F
● **Beaune** 1er Cru Clos du Roi★★★ £E 1er Cru Epenottes★★★ £E
● **Savigny-lès-Beaune** 1er Cru Les Lavières★★ £D
○ **Puligny-Montrachet**★★★ £E 1er Cru Les Perrières★★★★ £E 1er Cru Clos de la Mouchère★★★★ £E
○ **Puligny-Montrachet** 1er Cru Les Pucelles★★★★ £F
○ **Meursault** 1er Cru Les Genevrières★★★★ £F ○ **Savigny-lès-Beaune** 1er Cru Les Vergelesses★★★ £D

JEAN-MARC BOILLOT Pommard   A: RsW, BBR, DDr, L&S, Rae, F&R

Owner: Jean-Marc Boillot La Pommardière, 21630 Pommard
Jean-Marc Boillot seems equally at ease making both red or white, as indeed he needs to be with half of his 10 ha planted to Chardonnay. The wines have a fruit richness and depth to marry with the oak input. The reds range from a full Beaune to more structured Pommards, including a tiny amount of superb rich

Rugiens, and a Volnay-like Jarolières (contiguous with Volnay Frémiets) to stylish, perfumed Volnays. Even the village examples are very good. The whites if anything are even better. A string of Puligny *premiers crus* (the SAUZET inheritance) all have an intense pure fruit and great class, nowhere better expressed than in Les Combettes. There is also a little Bâtard-Montrachet. Some Rully and Puligny-Montrachet Les Pucelles have recently been made from bought-in fruit. Jean-Marc Boillot is now also making wine in the Coteaux du Languedoc (see Languedoc-Roussillon). (PW)

- ● **Pommard**★★★ £D 1er Cru Jarolières★★★ £E 1er Cru Rugiens★★★★ £F
- ● **Volnay**★★★ £E 1er Cru Carelle-sous-Chapelle★★★ £E 1er Cru Pitures★★★ £E
- ● **Volnay**1er Cru Le Ronceret★★★ £E ● **Beaune** 1er Cru Montrevenots★★ £D
- ○ **Puligny-Montrachet** 1er Cru Champ Canet★★★★ £F 1er Cru Les Combettes★★★★ £F
- ○ **Puligny-Montrachet** 1er Cru Les Referts★★★★ £F 1er Cru La Truffière★★★★ £F
- ○ **Puligny-Montrachet**★★★ £E 1er Cru La Garenne★★★ £F

LUCIEN BOILLOT ET FILS Gevrey-Chambertin A: CTy, Eno BBR, WSc

Owner: Lucien, Louis & Pierre Boillot 1 Rue Docteur Magnon Pujo, 21220 Gevrey-Chambertin
Though Gevrey-based, this domaine draws half of its grapes from original family vineyards in Volnay and Pommard. Lucien's sons Louis and Pierre haven't quite the sites or wines of other Boillot domaines (see Jean BOILLOT and Jean-Marc BOILLOT) but nonetheless have a diverse and interesting resource with which to work. The grapes are only partially destemmed and an extended maceration is favoured, resulting in wines with structure, breadth and flavour intensity, though not always with the concentration or fullness to match. A lack of ripeness and finesse in the tannins can also detract. Though reasonably priced, the wines can be disappointing, missing the fruit depth and richness in lighter years and some of the vintages of the late 1990s if less so more recently. In the future Louis Boillot, husband of Ghislaine BARTHOD will make his share of these parcels separately. (PW)

- ● **Gevrey-Chambertin** 1er Cru Les Cherbaudes★★★ £E 1er Cru Les Corbeaux★★★ £E
- ● **Gevrey-Chambertin**★★ £D Evocelles★★★ £D
- ● **Nuits-Saint-Georges** 1er Cru Les Pruliers★★★ £D ● **Beaune** Epenottes★ £C
- ● **Pommard**★ £C 1er Cru Les Croix Noires★★ £D 1er Cru Fremiers★★★ £D
- ● **Volnay**★ £C 1er Cru Angles★★ £D 1er Cru Brouillards★★ £D 1er Cru Caillerets★★ £D

DOM. BONNEAU DU MARTRAY A: HHC, BBR, L&W, HRp, L&S, JAr, F&R, C&R

Owner: Jean-Charles Le Bault de la Morinière 21420 Pernand-Vergelesses
An outstanding 11-ha domaine producing just two wines. The white Corton-Charlemagne comes from 9.5 ha of the best-sited part of the famous vineyard. The red comes from 1.5 ha at the base of the Corton hill. As good as the wines are now, the reputation of this domaine has only been fully re-established by Jean-Charles Le Bault de la Morinière, who has made tremendous progress since taking over from his father. The red, in particular, has improved; since 1995 a previously rather dilute, insubstantial wine has taken on greater flesh and extract without sacrificing its finesse. The white has long been a wine of tremendous richness and great depth and character that will keep for many years from the best vintages. It is also one of the few wines made from this large vineyard to show true *grand cru* class. (PW)

- ○ **Corton-Charlemagne** ✪✪✪✪✪ £F ● **Corton**★★★★ £F

BOUCHARD PÈRE ET FILS Beaune www.bouchard-pereetfils.com A: JEF, AAA

Owner: Joseph Henriot 15 Rue du Château, 21200 Beaune
This merchant is one of the best-known names in Burgundy, thanks in part to its substantial holdings. Domaine vineyards total 130 ha, including 12 ha of *grands crus* and 74 ha of *premiers crus* and two-thirds of the vineyards are planted to Pinot Noir. Its decline under family ownership and the scandal of its conviction for flouting legal winemaking practices have been well-documented. Yet from the time of the purchase by the much respected Champenois Joseph Henriot (see HENRIOT) in 1995, quality has dramatically improved. Despite the poor health of the vineyards, almost immediately the reds showed

greater richness and better structure and more recently have added more expression and individuality. The ongoing investment in both people and winemaking facilities is backed by a determination to maximise quality and consistency. In more difficult vintages, such as 2000 for red, Bouchard was prepared to sell off a large quantity of wine in order to maintain the progress made in re-establishing the integrity of its label. The best whites show superb fruit combined with excellent structure and concentration and are particularly fine in 2000. As with other leading *négociants* the range is quite vast. Nearly all the wines below are 'domaine' bottlings though one or two are made from purchased grapes such as the very fine Chambertin Clos-de-Bèze which shows fabulous breadth, depth and complexity. Excellent style and consistency here in 2002 though some will need more time than usual. (PW)

● **La Romanée**✪✪✪✪✪ £H   ● **Chambertin Clos-de-Bèze**✪✪✪✪✪ £H
● **Chambertin**★★★★★ £H   ● **Bonnes Mares**★★★★★ £G
● **Clos de Vougeot**★★★ £G   ● **Echezeaux**★★★ £G   ● **Le Corton**★★★★ £G
● **Monthelie**★ £C   1er Cru Les Duresses★★ £D   1er Cru Clos des Champs Fuillot★★ £D
● **Gevrey-Chambertin**★★ £E   1er Cru Les Cazetiers★★★ £F
● **Chambolle-Musigny**★★★ £E   ● **Vosne-Romanée** 1er Cru Aux Reignots★★★ £G
● **Nuits Saint-Georges** 1er Cru Clos des Argillières★★★ £E   1er Cru Les Cailles★★★★ £E
● **Nuits Saint-Georges**★★★ £E   1er Cru Clos Saint-Marc★★★ £E
● **Beaune** 1er Cru★★ £D   1er Cru Clos de la Mousse★★ £E   1er Cru Teurons★★★ £E
● **Beaune** 1er Cru Grèves Vigne de L'Enfant Jésus★★★ £E
● **Volnay** 1er Cru★★ £D   1er Cru Caillerets★★★★ £E   1er Cru Clos des Chênes★★★★ £E
● **Volnay** 1er Cru Fremiets Clos de la Rougeotte★★★ £E   1er Cru Taillepieds★★★ £E
● **Pommard** 1er Cru★★ £D   1er Cru Les Chanlins★★★ £E   1er Cru Pezerolles★★★★ £E
● **Pommard** 1er Cru Rugiens★★★★ £E   ● **Savigny-lès-Beaune**★ £C   1er Cru Les Lavières★★ £C
○ **Le Montrachet**✪✪✪✪✪ £H   ○ **Bâtard-Montrachet** ★★★★ £H
○ **Corton-Charlemagne**★★★★★ £F   ○ **Chevalier-Montrachet**★★★★★ £H
○ **Puligny-Montrachet**★★★ £E   1er Cru Champs Gains★★★★ £F
○ **Meursault** 1er Cru Genevrières★★★★★ £F   1er Cru Perrières★★★★★ £F
○ **Meursault** 1er Cru Les Gouttes d'Or★★★★ £E   1er Cru Les Bouchères★★★★ £E
○ **Meursault**★★ £E   Les Clous★★★ £E   1er Cru Charmes★★★ £E
○ **Beaune** 1er Cru★ £C   1er Cru Clos Saint-Landry★★★ £C   1er Cru Sur Les Grèves★★ £C
○ **Montagny** Les Platières★★ £C   ○ **Pouilly-Fuissé**★★ £C   ○ **Mâcon-Villages**★ £B

RENÉ BOUVIER   Gevrey-Chambertin   A: THt, DDr, UnC

Owner: Bouvier family   29 B Route de Dijon, 21220 Gevrey-Chambertin
This increasingly fine domaine based on 17 ha of vineyards has been transformed from a producer of fine Marsannay to one that includes many other fine *crus* from the Côtes de Nuits. Working in part in a négociant role Bernard Bouvier is expanding on his father's achievements. As well as good Gevrey-Chambertin recently there has been fine Chambolle-Musigny, Vosne-Romanée and even Echezeaux and Clos de Vougeot. Of the most recent vintages, the 2001s are atypically good for this vintage while the 02s provide further endorsement of the consistent high quality obtained. Some of the best value is at the lower levels: some of the *grands crus* while good aren't up there with those from the very best growers. In addtition to the wines below, following on from an excellent Clos Saint-Denis in 2001, very good Echezeaux and Vosne-Romanée Premier Cru Les Chaumes were made in 2002. (PW)

○ **Marsannay** Vieilles Vignes★★ £C   Le Clos★★ £C
● **Marsannay** Longeroies★★ £C   En Ouzeloy★★ £C   Clos du Roy★★ £C   Champs Salomon★★ £C
● **Fixin** Crais de Chêne★★ £C   ● **Côtes de Nuits-Villages**★★ £C
● **Gevrey-Chambertin** Jeunes Rois★★★ £D   Racines du Temps Très Vieilles Vignes★★★ £E
● **Gevrey-Chambertin** 1er Cru Petite Chapelle★★★★ £F   1er Cru Les Cazetiers £F
● **Charmes-Chambertin**★★★ £G   ● **Morey-Saint-Denis** 1er Cru Genevrières★★★ £E
● **Chambolle-Musigny** 1er Cru Les Noirots★★★ £F   ● **Clos de Vougeot**★★★★ £G

MICHEL BOUZEREAU ET FILS Meursault A: M&V, BBR, CTy, L&W, F&R

Owner: Michel & Jean-Baptiste Bouzereau 3 Rue de la Planche-Meunière, 21190 Meursault
Devotees of white Burgundy will recognise a Michel Bouzereau label as a good bet for ripe, full yet elegant Meursault and as Michel's son Jean-Baptiste assumes responsibility it seems certain to remain that way. The domaine comprises 12 ha, more than three-quarters of it white. Stylish and pure, the whites show good definition with subtle differences between the various *crus*. Most outstanding is the Meursault-Charmes. Meursault-Blagny can be the most austere but is deep and minerally, Genevrières is very suggestive of this *cru*, and there is plenty of style and fruit in the humbler village-level Limouzin and Les Tessons too. Caillerets is much the better of the two Pulignys but this is reflected in the price difference. There's only a little red and if it's not at the same level as the whites it is at least reasonably priced for the quality. Good value, too, are the basic Bourgogne Aligoté and Bourgogne Chardonnay. (PW)

O **Meursault** 1er Cru Blagny★★★★ £E 1er Cru Genevrières★★★★ £E 1er Cru Charmes★★★★★ £E
O **Meursault** Grands Charrons★★★ £D Limouzin★★★ £D Les Tessons★★★ £D
O **Puligny-Montrachet** 1er Cru Champ Gain★★★ £E 1er Cru Cailllerets★★★★ £F
O **Bourgogne Aligoté**★ £B O **Bourgogne Chardonnay**★★ £B
● **Beaune** Epenottes★ £C 1er Cru Vignes Franches★★ £D

BOYER-MARTENOT Meursault A: CTy, BBR, For, F&R

Owner: Yves Boyer 17 Place de l'Europe, 21190 Meursault
Yves Boyer who is now assisted by his son Vincent (fourth generation), makes classic rich, plump and full-flavoured Meursault, traditional in the best sense with a measure of restraint when young. A high average vine age in 10 ha of vines is maintained as is apparent in wines with plenty of personality and depth but that are also well-balanced with good definition. Les Narvaux vies with Les Tillets as the best of the village Meursault *climats* while Perrières is arguably the finest *premier cru* Meursault, with a little extra breadth and complexity characteristic of the vineyard. This in turn vies with an intense, refined and classy Puligny-Montrachet Le Cailleret as the top wine. All the better *crus* will keep for six to eight years but can readily be drunk with just two or three. Good Bourgogne Chardonnay can show good fruit and flavour, too, if in a simpler fashion. The 2002s show a classic combination of restraint and stylish complexity. (PW)

O **Meursault** 1er Cru Charmes★★★★ £F 1er Cru Genevrières★★★★ £F 1er Cru Perrières★★★★ £F
O **Meursault**★★ £D En L'Ormeaux★★★ £D Narvaux★★★ £E Tillets★★★ £E
O **Puligny-Montrachet** les Reuchaux★★★ £E 1er Cru Le Cailleret★★★★ £F
O **Bourgogne Blanc**★ £B

DOM. BRINTET Mercurey www.domaine-brintet.com A: DDr, Goe, OWL

Owner: Luc & Véronique Brintet Grande Rue, 71640 Mercurey
Luc Brintet's 13 ha are mostly red as would be expected in Mercurey but he makes a little white that is every bit as good. Reds are rigorously sorted and totally destemmed and a long *cuvaison* is sought with an extended period of pre-fermentation maceration. Both reds and whites are oakier than some but have ripe succulent fruit underneath and good structure and definition. The *premiers crus* are a definite notch up in quality and are among the best in the appellation. Whites are better with two or three years' age, reds with three to five. (PW)

● **Mercurey** 1er Cru Crêts★★ £C 1er Cru Vasées★★ £C 1er Cru Levrières★★★ £C
● **Mercurey**★ £B Charmée★ £B Perrières★ £B Vieilles Vignes★★ £C
O **Mercurey**★ £B Vieilles Vignes★★ £C 1er Cru Crêts★★★ £C

ALAIN BURGUET Gevrey-Chambertin A: HRp

Owner: Alain Burguet 18 Rue de l'Église, 21220 Gevrey-Chambertin
Already experienced, Alain Burguet first got a foothold of his own in Gevrey back in 1974 and has now progressed to 6 ha. His reputation is for being tough and intransigent both in personality and in his

approach to winemaking. Yet there is clearly a mellowing of sorts as he has modified and refined his vinification and ageing methods in the 1990s, including complete destemming and longer oak ageing. It has taken a couple of vintages to perfect but since 1998 the wines have been more stylish and complete though still with good richness and power. If most of the wines are only village level (there is now a little Premier Cru Champeaux), a Vieilles Vignes bottling (now labelled Mes Favorites) of great depth and richness is consistently of comparable quality to some of the best Gevrey made. All the wines show good classic Gevrey spice, strength and red and black fruit intensity. Older vintages can be slightly tougher, more rustic but can mellow and soften with age, too and are unlikely to disappoint from a good vintage. Bourgogne Rouge is a decent example too. (PW)

- **Gevrey-Chambertin** Vieilles Vignes Mes Favorites★★★★ £E 1er Cru Champeaux★★★ £E
- **Gevrey-Chambertin** Tradition★★ £D Billard★★★ £D Reniard★★★ £D
- **Bourgogne Rouge** Les Pince Vins★ £B

LOUIS CARILLON ET FILS Puligny-Montrachet　　　A: BBR, CTy, Fie, L&W, JNi, Maj, F&R

Owner: Carillon family 21190 Puligny-Montrachet
The wines of Louis Carillon et Fils are widely distributed and with good reason. This is a star Puligny domaine that has been making excellent wines for decades, with a lineage that goes back several centuries. The whites have great vibrancy, expressive fruit and in a way are more direct and easier to appreciate than others of comparable quality – but are not lesser wines for that. Out of a total of 12 ha, 3.5 ha are planted to Pinot Noir but the fuss is rightly about the Puligny *premiers crus*. Central to the style are low yields and minimal manipulation during both vinification and ageing. Champ Canet is the most elegant and approachable when quite young; Combettes is seductive and more immediate than the bigger, more structured Perrières; the citrusy, minerally Referts fattens up with age and like Perrières will benefit from extra bottle age. The *grand cru* Bienvenues is the most complex and refined of all, and while deserving of the most patience, shows great power and intensity when young. To an extent the prices reflect the high regard in which the wines are held, though the sound reds are much more affordable. (PW)

- O **Bienvenues-Bâtard-Montrachet**✪✪✪✪✪ £H
- O **Puligny-Montrachet** 1er Cru Perrières★★★★★ £F 1er Cru Referts★★★★ £E
- O **Puligny-Montrachet**★★★ £E 1er Cru Champ Canet★★★ £F 1er Cru Combettes★★★★ £F
- ● **Puligny-Montrachet**★ £C ● **Saint-Aubin** 1er Cru Pitangerets★ £C

SYLVAIN CATHIARD Vosne-Romanée　　　A: OWL, L&W, Res, BBR, HHC, SVS

Owner: Sylvain Cathiard 20 Rue de la Goillotte, 21700 Vosne-Romanée
Sylvain Cathiard makes very refined, subtle but harmonious wines. In the past some of the lesser wines needed a little more richness and ripeness but this is no longer the case, in fact they are superb examples of what generic or village-level wines should be. All the Vosne-Romanée wines (including an exceptional village example in 2002) have plenty of substance and are ripe with increasing intensity and length of flavour, culminating in an inspired *grand cru* Romanée-Saint-Vivant. Of the Vosne *premiers crus*, En Orveaux (nearest to Chambolle-Musigny) and Aux Reignots have lovely depth and complexity without the richness of the other two. The purity and intensity of Suchots contrasts with the bigger, more structured Malconsorts. A sophisticated Bourgogne Rouge and elegant Chambolle-Musigny apart, all the wines deserve to be kept for at least five or six years from the vintage date. Recent vintages have been outstanding with superb 2002s. (PW)

- ● **Romanée-Saint-Vivant**✪✪✪✪✪ £H
- ● **Vosne-Romanée** 1er Cru Les Malconsorts★★★★★ £F 1er Cru Les Suchots★★★★★ £F
- ● **Vosne-Romanée**★★★ £E 1er Cru Aux Reignots★★★★ £F 1er Cru En Orveaux★★★★ £F
- ● **Chambolle-Musigny** Clos de L'Orme★★★★ £E
- ● **Nuits-Saint-Georges** 1er Cru Aux Murgers★★★★ £E ● **Bourgogne Rouge**★★ £C

MAISON CHAMPY Beaune www.champy.com   A: HHC, Sav, Pol, ThP, F&R

Owner: Meurgey family   5 Rue Grenier à Sel, 21202 Beaune

This 280-year-old *négociant* house, the oldest in Burgundy, has been in the hands of the Meurgey family for a little over a decade, but how its fortunes have been revived. Quality has been good since the mid-1990s but the hiring of Dimitri Bazas is providing a further boost. As well as bought-in grapes, around 13 ha are now owned. The winemaking hand is light, allowing the individual *terroirs* to shine through. Among the many reds, Vosne-Romanée Les Suchots, from a well-established vineyard (35 to 40 years), always stands out with fine fruit, lots of class and great length; a Bonnes-Mares is more classy and complex again, as is the Romanée-Saint-Vivant. At a lower level, Beaune Champs Pimont is a consistently plump and approachable red full of raspberry fruit. The 2000 and 02 whites are the best yet and if not yet the equal of the top growers, are well-made and reasonably priced, particularly regular Savigny-lès-Beaune and Pernand-Vergelesses. Puligny Enseignères has nice richness for a village-level example, while Corton-Charlemagne adds more breadth; both can be drunk fairly young but will develop further with age. All in all this is a increasingly good, reliable source of Burgundy. Listed are most of the best wines that are regularly made. Other good examples may be encountered, though the basic generics are of more modest quality. (PW)

- ● **Bonnes Mares**★★★★ £G ● **Romanée-Saint-Vivant**★★★★ £G ● **Clos de Vougeot**★★★ £F
- ● **Vosne-Romanée** 1er Cru Les Beaumonts★★★ £F 1er Cru Les Suchots★★★★ £F
- ● **Gevrey-Chambertin** 1er Cru Les Cazetiers★★★ £E
- ● **Aloxe-Corton** 1er Cru Les Vercots★★ £D ● **Volnay** 1er Cru Les Caillerets★★★ £E
- ● **Beaune** Vieilles Vignes★★ £D 1er Cru Les Champs Pimont★★ £D 1er Cru Les Grèves★★ £D
- ● **Savigny-lès-Beaune** Aux Fourches★ £C 1er Cru Les Peuillets★★ £C 1er Cru Les Vergelesses★★ £C
- ○ **Corton-Charlemagne**★★★ £F
- ○ **Puligny-Montrachet** Les Enseignères★★★ £E 1er Cru Les Chalumeaux★★★ £E
- ○ **Meursault** Grand Charrons★★★ £E 1er Cru Genevrières★★★ £E ○ Pernand-Vergelesses★★ £C
- ○ **Savigny-lès-Beaune**★★ £C ○ **Saint-Aubin** 1er Cru Murgers Dents de Chien★★ £C

CHANDON DE BRIAILLES Savigny-lès-Beaune   A: HHC, CTy, BBR, L&S, L&W, Tan, F&M

Owner: De Nicolay family   Rue Soeur Goby, 21420 Savigny-lès-Beaune

A popular and fine domaine and a leading proponent of Savigny-lès-Beaune, Pernand-Vergelesses and Corton. François de Nicolay and his sister Claude Drouhin work with their mother to produce wines from low yields that favour elegance over power. Corton Clos du Roi is the top red, the most structured and profound. Corton-Bressandes has better dimension, weight and length than Les Maréchaudes, though the latter almost matches it for finesse and style. The Pernand-Vergelesses are only medium-bodied, though the racy, slender but classy and intense Île des Vergelesses adds a little more weight with age. Both Savigny wines can be good value, though Les Lavières has been a bit lean in recent vintages. 2000 reds were generally lighter as were the 01s if still with the characteristic intensity and style. 2002 promises a little more fullness. Whites are very good too, tight and minerally when very young but with real intensity and length, becoming quite rich with a little age. The Corton becomes fuller and broader than a deeper, more minerally Corton-Charlemagne. François de Nicolay also owns a vineyard in his own right, producing an aromatic, plump white Savigny. (PW)

- ● **Corton** Clos du Roi★★★★ £F ● **Corton** Bressandes★★★★ £E ● **Corton** Les Maréchaudes★★★★ £E
- ● **Pernand-Vergelesses** 1er Cru Les Vergelesses★★★ £D 1er Cru Île des Vergelesses★★★ £D
- ● **Savigny-lès-Beaune** 1er Cru Les Fourneaux★★ £C 1er Cru Les Lavières★★ £D
- ○ **Corton-Charlemagne**★★★★ £F ○ **Corton** Blanc★★★★ £F
- ○ **Pernand-Vergelesses** 1er Cru Île des Vergelesses★★★ £D
- ○ **Savigny-lès-Beaune** 1er Cru Aux Vergelesses★★★ £C

PHILIPPE CHARLOPIN Gevrey-Chambertin   A: IVV

Owner: Philippe Charlopin   18 Route de Dijon, 21220 Gevrey-Chambertin

Starting from a meagre 1.8 ha of family vineyards in 1976, Philippe Charlopin's holdings have since mushroomed to 15 ha. To the more humble village parcels have been added small segments of several *grands crus*. Harvesting often very late for Burgundy, Philippe subjects his very ripe grapes to a rigorous selection. Vinification involves a long maceration followed by minimal racking (sometimes leading to a measure of reduction in the wines) and quite liberal helpings of new oak; 100 per cent new oak in the case of the Vieilles Vignes Gevrey-Chambertin and the seven *grands crus*. They are also unfined and unfiltered. The result is usually richly textured, chewy, sometimes tannic wines, a style that does work (for the most part) and the wines still reflect the general style of their appellations. The regular village wines have plenty of immediate appeal and are for relatively early drinking. The top wines will keep for at least a decade. Of the simpler reds, the Marsannay and Bourgogne Rouge can be good value while the whites, too, can offer ample fruit and character. Bonnes Mares, Clos de Vougeot and Echezeaux are the newest of the *grands crus*. (PW)

● **Chambertin**★★★★ £G ● **Charmes-Chambertin**★★★★ £F ● **Mazis-Chambertin**★★★★ £F
● **Clos Saint-Denis**★★★★ £F ● **Bonnes Mares**★★★★ £G
● **Gevrey-Chambertin** La Justice★★ £D Vieilles Vignes★★★★ £E ● **Morey-Saint-Denis**★★ £D
● **Chambolle-Musigny**★★ £D Vosne-Romanée★★ £D ● **Fixin** Clos de Fixey★ £C
● **Marsannay** En Montchenevoy★★ £C ● **Bourgogne Rouge**★★ £C
○ **Fixin** Blanc★★ £C ○ **Marsannay** Blanc★ £C

GÉRARD CHAVY ET FILS Puligny-Montrachet   A: BBR, CTy, Eno, HRp, M&V, CPp

Owner: Chavy family   12 Rue de Château, 21190 Puligny-Montrachet
Alain and Jean-Louis, sons of Gérard, have made many changes at their family's small domaine, with the result that this is now one of the emerging stars of the appellation. Typical of small, well-run family domaines, there are no short cuts taken and every wine is given the same measure of respect. Bourgogne Blanc can be very good while the regular example of Puligny has some substance and style and a good example of Saint-Aubin is made too. But it is the *premiers crus* that are forging the reputation, including a very minerally, full Perrières and an elegant Clavoillons that contrasts with the firmer, more structured Folatières. An intense weighty Champs-Gain first made in 2002 shows real promise too. The wines can be a bit reduced if drunk very young but the generally excellent quality is matched by good prices. (PW)

○ **Puligny-Montrachet** 1er Cru Perrières★★★★ £E 1er Cru Clavoillons★★★★ £E
○ **Puligny-Montrachet**★★ £D Charmes★★★ £D 1er Cru Folatières★★★★ £E
○ **Saint-Aubin** 1er Cru En Remilly★★ £C ○ **Bourgogne Blanc**★ £B

ROBERT CHEVILLON Nuits-Saint-Georges   A: J&B, WTs, F&M, Sec, F&R, Maj

Owner: Chevillon family   68 Rue Félix Tisserand, 21700 Nuits-Saint-Georges
Robert Chevillon is one of the celebrated names of this appellation at the southern end of the Côte de Nuits, a village that is synonymous with red Burgundy. Robert is making way for his sons and Bertrand Chevillon now makes the wines from the vines tended by his older brother, Denis. There are no less than eight different *premiers crus* (six of them in the central section of Nuits, which has a higher clay content and is south of the town itself), all with a high average vine age. No two taste quite the same, each giving a different expression of its individual *terroir*. With relatively high fermentation temperatures and a small percentage of stems retained, the wines are fairly full-bodied and tannic but with the flesh, depth and fruit intensity to be very rich and satisfying with 8 to 10 years' age. The regular Nuits, Bousselots and to a lesser extent Chaignots (the Chevillons' two *crus* north of Nuits) can be a bit light in lesser vintages but the others regularly deliver the fruit to match their robust structures. The fullest and most structured are the Les Saint-Georges and Vaucrains, followed by Les Cailles. Also made is a little white Nuits-Saint-Georges with a very good reputation and some Bourgogne Rouge. (PW)

● **Nuits-Saint-Georges** 1er Cru Les Vaucrains★★★★ £E 1er Cru Les Saint-Georges★★★★ £E
● **Nuits-Saint-Georges** 1er Cru Les Perrières★★★ £E 1er Cru Les Pruliers★★★ £E
● **Nuits-Saint-Georges** 1er Cru Les Roncières★★★ £E 1er Cru Les Chaignots★★★ £E
● **Nuits-Saint-Georges** 1er Cru Les Cailles★★★ £E 1er Cru Les Bousselots★★ £D
● **Nuits-Saint-Georges** Vieilles Vignes★★ £D

DOM. DU CH. DE CHOREY Chorey-lès-Beaune www.chateau-de-chorey.com A: DDr

Owner: Germain family Château de Chorey-lès-Beaune, 21220 Beaune

The fine château of this domaine provides accomodation for those who have come in search of good red and white Burgundy. Formerly called Domaine Germain Père et Fils, the wines of the 17-ha estate have, over the last decade, increasingly been made by François Germain's son, Benoît, who now runs the estate with his sister, Aude. The wines are good rather than great, with full-flavoured, balanced white Pernand-Vergelesses and fairly full, sturdy yet not inelegant reds. The latter are completely destemmed and subject to a pre-fermentation maceration. Ratings apply to the best and most recent vintages of which 2002 is the best to date. Occasionally in the past some of the reds have been a little too extracted and lacked fully ripe tannins. As well as those listed, two other red *premiers crus* Beaunes (Boucherottes and Cent Vignes) and a little white (Sous les Grèves) are also made. A village Meursault, Les Pellans, has been made since 1999. (PW)

● **Beaune** 1er Cru Vignes Franches★★ £E 1er Cru Cras★★ £E 1er Cru Teurons★★ £E
● **Chorey-lès-Beaune**★ £C ○ **Pernand-Vergelesses**★★ £C

BRUNO CLAIR Marsannay A: J&B, Col, Tan, WSc, F&R

Owner: Bruno Clair 5 Rue du Vieux Collège, BP 22, 21160 Marsannay-la-Côte

Bruno Clair has been a style leader for a couple of decades, producing the mostly northern Nuits reds of great balance, harmony and elegance. One of the beneficiaries of the noted Clair-Daü estate (many of the prime vineyards went to Louis JADOT), he now commands 23 ha, nearly 5 ha of which are planted to Chardonnay. The classics are his Gevrey *premiers crus* Clos Saint-Jacques and Cazetiers, and the *grand cru* Chambertin Clos de Bèze. These are wines with great purity, elegance and with exceptional length of flavour. Not to be overlooked are the *monopole* Clos du Fonteny, a gutsy, meaty Savigny, La Dominode, and an increasingly classy Corton-Charlemagne. The best value lies in the three Marsannay reds (though a white can be good too), with the floral, intense Longeroies usually vying with the slightly darker-fruited Grasses Têtes as the best of these. While the reds have been generally less impressive in lighter vintages such as 1997, there are excellent 96s, 98s and 99s, and 00, 01 and 02 all look promising. All the reds can seem a little firm and austere when young and shouldn't be drunk with less than three or four years' age; seven or eight for the top examples. A rare Morey-Saint-Denis white is made from the same vineyard as the red, while a white Pernand-Vergelesses is a recent addition. (PW)

● **Chambertin Clos de Bèze**★★★★★ £G
● **Gevrey-Chambertin** 1er Cru Clos Saint-Jacques★★★★ £G 1er Cru Les Cazetiers★★★★ £F
● **Gevrey-Chambertin** 1er Cru Petite Chapelle★★★ £E 1er Cru Clos du Fonteny★★★ £F
● **Morey-Saint-Denis** En La Rue de Vergy★★ £E ● **Chambolle-Musigny** Véroilles★★ £D
● **Vosne-Romanée** Champs-Perdrix★★★ £E ● **Savigny-lès-Beaune** 1er Cru La Dominode★★★ £E
● **Marsannay** Grasses Têtes★★ £C Longeroies★★★ £C Vaudenelles★★ £C
○ **Corton-Charlemagne**★★★★ £G ○ **Pernand-Vergelesses**★★ £C ○ **Marsannay** Blanc★ £C

BRUNO CLAVELIER Vosne-Romanée A: Dec, HRp, OWL, Res, Sav

Owner: Bruno Clavelier 6 Route Nationale 74, 21700 Vosne-Romanée

Bruno Clavelier is a relatively new star who took over his grandfather's vines in 1987 and started bottling wine previously sold in bulk. He has since expanded into other Côte de Nuits communes. The domaine is now fully biodynamic and there has been a steady refinement in the wines while adding greater richness and expression, particularly in the most recent vintages. The amount of new oak used is low and the average vine age very high (most are either 50 or 65 years old), giving wines with delicious fruit, ample concentration and a real sense *terroir*. Of the *premiers crus*, Vosne-Romanée Beaux-Monts has the greater structure, Aux Brulées a touch more refinement. The Nuits-Saint-Georges, lying close to Vosne-Romanée, tastes like a cross between the two appellations. The Chambolle-Musigny is even better, combining grace with richness. From 2000 the regular Vosne-Romanée, from some of the highest slopes in the commune, has been bottled as La Combe Brulée and Les Hauts de Beaux Monts. A third of a hectare of Corton Rognets was purchased in

1999 and is also from old vines and has the potential to be the best wine of the lot, while Bruno's old-vine Aligoté is just about as good as it gets. (PW)

- **Vosne-Romanée** 1er Cru Les Beaux Monts★★★★ £F 1er Cru Aux Brulées★★★★ £F
- **Vosne-Romanée** Les Hauts Maizières★★★ £E La Montagne★★★ £E
- **Vosne-Romanée** La Combe Brulée★★★ £E Les Hauts de Beaux Monts★★★ £E
- **Gevrey-Chambertin** 1er Cru Les Corbeaux★★★ £E
- **Chambolle-Musigny** 1er Cru Combe d'Orveau★★★★★ £F
- **Nuits-Saint-Georges** 1er Cru Aux Cras★★★★ £E

CLOS DE TART   Clos de Tart   A: Cas, BBR, HRp, Res, WSc, F&R

Owner: Mommessin family   21220 Morey-Saint-Denis

Winemaker Sylvain Pitiot has made this 7.53-ha *grand cru monopole* great again. Lying between Bonnes Mares and Clos des Lambrays, Clos de Tart has remained intact since being named by Benedictine monks in the late 12th century. The wine is increasingly adding some of the succulence of Clos des Lambrays to the power and sturdiness of Bonnes Mares. There is greater depth and concentration than previously, together with the complexity, class and elegance of a *grand cru*. Yields are low, the vine age high and being such a large site, different parcels are vinified separately. Spice and red and black cherries are the predominant flavours if drunk fairly young but wait 10 years from a top vintage. While there are many good earlier vintages, buy to cellar from 1996 or later. (PW)

- **Clos de Tart**✪✪✪✪✪ £G

JEAN-FRANÇOIS COCHE-DURY   Meursault   A: BBR, Far, Res, Hrd, Sec, F&R

Owner: Jean-François Coche-Dury   9 Rue Charles Giraud, 21190 Meursault

An outstanding domaine. Jean-François's Meursaults are rivalled only by those from LAFON and perhaps one or two others. Yet apart from from a little *grand cru* Corton-Charlemagne and *premier cru* Perrières, his reputation has been established with village-level wines, an indication of his talent and dedication. There is great attention to detail in the vineyard and as at many top-quality estates vines are replaced one at time when necessary and from the best existing plant material. The approach to vinification is flexible to maximise the potential of each vintage and long fermentations are also favoured. What makes the wines so special? Well, a grace, subtlety and purity allied to a remarkably well-delineated complexity. The depth, length, structure and concentration are givens. The floral, fruit and mineral components, as well as a fine grilled nuts character that comes with age, give the wines extra finesse over most other examples. Of 11 ha, almost 2.5 are planted to Pinot Noir and a chance to try the Volnay Premier Cru shouldn't be passed up. A little red Auxey-Duresses and Monthelie are also made. The Meursault Vireuils is now being bottled separately as Vireuils Dessous and Vireuils Dessus. Nearly all the whites deserve five years' age but will keep for 10 or more. 2002, 00 and 99 are the best recent vintages but due to the demand, finding any of the wines at reasonable prices will be a minor miracle. (PW)

- O **Corton-Charlemagne**✪✪✪✪✪ £H O **Meursault** 1er Cru Perrières✪✪✪✪✪ £H Rougeots★★★★ £F
- O **Meursault** Vireuils★★★ £F Narvaux★★★★ £F Caillerets★★★★ £G Chevalières★★★★ £F
- O **Puligny-Montrachet** Les Enseignières★★★★ £F
- ● **Volnay** 1er Cru★★★ £F ● **Bourgogne Pinot Noir**★ £C
- O **Bourgogne Aligoté**★ £C ● **Bourgogne Chardonnay**★★ £D

DOM. MARC COLIN ET FILS   Saint-Aubin   A: CCC, RsW, F&R

Owner: Colin family   Gamay, 21190 Saint-Aubin

Marc Colin and his sons, Joseph, Pierre-Yves and Damien manage 20 ha and the domaine's reputation is built on its finest whites. These are rich, ripe wines with good complexity and a distinct and attractive minerality in the best examples. Several Chassagne-Montrachets, led by an intense, minerally Caillerets, are made to a high standard and there is a galaxy of really fine Saint-Aubin in both colours (more than a third of the estate is planted to Pinot Noir). A very minerally, stylish En Remilly vies with a slightly more structured La Chatenière and classy Les Charmes as the best Saint-Aubin white, though newish Sentier du Clou from old vines is very rich. For red, the Santenay Vieilles Vignes shows what is possible from that appellation, particularly when from an excellent vintage such as 1999. This still-expanding domaine also produces some *négociant* wines, including a Bâtard-Montrachet. (PW)

○ **Montrachet**★★★★ £H ○ **Chassagne-Montrachet** 1er Cru Caillerets★★★ £F
○ **Chassagne-Montrachet**★★ £E 1er Cru Champ Gain★★★ £E 1er Cru Vide Bourse★★★ £E
○ **Puligny-Montrachet** 1er Cru Garennes★★★ £E
○ **Saint-Aubin** 1er Cru Les Charmes★★★ £D 1er Cru La Chatenière★★★ £D 1er Cru En Remilly★★★ £D
○ **Saint-Aubin** 1er Cru Sentier du Clou★★★ £D 1er Cru Les Combes★★ £D 1er Cru En Montceau★★ £D
○ **Saint-Aubin** Fontenotte★★ £C ● **Saint-Aubin**★ £C 1er Cru★★ £C 1er Cru Frionnes★★ £D
● **Chassagne-Montrachet**★★ £D ● **Santenay** Vieilles Vignes★★★ £D

MICHEL COLIN-DELÉGER ET FILS A: BWC, BBR, MCW, HRp, L&W, F&R

Owner: Colin-Deléger family 3 Impasse des Crêts, 21190 Chassagne-Montrachet
As much of the wine here is red as white but, as so often with Chassagne producers, the attention they receive is based almost solely on the quality of the whites. The standard here is very high, with intense, concentrated but beautifully balanced wines produced from low-yielding vines. En Remilly heads a raft of fine Chassagne-Montrachet *premiers crus*. The reds used to be a little tough but are now richer with riper tannins, especially from a good red wine vintage such as 2002. Santenay Gravières and Chassagne-Montrachet Morgeots both stand out; Michel Colin is unusual in producing a fine example of both red and white Morgeots. The best reds, like the whites, will benefit from five or six years' age, sometimes more. Of a range of very fine Puligny-Montrachet *premiers crus* made in small quantities, Les Demoiselles is tucked up against a tiny amount of *grand cru* Chevalier-Montrachet. Other attractive whites are made on a *négociant* basis. (PW)

○ **Chassagne-Montrachet** 1er Cru Morgeots★★★★ £F 1er Cru En Remilly★★★★£F
○ **Chassagne-Montrachet** 1er Cru Les Chaumées★★★★ £F 1er Cru Vergers★★★★ £F
○ **Chassagne-Montrachet**★★★ £E 1er Cru La Maltroie★★★ £F 1er Cru Chevenottes★★★ £F
○ **Puligny-Montrachet**★★★ £E 1er Cru Les Demoiselles★★★★★ £G 1er Cru La Truffière★★★★ £G
○ **Saint-Aubin** 1er Cru Les Charmois★★★ £C
● **Chassagne-Montrachet** Vieilles Vignes★★ £C Morgeots★★★ £D
● **Santenay**★★ £B 1er Cru Gravières★★★ £C

DOM. JEAN-JACQUES CONFURON Nuits-Saint-Georges A: Bal, OWL, Eno, BBR, F&R

Owner: Alain & Sophie Meunier Prémeaux-Prissey, 21700 Nuits-Saint-Georges
Alain Meunier and his wife make increasingly good wines from 7 ha of their own vineyards in the heart of the Côte de Nuits. By following organic principles, much has been done to restore the health of the vineyard and yields are low. A cold pre-fermentation maceration is employed, with moderately high temperatures, and a lot of new oak is used in ageing the wines. Quite dense and concentrated when young, the powerful fruit unfurls with 5 to 10 years' age. The results can be a little uneven and the wines have occasionally suffered from a little reduction or too much oak. But if patience is needed there's great intensity and length of flavour, particularly in the *premiers* and *grands crus*. Alain Meunier also oversees production for the part-domaine, part-*négociant* Domaine Féry/Féry-Meunier label. (PW)

● **Romanée-Saint-Vivant**★★★★ £G ● **Clos Vougeot**★★★★ £G
● **Vosne-Romanée** 1er Cru Beaux Monts★★★★ £E ● **Chambolle-Musigny**★★★ £D 1er Cru★★★★ £E
● **Nuits-Saint-Georges** Fleurières★★★ £D Chaboeufs★★★ £E 1er Cru Boudots★★★★ £E
● **Côte de Nuits-Villages** Les Vignottes★★ £C

DOM. CONFURON-COTÉTIDOT Vosne-Romanée A: L&S, OWL

Owner: Jacky Confuron-Cotétidot 10 Rue de la Fontaine, 21700 Vosne-Romanée
The Confuron domaine was one of the original private estates in the Côtes de Nuits and Yves Confuron now maintains this fine 11-ha property, further building on his father's considerable achievements. Jacky

Confuron's dedication and skill as a *vigneron* has produced healthy vines of a high average age with really low yields. A so-called traditional approach has long been adhered to in the winemaking. There is no destemming (requiring ripe stalks as well as fruit), a long pre-fermentation maceration and lengthy *cuvaison*, while the subsequent ageing utilises a relatively low percentage of new oak, though this has recently been increased. This usually results in intense, deep and, at times, tannic Burgundies but there is more refinement in the latest releases. Across a range of appellations with good *terroir*, the wines show varied character but almost always good colour, body and ripe fruit. While not every wine in every vintage always achieves its full potential, each does require attention on the part of the drinker. These are wines that require assessment and often, patience; wines to devote cellar space to so they can be revisited over a period of years. Cellar some very good 2001s and 02s. A tiny amount of Mazis-Chambertin and only a little Clos de Vougeot are also made. Yves also makes some excellent Pommard at the De COURCEL estate. (PW)

- **Charmes-Chambertin★★★★** £F ● **Echezeaux★★★★** £F
- **Vosne-Romanée★★★** £E 1er Cru Suchots★★★★ £F
- **Gevrey-Chambertin★★★** £E 1er Cru Petite Chapelle★★★ £F 1er Cru Lavaux-Saint-Jacques★★★★ £F
- **Chambolle-Musigny★★★** £E ● **Nuits-Saint-Georges★★★** £E 1er Cru★★★ £F

DOM. DE COURCEL Pommard   A: HRp, OWL, L&S, Res, P&S, C&C

Owner: De Courcel family Place de l'Église, 21630 Pommard
As at his family's domaine, CONFURON-COTÉTIDOT, winemaker Yves Confuron favours whole-bunch fermentation after having harvested late for fully ripe grapes. Yields are low and the percentage of wine bottled by the domaine has gone from around half to the lion's share of what it grows. At the heart of the estate's 8 ha is 5 ha of Grand Epenots, supplemented by sometimes brilliant Rugiens and another classy *premier cru*, Fremiers. There were some fine wines made prior to Yves's arrival but the standard is even higher now. Recent vintages have been vigorous, sturdy, concentrated, more oaky than previously and capable of ageing for a decade; the Grand Clos des Epenots and the Rugiens need almost that long before they've even started to open up. The elegance and complexity of the Rugiens is only fully apparent with age. Consistently excellent Bourgogne Rouge deserves a couple of years' bottle-age, too. The wines make for an interesting comparison with those from Comte ARMAND and Jean-Marc BOILLOT. Another fine village Pommard, Valmuriens, has only been made since 1999. (PW)

- **Pommard** 1er Cru Rugiens★★★★ £F 1er Cru Grand Clos des Epenots★★★★ £F
- **Pommard** Croix Noires★★★ £E Les Valmuriens★★★ £E 1er Cru Fremiers★★★ £E
- **Bourgogne Rouge★★** £C

DOM. PIERRE DAMOY www.domaine-pierre-damoy.com   A: OWL, Res, Dec, JNi, L&W

Owner: Damoy family 11 Rue du Maréchal de Lattre de Tassigny, 21220 Gevrey-Chambertin
Under the direction of the young Pierre Damoy (the current generation Damoy who shares the domaine's name), this important 11-ha estate only started to realise its potential in the 1990s. A remarkable 5.3 ha are in Chambertin Clos-de-Bèze but as well as a decent chunk (2.2 ha) of Chapelle-Chambertin there's some Chambertin and a solely-owned village *lieu-dit*, Clos Tamisot from vineyards surrounding the cellar. The wines are harvested late and the yields are now low, considerably reduced from what they were prior to Pierre's stewardship. The wines are lush, powerful and concentrated, with good breadth and length, but are also oaky with a lot of tannin, particularly in a heavily structured and more austere Chambertin. There has been a lack of consistency, too, in recent years until 1999, which worked more in favour of the style of wines here. 2001s and 02s show promise too, though a little extra harmony and class is still required before the top wines rival the best in their respective *grands crus*. Ripe fruity Bourgogne Blanc and a lightish Bourgogne Rouge are also made. (PW)

- **Chambertin Clos-de-Bèze★★★★** £G ● **Chambertin★★★** £G ● **Chapelle-Chambertin★★★** £G
- **Gevrey-Chambertin★★** £E Clos Tamisot★★★ £E

DARVIOT-PERRIN Monthelie   A: HRp, A&B, JAr, Dec, L&W, May, T&W

Owner: Darviot-Perrin family Grande Rue, 21190 Monthelie

Didier Darviot's cellar is in the quiet pretty village of Monthelie but his 9.5 ha estate includes Volnay, Meursault and Chassagne-Montrachet, much of it inherited by his wife. The wines are elegant and racy with fine pure fruit, and are increasingly generous and complex with five years' age. *Premiers crus* Charmes and Perrières are excellent examples of their noble *terroirs*. Dark, deep and intense Volnay with classic perfumes and really delicious fruit show similarly sophisticated winemaking. Though not quite at the same level, this is, in fact, a very credible alternative if superstars like COCHE-DURY or COMTES LAFON remain out of reach due to the demand-inflated prices. Village-level Meursaults Clos de la Velle and Tessons have only been produced separately from 2000 and an excellent Meursault Premier Cru Genevrières since 01. A little Pommard is also made. (PW)

O **Chassagne-Montrachet** La Bergerie★★ £E 1er Cru Blanchots-Dessus★★★★ £F
O **Meursault** 1er Cru Genevrières★★★★ £F 1er Cru Perrières★★★★ £F
O **Meursault** Clos de la Velle★ £D Tessons★★★ £E 1er Cru Charmes★★★★ £E
● **Volnay** Les Blanches★★★ £D 1er Cru La Gigotte★★★ £E 1er Cru Santenots★★★★ £E
● **Chassagne-Montrachet** 1er Cru Les Bondues★★ £D ● **Monthelie**★★ £C

JOSEPH DROUHIN Beaune www.drouhin.com   A: DAy, OWL, L&W, Sav, C&R, MCW

Owner: Drouhin family 7 Rue d'Enfer, 21200 Beaune

An excellent high-profile domaine (owning over 60 ha) and *négociant* that combines integrity and know-how. Equally adept at producing red as white, Drouhin delivers good-quality wine at every level. As celebrated as any of the Drouhin wines are the red and white from the Beaune *premier cru* Clos des Mouches. While the red can be good, it can be surpassed by a Grèves bottling, but the white can be superb, with its delicate spice, flavour complexity, real presence on the palate and considerable elegance. Generally the wines are not big or overly powerful yet show good expression and are subtle and elegant. Occasionally wines miss a little extra concentration but it is important not to expect immediate gratification. The wines add weight and their centres usually fill in with the requisite bottle-age. Of the reds, the attractive Côte de Beaune (a Beaune appellation but usually including young-vine Clos des Mouches) and similarly-priced examples usually need three years' ageing; Vosne, Chambolle and other village-level wines and the Beaune *premiers crus* around six; the top *crus* 8 to 10 years. Not all the *grands crus* are of the same standard but Drouhin's versions of Griotte-Chambertin and Grands-Echezeaux, where good examples can be hard to find, are usually excellent. In Chablis, where Drouhin is an important vineyard owner (see Joseph DROUHIN CHABLIS), there are facilities to press the grapes, though vinification takes place in Beaune. Drouhin also make the wines for the Marquis de Laguiche including the brilliant Montrachet, which comes from the appellation's largest single parcel. DOMAINE DROUHIN is the company's quality outpost in Oregon, run by Veronique, daughter of Robert Drouhin. As well as those listed, a little of the *grands crus* Chambertin, Chambertin Clos de Bèze, Charmes-Chambertin, Clos Saint-Denis, Clos de la Roche, Romanée-Saint-Vivant, Corton and Bâtard-Montrachet are also made, as are generic examples of leading village appellations. (PW)

● **Musigny**❍❍❍❍❍ £H ● **Grands-Echezeaux**★★★★★ £G ● **Griotte-Chambertin**★★★★ £G
● **Bonnes Mares**★★★★ £G ● **Clos de Vougeot**★★★★ £F ● **Echezeaux**★★★ £F
● **Corton Bressandes**★★★★ £F
● **Morey-Saint-Denis** 1er Cru Clos Sorbé★★★ £E
● **Chambolle-Musigny**★★ £E 1er Cru★★★ £E 1er Cru Amoureuses★★★★ £F
● **Vosne-Romanée**★★★ £E 1er Cru Petits Monts★★★ £F
● **Beaune** 1er Cru Clos des Mouches★★★ £E 1er Cru Grèves★★★ £E
● **Volnay**★★ £D 1er Cru Chevret★★ £E 1er Cru Clos des Chênes★★★ £E
● **Côte de Beaune**★★ £D ● **Côte de Beaune-Villages**★ £C
● **Savigny-lès-Beaune**★ £C 1er Cru Serpentières★★ £D ● **Chorey-lès-Beaune**★★ £C
O **Montrachet** Marquis de Laguiche❍❍❍❍❍ £H O **Corton-Charlemagne**★★★★ £G

O **Beaune** I er Cru Clos des Mouches★★★★ £F O **Chassagne-Montrachet** Marquis de Laguiche★★★ £F
O **Puligny-Montrachet** I er Cru Folatières★★★★ £F O **Meursault**★★★ £E O **Côte de Beaune**★★ £D
O **Saint-Aubin**★ £D O **Saint-Romain**★ £C O **Rully**★ £B

CLAUDE DUGAT Gevrey-Chambertin   A: Eno, HRp, Hrd, Sec, F&R

Owner: Claude Dugat 1 Place de l'église, 21220 Gevrey-Chambertin
There are similarities between Claude Dugat and his cousin Bernard (Bernard DUGAT-PY). Both have small holdings (Claude has just 4 ha) and both make very rich, concentrated wines swaddled in, but not swamped by, new oak. In addition, yields are low, occasionally very low, and there is an intuitive feel for the vine that runs back a generation or two. Unsurprisingly perhaps, Claude Dugat's wines have gone down a treat in the US and their prices have soared (at first filling the pockets of the middlemen). The wines are rich with, in some instances, old-vine succulence as well as balancing fine ripe tannins and good acidities but how many of these wines get the 6 to 10 years' ageing they deserve, and occasionally need, I wouldn't hazard a guess at. A tiny amount of Chapelle-Chambertin is also made. As well as the *premiers crus* and *grands crus* there's very good if no longer inexpensive village-level Gevrey and Bourgogne Rouge. Oh, and both cousins have beautiful, restored medieval cellars. (PW)
● **Charmes-Chambertin**✪✪✪✪✪ £H ● **Griottes-Chambertin**✪✪✪✪✪ £H
● **Gevrey-Chambertin**★★★★ £F I er Cru★★★★ £G I er Cru Lavaux-Saint-Jacques★★★★★ £G
● **Bourgogne Rouge**★★ £D

BERNARD DUGAT-PY www.dugat-py.com   A: THt, BBR, Blx, Sec, JNi, F&R

Owner: Bernard Dugat Rue de Planteligone, BP 31, 21220 Gevrey-Chambertin
Bernard Dugat has been making wine since 1975 but only bottling his own since 1989. His 7.2 ha are planted exclusively to Pinot Noir. The concentration and richness of fruit, lush oak, silky textures and fine tannins make the wines irresistible. Nearly all the wines see 100 per cent new oak but only rarely does this or the amount of extract or tannin seem overdone. These are big, dense wines but in the best sense. The Lavaux-Saint-Jacques and the *grands crus* have extra class and dimension as well as concentration. The Chambertin is distinguished by very, very concentrated black fruits that make the structure difficult to assess, a testament to very low-yielding and very old, very densely planted vines. Gevrey-Chambertin Coeur de Roy also comes from a selection of very old vines. Vieilles Vignes Vosne-Romanée (from 70-year-old vines) has only been made since 1999. Only tiny amounts of Mazis-Chambertin and Chambertin are made. (PW)
● **Chambertin**✪✪✪✪✪ £H ● **Mazis-Chambertin**✪✪✪✪✪ £H
● **Charmes-Chambertin**✪✪✪✪✪ £H ● **Gevrey-Chambertin** I er Cru Petite Chapelle★★★★★ £G
● **Gevrey-Chambertin** I er Cru★★★★ £G I er Cru Lavaux-Saint-Jacques★★★★★ £G
● **Gevrey-Chambertin** Vieilles-Vignes★★★★ £F Coeur de Roy★★★★ £F Évocelles★★★★ £F
● **Vosne-Romanée** Vieilles-Vignes★★★★ £F

DOM. DUJAC Morey-Saint-Denis www.dujac.com   A: OWL, L&W, HRp, WSc, ABy, T&W

Owner: Jacques Seysses 7 Rue de la Bussière, 21220 Morey-Saint-Denis
Jacques Seysses is one of the best-known and most respected winemakers in Burgundy. His openness and generosity have helped many a fellow Burgundian and more than a few New World Pinot-phile winemakers along their way. Perhaps unsurprisingly the winemaking reflects modern influences as well as Burgundian traditions. There is great attention to detail, scrupulous hygiene and new oak is favoured for the top wines. A preference for clonal selection and cultured yeasts is offset by a desire for whole-bunch fermentation (no destemming). As a consequence the wines are never that deeply coloured but are intense, clean, elegant and perfumed. Now that Seysses is assisted by his son Jeremy, past criticisms of a lack of weight and occasionally too much oak have been countered with a slightly more flexible approach in recent vintages. At any rate the wines gain in richness and harmony with age, becoming ever more expressive of their *terroir*. Of the five *grands crus*, the Bonnes Mares is arguably the best, with remarkable breadth, power and flavour profile. An intense, vigorous Echezeaux and an expansive Clos de Roche are stylish examples of their respective

appellations but all are fine and individual, as are the Chambolle and Gevrey *premiers crus*. The splendid regular Morey-Saint-Denis *premier cru* comes from Ruchots and some younger vines in Clos de la Roche. Some Vosne-Romanée Premier Cru Les Beaumonts is also made on a sharecropping basis. A little of the estate's 12-odd ha is planted to Chardonnay for some white Morey-Saint-Denis, including some Monts Luisants since 2000. Wines made from bought-in grapes are sold under the label Dujac Fils et Père and include very good village level Gevrey-Chambertin, Morey-Saint-Denis and Chambolle-Musigny for red and Meursault and Puligny-Montrachet whites. (PW)

Domaine Dujac:
- **Bonnes Mares**✪✪✪✪✪ £H   ● **Clos de la Roche**★★★★★ £H   ● **Echezeaux**★★★★ £H
- **Clos Saint-Denis**★★★★★ £G   ● **Charmes-Chambertin**★★★★ £G
- **Gevrey-Chambertin** 1er Cru Aux Combottes★★★★ £G
- **Chambolle-Musigny**★★★ £E   1er Cru Les Gruenchers★★★ £G
- **Morey-Saint-Denis**★★★ £E   1er Cru★★★★ £F   O **Morey-Saint-Denis**★ £E

DOM. VINCENT DUREUIL-JANTHIAL   Rully   A: THt, CdP, OWL, Rae, Gau, CPp, Sel

Owner: Vincent Dureuil   10 Rue de la Buisserolle, 71150 Rully
Vincent Dureuil's 7-ha estate is planted to more red than white but the whites are the better suit and among the best made by a local grower. Having established his own domaine he is able to add to it bit by bit with plots inherited from his father, Raymond, who also makes attractive red and white Rully, albeit in a slightly less modern style. Greater use of new oak is apparent but whites have a depth and fullish fruit character as well as decent acidity to drink well with two or three years' ageing. The stars are *premiers crus* that come from low-yielding old vines. A departure is a little Nuits-Saint-Georges Clos des Argillières, first made in 1999. Bourgogne Rouge is good from vintages like 2002 (PW)

O **Rully**★★ £C   1er Cru Margotés★★★ £C   1er Cru Le Meix Cadot★★★ £C
● **Rully**★★ £C   Maizières★★★ £C   ● **Mercurey**★★ £C   ● **Bourgogne Rouge**★ £B
● **Nuits-Saint-Georges** 1er Cru Clos des Argillières★★★ £E

DOM. RENÉ ENGEL   www.domaine-engel.com   A: M&V, Con, Gau, HHB, HRp, F&M

Owner: Philippe Engel   3 Place de la Mairie, 21700 Vosne-Romanée
Over the past two decades Philippe Engel has steadily revived the estate established by his industrious and learned grandfather René. All 7 ha are in the commune of Vosne and neighbouring Flagey and Vougeot. The style is one of power, structure and richness and is achieved in part through destemming, high fermentation temperatures, long *cuvaisons* and a moderately high percentage of new oak. The wines are typically deep coloured, full and structured with a dark fruit richness and impressive depth and length. Older vintages had a tendency to be a bit too brutal but in the 1990s the wines gained better balance and now show more of their intrinsic quality and class, while retaining their muscular, concentrated stamp. Vosne-Romanée Les Brulées comes from very old vines and shows tremendous fruit quality and arguably represents the best value of this fabulous range. All the wines become ever richer and more luscious with age; the village Vosne-Romanée needs five years' ageing while the others are better with 10 years. Great 2002s. (PW)

● **Grands-Echezeaux**✪✪✪✪✪ £G   ● **Clos de Vougeot**★★★★★ £F   ● **Echezeaux**★★★★ £F
● **Vosne-Romanée**★★★ £E   1er Cru Les Brulées★★★★★ £F

ARNAUD ENTE   Meursault   A: M&V, Sec, Hrd

Owner: Arnaud Ente   12 Rue de Mazeray, 21190 Meursault
Arnaud Ente is a young grower able to make only a relatively small amount of wine but a lot of effort goes into each one. Yields are kept low and there is a good smattering of old vines. The wines are ripe, concentrated but not overdone with fine structures and good flavour intensity and depth. Of the two superior Meursaults, the Goutte d'Or has a more floral, exotic character in contrast to a citrusy but very concentrated Vieilles Vignes. The Puligny has a spicy intensity but less depth. Decent Bourgogne Blanc and

Bourgogne Aligoté usually show good fruit too. (PW)
O **Puligny-Montrachet** 1er Cru Les Referts★★★ £F
O **Meursault**★★★ £E Vieilles Vignes★★★★ £F 1er Cru Goutte d'Or★★★ £F
O **Bourgogne Chardonnay**★★ £C

FRÉDÉRIC ESMONIN Gevrey-Chambertin   A: JAr, HRp, Hrd

Owner: Frédéric Esmonin 1 Rue de Curley, 21220 Gevrey-Chambertin
This small estate only started bottling its own wines in the late 1980s after Frédéric's father, André, had
established a reputation as a top grower. Most of the wines here are made from leased vineyards on a
sharecropping basis; in addition some of the top *crus* are from bought-in grapes as this estate has also
established a separate small *négociant* operation. Most significant is 1 ha of the prized small *premier cru*
Estournelles; the wine's concentration, depth and refinement do justice to the *cru's* cachet. The other estate
wines show fine fruit and depth too. An intense, meaty, structured Ruchottes-Chambertin is rivalled by a
very powerful, black-fruited and classy Mazis-Chambertin, made from the Esmonin's share of that which
they cultivate for the Hospices de Beaune. A fine example of another *grand cru*, Griottes-Chambertin, was
made here until 1999. Wines made to a high standard from purchased grapes (or wine) include Clos de
Vougeot, Chambertin and Chambertin Clos-de-Bèze. Prices are very reasonable across the range. (PW)
● **Chambertin**★★★★★ £F   ● **Chambertin Clos-de-Béze**★★★★★ £F   ● **Mazis-Chambertin**★★★★★ £F
● **Ruchottes-Chambertin**★★★★ £F   ● **Charmes-Chambertin**★★★★ £F
● **Gevrey-Chambertin** 1er Cru Lavaux Saint-Jacques★★★★ £E 1er Cru Estournelles Saint-Jacques★★★★ £E
● **Gevrey-Chambertin** Clos Prieur★★★ £D

SYLVIE ESMONIN Gevrey-Chambertin   A: M&V, HHB, C&R

Owner: Sylvie Esmonin Clos Saint-Jacques, 1 Rue Neuve, 21220 Gevrey-Chambertin
This small 7-ha domaine, previously called Domaine Michel Esmonin et Fille (after Sylvie's father) makes
some splendid Gevrey-Chambertin. Prior to 1987 most of the wine was sold to *négociants* but the highly
trained Sylvie Esmonin has worked with her father for more than a decade and after making an immediate
impact has continued to improve the wines. There is an extra vigour and concentration in the most recent
vintages but this has been added whilst retaining their silky elegance. The wines can be drunk reasonably
young but the 1999s, in particular, need more time. (PW)
● **Gevrey-Chambertin**★★ £E Vieilles Vignes★★★ £E 1er Cru Clos Saint-Jacques★★★★ £F
● **Volnay** Santenots★★★ £E   ● **Côte de Nuits-Villages**★★ £C   ● **Bourgogne Rouge**★ £C

DOM. FAIVELEY Nuit-Saint-Georges   A: MMD, BBR, HHC, HRp, JAr, L&W

Owner: Faiveley 8 Rue de Tribourg, 21701 Nuits-Saint-Georges
Faiveley command more than 120 ha of vines in the Côte d'Or and Côte Chalonnaise. Nearly all the wines
of an extensive high-quality range come from their own vineyards, either owned or leased, and quality is
closely supervised by François Faiveley. A long *cuvaison* is favoured and temperatures are kept well below the
average for the red wine fermentation. The wines typically show fine perfumes combined with lots of depth
and dimension on the palate. They also add richness with age and are proven keepers at every level. The
character varies enormously from appellation to appellation, from intense, raspberryish Mercureys to burly,
meaty Nuits-Saint-Georges Clos de la Maréchale to deep, stylish Gevrey Cazetiers to splendid, classy Clos
des Cortons. The wines can be a little slight in lighter years such as 1997 or 00, though they will still keep
well. They are superb in the best years such as 99 and 02. The Clos des Cortons and most of the Mercureys
are *monopoles*. All the leading domaine wines are listed below but there are others. (PW)
● **Chambertin Clos-de-Bèze**✪✪✪✪✪ £H   ● **Corton** Clos des Cortons✪✪✪✪✪ £G
● **Mazis-Chambertin**★★★★★ £G   ● **Latricières-Chambertin**★★★★ £G
● **Clos de Vougeot**★★★ £G   ● **Echezeaux**★★★ £G
● **Gevrey-Chambertin** Les Marchais★★ £E 1er Cru Combe aux Moines★★★ £F 1er Cru Cazetiers★★★★£F
● **Chambolle-Musigny** 1er Cru La Combe d'Orveau★★★ £F 1er Cru Les Fuées★★★ £F

- **Nuits-Saint-Georges** 1er Cru Aux Chaignots★★★ £E 1er Cru Damodes★★★ £E
- **Nuits-Saint-Georges** 1er Cru Les Saint-Georges★★★ £F
- **Nuits-Saint-Georges** 1er Cru Porets Saint-Georges★★ £E 1er Cru Vignerondes★★ £E
- **Nuits-Saint-Georges** 1er Cru Lavières★★ £E 1er Cru Clos de la Maréchale★★ £E
- **Mercurey** Clos des Myglands★★ £C Clos du Roy★★ £C La Framboisière★★ £C
- **Mercurey** Domaine de la Croix Jacquelet★ £C Les Mauvarennes★ £C
- O **Corton-Charlemagne**★★★★ £H O **Mercurey** Les Mauvarennes★ £C Clos Rochette★ £C

JEAN-PHILIPPE FICHET   Meursault   A: M&V, Bal, HHB, Goe, WSc

Owner: Jean-Philippe Fichet   21190 Meursault

Jean-Philippe Fichet produces ever better white wines from a range of different *climats* in the Côte de Beaune. Most come from vineyards managed on a sharecropping basis but he is able to supplement his production by buying back the vineyard owners' share of the crop. Though most of the Meursault is village-level wine, individual *lieux-dits* are bottled separately and show definite stylistic differences from a ripe, typical Meursault Gruyaches through minerally Chevalières to a structured, classy Tessons that needs the greatest amount of time to show all its qualities. All contrast with a Puligny of real vigour and intensity. Without a superstar tag his wines are reasonably priced if made in fairly modest quantities. A little red wine is also made. (PW)

- O **Meursault** Meix sous le Château★★★ £E Gruyaches★★★ £E Chevalières★★★ £E Tessons★★★★ £E
- O **Meursault**★★★ £D Criots★★★ £E O **Puligny-Montrachet** 1er Cru Les Referts★★★★ £F
- O **Bourgogne Blanc**★★ £B O **Auxey-Duresses**★★ £B

RICHARD FONTAINE-GAGNARD   Chassagne-Montrachet   A: JAr, Dec, Maj

Owner: Richard Fontaine   19 Route de Santenay, 21190 Chassagne-Montrachet

Richard Fontaine married one of Jacques Gagnard's daughters, Jean-Marc Blain the other (see BLAIN-GAGNARD). Both make fine wines. There are three *grands crus* and a host of Chassagne *premiers crus* made to increasingly high standards from a 9-ha estate. The wines are full and ripe, with lots of fruit, good breadth and balanced acidities, not heavy or overoaked. All the *premiers crus* show fine citrus and mineral intensity when young but generally drink best with between four and eight years' age. The *grands crus* add more weight, breadth and class: the Criots has more finesse but the Bâtard more richness, while the Montrachet has both and then some. In addition to those listed, other fine *premier cru* Chassagne-Montrachet whites include La Grande Montagne, Les Murées, Chevenottes and Morgeots and new Clos Saint-Jean. Some Pommard is also made. (PW)

- O **Montrachet**⬢⬢⬢⬢⬢ £H O **Bâtard-Montrachet**★★★★★ £G O **Criots-Bâtard-Montrachet**★★★★★ £G
- O **Chassagne-Montrachet** 1er Cru La Boudriotte★★★★ £E 1er Cru La Maltroie★★★★ £E
- O **Chassagne-Montrachet** 1er Cru Caillerets★★★★ £F
- O **Chassagne-Montrachet**★★★ £E 1er Cru La Romanée★★★★ £E 1er Cru Vergers★★★★ £E
- ● **Volnay** 1er Cru Clos des Chênes★★★ £E
- ● **Chassagne-Montrachet**★ £C 1er Cru Clos Saint-Jean★★ £D 1er Cru Morgeots★★ £D

DOM. FOURRIER   Gevrey-Chambertin   A: THt, JAr, Ben, Gau, Goe, HRp, Hrd, Sel

Owner: Jean-Claude Fourrier   7 Route de Dijon, 21220 Gevrey-Chambertin

Since assuming control from his father in the mid-1990s, Jean-Marie Fourrier has determinedly pursued quality. Yields are kept low and while there is nothing unusual in a cold pre-fermentation maceration, minimal or no sulphur is utilised. A steady and gentle fermentation is sought in the pursuit of finer structures that allow the fruit to shine. To the same end, a relatively low percentage of new oak is used. He certainly has a good smattering of diverse *crus* from which subtle differences of *terroir* may be unearthed. All the wines are deep and ripe, with increasing concentration and complexity in the top wines. There is an excellent example of the would-be *grand cru*, Clos Saint-Jacques and very good Combe aux Moines too. All the wines are labelled 'Vieille Vigne' (sic). (PW)

● **Griotte-Chambertin**★★★★ £G
● **Gevrey-Chambertin** 1er Cru Clos Saint-Jacques★★★★★ £F 1er Cru Combe aux Moines★★★★ £E
● **Gevrey-Chambertin**1er Cru Cherbaudes★★★★ £E 1er Cru Champeaux★★★ £E
● **Gevrey-Chambertin**★★★ £D Aux Echezeaux★★★ £D 1er Cru Goulots★★★ £E
● **Chambolle-Musigny**★★★ £E 1er Cru Les Gruenchers★★★★ £E

JEAN-NOËL GAGNARD   Chassagne-Montrachet   A: GBa, JAr, Far, J&B, WSc

Owner: Jean-Noël Gagnard and family 21190 Chassagne-Montrachet
Caroline Lestimé has taken over the running of this domaine, one of the leading Chassagne estates, from her father, Jean-Noël Gagnard (whose brother is Jacques Gagnard – see BLAIN-GAGNARD). With half a dozen or so vintages to her credit, the wines have gained in both richness and finesse. As well as a fine village example, Les Masures, there are several *premiers crus*, from the lighter but elegant and more forward Chevenottes, through fuller Champgains, to rich, concentrated Blanchot-Dessus and Caillerets that need at least five or six years to reveal their full glory. The Bâtard-Montrachet adds more again but can usually be drunk from a similar age. The reds, including some Santenay Clos des Tavannes and Chassagnes Clos Saint-Jean and Morgeots, can be attractive but lack richness and depth, even in better years. In addition to those listed some Chaumées, Morgeots and La Maltroie white Chassagne *premiers crus* are made. (PW)
○ **Bâtard-Montrachet**★★★★★ £H ○ **Chassagne-Montrachet** 1er Cru Caillerets★★★★★ £F
○ **Chassagne-Montrachet** 1er Cru Champgains★★★★ £F 1er Cru Blanchots-Dessus★★★★ £F
○ **Chassagne-Montrachet** Les Masures★★★ £E Clos de la Maltroye★★★ £F 1er Cru Chevenottes★★★★ £E

GEANTET-PANSIOT   www.geantet-pansiot.com   A: DDr, HRp, EoR, F&R, C&R

Owner: Vincent Geantet 3 Route de Beaune, 21220 Gevrey-Chambertin
This 13-ha estate is a fine source for intense, concentrated and well-balanced northern Côte de Nuits reds. Vincent Geantet employs long macerations, but at a low temperature, prior to fermentation and has gone to great lengths to reduce yields and ensure optimum ripeness in his grapes. The very high average vine age shows in the wines, adding a succulence and intensity to the fruit. There are no poor wines here and they increasingly show well in lighter vintages as well the best years. The Charmes-Chambertin (from almost half a hectare) is a really fine example of how good this *grand cru* can be. Since taking full control in 1989, Vincent Geantet has steadily built up the estate and from 1999 has had a new cellar and some new wines following the sale of the Vachet-Rousseau domaine. New Gevrey-Chambertins En Champ, from a small parcel of extremely old vines, has been made since 2000. There's good value here, too. (PW)
● **Charmes-Chambertin**★★★★★ £F ● **Gevrey-Chambertin** En Champ★★★★ £E
● **Gevrey-Chambertin** Jeunes Rois★★★ £D Vieilles Vignes★★★★ £D 1er Cru Le Poissenot★★★★ £E
● **Chambolle-Musigny** Vieilles Vignes★★★ £E 1er Cru★★★★ £E
● **Marsannay** Champ-Perdrix★★ £C ● **Bourgogne Rouge**★ £C

DOM. HENRI GERMAIN ET FILS   Meursault   A: DDr, L&S, Tan, Adm, HRp

Owner: Henri Germain 4 Rue des Forges, 21190 Meursault
Henri Germain possesses just 5 ha, two of Pinot Noir and three of Chardonnay, but his son Jean-François continues the habit of making fine wines. Even the village Meursault is of good quality and exemplifies the efforts that go into every wine; its weight, structure and balance is particularly impressive so that it tastes attractive when fairly young, with pronounced citrus, spice and floral aspects, but it also has the capacity to keep far longer than average. Much is made of the importance of a cold cellar for the *élevage* and this does seem to be borne out here. The wines' slow development makes for late bottling. Reds are subject to both a cold maceration and long *cuvaisons,* evident in both the fine, complex, sappy but ripe, cherry, berry aromas and the real intensity and breadth on the palate. Both reds and whites are better with a little age and promise much more with six years or so. Some red Chassagne-Montrachet is also made, while more Meursault (Perrières) has been added as the estate expands a little. (PW)

O **Meursault**★★★ £D   Limozin★★★ £E   Chevalières★★★ £E   1er Cru Charmes★★★★ £E
O **Chassagne-Montrachet** 1er Cru Morgeot★★★★ £E   O **Bourgogne Blanc**★★ £B
● **Beaune** 1er Cru Bressandes★★★ £D

VINCENT GIRARDIN   Santenay   A: THt, CTy, OWL, BWC, HRp, Tan, JNi, Sel, WSc

Owner: Vincent Girardin   4 Route de Chassagne-Montrachet, 21590 Santenay
This dynamic Santenay-based grower acquired a *négociant*'s licence only in the mid-1990s but has rapidly expanded, requiring a second move to larger winemaking premises in 2002. From his own expanding estate he has made some brilliant affordable red and white Santenay. The wines are modern, fruit-rich and clean with a healthy but rarely excessive dose of new oak. There is an energy and zip about most of the wines, a certain style and precision, yet they are still indicative of their respective appellations. In his *négociant* role, only grapes (rather than wine) are bought in, for while the sources are good this allows for further sorting for quality. Girardin vinifies both red and white with equal ease and is as sucessful in producing both more humble village wines as *grands crus*, though some of the top wines fail to match the very best made. There is real consistency too, important in an extensive and growing range of wines. Despite the number of wines, most are made in relatively small quantities and Girardin's total production is dwarfed by the likes of JADOT or Louis LATOUR. The wines listed below are most of those that are regularly made. (PW)

O **Bienvenue-Bâtard-Montrachet**★★★★★ £H
O **Bâtard-Montrachet**★★★★ £H   O **Corton-Charlemagne**★★★★ £F
O **Puligny-Montrachet** Vieilles Vignes★★★ £E   1er Cru Champs Gain★★★ £E   1er Cru Folatières★★★★ £E
O **Chassagne-Montrachet** 1er Cru Le Cailleret★★★ £E   1er Cru Morgeots★★★★ £E
O **Meursault** Narvaux★★★ £D   1er Cru Poruzots★★ £E   1er Cru Charmes★★★ £E
O **Savigny-lès-Beaune** Vermots Dessus★★ £C   O **Santenay** 1er Cru Clos de Tavannes★★ £C
O **Santenay** 1er Cru Beaurepaire★★ £C   1er Cru Clos du Beauregard★★ £C
● **Charmes-Chambertin**★★★★★ £G   ● **Clos de la Roche**★★★★ £G   ● **Echezeaux**★★★★ £G
● **Corton** Renardes★★★★ £F   ● **Gevrey-Chambertin** Lavaux Saint-Jacques★★★★ £F
● **Pommard** 1er Cru Grands Epenots★★★ £E   1er Cru Rugiens★★★ £E
● **Beaune** 1er Cru Clos des Vignes Franches★★ £C
● **Volnay** 1er Cru Santenots★★★★ £F   ● **Chassagne-Montrachet** 1er Cru Clos de la Boudriotte★★★ £D
● **Santenay** 1er Cru Gravières Vieilles Vignes★★★ £C   ● **Maranges** Clos des Loyères★★ £C

DOM. HENRI GOUGES   www.gouges.com   A: OWL, CTy, HBJ, Res, NYg, Sec, HRp, Hrd

Owner: Gouges family   7 Rue du Moulin, 21700 Nuits-Saint-Georges
This famous 14.5-ha estate is run by two cousins. Pierre takes care of the vines, Christian the winemaking, but it was their grandfather, Henri, who first established the domaine and was one of the pioneers of domaine bottling in Burgundy. He amassed a full hand of some of Nuits' best *crus*, including Les Saint-Georges, Vaucrains and Pruliers as well as the 3.5-ha *monopole* of Clos des Porrets-Saint-Georges. The use of grasses to counter erosion has also made it possible to move slowly towards an essentially organic operation. The grapes are fully destemmed but the use of new oak is minimal (a maximum of 20 per cent). Christian makes powerful, structured wines with excellent definition but most of all with an intensity and a quality to the fruit (particularly in the Vaucrains and the Les Saint-Georges) that sets them apart from most other Nuits. This core of quality is evident even when young and relatively tannic. Lush, soft and easy thankfully they are not; all the wines deserve (demand) at least six to eight years' ageing. A further *premier cru*, Les Chaînes Carteaux is also made. The Nuits white (from a Pinot Noir mutation) is a treat with its spice, mineral and unusual exotic flavour intensity but benefits from a little age too. Prices are very good for the quality. (PW)

● **Nuits-Saint-Georges** 1er Cru Les Vaucrains★★★★★ £E   1er Cru Les Saint-Georges★★★★★ £F
● **Nuits-Saint-Georges** 1er Cru Les Pruliers★★★★ £E   1er Cru Les Chaignots★★★★ £E
● **Nuits-Saint-Georges**★★★ £D   1er Cru Clos des Porrets-Saint-Georges★★★★ £E
● **Bourgogne Rouge**★ £C   O **Bourgogne Pinot Blanc**★★ £C
O **Nuits-Saint-Georges** 1er Cru La Perrière★★★ £E

DOM. JEAN GRIVOT   Vosne-Romanée   www.grivot.com   A: RsW, Bal, BBR, Res, HRp, Sec

Owner: Grivot family   6 Rue de la Croix Rameau, 21700 Vosne-Romanée

A brilliant 15-ha estate whose wines are much sought after. In 1987 Étienne took over the already successful family domaine built up by his grandfather, Gaston Grivot, in the first half of the 20th century. He immediately embraced some of the principles of the controversial consultant enologist Guy Accad. After a period of adjustment, the wines since the mid-1990s have been better than ever. The use of a cold pre-fermentation maceration seems to have been the main legacy of Accad's input but much thought and precision goes into every aspect of both viticulture and vinification. The wines are marvellous, combining great richness and concentration, and despite their size avoid any heaviness, with an excellent balance of acidity and fine tannins. The wines can sometimes show a reductive quality when tasted young but this doesn't persist. They all need at least five years' age and will be better with 10 or more. The top Vosnes and *grands crus* are an excellent cellaring prospect if you can afford them. Tiny amounts of Vosne *premiers crus* Les Chaumes and Les Reignots are also made to a very high standard. (PW)

- **Richebourg**✪✪✪✪✪ £H   ● **Echezeaux**✪✪✪✪✪ £G   ● **Clos de Vougeot**★★★★ £F
- **Vosne-Romanée** 1er Cru Les Beaux Monts✪✪✪✪✪ £F   1er Cru Les Suchots✪✪✪✪✪ £F
- **Vosne-Romanée** 1er Cru Les Rouges★★★★ £E   1er Cru Aux Brulées★★★★★ £F
- **Vosne-Romanée**★★★ £D   Bossières★★★ £E
- **Nuits-Saint-Georges** 1er Cru Les Boudots★★★★ £F   1er Cru Les Pruliers★★★★ £F
- **Nuits-Saint-Georges** Les Charmois★★★ £E   Les Lavières★★★ £E   1er Cru Les Roncières★★★★ £E
- **Chambolle-Musigny** La Combe d'Orveaux★★★ £E

ROBERT GROFFIER   Morey-Saint-Denis   A: A&B, JAr, F&M, F&R, Blx

Owner: Robert Groffier   35 Route des Grands Crus, 21220 Morey-Saint-Denis

Since the late 1990s the wines have become very rich and concentrated, adding to their already intense and classy character. With 8 ha, Robert and his son Serge make a little wine across several different appellations. Most stunning are the *grands crus*; a small amount of Clos-de-Bèze and almost one hectare of Bonnes Mares are owned. There is also slightly over 1 ha (the largest holding) of the excellent *premier cru* Les Amoureuses from Chambolle-Musigny. While new oak contributes to the wines' lush texture, low yields of first-rate fruit is the underlying reason behind the quality. The whole range is impressive and only rarely is the oak excessive, with real charm and style in the Hauts Doix and Les Sentiers and greater richness, dimension and complexity in the top trio. The wines can be drunk fairly young but bring further rewards to the patient; wait eight years for the best. (PW)

- **Chambertin Clos-de-Bèze**✪✪✪✪✪ £H   ● **Bonnes Mares**✪✪✪✪✪ £G
- **Chambolle-Musigny** 1er Cru Les Amoureuses★★★★★ £G
- **Chambolle-Musigny** 1er Cru Les Hauts Doix★★★★ £F   1er Cru Les Sentiers★★★★ £F
- **Gevrey-Chambertin**★★★ £E   ● **Bourgogne Rouge**★★ £C

A F GROS & FRANÇOIS PARENT   Beaune   A: BSh, Dec, HHC, Res

Owner: Anne-Françoise Gros   La Garelle, 21630 Pommard

Anne-Françoise Gros is one of many family members involved in wine. Like brother Michel GROS she also includes some Vosne-Romanée in her range of wines. The wines are made by Anne-Françoise's husband, François Parent, and share the same cellar space as his wines, in Beaune. While the wines have very good depth and breadth, they had a tendency to be somewhat alike and indistinguishable. However, since 1999 there has been more finesse and flair, with particularly successful 2000s and 01s but fine 02s too. The Vosne-Romanée *lieux-dits* are reasonably priced, the Echezeaux rich and concentrated and the Richebourg really profound, intense and very powerful and long. François Parent, in addition to existing Beaune and Pommard vineyards, has recently acquired a further 12 ha from Pommard-based Raymond Launay. Some fine solid Beaune and Pommard are made under his label. (PW)

A.F Gros:
- **Richebourg**✪✪✪✪✪ £H ● **Echezeaux**★★★★★ £F
- **Vosne-Romanée** Clos de la Fontaine★★★ £D Aux Maizières★★★ £D Aux Réas★★★ £D
- **Chambolle-Musigny**★★★ £D ● **Savigny-lès-Beaune** 1er Cru Clos des Guettes★★★ £D
- **Bourgogne-Hautes Côtes de Nuits**★★ £B

F Parent:
- **Beaune** 1er Cru Les Boucherottes★★★ £D ● **Pommard** 1er Cru Les Arvelets★★★★ £E

ANNE GROS   Vosne-Romanée   www.anne-gros.fr   A: Adm, Lay, L&W, HRp, JAr

Owner: Anne Gros   11 Rue des Communes, 21700 Vosne-Romanée

Anne's 6.5 ha is the smallest of the various Gros estates but the wines are the most complete and refined of all. From Bourgogne Rouge to Richebourg, though deeply coloured with plenty of extract, there is a harmony and fruit quality that set the wines apart. A new cellar contains vats that can be adjusted in size according to the amount of wine to be vinified. Though only village-level, Chambolle-Musigny and Vosne-Romanée are lovely examples of their respective appellations. The outstanding Clos de Vougeot and Richebourg absorb the high percentage of new oak used and both have a wonderful, silky texture that belies an excellent structure. Not surprisingly the small quantities of wine are keenly sought after. In addition to some Bourgogne Blanc, a little Bourgogne-Hautes Côtes de Nuits Blanc has been made since 2000. Older wines will be labelled Domaine Anne et François Gros. (PW)

- **Richebourg**✪✪✪✪✪ £H ● **Clos de Vougeot** Grand Maupertuis★★★★★ £G
- **Vosne-Romanée** Les Barreaux★★★ £E ● **Chambolle-Musigny** La Combe d'Orveau★★★ £E
- **Bourgogne Rouge**★★ £C ● **Bourgogne Hautes-Côtes de Nuits**★ £C
- O **Bougogne Blanc**★★ £C O **Bourgogne Hautes-Côtes de Nuits**★★ £C

MICHEL GROS   www.domaine-michel-gros.com   A: THt, JNi, ABy, Tan, Res, Hrd

Owner: Michel Gros & Jean Gros family   7 Rue des Communes, 21700 Vosne-Romanée

For a time Michel Gros made wines both under his own name and those of his family's domain (Domaine Jean Gros). Now the estate of Michel Gros is, like those of his brother Bernard (Gros Frère et Soeur) and sister Anne-Françoise (A F GROS), a distinct entity. Michel has nearly 18 ha but much of it lies in the Hautes-Côtes de Nuits and only a little in the top sites. The real exception is the 2.12-ha *monopole* Clos des Réas, a Vosne-Romanée *premier cru*. A dedicated and skilled *vigneron*, Michel avoids green-harvesting by careful pruning earlier in the growing season. Quite a lot of new oak is used, with 100 per cent in the Clos de Vougeot. These are intense, elegant, very stylish wines, structured but not big or overpowering. Some Richebourg used to be made but this has now been relinquished. New is a Morey-Saint-Denis produced from young vines in En La Rue de Vergy. The Hautes Côtes de Nuits is a consistently good example. (PW)

- **Clos de Vougeot**★★★★ £F
- **Vosne-Romanée**★★★ £E 1er Cru Aux Brulees★★★★ £F 1er Cru Clos des Réas★★★★★ £F
- **Morey-Saint-Denis** En la Rue de Vergy★★ £E
- **Nuits-Saint-Georges**★★ £E Chaliots★★★ £E 1er Cru★★★ £F ● **Chambolle-Musigny**★★★ £E
- **Bourgogne Hautes-Côtes de Nuits**★★ £C ● **Bourgogne Rouge**★★ £C
- O **Bourgogne Hautes-Côtes de Nuits**★★ £C

DOM. ANTONIN GUYON   Savigny-lès-Beaune   www.guyon-bourgogne.com   A: Frw

Owner: Michel & Dominique Guyon   2 Rue de Chorey, 21420 Savigny-lès-Beaune

Two brothers, Michel and Dominique Guyon oversee this relatively large (48 ha), predominantly red wine domaine that has only recently moved up an extra notch or two in quality. They are now producing rich, clean, concentrated wines with an immediate appeal that is only partly due to a measure of new oak. While yields are high, wines since the late 1990s have shown an extra depth and intensity. The cellars are in Savigny but the extensive range of wines includes some of the best sites from the surrounding appellations, in some instances from old vines. If not of the very highest order, there are some very good medium-term reds and delicious whites. A little Corton Renardes is also made, as is some Gevrey-Chambertin and Chambolle-Musigny. (PW)

● **Corton** Bressandes★★★ £F ● **Corton** Clos du Roy★★★★ £F ● **Volnay** Clos des Chênes★★★ £E
● **Pernand-Vergelesses** I er Cru Fichots★★ £D I er Cru Vergelesses★★ £D
● **Aloxe-Corton** I er Cru Fournières★★ £E I er Cru Vercots★★★ £E ● **Savigny-lès-Beaune**★★ £D
● **Bourgogne Hautes-Côtes de Nuits** Dames de Vergy★ £C
O **Corton-Charlemagne**★★★★ £G O **Meursault** I er Cru Charmes Dessus★★★ £F
O **Pernand-Vergelesses** I er Cru Sous Frétille★★ £C

HUDELOT-NOËLLAT Chambolle-Musigny A: Dec, JAr, Res, HRp, Col, Tur, F&R

Owner: Alain Hudelot-Noëllat Ancienne Route Nationale, 21220 Chambolle-Musigny
Greater consistency has been a feature of this domaine in the 1990s and the latest vintages continue to endorse this view. The estate's 10 ha is planted entirely to Pinot Noir and the constancy of the landholding makes it possible to track older vintages of many of the wines. Recent vintages have had input from Pierre Nawrocki who has helped to reduce yields whilst maintaining good balance in the vineyard. A light but responsive hand can be seen in the winemaking, along with an adeptness at bringing out the best in the grapes. A small proportion of the stems are usually retained and 100 per cent new oak is used in the top wines. Some of the wines have a certain rigour and austerity when young but become supple, opulent, stylish wines with great depth and expression with the appropriate age; about eight years for the Vosne *premiers crus* and the *grands crus* but closer to five for the other wines. Only a little Richebourg (the top wine) and Vosne Malconsorts is made. Village wines and *premiers crus* are good value. (PW)

● **Romanée-Saint-Vivant**★★★★★ £H ● **Clos de Vougeot**★★★★ £G
● **Vosne-Romanée** I er Cru Malconsorts★★★★★ £F
● **Vosne-Romanée**★★★ £E I er Cru Beaux-Monts★★★★ £E I er Cru Suchots★★★★ £E
● **Chambolle-Musigny**★★★ £E I er Cru Charmes★★★★ £E ● **Vougeot** I er Cru★★★ £E
● **Nuits-Saint-Georges** I er Cru Murgers★★★★ £E

HENRI ET PAUL JACQUESON Rully A: THt, BWC, L&S, JNi, HHB

Owner: Henri & Paul Jacqueson 5-7 Rue de Chèvremont, 71150 Rully
This small domaine run by Paul Jacqueson (son of Henri) makes superb Rully in both colours. The 9 ha of vineyards are planted mostly to Pinot Noir and Chardonnay but also include a little Aligoté and Gamay. The wines are natural, pure and expressive, with delicious fruit. Of the whites a Pucelle is full and stylish, with a slightly floral, exotic character, while the Grésigny is more structured and minerally. Red Chaponnières has an enticing perfume and good depth but not the extra weight or class of Les Cloux. These delightful but not simple wines are also affordable, though due to a long-established reputation are not always that easy to find. Another white Rully, Raclot, is now also made, as is a rare, decent example of Bourgogne Passetoutgrains. (PW)

O **Rully** I er Cru Grésigny★★ £C I er Cru La Pucelle★★★ £C O **Bourgogne** Aligoté★ £B
● **Rully** Chaponnières★★ £C I er Cru Les Cloux★★ £C
● **Mercurey** I er Cru Les Naugues★★ £C

LOUIS JADOT Beaune www.louisjadot.com A: HMA, AAA

Owner: Kopf family 21 Rue Eugène Spuller, BP 117, 21203 Beaune
Under the direction of André Gagey, and more recently his son Pierre-Henry, and the winemaking mastery of Jacques Lardière, this giant (by Burgundian, not international standards) has made Burgundy of the highest order. Around half of the 144 ha is in the Côte d'Or, the rest in Beaujolais (see CHÂTEAU DES JACQUES). As well as a string of *grands crus*, there are many of the leading *premiers crus* and most of the top wines come from their own vineyards, comprising five separate domaines. The Domaine des Héritiers Louis Jadot provides Corton, Corton-Charlemagne and Chevalier-Montrachet *grands crus* and other important Côte de Beaune *premiers crus*. Domaine Louis Jadot includes the superb Côte de Nuits *grands crus* and

premiers crus, much of it from the original Clair-Däu domaine. Domaines André Gagey, Robert Tourlière and Duc de Magenta add further riches. The key is the know-how that ensures the highest possible quality from a diverse range of sources (including every village in the Côte d'Or) in every vintage, and the expert organisation of logistics. Destemming, a pre-fermentation maceration, high fermentation temperatures and long *cuvaisons* are important features of the red wine vinification. New oak, where it is used (up to 30 per cent), never takes on more than a supporting role. A flexibile, responsive but generally non-interventionist approach can similarly seen in the white winemaking. Reds nearly always have good colour, excellent breadth and depth and plenty of structure but also marvellous concentration, complexity and class in the top wines. Not every bottle is a great one but most will provide a very good example of its appellation and if your only experience of Jadot is one of the humble generics then try one of the many fine domaine wines listed below. There are also several other outstanding wines, including whites Bâtard-Montrachet, Bienvenues-Bâtard-Montrachet and Le Montrachet. (PW)

● **Musigny**✪✪✪✪✪ £H ● **Bonnes Mares**✪✪✪✪✪ £H ● **Chambertin Clos de Bèze**✪✪✪✪✪ £H
● **Clos Saint-Denis**★★★★ £G ● **Chapelle-Chambertin**★★★★ £G
● **Clos de Vougeot**★★★★ £G ● **Echezeaux**★★★★ £H
● **Gevrey-Chambertin** 1er Cru Clos Saint-Jacques✪✪✪✪✪£F
● **Gevrey-Chambertin** 1er Cru Estournelles-Saint-Jacques★★★★★ £F
● **Gevrey-Chambertin** 1er Cru Cazetiers★★★★ £F 1er Cru Lavaux-Saint-Jacques★★★★★ £F
● **Chambolle-Musigny** 1er Cru Les Baudes★★★ £F 1er Cru Les Amoureuses★★★★ £F
● **Nuits-Saint-Georges** 1er Cru Boudots★★★★ £F ● **Corton** Pougets★★★★ £F
● **Beaune** 1er Cru Clos de Couchereaux★★★ £E 1er Cru Clos des Ursules★★★ £E
● **Beaune** 1er Cru Cent Vignes★★★ £E ● **Beaune** 1er Cru Teurons★★★ £E
● **Beaune** 1er Cru Avaux★★★ £E 1er Cru Bressandes★★★ £E 1er Cru Grèves★★★ £E
● **Savigny-lès-Beaune** 1er Cru La Dominode★★★ £D ● **Santenay** Clos de Malte★★ £D
○ **Chevalier-Montrachet** Les Demoiselles✪✪✪✪ £H **Corton-Charlemagne**✪✪✪✪✪ £G
○ **Puligny-Montrachet** 1er Cru Champ Gain★★★ £G 1er Cru Les Folatières★★★★ £G
○ **Beaune** Grèves★★ £E ○ **Santenay** Clos de la Malte★★ £D ○ **Marsannay**★ £C

Duc de Magenta:
○ **Puligny-Montrachet** 1er Cru Clos de la Garenne★★★★ £G
○ **Chassagne-Montrachet** Morgeots Clos de la Chapelle★★★★ £G

PATRICK JAVILLIER Meursault   A: BBR, Res, L&W, OWL, Sel, N&P

Owner: Patrick Javillier 7 Impasse des Acacias, 21190 Meursault

Patrick Javillier produces a range of fine village Meursaults and bottles individually several different *lieux-dits*. The best of these actually taste like *premiers crus* and certainly offer better value than a top site from an underperforming producer. The wines are rich and ripe, with surprising class and depth for their origins. Though they can occasionally tend to be a bit too broad and slightly clumsy, Les Clous, Les Tillets and Les Narvaux always show a little more verve and racy minerality. Tête de Murgers is the richest, deepest and most complex of all. Two Bourgogne Blancs are also treated like Meursault – which the richer, more structured of the two, Cuvée Oligocène, effectively is. A village-level Puligny-Montrachet, in contrast, shows more of a Puligny style, with more finesse and delineation, if less character, than the Meursaults. There's good white Savigny-lès-Beaune, too. All the whites are now being vinified in two different ways before being blended back together prior to bottling. A little *grand cru* Corton-Charlemagne has been made since the 1999 vintage and a tiny amount of *premier cru* Meursault Charmes might also be found. An increasing amount of red is also being produced; Savigny-lès-Beaune Grand Liards and *premier cru* Serpentières are reasonable examples of their appellation. (PW)

○ **Corton-Charlemagne**★★★★★ £G
○ **Meursault** Tête de Murgers★★★★ £F Les Tillets★★★★ £E
○ **Meursault** Clos du Cromin★★★ £E Les Clous★★★ £E Les Narvaux★★★ £E
○ **Puligny-Montrachet** Levrons★★★ £E ○ **Savigny-lès-Beaune** Montchevenoy★★★ £D
● **Bourgogne Blanc** Cuvée des Forges★★ £C Cuvée Oligocène★★★ £C

FRANÇOIS JOBARD   Meursault   A: RsW, A&B, Rae, Hrd, Sec

Owner: François Jobard 2 Rue de Leignon, 21190 Meursault

François Jobard makes somewhat tighter, more traditional wines than his nephew, Rémi JOBARD. Low yields are achieved through rigorous pruning, while vinification is a relatively hands-off affair. While favouring long oak-ageing with extended lees contact, the percentage of new wood is kept low. A rather old-fashioned, heavy sulphur treatment can show in the wines when tasted young but they are meant to be aged. More austere and minerally but with underlying intensity when young, a deep, ripe, leesy nuttiness and flavour complexity develops with extended cellaring. In general the Blagny is usually deep and minerally, Poruzots is also minerally but peachier, Genevrières the more honeyed and the Charmes the most refined. The Meursaults, particularly the *premiers crus,* deserve at least five years' ageing but even the Bourgogne Blanc needs three or more. A little Puligny-Montrachet and some red Blagny are also made. (PW)

O **Meursault** 1er Cru Charmes★★★★ £F   1er Cru Genevrières★★★★ £F   1er Cru Poruzots★★★★ £F
O **Meursault** En la Barre★★★ £E   1er Cru Blagny★★★ £F   O **Bourgogne Blanc**★★ £C

RÉMI JOBARD   Meursault   A: L&S

Owner: Rémi Jobard 12 Rue Sudot, 21190 Meursault

Rémi Jobard has assumed the responsibility of running this 8-ha estate from his father, Charles (brother of François JOBARD). These are rich, ripe concentrated Meursaults with good depth and balance. The three *premiers crus* show more class and length but there is good style, too, in the village bottlings, even if the Sous la Velle and Chevalière tend to be broader and slightly heavy in warm years. The Charmes is consistently the finest Meursault with superb fruit, excellent balance and a long, intense finish. The most recent vintages, benefitting from later bottling after being refreshed in tank, show increasing finesse. Despite having so many different *cuvées* of Meursault, only around half the estate is planted to Chardonnay. Inexpensive Bourgogne Aligoté is regularly made and from 2.5 ha of Pinot Noir there is good Bourgogne Rouge and some Monthelie and Volnay Santenots. (PW)

O **Meursault** 1er Cru Charmes★★★★ £F   1er Cru Genevrières★★★★ £F
O **Meursault** En Luraule★★★ £E   1er Cru Poruzots-Dessus★★★★ £F
O **Meursault** Sous la Velle★★ £D   Chevalière★★★ £E   O **Bourgogne Blanc**★ £C

DOM. MICHEL JUILLOT   Mercurey   www.domaine-michel-juillot.fr   A: DDr, HHB

Owner: Juillot family 59 Grande Rue, BP 10, 71640 Mercurey

The Juillot vineyards comprise 21 ha of Pinot Noir and 9 ha of Chardonnay. Laurent Juillot has taken over from his father and there are some very attractive whites and excellent reds, including four *premiers crus* culminating in the well-sited Clos des Barraults. The latter is the most forbidding and structured red but all reveal good depth and richness with three years' age or more. Both pumping over and punching down are employed, no doubt contributing to some youthful austerity. As well as the reds listed below, some Combins and a few magnums of the highly regarded Clos du Roi (both *premiers crus*) are also made. Other than Mercurey, a little of the *grands crus* Corton Perrières (red) and Corton-Charlemagne together with some village-level Aloxe-Corton are produced. (PW)

● **Mercurey** 1er Cru Clos des Barraults★★ £D   1er Cru Champs-Martin★★ £D
● **Mercurey**★ £B   1er Cru Clos Tonnerre★★ £C   O **Mercurey** 1er Cru Clos des Barraults★★ £D
O **Mercurey** 1er Cru Clos des Barraults★★ £D   1er Cru Champs-Martin★★ £D
O **Mercurey**★ £B   1er Cru En Sazenay★ £C

MICHEL LAFARGE   Volnay   A: BBR GFy, Gau, HRp, Sec

Owner: Lafarge family Domaine Michel Lafarge, 21190 Volnay

Michel and his son Frédéric have an excellent and deserved reputation for Volnay and are as good a source of fine Côte de Beaune reds as anybody. The domaine is now farmed biodynamically and relatively old vines that give lowish yields are picked at full physiological ripeness to provide the fine raw materials, while care and consideration is evident at every step of the winemaking process. There is much experience to draw on in order to adapt to the particular conditions of each vintage. The wines are elegant and sophisticated, with magical aromas and superb fruit together with good structure and concentration; and vintages like 1993, 96, 99 or 02 show added intensity and concentration. Most of the wines can be drunk fairly young but will only really start to open out after five years or more; in the case of the Clos des Chênes this is a minimum. Otherwise some of the class and complexity is tantalising but remains partially hidden. A Lafarge bottle always delivers fine quality wine that is balanced and complete and a lovely expression of where it comes from. Only 8 ha of a total of 10 is planted to Pinot Noir and some Meursault is made. There's also a little Pommard Premier Cru Pézerolles. New is a small amount of Volnay Premier Cru Caillerets, which was purchased by Frédéric. Bourgogne Rouge is always a fine example. (PW)

● **Volnay** 1er Cru Clos du Château des Ducs★★★★ £F   1er Cru Clos des Chênes★★★★★ £F
● **Volnay**★★★ £E Vendange Sélectionée★★★ £E   1er Cru★★★★ £F   1er Cru Caillerets★★★★ £F
● **Beaune** 1er Cru Grèves★★★ £F ● **Côte de Beaune-Villages**★★ £C
● **Bourgogne Rouge**★★ £C

DOM. DES COMTES LAFON   Meursault   A: Adm, M&V, BBR, JAr, Far, F&M

Owner: Lafon family   Clos de la Barre, 21190 Meursault
The finest domaine in Meursault and one of the very best in the Côte d'Or, with some excellent Volnay as well as outstanding Meursault. Dominique Lafon has had the mastery of this 14-ha estate for two decades now and in recent years has converted its viticulture to a biodynamic regime. In the Meursault *premiers crus* the fruit is intense, rich and pure and encased in a precise but seamless structure. An opulent Gouttes d'Or, wonderfully expressive Charmes and remarkably profound Genevrières are only surpassed by a peerless Perrières. Yet even the village wines, such as the Clos de la Barre, show good dimension and a touch of class. The fine Volnays are crowned by a rich Santenots du Milieu, with great finesse and length. The acclaim for these wines adds a premium and they need to be bought before changing hands too many times if prices are to be remotely proportionate to their quality. Most expensive, from just a few barrels, is a Montrachet of exalted reputation. A little Puligny-Montrachet Premier Cru Champ Gain is also made and some very good wines are now being produced in the Mâconnais under the Domaine des HERITIERS COMTES LAFON. (PW)

O **Meursault** 1er Cru Perrières❂❂❂❂❂ £G   1er Cru Charmes★★★★★ £G
O **Meursault** 1er Cru Goutte d'Or★★★★ £G   1er Cru Genevrières★★★★★ £G
O **Meursault**★★★ £E Désirée★★★ £F Clos de la Barre★★★ £F
● **Volnay** 1er Cru Clos des Chênes★★★★ £E   1er Cru Santenots du Milieu★★★★★ £F
● **Volnay**★★★ £E   1er Cru Champans★★★★ £E ● **Monthelie** 1er Cru Les Duresses★★★ £D

FRANÇOIS LAMARCHE   www.domaine-lamarche.com   A: Col, Rae, RsW ,Sec

Owner: Lamarche family   9 Rue des Communes, 21700 Vosne-Romanée
Only recently much improved, this estate has some prized possessions in its patchwork of 10 ha, including all 1.65 ha of that wedge of *grand cru*, La Grande Rue, lying between La Tâche and La Romanée-Conti. The wines previously showed a certain finesse but missed their real potential but have become more concentrated and classy under François's direction. Yields have been reduced, the grapes are now fully destemmed and up to 60 per cent new oak is used but the wines still start out quite tight and tannic and this noble but at times slightly austere style demands patience. Deep and intense, La Croix Rameau and Malconsorts are arguably the finest Vosne *premiers crus*, which is reflected in their marginally higher prices. Yet there are currently even better examples of most of the *crus* to be had from other producers. La Grande Rue however, is not only unique but very fine indeed. In addition to the three other *grands crus*, a small amount of Grands-Echezeaux is made. Only the most recent vintages should be bought for cellaring. A decent example of inexpensive Hautes-Côtes de Nuits red can be found here too. (PW)

● **La Grande Rue**❂❂❂❂❂ £G ● **Echezeaux**★★★★ £F ● **Clos de Vougeot**★★★★ £F
● **Vosne-Romanée** 1er Cru La Croix Rameau★★★★ £E   1er Cru Malconsorts★★★★ £F
● **Vosne-Romanée**★★ £E   1er Cru Chaumes★★★ £E   1er Cru Les Suchots★★★★ £E

DOM. DES LAMBRAYS Morey-Saint-Denis   A: OWL, HRp, BBR, HHC, Res, Sel

Owner: Freund family 31 Rue Basse, 21220 Morey-Saint-Denis

The historic 8.8-ha Clos des Lambrays is almost entirely owned by Gunter Freund and, though relatively small, it is certainly a big chunk of *grand cru* under single ownership. After years of neglect, the Clos was partially replanted in 1981 and around the same time upgraded from *premier cru* to *grand cru*. Much effort and expense was poured into the estate under the guidance of winemaker Thierry Brouin, whose efforts have only really paid full dividends since 1996, coinciding with the most recent change of ownership. The wine is seductively plump and silky but with terrific class and complexity too, softer than adjoining Clos de Tart or indeed Bonnes Mares or Chambertin yet of true *grand cru* status. Morey-Saint-Denis (both in a village-level and a *premier cru* Les Loups bottling) shares the delicious fruit and superfine tannins if missing the depth and dimension of the *grand cru*. Small quantities of two very exciting whites are made from a few rows in top Puligny *premiers crus*. They have a depth, weight and structure allied to class, particularly the Clos du Cailleret which comes from a plot behind Les Pucelles adjoining Le Montrachet. (PW)

● **Clos des Lambrays**★★★★★ £F ● **Morey-Saint-Denis**★★★ £E 1er Cru Les Loups★★★★ £E
○ **Puligny-Montrachet** 1er Cru Clos du Cailleret★★★★★ £F 1er Cru Les Folatières★★★★ £F

HUBERT LAMY Saint-Aubin   A: BBR, DDr, HHB, L&S, L&W

Owner: Lamy family Le Paradis, 21190 Saint-Aubin

This is another estate where the input of a new generation has had a positive impact on quality. Already good Saint-Aubin whites have been honed into ripe, rich and stylish examples under the winemaking expertise of Hubert Lamy's son, Olivier. Only 5 of the 16.5 ha of vineyard are planted to Pinot Noir but the reds are increasingly ripe and concentrated too, especially from good years like 1999 or 02. This is a good source of both red and white Burgundy without silly prices. The bottling of Puligny, Les Tremblots, for instance, could pass for a *premier cru* wine. A very small amount of Criots-Bâtard-Montrachet is also made. (PW)

○ **Chassagne-Montrachet** 1er Cru Macherelles★★★ £F ○ **Puligny-Montrachet** Les Tremblots★★★ £E
○ **Saint-Aubin** 1er Cru En Remilly★★★ £D 1er Cru Murgers Dents de Chien★★★ £D
○ **Saint-Aubin** Princée★★ £C 1er Cru Les Frionnes★★★ £C 1er Cru Clos de la Chatenière★★★ £D
○ **Bourgogne Blanc**★★ £B
● **Saint-Aubin** 1er Cru Les Castets ★★ £C 1er Cru Derrière Chez Edouard★★★ £C
● **Chassagne-Montrachet** Goujonne Vieilles Vignes★★ £C

LOUIS LATOUR www.louislatour.com   A: LLt, Hay, BBR, C&R, MCW, F&M, Maj

Owner: Latour family 18 Rue des Tonneliers, 21200 Beaune

With an annual production of 5.5 million bottles, this historic Burgundy house (and domaine of 50 ha) is one of the most widely seen labels outside of France. Not only are wines made from Chablis down through the Côte d'Or to the Chalonnaise, Mâconnais and Beaujolais, but beyond into the Ardèche and the Var. The continued use of flash-pasteurisation for the red wines (in order to kill bacteria) and filtration remain the most controversial aspects of their production. In addition a short *cuvaison* (8 to 10 days) has long been favoured – in search of greater finesse it is argued – but too often the reds lack vigour, depth and vibrancy as well as the flavour amplitude they surely otherwise have the potential for. White grapes are harvested late for optimum ripeness, yields are low and plenty of new oak is used in their *élevage*. While generally better quality and value can be found elsewhere, some of the top *crus* (including all six white *grands crus*) can be astonishingly good, with great concentration, complexity and power. A selection of the best white wines is listed below. (PW)

○ **Bâtard-Montrachet**★★★★ £H ○ **Chevalier-Montrachet** Demoiselles★★★★ £H
○ **Corton-Charlemagne**★★★★ £G
○ **Meursault** 1er Cru Château de Blagny★★★ £E 1er Cru Goutte d'Or★★★ £E
○ **Puligny-Montrachet** 1er Cru Folatières★★ £E 1er Cru Truffières★★★ £E
○ **Chassagne-Montrachet** 1er Cru Morgeot★★ £E

LATOUR-GIRAUD Meursault   A: Bib, THt

Owner: Jean-Pierre Latour 21190 Meursault

This previously underperforming domaine is now making whites of a quality expected of its impressive holdings. Of 10 ha, 8 ha planted to Chardonnay, arguably the most prized is that of a large, 2.4 ha section of Genevrières. Recent vintages show great class and an elegant and intense expression that is true to its origins. Both this and the tiny production of a minerally Perrières shouldn't be rushed; the depth and intensity will slowly unfurl with up to 10 years' ageing. As well as some fine Charmes, two other *premiers crus*, Bouchères and Poruzots, are also made but there's also fine quality in Le Limozin and Cuvée Charles Maxine, which both give classic Meursault style and richness with less age and at a more affordable price. Besides a little Puligny some red is made, mostly from Maranges. (PW)

O **Meursault** 1er Cru Genevrières★★★★★ £F   1er Cru Perrières★★★★★ £F
O **Meursault** 1er Cru Charmes★★★★ £F   Charles Maxime★★★ £E   Le Limozin★★★ £E
O **Puligny-Montrachet** Champs Canet★★★★ £F

DOMINIQUE LAURENT Nuits-Saint-Georges   A: Far, HBJ, N&P, HRp, Hrd

Owner: Dominique Laurent 2 Rue Jacques-Duret, 21700 Nuits-Saint-Georges

Ex-pastry chef Dominique Laurent buys only the best small lots of young red wine made from old low-yielding vines, ages them himself, then sells the many individual *cuvées* for very high prices. His considerable following in both France and other premium wine markets stems in part from the support of Michel Bettane and *La Revue du Vin de France*. The wines are typically big, powerful and very concentrated, with lots of extract and tannin. Oak, and lots of it, was an early theme, resulting in some excessively oaky wines, though this is much less common in more recent releases. Now, in the same way that pastries can be butter-rich, many of the wines can be oak-rich (but without compromising the wine's structure with excessive oak tannins as is typical in a badly wooded wine) with the requisite balance of fruit richness and extract that is enriched and enhanced by the oak, resulting in a succulent creaminess. Quality is generally very high indeed but rare lapses can result in rather tough, chewy wines. Thanks, though, to the high prices obtained for other wines, even these can be declassified. Though all the wines are bought in, many of the exact same parcels can be acquired year after year. Some of the wines made fairly regularly include: (*grands crus*) Chambertin Clos de Bèze, Mazis-Chambertin, Le Musigny, Bonnes Mares, Clos de la Roche and Clos de Vougeot; (*premiers crus*) Vosne-Romanée Beaux Monts and Suchots, Chambolle-Musigny Charmes, Gevrey-Chambertin Clos Saint-Jacques, Nuits-Saint-Georges Les Saint-Georges, Vaucrains and Richemone, Volnay Clos des Chênes, Pommard Epenots, Beaune 1er Cru and Grèves as well as some excellent village examples designated Vieilles Vignes. If you like vibrant, rich, oaky Burgundy with often remarkable depth, length and intensity, never turn down the chance to taste any of the many varied offerings. Dominique applies some of the same methods in both the northern and southern Rhône (and beyond) where with Michel Tardieu he turns out small-volume, high-priced *cuvées* under the TARDIEU-LAURENT label. (PW)

OLIVIER LEFLAIVE Puligny-Montrachet www.olivier-leflaive.com   A: C&B, HHC, L&W, WSc

Owner: Olivier Leflaive (& others) Place du Monument 21190 Puligny-Montrachet

Olivier Leflaive set up this merchant house in 1984 and continued to co-manage the family domaine (Domaine Leflaive) until 1994. The company now has a small 12-ha domaine of its own, though the lion's share of production (three-quarters of a million bottles) is made from bought-in grapes. Franck Grux, the winemaker for more than a decade, has provided a largely consistent and sometimes enviable range of white Burgundy. Leading *premiers crus* from Puligny-Montrachet, Chassagne-Montrachet and Meursault can be good if a little variable. In addition, examples of all six Côte de Beaune *grands crus* are made, including very fine Criots-Bâtard-Montrachet and Le Montrachet. If at a lower level the wines can be a little dull, occasionally even dilute in a lesser vintage, the Côte Chalonnaise whites, Rully and Montagny, can be also be very good. A increasing amount of fine Chablis is being made, including a range of fine *premiers crus*. While more than 90 per cent of production is white, a relatively small range of reds is also made. The best, mostly Pommard and Volnays, are quite structured, with appreciable oak, but have the depth and richness to be very satisfying with five years' age or more. Bourgogne Blanc Les Sétilles is usually a good example of everyday white Burgundy. Listed are only some of the best wines that are regularly made. Franck Grux also makes some good Meursault Meix Chavaux under his own label. (PW)

O **Montrachet**✪✪✪✪✪ £H   O **Criots-Bâtard-Montrachet**★★★★★ £G

O **Puligny-Montrachet** 1er Cru Champ Canet★★★ £F   1er Cru Pucelles★★★★ £F

O **Puligny-Montrachet** 1er Cru Champs Gain★★★ £F   1er Cru Les Referts★★★ £F

O **Chassagne-Montrachet** 1er Cru Les Chaumées★★★ £E   1er Cru Abbaye de Morgeot★★★ £F

O **Meursault** Narvaux★★ £E   1er Cru Poruzots★★★ £F   1er Cru Perrières★★★★ £F

O **Chablis Premier Cru** Fourchaumes★★★ £D   Montée de Tonnerre★★★ £D   Vaillons★★★ £D

O **Saint-Aubin** 1er Cru Les Perrières★ £C   1er Cru En Remilly★★ £D

O **Rully** 1er Cru★ £C   1er Cru Les Clous★★ £C   1er Cru Rabourcé★★ £C

O **Montagny** 1er Cru★ £B   1er Cru Bonneveaux★★ £C

● **Volnay**★★ £D   1er Cru Clos des Angles★★★ £E   1er Cru Champans★★★ £E   1er Cru Santenots★★★ £E

● **Pommard**★★ £D   1er Cru Charmots★★★ £E   1er Cru Rugiens★★★ £E

● **Aloxe-Corton**★★ £D   ● **Santenay**★★ £C

DOM. LEFLAIVE   Puligny-Montrachet   www.leflaive.fr   A: JAr, BBR, Goe, L&W, HRp, Tan, Hrd

Owner: Leflaive family   Place des Marronniers, 21190 Puligny-Montrachet
Under the direction of Vincent Leflaive this estate gained a fabulous reputation during the 1960s and 70s, so much so that the wines have been both sought-after and very expensive for as long as many wine enthusiasts can remember. Under the direction of his daughter Anne-Claude, who initially worked with her cousin Olivier (dedicated to his own business OLIVIER LEFLAIVE since 1994), the unsurpassed holding of prime white Burgundy vineyard has become progressively biodynamic, totally so since 1998. Of the 23.5 ha, 11.5 ha are of *premiers crus*, 5 ha of *grands crus*, including nearly 2 ha each of Chevalier-Montrachet and Bâtard-Montrachet. Pierre Morey has made the wines in recent years and brought to an end some of the criticism directed at wines from vintages between the mid-1980s and early 90s, when yields were high and the wines' considerable reputation for ageing was tarnished. With the balance and the health of the vineyards now paramount, wines from recent vintages look set to rival past glories. No end of descriptions of flavour nuances can do them justice. The wines have wonderful purity and clarity, great concentration and intensity but almost perfect precision and poise, together with compelling complexity, dimension and length in the *grands crus*. (PW)

O **Le Montrachet**✪✪✪✪✪ £H   O **Chevalier-Montrachet**✪✪✪✪✪ £H

O **Bienvenues-Bâtard-Montrachet**✪✪✪✪✪ £H   O **Bâtard-Montrachet**✪✪✪✪✪ £H

O **Puligny-Montrachet** 1er Cru Les Pucelles★★★★★ £G   1er Cru Les Combottes★★★★★ £G

O **Puligny-Montrachet**★★★ £F   1er Cru Clavoillon★★★★ £F   1er Cru Les Folatières★★★★ £G

O **Bourgogne** Blanc★★ £D

DOM. LEROY   www.domaineleroy.com   A: JAr, BBR, C&R, Far, HRp, Sec, F&R

Owner: Leroy and Bize families   Rue du Pont-Boillot, 21190 Auxey-Duresses
Madame Lalou Bize-Leroy, one of the most formidable and dynamic wine personalities on the planet, directs one of Burgundy's most prestigious domaines. Built around the former Domaine Charles Noëllat (Vosne-Romanée) purchased in 1988, it now boasts 22 ha of some of the finest *crus* in the Côte d'Or. Lalou Bize has championed the cause of biodynamic viticulture and has built a domaine to rival the Domaine de la ROMANÉE-CONTI, which she co-managed until 1993. In terms of out and out quality there is arguably no finer estate. Yields are tiny (20–24 hl/ha is typical), and in common with Romanée-Conti there is no destemming, long *cuvaisons* and more than enough new oak to keep the *tonnelier* (barrelmaking) firms happy. The wines are distinguished by quite staggering concentration and richness, in some instances with almost overwhelming extract and structure, as well as great intensity, depth and length. Every wine needs the best part of a decade's age and they usually have the balance to keep for much longer. Due to insufficient repeated tastings of the wines they have not been rated individually but as an indication of their ratings

generally the *grands crus* (eight red and one white) are five stars, leading *premiers crus* four or five stars, and others at least three stars. Reds include: (*grands crus*) Chambertin, Latricières-Chambertin, Clos de la Roche, Musigny, Clos de Vougeot, Richebourg, Romanée-Saint-Vivant and Corton Renardes; (*premiers crus*) Gevrey-Chambertin Combottes, Chambolle-Musigny Charmes, Vosne-Romanée Aux Brulées and Beaux Monts, Nuits-Saint-Georges Boudots and Vignerondes, Volnay Santenots and Savigny-lès-Beaune Narbantons; (village-level) Chambolle-Musigny Fremières, Vosne-Romanée Genevrières, Nuits-Saint-Georges Au Bas du Combe, Aux Allots and Lavières and Pommard Les Vignots. The only white is some Corton-Charlemagne. Bize-Leroy's own domaine is Domaine D'AUVENAY, while Leroy SA is the *négociant* and distribution operation. (PW)

HUBERT LIGNIER   Morey-Saint-Denis   A: RRI, Eno, C&R, Far

Owner: Hubert Lignier   45 Grande Rue, 21220 Morey-Saint-Denis
Romain Lignier, Hubert's son, has gradually honed the quality of his family's wines over the last decade. Almost 8 ha include a decent amount of Clos de la Roche and five *premier cru* bottlings. There is also a tiny amount of Charmes Chambertin. Moderately low yields are maintained and good extraction is favoured; Romain aids the *pigéage* by entering the vats himself and physically agitating the grapes and pulp in what seems to be a family proclivity. The wines can start off quite tight but have real depth and intensity that more than covers their fine but abundant tannin. The wines don't lack for oak, particularly the Combottes, but this is generally better integrated than previously. The *premiers crus* are markedly more expensive than the village wines but this is where the real quality kicks in. The excellent Morey-Saint-Denis Premier Cru Vieilles Vignes combines the *crus* of Faconnières and Chenevery and is a little bolder and deeper than the other two Morey *premiers crus*. Chambolle-Musigny is the best of the three village-level wines. (PW)

- ● **Clos de la Roche**✪✪✪✪✪ £H
- ● **Morey-Saint-Denis** ler Cru La Riotte★★★ £F   ler Cru Vieilles Vignes★★★★ £F
- ● **Morey-Saint-Denis**★★ £E   ler Cru Les Chaffots★★★ £F   ler Cru Vieilles Vignes★★★★ £F
- ● **Gevrey-Chambertin**★★ £E   ler Cru Les Combottes★★★ £G
- ● **Chambolle-Musigny**★★★ £E   ler Cru Les Baudes★★★ £F

FRANÇOIS LUMPP   Givry   A: THt, L&S, N&P, JNi, Hrd

Owner: Isabelle & François Lumpp   Le Pied du Clou, 36 Avenue de Mortières, 71640 Givry
One of the best Givry producers (others include Joblot, René Bourgeon and Clos Salomon) with wines to match the best from the other Côte Chalonnaise appellations, too. From just 6.5 ha (5 Pinot Noir) François Lumpp keeps yields low and shows a light hand in the winemaking that results in supple, harmonious and balanced reds, especially with a couple of years' bottle-age. The red from Crausot is particularly impressive. Whites are fine, too, ripe but not overripe, with good intensity and balanced acidities and an elegant minerality in the Petite Marole. (PW)

- O **Givry** ler Cru Petit Marole★★★ £C   Clos des Vignes Rondes★★ £C   ler Cru Crausot★★ £C
- ● **Givry** ler Cru Clos du Gras Long★★ £C   ler Cru Clos Jus★★ £C   ler Cru Crausot★★★ £C
- ● **Givry** Pied du Clou★★ £C   ler Cru Petite Marole★★ £C

DOM. MICHEL MAGNIEN ET FILS   Morey-Saint-Denis   A: JAr

Owner: Michel & Frédéric Magnien   4 Rue Ribordot, 21200 Morey-Saint-Denis
Frédéric Magnien works with his father to make the wines on the family domaine but also makes a large number of *négociant* wines under his own label. The 11-ha domaine includes some excellent sites, mostly in the communes of Morey-Saint-Denis and Gevrey-Chambertin but they have only been bottling all of their production since 1994. The Magnien style is for richness and extract combined with lots of new oak. The wines are succulent, fleshy and richly fruity, with fine ripe tannins, at least in the best years. A lighter hand is needed in merely good years to avoid overly tannic, structured wines. The 1997s and 98s are not likely to be encountered due to their withdrawal following a bacterial contamination in the new cellars. With their

own premises sealed off, Frédéric was fortunate to be offered winemaking facilities *chez* DUJAC in 1999. The resulting wines show a lot of new oak but have the fruit to match. While the top reds will keep, the hedonistic pleasure that just five or six years' age brings, will sway many wine drinkers. The balance in the 2000s and 01s is less satisfactory and shows a marked contrast though the style is more likely to work in 02. A little Charmes-Chambertin and other Morey-Saint-Denis are also made. (PW)

Domaine Michel Magnien et Fils:
- **Clos de la Roche**★★★ £F ● **Clos Saint-Denis**★★★★ £G
- **Gevrey-Chambertin** Seuvrées★★★ £E Aux Echezeaux★★★ £E 1er Cru Les Cazetiers★★★ £F
- **Morey-Saint-Denis** 1er Cru Aux Charmes★★★ £E 1er Cru Les Milandes★★★ £E
- **Morey-Saint-Denis** Mont Luisants★★★ £E 1er Cru Les Chaffots★★★★ £E

DOM. MATROT Meursault   A: C&B, BBR, Gau, GFy, Con, T&W

Owner: Matrot family   12 Rue de Matray, 21190 Meursault
Thierry Matrot is a devoted *vigneron*, bestowing great care on his vines, ensuring low yields and harvesting as late as possible. He is not a huge fan of new oak and is not an advocate of *bâtonnage* but produces rich, powerful and structured whites, sometimes with more than a hint of sulphur when young. The wines can seem a little awkward at first, but all the *premiers crus* should have a minimum of five years' age before they are ready. Amongst the reds, both Volnay Santenots and Blagny are ripe, long and quite classy. The shape of this domaine is evolving as another Matrot estate, that of Thierry's sister, comes into existence. Domaine wines now appear under any of either of two labels (Pierre Matrot or Thierry Matrot). (PW)

O **Meursault** 1er Cru Perrières★★★★★ £F 1er Cru Blagny★★★★ £E 1er Cru Charmes★★★★ £F
O **Meursault**★★★ £E Chevalière★★★ £E
O **Puligny-Montrachet** 1er Cru Les Chalumeaux★★★★ £F 1er Cru Les Combettes★★★★ £F
● **Blagny** 1er Cru La Pièce sous le Bois★★★ £E ● **Volnay** 1er Cru Santenots★★★★ £E

MÉO-CAMUZET www.meo-camuzet.com   A: BBR, Fie, RsW, N&P, F&M, F&R

Owner: Jean Méo   11 Rue des Grands Crus, 21700 Vosne-Romanée
One of Burgundy's great 20th-century winemakers, Henri Jayer, made the wines from this Domaine between 1945 and 1988. The rich legacy of prime vineyards that belonged to Étienne Camuzet provided Jayer with the opportunity to make some magnificent wines both for himself and others. The Méo-Camuzet label has only been around since the 1980s but most of that Camuzet legacy is now in the hands of the current generation, who have built up the holdings to 15 ha. Jean-Nicolas Méo, son of Jean Méo, continues with the Jayer method, including total destemming, cold pre-fermentation maceration and an extended *cuvaison* and 100 per cent new oak. The new oak is nearly always in evidence but there is a polish and a completeness that is the hallmark of these wines. At a lower level there is not the purity or intensity of others, especially at comparable prices, but the Cros Parentoux and Richebourg and increasingly the Corton and Echezeaux are very classy, very exciting wines. They have always been expensive and as good as some of them are, there's better value to be had. (PW)

● **Richebourg**✪✪✪✪✪ £H ● **Clos de Vougeot**★★★★ £H ● **Echezeaux**★★★★ £H
● **Corton**★★★★ £H ● **Vosne-Romanée** 1er Cru Cros Parentoux★★★★★ £H
● **Vosne-Romanée**★★★ £F 1er Cru Les Chaumes★★★ £G 1er Cru Aux Brulées★★★★★ £H
● **Nuits-Saint-Georges**★★★ £F 1er Cru Aux Boudots★★★★ £G 1er Cru Aux Murgers★★★★ £G

FRANÇOIS MIKULSKI Meursault   A: Eno, GFy, Han, N&P, Sec, Blx

Owner: François Mikulski   5 Rue de Leignon, 21190 Meursault
François is one of the newest stars of the Côte de Beaune and makes the sort of wines that get noticed. He has 7 ha and concentrates on Meursault. The wines are ripe and full-bodied and develop a creamy, honeyed richness with even a little age. Most convincing and complete of three *premiers crus* is the Genevrières, which has the structure to match the concentration. Yet a deeply flavoured, citrusy Poruzots and a floral, exotic

old-vine Charmes are in much the same style. A regular Meursault is rich and ripe too but if you find the Meursaults out of reach then there's ripe, fruity Bourgogne Blanc and Aligoté that don't lack for flavour or character. Two reds, a Meursault and a Volnay, are also made but these don't as yet show the flair of the whites. (PW)

O **Meursault**★★★ £E 1er Cru Charmes★★★ £F 1er Cru Genevrières★★★★ £F 1er Cru Poruzots★★★★ £F
O **Bourgogne Blanc**★★ £B O **Bourgogne Aligoté**★ £B

HUBERT DE MONTILLE Volnay   A: HHB, OWL, HRp, CTy, GFy, Sel

Owner: Hubert et Étienne de Montille   Rue de Pied de la Vallée, 21190 Volnay
One of the leading producers of both Volnay and Pommard, Hubert de Montille was well-known for his dislike of high alcohol wines and has always kept chaptalisation to an absolute minimum. He also favoured fermentation at high temperatures and an extended *cuvaison* followed by a low percentage of new oak. The wines? They showed great dimension and depth but also tended to have a lot of extract and tannin, only opening out with 10 years' age, but vintages since 1998 have been made by Hubert's son Étienne. The wines are now a little less formidable, with finer tannin yet without sacrificing their elegance and individuality. They are now also produced biodynamically. Of the Pommards, the Rugiens is that little bit more intense and classy but all three are full and stylish. The Volnays can be a little lighter, though are full and concentrated in a year like 1999 or 02; the Taillepieds reveals great length and finesse. An extremely good Puligny Cailleret, made initially by Jean-Marc ROULOT, is now also made by Étienne. (PW)

● **Pommard** 1er Cru Rugiens★★★★ £F 1er Cru Grands Epenots★★★★ £F 1er Cru Pézerolles★★★★ £F
● **Volnay** 1er Cru Mitans★★★★ £F 1er Cru Taillepieds★★★★★ £F
● **Volnay** 1er Cru★★★ £E 1er Cru Champans★★★★ £F
O **Puligny-Montrachet** 1er Cru Cailleret★★★★★ £F

BERNARD MOREY Chassagne-Montrachet   A: BWC, A&B, Las, DDr, HHB, CTy

Owner: Bernard Morey   21190 Chassagne-Montrachet
Bernard Morey is a true *vigneron* and takes great pride in his vineyards. Vines are replaced individually and propagated from the best old vines rather than bought-in clones. As a result the average vine age is increasingly high as is the health and balance in the vineyards. He also favours late picking and produces ripe, ample and flavoursome whites with well-integrated oak. Of the consistently fine Chassagne-Montrachet, the Vieilles Vignes come from almost 80-year-old vines as does the Vide Bourse and both show very ripe fruit, with lots of depth and richness if not the definition and structure of the Caillerets or Morgeots. A rich powerful, minerally but stylish Puligny La Truffière can be even better. Several other Chassagne-Montrachets (including a good *premier cru* Les Macharelles) are made from grapes purchased as part of the *négociant* side of the business. A little Bâtard-Montrachet is also made. The reds, particularly both Chassagnes, can be good (promising in 2002) but suffered a little at the hands of the elements in 2000 and 01. (PW)

Domaine wines:

O **Chassagne-Montrachet** 1er Cru Caillerets★★★★ £E 1er Cru Morgeot★★★★ £E
O **Chassagne-Montrachet** 1er Cru Embrazées★★★ £E 1er Cru Vide Bourse★★★ £E
O **Chassagne-Montrachet** Vieilles Vignes★★★ £E 1er Cru Baudines★★★ £E
O **Puligny-Montrachet** 1er Cru La Truffière★★★★ £F O **Saint-Aubin** 1er Cru Charmois★★ £C
O **Santenay** 1er Cru Passetemps★★ £D
● **Chassagne-Montrachet** Vieilles Vignes★★ £C 1er Cru Clos Saint-Jean★★★ £D
● **Santenay** Vieilles Vignes★★ £C 1er Cru Passetemps★★ £D Grand Clos Rousseau★★ £D
● **Beaune** 1er Cru Grèves★★★ £E ● **Maranges** 1er Cru La Fuissière★ £C

DOM. MARC MOREY Chassagne-Montrachet   A: HHC, JAr, Gau

Owner: Bernard Mollard   3 Rue Charles Paquelin, 21190 Chassagne-Montrachet
Bernard Mollard, recently joined by his son Jerôme, makes outstanding whites from a small 9.5-ha domaine

that has improved year-on-year under his direction. All the vineyards lie within or close to Chassagne-Montrachet. An excellent, minerally village-level example is structured, with good citrus intensity and can be drunk young or kept for three or four years. The *premiers crus* are all classy, with depth, intensity and fine structure. Les Vergers is tight and minerally in contrast to a more forward, fatter, more obvious Virondot. Cailleret and Morgeot are both rich and concentrated. The top wine is a powerful, classy and complex Bâtard-Montrachet. A very respectable Bourgogne Blanc is always attractive and fruity with decent acidity. Some Saint-Aubin comes from the Les Charmois *premier cru* adjacent to Chassagne-Montrachet. Good Puligny-Montrachet is also made, some Pucelles and Champ-Gain. Prices are reasonable for the quality, with excellent 2002s and 00s but generally very good since 98. A significant amount of red is made too. These are slightly austere when young but, while the regular version can lack for ripeness, Morgeot has attractive red fruit and good breadth. (PW)

O **Bâtard-Montrachet**✪✪✪✪ £G
O **Chassagne-Montrachet** 1er Cru Morgeot★★★★ £E 1er Cru Cailleret★★★★ £E
O **Chassagne-Montrachet** 1er Cru En Virondot★★★ £E 1er Cru Les Vergers★★★★ £E
O **Chassagne-Montrachet**★★★ £E 1er Cru Les Chenevottes★★★ £E
O **Saint-Aubin** 1er Cru Charmois★★★ £E   O **Bourgogne Blanc**★ £B
● **Chassagne-Montrachet** 1er Cru Morgeot★★ £C

PIERRE MOREY/MOREY BLANC   Meursault   A: HRp, L&W, MCW, Res, Tan

Owner: Pierre Morey   13 Rue Pierre Mouchoux, 21190 Meursault
Pierre Morey is one of Burgundy's most highly regarded white winemakers, making the wines for Domaine Leflaive as well as those of his own. He has nearly 3 ha of Pinot Noir as well as 6 for whites, (predominantly Chardonnay but some Aligoté too). The wines build great richness and opulence with age, becoming nutty, buttery and peachy. Of his own estate wines there's intense minerally depth in the Meursault Perrières and indisputable class and complexity in the Bâtard-Montrachet. The wines can have quite a lot of sulphur and are generally quite closed when young. Buy these wines to cellar and give them at least five to six years from a good vintage. Good Bourgogne Blanc and Aligoté are usually better with a couple of years too. Reds include good Pommard Epenots. Morey Blanc is the label for the *négociant* wines, made to the same high standards but from bought-in grapes. (PW)

Pierre Morey:
O **Bâtard-Montrachet**✪✪✪✪✪ £H
O **Meursault**★★★ £E Tessons★★★★ £F 1er Cru Perrières★★★★★ £F
O **Bourgogne Blanc**★★ £B   O **Bourgogne Aligoté**★ £B
Morey Blanc:
O **Meursault**★★★ £E Navaux★★★ £E 1er Cru Genevrières★★★ £E
O **Saint-Aubin** 1er Cru★★ £C

DOM. ALBERT MOROT   Beaune   A: **Hal**, N&P, Res

Owner: Choppin family   Avenue Charles Jaffelin, 21200 Beaune
This 7-ha domaine, based on vineyards acquired in the 1890s, has until very recently been run by Mademoiselle Choppin, whose grandfather Albert Morot ran a *négociant* business. From the beginnning of the new millennium her nephew, Geoffroy Choppin de Janvry, has been in charge. The domaine is unusual in that it produces almost exclusively *premier cru* Beaune from the heart of the richest vein of *crus* on the slopes behind the town. The only exception is a sturdy but concentrated *premier cru* Savigny, with impressive depth and length for the appellation. All the wines see a percentage of new oak after an extended maceration, resulting in wines that can be quite robust and meaty when young but with a great propensity to age, especially in top vintages. All of the wines are of a high standard and all deserve at least five years' cellaring; a rich, concentrated and classy Teurons can be the most satisfying but is at least matched for complexity by an old-vine Bressandes. As well as three other *premiers crus*, a miniscule amount of Grèves is also made. New from the 2001 vintage is some Beaune Les Aigrots (white as well as red), sited closer to Pommard than the

existing *premiers crus.* (PW)

● **Beaune** I er Cru Bressandes★★★★ £E   I er Cru Teurons★★★★ £E   I er Cru Toussaints★★★ £E
● **Beaune** I er Cru Cent Vignes★★★ £E   I er Cru Marconnets★★★ £E   I er Cru Aigrots★★ £E
■ **Savigny-lès-Beaune** I er Cru Bataillère aux Vergelesses★★★ £E

DENIS MORTET   Gevrey-Chambertin   A: BBR, DDr, Sec, WSc, HHB

Owner: Denis Mortet   22 Rue de l'Église, 21220 Gevrey-Chambertin
One of the truly outstanding Gevrey estates, with 11 ha of fine *premiers crus* and some of the best
village *lieux-dits.* Denis Mortet's first vintage under his own name was as recent as 1992, after he and his
brother Thierry (who also makes fine Gevrey and Chambolle-Musigny) split up the former Domaine
Charles Mortet. After a flying start the wines have continued to improve. As with all the best *vignerons,* there
is attention to each and every vine. What matters is the yield and health of each individual plant rather than
an average low yield, which may disguise overbearing vines offset by poorly specimens. Rigorous selection,
total destemming, a pre-fermentation maceration and a long *cuvaison* are important to the style, while the
type and percentage of new oak is carefully adapted to each different *cuvée.* These are marvellously complete
wines, full, ripe and rich and with everything in balance. The one criticism, that the oak and extraction were
slightly overdone, has been countered in the most recent vintages, which show still greater refinement and
harmony. Apart from the regular Gevrey-Chambertin and the Marsannay, all the wines should be drunk
with five years' ageing or more, and closer to 10 from a vintage like 1999 or 02. Newish are a village Gevrey-
Chambertin En Derée from very old vines and a straight Gevrey-Chambetin Premier Cru, a blend of several
small *premiers crus* plots. A touch of reduction can be a problem if the reds are drunk very young. A little
Aligoté and Bourgogne Blanc are also made. (PW)

● **Chambertin**✪✪✪✪✪ £H   ● **Clos de Vougeot**★★★★ £G
● **Gevrey-Chambertin** I er Cru En Champeaux★★★★ £F   I er Cru Lavaux Saint-Jacques★★★★★ £F
● **Gevrey-Chambertin** Au Vellé★★★ £E   En Champs★★★ £E   En Motrot★★★ £E
● **Gevrey-Chambertin**★★★ £E   La Combe de Dessus★★★ £E   En Derée★★★ £E
● **Chambolle-Musigny** I er Cru Beaux Bruns★★★★ £F   ● **Marsannay** Les Longeroies★★ £D
● **Bourgogne Rouge**★★ £C

MUGNERET-GIBOURG/DR GEORGES MUGNERET   A: BWC, HRp, L&S, OWL

Owner: Mugneret family   5 Rue des Communes, 21700 Vosne-Romanée
Sisters Marie-Christine and Marie-Andrée, assisted by their mother, make consistently refined wines from
this 8.8-ha estate. The original vineyards of the property are sold under the Mugneret-Gibourg label while
those acquired by their widely respected late father, Dr Georges Mugneret, are sold under his name. Most
of the vineyards are taken care of by others on a sharecropping basis. The grapes are now fully destemmed
and the wine is given a maceration on the skins both before and after a fermentation at relatively high
temperatures. Up to 80 per cent new oak is used for the *grands crus* each one being made in small quantities,
but all the wines show a measure of oak. They also have a lovely ripe pure Pinot fruit within a firm structure
and there is real class, style and definition to each. The village wines and the elegant, seductive Chambolle-
Musigny need five years, the complex, refined Chaignots and the *grands crus* eight or more. (PW)

● **Clos de Vougeot**★★★★ £F   ● **Ruchottes-Chambertin**★★★★★ £F
● **Echezeaux**★★★★ £F   ● **Vosne-Romanée**★★★ £D
● **Chambolle-Musigny** I er Cru Les Feusselottes★★★★ £E
● **Nuits-Saint-Georges**★★★ £D   I er Cru Les Chaignots★★★★ £E
● **Bourgogne Rouge**★★ £C

JACQUES-FRÉDÉRIC MUGNIER   www.mugnier.fr   A: HHB, HRp, M&V, Sec, Las, F&R

Owner: Jacques-Frédéric Mugnier   Château de Chambolle-Musigny, 21220 Chambolle-Musigny
The early 18th-century Château de Chambolle-Musigny is rather at odds with the style of the wines here.
For me, the architecture of the building pales beside the elegance, finesse even grandeur of these, at times,

sublime wines. Since taking charge in 1984, Frédéric Mugnier has not only refined the practices on this small 4-ha estate (grape quality and selection are paramount and high fermentation temperatures are a feature of the vinification) but he has also pursued his passion for flying as a commercial airline pilot (as an aerial photo on the website shows). Don't come looking for powerful blockbusters; not even the more robust Bonnes Mares, the most sturdy of these wines, offers that. And if it's masses of oak, extract and flesh you want in your glass, then again look elsewhere. Building in richness and complexity with age, these are beautiful wines true to their appellations and with wonderful finesse and harmony. The regular Chambolle-Musigny can sometimes be a little slight but there's a hint of nobility even here. (PW)

● Musigny❋❋❋❋❋ £H ● Bonnes Mares★★★★★ £G
● Chambolle-Musigny★★★ £E 1er Cru Les Fuées★★★★ £F 1er Cru Les Amoureuses★★★★★ £G

MICHEL NIELLON   Chassagne-Montrachet   A: OWL, BBR, RRI, F&R, C&R, Sec

Owner: Niellon family   1 Rue du Nord, 21190 Chassagne-Montrachet
This domaine is remarkably small considering some of the plaudits it has received. The wines are made in quite a reductive manner (with minimal aeration), the oak is restrained and the wines tight and intense when young. The *grands crus* are usually brilliant but the *premiers crus*, while often very good, do not approach the same level in the way that that they do at other estates. At their best there is depth, fine fruit concentration and good style. When tasted young the wines can be a bit reduced but will usually come round with aeration. At any rate all the wines deserve at least five to six years' age. Some Chassagne-Montrachet Premier Cru Vergers used to be made but is currently being replanted. The *grands crus* are very expensive due to their scarcity and reputation; the *premiers crus* can be bought for prices more in line with their quality but don't offer better value than other examples. (PW)

O Chevalier-Montrachet❋❋❋❋❋ £H O Bâtard-Montrachet❋❋❋❋❋ £H
O Chassagne-Montrachet 1er Cru Les Chaumées★★★★ £F 1er Cru Clos de la Maltroie★★★★ £F
O Chassagne-Montrachet★★ £E 1er Cru Clos Saint-Jean★★ £F 1er Cru Champs Gain★★★ £F

JEAN-MARC PAVELOT   Savigny-lès-Beaune   A: DDr, L&W, Res

Owner: Pavelot family   1 Chemin des Guettottes, 21420 Savigny-lès-Beaune
A superior domaine in an appellation with a reputation for providing wines with plenty of fruit and body, though they can also be a bit coarse and simple too. Not so here. Jean-Marc Pavelot has *premiers crus* from Savigny's more northern band, where the wines are generally lighter and more elegant, but also in the southern group of *premiers crus* (nearer Beaune), where the wines are fuller but firmer yet all his wines have a grace and charm that sets them apart. From the northern band both a vigorous Guettes and a seductive Aux Gravains reveal delicious fruit and a stylish complexity with a little age; Narbantons and Peuillets from closer to Beaune are fuller, meatier but less stylish. La Dominode comes from very old vines and is the richest and most complete Savigny. Regular red and white Savigny have ample fruit and good structure and are great drinking with a little bottle-age. The *premiers crus* are capable of ageing for at least 8 to 10 years, though I doubt many are kept that long. Jean-Marc's son, Hughes, is now taking over the winemaking responsibility. (PW)

● Savigny-lès-Beaune 1er Cru La Dominode★★★★ £D
● Savigny-lès-Beaune 1er Cru Aux Gravains★★★ £D 1er Cru Narbantons★★★ £D
● Savigny-lès-Beaune★★ £C 1er Cru Peuillets★★ £D 1er Cru Guettes★★★ £D
● Pernand-Vergelesses 1er Cru Les Vergelesses★★ £C O Savigny-lès-Beaune★★ £C

DOM. PAUL PERNOT ET FILS   Puligny-Montrachet   A: JAr, Bal, L&S, HRp, Las, BWC, Sel

Owner: Pernot family   7 Place du Monument, 21190 Puligny-Montrachet
The owners of this relatively large estate of 19 ha only bottle a portion of the grapes they grow, but it is very good. The remainder must be gratefully received by the merchants. Paul Pernot is assisted by two of his sons and makes concentrated, powerful whites that become increasingly rich and honeyed with age. There's

arguably not the definition or poise of a Domaine Leflaive equivalent but there is wonderful proportion and balance despite the wines' size, and real finesse as well as great complexity in the *premiers* and *grands crus*. Reds have good intensity if not that much refinement. The *grands crus*, though hardly cheap, are better priced than most others and the village Puligny-Montrachet is remarkably good value. (PW)

○ **Bâtard-Montrachet❂❂❂❂❂** £G ○ **Bienvenues-Bâtard-Montrachet❂❂❂❂❂** £G
○ **Puligny-Montrachet★★★** £E 1er Cru Folatières★★★★ £F 1er Cru Les Pucelles★★★★ £F
○ **Bourgogne Blanc★** £C ● **Pommard** Noizons★★ £D ● **Volnay** 1er Cru Carelles★★★ £D
● **Beaune** Clos du Dessus des Marconnets★★ £C 1er Cru Teurons★★ £D 1er Cru Renversées★★ £D

PERROT-MINOT   Morey-Saint-Denis   www.perrot-minot.com   A: BWC, Bal, Blx, F&R, HHB

Owner: Henri Perrot-Minot   54 Route des Grands Crus, 21220 Morey-Saint-Denis
Christophe Perrot works with his father to produce wines less extracted than previously but still with impressive power and intensity. The wines can still be quite austere and firm when young but nearly always have the fruit richness underneath to reveal great style and individuality with seven or eight years' age or more. Though all the wines are true to the general style, they are also true to their appellations and individual *terroirs*. The Chambolle-Musigny Premier Cru La Combe d'Orveau, adjacent to Le Musigny, is arguably the most classy and complex wine of all, though the *grands crus*, particularly the Chambertin, contrast with greater power and structure. The standard of the range is consistently high, with good Bourgogne Rouge at a lower level. The purchase of the Pernin-Rossin domaine in Vosne-Romanée has enlarged the family's holdings to 14 ha. These exciting new wines include some old-vine Nuits-Saint-Georges La Richemone, some Vosne-Romanée Les Beaux-Monts and Gevrey-Chambertin Les Cazetiers. The first releases would seem to have already obtained the same balance, intensity and combination of elegance and vigour seen in the existing wines. (PW)

● **Chambertin★★★★** £G ● **Charmes-Chambertin★★★★** £G ● **Mazoyères-Chambertin★★★★** £G
● **Morey-Saint-Denis** En la Rue de Vergy★★★ £E 1er Cru La Riotte Vieilles Vignes★★★★ £F
● **Chambolle-Musigny** 1er Cru La Combe d'Orveau★★★★ £F
● **Chambolle-Musigny** Vieilles Vignes★★★ £E 1er Cru Les Fuées★★★★ £F
● **Vosne-Romanée** 1er Cru Les Beaux-Monts★★★★ £F
● **Nuits-Saint-Georges** 1er Cru La Richmone★★★★ £F
● **Gevrey-Chambertin★★★** £E ● **Bourgogne Rouge★★** £B

JEAN PILLOT ET FILS   Chassagne-Montrachet   A: C&C, Eno, BBR, Res, CTy, JNi, Hrd

Owner: Pillot family   Rue Combard, 21190 Chassagne-Montrachet
Jean-Marc Pillot runs this family domaine of 10 ha. The estate's reputation, like that of the commune (albeit only in modern times), is for whites, yet half the vines are Pinot Noir and this is an increasingly good source of red Chassagne. The whites have long been good but have become more consistent and richer, riper and oakier under Jean-Marc's hand. There is now marvellous concentration, breadth and depth in the top *premiers crus*. A bottle from a fine vintage is particularly rewarding. The reds show proper ripeness and richness too; a particularly oaky version (labelled L'Exception) of the otherwise very good Morgeots was made in 1999. The range is continuing to expand and, as well as very good estate wines, some very fine Puligny-Montrachet Premier Cru Les Caillerets and Chevalier-Montrachet is made from bought-in wine. Good Saint-Romain white, red Santenay and Bourgogne red and white are made in most vintages too. The wines have been labelled both as Jean Pillot et Fils and Jean-Marc Pillot. (PW)

○ **Chassagne-Montrachet** 1er Cru Les Chevenottes★★★★ £E 1er Cru Caillerets★★★★ £E
○ **Chassagne-Montrachet** 1er Cru Morgeots★★★★ £E 1er Cru Les Vergers★★★★ £E
○ **Chassagne-Montrachet★★★** £D 1er Cru Les Macherelles★★★ £E 1er Cru Les Champs Gain★★★ £E
○ **Puligny-Montrachet★★★** £D ● **Santenay** Champs Claude★★ £C
● **Chassagne-Montrachet★** £C 1er Cru Les Macherelles★★ £D 1er Cru Morgeots★★★ £D

DOM. PONSOT   www.domaine-ponsot.com   A: BBR, Bal, Goe, L&W, F&R, Sec

Owner: Ponsot family   17-21 Rue de la Montagne, 21220 Morey-Saint-Denis

This is a very serious traditional and historic family estate that places huge importance on *terroir* and respect for the soil and the natural order. Laurent Ponsot has gradually assumed control from his father, Jean-Marie over the past decade or so. Several decades of expertise and refinement can be seen in the wines. The Ponsots undertake to pick the grapes as late as possible from vines with an average age of 40 years, though some individual parcels are as much as twice that age. Yields are very low, and naturally so without any green harvesting, which is abhorred. The Ponsots do not have a high tolerance for new oak or sulphur either and their use is kept to a minimum. No two wines are quite alike but there is a strength underpinning the truly marvellous expression and fine, silky textures that can be spellbinding. Though a charge of inconsistency has often been levelled at the domaine's wines, there seems little evidence of this in recent vintages, particularly since the atypically good 1997s. The Morey-Saint-Denis white, made mostly from Aligoté in recent vintages, is very full and ripe but structured too, not remotely like most Aligoté. A very small amount of Chambertin is also made. Village Gevrey and Morey can be superb value. (PW)

● **Clos de la Roche** Vieilles Vignes❂❂❂❂❂ £H   ● **Clos Saint-Denis** Vieilles Vignes❂❂❂❂❂ £H
● **Griotte-Chambertin**❂❂❂❂❂ £G   ● **Chapelle-Chambertin**★★★★ £G
● **Morey-Saint-Denis** Cuvée des Grives★★★ £E   1er Cru Alouettes★★★★ £E
● **Gevrey-Chambertin** Cuvée de l'Abeille★★★ £D   ● **Chambolle-Musigny** 1er Cru Les Charmes★★★ £F
O **Morey-Saint-Denis** Clos des Mont-Luisants★★★ £E

NICOLAS POTEL   Nuits-Saint-Georges   A: GFy, Bib, BBR, L&W, Tan, Gau, JNi, WSc

Owner: Cottin Frères   21 Rue Thurot, 21700 Nuits-Saint-Georges

Nicolas Potel fashioned some seriously good reds with his late father at the Domaine de la POUSSE D'OR until 1997 and since then has been employing his talents on an extensive range of bought-in wines. Volnay is still a strength but now he makes a host of others to a generally high standard, though there is some variability, more perhaps as a result of the disparate sources than anything else. Already well-established are some stylish, fragrant Volnays, concentrated Pommards and full, quite classy Nuits-Saint-Georges. His Clos de Vougeot is a fine example of this frustratingly uneven *grand cru*. This is now an extensive range, only a selection are included below. It is to be hoped that the best sources become long-standing. Romanée Saint-Vivant and Vosne-Romanée *premiers crus* are also made and still newer wines include Charmes-Chambertin, Chambertin and other northern Côte de Nuits *premiers* and *grands crus*. (PW)

● **Clos de Vougeot**★★★★ £F   ● **Grands Echezeaux**★★★★★ £G   ● **Bonnes-Mares**★★★★★ £G
● **Echezeaux**★★★★ £F   ● **Clos de la Roche**★★★★★ £F
● **Nuits-Saint-Georges** 1er Cru Vaucrains★★★ £E
● **Nuits-Saint-Georges** 1er Cru Les Saint-Georges★★★ £E   1er Cru Roncières★★★ £E
● **Aloxe-Corton** 1er Cru Les Valozières★★★ £E   ● **Volnay** 1er Cru Santenots★★★ £E
● **Volnay** Vieilles Vignes★★ £D   1er Cru Champans★★★ £E   1er Cru Pitures★★★★ £E
● **Pommard** 1er Cru Epenots★★★ £E   1er Cru Rugiens★★★ £E
● **Beaune** 1er Cru Epenottes ★★ £D   1er Cru Grèves★★ £D
● **Savigny-lès-Beaune**★★ £C   ● **Bourgogne Rouge** Maison Dieu Vieilles Vignes★★ £B

FRANÇOIS RAQUILLET   Mercurey   A: THt, M&V, NYg, P&S, F&M, Sel

Owner: François Raquillet   19 Rue de Jamproyes, 71640 Mercurey

François Raquillet is a young vigneron who is turning his family's 11 ha of vineyards into some of the most prized in Mercurey. A series of *premiers crus* reds benefit from being part aged in new oak resulting in wines of good colour, intensity but also accessibility. The purity of fruit is retained but the firmness of some Mercurey is usually avoided. Naugues is the most sophisticated but there is good intensity and character in all the reds. 2001s are good in the context of the vintage but 2002s are richer and more promising. As well as the wines listed below a small amount of *premier cru* Clos l'Eveque is also made. Most recently a small amount of grapes is also being bought-in to supplement the existing grape supply. (PW)

● **Mercurey** Vieilles Vignes★★ £C I er Cru Vasées★★ £C I er Cru Veleys★★ £C
● **Mercurey** I er Cru Puillets★★ £C I er Cru Naugues★★★ £C O **Mercurey** I er Cru Veleys★★ £C

RAMONET Chassagne-Montrachet A: C&B, Far, OWL, Res, HRp, Sel

Owner: Ramonet family 21190 Chassagne-Montrachet
Ramonet is another of the great white Burgundy estates. There is a division of responsibilities between brothers Jean-Claude and Noël Ramonet but it is Noël who makes the wines. There are 17 ha of mostly first-rate Chassagne-Montrachet vineyard plus a little of three *grands crus* in Puligny, which makes for a fantastic array of wines. The winemaking is somewhat intuitive and responsive to the vintage conditions but usually results in wines that have an explosive concentration and breadth within a powerful structure. Only occasionally has anything less than very good wine been produced in the last couple of decades but there is some variability, with a tendency to be almost too structured and slightly hard in some instances. Others have lacked balance, with excess alcohol for the fruit concentration, and there can be a reductive quality in others. However these are the exceptions and can be avoided by taking the precaution of tasting and/or comparing notes of a specific wine and vintage before adding one or more of these great wines to a cellar (an approach advisable not just here but anywhere that involves the kind of sums the world's best wines now command). Reds play second fiddle to the whites but have been very good in recent good vintages including some Chassagne-Montrachet Premier Cru La Boudriotte (owned by Noël Ramonet and sold under his own label). A little Montrachet is made, as is some Puligny-Montrachet Premier Cru Champ Canet, while some Chevalier-Montrachet is produced from bought-in wine. (PW)

O **Bâtard-Montrachet**✪✪✪✪✪ £H O **Bienvenues-Bâtard-Montrachet**★★★★★ £H
O **Chassagne-Montrachet** I er Cru Caillerets★★★★ £F I er Cru Grandes Ruchottes★★★★★ £F
O **Chassagne-Montrachet** I er Cru Boudriottes★★★★ £F I er Cru Morgeots★★★★ £F
O **Chassagne-Montrachet**★★ £E I er Cru Les Chaumées★★★ £F I er Cru Les Vergers★★★ £F
O **Saint-Aubin** I er Cru Le Charmois★★ £D O **Bourgogne Aligoté**★ £B
● **Chassagne-Montrachet**★ £D I er Cru Clos Saint-Jean★★ £E I er Cru Morgeots★★ £E
● **Chassagne-Montrachet** I er Cru Clos de la Boudriotte★★★ £E

DOM. RAPET PÈRE ET FILS Pernand-Vergelesses A: Anl, Goe, Res, HRp

Owner: Rapet family Rue des Paulands, 21420 Pernand-Vergelesses
The input of Vincent Rapet over recent vintages has given a considerable boost to this long-established domaine. Though some two-thirds of the 18 ha are planted to Pinot Noir, the reputation rests as much with the whites as reds. The core of the production is very good Pernand-Vergelesses but fine examples of Corton and Corton-Charlemagne are also made. There is now better grape selection, the whites have longer lees-contact than previously and show good depth, richness and restrained oak. Reds can be sturdy, occasionally with slightly coarse tannins, but generally show more refinement and depth in the most recent vintages, particularly in the very stylish Pernand-Vergelesses. All the better reds should be drunk with five years or more, but whites can be drunk younger. New from 1999 is a second Beaune *premier cru*, Grèves. From the 2000 vintage white Pernand-Vergelesses is now being bottled as separate specified *premiers crus* (including Le Clos du Village, En Caradeux and Sous Frétille) following the recent promotion of some village land. (PW)

● **Corton**★★★★ £E ● **Corton** Pougets★★★★ £E
● **Pernand-Vergelesses** I er Cru Les Vergelesses★★ £D I er Cru Île de Vergelesses★★★ £E
● **Beaune** I er Cru Clos du Roi★★★ £D ● **Aloxe-Corton**★★ £D
O **Corton-Charlemagne**★★★★ £F O **Pernand-Vergelesses** I er Cru En Caradeux★★ £D
O **Pernand-Vergelesses** I er Cru Sous Frétille★★ £D I er Cru Clos du Village★★ £D

MICHÈLE & PATRICE RION Nuits-Saint-Georges A: M&V, NYg, UnC

Owner: Rion family 21700 Prémeaux-Prissey
Some very good wine was made by Patrice Rion for his own label even before he handed over the winemaking reins at the family domaine (Daniel RION ET FILS) to his two brothers. From 2000 the range

here has been greatly expanded to include bought-in wines but these are labelled as simply Patrice Rion. Given an insistence on high-quality fruit, this promises to be a good quality range of *négociant* wines. The estate range has been expanded too with recent additions including an intense, full Chambolle-Musigny Les Charmes and very classy Nuits-Saint-Georges Clos des Argillières. (PW)

Dom. Michèle & Patrice Rion:
● **Chambolle-Musigny** Les Cras★★★ £E 1er Cru Les Charmes★★★★ £F
● **Nuits-Saint-Georges** 1er Cru Clos des Argillières★★★★ £F
● **Bourgogne Rouge** Bons Batons★★ £C

Patrice Rion:
● **Nuits-Saint-Georges** Vieilles Vignes★★★ £E ● **Gevrey-Chambertin** Clos Prieur★★★★ £E

DOM. DANIEL RION ET FILS   Nuits-Saint-Georges   A: CTy, N&P, JNi, WSc

Owner: Rion family 21700 Prémeaux-Prissey
Christophe and Olivier are now making the wines here on their own after the departure of their brother, Patrice (Michèle & Patrice RION), following the 2000 vintage. Over the course of two decades Patrice had established a solid reputation for this estate created by his father. The 19 ha is based primarily on Nuits-Saint-Georges and Vosne vineyards and includes some Chardonnay and Aligoté as well as Pinot Noir. The wines have long been characterised by their strength and a certain firmness allied to depth and intensity. In recent years there has been a gradual shift to finer tannins and more immediate richness and the wines are particularly successful in the best years, if sometimes a little harsh or tough in lighter vintages. Produced since the 1998 vintage are an Echezeaux as well as Clos de Vougeot from a different source to that previously made. The reds shouldn't be rushed, in fact they can be transformed with a little extra bottle age. The rich creamy white Nuits is produced from Pinot Blanc. (PW)

● **Clos de Vougeot**★★★★★ £F
● **Vosne-Romanée**★★ £D 1er Cru Chaumes★★★★ £E 1er Cru Beaux-Monts★★★★★ £E
● **Nuits-Saint-Georges** 1er Cru Hauts-Pruliers★★★ £E
● **Nuits-Saint-Georges** 1er Cru Vignes Rondes★★★ £E Vieilles Vignes★★★ £E
● **Nuits-Saint-Georges** Lavières★★ £D Grandes Vignes★★★ £D
● **Côte de Nuits-Villages**★★ £C O **Nuits-Saint-Georges** 1er Cru Terres Blanches★★★ £E

ANTONIN RODET   Mercurey www.rodet.com   A: BBR, C&R, MCW, Las, N&P

Owner: Worms & Cie Antonin Rodet, 71640 Mercurey
Directed by Bertrand Devillard, this is a *négociant* house with substantial holdings in both the Côte d'Or and Côte Chalonnaise. The following estates are all either owned, partly owned or made and distributed by Antonin Rodet: Château de Rully (Rully), Château de Mercey (Maranges-based for Hautes Côtes de Beaune red and white, and Mercurey), Château de Chamirey (Mercurey), Domaine des Perdrix (Bertrand Devillard's own 12-ha property in Nuits-Saint-Georges) and the Meursault-based Domaine Jacques Prieur. The later is run in conjunction with co-owner Martin Prieur and its previously flagging reputation has been at least partly restored in recent years by Rodet's winemaker, Nadine Gublin. The Jacques Prieur whites are rich, ripe and powerful though sometimes at the expense of expression and finesse and include *grands crus* Le Montrachet, Chevalier-Montrachet and Corton-Charlemagne. Reds include *grands crus* Musigny, Echezeaux, Chambertin, Clos de Vougeot and Corton Bressandes; and *premiers crus* from Volnay (Santenots and *monopole* Clos des Santenots) and Beaune (Grèves and *monopole* Clos de la Féguine). Both reds and whites are much improved if still somewhat uneven. The best wines under the Antonin Rodet label (many of them designated Cave Privée) are consistently very good indeed, at times quite oaky but rich and ripe, with great depth and complexity. Those listed include some of the best wines made on a regular basis. At a humbler level there are some remarkably good Côte Chalonnaise wines under the respective estate labels. In addition, as well as a range of Vin de Pays d'Oc varietals Antonin Rodet also owns the Domaine de l'AIGLE in Limoux, Languedoc-Roussillon. (PW)

Antonin Rodet:
- **Charmes-Chambertin★★★★** £G ● **Clos de Vougeot★★★★** £G
- **Gevrey-Chambertin** 1er Cru Estournelles★★★★ £F
- **Nuits-Saint-Georges** 1er Cru Les Saint-Georges★★★ £F 1er Cru Porêts-Saint-Georges★★★★ £F
- **Meursault** 1er Cru Perrières★★★★ £F ○ **Bourgogne Blanc** Vieilles Vignes★★ £C

Domaine des Perdrix:
- **Echezeaux★★★★** £G ● **Vosne-Romanée★★★** £E
- **Nuits-Saint-Georges★★★** £E 1er Cru Aux Perdrix★★★★★ £F

Château de Chamirey:
- ○ **Mercurey★** £C 1er Cru La Mission★★ £D ● **Mercurey★★** £C 1er Cru Les Ruelles★★★ £D

Château de Mercey:
- ○ **Bourgogne Hautes-Côtes de Beaune★** £B ○ **Mercurey★** £C
- **Bourgogne Hautes-Côtes de Beaune★** £B ● **Mercurey** 1er Cru En Sazenay★★ £C

Château de Rully:
- ○ **Rully★★** £C ● **Rully★** £C

DOM. DE LA ROMANÉE-CONTI   Vosne-Romanée   A: **C&B**, BBR, F&M, Hrd, F&R

Owner: de Vilaine and Leroy/Bize/Roch families   1 Rue Derrière le Four, 21700 Vosne-Romanée
DRC, as it referred to by both devotees and novices alike, is considered by many to be Burgundy's greatest domaine. The history and nobility of these famous *grand cru* vineyards make this a difficult assertion to refute, though over the past decade this domaine has been seriously challenged by part-owner Lalou Bize-Leroy's own estate, Domaine LEROY. Any serious text on Burgundy will provide background on both the estate and individual wines. Currently yields are lower than previously, the average vine age is now high across all the wines and the viticulture is now essentially biodynamic (in practice if not in name), making for healthier soils than previously. The most distinctive features of the vinification are that there is little or no destemming and automatic punching down is carried out. All the wines see 100 per cent new oak. Individual wines seem to have had slight ups and downs but when on form they all rate five stars. Montrachet apart, all are made in decent quantities by Burgundian standards, assuming, that is, you can afford them. The holdings are: La Romanée Conti (1.81 ha), La Tâche (6.06 ha), Richebourg (3.51 ha), Romanée-Saint-Vivant (5.28 ha), Echezeaux (4.67 ha), Grands-Echezeaux (3.53 ha) and the solitary white, Le Montrachet (0.68 ha). All the wines are £H. The first two are *monopoles* and are considered the brightest stars in the firmament, while the other reds account for a substantial proportion of the vineyard area of their respective appellations. (PW)

EMMANUEL ROUGET   Vosne-Romanée   A: J&B, RsW, BBR, F&R, Sec

Owner: Emmanuel Rouget   Flagey-Echezeaux, 21700 Vosne-Romanée
Emmanuel Rouget is the nephew of Henri Jayer and has retained a portion of the vineyards that Jayer, one of the great 20th-century figures in Burgundy, made famous. Jayer's use of a cold pre-fermentation maceration, 100 per cent destemming, plenty of new oak, no filtration and rigorous attention to hygiene transformed the face of Burgundy as many others followed in his footsteps. Rouget's early efforts looked promising but some of the wines from vintages in the late 1990s and more recently seem to have lost a bit of the vigour and concentration of old. Yet quality is still good with no lack of style or class. Prices however are very high. (PW)

- **Echezeaux★★★★** £H
- **Vosne-Romanée★★** £G 1er Cru Les Beaumonts★★★ £H 1er Cru Cros Parentoux★★★★ £H
- **Nuits-Saint-Georges★★** £F ● **Bourgogne Rouge★** £C

DOM. ROULOT Meursault www.domaineroulot.com A: DDr, HHC, HRp, Res, JAr, BWC

Owner: Roulot family 1 Rue Charles Giraud, 21190 Meursault

Since 1989 Jean-Marc Roulot has run this highly respected domaine with a hatful of Meursault *crus*, built up by his father Guy some 30 years earlier. The wines show something of a leesy character and and some new oak influence but neither dominate and the percentage of new oak is sometimes less than 20 per cent. The *premiers crus* Charmes, Perrières (and more recently, Bouchères) are the top wines, the Perrières easily the most complex and complete of the three, but this is reflected in their prices. The most significant proportion of the estate's 12 ha comes from vineyards lying on higher slopes running towards Auxey-Duresses. Les Tessons and Les Tillets (from vines with a high average age) are arguably the pick of these and offer relatively good value for Meursault. Though majoring on Meursault, Roulot also produces an intense, vibrant, minerally Monthelie *premier cru* that adds richness with two or three years' age. Bourgogne Aligoté and a flavoursome, scented Bourgogne Blanc are more than dependable. (PW)

O **Meursault** 1er Cru Bouchères★★★★ £F 1er Cru Charmes★★★★ £F 1er Cru Perrières★★★★★ £F
O **Meursault** Meix Chavaux★★★ £D Les Luchets★★★ £D Les Tillets★★★★ £D Les Tessons★★★★ £D
O **Meursault** Les Vireuils★★★ £D O **Monthelie** 1er Cru Champs Fulliot★★ £C
O **Bourgogne Blanc**★★ £B O **Bourgogne Aligoté**★ £B

DOM. ROUMIER www.roumier.com A: JAr, HHC, DDr, HRp, M&V, Tan, Res

Owner: Christophe Roumier Rue de Vergy, 21220 Chambolle-Musigny

A fabulous domaine whose wines express the essence of Chambolle-Musigny. Christophe Roumier has now had two decades of input, achieving ever better balance in his vineyards and maximising the potential of each site. The vines are of a high average age and low-yielding, but naturally so without the need for the excessive pruning or green harvesting required elsewhere. Quality is consistently high but that is not to say the wines are the same year in, year out; rather each expresses something of the vintage without its defects. What is most impressive is the structure of the wines; always there's a dimension and depth without a trace of hardness, allied to harmony and persistence. The Chambolles, in particular, are fragrant and elegant with more power, depth and concentration in the *premiers crus*. In the *grands crus* the power and elegance of Le Musigny contrasts with the muscle, intensity and grip of Bonnes Mares. From outside Chambolle-Musigny, the 2.5-ha *monopole* Clos de la Bussière in Morey-Saint-Denis produces a firmer, tighter wine, now showing more refinement and class than previously, and it can be very good value. Tiny amounts of very high quality Ruchottes-Chambertin and Charmes-Chambertin are also made, as is a little Corton-Charlemagne. (PW)

● **Le Musigny**❂❂❂❂❂ £H ● **Bonnes Mares**❂❂❂❂❂ £H
● **Chambolle-Musigny**★★★ £D 1er Cru Les Cras★★★★★ £F 1er Cru Les Amoureuses❂❂❂❂❂ £G
● **Morey-Saint-Denis** 1er Cru Clos de la Bussière★★★ £E ● **Bourgogne Rouge**★★ £B

DOM. A ROUSSEAU www.domaine-rousseau.com A: HRp, BBR, HBJ, OWL, Res, F&M, Hrd

Owner: Charles Rousseau 1 Rue de l'Aumônerie, 21220 Gevrey-Chambertin

Eric Rousseau and his sister, Corinne are gradually assuming control of this the most famous Gevrey-Chambertin domaine that has been directed by their father, Charles Rousseau, for more than 40 years. The estate was built up in the early part of the 20th century by their grandfather Armand but was further enlarged by Charles. A remarkable 8 ha of the 14 ha planted exclusively to Pinot Noir are *grands crus*. Only a small percentage of the stems are retained to assist a moderately long vinification complete with automatic *pigeage*. The top wines, Chambertin and Chambertin Clos-de-Bèze, show all the class and breed of great *grand cru* Burgundy, with a breadth and presence in the mouth that even the very best *premiers crus* lack. These and the Clos Saint-Jacques receive 100 per cent new oak but the oak treatment is rarely, if ever, excessive, though shows more in the Clos-de-Bèze than the Chambertin. Other *crus* receive at most 30 per cent new oak. In the Charmes-Chambertin and Mazy-Chambertin finesse and elegance are emphasised yet there is a vigour and intensity about all the wines. The textures of all the Rousseau wines are very impressive too, even if other wines may provide greater richness and extract. All the wines need five years, the top wines

10 or more. The *premier cru* Lavaux Saint-Jacques, previously part of the regular Gevrey, has been bottled separately since 1999. The 2002s are superlative with splendid Clos des Ruchottes and stunning Chambertin. (PW)

- **Chambertin**✪✪✪✪✪ £H
- **Chambertin Clos-de-Bèze**✪✪✪✪✪ £H
- **Ruchottes-Chambertin** Clos des Ruchottes✪✪✪✪✪ £G
- **Mazy-Chambertin**★★★★★ £F
- **Charmes-Chambertin**★★★★ £F
- **Clos de la Roche**★★★★★ £F
- **Gevrey-Chambertin** 1er Cru Les Cazetiers★★★★★ £F 1er Cru Clos Saint-Jacques✪✪✪✪✪ £F
- **Gevrey-Chambertin**★★★ £E 1er Cru Lavaux-Saint-Jacques★★★★ £F

ETIENNE SAUZET   www.etienne-sauzet.com   A: HHC, OWL, BBR, Hrd, Res, Tan, JAr, Maj

Owner: Gérard & Jeanine Boudot   11 Rue de Poiseul, 21190 Puligny-Montrachet

This estate has a fabulous reputation and highly respected winemaker in Gérard Boudot. However it is now significantly smaller than it once was. Gérard's wife, Jeanine Boudot, grand daughter of Étienne Sauzet, has retained only a third of the vines, though their company has another third under contract for some time to come (the rest of the legacy has gone to brother Jean-Marc BOILLOT). There are now 8 ha (but much boosted by bought-in grapes) with small amounts of four *grands crus* (Bâtard-Montrachet, Bienvenues-Bâtard-Montrachet, Le Montrachet and Chevalier-Montrachet) and more significant amounts of some of Puligny's best *premiers crus*. Form in the 1990s was irregular, the winesometimes lean and slightly undistinguished - missing some of the class and finesse for which they are famous. Nor have they always aged as well as previously. High demand has of course contributed to high prices but some caution should be taken before investing heavily. Ratings are based on the best recent vintages, 1999 and 2002. (PW)

- O **Le Montrachet**★★★★★ £H
- O **Chevalier-Montrachet**★★★★★ £H
- O **Bienvenue-Bâtard-Montrachet**★★★★★ £H
- O **Bâtard-Montrachet**★★★★ £H
- O **Puligny-Montrachet** 1er Cru Champ-Canet★★★★ £F 1er Cru Les Perrières★★★★ £F
- O **Puligny-Montrachet** 1er Cru Les Combettes★★★★ £F 1er Cru Les Referts★★★★ £F
- O **Puligny-Montrachet**★★★ £E 1er Cru Les Folatières★★★ £F 1er Cru La Garenne★★★ £F

COMTE SENARD   Aloxe-Corton   A: Anl, F&R

Owner: Senard family   21420 Aloxe-Corton

Philippe Senard was one of those to work with the controversial consultant Guy Accad in the early 1990s, aiming for more colour and greater aroma and fruit intensity, in part from an extended cold maceration on skins prior to fermentation. Like other producers advised by Accad, he gradually incorporated the best of his advice to make stylish, aromatic and intensely fruity red Burgundies. More recently he has been assisted by his daughter, Lorraine. Some of the lesser wines can struggle for full ripeness but typically there is a cool, pure vibrant fruit intensity to which is added more breadth, length and elegance in the various Cortons. This is a good cellar from which to compare several different Cortons. Bressandes and Clos du Roi show lots of intensity and depth, En Charlemagne a cool, classy fruit and good dimension. All deserve at least five years' age. Good whites are also made, including an Aloxe-Corton from old-vine Pinot Gris, while a Corton Blanc is gaining in richness and complexity. Other reds include a Chorey-lès-Beaune and a *premier cru* Beaune. The Senards also make the wines of Domaine des Terregelesses. (PW)

- **Corton** Bressandes★★★ £F
- **Corton** Clos du Roi★★★ £F
- **Corton** Clos de Meix★★★ £F
- **Corton** En Charlemagne★★★ £F
- **Aloxe-Corton**★★ £D 1er Cru Les Valozières★★ £E
- O **Corton** Blanc★★★ £F
- O **Aloxe-Corton**★★ £D

CHRISTIAN SÉRAFIN   Gevrey-Chambertin   A: Eno, Goe, BBR Res, F&R

Owner: Christian Sérafin   7 Place du Château, 21220 Gevrey-Chambertin

Christian Sérafin has been quietly working away on his family's small 5-ha estate, gradually refining his winemaking practices and producing ever more satisfying and consistently good wines. His signature is the power that might be expected from Gevrey together with plenty of oak and spice that embellish wines that are lush and fruit-rich, with lots of obvious appeal. The top *crus* add more class and breadth. The best wine made in any real quantity is the Vieilles Vignes bottling, which is meaty and full of ripe fruit, with plenty of depth. All the wines show very well with just five years' age. A tiny amount of top-quality Charmes-Chambertin is also made but is likely to be hard to find. (PW)

- **Gevrey-Chambertin** 1er Cru Les Cazetiers★★★★★ £F 1er Cru Les Corbeaux★★★★ £F
- **Gevrey-Chambertin**★★★ £E Vieilles Vignes★★★★ £E 1er Cru Fontenys★★★★ £F
- **Chambolle-Musigny** 1er Cru Les Baudes★★★★ £F
- **Morey-Saint-Denis** 1er Cru Les Millandes★★★★ £F

TOLLOT-BEAUT   Chorey-lès-Beaune   A: DDr, Adm, L&W, OWL, Tan, HHB

Owner: Tollot families   Rue Alexandre Tollot, 21200 Chorey-lès-Beaune

Tollot-Beaut's 24-ha estate includes some of the northern Côte de Beaune's lesser but better-value appellations. With lots of new oak and ripe, forward fruit, the wines have had plenty of appeal in the past but also a tendency to lack a little structure despite some firm tannins and some have aged quite quickly. However since 1999 the wines have shown better definition and balance and, if less upfront, will have much more to offer with four or five years' age than previously. It has always been a team effort but the current members in charge, Nathalie, Jean-Paul and Olivier, look set to make better wines than ever before. Yields have been lowered, though they were never high. The Chorey-lès-Beaune is a very attractive, relatively inexpensive red Burgundy. Only a little white is made but includes some Corton-Charlemagne. There are new labels but prices remain much the same. Ratings apply to the most recent vintages only. (PW)

- **Corton**★★★★ £F • **Corton** Bressandes★★★★ £F
- **Aloxe-Corton**★★ £D 1er Cru Vercots★★★ £E 1er Cru Fournières★★★ £E
- **Beaune** 1er Cru Clos du Roi★★★ £E 1er Cru Grèves★★★ £E • **Chorey-lès-Beaune**★★ £C
- **Savigny-lès-Beaune** 1er Cru Champs Chevrey★★ £D 1er Cru Lavières★★★ £D

DOM. TRAPET PÈRE ET FILS   www.domaine-trapet.com   A: C&B, C&C, Res, Hrd, F&R

Owner: Jean et Jean-Louis Trapet   53 Route de Beaune, 21220 Gevrey-Chambertin

The original Domaine Louis Trapet (source of some famous bottles from the 1950s and 60s) was built up from the late 19th century before being divided in 1990 between Jean and his sister (ROSSIGNOL-TRAPET). Jean's son, Jean-Louis, has revived their venerable vineyards, which include nearly 2 ha of Chambertin and decent segments of Chapelle-Chambertin and Latricières-Chambertin. The raw material is now of much higher quality than previously, with reduced yields from higher than typical vine densities under a regime that became progressively more biodynamic in the late 1990s. The 13 ha also includes some excellent *premier cru* Petite Chapelle and Clos Prieur as well as village Gevrey-Chambertin and Marsannay. There is a measured use of new oak but the accent is on the quality of the fruit and producing wines of finesse and real class. There is great depth and dimension as well as a particular strength and definition characteristic to the wines, which require patience. Five years' is needed for Gevrey, five to 10 for the *premiers crus*, and a minimum of 10 for Chambertin. Given time these wines are some of the very best from Gevrey and are reasonably priced in that context. (PW)

- **Chambertin**★★★★★ £G • **Latricières-Chambertin**★★★★★ £G
- **Gevrey-Chambertin**★★★ £D 1er Cru Petite Chapelle★★★★ £F 1er Cru Clos Prieur★★★★ £F
- **Marsannay**★★ £C

VERGET   A: Far, L&S, L&W, BBR, Odd, F&R, C&R

Owner: Jean-Marie Guffens-Heynen & others   71960 Sologny

In just over a decade Jean-Marie Guffens has constructed a merchant house of remarkable constitution. It is not built around the great *crus* of the Côte de Beaune, though there are some of those, but rather the less hallowed vineyards of the Mâconnais and increasingly Chablis, where a new winemaking base has been established in conjunction with Olivier LEFLAIVE for their joint but independent use. The Mâconnais wines (including Pouilly-Fuissé, Saint-Veran and various Mâcon-Villages) are covered, together with the wines of his own private estate, GUFFENS-HEYNEN in the Mâconnais section. The wines from the Côte d'Or are true to the Verget style, which is one of great extract, concentration and richness, made from fully ripe grapes sourced from low-yielding vineyards. The wines from Chablis are also deep and concentrated but a little tighter, cooler and more minerally than his other wines (particularly in contrast to the Mâconnais wines). Largely eschewing the use of oak here, the wines are riper and fuller, if slightly less steely, than examples from other producers but nevertheless archetypal Chablis and very fine. Almost all of the Verget wines can be broached fairly young but should keep for a decade. (PW)

O **Bâtard-Montrachet**★★★★ £H   O **Corton-Charlemagne**★★★★ £E
O **Meursault** Tillets★★★★ £E   Rougeots★★★ £E   O **Chassagne-Montrachet** Franchemont★★★ £E
O **Puligny-Montrachet** Enseignières★★★ £F   1er Cru Sous le Puits★★★ £F
O **Chablis Grand Cru** Bougros Côte de Bougueyraud★★★★ £F
O **Chablis Premier Cru** Les Forêts★★★ £D   Montée de Tonnerre★★★ £E   Vaillons★★★★ £D

AUBERT ET PAMÉLA DE VILLAINE   Bouzeron   A: **C&B**, ACh

Owner: Aubert et Paméla de Villaine   2 Rue de la Fontaine, 71150 Bouzeron
It still seems remarkable that the co-director of the Côte d'Or's most prestigious estate (Domaine de la ROMANÉE-CONTI) should choose to make wine in the Côte Chalonnaise but Aubert de Villaine and his wife Paméla have done so to great acclaim. More than half of 21 ha is planted to Aligoté (the grape which dominates the appellation) and a fine characterful example - as good as any produced - is made along with some red Mercurey and white Rully. The wines are elegant and harmonious with real depth and intensity in the Mercurey Montots. All are better with two or three years' age, including the Aligoté. (PW)

● **Mercurey** Montots★★ £C   ● **Bourgogne Pinot Noir** La Digoine★★ £C
O **Rully** Saint-Jacques★★ £C   O **Bouzeron Aligoté**★★ £B

DOM. COMTE GEORGES DE VOGÜE   A: Men, DWS, JAr, BBR, F&M, Far, Sec, Hrd, N&P

Owner: Ladoucette family   Rue Sainte Barbe, 21220 Chambolle-Musigny
This estate is known for one of the single greatest red Burgundies made. The Musigny has an exalted reputation based in part on the on-going quality of the wine but also on some legendary old vintages (including 1945, 47, 59, 69 and 72). The domaine owns 7.2 ha of the 10.7 ha *grand cru*, though this includes 0.5 ha of Musigny Blanc (recently sold as Bourgogne Blanc), the only place in the commune of Chambolle-Musigny where Chardonnay is permitted to be grown. François Millet has made the wines here since the Comte died in 1986 and his daughter took over the running of the estate. Vine age is high and yields vary but are kept low; adjustments are made where necessary in response to vintage conditions. The approach to vinification is also vintage-responsive, with individual parcels of vineyard treated in different ways, though a long *cuvaison* is favoured. Since 1990 few if any expert tasters have been left in any doubt about the true greatness of the Musigny Vieilles Vignes after some leaner offerings in the 1970s and 80s. The wine is now more deeply coloured than previously and its extraordinary aromatics, with preserved fruits and floral notes, precede a considerable structure that underpins the silky texture, wonderful definition and mouthfilling dimension on the palate that becomes increasingly opulent with age, the intense flavours being sustained long on the finish. Its remarkable longevity from top vintages make it a cellaring must for the few who can afford it. There is wonderful class, intensity and concentration in the Amoureuses too; and a rich, sturdy, darker fruit density to the Bonnes Mares. (PW)

● **Musigny** Vieilles Vignes❂❂❂❂❂ £H   ● **Bonnes Mares**★★★★★ £H
● **Chambolle-Musigny**★★★ £F   1er Cru Les Amoureuses★★★★★ £H

DOM. DE LA VOUGERAIE   www.domainedelavougeraie.com   A: Hay, M&V, L&W, BWC

Owner: Boisset   Rue de l'Église, 21700 Premeaux-Prissey
This newcomer is a southern Côte de Nuits-based estate that comprises all of Boisset's (Burgundy's single biggest producer) own vineyards. Boisset recruited Pascal Marchand, the very highly regarded winemaker of

the Clos des Epeneaux (Comte ARMAND) in Pommard, to direct operations. He made the wines in 1999 but has only assumed full responsibility for both viticulture and winemaking from 2000. The vineyards total an impressive 37 ha, which are certified organic and now treated biodynamically, predominantly planted to Pinot Noir and much of it in the Côte de Nuits. Yields are low (less than 30 hl/ha in the reds), which is immediately apparent in wines of richness, depth and class. Gevrey-Chambertin and Nuits-Saint-Georges feature, including some *premier cru* sites, while *grands crus* run to Corton Clos du Roi, Clos de Vougeot, Bonnes Mares, Charmes-Chambertin and a third of a hectare of Musigny. Nearly all the wines are proving to be, at the very least, good examples of their respective appellations. Corton-Charlemagne and the solely-owned Vougeot *cru* are already very good whites. (PW)

● **Clos de Vougeot**★★★★ £F ● **Charmes-Chambertin**★★★★ £F
● **Vougeot** 1er Cru Les Cras★★★ £F ● **Vougeot** Clos du Prieuré★★★ £E
● **Gevrey-Chambertin** 1er Cru Les Evocelles★★★★ £F
● **Chambolle-Musigny**★★★ £E ● **Pommard** Les Petit Noizons★★★ £E
● **Côtes de Beaune** Les Pierres Blanches★★ £C ● **Bourgogne Rouge** Terres de Famille★★ £C
○ **Vougeot** 1er Cru Clos Blanc de Vougeot★★★★ £F
○ **Corton-Charlemagne**★★★★ £G

CÔTE D'OR & CÔTE CHALONNAISE/OTHER WINES OF NOTE

This list includes notable wines from a range of producers but is not intended to be a comprehensive list of a given producer's wines; just those that we have encountered. In some instances there may be several more good wines.

STÉPHANE ALADAME ○ **Montagny** 1er Cru £C 1er Cru Cuvée Selection £C 1er Cru Les Coères £C
FRANÇOIS D'ALLAINES ○ **Montagny** £C ○ **Rully** Saint-Jacques £C
○ **Saint-Aubin** 1er Cru En Remilly £D
ROBERT AMPEAU ○ **Puligny-Montrachet** 1er Cru Combettes £F
○ **Meursault** £E 1er Cru Pièce sous le Bois £F 1er Cru Perrières £F
○ **Auxey-Duresses** 1er Cru Ecusseaux £D ● **Volnay** 1er Cru Santenots £F
● **Savigny-lès-Beaune** 1er Cru Lavières £D
HERVÉ ET CYPRIEN ARLAUD ● **Charmes-Chambertin** £F
● **Morey-Saint-Denis** £E 1er Cru Ruchots £F
ARNOUX PÈRE ET FILS ● **Beaune** 1er Cru Cent Vignes £D ● **Savigny-lès-Beaune** £C
● **Savigny-lès-Beaune** 1er Cru Vergelesses £D ● **Chorey-lès-Beaune** Confrelins £C
JEAN-CLAUDE BACHELET ○ **Saint-Aubin** 1er Cru Les Champlots £C
○ **Puligny-Montrachet** £E 1er Cru Sous le Puits £E
BACHELET-RAMONET ○ **Chassagne-Montrachet** £D 1er Cru Caillerets £E 1er Cru Grde Montagne £E
● **Chassagne-Montrachet** 1er Cru Clos Saint-Jean £D
DOM. BERTAGNA ● **Vougeot** 1er Cru Petits Vougeots £F 1er Cru Clos de la Perrière £F
PIERRE BERTHEAU ● **Chambolle-Musigny** 1er Cru £E 1er Cru Charmes £F
BILLARD-GONNET ● **Pommard** £D 1er Cru Chaponnières £E 1er Cru Pezerolles £E
● **Pommard** 1er Cru Rugiens £F
VINCENT BITOUZET-PRIEUR ○ **Meursault** Clos du Cromin £E 1er Cru Perrières £F
● **Volnay** £D 1er Cru Pitures £E
JEAN-MARC BOULEY ● **Volnay** £ D 1er Cru Clos de la Cave £D 1er Cru Caillerets £D
● **Pommard** 1er Cru Frémiers £E 1er Cru Rugiens £E
RENÉ BOURGEON ● **Givry** £B Baraude £C ○ **Givry** Clos de la Brulée £B
DENIS BOUSSEY ○ **Meursault** 1er Cru Charmes £E
JEAN-CLAUDE BRELIÈRE ○ **Rully** 1er Cru Margotée £C
● **Rully** 1er Cru Préaux £C 1er Cru Montpalais £C
DOM. MICHEL BRIDAY ○ **Rully** Bergerie £B 1er Cru Grésigny £C

● **Rully** Quatre Vignes £B   1er Cru Champs-Cloux £C
CAVE DES VIGNERONS DE BUXY O **Montagny** Domaine des Pierres Blanches £C
O **Montagny** 1er Cru Cuvée Speciale £C   1er Cru Chaignots £C
DOM. CAILLOT O **Meursault** £D   Limozin £E   O **Bourgogne Blanc** £B
LUCIEN CAMUS-BRUCHON ● **Savigny-lès-Beaune** Liards Vieilles Vignes £C   1er Cru Lavières £D
● **Beaune** 1er Cru Clos du Roi £D   ● **Pommard** 1er Cru Arvelets £E
O **Savigny-lès-Beaune** Goudelettes £D
DOM. CARRÉ-COURBIN ● **Pommard** £D   1er Cru Grands Epenots £F
● **Volnay** £D   Vieilles Vignes £E   1er Cru Les Lurets £E   1er Cru Robardelle £E
● **Volnay** 1er Cru Clos de la Cave des Ducs £E   1er Cru Taillepieds £E
CHANSON PÈRE ET FILS O **Beaune** Clos des Mouches £F   O **Pernand-Vergelesses** Caradeux £E
● **Beaune** 1er Cru Grèves £E   1er Cru Clos des Fèves £F   ● **Côte de Beaune-Villages** £C
CHARTRON & TRÉBUCHET O **Puligny-Montrachet** 1er Cru Clos des Caillerets £F
O **Saint-Aubin** 1er Cru Châtenière £D   O **Bourgogne Chardonnay** Jean Chartron Vieilles Vignes £C
CHÂTEAU DE LA MALTROYE O **Chassagne-Montrachet** 1er Cru Clos du Château de Maltroye £E
O **Chassagne-Montrachet** 1er Cru Le Dent de Chien £F   1er Cru Grandes Ruchottes £F
● **Chassagne-Montrachet** 1er Cru Clos du Château de Maltroye £E   ● **Santenay** 1er Cru Comme £D
CHÂTEAU DE PULIGNY-MONTRACHET O **Puligny-Montrachet** £E   1er Cru Les Folatières £F
O **Meursault** 1er Cru Les Poruzots £F
CHÂTEAU DE LA SAULE O **Montagny** 1er Cru £C   1er Cru Vignes sur les Cloux £C
JEAN CHAUVENET ● **Nuits-Saint-Georges** £D   1er Cru Bousselots £E   1er Cru Damodes £E
● **Nuits-Saint-Georges** 1er Cru Vaucrains £F
HUBERT CHAUVENET-CHOPIN ● **Nuits-Saint-Georges** £C   1er Cru Murgers £D
● **Côte de Nuits-Villages** £B
CHOFFLET-VALDENAIRE ● **Givry** £B   1er Cru Clos de Choué £C   1er Cru Clos Jus £C
O **Givry** Galaffres £B
DENIS ET FRANÇOISE CLAIR ● **Santenay** Clos Genet £C   1er Cru Clos de la Comme £C
● **Santenay** 1er Cru Clos des Tavannes £C
DOMAINE DES CLOS ● **Beaune** 1er Cru Les Avaux £D   ● **Nuits-Saint-Georges** Les Crots £D
CLOS SALOMON ● **Givry** 1er Cru £C
DOM. ALAIN COCHE-BIZOUARD O **Meursault** Luchets £D   1er Cru Charmes £E
O **Meursault** 1er Cru Gouttes d'Or £E   O **Bourgogne Blanc** £B
VINCENT DANCER O **Meursault** Grands Charrons £E   1er Cru Perrières £F
O **Chassagne-Montrachet** 1er Cru Romanée £F
JEAN-YVES DEVEVEY/DOM. DU BOIS GUILLAUME ● **Beaune** 1er Cru Pertuisots £D
O **Hautes-Côtes de Beaune** Les Champs Perdrix £B   Les Chagnots £C
JEAN-PIERRE DICONNE ● **Auxey-Duresses** 1er Cru Duresses £C   O **Auxey-Duresses** £C
DIGIOIA-ROYER ● **Chambolle-Musigny** Vieilles Vignes £E   1er Cru Groseilles £E   1er Cru Gruenchers £E
DAVID DUBAND ● **Nuits-Saint-Georges** £D   1er Cru Procès £E   1er Cru Pruliers £E
● **Bourgogne-Hautes Côtes de Nuits** £B
MAURICE ECARD ET FILS ● **Savigny-lès-Beaune** 1er Cru Narbantons £D   1er Cru Jarrons £D
● **Savigny-lès-Beaune** 1er Cru Serpentières £D
BENOÎT ENTE O **Puligny-Montrachet** £E   1er Cru Champ-Gain £F   1er Cru Les Folatières £F
DOM. FOREY PÈRE ET FILS ● **Echezeaux** £F   ● **Vosne-Romanée** 1er Cru Gaudichots £F
FOUGERAY DE BEAUCLAIR ● **Fixin** Clos Marion £D   ● **Marsannay** Saint Jacques £C
DOMINIQUE GALLOIS ● **Gevrey-Chambertin** 1er Cru Combe aux Moines £E
ALEX GAMBAL O **Chassagne-Montrachet** 1er Cru La Maltroie £E
O **Meursault** Clos du Cromin £E   O **Bourgogne Chardonnay** £B
PAUL GARAUDET ● **Monthelie** £C   1er Cru Clos Gauthey £C   1er Cru Duresses £D   ● **Volnay** £D
JEAN-MICHEL GAUNOUX O **Meursault** £D   1er Cru Gouttes d'Or £E   1er Cru Perrières £E
O **Meursault** 1er Cru Genevrières £E
GÉNOT-BOULANGER O **Chassagne-Montrachet** 1er Cru Chevenottes £E   1er Cru Vergers £E
JEAN-JACQUES GIRARD ● **Savigny-lès-Beaune** 1er Cru Lavières £D   1er Cru Peuillets £D
● **Savigny-lès-Beaune** 1er Cru Serpentières £D   1er Cru Fourneaux £D   1er Cru Vergelesses £D
O **Savigny-lès-Beaune** £C   O **Pernand-Vergelesses** Belles Filles £C

CAMILLE GIROUD ● **Beaune** 1er Cru Avaux £D   1er Cru Cras £D
● **Volnay** Clos des Chênes £E   1er Cru Carelles £E
ALBERT GRIVAULT ○ **Meursault** £D   1er Cru Perrières £E
GROS FRÈRE ET SOEUR ● **Clos de Vougeot** Musigni £F   ● **Bourgogne-Hautes Côtes de Nuits** £B
HERESZTYN ● **Gevrey-Chambertin** £D   1er Cru Champonnets £E   ● **Chambolle-Musigny** £D
● **Morey-Saint-Denis** 1er Cru Milandes £E
HUMBERT FRÈRES ● **Gevrey-Chambertin** £D   1er Cru Poissenots £E
DOM. LUCIEN JACOB ● **Savigny-lès-Beaune** £C   ○ **Savigny-lès-Beaune** £C
DOM. JAYER-GILLES ● **Echezeaux** £H   ● **Hautes Côtes de Nuits** £D
○ **Bourgogne-Hautes Côtes de Nuits** £D
DOM. JEANNIN-NALTET ● **Mercurey** Clos des Grands Voyens £C
DOM. JOBLOT ● **Givry** Pied de Chaume £C   1er Cru Servoisine £C
○ **Givry** Pied de Chaume £C   ○ **Givry** 1er Cru Servoisine £C
VINCENT ET FRANÇOIS JOUARD ○ **Chassagne-Montrachet** 1er Cru Champ Gain £E
○ **Chassagne-Montrachet** 1er Cru Chaumées £E   1 er Cru Maltroie £E   1er Cru Morgeot Fairendes £E
○ **Bâtard-Montrachet** £F
DOM. ÉMILE JUILLOT ● **Mercurey** £B   1er Cru Cailloute £C   1er Cru Croichots £C
● **Mercurey** 1er Cru Combins £C   ○ **Mercurey** £B   1er Cru Cailloute £C
RENÉ LAMY-PILLOT ○ **Chassagne-Montrachet** £D   1er Cru Morgeots £E;
● **Chassagne-Montrachet** 1er Cru Clos Saint-Jean £E   1er Cru Morgeots £E
DOM. LARUE ○ **Saint-Aubin** 1er Cru Vieilles Vignes £D   1er Cru En Remilly £D
○ **Saint-Aubin** 1er Cru Murgers des Dents de Chien £D
○ **Chassagne-Montrachet** £E   ○ **Puligny-Montrachet** 1er Cru La Garenne £D
DOM. ALETH LE ROYER-GIRARDIN ● **Pommard** £D   1er Cru Charmots £E
● **Beaune** Clos des Mouches £D
DOM. LECHENAUT ● **Nuits-Saint-Georges** £D   1er Cru Cailles £F   ● **Morey-Saint-Denis** £D
● **Vosne-Romanée** £E
DOM. LORENZON ● **Mercurey** £C   1er Cru Champs-Martin £C
○ **Mercurey** 1er Cru Croichots £C   1er Cru Champs Martin £C
JEAN-PAUL MAGNIEN ● **Morey-Saint-Denis** 1er Cru Faconnières £D   ● **Chambolle-Musigny** £D
JEAN-PHILIPPE MARCHAND ● **Gevrey-Chambertin** Vieilles Vignes £D
● **Gevrey-Chambertin** 1er Cru Lavaux Saint-Jacques £E
MAROSLAVAC-LEGER ○ **Puligny-Montrachet** 1er Cru Combettes £E   1er Cru Champgains £E
BERTRAND MAUME ● **Gevrey-Chambertin** 1er Cru £D   1er Cru Champeaux £D
● **Gevrey-Chambertin** 1er Cru Lavaux Saint-Jacques £E
PRINCE FLORENT DE MÉRODE ● **Corton Bressandes** £F   ● **Corton Clos du Roi** £F
ALAIN MICHELOT ● **Nuits-Saint-Georges** 1er Cru Chaignots £E   1er Cru Vaucrains £E
● **Nuits-Saint-Georges** 1er Cru Champs Perdrix £E   ● **Morey-Saint-Denis** 1er Cru Charrières £E
JEAN-MARC MILLOT ● **Echezeaux** £F   ● **Vosne-Romanée** £D
DOM. BERNARD MOREAU ET FILS ○ **Chassagne-Montrachet** 1er Cru Chevenottes £E
○ **Chassagne-Montrachet** 1er Cru Maltroie £E
DOM. MICHEL MOREY-COFFINET ○ **Chassagne-Montrachet** £D   1er Cru En Remilly £E
○ **Chassagne-Montrachet** 1er Cru Fairendes £E   1er Cru Romanée £E   1er Cru Caillerets £F
○ **Bâtard-Montrachet** £H
THIERRY MORTET ● **Gevrey Chambertin** £D   1er Cru Clos Prieur £E
● **Chambolle-Musigny** £D   1er Cru Beaux Bruns £E
GÉRARD MOUTON ● **Givry** 1er Cru Clos Jus £C
GÉRARD MUGNERET ● **Vosne-Romanée** £D   ● **Nuits-Saint-Georges** 1er Cru Boudots £E
● **Bourgogne Rouge** £B
DOM. LUCIEN MUZARD ET FILS ● **Santenay** 1er Cru Beauregard £C   1er Cru Clos Faubard £C
● **Santenay** 1er Cru Clos des Tavannes £C
PHILIPPE NADDEF ● **Gevrey-Chambertin** Vieilles Vignes £D   1er Cru Cazetiers £E
DOM. JEAN ET ANNICK PARENT ● **Monthelie** 1er Cru Duresses £C
● **Pommard** 1er Cru Rugiens £E
DOM. PARIZE PÈRE ET FILS ● **Givry** Champ Nalot £B   1er Cru Grandes Vignes £C

O **Givry** 1er Cru Grandes Vignes £C
DOM. JEAN PASCAL ET FILS O **Puligny-Montrachet** 1er Cru Hameau de Blagny £E
FERNAND & LAURENT PILLOT O **Chassagne-Montrachet** 1er Cru Vergers £E 1er Cru Morgeots £E
O **Chassagne-Montrachet** 1er Cru Vide Bourse £E 1er Cru Grande Ruchottes £E
O **Meursault** 1er Cru Caillerets £E ● **Pommard** 1er Cru Rugiens Peregrinus £F
PAUL PILLOT O **Chassagne-Montrachet** 1er Cru Caillerets £F O **Saint-Aubin** 1er Cru Charmois £D
DOM. DE LA POUSSE D'OR ● **Volnay** 1er Cru Clos de la Bousse d'Or £E
● **Volnay** 1er Cru Clos des 60 Ouvrées £E
HENRI PRUDHON O **Puligny-Montrachet** Les Enseignières £E
● **Saint-Aubin** Les Argillers £C 1er Cru Sentier du Clou £C
MICHEL PRUNIER O **Auxey-Duresses** Vieilles Vignes £C
DOM. RAGOT ● **Givry** 1er Cru Grande Berge £C
HENRI ET GILLES REMORIQUET ● **Nuits-Saint-Georges** Allots £D 1er Cru Damodes £E
● **Nuits-Saint-Georges** 1er Cru Les Saint-Georges £E
ROBLET-MONNOT ● **Volnay** 1er Cru Brouillards £E 1er Cru Taillepieds £E
ROSSIGNOL-TRAPET ● **Gevrey-Chambertin** £E 1er Cru Petite Chapelle £E
JOSEPH ROTY ● **Charmes-Chambertin** Tres Vieilles Vignes £G
● **Gevrey-Chambertin** 1er Cru Fontenys £F
DOM. MICHEL SARRAZIN ET FILS ● **Givry** Clos de la Putin £C 1er Cru Grands Pretants £C
O **Givry** Grognots £C
DOM. DE SUREMAIN ● **Monthelie** Château de Monthelie £C 1er Cru Sur La Velle £E
O **Rully** 1er Cru £C
H ET Y DE SUREMAIN ● **Mercurey** 1er Cru En Sazenay £C
JEAN TARDY ● **Clos de Vougeot** £G ● **Vosne-Romanée** Chaumes £F
DOM. CHARLES THOMAS ● **Romanée-Saint-Vivant** £G ● **Bonnes Mares** £G
● **Chambertin Clos-de-Bèze** £G ● **Vosne-Romanée** 1er Cru Les Malconsorts £F
● **Nuits-Saint-Georges** 1er Cru Clos de Thorey £E
GÉRARD THOMAS O **Saint-Aubin** £C 1er Cru Murgers des Dents de Chien £D
JOSEPH VOILLOT ● **Volnay** £D ● **Pommard** £D

Author's Choice for Côte d'Or & Côte Chalonnaise (PW)

30 classic red Burgundies
MARQUIS D'ANGERVILLE ● **Volnay** 1er Cru Clos des Ducs
DOM. DE L'ARLOT ● **Nuits-Saint-Georges** 1er Cru Clos des Forêts-Saint-Georges
COMTE ARMAND ● **Pommard** 1er Cru Clos des Epeneaux
DOM. ROBERT ARNOUX ● **Vosne-Romanée** 1er Cru Les Suchots
GHISLAINE BARTHOD ● **Chambolle-Musigny** 1er Cru Les Charmes
BOUCHARD PÈRE ET FILS ● **Pommard** 1er Cru Rugiens
SYLVAIN CATHIARD ● **Romanée-Saint-Vivant**
ROBERT CHEVILLON ● **Nuits-Saint-Georges** 1er Cru Les Saint-Georges
BRUNO CLAIR ● **Gevrey-Chambertin** 1er Cru Les Cazetiers
CLOS DE TART ● **Clos de Tart**
DOM. DE COURCEL ● **Pommard** 1er Cru Grand Clos des Epenots
DOM. DUJAC ● **Clos de la Roche**
DOM. RENÉ ENGEL ● **Clos de Vougeot**
DOM. FAIVELEY ● **Chambertin Clos-de-Bèze**
GEANTET-PANSIOT ● **Charmes-Chambertin**
DOM. HENRI GOUGES ● **Nuits-Saint-Georges** 1er Cru Les Vaucrains
DOM. JEAN GRIVOT ● **Vosne-Romanée** 1er Cru Les Beaux Monts
ANNE GROS ● **Richebourg**
LOUIS JADOT ● **Gevrey-Chambertin** 1er Cru Clos Saint-Jacques
MICHEL LAFARGE ● **Volnay** 1er Cru Clos des Chênes
DOM. DES LAMBRAYS ● **Clos des Lambrays**

MÉO-CAMUZET ● **Vosne-Romanée** 1er Cru Cros Parentoux

HUBERT DE MONTILLE ● **Volnay** 1er Cru Taillepieds

DENIS MORTET ● **Gevrey-Chambertin** 1er Cru Lavaux Saint-Jacques

JACQUES-FRÉDÉRIC MUGNIER ● **Musigny**

DOM. PONSOT ● **Griotte-Chambertin**

DOM. ROUMIER ● **Bonnes Mares**

DOM. ARMAND ROUSSEAU ● **Chambertin**

DOM. TRAPET PÈRE ET FILS ● **Gevrey-Chambertin** 1er Cru Petite Chapelle

DOM. COMTES GEORGES DE VOGÜÉ ● **Musigny** Vieilles Vignes

15 consistently fine Côte de Beaune whites

DOM. GUY AMIOT ET FILS ○ **Chassagne-Montrachet** 1er Cru Les Caillerets

ROGER BELLAND ○ **Chassagne-Montrachet** 1er Cru Morgeot Clos Pitois

DOM. BONNEAU DU MARTRAY ○ **Corton-Charlemagne**

MICHEL BOUZEREAU ET FILS ○ **Meursault** 1er Cru Genevrières

LOUIS CARILLON ○ **Puligny-Montrachet** 1er Cru Perrières

GÉRARD CHAVY ET FILS ○ **Puligny-Montrachet** 1er Cru Folatières

JEAN-FRANÇOIS COCHE-DURY ○ **Meursault** 1er Cru Perrières

MICHEL COLIN-DELÉGER ET FILS ○ **Puligny-Montrachet** 1er Cru Les Demoiselles

JEAN-PHILIPPE FICHET ○ **Meursault** Tessons

VINCENT GIRARDIN ○ **Chassagne-Montrachet** 1er Cru Morgeot

PATRICK JAVILLIER ○ **Meursault** Les Tillets

DOM. DES COMTES LAFON ○ **Meursault** 1er Cru Charmes

DOM. LEFLAIVE ○ **Puligny-Montrachet 1er Cru** Les Pucelles

BERNARD MOREY ○ **Chassagne-Montrachet** 1er Cru Caillerets

DOM. ROULOT ○ **Meursault** 1er Cru Perrières

20 value for money Burgundies

DOM. ARLAUD ● **Bourgogne** Roncevie

DENIS BACHELET ● **Côtes de Nuits-Villages**

GHISLAINE BARTHOD ● **Chambolle-Musigny**

ROGER BELLAND ○ **Santenay** 1er Cru Beauregard

ROGER BELLAND ● **Santenay** 1er Cru Beauregard

BOUCHARD PERE ET FILS ○ **Beaune** 1er Cru Clos Saint-Landry

DOM. CARRÉ-COURBIN ● **Volnay** Vieilles Vignes

SYLVAIN CATHIARD ● **Bourgogne Rouge**

MICHEL COLIN-DELÉGER ○ **Chassagne-Montrachet**

JEAN-JACQUES CONFURON ● **Côtes de Nuits-Villages** Les Vignottes

VINCENT DUREUIL-JANTHIAL ○ **Rully** 1er Cru Les Margotés

JEAN-JACQUES GIRARD ○ **Pernand-Vergelesses** Les Belles Filles

PATRICK JAVILLIER ○ **Bourgogne** Cuvée Oligocène

DOM. DES COMTES LAFON ● **Monthelie** 1er Cru Les Duresses

HUBERT LAMY ○ **Bourgogne Blanc**

FRANÇOIS LUMPP ○ **Givry** 1er Cru Petite Marole

JEAN-MARC PAVELOT ● **Savigny-lès-Beaune** 1er Cru La Dominode

FRANÇOIS RAQUILLET ● **Mercurey** 1er Cru Les Naugues

MICHELE & PATRICE RION ● **Bourgogne Rouge** Bons Bâtons

AUBERT ET PAMÉLA DE VILLAINE ○ **Bouzeron Aligoté**

The Mâconnais is Burgundy's frontier region where the full potential of the Chardonnay grape is only just beginning to be realised. Thanks in part to a new wave of producers Pouilly-Fuissé is now at an unprecedented level of quality, increasingly expressed in individual climats that make this region so complex and fascinating. Not only is the trend swinging away from overblown high-octane examples but a handful of growers are also revitalising the soils of vineyard plots scattered wide across the Mâconnais.

Village secrets

The Mâconnais produces as much wine as the Côte d'Or and Côte Chalonnaise combined, though much of it is pretty ordinary. Red under the **Mâcon** and **Mâcon Supérieur** ACs is usually poor and Gamay-based; any better reds are likely to be sold as Bourgogne Rouge. Limestone soils are important to the increasing percentage of Chardonnay planted in the region and much of what is produced is sold as **Mâcon-Villages** or hyphenated with the name of the individual village (such as Uchizy or Chardonnay). From the best growers this is a source of inexpensive and increasingly good-quality white Burgundy. Since 1998, **Viré-Clessé** has been a separate appellation for a stretch of vineyards near the eastern edge of the Mâcon centred on the villages of Viré and Clessé.

Heart of the Mâconnais

For long the greatest interest has been centred around four communes in the very south of the Mâconnais. Chaintré, Fuissé, Solutré and Vergisson comprise **Pouilly-Fuissé**, the latter two famous for the rock bluffs that proved useful in prehistoric times for herding and killing wild animals. Now the slopes that run down from the foot of the cliffs are some of the best in the region for producing rich, ripe, full-bodied whites. There are still some heavy, alcoholic whites but radical improvement over the last decade or so has seen the emergence of wines to rival all but the most elegant, refined and complete Côte de Beaune. As well as displaying increasing balance and harmony there is definite refinement and elegance from the top sites. At a lower level the wines are more immediate and obvious than something from the Côte de Beaune. North of Chaintré at the eastern limit of these hills are the separate villages of **Pouilly-Loché** and **Pouilly-Vinzelles**. Bret Brothers/La Soufrandière show the quality that is possible here. **Saint-Véran** encompasses Chardonnay vineyards from villages to the north and south of Pouilly-Fuissé. Its quality is very producer-dependent, ranging from the lean and angular to a fine Pouilly-Fuissé substitute at considerably lower prices. Jean Rijckaert has shown what is possible both at Leynes and from further afield. More potential is also beginning to be exploited from other sites further along a north-west axis from Pouilly-Fuissé, including Merlin at La Roche Vineuse, Guffens-Heynen/Verget at Sologny and Héritiers du Comte Lafon at Milly Lamartine.

Mâconnais vintages

The ageing potential of the finest white Burgundy from the Mâconnais varies greatly, even within Pouilly-Fuissé. Most regular examples will only improve for two or three years' from the vintage date. Vineyard-designated or special *cuvées* however might improve for 5 to 10 years. However, not only does quality vary from producer to producer but so does style and the structure, and consequently it is difficult to generalize about ageing potential. Of recent vintages, 2002 is the star. Despite changeable weather conditions healthy grapes were harvested with excellent balance between ripeness and acidity. There are many good wines, vibrant with marvellous fruit and style. By contrast the extreme heat of 2003 means producers will have to battle to produce balanced, harmonious wines. Conditions in 2001 were also much more difficult with an unsettled growing season and a struggle to achieve ripeness and avoid rot due to damp, warm conditions. Despite this the best 2001s, if sometimes leaner, can show good minerality and ripe fruit. There's plenty of excellent wine from 2000 due to a favourable growing season and harvest.

AUVIGUE Pouilly-Fuissé A: **WSS**, P&S

Owner: Jean-Pierre Auvigue   Le Moulin du Pont, 71850 Charnay-lès-Mâcon
Based outside Pouilly-Fuissé at Charnay-lès-Mâcon, Auvigue produces less than 20,000 cases of a range of Mâcon whites. Top wines show particularly good structure. All the grapes are hand-harvested, with the estate vineyards supplemented by bought-in grapes for the lesser *cuvées*. Mâcon-Fuissé is a good example of round, plump, fruity white Burgundy, while the Les Chênes version of Saint-Véran has well-integrated oak with its lemony fruit. *Cru* Pouilly-Fuissé show good restraint if not the concentration of some examples but the most remarkable wines are the Vieilles Vignes and Hors Classé versions. The Vieilles Vignes adds much more depth and intensity and a structure that calls for at least four or five years' age. The Hors Classé is only made when conditions are right, and is late-picked – while in the rich blockbuster style, it is balanced by excellent strucure. (PW)

O **Pouilly-Fuissé** La Frairie★★ £C Les Chailloux★★ £C Vieilles Vignes★★★ £D Hors Classé★★★★ £D
O **Saint-Véran** Moulin du Pont★★ £B Les Chênes★★ £B
O **Mâcon-Solutré** Moulin du Pont★ £B O **Mâcon-Fuissé** Moulin du Pont★★ £B

DANIEL ET MARTINE BARRAUD Pouilly-Fuissé A: **L&S**, NYg

Owner: Daniel et Martine Barraud   Le Bourg, 71960 Vergisson
This couple are leaders in differentiating and better defining the various *terroirs* of Pouilly-Fuissé. This large appellation has a little over twice the vineyard area of Meursault and there are considerable differences in both quality and style across the four communes it covers. Most of the Barrauds' 7 ha of vines are on the higher slopes of Vergisson, beneath the dramatic rock itself, where the grapes generally ripen a little later than in lower-lying vineyards. While new oak is employed, it is usually well-judged. Wines from vineyards with an average vine age in excess of 40 years are designated Vieilles Vignes. The En Buland is the richest, most full-bodied of the various *cuvées*, though the Les Crays shows great concentration, intensity and a mineral influence, La Roche more of a piercing mineral elegance. Of two Saint-Vérans, the lighter En Crèches shows more style than a fatter, more four-square Les Pommards. The Mâcon-Vergisson also comes from Vergisson vineyards but from just outside the Pouilly-Fuissé boundaries. The 2000s are particularly rich and powerful but with the fruit and structure to keep for the best part of a decade (in the top *cuvées*) while the 2001s are atypically good for the vintage and 2002s excellent. The wines remain reasonably priced for their quality. (PW)

O **Pouilly-Fuissé** La Roche★★★ £C Les Crays Vieilles Vignes★★★ £D En Bulands Vieilles Vignes★★★★ £D
O **Pouilly-Fuissé** En France★★ £C La Verchère Vieilles Vignes★★ £C
O **Saint-Véran** En Crèches★★ £B Les Pommards★★ £C
O **Mâcon-Vergisson** La Roche★★ £B

ANDRÉ BONHOMME Viré-Clessé A: **DDr**, WSc

Owner: André Bonhomme   71260 Viré
In an attempt to become profitable rather than just accepting what the *négociants* were prepared to pay, André Bonhomme was the first to bottle his own wines in the Mâcon-Villages area in 1957. He has long held a reputation as a reliable source for fine inexpensive white Burgundy. His 9 ha are manually harvested and there has always been a willingness to wait until the grapes are fully ripe. The wines are now made by André's son, Pascal, but this domaine has been one of the few steady alternatives to the lean, acidic wines that are still too prevalent in the Mâconnais. The regular *cuvée* is vinified solely in vats but oak is used in part for the Cuvée Speciale and Vieilles Vignes, around a quarter new for the latter. Older wines (they can keep for up to five years) made before the new Viré-Clessé appellation came into being, are labelled as Mâcon-Viré. (PW)

O **Viré-Clessé**★ £B Cuvée Spéciale★★ £C Vieilles Vignes★★ £C

CH. DE FUISSÉ   Pouilly-Fuissé   www.chateau-fuisse.fr   A: **ABy**, BBR, Res, Hrd

Owner: Vincent family   Château de Fuissé, 71960 Fuissé
Arguably Pouilly-Fuissé's most famous estate, if no longer one of the very best. It has been in the Vincent family since 1852 but has come to prominence under Jean-Jacques Vincent since he assumed control of the domaine in 1966. There are now 30 ha, mostly in the commune of Fuissé from which a number of different Pouilly-Fuissé *cuvées* are made, including three separate *climats* (Le Clos, Les Brûles, Les Combettes). All are vinified in oak followed by nine months' ageing in barrel. At their best, the top wines combine a ripe fruit intensity with excellent structure and depth and usually come into their own with at least five years' age. Recent tastings reveal a slight lack of intensity, even hollowness, with the Vieilles Vignes easily the most convincing wine. Saint-Véran, Mâcon-Villages and Mâcon-Fuissé are also made under the Château-Fuissé label. A second range of wines is made under the Vincent label, in part from family domaines and in part from bought-in grapes. These include Pouilly-Fuissé, Saint-Véran (Domaine des Morats), Mâcon-Villages, Mâcon-Fuissé and two Beaujolais, Morgon Les Charmes and Juliénas Domaine le Cotoyon. (PW)

Château-Fuissé:
O **Pouilly-Fuissé**Vieilles Vignes★★★ £E
O **Pouilly-Fuissé**★★★ £D   Les Combettes★★ £D   Le Clos★★ £E   Les Brûles★★★ £E
O **Saint-Véran**★ £C

CH. DES RONTETS   Pouilly-Fuissé   A:VTr, C&R

Owner: Gazeau family   Château des Rontets, 71960 Fuissé
Claire Gazeau and her Italian husband, Fabio Montrasi, have transformed the wines from this old family property since the mid-1990s. There are just 6 ha but all are planted to Chardonnay. Being well-established, the average vine age is high (45 years in the Clos Varambon, 70 in Les Birbettes). The Clos Varambon is a fine example of Pouilly aged exclusively in large wood. Pierrefolle adds more depth and interest and a spicy component which derives in part from a small percentage of new oak. The top *cuvée*, Les Birbettes, has really superb fruit which easily takes up the new oak (30 per cent) as well as excellent depth and is one of the most stylish examples of Pouilly-Fuissé. Though it is not inexpensive it outperforms many a more expensive village-level Chassagne or Puligny-Montrachet. (PW)
O **Pouilly-Fuissé** Clos Varambon★★ £C   Pierrefolle★★★ £D   Les Birbettes★★★ £D

DOM. CORDIER PÈRE ET FILS   Pouilly-Fuissé   A: HHB, L&S, Maj, WSc

Owner: Cordier family   Les Molards, 71960 Fuissé
Since Christophe Cordier joined his father Roger, this estate's inherent potential has been further realised. Their vineyards are in the commune of Fuissé, where some of other big Pouilly-Fuissé names such as J A FERRET and CHÂTEAU DE FUISSÉ are to be found. The 14.5 ha also includes some Saint-Véran. The wines are very powerful, many of them high in alcohol – being made from very ripe, low-yielding fruit – but are still remarkably well-balanced. There is progressively more concentration and depth, as well as power, in the top *cuvées*. An intense minerality complements a preserved citrus character and oak-derived spiciness in many of the wines. Prices are now high, even in the context of the prices Pouilly-Fuissé now commands, but so is the quality. Most of the wines can be drunk young for their dramatic, exuberant richness, though the most structured and profound, Vers Cras and Vers Pouilly, will be better with four or five years' age. As well as some Bourgogne Blanc (Jean de la Vigne) and other *cuvées* of Pouilly-Fuissé (Au Métertière and *cuvées* from individually numbered barrels), a little of an exotic blockbuster, Juliette la Grande, is also made. (PW)
O **Pouilly-Fuissé** Vignes Blanches★★★★ £E   Vers Cras★★★★ £E   Vers Pouilly★★★★ £E
O **Pouilly-Fuissé**★★★ £C   Vieilles Vignes★★★ £D   La Vigne de Monsieur Marguin★★★★ £E
O **Saint-Véran** Clos à la Côte★★★ £C   En Faux★★★ £C   Les Crais★★★★ £D
O **Pouilly-Loché**★★★ £C   O **Mâcon-Fuissé**★★ £C   O **Mâcon Blanc**★★ £B

CORSIN Pouilly-Fuissé www.domaine-corsin.com A: **SsG**, E&T

Owner: Corsin family Les Plantés, 71960 Davayé
Gilles and Jean-Jacques Corsin are the current generation making the wines at this long-established Pouilly-Fuissé estate. The 12 ha are split between Pouilly-Fuissé and Saint-Véran. The wines are fermented and aged both partly in vats and partly in oak, and typically show concentrated ripe fruit and a well-integrated oak character. They can provide excellent, relatively inexpensive drinking with two or three years' age. A Cuvée Précoce bottling of Saint-Véran comes from younger vines, is bottled sooner and can be drunk earlier. (PW)
O **Pouilly-Fuissé★★** £D O **Saint-Véran★★** £C O **Mâcon-Villages★** £B

DOM. DE LA CROIX SENAILLET Saint-Véran A: OWL, CTy, B&T,Goe, P&S, CeB

Owner: Richard et Stéphane Martin En Coland, 71960 Davayé
The Martins have 22 ha, the majority of which fall in Davayé (part of Saint-Véran) but on the lower slopes of Vergisson and Solutré. The regular Saint-Véran is an excellent example, ripe and intense with a refined floral and mineral character – what more Saint-Véran should taste like. Les Rochats, one of two *crus* (the other is La Grande Bruyère), shows more depth and a touch of class but needs three to four years' age. A basic Mâcon Blanc is also attractive with a leesy, citrusy character. As well as a little rich, ripe old-vines Pouilly Fuissé (from the *lieu-dit* En Pommard), some red Mâcon is also produced. (PW)
O **Pouilly-Fuissé★★★** £C O **Saint-Véran★★** £B Les Rochats★★★ £C
O **Mâcon Blanc★** £B

DOM. DES DEUX ROCHES Saint-Véran A: **BBR**, ThP

Owner: Christian Collovray & Jean-Luc Terrier Domaine des Deux Roches, 71960 Davayé
Increasing amounts of very good whites are being made outside the quality heart of Mâconnais, Pouilly-Fuissé. Saint-Véran lies both to the north and south but this estate has long shown that high quality is possible here too. While a number of Pouilly-Fuissé estates make fine Saint-Véran in addition to their top whites, the 35-ha Deux Roches majors on Saint-Véran. As well as attractive, fruity regular *cuvées*, a percentage of new oak is used for fermenting and ageing the top wines. Generally there is good ripeness as well as a mineral aspect to most of the wines. There is also a little Pouilly-Fuissé La Roche. Owners Christian Collovray and Jean-Luc Terrier also produce some very good wines from Chardonnay at Domaine d'ANTUGNAC in the Limoux AC in the Languedoc-Roussillon. (PW)
O **Saint-Véran★** £B Vieilles Vignes★★ £C Terres Noires★★ £C Cras★★★ £D
O **Mâcon-Villages★** £B

DOM. J A FERRET Pouilly-Fuissé A: Bal, JAr, Lay, Rae

Owner: Colette Ferret Le Plan, 71960 Fuissé
This domaine has been bottling its own wine for 60 years, though it had its beginnings more than two decades before the French Revolution. Colette Ferret's Pouilly-Fuissés, made famous by her mother before she died in 1993, have been compared not just to *premier cru* but also *grand cru* Côte de Beaune whites. They are certainly very full-bodied with remarkable concentration and extract and with added finesse and purity in the best examples. As might be expected, yields are low, the average vine age high and the grapes are manually harvested. The wines are barrel-fermented and aged with extended lees-contact for maximum enrichment. From 15 ha are fashioned four great *crus*: Le Clos, Les Ménétrières, Les Perrières and Tournant de Pouilly. These are given the greatest amount of new oak and the longest period of ageing. Other bottlings are also made including three other *crus*, Les Sceles, Les Vernays and Les Moulins, which are sold only in the US. Rich and honeyed, the wines also display fine floral, mineral aspects as well as a classic grilled nuts character. The Hors Classé designation applies only to a selection of old vines in the best years and these wines are slightly more expensive than the Tête de Cru bottlings. Prices reflect what top Pouilly-Fuissé ought to command and are no longer anything like the most expensive from the appellation. (PW)

○ **Pouilly-Fuissé** Ménétrières Hors Classé★★★★ £D Tournant de Pouilly Hors Classé★★★★ £D
○ **Pouilly-Fuissé** Le Clos Tête de Cru★★★ £D Perrières Tête de Cru★★★ £D

DOM. DES GERBEAUX Pouilly-Fuissé   A: **WTs**, BBR

Owner: Beatrice et Jean-Michel Drouin   71960 Solutré
The husband-and-wife team of Beatrice and Jean-Michel Drouin make excellent examples of Mâcon, Saint-Véran and Pouilly-Fuissé whites which are not that widely seen on account of the production always selling out. The wines show excellent intensity, texture and structure and have balanced alcohol. There is attractive minerality even in Mâcon-Solutré, a lively intensity to ripe Saint-Véran and more depth and richness in Pouilly-Fuissé. The wines are also very reasonably priced without the premiums that the wines of more high-profile producers have acquired. All the wines can be drunk fairly young but the Pouilly-Fuissé in particular will also repay keeping. Two other special *cuvées* of Pouilly-Fuissé are also made, En Champs Roux and Jacques Charvet. (PW)
○ **Pouilly-Fuissé** Terroir de Solutré Vieilles Vignes★★★ £C
○ **Saint-Véran**★★ £B ○ **Mâcon-Solutré** Le Clos★★ £B ○ **Mâcon-Chaintré**★★ £B

DOM. GUFFENS-HEYNEN Mâcon-Villages   A: L&W, L&S, Far, C&R, Odd

Owner: Jean-Marie Guffens-Heynen   Domaine Guffens-Heynen, 71960 Vergisson
Jean-Marie Guffens is one of the wine world's larger-than-life characters but also one of its most exciting winemakers. Both through the substantial *négociant* VERGET operation and a small number of wines made at this, his own private 3-ha estate, he has made a significant impact on the fine wine scene. The grapes are picked very ripe from low-yielding vines that have been meticulously cared for, before being pressed very slowly in an old-fashioned vertical press. A mix of oak, both new and used, small and large, is used in their fermentation and ageing. Not only do the wines have fantastic richness, depth and substance but they also show finesse and elegance. They are not as consistent as some but neither is there uniformity; when these wines are particularly successful (there is brilliant quality in most 2002, 01 and 00s) they will provide memorable drinking for up to a decade. Guffens-Heynen *cru* bottlings of Pouilly-Fuissé have included Les Croux, Roche and Hauts de Vignes. The Verget Mâconnais wines are included below, for others see the Côte d'Or section. (PW)

Guffens-Heynen:
○ **Pouilly-Fuissé**★★★★ £E
○ **Mâcon-Pierreclos**★★★ £C En Chavigne★★★★ £D

Verget:
○ **Pouilly-Fuissé** Terroir de Vergisson★★★ £D ○ **Pouilly-Vinzelles** Les Quarts★★ £B
○ **Saint-Véran** Terroirs de Davayé★★ £C Terres Noires★★★ £C Vignes de Saint-Claude★★★ £C
○ **Mâcon-Bussières** Vieilles Vignes de Montbrison★★★ £B Les Prusettes★★ £C
○ **Mâcon-Burgy** Les Prusettes★★ £C En Chatelaine★★★ £C
○ **Mâcon-Vergisson** La Roche★★★ £B ○ **Mâcon-Charnay** Clos Saint-Pierre★★ £B

HÉRITIERS DU COMTE LAFON Macon-Villages   A: **M&V**, BBR, P&S

Owner: Lafon family   Cartelées, 71960 Milly Lamartine
Dominique Lafon's arrival in the Mâcon may not have aroused much interest amongst those who regularly jostle for his marvellous Meursaults (see Domaine des Comtes LAFON) but taste these wines and you'll see there is much more to this than a source of (somewhat) cheaper, more everyday white Burgundy. The wines have already improved considerably since the debut 1999s and now the potential quality that is possible in the Mâcon is increasingly apparent. The Mâcon Milly Lamartine shows a pure elegant minerally fruit and is very stylish and expressive. Clos du Four has more of everything – more depth, more mineral, more structure – and consequently needs more time. Mâcon-Bussières Le Monsard starts out austere but has real intensity of ripe citrus with a stony aspect, best with four or five years' age from a fine vintage like 2002.

New vineyards from the villages of Chardonnay and Uchizy will augment production from the 2003 vintage. (PW)

O **Mâcon Milly Lamartine**★★★ £C Clos du Four★★★ £D
O **Mâcon-Bussières** Le Monsard★★★ £D O **Mâcon Villages**★★ £C

DOM. ROGER LASSARAT Pouilly-Fuissé www.roger-lassarat.com A: **THt**, Mar, Sel

Owner: Roger Lassarat Le Martelet, 71960, Vergisson

Roger Lassarat was inspired by Château de Fuissé and J A FERRET and set out to emulate them as he established his own estate more than 30 years ago. Here as at so many of the best Pouilly-Fuissé estates the secret to the quality of the fruit is manual picking of carefully maintained, low-yielding old vines. The grapes receive a gentle pressing and partial barrel-fermentation with prolonged lees-enrichment in barrel before the wines are bottled unfiltered. The wines are ripe and richly textured, with increasing definition and better balance and structure in the most recent vintages. The range of wines has very recently been expanded to single out more individual *climats*. (PW)

O **Pouilly-Fuissé** Clos de France★★ £C Cuvée Prestige★★★ £D
O **Saint-Véran** Fournaise★★ £C Cuvée Prestige★★★ £C O **Mâcon-Vergisson** La Roche★★ £B

OLIVIER MERLIN Mâcon-Villages A: **M&V**, P&S, Hrd, WSc

Owner: Olivier Merlin Domaine du Vieux Saint-Sorlin, 71960 La Roche Vineuse

Olivier Merlin's Domaine du Vieux Saint-Sorlin has built a reputation since the late 1980s as one of the Mâcon's most reliable as well as exciting producers. For long this took the form of excellent white Mâcon-La Roche Vineuse but more recently he has made wines to the same high standards from Pouilly-Fuissé. His own 7.5 ha includes a little Pinot Noir for some red Mâcon but is mostly Chardonnay, from which he makes rich, full-bodied whites with deep ripe fruit and a certain finesse and complexity, particularly in the very complete, old-vine Les Cras. Three Pouilly-Fuissé show good structures and in Vergisson and Fuissé the capacity to age for at least five years. The Vergisson, with a fine mineral streak, is most individual, Fuissé the most classic, and the creamy Chaintré a good alternative to a fat village Meursault. A sophisticated Moulin-à-Vent is also made, as is Bourgogne Rouge. (PW)

O **Mâcon-La Roche Vineuse**★★ £B Vieilles Vignes★★★ £C Les Cras★★★ £C
O **Pouilly-Fuissé** Terroir de Chaintré★★★ £D Terroir de Fuissé★★★ £D Terroir de Vergisson★★★ £D
O **Saint-Véran** Grand Bussière★★★ £C ● **Moulin-à-Vent**★★ £C

DOM. RIJCKAERT Viré-Clessé A: JAr, Far, BBR, Odd

Owner: Jean Rijckaert En Correaux, 71570 Leynes

Jean Rijckaert is one of the Mâconnais' most exciting new producers. He used to work with Jean-Marie Guffens (GUFFENS-HEYNEN) but he is now giving the Mâconnais a further boost with his own range of wines. Having helped mould the VERGET style, it is no surprise that the same principles of slow pressings, enhanced lees-enrichment and intelligent oak-ageing, are being continued here. Rijckaert also believes passionately in restoring life to the soils and the importance of promoting deep roots in the vines. He makes more than two dozen individual *cuvées*, mostly from 35- to 40-year-old vines, both from his own 4 ha of vineyards and for other small growers. He seeks precision and minerality in his wines and achieves it with some superb aromatic, concentrated wines that show excellent definition and purity. Also made are a number of excellent whites from the Jura where he has another 4 ha of vineyard and a winery facility. Many are of an unprecedented level of quality for the region, both those based on Chardonnay and those from Savagnin. Particularly good and relatively inexpensive are Arbois Pre-Leveron Vieilles Vignes (Chardonnay), Côtes de Jura Vignes des Voies (Chardonnay), Côtes du Jura Les Sarres (both Chardonnay and Savagnin), Arbois Chante-Merle (Chardonnay) and Arbois En Paradis Vieilles Vignes (both versions). Rarely is there any need to hurry to drink these wines, as most will be better with three or four years' age. A brown label indicate a grower's wine (and also includes their name), while a green label is used for the domaine wines.

Only a selection are listed below. The 2002s are particularly fine. (PW)

O **Pouilly-Fuissé** Vers Chânes Vieilles Vignes★★★ £C
O **Saint-Véran** En Avonne★★ £C L'Epinet★★ £C En Faux Vieilles Vignes★★★ £C
O **Viré-Clessé** Les Vercherres Vieilles Vignes★★ £C En Thurissey Vieilles Vignes★★★ £C
O **Saint-Aubin** En Monceau★★★ £D O **Mâcon Montbellet** En Pottes★★ £C

DOM. ROBERT-DENOGENT Pouilly-Fuissé www.robert-denogent.com A: Bib, Gau

Owner: Jean-Jacques Robert Domaine Robert-Denogent, 71960 Fuissé
Jean-Jacques Robert has rapidly improved quality at this small 5-ha estate since taking over in 1988. There is a tremendous resource of old vines and yields are further reduced through careful pruning. Though new oak is used, all the wines show lovely fruit intensity and fine structures with pronounced minerally, *terroir*-given definition; no two are quite alike. Even the Mâcon-Solutré shows some style, more floral in character than the various Pouilly-Fuissé. The La Croix has a striking mineral component due to more schistous soils, while the Claude Denogent wine is an old-vine selection and Les Carrons comes from an exceptional site with a higher clay content and very old vines. The top wines benefit from at least three to four years' ageing. As well as those listed below, another *cuvée*, Les Taches, is also made. (PW)

O **Pouilly-Fuissé** La Croix★★ £C Les Reisses★★ £C Claude Denogent★★★ £D Les Carrons★★★★ £E
O **Mâcon-Solutré** Clos Bertillonnes★★ £C

SAUMAIZE-MICHELIN Pouilly-Fuissé A: **Eno, CTy**, Rae, SVS

Owner: Roger & Christine Saumaize Le Martelet, 71960 Vergisson
Like the wines of Daniel et Martine BARRAUD and others, these wines show that Vergisson has the potential to equal Pouilly-Fuissé's more established and generally most highly regarded commune, Fuissé. The Saumaize estate extends to 9 ha and as well as several different *cuvées* of Pouilly-Fuissé, some fine Saint-Véran and Mâcon-Villages are made. There is the utmost attention to detail and hygiene and the resulting consistency, both from year to year and across the range, is very impressive. The wines see some oak. They can be quite firm and steely when very young but they have good definition and added richness with age. The best Pouilly-Fuissé *cuvées* come from old vines, including a very small amount of the top wine, Ampelopsis, which is remarkably concentrated and proportioned. The Saint-Vérans are two more of an increasing number of good examples from this previously under-performing appellation. (PW)

O **Pouilly-Fuissé** Ampelopsis★★★ £D
O **Pouilly-Fuissé** Vigne Blanche★★ £C Clos sur la Roche★★★ £C Ronchevats★★★ £C
O **Saint-Véran** Crêches★★ £B Vieilles Vignes★★ £B O **Mâcon-Villages** Les Sertaux★★ £B

DOM. DE LA SOUFRANDIÈRE Pouilly-Vinzelles A: **M&V**, BBR, F&M, WSc

Owner: Jean-Guillaume & Jean-Philippe Bret Domaine La Soufrandière, 71680 Vinzelles
These two young *vigneron* brothers have made the finest wines ever under the small Pouilly-Vinzelles AC, which together with the contiguous Pouilly-Loché AC has less than 100 ha of vines. The Brets have less than 5 ha but their rich, ripe, structured wines have finally shown that these separate zones at the south-eastern end of Pouilly-Fuissé have similar exciting potential to that being realised elsewhere in the region. All the grapes are picked by hand and the wines are ripe and concentrated, verging on being overdone in both the regular bottling and Les Quarts, which comes from older vines. The top *cuvée* Millerandée show tremendous richness, coming from very small (*millerandé*) grapes from 70-year-old vines. While there is not the finesse of a top Côte de Beaune white it is well-proportioned and deserves to be drunk with five years' age. A series of wines is also are made from bought-in grapes and sold under the Bret Brothers label including Mâcon-Cruzilles and examples of Viré-Clessé, Saint-Véran and Pouilly-Fuissé. (PW)

Dom. de la Soufrandière:
O **Pouilly-Vinzelles**★★ £B Les Quarts★★★ £D Les Quarts Millerandée★★★ £E

Bret Brothers:
O **Pouilly-Vinzelles** Les Remparts★★★ £D

JEAN THÉVENET Macon-Villages www.bongran.com A: L&S, GBa, Adm, HHB, JNi, T&W

Owner: Jean Thévenet Domaine de la Bongran, Quintaine, 71260 Clessé
Jean Thévenet's wines are like no one else's – atypically rich, very ripe and honeyed but with great structure and vibrancy. The wines from 15 ha of vineyards are the products of two separate domaines, Domaine de la Bongran and Domaine Emilian Gillet. Yields are low and the grapes are harvested manually. The Emilian Gillet is more floral than the Bongran but similarly strikingly honeyed. Previously labelled Mâcon-Clessé and Mâcon-Viré, the wines are now simply labelled Mâcon-Villages as, with a degree of residual sugar, they were denied promotion to the new Viré-Clessé AC despite their evident quality. A Cuvée Levroutée is made from selected overripe grapes in certain years, while a little Cuvée Spéciale Botrytis (from botrytised grapes) is made when exceptional conditions permit (such as 2000 and 1995). This is a wine of exceptional richness and honeyed, preserved and tropical fruits but with excellent acidity and the ability to keep for more than a decade. (PW)
O **Mâcon-Villages** Tradition Sélection EJ Thévenet Domaine de la Bongran★★★ £D
O **Mâcon-Villages** Quintaine Domaine Emilian Gillet★★★ £C

DOM. THIBERT Pouilly-Fuissé A: **ABy**, Dec, CRs

Owner: Thibert family Le Bourg, 71960 Fuissé
Christophe Thibert and his wife Catherine run this 16-ha estate, which has around half its vineyards in Pouilly-Fuissé. The wines show more finesse and less upfront richness than some but combine a minerally intensity with good concentration in the best years. Oak is used to enhance structure and is considerably less overt in most of the wines than in many a Pouilly-Fuissé. Though less immediate, the wines have excellent ageing potential, especially the top *cuvées*. Recent releases have been a little uneven but always elegant. In addition, as well as some Pouilly-Vinzelles, a little of a prestige *cuvée*, Vignes de la Côte, is made. (PW)
O **Pouilly-Fuissé★★** £C Vieilles Vignes★★★ £C Vignes Blanches★★★ £D
O **Mâcon-Fuissé★** £B O **Mâcon-Prissé** En Chailloux★ £B

DOM. VALETTE Pouilly-Fuissé A: M&V, WSc

Owner: Valette family Vercheres, 71570 Chaintré
No list of the Mâconnais' best producers would be complete without Gérard Valette. Gérard and his son Philippe run what is effectively an organic estate of 17 ha. Although more than half of it is in Mâcon-Chaintré, the rest is in Pouilly-Fuissé, producing full-bodied, very ripe-fruited blockbusters. The grapes are harvested very late from often very low-yielding old vines and a percentage of new oak is used for fermenting the two Réserve *cuvées*, resulting in very powerful oaky wines. Despite the rich, almost overwhelming fruit and lees-enriched character, the wines usually have the necessary balance to provide heady, complex drinking soon after their release and often for another five years' or more. The extended ageing of these *cuvées* before bottling means they become available a year or two later than other top Pouilly-Fuissé releases – but in the meantime you can enjoy the fresh, fruit-filled Mâcon-Chaintré made for relatively early drinking. A little Pouilly-Vinzelles is also made. (PW)
O **Pouilly-Fuissé** Tradition★★★ £D Clos Reyssie Réserve★★★★ £E
O **Pouilly-Fuissé** Clos de Monsieur Noly Vieilles Vignes Réserve★★★★ £F
O **Mâcon-Chaintré** Vieilles Vignes★★ £B

Also see the following Burgundy producers with an entry in the section *Côte D'Or & Côte Chalonnaise:*
BOUCHARD PERE ET FILS
as well as Beaujolais producers with an entry in the *Beaujolais* section:
GEORGES DUBOEUF

MÂCONNAIS/OTHER WINES OF NOTE

CH. DE BEAUREGARD/JOSEPH BURRIER O **Pouilly-Fuissé** £C Les Châtaigniers £D
CORINNE ET THIERRY DROUIN O **Pouilly-Fuissé** Vieilles Vignes £C
MICHEL FOREST O **Pouilly-Fuissé** £C La Roche £C Les Crays £D Vieilles Vignes £D
O **Mâcon-Vergisson** £B
DOM. DE FUSSIACUS O **Pouilly-Fuissé** Vieilles Vignes £C   O **Mâcon-Fuissé** £B
PIERETTE ET MARC GUILLEMOT-MICHEL O **Mâcon-Villages** Quintaine £B
MAURICE LAPALUS ET FILS O **Mâcon Pierreclos** £B
NICOLAS MAILLET O **Mâcon-Verzé** £B Le Chemin Blanc £B
JEAN MANCIAT O **Mâcon-Charnay** £B
MANCIAT-PONCET O **Pouilly-Fuissé** La Roche Vieilles Vignes £C Vieilles Vignes £C
O **Pouilly-Fuissé** Les Crays Vieilles Vignes £C
GILLES NOBLET O **Pouilly-Fuissé** £C Vieilles Vignes Les Champs £C   O **Mâcon-Fuissé** £B
DOM. ALAIN NORMAND O **Mâcon La Roche Vineuse** £B
CAVE DE PRISSÉ O **Saint-Véran** Les Pierres Blanches £B   O **Mâcon Milly Lamartine** £B
DOM. DE ROALLY O **Mâcon-Montbellet** £B   O **Mâcon-Villages** £B
JACQUES ET NATALIE SAUMAIZE O **Pouilly-Fuissé** Vieilles Vignes £C
DOM. LA SOUFRANDISE/MELIN O **Pouilly-Fuissé** Vieilles Vignes £C   O **Mâcon-Fuissé** £B
DOM. GÉRALD ET PHILIBERT TALMARD O **Mâcon-Uchizy** £B   O **Mâcon-Chardonnay** £B
DOM. PAUL ET MALLORY TALMARD O **Mâcon-Uchizy** £B
DOM. VESSIGAUD O **Pouilly-Fuissé** Vieilles Vignes £C

Author's Choice for Mâconnais (PW)

15 Great Mâcon whites
DANIEL ET MARTINE BARRAUD O **Pouilly-Fuissé** En Buland Vieilles Vignes
CH. FUISSÉ O **Pouilly-Fuissé** Vieilles Vignes
CH. DES RONTETS O **Pouilly-Fuissé** Les Birbettes
DOM. CORDIER PÈRE ET FILS O **Pouilly-Fuissé** Vignes Blanches
HÉRITIERS DU COMTE LAFON O **Mâcon Milly Lamartine** Clos du Four
DOM. DES DEUX ROCHES O **Saint-Véran** Cras
DOM. J A FERRET O **Pouilly-Fuissé** Ménétrières Hors Classé
DOM. GUFFENS-HEYNEN O **Pouilly-Fuissé**
OLIVIER MERLIN O **Pouilly-Fuissé** Terroir de Vergisson
DOM. RIJCKAERT O **Viré-Clessé** En Thurissey Vieilles Vignes
DOM. ROBERT-DENOGENT O **Pouilly-Fuissé** Claude Denogent
DOM. LA SOUFRANDIÈRE O **Pouilly-Vinzelles** Les Quarts Millerandée
DOM. LA SOUFRANDISE/MELIN O **Pouilly-Fuissé** Vieilles Vignes
JEAN THÉVENET O **Mâcon-Villages** Quintaine Domaine Emilian Gillet
DOM. VALETTE O **Pouilly-Fuissé** Clos de M Noly Vieilles Vignes Réserve

10 Value for money Mâcon whites
AUVIGUE O **Mâcon-Fuissé** Moulin du Pont
ANDRÉ BONHOMME O **Viré-Clessé** Cuvée Speciale
DOM. DE LA CROIX SENAILLET O **Saint-Véran**
DOM. DES GERBEAUX O **Saint-Véran**
MAURICE LAPALUS & FILS O **Mâcon Pierreclos**
NICOLAS MAILLET O **Mâcon-Verzé**
OLIVIER MERLIN O **Mâcon-La Roche Vineuse** Vieilles Vignes
ALAIN NORMAND O **Mâcon-La Roche Vineuse**
SAUMAIZE-MICHELIN O **Mâcon-Villages** Les Sertaux
VERGET O **Mâcon-Charnay** Clos Saint-Pierre

France/Beaujolais

Now that the cheap trick that was Beaujolais Nouveau seems pretty much played out the world over, more seems set to be made of the region's real strengths. Its crus, the Gamay grape, the old vines, its granite, schist and sandy soils, its many small estates and some dedicated vignerons are the fundamentals. Add improved vinification, breathe life back into the soils and promote a willingness to explore different interpretations of just what Beaujolais can be (both a quaffer and something more serious) and more wine lovers might just add it to their shopping lists.

Beaujolais by village

Burgundy's Mâconnais melts into Beaujolais where a few Chardonnay vines qualify to be sold as Beaujolais Blanc. But the real story concerns the Gamay grape and its predisposition for a radically different growing environment as granite, schist (and in places sand or clay) soils take over from the limestone-based soils of Burgundy proper. In these soils old vines seem to count for more than low yields and grapes must be hand-picked as they are subject (in most instances) to a vinification that involves semi-carbonic maceration of whole bunches of grapes. The quality of the fruit can leave much to be desired and too much Beaujolais finishes abruptly with a hard, green edge. Better examples are richly fruity but relatively short-lived with little real structure but easy drinkability. Different interpretations of style do exist however, and some producers get more structure into the wines without losing too much of their charm and quaffability. Jadot and one or two others make the wines in the style of red Burgundy with a similar vinification and oak-ageing as for Pinot Noir-based reds. Though it may not seem worth the effort the difference a dedicated progressive grower can make to the quality of Beaujolais can be a revelation.

The best Beaujolais comes from the northern or Haut-Beaujolais, with purer soils and better slopes. It is sold as **Beaujolais-Villages** or better still as one of ten recognised *crus* from within this area. There is a trend to increasing identification of individual *climats* within the *crus*. The vineyards of **Saint-Amour**, where Beaujolais takes over from Mâconnais, are on rather mixed soils and are generally a little unexciting. **Juliénas** in contrast, from well-positioned slopes and a significant clay component in its soils, is a consistent provider of wines with better depth and intensity than most. Lighter **Chénas** occupies higher ground than the adjoining **Moulin-à-Vent** and it is the latter that has the most strength, structure and longevity of all the *crus*. Its prices are matched only by **Fleurie**, the best examples of which are perfumed but also often unequalled for their density of fruit and lush texture. **Chiroubles** has some of the most elevated vineyards in the region; the best wines are light but as refined as they get. At the heart of **Morgon** is the Côte de Py with its distinctive *roches pourries* soils of friable schist, the wines are dense and intensely cherryish. **Regnié** is the most recent *cru* and rarely exciting. The large **Brouilly** *cru* surrounds the hill of Mont Brouilly whose slopes provide **Côte de Brouilly**. The best Brouilly can have attractive fruit but much of it is poor, while Côte de Brouilly is usually marginally better.

Beaujolais vintages

Do vintages in Beaujolais matter with most of the wines being drunk so young? Apart from the fact that most of the better quality *cru* Beaujolais need at least two or three years' age, in terms of the quality in your glass choosing one vintage over another can make a big difference. Take 2003 and 2002. The latter was spoilt by late rains and many a supposedly better cru is marred by poor quality fruit. Even when the wines do have sound ripe fruit they tend to be a little dull and inspiring. By contrast from the 2003 vintage there are some super wines with thrilling vibrant fruit, in many instances without the low acidities (and the consequent need for acidification) that might have been expected. While some are over-ripe and others show green tannins, look out for some real gems. While 2001 has turned out better than first expected most producers' 2000s and 1999s are far superior.

DOM. F ET J CALOT Morgon

A: **HHB**, BBR, SVS

Owner: François et Jean Calot Le Bourg, 69910 Villié-Morgon

This 11.5-ha estate has long been an excellent source of ripe, concentrated and characterful Morgon. There are several *cuvées*, from a supple, fruity regular Cuvée Tradition to a deep, intense Vieilles Vignes that needs three years or so in order to soften a little. Vinification is traditional and not the semi-carbonic maceration favoured by most. An old-fashioned vertical press is employed and both small and large oak are used for ageing. A small amount of Tête de Cuvée and an intense, complex Cuvée Jeanne have also been made in recent vintages. All are very reasonably and honestly priced for the quality – there has been no attempt to sell any of the wines at a premium to enhance the domaine's status or cash flow as some growers in the region have done. (PW)

● **Morgon** Tradition★★ £B Vieilles Vignes★★ £B Tête de Cuvée★★ £B Cuvée Jeanne★★★ £B

CH. DES JACQUES Moulin-à-Vent www.louis-jadot.com

A: **HMA**

Owner: Louis Jadot Château des Jacques, 71570 Romanèche-Thorins

Long before its recent purchase by Louis JADOT, this was the leading estate in the Beaujolais region. Singular in its approach to vinification, with a Pinot-like destemming followed by fermentation in open tanks and *pigeage*, the wines have been richer and fuller with none of the woodiness or greenness that the whole-bunch fermentation practised by others can bring. Following the arrival of Jadot's Jacques Lardière, maceration times have been extended and there is some use of automatic *pigeage*. In addition, five separate sites have been isolated from within the estate's 27 ha of Gamay vines and each of these is aged in new oak (Clos du Grand Carquelin, Grand Clos de Rochegrès, Champ de Cour, La Roche and Clos des Thorins). So the Côte d'Or has come to Beaujolais and with some clout, in order to promote further efforts towards higher quality (and higher prices). The wines show a previously unseen sumptuous, velvety quality and in the case of the Grand Carquelin and the Rochegrès at least also show promising complexity and structure, while Champ de Cour is arguably the most refined. There are also 9 ha of Chardonnay from which the white Beaujolais (stainless steel-vinified) and Bourgogne Blanc (barrel-fermented and aged) are made. Combe aux Jacques is a separate facility dedicated to producing high-quality Beaujolais-Villages in conjunction with local growers. In 2001 Jadot added Château Bellevue, one of Morgon's most prized estates, where a similar prestigious string of *crus* is being made along the same lines as at Château des Jacques. (PW)

Château des Jacques:
● **Moulin-à-Vent** Clos du Grand Carquelin★★★ £C Champ de Cour★★★ £C
● **Moulin-à-Vent**★★ £C Grand Clos des Rochegrès★★ £C
○ **Beaujolais-Villages** Chardonnay★★ £B ○ **Bourgogne Blanc** Clos de Loyse★★ £B

Château de Bellevue:
● **Morgon**★★ £C

DOM. DE LA CHANAISE Morgon

A: **MPe**, F&M

Owner: Dominique Piron Domaine de la Chanaise, Morgon, 69910 Villié-Morgon

Descended from a long line of grape growers stretching back to the mid-17th century, Dominique Piron has put much effort into improving viticulture and the quality of his grapes. His 22 ha of vineyard with an average vine age of 40 years are composed of the 17 ha Domaine de la Chanaise and 5 ha Domaine de Combiaty. The best wines can show a minerality that, given the soils, ought to be seen in more Beaujolais – yet most simply exhibit attractive fruit and floral characters. This is most evident in the Morgon Côte de Py, the only one of six *climats* bottled separately. Given a relatively long maceration, this is usually the top wine but Brouilly can also be very good, although quality of the sometimes complex Moulin-à-Vent is a little more irregular. Good Beaujolais-Villages and a little Beaujolais Blanc (from Chardonnay) are also made. As well as the Domaine de la Chanaise wines, Dominique Piron acts as a *négociant* producing wines under his own name and own-label Beaujolais for Fortnum & Mason in London. (PW)

● **Morgon**★★ £B Côte du Py★★★ £B ● **Moulin-à-Vent** Les Vignes du Vieux Bourg★★★ £B
● **Brouilly** Château du Prieuré ★ £B ● **Regnié**★ £B ● **Beaujolais-Villages** Les Vignes de Pierreux★ £B

CH. THIVIN Côte de Brouilly www.chateau-thivin.com A: RHW, GWW, VTr, Wse

Owner: Claude & Evelyne Geoffray Château Thivin, 69460 Odenas
Château Thivin is renowned for its Côte de Brouilly and is one of Beaujolais' historic properties, with medieval origins. The top *cuvée*, Zaccharie Geoffray, is named for one of Claude Geoffray's ancestors who purchased the property in 1877. The 24 ha include a second domaine, Manoir du Pavé (from his wife's family), which is the source of a good Beaujolais-Villages. While ripe and supple with fine structures, the wines show real individual expression and distinctive fruit, with a mineral, floral and herbal quality that is unique to the local soils. Other *cuvées* now bottled separately and made to the same standards, include Clos Bertrand and La Croix Dessaigne. Prices are reasonable for the quality. (PW)

● **Côte de Brouilly**★★ £B La Chapelle★★★ £B Zaccharie Geoffray★★★ £B
● **Brouilly**★ £B ● **Beaujolais-Villages** Manoir du Pavé★ £B

CLOS DE LA ROILETTE/COUDERT Fleurie A: DDr, L&W, Sav, L&S

Owner: Coudert family Clos de la Roilette, La Roilette, 69820 Fleurie
Within their 9.5 ha of vineyard, the Couderts possess the best part of La Roilette, the finest *climat* in Fleurie. The site gives Fleurie of more body, depth and complexity than is typical and theirs is a parcel of very old vines. The grapes are harvested very ripe and in the small amount of a special bottling called Cuvée Tardive there is more intensity and richness. The wines are sleek and supple, with a black fruit character and a subtle mineral streak. Both are consistently fine yet reasonably priced Beaujolais that drink well with anything from one to three years' age, occasionally more. The newish Cuvée Christal is even more accessible. (PW)

● **Fleurie** Cuvée Christal★★ £B ● **Fleurie** Clos de la Roilette★★★ £B Cuvée Tardive★★★ £C

DOM. LOUIS-CLAUDE DESVIGNES Morgon A: Sav, BBR

Owner: Louis-Claude Desvignes 135 Rue de la Voûte, 69910 Villié-Morgon
Louis-Claude Desvignes was one of the first in Beaujolais to produce separate *cuvées* from the best parcels in his estate. From 1.5 ha of Côte de Py and 2 ha of Javernières (from different soils within the Côte de Py) are regularly produced two rich vibrant, aromatic and distinctly different Morgons that bear little resemblance to most of what comes out of the Beaujolais region. There is undoubted skill and care in their production; low yields and a cold pre-fermentation maceration are just two contributing factors. Though there are now several other versions of Côte de Py (including Jean FOILLARD'S), few rival this one and none at the price, which remains low. These are wines to drink with at least three or four years' age if their full potential is to be realised. (PW)

● **Morgon** La Voûte Saint-Vincent★★ £B Javernières★★ £B Côte de Py★★ £B

GEORGES DUBOEUF Beaujolais www.duboeuf.com A: BWC, JNi, Maj

Owner: Georges Duboeuf 71570 Romanèche-Thorins
For many around the world Duboeuf represents Beaujolais, or at least the decent stuff. A production of 30 million bottles is one of the reasons why it can be found in local wine shops and supermarkets almost everywhere. Duboeuf has been admirably consistent despite the phenomenal growth over more than three decades. Many small domaines, including some in every *cru*, come under the Duboeuf umbrella and are marketed and bottled accordingly. Though some of the *cuvées*, especially the generic *crus*, are simple and rather short and firm on the finish, others show more expression, and more succulence and finesse in their structures. The individual *cuvées* (most from single domaines) are nearly always worth the small premium they command, particularly those from Moulin-à-Vent and Fleurie, when compared to regular examples of

the more southerly Beaujolais *crus*, Brouilly or Régnié. Individual *crus* can be drunk with a couple of years' ageing but don't need it. Prices of fine wines around the globe may have escalated but those of most of these Beaujolais, like their quality, have remained steady. Some fresh, attractive whites with good substance are also made, as are many Rhône wines and vins de pays from the Languedoc-Roussillon. Below are some of the very best of Duboeuf's Beaujolais/Mâconnais wines. (PW)

● **Moulin-à-Vent**★★ £B Fût de Chêne★★ £B Domaine des Rosiers★★ £B Prestige★★★ £B
● **Moulin-à-Vent** Domaine de la Tour de Bief★★★ £B
● **Fleurie**★ £B Domaine des Quatre Vents★★ £B La Madone★★ £B Château des Déduits★ £B
● **Fleurie** Château des Bachelards★ £B ● **Chiroubles** Domaine des Tilleuls★★ £B
● **Saint-Amour** Domaine des Sablons★ £B Domaine du Paradis★★ £B
● **Morgon**★ £B Domaine Jean Descombes★★ £B ● **Juliénas** Domaine de la Seigneurie★ £B·
● **Brouilly** Domaine de Combillaty★ £B ● **Beaujolais-Villages** Château de Varennes★★ £B
○ **Pouilly-Fuissé** Fût de Chêne★ £B Prestige★★ £B ○ **Saint-Véran** Domaine Saint-Martin★ £B
○ **Mâcon-Villages** Prestige★ £B

HENRY FESSY Beaujolais www.vins-henry-fessy.com A: **Cib**, For, Frw

Owner: Henry Fessy Bel Air, 69220 Saint-Jean d'Ardières

With both a domaine of 12 ha and a *négociant* business, Henry and Serges Fessy make a number of ripe, vigorous, perfumed Beaujolais. The estate vineyards are confined to Brouilly and Beaujolais but some fine examples are made from other *crus*. The Brouilly wines are particularly good for this *cru*, with both intensity and length of flavour in a forward, supple Cuvée Georges Fessy and a richer Pur Sang. Other wines listed are those regularly encountered but the standard of Beaujolais seems good throughout. Prices are not excessive for the quality. Some white Beaujolais, Saint-Véran and Pouilly-Fuissé are also made but have not been tasted. (PW)

● **Brouilly** Cuvée Georges Fessy★★ £B Domaine du Plateau de Bel Air★★ £B Pur Sang★★ £B
● **Morgon** Cuvée Luquet★★ £B ● **Fleurie** Mauriers ★★ £B

JEAN FOILLARD Morgon A: **HHB**

Owner: Jean Foillard Le Clachet, 69910 Villié-Morgan

Jean Foillard is a disciple of Jules Chauvet, a noted enologist who believed in fashioning Beaujolais in an altogether different way from the modern standard of semi-carbonic maceration. Foillard's 8 ha include one of the best sites in the whole Beaujolais region, Morgon's Côte du Py. Important to the style are low yields and very ripe grapes, which are subject to a long cool vinification, practically zero use of sulphur and minimal or no filtration. It's not what you would normally associate with Beaujolais; an intense, spice- and mineral-rich structured wine that needs five years or more before it is ready. Light years from simple, fruity quaffing Beaujolais, it does achieve real harmony in the best years. (PW)

● **Morgon** Première★★ £B Côte du Py★★★ £C

DOM. PAUL ET ERIC JANIN Moulin-à-Vent A: DDr, L&S, CPp, Rae, SVS

Owner: Janin family 71570 Romanèche-Thorins

Eric Janin makes excellent Moulin-à-Vent to a biodynamic recipe. The domaine of 10 ha of old vines are carefully nurtured by father and son and the result is a marvellous fruit quality and good concentration and depth in the wines. Occasionally the tannins can be a little firm in the finish but the Clos du Tremblay (which is a selection of the very best old vines) in particular benefits from a couple of years' age. Two-thirds of production is Moulin-à-Vent, the rest Beaujolais-Villages from the smaller Domaine des Vignes des Jumeaux. Prices, as so often from those most dedicated to the land, are very reasonable. (PW)

● **Moulin-à-Vent** Clos du Tremblay★★★ £C Vignes du Tremblay★★ £B
● **Beaujolais-Villages** Domaine des Vignes du Jumeaux★ £B

JACKY JANODET/DOM. LES FINE GRAVES   A: **THt**, BBR, Tan, UnC, Sel

Owner: Jacky Janodet   Les Garniers, 71570 Romanèche-Thorins
Jacky Janodet is one of the best-known growers based in Moulin-à-Vent. He has just over 10 ha, of which
6.5 ha are in Moulin-à-Vent itself and much is planted to very old vines. The wine is classically powerful
with good depth, its concentration, structure and texture owed in part to ageing in small barrels. The 2003
shows the intensity, vibrancy and ripeness of the vintage but as with other years will be at its best with three
to four years' age. Some Chénas, Beaujolais-Villages and a tiny amount of white is also made. (PW)
● **Moulin-à-Vent** Vieilles Vignes★★★ £B

DOM. DE LA MADONE   Fleurie   A: **OWL**, THt, Ear, RHW, NDb

Owner: Despres family   La Madone, 69820 Fleurie
Jean-Marc Despres and his son Arnaud consistently produce benchmark Fleurie from almost 9 ha of vines
on south-west facing slopes. The regular *cuvée* is supple and smooth with raspberry, cherry and refined floral
characters. There is no hardness or greenness even in a vintage like 2002, and there is depth and breadth
without being overdone. The Vieilles Vignes offers more complexity and refinement (as well as density in
the 2003 vintage). This ability to respond to the vintage conditions marks these wines out; too many others
are overextracted and unbalanced in all but the best years. Another *cuvée* of old vines, Grille Midi, comes
from a particularly warm part of the vineyards and can be more fleshy, more structured but displays a fine
minerality. Also made are a little Juliénas, an oak-aged Fleurie and some Beaujolais-Villages. (PW)
● **Fleurie**★★ £B Vieilles Vignes★★★ £C Grille Midi Vieilles Vignes★★★ £C

DOM. DES TERRES DORÉES   Beaujolais   A: **Sav**

Owner: Jean-Paul Brun   Crière, 69380 Charnay-en-Beaujolais
Jean-Paul Brun's domaine is situated in the south of the Beaujolais region, known as the Pierres Doreés. His
wines are the exception in what is otherwise a sea of inferior plonk (most of which appears under a simple
'Beaujolais' label). Soils in these parts are predominantly limestone, and that part of Brun's 20 ha of vineyards
with calcareous soils is planted not to Gamay but instead to Chardonnay and Pinot Noir. Therefore as well
as producing pure, intense Beaujolais that really tastes of its origins there's both a light Bourgogne Grand
Ordinaire (Pinot Noir) and Beaujolais Blanc (En Fût is a *barrique*-fermented version) that are intense and
original. Late-harvested wines are also produced including Labeur d'Octobre and 'E sens de chardon né',
from botrytis-affected Chardonnay grapes. Good Côte de Brouilly and Moulin-à-Vent are also made. (PW)
● **Beaujolais** Cuvée à l'Ancienne★★ £B ● **Côte de Brouilly**★★ £B ● **Moulin-à-Vent**★★ £C
● **Bourgogne Grande Ordinaire**★ £B O **Beaujolais Blanc**★ £B

DOM. DU VISSOUX   Beaujolais   A: **Eno**, Vne, Hrd

Owner: Pierre-Marie Chermette   Domaine du Vissoux, 69620 Saint-Vérand
The wines from this 30-ha estate continue to improve and include excellent examples of both Fleurie and
Moulin-à-Vent. Fleurie has lovely style and intensity, the Garants showing the lusher texture of the two
bottlings. Moulin-à-Vent, both Rochegrès and slightly superior Rochelle, show more spice, mineral and
greater breadth though have been slightly less consistent quality-wise. That said, in 2002 these were more
successful than the Fleurie, which shone more in 2001. The regular Beaujolais Traditionelle, sourced from
the southern Beaujolais, is not of the same ilk. (PW)
● **Fleurie** Poncié★★ £B Les Garants★★★ £C ● **Moulin-à-Vent** Rochegrès★★ £C Rochelle★★★ £C

BEAUJOLAIS/OTHER WINES OF NOTE

RENÉ BERROD ● Fleurie £B

JEAN-MARC BURGAUD ● Morgon Côte du Py £B Les Charmes £B

NICOLE CHANRION/DOM. DE LA VOÛTE DES CROZES ● Côte de Brouilly £B

FERNAND CHARVET/DOM. DES VIEILLES CAVES ● Chénas Vieilles Vignes £B
● Moulin-à-Vent Vieilles Vignes £B

GÉRARD CHARVET/DOM. DES ROSIERS ● Moulin-à-Vent £B

CH. DE BEAUREGARD/JOSEPH BURRIER ● Moulin-à-Vent £C

CH. DE LA CHAIZE ● Brouilly £B

CH. DE PIERREUX ● Brouilly £C La Réserve du Château £C

DOM. ÉMILE CHEYSSON ● Chiroubles £B Prestige £B

MICHEL CHIGNARD ● Fleurie Les Moriers £B Spéciale Vieilles Vignes £C

ANDRÉ COLONGE ● Fleurie £B

JOELLE ET GÉRARD DESCOMBES ● Beaujolais-Villages Ch. de la Roche £B ● Juliénas £C

DOM. DIOCHON ● Moulin-à-Vent Vieilles Vignes £B

DOM. DUBOST ● Brouilly La Bruyère Vieilles Vignes £B

CAVE COOPÉRATIVE DE FLEURIE ● Fleurie Cuvée Millésimé £B

JACKY GAUTHIER ● Regnié Domaine de Colette £B

DOM. GAY-COPERET ● Moulin-à-Vent Réserve Vieilles Vignes £B

PASCAL GRANGER ● Chénas £B ● Juliénas Cuvée Speciale £B

DOM. DE GRY-SABLON ● Morgon £B

MARCEL LAPIERRE ● Morgon £B

HUBERT LAPIERRE ● Chénas Vieilles Vignes £B ● Moulin-à-Vent Vieilles Vignes £B

JEAN-PIERRE MARGERAND ● Juliénas £B

LAURENT MARTRAY ● Brouilly Vieilles Vignes £B

DOMAINE BERNARD MÉTRAT ● Fleurie Roilette Vieilles Vignes £B

ALBERT MOREL ● Fleurie £B

CHÂTEAU DU MOULIN-À-VENT ● Moulin-à-Vent £B Cuvée Exceptionelle £B

ALAIN PASSOT/DOM. DE LA GROSSE PIERRE ● Chiroubles £B

JEAN-CHARLES PIVOT ● Beaujolais-Villages £B

POTEL-AVIRON ● Morgon Côte du Py Vieilles Vignes £C ● Fleurie Vieilles Vignes £C
● Moulin-à-Vent Vieilles Vignes £C

DOM. LES ROCHES BLEUES ● Côte de Brouilly £B

BERNARD SANTÉ ● Chénas £B

MICHEL TÊTE/DOM. DU CLOS DU FIEF ● Juliénas £B Cuvée Prestige £C
● Saint-Amour £B

DOM. GEORGES VIORNERY ● Côte de Brouilly £B

France/Alsace

This is one of France's most unusual and exciting regions. Culturally it is as much German as it is French and twice during the last 130 years or so has been a part of the former. It is one of France's most spectacular regions to visit, with the splendour of the Vosges mountains complemented by the medieval architecture of many towns and villages. Unlike in other regions, the grape varietal plays a key element in wine labelling. The wines themselves can be piercingly aromatic and are quite unique in style. Although there are some substantial merchant operations and large co-ops the area is not a purveyor of bulk wine. However there is still a wide variation in quality and yields generally throughout the region are too high, with most wine still coming from over-productive sites on the plains. As elsewhere, who produced the wine is the key.

Geography

The region of Alsace is a narrow stretch of vineyards running north-south at the base of and nestled into the eastern foothills of the Vosges mountains. These, along with the Rhine just to the east of the *vignoble*, provide the region with an impressively favourable climate for such a northerly latitude. Sunshine hours are high during the growing season and rainfall low. The vineyard area stretches from just west of Strasbourg in the north to Mulhouse in the south, with the heart of the region centred around the town of Colmar. This is where the greatest concentration of top villages and vineyard sites, particularly *grands crus,* is to be found. These southern stretches are known as the **Haut Rhin**; the northern part is the **Bas Rhin**. There are fewer great sites in the Bas Rhin but some very fine wine is produced nonetheless. In some respects the region resembles the Côte d'Or. The finest sites are inevitably on the slopes of the Vosges, with well-drained, meagre soils. By contrast those vineyards planted on the fertile, heavy alluvial soils on the plains towards the Rhine are far less propitious for quality wine production.

Wine Styles

The generic appellation of the region is simply **Alsace** AC. The vast majority of wine is labelled by its grape variety. There is an ongoing debate in the region about the importance of the varieties themselves, as opposed to site and *terroir,* in determining style. There is just one permitted red grape, Pinot Noir, which can be good but is often light and insubstantial, needing a good vintage. The white varietals are the fairly neutral Pinot Blanc and Sylvaner (although there are some impressive old-vine examples) and the more aromatic Riesling, Muscat, Tokay Pinot Gris and Gewürztraminer. There is some Chasselas producing the odd varietal wine, as well as Auxerrois, but both will generally be used with Sylvaner and Pinot Blanc in generic blends. These are covered by the Alsace AC and are labelled either Edelzwicker or Gentil. An unusual rarity in the higher reaches of the Bas Rhin is the Klevner de Heilegenstein. No wines of real note have been produced from it. Confusingly, Auxerrois is often referred to as Klevner.

The 50 *grands crus* here were established in 1983. Wines produced from these are classified **Alsace Grand Cru** AC. The majority of these sites can be found in the heart of the Haut Rhin and were created to pinpoint the best vineyards. Much work still needs to be done with the region's labelling system and although there is talk of it, there is no further official classification. Many wines make reference to their *lieux-dits* in order to emphasise potential quality. A number of these sites produce wines that are comfortably a match for many *grands crus.* The vineyards of the latter must be planted to Gewürztraminer, Muscat, Riesling or Tokay Pinot Gris.

Almost all wines are varietal but there are experiments, particularly those by Jean-Michel Deiss, in establishing field blends.

Some of the region's greatest wines are the late-harvested wines, *Vendange Tardive* (VT) and *Sélection de Grains Nobles* (SGN). Being made from late-harvested grapes, these are generally sweet styles. Noble rot may occur, particularly in the SGNs, but not always. However, the classification is based on grape ripeness at harvest and some *Vendange Tardive* wines can be surprisingly dry. Indeed the whole question of levels of residual sugar can be confusing. Some producers tend towards a very steely, dry style, while others prefer to let nature take its course, with fermentation stopping naturally. The results in the latter case are wines with often surprising levels of sugar and extract. The best, though, are very well balanced with sometimes remarkable depth. In order to help with this confusion a scale has been established, indicating on the back label the degree of sweetness.

The final style is **Crémant d'Alsace** AC. These are made by the traditional method and are mostly produced from Pinot Blanc and Riesling, although Auxerrois, Pinot Noir and Tokay Pinot Gris are also permitted. The best examples have reasonable depth and structure, often with marked acidity.

Alsace vintages

The region is sunny and warm and, like many of the top areas of France, governed by a marginal climate. While this is important in the development of great wines, there will inevitably be some vintage variation. The lesser whites should be drunk young and certainly by the time they have had four or five years' ageing. Riesling is better in slightly cooler years, Gewürztraminer and Tokay Pinot Gris add dimension in warmer years. The chart below will provide a reliable guide as to what you should expect. The very best *grand cru* and late-harvest styles are remarkably ageworthy. Of the great earlier years to consider are 1983, 1976 and for very top wines 1971 and 1967.

Alsace vintage chart

	Riesling Grand or Top Cru	Pinot Gris Grand or Top Cru	Gewürztraminer Grand or Top Cru	Late-Harvest Wines Vendange Tardive or SGN
2003	★★★★ A	★★★★ A	★★★★ A	★★★/★★★★ A
2002	★★★★ A	★★★★/★★★★★ A	★★★★/★★★★★ A	★★★★ A
2001	★★★★ A	★★★★ A	★★★★ A	★★★★ A
2000	★★★★ A	★★★★ A	★★★★ A	★★★★ A
1999	★★★★ A	★★★/★★★★ B	★★★/★★★★ B	★★★★ A
1998	★★★★/★★★★★ A	★★★★ B	★★★★ B	★★★★/★★★★★ A
1997	★★★★ B	★★★★/★★★★★ B	★★★★/★★★★★ B	★★★★/★★★★★ A
1996	★★★★/★★★★★ B	★★★★/★★★★★ B	★★★★ B	★★★★/★★★★★ B
1995	★★★★/★★★★★ B	★★★★/★★★★★ B	★★★★ C	★★★★/★★★★★ B
1994	★★★ C	★★★ C	★★★ C	★★★★ B
1990	★★★★/★★★★★ C	★★★★/★★★★★ C	★★★★/★★★★★ C	★★★★/★★★★★ B
1989	★★★★ C	★★★★/★★★★★ C	★★★★/★★★★★ C	★★★★/★★★★★ B
1988	★★★★/★★★★★ C	★★★★ C	★★★★ C	★★★★ B
1985	★★★★ C	★★★★/★★★★★ C	★★★★ C	★★★★ C

DOM. JEAN-BAPTISTE ADAM Ammerschwihr www.jb-adam.com A: All

Owner: Jean-Baptiste Adam 5 Rue Aigle, 687700 Ammerschwihr
Long-established Alsace producer, founded in 1614. There are just 15 ha of vineyards but fruit is bought in to produce no fewer than 80,000 cases a year, making this one of the largest operations in the region. The generic Sélection and Réserve wines offer reliable drinking but better are the Jean-Baptiste labels, including decent Pinot Noir in warmer years. The heart of the Adam estate is based on the *lieux-dits* Letzenberg and Kaefferkopf and Riesling also comes from the Grand Cru Winneck-Schlossberg. Letzenberg is just 2.5 ha of mass-selected Riesling and Pinot Gris grown on mainly clay soils. The top site, the Kaefferkopf, has been cultivated by the Adam family since the early 1800s. Finely drained granite soils produce excellent Riesling and Gewürztraminer as well as the Traditional Kaefferkopf Cuvée, a blend of both varieties. Occasional Vendange Tardive and SGN bottlings are released as well as some sound Crémant d'Alsace, both Brut and Extra Brut. (DM)

O **Gewürztraminer** Kaefferkopf Jean-Baptiste★★★ £C Vendange Tardive★★★ £D
O **Riesling** Letzenberg★★ £B Kaefferkopf Vieilles Vignes★★★ £C Grand Cru Winneck-Schlossberg★★★ £C
O **Tokay Pinot Gris** Letzenberg★★★ £C
O **Muscat** Reserve★ £B

DOM. LUCIEN ALBRECHT Orschwihr www.lucien-albrecht.fr A: Eno

Owner: Jean Albrecht 9 Grand-Rue, 68500 Orschwihr
There are just over 30 ha of vineyards at this property. The regular wines are simple, straightforward and emphasise their varietal character well. The best wines are from Grand Cru Pfingstberg, particularly the special bottlings labelled Cuvée A de Albrecht. Vendange Tardive and SGN can be impressive as well. Top Pinot Gris and Gewürztraminer are quite opulent and reasonably approachable; Riesling is in a tighter, more structured mould – citrusy and intense with some age but relatively austere when young. Prices are very reasonable. (DM)

O **Gewürztraminer** Cuvée Martine Albrecht★★★ £B Pfingstberg Grand Cru Cuvée A de Albrecht★★★ £C
O **Riesling** Pfingstberg Grand Cru Cuvée A de Albrecht★★★ £C Vendange Tardive★★★ £C
O **Tokay Pinot Gris** Grand Cru Pfingstberg★★★ £C Vendange Tardive★★★★ £D
O **Muscat** Bollenberg★★ £B

DOM. JEAN BECKER Zellenberg vinsbecker@aol.com

Owner: Marie-José Becker 4 route d'Ostheim, 68340 Zellenberg
Fine old family domaine established in 1610, which now has 18 ha of vineyards in the villages of Zellenberg, Riquewihr, Beblenheim and Ribeauvillé. Of these, 4 ha are *grand cru* and a small amount of fruit is bought in from other growers around Zellenberg. Among the *grands crus*, floral, elegant Riesling, Tokay Pinot Gris, Muscat and Gewürztraminer come from Froehn. Riesling and Gewürztraminer from the marl soils of Schoenenbourg can produce excellent late-harvest wines. Gewürztraminer is also grown at the Sporen, Sonnenglanz and Praelatenberg sites. Among the *lieux-dits*, fresh fruity Riesling comes from Hagenschlauf and Tokay Pinot Gris and Gewürztraminer, often produced as Vendange Tardive and occasionally as SGN, from Rimelsberg. Good fruit-driven Pinot Blanc and regular Tokay Pinot Gris are produced organically. The style of the wines is traditional but they all show good fruit intensity. The top *crus* have a fine mineral complexity to them and you can expect them to age well. (DM)

O **Gewürztraminer** Grand Cru Sonnenglanz★★ £C Vendange Tardive★★★★ £D
O **Gewürztraminer** Grand Cru Schoenenbourg SGN★★★★ £E
O **Riesling** Hagenschlauf★★ £C Grand Cru Froehn★★★ £C
O **Tokay Pinot Gris★★** £B Grand Cru Froehn★★★ £C
O **Muscat** Grand Cru Froehn★★★ £C
O **Pinot Blanc★** £B

DOM. CÉCILE BERNHARD-RIEBEL   Châtenois   A:SVS

Owner: Cécile Bernhard-Riebel   20 Rue de Lorraine, 67730 Châtenois

Small to medium-sized producer with an output of around 8,000 to 9,000 cases a year from 17 ha of vineyards planted to Riesling, Tokay Pinot Gris, Gewürztraminer, Pinot Blanc and a little Sylvaner planted in well-drained granite soils. Unusually the domaine is run by mother Cécile and son Pierre. There are no *grand cru* vineyards but they have small holdings in the *lieux-dits* Weingarten, Hahnenberg and Rittesberg. The Rieslings are the best bets, very pure with classic varietal character, while the Tokay Pinot Gris are rich and weighty wines that go through malolactic fermentation. Vendanges Tardives are produced from Riesling, Gewürztraminer and Pinot Gris. Prices are very reasonable. (DM)

O **Riesling** Vieilles Vignes★★ £B Weingarten★★★ £C
O **Tokay Pinot Gris** Tradition★★ £B Hahnenberg★★★ £C
O **Pinot Blanc**★ £B

LÉON BEYER   Eguisheim   www.leonbeyer.fr   A: Hal, BBR

Owner: Léon Beyer   2 Rue de la Première-Arnée, 68420 Eguisheim

This is quite a substantial property producing wines from its own 20 ha of vineyards and also buying in grapes for its *négociant* wines. Vineyard holdings include the Grands Crus Eichberg and Pfersigberg but as at HUGEL no wines are released as such. Output is around 60,000 cases a year. As one would expect, the generic bottlings do not set the world on fire but are generally well crafted and offer a particularly dry, almost austere style. They will develop well in bottle. Better are the Grandes Cuvées Comtes d'Eguisheim labels, which are rich and reasonably concentrated. Riesling Ecaillers and Gewürztraminer Réserve also stand out. Vendange Tardive Gewürztraminer is good but just lacks some of the weight one might hope for. Sélection de Grains Nobles from the same variety is very impressive. The Pinot Gris SGN is remarkable: structured, rich and very ageworthy. (DM)

O **Gewürztraminer** Comtes d'Eguisheim★★ £D Vendange Tardive★★★ £E SGN★★★★ £F
O **Riesling** Ecaillers★★ £C Comtes d'Eguisheim★★ £D
O **Tokay Pinot Gris** SGN✪✪✪✪✪ £F

DOM. PAUL BLANCK   Kaysersberg   www.blanck.com   A: Lay

Owner: Blanck family   32 Grand-Rue, 68240 Kientzheim

Medium-sized family producer with an output approaching 20,000 cases a year. Quality is generally good to very good across the board and the wines tend to be made in an opulent, rich vein. Often quite marked levels of residual sugar can be found in the drier styles. Generic labels including Riesling and Pinot Blanc are sound but can be a little simple. Very good is an intense, green-apple Sylvaner from old vines. There are a range of *vieilles vignes, grand cru*, VT and SGN bottlings. You can expect almost all *grand cru* bottles to be at least three stars. Very good examples are produced from the Grands Crus Furstentum, Sommerberg and Schlossberg and there are fine wines produced from other *lieux-dits* as well. Fine VT is almost invariably of four-star quality and there is an explosively rich and opulent Pinot Gris SGN. Make sure you get the right address; there is more than one Blanck in Kientzheim. (DM)

O **Pinot Auxerrois**★ £B
O **Gewürztraminer** Furstentum Grand Cru Vieilles Vignes★★★★ £E
O **Gewürztraminer** Furstentum Grand Cru Vendange Tardive★★★★★ £E
O **Riesling** Rosenbourg★★ £B Patergarten★★★ £C
O **Riesling** Furstentum Grand Cru★★★★ £D Schlossberg Grand Cru★★★★ £D
O **Tokay Pinot Gris** Patergarten★★ £B Furstentum Grand Cru★★★ £E SGN✪✪✪✪✪ £G

DOM. BOTT-GEYL Beblenheim bottgeyl@libertysurf.fr A: CTy

Owner: Bott-Geyl family 1 Rue du Petit-Château, 68980 Beblenheim

Impressive small family domaine that has some 12.5 ha of estate vineyards producing close to 8,000 cases a year. The quality is nearly always very sound right across the range. The style is almost explosively rich and the wines will often have marked residual sugar. Harvesting as ripe as possible and letting nature and indigenous yeasts run their natural course produces such results. Good generic Pinot Auxerrois and Gewürztraminer Beblenheim as well as Muscat Riquewihr offer very good value. There are also considerable *grand cru* holdings. Gewürztraminer and Pinot Gris from Grands Crus Furstentum and Sonnenglanz are always three stars, often better, and also come from the excellent *lieu-dit* of Schlosselreben. Riesling comes from Mandelberg, Schoenenbourg and Grafenreben. The Mandelberg tends to be fullest – rich and weighty with a marvellously pure mineral core. While the Gewürztraminer VT is quite tight and restrained in style, the Pinot Gris SGN from Sonnenglanz can be explosive, rich and sumptuous but with a marvellous fresh, structured backbone. The top wines will inevitably age extraordinarily well. Most offer very good value. (DM)

O **Pinot d'Alsace** Beblenheim★ £B O **Muscat** Riquewihr★★ £B
O **Riesling** Mandelberg Grand Cru★★★★ £C
O **Gewürztraminer** Furstentum Grand Cru★★★ £C Sonnenglanz Grand Cru Vieilles Vignes★★★★ £D
O **Gewürztraminer** Sonnenglanz Grand Cru Vendange Tardive★★★★★ £E
O **Tokay Pinot Gris** de Beblenheim★★★ £B Furstentum Grand Cru★★★★ £C
O **Tokay Pinot Gris** Sonnenglanz Grand Cru Vendange Tardive★★★★★ £E SGN✪✪✪✪✪ £F

ALBERT BOXLER Niedermorschwihr albert.boxler@9online.fr A: Gau

Owner: Jean-Marc Boxler 78 Rue des Trois-Epis, 68230 Niedermorschwihr

Jean-Marc Boxler's small domaine, nearly 14 ha, produces just over 4,000 cases across a small but well-made range. Generics including Riesling and Pinot Blanc are very good, but Gewürztraminer can occasionally disappoint. Top Gewürztraminer and Pinot Gris comes from the Brand vineyard, Riesling from Brand and Sommerberg. The Rieslings particularly stand out. The style is for very dry, almost austere wines with a restrained, youthful, green-apple and markedly mineral character. Pinot Gris and Gewürztraminer, even at *grand cru* level, do not have the formidable structure and depth of the Rieslings. They tend more towards a simpler, riper if more opulent style. Riesling VT and SGN can be stunning as can a very impressive Pinot Gris – all are four stars, often five or occasionally super-five. The top Rieslings will age magnificently and should not be broached without six or seven years' ageing. (DM)

● **Pinot Blanc★★** £B
● **Gewürztraminer** Brand Grand Cru★★★ £D
O **Riesling★★** £B Brand Grand Cru★★★ £D Sommerberg Grand Cru★★★★ £D
O **Tokay Pinot Gris★** £B Brand Grand Cru★★★ £C

ERNEST BURN Gueberschwihr www.domaine-burn.fr A: Has, HHB, NYg, Gau

Owner: Joseph et Francis Burn 8 Rue Basse, 68420 Gueberschwihr

This is a very impressive small, traditional domaine with a holding of just 10 ha. The wholly owned *monopole* Clos Saint Imer is part of the Grand Cru Goldert and this accounts for over half the vineyard holdings. A fine Pinot Blanc is joined by some very well-crafted rich and stylish Muscat, Pinot Gris, Gewürztraminer and Riesling. The style of the *grand cru* wines is for rich, very late-harvested fruit with real density and imense depth. They can almost seem overblown but always retain a fine, structured undercurrent. Riesling can be a touch overwhelmed in this style when the vintage produces very ripe, soft wines, as in 1997, and tends to be at its best in the cooler years. Some very fine, sumptuous and honeyed VT is made from Gewürztraminer and Pinot Gris. (DM)

O **Pinot Blanc★★** £B
O **Gewürztraminer** Goldert Grand Cru Cuvée de la Chapelle★★★★ £E
O **Riesling** Goldert Grand Cru Cuvée de la Chapelle★★★ £D
O **Tokay Pinot Gris★★** £B Goldert Grand Cru Cuvée de la Chapelle★★★★ £D

CAVE DE CLEEBOURG Cleebourg www.cave-cleebourg.com A: **C&B**

Owner: 'Co-Operative' Route du Vin, 67160 Cleebourg

An extensive range is made at this sizeable co-op established in 1946. There are 192 member growers with a total of 180 ha of vineyard holdings in the extreme north of the Alsace region. The vineyard area was destroyed during the Second World War but has been progressively built up since and some of the plantings are now of considerable age. Some excellent, pure and intense single-vineyard Gewürztraminer, Riesling and Tokay Pinot Gris are produced as well as good examples of Muscat and Pinot Auxerrois and a clean, fresh Crémant d'Alsace. Vendanges Tardives are released occasionally. They are sound but do not offer the same value as the other wines. (DM)

- O **Gewürztraminer**★ £B Reiffenberg★★ £B
- O **Riesling** Hannesacker★★★ £B
- O **Tokay Pinot Gris** Vieilles Vignes★★ £B Karchweg★★ £B
- O **Muscat** Sigille★ £B
- O **Pinot Blanc/Auxerrois**★ £B
- O **Cremant d'Alsace** Clerostein★ £B

MARCEL DEISS Bergheim www.marceldeiss.com A: Res, Bal, L&S

Owner: Deiss family 15 Route du Vin, 68750 Bergheim

The Deiss family has been producing wines here for over 50 years. Jean-Michel Deiss is now in charge of the property and runs the domaine along biodynamic lines. He is unquestionably now one of the three or four best producers in the entire region. An exemplary range of wines is made from very low yields from a range of sites including *grand cru* holdings at Altenberg, Mambourg and Schoenenbourg. A very good generic Pinot Blanc is made, as well as Riesling from Saint-Hippolyte and Pinot Gris and Gewürztraminer from Bergheim. The *grands crus* are very fine. Riesling comes from Altenberg and Schoenenbourg, Gewürztraminer and Pinot Gris from Altenberg. Deiss also produces three remarkable and very rich *grands crus* from Altenberg, Mambourg and Schoenenbourg that are field blends of the noble varieties. As well as these, there is a very good Gentil from the Burg site. The intention is to increase the complexity of the wines and emphasise their *terroir* rather than their varietal character. The approach throughout is to achieve very ripe fruit and the wines regularly have very marked sugar levels. Occasional super-rich VT and SGN are made. (DM)

- O **Pinot Blanc**★★★ £C   O **Altenberg Grand Cru**OOOOO £F
- O **Gewürztraminer** Bergheim★★★★ £D Altenberg Grand Cru★★★★ £F
- O **Riesling** Saint-Hippolyte★★★ £C Altenberg Grand Cru OOOOO £F
- O **Tokay Pinot Gris** Bergheim★★★★ £E Altenberg Grand Cru★★★★★ £F

DOM. DIRLER-CADÉ Bergholz jbdirler@terre-net.fr

Owner: Jean & Ludivine Dirler 5 Rue d'Issenheim, 68500 Bergholz

The Dirlers produce an excellent range of traditionally made wines from all the major Alsace varieties. The property was founded in 1871 and there are some 16 ha of producing vineyards, which since 1998 have been farmed biodynamically. Over 40 per cent of the family holding is *grand cru* with vines planted in the Saering, Spiegel, Kessler and Kitterlé sites. The Dirlers also have holdings in the *lieux-dits* Scwarzberg, Bux, Bollenberg, Schimberg and Belzbrunnen. While the wines are traditional in style, dry and tightly structured with a real mineral component running through them, vinification benefits from modern equipment, with temperature control for fermentation in *inox* as well as wood. Muscat in particular is very striking here and the Grand Cru Spiegel bottling is one of the very finest in the appellation. Some truly excellent *grand cru* Riesling and Gewürztraminer are produced as well as rich and pure VT and an exquisite Gewürztraminer Spiegel SGN. Expect the wines to develop very well in bottle, particularly the top *crus*. (DM)

- O **Gewürztraminer** Grand Cru Kessler★★★★ £C Grand Cru Spiegel SGN★★★★★ £F
- O **Riesling** Grand Cru Kessler★★★ £C Grand Cru Spiegel★★★★ £C Grand Cru Saering★★★★ £C

O **Tokay Pinot Gris** Reserve★★★ £B Schwarzberg Vendanges Tardives★★★★ £E
O **Muscat**★★ £B Grand Cru Spiegel★★★★ £C
O **Sylvaner** Vieilles Vignes★★ £B

DOM. PIERRE FRICK Pfaffenheim pierre.frick@wanadoo.fr A:Vcs

Owner: Chantal & Jean-Pierre Frick 5 Rue de Boer, 68250 Pfaffenheim
An impressive and diverse range is produced by the Fricks at their biodynamically farmed 12-ha property, which they inevitably harvest solely by hand. In the winery chaptalisation is strictly avoided and fermentation is carried out naturally without interference. Ageing takes place in large cask. The resulting wines often have some degree of residual sugar but are rich, opulent and, crucially, always balanced. There is a range of good generic Cuvées Classiques but it is the single-vineyard and *grand cru* wines as well as the special Précieuse selections which really stand out here. The Pinot Blanc Précieuse is a benchmark for the variety in Alsace. The domaine possesses holdings in the *lieux-dits* Bergweingarten, Bihl, Rot Murle and Strangenberg as well as Grands Crus Steinert, Vorbourg and Eichberg. Both Vendange Tardive and SGN wines are released in propitious vintages. All the top wines here will develop very well in bottle. (DM)
O **Gewürztraminer** Grand Cru Steinert★★★★ £C
O **Riesling** Précieuse★★★ £C Vendange Tardive★★★★ £C
O **Pinot Blanc** Précieuse★★★ £C
O **Sylvaner** Bihl★★ £B Bergweingarten★★★ £D
● **Pinot Noir** Rot Murle★★★ £C

DOM. PAUL GINGLINGER Eguisheim ginglin@club-internet.fr

Owner: Paul Ginglinger 8 Place Charles de Gaulle, 68420 Eguisheim
This ancient domaine dates back to 1636. Paul Ginglinger, who heads the latest generation, now possesses some 12 ha, 1.5 ha being Pinot Noir, although it is his excellent whites that stand out. Decent enough Muscat and a Clevner are released but it is the classic Alsace varieties of Riesling, Gewürztraminer and Tokay Pinot Gris that impress most as well as a very good, piercing, finely structured, appley Pinot Blanc. Vinification is strictly non-interventionist and the wines often have a touch of residual sugar. The Rieslings have a penetrating mineral quality and demand cellaring, particularly the *grand cru* bottlings which come from Eichberg as well as Pfersigberg. Both the Tokay Pinot Gris and Gewürztraminer tend towards the opulent, again with that degree of residual sugar often apparent, but the Pinot Gris in particular is also tight and structured when young, with a marked mineral quality. The Gewürztraminer, notably the Pfersigberg, is opulent and classically full of lychee and spice – full, deep and very pure. Expect to age the top wines here for at least five or six years. (DM)
O **Gewürztraminer** Wahlenbourg★★★ £C Grand Cru Pfersigberg★★★★ £C
O **Riesling** Cuvee Drei Exa★★★ £C Grand Cru Pfersigberg★★★ £C
O **Tokay Pinot Gris** Grand Cru Eichberg★★★ £C
O **Pinot Blanc**★★ £B

DOM. ANDRÉ ET RÉMY GRESSER Andlau remy.gresser@wanadoo.fr A: SVS

Owner: Rémy Gresser 2 Rue de l'Ecole, 67140 Andlau
Rémy Gresser produces an exemplary small range of wines, almost exclusively sourced from *grand cru* sites. The Gresser domaine is one of a number of ancient Alsace properties, dating from 1667, and now has a holding of just over 10 ha, prodicing a total of 5,000 cases a year. Almost all is white but there is just 0.65 ha of Pinot Noir as well. The vineyard is currently being converted to biodynamic farming. Andlau is in the centre of the Bas-Rhin, so is cooler than most areas in the region and as such strongly favours the production of tight, minerally, pure Rieslings of classic structure and dimension. Inevitably they are relatively austere when young. The Grand Cru Kastelberg is notable for its slatey, schistous soils which encourage late-season ripening. Riesling also comes from the Grand Cru Moenchberg , with warmer years often producing wines of Vendange Tardive ripeness. Gewürztraminer and Tokay Pinot Gris will evolve well

in bottle for at least six or seven years, the Rieslings often longer. (DM)
- O **Gewürztraminer** Duttenberg Vieilles Vignes★★★ £C
- O **Riesling** Grand Cru Wiebelsberg★★★ £C Grand Cru Kastelberg Vieilles Vignes★★★★ £C
- O **Tokay Pinot Gris** Brandhof Vieilles Vignes★★★★ £C

HUGEL ET FILS Riquewihr www.hugel.fr   A: **Day**,OWL,BBR,PFx,WSc,Har

Owner: Hugel family 3 Rue de la Premiere-Armee-Française, B.P. 32, 68340 Riquewihr
Along with TRIMBACH one of the two best-known names in the region. As well as being a substantial
merchant operation Hugel also has extensive vineyard holdings – some 127 ha. The top wines here are good
to exceptional and are excellent, structured examples of the region. What disappoints most is the very
average, at times downright poor, quality of the generics. The Gentil basics and the Tradition *cuvées* struggle
to stand up to much of their competition. Gewürztraminer Tradition is sound with good varietal character,
as is Pinot Gris. The Jubilee wines and the VT and SGN *cuvées* are of an entirely different class. Riesling
Jubilee is taut and intense, minerally with great structure; Pinot Gris is powerful with subtle, honeyed notes;
the Jubilee Gewürztraminer floral and spicy with classic but youthfully restrained lychee character. These
are wines that should be cellared for at least four or five years as they will continue to develop very well in
bottle. Pinot Noir is less successful. VTs are very intense. The style tends towards the drier end of the
spectrum but they have remarkable depth. Both Pinot Gris and Riesling SGN are quite splendid wines with
remarkable depth and complexity. The Riesling is perhaps the finest, with astonishing toasty, citrus and
mineral character. (DM)
- O **Gewürztraminer** Tradition★★ £B Jubilee★★★ £F Vendange Tardive★★★★ £F
- O **Riesling** Jubilee★★★ £C Vendange Tardive★★★★ £F SGN⚫⚫⚫⚫⚫ £H
- O **Tokay Pinot Gris** Tradition★ £B Jubilee★★★ £F Vendange Tardive★★★★ £F SGN⚫⚫⚫⚫⚫ £H

JOSMEYER Wintzenheim www.josmeyer.com   A: **Pol**,May,Res,Vts

Owner: Jean Meyer 76 Rue Clemenceau, 68920 Wintzenheim
Long-established top-quality producer whose origins date back to 1854. Output at a little over 20,000 cases
a year is sizeable for the region but dwarfed by some of the larger merchant houses. The Meyer family
possess some 31 ha of vineyard which form the base for an extensive collection of six small ranges. The
Classic labels are straightforward and easy drinking, the Artist Label series a step up, of which the Riesling
Kottabe, Pinot Gris Fromenteau and Gewürztraminer Folastries stand out. Muscat, Riesling and Pinot Noir
are all produced from the Herrenweg site, the Riesling labelled Dragon. Of particular interest, though, are
the prestige selections which include not only fine, pure Pinot Gris Foundation 1854 and opulent, spice-
strewn Gewürztraminer Archenets but also very intense Pinot Blanc Les Lutins. *Grand cru* holdings include
plots on both Brand and Hengst. Vendanges Tardives are produced from Pinot Gris and Riesling, SGN
from Pinot Gris and Gewürztraminer. Particularly rare and unusual is the late-harvest Pinot Blanc Derriere
La Chapelle, probably the best example of the variety in the region. All the top wines are very ageworthy.
(DM)
- O **Gewürztraminer** Les Folastries★★ £C Les Archenets★★★★ £E Grand Cru Hengst★★★★ £E
- O **Riesling** Le Kottabe★★ £C Grand Cru Hengst★★★★ £E
- O **Tokay Pinot Gris** Le Fromenteau★★ £C Foundation 1854★★★★ £E
- O **Pinot Auxerrois** H Vieilles Vignes★★★ £C
- O **Pinot Blanc** Les Lutins★★★ £C

ANDRÉ KIENTZLER Ribeauvillé   A: JAr, Res, HHB

Owner: André Kientzler 50 Route de Bergheim, 68150 Ribeauvillé
André Kientzler makes around 6,500 cases across a small but very impressive range of wines. They are
marked by their purity of fruit and elegant structure at all levels. The top *grand cru* bottles are very
ageworthy and require cellaring. No varieties stand out but the Rieslings, particularly from the Grands Crus
Geisberg and Osterberg, are truly profound. On occasion Geisberg produces a Riesling VT and SGN.

These are wines of remarkable complexity: the latter is astonishingly rich while the former is very structured, almost dry. You can expect them to be four stars, often five or super-five. Very good Muscat and Pinot Gris is made from Kirchberg. Gewürztraminer is not *grand cru* but there are occasional bottles of VT and SGN. Even the lesser Pinot Blanc, Auxerrois and Chasselas offer excellent quality and value. (DM)

O **Chasselas★** £B O **Auxerrois★★** £B O **Pinot Blanc★★** £B
O **Gewürztraminer★★** £B Vendange Tardive★★★★ £E
O **Riesling** Réserve Particulière★★★ £B Geisberg Grand Cru★★★★ £D
O **Tokay Pinot Gris★★** £B Kirchberg Grand Cru★★★★ £E

MARC KREYDENWEISS Andlau   marc.kreydenweiss@wanadoo.fr   A: C&C, Har

Owner: Marc Kreydenweiss 12 Rue Deharbe, 67140 Andlau
Marc Kreydenweiss's 12-ha domaine is in the north of the region in the Bas Rhin. He produces around 5,000 cases using biodynamic principles in the vineyard. In addition to the Alsace property, Marc and his wife Emmanuelle own the Costières de Nîmes property Domaine des PERRIÈRES (see Languedoc-Roussillon & Provence). The approach at both properties is the same: to achieve elegance and refinement rather than weight and power. The wines here are marked most by their intense fruit purity. Taut and with an almost gripping structure the top wines should be cellared for six or seven years, sometimes more. Marc produces an unusual blend of mainly Riesling and some Pinot Gris labelled Le Clos du Val d'Eléon, which technically is an Edelzwicker but is unlike almost all you're likely to encounter elsewhere. Plots are farmed in a considerable number of sites, both *lieux-dits* and *grands crus*. Supreme examples include Tokay Pinot Gris from Moenchberg, and Riesling from Kastelberg and Wiebelsberg. Among the great *lieux-dits* are Gewürztraminer from Kritt and Pinot Gris from both Rebberg and Lerchenberg. Fine Muscat Clos Rebgarten is intense, floral and musky and there is also a most unusual, very impressive Klevner from the Kritt site. Very stylish VT and SGN are produced from Gewürztraminer and VT Riesling comes from Kastelberg. (DM)

O **Le Clos du Val d'Eléon★★★** £D O **Klevner** Kritt★★★ £C
O **Gewürztraminer** Kritt★★★ £C
O **Riesling** Wiebelsberg Grand Cru★★★ £E Kastelberg Grand Cru★★★★ £E
O **Tokay Pinot Gris** Rebberg★★★ £C Lerchenberg★★★ £C Moenchberg Grand Cru★★★★ £E

KUENTZ-BAS Husseren-les-Châteaux www.kuentz-bas.fr

Owner: Christian Bas 14 Route du Vin, 68420 Husseren-les-Châteaux
Solidly established old family merchant business with an output now approaching 40,000 cases a year. There are 11 ha of owned vineyards including plots in the Grands Crus Eichberg and Pfersigberg. As well as this a considerable volume of grapes are also bought in. Quality, particularly when contrasted with other *négociants*, is very good across the board, the best wines being rich, full and long-lived. The style can vary: some bottlings are relatively dry, while others can have a touch of residual sugar. The regular varietal bottlings are labelled Tradition, of which the Pinot Gris stands out. The Collection wines are a step up and made from the family's own vineyards. The Muscat and Gewürztraminer have impressive depth and substance. The Collection Rare wines come from a selection of the best plots and the Tokay Pinot Gris combines pungency with real intensity and finesse. A range of first-class wines is produced from the Eichberg and Pfersigberg. Riesling is minerally and finely structured, Pinot Gris more opulent. Riesling also comes from the Grand Cru Brand. Very good Cuvée Caroline Vendange Tardive is produced as Gewürztraminer, Riesling and Tokay Pinot Gris. Quite exceptional is the rich, fine and intense Cuvée Jérémy Tokay Pinot Gris. All the top wines will age well, the late-harvest bottlings for up to a couple of decades. (DM)

O **Gewürztraminer** Collection★★ £B Cuvée Caroline Vendange Tardive★★★★ £E
O **Riesling** Collection★ £C Grand Cru Eichberg★★★ £D Grand Cru Pfersigberg★★★ £D
O **Riesling** Cuvée Caroline Vendange Tardive★★★★ £E
O **Tokay Pinot Gris** Tradition★ £B Grand Cru Eichberg★★★ £D Collection Rare★★★★ £D

O **Tokay Pinot Gris** Cuvée Jérémy SGN★★★★★ £G
O **Muscat** Collection★★ £B

DOM. SEPPI LANDMANN Soultzmatt www.seppi-landmann.fr A: Tra

Owner: Seppi Landmann 20 Rue de la Vallée, 68570 Soultzmatt
With a total output of only a little over 5,000 cases a year and vineyard holdings of just 8.5 ha, Seppi
Landmann produces a bewildering array of wines of exemplary quality. Good examples are made from
lowly varieties such as Sylvaner and Pinot Blanc and a range of Crémant d'Alsace is produced, the Brut Clos
des Paiens being the top label. Sylvaner Z comes from the Grand Cru Zinnekoepflé like the best of
Landmann's wines but this variety is not allowed *cru* status. The regular wines are labelled Vallée Noble and
these range from good to very fine in the case of the Gewürztraminer Vendange Tardive. A number of
special selections are released as Hospices de Strasbourg, where the wines are matured. Gewürztraminer,
Riesling and Tokay Pinot Gris are produced from the Zinnekoepflé site and occasional Vendange Tardive
and SGN are released. A real purity and character can be found in all the wines and you can expect the top
wines to age very well. (DM)

O **Gewürztraminer** Vallée Noble Vendange Tardive★★★★ £E
O **Gewürztraminer** Grand Cru Zinnekoepflé Vendange Tardive★★★★★ £E
O **Gewürztraminer** Vallée Noble Sigilé★★ £C Grand Cru Zinnekoepflé★★★ £E
O **Riesling** Grand Cru Zinnekoepflé★★★ £C
O **Tokay Pinot Gris** Grand Cru Zinnekoepflé★★★ £C Hospices de Strasbourg★★★ £C
O **Tokay Pinot Gris** Vallée Noble Sigilé★★ £C
O **Pinot Blanc** Vallée Noble★ £B
O **Cremant d'Alsace** Brut★ £B

DOM. FRANÇOIS LICHTLÉ Husseren-les-Châteaux hlichtle@aol.com

Owner: Lichtlé family 17 Rue des Vignerons, 68420 Husseren-les-Châteaux
Hervé Lichtlé has progressively improved quality at this small family domaine and it is a property to watch.
There are currently 6 ha of vineyards spread across 33 separate plots. Sylvaner, Pinot Blanc, Gewürztraminer
and Pinot Noir are grown in the *lieu-dit* of Horain and are some of the oldest vines of the property. There
is a small holding of Riesling in the Grand Cru Pfersigberg as well as a little Chardonnay which is used in
the Crémant d'Alsace. The wines all display pure varietal characters with good depth and intensity,
particularly in the Réserve and Vieilles Vignes bottlings. Pinot Gris Leo is rich and pungent, in marked
contrast to the fine, minerally, steely Riesling Pfersigberg. Good to very good examples of both Vendange
Tardive and SGN are produced from Gewürztraminer and Pinot Gris and there is a fine, elegant and
intense Riesling SGN too. Expect the top wines here to develop well in bottle over the medium term. Prices
are very reasonable. (DM)

O **Gewürztraminer**★★ £B Réserve★★★ £C Vieilles Vignes★★★ £C
O **Riesling** Grand Cru Pfersigberg★★★ £D SGN★★★★ £E
O **Riesling**★★ £B
O **Tokay Pinot Gris**★ £B Réserve★★ £C Cuvée Leo★★★★ £D
O **Pinot Blanc**★ £B

DOM. ALBERT MANN Wettolsheim vins@mann-albert.com A: NYg

Owner: Barthelmé family 13 Rue du Château, 68920 Wettolsheim
Very fine producer with a bewildering array of wines from just under 19 ha of vineyards, which are now,
like so many others, being tended organically. The style is for very ripe, full-bodied, traditional wines.
Generics can be very good: Pinot Blanc/Auxerrois is one of the best in the region. Gewürztraminer at the
generic level also impresses and the 2001 was three stars. Rieslings have considerable weight and depth –
more so than most – and they work best in a cooler vintage. The great Grand Cru Furstentum is a source
not only of Riesling but of very rich and concentrated Gewürztraminer too, full of lychee and spice. Pinot

Gris is very important and there is an excellent regular *cuvée* from old vines as well as first-class bottles from Altenbourg, Furstentum and Hengst. VT can be stunning and both the Grand Cru Hengst and Furstentum SGNs are remarkable wines, immensely rich and concentrated with substantial toffee, honey and peach. The style throughout is rich, opulent, almost extracted and the wines can be approached quite young, though the top examples age very well indeed. Prices are very fair. (DM)

○ **Pinot Blanc /Auxerrois** Vieilles Vignes★★ £B ○ **Muscat**★★ £B
○ **Gewürztraminer**★★ £B Steingrubler Grand Cru★★★★ £D
○ **Gewürztraminer** Furstentum Grand Cru Vieilles Vignes★★★★ £D
○ **Riesling** Schlossberg Grand Cru★★★ £C Furstentum Grand Cru★★★ £D
○ **Riesling** Pfleck Vendange Tardive★★★ £D
○ **Tokay Pinot Gris** Vieilles Vignes★★★ £C Hengst Grand Cru★★★★ £C
○ **Tokay Pinot Gris** Altenbourg Vendange Tardive★★★★ £D
○ **Tokay Pinot Gris** Hengst Grand Cru SGN✪✪✪✪✪ £E Furstentum Grand Cru SGN✪✪✪✪✪ £E
● **Pinot Noir** Vieilles Vignes★★ £D

RENÉ MURÉ Rouffach www.mure.com A: BWC, Gau

Owner: Muré family Clos Saint Landelin, Route du Vin, 68250 Rouffach
René Muré's total production is not vast but sizeable for the area, at close to 25,000 cases per year. There are two distinct sides to the operation here. Domaine wines are labelled Clos Saint-Landelin and produced from 20 ha of estate vineyards at the Grand Cru Vorbourg and a number of neighbouring sites. The Muré family solely own the Clos Saint-Landelin vineyard, a *monopole* within the Vorbourg. The quality and prices of the wines are substantially above those of the *négoçiant* wines under the René Muré label. These are a range of generics which generally offer good value along with a decent Crémant d'Alsace. Superior bottlings of varieties go under the Côte de Rouffach label. Among the Domaine wines there is impressively steely Sylvaner from the *clos* which is full of ripe, green fruits and minerals and one of the finest examples in the region. Intense, long-lived Riesling comes from Vorbourg and Clos Saint-Landelin, while rich, spicy and opulent Gewürztraminer hails from the *lieu-dit* Schultzengass as well as Vorbourg and Pinot Gris comes from Lutzeltal as well as the *clos*. Some better-than-average Pinot Noir is also produced, plus some very fine Muscat, as both VT and SGN, along with Riesling, Gewürztraminer and Tokay Pinot Gris. Clos Saint-Landelin is favoured by the regular occurrence of noble rot. The Gewürztraminer and Pinot Gris are more approachable than the Rieslings, which really will benefit from six or seven years in bottle. The generic René Muré labels will be enjoyable on release, the Côte de Rouffach wines will be better for two or three years' ageing. (DM)

Domaine du Clos Saint-Landelin
○ **Sylvaner** Cuvée Oscar★★ £B
○ **Gewürztraminer** Schulzengass★★★ £C Vorbourg Grand Cru★★★ £D
○ **Riesling** Vorbourg Grand Cru★★★ £C Clos Saint Landelin Vorbourg Grand Cru★★★★ £E
○ **Tokay Pinot Gris** Lutzeltal★★ £D Clos Saint Landelin Vorbourg Grand Cru★★★ £D
● **Pinot Noir** V★★ £D

René Muré
○ **Muscat** Côte de Rouffach★★ £C
○ **Gewürztraminer**★ £B Côte de Rouffach★★ £C
○ **Riesling** Côte de Rouffach★★ £C
○ **Tokay Pinot Gris** Côte de Rouffach★★ £D
○ **Crémant d'Alsace**★★ £C
● **Pinot Noir** Côte de Rouffach★★ £C

OSTERTAG Epfig A: M&V, Har

Owner: André Ostertag 87 Rue Finckwiller, 67680 Epfig
For more than 10 years André Ostertag has taken a radical approach to winemaking in the region. The vineyards are now farmed biodynamically but of greater significance has been the creation of wines that are

given *barrique* treatment, including Pinot Blanc, Pinot Gris and Pinot Noir. Some of his experiments have brought him into open conflict with the appellation bureaucrats in the past. The generic labels he classifies as *vins du fruit*, the *lieux-dits* and *grands crus* as *vins du terroir,* and his late-harvest bottlings are *vins du temps*. In general the oak-handled wines work well. He also makes very good Rieslings with no recourse to wood, most notably from the Grand Cru Muenchberg, and some very fine Gewürztraminer. Ostertag favours producing a dry style but the Gewürztraminer will often have a touch of residual sugar for balance. Sylvaner from very old vines is arguably the best example in the region. Top wines are not only very ageworthy but require five or six years' cellaring at a minimum. (DM)

O **Sylvaner** Vieilles Vignes★★ £B O **Pinot Blanc** Barriques★ £B
O **Gewürztraminer** d'Epfig★★★ £C Fronholz Vendange Tardive★★★★ £E
O **Riesling** Fronholz★★★ £D Muenchberg Grand Cru★★★★ £E
O **Riesling** Muenchberg Grand Cru Vendange Tardive★★★★ £F
O **Tokay Pinot Gris** Barriques★★ £C Zellberg★★★ £E Muenchberg Grand Cru★★★★ £E

CAVE DE RIBEAUVILLÉ   Ribeauvillé   www.cave-ribeauville.com

Owner: 'Co-operative'   2 Route de Colmar, 68150 Ribeauvillé
Founded in 1895, this is the oldest wine co-operative in France. Its 110 members provide up to 270 ha of vineyards and output is sizeable for the region at upwards of 200,000 cases a year. As well as a good range of generic varietal wines the Ribeauville co-op has just released a series of exciting bio-dynamically producers wines which are quality benchmarks for large producers throughout the region. An extensive range of well-priced *grand cru* wines is available: Gewürztraminer comes from Gloekelberg and Osterberg, Pinot Gris from Gloekelberg and Riesling from Altenberg de Bergheim, Kirchberg, Osterberg and Rosacker. A range of wines is also released under the Collection d'Artistes label which supports local arts and culture, notably for blind people. The wines will develop well in the short to medium term, the *grand cru* labels keeping longer. (DM)

O **Gewürztraminer**★★ £B Weingarten Collection d'Artistes★★ £B
O **Riesling**★★ £B Steinacker Collection d'Artistes★★ £B Martin Zahn★★★ £B
O **Tokay Pinot Gris**★★ £B Weingarten Collection d'Artistes★★ £B Martin Zahn★★★ £B
O **Pinot Blanc** Prestige★ £B Martin Zahn★★★ £B
O **Clos du Zahnacker**★★ £B

ROLLY-GASSMANN   Rorschwihr   rollygassmann@wanadoo.fr   A: RsW, Bib, Rae, WSc

Owner: Rolly-Gassmann family   2 Rue de l'Eglise, 68950 Rorschwihr
An extensive range of very good, traditionally produced wines emerges from this family domaine. There are no *grand cru* vineyards but a number of wines from some excellent *lieux-dits*. As well as the varietal and vineyard-labelled wines, including a good Edelzwicker, there are some particularly fine Vendange Tardive and SGN bottlings. The Muscat, Pinot Gris and Gewürztraminer are marked by pungent and concentrated varietal character. Riesling is intense and lightly mineral in style but with a piercing citrus character regularly showing through. The top wines need some cellaring to show at their best. Release dates can be confusing with a number of bottlings held back in the cellar and released with several years' age. This is is however a rare source for purchasing top wines approaching their peak. (DM)

O **Pinot Blanc Auxerrois** Moenchreben★★ £B
O **Muscat** Moenchreben★★★ £C Moenchreben Vendange Tardive★★★★ £E
O **Gewürztraminer** SGN★★★★ £F
O **Riesling** Kappelweg★★★ £C Kappelweg Vendange Tardive★★★★ £E Pflaenzereben★★★ £C
O **Tokay Pinot Gris**★★ £B Réserve★★★ £C

DOM. SCHLUMBERGER   Guebviller   www.domaines-schlumberger.com

Owner: Sclumberger family   100 Rue Théodore-Deck, 68500 Guebviller
This is the largest domaine in the region in terms of vineyard holdings, which at some 140 ha rival some

of the larger co-ops. Of particular significant are the terroirs of the various plots spread across a five kilometre stretch of the southern Vosges. The vineyards are planted in sandstone at an altitude of 250 to 380 metres with a south-easterly aspect. Amongst the plots are holdings in the Grands Crus Kitterle, Kessler, Saering and Spiegel. Rich, perfumed and opulent Gewürztraminer and Tokay Pinot Gris from these sites are especially good. Riesling tends to impress less in this southerly location and among the regular Les Princes Abbés labels it is the Gewürztraminer which stands out. Some very fine late-harvest wines are also produced. In addition to the Cuvée Christine Vendange Tardive Gewürztraminer, SGNs Cuvée Anne (Gewürztraminer), Cuvée Clarisse (Pinot Gris) and Cuvée Ernest (Riesling) are also produced in exceptional vintages, generally only once or twice a decade. The top wines are firmly structured and require at least five or six years' cellaring. (DM)

O **Gewürztraminer** Grand Cru Kitterelé★★★★ £D Cuvée Christine Vendange Tardive★★★★ £E
O **Gewürztraminer** Grand Cru Kessler★★★ £D Grand Cru Saering★★★ £D
O **Gewürztraminer** Les Princes Abbés★★ £B
O **Riesling** Les Princes Abbés★ £B Grand Cru Kitterelé★★ £D Grand Cru Saering★★★ £D
O **Tokay Pinot Gris** Grand Cru Spiegel★★★ £D Grand Cru Kitterelé★★★ £D Cuvée Clarisse★★★★ £F
O **Tokay Pinot Gris** Les Princes Abbés★ £B

DOM. SCHOFFIT Colmar   A: HBJ,BBR,Gau,Har

Owner: Schoffit family 66-68 Nonnenholzweg, 6800 Colmar
There are some 16 ha planted at this brilliant domaine based in Colmar, with production now running at around 8,000 cases a year. The regular bottlings are all very good. Pinot Blanc and particularly the humble Chasselas produced from venerable vines really stand out. A significant part of the Schoffits' vineyard holding is in lesser sites but quality is still admirable. The focal point of the domaine, though, is the fine volcanic soil of the Clos Saint-Théobald in the Grand Cru Rangen, which yields wines that are structured but with a remarkable array of exotic fruit aromas and always a pure mineral undercurrent. VT and SGN are very fine to exceptional. Given the extraordinary quality, the entire range represents excellent value for money. (DM)

O **Pinot Blanc** Cuvée Caroline★★ £B O **Muscat** Tradition★★ £B
O **Chasselas** Vieilles Vignes★★ £B
O **Gewürztraminer** Harth Cuvée Alexandre Vieilles Vignes★★★ £C
O **Gewürztraminer** Clos Saint-Théobald Rangen Grand Cru★★★★ £E
O **Gewürztraminer** Clos Saint-Théobald Rangen Grand Cru Vendange Tardive★★★★★ £F
O **Riesling** Harth Cuvée Alexandre★★ £B Clos Saint-Théobald Rangen Grand Cru★★★★ £E
O **Riesling** Clos Saint-Théobald Rangen Grand Cru Vendange Tardive✪✪✪✪✪ £F
O **Tokay Pinot Gris** Cuvée Alexandre Vieilles Vignes★★★ £C
O **Tokay Pinot Gris** Clos Saint-Théobald Rangen Grand Cru★★★★★ £E
O **Tokay Pinot Gris** Clos Saint-Théobald Rangen Grand Cru SGN✪✪✪✪✪ £F

DOM. BRUNO SORG Eguisheim   A: THt,BBR

Owner: Sorg family 8 Rue Mgr-Stumpf, 68420 Eguisheim
Very fine small grower, based just to the south of Colmar with 10 ha of well-sited vineyards which include holdings in the Grands Crus Eichberg, Florimont and Pfersigberg. François Sorg is one of the best producers of Muscat in Alsace. The wines are always pure, musky and complex and the dry Pfersigberg is a benchmark example. Riesling is steely and minerally with a real intensity, particularly the finely structured and very ageworthy Vieilles Vignes. Pinot Gris and Gewürztraminer are richly textured and opulent, the latter full of concentrated lychee and tropical spices, but the wines always have great varietal purity and are impeccably balanced. The regular and old-vine bottlings will drink well with two or three years' age but will keep very well. Its best to leave the *grands crus* for five or six years, particularly the Rieslings. (DM)

O **Gewürztraminer** Vieilles Vignes★★★ £C
O **Riesling**★★ £B Grand Cru Pfersigberg★★★ £C Grand Cru Pfersigberg Vieilles Vignes★★★★ £D

O **Tokay Pinot Gris** Vieilles Vignes★★★ £C Grand Cru Florimont★★★★ £D
O **Muscat**★★ £B Grand Cru Pfersigberg★★★ £C

TRIMBACH Ribeauvillé www.maison-trimbach.fr   A: **Par**,BBR,WSc,Sel,Har

Owner: Trimbach family 15 Route de Bergheim, 68150 Ribeauvillé
Large well-established merchant house producing close to 100,000 cases a year. As at HUGEL, the top wines
are very impressive, although perhaps of not quite the same dimension. This is with the exception of the
remarkable Riesling Clos Sainte-Hune, arguably the greatest dry expression of the variety in the region and
one of the greatest anywhere in the world. Indeed, the Rieslings are the most successful of the varietals. They
are structured, very dry in style and have a pure and intense mineral depth. They age remarkably well. The
Gewürztraminer Seigneurs de Ribeaupierre is in a similarly dry, structured style. Rich, aromatic, lychee
notes and an increasingly honeyed character will emerge with five or six years' cellaring. VT and SGN
bottlings are certainly impressive. They are structured and rich, just a little way short of the very best. The
generics are less exciting than many equivalents you may find from smaller domaines and the prices for these
are quite steep. (DM)
O **Muscat** Réserve★ £B
O **Gewürztraminer**★ £C Seigneurs de Ribeaupierre★★★ £E Vendange Tardive★★★★ £F
O **Riesling**★★ £B Réserve★★ £C Clos Sainte-Hune❍❍❍❍❍ £G
O **Riesling** Cuvée Frédéric Émile★★★★ £E
O **Tokay Pinot Gris** Réserve★★ £B Réserve Personnelle★★★ £C SGN★★★★ £G

CAVE DE TURCKHEIM Turckheim www.cave-turckheim.com   A: **PBW**

Owner: 'Co-operative' 16 Rue des Tuileries, 68230 Turckheim
Another fine co-op in a region that features an impressive number of such quality-conscious operations.
Turckheim's co-op is one of the more recently established, dating from 1956. The Cave can call on 310 ha
of vineyards owned by its members and output is sizeable, approaching 300,000 cases annually. There are
some sound generic wines under the Tradition label, in particular Gewürztraminer and Tokay Pinot Gris.
The Réserves are a step up. The best part of the operation is a solid range of single-vineyard and *grand cru*
wines along with some excellent Vendange Tardive bottlings, particularly the Gewürztraminer. Both Tokay
Pinot Gris and Gewürztraminer from the great Hengst and Brand sites stand out. Gewürztraminer is
opulent and spicy with real depth, the Hengst offering a subtle extra dimension, while Tokay Pinot Gris is
rich and honeyed with a fine mineral structure. Riesling tends to pale by comparison and lacks the depth
and intensity of the other varieties. The Brand bottling is sound but you feel there should be more. Top
Pinot Gris and Gewürztraminer will develop very well in bottle. (DM)
O **Gewürztraminer** Grand Cru Brand★★★ £C Grand Cru Hengst★★★★ £C Vendange Tardive★★★★★ £E
O **Gewürztraminer** Tradition★ £B Reserve★★ £B
O **Riesling** Grand Cru Brand★★ £C
O **Tokay Pinot Gris** Grand Cru Hengst★★★ £D Vendange Tardive★★★★ £E
O **Tokay Pinot Gris** Tradition★ £B Reserve★★ £B Heimbourg★★ £C
O **Cremant d'Alsace** Mayerling★ £B

DOMAINE WEINBACH Kaysersberg www.domaineweinbach.com   A: **J&B**, Tan, NYg

Owner: Mme Faller & family 25 route du Vin, 68240 Kaysersberg
Weinbach is one of the great names of Alsace. Madame Faller and her daughters run an impressive 26-ha
estate partly converted to biodynamic cultivation since 1998. The wines are stylistically different from those
of Trimbach or Zind-Humbrecht, offering neither the elegance or reserve of the former nor the same degree
of definition and nuance of terroir seen in the Zind-Humbrecht wines, yet they are rich, powerful and
complex, particularly concentrated and impressive in the top *cuvées*, and they are rarely disappointing. The
richest styles can be magnificent. The two most important holdings are those of the 5-ha walled Clos des
Capucins and 10 ha in the Grand Cru Schlossberg, but outstanding wines are also made from *lieu-dit*

Altenbourg. The number of bottlings is extensive and somewhat complicated with special *cuvées* named after family members. Cuvée Theo Gewürztraminer and Riesling (named after the late Theo Faller) come only from the Clos. Cuvée Sainte-Catherine is a rich Riesling from the lower part of Schlossberg, usually harvested in late November, but a more select bottling is additionally labelled Grand Cru Schlossberg while L'Inédit represents the very best selection of this vineyard. Regular Cuvée Laurence Tokay Pinot Gris and Gewürztraminer comes from the foot of Altenbourg, while those additionally labelled Altenbourg come from the vineyard itself. A small amount of Gewürztraminer also comes from the Grand Cru Furstentum. VT and SGN styles add more sweetness to the usual Weinbach concentration and depth whilst retaining good balance. Cuvée d'Or Quintessence SGN is reserved for formidable rich and sweet *cuvées* made when conditions allow it, such as an intensely sweet and spicy botrytised Gewürztraminer. A scented, stylish Muscat Réserve Personelle is also very good if drunk fairly young. (PW)

O **Riesling** Cuvée Theo★★★ £C Schlossberg Grand Cru Cuvée Sainte-Catherine★★★★★ £E
O **Riesling** Schlossberg Grand Cru Cuvée Sainte-Catherine l'Inédit★★★★★ £F Vendange Tardive★★★★★ £F
O **Gewürztraminer** Cuvée Theo★★★ £D Altenbourg Cuvée Laurence★★★★ £E
O **Gewürztraminer** Furstentum Vendange Tardive✪✪✪✪✪ £F
O **Gewürztraminer** Cuvée d'Or Quintessence SGN✪✪✪✪✪ £G
O **Tokay Pinot Gris** Cuvée Sainte-Catherine Fut II★★★★ £E O **Pinot Blanc** Réserve★★ £C
O **Muscat** Réserve Personelle★★★ £D

ZIND-HUMBRECHT Turckheim o.humbrecht@wanadoo.fr A: ABy,BBR,Har,Gau,Coe

Owner: Olivier Zind-Humbrecht 4 Route de Colmar, 68230 Turckheim

It is very easy to eulogise both the wines and the winemaking ethos of Olivier Humbrecht. The family's 40 ha of vineyards cultivated by Olivier's father Léonard (and biodynamic since 1997) offer an enviable resource from which individual *terroirs* have been given expression. In fact, from a combination of several different grape varieties and many excellent sites, one of France's, indeed the world's great white wine producers has created a miniature vinous wonderland. More than 30 wines are produced in every vintage – multiply that by the different vintage permutations that a non-interventionist winemaking approach emphasises and you might not ever find time to taste anything else. The wines, made only from fully ripe grapes, are full, concentrated and intense, each expressing something of the essence of their origins. Some of Zind-Humbrecht's *crus* are also produced in late-harvested VT and SGN styles and although even regular versions can vary in the degree of residual sugar there is almost always the necessary balance between sweetness and acidity. If the range and variable levels of sweetness can make it difficult to choose an individual bottle, the new scale of sweetness being introduced in Alsace will help make it a little less bewildering. Highlights include a fascinating array of fine Riesling: Clos Saint-Urbain combines breadth and a fine minerality; Brand has great structure and power that unfurls slowly with age; Clos Windsbuhl shows an intense fruit depth; while Clos Hauserer can be more classically crisp and stimulating. Fine Pinot Gris include a very rich, creamy Vieilles Vignes example, potent Rotenberg, vibrant and deeply fruity Clos Windsbuhl and the smoky, minerally Clos Saint-Urbain, all of which are surpassed by the Clos Jebsal for sheer richness and substance. Impressively rich and aromatic Gewürztraminers include fine, minerally Wintzerheim, broad and powerful Herrenweg, rich, almost overwhelming Heimbourg, exotic Goldert and marvellously deep and concentrated Clos Windsbuhl. There is also a very small amount of Grand Cru Rangen Clos Saint-Urbain. Fine Muscat is also made, both deeply grapey Herrenweg and a more expressive, floral Goldert. Muscat excepted, almost all the wines need a decent amount of bottle-age to show at their best. Regular bottlings should have at least two or three years' ageing; most *lieu-dits* or *grands crus* (whether in regular versions or either VT or SGN styles) deserve at least five or six years. The list below includes most but not all of the extensive range. VT and SGN bottlings add a considerable premium to prices, especially the latter style. (PW)

O **Riesling** Rangen Grand Cru Clos Saint-Urbain★★★★ £F Brand Grand Cru✪✪✪✪✪ £F
O **Riesling** Turckheim★ £B Clos Hauserer★★★★ £E Clos Windsbuhl★★★★ £E
O **Tokay Pinot Gris** Rangen Grand Cru Clos Saint-Urbain★★★★★ £F Clos Windsbuhl★★★★★ £F
O **Tokay Pinot Gris** Vieilles Vignes★★★ £C Rotenberg★★★ £E Heimbourg★★★ £E Clos Jebsal★★★★ £E

O **Gewürztraminer** Heimbourg★★★★ £E Goldert Grand Cru★★★★ £E Clos Windsbuhl★★★★ £E
O **Gewürztraminer** Herrenweg★★★ £D Wintzenheim★★★ £D Hengst Grand Cru★★★★★ £F
O **Muscat** Herrenweg★★★ £D Goldert Grand Cru★★★★ £D
O **Pinot d'Alsace** ★★ £C O **Sylvaner**★ £B

OTHER WINES OF NOTE

ALLIMANT-LAUGNER O **Muscat** £B O **Riesling** £B O **Gewürztraminer** £C
DOM. AUTHER O **Muscat** £B O **Riesling** £B
DOM. BARMES-BUECHER O **Gewürztraminer** Wintzenheim £D
JEAN-PIERRE BECHTOLD O **Gewürztraminer** Silberberg £C O **Riesling** Engelberg Grand Cru £C
LÉON BOESCH O **Sylvaner** £B O **Gewürztraminer** Zinnkoepflé Grand Cru £D
DOPFF & IRION O **Tokay Pinot Gris** Maquisards £B Vorbourg Grand Cru £F
DOPFF AU MOULIN O **Gewürztraminer** Brand Grand Cru £D
CAVE DE HUNAWIHR O **Muscat** Réserve £B O **Gewürztraminer** Rosacker Grand Cru
O **Riesling** Rosacker Grand Cru £C O **Tokay Pinot Gris** Réserve £B Rosacker Grand Cru £C
DOM. ROGER JUNG O **Riesling** VV £B Schoenenbourg Grand Cru £C
O **Tokay Pinot Gris** Schoenenbourg Grand Cru £C
DOM. CLEMENT KLUR O **Cremant d'Alsace** £B O **Pinot Blanc** Grain d'Or £B
O **Tokay Pinot Gris** Vieilles Vignes £C O **Riesling** Sommerberg Grand Cru £C
O **Gewürztraminer** Grand Cru Sclossberg £C
JEAN-LUC MADER O **Pinot Blanc** Théophile £B O **Gewürztraminer** Théophile £B
DOM. JEAN-LOUIS & FABIENNE MANN O **Sylvaner** Vieilles Vignes £B
O **Gewürztraminer** Pfersigberg Grand Cru £C
DOM. DES MARRONNIERS O **Riesling** Moenchberg Grand Cru £C Kastelberg Grand Cru £C
DOM. MATERNE-HAEGELIN O **Gewürztraminer** £B O **Riesling** Bollenberg £B
MEYER-FONNÉ O **Riesling** Katzenthal £B Winneck-Schlossberg Grand Cru £C
O **Gewürztraminer** Winneck-Schlossberg Grand Cru £C
DOM. MITTNACHT-KLACK O **Riesling** Muhlforst £B Schoenenbourg Grand Cru £C
CAVE DE PFAFFENHEIM O **Riesling** Goldert Grand Cru £C Zinnkoepflé Grand Cru £C
DOM. RIEFLÉ O **Gewürztraminer** Steinert Grand Cru £E O **Riesling** £C Steinert Grand Cru £C
O **Tokay Pinot Gris** Côte de Rouffach £C Steinert Grand Cru £C
DOMAINE MARTIN SCHAETZEL O **Pinot Blanc** Réserve £B O **Riesling** Réserve £B
O **Tokay Pinot Gris** Réserve £B O **Gewürztraminer** Kaefferkopf £C
ANDRÉ SCHERER O **Riesling** Pfersigberg Grand Cru £C
DOM. CHARLES SCHLERET O **Sylvaner** £B O **Riesling** Herrenweg £C
O **Tokay Pinot Gris** Herrenweg £C
DOM. ROLAND SCHMITT O **Riesling** Altenberg de Bergheim Grand Cru Cuvée Roland £C
GÉRARD SCHUELLER O **Muscat** Reserve £B O **Tokay Pinot Gris** Trottacker £C
DOM. JEAN SIPP O **Gewürztraminer** Vieilles Vignes £B O **Tokay Pinot Gris** Trottacker £C
LOUIS SIPP O **Gewürztraminer** £B O **Riesling** Réserve Personelle £C
O **Tokay Pinot Gris** Réserve Personelle £C
PIERRE SPARR O **Gewürztraminer** GC Mambourg £C O **Tokay Pinot Gris** Réserve £B
DOM. SYLVIE SPIELMANN O **Gewürztraminer** Blosenberg Bergheim £C
O **Gewürztraminer** Grand Cru Altenberg de Bergheim £D
DOM. STOEFFLER O **Tokay Pinot Gris** £B O **Riesling** Kronenbourg £B
MARC TEMPÉ O **Pinot Blanc** Zellenberg £B O **Riesling** Zellenberg £B
PAUL ZINCK O **Riesling** Prestige £B Rangen Grand Cru £C O **Tokay Pinot Gris** Prestige £B
O **Gewürztraminer** Prestige £B Eichberg Grand Cru £C

Author's choice (DM)

A dozen striking dry whites

DOM. PAUL BLANCK ○ **Gewürztraminer** Grand Cru Furstentum Vieilles Vignes

DOM. BOTT-GEYL ○ **Riesling** Mandelburg Grand Cru

ERNEST BURN ○ **Tokay Pinot Gris** Goldert Grand Cru Cuvée de la Chapelle

MARCEL DEISS ○ **Altenberg Grand Cru**

MARC KREYDENWEISS ○ **Le Clos du Val d'Eléon**

DOM. ALBERT MANN ○ **Pinot Blanc/Auxerrois** Vieilles Vignes

RENÉ MURÉ ○ **Riesling** Clos Saint Landelin Vorbourg Grand Cru

OSTERTAG ○ **Sylvaner** Vieilles Vignes

DOM. SCHOFFIT ○ **Gewürztraminer** Harth Cuvée Alexandre Vieilles Vignes

TRIMBACH ○ **Riesling** Clos Sainte-Hune

DOM. WEINBACH ○ **Muscat** Réserve Personelle

ZIND-HUMBRECHT ○ **Tokay Pinot Gris** Clos Windsbuhl

An exciting selection of late harvest whites

DOM. JEAN BECKER ○ **Gewürztraminer** Schoenenbourg Grand Cru SGN

DOM. LÉON BEYER ○ **Tokay Pinot Gris** SGN

DOM. BOTT-GEYL ○ **Tokay Pinot Gris** Sonnenglanz Grand Cru SGN

HUGEL ET FILS ○ **Riesling** SGN

ANDRÉ KIENTZLER ○ **Gewürztraminer** Vendange Tardive

DOM. ALBERT MANN ○ **Tokay Pinot Gris** Hengst Grand Cru SGN

OSTERTAG ○ **Gewürztraminer** Fronholz Vendange Tardive

ROLLY-GASSMANN ○ **Muscat** Moenchreben Vendange Tardive

DOM. SCHOFFIT ○ **Riesling** Clos Saint Théobald Rangen Grand Cru Vendange Tardive

DOM. WEINBACH ○ **Gewürztraminer** Cuvée d'Or Quintessence SGN

The name Champagne carries almost mystical properties for a vast number of people. However, there are a bewildering number of Champagne houses, co-operatives and growers bottling wine under their own labels and a further huge own-label business with wines of immensely variable quality all being bottled under the auspices of just one appellation. The great Champagne houses virtually invented the concept of the brand in winemaking and in most cases they do a very acceptable job. Nonetheless, in the absence of a better classification system the area remains a minefield for consumers. There are some 30,000-plus ha under vine with many of the 19,000 growers cultivating no more than a hectare or two. Both in the cellars of the region and in the vineyards there are inevitably substantial variations in quality.

The appellation and its districts

Making sparkling wine is realistically the only consistent vinegrowing activity that can be undertaken here, among the windswept rolling hills of the most northerly of France's wine regions. Alsace may be on a not dissimilar latitude but crucially it is protected by the Vosges Mountains. Ripening the three varieties Pinot Meunier, Pinot Noir and Chardonnay is by no means easy. Pinot Noir and Chardonnay are at their optimum in the production of the great wines of the Côte d'Or some 240 km (150 miles) to the south. The vital requirement here is to provide grapes that are physiologically ripe and of sufficient intensity to produce at least good wine. That means controlling yields and harvesting properly ripened fruit, which remains a problem.

Within the appellation the communes have been classified as Grand Cru, Premier Cru or Deuxième Cru. This does not however give an indication of quality or the potential of a given *terroir* as it does in Burgundy but works more as a means by which to establish the price a grower gets for his harvest. You may have an outstanding performer in a second-classed village and a moderate grower in a *grand cru*.

The appellation falls into five main districts, which account for some two-thirds of the working vineyard area. These five districts may yet become their own sub-appellations in a desired move to establish better regional identity within this geographically extensive AC. The rest of the appellation is spread across a vast area. Indeed the idea that all Champagne comes from fabled chalk soils is not the case. Much of the *vignoble* is clay, sand or marl. The **Montagne de Reims** is just to the south of that city and the aspect of the vineyards improves as it extends southwards. Pinot Noir and Pinot Meunier are the predominant varieties here and are famed for producing rich, full-bodied Champagnes. The village of **Bouzy** is as well known for producing the best still Coteaux Champenois reds as it is sparkling wines.

The **Vallée de la Marne** to the north-west of the Montagne de Reims stretches east along the River Marne. The centre of the district is the town of Épernay and the best vineyard sites are to the east. Red grapes are predominant here and the wines tend to be a touch lighter than those from the Montagne de Reims, with more elegance and refinement. The **Côte des Blancs** is, as the name suggests, white wine territory. Chardonnay is virtually the exclusive grape here with very few red plantings. The vineyards are largely sited with an easterly aspect. The great Chardonnay villages of Avize, Le Mesnil-sur-Oger and Vertus are found here.

In the far south-west of the main Champagne area, north of Troyes, is the **Côte de Sézanne**, with the small town of the same name at its heart. The vineyards are dominated by Chardonnay, which accounts for some seven out of every 10 vines. As in the Côte des Blancs there is extensive chalk in the soil but not to the same degree. Way to the south of Troyes and away from the main Champagne appellation boundaries is the **Aube**. The area is one hundred miles from Reims. The soil is different, there is no chalk but more of the Kimmeridgian clay and limestone soils of Sancerre and Chablis. The latter is in fact a good deal closer to the Aube than any of the other Champagne vineyards.

At present the Aube is largely planted to Pinot Noir. There is a case for a considerable increase in Chardonnay. The area could potentially make extremely rich and powerful Blanc de Blancs.

The styles

The range of different styles available takes in sparkling white and rosé along with the still red wines which use the Coteaux Champenois appellation. While the role of the master blender in Champagne remains as significant as ever, the development of wines that come from single *terroirs* or from the same, very specific sources when vintage conditions favour – like the great Salon wines – seems likely to accelerate as time goes on. The sheer quality of many of the emerging small growers is a signal of things to come.

The styles and method outlined below should only be used as a very general guide; there can be significant variation within these. It is quite possible to find deluxe super-premium *cuvées* that are non-vintage, Blanc de Blancs that may be from a single vineyard or a blend of many, or Blanc de Noirs in vintage and non-vintage versions.

Most common and providing the bulk of the output of the great Champagne houses are the regular **non-vintage** blends. The use of reserve wine stocks is an undoubted asset, but a huge variation in quality exists. Available vineyard resources (and consequent fruit quality) and the length of time on lees in bottle are just two of the factors that affect the style of these wines. You should expect **vintage** *cuvées* to be a significant step up. They should be denser and richer with significantly greater structure. Inevitably there will be more variation in style with these as they reflect the nature of the year. Generally they should only be released after good harvests.

Blanc de Blancs is produced solely from Chardonnay while **Blanc de Noirs** is produced from Pinot Noir and/or Pinot Meunier, to the complete exclusion of Chardonnay. Blanc de Blancs is more refined and elegant and often has a tighter structure when young, whereas a Blanc de Noirs is fuller, with richer, more opulent flavours. The pink **Rosés** can be made either by blending in a little red wine (the only AC where this is permitted) or, and generally with better results, by the normal manner of a short maceration on skins. The best rosé generally comes from pure Pinot Noir.

The most expensive Champagnes are the deluxe bottlings. There is a wide range of styles but the best are among the finest white or rosé wines in the world. The latter are generally more expensive and made in minute quantities.

Champagne vintages

Because of the variable and challenging climate there is much vintage variation. Vintage wines are only produced when conditions permit. Among recent years 2003 may produce some excellent vintage bottles but balance will be a problem with many wines after a very hot summer. 2002 looks to be very promising. 2001, though, was a disaster with unprecedented rainfall. From 1995 to 2000 the Champenois were very lucky, having a string of good to very good vintages. 1996 and 1998 were outstanding. 1996 was uniformly good, very warm and sunny with ideal ripening conditions. There was some variation in 1998. 1996 and 1997 are now emerging on the market. Prior to 1995 the only really halfway presentable year was 1993. There were an alarming number of 1992s which were green and hard. 1990 is a classic. There are fine wines on release now, like the Bollinger RD 1995. 1989 and 1988 were both very good but not quite on a par with 1990. 1989 has less structure and should be drunk now. 1985, 1983 and 1982 are all great earlier years and top wines encountered from these will be worth considering, although 1985 and 1983 particularly do need drinking now.

AGRAPART   www.champagne-agrapart.com

Owner: Agrapart family   57 Ave Jean Jaures, 51190 Avize

Impressive small family-owned producer run by brothers Pascal and Fabrice with 9.6 ha of vineyards on the Côte des Blancs, almost half of which are at Avize. Other plots are in the *grand cru* villages of Oger, Cramant and Oiry. The Agraparts' holding is exclusively Chardonnay, traditionally established by mass selection and crucially the vines are of significant age: the oldest parcels over 55 years. This is clearly perceptible in the wines which have great purity and intensity. The non-vintage Brut Reserve is partly wood-aged and gets four years on its lees. The Brut Millésime is vinified in *demi-muids* and comes from calcareous soils at Avize and argilo-calcareous soils at Cramant. Both richness and complexity are gained from six years on lees. The top wine, the marvellously intense, citrus and mineral-laden L'Avizoise gets a similar period of lees-ageing and comes from the oldest vines. It will age very well in bottle. (DM)

O **Brut Réserve Grand Cru** Non-Vintage★★ £C   O **Brut Grand Cru** Vintage★★★ £D
O **L'Avizoise Brut Grand Cru** Vintage★★★★ £E

AYALA   www.champagne-ayala.fr   A: **Lib**

Owner: Ducellier family   2 Boulevard du Nord, 51160 Aÿ

Jean-Michel Ducellier owns this recently improved small house as well as the Haut-Médoc classed growth Château LA LAGUNE. Ayala is now run by his son Alain. Recent releases have been showing greater richness, weight and concentration than a decade ago. These are very ripe, almost rustic styles of Champagne. The non-vintage Brut is dominated by Pinot Noir with a fair proportion of Pinot Meunier as well. The vintage Brut is again dominated by Pinot Noir with sufficient Chardonnay to provide additional complexity and intensity. The Blanc de Blancs is rich and weighty for the style with surprising opulence. There is also a light, fruit-driven rosé and also a special prestige bottling Grand Cuvée. (DM)

O **Brut** Non-Vintage★★ £D   O **Brut** Vintage★★★ £E   O **Brut Blanc de Blancs** Vintage★★★ £E
◉ **Brut** Non-Vintage★ £D

PAUL BARA   A: OWL

Owner: Bara family   4 Rue Yvonnet, 51150 Bouzy

Very good small and traditional producer with vineyard holdings in the *grand cru* village of Bouzy. The wines have a high level of Pinot Noir in the blend and this tends to show through with weight and substance. The Grand Cru Vintage is rich and bready, the Vintage Club shows extra depth and there is a very impressive, intense rosé. The Comtesse Marie de France is lighter and more elegant. The wines are all good value. (DM)

O **Brut Réserve Grand Cru** Non-Vintage★★ £C   O **Brut Grand Cru** Vintage★★★ £D
O **Brut Grand Cru Comtesse Marie de France** Vintage★★★★ £E
O **Grand Cru Vintage Club** Vintage★★★★ £E
◉ **Brut Grand Cru Grand** Rosé de Bouzy★★★ £D

EDMOND BARNAUT   www.champagne-barnaut.com   A: L&S, GFy

Owner: Philippe Secondé   2 Rue Gambetta, BP 19, 51150 Bouzy

The 14 ha of vineyards are, like those of the Bara family, planted around the village of Bouzy. Unlike the Bara vineyards, though, they contain a high proportion of Chardonnay. This gives an added finesse and grip although the wines are of an impressively weighty, substantial style. There are two fine non-vintage wines: the Sélection-Extra and Grand Réserve. The former has a higher proportion of Pinot Noir which is evident, as it is in a rich, bready Blanc de Noirs. The Authentique Rosé gains its colour from the Pinot Noir skins rather than from blending with red base wine. There is also a limited-production special Cuvée Edmond Brut (1995 is the latest release), a Cuvée Douceur Sec and a fruity Bouzy Rouge. (DM)

O **Brut Sélection-Extra** Non-Vintage★★★ £D   O **Grand Réserve** Non-Vintage★★★ £D

O **Blanc de Noirs** Non-Vintage★★★ £D
◉ **Brut Authentique** Non-Vintage★★ £D

BEAUMONT DES CRAYERES   www.champagne-beaumont.com   A: Tan, Res

Owner: Co-operative   BP 103, 51318 Epernay
This small, quality-concious co-op has over 200 growers who between them have only 80 ha of vineyards. Output for a co-op is also fairly low at just 50,000 cases a year and prices are generally very fair. The Grande Réserve is a soft, forward and fruity non-vintage blend dominated by Pinot Meunier and including a fair dollop of reserve wine. The Grand Prestige is again fruit-driven in style, but subtler and more elegant with a light citrus and bready character from 40 per cent Chardonnay as well as the Pinots. The Fleur de Prestige is particularly good value, with 60 per cent Chardonnay adding intensity and elegance. The top cuvee, Nostalgie, again has 60 per cent Chardonnay and 40 per cent Pinot Noir and is richer and fuller with surprising opulence for such a blend. The 1996 was rich and softly structured. (DM)

O **Brut Grande Réserve** Non-Vintage★ £C   O **Brut Grand Prestige** Non-Vintage★★ £C
O **Fleur de Prestige** Vintage★★★ £D   O **Nostalgie** Vintage★★★ £E

BILLECART-SALMON   www.champagne-billecart.fr   A: **B-S**

Owner: Billecart family   40 Rue Carnot, 51160 Mareuil-sur-Aÿ
A medium-sized and very impressive house, family-owned Billecart-Salmon produces 100,000 cases a year. The house was founded in 1818. The Brut Réserve non-vintage is classy stuff at this level and the top wines are very intense and marvellously refined. A sizeable proportion of Chardonnay is used and this helps the wines' balance and classic Champagne structure. The elegant non-vintage Blanc de Blancs is sourced from Le Mesnil-sur-Oger and is normally a blend of two vintages. The super Cuvée Nicolas-François Billecart is a very complex and elegant blend of 40 per cent Chardonnay and 60 per cent Pinot Noir. A vintage Blanc de Blancs is also produced along with a vintage Grande Cuvée, the current release of which is 1990. There is also a tiny amount of prestige rosé Cuvée Elisabeth Salmon. (DM)

O **Brut Réserve** Non-Vintage★★★ £E   O **Blancs de Blancs Grand Cru** Non-Vintage★★★★ £F
O **Brut Cuvée Nicolas-François Billecart** Vintage★★★★★ £F
◉ **Brut Rosé**★★★ £F

BOLLINGER   www.champagne-bollinger.fr   A: **Men**

Owner: Bollinger family   16 Rue Jules-Lobet, BP4, 51160 Aÿ
One of the greatest names in sparkling wine production. Bollinger produces around 150,000 cases a year. It is one of just a handful of producers here to still ferment base wines in wood. A high proportion of Pinot Noir is used and the non-vintaged Special Cuvée is always full and rich in style. The vintage Grande Année can almost take on a hint of Burgundian gaminess with age, as can the remarkable RD *(récemment dégorgé)*. This wine is kept in bottle on its yeast sediment for up to 10 years and possesses a rich toastiness; it is both concentrated and exceptionally well balanced. 1995 is the current release. A tiny amount of a 100 per cent Pinot Noir *cuvée*, Vieilles Vignes, is made from ungrafted, very low-yielding old vines and there is a decent Coteaux Champenois red, Côte aux Enfants. (DM)

O **Brut Spécial Cuvée** Non-Vintage★★★ £E
O **Brut Grande Année** Vintage★★★★★ £G   O **RD**✪✪✪✪✪ £H
◉ **Brut Grande Année** Rosé Vintage★★★ £G

DEUTZ   www.champagne-deutz.com   A: BWC, Lay

Owner: Louis Roederer   16 Rue Jeanson, BP 9, 51160 Aÿ
Now owned by Louis Roederer, Deutz also has a successful sparkling wine partnership in New Zealand with MONTANA. By comparison with many of the other great houses the annual production here is relatively modest at some 80,000 cases or so. Quality is generally good to very good indeed and the wines are well

priced, perhaps with the exception of the luxury *cuvées* William Deutz and Blanc de Blancs Amour de Deutz. The non-vintage Brut Classic is a good and well-structured, yeasty style; the vintage wines are tighter, more refined. (DM)

O **Brut Classic** Non-Vintage★★★ £E
O **Brut** Vintage★★★★ £F   O **William Deutz** Vintage★★★★★ £G
O **Blanc de Blancs** Vintage★★★★ £F
◉ **Brut** Rosé Vintage★★★★ £F

DOQUET-JEANMAIRE

Owner: Pascal Doquet   44 Chemin de Moulin de la Cense Bizet, 51130 Vertus
Relatively small family-owned domaine with 10 ha of vineyards on the Côte des Blancs, as well as a further 5.6 ha at Epernay and Perthois. There are 2.5 ha of *grand cru* vineyards at Le Mesnil-sur-Oger and a further 7.5 ha of *premier cru* vineyards. The huge majority of the plantings (99 per cent) are Chardonnay and the wines surprisingly show quite a forward opulent character. The best bottles, though, do show a real propensity to age. This is one of the rare cellars in the region where you can acquire very old bottles. There are vintage releases of both Premier Cru and the more expensive Premier Cru Coeur de Terroir. At the time of writing vintages available included Premier Cru 1990, 1985 and a surprisingly fresh but not terribly complex 1970. Coeur de Terroir releases currently available are 1993, probably the best structured, as well as 1989, 1988 and 1985. The Brut rosé is also exuberantly fruity and forward. A Coteaux Champenois is also produced. (DM)

O **Blanc de Blancs Premier Cru Coeur de Terroir** Vintage★★★ £D
O **Blanc de Blancs Premier Cru** Vintage★★ £D
O **Blanc de Blancs Premier Cru Sélection** Non-Vintage★★ £C
O **Blanc de Blancs Carte d'Or** Non-Vintage★★ £C
◉ **Brut Premier Cru** Rosé Non-Vintage★★ £C

EGLY-OURIET

Owner: Michel et Francis Egly-Ouriet   9-15. Rue de Trépail, 51150 Ambonnay
Very impressive, small family-run property with some 7 ha of Pinot Noir and 2 ha of Chardonnay. Production is tiny at some 5,500 cases a year. Quality is high, with well-aged vineyards that are over 30 years old and a dedicated, generally organic approach to viticulture. Yields are carefully tempered and a partial *vendange vert* is practised. In the cellar minimal handling extends to an absence of both fining and filtration for the base wines. The result is wonderfully pure, full-bodied wines of great character. A very good example of Coteaux Champenois is also produced but available only in very limited quantities. (DM)

O **Brut Tradition** Non-Vintage★★★ £D   O **Grand Cru** Vintage★★★★★ £E
O **Blanc de Noirs Vieilles Vignes** Non-Vintage★★★★ £E
◉ **Brut** Rosé Non-Vintage★★★ £D

PIERRE GIMONNET ET FILS   www.champagne-gimmonet.com   A: Oas

Owner: Gimonnet family   1 Rue de la République, 51530 Cuis
Family domaine that possesses 26 ha of very well-sited vineyards in the Côte des Blancs populated exclusively with old Chardonnay vines. Part of the vineyard holding is *premier cru* and part *grand cru*. This provides the property with a superb resource of base wine material. The style varies from the fresh, taut and lightly toasty Cuis Premier Cru to the weightier and richer Fleuron and Club Premier Cru labels. The Extra-Brut Oenophile, bottled without *dosage*, is very tight and lean but elegant. (DM)

O **Blanc de Blancs Cuis** Premier Cru Non-Vintage★★ £D
O **Brut Fleuron** Premier Cru Vintage★★★ £E   O **Brut Club** Premier Cru Vintage★★★ £E
O **Brut Gastronome** Vintage★★ £D
O **Extra-Brut Oenophile** Vintage★★★ £E

GOSSET www.champagne-gosset.com   A: McK

Owner: Cointreau family   69 Rue Jules-Blondeau, 51160 Aÿ
This is among the very oldest of the Champagne houses, its commercial origins going back to 1584. The regular non-vintage Excellence is generally very reliable. The Grande Réserve and Grand Rosé, both non-vintage, and the vintage offerings here are a step up. The style is one of weight and a rich toastiness in the top wines but unfortunately a lack of elegance can creep in as well. Celebris is clearly a cut above the rest. (DM)

O **Brut Excellence** Non-Vintage★★ £D
O **Grande Réserve** Non-Vintage★★★ £F   **Grande Millésime** Vintage★★★ £F
O **Celebris** Vintage★★★★ £G
◉ **Grand Rosé** Non-Vintage★★★ £F

ALFRED GRATIEN www.alfredgratien.com   A: Wit, WSc

Owner: Henkell and Sohnlein   30 Rue Maurice Cerveaux, BP 3, 51201 Épernay
Very good, small, traditional house which produces barely 15,000 cases a year. The base wines are vinified in wood and all cellar operations are still carried out by hand. The malolactic fermentation is blocked and this provides the taut, structured style. The wines, even the non-vintage, are ageworthy. The purchase by German *sekt* producer Henkell and Sohnlein is a recent development and it remains to be seen whether the house style will remain faithful and equally whether production will soar. (DM)

O **Brut** Réserve Non-Vintage★★★ £E   O **Paradis** Non-Vintage★★★★ £F
O **Brut** Vintage★★★★★ £F
◉ **Brut Rosé Paradis** Non-Vintage★★★ £F

CHARLES HEIDSIECK www.charlesheidsieck.com   A: Max

Owner: Remy Cointreau   4 Boulevard Henri-Vasnier, 51100 Reims
Under the ownersip of Remy-Cointreau, the quality of the wine at this house over the past 15 years has been very impressive. The non-vintaged Brut Réserve Mis-en-Cave is arguably the best of its style in the appellation. The wine draws on a considerable amount of reserve wine and unusually gives the date of bottling so that the consumer has some idea of the age of the wine. Much of the consummate skill in creating this wine was achieved by the late Daniel Thibaut, one of the great modern master blenders of Champagne. There are two first-class vintage reserves: the elegant, superbly-crafted Blanc des Millénaires made from Chardonnay and the Pinot-dominated Charlie, a powerful, concentrated, weighty but very refined wine. (DM)

O **Brut Réserve Mis-en-Cave** Non-Vintage★★★★ £E   O **Charlie** Vintage★★★★★ £G
O **Blanc des Millénaires** Vintage★★★★★ £G   ◉ **Brut** Rosé Vintage★★★★ £G

HENRIOT contact@champagne-henriot.com   A: JEF

Owner: Joseph Henriot   81 Rue Coquebert, 51100 Reims
Medium-sized producer accounting for some 80,000 cases a year of moderately priced Champagne. The price reflects the quality here but the top vintage wines are reasonably impressive. The wines, including the straightforward Brut Souverain non-vintage, are weighty enough but lack a certain amount of refinement. The Cuvée des Enchanteleurs is a marked step up in both elegance and depth. (DM)

O **Blanc de Blancs** Non-Vintage★★ £D   O **Brut Souverain** Non-Vintage★★★ £E
O **Brut** Vintage★★★ £E
O **Cuvée des Enchanteleurs**★★★★ £F   ◉ **Brut** Rosé Vintage★★★★ £E

JACQUESSON champagne.jacquesson@wanadoo.fr   A: **May**

Owner: Chiquet family   68 Rue du Colonel-Fabien, 51530 Dizy

This is a good small-scale, family-run operation producing around 25,000 cases a year of good to very good quality. Barrel-fermentation is used for the base wine and the resulting Champagnes are characterful and refined. The style is rich, full-bodied and harmonious. The Brut Signature vintage bottlings are very serious and structured and there is a very impressive vintage Blanc de Blancs as well. A complex and very pricey Dégorgement Tardif is now being produced, which is given extended ageing on lees. (DM)

O **Brut Perfection** Non-Vintage★★ £E   O **Grand Vin Signature** Vintage★★★★ £G
O **Blanc de Blancs Vintage**★★★★ £G
◉ **Brut Perfection Rosé** Non-Vintage★★ £E   ◉ **Grand Vin Signature** Vintage★★★ £E

KRUG krug@krug.fr   A: **Par**

Owner: LMVH   5 Rue Coquebert, 51100 Reims

Still run by Rémy Krug, this is arguably the most prestigious of all the great Champagne houses. However, production remains quite small at just over 40,000 cases a year. It is to be hoped that the exceptional quality standards here will remain under LMVH ownership and that volume will not escalate. These are quite remarkably impressive and structured wines. Tight and very restrained, perhaps more so than all other Champagnes, they demand cellaring. Even the non-vintage Grande Cuvée, a wine often on the cusp of a super-five rating, will benefit from at least five years after release. The Clos du Mesnil is that rare breed in this appellation, a wine from a small single vineyard. The range is completed by the tiny-production and undoubtedly very fine non-vintage Rosé. (DM)

O **Grande Cuvée** Non-Vintage★★★★★ £H   O **Clos du Mesnil** Vintage✪✪✪✪✪ £H
O **Vintage**✪✪✪✪✪ £H

LANSON www.lanson.fr   A: **MCD**

Owner: Marne et Champagne   12 Boulevard Lundy, 51100 Reims

Production here is vast at close to some 600,000 cases a year. In the light of that, quality has been at least solid. The Black Label Brut is probably the best-known Champagne brand after the MOËT ET CHANDON Brut Impérial; recent releases have shown a sound upturn in form – by no means where it could be, but a marked improvement. As well as the big brand a non-vintage rosé is fairly unexciting but there is a stylish Blanc de Blancs vintage and a decent enough Ivory Label Demi-Sec. The Brut Gold Label vintage was good rather than spectacular in 1995 but the quality of the current wines does seem to indicate real progress. The Noble Cuvée is a seriously structured and impressive Champagne. (DM)

O **Brut Black Label** Non-Vintage★ £D   O **Gold Label** Vintage★★ £E
O **Blanc de Blancs** Vintage★★★ £F
O **Noble Cuvée** Vintage★★★★ £G

LARMANDIER-BERNIER larmandier@terre-net.fr   A:VTr

Owner: Larmandier-Bernier family   43 Rue de 28 Août, 51130 Vertus

Small, top-class grower based in the Côte des Blancs, with an understandably large proportion of Chardonnay plantings. Like most really quality-conscious winemakers around the world, Pierre Larmandier keeps the human input to a minimum. The style is for very structured, minerally, intense Champagnes that have been given extra weight and depth through cask-ageing (no new wood is used) prior to bottling and further cellaring prior to release. Very low *dosage* is the approach here, with the Né d'Un Terre de Vertus being bone dry. The wines have the depth and texture to support the style but will reward cellaring, the vintage wines for many years. A very small amount of red Coteaux Champenois is also produced and is among the very best examples of the style. The fact that the wines are excellent value is another plus. (DM)

O **Brut Tradition** Non-Vintage★★ ★ £D   O **Blanc de Blancs** Non-Vintage★★★ £D

O **Extra Brut Vieille Vignes de Cramant** Vintage★★★★★ £E
O **Né d'Un Terre de Vertus Non Dosé** Non-Vintage★★★★ £D
◉ **Brut Rosé** Non-Vintage★★ £D

LAURENT-PERRIER   www.laurent-perrier.co.uk   A: **L-P**

Owner: De Nonancourt family   151150 Tour-sur-Marne
Still very much a family-run operation, although interests also include the other Champagne houses of DE
CASTELLANE, DELAMOTTE and the super-prestige SALON. The great wines here are the Grand Siècle
labels, which are all immensely refined. The two whites have a rich, powerful, bready character underpinned
by a pure mineral structure. The rosé is very complex with a remarkable array of berry fruit aromas. The
regular Brut non-vintage is sound with quite a heavy *dosage* but lacks a bit of grip. The non-vintaged rosé,
though, is stylish and fresh, with attractive fruit. The Ultra Brut is impressively piercing and will develop
well with some bottle-age. (DM)
O **Brut LP** Non-Vintage★ £E   O **Vintage**★★ £F   O **Ultra Brut** Non-Vintage★★★ £F
O **Grand Siècle La Cuvée** Non-Vintage★★★★ £G
O **Grand Siècle** Vintage★★★★★ £H
◉ **Brut Rosé** Non-Vintage★★★ £H
◉ **Grand Siècle Alexandra Rosé** Vintage★★★ £H

SERGE MATHIEU   champagne.mathieu@wanadoo.fr

Owner: Mathieu family   6 Rue des Vignes, 10340 Avirey-Lingey
Small but very good property based in the Aube. Pinot Noir is the key component here and the wines
certainly display a real weight and concentration. However, what marks them out is their elegance and
refinement, something that a great many of the family's near neighbours struggle to achieve. The vintage
Brut is impressively concentrated, rich, bready and toasty but with a fine mineral backbone. The Tête de
Cuvée is subtler, more refined, with a higher proportion of Chardonnay and a shorter period on lees. Both
are ageworthy. (DM)
O **Brut Tradition** Non-Vintage★★ £C   O **Brut Prestige** Non-Vintage★★ £D
O **Brut Millésime** Vintage★★★ £E   O **Tête de Cuvée** Non-Vintage★★★ £E
O **Blanc de Noirs** Non-Vintage★★★ £D
◉ **Brut Rosé** Non-Vintage★★ £D

MOËT ET CHANDON   www.moet.com   A: **MHn**

Owner: LMVH   20 Rue avenue de Champagne, 51220 Épernay
Of all the Champagne houses this is the one that most readily comes to most consumers' minds. The
tendency among the majority of occasional wine drinkers is to think of Moët as a brand rather than
understanding it as a great Champagne house. Production is considerable, around 2,500,000 cases a year.
Brut Impérial can be a lot more impressive than it is often given credit for. The White Star is marketed in
the US and contains a higher *dosage*. The vintage Brut is well made with reasonable yeasty complexity and
will age well over the medium term. Like the house itself, Dom Pérignon is the most established of the
region's luxury *cuvées* and production is not small. The wine is very good and consistent, becoming
increasingly complex and harmonious with age. There is a fine vintage rosé and a very small amount of the
Dom Perignon Rosé, every bit as impressive as the white. Three expensive additions have also been made
from *grand cru* villages: Champs de Romont is based on Pinot Meunier, Vignes de Saran is from
Chardonnay and Sarment d'Aÿ is a Pinot Noir. All are non-vintage. There is also now a non-vintage *premier
cru* bottling blended from all three Champagne varieties. (DM)
O **Brut Impérial** Non-Vintage★★ £E   O **Brut White Star** Non-Vintage★ £E
O **Brut Impérial** Vintage★★★ £E
O **Dom Pérignon** Vintage★★★★★ £E
◉ **Brut Rosé** Vintage★★ £H

PIERRE MONCUIT — A: HHB

Owner: Nicole & Yves Moncuit   11 Rue Persault-Maheu, 51190 Le Mesnil-sur-Oger
The Moncuits produce two very fine Blanc de Blancs at their 20-ha property at Le Mesnil-sur-Oger. The Grand Cru Vintage bottling is superbly crafted, intense and refined with not a hint of austerity, rather a rich, biscuity approachability. The Vieilles Vignes is a very fine expression of Champagne hand-crafted from Chardonnay – intense, refined and very ageworthy. Sadly very little is made. What makes these wines all the more remarkable is the reasonable prices. (DM)
O **Blanc de Blancs** Grand Cru Vintage★★★ £D   O **Nicole Moncuit Vieilles Vignes** Vintage★★★★ £E

G H MUMM   www.mumm.com — A: ADo

*Owner: **Allied Domecq**   29 Rue du Champs-de-Mar, 51100 Reims*
Allied Domecq purchased this old house in 2001 and it now joins PERRIER-JOUËT in the same stable. It will be interesting to see how the operations perform. The main brand, Cordon Rouge, was for a long time a serious underperformer. However during the late 1990s the quality has been altogether sounder. The wine is not complex but has a good core of appley fruit and is bottled with quite a high *dosage*. The vintage bottling is really only marginally better but the Grand Cordon vintage is a classier proposition. There is also now a vintage Grand Cru, a decent Brut Rosé and of course the prestige, non-vintaged Mumm de Cramant. (DM)
O **Cordon Rouge** Non-Vintage★ £E   O **Cordon Rouge** Vintage★ £E
O **Grand Cordon** Vintage★★★ £F   O **Grand Cru** Vintage★★ £E
O **Mumm de Cramant** Non-Vintage★★★★ £G
◉ **Brut Rosé** Non-Vintage★ £E

BRUNO PAILLARD   www.champagnebrunopaillard.com — A: Bib

Owner: Bruno Paillard   Avenue de Champagne, 51100 Reims
Bruno Paillard runs a modern, well-organised cellar producing nearly 45,000 cases a year. The style is relatively austere but these are wines, particularly the vintage *cuvées*, that should develop well in bottle. The prestige NPU (Nec Plus Ultra) is undoubtedly a serious step up from the rest of the range but is also very pricey. The wines are labelled with a date of disgorging which gives a clear idea about when to drink the non-vintaged wines. (DM)
O **Brut Première Cuvée** Non-Vintage★ £E   O **Brut Millésime** Vintage★★★ £F
O **Chardonnay** Réserve Privée★★ £E
O **Nec Plus Ultra** Vintage★★★★ £H
◉ **Brut Rosé Première Cuvée** Non-Vintage★ £E

JOSEPH PERRIER   josephperrier@wanadoo.fr — A: CHk, FSA, GWW

Owner: Alain Thienot   69 Avenue de Paris, 51016 Châlons-en-Champagne
Relatively small among the big Champagne houses, Joseph Perrier is noted for traditional, medium- to full-bodied wines. The Brut Royale non-vintage has a considerable amount of both Pinot Meunier and Pinot Noir in the blend, resulting in a full, fruity style. The vintage Royale is more complex. There is no Pinot Meunier and the wine is tighter, more structured. The Joséphine vintage is of a different order. The concentrated Pinot fruit is beautifully balanced by a refined, nutty quality with its Chardonnay component providing finesse and a real depth and mineral purity. This will cellar well. (DM)
O **Brut Royale** Non-Vintage★★ £E   O **Brut Royale** Vintage★★★ £F
O **Joséphine** Vintage★★★★ £G
◉ **Brut Royale** Non-Vintage★★ £E

PERRIER-JOUËT www.perrier-jouet.com   A: ADo

Owner: Allied Domecq 51201 Epernay

Like G H MUMM this house, nearly 200 years old, has only been under the Allied Domecq banner since 2001. The wines have a relatively high proportion of Chardonnay but at the lower level they struggle to offer a great deal. The basic non-vintage Brut is a straightforward and simple offering with more green apple than complex, yeast-developed flavours. The Brut Rosé is a touch more impressive and there is a non-vintaged Blason white which provides a hint of bready complexity with a little time in bottle. The Blason Rosé is marked by very simple, straightforward fruit, no more. The vintage Brut has better depth than the regular and a hint of toastiness but there should be greater dimension. The prestige *cuvée* La Belle Époque has a stylish bottle design and impressively tight, Chardonnay-based fruit. It achieves good to very good complex characters with age. There's a very good Belle Époque rosé as well. (DM)

O **Brut Blason de France** Non-Vintage★ £E O **Grand Brut** Vintage★ £F
O **La Belle Époque** Vintage★★★★ £G
◉ **Grand Brut** Non-Vintage★★ £E

PHILIPPONNAT www.champagnephilipponnat.com   A: Eur

Owner: Bruno Paillard 13 Rue du Pont, 51160 Mareuil-sur-Aÿ

This is a relatively small *négociant-manipulant* with an output of just 50,000 cases a year. Until its acquisition by Bruno PAILLARD, the range was decidedly ordinary – with the exception of the great prestige *cuvée* Brut Clos de Goisses, a wine of super-five quality in extravagant vintages like 1990. However things appear to be taking a turn for the better. A good, attractive, strawberry-fruited rosé is joined by the Royale Réserve, which has reasonable depth and a light nutty, biscuity character. The vintage is clearly a step up, more complete and complex, while the impressive Grand Blanc is a tight and structured Blanc de Blancs that needs time. The Clos des Goisses should be given additional cellaring – up to five years' ageing after release. (DM)

O **Brut Royale Réserve** Non-Vintage★ £E O **Brut Réserve Spécial** Vintage★★ £F
O **Grand Blanc** Vintage★★★ £F O **Clos des Goisses** Vintage★★★★★ £H
◉ **Brut Réserve** Non-Vintage★ £E

PIPER-HEIDSIECK www.piper-heidsieck.com   A: Max

Owner: Remy Cointreau 52 Boulevard Henry-Vasnier, 51100 Reims

Under the same ownership as Charles HEIDSIECK but the Champagne here is a very different proposition. The non-vintage Brut is a simple, fruit-driven style, now produced without malolactic fermentation to retain its fresh, forward character. In recent years it has been better than of old – some releases used to be basically dilute. The Brut Rosé is simple and straightforward, with some pleasant red berry fruit showing through. The Brut vintage is a good deal better – the wine has structure and depth with some complex toasty, yeasty notes evolving – while the Rare prestige *cuvée* is tight, structured and displays some real class. (DM)

O **Brut** Vintage★★ £F O **Rare** Vintage★★★★ £G

POL ROGER www.polroger.co.uk   A: Pol

Owner: Pol Roger family 1 Rue Henri-de-Large, 51206 Epernay

Family-owned, sizeable house with production approaching some 125,000 cases a year. The non-vintage White Foil is now consistently good, a style with real depth and a refined biscuity character but, like all the wines here, elegance and intensity is displayed more than weight. The vintage is just that little bit more complex and structured, very good and intense. There is a first class Blanc de Blancs Chardonnay vintage offering which is lighter still in style but impeccably balanced. Sir Winston Churchill is a very impressive prestige *cuvée* which demands to be cellared. (DM)

○ **Brut White Foil** Non-Vintage★★★ £E ○ **Brut** Vintage★★★★ £F
○ **Brut Chardonnay** Vintage★★★ £F ○ **Sir Winston Churchill** Vintage★★★★★ £H
◉ **Brut** Vintage★★★ £F

POMMERY www.pommery.fr A: Eve,PFx

Owner: Vranken 5. Place du Général Gouraud, 51100 Reims

Production is considerable at this large house, with a volume of some 500,000 cases a year. However the LMVH group has sold its interest to Vranken who, while commercially successful throughout the appellation, have not so far established themselves as a beacon of top quality. Under LMVH ownership the quality throughout the range has been at least sound. There is a straightforward non-vintage Brut Royal – biscuity with a slightly raw edge to it – a better non-vintage Apanage and a sound rosé. The Blanc de Blancs Summertime is tight and structured, really quite elegant, while the Blanc de Noirs Wintertime is fuller and weightier. The vintage Grand Cru is refined and very well balanced in the best years, not overly weighty but long and intense. The Cuvée Louise is very impressive, not a full style but very long, harmonious and ageworthy. There is also a very fine Louise Rosé. Time will tell how the style and quality of the house will develop as a part of the Vranken empire. (DM)

○ **Brut Royal** Non-Vintage★★ £E ○ **Brut Apanage** Non-Vintage★★ £E
○ **Blanc de Blancs Summertime** Non-Vintage★★★ £E
○ **Blanc de Noirs Wintertime** Non-Vintage★★★ £E
○ **Brut Grand Cru** Vintage★★★ £F ○ **Louise** Vintage★★★★ £G
◉ **Brut Non-**Vintage★ £E

LOUIS ROEDERER www.champagne-roederer.com A: **MMD**

Owner: Champagne Louis Roederer 21 Boulevard Lundy, 51100 Reims

This has long been established as one of the great Champagne houses. It is still family-owned and the company has invested heavily in other projects. As well as the ROEDERER ESTATE venture in California's Anderson Valley (see California North Coast), much closer to home it has acquired DEUTZ, along with Château de PEZ in the Médoc and in Portugal the Port house RAMOS PINTO. The style here is weighty and rich with a considerable Pinot Noir influence. The Blanc de Blancs is the most obviously restrained style and has its malolactic blocked for freshness and to achieve balance and harmony. A considerable holding of reserve wine helps the non-vintage Brut Premier, while the Cristal prestige *cuvée* is one of the greatest and most refined sparkling wines in the world. It needs time. (DM)

○ **Brut Premier** Non-Vintage★★★ £E ○ **Brut** Vintage★★★★ £F
○ **Blanc de Blancs** Vintage★★★ £F
○ **Cristal** Vintage○○○○○ £H
◉ **Brut** Vintage★★★ £F

RUINART www.ruinart.com A: **Rui**

Owner: LMVH 4 Rue des Crayères, BP 85, 51053 Reims-Cedex

Among the big houses Ruinart has maintained a relatively low profile in recent years despite being under the same ownership as MOËT ET CHANDON and more recently KRUG. Surprisingly its production is relatively large at close to 200,000 cases a year. The wines, though, are good to excellent, with the prestige *cuvées* (both Blanc de Blancs Dom Ruinart and the Rosé) worthy of a super-five rating on occasion. Chardonnay is an important part of the blending equation here and the wines are both refined and powerful, particularly the vintage *cuvées,* due to some extended ageing of the base wines. The non-vintage Brut is consistently one of the best of its kind. Newly added is a luxury blend of six *grands crus* and five vintages all from Chardonnay, the rare and pricey l'Exclusive de Ruinart. (DM)

○ **Brut R de Ruinart** Non-Vintage★★★ £E ○ **Brut R de Ruinart** Vintage★★★★ £F
○ **Blanc de Blancs** Non-Vintage★★★ £F
○ **Dom Ruinart** Vintage★★★★★ £H
◉ **Brut R de Ruinart** Non-Vintage★★ £F ◉ **Dom Ruinart** Vintage★★★★★ £H

SALON

A: **C&B**

Owner: Laurent-Perrier 5 Rue de la Brèche-d'Oger, 51190 Le Mesnil-sur-Oger
Now owned by Laurent-Perrier. Just one exceptional wine is produced here: a Blanc de Blancs, in fact the first created, sourced entirely from selected vineyard plots in the village of Le Mesnil. Only bottled in the very best vintage years (the average through the last century was just over one year in four), an exceptional 1995 is the current release. Surprisingly rich and intense, but of course as well structured as one would expect, the wine should be cellared for at least a decade after release. (DM)
O Salon Vintage✪✪✪✪✪ £H

FRANÇOIS SECONDÉ

Owner: François Secondé 6 Rue des Galipes, 51500 Sillery
Based in the Marne village of Sillery, Francois Secondé produces very well-priced and finely structured Champagne from just 5 ha. Around three-quarters of the vineyard is planted to Pinot Noir with the balance Chardonnay, but the style is for tight, restrained, wines which need a little time to show at their best. The vineyards are farmed organically and the vines are approaching 35 years age, all of which helps in providing excellent raw material. The wines are traditionally made with manual *remuage*. They offer very good value. (DM)
O **Brut** Non-Vintage★★★ £C   O **Brut Clavier** Non-Vintage★★★ £D
◉ **Brut Rosé** Non-Vintage★★ £C

JACQUES SELOSSE

A: **O-F**

Owner: Corinne & Anselme Selosse 22 Rue Ernest-Vallé, 51190 Avize
Remarkable small producer. Anselme Selosse bottles less than 4,000 cases of very impressive Champagne every year. The approach in the vineyard is biodynamic and yields are severely resticted to provide the purest, greatest intensity of fruit possible. What makes the approach here radical is the use of new as well as old oak to barrel-ferment the base wine. Extensively aged prior to release, these are massive and powerful wines for Champagne but no less impressive for that. On occasion the presence of oak can almost overwhelm, particularly in young or newly released wines, but there is no doubt that they are some of the most exciting and original wines of the appellation. (DM)
O **Blanc de Blancs Tradition** Non-Vintage★★★ £E   O **Originale** Extra-Brut Non-Vintage★★★★ £E
O **Grand Cru Substance** Non-Vintage★★★★ £E
O **Blanc de Noirs Contraste** Non-Vintage★★★★ £E   O **Blanc de Blancs** Vintage★★★★★ £F

TAITTINGER   www.taittinger.com

A: **HMA**

Owner: Taittinger family 9 Place Saint-Nicaise, 51100 Reims
A large house producing around 400,000 cases a year of generally reliable if rather unexciting non-vintage Brut Réserve. Better are some really very fine vintage wines and an exceptional Blanc de Blancs prestige *cuvée* Comtes de Champagne, matched by an equally exquisite and very rare rosé. Taittinger also owns the Loire Valley sparkling wine house BOUVET-LADUBAY and Domaine CARNEROS in California. (DM)
O **Brut Réserve** Non-Vintage★ £E   O **Brut Millésime** Vintage★★★ £F
O **Blanc de Blanc Comtes de Champagne** Vintage✪✪✪✪✪ £H
◉ **Brut Prestige** Non-Vintage★ £E   ◉ **Comtes de Champagne** Vintage★★★★★ £H

VEUVE CLICQUOT   www.veuve-clicquot.fr

A: **Par**

Owner: LVMH 12 Rue du Temple, 51100 Reims
Second to MOËT ET CHANDON in the LVMH hierarchy in terms of volume but most certainly ahead in terms of quality. Throughout the last five or six years the quality here has always been good, even for the

regular Carte Jaune (Yellow Label). The vintage wines have weight and structure and are full of rich, toasty character. La Grande Dame is an exceptional wine, both the more easily available white and the scarce rosé. Both are rich, heady blends of Pinot Noir and Chardonnay. A number of prestige wineries around the world originally purchased by Veuve Clicquot now fall within the LVMH banner. These include CLOUDY BAY in New Zealand, CAPE MENTELLE in Western Australia and NEWTON in the Napa Valley. The house of Canard-Duchêne, which continues to disappoint of late, has long been under the Clicquot wing. (DM)

○ **Brut Carte Jaune** Non-Vintage★★★ £E
○ **Vintage Réserve**★★★ £F   ○ **Rich Réserve** Vintage★★★ £F
○ **La Grande Dame** Vintage✪✪✪✪✪ £H
◉ **Rosé Réserve** Vintage★★★ £F

OTHER WINES OF NOTE

H BLIN ○ **Brut** Vintage £E
BOIZEL ○ **Brut Réserve** Non-Vintage £C   ○ **Brut Grand** Vintage £E
◉ **Brut Rosé** Non-Vintage £D
ALEXANDRE BONNET ○ **Madrigal** Vintage £E
PHILIPPE BRUGNON ○ **Brut** Non-Vintage £D
ROGER BRUN ○ **Brut Réserve** Non-Vintage £D
CHARLES DE CAZENOVE ○ **Brut Azur Premier Cru** Non-Vintage £E
GUY CADEL ○ **Carte-Blanche** Non-Vintage £C   ○ **Brut** Vintage £E
◉ **Brut Rosé** Non-Vintage £D
GUY CHARLEMAGNE ○ **Blanc de Blancs Grand Cru** Vintage £E
JACKY CHARPENTIER ○ **Brut Prestige** Non-Vintage £D   ○ **Brut** Vintage £E
◉ **Brut Rosé** Non-Vintage £E
DE CASTELLANE ○ **Cuvée Florens** Vintage £F
DELAMOTTE ○ **Brut** Vintage £E
DELBECK ○ **Brut** Vintage £E
DE SOUSA ○ **Blanc de Blancs** Réserve £D   ○ **Brut** Vintage £F
PAUL DÉTHUNE ○ **Grand Cru** Non-Vintage £C
DE VENOGE ○ **Blanc de Noirs** Non-Vintage £D
DRAPPIER ○ **Brut Carte d'Or** Vintage £F   ○ **Grande Sendrée** Vintage £G
JACKY DUMANGIN ○ **Brut Grande Réserve Premier Cru** Non-Vintage £D
DUVAL-LEROY ○ **Fleur de Champagne Blanc de Chardonnay** Vintage £E
◉ **Fleur de Champagne Rosé de Saignée** Non-Vintage £E
GARDET ○ **Brut Cuvée Charles Gardet** Vintage £E
GATINOIS ○ **Grand Cru** Vintage £E
RENE GEOFFROY ○ **Brut Réserve** Non-Vintage £D
HENRI GIRAUD ○ **Brut Grand Cru Tradition** Non-Vintage £D
MICHEL GONET ○ **Brut Réserve** Non-Vintage £D   ○ **Cuvée Prestige** Vintage £E
GEORGES GOULET ○ **Brut** Non-Vintage £D
HENRI GOUTORBE ○ **Brut Cuvée Tradition** Non-Vintage £D
JACQUART ○ **Blanc de Blancs Mosaïque** Vintage £E
A. JACQUART ○ **Blanc de Blancs** Vintage £E
JEAN LALLEMENT ○ **Brut Réserve** Non-Vintage £D
J. LASSALLE ○ **Cuvée Imperial Préférence** Non-Vintage £D   ○ **Cuvée Special Club** Vintage £E
◉ **Premier Cru** Non-Vintage £D
LECLERC BRIANT ○ **Brut Réserve** Non-Vintage £D
LEGRAS ○ **Blanc de Blancs Grand Cru** Non-Vintage £D
LE MESNIL ○ **Blanc de Blancs Grand Cru** Non-Vintage £D   ○ **Blanc de Blancs Grand Cru** Vintage £E
LILBERT ○ **Blanc de Blancs Grand Cru** Non-Vintage £D
MAILLY GRAND CRU ○ **Brut Réserve** Non-Vintage £D   ○ **Brut Grand Cru** Vintage £E
○ **Echansons** Vintage £G   ◉ **Grand Cru** Non-Vintage £E
MARGAINE ○ **Brut Premier Cru** Non-Vintage £C   ○ **Special Cuvée Club** Vintage £E

◉ **Brut** Non-Vintage £D

HENRI MANDOIS O **Brut** Non-Vintage £C   O **Brut Cuvée Victor Vieilles Vignes** Vintage £E

◉ **Brut Premier Cru** Non-Vintage £D

JEAN MOUTARDIER O **Brut Carte d'Or** Non-Vintage £C   O **Brut Selection** Non-Vintage £C

NICOLAS FEUILLATTE O **Cuvée Spéciale** Vintage £F   O **Cuvée Palmes d'Or** Vintage £G

PALMER O **Amazone de Palmer** Non-Vintage £D

ROGER POUILLON O **Brut Réserve** Non-Vintage £C   O **Fleur de Mareuil** Non-Vintage £C

ALAIN ROBERT O **Blanc de Blancs Le Mesnil** Vintage £F

J.P. SECONDÉ O **Brut Grand Cru** Non-Vintage £C   O **Brut** Vintage £E

◉ **Brut Rosé** Non-Vintage £D

SOUTIRAN-PELLETIER O **Blanc de Blancs Grand Cru** Non-Vintage £E

TARLANT O **Brut Réserve** Non-Vintage £D   **Brut** Vintage £E

PIERRE VAUDON O **Brut Premier Cru** Non-Vintage £C   O **Brut Premier Cru** Vintage £D

JEAN VESSELLE O **Brut Réserve** Non-Vintage £D

VEUVE A DEVAUX O **Blanc de Noirs** Non-Vintage £E

VILMART O **Grand Cellier** Non-Vintage £D   O **Grand Cellier d'Or** Vintage £D

O **Coeur de Cuvée** Vintage £F

Work in progress!!

Wines from the following producers under consideration for the next edition

BARON FUENTÉ

PIERRE CALOT

LAMIABLE

MARIE-NOËLLE LEDRU

PANNIER

SADI MALOT

SANT-GALL

Author's Choice (DM)

A selection of lesser known Champagnes

PAUL BARA   O **Brut Grand Cru** Vintage

EDMOND BARNAUT   O **Blancs de Noirs** Non-Vintage

EGLY-OURIET   O **Brut Tradition** Non-Vintage

PIERRE GIMONNET ET FILS   O **Blanc de Blancs Cuis** Premier Cru Non-Vintage

ALFRED GRATIEN   O **Paradis** Non-Vintage

LARMANDIER-BERNIER   O **Blanc de Blancs** Non-Vintage

SERGE MATHIEU   O **Brut Millésime** Vintage

PIERRE MONCUIT   O **Blanc de Blancs** Grand Cru Vintage

FRANÇOIS SECONDÉ   O **Brut Clavier** Non-Vintage

JACQUES SELOSSE   O **Blanc de Blancs Tradition** Non-Vintage

Pick of the luxury cuvée's

BILLECART-SALMON   O **Brut Cuvée Nicolas-François Billecart** Vintage

BOLLINGER   O **RD** Vintage

CHARLES HEIDSIECK   O **Charlie** Vintage

KRUG   O **Clos du Mesnil** Vintage

LAURENT-PERRIER   O **Grand Siécle** Vintage

MOËT ET CHANDON   O **Dom Pérignon** Vintage

POL ROGER   O **Sir Winston Churchill** Vintage

LOUIS ROEDERER   O **Cristal** Vintage

SALON   O **Salon** Vintage

VEUVE CLICQUOT   O **La Grande Dame** Vintage

The Loire is perhaps the most diverse and certainly geographically the most extensive of all France's classic wine regions. Inevitably there is a vast difference in styles from Nantes on the Atlantic coast to the heart of the Auvergne. Much of the region is steeped in tradition but, while you won't find the wave of new developments that is happening in the Midi for instance, there are new high-quality producers emerging in almost all appellations. A number of them are committed to either organic farming practices or indeed biodynamic viticulture. Applying these principles in this northerly climate is a far taller order than in, say, dry and sunny Provence.

Pays Nantais

The Pays Nantais generally means just one wine to the majority of people: Muscadet. Generic **Muscadet** can be pretty dire stuff, but there are a number of beacons of quality; names like Domaine de l'Ecu and Louis Métaireau. From a quality perspective the most important appellation is **Muscadet de Sèvre-et-Maine** with the best wines bottled *sur lie*. This means the wine spends a period of time on its lees for added richness. There are two other superior ACs, **Muscadet-Coteaux de la Loire** and **Muscadet Côtes de Grandlieu**. Covering the same area is the **Gros Plant VDQS**, producing simple, austere wines and to the south is the **Fiefs Vendéens VDQS** – you are most likely to encounter these on holiday in the area and the odd exciting example is emerging. Further east and stretching towards the south of Anjou and Saumur is the heart of the **Vin de Pays du Jardin de la France**, although this covers the whole of the valley; the odd fine white is appearing here. To the south is the VDQS of **Haut-Poitou**, where there are some relatively unexciting whites in vineyards surrounding the town of Poitiers. Good Muscadet can be crisp, minerally and with a real green-fruited depth, not dissimilar to sound village Chablis.

Anjou and Saumur

The **Anjou** appellation includes red, rosé and white wines. It covers a vast area north and south of the River Loire, from the west of Angers east to beyond Saumur. The quality can range from dire to very impressive, with some stylish barrel-fermented whites from the major white variety of the region, Chenin Blanc. Reds tend to be light, but the best are ripe and juicy with the odd more serious example and can be made from Gamay, Cabernets Sauvignon and Franc and Pineau d'Aunis. The medium to sweet rosé is generally very average, but well-made examples occasionally turn up under the Cabernet d'Anjou AC. The best red now has its own AC, **Anjou-Villages** and some very good wines are being made from Cabernet Franc and Cabernet Sauvignon. New oak is increasingly favoured.

The great wines here, though, are the steely, intense dry whites of **Savennières** and the sweet botrytised wines of the **Coteaux du Layon**. Those from the **Coteaux de l'Aubance** are less impressive but there are good examples. Within the Coteaux du Layon are the ACs of **Quarts de Chaume** and **Bonnezeaux** along with a number of communes which may append their names. These sweet wines tend to be traditional, quite restrained and very ageworthy or, increasingly, wines of immense extract and honeyed richness. Producers of the latter have become known as the sugar hunters. The best of these wines are marvellously rich and refined but some seem overblown and not entirely balanced and you have to wonder how they will age. A small amount of fine sweet Chenin Blanc is also made at Saumur and labelled as **Coteaux de Saumur.**

The vineyards of Saumur are also a haven for sparkling wine production. As well as sparkling Saumur there is also the catch-all appellation of **Crémant de Loire**. The attraction in making sparkling Chenin, as opposed to still, is the option it offers in poor vintages like those of the late 1990s. Many small producers take this route and there are some sizeable merchant houses and commercial offshoots of the big Champagne houses in Saumur. Quality can be quite good. The wines are generally more green apple in character than rich and biscuity in the manner of Champagne.

The best wines from Saumur, though, are the impressive barrel-fermented still white Chenin Blancs of the **Saumur** AC and the rich, ripe and supple reds of **Saumur-Champigny** produced from Cabernet Franc and

Cabernet Sauvignon. These tend to be softer and lusher in texture than the equally impressive reds from Bourgueil, Chinon and Saint-Nicolas-de-Bourgueil. Chinon is produced exclusively from Cabernet Franc and tends to be tighter and leaner. However, that said, there is still an alarming amount of dull, over-sulphured white and under-ripe, green-flavoured red throughout Anjou. The producer rather than the appellation is all-important.

Touraine

As in Anjou there is a catch-all **Touraine** AC that encompasses most of the region. Sauvignon Blanc is as important for whites here as Chenin and is common under the Touraine banner. In the far west of the region are the red wine appellations of **Bourgueil** and **Saint-Nicolas-de-Bourgueil** north of the river Loire and **Chinon** just to the south. The best of these wines are very good indeed and new oak is increasingly favoured. Bourgueil tends to be the fullest, while Saint-Nicolas often shows greater elegance and Chinon grown on the limestone *coteaux* is equally refined.

Just to the east of the city of Tours are the vineyards of **Vouvray** amd **Mountlouis**. Vouvray is found on the north of the river, Montlouis just to the south. Depending on the vintage conditions – and there have been some very moderate recent years although 2002 and particularly 2003 have been favourable – dry, *demi-sec* and *moelleux* styles are all created. The latter can be some of the greatest and longest-lived sweet wines in the world. Green and minerally in their youth, the dry and medium styles become increasingly rich and honeyed with age. The dry styles can be very austere when young and the searing acidity can be almost overwhelming. This can be the same with the *moelleux* wines – it's just better disguised by the residual sugar. Like many of the sweet wines along the valley the dependence on liberal sulphur additions is beginning to wane and you don't need to wait 20 years now for it to dissipate.

There are a number of lesser Touraine appellations. To the west of Tours can be found **Touraine Azay-le-Rideau** and to the immediate east of Vouvray and Montlouis **Touraine-Amboise** and **Touraine-Mesland**. Gamay, Cabernet Franc and Cabernet Sauvignon feature for the reds and Chenin Blanc for the whites. There are a few good examples. To the south of Blois are the regions of **Cheverny** and **Cour-Cheverny**. Similar reds are planted at Cheverny but the whites include Sauvignon Blanc and the unusual Romorantin. Cour-Cheverny is a white-only appellation planted to Romorantin.

To the north of Tours and the Touraine appellation are the regions of the **Coteaux du Loir** and its sub-region of **Jasnières**. The climate here is extremely marginal. The best wines – dry and late-havested Chenin Blancs – are Jasnières from vines planted on south-facing aspects with a protected mesoclimate. A handful of very good wines are made.

Central Vineyards and the South

The main wines of consequence are the Sauvignon Blancs from **Quincy**, **Reuilly**, **Menetou-Salon**, **Sancerre** and **Pouilly-Fumé**. Good Pinot Noir is also made at Sancerre and to a lesser extent at Menetou-Salon. While a considerable amount of very average white wine is made from these appellations there are some seriously good wines too. Those whites that are barrel-fermented and kept on lees are capable of considerable age and bottle development.

To the south is the Auvergne. The best wines come from the **Côte Roannaise**, where the odd decent example of Gamay is produced. Indeed the vineyards are nearer to and have more similarity geographically with Beaujolais than the rest of the Loire. Gamay is also produced in the **Côtes du Forez**.

A-Z of producers by appellation/region

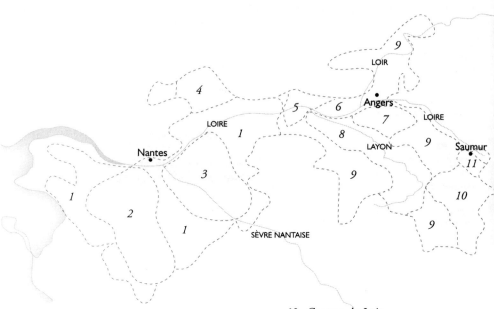

1   Muscadet
2   Muscadet Côtes de Grand Lieu
3   Muscadet de Sèvre-et-Maine
4   Muscadet des Coteaux de la Loire
5   Anjou Coteaux de la Loire
6   Savennières
7   Coteaux de l'Aubance
8   Coteaux du Layon
9   Anjou
10 Saumur
11 Saumur-Champigny
12 Jasnières

13 Coteaux du Loir
14 Saint-Nicolas-de-Bourgeuil
15 Bourgeuil
16 Chinon
17 Vouvray
18 Montlouis
19 Touraine
20 Cheverny, Cour Cheverny
21 Reuilly
22 Quincy
23 Menetou-Salon
24 Sancerre
25 Pouilly-Fumé

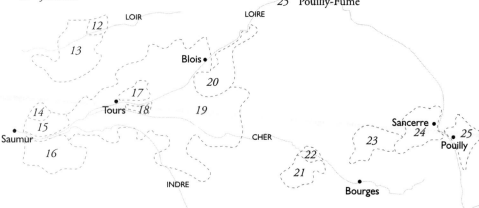

Loire Valley vintages

With an area as geographically extensive and as diverse in climate as the Loire it is difficult to generalise about its wines or individual years. Cooler conditions in a given year may favour dry whites, while sweet whites and reds need warm vintages. The heat of 2003 will produce some exceptional sweet whites and good reds. 2002 has turned out to be very good across the region. A huge amount of the general output of the region is best drunk young. You will, though, find the odd top Muscadet which will age well (2000 and 1997 were good) as well as those wines listed below.

The best red and white wines will age very well. They have great structure and the intense acidity that is characteristic of such a marginal climate. The reds are more marked by their acidity than their tannin. The great dry whites of Savennières and top *demi-secs* from Vouvray and Montlouis are capable of being held in your cellar for well over three decades. They will generally need at least six to seven years before they show their more exotic honeyed characters, though increasing use of oak, new and old, and *macération pelliculaire* are providing more accessible styles. Top Sancerre and Pouilly-Fumé, particularly those wines that are barrel-fermented, are surprisingly ageworthy and a far cry from the kind of tropical, gooseberry-laden examples of Sauvignon Blanc from the southern hemisphere that will barely make it past their first birthday.

Of the great earlier vintages Savennières was particularly impressive in 1985, 1983, 1982, 1978 and 1976. The great sweet wine vintages to consider were 1985, 1983, 1982, 1976, 1971, 1959, 1949, 1947 and 1921. Top reds were made in 1986, 1985, 1983, 1982, 1978 and 1976.

Loire Valley vintage chart

	Anjou & Touraine	Anjou & Touraine	Saumur & Touraine	Sancerre & Pouilly-Fume
	Top Dry Whites inc Savennières	Sweet Whites	Top Red Cuvees	Whites
2003	★★★★/★★★★★★ A	★★★★★ A	★★★★/★★★★★★ A	★★★/★★★★ A
2002	★★★★ A	★★★★ A	★★★/★★★★ A	★★★★/★★★★★★ A
2001	★★★ A	★★★/★★★★ A	★★★/★★★★ A	★★★ A
2000	★★★/★★★★ A	★★★ A	★★★ A	★★★★/★★★★★★ A
1999	★★★ B	★★★ B	★★★ A	★★★★/★★★★★★ B
1998	★★★ B	★★★ B	★★★ B	★★★★/★★★★★★ B
1997	★★★/★★★★ B	★★★★/★★★★★★ A	★★★★ B	★★★★ C
1996	★★★★/★★★★★ A	★★★★/★★★★★ A	★★★★/★★★★★★ B	★★★★ C
1995	★★★★ B	★★★★ A	★★★★/★★★★★ B	★★★★ C
1993	★★★ C	★★/★★★ C	★★★ D	★★★ D
1990	★★★★/★★★★★★ B	★★★★/★★★★★ B	★★★★/★★★★★★ C	★★★★/★★★★★ D
1989	★★★★/★★★★★★ C	★★★★★ A	★★★★/★★★★★ C	–
1988	★★★★ C	★★★★ B	★★★★ C	–

PHILIPPE ALLIET Chinon   A: Lay

Owner: Philippe Alliet L'Ouche Monde, 37500 Cravant-les-Coteaux
One of the very best producers in Chinon with 9 ha of Cabernet Franc planted on the *coteaux* at Cravant.
In the vineyard Alliet severely restricts his yields and looks to produce a full, powerful style with an extended
fermentation and maceration. The resulting wines possess marvellously pure blackcurrant and cedar fruit
all underpinned by supple, velvety tannins. New oak is avoided as are fining and filtration. The top wines
possess additional depth and weight. The Coteau de Noiré and Vieilles Vignes are the sturdiest and
longest-lived. (DM)
● **Chinon**★★ £B Coteau de Noiré★★★★ £C Vieilles Vignes★★★★ £C

YANNICK AMIRAULT Bourgueil   A: L&S, SVS

Owner: Yannick Amirault 5 Pavillon du Grand Clos, 37140 Bourgueil
The Amirault family domaine possesses some 17 ha spread throughout both Bourgueil and Saint-Nicolas-
de-Bourgueil. The wines are among the very best produced in either appellation. The Bourgueils are
marginally deeper, more brawny wines, the Saint-Nicolas bottlings a touch more elegant and tightly
structured. La Petite Cave is a splendid, dark and complex wine produced from old vines. Malgagnes is the
denser, more tannic of the two Saint-Nicolas-de-Bourgueils. Young-vine *cuvées* of both are also produced.
The top wines are very ageworthy and will improve in bottle for 10 years or more. (DM)
● **Bourgueil** Quartiers★★★ £B La Petite Cave★★★ £C
● **Saint Nicolas-de-Bourgueil** Graviers★★★ £B Malgagnes★★★★ £C

DOM. DES AUBUISIÈRES Vouvray www.vouvrayfouquet.com   A: C&R

Owner: Bernard Fouquet Rue de la Vallée-de-Nouy, 37210 Vouvray
Very good Vouvray from bone dry to lusciously sweet is made at this 22-ha domaine. Production is relatively
small at around 9,000 cases a year and an extensive range is produced when conditions are favourable. Silex
is dry, almost austere and very pure, while the stylish Marigny Sec is barrel-fermented. The Girardières
shows a sweet citrus and mineral style and is refined and well balanced. Currently available vintages haven't
favoured the production of any sweet Moelleux. When the right conditions do occur, as in 2003, the
magnificent top bottling is the Cuvée Alexandre. All of the wines will age very well. (DM)
O **Vouvray** Silex Sec★★ £B Marigny Sec★★★ £C
O **Vouvray** Girardières Demi-Sec★★★ £B
O **Vouvray** Brut★★ £C

PATRICK BAUDOUIN Coteaux du Layon www.patrick-baudouin-layon.com   A: WTs

Owner: Patrick Baudouin Princé, 49290 Chaudefonds-sur-Layon
Baudouin is one of the Layon's "sugar hunters", and the style here is rich, heady and unctuously sweet. What
impresses, though, is the balance and elegance achieved at the same time. He also produces two very decent
reds. The Anjou is solely from Cabernet Franc and displays some attractive berry and leafy notes. The
Anjou-Villages is more serious and structured; a blend of both Cabernets, it is part oak-aged. Neither is
filtered. Of the great sweet wines the regular Bruandières is intense and honeyed and it just needs a little
extra dimension for true class. The Grains Nobles and Maria Juby are seriously impressive. Both are
honeyed with marked botrytis and the Maria Juby has a marvellously fresh mineral balance. Aprés Minuit,
made in tiny quantities, is an astonishing wine. Selected berry by berry it is very opulent, concentrated and
complex. It should not only age well but is surprisingly approachable when young. (DM)
● **Anjou**★ £B ● **Anjou-Villages**★★ £B
O **Coteaux du Layon** Les Bruandières★★★ £D Grains Nobles★★★★ £F
O **Coteaux du Layon** Maria Juby★★★★★ £F Aprés Minuit✪✪✪✪✪ £G

BERNARD BAUDRY   Chinon   www.bernard-baudry@chinon.com   A: L&S

Owner: Bernard Baudry   13 Coteau de Sonnay, Cravant-les-Coteaux, 37500 Chinon
Bernard Baudry has 25 ha under vine at Chinon with a tiny amount planted to Chenin Blanc, from which
he makes an impressive white Chinon Croix Boisée. Good regular red Chinon is marked by approachable
leafy, berry fruit and a hint of spiciness. Les Granges is soft, vibrant and forward. The three top *cuvées* that
stand out. Clos Guillot is sturdy and dense, Grézeaux deep and extracted but supple and sufficiently soft
too. The top red Croix Boisée is dark, dense and complex and needs three to four years' ageing. (DM)
● **Chinon**★★ £B Les Granges★★ £B Clos Guillot★★★ £C Grézeaux★★★ £C Croix Boisée★★★★ £C

DOM. DES BAUMARD   Anjou-Saumur   www.baumard.fr   A: Res

Owner: Florent Baumard   8 Rue de l'Abbaye, 49190 Rochefort-sur-Loire
One of the Loire Valley's great and noble properties and among Anjou's best producers of dry and sweet
wines. The range is fairly extensive despite a production of barely more than 10,000 cases a year. Anjou red
and white, Rosé de Loire, Cabernet d'Anjou rosé and Crémant de Loire are all produced. The latter can be
good but on the whole are somewhat unexciting. The real gems here are the Layon sweet wines and the
various *cuvées* of Savennières. The latter are impressively steely and formidably structured in great years. Top
years also see the release of a Trie Spéciale. Among the sweet whites there are four Layons, including the
impressive Cuvée Le Paon and Clos Sainte-Catherine bottlings, as well as the unquestioned star, the
magnificent Quarts de Chaumes – a sublime, restrained and extraordinarily subtle sweet wine, a super-five
in great years. (DM)
○ **Savennières**★★ £B Clos du Papillon★★★★ £C
○ **Coteaux du Layon** Carte d'Or★★ £B Clos Sainte-Catherine★★★★ £D
○ **Quarts de Chaume**★★★★★ £E

DOM. HENRI BOURGEOIS   Sancerre   www.bourgeois-sancerre.com   A:WSS

Owner: Jean-Marie Bourgeois   Chavignol, 18300 Sancerre
This is a reasonably substantial but very impressive Sancerre producer and *négociant*. The domaine covers a
total of some 60 ha with 50 ha planted to Sauvignon Blanc, the balance Pinot Noir. The Bonnes Bouches
and Grande Réserve are the regular *cuvées* of Sancerre, while the MD de Bourgeois (named after the local
Monts Damnés slopes) and Bourgeoise are a level up. There is a good Pouilly-Fumé as well. Among the top
cuvées d'Antan is very concentrated, made from 65-year-old vines, while Jadis is intense and minerally from
vines planted in Kimmeridgian marl. The top wine, produced in extremely small quantities, is the very
intense, flinty and lightly nutty Étienne Henri, vinified in oak for 12 months on fine lees. The red Sancerre
Bourgeoise can be good but needs the benefit of a warm, sunny vintage. (DM)
● **Sancerre** Bourgeoise★★ £C
○ **Pouilly Fumé**★★ £B Demoiselle de Bourgeois★★★ £C
○ **Sancerre** Grande Réserve★★ £B Bonne Bouches★★ £B La Côte des Monts Damnés★★★ £C
○ **Sancerre** Bourgeoise★★★ £C Jadis★★★★ £D d'Antan★★★★ £E

DOM. BOURILLON-DORLÉANS   Vouvray   www.bourillon.com   A:TWS, M&V

Owner: Frédéric Bourillon-Dorléans   4 Rue de Chalateau, 37210 Rochcordon
There are some 18 ha at this Vouvray property where the emphasis is on dry and *demi-sec* Chenin wines.
Two *moelleux* bottlings are made when the vintage conditions allow, most recently in 2003. Art'ronia is
produced in reasonable volume and the top wine La Coulée d'Or is much rarer. The range is also buoyed
up by a regularly produced sparkling Brut. The dry styles are very tight and minerally in their youth with
piercing green-apple aromas. The Coulée d'Argent gets a touch more oak during vinification, some of it
new. The Demi-Sec is minerally and honeyed; it will become rich and profound with age. Handling is kept
to a minimum and there is just a light filtration prior to bottling. (DM)

O **Vouvray** Argilo Sec★★ £B Coulée d'Argent Sec★★★ £C
O **Vouvray** Cuvée Gaston Dorléans Demi-Sec★★★ £C

ALAIN CAILBOURDIN Pouilly-Fumé   A:THT

Owner: Alain Cailbourdin Maltaverne, 58150 Tracy-sur-Loire

Alain Cailbourdin has 16 ha under vine at Pouilly Fumé from which he produces around 8,000 cases a year
of fine, tight, minerally white. The vineyards, some up to 65 years old, are tended as naturally as possible
and there are varied soils including limestone and flint. Temperature control is used during fermentation
and the wines are very lightly filtered before bottling. The Cuvée de Boisfleury is the lightest and most floral
of the three bottlings; Les Cris is fuller and more structured, becoming lightly tropical and richer with two
or three years' age. Les Cornets, grown in clay-limestone is the sturdiest and most backward when young.
All will evolve well over five years or more.

O **Pouilly Fumé** Les Cris★★★ £C Cuvée de Boisfleury★★★ £C Les Cornets★★★ £C

DIDIER CHAMPALOU Vouvray champalou@wanadoo.fr   A:GWW,Tan,Sel

Owner: Didier et Cathérine Champalou 7 Rue du Grand Ormeau, 37210 Vouvray

The Champalous run a model Vouvray property with 20 ha of vineyards. Total output is around 8,000 to
8,500 cases a year. The regular Vouvray and the Fondraux are vinified in stainless steel and aged in old
wooden casks. They are generally *sec* in style but can have a fair level of residual sugar depending on the
nature and conditions of the vintage. In cooler years such as 2000 a stylish sparkling Brut is produced and
in great years for sweet wines, such as 1995, 1997 and most recently 2002, a *moelleux* style labelled
La Moelleuse is produced. Very occasionally a very sweet and late-harvested Trie de Vendange is released.
Both of these sweet wines are rich, honeyed and extremely long-lived. (DM)

O **Vouvray**★★ £B Fondraux★★★ £B

LAURENT CHATENAY Montlouis www.laurentchatenay.com   A:

Owner: Laurent Chatenay 41 route de Montlouis, 37270 Saint-Martin-le-Beau

Laurent Chatenay has been farming his family's vineyards since 1996. Their holdings have now grown to a
total of 13 ha of which the great majority are planted to very old vines ranging from 40 to 80 years of age.
This priceless raw material allied to low yields of less than 35 hl/ha is resulting in some of the finest wines
of the Mountlouis appellation. Les Maisonnettes is a tight, steely dry style with classic Chenin Blanc varietal
character. The La Vallée is *demi-sec* but the piercing fruit and high acidity tend to mask the sweetness.
Backward and restrained, the wine ideally needs six or seven years to add some flesh; expect it to become
increasingly honeyed with time. In the cellar SO_2 additions are kept to a minimum and the wines are never
chaptalised. The propitious conditions of 2001 and 02 have yielded a *moelleux* La Vallée aux Prêtres and 01
and 03 will see the release of the *liquoreux* Clos Michet. (DM)

O **Montlouis** Les Maisonnettes★★ £B La Vallée★★★ £B

JEAN-CLAUDE CHATELAIN Pouilly-Fumé jean-claude.chatelain@wanadoo.fr   A: CTy

Owner: Jean-Claude Chatelain Les Berthiers, 58150 Saint-Andelain

Father and son Jean-Claude and Vincent have 20 ha of vines in the Pouilly-Fumé AC and act as small-scale
négociants, buying in fruit to supplement their needs. They are now producing a regular Sancerre as well as
the Pouilly and if anything it's the better of the two. Les Charmes is a level up, richer and with a hint of oak
(10 per cent is barrel-fermented), while the top *cuvée,* the Prestige, from old vines is tight and structured
and very classy. It is vinified in stainless steel but gets six to seven months on lees. Pilou, an unusual and
concentrated barrel-fermented style, is occasionally produced from late-harvest dried grapes if vintage
conditions permit. (DM)

O **Pouilly Fumé**★★ £B Les Charmes★★★ £C Préstige★★★★ £D
O **Sancerre**★★ £B

CH. D'EPIRÉ Savennières www.chateau-epire.com

Owner: Luc Bizard 49170 Savennières

Luc Bizard produces only Savennières, around 4,000 to 5,000 cases a year, from his 11 ha of vineyards. Viticulture is traditional and the harvest is hand-picked with up to three *tries*. The wines are vinified in *inox* and aged on lees in barrel. A small-production bottling, Hu-Boyau, is sourced from the oldest parcel in the vineyard and is barrel-aged for nine months. Cuvée Spéciale is usually just 15 per cent of the harvest and is generally sourced from parcels that are closest to COULÉE DE SERRANT. These are fine, tightly structured, minerally examples and all show impressive depth and intensity. They are also very fairly priced. (DM)

O **Savennières**★★ £B Cuvéé Spéciale★★★ £C Moëlleux★★★ £C

CH. DE FESLES Bonnezeaux www.vgas.com A:Bsh, BBR, WTs

Owner: Bernard Germain Château de Festes, 49380 Thouarcé

Bordeaux *négociant* Bernard Germain purchased Château de Fesles in 1996. At that time the property had been through a period of serious decline. In the 1970s and 1980s the top Bonnezeaux had been labelled La Chapelle and if you encounter any old vintages prior to 1985 they can be superb. The Bonnezeaux is now just labelled as such and is very good once more despite poor recent vintages. Two other properties also acquired by Germain, the Châteaux de la Guimonière and de la Roulerie, are both turning out impressive Coteaux du Layon and there are some classy reds from Anjou, particularly the dense and chunky Fesles Anjou-Villages. There is also a very stylish, minerally Savennières Clos de Varennes made from 7 ha of vines that Germain has bought from Pierre SOULEZ at Château de Chamboreau. (DM)

Château de Fesles
● **Anjou** Vieilles Vignes★★ £B ● **Anjou-Villages**★★★ £C
O **Bonnezeaux**★★★★★ £F

Château de la Guimonière
● **Anjou**★ £B
O **Coteaux du Layon Chaume** Julines★★★ £E

Château de la Roulerie
● **Anjou**★ £B
O **Coteaux du Layon Chaume** Aunis★★★★ £E

Clos de Varenne
O **Savennières**★★★ £C

CH. DU HUREAU Saumur-Champigny www.domaine-hureau.fr A:GWW

Owner: Philippe Vatan Dampierre-sur-Loire, 49400 Saumur

Philippe Vatan produces excellent Saumur Blanc and sumptuous and supple Saumur-Champigny. He possesses 21 ha planted in tufa/limestone soils, which are particularly suitable for producing first-rate Cabernet Franc. As well as the regular red *cuvée* there are two very fine wines produced from old vines. Cuvée des Fevettes gets new wood treatment, whereas the Lisgathe has more exuberant, fleshy dark berry fruit and is aged in old barrels. The white is everything that good dry Chenin Blanc should be. Minerals, citrus and honey are all in evidence. These are approachable but ageworthy wines, keeping well for 10 years and more in the best vintages. (DM)

● **Saumur-Champigny** Grande Cuvée★★ £B Fevettes★★★ £C Lisgathe★★★★£C
O **Saumur**★★★£B

CH. PIERRE-BISE Coteaux du Layon A: L&S

Owner: Claude Papin 49750 Beaulieu-sur-Layon

Based in sleepy Beaulieu-sur-Layon, Claude Papin possesses 53 ha of vines spread across the Anjou-Villages, Coteaux du Layon and Savennières appellations. He is one of the best-established quality producers in the region. The wines are well-crafted and offer great value for money. The reds are full of rich blackberry and mulberry fruit and are aged in a small proportion of new oak. The Coteaux du Layon *cuvées* are full of peach, honey and nutmeg in the best years and are always well structured, refined and ageworthy. The Quarts de Chaume is richer still, with formidable depth. The intense, ageworthy, Clos de Coulaine Savennières is not only remarkably well-priced but it has marvellous citrus and mineral aromas. It will be better with five or six years' cellaring. (DM)

● **Anjou-Villages** Clos de Coulaine★★ £B Sur Spilite★★★ £B
○ **Anjou** Haut de la Garde★★ £B ○ **Savennières** Clos de Coulaine★★★ £B
○ **Coteaux du Layon-Beaulieu** Rouannières★★★★£D
○ **Coteaux du Layon-Rochefort** Rayelles★★★★ £D
○ **Quarts de Chaume**★★★★★ £F

CH. DE TRACY Pouilly-Fumé tracy@wanadoo.fr A: JBa, Lay

Owner: Comtesse Alain d'Estutt d'Assay Château de Tracy, 58150 Tracy-sur-Loire
Historic property with a Renaissance château whose origins date back to 1396. There are approximately 31 ha under vine, all of which are Sauvignon Blanc. Just the one wine is made and output is by no means small, approaching 20,000 cases a year. Despite this the wine has been consistently good in recent vintages. It is a steely, flinty style with surprisingly exotic fruit emerging with age. Structured and refined it needs at least a year or two in your cellar. (DM)

● **Pouilly-Fumé**★★★ £D

CH. DE VILLENEUVE Saumur-Champigny www.chateau-de-villeneuve.com A: THt

Owner: Jean-Pierre Chevallier Château de Villeneuve, 49400 Souzay-Champigny
Very good property producing red and white from the Saumur-Champigny and Saumur ACs. The vineyards are run organically and partly on biodynamic principles. The focus here is the quality of the fruit, its intensity and concentration achieved through careful viticulture, a tight control on yields and minimal handling in the cellar. The white Cormiers is subtly oaked and barrel-fermented with a period on lees. The reds are concentrated, dark and spicy examples of the very best Loire Cabernet Franc. A special *cuvée*, Grand Clos, is a super-rich special bottling made in the greatest years only. These are all very ageworthy, improving in bottle for 5 to 10 years. (DM)

● **Saumur-Champigny**★★ £B Vieille Vignes★★★ £C
○ **Saumur**★★★ £B Cormiers★★★ £C

CLOS DE LA COULÉE DE SERRANT Savennières www.coulée-de-serrant.com A: Yap

Owner: Nicolas Joly Château de la Roche-aux-Moines, 49170 Savennières
Nicolas Joly has 14.5 ha of Chenin Blanc which is tended biodynamically. Indeed, Joly is one of the most outspoken proponents of this concept of organic farming. In the past he has been criticised for being more concerned with the application of biodynamic principles than in his wines. This would appear to be unjustified because these are some of the finest expressions of dry Chenin to be found anywhere. The supremely structured and refined Coulée de Serrant is loaded with subtle citrus, mineral and flint. This is a very fine wine with a remarkable capacity to age: it is not really ready for 10 years and will keep with ease for more than twice that time. The Clos de la Bergerie is also impressive and more accessible although it still ages very well. When vintage conditions allow, there is a small amount of Moelleux. (DM)

○ **Savennières**★★★ £D
○ **Savennières Coulée de Serrant**✪✪✪✪✪ £F
○ **Savennières Roches aux Moines** Clos de la Bergerie★★★★ £E

DOM. DU CLOS NAUDIN Vouvray   A: Gau, SVS

Owner: Philippe Foreau   14 Rue de la Croix Buisée, 37210 Vouvray
A marvellous traditional producer of the some of the greatest Vouvrays made in recent decades. Only the wines of HUËT L'ECHANSONNE bear comparison. Intense and very well-crafted *sec* and *demi-sec* wines are tight, very minerally and superbly structured. They need time to emerge from their shell and will age for decades. Very good sparkling Méthode Traditionelle Réserve and a limited amount of a vintage sparkler are also made. When the gods are favourable in this most marginal of climates for great sweet wines, Foreau produces precisely that: magnificent Moelleux, as he did in 2002, and Moelleux Réserve. (DM)
O **Vouvray** Sec★★★ £B Demi-Sec★★★ £B Méthode Traditionelle Réserve★★★ £C

CLOS ROUGEARD   Saumur-Champigny   A: HHB

Owner: Foucault family   15 Rue de l'Église, 49400 Chacé
There are 10 ha under vine and just one of those is planted with Chenin Blanc, the balance being Cabernet Franc. Inevitably the impressive Saumur Blanc Brezé is very rarely encountered. It is a subtly barrel-fermented style and strikingly intense. There is a very good regular Saumur-Champigny with ripe, dark fruit and soft and supple tannins. The two superior *cuvées*, Bourg and Poyeux, are equally velvety in texture but with greater depth and power. Le Bourg offers slightly darker and more overt notes of cassis while the Poyeux is the more elegant with classic leafy, Loire spice. (DM)
● **Saumur-Champigny**★★★ £B Bourg★★★★ £C Poyeux★★★★ £C

DOM. DU CLOSEL   Savennières   www.savennieres-closel.com   A: Yap, BBR

Owner: De Jessey family   Château des Vaults, 1 Place du Mail, 49170 Savennières
The de Jessey family produce decent, solid, fruity Anjou-Villages red and more importantly some impressive, rich, and mineral-laden Savennières. The regular Savennières is good if lacking real depth; the Caillardières is a solid step up. The Clos du Papillon is very impressive indeed; intense and minerally but with a remarkable depth of citrus and rich honeyed aromas emerging with age. These are cellarworthy, particularly the Clos du Papillon. An occasional Vieilles Vignes bottling is produced in the best years as well as a *moelleux* labelled Cuvée Isa. (DM)
● **Savennières** Les Vaults★★ £B Caillardières★★★ £C Clos du Papillon★★★★ £C

PASCAL COTAT   Sancerre   A: Bal, Gau, Rae, SVS

Owner: Pascal/Francis Cotat   98 Chemin de Grous, 18300 Sancerre
The Cotats make some of the very finest Sancerre. Their production is tiny at just 1,200 to 1,300 cases a year with minimal intervention in both vineyard and cellar. Their sites are superb and naturally low-yielding and all that is required is to ensure that the vines stay in balance. The wine is fermented naturally and no fining or filtration is undertaken. These are rich, explosive Sauvignon Blancs which need at least a year or two to show at their best. Remarkable Cuvée Spéciale is produced in the greatest years for both wines. (DM)
O **Sancerre** Grande Côte★★★★ £C Monts Damnés★★★★ £D

LUCIEN CROCHET   Sancerre   lcrochet@terres-net.fr   A: BSh, EoR

Owner: Gilles Crochet   Place de l'Église, 18300 Bué
The Crochets have 35 ha of their own vineyards in Sancerre and also act as *négociants*. Inevitably the best wines here are from their own vineyards. As well as the white Sancerre, which is vinified without new oak, the reds are also noteworthy. So often Pinot Noir fails to perform in this climate and red   Sancerre is frequently light and insubstantial, but not here. Late harvesting and ripe fruit is always the key to quality. The Cuvée Prestige white and red are both old-vine bottlings and most impressive. The white Le Chêne Marchand is lighter but very intense and minerally. The Prestige labels will be better given four or five years' ageing. (DM)

O **Sancerre** Le Chêne Marchand★★★ £C Cuvée Prestige★★★ £D
● **Sancerre** Le Croix du Roy★★ £C Cuvée Prestige★★★ £D

DIDIER DAGUENEAU Pouilly-Fumé silex@wanadoo.fr A: HHB, Tan, BBR

Owner: Didier Dagueneau Le Bourg, 58150 Saint-Andelain
Didier Dagueneau is the finest producer in Pouilly Fumé and while he has a few rivals in Sancerre he stands out as the region's standard bearer for magnificent, complex and very ageworthy Sauvignon Blanc. These wines are light years away from the simple gooseberry and tropical flavours many associate with the variety. Immense care is taken in the vineyard, yields are low, harvesting is only at peak maturity with several passes through the vines and handling in the cellar is kept to an absolute minimum. Buisson Renard, Pur-Sang and the magnificent Silex are all barrel-fermented but in no way does the oak become intrusive. What you are left with is an intense and very complex mix of green fruits and minerals. Superbly structured, these are wines that demand cellaring for half a dozen years or more. (DM)

O **Pouilly-Fumé** En Chailloux★★★★ £E Buisson Renard★★★★★ £E
O **Pouilly-Fumé** Pur-Sang★★★★★ £E Silex✪✪✪✪✪ £F

PHILIPPE DELESVAUX Coteaux du Layon dom.delesvaux.philippe@wanadoo.fr A:Gau

Owner: Philippe et Catherine Delesvaux 49190 Saint-Aubin-de-Luigné
Philippe Delesvaux is one of a small new group of dedicated and quality-conscious wine producers in the sleepy Coteaux du Layon. Recent vintages have not been kind to sweet wine makers here but Delesvaux continues to handcraft intense, stylish examples. The Anjou reds are deeper and with better grip and structure than most. The Anjou bottling is Cabernet Franc; the more substantial Anjou-Villages is Cabernet Sauvignon. Both are vinified in *inox*. In whites there is a very stylish barrel-fermented Anjou Blanc as well as the sweet Layons. What marks these wines out is not just their rich, honeyed botrytised character but their intensity, refinement and balance. In exceptional vintages two remarkable special *cuvées*, Anthologie and Carbonifera, are produced, both comfortably five-star wines. The former is just that touch more unctuous and heady. (DM)

● **Anjou**★★ £B ● **Anjou-Villages**★★ £B
O **Anjou** Feuille d'Or★★★ £B
O **Coteaux du Layon**★★★ £C
O **Coteaux du Layon-Saint-Aubin** Clos de la Guiberderie★★★★ £D
O **Coteaux du Layon** Grains Nobles★★★★ £E

OLIVIER DELÉTANG Montlouis www.domaine-deletang.com

Owner: Olivier Delétang 19 Rue d'Amboise, 37270 Saint-Martin-Beau
Olivier Delétang produces very good Montlouis from three different sites – his own 20 ha vineyard, Les Batisses and Les Petits Boulay. The vineyard and the climate conditions are the key here rather than individual wines. He produces *sec* and often *demi-sec* regularly from each site. Some very special sweet wines have been made in great years but none since 1997, when great Moelleux, Moelleux Réserve and Garde Réserve of very fine quality indeed were produced. As well as the Montlouis bottlings there are some simple straightforward Touraines, a white from Sauvignon Blanc and a red from Cabernet Franc. There is also a regular sparkling Brut, called Effervescent, which is clean, appley and fresh. (DM)

O **Montlouis** Sec★★ £B Demi-Sec★★★ £B Les Batisses Sec★★★ £B Les Batisses Demi-Sec★★★ £B
O **Montlouis** Les Petits Boulay Sec★★ £B

PIERRE-JACQUES DRUET Bourgueil A: J&B, Bal, HHB, ABy, Har

Owner: Pierre-Jacques Druet 7 Rue de la Croix-Rouge, 37140 Benais
A brilliant source of top Cabernet Franc. The Bourgueil rosé is delicious and fruity, far better than most of its kind. There are three *cuvées* of Bourgueil as well as the marvellously elegant and pure Chinon Clos de

Danzay, which is aged in *demi-muids*. The Bourgueil Cent Boisselées is handled entirely in stainless steel and displays classic blackcurrant fruit and just a subtle hint of leafiness. The Grand Mont is refined and elegant with hints of cassis and cedar. Produced from chalk vineyards the tannin is supple and well balanced. The top red Vaumoreau comes from nearly 100-year-old vines. It is an unfiltered, dense, very powerful and concentrated red, full of ripe intense cassis and cedar. A wine of immense class and finesse, it is only produced in top years. (DM)

● **Bourgueil** Cent Boisselées★★ £B   Grand Mont★★★ £C Vaumoreau★★★★ £E
● **Chinon** Clos de Danzay★★★ £C
◎ **Bourgueil★** £B

DOM. DES FORGES   Coteaux du Layon   A: M&V, Tan, SVS

Owner: Branchereau family   Vignoble Branchereau, 49190 Saint-Aubin-de-Luigné
A wide range of Anjou wines are made at this underrated property: good straightforward Sauvignon Blanc and Chardonnay Vin de Pays de la Jardin de France along with supple, fruity Anjou reds and some decent Anjou white. But best of all are the impressive sweet whites – stylish, rich but restrained Coteaux du Layon and Quarts de Chaume. The top wines are the Quarts de Chaume and Coteaux du Layon-Chaume. There is also a good well-crafted Savennières which is tight and flinty. Recent moderate vintages have prevented the domaine from producing great sweet wines. (DM)

O **Coteaux du Layon★★** £C Coteaux du Layon-Saint-Aubin★★★ £C
O **Coteaux du Layon-Chaume★★★★** £D   Les Onnis★★★★ £E
O **Quarts de Chaume★★★★** £F
O **Savennières** Clos des Mauriers★★ £B

JOËL GIGOU/DOM. DE LA CHARRIÈRE   Jasnières   joel-gigou@libertysurf.fr   A: Yap

Owner: Joël Gigou   4 Rue des Caves, 72340 La Chartre-sur-le-Loir
Joël Gigou is an immensely dedicated grower in this most marginal and extreme of Loire Valley climates. The vineyard is close to organic, yields are kept in check and balanced vines mean no *vendange vert*. There are two intense and almost austere dry whites. A real mineral backbone runs through the wines and they have piercing acidity but are very ageworthy. The Clos Saint-Jacques will take on a marvellously rich citrus and honeyed character with age. Also produced is a very fine late-harvest white which is far removed from a Bonnezeaux or a Quarts de Chaume. The wine is tightly structured, lightly honeyed but very long and intense. It is extraordinarily long-lived. (DM)

O **Jasnières** Cuvée Trois Clos★★ £B   Cuvée Clos Saint-Jacques Vieilles-Vignes★★★ £C
O **Jasnières** Sélection de Grains Nobles★★★★ £D

DOM. GUIBERTEAU-EGGERTON   Saumur   A: Sav

Owner: Roman Guiberteau & Stephen Eggerton   3 Impasse du Cabernet, 49260 Saint-Just-sur-Dive
Roman Guiberteau established this excellent small domaine in 1996 and has sinced been joined by partner, Englishman Stephen Eggerton. Their small property consists of 2.5 ha of Chenin Blanc and just under 6 ha of Cabernet Franc. Output is small, barely more than 2,000 cases a year, but quality is very impressive. The low-yielding vineyards are now handled organically and great pains are taken to work the soil effectively to ensure deep-rooting vines and top-quality fruit, even in difficult years. In the winery minimal handling is the order of the day, although some micro-oxygenation is used to help ensure rich, supple wines. The regular red Saumur is elegant and intense with classic Cabernet Franc fruit; the Motelles has that extra dimension with piercingly intense red berry fruit and the firm structure to develop very well in bottle for six or seven years. We will be looking to assess the white Saumur Le Clos for the next edition but it should be well worth trying. (DM)

● **Saumur★★** £B Motelles★★★ £C

HUET L'ECHANSONNE   Vouvray   www.huet-echansonne.com   A: RsW,WSc,Sel,Har

Owner: Huet family/Antony Hwang   11–13 Rue de la Croix Buisée, 37210 Vouvray
There may be a rising tide of new quality-conscious producers in Vouvray but this biodynamically farmed domaine remains the standard-bearer for the appellation. The property has a total of 40 ha and sources its fruit from three different sites; Clos du Bourg, Haut-Lieu and Le Mont. Eighty per cent of the domaine has now been purchased by the partnership of Istvan SZEPSY and American financier Antony Hwang, who are helping to revolutionise sweet-wine production in Hungary's Tokaji region. The wines are made as *sec*, *demi-sec* and when conditions allow, like those in 1997, some magnificent *moelleux* including the extraordinary Cuvée Constance. The dry wines are intense, minerally and very backward when young. They will, though, evolve into superb, complex, honeyed masterpieces with time, but you have to be patient. The *demi-sec* and *moelleux* are more immediately approachable, drinking with three or four years' ageing but very fine indeed. (DM)

O **Vouvray** Clos du Bourg Sec★★★ £B Clos du Bourg Demi-Sec★★★ £C
O **Vouvray** Clos du Bourg Moelleux★★★★★ £E
O **Vouvray** Haut-Lieu Sec★★★ £B Haut-Lieu Demi-Sec★★★★ £C Haut-Lieu Moelleux★★★★★ £E
O **Vouvray** Le Mont Sec★★★ £B Le Mont Demi-Sec★★★ £C Le Mont Moelleux★★★★★ £E
O **Vouvray** Cuvée Constance❂❂❂❂❂ £F

DOM. CHARLES JOGUET   Chinon   A: M&V,SVS,OWL

Owner: Jacques Genet   La Dioterie, 37220 Sazilly
The Joguet domaine is mainly planted to Cabernet Franc with 37 ha under vine and just 3 ha of Chenin Blanc. Jacques Genet now owns the estate and he is ably assisted by Alain Delaunay and cellarmaster Michel Pinarde. Seven and sometimes eight different *cuvées* are made each year and these are based on both vine age and soil type. The Terroir and Clos de la Cure bottlings are relatively soft and forward, the most approachable of these most traditional of Chinons. The Varennes du Grand Clos is grown in limestone soils and produced from a yield of 40 hl/ha. The top two wines the Clos du Chene Vert and Clos de la Dioterie come from lower-yielding plots, barely 30 hl/ha. The wines are marked by their traditional vinification with fermentation being instigated in the high 30s celsius, and are correspondingly backward when young. Even the lesser *cuvées* can seem angular and awkward before gaining richness with age. Chenin Blanc was planted in the early to mid-1990s and now makes a decent Touraine white Clos de la Plante Martin. (DM)

● **Chinon** Clos du Chêne Vert★★★ £C Clos de la Dioterie★★★ £C
● **Chinon** Terroir★★ £B Clos de la Cure★★ £B Les Varennes du Grand Clos★★★ £C

DOM. FRÉDÉRIC MABILEAU   Saint-Nicolas-de-Bourgueil   A: Cam

Owner: Frédéric & Nathalie Mabileau   17-19 Rue de la Treille, 37140 Saint-Nicolas-de-Bourgueil
Frédéric Mabileau has been running his small domaine with his wife Nathalie since the early 1990s. He now has some 9 ha under vine planted to a combination of Cabernet Franc (90 per cent) and Cabernet Sauvignon. There is a softly fruity Cabernet Sauvignon Anjou made from younger vines and a Bourgueil, Les Racines, has also been added. Saint-Nicolas-de-Bourgueil stands out and there are three good to very good and pure bottlings, marked more by their elegance and refinement than by their weight. The Mabileaus possess plots across the AC in a range of *terroirs*. Les Rouillères is the softest of the trio, sourced from sandy/gravel soils where the vines are relatively young. Les Coutures is fuller and firmer, sourced from older vines (over 40 years) grown in gravel. The wine gets a brief cold soak, 20 day maceration and is aged for 12 months in oak. The brilliant, piercingly intense top wine, Éclipse, comes from the lowest-yielding plots of clay/gravel over limestone. The wine gets 12 months in oak, a proportion new, and malolactic takes place in barrel. The top two wines in particular will benefit from five or six years' ageing. (DM)

● **Saint-Nicolas-de-Bourgueil** Les Coutures★★★ £C Éclipse★★★★ £C
● **Saint-Nicolas-de-Bourgueil** Rouillères★★ £B

ALPHONSE MELLOT   Sancerre   mellot@sifiedi.fr   A: **Hal**, GVF

Owner: Alphonse Mellot   La Moussière, 18300 Sancerre

Mellot is one of the leading producers in Sancerre. There are *négociant* wines including good Menetou-Salon and Pouilly-Fumé but the domaine wines are of a different order, particularly the top *cuvées*. The white Edmond and Génération XIX, made from very old vines and vinified in oak, are wines of real dimension, the latter often on the cusp of five stars. The Pinot Noirs are increasingly impressive, displaying considerable depth and a round, supple texture, especially the brilliant, subtly oaked Génération XIX. The top wines will undoubtedly develop very well in bottle. (DM)

O **Sancerre** La Moussière★★★ £C   Edmond★★★★ £E   Génération XIX★★★★ £E
● **Sancerre** Génération XIX★★★★ £F

DOM. HENRY NATTER   Sancerre   www.henrynatter.com   A: **L&W**

Owner: Henry Natter   Place de l'Eglise, 18250 Montigny

Established in 1974, this domaine based in the top village of Montigny is now one of the best for fine-quality white Sancerre. As well as the regular white there is a small-volume special bottling, Cuvée François de la Grange de Montigny, and a fruity red and rosé. Vinification of the whites is traditional with fermentation in large oak vats. The regular version is then aged in stainless steel, while François de la Grange de Montigny sees 12 months in oak. The wines have been consistently good in recent years and will develop well with short bottle age. (DM)

O **Sancerre**★★★ £C   Cuvée François de La Grange★★★ £C

DOM. OGEREAU   Anjou   A: CdP

Owner: Vincent Ogereau   44 Rue de la Belle-Angevine, 49750 Saint-Lambert-du-Lattay

Vincent Ogereau produces very good Anjou-Villages reds, decent minerally dry white Anjou and rich, well-crafted Coteaux du Layon. The regular Anjou-Villages is a blend of Cabernet Franc and Cabernet Sauvignon, whereas the Côte de la Houssaye is a dense and powerful, brambly Cabernet Sauvignon. Both will be the better for five years' ageing. The Coteaux du Layon is powerful, sweet and unctuous and achieves a really intense botrytised peachy character in the very best years. A special selection, Clos de Bonnes Blanches, is also produced. (DM)

● **Anjou**★★ £B   ● **Anjou-Villages**★★★ £B   Côte de la Houssaye★★★ £C
O **Anjou** Prestige Sec★★ £B
O **Coteaux du Layon-Saint-Lambert-du-Lattay** Prestige★★★★ £C

DOM. DES OUCHES   Bourgueil   perso.wanadoo.fr/gambier   A: THT

Owner: Denis Gambier   3 Rue des Ouches, 37140 Ingrandes-de-Touraine

First class Bourgueil producer offering classic, restrained and ageworthy examples of the appellation at very keen prices indeed. The style is tighter and more backward than many, even from this cool-climate region. All the wines have an angular character in their youth, as much from their high acidity as from their tannin, and require a few years' ageing to add flesh. The top two *cuvées* in particular should be cellared for at least four to five years. Cabernet Franc is the main variety but there is a little (10 per cent) Cabernet Sauvignon in the Grande Réserve. Some of the vines are remarkably old here, up to 100 years, and this undoubtedly contributes to quality. With the exception of the Grande Réserve, which is aged in new oak (50 per cent) with malolactic in barrel, the wines are traditionally vinified and aged in *foudres*. (DM)

● **Bourgueil**★★ £B   Clos Princé★★ £B   Vieilles Vignes★★★ £B   Grande Réserve★★★★ £C

HENRY PELLÉ   Menetou-Salon   www.henry-pelle.com   A: PBW,M&V,HHB,GVF,Sel

Owner: Pellé family   18220 Morogues

The leading estate in Menetou-Salon and a producer of Sancerre as well. There are some 40 ha under vine and these split roughly two-thirds to one-third Sauvignon Blanc to Pinot Noir. The vineyards in Menetou-Salon are planted on Kimmeridgian clay and tended organically, and green harvesting is practised. Straightforward Menetou-Salon and Sancerre white and red now come from a mix of estate and bought-in grapes. Of the estate-grown wines, the white Menetou-Salon tends to impress more than the Sancerre, the vineyards of which are younger, although the Sancerre is increasingly improving as the vines mature. 2002 was very good here. White Clos de Ratier is from a single parcel as is the rich and intense Clos des Blanchais, which is from the domaine's oldest vines and posseses an impressive depth of ripe gooseberry fruit and a fine, mineral structure. The reds, while fruity enough, can be insubstantial. (DM)

● **Menetou-Salon** Les Cris★ £B ●Sancerre La Croix au Garde★ £C
O **Menetou-Salon** Morogues★★ £B Clos de Ratier★★ £B Clos des Blanchais★★★ £C
O **Sancerre** La Croix au Garde★★ £C

VINCENT PINARD Sancerre   A: GWW, HHB, Han

Owner: Vincent Pinard 42 Rue Saint-Vincent, 18300 Bué
There are some 15 ha at this model Sancerre domaine where Vincent Pinard produces good to very good white and red Sancerre. The regular red is good, light but exuberantly fruity with attractive berry fruit. Charlouise is denser, richer. Of the whites the Cuvée Florès emphasises ripe classic gooseberry fruit. The two top whites are fuller and more complex, and both are vinified in wood. Harmonie in particular is spicy and toasty in its youth, needing three or four years to achieve a balance of fruit and oak. (DM)

● **Sancerre**★★ £C Charlouise★★★ £D
O **Sancerre** Cuvée Florés★★£D Nuance★★★ £C Harmonie★★★ £D

DOM. DES ROCHES NEUVES Saumur-Champigny www.roches-neuves.com

Owner: Thierry Germain 56 Boulevard Saint-Vincent, 49400 Varrains
Thierry Germain's father Bernard has owned CHÂTEAU DE FESLES in Bonnezeaux since 1996 but his son has been established in Anjou for longer. He produces opulent, powerful, ripely extracted reds from Cabernet Franc. The wines are deeply coloured, dense and oaky. Vinification is aimed at maximum extraction, with the fruit getting a pre-fermentation cold soak and the wine staying on its skins in order to achieve rounded, supple tannins. He notably succeeds in reducing some of the austere youthful characteristics that can often show in other Loire Cabernets. He also makes a very good barrel-fermented white Saumur which is stylish and refined with a nice balance of toasty, citrus fruit and a fresh mineral structure. The Terres Chaudes and the Marginale are the two top reds. The latter is marked by new oak in its youth and needs time. (DM)

● **Saumur-Champigny**★★ £B Terres Chaudes★★★ £C Marginale★★★ £C
O **Saumur** Insolite★★★ £C

DOM. DE LA SANSONNIÈRE Anjou   A: Har

Owner: Marc Angeli 49380 Thouarcé
Marc Angeli farms his 7 ha biodynamically and he makes some of the very finest examples of the humble Anjou AC. He has also produced tiny amounts (from less than a hectare) of exquisite Bonnezeaux that are released as Les Blanderies and Le Coteau du Houet. The largest volume here is saved for his Anjou La Lune which accounts for nearly half his holding at 3.10 ha. The wine is produced from low yields and is vinified in 400- to 600-litre barrels. It is remarkably pure with an intense mineral quality amidst complex, very subtly tropical fruit. It is occasionally bottled with just a hint of residual sugar. Les Fouchardes and Les Vieilles Vignes des Blanderies are produced from much smaller holdings and therefore very hard to find. The range is completed by a Cabernet Sauvignon Les Gelinettes and a Rosé d'Anjou, Coteau du Houet. (DM)

O **Anjou** La Lune★★★★ £E

SILICES DE QUINCY Quincy   A: Gau,Har,THT

Owner: Jacques Sallé   Place de L'Echuzeau, 18120 Quincy
From his tiny holding of 5.5 ha, Jacques Sallé produces around 1,000 cases of Quincy which is the
benchmark for the appellation. In order to ensure the integrity of the main wine a second label Silicette is
also made. The vineyard is tended biodynamically and the vines are very old. The wine possesses an intense
mineral, green-fruit character underpinned by tight gripping acidity. The depth and structure here suggest
the top wine will develop surprisingly well over at least four or five years. (DM)
O **Quincy★★★** £C

YVES SOULEZ/CH. DE LA GENAISERIE Coteaux du Layon   A: GVF

Owner: Yves Soulez   Ch. de la Genaiserie, 49190 Saint-Aubin-de-Luigné
Yves Soulez makes very good, stylish and refined Coteaux du Layon in a more restrained style than most of
his peers. His wines are quite different from the new wave of super-ripe and unctuous styles achieved
elsewhere by the likes of Patrick BAUDOUIN or Jo PITHON. They are tight and often quite backward when
young but have a real intensity and finesse also. There are three very fine special *cuvées* in addition to the
regular bottling. Les Simonelles is elegant and minerally with subtle botrytis and comes from vines grown
on volcanic, schistous soils. La Roche is from a vineyard with a high charcoal content and is very restrained.
Les Tetuères is the fullest and most obviously honeyed of the three and generally has more marked botrytis
character. There are also good Anjou reds from Gamay and Cabernet Franc and a fruity, fresh medium-
sweet Cabernet d'Anjou; a revelation in comparison with so many wines sold under this label. (DM)
● **Anjou★** £B O **Coteaux du Layon-Chaume★★★** £C
O **Coteaux du Layon-Chaume** Les Simonelles★★★★ £D La Roche★★★★ £D Les Tetuères★★★★ £D

TAILLE AUX LOUPS Montlouis   A: M&V

Owner: Jacky Blot   8 Rue des Aitres, Husseau, 37270 Montlouis-sur-Loire
One of the best domaines in Montlouis. A varying small range of *sec, demi-sec* and sweet wines are made
both in Montlouis and Vouvray. Recent vintages have seen the production of mainly dry and medium styles
along with good sparkling wines including Brut Tradition and a very dry Pétillant, although some brilliant
late-harvest wines emerged in 2002. The Montlouis Remus *sec* is barrel-fermented in new oak and aged on
lees with *bâtonnage*. The impressive *demi-sec* is not oversweet and when nature is kind *moelleux* are very
impressive indeed. The Montlouis Cuvée des Loups and particularly Montlouis Cuvée Romulus can be
explosively rich. Vouvray is also now produced from Clos de Venise as well as some fine bottlings of
Bourgueil. (DM)
O **Montlouis** Brut Tradition★★ £B Pétillant★★ £B Sec★★ £B Demi-Sec★★★ £C
O **Montlouis** Moelleux★★★ £D Cuvée des Loups★★★★ £E
O **Vouvray** Clos de Venise Sec★★★ £C

DOM. VACHERON Sancerre   A: E&T, SsG, TWS

Owner: Vacheron family   1 Rue du Puis Poulton, 18300 Sancerre
The Vacherons have some 37 ha under vine with no less than 11 ha planted to Pinot Noir. They are one
of only a handful of growers in Sancerre to make impressive red wines. There are regular red and white
Sancerres and two very impressive reserve *cuvées*; the white Romains and the dense and surprisingly
powerfully structured red Belle Dame. Good rosé is also produced. The white Sancerre has fine grass and
mineral notes and the Romains an impressive depth with subtle, nutty, oak-derived notes and real finesse.
Both the top wines have the structure to develop well with five years' cellaring. (DM)
● **Sancerre★★** £C Belle Dame★★★ £C
O **Sancerre★★** £C Romains★★★ £D

OTHER WINES OF NOTE

PIERRE AGUILAS ○ Coteaux du Layon Cuvée Claire £D
DOM. DE BABLUT ○ Coteaux de l'Aubance Vin Noble £D
DOM. JEAN-PAUL BALLAND ○ Sancerre £B Grand Cuvee £C ● Sancerre £B
BALLAND-CHAPUIS ○ Sancerre Le Chêne Marchand £B
DOM. J & C BAUDRY ● Chinon £B
DOM. DE BELLIVIÈRE ○ Coteaux du Loir Vieilles-Vignes Eparses £C ○ Jasnières Les Rosiers £C
BOUVET-LADUBAY ○ Saumur Mousseux Crémant Excellence Brut Saphir Vintage £B
○ Saumur Mousseux Brut Trésor £B ● Saumur Mousseux Brut Rubis £C
DOM. BRETON ● Bourgueil Clos Senechal £B
CH. DE L'AULÉE ● Chinon Cèdre £B
CH. DE BROSSAY ○ Coteaux-du-Layon Vieilles-Vignes Eparses £C
CH. DE COULAINE ● Chinon La Diablesse £C
CH. DAILLARD ○ Touraine-Mesland £B
DOM. DE CH. DAILLARD ● Saumur £B
CH. GAUDRELLE ○ Vouvray Réserve Spéciale £B
CH. LA VARIÈRE ● Anjou-Villages-Brissac Grand Chevalerie £B
CH. DE LA RAGOTIÈRE ○ Muscadet-de-Sèvre-et-Maine Sur Lie Auguste Couillaude £B
CH. DE SAINTE-LOUAND ● Chinon Réserve des Trompegueux £B
CH. DE SOUCHERIE ○ Coteaux du Layon-Beaulieu £E
CH. DE SURONDE ○ Quarts de Chaume £E
CH. DE TIGNÉ ● Anjou-Villages Mozart £C Cyrano £C
DOM. DE CHATENOY ○ Menetou-Salon £B
CHÉREAU-CARRÉ ○ Muscadet-de-Sèvre-et-Maine Chateau Chasseloir £B
PAUL CHERRIER ○ Sancerre £B
FRANÇOIS CHIDAINE ○ Montlouis Demi-Sec Clos Habert £B
CLOS BAUDOIN ○ Vouvray Aigle Sec £B
CLOS DE LA BRIDERIE ○ Touraine-Meslands Vieilles-Vignes £B
CLOS ROCHE BLANCHE ● Touraine Cabernet £B Closerie £B
MAX COGNARD ● Saint-Nicolas-de-Bourgueil Malgagnes £B
DOM. DE CORBILLÈRES ○ Touraine Sauvignon £B
COULY-DUTHEIL ● Chinon Clos de l'Echo £B
JEAN-CLAUDE DAGUENEAU ○ Pouilly-Fumé £C
VINCENT DELAPORTE ○ Sancerre £C
DOM. DELAUNAY ● Bourgueil Prestige £B
DOM DES DORICES ○ Muscadet-de-Sèvre-et-Maine Sur Lie £B
DOM. DE L'ÉCU ○ Muscadet-de-Sèvre-et-Maine Sur Lie £B Expression de Gneiss £B
ANDRE DÉZAT ○ Sancerre £C ● Sancerre £C Vieilles-Vignes £C Fûts de Chêne £C
PIERRE ET ALAIN DÉZAT ○ Sancerre £C
FILLIATREAU ● Saumur-Champigny £B ● Saumur-Champigny Vieilles-Vignes £C
DOM. FOURNIER ○ Menetou-Salon £B
DOM. GADAIS ○ Muscadet-de-Sèvre-et-Maine Sur Lie Vieilles Vignes £B
PIERRE GIRAULT ○ Sancerre Chêne du Roy £C
DOM. GITTON ○ Sancerre Les Belles Dames £C
GRATIEN & MEYER ○ Crémant de Loire £B
DOM. GUINDON ○ Muscadet-Coteaux de la Loire Sur Lie Tradition £B
DOM. JEAN-CLAUDE GUYOT ○ Pouilly-Fumé Les Loges £C
DOM. DE LA HAUTE BORNE ○ Vouvray Sec £B Tendre £B
DOM. DES HAUTES PEMIONS ○ Muscadet-de-Sèvre-et-Maine £B
DE LADOUCETTE ○ Pouilly-Fumé £C Baron de L £E
DOM. LAME DELISLE BOUCARD ● Bourgueil Prestige £B Vieilles Vignes £B
LANGLOIS-CHÂTEAU ○ Saumur Vieilles-Vignes £B ● Saumur-Champigny Château de Varrains £B
DOM. LA ROCHE RENARD ○ Muscadet-de-Sèvre-et-Maine £B
LA TOUR SAINT MARTIN ○ Menetou-Salon Morogues

RENÉ-NOËL LEGRAND ● **Saumur-Champigny** Terrages £B Rogelins £B
J Y LEBRETON ● **Anjou-Villages** Croix de Mission £B
DOM. DES LIARDS O **Montlouis** Demi-Sec Vieilles-Vignes £B
PIERRE LUNEAU O **Muscadet-de-Sèvre-et-Maine** Le L d'Or £B
ALAIN MARCADET ● **Touraine** Sauvignon £B
HENRY MARIONNET ● **Touraine** Premiere Vendange £B O **Touraine** M de Marionnet £C
MASSON-BLONDELET O **Pouilly-Fumé** Angelots £C Cullus £D
DOM. MERLIN CHERRIER O **Sancerre** £B
LOUIS MÉTAIREAU O **Muscadet-de-Sèvre-et-Maine** Cuvée LM £B
FLORIAN MOLLET O **Sancerre** £C O **Pouilly-Fumé** £C
DOM. DE MONTGILET O **Coteaux de l'Aubance** £B Les Trois Schistes £C Le Tertereaux £D
Clos des Huittières £D
DOM. AUX MOINES O **Savennières Roches-aux-Moines** £C
DOM. DE LA MONNAIE O **Savennières** £C
ROGER NEVEU O **Sancerre** £B
DOM. JEAN PABIOT O **Pouilly-Fumé** £C
DOM. DU PETIT VAL O **Bonnezeaux** La Montagne £D
DOM. DES PETITS QUARTS O **Bonnezeaux** £D
DOM. PICHOT O **Vouvray** Sec Coteau de la Biche £B Demi-Sec Peu de la Moriette £B
DOM. PINON O **Vouvray** Sec Tradtion £B
JO PITHON O **Coteaux du Layon-Lambert** Clos des Bonnes Blanches £E O **Quarts de Chaume** £G
DOM. DE LA PRESLE O **Touraine** Sauvignon Blanc £B
DOM. PAUL PRIEUR O **Sancerre** £B ● **Sancerre** £B
DOM. RAIFAULT ● **Chinon** £B Allets £B
DOM. MICHEL REDDE O **Sancerre** Les Tuilières £C O **Pouilly-Fumé** La Moynerie £C
DOM. ROY RENÉ O **Coteaux du Layon-Lambert** Le Cormier £C
RENÉ RENOU O **Bonnezeaux** Les Mellereses £D
PASCAL ET NICOLAS REVERDY O **Sancerre** Vieille-Vignes £C
DOM. RICHOU O **Coteaux de l'Aubance** Cuvée Les Trois Desmoiselles £C
CLAUDE RIFFAULT O **Sancerre** Cuvée Antique £C
JEAN-MAX ROGER O **Sancerre** Cuvee CM £C O **Menetou-Salon** £B
DOM. DU RONCÉE ● **Chinon** Clos des Marronniers £B
DOM. DES SABLONNETTES ● **Anjou** £B O **Anjou** Genêts £B
O **Coteaux du Layon** Champ du Cygne £E
DOM. SAUTEREAU O **Sancerre** Vieilles Vignes £C
PIERRE SOULEZ O **Savennières** Château de Chamboreau £C
JOËL TALUAU ● **Saint-Nicolas-de-Bourgueil** Vieilles-Vignes £B
DOM. THIBAULT O **Pouilly-Fumé** £C
DOM. ANNICK TINEL O **Pouilly-Fumé** £C
DOM. ANDRE VATAN O **Sancerre** Les Perriers £C
DOM. VIGNEAU-CHEVREAU O **Vouvray** Sec £B Sec Clos de Rougemont £C Demi-Sec £B
Moelleux £D

Work in progress!!

Wines from the following producers under consideration for the next edition
ADÉÂ CONSULES (VIN DE PAYS - LOIRE)
AMPELIDÆ (ANJOU SAUMUR)
CH. DE PASSAVANT (ANJOU)
CH. YVONNE (SAUMUR)
DOM. DE LA CHEVALERIE (BOURGUEIL)
DOM. DU COLLIER (SAUMUR)
DOM. DAVIAU (ANJOU-VILLAGES)
DOM DE LA GARRELIÈRE (TOURAINE)
DOM. DES GRIOTTES (ANJOU)

DOM. LES GRANDES VIGNES (ANJOU-VILLAGES)
DOM. RICHARD LEROY (ANJOU/COTEAUX-DU-LAYON)
DOM. MOSSE
DOM. SAINT-NICOLAS (FIEFS-VENDÉENS)
DOM. SAINT-VINCENT (SAUMUR-CHAMPIGNY)

Author's choice (DM)
A diverse selection of sweet whites
PATRICK BAUDOUIN O **Coteaux du Layon** Aprés Minuit

DOM. DES BAUMARD O **Quarts de Chaume**

CH. DE FESLES O **Bonnezeaux**

DOM. DU CLOS NAUDIN O **Vouvray** Moelleux

PHILIPPE DELESVAUX O **Coteaux du Layon** Grains Nobles

OLIVIER DELÉTANG O **Montlouis** Les Petits Boulay Garde Réserve

JOËL GIGOU O **Jasnières** Sélection de Grains Nobles

HUET L'ECHANSONNE O **Vouvray** Haut-Lieu Moelleux

YVES SOULEZ O **Coteaux du Layon** Les Tetuères

TAILLE AUX LOUPS O **Montlouis** Cuvée Romulus

A choice of individual dry whites
DOM. HENRI BOURGEOIS O **Sancerre** Jadis

CH. D'EPIRÉ O **Savennières** Cuveé Spéciale

CH. DE VILLENEUVE O **Saumur** Cormiers

JEAN-CLAUDE CHATELAINE O **Pouilly Fumé** Prestige

CLOS DE LA COULÉE DE SERRANT O **Savennières Coulée de Serrant**

PASCAL COTAT O **Sancerre** Monts Damnés

DIDIER DAGUENEAU O **Pouilly Fumé** Silex

HENRY PELLÉ O **Menetou-Salon** Clos des Blanchais

DOM. DE LA SANSONNIÈRE O **Anjou** La Lune

SILICES DE QUINCY O **Quincy**

The best of the reds
PHILIPPE ALLIET ● **Chinon** Vieilles-Vignes

YANNICK AMIRAULT ● **Saint-Nicolas-de-Bourgueil** Malgagnes

BERNARD BAUDRY ● **Chinon** Croix Boisée

CH. DU HUREAU ● **Saumur-Champigny** Lisgathe

CLOS ROUGEARD ● **Saumur-Champigny** Poyeux

PIERRE-JACQUES DRUET ● **Bourgueil** Vaumoreau

DOM. OGEREAU ● **Anjou-Villages** Côte de la Houssaye

DOM. DES OUCHES ● **Bourgueil** Grande Réserve

DOM. DES ROCHES NEUVES ● **Saumur-Champigny** Marginale

JOËL TALUAU ● **Saint-Nicolas-de-Bourgueil** Vieilles-Vignes

No longer undiscovered gems of French wine, the top vineyards of the Rhône are producing increasingly widely distributed wines of world class. The established and increasing number of Rhône super-cuvées are now some of the most exciting as well as expensive wines in the world. However, there remains a vast sea of simple, sometimes disappointingly poor wine at the bottom end of the market. Two-thirds of all wine made throughout the Rhône Valley is generic AC Côtes du Rhône, although the region is improving fast and smart and slick generic marketing is being allied to generally higher quality standards. It is worth seeking out the ever-increasing number of young growers, mainly in the south, who are endeavouring to produce wines of quality and style at still very fair prices, rather than selling to the co-ops or large négociants.

The Northern Rhône

The northern and southern parts of the valley are very different geographically. The Northern Rhône stretches south down the narrow valley of the River Rhône, from Vienne in the north to Valence in the south. The vineyards of **Côte-Rôtie** are on steep, precipitous terraces and provide some of the world's most challenging viticultural conditions. The name Côte-Rôtie means 'roasted slope'. This may be the most northerly of the Rhône appellations, but the vineyards have a superb aspect facing south-east and the soils are ideal for viticulture – high in minerals, relatively infertile and very well drained.

There are only some 200 ha under vine, with a number of *cru* sections identified. The best quality wine comes from the centre of the appellation. Côte Brune to the north of Ampuis produces wines of fuller body, the Côte Blonde to the south lighter more elegant wines often with Viognier blended in, which is permitted here. The style of Côte-Rôtie is perhaps less overtly muscular than the wines of Hermitage and Cornas and its climate can be very marginal in achieving full ripeness. In great years, when everything comes together at vintage, these wines at their best are quite sublime.

Immediately south of Côte-Rôtie, the vineyards of **Condrieu** continue on the western bank of the river. They are planted on granite and sandstone rather than on the schistous soils to the north. The slope becomes less precipitous and the conditions are more suitable for that uniquely perfumed, aromatic variety Viognier. Widely planted now further afield, from the Languedoc to California, the variety has only come into vogue in the last decade or so. While the weight and aromatic power of the wines can be almost overwhelming, Viognier is a difficult variety to grow and Condrieu lacks the structure of other great French whites. The majority are best drunk in their first two or three years. An increasing number are now barrel-fermented on lees with *bâtonnage* and a few more are produced as late-harvest and very occasionally botrytis-affected wines. The best of these can be stunning.

The most extensive appellation in the north is **Saint-Joseph**. It encompasses the southern part of Condrieu and runs right down the western bank of the river to the borders of Cornas, just to the north of Valence. The reds are produced from Syrah, while the whites are a blend of Marsanne and Roussanne. The best wines are produced from the gravel-based soils close to the river. An impressive number of very good wines, both red and white, have been made in recent years and prices are rising. The best sites have real potential.

The great hill of **Hermitage** and its wines, dark, brooding and powerful, are perhaps the quintessential expression of classic northern Rhône reds. There are many fewer producers here than at Côte-Rôtie and a mere 131 ha of vineyards. The hill is split up into seven different *crus* or *lieux-dits* with varying soil types. One grower, Jean-Louis Chave, is able to draw on all seven in blending his reds. The Syrah is joined by whites based on Marsanne with some Roussanne. These can be remarkably long lived, often more so than the reds. New oak and destemming in the cellar are playing an increasing role and the whites often see barrel-fermentation. More often than not here though, the oak is used rather than new. Red Hermitage should be cellared, as it is slow-developing. The white, too, needs years to show at its best. It can be approachable for a couple of years and then mysteriously close up, so if you plan to drink it young, do so within a year or two or else you will be very disappointed.

Surrounding the hill of Hermitage are the vineyards of **Crozes-Hermitage**. The same grapes are used but the vineyard area is much larger and encompasses some 1,238 ha of vines. The better wines are made on isolated outcrops of granite and there can be a wide variation in quality. The best are very good and generally well-priced and there are an increasing number of relatively highly priced special *cuvées*.

To the south and on the west bank of the river opposite Valence, are the appellations of **Cornas**, which borders southern Saint-Joseph, and immediately to its south Saint-Péray. Cornas is dense and muscular Syrah. It shares more in common with Hermitage than Côte-Rôtie, which is not surprising given its near proximity. A wide range of styles are produced, from the modern oak-influenced wines of Jean-Luc Colombo to the fiercely traditional style of Auguste and Pierre-Marie Clape. At their finest, these are dark-fruited, intense and splendidly long-lived expressions of Syrah.

Many of the Cornas growers also produce the still and sparkling wines of **Saint-Péray**; the still having greater potential on the whole. They are blended from Marsanne and Roussanne, like their white counterparts to the north. A further sparkling wine comes from a little further south-east under the **Clairette de Die** AC, which produces lighter semi-sweet sparkling Muscats. **Crémant de Die** is now the AC for dry sparklers from Clairette. At best they are crisp and fresh. There also some dry white still wines produced under the **Châtillon-en-Diois** appellation, from cool-planted Chardonnay and Aligoté in the same area.

The Southern Rhône

While the north meanders down a narrow river valley, giving it its unique viticultural environment, the southern Rhône covers a much greater area, and is extensively planted with vines. The total vineyard area planted in the north is just under 2,700 ha, whereas the total for the whole region is some 75,000 ha and nearly 42,000 ha of that Côtes du Rhône. The climate is altogether warmer in the south and Grenache is the mainstay variety. There can be a significant influence on the region from the cold Mistral wind, which blows down out of the Alps. While it has some influence in the north, it can cause devastation in the south, with not only physical damage to vineyards but stressing of the vines, causing them to shut down. The same Mistral can on occasion help in ripening fruit close to *vendange* and keeping cellars free of humidity.

The most important quality region in the south is **Châteauneuf-du-Pape**. This is a sizeable appellation with some 3,084 ha of vineyards. Quality has soared in recent very good vintages and an increasing number of growers are now bottling their own wine. The main Châteauneuf variety is Grenache, but there are 13 permitted varieties in the red blend, a number of them white. Syrah and Mourvèdre are also very important in lending structure and grip. The Châteauneuf soils are varied with clay, gravel and stone all playing a role. The larger *galets roulés*, the famous round stones that store up heat and reflect it onto the vines at night are not universally found throughout the appellation and many consider the clay to be the key component in controlling moisture supply.

Among current trends an increasing number of growers are making limited-production special *cuvées* from old vines. While some of these are very splendid wines, there is some question as to whether the quality of the regular bottlings suffers as a consequence. The best red Châteauneuf is rich, heady, almost exotic and very ageworthy. The best will easily continue to improve for a decade or more. The white can be good, floral and nutty and there are some more serious structured wines as well, with oak playing a limited role. In general the whites should be drunk young.

To the north and west of Châteauneuf-du-Pape and the ancient Roman town of Orange are the **Côtes du Rhône-Villages** and the separate appellations of **Gigondas** and **Vacqueyras**. The best vineyards of Gigondas are planted on the slopes of the Dentelles de Montmirail, the small range that merges into the hills of the Vaucluse. The wines are dense, massive and brooding. They tend to lack the refinement of the very greatest Châteauneufs, but they can offer not only excellent quality but also value for money. Like Gigondas, Grenache is the most important variety in Vacqueyras, which was awarded its own AC in 1990. The wines are generally lighter than Gigondas and an increasing amount of Syrah is now being used. There are even some varietal wines being produced. The best have an intoxicating combination of ripe dark berry fruit and a marked *garrigues* character.

There are 16 villages which can append their names after the Côtes du Rhône-Villages name. Among these are **Cairanne**, **Rasteau**, **Sablet** and **Beaumes-de-Venise** to the south and **Valréas**, **Vinsobres** and **Saint-Maurice** further north where, unsurprisingly, the Syrah is planted with greater success. It is the southern villages, though, and particularly Cairanne, which are producing the greatest number of stylish wines. At their best these express vibrant and complex dark fruit and subtle herbal notes. Those wines produced from old vines can be both excellent value and remarkably impressive. Outside these 16 villages there are several thousand hectares of vines producing straight Côtes du Rhône-Villages. A number of very good wines under both this appellation and the humble **Côtes du Rhône** label are now being produced. The latter tend to emphasise their forward fruit, but there are also some very serious and ageworthy wines being produced. Some of the better Rhône-Villages domaines may also have vineyards outside the appellation boundaries, or may chose to label younger-vine *cuvées* as Côtes du Rhône.

There are also two regional specialities, which have their own appellations. **Muscat de Beaumes de Venise** is a floral, grapey fortified Muscat. It is not late-harvested and tends to lack the quality found in the Muscat de Rivesaltes wines of the Roussillon. **Rasteau** is a fortified red *vin doux naturel* produced from Grenache that can develop marked *rancio* notes with cask age. This AC should not be confused with Côtes du Rhône-Villages Rasteau, where some of the best modern southern reds are being made.

To the west of Châteauneuf-du-Pape are the appellations of **Lirac** and **Tavel**. The latter is for rosé only, Lirac for both rosé and, of greater importance from a quality point of view, some very good Grenache-based reds planted in the limestone-rich soils. The rosé can often be excessively high in alcohol and dull. Further to the east is the newly developed appellation of the Costières de Nîmes

Towards the outer extremities of the Rhône are four other appellations. To the north of the Côtes du Rhône-Villages sector, west and east respectively of the River Rhône, are the **Côtes du Vivarais** and the **Coteaux du Tricastin**. To the south in the Vaucluse are the vineyards of the **Côtes du Ventoux**, where encouraging progress is being made by a number of domaines and reds of some substance are being produced. Immediately south again, on the borders of Provence, is the **Côtes du Lubéron**. The odd exciting red is beginning to emerge and there are some stylish whites as well. To the far east towards the Alpes some good reds and whites are also emerging from the **Coteaux de Pierrvert**.

There are a number of *vin de pays* classifications. In the northern Rhône the important one is the **Vin de Pays des Collines Rhodaniennes**, under which some impressive red and white is produced. Two important southern *vins de pays* offering wines largely based on Grenache (but also Cabernet Sauvignon in the case of the former) are the **Vin de Pays de la Principauté d'Orange** and further south the **Vin de Pays de Vaucluse**.

Just to the west of the River Rhône is the emerging region of the **Costières de Nîmes**. Not surprisingly the wine here has more in common with the blends of the southern Rhône than the rest of the Languedoc and for this reason is covered here. Intense, strawberry-scented, Grenache-based reds are being produced by a number of good domaines and increasing use is being made of Mourvèdre. Many of these properties are also making rich, stylish blends of Cabernet Sauvignon and Syrah, generally labelled as **Vin de Pays du Gard**.

A-Z of producers by appellation/commune

NORTHERN RHÔNE

1   Côte Rôtie
2   Château Grillet
3   Condrieu
4   Saint-Joseph
5   Crozes-Hermitage
6   Hermitage
7   Cornas
8   Saint-Péray
9   Côtes du Rhône

SOUTHERN RHÔNE

RHÔNE

1

● Valréas

2

ARDÈCHE

● Nyons

● Visan

● Vinsobres

Saint-Maurice-sur-Eygues

● Bollène

● Cairanne   *3*

Sablet ●

4

● Bagnols-sur-Cèze

● Orange

5

6

2

7

● Châteauneuf-du-Pape   ● Carpentras

8

9

11

● Avignon

GARD

RHÔNE

DURANCE

12

● Nîmes

10

RHÔNE

1	Coteaux du Tricastin
2	Côtes du Rhône/Villages
3	Rasteau
4	Gigondas
5	Vacqueyras
6	Muscat de Beaumes-de-Venise
7	Châteauneuf-du-Pape
8	Lirac
9	Tavel
10	Costières de Nîmes
11	Côtes du Ventoux
12	Côtes du Luberon

● Arles

Rhône Valley vintages

The run of vintages from 1998 to 2001 was remarkable in both the north and south of the Rhône Valley. The wines were either very good or excellent. The best wines from these years are becoming extraordinarily scarce but it is still well worth your while to hunt around for them. 2003 is likely to be worth following as well. Over the same period, the lesser Rhône-Villages wines have performed in a similarly impressive manner to those at Châteauneuf-du-Pape. The top wines will keep very well, 10 even 20 years in the best examples. The lesser wines from recent years will last comfortably for five years or more.

2003: The super warm summer of may result in some superb wines from this vintage in the north. The key will be who has harnessed the ripening of their grape tannins best. Potentially great in the south, some wines will be very alcoholic though and achieving balance with Grenache will be the key.

2002: After the previous four bountiful vintages this was a disappointment. There was very heavy rain in the north requiring extreme care and selectivity by growers to achieve any real quality. In the south it was a similar tale of woe with heavy flooding. The wines are likely to be for early drinking.

2001: This was very good throughout the valley, if not quite hitting the heights of 1999 for the northern appellations or 2000 for the south. Nevertheless these are impressive and cellarworthy examples, a smaller than normal yield helping to ensure this. White Hermitage is very ageworthy.

2000: A generally very good year, particularly in the south with good crop levels and some very rich, profound and complex wines being made. The best are ripe, very full and approachable. Not quite the same quality in the north, but good and very ageworthy wines were produced. Côte-Rôtie is the most successful among the reds.

1999: A very good year throughout the north, with well-structured, opulent and heady wines being produced in all the major appellations. Conditions were excellent with a balmy and dry summer and adequate rainfall. The wines are surprisingly forward and approachable but should be long-lived. The south was good to very good but lacked the sheer quality of 1998 and 2000. The wines will be a little lighter but the best will age very well.

1998: The northern appellations fared well, producing very good results after a solid 1997. The wines are generally sizeable and and masculine in structure. They should turn out to be very good cellaring prospects but without the opulence or elegance of 1999. In the south the vintage was spectacularly good. The wines are immensely opulent, ripe and exotic but have a fine balance and structure. They will be enjoyable in their relative youth but are excellent cellaring prospects.

1997: A generally average year at best in the south after spring frost damage. The summer was very hot and the wines have neither perfect balance nor ripeness. Almost all should be drunk now. The north fared better, with good quality. Saint-Joseph and Crozes-Hermitage are drinking well now.

1996: A pretty moderate year with the best results in the north, where the top wines have higher than normal acidity after a cold wet summer and windy ripening period. Some good wines were produced in a relatively austere style. The south produced soft, forward reds somewhat lacking in structure. They are drinking now and are not for ageing.

1995: Generally the best year since 1990 for reds with the exception of the magnificent 1991 Côte-Rôties. Yields were low but a warm and propitious summer and favourable harvest produced wines of impressive density and extract both in the north and the south. Whites were somewhat less impressive and will be surprisingly short-lived. They should be drunk soon except for the best white Hermitage.

1994: Neither north nor south produced wines with the density or structure of the 95s. They are marked more by their soft tannins and elegance than their power and are for the mid-term. Many are drinking well now.

1993: For much of the north this was a disastrous vintage. Côte-Rôtie was a little better but not much. Châteauneuf-du-Pape produced some soft agreeable reds which need finishing up.

1992: Sadly the vintage was badly affected by rain in September and most wines were light and soft. Most should have been drunk by now.

1991: This was a good to very good year in the northern Rhône and in Côte-Rôtie in particular. There was quite marked variation and some producers were more successful than others, particularly in Cornas and Hermitage. The south was disappointing and the wines should by now have been drunk.

1990: A superb year for great long-lived Hermitage. These will need more time to achieve their full potential. Côte-Rôtie did not quite match the superb 91s. Cornas and Côte-Rôtie are both drinking well now, as are some of the excellent wines produced at Châteauneuf-du-Pape.

1989: A good to very good vintage, particularly at Hermitage and Cornas and in the south for top reds. White Hermitage was also good and is drinking well now as are the generally fleshy reds. These are not the great structured wines of 1990 but are perfect now if you have them cellared or come across them.

1988: This was a very good year for classic northern Rhône reds; the best Hermitage will probably benefit from a little more time. Also tremendous exotic white Hermitage which is drinking well now. Impressive in the south but only the top wines will still be at their best.

Earlier Years: 1985 was good in both the north and the south. 1983 produced some excellent long-lived Hermitage. Châteauneuf-du-Pape in 1981 is worth considering from very top producers. A few good 1979s from both north and south are still drinking well. 1978 was a truly great year in the north, with some very fine Châteauneuf also. Other very good earlier years for the north were 1971, 1970, 1969, 1966, 1964 and 1961.

Rhône Valley vintage chart

	Côte-Rôtie	Red Hermitage	White Hermitage	Châteauneuf-du-Pape
2003	★★★★ A	★★★★ A	★★★★ A	★★★★ A
2002	★★ A	★★ A	★★/★★★★ A	★★ A
2001	★★★★ A	★★★★ A	★★★★/★★★★★ A	★★★★ A
2000	★★★★/★★★★★ A	★★★★ A	★★★★ A	★★★★/★★★★★ A
1999	★★★★/★★★★★ A	★★★★/★★★★★ A	★★★★/★★★★★ A	★★★★ B
1998	★★★★ A	★★★★ A	★★★★ A	★★★★★ B
1997	★★★/★★★★ B	★★★/★★★★ A	★★★/★★★★ A	★★★ C
1996	★★★ B	★★★ B	★★★/★★★★ A	★★/★★★ C
1995	★★★★ B	★★★★ B	★★★/★★★★ C	★★★★ C
1994	★★★/★★★★ C	★★★/★★★★ C	★★★/★★★★ C	★★★ C
1991	★★★★/★★★★★ B	★★★★ B	★★★★ C	★/★★ D
1990	★★★★ C	★★★★★ B	★★★★/★★★★★ B	★★★★/★★★★★ C
1989	★★★★ C	★★★★/★★★★★ C	★★★★ C	★★★★/★★★★★ C
1988	★★★★ C	★★★★ C	★★★★/★★★★★ C	★★★★ C

Northern Rhône

THIERRY ALLEMAND   Cornas   A:**RsW**,Sec,Rae

Owner: Thierry Allemand   22 Impasse des Granges, 07130 Cornas
Small Cornas domaine with just over 3 ha, producing two rich, sturdy and powerful Syrah wines. Total production is tiny at a mere 1,000 cases a year but the quality is very good to exceptional and among the best in the appellation. Vinification is traditional with a long *cuvaison* at high temperatures to extract both flavour and supple, well-rounded tannins. The resulting wines are impressive, concentrated and very elegant. They are both bottled unfiltered. Reynard, made from vines that are over 80 years old, is very ageworthy and will continue to improve for up to a decade, sometimes longer in the best years. (DM)
● **Cornas** Chaillot★★★★ £E Reynard★★★★★ £F

DOM. BALTHAZAR   Cornas   A:**Has**,SVS

Owner: René Balthazar   07130 Cornas
Balthazar produces traditionally vinified and aged Cornas that is generally very good. 2002, 01 and 00 are all ripe and structured, with the depth and complexity of dark berry fruit that can only be coaxed from a vineyard planted with very old vines. Aged in large old wood the wine is nevertheless surprisingly ripe, forward and approachable with just four or five years' ageing. Like many producers in this village Balthazar offers very good value. (DM)
● **Cornas**★★★ £D

GILLES BARGE   Côte-Rôtie   A: C&B,Bib,Tan,SVS,Rae,Sec

Owner: Gilles Barge   8 Boulevard des Allées, 69420 Ampuis
Gilles Barge took over from his father Pierre in the mid-1990s and is now producing excellent Côte-Rôtie, if not in the absolute top flight. He has not only reduced yields from his holdings of around 7 ha but has refined the approach in the cellar as well. The wines are still vinified with stems but the tannins are riper and suppler. They are characterised by elegance and finesse rather than by raw power and are bottled unfiltered. The Cuvée du Plessy is the lighter, more forward of the two, elegant and approachable. Both wines are impressively ageworthy and will improve in bottle for 7 to 10 years. Enjoy his peachy Condrieu and straightforward spicy, berry-fruited Saint-Joseph young. (DM)
● **Côte-Rôtie** Cuvée du Plessy★★★ £E Côte Brune★★★★ £F

ALBERT BELLE   Hermitage   A: **Ear**,Cdp

Owner: Albert Belle   Quartier les Marsuriaux, 26600 Larnage
This young domaine which has been producing good red and white for upwards of a decade. Total vineyard holdings are now close to 18 ha, almost all in Crozes-Hermitage. Reds are made traditionally and destemming is avoided. Good, structured, ageworthy wines result in the best years but there can be an occasional green hint in cooler vintages. The key here is to get the stems as well as the fruit fully ripe at harvest. The white is fully or part-fermented in oak and the Hermitage is fat and toasty with real depth and concentration. The top wines will be all the better for five or six years' cellaring. (DM)
● **Hermitage**★★★ £E
● **Crozes-Hermitage** Les Pierelles★★ £B Cuvée Louis Belle★★★ £C
O **Hermitage**★★★ £D O **Crozes-Hermitage**★ £B

DOM. BONNEFOND   Côte-Rôtie   A:Goe,GWWSVS,Odd,N&P,WAe

Owner: Patrick & Christophe Bonnefond   Mornas, 69420 Ampuis
From their small holding of 6 ha, the Bonnefond brothers produce very good Condrieu and – in their top bottling, Les Rochains – one of the finest of all Côte-Rôties. The style of the reds is modern, with

destemming and new oak in the top *cuvée,* and a really elegant spicy, mineral character shows through in all the wines. The regular bottling is a little light in comparison to Côte Rozier and Les Rochains but is nonetheless ripe and well-structured with the slightest hint of green pepper. Côte Rozier, with 10 per cent Viognier has a characteristic floral undercurrent but with depth and real dimension. Les Rochains is rich, opulent and firmly structured, needing two to three years longer in bottle than the other reds, and should not be broached without five or six years' ageing. Condrieu is opulent, peachy and immediately accessible. (DM)

● **Côte-Rôtie★★★** £E Côte Rozier★★★★ £E Les Rochains★★★★★ £F
○ **Condrieu★★★** £D

DOM. DE BONSERINE Côte-Rôtie   A:Ear

Owner: Richard Dommerc Verenay, 69420 Ampuis
This is a large property for the appellation, which has been developed with considerable outside investment from Georges DUBOEUF among others. It is now the second-largest vineyard owner after GUIGAL with a total of just under 10 ha of Syrah (95 per cent) and Viognier (5 per cent) spread across 17 different parcels. Vinification is modern and the fruit is all destemmed before ageing in barrel. The regular *cuvée,* La Sarrasine, has 5 per cent Viognier blended in whereas the two top wines, Les Moutonnes and La Garde, are both 100 per cent Syrah and are aged in new oak for 24 months, which tends to show through when the wine is very young. These are impressive, modern and opulent examples of the appellation which should be aged for five, even as much as seven, years. (DM)

● **Côte-Rôtie★★★** £D Les Moutonnes★★★ £E La Garde★★★★ £E

BERNARD BURGAUD Côte-Rôtie   A: J&B, BBR, Yap, SVS

Owner: Bernard Burgaud Le Champin, 69420 Ampuis
Just one wine is produced here but it is among the better examples in the appellation. It is made from a number of different sites that are always vinified separately to maximise the wine's complexity. Bernard Burgaud maintains strict control of yields, and a portion of the harvest is regularly sold off after careful sorting. Finally a *saignée* of up to 20 per cent of the juice prior to fermentation results in a wine that is both concentrated and full of character, and which benefits from four to five years' ageing. It always offers good value. (DM)

● **Côte-Rôtie★★★** £E

M CHAPOUTIER Hermitage www.chapoutier.com   A: **Men**, Tan, Sel, BBR, F&M

Owner: Chapoutier family   18 Avenue Dr Paul Durand, 26600 Tain-l'Hermitage
One of the most important *négociants* in the northern Rhône, with the largest vineyard holding on the great Hermitage hill. Interests are not restricted to the Rhône but also include Domaine des BÉATES in Provence and M CHAPOUTIER AUSTRALIA at Mount Benson in South Australia, as well as some fine, chunky Collioure, rich Banyuls and Muscat de Rivesaltes from Roussillon. Côtes du Roussillon is also the source of new reds from Domaine Bila, with a top label Occultum Lapidem, as the Chapoutiers have not been slow to realise the potential of the Agly Valley. Amidst the vast array of Rhône labels the top wines are superbly crafted examples of their appellations. New benchmarks have been set in both Crozes-Hermitage – with the dense, muscular and very concentrated Les Varonniers – and Saint-Joseph, with both red and white Les Granits. These are not cheap but have established new standards that others are following. Côte-Rôtie La Mordorée is a magnificent example of the appellation; even though not quite of the order of the three GUIGAL *super-cuvées* it is still very impressive. Hermitage red and white now comes in a number of guises. Pavillon and L'Ermite are perhaps the finest among the reds and the former is the weightiest and most powerful of the trio. Of the whites Cuvée de l'Orée is now joined by Le Méal. There is no doubting the supreme quality at this level. The wines are remarkably plush, even when relatively young, and very different to a Jean-Louis CHAVE Hermitage. The regular Hermitage Monier de la Sizeranne and Chante Alouette

white pale a little in comparison, but at least won't break the bank. In the south, Châteauneuf-du-Pape is good to very good and Barbe Rac is 100 per cent Grenache. New is the Coteaux du Tricastin Château des Estubiers,with a very good red example of that appellation. At a lower level the wines from lesser appellations can be disappointing. The generic Côtes du Rhône Belleruche labels are light and insubstantial. The top Hermitage wines are labelled with the traditional spelling, Ermitage. (DM)

- ● **Côte-Rôtie** Les Bécasses★★★ £E La Mordorée✪✪✪✪✪ £H
- ● **Hermitage** Monier de la Sizeranne★★★★ £E Le Meal✪✪✪✪✪ £H L'Ermite✪✪✪✪✪ £H
- ● **Hermitage** Le Pavillon✪✪✪✪✪ £H
- O **Hermitage** Chante Alouette★★★★ £E Cuvée de l'Orée✪✪✪✪✪ £H Le Meal✪✪✪✪✪ £H
- O **Hermitage Vin de Paille**✪✪✪✪✪ £H   O **Condrieu**★★ £D
- ● **Crozes-Hermitage** La Petite-Ruche★★ £B Les Meysonniers★★ £C
- ● **Crozes-Hermitage** Les Varonniers★★★★ £E
- O **Crozes-Hermitage** La Petite-Ruche★ £B Les Meysonniers★ £B
- ● **Cornas**★★★ £D   ● **Saint-Joseph** Deschants★★ £C Les Granits★★★★ £E
- O **Saint-Joseph** Deschants★★ £C Les Granits★★★ £D
- ● **Chateauneuf-du-Pâpe** La Bernadine★★★ £D Croix de Bois★★★★ £E Barbe Rac★★★★★ £G
- O **Chateauneuf-du-Pâpe** La Bernadine★★ £D
- ● **Côtes-du-Rhône Villages Rasteau**★ £B   ● **Côtes-du-Rhône Villages Valréas**★ £B
- ● **Coteaux du Tricastin** Ch. des Estubiers★★ £B
- ● **Collioure**★★ £B   ● **Banyuls**★★★ £C Terra Vinya★★★★ £D
- ● **Cotes du Roussillon-Villages** Dom. Bila★★ £B Occultum Lapidem★★★ £C
- O **Muscat de Beaumes-de-Venise**★★ £C   O **Muscat de Rivesaltes**★★★ £C

CH. D'AMPUIS Côte-Rôtie www.guigal.com   A: **JEF**,BBR,C&B

Owner: Marcel Guigal   Château d'Ampuis, 69420 Ampuis

Guigal is rightly famed for the resurrection of the wines of Côte-Rôtie during the 1970s and 80s. His top three red *cuvées*, La Mouline, La Landonne and La Turque, are now sold under the Château d'Ampuis rather than E. GUIGAL label. Super-rich, very extracted and with loads of new oak, they are produced in very limited quantities and not surprisingly sell for stratospheric prices. However, their balance and extraordinary finesse is more important still. All three are truly profound wines with that extra dimension and depth found in only a handful of truly great wines. Perhaps La Turque is the finest. The vinification of each is quite unique. The Côte-Rôtie Château d'Ampuis and Condrieu La Doriane are very good but not of the same order. In 2001 Marcel Guigal purchased the domaine and vineyards of Jean-Louis GRIPPAT, embellishing his estate with top-class sites in both Saint-Joseph and Hermitage. These wines are now labelled Lieu-Dit Saint Joseph and are released under the d'Ampuis label. The Vignes de l'Hospice red remains particularly striking under the new ownership. (DM)

- ● **Côte-Rôtie** Ch. d'Ampuis★★★★★ £E La Mouline✪✪✪✪✪ £H La Turque✪✪✪✪✪ £H
- ● **Côte-Rôtie** La Landonne✪✪✪✪✪ £H
- O **Condrieu** La Doriane★★★★★ £F

CH. GRILLET Château Grillet   A: **Yap**, BBR,Sel,F&M

Owner: Neyret-Gachet family   42410 Vérin

This is in fact a tiny appellation as well as a single estate and one of the smallest in France at around 3 ha. Like Condrieu the wine is produced solely from Viognier and has always been vinified in barrel on its *lees*. Unlike many Viogniers, at its best this wine can be aged. After a period in the doldrums the quality at Grillet has improved somewhat. However there is some way to go before the wine offers the same quality and dimension of the best examples in Condrieu. (DM)

- O **Château Grillet**★★★ £F

DOM. YANN CHAVE Hermitage

A: **GrD**,HHB,L&W,SVS,Gau

Owner: Yann Chave La Burge, 26600 Mercurol
Fine, improving small domaine with 16 ha of Syrah and a tiny amount of Marsanne and Roussanne producing increasingly impressive supple and structured red wines. Vinification is modern and more new wood is being used both for red and white. These are now wines of finesse and depth and the top reds need cellaring. The Crozes-Hermitage Tête de Cuvée and Hermitage will improve in bottle for up to 10 years, the latter for even longer in great years. (DM)

● **Hermitage★★★★** £E
● **Crozes-Hermitage★★** £B Tête de Cuvée★★★ £C
O **Crozes-Hermitage★★** £B Le Rouvre★★★ £C

JEAN-LOUIS CHAVE Hermitage

A: Yap,Adm,BBR,WSc,C&BTan,Sel,F&M

Owner: Gérard et Jean-Louis Chave 37 Avenue de St-Joseph, 07300 Mauves
Utterly splendid ancient domaine, perhaps the finest in the northern Rhône and among the best in France. The Chave family own plots in all seven *lieux-dits* on the Hermitage hill, which contributes to the marvellous complexity and finesse of their wines. Any of the components felt to be below standard will be sold off in order to protect the integrity of the wine. Cuvée Cathelin is a special selection which sees more new wood and is produced only in top years. Both red and white are extraordinarily ageworthy and are not wines to approach in their youth. Also produced are a very good Saint-Joseph and an extraordinary *vin de paille,* the latter only in tiny quantities. (DM)

● **Hermitage**✪✪✪✪✪ £F Ermitage Cuvée Cathelin✪✪✪✪✪ £H
O **Hermitage**✪✪✪✪✪ £F
● **Saint-Joseph★★★** £C

DOM. DU CHÊNE Côte-Rôtie

A: Rev,F&M

Owner: Marc & Dominique Rouvière Le Pêcher, 42410 Chavanay
Marc Rouvière makes small but impressive quantities of both red and white Saint-Joseph, as well as a striking and intensely peachy, honeyed Condrieu. Medium- rather than full-bodied, with a fine lightly mineral structure, this will drink well over three to four years. 2002 was impressively concentrated despite the vintage. In addition to the regular Saint-Joseph bottlings – a good fruit-driven white produced from Marsanne and a medium-weight, spicy, strawberry-scented red – there is a much deeper special Cuvée Anais. Firm and structured in its youth, with rich, dark berry fruit and spicy oak, it should be aged for three or four years to show at its best. (DM)

O **Condrieu★★★★** £E O **Saint-Joseph★★** £C
● **Saint-Joseph★★** £C Cuvée Anais★★★ £D

DOM. LOUIS CHÈZE Condrieu

A:**C&C**,N&P

Owner: Louis Chèze Les Chênes Verts, 26600 Pont-de-l'Isère
Louis Chèze has gradually built up a small domaine of some 20 ha, with the largest plots planted to Syrah in Saint-Joseph. His holding of Viognier in Condrieu is mainly young vines but the wines are stylish and well-crafted with good, nicely integrated oak. The Coteau de Brèze in particular is very fine with rich, peachy, opulent fruit. The white Saint-Joseph emphasises Marsanne's broad, nutty character. The top reds are supple and sufficiently structured to provide excellent drinking with a few years' cellaring. (DM)

O **Condrieu★★★** £D Coteau de Brèze★★★★ £E
● **Saint-Joseph** Ro-Rée★★ £C Cuvée des Anges★★★ £C Caroline★★★ £C
O **Saint-Joseph★★** £B Ro-Rée★★ £C

AUGUSTE CLAPE Cornas A: Yap, Sel, F&M

Owner: Auguste et Pierre-Marie Clape RN 146, 07130 Cornas
Pierre-Marie now makes the wine at this domaine, an established leader in the appellation. The winemaking is fiercely traditional and no new wood is used whatsoever. However, any stems retained during vinification are always fully ripened and the the wines are supple with harmonious tannin and fruit, balanced and very refined. Vines that date from the 1890s contribute to the impressive quality. Cuvée Renaissance is a second wine, made to help maintain the quality of the Cornas. Inevitably from younger vines, it lacks the weight and power of the *grand vin*. Both the spicy Côtes du Rhône red and Saint-Péray offer good value. (DM)

● **Cornas★★★★★** £D Cuvée Renaissance★★ £C
O **Saint-Péray★★** £B
● **Côtes du Rhône★★** £B

CLUSEL ROCH Côte-Rôtie A: L&S, VTr

Owner: Gilbert Clusel et Brigitte Roch 15 Route du Lacat, Verenay, 69420 Ampuis
Among the leading handful of small domaines in Côte-Rôtie, this tiny operation with just 4 ha of Syrah and Viognier produces barely more than 1,000 cases a year. The Côte-Rôties are powerful and structured for the long haul, particularly Les Grandes Places, made from 65- to 70-year-old vines and occasionally of super-five quality. Neither is for drinking young. The Condrieu is good, with attractive peachy Viognier fruit, but lacks the intensity and depth of the reds. (DM)

● **Côte-Rôtie★★★★** £D Les Grandes Places★★★★★ £F
O **Condrieu★★★** £D

DOM. DU COLOMBIER Hermitage A: Bib, Gau, J&B, Tan, HHB, BBR, Bal, SVS

Owner: Florent Viale 2 Route de Chantemerle, 26600 Tain L'Hermitage
Another small, improving northern Rhône domaine. The Viale family own just over 15 ha of vineyards, some with very old vines on the Hermitage hill. They produce around 6,000 cases of wine including a cool-fermented white Crozes-Hermitage, vinified with a touch of oak, and three stylish, complex reds. The Crozes-Hermitage Cuvée Gaby and in particular the Hermitage are powerful, structured reds that benefit from five or six years' cellaring. The Hermitage keeps extremely well. Prices are very fair indeed. (DM)

● **Crozes-Hermitage★★★** £B Cuvée Gaby★★★ £C ● **Hermitage★★★★** £D
O **Crozes-Hermitage★★** £B

JEAN-LUC COLOMBO Cornas A: L&W, HHB, N&P

Owner: Jean-Luc Colombo Chemin Pied la Vigne, 07130 Cornas
This operation is essentially split into two. Domaine Jean-Luc Colombo produces wines from vineyards in and around Cornas and Saint-Péray, whereas the Jean-Luc Colombo label is reserved for an extensive range of *négociant* wines. There are also two separate domaines in the Midi. Domaine de Salente in the Languedoc produces red and white Vins de Pays d'Oc from Syrah and Viognier as well as a Coteaux du Languedoc red, L'Ame de Salente, a structured blend of Syrah, Carignan, Grenache and a smattering of Mourvèdre. Good red Côtes du Roussillon and Muscat de Rivesaltes are produced at Domaine de Saint-Luc and a premium red, La Mission Saint-Luc, has been added here. New reds are also now produced from vineyards in Provence's Coteaux d'Aix-en-Provence and there is a good white Vin de Pays des Bouches-du-Rhône, Les Pins Couchés. The wines are labelled Domaine de la Côte Bleue. Of the Rhône *négociant* wines, which range from ordinary to very good, the Châteauneuf-du-Pape Bartavelles stands out, a powerful, dense, Grenache-based red. Top Cornas *cuvées* Les Ruchets and La Louvée are most impressive. Aged in new oak, the wines are always well-balanced and are some of the best in the appellation. (DM)

Domaine Jean-Luc Colombo
● **Cornas** Les Mejeans★★★ £E Terres Brûlées★★★ £E Les Ruchets★★★★ £F La Louvée★★★★★ £F
Jean-Luc Colombo
● **Hermitage** Le Louet★★★ £E O **Hermitage** Le Louet★★★ £E
● **Saint-Joseph** Le Prieuré★★ £C Les Lauves★★ £C
O **Condrieu**★★★ £E O **Vin de Pays Viognier** Les Ramilles Blanche★★ £B
● **Crozes-Hermitage** La Tuilière★★ £B O **Crozes-Hermitage**★ £B
● **Vin de Pays des Collines Rhodaniennes** Collines de Laure★ £B Syrah la Serine Pointue★★ £B
● **Chateauneuf-du-Pape** Les Bartavelles★★★★ £D
● **Côtes du Rhône** Abeilles★★ £B Les Forots★★★ £C O **Côtes du Rhône** Les Figuières★★ £B
● **Vin de Pays Syrah** Les Ramilles★★ £B
Domaine de Saint-Luc
● **Côtes du Roussillon** La Chance de Saint-Luc ★★ £B O **Muscat de Rivesaltes** Les Saintes★★★ £C

DOM. COMBIER Crozes-Hermitage   A: **Eno**

Owner: Maurice et Laurent Combier RN 7, 26600 Pont de l'Isère
Good stylish and concentrated wines are made at this recently established domaine. The regular red and white wines are well crafted and see some new wood during maturation. The Clos des Grives is altogether more serious and amongst the best in the appellation. The red, which is macerated for around 30 days on skins, is dense and muscular, with refined fruit and supple, balanced tannins. The wine is aged in new oak and requires a little patience before it is ready. The whites are mainly Roussanne, barrel-fermented and kept on their lees with *bâtonnage*. Both will develop well in the medium term. (DM)
● **Crozes-Hermitage**★★ £B Clos des Grives★★★ £C
O **Crozes-Hermitage**★★ £B Clos des Grives★★★ £C
● **Saint-Joseph**★★ £C

DOM. COURBIS Saint-Joseph   A: **Ege**,HHB,Res,SVS

Owner: Dominique Courbis Les Ravières, 07130 Chateaubourg
The bulk of this estate's 26 ha is in Saint-Joseph, with 5 ha planted to white varieties. The average vine age is fairly young. This is to some extent illustrated in the wines, which as yet do not have quite the density or complexity of the best in the appellation. The Cornas bottlings, though, are of a different order. Les Eygats and La Sabarotte are wines of dense muscular power. The latter comes from old vine plantings and is very ageworthy. It is close to five stars in top years like 2001. Both top Cornas will improve for up to a decade with ease. (DM)
● **Saint-Joseph**★★ £B Domaine Les Royes★★★ £C
O **Saint-Joseph**★★ £B
● **Cornas** Champelrose★★★ £C Les Eygats★★★★ £E La Sabarotte★★★★ £E

DOM. PIERRE COURSODON Saint-Joseph   A: **Win**,WSc,BRW

Owner: Pierre et Gilbert Coursodon 3 place du Marché, 07300 Mauves
During the early to mid-1990s the Coursodon wines were sound enough but often possessed a raw, harsh undercurrent. Destemming was not practised and old *foudres* were the order of the day. Jérôme Coursodon has now taken over the winemaking and the results in the late 90s have been impressive, particularly with the top red *cuvées*. The wines have concentrated dark fruit but are more refined and better balanced than of old. The very fine bottling of La Sensonne is produced in association with Patrick LESEC. (DM)
● **Saint-Joseph**★★ £B L'Olivaie★★★ £C Le Paradis St-Pierre★★★ £C La Sensonne★★★★ £D
O **Saint-Joseph**★ £B Le Paradis St-Pierre★★ £C

YVES CUILLERON   Condrieu   www.cuilleron.com   A: **Eno**,A&B,BBR,Swg,P&S,Las,But

Owner: Yves Cuilleron   Verlieu, 42140 Chavanay

One of the new younger superstars of the northern Rhône, Cuilleron is best known for superb Condrieu made in a number of guises including Fleur d'Automne, a very intense and distinctive sweet botrytised example that spends eight months in wood. A new dry wine labelled Vertige was added to the range of Condrieus with the 2001 vintage, which like the others is barrel-fermented and aged on lees. He also produces a small range of first-class Saint-Joseph, both red and white. The whites are barrel-fermented and aged and the reds macerated for three to four weeks and aged in oak. He is also working with François VILLARD and Pierre GAILLARD in a new small-scale *négociant* venture, Les VINS DE VIENNE. An additional Côte-Rôtie and a small range of *vins de pays* are the latest additions. The wines offer generally very good value. (DM)

● **Côte-Rôtie** Coteau de Bassenon★★★★ £E Terres Sombres★★★★★ £F
○ **Vin de Pays Marsanne**★ £B
○ **Condrieu** La Petite Côte★★★★ £D Chaillets Vieilles Vignes★★★★★ £E
○ **Condrieu** Les Ayguets✪✪✪✪✪ £F Fleur d'Automne✪✪✪✪✪ £G
● **Saint-Joseph** Les Pierres Sèches★★ £C Les Serines★★★ £C L'Amarybelle★★★ £C
○ **Saint-Joseph** Coteaux Saint-Pierre★★★ £C Le Lombard★★★★ £C Lyseras★★★ £C

DELAS FRÈRES   Hermitage   A: **BWC**, BBR

Owner: Maison Louis Roederer   2 Allée de l'Olivet, 07300 Saint-Jean-de-Muzols

Once one of the northern Rhône's under-performers, Delas is now a serious player among the top Rhône *négociants*. With the purchase by leading Champagne house Louis ROEDERER and the arrival of Jacques Grange as winemaking chief, the wines have radically improved. The range is comprehensive and even the humbler wines are now sound and well-crafted. Far better fruit quality and well-handled new oak in the better wines are just two of the keys here to the transformation in fortune and quality. Star turns are the top *cuvées*, which are densely textured and explosively rich and concentrated. The outstanding Hermitage Les Bessards and Côte-Rôtie La Landonne are remarkably ageworthy propositions now, demanding at least six to seven years' cellaring. The other top reds and white Hermitage also deserve cellaring. (DM)

● **Côte-Rôtie** Seigneur de Maugiron★★★★ £E La Landonne★★★★★ £G
○ **Condrieu** Galopine★★★ £D Clos Boucher★★★★ £F
○ **Condrieu** Vendange Tardive Brumaire de Bruyère★★★★ £F
● **Hermitage** Marquise de la Tourette★★★ £E Les Bessards✪✪✪✪✪ £H
○ **Hermitage** Marquise de la Tourette★★★ £E
● **Crozes-Hermitage** Les Launes★★ £B Tour d'Albon★★★ £D Le Clos★★★★ £E
○ **Crozes-Hermitage** Les Launes★★ £B
● **Saint-Joseph** François de Tournon★★★ £C Les Challeys★★★ £C Sainte-Épine★★★ £D
○ **Saint-Joseph** François de Tournon★★ £B Les Challeys★★★ £C
● **Cornas** Chante Perdrix★★★ £D
● **Châteauneuf-du-Pape**★★ £C ● **Gigondas**★★★ £C
● **Vacqueyras** Domaine des Genêts★ £B ● **Côtes du Ventoux**★ £A ● **Côtes du Rhône** Saint-Esprit★£B
○ **Côtes du Rhône** Saint-Esprit★ £A

PIERRE DUMAZET   Condrieu   A: **Bib**

Owner: Pierre Dumazet   RN 86, 07340 Limony

Somewhat controversial among Condrieu producers, Dumazet produces wines which are rich, dense and full of classic Viognier dried peaches, spices and minerals. Don't expect modern squeaky-clean fruit-driven wines here. The *vin de pays* and Cuvée du Zenith offer a similar style at a lower level than the Condrieus. Old-fashioned and quite heavily oaked, the Condrieus are at times almost rustic. However they are also characterful, powerful and structured. This is an excellent source of traditional wines from the appellation. (DM)

O **Condrieu**★★★ £D Côte de Fournet★★★★ £E
O **Vin de Pays Viognier**★★ £B   O **Côtes du Rhône** Cuvée du Zenith★★ £B

ERIC ET JOËL DURAND   Cornas
A: N&P,NYg

Owner: Eric et Joël Durand   07130 Châteaubourg
Just two reds are made here from a small holding of some 7 ha. They are traditionally vinified and are bottled unfiltered. Ageing at present is in older barrels and, while the wines are dense and impressively concentrated, they are not quite in the first division. However, the vineyard is still relatively young and the best has probably yet to emerge. Both wines are firmly structured and will age well in the medium term. The Cornas requires four to five years at a minimum. (DM)

● **Cornas**★★★ £C   ● **Saint-Joseph** Les Coteaux★★★ £C

BERNARD FAURIE   Hermitage
A: THt,J&B,HHC

Owner: Bernard Faurie   27 Avenue Hélène de Tournon, 07300 Tournon
Producer of old-style Hermitage and Saint-Joseph from a tiny holding of just 3 ha of vines. The wines are at their best in great years, when they are both ripe and powerful. In lesser vintages the odd green note can creep in. The Hermitage Le Méal packs a real punch of complex old-vine fruit. They demand cellaring for 10 years or more. (DM)

● **Hermitage**★★★ £D   Le Méal★★★★ £E   O **Hermitage**★★★ £D
● **Saint-Joseph**★★ £B   Cuvée Vieilles-Vignes★★★ £D

DOM. DE FAUTERIE   Cornas
A: M&V, Yap

Owner: Sylvain Bernard   07130 Saint-Péray
This is a recently established domaine but assuredly traditional in its approach to viticulture. Sylvain Bernard trained with Jean-Louis CHAVE before establishing his own small holding of vineyards in Saint-Peray, Saint-Joseph and now of most interest in Cornas. The vines in the latter, leased from Guy de Barjac, are around 100 years old and are grown in ideal sandy granite soils with an exceptional and very sunny mesoclimate. The result is a wine with considerable depth, complexity and some power. It will be all the better for five years' ageing. Top recent vintages are particularly impressive. (DM)

● **Cornas**★★★★ £D   O **Saint-Péray** Les Hauts de Fauterie★★ £B

PIERRE GAILLARD   Saint-Joseph
A: HHB,Cav,J&B,L&S,Sel

Owner: Pierre Gaillard   Chez Favier, 42520 Malleval
A diverse range of wines from a scattered 17 ha in Saint-Joseph, Côte-Rôtie and Condrieu. Gaillard also runs to a good Côtes du Rhône Viognier and, when conditions permit, an excellent late-harvest Condrieu and a rare *vin de paille* Jean-Elise. Though small, this is an expanding domaine. The wines are modern and stylish and, given the relative youth of the vines, it is clear that the best is yet to come. New oak is present but not overdone in the best reds. The regular Côte-Rôtie is lighter and more elegant, with the inclusion of Viognier. It like the Saint-Joseph Les Pierres and Clos du Cuminaille is a good medium-term cellaring prospect. The Rose Pourpre is altogether denser and more firmly structured. It requires five or six years' cellaring at a minimum. Gaillard is also the inspiration and one of the partners behind the excellent range at LES VINS DE VIENNE. (DM)

● **Côte-Rôtie**★★★ £D   Rose Pourpre★★★★ £E
O **Condrieu**★★★★ £E
● **Saint-Joseph**★★★ £C   Les Pierres★★★ £C   Clos du Cuminaille★★★★ £C
O **Saint-Joseph**★★★ £C   O **Côtes du Rhône** Viognier★★★ £C

DOM. YVES GANGLOFF   Condrieu   A: **Rae**,M&V,F&M

Owner: Mathilde & Yves Gangloff 2 Rue de la Garenne, 69420 Condrieu

Yves Gangloff has been established here for nearly 20 years and has gradually built up a small holding in the same way as many of his neighbours. He now has 3.5 ha. The rich and opulent Condrieu is sourced from two separate parcels, La Bonnette and Chéry, adding to the wine's complexity. For Viognier it is finely structured with sufficient grip to develop well over four or five years. There are two Côte-Rôties, Barbarine, which is blended with a little Viognier and produced from younger vines, and the sturdier Sereine Noir, which is partly aged in new wood. Both are very impressive, with the Sereine Noir requiring five years or so to show at its best. (DM)

● **Côte-Rôtie** Barbarine★★★★ £D Sereine Noir★★★★★ £E
O **Condrieu**★★★★ £E

JEAN-MICHEL GERIN   Côte-Rôtie   A: **C&C**,IVV,Blx

Owner: Jean-Michel Gerin 19 Rue de Montmain, Verenay, 69420 Ampuis

Jean-Michel Gerin's 9 ha are the source of some fine rich and modern Côte-Rôtie with an emphasis on dark, brambly and chocolaty fruit. New oak is not used sparingly either. Champin Junior and Champin Le Seigneur are a little light but La Landonne and Les Grandes Places, which is produced from vines that are over 80 years old, are very good indeed. Modern and oaky they may be but the wines are superbly crafted and display a fine balance of complex fruit and firm but supple rounded tannins. These top *cuvées* need five years or so of ageing at a minimum and will keep much longer. (DM)

● **Côte-Rôtie** Champin Junior★★ £C Champin Le Seigneur★★★ £E
● **Côte-Rôtie** Les Grandes Places★★★★★ £F La Landonne★★★★★ £F
O **Condrieu** Coteau de la Loye★★ £D
● **Côtes du Rhône**★ £B

ALAIN GRAILLOT   Crozes-Hermitage   A:Yap, L&W, ABy,Sel

Owner: Alain Graillot Les Chênes Verts, 26600 Pont-de-l'Isère

In barely two decades Alain Graillot has become a benchmark, if not *the* benchmark, producer of Crozes-Hermitage, both white and red. Others are now emerging and new special bottlings from the likes of CHAPOUTIER may challenge him but he has been the inspiration for an appellation that for too long represented mediocrity. Yields are kept in check but green harvesting is not practised. Graillot considers winter pruning sufficient to set the yield for the year, the productivity of his vineyard being fully in balance. The white is vinified in wood and *inox* and kept on lees and the reds given an extended maceration of up to 21 days. The special *cuvée* La Guiraude is a very impressive barrel selection. The reds, particularly La Guiraude, will age very well. (DM)

● **Crozes-Hermitage**★★★ £B La Guiraude★★★★ £C   O **Crozes-Hermitage**★★ £B
● **Hermitage**★★★ £D **Saint-Joseph**★★★ £C

E GUIGAL   Côte-Rôtie   www.guigal.com   A: **JEF**,AAA

Owner: Marcel Guigal Château d'Ampuis, 69420 Ampuis

The E. Guigal label covers an extensive range produced from the length and breadth of the Rhône Valley. The firm is far and away the largest producer of Côte-Rôtie and also owns Domaine de VALLOUIT as well as the merchant house of VIDAL FLEURY. The vibrant red Côtes du Rhône, if not quite of the quality of a decade ago, remains a model of consistency. The Côte-Rôtie Brune et Blonde, which is sourced mainly from bought-in fruit, is good rather than great. More impressive is the Hermitage, which is dense and concentrated. It generally offers very fair value for the appellation. The southern Rhône wines in general lack the quality and refinement of their northern counterparts. The top Guigal wines appear under the separate CHÂTEAU D'AMPUIS label. (DM)

● **Côte-Rôtie** Brune et Blonde★★★ £D O **Condrieu**★★★ £D
● **Hermitage**★★★★ £D O **Hermitage**★★★ £D
● **Châteauneuf-du-Pape**★★★ £D ● **Gigondas**★★ £C
● **Côtes du Rhône**★ £B O **Côtes du Rhône**★ £B

PAUL JABOULET AINÉ   Hermitage   www.jaboulet.com   A: **DAy**,Tan,BBR,WSc,F&M

Owner: Jaboulet family   Les Jalets, La Roche-sur-Glun, 26600 Tain-l'Hermitage

Large *négociant* operation with some 100 ha of their own vineyards, 84 of which are planted to Syrah. As such they have the largest holding of vineyards producing under their own label of the big Rhône merchant houses. An extensive range is produced but the main focus is the northern Rhône appellations. The Jaboulet name is most famous for one massive and very ageworthy *cuvée* of red Hermitage, La Chapelle. With dense and dark fruit, the wine is more approachable than, say, a Jean-Louis CHAVE but not as modern and opulent as a top CHAPOUTIER. Recent vintages have not been quite so good, although 2000 looks to be back on fine form. There is also a much lighter second red Hermitage, Le Pied de la Côte, produced from younger vines. During the 1990s the Raymond Roure property was added to the portfolio and with the dense and chocolaty Thalabert offers good to very good quality in Crozes-Hermitage. Domaine de Saint-Pierre Cornas is powerful and tannic in its youth and the Châteauneuf-du-Pape Les Cèdres has been better of late. Top wines are ageworthy but the lesser appellations should be approached young. (DM)

● **Côte-Rôtie** Les Jumelles★★ £E
O **Condrieu** Les Cassines★★ £D
● **Hermitage** La Chapelle✪✪✪✪✪ £G O **Hermitage** Chevalier de Sterimberg★★★★ £E
● **Crozes-Hermitage** Les Jalets★ £B Raymond Roure★★★ £C Thalabert★★★ £C
O **Crozes-Hermitage**★ £B Raymond Roure★★ £C Mules Blanche★★ £C
● **Cornas** Les Grandes Terrasses★★ £C Domaine de St Pierre★★★ £D
● **Saint-Joseph** La Grand Pompée★ £B O **Saint-Joseph** La Grand Pompée★★ £B
● **Châteauneuf-du-Pape** Les Cèdres★★★ £D ● **Vacqueyras**★★ £B
● **Gigondas** Pierre Aiguille★★ £C
O **Muscat de Beaumes-de-Venise**★★★ £C

DOM. JAMET   Côte-Rôtie   A: **Bib**,C&B,IVV

Owner: Jean-Paul et Jean-Luc Jamet   Le Vallin, 69420 Ampuis

Brothers Jean-Luc and Jean-Paul Jamet own 6.5 ha of Syrah and a tiny amount of Viognier. They make a sumptuous, almost opulent Côte-Rôtie which has marvellous balance and poise. The oak is seamlessly handled and the wine is bottled unfiltered. Not only is this one of the finest examples of the appellation but it also represents excellent value for money. 1999 was of super-five quality. An attractive light and vibrant Syrah is also produced from young vines and classified as Vin de Pays des Collines Rhodaniennes. (DM)

● **Côte-Rôtie**★★★★ £E

DOM. JASMIN   Côte-Rôtie   A:**Yap**,F&M

Owner: Patrick Jasmin   14 Rue des Maraîchers, 69420 Ampuis

Patrick Jasmin took over the running of this fine, traditional domaine after his late father Robert's early death. Patrick continues to make the wines in a traditional and elegant style. However destemming is now employed, which helps in lesser years, and the wine is aged for around two years in mainly old wood. Never blockbusters, there is always great purity of fruit and impressive intensity and depth in these wines. Top years like 2001 and 00 require 7 to 10 years' ageing. (DM)

● **Côte-Rôtie**★★★★ £

DOM. DU MONTEILLET   Condrieu   A: Cdp,Goe,GWW,Gau,SVS

Owner: Antoine et Stéphane Montez   Le Montelier, 42140 Chavanay

Stéphane Montez runs this small family domaine in Condrieu. The property consists of some 7 ha in

Condrieu, Côte-Rôtie and Saint-Joseph. Vinification is modern and plenty of new oak is used in the top *cuvées*. The Condrieu is rich and peachy but has a fine minerally backbone. The top *cuvée* Les Grandes Chaillées is particularly impressive. Both should develop well over three or four years. A late-harvest label, Tries Grains de Folie, is also produced when conditions permit. The reds are ripe and spicy; both the Cuvée Papy and Côte-Rôtie are wines of considerable dimension and should be cellared for a good four or five years. (DM)

● **Côte-Rôtie** Fortis★★★★ £E
O **Condrieu**★★★★ £D Les Grands Chaillees★★★★★ £E Tries Grains de Folie★★★★★ £F
● **Saint-Joseph** Fortior★★★ £C Cuvée Papy★★★ £C O **Saint-Joseph**★★ £C

DOM. DU MURINAIS   Crozes-Hermitage   A: OWL, GVV

Owner: Catherine & Luc Tardy   Quartier Champ Bernard, 26600 Beaumont-Monteux
This is an impressive producer of well priced Crozes-Hermitage with 12.5 ha of Syrah and a mere 0.5 ha planted to Marsanne. The Tardys produce a little under 4,000 cases a year. The white is good and lightly nutty with moderate depth and intensity. The 2001 was particularly successful. The reds are a step up, particularly the densely structured Vieilles Vignes bottling from vines that are over 30 years old. A special selection Cuvée Valentin will also now be produced in exceptional years. (DM)

● **Crozes-Hermitage** Cuvée Amandier★★ £B Vieilles Vignes★★★ £C
O **Crozes-Hermitage** Cuvée Marine★★ £B

DOM. NIERO-PINCHON   Condrieu   A: **M&V**, SVS, PWa

Owner: Robert Niero   20 Rue Cuvillère, 69420 Condrieu
Robert Niero has been in charge of this fine domaine since the 1980s. The vineyard holding is typically small, with some 3 ha in Condrieu and a small parcel within Les Viaillères in Côte-Rôtie. Insecticides are never used and the vines tended as naturally as possible. Les Ravines is part vinified in *inox* and part in old wood and is elegant and lightly mineral with less overt peachy, honeyed character than others. The Coteau de Chéry comes from old vines, some approaching 60 years, and the wine is fuller and more opulent with an added dimension and greater weight and concentration. The Côte-Rôtie is lighter than some of his neighbours' examples but very elegant, not least because of the 10 per cent Viognier in the blend. Both Condrieus should be drunk young but the Côte-Rôtie will benefit from five years' cellaring. (DM)

● **Côte-Rôtie**★★★★ £E
O **Condrieu** Les Ravines★★★ £E Coteau de Chéry★★★★ £E

DOM. MICHEL OGIER   Côte-Rôtie   sogier@club-internet.fr   A: **CTy**, BBR, N&P

Owner: Michel & Stephane Ogier   3 Chemin du Bac, 69420 Ampuis
Some exceptional Côte-Rôtie is made at this 3.5 ha property as well as very good *vin de pays* La Rosine from vineyards just to the south of Ampuis towards Condrieu. Winemaking is modern and the fruit is always destemmed prior to fermentation. New oak is used both for the regular Côte-Rôtie as well as for the limited-release special bottlings, Belle Hélène, Les Embruns and Lancement, the latter two released for the first time with the 2001 vintage. The wines are supple and velvety, with a real dimension to the fruit. The Belle Hélène has become established as one of the *super-cuvées* of the appellation and as such is very pricey. (DM)

● **Côte-Rôtie**★★★★ £E ● **Vin de Pays des Collines Rhodaniennes** La Rosine★★★ £C

DOM. ANDRÉ PERRET   Côte-Rôtie   A: VTr, L&W, CTy, WTs, M&V

Owner: André Perret   Verlieu, 42410 Chavanay
André Perret took over the family domaine in 1982 and now has some 10 ha of vines from which he produces Condrieu, Saint-Joseph, Côtes du Rhône and varietals. The Condrieus are some of the finest of the AC. These and the white Saint-Joseph are vinified in a combination of *inox* and oak, some of it new

and kept on lees. The reds are fully destemmed and spend two to three weeks on their skins. Some late-harvest grapes are also included in the blend, adding greater complexity. Les Grissières is dense and dark with ripe, black pepper notes. It will age well. Varietal Syrah and Marsanne are produced as *vins de pays* and offer attractive early drinking. (DM)

O **Condrieu**★★★ £D   Clos Chanson★★★★ £E   Coteau du Chéry★★★★★ £F
● **Saint-Joseph**★★ £B   Les Grissières★★★ £C   O **Saint-Joseph**★★ £B

DOM. ÉTIENNE POCHON   Crozes-Hermitage   A:J&B,GBa,L&W,WSc

Owner: Etienne Pochon   Château de Curson, 26600 Chanos Curson
Étienne Pochon makes straightforward, attractively fruity regular red and white Crozes-Hermitage and a special Château de Curson bottling of each. Theses are vinified using more oak and are a significant step up in quality. The property consists of a total of 18 ha with 14 planted to Syrah plus around 3 ha of Roussanne and a single hectare of Marsanne. The Curson white is dominated by Roussanne and is enticingly floral as well as lightly toasty and spicy. The red Curson is weighty but supple and will benefit from two or three years' cellaring. (DM)

● **Crozes-Hermitage**★★ £B   Cuvée Château de Curson★★★ £C
O **Crozes-Hermitage**★ £B   Cuvée Château de Curson★★★ £C

DOM. DES REMIZIÈRES   Crozes-Hermitage   A: Bib, SVS

Owner: Philippe Desmeure   Route de Romans, 26600 Mercurol
This 27-ha property has greatly improved in recent vintages. At best the wines used to be no more than middle-ranking examples of their appellations. The reds are now deep and intense. The Hermitage Émilie is powerful and structured with considerable grip but there is also real concentration and old-vine complexity here. Patrick LESEC also produces his own *cuvée* of the same wine in association with Philippe Desmeure. The Cuvée Christophe red is ripe and full of dark fruit, needing three or four years' ageing, while the whites display all the nutty, pure character of Marsanne at its best. The wines also represent very good value. (DM)

● **Hermitage** Cuvée Émilie★★★★ £E   O **Hermitage** Cuvée Émilie★★★★ £E
● **Crozes-Hermitage** Cuvée Christophe★★★ £C   O **Crozes-Hermitage** Cuvée Christophe★★★ £B
● **Saint-Joseph**★★ £C

RENÉ ROSTAING   Côte-Rôtie   A: **Mis**, BBR, J&B, HHB, GBa,SVS

Owner: René Rostaing   69420 Ampuis
Rostaing is now one of the very best producers of great Côte-Rôtie. He is continually seeking to keep yields in check, to harvest at optimum ripeness and to minimize handling in the cellar. The wines are uniformly bottled without filtration. He has tremendous vineyards to draw upon, having taken over the running of those of Albert Dervieux-Thaize as well as Marius Gentaz-Dervieux. The wines are deep and extracted but always refined and with supple, finely crafted, velvety tannins. The top *cuvées* are very ageworthy. They will improve in bottle for a decade or more. La Landonne is dense, massive in its youth, while the Côte Blonde is lighter and typically more elegant as one might expect from vines planted in these soils. The Condrieu is marked by glorious ripe, peachy varietal fruit and should be drunk young. (DM)

● **Côte-Rôtie**★★★ £D   Classique★★★ £E   La Viallières★★★★ £E
● **Côte-Rôtie** La Landonne★★★★★ £F   Côte Blonde❂❂❂❂❂ £G
O **Condrieu** La Bonnette★★★★ £E

MARC SORREL   Hermitage   marc.sorrel@wanadoo.fr   A: CTy,Gau,NYg

Owner: Marc Sorrel   Avenue Jean-Jaurès, 26600 Tain-l'Hermitage
The top *cuvées*, both red and white, are some of the finest expressions of the great wines of the Hermitage hill. The regular bottlings, in particular the red, can be a touch disappointing and should often have more

depth and substance. 2001, though, looks to be more impressive and Le Gréal potentially exceptional. The red Crozes-Hermitage is a reasonable example with moderately intense, dark berry fruit in a lighter style than some but stylish for what it is. What marks out Le Gréal is its powerful, dense and complex fruit and backward structure. If you give it seven or eight years at least you'll be rewarded with a great example of the appellation. In exceptional years, among them 1998, 91 and 90, this can be legendary. Les Rocoules is an equally fine, but equally backward example of great Marsanne. Honeyed, nutty and complex with age, this really needs at least ten years. (DM)

● **Hermitage★★★** £D Le Gréal★★★★★ £F
O **Hermitage★★★** £D Les Rocoules★★★★★ £F
● **Crozes-Hermitage★★** £B   O **Crozes-Hermitage★** £B

CAVE DE TAIN L'HERMITAGE   Hermitage   A: **PBW**,AAA

Owner: Co-operative members   22 Route de Larnage, BP 3, 26601 Tain-l'Hermitage Cedex
The growers belonging to this co-operative have a considerable holding, in total some 1,000 ha, planted throughout the region and production is around 475,000 cases a year. The range is fairly extensive and there are varietal *vins de pays* as well as AC bottlings. These are sound but relatively unexciting. It is the top bottlings within each appellation, labelled as Nobles Rives, which particularly stand out. There are also special superior *cuvées* of Hermitage and Crozes-Hermitage red. The former, Gambert de Loche, is from an individual plot of old vines. It is dense, rich and very complex, impressive indeed for a co-op wine. A further special bottling from Saint-Joseph, Esprit de Granit, has also been added to the range and this should enhance the quality of the somewhat disappointing regular Saint-Joseph. Occasionally a little *vin de paille* is also produced, which is rich, intense and nutty. (DM)

● **Hermitage** Les Nobles Rives★★ £D Gambert de Loche★★★ £E
O **Hermitage** Les Nobles Rives★★★ £D
● **Crozes-Hermitage** Les Nobles Rives★ £B Les Hauts du Fief★★ £C
O **Crozes-Hermitage** Les Nobles Rives★ £B
● **Cornas** Les Nobles Rives★★ £C
● **Saint-Joseph** Les Nobles Rives★ £B

DOM. DU TUNNEL   Saint-Péray   A:HHB,Gau,Lib,FCA

Owner: Stéphane Robert   20 Rue de la République, 07130 Saint-Péray
Very good Saint-Péray as well as Cornas are made at this 3.5-ha property which was established as recently as 1996. The regular Saint-Péray is fresh, forward and attractively nutty, while the Prestige is denser and altogether more concentrated. The two Cornas are both splendid wines made from ancient vineyard plantings; the Prestige comes from a parcel of 80-year-old vines originally farmed by Marcel JUGE. The wines are dense, sumptuous and full of classic dark fruit, spice and black pepper, the Prestige characterised by complex old-viney fruit. The 2001 was particularly impressive. A small amount of well-crafted Saint-Joseph is also made. (DM)

● **Cornas★★★** £D Prestige★★★★ £E   ● **Saint-Joseph★★★** £C
O **Saint-Péray★★** £B Prestige★★★ £C

DOM. GEORGES VERNAY   Condrieu   A:Yap,Win, Cco

Owner: Georges Vernay   1 Route National, Condrieu 69420
Vernay is one of the great Condrieu producers. His daughter Christine now runs the domaine and they possess some 9 ha of Viognier and a further 7 ha of Syrah from which they are making increasingly impressive Côte-Rôtie, an appellation they used to struggle with. There has been some consultancy for the reds from Jean-Luc COLOMBO. Other reds are a simple red *vin de pays*, a sound fruit-driven Côtes du Rhône and a Saint-Joseph that as yet lacks the depth of the Côte-Rôties. Good white *vin de pays* Viognier is made from the youngest vines but it is the three Condrieus that are the main focus here. Terasses de l'Empire, the regular bottling, is well-crafted but lacks a little depth. The other two wines are part barrel-

fermented and of serious depth and weight; Chaillées de L'Enfer is just a little more opulent and heady. Both will develop well in the short term. (DM)

● **Côte-Rôtie** Blonde du Seigneur★★★ £E Cuvée Maison Rouge★★★★ £E
O **Condrieu** Les Terrasses de L'Empire★★★ £D Les Chaillées de L'Enfer★★★★ £E
O **Condrieu** Coteau du Vernon★★★★ £E   O **Vin de Pays** Viognier Le Pied de Samson★★ £C
● **Saint-Joseph**★ £B

FRANÇOIS VILLARD   Condrieu   A: **HHB**,

Owner: François Villard   Montjoux, 42410 Saint-Michel-sur-Rhône
Out of a total of 9 ha of vineyards, 3.5 ha are in Condrieu, where three fine dry examples of the appellation are produced. Vinified in new oak on their lees with careful *bâtonnage*, they have considerable depth and structure for Viognier and age uncharacteristically well. A sweet Condrieu, Quintessence, is also made as are very good Côte-Rôtie and red and white Saint-Joseph. The range is completed by *vin de pays* bottlings of impressive quality. A Merlot has been introduced to join the Syrah and Viognier. François is involved with Pierre GAILLARD and Yves CUILLERON in Les VINS DE VIENNE. (DM)

● **Côte-Rôtie** la Brocarde★★★★★ £E
● **Vin de Pays des Collines Rhodaniennes** Syrah★★ £B
O **Vin de Pays des Collines Rhodaniennes** Viognier Contours de Deponcins★★★ £C
O **Condrieu** Grand Vallon★★★ £E Les Terrasses du Palat★★★★ £E Coteaux de Poncin★★★★★ £E
O **Condrieu** Quintessence✪✪✪✪✪ £G
● **Saint-Joseph** Côtes de Mairlant★★★ £C Reflet★★★★ £D
O **Saint-Joseph** Côtes de Mairlant★★★★ £C

LES VINS DE VIENNE   Côte-Rôtie   A: **Goe**,C&B,BBR,Lay

Owner: Yves Cuilleron, Pierre Gaillard & François Villard   Le Bas de Seyssuel, 38200 Seyssuel
A recently established small-scale operation that is part domaine and part *négociant*. The three partners are re-establishing the pre-phylloxera vineyards of the Côteaux du Seyssuel to the west of Vienne. This once famous area, known to Pliny and Plutarch, produces the red Sotanum, a wine of real potential, and a partially barrel-aged Viognier, Taburnum. The vines are as yet very young at six years and the wines are likely to improve considerably as they age. The *négociant* offerings range from good to exciting. New oak is evident in all the wines but is well handled. One criticism might be that the character of the individual appellations can struggle to show through. The Côte-Rôtie Les Essartailles and Condrieu La Chambée particularly stand out. The best are undoubtedly very ageworthy. (DM)

● **Vin de Pays des Collines Rhodaniennes** Sotanum★★★★ £C
O **Vin de Pays des Collines Rhodaniennes** Taburnum★★★ £C
● **Côte-Rôtie** Les Essartailles★★★★★ £E
O **Condrieu** La Chambée★★★★ £E
● **Hermitage** Les Chirats de Saint-Christophe★★★ £E
O **Hermitage** La Bachole★★★ £E
● **Crozes-Hermitage** Les Palignons★★ £C   O **Crozes Hermiotage** Les Chaponnières★★ £C
● **Cornas** Les Barcillants★★★ £D
● **Saint-Joseph** L'Arzelle★★ £C   O **Saint-Joseph** L'Elouède★★ £C
O **Saint-Péray** Les Bialères★★★ £B
● **Châteauneuf du Pape** Les Oteliées★★★ £C
● **Gigondas** Les Pimpignoles★★★ £D   ● **Vacqueyras** La Sillote★★ £B
● **Côtes du Rhône-Villages Visan** La Tine★★★ £B   ● **Cairanne** La Perpendaille★★★ £B
● **Côtes du Rhône** Les Cranilles★★ £B   O **Côtes du Rhône** Les Laurelles★★ £B

ALAIN VOGE   Cornas   A: GWW, VTr, SVS

Owner: Alain Voge   4 Rue de l'Equerre, 07130 Cornas
As well as his very powerful and muscular Cornas, Alain Voge also produces some of the best Saint-Péray,

both dry and sparkling. The Mélodie William and Harmonie are unoaked and marked by impressive nutty Marsanne fruit, while the Cuvée Boisée sees some new oak. The top Fleur du Crussol is amongst the very finest in the appellation. His Cornas vineyards are of increasingly venerable age and this is showing through in the wines with immensely complex smoky dark fruits and black spices emerging in the Vieilles Vignes and Vieille Fontaines bottlings. A very small amount of new oak is used to barrel-age the wines, which you should expect to cellar for five years or more. (DM)

● **Cornas**★★★ £D Vieilles Vignes★★★★ £E Vieilles Fontaines★★★★★ £E

○ **Saint-Péray** Cuvée Mélodie William★★ £B Cuvée Harmonie★★ £B Cuvée Boisée★★★ £B

○ **Saint-Péray** Cuvée Fleur du Crussol★★★ £B Dry Vintage★ £B

NORTHERN RHÔNE/OTHER WINES OF NOTE

GUY DE BARJAC ● **Cornas** £D

DOM. DE BIGUET ● **Cornas** £D

DOM. BOISSEYT-CHOL ● **Côte-Rôtie** £E

DOM. FRÉDÉRIC BOISSONET ○ **Condrieu** £E Les Rochains £E

JOEL CHAMPET ● **Côte-Rôtie** £E

CH. MONTLYS ● **Côte-Rôtie** £E

CH. DU ROZAY ○ **Condrieu** £D

CAVE DES CLAIRMONTS ● **Crozes-Hermitage** £B ○ **Crozes-Hermitage** £B

MARTIN DAUBRÉE ● **Côte-Rôtie** Côte Brune £D

EDMOND ET DAVID DUCLAUX ● **Côte-Rôtie** £E

OLIVIER DUMAINE ● **Crozes-Hermitage** £B ○ **Crozes-Hermitage** £B

DOM. DUMIEN-SURETTE ● **Cornas** Vieilles Vignes £D

DOM. DES ENTREFAUX ● **Crozes-Hermitage** £B Les Marchonnières £D

CHRISTIAN FACCHIN ○ **Condrieu** Les Grands-Maison £E

PHILIPPE FAURY ● **Saint-Joseph** £C ● **Côte-Rôtie** £E ○ **Condrieu** La Berne £E

CAVE FAYOLLE ● **Hermitage** £D ○ **Hermitage** £D

DOM. FERRATON ● **Hermitage** Les Miaux £E Le Méal £F ○ **Hermitage** Le Reverdy £F

GILLES FLACHER ● **Saint-Joseph** Prestige £C ○ **Condrieu** £D Cuvée Lea £E

DOM. GACHON ● **Saint-Joseph** £C

HENRI GALLET ● **Côte-Rôtie** £E

VINCENT GASSE ● **Saint-Joseph** £C ● **Côte-Rôtie** £D Vieilles Vignes £E

DOM. GONON ● **Saint-Joseph** £C ○ **Saint-Joseph** Les Oliviers £C

DOM. BERNARD GRIPA ● **Saint-Joseph** £C Le Berceau £C ○ **Saint-Joseph** Le Berceau £C
○ **Saint-Péray** £B Les Figuières £C

DOM. MARCEL JUGE ● **Cornas** Cuvée C £D

JACQUES LEMENCIER ● **Cornas** £D

BERNARD LEVET ● **Côte-Rôtie** £D La Chavaroche £E

DOM. JEAN LIONNET ● **Cornas** £C Rochepertuis £E

ROBERT MICHEL ● **Cornas** Cuvée de Coteaux £C La Geynale £D

DOM. MOUTON ● **Côte-Rôtie** £E ○ **Condrieu** Côte Bonnette £E Côte Chatillons £E

ALAIN PARET ● **Côtes du Rhône** Valvigneyre £B ○ **Condrieu** Lys de Volan £D

VINCENT PARIS ● **Cornas** Granit 60 £E

DOM. PAVILLON-MERCUROL ● **Crozes-Hermitage** £B

CHRISTOPHE PICHON ● **Saint-Joseph** £C ○ **Condrieu** £D

PHILIPPE PICHON ● **Saint-Joseph** £C ○ **Condrieu** £D

JEAN-PAUL REMILLIER ● **Côte-Rôtie** £E

HERVÉ RICHARD ● **Côte-Rôtie** L'Amarage £D

GILLES ROBIN ● **Crozes-Hermitage** Alberic Bouvet £B ● **Crozes-Hermitage** Les Marelles £B

DOM. ERIC ROCHER ● **Saint-Joseph** Terroir de Champal £C

CAVE CO-OPÉRATIVE DE SAINT DÉSIRAT ● **Saint-Joseph** £B

JEAN-MICHEL STEPHAN ● **Côte-Rôtie** £D Coteau de Tupin £E Vieilles Vignes En Coteau £F

JEAN-LOUIS THIERS ● **Cornas** £D
DOM. DE VALLOUIT ● **Côte-Rôtie** Les Roziers £E ● **Hermitage** Les Greffières £F
DANIEL VERNAY ● **Côte-Rôtie** £D
NOËL VERSET ● **Cornas** £E
VIDAL FLEURY ● **Côte-Rôtie** £E La Chatillon £F ● **Cairanne** £B ○ **Condrieu** £E

Author's choice (DM)

10 of the Northern Rhone's most distinguished reds
THIERRY ALLEMAND ● **Cornas** Reynard
M CHAPOUTIER ● **Hermitage** Le Pavillon
CH. D' AMPUIS ● **Côte-Rôtie** La Turque
JEAN-LOUIS CHAVE ● **Hermitage** Ermitage Cuvée Cathelin
AUGUSTE CLAPE ● **Cornas**
CLUSEL ROCH ● **Côte-Rôtie** Les Grandes Places
PAUL JABOULET AINÉ ● **Hermitage** La Chapelle
DOM. JAMET ● **Côte-Rôtie**
RENÉ ROSTAING ● **Côte-Rôtie** Côte Blonde
MARC SORREL ● **Hermitage** Le Gréal

A choice of opulent dry whites
M CHAPOUTIER ○ **Hermitage** Cuveé de l'Orée
JEAN-LOUIS CHAVE ○ **Hermitage**
DOM. DU CHENE ○ **Condrieu**
YVES CUILLERON ○ **Condrieu** Chaillets Vieilles Vignes
DOM. YVES GANGLOFF ○ **Condrieu**
DOM. DU MURINAIS ○ **Crozes Hermitage** Vieilles Vignes
ANDRÉ PERRET ○ **Condrieu** Coteaux du Chéry
GEORGES VERNAY ○ **Condrieu** Les Chaillées de L'Enfer
FRANÇOIS VILLARD ○ **Saint-Joseph** Côtes de Mairlant
ALAIN VOGE ○ **Saint-Péray** Cuvée Fleur du Crussol

A selection of up and coming reds and whites
ALBERT BELLE ● **Crozes-Hermitage** Cuvée Louis Belle
M CHAPOUTIER ● **Saint-Joseph** Les Granits
YANN CHAVE ● **Crozes-Hermitage** Tête de Cuvée
JEAN-LUC COLOMBO ○ **Hermitage** Le Louet
DOM. COMBIER ○ **Crozes-Hermitage** Clos des Grives
YVES CUILLERON ○ **Saint-Joseph** Le Lombard
DELAS FRÈRES ● **Crozes-Hermitage** Le Clos
PIERRE GAILLARD ○ **Côtes du Rhône** Viognier
DOM. MICHEL OGIER ● **Vin de Pays des Collines Rhodaniennes** La Rosine
DOM. DU TUNNEL ○ **Saint-Peray** Prestige

Southern Rhône

DANIEL ET DENIS ALARY Cairanne   A: HHB,Sel

Owner: Daniel & Denis Alary   Font d'Estevenas, Route de Rasteau, 84290 Cairanne

A comprehensive and impressive range of Côtes du Rhône and Cairanne village wines are made here from the Alarys' 25 ha. Nearly 90 per cent of the vineyard is planted to red varieties, with some of the plantings now of notable age. The floral, forward white Côtes du Rhône blends Clairette with Bourboulenc. The Font d'Estevenas white is a step up, a rich, nutty and complex blend of Roussanne with some Viognier. The reds are unfiltered, full of dense and aromatic *garrigue* scents and complex, heady, berry fruit. The Font d'Estevenas and Jean de Verde are among the best expressions of old-vine Grenache outside Châteauneuf-du-Pape. The former usually has a proportion of Syrah, whereas La Jean de Verde is 100 per cent Grenache. The overall quality across all the wines is very good indeed as are the prices. The top two reds will age well. (DM)

● **Côtes du Rhône★** £B ● **Côtes du Rhône-Villages Cairanne★★** £B
● **Côtes du Rhône-Villages Cairanne** Réserve du Vigneron★★★ £B
● **Côtes du Rhône-Villages Cairanne** La Jean de Verde★★★ £C
● **Côtes du Rhône-Villages Cairanne** La Font d'Estevenas★★★★ £C
O **Côtes du Rhône** La Chevre d'Or★★ £B
O **Côtes du Rhône-Villages Cairanne** La Font d'Estevenas★★★ £C
◉ **Côtes du Rhône★** £A

DOM. DES AMADIEU Cairanne www.achiary.com   A:P-F

Owner: Marylène & Michel Achiary   Quartier Beauregard, 84290 Cairanne
Small 7-ha domaine established in 1984 which produces some excellent-value Cairanne. The property is planted to Grenache, Syrah and Mourvèdre and the Grenache vines now average 50 years of age. Yields are restricted to an average of 35 hl/ha and *pigeage* is employed during vinification. With output a mere 1,500 cases or so the wines will not be the easiest to find. The small range consists of two wines which are labelled Vitalis and Vieilles Vignes. Vitalis generally blends all three of the varieties planted and is the softer, more vibrantly fruit-driven example of the two. The Vieilles Vignes is usually crafted from an equal amount of Syrah and Grenache. It is denser and firmer and will age well in the medium term. The 2001 was nudging three stars. (DM)

● **Côtes du Rhône-Villages Cairanne** Vitalis★★ £B
● **Côtes du Rhône-Villages Cairanne** Vieilles Vignes★★ £B

DOM. AMIDO Tavel

Owner: Christian Amido   Rue des Carrières, 30126 Tavel
This is the most significant domaine in Tavel from a quality point of view, producing one of the best examples of the appellation. The wine undergoes a 36 hour pre-fermentation maceration and is fermented cool to preserve its attractive fresh berry fruit, something many in the AC fail to achieve. More important from a quality perspective are a fine Côtes du Rhône-Villages blended from Grenache (70 per cent) and Syrah (30 per cent) and a benchmark red Lirac. This is produced from 50-year-old Grenache (just over 50 per cent) plus Syrah and Mourvèdre. It is aged first in cement tanks and then transferred to used oak. The wine shows rich dark berry fruit and classic southern herbal spice and will benefit from a year or two of bottle age. (DM)

● **Lirac★★★** £B ● **Côtes du Rhône-Villages★★** £B
◉ **Tavel** Les Amandines★★ £B

DOM. DES AMOURIERS Vacqueyras   A: EoR, HHB

Owner: Patrick Gras   Les Garrigues, 84260 Sarrians
First-class operation run by Patrick Gras, producing very stylish, balanced wines. There are 34 ha all planted to reds, half Grenache with the balance a mix of Mourvèdre, Syrah and Carignan. Up until the mid-1990s the estate fruit was sold on but in only a few years this has become one of the finest sources in the AC. The Vacqueyras are wines of depth and rich savoury fruit and considerable structure, with new oak playing a large part in the style. The 1998, 99, 2000 and now 01 Genestes are benchmarks for the appellation and will age very well. Both Les Hautes Terasses and Les Genestes are ageworthy, the latter rising four stars in recent vintages. (DM)

● **Vin de Pays du Vaucluse★** £A ● **Côtes du Rhône★** £B
● **Vacqueyras★★** £B Signature★★ £B Les Hautes Terrasses★★★ £C Les Genestes★★★ £C

DOM. PAUL AUTARD Châteauneuf-du-Pape

Owner: Autard family Route de Châteauneuf-du-Pape, 84350 Courthézon
A small but impressive range of wines is made by Jean-Paul Autard at his 12-ha family domaine. The winemaking style has become more modern over the last decade: the fruit is not only carefully sorted at harvested but the reds are now fully destemmed as well. The good, sound, forward Côtes du Rhône red blended from Syrah and Counoise should be drunk young. More serious are the red Châteauneuf-du-Papes. The Traditionelle *cuvée* blends 70 per cent Grenache with Syrah, Counoise and Mourvèdre and is aged in a mix of *foudres* and *barriques*. It is marked by its peppery, herbal *garrigue* notes and approachable berry fruit. The Côte Ronde is considerably fuller and richer with a firmer structure. It demands five years' ageing, particularly in top years like 2000 and 01. A blend of Grenache and Syrah, it is aged in part new and part used *barriques* for up to 18 months. Two whites are produced, a nicely concentrated, nutty and toasty barrel-fermented white Châteauneuf-du-Pape from Grenache Blanc, Clairette and Roussanne and a late-harvest *vin de pays*, Je ne Souvione, produced solely from Viognier. Rich, sweet and not at all cloying, it has sufficient fresh acidity to offer a fine balance of honey, peach and citrus flavours and should be drunk young. (DM)

● **Châteauneuf du Pape** Traditionelle★★★ £D La Côte Ronde★★★★ £E
O **Châteauneuf du Pape**★★★ £D O **Vin de Pays** Je ne Souvione★★★ £D

DOM. LUCIEN BARROT Châteauneuf-du-Pape A: M&V, Maj, Bal

Owner: Barrot family Chemin du Clos, 84230 Châteauneuf-du-Pape
This is a small family-run operation with 20 ha of vineyards spread across the Châteauneuf-du-Pape appellation. The Barrots have been established as winemakers here since the late 17th century. The vines are old, approaching 50 years, planted on limestones soils with a *galets roulés* stone topsoil. The resulting wine is dense, complex and stylish and possesses a classic rich, savoury, *garrigue*-scented character. It is blended from Grenache, Syrah, Mourvèdre and Cinsault and vinification is traditional: the grapes are not destemmed and maceration lasts up to four weeks in top years. The wine is then aged in *foudres* for around 18 months. Firmly structured when young, it will drink well at five years or so. Excellent value for the appellation. (DM)

● **Châteauneuf du Pape**★★★ £C

DOM. DE BEAURENARD Châteauneuf-du-Pape www.beaurenard.fr A: BWC

Owner: Paul Coulon Avenue Pierre-de-Luxembourg, 84231 Châteauneuf-du-Pape
The Coulon family make an impressive range of stylish reds and whites in modern, well-equipped cellars. The lighter reds and white Châteauneuf-du-Pape are forward and full of fruit, the latter enjoying some lees-enrichment. The Côtes du Rhône Rasteau has 20 per cent Syrah blended into the Grenache, to add to the wine's structure. The regular Châteauneuf-du-Pape red is supple, rich and forward, whereas the Boisrenard is a dense, powerful wine produced from very low yields of 15 to 20 hl/ha. It requires six or seven years' ageing in years such as 1998, 99 and 2000. The fortified Rasteau is one of the better examples. (DM)

● **Châteauneuf du Pape**★★★ £D Boisrenard★★★★★ £F
● **Côtes du Rhône**★ £A ● **Côtes du Rhône-Villages Rasteau**★★ £B
● **Rasteau**★ £B
O **Châteauneuf du Pape**★★★ £C

DOM. BERTHET-RAYNE Châteauneuf-du-Pape

Owner: Berthet-Rayne family 2334 Route de Caderousse, 84350 Courthézon
The Berthet-Rayne family produce a small range of good middle-grade Châteauneuf-du-Pape and sound red and white Côtes du Rhône from their property in the north of the appellation, where the limestone soils are covered by the famous *galet* stones. Of the Rhônes, the white offers straightforward light, nutty

fruit, while the red is more intense, a blend dominated by Grenache and sourced from vineyards just on the Châteauneuf appellation boundary. Among the Châteauneuf labels, the white is in a clean fresh, fruit-driven style and should be drunk within a couple of years of release. The regular red is in a modern, fleshy mould with bright berry fruit and soft, easy tannins. It will drink well young. Vieilli en Fûts de Chêne was added with the successful 2000 vintage and produced again in 01. It will only be released in similarly good vintages and blends Grenache with Mourvèdre and Syrah. Cadiac is the most structured and dense of the wines, rich and impressively concentrated. Produced from equal proportions of Grenache and Mourvèdre it is relatively backward and firm young and will benefit from four or five years' cellaring. (DM)

● **Châteauneuf du Pape★★★** £D Vieilli en Fûts de Chêne★★★★ £E Cuvée Cadiac★★★★ £F
● **Côtes du Rhône★** £B
○ **Châteauneuf du Pape★★** £C

BOIS DE BOURSAN   Châteauneuf-du-Pape   A: Tur

Owner: Jean et Jean-Paul Versino   Quartier Saint-Pierre, 84230 Châteauneuf-du-Pape
Small, extremely quality-conscious Châteauneuf producer, located just on the edge of the village itself, with around 15 ha planted mainly to Grenache, Syrah and Mourvèdre. The white is relatively unexciting but both the reds are dense, powerful wines needing time to soften their youthful tannins and fiery character. Both are bottled without filtration. The Cuvée Felix is aged in part in smaller oak and offers more opulent and exotic characters. Both wines are finely structured and notably ageworthy. (DM)

● **Châteauneuf du Pape★★★★** £D Cuvée des Felix★★★★★ £E

HENRI BONNEAU   Châteauneuf-du-Pape   A: HHB, BBR, Sec

Owner: Henri Bonneau   35 Rue Joseph-Ducos, 84230 Châteauneuf-du-Pape
A somewhat controversial producer, M. Bonneau is, as was the late Jacques Reynaud at CH. RAYAS, one of Châteauneufs more interesting characters. The two special *cuvées*, which are produced from a high proportion of Grenache, are generally only bottled if the vintage justifies it – otherwise a regular Châteauneuf-du-Pape is produced – and he sells to *négociants* to maintain quality. Both the Marie Beurrier and Réserve des Célestins wines will improve with a decade or more in bottle. (DM)

● **Châteauneuf du Pape★★** £C Marie Beurrier★★★★★ £F Réserve des Célestins❂❂❂❂❂ £G

BOSQUETS DES PAPES   Châteauneuf-du-Pape   A: Cty, HHB, Res, SVS, OWL

Owner: Boiron Family   18 Route d'Orange, BP 50, 84232 Châteauneuf-du-Pape
The Boiron family own 8 ha of vineyards but also lease from other properties, working with close to 30 ha in total. There is a relatively dull white as well as three potentially classic dense and rich reds. Vinification is traditional and the fruit is not destemmed. They can be some of the most impressive traditional Châteauneufs, particularly the old-vine Cuvée Chantemerle. Bottling is carried out according to demand, so beware, there can be considerable variation. Tasting can reveal wines of extraordinary richness and also others bottled later that show excessive oxidation. The best advice is to buy as close to the vintage as possible. (DM)

● **Châteauneuf -du-Pape★★★** £C Cuvée Grenache★★★★ £E Cuvée Chantemerle★★★★★ £F

DOM. BRUSSET   Cairanne   www.domaine brusset.fr   A: Eno, NYg,Sel

Owner: Daniel & Laurent Brusset   Le Village, 84290 Cairanne
The Brusset family make an excellent range of wines, producing some 30,000 cases annually from a sizeable vineyard holding of 84 ha. The top wines are modern in style with pre-fermentation maceration, ageing on lees and no filtration. They are marked by rich, concentrated fruit and ripe but powerful tannins; they need to be cellared to show of their best but are less backward than some, particularly in Gigondas. Les Hauts de Montmirail is a magnificent, complex old-vine *cuvée* mainly from Grenache. In contrast lesser *cuvées* exhibit

vibrant juicy fruit and are great youthful gluggers. (DM)
- ● **Gigondas** Le Grand Montmirail★★★ £C   Les Hauts de Montmirail★★★★ £D
- ● **Côtes du Rhône-Villages Cairanne** Travers★★ £B Hommage à André Brusset★★★★ £D
- O **Côtes du Rhône-Villages Cairanne**★ £B
- ● **Côtes du Rhône** Laurent Brusset★ £A   O **Côtes du Rhône** Viognier★★ £C
- ● **Cotes du Ventoux** La Boudale★ £A

CAVE DE CAIRANNE Cairanne   A: RSo

Owner: Co-operative members 84290 Cairanne
Very good modern co-op producing an extensive range of wines from this important southern Rhône
village as well as decent straightforward Côtes du Rhône. The basic *cuvées* represent good value with
attractive berry fruit and are best drunk young, while the top wines are a notch up in quality. The Réserve
des Voconces is made from 40-year-old vines. The red Cuvée Salyens sees 30 per cent new oak while the
Cuvée Antique is quite firmly structured and will benefit from three or four years of ageing. The top reds
are bottled unfiltered and represent very fair value for money. (DM)
- ● **Côtes du Rhône-Villages Cairanne** Temptation★ £B Grand Réserve★ £B
- ● **Côtes du Rhône-Villages Cairanne** Réserve des Voconces★★ £B
- ● **Côtes du Rhône-Villages Cairanne** Cuvée Antique★★ £B Cuvée Salyens★★ £B
- O **Côtes du Rhône-Villages Cairanne** Cuvée Salyens★★ £B

DOM. DU CAYRON Gigondas   A: JAr

Owner: Michel Faraud 84190 Gigondas
Just one wine is made at this traditional estate, and very good it is in most years. The vineyard holding is
not small at 15 ha, split between Grenache (70 per cent) and an equal amount of Cinsault and Syrah, and
yields 5,000 cases a year. With vines close to 50 years old and very well-drained stony soils producing fruit
of exceptional quality, this is one of the best estates in the appellation. Odd years like 1998 can be a bit
disappointing, but most recent vintages have been on good form. 2002 has yet to be tasted. (DM)
- ● **Gigondas**★★★ £C

DOM. DE LA CHARBONNIÈRE Châteauneuf-du-Pape   A: GWW,VWs, BBR

Owner: Michel Maret 84230 Châteauneuf-du-Pape
Generally good, if not in the top division. The wines are produced from a total of 21 ha of vines. Michel
Maret avoids filtration and in the best years the results are very impressive. The Mourre de Perdrix is partially
aged in new wood, but it is the impressively concentrated Haut Brusquières (blending a proportion of Syrah
with Grenache) and Vieilles Vignes bottlings that really stand out. The Vacqueyras is a good chunky, earthy
example and represents good value for money. (DM)
- ● **Vacqueyras**★★ £B
- ● **Châteauneuf-du-Pape**★★£C Mourre des Perdrix★★★ £D
- ● **Châteauneuf-du-Pape** Haut Brusquières★★★★ £E Vieilles Vignes★★★★ £E
- O **Châteauneuf-du-Pape**★ £C

GÉRARD CHARVIN Châteauneuf-du-Pape   A:VTr

Owner: Gérard Charvin Quartier Maucoil, 84100 Orange
Small, high-quality domaine now run by Laurent Charvin, producing full-blown, rich spicy reds. Both the
Côtes du Rhône and the Châteauneuf-du-Pape offer quality and value. The latter is a blend of Grenache
with a little Syrah, Mourvèdre and Vaccarese adding both definition and a firm youthful structure. The wine
has been particularly impressive in the current run of fine vintages – a real blockbuster style, it will age
very well. (DM)
- ● **Côtes du Rhône**★★ £B   ● **Châteauneuf-du-Pape**★★★★ £D

CH. DE BEAUCASTEL Châteauneuf-du-Pape   A: Mis,Far,Tan,Rae,F&M

Owner: Perrin family 84350 Courthezon
Among the very top echelon of producers in the southern Rhône. Notable for the organic approach in their 131 ha estate vineyards, where all 13 permitted varieties are planted, the Perrins also employ a process called *vinification à chaud* for their red Châteauneuf, which extracts good colour and fruit and guards against bacteria and oxidation. The very finest quality is achieved in both red and white, the former unusually dominated by Mourvèdre and Syrah, and there is a good second label Coudoulet de Beaucastel. The red is not filtered but is given a light fining to help soften the very firm structure of the wine in its youth. Also produced are a range of *négociant* wines under the Domaines PERRIN label, while the Côtes du Rhône property Château du Grand Prebois is a recent acquisition. Further afield the Perrins have a partnership in the Californian Paso Robles winery TABLAS CREEK. Both the Châteauneuf red and white must be cellared, up to 8 to 10 years in top vintages. (DM)
- **Châteauneuf-du-Pape★★★★★** £E Homage à Jacques Perrin✪✪✪✪✪ £H
- **Châteauneuf-du-Pape★★★★** £E Vieilles Vignes✪✪✪✪✪ £G
- **Côtes du Rhône** Coudoulet du Beaucastel★★★ £C
- **Côtes du Rhône** Coudoulet du Beaucastel★★ £C

CH. DE FONSALETTE Côtes du Rhône   A: Sec, Blx

Owner: Reynaud family 84290 Lagarde-Pareol
Benchmark 11-ha Côtes du Rhône property owned by the Reynaud family of CHÂTEAU RAYAS. Emmanuel Reynaud now also undertakes vinification here as well as at Rayas and his own Vacqueyras property, CHÂTEAU DES TOURS. The regular bottling is a blend of Grenache with a sizeable dollop of Cinsault. The Syrah is a varietal bottling. These fine, intense and firmly structured wines are long-lived albeit expensive examples of the AC. (DM)
- **Côtes du Rhône★★★** £C Syrah★★★★ £D
- **Côtes du Rhône★★★** £C

CH. LA GARDINE Châteauneuf-du-Pape www.gardine.com   A:T&W

Owner: Brunel family Route de Roquemaure, BP 35, 84231 Châteauneuf-du-Pape
A modern approach to vinification here allied to a dedication to *terroir* results in an impressive range of wines. The reds are dense and deeply coloured when young but supple and impeccably balanced. In their youth they are sturdy and firm and they require several years' ageing. Temperature control is used in producing fruity, gloriously nutty whites, with new oak in abundance in the top *cuvées*. The Brunels purchased the Lirac property Domaine SAINT-ROCH in 1998 and have started to bring about improvements. (DM)
- **Côtes du Rhône-Villages★** £B
- **Châteauneuf-du-Pape** Tradition★★★★ £D Cuvée des Générations Gaston Philippe★★★★★ £F
- **Châteauneuf-du-Pape** Tradition★★★ £D Cuvée des Generations Marie-Léoncie★★★★ £E

CH. LA NERTHE Châteauneuf-du-Pape   A: BBR, C&C

Owner: LVMH Route de Sourgues, 84230 Châteauneuf-d-Pape
This large (for Châteauneuf) property has been performing at a high level since it was purchased by the Richard family in the mid-1980s. Annual production is now around 25,000 cases. There tends to be less Grenache in the reds here than elsewhere. The Cadettes, a sturdy blend of 100-year-old Grenache and Mourvèdre, is right on the edge of five stars and was undoubtedly so in 2000. Throughout the small range a modern, sophisticated approach to vinification has produced excellent results, with destemming and extended vatting for reds and increasing use of *barriques* for both reds and whites. (DM)
- **Châteauneuf-du-Pape★★★★** £D Cuvée des Cadettes★★★★ £E
- **Châteauneuf-du-Pape★★★** £C Clos de Beauvenir★★★★ £D

CH. MAS NEUF   Costières de Nîmes   www.chateaumasneuf.com

Owner: Luc Baudet   30600 Gallician

Luc Baudet has a sizeable property of 60 ha, 53 ha of which are planted to red varieties. Of the whites the regular Costières de Nîmes is straightforward and fruity with some nutty, spicy tones. Richer and fuller are the Compostelle Blanc, a blend of Grenache Blanc and Roussanne which is lent some additional weight from ageing in oak, and the *vin de pays* Chardonnay/Viognier blend which is leaner but more aromatic. The regular red is a sturdy, forward blend of Syrah, Grenache and Mourvèdre with a hint of Carignan adding some herbal spice notes. The Compostelle red, a blend of Syrah, Grenache and Mourvèdre, is a serious step up. There are two very good *vin de pays* varietal reds and new is a limited-production red *super-cuvée*, Armonio, made in association with Louis Mitjavile of CH. TERTRE-RÔTEBOEUF in Saint-Emilion. None of the top wines is either fined or filtered after a long 30-day maceration and ageing is in *barriques* for 8 to 12 months. These will benefit from at least two or three years' further cellaring after release. (DM)

● **Costières de Nîmes**★★ £B Compostelle★★★ £C
● **Vin de Pays d'Oc** Merlot★★★ £C Syrah★★★ £C
O **Costières de Nîmes** Compostelle★★ £B   O **Vin de Pays d'Oc** Chardonnay/Viognier★★ £B

CH. MONT-REDON   Châteauneuf-du-Pape   www.chateaumontredon.fr   A: PFx,Sel

Owner: Abeille-Fabre family   BP 10, 84321 Châteauneuf-du-Pape

By the standards of the appellation this is a large property producing good to very good rather than exceptional wines. Vinification is now modern, using a mix of *inox* and some *barriques* for the Châteauneuf bottlings. A Lirac property, Château Cantegril, has recently been purchased and these wines are now to be marketed under the Mont-Redon label. Expect quality at Cantegril to improve. The red Châteauneuf ages well over the medium term, acquiring additional depth and finesse. These are very fairly priced wines. (DM)

● **Côtes du Rhône**★★ £B ● **Châteauneuf-du-Pape**★★★ £D ● **Lirac**★★ £B
O **Châteauneuf-du-Pape**★★★ £C
O **Côtes du Rhône**★ £B Viognier★ £B

CH. MOURGUES DU GRÈS   Costières de Nîmes   mourguesdugres@wanadoo.fr

Owner: François Collard   Route de Bellegarde, 30300 Beaucaire

Some 20,000 cases of red, white and rosé are now made here each year. As one would expect the majority of the planting is to red varieties, which make up 34 ha of the 40 ha. Of these Syrah accounts for 70 per cent, the balance being mainly Grenache with a small amount of Carignan and Mourvèdre. Whites consist of Grenache (40 per cent), Roussanne (40 per cent) and Viognier. Galets is the label for the basic red, white and rosé and these are straightforward wines characterised by their approachable, forward fruit. The second tier Terre d'Argence wines are more serious. There is a nutty, floral white dominated by Roussanne and a dense, powerful red. The top wine is Capitelles des Mourgues, which spends a year in barrel. There is also a premium rosé under the same label. The top reds will improve with short ageing. (DM)

● **Costières de Nîmes** Galets Rouge★★ £B Terre d'Argence★★★ £B Capitelles des Mourgues★★★ £C
O **Costières de Nîmes** Terre d'Argence★★ £B

CH. D'OR ET DE GUEULES   Costières de Nîmes   www.chateau-or-et-gueules.com   A:Maj

Owner: Diane de Puymorin   Chemin des Cassagnes, Route de Générac, 30800 Saint-Gilles

This property was very recently established (in 1998) and the wines appear to be improving with every vintage. The vineyards have an excellent south to south-east exposure and its large pebbles and stones retain heat well, aiding ripening. A couple of rosés are produced including a Cuvée Trassegum which is part barrel-fermented. The Cep de Diane Chardonnay is full, rich and toasty, with an almost toffeed character. It is vinified in barrel on lees. There are two lower-level Costières de Nîmes reds, of which the Tradition, a blend of Grenache, Carignan and Mourvèdre, has more dimension than the Classique. Some of the Carignan is very old and adds dark and spicy complexity. Les Cimels is a blend of Syrah with very old Carignan with yields restricted to 35 hl/ha. The wine is dark, spicy and full of old-viney character. Top of the line are the Cuvée Trassegum red (formerly Cuvée Prestige) and La Bolida. Trassegum is now aged in less oak than in the debut 1998 vintage and is the better for it. La Bolida is a blend of 90 per cent very old Mourvèdre and 10 per cent Syrah. Rich and supple it could do with just a little more refinement but is a wine of great potential. (DM)

● **Costières de Nîmes** Tradition★★ £B Les Cimels★★ £B Cuvée Trassegum★★★ £C
● **Costières de Nîmes** La Bolida★★★ £D
○ **Vin de Pays d'Oc** Le Ceps de Diane★★★ £C

CH. PESQUIÉ Côtes du Ventoux   A: VWs, OWL

Owner: Chaudière Bastide family 84570 Mormoiron
Medium-sized property with over 70 ha of vineyards producing some 25,000 cases a year. Quality is generally good across the board, with attractive forward, fruit-driven styles being the order of the day. The Terrasses labels are simple and straightforward and there is a very decent fresh and characterful rosé, Perle de Roses. The real stars here, though, are the Prestige and Quintessence. These are a serious step up and are among the best examples of the appellation. Prestige is dominated by Syrah with some old-vine Grenache lending opulence and complexity. Quintessence is 80 per cent Syrah but the small proportion of Grenache is 70 years old. The wines are aged in small barrels, around 30 to 35 per cent new. Both are impressively cellarworthy. Ageing for four or five years is advisable. (DM)

● **Cotes du Ventoux** Terre Précieuse★ £B Prestige★★★ £B Quintessence★★★ £B
◉ **Cotes du Ventoux** Perle de Roses★ £A
○ **Vin de Pays** Chardonnay du Pesquié★ £B Viognier du Pesquié★ £B

CH. RAYAS Châteauneuf-du-Pape   A: OWL, BBR

Owner: Reynaud family Route de Courthézon, 84230 Châteauneuf-du-Pape
Legendary estate, which produced stunning red and white Châteauneuf for decades under the late Jacques Reynaud. The second label, Pignan, is also very impressive and comes from a separate plot rather than a selection. The property consists of just under 14 ha with old vines planted on sand and clay/limestone soils, rather than on *galets roulés*. The red is made solely from Grenache while an even split of Clairette and Grenache Blanc contribute to the very ageworthy white. The wines are now vinified by Jacques' nephew, Emmanuel Reynaud of CHATEAU DES TOURS, who also produces the wines at the Rayas sister property CHATEAU DE FONSALETTE. They have unquestionably been very fine in the late 1990s but lack some of the sublime quality of earlier years. (DM)

● **Châteauneuf-du-Pape**✪✪✪✪✪ £F Pignan★★★★★ £E
○ **Châteauneuf-du-Pape**★★★★★ £E

CH. REDORTIER Gigondas   A: BRW

Owner: Étienne & Sabine de Menthon 84190 Suzette
Although a little white is produced it is the reds that show real refinement and class at this excellent property. As yet the overall vine age, at around 25 years, is younger than at some other estates, so there should be more to to look forward to. The blend for the Gigondas is dominated by Grenache but there is a hefty dollop of Syrah as well. The wine is firmer and more structured than some of its neighbours. It undergoes extended cask-ageing and requires a few years of patience. The Beaumes-de-Venise Cuvée Prestige is an undoubted star of that village. (DM)

● **Cotes du Rhone-Villages Beaumes-de-Venise**★★ £B Cuvée Prestige★★ £C
● **Gigondas**★★★ £C

CH. SAINT-COSME Gigondas louis@chateau-st-cosme.com A: Dec, NYg, Han

Owner: Louis Barruol 84190 Gigondas

Louis Barruol owns vines only in Gigondas but in recent years he has made an excellent small range of *négociant* wines as well. The Côtes du Rhône offerings represent excellent value, notably the reds, whereas the Gigondas Cuvée Valbelle, Châteauneuf-du-Pape and Côte-Rôtie are all impressively concentrated and ageworthy. The Gigondas bottlings are dense and powerful and quite marked by youthful new oak. At their best they are both intense and complex. There is also decent if not yet top-flight Condrieu but the potential here is exciting and current releases are very fairly priced. (DM)

● **Côtes du Rhone★★** £B Les Deux Albions★★ £B
O **Côtes du Rhone★** £A
● **Gigondas★★** £C Cuvée Valbelle★★★ £D
● **Châteauneuf-du-Pape★★★** £E
● **Côte-Rôtie★★★** £E
O **Condrieu★★** £E

CH. SAINT-ESTÈVE D'UCHAUX Côtes du Rhône-Villages A:HBJ

Owner: Marc Français Route de Sérignan, 84100 Uchaux

Some very good reds and whites are made at this sizeable 60-ha property in the northern Vaucluse, at the southern limit of the Côtes du Rhône-Villages appellation. There are three regular reds and the same number of whites. The straightforward white Côtes du Rhône is a blend of mainly Grenache Blanc and Roussanne. There are also two fine Viognier-based whites, one from young vines which is blended with a little Grenache Blanc and a very striking top *cuvée*, Dionysos, which is 100 per cent varietal. In reds, there is a good straightforward fruit-driven Côtes du Rhône as well as two more serious Côtes du Rhône-Villages. Grande Réserve is 60 per cent Grenache and 40 per cent Syrah whereas the dense and impressively structured Vieilles Vignes is the reverse blend. The range is completed by a straightforward juicy rosé and a Méthode Traditionelle Blanc de Blancs sparkler. There is also a very limited production pricey oak-aged Viognier Cuvée Thérèse. Top reds will benefit from two or three years' ageing. (DM)

● **Côtes du Rhône** Tradition★ £B
● **Côtes du Rhône-Villages** Grande Réserve★★ £C Vieilles Vignes★★★ £C
O **Côtes du Rhône★** £B Viognier Jeune Vignes★★ £B
O **Côtes du Rhône-Villages** Dionysos★★★ £C

CH. DES TOURS Vacqueyras A:Yap, Bib, Rae

Owner: Emmanuel Reynaud Quartier des Sablons, 84260 Sarrians

As well as owning this excellent 40-ha property, Emmanuel Reynaud, the nephew of the late Jacques Reynaud, is now vinifying the wines at Château RAYAS and Château de FONSALETTE. His Vacqueyras has long been a yardstick example for the AC and is produced from mainly Grenache from very low-yielding old vines. Always emphasising classic *garrigue* aromas, these are complex, even refined wines, in marked contrast to some of the more extracted examples of some of his neighbours. A ripe and fruit-laden red and nutty white *vin de pays* complete the small range. (DM)

● **Côtes du Rhône★★** £B ● **Vacqueyras★★★** £C
O **Côtes du Rhône★** £B

DOM. CHAUME-ARNAUD Vinsobres A:M&V

Owner: Valérie & Philippe Chaume-Arnaud 26110 Vinsobres

This is a good source of well-priced southern Rhône red and white. The domaine is small with 13.5 ha situated around the lesser-known village of Vinsobres. Reds are dominated by Grenache and Syrah and there is a little Viognier and Marsanne for the white. Quality is key, yields are kept low and no artificial fertilizers are used on the soil. The property also benefits from some very old vines. The small amount of

Carignan used in the Vinsobres red is now over 60 years old. Both the Vinsobres reds will develop well in bottle with three or four years' age. (DM)

● **Côtes du Rhône★★** £B
● **Côtes du Rhône-Villages Vinsobres★★** £B La Cadene★★★ £C
○ **Côtes du Rhône-Villages Vinsobres★★** £B

CLOS DU CAILLOU   Châteauneuf-du-Pape   A: HHB, BBR, NYg

Owner: Jean-Denis Vacheron 84350 Courthezon
Jean-Denis Vacheron (related to the VACHERONS of Sancerre) has been in charge of the winemaking at this domaine since the late 1990s and quality has gone from strength to strength. Careful vineyard management, modern vinification with some malolactic in cask and a tight control of yields are producing excellent results. Les Quartz is tight and firmly structured, the Réserve bottling richer and more opulent with added dimension from a large dollop of Mourvèdre. The top two *cuvées* will age very well. (DM)

● **Côtes du Rhône** Bouquet des Garrigues★ £B
● **Châteauneuf-du-Pape★★★** £D Les Quartz★★★★ £E Réserve Clos du Caillou★★★★★ £F

CLOS DES CAZAUX   Vacqueyras   A: CBg, Lay, VWs, Tan

Owner: Jean-Michel & Frédéric Archimbaud-Vache 84190 Vacqueyras
The Archimbaud-Vache family make a surprisingly diverse range of wines from their holdings in Vacqueyras and Gigondas. There is a very good nutty white Vacqueyras, a blend of Clairette, Roussane and Grenache Blanc which is aged in *cuve* to emphasise its fruit. The Blanc Barrique is vinified in wood and has a small portion of Viognier to add fragrance. A very small amount of a 100 per cent Grenache Blanc Quintessence is also made. The red Cuvées Saint-Roche and Reservé are mainly Grenache with some Syrah. The former has 5 per cent Mourvèdre and comes from marginally older vines. The Templiers is dominated by Syrah whereas the Prestige is solely Syrah. Green harvesting is practised and there is minimal intervention in the cellar. Particularly unusual and generally successful is a late-harvest Vacqueyras produced from Grenache infected by noble rot. It has great depth and intensity. Expect the reds to develop well in the medium term, particularly the Syrah based *cuvées*. (DM)

● **Vacqueyras** Cuvée des Templiers★★★ £B Réserve★★★ £C Grénat Noble★★★★ £C
● **Vacqueyras** Cuvée St Roche★★★ £B Réserve★★★ £B
○ **Vacqueyras** Cuvée des Clefs d'Or★★ £B Blanc Barrique★★ £B
● **Gigondas** La Tour Sarrazine★★★ £C

CLOS DU MONT OLIVET   Châteauneuf-du-Pape   A: Hal, Res, Rae

Owner: Sabon family Chemin Bois la Ville, 84230 Châteauneuf-du-Pape
These are very traditional, old fashioned examples of the appellation. The regular bottling is moderately dense with some marked dark fruit and herbal scents and reasonable depth. The Cuvée du Papet is bigger and fuller. The fruit is not destemmed, which works very well in the best years, but occasionally the wines can show a marked rusticity and some hard and green tannin in more challenging years. Bottling occurs in several stages, so the fruit will not be consistent. Buy as soon after the vintage as you can. (DM)

● **Châteauneuf-du-Pape★★★** £C Cuvée du Papet★★★★ £E
○ **Châteauneuf-du-Pape★★** £C

CLOS DES PAPES   Châteauneuf-du-Pape   A: RsW, Rae, SVS, BBR

Owner: Avril family 13 Avenue Pierre-de-Luxembourg, BP 8, 84231 Châteauneuf-du-Pape
One of the great benchmark names in Châteauneuf-du-Pape, producing just one white and one red. The Avrils have 32 ha of which 29 ha are planted to reds. Considerable investment in the cellar during the 1990s has enabled the property to go from strength to strength. The red is a very structured, ageworthy example of the AC. It is always destemmed and the different varieties are fermented together, which the Avrils feel

adds complexity. The red needs five or six years' patience and the white will also age well, which is unusual for a white Châteauneuf. Vincent has now taken over the winemaking from his father Paul. (DM)

● **Châteauneuf-du-Pape★★★★★** £E ○ **Châteauneuf-du-Pape★★★★** £D

CLOS PETITE BELLANE Valréas   A:Odd

Owner: Olivier Peuchot Chemin de Sainte-Croix, 84600 Valréas

Impressive property producing modern, stylish wines with classic Rhône fruit. The vineyard covers an area of 44 ha and some of the vines, particularly the Grenache, are up to 65 years old. The white Côtes du Rhône is half Roussanne and half Viognier and like all the whites is given a period of *macération pelliculaire*. The white Les Echalas is finer and purer, produced from 100 per cent Roussanne. The red Côtes du Rhône is ripe, forward and brambly, the Valréas bottlings fuller and more concentrated. The top two reds have real depth and concentration. Les Echalas is 100 per cent Syrah and can show a hint of reduction when young. Vieilles Vignes is very fine and complex, full of old-viney character and spicy, herbal scents. Both will age well. (DM)

● **Côtes du Rhône★★** £B ● **Côtes du Rhône Valréas★★** £B
● **Côtes du Rhône Valréas** Les Echalas★★★ £D Vieilles Vignes★★★★ £D
○ **Côtes du Rhône★★** £B ○ **Côtes du RhôneValréas** Les Echalas★★★ £D

DOM. COTEAUX DES TRAVERS Rasteau

Owner: Robert Charavin 84110 Rasteau

Robert Charavin produces some of the best examples from this Rhône village, which is now a candidate for its own appellation for dry wines as well as for the fortifieds that the Rasteau AC currently covers. He has 20 ha under vine, including a sizeable planting of old vines, and produces around 5,000 cases a year. In the vineyard everything is as natural as possible and no fertilizers are used on the soil. There is a good, nutty white which blends equal parts of Marsanne, Grenache Blanc, Roussanne and Viognier. The soft, forward red Côtes du Rhône is produced from young vines and is mainly Grenache with some Carignan. More serious are the Rasteau reds. Prestige is made from 60-year-old vines, a blend of Grenache, Syrah and Mourvèdre which gets 12 months in wood. The top wine is the complex, structured Cuvée Paul, full of old-vine character and very ageworthy. Produced from 50- to 100-year-old vines it blends Syrah with a little Mourvèdre and Grenache. It needs a year or two of bottle-ageing to integrate the 24 months spent in oak. (DM)

● **Côtes du Rhône★** £B
● **Côtes du Rhône Rasteau★★** £B Prestige★★★ £C Cuvée Paul★★★ £C
○ **Côtes du Rhône Rasteau** Cuvee Marie★★ £D

DOM. DE CRISTIA Châteauneuf-du-Pape

Owner: Grangeon family 84350 Courthézon

Baptiste Grangeon makes very good red Côtes du Rhône and Châteauneuf-du-Pape in a modern accessible style. The Côtes du Rhône is aged in *cuve* and is light, soft and fruit-driven, whereas the Côtes du Rhône Villages is richer and sturdier. A blend of mainly Grenache with 20 per cent Syrah, it is aged in a combination of *cuve* and used barrels. The white Châteauneuf-du-Pape is a fairly even blend of Grenache Blanc, Clairette, Bourboulenc and Roussanne. Vinified in stainless steel it possesses very fresh fruit, full of citrus, nutmeg and herbs. Drink it young. The regular red Châteauneuf is mainly Grenache but has 15 per cent Syrah and just 5 per cent Mourvèdre blended in. Finely crafted, with attractive bright berry fruit, it has a firm but supple structure which will enable it to develop well over five to seven years and to keep for longer. The 2001 was right on the edge of four stars and the 2003 looks to have similar potential. The top wine, Cuvée Renaissance, is mainly sourced from a 100-year-old vineyard of Grenache with a small amount of Mourvèdre and Syrah added. Aged in old oak to preserve the remarkable intensity and character of the fruit it needs a minimum of 8 to 10 years to show at its best. In 2003 Baptiste also experimented with a

50/50 blend of Syrah and Grenache, vinified with no sulphur. It will have minimal handling and exposure to oxygen and it will be very interesting to see how it develops. (DM)

● **Châteauneuf du Pape★★★** £D   Cuvée Renaissance★★★★★ £E
● **Cotes du Rhone★** £B   ● **Côtes du Rhône-Villages★★** £B

CROS DE LA MÛRE   Côtes du Rhône   A: JAr, CBg

Owner: Eric Michel   Hameau de Derboux, 84430 Mondragon
Small estate making stylish, elegant Côtes du Rhône, Côtes du Rhône-Villages and denser fuller Gigondas. These wines are not blockbusters but display very good classic *garrigue*-scented red berry fruit. The Côtes du Rhône has a high proportion of old-vine Grenache and will drink well in the short to medium term. The Villages bottling has a higher proportion of Syrah and a touch more density and structure. The Gigondas is the sturdiest of the wines and will benefit from tucking away for four or five years. All the wines offer good value. (DM)

● **Cotes du Rhone★★** £B   ● **Côtes du Rhône-Villages★★★** £B
● **Gigondas★★★** £B

DOM. DE DEURRE   Vinsobres   A: MtC, SVS

Owner: Hubert Valayer   26110 Vinsobres
Hubert Valayer's property is newly established but the results are very promising and the wines show increasing potential with every vintage. The 2001s and 00s are all stunning and a marked step up on earlier vintages. As well as the southern Rhône wines a Cornas is produced thanks to a leasehold agreement with a cousin. As yet it does not show the same potential as Valayer's other wines. The Saint-Maurice is supple and well-structured, with around 30 per cent Syrah in the blend, and the Vinsobres richer, more savoury, with a touch of Mourvèdre. Both are edging towards three stars. There are two splendid Côtes du Rhônes. Les Oliviers is 100 per cent Syrah and the brilliant Les Rabasses 100 per cent Grenache. In 2000 the Rabasses was right on the edge of four stars. Newly added Cuvée J.M. Valayer, which is aged in used barriques, resembles a very good Châteuneuf-du-Pape. (DM)

● **Côtes du Rhône★** £B   Les Oliviers★★★ £C   Les Rabasses★★★ £C
● **Côtes du Rhône-Villages Saint-Maurice★★** £B
● **Côtes du Rhône-Villages Vinsobres★★** £B   Cuvee JM Valayer★★★★ £C
● **Cornas★★** £C

DOM. DURBAN   Beaumes-de-Venise   A: Yap, BBR

Owner: Jean-Pierre Leydier   84190 Beaumes-de-Venise
The Beaumes-de-Venise Vieilles Vignes at this sizeable 57-ha property is a good, spicy, nicely intense red dominated by Grenache, with some Syrah and Mourvèdre. Made from 50-year-old vines, it is traditionally vinified and aged in *cuve*. However, it is the fortified Muscat de Beaumes-de-Venise that marks out this estate. One of the very best examples made, it is richly intense and gloriously honeyed but has a real finesse and elegance very rarely encountered in these wines. It should, though, in the style of the appellation, be drunk young and fresh. (DM)

● **Côtes du Rhône-Villages Beaumes-de-Venise** Vieille Vignes★★ £B
O **Muscat de Beaumes-de-Venise★★★** £C

DOM. DES ESPIERS   Vacqueyras   A: Bal

Owner: Philippe Cartoux   84190 Vacqueyras
With cellars based in the village of Vacqueyras, Philippe Cartoux crafts his excellent wines from parcels totalling some 10 ha around Gigondas and Sablet. A little white and rosé Côtes du Rhône is produced but it is the top reds that particularly impress. The Cuvée des Blâches is wonderfully dense and gamey with some attractive herbal *garrigue* notes. It is produced from 35-year-old vines. Both Gigondas

cuvées will be the better for four or five years' cellaring; the Sablet too will benefit from short ageing. (DM)

● **Côtes du Rhône**★ £B ● **Côtes du Rhône-Villages Sablet**★★ £B
● **Gigondas**★★★ £B Cuvée des Blâches★★★★ £C

FERAUD-BRUNEL Châteauneuf-du-Pape

Owner: Feraud/Brunel families 84230 Châteauneuf-du-Pape

Fine quality small *négociant* operation run by Laurence Feraud of Domaine du PEGAÜ and André Brunel of LES CAILLOUX in Châteauneuf-du-Pape. The traditional-style wines are vinified by the Brunel *oenologue*, Philippe Cambie, in a manner similar to that at Pegaü and Les Cailloux. Results are impressive across the board. The *vin de table*, Images du Sud, is an attractive, spicy, forward red blend. All represent good value. (DM)

● **Vin de Table** Image du Sud★★ £B
● **Côtes du Rhône-Villages Cairanne**★★★ £B
● **Côtes du Rhône-Villages Rasteau**★★ £B ● **Vacqueyras**★★ £B
● **Gigondas**★★★ £C ● **Châteauneuf-du-Pape**★★★ £C

DOM. DE FONDRÈCHE Côtes du Ventoux   A: N&P

Owner: Sébastien Barthélémy Quartier Fondrèche, 84380 Mazan

With their 30-odd ha Sébastien and Nanou Barthélémy are rivals to CHÂTEAU PESQUIÉ – both are making benchmark wines for the appellation. Careful viticulture with increasingly old vines (now averaging 40 years) and minimal interference throughout vinification and *élévage* is paying off with an impressive range. The regular red, blended from Grenache, Syrah and Cinsault, is silky and forward. The Fayard, similarly aged in tank, adds Carignan to Grenache and Syrah. The Persia red is mainly Syrah and aged in *barriques*, some new. Nadal is roughly equal proportions of Syrah and Grenache, a blockbuster style often marked by alcohol but generally well-balanced. A number of single varietal bottlings of reds have also been produced in recent vintages. Roussanne is an important component of the two whites. The regular bottling blends in some Clairette as well, whereas the Persia is almost exclusively Rousanne aged in barrel on its lees. The wines are well worth seeking out and very good value. (DM)

● **Côtes du Ventoux**★ £A Cuvée Fayard★★ £B Cuvée Persia★★★ £B
● **Côtes du Ventoux** Cuvée Carles Nadal★★★ £B
O **Côtes du Ventoux**★ £A Cuvée Persia★★ £B

FONT DE MICHELLE Châteauneuf-du-Pape   A: JAr, Yng, Tan, WSS

Owner: Gonnet family 14 Impasse de Vignerons, 84370 Bedarrides

There has been a marked step up in quality here since the late 1990s, not least because of considerable investment in the cellar. The Côtes du Rhone and Rhône-Villages reds are fruity and approachable. Les Promesses is dominated by Grenache with some Carignan and Cinsault, while Notre Passion blends Syrah and Grenache in equal parts. It is understandably denser and fuller but ripe and forward too. Both are 80 per cent destemmed and get a two week maceration. A small portion Notre Passion is aged in oak. The Font de Viognier is 100 per cent varietal, cool-fermented and marked by clean, lightly perfumed peach fruit. It should be drunk young and fresh. White Châteauneuf-du-Pape is also for early drinking, although the stylish Cuvée Etienne Gonnet, vinified with a high proportion of Rousanne, will develop well over the short term. The regular red Châteauneuf used to lack real depth and substance, with part being vinified by carbonic maceration. The style now, though, is for sturdier, longer-lived wines and the Gonnets have produced serious wines in recent vintages. Part of the key is some very old Grenache: 50-year-old vines go into the regular wine and 90-year-olds into the *barrique*-aged (part new) Etienne Gonnet, which is now very cellarworthy and will improve for a decade or more. (DM)

● **Côtes du Rhône** Font du Vent Les Promesses★★ £B
● **Côtes du Rhône-Villages** La Font du Vent Notre Passion★★ £B

O **Côtes du Rhône** F de Font Viognier★★ £B
● **Châteauneuf-du-Pape**★★★ £D Cuvée Etienne Gonnet★★★★★ £F
O **Châteauneuf-du-Pape**★★ £C Cuvée Etienne Gonnet★★★★ £E

DOM. DE FONT SANE   Gigondas   A: Bib, GBa

Owner: Peysson family   Route Sablet, 84190 Gigondas
First-class producer of both Gigondas and Côtes du Ventoux with 14 ha of very low-yielding vineyards. The
Ventoux is among the better examples in that AC and excellent value for money. The vineyards are planted
on the lower slopes of the Dentelles and the climate is warmer than most in the appellation. The regular
Gigondas is a spicy herb-laden blend of Grenache, Syrah, Mourvèdre and Cinsault, while the oak-aged
barrel selection Cuvée Futée is dense, powerful and very ageworthy. It is generally made from the oldest
vines on the property and requires five years' patience to show at its best. (DM)
● **Cotes du Ventoux**★ £A
● **Gigondas**★★★ £C Cuvée Futée★★★★ £C

DOM. LA GARRIGUE   Vacqueyras

Owner: Bernard family   84190 Vacqueyras
Very good traditional domaine with 65 ha of vineyard spread across Vacqueyras and Gigondas and
additional holdings simply classified as Côtes du Rhône. Clairette and Grenache Blanc make up the blend
of the white Vacqueyras but the main focus of the property is on red Vacqueyras and Gigondas from
plantings dominated by Grenache with a smattering of Syrah, Mourvèdre and Cinsault. Vinification is
traditional, with no destemming and no fining or filtration. There is a 20 day *cuvaison* and the resulting
wines are sturdy and powerful. The Cuvée de Hostellerie is particularly fine and in 2001 was close to four
stars. (DM)
● **Vacqueyras**★★★ £B Cuvée de Hostellerie★★★ £C
● **Gigondas**★★★ £C

GOURT DE MAUTENS   Rasteau   A: Rae, SVS

Owner: Jérôme Bressy   84110 Rasteau
Enormously impressive producer with some 14 ha planted almost exclusively to red varieties: Grenache,
Carignan, Syrah, Mourvèdre and a few others. The rich, dense and ageworthy red is produced from vines
that are up to 80 years old. The Bressy style is to create wines with considerable extraction, producing fiery
almost ferocious examples which always not only show concentration but are complex, dark and spicy too.
In recent vintages it has been quite as good as many a top Châteauneuf. The white, a blend of Bourboulenc
and Grenache Blanc, doesn't quite hit the same stellar heights but is still among the most interesting and
structured examples of the region. In keeping with the approach, the wines are bottled unfiltered. (DM)
● **Côtes du Rhône-Villages Rasteau**★★★★ £D
O **Côtes du Rhône-Villages Rasteau**★★★★ £D

DOM. GRAMENON   Côtes du Rhône   A: BRW, HHB, Rae, SVS

Owner: Laurent family   26770 Monbrison-sur-Lez
Long established as one of the great producers in the lesser area of the Côtes du Rhône. Michèle Laurent
has now taken over the running of this domaine from her late husband. The vineyard is planted to
Grenache and Syrah with a little Cinsault and Carignan for the reds and a little Clairette and Viognier
for the whites. Yields are very low and minimal handling and an absence of filtration in the cellar produces
wines of density, concentration and finesse. The remarkable Ceps Centenaires Cuvée Mémé, produced
from very old vines, is as fine as the very best from the southern Rhône. Prices are very reasonable
as well. (DM)
● **Côtes du Rhône** Le Gramenon★★ £B Les Laurentides★★★ £B

● **Côtes du Rhône** La Sagesse★★★ £B La Sierra du Sud★★ £B
● **Côtes du Rhône** Ceps Centenaires Cuvée Mémé★★★★ £C
● **Côtes du Rhône-Villages** Les Hauts de Gramenon★★★ £C
O **Côtes du Rhône** Vie on y est★ £B

DOM. DE GRAND TINEL Châteauneuf-du-Pape   A: NoG, EoR, OWL, WSc

Owner: Jeune family   Route de Bedarrides, 84230 Châteauneuf-du-Pape
Fine, traditional old Châteauneuf property producing earthy, robust reds, albeit without the power of their counterparts a decade ago. Alexis Establet is produced from the family's parcels of particularly old vines and shows greater complexity. Bottling here is staged and it's worth trying to purchase as close to the vintage as possible. (DM)
● **Châteauneuf-du-Pape Traditionelle★★★** £C Cuvée Alexis Establet★★★ £D

DOM. GRAPILLON D'OR Gigondas   A: CTy

Owner: Bernard Chauvet 84190 Gigondas
Bernard Chauvet produces good traditional wines from around 15 ha in Gigondas, including several different parcels, and a further 9 ha in Vacqueyras. Plantings are dominated by Grenache but also include Syrah and Cinsault and, as is the practice in a number of properties, they are vinified together. The fruit is not destemmed and there is a long *cuvaison* of up to 20 days for the Gigondas. The Vacqueyras is the lighter of the wines and will drink well with two or three years age, while the Gigondas is sturdy and masculine, and will add increasing complexity with up to 10 years' age. The wines are bottled without filtration after ageing in old *foudres*. (DM)
● **Gigondas★★★** £C ● **Vacqueyras★★** £B

DOM. DE LA JANASSE Châteauneuf-du-Pape   A: Eno, N&P, NYg, WSc

Owner: Aimé Sabon   27 Chemin de Moulin, 84350 Courthezon
Splendid, medium-sized domaine producing good to excellent wines across the board. A total of some 12,500 cases are produced annually from 50 ha of vines. The Châteauneuf vines are planted on ideal, free-draining stony soils and this, together with a vine age averaging over 60 years, results in lovely supple, dense and powerful wines. Vinification is a good deal more modern than at some properties in the region. Jean-Luc COLOMBO has consulted here and part of the red crop is always destemmed. Ageing is in an assortment of vessels with some new oak being used for the red and white Châteauneuf-du-Pape. The Chaupin and Vieilles-Vignes reds develop very well in bottle and should be given at least four or five years. (DM)
● **Côtes du Rhône** Tradition★ £B Les Garrigues★★ £B O **Côtes du Rhône★** £B
● **Châteauneuf-du-Pape★★★★** £D Cuvée Chaupin★★★★★ £E Vieilles Vignes★★★★★ £F
O **Châteauneuf-du-Pape** Tradition★★★ £C Prestige★★★★ £F
● **Vin de Pays de la Principaute d'Orange** Terre de Buissiere★★ £B
O **Vin de Pays de la Principaute d'Orange** Viognier★★ £B

DOM. LA BLAQUE Coteaux de Pierrevert

Owner: M. Pampus Route de la Bastides-des-Jourdans, 04860 Pierrevert
As well as being the leading property in size at 62 ha, Domaine la Blaque is also the beacon for quality in this small (450 ha), little-known but potentially fine appellation. A range of AC wines are joined by a couple of *vin de pays* labels, a fresh fragrant Viognier and a Pinot Noir. The vineyards are planted at altitude, 450 to 550 m up in the Alpes de Haute Provence, and the Alps proper can be seen in the distance from the vineyards. The climate, though, is very benign for wine-growing. There are up 320 sunny days a year and during the summer the diurnal swing in temperature between day and night ensures good acidity in the fruit. The regular AC labels are vinified to emphasise their fruit, although the red has the structure to stand

a little age. Both the red and white Reserves will develop well in bottle. The white, a blend of Grenache Blanc, Vermentino and Roussanne is barrel-fermented with rich, concentrated honey, citrus and nutmeg aromas and impressive structure. It will develop well over 5 years or so. The dense and structured Reserve red is mainly Syrah with carefully selected Grenache. Aged in oak for 12 months, it is dense and structured, full of black pepper and rich blackberry fruit and just a hint of herb spice. The top wine, Cuvée Collection, is dominated by old-vine Syrah. Vinified with whole bunches and macerated for 4 weeks before ageing in new oak, it is rich, pure and ageworthy. (DM)

- ● **Coteaux de Pierrevert★★** £B Reserve★★★ £C
- O **Coteaux de Pierrevert★★** £B Reserve★★★ £C
- ◉ **Coteaux de Pierrevert★** £B

DOM. LAFOND-ROC-EPINE Tavel www.lafond.roc-epine.com A:CTy, BBR

Owner: Jean-Pierre & Pascal Lafond Route des Vignobles, 30126 Tavel
Excellent-value wines produced from Lirac, Châteauneuf-du-Pape and the Côtes du Rhône as well as one of the better Tavels, which shows some vibrant fresh fruit. The Lirac and Châteauneuf-du-Pape are blended from a mix of Grenache, Syrah and Mourvèdre, while the Côtes du Rhône is just Grenache and Syrah. Vinification of the reds is modern with fermentation in stainless steel before ageing in a mix of large and small oak. In addition, the Lafonds produce a straightforward, pleasant white Lirac from a blend of Grenache Blanc, Viognier and Roussanne and a sumptuously rich special *cuvée* La Ferme Romaine, which is aged in small oak for a year. The Liracs and Châteauneuf-du-Pape will evolve well in the medium term. (DM)

- ● **Lirac★★** £B La Ferme Romaine★★★ £C
- ● **Châteauneuf-du-Pape★★★** £D
- ● **Côtes du Rhône★★** £B
- O **Lirac★** £B

DOM. LA GUINTRANDY Visan

Owner: Olivier Cuilleras 84820 Visan
Olivier Cuilleras is emerging as one of the new stars of the southern Rhône. His family possesses 28 ha of vineyards, all but 1 ha being planted to reds, and produces 4–5,000 cases a year. The domaine is characterised by the extent of its old-vine plantings, which contribute greatly to the quality of the wines. As well as the three fine bottlings from Visan there is an improving Côtes du Rhône, which includes 70 per cent of 30-year-old Grenache and some very old Carignan. The *vin de pays* red, generally 50/50 Grenache and Syrah, is produced from some of the youngest vines on the property. The Visan Vieilles Vignes is a blend of mainly 50-year-old Grenache with a little Carignan and Syrah. The Cuvee Les Devès and top Cuvee Louise Amelie are both aged in oak, the Louise Amelie seeing some new wood. These wines are marked out by pure, rich and complex old-vine character. Expect all the Visan bottlings to develop well over five years or more. (DM)

- ● **Côtes du Rhône-Villages Visan** Les Devès★★★ £B Vieilles Vignes★★★ £B
- ● **Côtes du Rhône★★** £B ● **Côtes du Rhône-Villages Visan** Louise Amelie★★★ £C
- ● **Vin de Pays de Comté de Grignan★** £A

DOM. LA ROQUETTE Châteauneuf-du-Pape www.vignoblesbrunier.fr A:L&W, BBR

Owner: Brunier family Avenue Louis Pasteur, 84230 Châteauneuf-du-Pape
While this property is owned by the Bruniers it is quite separate from VIEUX-TÉLÉGRAPHE. Produced from vineyard parcels spread throughout the appellation, these are unfiltered modern wines of some class and finesse. The average vine age is now around 40 years and this undoubtedly helps quality. The white should be broached young, the red with a little age. It is marked particularly by its vibrant, attractive, dark, spicy fruit character, supple velvety tannin and approachable style. (DM)

- ● **Châteauneuf-du-Pape★★★** £D O **Châteauneuf-du-Pape★★★** £D

DOM. LA SOUMADE Rasteau A: BBR,HHB, NYg, Hal

Owner: André Romero 84110 Rasteau
A great range of wines, especially the impressive red Côtes du Rhône, Rasteau and Gigondas. These are vinified as true *vins de garde*. Romero goes for maximum extraction but the results are almost always very good indeed. Even the lesser wines have an abundance of vibrant, crunchy fruit. With the best *cuvées* the lengthy vatting, allied to extensive parcels of old vines (some up to 100 years), provides for dense, chewy, powerful reds in need of five years' cellaring. Romero also produces fine *vins doux naturels* under the Rasteau AC. (DM)
● **Vin de Pays de la Principauté d'Orange** Prestige★★ £B   ● **Vin de Pays** Cabernet Sauvignon★ £B
● **Côtes du Rhône** Les Violettes★★★ £C
● **Côtes du Rhône-Villages Rasteau** Prestige★★★ £C Confiance★★★★ £D
● **Côtes du Rhône-Villages Rasteau** Fleur de Confiance★★★★★ £E
● **Gigondas★★★★** £C   ● **Rasteau★★** £C

DOM. LEA Vin de Pays de Gard www.domaine-lea.com A: Vne

Owner: Vincent Auquier 30260 Cannes et Clairan
Very new small property of some 18 ha planted to a range of varieties including Cabernet Sauvignon, Syrah, Grenache, Cinsault and Carignan among the reds, along with Sauvignon Blanc, Chardonnay and Ugni Blanc. At present two wines are produced. The excellent-value domaine wine is a blend of Merlot and Syrah. Broad, fleshy and approachable with black fruits, pepper and spice, it is marked by its fruit more than anything. The Terres Blanches is dominated by old-vine Carignan with a little Syrah. Vinification is carefully controlled and temperature during the maceration is restricted to ensure a rich but fruit-driven style. (DM)
● **Vin de Pays d'Oc★★** £B Terres Blanches★★ £B

DOM. LES APHILLANTHES Travaillan A:Sec

Owner: Daniel Boulle Quartier Saint Jean, 84850 Travaillan
This is one of the new rising stars of the southern Rhône based in the village of Travaillan. R & R is the most accesible of the wines but Les Galets, which is mainly Grenache, is similarly open and approachable. The more seriously structured Trois Cepages blends Grenache, Syrah and Mourvèdre. The Cuvée du Cros is produced solely from Syrah, while the Vieilles Vignes is made from very old Grenache with around 20 per cent Mourvèdre. Bottled with neither fining nor filtration all the wines show real depth and impressive concentration and will develop very well in bottle. A Côtes du Rhône-Villages made from pure low-yielding Mourvèdre is also now produced. (DM)
● **Côtes du Rhône-Villages** Cuvée du Cros★★★★ £C Vieilles Vignes★★★★ £C
● **Côtes du Rhône-Villages** Les Galets★★★ £C Trois Cépages★★★ £C
● **Côtes du Rhône-Villages** R & R★★ £B

LES CAILLOUX Châteauneuf-du-Pape A: Hal, SVS

Owner: André Brunel 84230 Châteauneuf-du-Pape
Very fine traditional producer of Côtes du Rhône and Châteauneuf-du-Pape. The Côtes du Rhônes are produced at the Brunel family property Domaine de l'Enclos. The profound Cuvée Centenaire produced from 100-year-old vines is one of the great wines of the appellation, while the regular red Châteauneuf is dense and powerful and lacks just a little of the depth of the centenarian. The Brunel family are also involved with the Feraud family of Domaine du PEGAÜ in an excellent small-scale *négociant* venture, FERAUD-BRUNEL. (DM)
Domaine de l'Enclos
● **Côtes du Rhône★★**£B Cuvée Sommelongue★★★ £B

Les Cailloux
● Châteauneuf-du-Pape★★★★ £C Cuvée Centenaire❂❂❂❂❂ £E

PATRICK LESEC SELECTIONS   A: Gau,NYg

Owner: Patrick Lesec 15 bis, Rue Hégésippe Moreau, 75018 Paris
As well as a portfolio that now covers Alsace, Bordeaux, Burgundy, the Rhône, Languedoc and Roussillon, the Loire, the South-West and Italy, wine broker Patrick Lesec also works in association with fine quality-conscious domaines in Languedoc and Roussillon and particularly in the Rhône Valley to produce wines which are released under his own label. As a part of his portfolio he produces top *cuvées* from a number of properties, such as Dom. des Remizières with their Cuvée Emilie and Dom. Coursodon with the La Sensonne. His approach is to vary these slightly to match his own style of ripe, elegant and above all approachable wines. Some of the Rhône *cuvées* are very, very good indeed and there is real potential here at all levels. Excellent results were produced throughout his range for the 2001 vintage and it remains to be seen how well the difficult 02s will fare. (DM)

● **Coteaux du Languedoc** Château Roumanière Tonneaux★★ £C Domaine de Granoupiac★★★ £C
● **Saint-Chinian** Domaine Rouanet Tonneaux★★ £C ● **Faugères** J.C. Estève Tonneaux★★★ £C
● **Hermitage** Domaine des Remizières Cuvée Émilie★★★★★ £E
● **Saint-Joseph** Domaine Coursodon La Sensonne★★★★ £C
● **Cornas** Domaine Michel Perraud Sarah★★★ £D Domaine Michel Perraud Le Vignon★★★★ £E
● **Châteauneuf-du-Pape** Marquis★★★★ £E Marquis Tonneaux★★★★★ £E
● **Châteauneuf-du-Pape** Chasse-Temps★★★★ £E Les Galets Ronds★★★★★ £F
● **Gigondas** Cuvée l'Estrale★★★ £C Les Blaches★★★★ £C
● **Côtes du Rhône-Villages Cairanne** Vieilles Vignes★★★ £C
● **Côtes du Rhône-Villages Rasteau** Vieilles Vignes★★ £B
● **Côtes du Rhône** Bouquet★★ £B

DOM. LES GOUBERT Gigondas   A: BRW

Owner: Jean-Pierre Cartier 84190 Gigondas
An extensive range of Côtes du Rhône and Rhône-Villages wines is made by this domaine and the quality is generally good, sometimes very good. There are 23 ha under vine, of which 20 or so are red, with the majority Grenache but a decent planting of Syrah as well. Barrel-fermentation is used to produce the Viognier, which has real depth and some gloriously ripe, peachy fruit. It is best drunk young. Vinification of the reds is modern without a hint of rusticity emerging in the wines and new oak is used to age the Gigondas Cuvée Florence. Both Gigondas wines are good cellaring prospects. (DM)

● **Gigondas★★** £C Cuvée Florence★★★ £C
● **Côtes du Rhône-Villages Sablet★★** £B
● **Côtes du Rhône-Villages Beaumes de Venise★★** £B
● **Côtes du Rhône★** £B
O **Cotes du Rhone-Villages Sablet★** £B
O **Côtes du Rhône★** £B Viognier Cuvée de V★★ £C

LES PALLIÈRES Gigondas www.vignoblesbrunier.fr   A: THt,F&M

Owner: Brunier family/Kermit Lynch 84190 Gigondas
Now owned as a joint venture between the Bruniers of VIEUX-TÉLÉGRAPHE and US wine merchant Kermit Lynch. The potential of the *terroir* is beginning to be fully explored – the 25 ha of vineyards are ideally located in limestone soils on the precipitous slopes of the Dentelles de Montmirail. The 50-year-old vines produce wines which are now less rustic and increasingly impressive. Some destemming has been introduced and there is careful control in the cellar. The wines are bottled without filtration after 15 months in *cuve* and *foudres*. (DM)

● **Gigondas★★★** £C

DOM. DE MARCOUX Châteauneuf-du-Pape   A: HHB, CCC, Alo

Owner: Armenier family Chemin de la Gironde, 84100 Orange
Model 24-ha property run on biodynamic lines since 1990. There are 16 ha of red grapes planted and just 1 ha of Roussanne and Bourboulenc, which adds a refreshing grip to the white Châteauneuf. The main purpose of the viticultural approach is to optimise the fruit quality of the late-ripening Grenache and Mourvèdre in particular. There can be no question about the results. Vieilles Vignes has for a decade been one of the benchmark wines of the appellation: very ageworthy and extraordinarily complex. (DM)
● **Châteauneuf-du-Pape★★★★** £E Vieilles Vignes✪✪✪✪✪ £F
O **Châteauneuf-du-Pape★★★** £D

DOM. DE LA MONARDIÈRE Vacqueyras

Owner: Martine & Christian Vache Les Grès, 84190 Vacqueyras
A good, small range of wines is produced by Christian Vache at this well-established Vacqueyras property. Volume is accounted for by the reds but a small amount of a fairly pricey and oaky white Vacqueyras is produced from less than 1 ha of Grenache Blanc, Roussanne and Viognier. The regular red, Les Calades, is soft, forward and approachable, whereas the Reserve des Deux Monardes and in particular the dense and complex Vieilles Vignes are wines of greater depth, substance and structure. The Monardes is full of dark cherry character and hints of *garrigue;* the Vieilles Vignes, dense and more imposingly structured, is a wine of real depth and intensity. Both the top reds will benefit from four or five years' patience. (DM)
● **Vacqueyras** Calades★★ £B Réserve des Deux Monardes★★ £C Vieilles Vignes★★★ £C
O **Vacqueyras★★** £C

DOM. MONTIRIUS Vacqueyras

Owner: Christine & Eric Saurel Le Devés, 84260 Sarrians
One of the better properties in Vacqueyras, Montirius has been run on biodynamic lines since the 1999 vintage and is operating from a new winery since 2002. The Saurels have over 50 ha of vineyard of which 35 ha are in Vacqueyras. The white Vacqueyras blends Grenache Blanc, Roussanne and Bourboulenc, which adds a refreshing acidity, and should be drunk within a year or two. The Côtes du Rhône is sourced from vineyards just outside the village of Sablet. Soft and accesible it too should be broached when young and full of fruit. The Gigondas comes from a 16-ha plot of which 12 ha date from 1925 and which is planted in five different soil types. Rich and complex at best, the wine has impressive substance even in a difficult year like 2002. Of the two red Vacqueyras, the regular bottling comes from vines which average 40 years. It is a blend of 70 per cent Grenache and 30 per cent Syrah. The Clos Montirius comes from a particular 8.5 ha sector of the Vacqueyras vineyard which enjoys a very localised drier mesoclimate. From a blend of 50/50 Grenache and Syrah it undoubtably has an extra level of depth and complexity. (DM)
● **Vacqueyras★★** £B Clos Montirius★★★ £C
● **Côtes du Rhône★★** £B ● **Gigondas★★★** £C
O **Vacqueyras★** £B

DOM. DE MONTPERTUIS Châteauneuf-du-Pape   A: L&W, SVS

Owner: Paul Jeune 84230 Châteauneuf-du-Pape
Paul Jeune produces impressively deep and concentrated red Châteauneuf-du-Pape, which is occasionally labelled Domaine de Croze. The wine, a blend of Grenache, Mourvèdre, Syrah and Cinsault, is a powerful, structured example with intense dark berry fruit and spicy, herbal *garrigue* scents. A white Châteauneuf produced from Clairette, Bourboulenc, Grenache Blanc and Roussanne is full, weighty and soft. It should be drunk relatively young. Forward, fruit-driven Côtes du Rhône and *vin de pays* are also produced. Paul Jeune now has an interest in the Côtes du Ventoux property Château de Valcombe, where some increasingly impressive dense and structured examples of this lesser appellation are being made. The

Cuvée Genevrières is very good. Montpertuis's winemaker, Gilles Basq, is also making a dense, richly concentrated new Côtes du Rhône under his own label, Domaine La Manarine. (DM)

Domaine de Montpertuis
● **Châteauneuf-du-Pape**★★★ £D ● **Vin de Pays du Gard** Counoise★ £B ● **Cotes du Rhone**★ £B
○ **Châteauneuf-du-Pape**★★ £C ○ **Côtes du Rhône**★ £B

Château de Valcombe
● **Côtes du Ventoux** Signature★ £B Cuvée Genevrières★★ £B

Domaine La Manarine
● **Côtes du Rhône**★★ £B

DOM. DE LA MORDORÉE Tavel A: L&S, Bal, Box, Rae, HHB

Owner: Christophe Delorme Chemin des Oliviers, 30126 Tavel
Christophe Delorme produces an extensive and impressive range of wines from his fully biodynamic domaine in Tavel. A total of over 55 ha spread across Lirac, Tavel and Châteauneuf-du-Pape yields an excellent range of wines. An impressive number of varieties are planted, particularly white. The Tavel is a benchmark wine, arguably the best of the appellation, and the various Reine des Bois *cuvées* are very refined and characterful and will improve in bottle for five to ten years, the Châteauneuf almost certainly longer. A superb source of very well-priced wines, although some recent very high scores from a well-known American wine critic are bound to put inflationery pressure on them. (DM)
● **Côtes du Rhône**★★ £B ○ **Côtes du Rhône**★ £B
● **Lirac**★★★ £C Reine des Bois★★★★ £C ○ **Lirac** Reine des Bois★★★ £C
● **Châteauneuf-du-Pape**★★★★ £D Reine des Bois★★★★★ £F
◉ **Tavel**★★ £B

MOULIN DE LA GARDETTE Gigondas A: A&B

Owner: Jean-Baptiste Meunier Place de la Mairie, 84190 Gigondas
These are powerful, traditionally slightly rustic styles of Gigondas. Grenache (90 per cent) and Mourvèdre comprise the blend of the regular *cuvée*, whereas Syrah is blended with Grenache and Cinsault in the Ventabren, which is also aged in *barrique* rather than the larger vats used for the regular bottling. Only a relatively small proportion is new and the wine is not overwhelmed by the wood, although some vintages need time for the fruit to show through. There is a general dedication to quality – the wines are neither fined nor filtered and are produced from vines that are over 50 years old. Fine and very intense, they drink very well over the medium term. (DM)
● **Gigondas**★★ £C Cuvée Ventabren★★★ £C

DOM. DE L'ORATOIRE SAINT-MARTIN Cairanne A: Car

Owner: Frédéric and François Alary Route de Saint-Roman, 84290 Cairanne
Frédéric and François are cousins of Daniel and Denis ALARY and produce equally exciting results in this outperforming Rhône village. The main Rhône varieties are planted and there are various blends. All the Cairanne bottlings are very impressive. The white Haut Coustias is a rich, nutty, almost honeyed blend of Marsanne, Roussanne and Viognier. The lesser reds have a high proportion of Grenache but are intense and heady. The Haut Coustias red is lent considerable depth and structure by its large Mourvèdre/Syrah component (60 and 20 per cent respectively). It can hold its own against top-quality Châteauneuf-du-Pape and is rich, concentrated, powerful and very ageworthy. (DM)
● **Côtes du Rhône-Villages Cairanne** Haut Coustias★★★★ £C
● **Côtes du Rhône-Villages Cairanne** Prestige★★★ £B Réserve des Seigneurs★★★ £C
● **Côtes du Rhône**★★ £B ○ **Côtes du Rhône**★ £B
○ **Côtes du Rhône-Villages Cairanne** Haut Coustias★★★ £C

DOM. DU PEGAÜ   Châteauneuf-du-Pape   www.pegau.com   A: Gau, H&B, GrD,SVS, NYg

Owner: Feraud family   Avenue Impériale, 84230 Châteauneuf-du-Pape
Very fine traditional domaine now run largely by Laurence Feraud. The *vin de table* Plan Pegaü is good, if a little light, but in the traditional style of the property. The white Châteauneuf-du-Pape is honeyed, nutty and concentrated. The reds are classic, formidably structured wines. Cuvée Réservée is in fact the regular red bottling but is full of impressive super-ripe, dark berry Grenache character and loaded with muscular tannin in its youth. The immensely concentrated Cuvée da Capo has emerged as one of the Rhône Valley's great reds – dense, massively powerful but refined and very pure as well. The Ferauds are also involved with André Brunel of LES CAILLOUX in a fine new *négociant* venture (FERAUD-BRUNEL). (DM)

- ● **Vin de Table** Plan Pegau Non-Filtré★★ £B
- ● **Châteauneuf-du-Pape** Cuvée Réservée★★★★★ £E   Cuvée da Capo✪✪✪✪✪ £G
- O **Châteauneuf-du-Pape** Cuvée Réservée★★★ £D

DOM. DES PERRIÈRES   Costières de Nîmes

Owner: Emmanuelle & Marc Kreydenweiss   30129 Manduel
Marc Kreydenweiss and his wife Emmanuelle are better known for their stylish Alsace domaine but here in the Costières de Nîmes they produce two good to very good elegant reds in quite marked contrast to many of their neighbours. The approach is one of refinement not muscle. Marc Kreydenweiss feels many of the current new wave of Mediterranean reds are over-extracted and alcoholic. How will they age? The Domaine de Grimaud bottling is Emmanuelle's baby and comes from its own 7-ha vineyard. Blended from 50 per cent Carignan, 25 Cinsault and 25 Grenache, it is full of upfront brambly fruit. Domaine des Perrières is a refined and harmonious blend of Carignan, Syrah and Grenache with vines ranging from 25 to 70 years. It has more depth and a firmer structure and will age well for five or six years. (DM)

- ● **Costières de Nîmes** Domaine des Perrières★★★ £C   Domaine de Grimaud★★ £B

DOM. PERRIN   Côtes du Rhône   www.beaucastel.com   A:Bib, JAr, Mis, BRW, BBR

Owner: Perrin Brothers   84350 Courthezon
This is the *négociant* arm of the Perrin brothers of CHÂTEAU DE BEAUCASTEL. Production is now considerable at over 300,000 cases a year. Most famous among the wines is the long-established brand, La Vieille Ferme, an original trendsetter for quality in the Côtes du Ventoux, although other producers have now taken quality there to higher levels. They also now produce reliable to good examples from a number of southern Rhône ACs along with a sound Crozes-Hermitage. The wines offer an attractive, approachable style with forward, juicy fruit but fail to sing in the way that some of the best small growers in these appellations now do. (DM)

- ● **Crozes-Hermitage**★ £B
- ● **Vacqueyras**★★ £B   ● **Gigondas**★★ £C   ● **Châteauneuf-du-Pape** Les Sinards★★ £C
- ● **Côtes du Rhône**★ £B   ● **Côtes du Rhône-Villages** Réserve★ £B
- O **Côtes du Rhône-Villages** Réserve★ £B

DOM. DE PIAUGIER   Sablet   piaugier@wanadoo.fr   A: GVF

Owner: Jean-Marc Autran   3 Route de Gigondas, 84110 Sablet
Jean-Marc Autran possesses some 30 ha of vineyards in Sablet and Gigondas, almost all of which are planted to red varieties. A very small amount of very good, nutty and lightly herbal white Sablet is made from Grenache Blanc, Roussanne, Viognier and Clairette, which lends a fresh grip to the wine. Among the reds the real star turns are the special *cuvées* from Sablet. All of these are dense, rich, powerful and very impressive for the appellation. Ténébi is an unusual 100 per cent Counoise, Réserve de Maude 100 per cent Syrah. The other Sablets blend Grenache with Mourvèdre. The approach to vinification is traditional and the fruit is not destemmed. The result, though, is never rustic. In the lesser regular Sablet, Côtes du Rhône and even

the Gigondas – which are all lighter – a green undercurrent can occur in poorer vintages. However the Gigondas was very good in 2001. The top Sablet reds and the Gigondas all improve with three or four years' ageing. (DM)

● **Côtes du Rhône★** £A   ● **Côtes du Rhône-Villages Sablet★** £B
● **Côtes du Rhône-Villages Sablet** Montmartel★★★ £C Ténébi★★★ £C Les Briquières★★★★ £C
● **Côtes du Rhône-Villages Sablet** Réserve de Maude★★★★ £D Réserve Alphonse Vautour★★★★ £D
● **Gigondas★★** £C

DOM. RABASSE-CHARAVIN   Cairanne   A:THt

Owner: Corinne Couturier   La Font d'Estevenas, 84290 Cairanne
A good small range here with fairly extensive vineyards (over 65 ha) and a surprisingly large annual production of around 15,000 cases. All but 2 ha are planted to red varieties. The average vine age is now over 50 years, which no doubt ably assists in maintaining wine quality. The approach to vinifying the reds is traditional, with no destemming and ageing in vat. The wines are well made, with good dark berry fruit and a typically intense herbal component. Cuvée Estevenas has impressive depth and firm tannin in its youth. It is a good medium-term cellar prospect. (DM)

● **Côtes du Rhône-Villages Cairanne★★** £B Estevenas★★★ £B
● **Côtes du Rhône-Villages Rasteau★★** £B
○ **Côtes du Rhône-Villages Cairanne★** £B

DOM. RASPAIL-AY   Gigondas   A: Has

Owner: Dominique Ay   Le Colombier, 84190 Gigondas
Dominique Ay produces just two wines from his 18 ha in Gigondas. There is a little rosé but the real interest here is the burly, powerful but elegant and very ageworthy Gigondas. The fruit is all destemmed and the result is not at all rustic. The wine is aged in large vats rather than in *barrique* but is none the worse for that. On occasion the wine can lack the intensity and power of the very best. 2000 lacked a touch of ripeness whereas 01 was very impressive indeed, clearly four stars. (DM)

● **Gigondas★★★** £C

DOM. RÉMÉJEANNE   Côtes du Rhône-Villages   remejeanne@wanadoo.fr   A: CTy

Owner: Remy Klein   Cadignac, 30200 Sabran
A real benchmark for other Côtes du Rhône properties. This medium-sized domaine makes some 12,500 cases annually, 90 per cent of it red, from 35 ha of vineyards. Les Arbousiers red and white are classic southern Rhône blends – the red is vibrant and spicy, the white subtly nutty. Les Chevrefeuilles adds Carignan and Counoise from old vines to Syrah and Grenache. The top two *cuvées* are Les Églantiers (100 per cent Syrah) and Les Génevriers, a blend of Grenache, Syrah and Mourvèdre. Vinification is high-tech and modern and micro-oygenation is used during *élevage*. The top wines are rich, concentrated and develop well in bottle after three to five years' ageing. A powerful white Les Eglantiers, currently labelled as a *vin de table*, has recently been added. (DM)

● **Côtes du Rhone** Les Arbousiers★★ £B Les Chèvrefeuilles★★★ £B Les Églantiers★★★★ £C
○ **Côtes du Rhone** Les Arbousiers★ £B
● **Côtes du Rhône-Villages** Les Génevriers★★★ £B

DOM. DE RENJARDE   Côtes du Rhône   www.chateau-la-nerthe.com   A: BBR, C&C

Owner: LVMH   Route d'Uchaux, 84830 Serignan du Comtat
Good, well-priced reds from a sister property to CHÂTEAU LA NERTHE. There are 50 ha under vine so this is quite a substantial operation with an annual output of around 20,000 cases in all. The vineyard is planted to a blend of Grenache, Syrah, Cinsault, Carignan and Mourvèdre. Alain Dugas, the director of Château La Nerthe, also guides operations here. Unlike at its sister property, vinfication of each variety is

separate, emphasising the quality of the fruit, with *assemblage* prior to bottling. Undoubtedly the quality stamp of the Richard family shows through, with a good, medium-weight, attractive fruit-driven Côtes du Rhône of some style and the Réserve de Cassagne, which is a particularly well-priced concentrated and structured red. (DM)

● **Côtes du Rhône**★★ £B
● **Côtes du Rhône-Villages** Réserve de Cassagne★★★ £B

MARCEL RICHAUD   Cairanne   A: Lib

Owner: Marcel Richaud   Route de Rasteau, 84290 Cairanne

Marcel Richaud is one of a number of excellent producers from this top-performing village. He has a reasonably sizeable vineyard holding of over 40 ha, some of which dates back over 100 years, so the potential of his raw material is remarkable and this shows through in his wines. All have impressive, spicy berry fruit with intense notes of thyme and the classic scent of *garrigues* from a range offering very fair prices. The top two *cuvées* are impressively structured; the Estrambords is aged in *barriques*, while the Côtes du Rhône Les Garrigues is particularly good value. In the difficult 2002 vintage only the Côtes du Rhône labels were released – no Cairanne – with quality holding up reasonably well. (DM)

● **Côtes du Rhône**★ £B Terres d'Aigues★★ £B Les Garrigues★★★ £B
O **Côtes du Rhône**★ £B
● **Côtes du Rhône-Villages Cairanne**★★★ £B L'Ebrescade★★★★ £C Les Estrambords★★★★ £C
O **Côtes du Rhône-Villages Cairanne**★★ £B

DOMINIQUE ROCHER   Cairanne   www.rochervin.com   A:WTs

Owner: Dominique Rocher   Route de Saint-Roman, 84290 Cairanne

Stylish modern domaine with some superbly sited vineyards totalling around 14 ha. The Côtes du Rhône wines are both full of fruit, the red as appealing in its youth as the nutty, herbal white. The Cairanne labels are more serious. Cuvée Monsieur Paul is firmly structured, but it can appear a touch over-extracted on occasions. The vinification is modern – virtually all the crop is destemmed and many of the cellar operations are carried out by gravity. This is a good source and the Cairanne wines will improve for several years. (DM)

● **Côtes du Rhône-Villages Cairanne**★★ £B Cuvée Monsieur Paul★★ £B
● **Côtes du Rhône**★ £B O **Côtes du Rhône**★ £B

DOM. ROUGE GARANCE   Côtes du Rhône-Villages

Owner: Jean-Louis Trintignant/Claudie et Bertrand Cortellini   30210 Saint-Hilaire d'Ozhilan

This is a small 5 ha estate run by the Cortellinis and jointly owned with the French comedy film actor Jean-Louis Trintignant. They own a total of 28 ha spread across various vineyards in the communes of Castillon du Gard and Saint-Hilaire d'Ozilhan. Only a relatively small part of the harvest each year is vinified as Rouge Garance. Some will go into the second label, Garances, which protects the integrity of the estate wine and fruit may also be sold off. With the trials of the 2002 vintage no Rouge Garance was made at all. Typically, in a good year like 03, the Garances has a lot of very old vine Carignan in the blend, whereas the Rouge Garance will be dominated by Grenache. The wines will age well over the short to medium term. There is a further straightforward fruit-driven Côtes du Rhône Feuilles de Garance and a well-priced ripe and forward easy-drinking white. (DM)

● **Côtes du Rhône-Villages**★★★ £B Garances★★ £B

ROGER SABON   Châteauneuf-du-Pape   A: Gau, Rae, BBR, Bal,Sel

Owner: Roger Sabon   Avenue Impérial, BP 57, 84230 Châteauneuf-du-Pape

While there is good to very good regular Lirac and Châteauneuf-du-Pape here it is the marvellous old-vine Cuvée Prestige and Le Secret de Sabon that show real intensity and sheer class. They are produced from very low-yielding, superbly sited, venerable vines. The latter is one of the great wines of the appellation. The wines are all bottled without filtration. (DM)

- **Châteauneuf-du-Pape** Les Olivets★★ £D Cuvée Réservée★★★ £D
- **Châteauneuf-du-Pape** Cuvée Prestige★★★★ £E Le Secret de Sabon★★★★★ £F
- **Lirac**★★ £B

SANG DES CAILLOUX Vacqueyras   A: CPp

Owner: Serge Férigoule 84260 Sarrians

The performance at this estate represents one of the region's notable turnarounds in recent years. Quality in the early to mid-1990s was acceptable but only just. The wines were light, lacked dimension and appeared heavily processed. Now, though, they have minimal manipulation and are all the better for it. A barrel-fermented white is made from Grenache Blanc, Bourboulenc, Clairette and Roussanne but in tiny quantities, fewer than 200 cases a year. It is the two excellent-value reds which demand attention, particularly for their availability. They are now rich, dense and loaded with black fruit and spicy *garrigue* scents. The Classique has been variously named Doucinello, Azalais and Floureto over recent vintages (since 1995). It is blended from Grenache, Syrah, Mourvèdre and Cinsault and is the mainstay of the domaine. The Cuvée Lopy is produced from the oldest vines of Grenache (75 years) and Syrah. It is firmly structured and requires three or four years. Both reds keep very well. (DM)

- **Vacqueyras** Classique★★★ £B Cuvée Lopy Vieilles Vignes★★★★ £C

DOM. SANTA DUC Gigondas   A: Bib,Rae,HHB,F&M

Owner: Yves Gras 84190 Gigondas

For the past decade or more Santa Duc has been one of the finest and most reliable names in Gigondas. Even in some of the lesser vintages of the 1990s the wines showed impressively well. Just over half of Yves Gras's holding is in Gigondas and of other wines the red *vin de pays* is attractively fruity with crunchy strawberry and dark cherry flavours to the fore, while the Côtes du Rhône is lighter than some but has intensity and a marked scent of *garrigues*. The wines are given a cold soak prior to fermentation and are bottled unfined and unfiltered after being aged on lees. In Gigondas there is a solid *negoçiant* wine, La Garancières, but it is the two domaine wines which really stand out. The regular *cuvée* is the softer, more forward of the two, with the more structured and very, very fine Les Hautes Garrigues seeing around one-third new oak. The balance is aged in *foudres*. A small range of *negoçiant* offerings from the southern Rhône is also now being offered, labelled Santa Duc Selections. (DM)

- **Vin de Pays de la Principauté d'Orange**★ £B ● **Côtes du Rhône**★★ £B
- **Gigondas**★★★ £C La Garancières★★ £B Les Hautes Garrigues★★★★ £D

DOM. SAINTE-ANNE Côtes du Rhône   A: OWL,Tan, SVS, BBR

Owner: Steinmaier family Les Cellettes, 30200 Saint-Gervais

Quality has been of a high order here throughout the 1990s but the wines still remain very good value. There are some 33 ha under vine and Syrah and Mourvèdre as well as Grenache are important in shaping the style of the reds. These are full-bodied and dense; the top two *cuvées* in particular will benefit from medium-term ageing. The Viognier is important here and is one of the better southern Rhône examples. It should always be enjoyed young and fresh, when it will be both exotic and peachy. (DM)

- **Côtes du Rhône-Villages**★★ £B Cuvée St Gervais★★★ £B Cuvée Notre-Dame des Celettes★★★ £B
- O **Côtes du Rhône** Viognier★★ £C

TARDIEU-LAURENT   A: HBJ,Vig, Rae, BBR

Owner: Michel Tardieu/Dominique Laurent Qtr. Les Ferailles, Route de Cucuron, 84160 Lourmarin

An exceptional range of wines from throughout the Rhône Valley is produced by the partnership of Michel Tardieu and Dominique LAURENT of Burgundy. Along with wines from the Rhône there are selected bottlings from the Costières de Nimes, Provence and the Languedoc. Almost everything is of at least two to three-star quality. Top wines from Hermitage, Côte-Rôtie and Cornas in the north and Châteauneuf-du-Pape, Gigondas and Vacqueyras in the south invariably rate at least three and often four stars, particularly the Vieilles Vignes labels. (DM)

● **Côtes du Rhône** Guy Louis★★★ £C   ● **Saint-Joseph** Vieilles Vignes★★★ £D
● **Côtes du Rhône-Villages Rasteau** Vieilles-Vignes★★★ £C
● **Costieres de Nimes**★★★ £B   ● **Corbieres** Roquefort★★★ £B

DOM. DU TRAPADIS   Rasteau   A: GrD, H&B, VTr, SVS

Owner: Michèle Charavin & Helen Durand   Route d'Orange, 84110 Rasteau
Helen Durand has been in charge here since 1994 and the estate is now run with minimal interference in vineyard or cellar. Les Adrès is a classic, Grenache-based southern Rhône blend while Harys is produced from Syrah. Traditional vinification (no destemming) produces wines which are both rich and structured. Even the Côtes du Rhône will benefit from short cellaring. In short these are powerful and complex wines. (DM)

● **Côtes du Rhône**★★ £B
● **Côtes du Rhône-Villages Rasteau**★★★ £B   Les Adrès★★★ £C   Harys★★★ £C

PIERRE USSEGLIO   Châteauneuf-du-Pape   A: Gau, BBR

Owner: Jean-Pierre & Thierry Usseglio   Route d'Orange, 84230 Châteauneuf-du-Pape
Jean-Pierre and Thierry are now running their father's property of some 23 ha, where they produce around 4,500 cases a year. The white is sound but it is the reds which excel. They include very good regular red Châteauneuf as well as the super-dense and rich old-vine Mon Aïeul and an exceptional Cuvée Cinquantenaire which was produced in 1999. Réserve des Deux-Frères, an expensive special bottling that replaces the Cinquantenaire as the top label, was made in 2000 and 01. (DM)

● **Châteauneuf-du-Pape** Tradition★★★ £C   Cuvée de Mon Aïeul★★★★ £E
O **Châteauneuf-du-Pape** Tradition★★ £C

DOM. DE LA VIEILLE-JULIENNE   Châteauneuf-du-Pape   A: SVS, OWL, Sel

Owner: Jean-Paul Daumen   84100 Orange
The wines here are now of a different order to those of a few years back. The *vin de pays* is still from relatively young vines but for the Côtes du Rhône and Châteauneuf-du-Pape bottlings the vines are old to very old. The Vieilles Vignes Côtes du Rhône is produced from 60-year-old plantings and is a blend of Grenache, Syrah and Mourvèdre. It is very intense and complex. The regular Châteauneuf-du-Pape is sweet, spicy and intense, full of *garrigue* and super-ripe dark berry fruit – the 2000 rated four stars. The top two *cuvées* are remarkable. The Vieilles Vignes is immensely powerful and structured and it needs time. The Vieilles Vignes Réservé is extraordinary – ninety-five per cent Grenache, heady and super-rich, it's the more open and approachable of the two but immensely ageworthy. (DM)

● **Châteauneuf-du-Pape**★★★ £C   Vieilles Vignes★★★★★ £F   Vieilles Vignes Réservé✪✪✪✪✪ £H
● **Cotes du Rhone**★★ £B   Vieilles Vignes★★★ £B
● **Vin de Pays de la Principauté d'Orange**★ £B

DOM. DU VIEUX-TÉLÉGRAPHE   Châteauneuf-du-Pape   A: J&B, BBR, THt, Sel, Tan, SVS, F&M

Owner: Brunier family   3 Route de Châteauneuf-du-Pape, 84370 Bedarrides
The Bruniers have been benchmark producers here for two decades. They now own the Domaine LA ROQUETTE also in Châteauneuf, and have an interest in the revitalised LES PALLIÈRES in Gigondas. The 70-ha estate is planted largely to reds, understandably, with a little Clairette, Grenache Blanc, Bourboulenc and Roussanne, which are used to produce a spicy, intensely nutty and surprisingly refined white Châteauneuf. The Vieux Mas des Papes is a very impressive second wine. The approach is to maximise the potential of the *grand vin*, rather than bottling small plots as special individual *cuvées*. The

Châteauneuf-du-Pape red is now denser and more powerful than of old but with marvellous depth and refinement. There have been significant improvements at many properties throughout the appellation in recent years but few of these wines can achieve the balance and harmony of those of the Bruniers. (DM)

● **Châteauneuf-du-Pape❂❂❂❂❂** £E Le Vieux Mas des Papes★★★ £C
○ **Châteauneuf-du-Pape★★★★** £E
● **Vin de Pays de Vaucluse** Le Pigeoulet★★ £B

SOUTHERN RHÔNE/OTHER WINES OF NOTE

DOM. D'AÉRIA ● **Côtes du Rhône-Villages Cairanne** Tradition £B
DOM. DE L'AMEILLAUD ● **Côtes du Rhône-Villages Cairanne** £B
DOM. DES ANGES ● **Côtes du Ventoux** £A Clos de l'Archange £B
LES DOMAINES BERNARD ● **Châteauneuf-du-Pape** Louis Bernard £C
DOM. DES BERNARDINS ○ **Muscat de Beaumes-de-Venise** £C
BOIS DAUPHIN ● **Châteauneuf-du-Pape** £C
DOM. DES BOSQUETS ● **Gigondas** £C
DOM. BOUCHASSY ● **Lirac** £B
DOM. DE LA BOUISSIÈRE ● **Gigondas** £B Cuvée La Font du Tonin £C
DOMAINES BOUR ● **Coteaux du Tricastin** Vieilles Vignes £B La Truffière £B
DOM. BRESSY MASSON ● **Côtes du Rhône-Villages** Envée Paul-Emile£B
DOM. DES BUISSERONS ● **Côtes du Rhône-Villages Cairanne** £B
DOM. DE CABASSE ● **Côtes du Rhône-Villages Séguret** £B Casa Bassa £B ● **Gigondas** £C
DOM. DE CASSAN ● **Gigondas** £B
DOM. DE CHANABAS ● **Châteauneuf-du-Pape** £C
CHANTE PERDRIX ● **Châteauneuf-du-Pape** £C
DIDIER CHARAVIN ● **Côtes du Rhône Villages Rasteau**£B Prestige£B
CH. D'ACQUERIA ◉ **Tavel** £B ● **Lirac** £B
CH. BEAUBOIS ● **Costières de Nîmes** £B Barriques £B
CH. CABRIÈRES ● **Châteauneuf-du-Pape** £C Tête de Cru £E
CH. CAMPUGET ● **Costières de Nîmes** Cuvée Prestige £B
CH. FONTSÉGUGNE ● **Côtes du Rhône** £B Santo Estello £B
CH. FORTIA ● **Châteauneuf-du-Pape** £C
CH. DE GRAND MOULAS ● **Côtes du Rhône** £B ● **Côtes du Rhône-Villages** £B
CH. GRANDE-CASSAGNE ● **Costières de Nîmes** £B
CH. LA CANORGUE ● **Côtes du Luberon** £B ● **Côtes du Rhône** £B
● **Côtes du Rhône-Villages Laudun** £B
CH. MAUCOIL ● **Châteauneuf-du-Pape** £C Cuvée Privilège £C
CH. LA TUILERIE ● **Costières de Nîmes** Cuvée Eole £B
CH. DE MONTMIRAIL ● **Vacqueyras** l'Ermite £B St Papes £B ● **Gigondas** Beauchamp £B
CH. DE NAGES ● **Costières de Nîmes** £B Vieilles Vignes £B
CH. DE ROUANNE ● **Côtes du Rhône-Villages Vinsobres** £B
CH. DES ROQUES ● **Vacqueyras** £B
CH. SAINT-ROCH ● **Lirac** Cuvée Confidentielle £C
CH. DE SEGRIES ● **Côtes du Rhône** Clos de l'Hermitage £B ● **Lirac** Cuvée Reservée £C
CH. SIGNAC ● **Côtes du Rhone-Villages** £B Combe d'Enfer £B Terra Amata £B
CH. DU TRIGNON ● **Côtes du Rhône-Villages Sablet** £B ● **Gigondas** £C
CH. VAL JOANIS ● **Côtes du Luberon** Réserve Les Griottes £B
CH. DE VALCOMBE ● **Costières de Nîmes** Cuvée Prestige £B
CH. DE LA VERRERIE ● **Côtes du Luberon** £B
CH. VIRGILE ● **Costières de Nîmes** £B
DOM. DE LA CITADELLE ● **Cotes du Luberon** £B Cuvée de Gouverneur £C
CLOS DU JONCUAS ● **Gigondas** Esprit de Grenache £B
CLOS DE L'ORATOIRE DES PAPES ● **Châteauneuf-du-Pape** £C
CLOS SAINT-MICHEL ● **Châteauneuf-du-Pape** £C Cuvée Réservée £D
DOM. DES CORIANCON ● **Côtes du Rhône-Villages Vinsobres** £B Cuvée Claude Vallot £B

DOM DU CORNE-LOUP ● **Lirac** £B

DOM. DU COUROULU ● **Vacqueyras** £B Vieilles Vignes £B

DOM. DE LA DAYSSE ● **Gigondas** £B

DIFFONTY ET FILS ● **Châteauneuf-du-Pape** £C Réserve Sixteen £D

DOMAINE DUCLAUX ● **Châteauneuf-du-Pape** £C

CAVE D'ESTÉZARGUES ● **Côtes du Rhône** Dom. d'Andezon £B
● **Côtes du Rhône-Villages** Dom. d'Andezon £B

DOM. DE FERRAND ● **Châteauneuf-du-Pape** £C

DOM. DE FONTENILLE ● **Côtes du Luberon** £B Vieilles Vignes £B Prestige £B

DOM. LOU FREJAU ● **Châteauneuf-du-Pape** £C

GALET DES PAPES ● **Châteauneuf-du-Pape** £C Vieilles Vignes £D

DOM. GRAND BOURJASSOT ● **Gigondas** £B

DOM. DES GRAND DEVERS ● **Côtes du Rhône** Enclave des Papes £B La Suranne £C
● **Côtes du Rhône-Villages Valreas** £B ● **Côtes du Rhône-Villages Visan** £B

DOM. GRAND VENEUR ● **Châteauneuf-du-Pape** £C Cuvée Les Origines £D

DOM. DE GRANGENEUVE ● **Coteaux du Tricastin** Vieilles Vignes £B La Truffiere £B

DOM. DU JONCIER ● **Lirac** £B

DOM. LA BASTIDE SAINT DOMINIQUE ● **Châteauneuf-du-Pape** £C

DOM. LA CABOTTE ● **Côtes du Rhône-Villages** £B Élevé en Futs de Chene £B

DOM. LA FOURMONE ● **Vacqueyras** £B ● **Gigondas** l'Oustau Fauquet £B

DOM. LA NAVETTE ● **Gigondas** £C

DOM. LA ROCALIÈRE ● **Lirac** Cuvée Prestige £B

DOM. LE CLOS DE CAVEAU ● **Vacqueyras** £B Cuvée Lao Muse £C

DOM. CATHERINE LEGOEUIL ● **Côtes du Rhône-Villages Cairanne** Cuvée Lea Felsch £B
● **Côtes du Rhône-Villages Cairanne** Cuvée Marie Rouvière £B Les Beauchières £B

DOM. LES CLEFS D'OR ● **Châteauneuf-du-Pape** £C

DOM. LES GRANDS BOIS ● **Côtes du Rhône-Villages Cairanne** Cuvée Mireille £B
● **Côtes du Rhône-Villages Cairanne** Cuvée Eloise £B

DOM. LES HAUTES CANCES ● **Côtes du Rhône-Villages Cairanne** £B Vieilles Vignes £B

LE VIEUX DONJON ● **Châteauneuf-du-Pape** £D

DOM. LONGUE TOQUE ● **Gigondas** £C

MAS DE BOISLAUZON ● **Châteauneuf-du-Pape** £C

MAS DES BRESSADES ● **Costières de Nîmes** £B ● **Vin de Pays du Gard** Cabernet/Syrah £B

DOM. DU MAS CARLOT ● **Costières de Nîmes** £B

MAS DE GUIOT ● **Vin de Pays du Gard** Cabernet Syrah £B

MAS DE LIBIAN ● **Côtes du Rhone** £B ● **Côtes du Rhône-Villages** £B La Calade £C

DOM. MATHIEU ● **Châteauneuf-du-Pape** £C Marquis Anselm Mathieu £D

DOM. DE MONTVAC ● **Vacqueyras** £B Cuvée Vincilan £C ● **Gigondas** £C

DOM. DU MOULIN ● **Côtes du Rhône-Villages Vinsobres** Charles Joseph £B
O **Côtes du Rhône-Villages Vinsobres** £B

DOM. DE NALYS ● **Châteauneuf-du-Pape** £C

DOM. PÉLAQUIÉ ● **Lirac** £B O **Côtes du Rhône-Villages Laudun** £B

DOM. PÈRE CABOCHE ● **Châteauneuf-du-Pape** £C Cuvée Elisabeth Chambellan £C

DOM. DU PÈRE PAPE ● **Châteauneuf-du-Pape** £C La Crau de Ma Mère £D

ROGER PERRIN ● **Côtes du Rhône** £B Prestige £B ● **Châteauneuf-du-Pape** £C Vieilles Vignes £E

DOM. PESQUIER ● **Gigondas** £C

DOM. DES RELAGNES ● **Châteauneuf-du-Pape** £C Cuvée Vigneronne £D

DOM SAINT-AMANT ● **Côtes du Rhône** Les Clapas £B
● **Côtes du Rhône-Villages Rasteau** Grangeneuve £C O **Côtes du Rhône** La Borry £B
O **Côtes du Rhône-Villages Rasteau** La Tabardonne £C

DOM. SAINT-ANTOINE ● **Costières de Nîmes** Cuvée des Oliviers £B

DOM. SAINT-GAYAN ● **Côtes du Rhône-Villages Rasteau** £B ● **Gigondas** £C Fontmaria £C

DOM. SAINT-ROCH O **Lirac** Cuvée Boisée £C ● **Lirac** £B ● **Châteauneuf-du-Pape** £D

DOM. DE LA SOLITUDE ● **Châteauneuf-du-Pape** £C

DOM. SAINT-BENOIT ● **Châteauneuf-du-Pape** £D La Truffière £E Grand Garde £E

DOM. DE SAINT-LUC ● **Coteaux du Tricastin** Syrah £B ● **Côtes du Rhône-Villages** £B

DOM. DES SAINT-SIFFREIN ● Châteauneuf-du-Pape £C

DOM. DU TERME ● Gigondas £C

DOM. LES TEYSSONIERES ● Gigondas Cuvée Alexandre £C

DOM. LES TOURELLES ● Gigondas £B

DOM. DE LA TOURADE ● Gigondas £B ● Vacqueyras £B

DOM. DE VERQUIERE ● Côtes du Rhône-Villages Sablet £B

DOM. DE VILLENEUVE ● Châteauneuf-du-Pape £D Vieilles Vignes £E

DOM. RAYMOND USSEGLIO ● Châteauneuf-du-Pape Girard £C Impériale £E

DOM VERDA ● Lirac Cuvée Prestige £B

DOM. DE LA VERRIÈRE ● Côtes du Ventoux £B

DOM VIRET ● Côtes du Rhône-Villages Saint-Maurice Renaissance £C Les Colonnades £C Emergence £D

Author's choice (DM)

12 benchmark Châteauneuf-du-Papes

DOM. DE BEAURENARD ● Châteauneuf du Pape Boisrenard

M CHAPOUTIER ● Châteauneuf du Pape Barbe Rac

CH. DE BEAUCASTEL ● Châteauneuf du Pape Hommage à Jacques`Perrin

CH. LA NERTHE ● Châteauneuf du Pape Cuvée des Cadettes

CH. RAYAS ● Châteauneuf du Pape

CLOS DES CAILLOU ● Châteauneuf du Pape Réserve

CLOS DES PAPES ● Châteauneuf du Pape

DOM DE LA JANASSE ● Châteauneuf du Pape Vieilles Vignes

DOM. DE MARCOUX ● Châteauneuf du Pape Vieilles Vignes

DOM. DE LA MORDORÉE ● Châteauneuf du Pape Reine des Bois

DOM. DE LA VIEILLE-JULIENNE ● Châteauneuf du Pape Vieilles Vignes Réservé

DOM. DU VIEUX TÉLÉGRAPHE ● Châteauneuf du Pape

A diverse selection of a dozen emerging reds

DANIEL ET DENIS ALARY ● Côtes du Rhône-Villages Cairanne La Font d'Estevenas

DOM. BRUSSET ● Gigondas Les Hauts de Montmirail

CLOS DES CAZAUX ● Vacqueyras Grénat Noble

CLOS PETITE BELLANE ● Cotes du Rhone Valréas Vieilles Vignes

DOM. DE DEURRE ● Côtes du Rhône Les Rabasses

GOURT DE MAUTENS ● Côtes du Rhône-Villages Rasteau

DOM. LA SOUMADE ● Côtes du Rhône-Villages Rasteau Fleur de Confiance

DOM. LES APHILLANTHES ● Côtes du Rhône-Villages Vieilles Vignes

DOM. DE L'ORATOIRE SAINT-MARTIN ● Côtes du Rhône-Villages Cairanne Haut Coustias

DOM. DE PIAUGIER ● Côtes du Rhône-Villages Sablet Réserve Alphonse Vautour

MARCEL RICHAUD ● Côtes du Rhône-Villages Cairanne Les Estrambords

DOM. SANTA-DUC ● Gigondas Les Hautes Garrigues

A selection of good value reds and whites

CH. SAINT-COSME ● Côtes du Rhone Les Deux Albions

DOM. CHAUME-ARNAUD ○ Côtes du Rhône-Villages Vinsobres

CROS DE LA MÛRE ● Côtes du Rhône-Villages

DOM. DE FONDRÈCHE ● Côtes du Ventoux Cuvée Persia

FONT DE MICHELLE ○ Côtes du Rhône F de Font de Michelle

DOM. LA GARRIGUE ● Vacqueyras

DOM. GRAMENON ○ Côtes du Rhône Vie on y est

DOM. GRAPILLON D'OR ● Gigondas

DOM. RABASSE-CHARAVIN ● Côtes du Rhône-Villages Cairanne Estevenas

DOM. DE RÉMÉJEANNE ● Côtes du Rhone Les Génevriers

SANG DES CAILLOUX ● Vacqueyras Classique

DOM. SAINTE-ANNE ○ Côtes du Rhône Viognier

DOM. DE LA VERRIÈRE ● Côtes du Ventoux

France/Languedoc & Roussillon

The focus here is on established pioneers, as well as the many new small domaines now placing Languedoc-Roussillon solidly on the country's quality wine map. Although many appellations here are of long standing only recently have widespread improvements been made in the standard of the wines. While many high quality domaines are emerging, in the Languedoc in particular many of the wines are over-extracted. There are many fewer new names in the Roussillon but these have been producing wines of a uniformly impressive quality. Many vineyards originally used for fortifieds are now providing some great reds in particular. While prices generally remain very fair some are creeping up significantly. The transformation here is unique in France.

Languedoc

Some truly great wine is now being made in the Languedoc. Most but by no means all of this is produced under a number of different appellations. For reasons of practicality and location a number of splendid new-wave wines, particularly red, are being produced as *vins de pays*. A number are **Vins de Pays d'Oc** but **Vin de Pays de l'Hérault** also features, including two of the greatest properties in the Languedoc, Mas de Daumas Gassac and Domaine de La Grange des Pères.

To the west of the Costières de Nîmes (see Rhône Valley) is the giant spread of the **Coteaux du Languedoc** AC. Vast and sprawling, it stretches from Nîmes in the east around the coastline to Narbonne and a considerable distance into the hills of the Gard and Hérault *départements*. There are twelve communes which are allowed to add their village names as *crus* and these include **La Clape, Picpoul de Pinet, Cabrières, Montpeyroux, Pic-Saint-Loup** and **Saint-Drézéry**. At best there are some splendid wines, generally blends of Syrah, Grenache and Mourvèdre for the reds with whites from a host of varieties including Roussanne, Grenache Blanc and Clairette. Sadly, you are also likely to encounter a great many moderate to average bottles, so always try to buy from a good source.

Just to the north of Béziers and to the west of the Coteaux du Languedoc are the small appellations of **Faugères** and **Saint-Chinian**. Some very fine small properties are now producing great reds, the most important variety being Syrah (which performs superbly in the schistous soils of Faugères) although Grenache, Mourvèdre and old-vine Carignan all play an important role in the local viticulture. There are a number of Muscat-based *vins doux naturels* as well but none are comparable to their peers from Muscat de Rivesaltes in the Roussillon. They include **Muscat de Frontignan, Muscat de Mireval** and **Muscat de Lunel**.

South of Narbonne and stretching down to the hills of the Roussillon are a number of key appellations. **Minervois, Corbières** and **Fitou** had for a long time been regarded as little more than Midi workhorse wines, vinified by unambitious local co-ops or volume *négociants*. This has to a large extent changed for the better. The wines of Minervois have shown the most potential and within that appellation is the new *cru* sub-zone of **La Livinière**, the source of generally the densest and most substantial wines of the AC. Old-vine Carignan plays an important role here although plantings of the Rhône *cépages améliorateurs* continue apace with some vineyards now possessing some increasingly old Syrah, Grenache and Mourvèdre. Carbonic maceration is widely used for Carignan, particularly in Corbières.

To the west of Minervois, the smaller new AC of **Cabardès** has real potential and the Bordeaux varieties Cabernet Sauvignon, Merlot and Cabernet Franc are important here. The biggest disappointment over the past decade has been the performance of Fitou, one of the first ACs established in the region. The co-op at Mont-Tauch has always been a solid source but other promising new producers are emerging.

To the west of Fitou, in the hills around the town of **Limoux**, cool hillside vineyards are planted to Chardonnay and Mauzac. Good sparkling wine is made here, both **Blanquette de Limoux** and **Crémant de Limoux**, but it is the barrel-fermented Chardonnays that have come to prominence in recent years that impress most.

Roussillon

Until recently the vineyards in the Pyrenées-Orientales *département* were best known in quality wine terms for the production of fine *vins doux naturels*. This situation is changing apace though, and there seems perhaps even more potential here than in the Languedoc. Some stunning reds have appeared over the past decade and the emergence of exciting new small producers continues unabated. One of the region's great strengths is the extensive hillside vineyards planted to both old-vine Carignan and equally importantly Grenache. This is because of the traditional importance of fortified Rivesaltes and Maury, from north of Perpignan, and of Banyuls-sur-Mer, another fortified wine further south on the coast.

Exciting wines are being made throughout the **Côtes du Roussillon** and the **Côtes du Roussillon-Villages** ACs. As well as Grenache, the other Rhône varieties are important too, and a number of top *cuvées* vinified largely from Syrah and aged in high-quality new oak are also emerging, along with the occasional exceptional blend dominated by Mourvèdre. On the coast around the village of Banyuls-sur-Mer the **Collioure** appellation shares the same vineyard area as **Banyuls**. Syrah, Carignan, Mourvèdre and Cinsault are all cultivated here but interestingly it is Mourvèdre planted in close proximity to the sea that has performed particularly well, as it does in Bandol. The **Vin de Pays des Côtes Catalanes** is also increasingly important for red blends and these include Cabernet Sauvignon and Merlot. A new and very exciting region that covers much of the physical area shared by the Maury sweet wine appellation is the newly established **Vin de Pays des Coteaux de Fenouillèdes** in the Agly Valley in the north western section of the Côtes du Roussillon. There is a tremendous resource of old vine Grenache and Carignan. A number of top producers have emerged, although not all use the Vin de Pays classification.

The great traditional wines of the Roussillon are the fortified **Maury**, **Rivesaltes** and **Banyuls**, which in their most exquisite and aged manifestations are characterised by an intense baked, raisiny, *rancio* character. A whole range of styles are produced, with small differences between the appellations. Almost all these wines depend on Grenache as the backbone of the blend; indeed, many are produced solely from the variety. There are youthful, fruit-driven styles that spend only a limited time in cask, wines that are aged for an extended time and wines that are made from a blend of vintages very much in a *solera*-style system. The wines of Maury tend to be more overtly tannic when young and those earlier-released vintages will need more cellaring. Most wines are aged in cool cellars but in Rivesaltes they are also left out for a period in the summer sun in large glass containers – *bonbonnes* – to encourage the development of those complex *rancio* aromas.

As well as the Grenache-based wines there is some very impressive **Muscat de Rivesaltes**, which is markedly different in style. At their best these wines emphasise Muscat's rich grapy character, and are heady and impressively perfumed. Indeed, the best examples are better generally than their equivalents in the Languedoc and the Rhône Valley at Beaumes-de-Venise.

A-Z of producers by appellation

1   Muscat de Lunel
2   Coteaux du Languedoc
3   Coteaux du Languedoc Pic Saint-Loup
4   Coteaux du Languedoc Montpeyroux
5   Muscat de Mireval
6   Muscat de Frontignan
7   Coteaux du Languedoc Picpoul de Pinet
8   Faugères
9   Saint-Chinian
10 Muscat de Saint-Jean de Minervois
11 Minervois
12 Coteaux du Languedoc La Clape
13 Cabardès
14 Côtes de la Malepère
15 Limoux
16 Corbières
17 Fitou
18 Maury
19 Côtes du Roussillon-Villages
20 Côtes du Roussillon
21 Rivesaltes, Muscat de Rivesaltes
22 Banyuls, Collioure

Languedoc & Roussillon vintages

It is extremely difficult in a vast region such as this to make specific vintage assessments. Also much of the development that has been made in recent years makes a longer term assessment of the wines more erratic. However, there have been significant changes in vintage conditions from one year to another throughout the region. These variations are more pronounced as you move further inland. Vineyards nearer the coast benefit from a benign maritime climate and are more consistent.

In terms of the wines, the best red examples from year to year have the potential to age. Some red Languedoc wines have shown a recent tendency to fade prematurely, particularly those from the Coteaux du Languedoc. As producers become more successful in unleashing the best character from their grapes this should improve. The *cépages améliorateurs* varieties planted in the Languedoc are also generally still young and the wines made from them can easily be over-extracted. There is no question that as these vines age and the Midi's keen young producers develop their craft the wines will become increasingly refined and cellarworthy.

Languedoc & Roussillon vintage chart

	Corbieres & Minervois	Coteaux du Languedoc	Côtes du Roussillon-Villages including Collioure
2003	★★★★ A	★★★★ A	★★★★/★★★★★ A
2002	★★★ A	★★★ A	★★★/★★★★ A
2001	★★★★/★★★★★ A	★★★★/★★★★★ A	★★★★/★★★★★ A
2000	★★★★/★★★★★ B	★★★★/★★★★★ A	★★★★ A
1999	★★★/★★★★ B	★★★/★★★★ B	★★★★ B
1998	★★★★/★★★★★ B	★★★★/★★★★★ B	★★★★★ B
1997	★★/★★★ D	★★/★★★C	★★★ C
1996	★★★ C	★★★ C	★★★ C
1995	★★★★ C	★★★★ C	★★★★ C
1994	★★★ D	★★★ D	★★★/★★★★ C
1993	★★★/★★★★ D	★★★/★★★★ C	★★★/★★★★ C
1991	★★/★★★ D	★★/★★★ D	★★/★★★ D
1990	★★★★★ D	★★★★ D	★★★★ C

Languedoc

JEAN-MICHEL ALQUIER   Faugères   A: Rae

Owner: Alquier family   4 Route de Pézenes-les-Mines, 34600 Faugères

Long-established quality producer in this appellation. These are impressive wines, almost rustic in the case of the reds – but in the best sense. There are some 12 ha under vine with the vast majority of this planted to red varieties. Syrah accounts for 40 per cent of the *vignoble* and does very well in the meagre, well-drained, soils. The average vine age of the *cépages ameliorateurs* is increasing and this along with a healthy planting of very old Carignan provides tremendous raw material. The regular red Faugères Les Premières, a blend of Syrah, Grenache and Carignan, is good if austere when very young, while there is an extra dimension in the two top reds. La Réserve La Maison Jaune is a mix of Syrah and Mourvèdre whereas Les Bastides is aged in some new oak and has a smattering of Grenache adding a touch of red-berry character. These two wines will age well over six or seven years. The basic white *vin de pays* Roussanne/Marsanne is attractively fruity while the Domaine Jean-Michel Alquier bottling is a gloriously nutty and complex southern-style white. Both of these should be drunk young. (DM)

● **Faugères** Les Premières★★ £B   La Réserve La Maison Jaune★★★ £C   Les Bastides★★★ £C
O **Vin de Pays de l'Hérault** Roussanne/Marsanne★ £B   Domaine Jean-Michel Alquier★★★ £C

DOM. L'AIGUELIÈRE   Coteaux du Languedoc Montpeyroux   A: GVF, N&P

Owner: Aimé Commeyras   2 Place du Square, 34150 Montpeyroux

One of the finest properties in the Languedoc, producing top class reds of impressive depth and raw power. Even in the tricky 2002 vintage the wines are of very sound quality. There are 25 ha planted, nearly 90% being Syrah. A small parcel of Viognier and Sauvignon Blanc results in a fresh, fruit driven white Sarments, produced for the first time in 1999. Fermented and vinified in tank, the wine is best enjoyed within a couple of years of the vintage. Tradition, which blends around 40% Grenache with Syrah, is aged in *cuve* and offers ripe, vibrant upfront dark berry fruit supported by soft youthfully accesible tannins. The two 100% Syrah *cuvées* are of an entirely different order, dense and powerful, with an underlying elegance and refinement often missing in the region. Produced from yields of barely 20hl/ha the opulent Côte Dorée comes from gravel soils, the more structured and backward Côte Rousse from limestone. Both will benefit from five years' ageing. (DM)

● **Coteeaux du Languedoc Montpeyroux** Côte Dorée★★★★ £B   Côte Rousse★★★★★ £B
● **Coteaux du Languedoc Montpeyroux** Tradition★★ £B
O **Vin de Pays d'Oc** Sarments★★ £B

DOM. DES AIRES HAUTES   Minervois   A: Gau, Maj, Gar

Owner: Gilles Chabbert   34210 Siran

This property stands out in an appellation that often disappoints more than it should. Gilles Chabbert produces just over 12,000 cases a year from his 30 ha of organically farmed vines, the vast majority of which are planted to red varieties. As well as the regular forward, fruit-driven Minervois Tradition there is a spicy Vin de Pays d'Oc Malbec and a little Chardonnay. The top two reds are from the sub-appellation of La Livinière and both are blended from Syrah, Grenache and Carignan. Vinification is traditional with an extended *cuvaison* and for the Carignan carbonic maceration is employed to emphasise the fruit. The La Livinière is aged partly in used oak and partly in *cuve*; the Clos de l'Escandil sees around one-third new wood. These are impressive and finely structured examples. The l'Escandil in particular will be all the better for three or four years' cellaring. (DM)

● **Minervois La Livinière**★★ £B   Clos de l'Escandil★★★ £C
● **Minervois** Tradition★ £B

DOM. D'ANTUGNAC Limoux   A: BBR

Owner: Jean-Luc Terrier & Christian Collovray   4 Rue du Château, 11190 Antugnac
Jean-Luc Terrier and Christian Collovray also own the Mâconnais property DOMAINE DES DEUX
ROCHES and Chardonnay is their most successful variety at Limoux. They have a substantial holding of
60 ha, half of which is planted to Chardonnay, Mauzac, Sauvignon and Chenin among white varieties and
half to Pinot Noir, Merlot, Cabernet Franc, Syrah, Cabernet Sauvignon and a smattering of lesser-known
red grapes. The vineyard is planted at altitude and warm summer days and cool nights contribute to the
fresh style. There is a decent vibrant, fruit-driven Merlot, a light and relatively simple Pinot Noir and a red
blend Planal but the whites, particularly the Limoux bottlings, are the wines to go for. Rich and very
Burgundian in style, they are traditionally vinified, offering opulent citrus and nutmeg character with subtle
creamy vanilla oak in the background. The Gravas bottling is a step up from the standard wine but both
will develop well in the short term. (DM)

O **Limoux**★★ £B Gravas★★★ £B
O **Vin de Pays de la Hautee Vallée de l'Aude** Les Grands Penchants★ £B
O **Chardonnay** Vin de Pays d'Oc★ £B
● **Pinot Noir** Vin de Pays de la Haute Vallée de l'Aude★ £C   ● **Merlot** Vin de Pays d'Oc★ £B

DOM. LES AURELLES Coteaux du Languedoc   A:Bal, Han

Owner: Karl Mauguin et Basil Saint-Germain   34720 Caux
Although this property was only established in 1994 some of the vines are up to 70 years old. The vines are
planted in ancient sand and gravel terraces providing for a meagre yield of around 25 hl/ha. The owners
were both classically trained in Bordeaux and this seems to come through in wines which are tight,
well-structured and elegant. Varieties are vinified separately and the vatting for the reds lasts between three
and five weeks. They get a light egg-white fining but filtration is avoided. The Deella, a blend of Carignan,
Grenache, Mourvedre and Syrah is soft, forward and fruit-driven. Solen and Aurel are much more seriously
structured and will develop well over five or more years. Solen is 65% Carignan with the balance Grenache,
rich and full with complex old-vine character. Aurel is a blend of Grenache, Mourvedre and Syrah. Very
fine, elegant and pure, it is tight and closed in its youth and will open up and add real complexity and depth
with age. The Aurel Blanc, which is 100% Roussanne, is barrel-fermented but not in new wood and is
loaded with subtle, complex spicy, nutty southern fruit. Drink it young or with a little age. (DM)

● **Coteaux du Languedoc** Déella★★ £B Solen★★★ £C Aurel★★★★ £D
O **Coteaux du Languedoc** Aurel★★★★ £D

BARON' ARQUES Limoux   A:Par, FWC,PWa, B&B

Owner: Baron Philippe de Rothschild SA/Vignerons du Sieur d'Arques   11250 Gardie
Newly established joint venture producing just one red wine from vineyards planted in the Limoux region.
Early releases have been labelled Vin de Pays until Limoux gained its own red wine appellation in 2003.
Currently produced from just under 35 ha of vineyard the partnership has identified 150 ha which should
be suitable for producing top-quality red wine. Baron'Arques is a blend of 60 to 70% Bordeaux varieties
Merlot, Cabernets Sauvignon and Franc and 30 to 40% Grenache, Syrah and Malbec. The wine currently
shows much more in common with Bordeaux than with other Languedoc reds. The first vintage was 1998,
which was relatively light but there was a marked increase in quality with both the 1999 and 2000 on which
the rating is based. It is to be hoped that the wine will improve further to correspond with its price tag.
Cellaring for five or more years will add weight and complexity. (DM)

● **Baron'arques** Vin de Pays de la Haute Vallée de l'Aude★★★ £E

DOM. LEON BARRAL Faugères A: WTr, A&B, P&S

Owner: Didier Barral Rue de la Sellele, 34210 Felines-Minervois
Impressive, small Faugères domaine producing wines with all the raw, spicy, meaty character of the appellation. The regular bottling is a blend of mainly Carignan along with Grenache and Cinsault. The Cuvee Jadis is a step up in quality and is a supple, structured and enticingly perfumed blend of Carignan (50%), Syrah (40%) and a smattering of Grenache. Barral's top red Valinière is outside appellation regulations and is simply labelled, like the wines of TERRE INCONNUE, *vin de table*. A heady, rich, ripe and powerful blend of 80% of Mourvedre plus Syrah, it is by no means cheap. The wines are structured and ageworthy. (DM)
● **Faugères★★** £C Cuvée Jadis★★★ £D ● **Valinière** Vin de Table★★★★ £F

DOM. BORIE DE MAUREL Minervois A: Odd, CdP

Owner: Michel Escande Rue de la Sellele, 34210 Felines-Minervois
Sizeable Minervois property producing close to 12,000 cases a year across the appellation. There are 30 ha under vine with just two planted to whites Marsanne and Muscat à Petits Grains. The white Aude is broad and fat with rich nutty fruit. Esprit d'Automne is a straightforward fruit-driven blend of Grenache, Syrah and Carignan, whereas Belle de Nuit is solely Grenache which should also be enjoyed young for its vibrant fruit but has added weight and concentration. More seriously structured is the La Livinière bottling, La Féline. Spicy dark berry fruit and a dense, rich texture are provided from 70% Syrah. The Cuvée Léopold is 100% Cabernet Sauvignon. Ripe and elegant it avoids some of the green notes found in other Languedoc examples. Of the top two Minervois reds, Maxim is 100% Mourvèdre, Sylla 100% Syrah. Both are finely structured and will develop well with four or five years in bottle. Exclusive to the UK is a varietal Carignan, La Rêve de Carignan, dark, dense and with an attractive spicy edge to the fruit. (DM)
● **Minervois** Cuvee Maxim★★★ £C Cuvee Sylla★★★★ £D
● **Minervois** Esprit d'Automne★ £B Belle de Nuit★★ £C
● **Minervois** La Rêve de Carignan★★ £C
● **Minervois La Liviniere** La Féline★★★ £B
● **Vin de Pays d'Oc** Cuvée Léopold★★★ £C
○ **Minervois** Aude★★ £B

DOM. BORIE LA VITARÈLE Saint-Chinian A: GVF, Por

Owner: Jean-François Izarn & Cathy Izarn Plane 34490 Saint-Nazaire de Ladarez
The Izarns have some 30 ha under vine now, of which a mere 2 ha are planted with white varieties. Most are in Saint-Chinian but some extend into the Coteaux du Languedoc. Powerful, dense and muscular reds are the order of the day, achieved through controlling yields, which rarely exceed 30 hl/ha. Coteaux du Languedoc Les Terres Blanches is supple, approachable and full of spicy dark fruit, whereas the *vin de pays* bottlings, including Cabernet Sauvignon and Merlot, are softer and show more overt fruit character. La Combe is the more serious and structured of the two. Of the two Saint-Chinians Les Schistes, mainly Grenache with Syrah and a touch of Carignan, has depth and a firm structure. Give it two or three years. The top wine Les Crès, like all the wines here, is named after the soil in which the vines are grown; in this case it is formed of the *galet*-type stones found at Châteauneuf-du-Pape. The wine is a blend of Syrah, Grenache and Mourvèdre and comes from vines yielding less than 20 hl/ha. No new wood is used and it is all the better for it, emphasising its dark, brooding, spicy fruit character. There is real depth and concentration with the structure to ensure ageing for up to a decade or more. (DM)
● **Saint-Chinian** Les Schistes★★★ £C Les Crès★★★★ £C
● **Coteaux du Languedoc** Les Terres Blanches★★ £B
● **Vin de Pays Coteaux de Murviel** Bouïsset★ £B La Combe★★ £B

DOM. CANET-VALETTE   Saint-Chinian   earl-canet-valette@wanadoo.fr   A: C&C, SVS

Owner: Marc Valette   Route de Causses-et-Veyran, 34460 Cessenon
There are 18 ha under vine here, all of it planted to red varieties. Along with BORIE LA VITARÈLE this is a benchmark for Saint-Chinian and the top red here, Le Vin Maghani, is arguably the finest in the AC. Minimal handling in the cellar with neither fining nor filtration helps to achieve this. No new oak is used and as a result the character of the impressively intense fruit really shines through in the wines. Une et Mille Nuits is a blend of Grenache, Mourvèdre, Syrah, Carignan and Cinsault. Aged in a mix of *inox* and older oak it is vibrant and approachable, but with sufficient structure to develop well over four or five years. Le Vin Maghani is more serious; dense, rich and very complex, the wine is full of dark fruits, spice and black pepper. Cellaring for five years is a must to enjoy this at its best. (DM)
● **Saint-Chinian** Une et Mille Nuits★★ £B Le Vin Maghani★★★★ £D

CH. CAPITOUL   Coteaux du Languedoc La Clape   www.chateau-capitoul.com   A: BFs

Owner: Charles Hock   Route de Gruissan, 11000 Narbonne
The bulk of the production at this organically farmed 65-ha property is red and white Coteaux du Languedoc La Clape, with some rosé produced as well under the same appellation. The Lavandines white blends Marsanne and Roussanne while the more complex barrel-aged Rocailles adds Viognier, to mostly Roussanne. The Les Lavandines red is almost equal proportions of Grenache, Syrah and Carignan whereas the striking and very good-value Les Rocailles is 40 per cent Grenache and 40 per cent Mourvèdre with 20 per cent Carignan adding some peppery spice. Richly concentrated, the wine is given a very lengthy period on skins for up to 45 days and is aged in *cuve* using micro-oxygenation rather than racking during *élevage*. A small-volume red, Maelma, is produced from mainly Mourvèdre and Carignan and there are two luscious late-harvest Viogniers, Les Oubliées and Les Tardives. The yield for Les Oubliées is barely more than 5 hl/ha. Not surprisingly fewer than 60 cases are produced. (DM)
● **Coteaux du Languedoc Pic Saint-Loup** Les Lavandines★ £B Les Rocailles★★★ £C
○ **Coteaux du Languedoc** Les Rocailles★★ £B

CH. DE CAZENEUVE   Coteaux du Languedoc Pic Saint-Loup   A: CBg,Bal,Lay,BBR,SVS

Owner: André Leenhardt   34270 Lauret
First class Languedoc property with some 20 ha under vine. Since acquiring Cazeneuve in the late 1980s André Leenhardt has been actively planting the top red Rhône varieties which are now dominated by Syrah. Output is still low for the area at just over 4,000 cases a year. His reds come in a number of guises. Syrah features strongly in the blend of Les Calcaires and the oak-aged Le Roc des Mates. Le Sang du Calcaire, now the top red, is an individual selection of the best the harvest has to offer. It too is aged in oak. The white is a stylish, nutty barrel-fermented blend of Roussanne, Grenache Blanc and Viognier. Top reds are ageworthy. (DM)
● **Coteaux du Languedoc Pic Saint-Loup** le Roc des Mates★★★ £C Le Sang du Calvaire★★★ £D
● **Coteaux du Languedoc Pic Saint-Loup** Les Terres Rouges★ £B Les Calcaires★★ £B
○ **Coteaux du Languedoc Pic Saint-Loup**★★ £B

CH. CAZAL VIEL   Saint-Chinian   A: HWC,Wai

Owner: Miquel Family   34460 Cessenon-sur-Orb
Large Saint-Chinian domaine producing around 75,000 cases of sturdily traditional Saint-Chinian under the Château Cazal Viel label and a range of mainly varietal Vin de Pays d'Oc under the Laurent Miquel label. Of the latter look out for simple, attractively fruity and well-priced Nord Sud Syrah and Viognier, as well as a Chardonnay/Viognier. Of a completely different order though is a fine, opulently rich, fleshy and spicy Saint-Chinian, Bardou, sourced from a single block of the finest Syrah on the Cazal Viel estate. Aged in new and one-year-old oak, all seamlessly integrated, the wine offers both density and finesse. The

Château Cazal Viel Saint-Chinians are more traditional in style, although Syrah is an important component at 65% of the estate vineyards. Both the l'Antenne and pricey Larmes des Fées are dense, structured and capable of developing well in bottle with five or more years of age. The 2000 Larmes des Fées was right on the cusp of four stars. (DM)

Château Cazal Viel
● **Saint-Chinian** Vielles Vignes★★ £B   Cuvée des Fées★★ £B   l'Antenne★★ £C   Larmes des Fées★★★ £E
Laurent Miquel
● **Saint-Chinian** Bardou★★★ £E

CH. DES ESTANILLES   Faugères   A: THt, Ter, C&R
Owner: Michel Louison   Lenthéric, 34480 Caberolles
Michel Louison produces upwards of 15,000 cases of Faugères and a white Coteaux du Languedoc each year, a sizeable production for a high-quality Midi property. Syrah now dominates the plantings and, as with the wines of Jean-Michel ALQUIER, the variety is notably successful here. Grenache and Mourvèdre are also important among the reds and the white is a blend of Marsanne, Roussanne and Viognier. The Préstige and Syrah *cuvées*, the latter seeing around a year in oak, will both stand some age, while the other wines are best approached young. (DM)
● **Faugères** Tradition★ £B   Préstige★★★ £B   Cuvée Syrah★★★ £C
○ **Coteaux du Languedoc**★★ £B
◉ **Faugères**★ £B

CH. L'EUZIÈRE   Coteaux du Languedoc Pic Saint-Loup   A: Lib, Gar, But
Owner: Michel & Marcel Causse   34270 Fontanes
The Causse siblings are, in fact, the fourth generation of vinegrowers at this impressive Languedoc property but it is only much more recently that they have established themselves as quality wine producers. They have some 22 ha under vine and produce around 5,000 cases a year. A good nutty, lightly floral white, Grains de Lune, is an unusual blend of Roussanne, Vermentino, Rolle and Grenache Blanc produced from young vines – the average age is still only eight years. After *macération pelliculaire* it is cool-fermented with limited lees-ageing. Of the three reds, Cuvée Tourmaline is a blend of Syrah and Grenache, whereas the more serious and structured Cuvées l'Almandin and Les Escarboucles are neither fined nor filtered and have a small dollop of Mourvèdre. They are both marvellously expressive with a fine balance of herb, spice and complex berry fruits and each will benefit from three or four years' ageing. (DM)
● **Coteaux du Languedoc** La Tourmaline★★ £B
● **Coteaux du Languedoc Pic Saint-Loup** Cuvée l'Almandin★★★ £B   Cuvée Les Escarboucles★★★ £C
○ **Coteaux du Languedoc** Grains de Lune★★ £B

CH. GRÈS SAINT-PAUL   Coteaux du Languedoc   www.gres-saint-paul.com   A: FCA, Gar, Idg
Owner: Jean-Philippe Servière   Route de Restinclières, 34400 Lunel
Small to medium-sized property with 24 ha of vineyards farmed along organic lines. Total production is now around 10,000 cases a year. An extensive range of wines is produced including some straightforward well-priced, fruit-driven *vin de pays* Chardonnay, Sauvignon Blanc and Merlot. It is the red Coteaux du Languedoc wines that are most important though from a quality point of view. Of the four *cuvées* La Grange Philippe is 90% Syrah and 10% Grenache and is vinified with some *macération carbonique* for the Syrah. It is soft, brambly and forward. Romanis, like all the red Languedocs, is dominated by Syrah with Grenache and Mourvèdre. Aged for 12 months in *cuve*, it is denser, more structured. The excellent-value Antonin is between 80 and 90% Syrah, the balance Grenache and Mourvèdre, produced from yields of 25 to 30 hl/ha. It is dark, concentrated and spicy with subtle hints of black pepper and just a touch of oak spice from the 16 months spent in one-third new barrels. The top wine is the impressive Sirius, a varietal Syrah produced from a yield of less than 20 hl/ha. It needs two or three years' cellaring to integrate the 100% new oak. Of the sweet white Muscats the Bohémienne has moderate depth, the Sévillane greater weight and

intensity. These are well made but lack the depth of a good Muscat de Rivesaltes. (DM)

● **Coteaux du Languedoc** Sirius★★★★ £D Antonin★★★ £C Romanis★★ £B La Grange Phlippe★★ £B
○ **Muscat de Lunel** Sévillane★★ £B ○ **Muscat Moelleux** Bohémienne★ £B

CH. DE JONQUIÈRES Coteaux du Languedoc   A:Vne, Vnf

Owner: Isabelle & François de Cabissole 34725 Jonquières
This 23-ha property located in the foothills of the Plateau de Gassac now has 19 ha planted to vines. The small range includes a good straightforward white, which is barrel-fermented and aged with *bâtonnage* and has the malolactic blocked to preserve freshness. It is a blend of Grenache Blanc, Chenin Blanc, Roussanne and Viognier. its red partner is a juicy, soft, easygoing Vin de Pays de l'Hérault red Domaine de Jonquières dominated by Cinsault and Carignan. More serious are the red Coteaux du Languedoc which blends Mourvèdre with lesser amounts of Syrah, Carignan and Grenache and the Syrah-dominated Renaissance. These top two red labels are dark, powerful and supple wines with a sufficiently firm structure and depth to ensure limited bottle-development with age, while at the same time retaining their core vibrant fruit quality. (DM)

● **Vin de Pays de l'Hérault** Domaine de Jonquières★★ £B
● **Coteaux du Languedoc**★★★ £C
○ **Coteaux du Languedoc**★ £B

CH. LA BARONNE Corbières   A:Lib, AoW

Owner: Andre Lignères 11700 Fontcouverte
A source of good well-priced examples of the Corbières appellation, this 80-ha domaine is in the Montagne d'Alaric sub-zone, arguably the best in this sizeable AC. The fine, ripe and supple standard Corbières is produced from a blend of 50% Carignan, 20% each of Grenache and Mourvèdre and 10% Syrah. Low yields of 25 to 35 hl/ha and vineyards planted at an altitude of 150 metres help to contribute to quality and carbonic maceration emphasises the fruit of the Carignan without compromising the wine's depth and intensity. The unfiltered bottling is a step up and will keep for a year or two. (DM)

● **Corbières** Montagne d'Alaric★★ £B Montagne d'Alaric Unfiltered★★ £B

CH. DE LASCAUX Coteaux du Languedoc   A: BBR, Gar, L&S

Owner: Jean-Benoit Cavalier 34270 Valflaunès
Jean-Benoit Cavalier established his Languedoc domaine located between Montpellier and Nîmes as long ago as 1984. The vineyards are planted at an altitude of 150 metres on a mix of gravel and limestone, ensuring some excellent growing conditions for the 26 ha of red varieties and 9 ha of whites. Syrah dominates the red plantings with a balanace of 30% Grenache. Whites consist of Roussanne, Marsanne, Viognier and Rolle and tend to be cropped at a lower yield of 25 to 30 hl/ha. A good regular white Coteaux du Languedoc blended from Roussanne, Marsanne and Rolle is joined by a stylish, subtly oaked, nutty white Pierres d'Argent which also includes Viognier. Both should be enjoyed young. The Coteaux du Languedoc red is a soft approachable blend of Syrah and Grenache, while the top two reds are largely Syrah and aged in oak. All of the wines offer a marked *garrigue* character that underpins their dark berry fruit. Both richly sumptuous Les Secrets and the leaner Nobles Pierres will benefit from three or four years' age. (DM)

● **Coteaux du Languedoc**★★ £B Nobles Pierres★★ £C Les Secrets★★★★ £D
○ **Coteaux du Languedoc**★ £B Pierres d'Argent★★ £C
◎ **Coteaux du Languedoc**★ £B

CH. LA VOULTE-GASPARETS Corbières   A:C&C

Owner: Patrick Reverdy 11200 Boutenac
One of the longer-established quality producers in Corbières, whose wine is distributed and

marketed by VAL D'ORBIEU. There are 42 ha under vine and decent regular red and white are produced along with two special *cuvées,* Réservée and Romain Pauc. The Réservée is good, stylish and shows some class and refinement but the Romain Pauc is clearly the benchmark wine here. Quality is helped by some very old vines, and the wine displays a rich, savoury concentration with marked vanilla oak and real complexity: a powerful spicy red that will age well in the medium term. (DM)
● **Corbières** Cuvée Réservée★★ £B Cuvée Romain Pauc★★★ £C

CH. LE THOU Coteaux du Languedoc   A:A&B
Owner: Comtesse de Ferrier de Montal 34410 Sauviau
This 24-ha estate on the outskirts of Béziers is planted largely to Syrah. Significant improvements have been seen in the wines since the 2000 vintage, particularly the top *cuvée* Georges et Clem. Blended from Syrah(at least 70%) with the balance Grenache, Mourvèdre and a little spicy Carignan, the wine is rich, fleshy and opulent. Ageing takes place in both *barrique* and tank. Even the 2002 vintage which was far from ideal looks highly promising thanks to very rigorous selection in both vineyard and winery. (DM)
● **Coteaux du Languedoc**★★ £B Georges et Clem★★★ £C

CH. MANSENOBLE Corbières mansenoble@wanadoo.fr   A:RMe
Owner: Jansegers et De Witte 11700 Moux
Fine, modern Corbières property with 20 ha planted to Carignan, Grenache, Syrah and a small amount of Mourvèdre. Production runs at just under 10,000 cases a year. Three red Corbières are produced. In addition to those rated below a small amount of a special limited *cuvée* Marie-Annick (named after one of the owners, Marie-Annick de Witte) is produced. The Montagne d'Alaric bottling is ripe, spicy and forward. The Reserve is rich and opulent, with creamy new oak underpinning the wine's dark and spicy berry fruit. Both wines are approachable on release although the Reserve has a sufficiently firm structure to enable short-term ageing. (DM)
● **Corbières** Montagne d'Alaric★★ £B Réserve★★★£C

CH. DE MONTPEZAT Coteaux du Languedoc   A:Vnf
Owner: Christophe Blanc 34120 Pezenas
Vineyards have been planted at this estate to the west of Montpellier for over 100 years. The stone and clay/limestone soils provide the successful growing conditions for both AC Coteaux du Languedoc as well as *vin de pays* reds and some Sauvignon Blanc. Future plans include a vineyard Les Epines from which a traditional Carignan/Grenache red blend and a white mix of Grenache Blanc and Marsanne will be produced. The Domaine de Montpezat-labelled *vin de pays* bottles are as striking as their Coteaux du Languedoc stablemates. Les Enclos is a soft, vibrant lightly plummy blend of mainly Merlot with some Cabernet Sauvignon, which gets 12 months in cask. The Cuvée Prestige is bigger, and considerably more concentrated. Blending Cabernet Sauvignon (60%) with Syrah, the wine posseses both depth and surprising finesse. The Palombières is an approachable blend of Grenache, Syrah and Mourvèdre. Pharaonne is big, firm and impressively structured. A mix of Mourvèdre and Grenache, it needs four or five years to bring out all its rich brambly fruit potential. The top wines get a light fining but are not filtered. (DM)
● **Coteaux du Languedoc** Les Palombières★★ £B La Pharaonne★★★ £C
● **Vin de Pays d'Oc** Domaine de Montpezat Les Enclos★★ £B
● **Vin de Pays d'Oc** Domaine de Montpezat Cuvee Prestige★★★ £C

CH. DE LA NÉGLY Coteaux du Languedoc La Clape lanegly@wanadoo.fr   A: THt
Owner: Jean Paux-Rosset 11560 Fleury d'Aude
Medium-sized but consistently excellent Languedoc domaine producing sound quality at all price levels. Since taking over the family property in 1992 Jean Paux-Rosset has single-mindedly dedicated himself to

producing wines of interest and excitement. He is aided by consultant Claude Gros and produces the *super-cuvée* Clos du Truffière from a small plot of exceptional Syrah near Pezenas, which is part owned by Bordeaux wine merchant Jeffrey Davies. The white Brise Marine blends Bourboulenc with Marsanne and Roussanne and has a fresh cutting edge to its nutty fruit. Les Embruns is ripe and full flavoured with hints of strawberry and spice, Palazy, a *vin de pays*, is the lighter of the two rosés. Two wines are released under the Domaine de Boède label. Le Pavillon is a soft fruit-driven blend of Carignan and Grenache, whereas Le Grès is a firmer richer blend of Syrah and Grenache. It gets a 45-day vatting and is aged in *cuve* for 14 months. La Côte is mainly Carignan. It has a fine, spicy, dark-berried character and drinks well young. La Falaise is sourced from south-east limestone slopes on the Massif de la Clape. A blend of Syrah, Grenache and Mourvèdre, it is aged in a mix of new and one-year-old oak and needs a year or two to find its equilibrium. All of these wines are excellent value. Less so, perhaps understandably given their small production and meagre yields, are the top three reds. L'Ancely is a rich, powerful and highly characterful blend of 95% Mourvèdre with Grenache. You'll struggle to find a Bandol sold at this price but similarly it is rare to find wines of this quality in that appellation. Finally there are two remarkably pure, powerful and very intense 100% Syrahs. Porte au Ciel is marked by its density and sheer power. The Clos du Truffière is finer, with greater elegance and sheer harmony. It vies for the title of finest red in the Languedoc. Both require cellaring for upwards of six or seven years and will age gracefully. All the reds here are bottled unfined and unfiltered. (DM)

- ● **Coteaux du Languedoc** Porte au Ciel★★★★★ £G Clos du Truffière★★★★★ £G
- ● **Coteaux du Languedoc** La Falaise★★★ £C L'Ancely★★★★ £F
- ● **Coteaux du Languedoc** La Côte★★ £B Domaine de Boède Le Grès★★★ £C
- ● **Vin de Pays des Côtes de Perpignan** Domaine de Boède Le Pavillon★ £B
- ◉ **Coteaux du Languedoc** Les Embruns★★ £B
- ○ **Coteaux du Languedoc** La Brise Marine★ £B

CH. SAINT-JACQUES D'ALBAS Minervois www.chateaustjacques.com A:Han,Goe

Owner: Graham Nutter 11800 Laure Minervois

The harvest at this small Minervois domaine used to be sold to the co-op. However, since the 2001 vintage new owner Graham Nutter has been releasing two impressive examples of the appellation. Winemaking expertise is provided by Australian Chester Osborne and the wines clearly have real potential. The Domaine wine is a blend of Syrah with older vines Grenache and Carignan. The grapes are all destemmed and carbonic maceration is not employed but the must gets a short cold soak prior to fermentation to ensure some attractive bright dark-fruit character. The Château label has a higher proportion of Syrah, part of which is vinified without a pre-fermentation maceration. Sturdier, deeper and more firmly structured the wine is aged for around a year in a mix of new, one- and two-year-old barrels of Russian and American as well as French origin. The Château label will keep well for four or five years; the Domaine label should be drunk young. (DM)

- ● **Minervois** Domaine Saint-Jacques d'Albas★★ £B Château Saint-Jacques d'Albas★★★ £C

DOM. CLAVEL Coteaux du Languedoc A: CBg,N&P, Odd,Tan,Adm,NYg

Owner: Pierre Clavel 34160 Saint-Bauzilles de Montimes

This property is situated just beyond the suburbs of the city of Montpellier. Some 40 ha are planted to Syrah, Grenache, Mourvèdre and Carignan among the reds, along with white varieties Roussanne, Grenache Blanc and Rolle. The latter are blended into a lightly herb-scented, nutty, fruit-driven white. It is the reds, though, that stand out here. Both Le Mas and Les Garrigues are ripe and sturdy with well-integrated, dark blackberry and herb-spiced fruit and supple tannins, while the old-vine Copa Santa, regularly on the cusp of four stars, is a splendid ageworthy blend of Syrah, Grenache and Mourvèdre. (DM)

- ● **Coteaux du Languedoc** Le Mas★★ £B Les Garrigues★★ £B Copa Santa★★★★£C

CLOS DE L'ANHEL Corbières www.anhel.fr A: L&W,SVS

Owner: Sophie Guiraudon et Philippe Mathias 11220 Lagrasse

Small 7-ha property making some of the very best wine in Corbières. Planted at an altitude of over 200 metres the vineyard comprises 2 ha each of Carignan and Grenache planted in clay/limestone soils and small 0.4 ha plots of both Syrah and Cinsault planted in a more gravelly/limestone soil which provides good water retention for the Syrah. Cultivation follows organic principles and harvesting is by hand. Characterful, supple, spicy and approachable red Les Terrassettes blends 60-year-old Carignan with Grenache, Syrah and Cinsault and is aged in cask with micro-oxygenation employed prior to the malolactic. Les Dimanches is a serious and more backward blend of just Carignan and Grenache. It gets a vatting of up to three weeks and is aged in a portion of new wood, again with micro-oxygenation rather than racking employed during *élevage*. Rich and concentrated with dark fruit and black pepper notes, it will benefit from four or five years' patience. (DM)

● **Corbières** Les Terrassettes★★ £B Les Dimanches★★★£C

CLOS BAGATELLE Saint-Chinian closbagatelle@libertysurf.fr A: Han,ACH,Ter

Owner: Luc & Christine Simon 34360 Saint-Chinian

With over 50 ha, the Simons are one of the larger Saint-Chinian growers but also one of the best. 47 ha is planted to Carignan, Grenache, Mourvèdre and Cinsault. For white they have a small holding of just 7 ha of Muscat. Production is now around 20,000 cases a year. There are four straightforward fruit-driven Vin de Pays d'Oc bottlings: a Sauvignon and a Chardonnay along with a red blend La Tuilière and a Merlot. It is though the Saint-Chinians that mark out this estate. A characterful rosé, Donnadieu Camille et Juliette, is produced from young vines and there are no fewer than five red labels. The Tradition is crafted from some of the younger Carignan vines along with Grenache, Syrah and Cinsault. No carbonic maceration is used and the wine shows some really attractive and vibrant spicy, brambly fruit. The Donnadieu labels are sourced from some of the higher-altitude plots and are harvested a little later. Camille et Juliette is 50% Carignan put through carbonic maceration, with Grenache, Syrah and a further small proportion of Carignan vinified traditionally. Vibrant and powerful but with a firm structure, it should develop well in the short term. In the Marie et Mathieu, a small (15%) portion of Syrah goes through *macération carbonique*, with the balancing Syrah, Grenache and Mourvèdre vinified traditionally. Yields of less than 30 hl/ha ensure a rich, stylish but accessible red. The Veillée d'Automne and premium *cuvée* La Gloire de Mon Père are more seriously structured and ageworthy examples. Both blend Mourvèdre, Syrah and Grenache, the Mourvèdre being the more important component of La Gloire Mon Père. The former is refined, well structured and intense with hint of new oak showing through; the latter is richer, purer and finer and is very intense and complex. Both need four to five years but the Gloire Mon Père will benefit from further age. An excellent range is completed by a honeyed and grapey sweet Muscat of impressive poise and class. (DM)

● **Saint-Chinian** Veillée d'Automne★★★ £B La Gloire de Mon Père★★★★ £D
● **Saint-Chinian** Tradition★ £B Donnadiieu Camille et Juliette★★ £B Donnadieu Mathieu et Marie★★ £B
O **Muscat de Saint-Jean de Minervois**★★ £B
◉ **Saint-Chinian** Donnadiieu Camille et Juliette★ £B

CLOS CENTEILLES Minervois A:Ter

Owner: Daniel & Patricia Domergue 34210 Siran

Stylish Minervois has been produced at this property for a decade and the Domergues have been established considerably longer than some of their competitors who opt, not often wisely, for a much fuller and more extracted style. There is a minimum of new wood here and the wines are restrained, intentionally so, but are good and well-crafted, with elegant fruit and well-honed, ripened tannins. A number of *cuvées* are produced. Carignanissime is made from 100% old-vine Carignan vinified in part by *macération carbonique*. It shows just what old-vine Carignan properly ripened can achieve. Capitelle de Centeilles is a juicy, vibrant 100%t Cinsault that, like Carignanissime, is aged for a couple of years in *cuve* before bottling. Campagne de Centeilles is a straightforward soft, fruit-driven blend of Cinsault and a little Syrah. The top wine is the Minervois La Livinière which is structured and refined and needs three to four years. The Guigniers de Centeilles Pinot Noir is less impressive and a touch one dimensional, possessing relatively simple red-berry fruit. (DM)

● **Minervois** Campagne de Centeilles★ £B Carignanissime★★ £B Capitelle de Centeilles★★ £B
● **Minervois** La Livinière★★ £C

CLOS MARIE Coteaux du Languedoc Pic Saint-Loup

Owner: Françoise Julien et Christophe Peyrus 34230 Saint-Pargoire
Some of the best and priciest wines in the Coteaux du Languedoc are now emerging from this 17 ha property which has 15.5 ha planted to mainly Grenache and Mourvèdre with some Carignan and a little Syrah. There is also a small white holding of Grenache, Roussanne and Clairette which is used to produce a fine nutty white Manon. The four reds take pride of place and all are serious, dense and powerful examples. Vinification is traditional, with no carbonic maceration and only a small amount of new oak in the top wines. L'Olivette is ripe and forward, Simon and Métairie du Clos more structured and firm. The top label Les Glorieuses is rich and concentrated but like all the wines refined with an elegance and purity rarely encountered in the Languedoc. L'Olivette will drink well young but the other *cuvées*, particularly Les Glorieuses, should be given five years or so of ageing. (DM)

● **Coteaux du Languedoc Pic Saint-Loup** Métairie du Clos★★★★ £E Glorieuses★★★★£F
● **Coteaux du Languedoc Pic Saint-Loup** L'Olivette★★★ £C Simon★★★£D
○ **Coteaux du Languedoc Pic Saint-Loup** Manon★★ £C

DOM. DE LA CROIX-BELLE Vin de Pays des Côtes de Thongue   A:Gar,L&S

Owner: Jacques et Françoise Boyer 34480 Puissalicon
The fairly extensive range of wines made at this property all offer good value for money. The mix of clay, limestone, silt and gravel soils have excellent drainage and assist in keeping yields down to around 45 hl/ha, helped by a green harvest. Although most of the vineyard is machine-harvested this is generally done at night to keep the fruit, particularly from the white varieties, as fresh as possible. The straightforward varietal wines are soft and fruity but it is the Champs, No 7 and Cascaillou wines that stand out here. Les Champs are fruit-driven styles which see no wood. Les Champ du Lys is blended from Grenache, Viognier and Sauvignon Blanc and is aged on lees for six months to add weight to its spicy, floral fruit. The red Champ du Coq combines Syrah, Grenache and Merlot and works better than Les Calades, which is Syrah, Mourvèdre and Carignan aged in oak for a year. The No 7 red and white are a clear step up, the former an unusual barrel-fermented blend of Viognier, Chardonnay, Grenache Blanc, Sauvignon Blanc, Carignan Blanc and Muscat à Petits Grains; the latter, comprising a varied mix of Syrah, Grenache, Mourvèdre, Cinsault, Merlot and Cabernet Sauvignon, is bottled unfiltered after 12 months in oak. Top of the range Cascaillou, an elegant blend of Grenache, Syrah and Mourvèdre, is bottled after just eight months in cask in order to emphasise its fruit. (DM)

● **Vin de Pays des Côtes de Thongue** no 7★★ £B Cascaillou★★★ £C
● **Vin de Pays des Côtes de Thongue** Le Champ du Coq★ £B Les Calades★ £B
○ **Vin de Pays des Côtes de Thongue** Les Champ des Lys★ £B no 7★★ £B

DOM. JEAN-LOUIS DENOIS Vin de Pays d'Oc jl.denois@wanadoo.fr   A: BBR, Gar

Owner: Jean-louis Denois Borde Longue, 11300 Roquetaillade
Jean-Louis Denois formerly owned the Limoux property DOMAINE DE L'AIGLE but sold up in frustration at the intransigent bureaucracy of the appellation authorities. He now cultivates four hectares of red and four hectares of white varieties from which he produces a range of *vins de pays* as well as Limoux wines of good to excellent quality. He blends traditional southern varieties with those from Bordeaux for his reds. The more forward of the two is a finely structured, supple, lightly cedary blend of Merlot, Cabernet

Sauvignon and Grenache which will benfit from three or four years' patience. Richer and fuller is the *cuvée* Chloé, a full-blown Right Bank blend of Merlot and Cabernet Sauvignon, aged in oak. Taut and firmly structured when young but with impressive weight and concentration it will benefit from five years' ageing. Neither of the wines is fined or filtered. He also makes a fine sparkling white Tradition Brut. Fermented in small oak, it is a blend of Pinot Noir and Chardonnay and rivals any of the current offerings from Limoux as well as many lesser Champagnes. Of perhaps greatest interest though are two excellent barrel-fermented still whites. La Rivière is a taut mineral-scented Chenin Blanc, Sainte-Marie an elegant and finely structured Chardonnay. Both possess a piercing intensity rare in this southerly region. Expect them to evolve well with three or four years' age. A very pricey late-harvest Limoux Vendanges d'Octobre Vieilles Vignes is sold at the domaine. (DM)

● **Vin de Pays d'Oc** Grande Cuvée★★ £B   Chloé★★★ £C
O **Vin de Pays d'Oc** Sainte Marie★★★ £C
O **Limoux** La Rivière★★★ £C
O **Tradition Brut**★★ £B

DOM. ALAIN CHABANON   Coteaux du Languedoc Montpeyroux   A:N&P,Ter

Owner: Alain Chabanon 34150 Lagamas
From his small Montpeyroux property, formerly known as Domaine Font Caude, Alain Chabanon produces somewhat less than 3,000 cases a year of three very good reds and a tiny amount of a white labelled Trelans, which is classified as *vin de table*. The reds are vinified with long macerations, often over a month, and are aged in wood, not all new. The Vin de Pays d'Oc Merle aux Alouettes is a fleshy, vibrant Merlot loaded with ripe plum and blackberry fruit, nicely supported by fine, supple, well-rounded tannins. The more powerfully structured Les Boissières is produced from Grenache. It is ripe and bold with an impressive depth of fruit. The third red is L'Esprit de Font Caude. Generally produced from a blend of Syrah and Mourvèdre this is a marvellously rich, dense red, full of smoky dark berry fruit and just a subtle hint of oak. In some vintages the wine has had more Mourvèdre than Syrah, when it tends to show more elegance and less overt concentration and extract. It will be interesting to see how the style develops here. (DM)

● **Coteaux du Languedoc Montpeyroux** Les Boissieres★★★★ £E   L'Esprit de Font Caude★★★★ £E
● **Vin de Pays d'Oc** Merle aux Alouettes★★★ £E

DOM. DE LA GRANGE DES PÈRES   Vin de Pays de l'Hérault   A:Gun

Owner: Laurent Vaillé 34150 Aniane
The wine here now rivals the long-established leader among Languedoc-Roussillon producers, MAS DE DAUMAS GASSAC. There is no doubt that Grange des Pères is every bit as impressive as its near neighbour. The production is much smaller, though, and Laurent Vaillé has just 10 ha under vine, the majority planted to Mourvèdre, Syrah and Cabernet Sauvignon farmed to almost organic standards. The wine is surprisingly approachable in its youth but has all the density, velvety tannin and class to age gracefully. Although matured in 100% new oak this is very well integrated and the wine is, of course, bottled without fining or filtration. There is a tiny amount of a very fine Roussanne-based white with equally deftly handled oak. (DM)

● **Vin de Pays de l'Hérault**★★★★ £F

DOM. DE L'HORTUS   Coteaux du Languedoc Pic Saint-Loup   A: CdP, L&S, HHB, Ter

Owner: Jean Orliac 34270 Valflaunes
Jean Orliac established this 54-ha property in the late 1970s but only began producing wine himself in 1990. This is now one of the benchmark producers for Pic Saint-Loup, an appellation with a depressingly large number of average wines that should be better. The red Grande Cuvée, blended mainly from Syrah and Mourvèdre, is aged in two-thirds new wood but is surprisingly tight and restrained in its youth. The Grande Cuvée white is ripe, almost tropical and produced from barrel-fermented and aged Viognier and Chardonnay. There is a second label, Bergerie de l'Hortus which offers decent value with an approachable

straightforward red and white. (DM)

● **Coteaux du Languedoc Pic Saint-Loup** Grande Cuvée★★★ £C
O **Vin de Pays Val de Montferrand** Grande Cuvée★★★ £C

DOM. DES JOUGLA Saint-Chinian   A:THt,BBR,But

Owner: Alain Jougla 34360 Prades-sur-Vernazobre
Alain Jougla has a reasonable holding of 40 ha from which he produces good earthy examples of Saint-Chinian. The vineyards are partly comprised of clay/limestone soils and partly more schistous. The Classique is the regular bottling, a blend of Grenache, Syrah, Mourvèdre, Carignan and Cinsault. It is soft, supple and immediately approachable, with aromas of dark fruits and spicy herbs. Les Tradition is Grenache, Mourvèdre and Syrah. It is a clear step up in quality, with an almost *sauvage* quality with a mineral undercurrent and firmly structured, well-rounded tannins. Best of all is the oak aged Cuvée Signée which has a rich and concentrated old-vine character. It is produced from Grenache, Syrah and Carignan grown on some the property's higher schistous slopes. A Vin de Pays d'Oc Viognier and white Coteaux du Languedoc are also produced. All of the wines offer very good value. The top two reds will keep well in the short term. (DM)

● **Saint-Chinian** Classique★★ £B Les Tradition★★★ £B Cuvee Signée★★★ £B

DOM. LACOSTE Muscat de Lunel

Owner: Francis Lacoste Mas de Bellevue 34400 Lunel
This domaine is very unusual in being planted solely to Muscat à Petits Grains. Sweet and late-harvest wines are the speciality here although a dry Vin de Pays d'Oc Muscat is produced from the estate's youger vines and cool-fermented for immediate appeal. Of the two Muscat de Lunel bottlings, the Lacoste is forward and richly grapey, full of simple luscious fruit but with a finesse often absent in such wines. Yields of less than 30 hl/ha no doubt help in achieving this. The Clos Bellevue is rich and very intense with great poise and refinement. Produced from a yield of less than 20 hl/ha and from some of the estate's oldest vines it is a beguiling example of sweet fortified Muscat. A small quantity of a very late-harvested white is also produced. This Muscat Passerillé Vendange d'Octobre is simply labelled *vin de table*. Produced from a microscopic yield of barely 6 hl/ha from both botrytis-affected and very late-harvested grapes it is aged solely in new oak. (DM)

O **Muscat de Lunel** Lacoste★★ £B Clos Bellevue★★★£B

DOM. LACROIX-VANEL Coteaux du Languedoc

Owner: Jean-Pierre Vanel 46 bd du Puits-Allier, 34720 Lunel
Fine, newly established small domaine with just over 8 ha of Grenache, Syrah, Carignan and Cinsault and a tiny holding of Grenache Blanc near Pezenas. Two reds are produced at present. The Clos Fine Amor is soft, round and forward: an immediately appealing red. The Clos Melanie is fuller, richer and more opulent. Principally from Syrah, with Grenache and old-vine Carignan, the wine is a full, rich, fleshy and quite extracted style with sufficiently firm and supple tannins to develop in the short term. Both wines will drink well young. (DM)

● **Coteaux du Languedoc** Clos Fine Amor★★ £B Clos Mélanie★★ ★£C

LA GRANGE DE QUATRE SOUS Vin de Pays d'Oc

Owner: Hildegard Horat 34360 Assignan
The first vineyards at this property were established in the early 1980s and the age of the vines is beginning to show through in the quality of the wines. The holding is small with 6 ha of red and just 2 ha of white varieties. The viticultural approach is essentially organic and no herbicides are used. As well as the Jeu du Mail, a little Chardonnay is also made. Jeu du Mail is an aromatic blend of Viognier and Marsanne, lent

additional structure from ageing in oak. Les Serrottes is a southern-style blend of Syrah and Malbec, whereas the Lo Molin is a fine and elegant Bordeaux blend of Cabernet Sauvignon and Cabernet Franc. Both reds will evolve well with three or four years' age. (DM)

● **Vin de Pays d'Oc** Lo Molin★★★ £C Les Serrottes★★★£C
○ **Vin de Pays d'Oc** Jeu du Mail★★ £B

DOM. LA TOUR BOISÉE Minervois   A: The, HKW, Wat

Owner: Jean-Louis Poudou 11800 Laure-Minervois
This is among the very best estates in Minervois, producing wines of density and real class. Production is sizeable for the appellation at 40,000 cases a year from 80 ha of estate vineyards. In addition to the top Minervois labels there is some decent regular white and rosé Minervois as well as Merlot, Cabernet Sauvignon and Chardonnay Vin de Pays d'Oc and a straightforward range of wines under the Domaine de Subremont label. The white Minervois Marie-Claude is dominated by Marsanne, with some Maccabeo and a little Muscat adding a touch of perfume to the wine's youthful oak. The regular red Minervois is a blend of Carignan, Grenache, Syrah and Cinsault. Fully de-stemmed prior to fermentation it is soft and rounded with lively blackberry fruit. The top Minervois *cuvées* are more seriously structured. Marie-Claude blends Syrah with Grenache and Carignan; Marielle et Frédérique adds in some Mourvèdre. Marie-Claude is a little firmer with some press wine and a touch of oak. The top wine Jardin Secret is an opulently rich Grenache aged in new oak. Expect all the top reds to develop well with short to mid-term ageing. The range is now completed by the 1905 which is produced from some of the very oldest vines in the appellation. (DM)

● **Minervois** Marielle et Frédérique★★★ £B Jardin Secret★★★★ £D
● **Minervois**★★ £B La Marie-Claude★★★ £B
○ **Minervois** La Marie-Claude★★ £B

DOM. LES CREISSES Vin de Pays de l'Hérault

Owner: Philippe Chesnelong 34290 Valros
Recently established domaine just outside the village of Valros, inland to the north-east of Béziers. Just two reds are produced here. The regular Domaine Les Creisses bottling is a blend of Syrah, Grenache and Cabernet Sauvignon. Produced from grapes grown in calcareous soils, the wine has excellent definition and structure with just a slight raw edge to its youthful tannin. It will be better with two or three years' ageing. Les Brunes is a considerable step up in quality and has a price tag to match. This richly textured dense, and cedary blend of Cabernet Sauvignon and Syrah should age well. As yet there is a feeling that the structure overpowers the wine. Great potential here, though. (DM)

● **Vin de Pays d'Oc** Les Creisses★★ £B Les Brunes★★★★ £D

DOM. DE LA MARFÉE Coteaux du Languedoc   A: Han

Owner: Thierry Hasard 34570 Murviel-lès-Montpellier
Very small new property: the first vintage was in 1997, with just 6-ha of vines. Two wines are produced and they are sturdy, powerful and very extracted in style. There is no doubt that there is real depth and power and an absolute commitment to quality but on occasion the tannin plays a greater role than it should. Les Champs Murmurés is a southern Rhône-style blend with some Cabernet Sauvignon thrown in, while Les Vignes qu'on Abat is dominated by old-vine Carignan. There is the potential here for these to be very classy wines indeed. (DM)

● **Coteaux du Languedoc** Les Champs Murmurés★★★ £E Les Vignes qu'on Abat★★★ £D

MAS BRUGUIÈRE Coteaux du Languedoc Pic Saint-Loup   A: HHB

Owner: Guilhem Bruguière La Plaine, 34270 Valflaunes
Guilhem Bruguière is one of the best producers in the Pic Saint-Loup sub-region. This is a small property of around 13 ha and Guilhem now produces close to 6,000 cases a year. Syrah, Grenache and Mourvèdre

are grown, along with Roussanne for the white Les Muriers; a nutty, floral, medium-weight spicy white. The basic Cuvée Calcadiz is well-priced but can be raw with some aggressive green notes creeping through. L'Arbouse though is round, suppler and fuller while the flagship La Grenadière is a blockbuster red: spicy and dense, with a solid chunk of vanilla oak. The top wine will keep well over five or six years. (DM)

● **Coteaux du Languedoc Pic Saint-Loup** Cuvée Calcadiz★ £B L'Arbouse★★ £B La Grenadière★★★ £C
○ **Coteaux du Languedoc Pic Saint -Loup** Les Muriers★★ £B

MAS CAL DEMOURA   Coteaux du Languedoc   A: GVF

Owner: Jean-Pierre Jullien   Chemin du Mas Jullien, 34725 Jonquières
Like so many growers, Jean-Pierre Jullien used to sell his grapes to the local co-op. Now he produces a very good red and a simple, vibrant, berry-fruited rosé from his 6 ha or so, which are all planted to red varieties. It is the *cuvée* L'Infidèle, though, that is the serious business here, a blend of Syrah, Mourvèdre, Grenache, Cinsault and Carignan, of which the Syrah, Grenache and Mourvèdre see some new oak during the 12 months of ageing. The wine is full, rich and quite extracted, with supple tannins and real depth. The 1999 and 2001 were particularly good. It will be interesting to see how they develop with age. (DM)

● **Coteaux du Languedoc** L'Infidèle★★★ £D
◉ **Coteaux du Languedoc** Qu'es Aquo★★ £B

MAS CHAMPART   Saint-Chinian   A:RsW, SVS, Ter

Owner: Isabelle & Matthieu Champart   34360 Saint-Chinian
There are now 16 ha planted at this fine Saint-Chinian property where the Champarts produce a fruity rosé and a rich, lightly oaked white from Roussanne, Marsanne, Viognier, Bourboulenc and Grenache, as well as four reds. Up until 1988 they sold their crop to the local co-op and a small proportion of the harvest is still sold on. The four reds are blends of different *terroirs* across the property. The wines are only lightly fined with egg whites and the top two reds are bottled without filtration. The Vin de Pays d'Oc is an unusual blend of 80% Cabernet Franc with the balance Syrah. It is lightly leafy with attractive ripe berry fruit. The brambly, forward Côte d'Arbo comprises Syrah, old vine Carignan, young Grenache and a tiny amount of Graciano. The top two wines are more serious and firmly structured. Causse du Bouquet blends Syrah with Mourvèdre, Grenache and, in certain vintages, some Carignan. It is aged for a year in barrel and then six months in vat. The impressively dense and concentrated Clos de la Simonette is mainly Mourvèdre with some Grenache. It is aged in oak, some new, for around 18 months. The top two reds will develop well for a decade at least. (DM)

● **Saint-Chinian** Côte d'Arbo★★ £B Causse de Bousque★★★ £B Clos de La Simonette★★★★ £C
● **Vin de Pays d'Oc★** £B

MAS DE DAUMAS GASSAC   Vin de Pays de l'Hérault   www.daumas-gassac.com   A: Adm

Owner: Aimé & Véronique Guibert   Guibert de la Vaissière, 34150 Aniane
Undoubtedly the most famous property in the Midi and the inspiration for the many high-quality winemakers now spread throughout Languedoc and Roussillon. There are some 26 ha of red varieties and 12 ha of white. The vineyard potential here in the upper Gassac Valley was discovered in 1970. The key is soil that is mineral-rich, superbly drained and that stresses the vines just sufficiently to produce grapes of remarkable flavour, the key to all great wine. The red is a dense and immensely powerful but refined blend of mainly Cabernet Sauvignon (80%) blended with a plethora of other varieties. Very backward and even austere when young this is best left for a decade or more. The white is an intense, nutty, complex blend dominated by Viognier, Petit Manseng and Chardonnay. Finely structured with a piercing mineral core the wine needs three or four years and will keep comfortably for a great deal longer. A tiny amount of a limited red *cuvée* Emile Peynaud, in honour of the great Bordeaux enology professor, was produced in 2001. Aimé Guibert also produces a range of simple and straightforward wines under the Terrasses label. (DM)

● **Vin de Pays de l'Hérault★★★★★** £F ○ **Vin de Pays de l'Hérault★★★★★** £F

MAS D'ESPANET Vin de Pays d'Oc

Owner: Agnès & Denys Armand 30730 Saint-Mamert-du-Gard
The Armand property is located just inland between Picpoul de Pinet and Nîmes. Production is spread across two reds and a white, all of which take the Vin de Pays d'Oc classification. The white Eolienne is a part tank- and part barrel-fermented blend of Sauvignon Blanc, Grenache Blanc and Viognier. The vines are grown in calcareous soils and from a yield of just 25 hl/ha the wine has a fine grassy, nutty intensity and is best enjoyed young. Les Lens is an exuberant, fruit-driven blend of Cinsault, Grenache and Syrah. It displays a marvellous pure strawberry character and will drink well over three to four years. The top red, Bois du Roi, is a Syrah-based oak-aged red. The blend has varied including Grenache, and on occasion some Carignan providing a real black pepper and spice character. It is an impressive wine with complexity, a fine balance of dark berry fruit and herbs, subtly oaked with a supple tannic structure. The Carignan adds a greater depth to the wine. (DM)

● **Vin de Pays d'Oc** Les Lens★★ £B Bois du Roi★★★ £C
○ **Vin de Pays d'Oc** Eolienne★★ £B

MAS DE L'ECRITURE Coteaux du Languedoc www.masdelecriture.fr A:Han,Ter

Owner: Pascal Fulla Rue de la Font du Loup, 34725 Jonquières
Top-quality small Languedoc domaine producing around 2,000 cases of some of the finest red wines in the appellation. Located in the commune of Jonquières, the vineyards are planted on elevated limestone and gravel terraces providing the property with an excellent *terroir*. Yields are purposely restricted below 20 hl/ha and both leaf-thinning and a limited green harvest are carried out to optimise the balance of the vineyard. Just two wines are produced. Les Pensées is the more approachable and forward of the two. A blend of Grenache with smaller proportions of Syrah, Cinsault and Carignan. L'Ecriture is a denser, firmer blend of mainly Syrah with some Grenache and Mourvèdre. Both wines are given a lengthy vatting and aged in new and one-year-old oak of differing sizes for up to 12 months. The wines complete their *élevage* in *cuve* for a further three months before final blending. Neither is fined nor filtered. Both will age well, with L'Ecriture gaining further complexity for up to a decade. (DM)

● **Coteaux du Languedoc** Les Pensées★★★ £D L'Ecriture★★★★ £E

MAS FOULAQUIER Coteaux du Languedoc Pic Saint Loup A:THt,BBR

Owner: Jequier, Stolt, Fallot 34270 Claret
Another top-quality small Languedoc producer with 8 ha planted equally to Syrah and Grenache. The operation is very new with the first vintage emerging in 1999. Swiss winemaker Pierre Jequier makes wines which are richly concentrated and well crafted with great fruit definition and purity. They are marked by the composition of their blends. L'Orphée is the most approachable and is dominated by Grenache, with powerful scents of ripe berries and spice. Le Rollier is a roughly equal blend of the two varieties, full of licorice and dark cherry character. Les Calades is mainly Syrah with a touch of oak ageing, it is the most firmly structured of the trio, it needs a minimum of four to five years to evolve. The wine has a marvellous mineral purity. Handling is kept to a minimum and inevitably filtration avoided. (DM)

● **Coteaux du Languedoc Pic Saint-Loup** L'Orphée★★★ £B Le Rollier★★★ £C
● **Coteaux du Languedoc Pic Saint-Loup** Les Calades★★★★ £C

MAS DE FOURNEL Coteaux du Languedoc Pic Saint Loup A:M&V,Han

Owner: Gerard Jeanjean 34270 Valflaunès
Gerard Jeanjean has only been bottling his own wine since 1997 but he produces two of the more striking examples in Pic Saint-Loup. The soils are a combination of gravel/pebbles and some clay/limestone particularly suitable for Syrah. He has just 8 ha and only 3 ha of Syrah and some old Grenache vines are currently in production, with 5 ha having recently been replanted with Syrah and Grenache as well as

Mourvèdre. Harvesting is by parcel rather than by variety to ensure maximum ripeness and all the fruit is destemmed before fermentation. The Pic Saint-Loup is 70% Syrah and 30% Grenache, ripe and supple with richly concentrated dark berry, mint, herb and spice-scented fruit and a sufficiently firm structure to suggest further development with four or five years in bottle. The Cuvée Pierre is a post-fermentation vat selection aged in small oak, a proportion of it new, and adds some rich creamy vanilla notes to the excellent fruit of the regular bottling. (DM)

● **Coteaux du Languedoc**★★ £B Pierre★★★ £B

MAS HAUT BUIS Coteaux du Languedoc

Owner: Olivier Jeantet 34520 Lavacquerie-et-Saint-Martin
The production at Olivier Jeantet's property is tiny, barely more than 1,200 cases a year for just one wine. It is, though, among the better examples in the appellation. Costa Caoude is a blend of Syrah, Grenache and Cabernet Sauvignon, of which 70% is aged in barrique and 30% in *cuve* for up to 12 months. It is then aged for a further year in *demi-muids* before bottling. Deep, dense and powerful but with well-judged oak and supple, well-rounded tannins, this is balanced and surprisingly refined wine. (DM)

● **Coteaux du Languedoc** Costa Caoude★★★ £D

MAS JULLIEN Coteaux du Languedoc   A: Ter,Gun,Han

Owner: Olivier Jullien 34725 Jonquières
Now one of the most established properties in the Coteaux du Languedoc. The wine style and indeed the labels have changed over the years. Olivier Jullien's vineyards are now farmed biodynamically and the oldest vines are approaching 50 years of age, which will improve his potential further. Two reds and a floral white Vin de Pays de l'Hérault are produced and the approach is one of restraint, in quite marked contrast to some of the extracted wines of his neighbours. The top Coteaux du Languedoc is tight and restrained, with a refined, intense mineral quality, whereas the États d'Âme is in a supple and forward fruit-driven style. The reds, particularly the Coteaux du Languedoc, should age very well. (DM)

● **Coteaux du Languedoc**★★★ £D États d'Âme★★★£C
O **Vin de Pay de l'Hérault**★★ £C

MAS LUMEN Coteaux du Languedoc

Owner: Pascal Perret 34120 Pezenas
Tiny and newly established 6-ha domaine which has just over 3.5 ha planted, mainly to Syrah, Carignan and Grenache. There is also half a hectare planted to the white Terret variety. Two reds are produced, the first vintage being in 2001. The organically handled terroir appears to be potentially exceptional and Pascal Perret also believes in minimal handling in the cellar. The wines are rich, concentrated and very pure. Although possessing immediate appeal, the exceptional La Sylve is firm but supple and will develop greater complexity with five years or so of cellaring. (DM)

● **Coteaux du Languedoc**★★★ £B La Sylve★★★★ £C

MAS DE MORTIÈS Coteaux du Languedoc   A: HHB

Owner: Isabelle & Rémi Duchemin Route de Cazevieille, 34270 Saint-Jean-de-Cuculles
This is a very good property with some 20 ha under vine in the southern sector of the Pic Saint-Loup sub-region. The estate has been continually improved over the last six or seven years with a careful replanting programme to improve quality in the vineyard. Good white as well as vibrant dark and chunky Coteaux du Languedoc are produced and Syrah Que Sera Sera is first class. The wines here are very reasonably priced. (DM)

● **Coteaux du Languedoc Pic Saint-Loup** Que Sera Sera★★★ £B

MAS MOURIES Coteaux du Languedoc   A: Vne

Owner: Solange & Eric Bouet 30260 Vic le Fesq
Fine new property located 25 km north-west of Nîmes with organically tended vineyards planted in well-drained calcareous soils. Two wines are produced, both red. Mas Mouries Coteaux du Languedoc is a blend of Syrah and Grenache. The varieties are vinified separately before blending and ageing in *cuve*. The fruit is forward and accessible, but the tannin is just a touch hard – perhaps 30 days vatting is too much here. The top *cuvée* Les Myrthes, which is aged in part new wood, is again a blend of Syrah and Grenache but at a lower yield – some 25 hl/ha rather than 40. The wine displays excellent black fruits with nicely handled vanilla oak; in short plenty of depth and class. (DM)
● **Coteaux du Languedoc**★★ £B Les Myrthes★★★ £C

MAS PLAN DE L'OM Coteaux du Languedoc

Owner: Joël Foucou 34700 Saint-Jean-de-la-Blaquière
Another fine emerging Languedoc domaine producing three reds and a white of impressive class and style. The estate's vineyards are planted at an altitude of 200 metres and benefit from a swing in temperature during the summer months which promotes acidity and freshness in the fruit. Well-drained schistous soils with interspersed *galets roulés* (similar to Châteauneuf-du-Pape) along with controlled yields of 15 to 25 hl/ha ensure excellent-quality fruit. The white Feuillage, blending Roussanne with Grenache Blanc and fermented partly in new barrels, is really refined with well-judged oak underpinning an intense nutty, citrus character. Vinification for the reds is traditional with a long maceration of 30 to 40 days. Œillade is sufficiently firmly structured for a little age and development but has immediate forward blackberry and bramble fruit. Aged partly in *cuve* and partly in old oak it is a mix of Cinsault, Grenache, Carignan and Syrah. The top two reds both require a little patience. Miéjour combines Grenache, Syrah and Carignan and the low-yielding fruit offers firm but supple youthful tannins and a mineral undercurrent to its dark, spicy, herbal character. The wine is solely aged in tank. Roucan, by contrast, sees only oak for ageing, part of which is new, and offers a rich, almost creamy, character to the fruit which is a blend of Syrah, Grenache and Carignan. Ageing both the Miéjour and Roucan for four or five years will be rewarded with bottles of greater depth and complexity. (DM)
● **Coteaux du Languedoc** Œillade★★ £B Miéjour★★★ £C Roucan★★★ £D
○ **Coteaux du Languedoc** Feuillage★★★ £B

DOM. DE MONTCALMES Coteaux du Languedoc   A: THt

Owner: Frederic Poutalie 34150 Puechabon
This very impressive new Languedoc red by Frederic Poutalie is produced from a mere 2.8 ha. The vineyards are now established by mass-selection and exceptionally well-drained calcareous topsoils with *galets roulés* provide the base for raw material of outstanding quality. Green harvesting is practiced and yields are resticted to barely more than 20 hl/ha. Just one wine is made here, a dense, fleshy modern blend of Syrah, Grenache and Mourvèdre. In the winery all operations are carried out by gravity and individual plots are vinified separately. The wine possesses real depth and intensity as well as a piercing mineral purity to its fruit. There is a balance and harmony here so often lacking in the appellation. Deep and concentrated dark berry fruit is subtly underpinned by a grip of creamy new wood and supple, well-rounded tannins. There is no doubt that five or so years' patience will provide both weight and additional complexity. (DM)
● **Coteaux du Languedoc**★★★★ £D

MOULIN DE CIFFRE Saint-Chinian www.moulindeciffre.com   A:BBR,OddL&W,WSc,Ter

Owner: Bernadette & Jacques Lesineau 34480 Autignac
Small to medium-sized estate producing around 10,000 cases a year from 30 ha across a number of appellations. The vineyards are dominated by red varieties with just 1.5 ha planted to Viognier, from which

a good spicy barrel-fermented *vin de pays* is produced. Ageing on lees with *bâtonnage* adds extra richness. Reds are produced under three appellations, Coteaux du Languedoc, Saint-Chinian and Faugères. A richly textured *vin de pays* red Val Taurou is also produced from a blend of Cabernet Sauvignon, Syrah and Grenache. The oak aged Saint-Chinian and Faugères *cuvées* add a rounder, suppler character, while the Eole is a step up. Firmly structured when young, this blend of Syrah, Grenache and Mourvèdre from the best parcels the estate has in the AC is aged in a mix of new and old barriques. The wines offer good value and the Eole and Val Taurou will develop well with three to five years' ageing. (DM)

● **Faugères★★** £B Élevé en Fûts de Chêne★★ £B Eole★★★ £C
● **Saint-Chinian★★** £B Élevé en Fûts de Chêne★★ £B
● **Coteaux du Languedoc★★** £B ● **Vin de Pays des Coteaux de Murviel** Val Taurou★★★ £C
○ **Vin de Pays des Coteaux de Murviel** Viognier★★ £C

DOM. GUY MOULINIER   Saint-Chinian

Owner: Moulinier Family   Pierrerue, 34360 Saint-Chinian
Among a wave of new domaines being established, the Moulinier family continue to produce some of the better wines in this potentially great appellation at their new winery completed in 1999. Their 24 ha of vineyards are spread across three communes and planted on a mix of clay/limestone, schist and sandstone soils to provide a diverse array of raw material. The bulk of the vineyards are planted at altitudes of 100 to 200 metres and low yields of 15 to 25 hl/ha are easy to achieve. Tradition, a blend of Grenache, Syrah and Mourvèdre aged in *cuve* is the most accessible of the wines, fruit-driven but traditionally firm. Les Sigillaires, an unusual blend of 70% Mourvèdre with Syrah aged in used barrels, is rich and full of dark, spicy herb-strewn fruit. The top wine Les Terrasses Grillées gets full oak ageing (40% new). A blend of 95% Syrah and a tiny proportion of Grenache and Mourvèdre, it positively demands five or so years to pull it all into balance. (DM)

● **Saint-Chinian** Tradition★★ £B Les Sigillaires★★★ £B Les Terrasses Grillées★★★ £B

DOM. DE PEYRE ROSE   Coteaux du Languedoc   A:Ter

Owner: Marlène Soria   34230 Saint-Pargoire
This 25-ha property is responsible for two of the most renowned reds in the Languedoc and they certainly have a price tag to match their reputation. The vineyard is planted in ideal sparse, rocky soils and there is a commitment to low-yielding fruit of the highest quality. Of the two reds Clos des Cistes has a hint of Grenache and is the more forward of the two. It is supple and full of piercing spicy, black fruit. Clos Syrah Léone is the more structured, denser, darker and on occasion shows real animal aromas. The wines are certainly very impressive in their youth, although it has to be said very marked by oak and highly extracted in style. It remains to be seen how they will develop. Some earlier bottles seemed prematurely evolved with five or six years' age. A stylish, nutty white is also now produced from Rolle, Roussanne and Viognier. (DM)

● **Coteaux du Languedoc** Clos de Cistes★★★ £E Clos Syrah Léone★★★★ £E

PRIEURÉ DE SAINT-JEAN-DE-BÉBIAN   www.bebian.com   A:RsW,Ter

Owner: Chantal Lecouty & Jean-Claude Lebrun   Route de Nizas, 34120 Pezenas
This has long been one of the esteemed names of the Languedoc but it is only in the last few years, under the stewardship of Chantal Lecouty and Jean-Claude Lebrun, that quality has been back to where it was in the mid- to late 1980s. The early 90s were vintages to avoid here. The current bottlings of both red from Syrah, Grenache and Mourvèdre and white from mainly Roussanne are very rich and stylish, especially the white. Perhaps the real disappointment is the Chapelle de Bébian, a second wine that has on occasion shown a fierce angular austerity. (DM)

● **Coteaux du Languedoc★★★** £D Chapelle de Bébian★ £B ○ **Coteaux du Languedoc★★★★** £D

DOM. RIMBERT Saint-Chinian www.domainerimbert.com A:FWW,Gar,SVS,Ter

Owner: Jean-Marie Rimbert 4 Avenue des Mimosas, 34360 Berlou

Jean-Marie Rimbert's domaine was only established in 1997 but he is proving to be one of the really exciting producers of the appellation. He now has 20 ha under vine and is producing between 7,000 and 8,000 cases per year. He has some very well sited vineyards with impoverished schistous soils planted to Carignan, Syrah, Grenache, Cinsault and Mourvèdre. Most of the vines are over 40 years old and some Carignan is extremely venerable. Three wines are made. The good regular Saint-Chinian Les Travers de Marceau is blended from 40 per cent each of Carignan and Cinsault, 15 per cent Syrah and 5 per cent Grenache. It is a finely structured, elegant example, not at all over-extracted and with a pure mineral undercurrent running through it. There are also two very fine pure Carignan wines which are simply labelled as *vin de table*. Le Chant de Marjolaine comes from old vines in some of the best parcels, whereas the extraordinary Carignator, blended from two vintages, is sourced from 50- to 70-year-old vines and fermented in *barriques*. Heady and exotic it is one of the most characterful wines of the region. (DM)

● **Carignator**★★★★ £D   ● **Le Chant de Marjolaine**★★★ £C
● **Saint Chinian** Les Travers de Marceau★★ £B

SIEUR D'ARQUES Limoux A: PVF

Owner: 'Co-operative' Avenue de Mauzac, 11303 Limoux

A very sizeable but well-organized co-op that produces close to a million cases a year. Its membership controls around 3,000 ha of vineyards, the vast majority of the whole Limoux appellation. Good, well-made Blanquette de Limoux is produced as well as Crémant de Limoux. There is a good lightly oaked regular Chardonnay but the top wines are four well-crafted Toques et Clochers bottlings, which are barrel-fermented and aged partly in new wood, on lees and with *bâtonnage*. With a number of decidedly cool mesoclimates within the AC these are surprisingly elegant and tight, with a fine piercing mineral undercurrent to the fruit. (DM)

Toques et Clochers
O **Chardonnay** Terroir Océanique★★★ £B Terroir d'Autan★★ £B Terroir Haute Vallée★★ £B
O **Chardonnay** Terroir Méditerranéen★★ £B

DOM. TERRE INCONNUE Gard

Owner: Robert Creus 62 Rue des Albizzias, 34400 Saint Séries

Robert Creus is based in the eastern borders of the Coteaux du Languedoc but has little interest in the bureaucracy of appellation regulations. As a result his garage-style wines are simply labelled as *vin de table*. His production is still very small but jumped dramatically in 2003, rising to 1,000 cases from the previous vintage of a mere 300 or so. He now has 4 ha of vines and these are handled as naturally as possible although he has no truck with biodynamism. The wines are vinified with a minimum of sulphur and aged in *barriques* for 16 to 18 months. Handling is by gravity, fining is avoided and the wines are bottled without filtration. There are three main *cuvées* as well as a second wine, Les Bruyères, for lots which are not felt to be up to scratch. Léonie is an astonishingly heady and rich 100% Carignan, in many ways the most exciting and shocking of Creus's wines. Los Abuelos is 100% Grenache, rich and characterful, always super-ripe. Alcohol levels for any of the top *cuvées* can easily be 15% or more but balance and purity are always maintained. Sylvie is dominated by Syrah with 12% Grenache and 5% Carignan blended in. More opulent than the wines of the northern Rhône and loaded with super-ripe fruit, perhaps a slightly firmer structure would add a further dimension. The wines are very good value. (DM)

● **Los Abuelos**★★★★ £E   ● **Léonie**★★★★★ £E   ● **Sylvie**★★★★★ £E

VAL D'ORBIEU Narbonne | A:VOC

Owner: Les Vignerons du Val d'Orbieu 11100 Narbonne
This vast organisation has among its membership many of the major co-ops of the Midi as well as a number of individual growers. Interests spread as far as Bordeaux, where Val d'Orbieu now owns GRAND-PUY-DUCASSE and RAYNE-VIGNEAU among others. It is responsible as well for the marketing and distribution of a number of small quality domaines. These include the CH. DE JAU in the Roussillon, CLOS DE PAULLILES in Collioure and fine Corbières produced at CH. LA VOULTE GASPARETS. The prestige Val d'Orbieu label is the Cuvée Mythique, a red blend from varying sources and varieties. It is inevitably labelled as Vin de Pays d'Oc. Good stylish and moderately fleshy, it has reasonable depth for drinking over the short to medium term. (DM)

Val d'Orbieu
● **Vin de Pays d'Oc** Cuvée Mythique★★ £C
○ **Vin de Pays d'Oc Chardonnay** Réserve Saint-Martin Vin de Pays d'Oc★ £B

Also see the following Rhône *négociants* with an entry in the section *Rhône Valley:*
M CHAPOUTIER
JEAN-LUC COLOMBO
TARDIEU-LAURENT

LANGEDOC OTHER WINES OF NOTE

L'ABBAYE SYLVA PLANA ● **Faugères** La Closeraie £B
ABBAYE DE THOLOMIES ● **Minervois** £B ● **Minervois La Livinière** £C
ABBOTTS WINES ● **Minervois** Cumulo Nimbus £B
DOM. DE L'AIGLE ○ **Limoux** les Aigles £C
DOM. DE L'ARJOLLE ● **Vin de Pays Côtes de Thongue** Cabernet £B Paradoxe £C
DOM. D'AUPILHAC ● **Coteaux du Languedoc-Montpeyroux** £C
DOM. BERTRAND BERGÉ ● **Fitou** Ancestrale £B
DOM. DE CABROL ● **Cabardès** Vent d'Ouest £B
DOM. CAPION ● **Syrah** Vin de Pays de l'Hérault £B ○ **Chardonnay** Vin de Pays de l'Hérault £B
CAVES DE CASTELMAURE ● **Corbières** Cuvée No 3 £D
DOM. DE CLOVALLON ● **Vin de Pays d'Oc** Pinot Noir £B ○ **Vin de Pays d'Oc** Viognier £B
CH. BONHOMME ● **Minervois** Les Amandiers £B Les Oliviers £C
CH. CABEZAC ● **Minervois** Belvèze Grand Cuvée £C Arthur Cuvée £B
CH. CAMPLAZENS ● **Coteaux du Languedoc La Clape** La Reserve £B
CH. CASCADAIS ● **Corbières** £B
CH. DE COMBEBELLE ● **Saint-Chinian** Tradition £B Réserve £C
CH. COUPE ROSES ● **Minervois** La Bastide £B Les Plots £B Orience £C Granaxa £C
CH. FLAUGERGUES ● **Coteaux du Languedoc** £B
CH. GLÉON MONTANIE ● **Corbières** Gaston Bonnes £C Combe de Berre £B
CH. DE GOURGAZAUD ● **Minervois** Quintus MMI £B ● **Minervois La Livinière** Réserve £B
CH. GRAND MOULIN ● **Corbières** Vieilles Vignes £B
CH. GRÉZAN ● **Faugères** Cuvée Arnaud Lubac £B
CH. HAUT-GLÉON.. ● **Corbières** £B ○ **Corbières** £B
CH. LA BASTIDE ● **Corbières** Optimé £B
CH. LA SAUVAGEONNE ● **Coteaux du Languedoc** Cuvée Prestige £C
CH. DE LASTOURS ● **Corbières** Cuvée Simon Descamps £B Fûts de Chêne £B
CH. LES PALAIS ● **Corbières** Les Randolin Vieille Vignes £B
CH. DE LA LIQUIERE ● **Faugères** Cistus £B
CH. MARIS ● **Minervois La Livinière** £C Vieilles Vignes £C
CH. DE NOUVELLES ● **Fitou** Vieilles Vignes £B

CH. D'OUPIA ● **Minervois** Les Barons £B
CH. PECH-CELEYRAN ● **Coteaux du Languedoc La Clape** Réserve £C
CH. PECH-LATT ● **Corbières** Cuvée Vieille Vignes £B Cuvée Alix £C
CH. PUECH-HAUT ● **Coteaux du Languedoc** Tête de Cuvée £D
CH. LA ROQUE ● **Coteaux du Languedoc Pic Saint-Loup** Cuvée Mourvèdre £B
CH. ROUMANIÈRES ● **Coteaux du Languedoc** £B
CH. SAINT-AURIOL ● **Corbières** Les Terrassettes £B
CH. SAINTE-EULALIE ● **Minervois La Livinière** £B
CH. VEYRAN ● **Saint-Chinian** Cuvée Henri £B
CH. VILLERAMBERT-JULIEN ● **Minervois** £C O Minervois £B
DOM. DE LA COMBE-BLANCHE ● **Minervois** La Chandelière £B
● **Vin de Pays d'Oc** Le Dessous de l'Enfer £B
DOM. DE COURTILLES ● **Corbières** £C Côte 125 £B
DOM. ERMITAGE DU PIC SAINT LOUP ● **Coteaux du Languedoc**
Pic Saint-Loup Cuvée Saint-Agnes £C
DOM. FONTEDICTO ● **Coteaux du Languedoc** Coulisses £C Cuvée Promise £D
DOM. DU GRAND ARC ● **Corbières** Cuvée des Quarante £C
DOM. DES GRECAUX ● **Coteaux du Languedoc** Hemera £D
DOM. HENRY ● **Coteaux du Languedoc** Les Chailles £D
DOM. VIRGILE JOLY ● **Coteaux du Languedoc** £D
DOM. DE LA GARANCE ● **Vin de Pays de l'Hérault** Les Armières £C
LA JASSE CASTEL ● **Coteaux du Languedoc** £C
DOM. LUC LAPEYRE ● **Minervois** L'Amourier £B
DOM. LA TERRASSE D'ELISE ● **Vin de Pays de l'Herault** £E
MAS DES CHIMÈRES ● **Vin de Pays du Salagou** Oeillades £B Marie et Joseph £B
MAS GRANIER ● **Coteaux du Languedoc** Les Gres £B
MAS DE MARTIN ● **Coteaux du Languedoc** £B
CAVES DU MONT TAUCH ● **Fitou** Les Crouzels £B Terroir de Tuchan £B
DOM. PICCININI ● **Minervois La Livinière** Line et Laetitia £B
DOM. DE LA PROSE ● **Coteaux du Languedoc** Cuvée Prestige £B Les Embruns £B
DOM. DE RAVANES ● **Vin de Pays de Coteaux de Murviel** Merlot Les Gravieres du Taurou £D
● **Vin de Pays de Coteaux de Murviel** Le Prime Verd £D Cinq Seaux d' OEillade £D
O **Vin de Pays de Coteaux de Murviel** L'ille £D
ROC D'ANGLADE ● **Coteaux du Languedoc** £E
DOM SAINT-ANDRIEU ● **Coteaux du Languedoc** Les Roches Blanches £B
DOM. SAINT-MARTIN LA GARRIGUE ● **Coteaux du Languedoc** £B
DOM. SERRES MAZARD ● **Corbières** Cuvée Henri Serres £B
SKALLI-FORTANT DE FRANCE ● **Cabernet Sauvignon** Réserve Édition Limité F £C

Author's choice (DM)

The new wave from the Languedoc

DOM. CANET-VALETTE ● **Saint-Chinian** Le Vin Maghani
CH. L'EUZIÈRE ● **Coteaux du Languedoc Pic Saint-Loup** Cuvée Les Escarboucles
CH. DES ESTANILLES ● **Faugères** Cuvée Syrah
CH. MOURGUES DU GRÈS ● **Costières de Nîmes** Capitelles des Mourgues
DOM. CLAVEL ● **Coteaux du Languedoc** Copa Santa
DOM. FONT CAUDE ● **Coteaux du Languedoc Montpeyroux** L'Esprit de Font Caude
DOM. DE LA GRANGE DES PÈRES ● **Vin de Pays de l'Hérault**
DOM. DE L'HORTUS O **Vin de Pays Val de Montferrand** Grande Cuvée
MAS CHAMPART ● **Saint-Chinian** Clos de La Simonette
MAS DE DAUMAS GASSAC O **Vin de Pays de l'Hérault**
PRIEURÉ DE SAINT-JEAN-DE-BÉBIAN O **Coteaux du Languedoc**
DOM. RIMBERT ● **Carignator**
DOM. TERRE INCONNUE ● **Sylvie**

Roussillon

DOM. CALVET-THUNEVIN Maury

Owner: Jean Roger Calvet & Jean-Luc Thunevin 66000 Maury
This partnership, Jean-Luc Thunevin is the owner of Château de VALANDRAUD in Saint-Émilion, purchased their small property in Maury in 2000 and the first bvintages were 2001. The terroir is ideal for producing red wines of the highest calibre from the naturally low yielding vines. Early yields from the vineyards have been just 18 hl/ha. The soils are very finely drained black schist which produce a real piercing minerality in the wines. You are struck as with some top Priorats by the mineral character of the wines rather than by their fruit. The Vin de Pays d'Oc bottling is a blend of 60 per cent Carignan and 40 per cent Syrah. The Cotes du Roussillon-Villages blends 45% each of Grenache and Carignan with 10 per cent Syrah. It offers the more approachably fruit driven style of the two and greater depth and complexity. Aged in 100 per cent new oak these are wines that will both evolve very well with five or six years cellaring. (DM)
● **Côtes du Roussillon-Villages★★★★** £E
● **Vin de Pays d'Oc★★★★** £D

DOM. DE CASENOVE Côtes du Roussillon

Owner: Etienne Montes Mas Sabole, 66300 Trouillas
An ancient estate which, unlike many in the Midi, has been in the same family for generations. However, impressive modern fruit-driven wines are now being made at this fine property, where owner Etienne Montes has enjoyed consultancy input from Jean-Luc COLOMBO. A total of some 50 ha of vines are planted, including 16 ha of whites comprising Grenache Blanc, Maccabeo, Muscat and the rare Torbat. Rich, honeyed Muscat de Rivesaltes and raisiny Rivesaltes are produced as well as a rather dull Côtes du Roussillon white. The red Commandant François Jaubert, produced from mainly Syrah and partly aged in new oak, is powerful, dense and smoky. The Garrigue bottling is spicy and approachable. Newly added are a rich and spicy red Torrespeyes and a very limited production *super-cuvée* Domaine Saint-Luc Pla del Rei, which is extremely expensive. (DM)
● **Côtes du Roussillon** Garrigue★★ £B Commandant François Jaubert★★★★ £E

DOM. CAZES Rivesaltes www.cazes-rivesaltes.com   A:Eno,Luv

Owner: André & Bernard Cazes 4 Rue Francisco-Ferrer, BP 61, 66602 Rivesaltes
In a region marked by new arrivals and vinegrowers becoming winemakers, this venerable and substantial property with some 160 ha of vineyards produces close to 70,000 cases of both table and fortified wines a year and has done so consistently for decades. An extensive range is produced here, including good red Vin de Pays des Côtes Catalanes. Le Credo is a decent blend of Cabernet Sauvignon and Merlot. There are red and white Côtes du Roussillons, red Côtes du Roussillon-Villages and Muscat de Rivesaltes, with some splendid aged examples, along with very good Rivesaltes. These have an intense nutty complexity and will keep very well. There are some remarkable and expensive limited-release old vintages available under the Aimé Cazes label. (DM)
● **Côtes du Roussillon★** £B ● **Côtes du Roussillon-Villages** Alter★★ £B Trilogy★★ £C
● **Vin de Pays des Côtes Catalanes** Le Credo★★ £C
● **Rivesaltes** Tuilé★★★ £C Ambré★★★ £C
○ **Muscat de Rivesaltes★★★** £B

CELLIER DES TEMPLIERS Banyuls & Collioure

Owner: 'Co-operative' Route du Mas-Reig, 66650 Banyuls-sur-Mer
This is the largest co-operative in the Banyuls and Collioure regions, producing traditional Collioure and some impressive fortifieds. The ownership consists of over 750 growers who between them farm close to

900 ha in Banyuls and Collioure, producing wines under both appellations along with a *vin de pays* white. The majority of the fortified production is relatively ordinary and the Collioure bottlings are sound rather than really inspiring, although the domaine wines are altogether more serious. The top Banyuls Grand Cru *cuvées*, though, are a big step up in quality and are labelled Cuvées de Prestige. These are wines with a real nutty complexity and often marked by a dry tangy finish. The Henri Caris is a *demi-sec* style. (DM)

● **Collioure** Château des Abelles★★ £C Abbaye de Valbonne★★ £C
● **Banyuls Grand Cru** Henri Caris★★★ £E Henri Vidal★★★★ £E Vivianne Leroy★★★ £E

CH. DE CALADROY Côtes du Roussillon-Villages

Owner: Michel Mezerette 66720 Belesta-de-la-Frontière
Sizeable well established Roussillon property with a fine range of dry reds, a Muscat de Rivesaltes, a relatively light red Rivesaltes and a barrel-fermented white dominated by Chardonnay. It is a vin de pays and has a balance of Maccabeu and Muscat in the blend. Indeed there is a surprisingly forceful floral, grapey character to the wine. The reds are particularly impressive and very fairly priced. Les Schistes, the lightest and softest is a blend of Syrah, Carignan and Grenache. Les Grenats is more densely structured, a blend of mainly Syrah with Mourvedre and Grenache. La Juliane is of a similar blend with just 5 per cent of Carignan as well and adding flesh through maturation in *barrique*. Particularly dark, spicy and characterful is the Cour Carrée which is an equal blend of Carignan (its dark, peppery character very evident), Syrah, Mourvedre and Grenache. There is also a small quantity of a Mourvedre dominant top *cru*, Cuvée Saint Michel. With the exception of the forward Les Schistes the reds will all benefit from a little age. (DM)

● **Côtes du Roussillon-Villages** Les Schistes★★ £B La Cour Carrée★★★ £B Les Grenats★★★ £B
● **Côtes du Roussillon-Villages** La Juliane★★★ £C
● **Rivesaltes** Tuilé★★ £B
O **Muscat de Rivesaltes★★** £B
O **Vin de Pays des Cotes Catalanes** Expression de Caladroy★★ £B

CH. DE JAU Côtes du Roussillon-Villages   A: GVF

Owner: Estelle Dauré 20 Rue du Colombier, 66600 Case-de-Pene
This is one of the largest properties in the Roussillon, just to the south of Corbières in the heart of the increasingly important Agly Valley. The origins of the château date back to the 12th century and one of the original towers remains today. The estate covers a massive 500 ha of *garrigue*-strewn landscape with 134 ha planted to vines in clay/limestone, marl and schistous soils, 110 ha being red and 24 ha white varieties. Production is considerable for the area at almost 80,000 cases a year and to some extent this is reflected in the regular red Tradition bottling which although relatively characterful is lighter than many other examples from the region. Talon Rouge, though, is a serious step up in quality, full of black fruits, licorice and dark tar flavours. Blended mainly from Syrah, along with Mourvèdre and Grenache it is dense, rich and very powerful. It should continue to develop well in bottle for four or five years. A white Côtes du Roussillon is also produced along with a Muscat de Rivesaltes. The Daure family also own the Collioure property CLOS DES PAULILLES and Mas Cristine in the Rivesaltes. (DM)

● **Côtes du Roussillon-Villages** Tradition★ £B Talon Rouge★★★ £D

DOM. DES CHÊNES Côtes du Roussillon-Villages   A: L&S

Owner: Razungles & Fils 7 Rue de Maréchal-Joffre, 66600 Vingrau
The 38 ha under vine here is fairly evenly divided between red and white and 8,000 or so cases are produced. Sturdy Côtes du Roussillon-Villages red Alzines is a blend of varieties, Grands Mères is vinified from Carignan and the rich and spicy Tautavel is Syrah and Mourvèdre. A limited-release Carissa is produced from the latter variety. Stylish barrel-fermented white *vin de pays* is joined by an impressive white Côtes du Roussillon Magdaleniens. The range is completed by a Muscat and two well-priced Rivesaltes fortifieds. (DM)

● **Côtes du Roussillon-Villages** Grands Mères★ £B Alzines★★ £B Tautavel★★★ £C
● **Rivesaltes** Ambré★★ £B Tuilé★★★ £C
O **Vin de Pays** Val d'Agly Sorbiers★★ £B
O **Muscat de Rivesaltes★★★** £B

DOM. DU CLOS DES FÉES   Côtes du Roussillon-Villages   www.closdesfees.com   A: Odd

Owner: Claudine & Hervé Bizeul   69 Rue du Maréchal-Joffre, 66600 Vingrau
Very impressive newly established domaine producing good to stunning red Roussillons from 11 ha of
Carignan, Grenache, Syrah, Mourvèdre and Lladoner Pelut; the latter is not exactly a regular point of
discussion around most dinner tables. Even the entry level Les Sorcières is full of dark, spicy bramble and
herbs. Approachable and supple, it is mainly aged in *cuve* with a small portion put in new oak. The Vieilles
Vignes, a blend produced from very old vines, many 50 to 100 years old, is not racked; instead
micro-oxygenation is used, as it is with Le Clos des Fées, the domaine's flagship wine. The latter is a blend
of Syrah, Mourvèdre, Grenache and Carignan aged in oak for 18 months. A tiny amount of a remarkable
100 per cent Grenache, La Petite Sibérie, is also produced. Very intense and concentrated, it displays more
piercing pure berry-fruit intensity than a top Châteauneuf-du-Pape but is softer and more approachable and
is very stylish indeed. The vineyard plot of some 1 ha and 17 ares yields a mere 175 cases of this wine a year.
Not surprisingly the price has now gone through the roof. (DM)
● **Côtes du Roussillon-Villages** Les Sorcières★★ £B Vieilles Vignes★★★★ £E
● **Côtes du Roussillon-Villages** Clos des Fées★★★★ £F La Petite Sibérie★★★★★ £H

CLOT DE L'OUM   Côtes du Roussillon-Villages

Owner: Eric Monne & Leia Obara   66720 Belesta
This is among the new wave of exciting new arrivals in the Agly Valley. The original vineyard owners here,
like many before, were happy to sell the fruit from their overcropped vines to the local co-op, unaware of
the tremedous potential of the area. The three reds now produced at Clot de l'Oum are wines of great finesse
and real style and purity, not in any way over-extracted or overdone. The high altitude vineyards are planted
at between 200 and 500 metres on a mix of granite, gneiss and schistous soils. Drainage is excellent and the
potential of the *terroir* is now being handled entirely naturally with no recourse to chemicals or fertilizers.
The excellent-value La Compagnie des Papillons is produced from Grenache and Carignan with some of
the vines up to 50 years old. Fruit is vinified by the parcel to ensure maximum ripeness and ageing is in
used oak. The Saint-Bart Vieilles Vignes is produced from equal proportions Syrah (known here as Shiraz),
Grenache Velu (known as Lladoner Pelut and closely related to Grenache Noir) and Carignan from the
highest parcels on the property. The wine is given a cold-maceration prior to fermentation resulting in a
dense and opulent red that nevertheless retains a fine, elegant mineral core to its fruit. Numero Uno is
named after the famous Berlin restaurant. Dominated by Syrah it is also blended with the best barrel of
Carignan. Once again used oak is preferred to age the wine for 15 months and there is a remarkable depth,
purity and complexity. It is certainly likely to be of five-star quality in a great vintage. All the wines have the
structure and refinement to evolve very well in bottle. Numero Uno particularly will reward the patient. (DM)
● **Côtes du Roussillon-Villages** Saint-Bart Vieilles Vignes★★★★ £C Numero Uno★★★★ £D
● **Côtes du Roussillon-Villages** Las Compagnie des Papillons★★★ £C

CLOS DE PAULILLES   Banyuls & Collioure   A:GVF, P&S

Owner: Estelle Dauré   66660 Port-Vendres
Like CHÂTEAU DE JAU this domaine is owned by the Dauré family. There are 90 ha of vineyards planted
in slate soils with the climate moderated by regular sea breezes. Both Collioure and Banyuls are produced.
Among the Collioures there is a soft fruity rosé and a barrel fermented white. It is the red though that stands
out. Quality has improved significantly in recent vintages and despite the size of the estate this is one of the
better examples of the appellation. It is dominated by Mourvèdre with the balance Syrah. Fermentation and

maceration is lengthy at three weeks before ageing in one-third new oak, one-third used oak and one-third in larger vats. The wine gets a light egg-white fining before bottling. Dense and finely structured, it will develop further with four or five years' age. Three Banyuls are produced solely from Grenache, of which the Rimage Mise Tardive and Cap Bear stand out. Mise Tardive gets up to two and a half years' ageing to add structure and depth. The Cap Bear is aged traditionally in glass demijohns for a year and a half before spending a final three months in in barrel in the cellars. The Mas Cristine Rivesaltes is produced from fruit grown on a separate property also with slate soils. Yields are easily kept naturally at less than 30 hl/ha and the wine is produced from 100% Grenache Blanc. Vinification is halted at 9% alcohol and fortified before being aged for two and a half years. It is rich, full of dark honeyed aromas and impressively complex on release. (DM)

Clos des Paulilles
● **Collioure**★★★ £C
● **Banyuls** Rimage Mise Tardive★★★ £E Cap Bear★★★ £E
Mas Christine
● **Rivesaltes**★★★ £E

DOM. DEPEYRE Côtes du Roussillon   A: SVS

Owner: Brigitte Bile & Serge Depeyre 1 Rue Pasteur, 66600 Cases-de-Pène
Small emerging Roussillon property with 7 ha under vine, 6 ha of which are red. The first vineyard was purchased in 1997 and Serge Depeyre has used his winemaking experience gained at first MAS AMIEL and then CLOS DES FÉES to very good effect. The white *vin de pays* is a blend of both Grenache Gris and Blanc as well as Muscat à Petits Grains. It is barrel-fermented and aged in oak, a small portion of which is new, and the wine absorbs it easily. Both reds are traditionally vinified getting a maceration of up to a month. The regular Roussillon is dominated by Carignan, with a little Syrah and Grenache whereas the Sainte-Colombe is mainly Grenache and aged in a combination of *cuve* and small oak. Although both will cellar well, the Sainte-Colombe just has that extra dimension. (DM)
● **Côtes du Roussillon-Villages**★★★ £B Sainte-Colombe★★★★ £C
○ **Vin de Pays Cotes Catalanes** Eleve en Futs de Chene★★ £B

DOM. FONTANEL Côtes du Roussillon-Villages   A: SVS, ldg

Owner: Pierre Fontanel 25 avenue Jean-Jaurés, 66720 Tautavel
A good small range of wine is produced in the commune of Tautavel by the Fontanels, who have a total of some 35 ha from which they produce approaching 15,000 cases a year. Rich and heady fortifieds are fine examples and good value for money, as are the three Roussillon reds. The regular Roussillon is soft, forward and juicy, while Cistes is rich and opulent with upfront, nicely ripe brambly, spicy fruit. The Prieuré is denser and more powerful, a real medium-term cellaring prospect. However it shows remarkably well in its youth, with opulent dark-berry fruit and a velvety, rounded, supple texture. (DM)
● **Côtes du Roussillon-Villages**★★ £B Cistes★★★ £B Prieuré★★★★ £C
● **Rivesaltes** ★★★ £C ○ **Muscat de Rivesaltes**★★★ £B

DOM. GARDIES Côtes du Roussillon-Villages   A: GVF, Bal, Jer

Owner: Jean Gardies 1 Rue Millères, 66600 Vingrau
A really first-class 30-ha property among a seemingly ever increasing number in this exciting appellation. Some good Muscat de Rivesaltes is produced here and now two excellent dry whites from the 5 ha of mainly Grenache Blanc and a little Roussanne. It is however the reds that are particularly noteworthy. There are 25 ha of Grenache, Syrah, Mourvèdre and Carignan and the property has superbly drained limestone and schistous soils and these provide ideal growing conditions. The Millères, a blend of all four red varieties, is vibrant and approachable. The Vieilles Vignes has a high proportion of Grenache from old vines while La Torre is a massive and dense dark, brooding mix of Mourvèdre and Carignan. The most expensive wine,

La Falaise is an extremely ageworthy and powerful expression of Syrah. (DM)

● **Côtes du Roussillon-Villages** La Torre★★★★ £E Falaises★★★★★ £E
● **Côtes du Roussillon-Villages** Millères★★★ £B Vieilles Vignes★★★ £C
O **Côtes du Roussillon** Glacières★★ £B Vieilles Vignes★★★ £C

DOM. GAUBY Côtes du Roussillon-Villages   A: A&B, F&R, Rae

Owner: Gérard Gauby La Faradjal, 66600 Calce

Gérard Gauby and his wife Ghislaine produce a stunning range of reds and whites from the Roussillon. They are also now involved with the equally thrilling wines of DOM. LE SOULA in the high-altitude vineyards of the Agly Valley and are a source of inspiration for the remarkable new domaines emerging from those vineyards. The white Gauby La Jasse is a crisp, piercing dry Muscat, while the Vieilles Vignes is a powerful nutty blend of southern varieties including Grenache Blanc, Maccabeo and Viognier, a wine of depth and great value for money. The top white Coume Gineste is sourced from a single vineyard and is produced from Grenache Blanc. Among the reds Les Calcinaires is a juicy, vibrant red made from Grenache, Syrah and Carignan and laden with sumptuous raspberry fruit, while the marvellous Vieilles Vignes is a structured, dense, powerful expression of intensely complex old-vine Grenache and Carignan with a smattering of Syrah, Mourvèdre and Cinsault. The top red, and among the most expensive wines in the South of France, is the magnificent Muntada. This is a superbly crafted Syrah, very rich, concentrated and powerful but increasingly refined and no doubt very long lived. (DM)

● **Côtes du Roussillon** Les Calcinaires★★ £B
● **Côtes du Roussillon-Villages** Vieilles Vignes★★★★ £D Muntada★★★★★ £F
O **Vin de Pays de Côtes Catalanes** La Jasse★★ £B Vieille Vignes★★★ £C Coume Gineste★★★★ £E

DOM. LAGUERRE Côtes du Roussillon   A:RSW

Owner: Eric Laguerre 66220 Saint-Martin-de-Fenouillet

Eric Laguerre, the former head of the Saint-Martin de Fenouillet co-op, is also involved with Gérard GAUBY at DOM. LE SOULA but has his own small 15-ha domaine with high-altitude biodynamically farmed vineyards where he produces both red and white Côtes du Roussillon. We have not yet tasted the red in depth but it is likely to show the same potential as the richly complex, nutty, mineral-scented white. The style here is influenced not only by the 600 m vineyards but also by vines that range from 20 to 50 years of age and the well-drained granite soils. The white Le Ciste blends Marsanne, Roussanne and Grenache Gris; the red is Grenache, Syrah and unusually Cabernet Sauvignon. The wines offer both excellent quality and very good value for money. (DM)

O **Côtes du Roussillon** Le Ciste★★★ £B

LA PASSION D'UNE VIE Côtes du Roussillon-Villages

Owner: Henri Despeaux c/o Terroirs d'Exception, 33330 Saint-Christophe des Bardes

First class Roussillon property owned by Henri Despeaux and Bernard Magrez in Bordeaux, the owner of PAPE-CLEMENT and much else besides. With consultancy advice from Michel Rolland as in all of the wines marketed under the Terroirs d'Exception banner this is a rich, opulent, fruit-driven red but of impressive grip and structure also. The vineyards are planted at an altitude of 180 to 250 metres above sea level on free-draining shale slopes. With an average vine age of over 30 years and some vines up to 100 years there is great potential here. Yields are naturally low, barely more than 20 hl/ha and a green harvest is also practised. In the winery everything is handled by gravity with a traditional vinification and ageing in 400-litre casks. Expect to be able to age the wine for five or more years and gain additional complexity. (DM)

● **Côtes du Roussillon-Villages**★★★★ £D

DOM. LE SOULA Vin de Pays des Côteaux des Fenouillèdes A:RSW,BBR

Owner: G Gauby, E Leguerre, R Richard 66220 Saint-Martin-de-Fenouillet

The white and the red here are labelled under the new Vin de Pays des Fenouilledes in the Agly Valley. Both wines are excellent and are indicative of the long-term potential of these high-altitude vineyards. The property has been developed by Gérard GAUBY, Eric Laguerre, who has his own property at DOM. LAGUERRE, and UK wine importer Roy Richards. The key to quality is the 600 m elevation of the vineyards, at the limit of ripening but where the south-facing aspect creates a sun trap. The red Le Soula blends Grenache and Syrah and the wine is extraordinarily dense, very backward young but with the potential to add layers of complex dark mineral fruit with age. The brilliantly intense, mineral and citrus white is a blend of Roussanne and Grenache Gris. It is a benchmark Roussillon white. The vineyards are all farmed biodynamically. (DM)

● **Vin de Pays des Côteaux des Fenouillèdes** Le Soula★★★★★ £E
○ **Vin de Pays des Côteaux des Fenouillèdes** Le Soula★★★★ £E

DOM. LA TOUR VIEILLE Banyuls & Collioure A: Yap

Owner: Vincent Cantié & Christine Campadieu 66190 Collioure

Well-established producer of both Collioure and Banyuls, the quality of which is consistently good. There are three red labels as well as a nutty honeyed white, Les Canadells, blended from Grenache Gris and Blanc as well as some Maccabeo. The red La Pinède, from Grenache, Carignan and Mourvèdre is a full, dense, spicy black-fruit style, while the Puig Oriol, which is 70% Grenache and the balance Syrah, is more fragrant with a marvellous *garrigue* scent to the deep berry fruit, the Grenache very prominent. A further red Collioure, Puig Ambeille has recently been added. Good Banyuls comes in two guises: the Cuvée Francis Cantié is the more serious with sophisticated nutty *rancio* characters from extended time in cask. (DM)

● **Collioure** La Pinède★★ £B Puig Oriol★★★ £C
● **Banyuls** Cuvée Francis Cantié★★★ £C
○ **Vin de Pays de la Côte Vermeille** Les Canadells★★★ £C

MAS AMIEL Maury A: L&S,HHB

Owner: Olivier Decelle 66460 Maury

A historic 155-ha property that is understandably best known for its remarkable range of Maury *vins doux naturels*. Two stylish and impressive red Côtes du Roussillons are also produced here in addition to a well-priced, vibrant *vin de pays*, Plaisir, and a white Côtes du Roussillon. The two Roussillon reds are impressively large, structured wines. The range of fortified Maury is extensive, from young minimally aged current vintages through to old vintage bottles. The top *cuvées* are Réserve, Privilège and the immensely rich Charles Dupuy. The wines are marked by a classic burnt raisiny, toffeed *rancio* character. The top wines are extraordinarily intense. Olivier Decelle now has a number of interests in Bordeaux. (DM)

● **Côtes du Roussillon** Hautes Terres★★★ £B ● **Côtes du Roussillon-Villages** Carrerades★★★ £C
● **Vin de Pays des Côtes Catalanes** Plaisir★★ £B
● **Maury** 10 Ans d'Age★★★ £C 15 Ans d'Age★★★★ £E
● **Maury** Vintage★★ £C Vintage Réserve★★★ £D Privilège★★★★ £E Charles Dupuy★★★★★ £E
○ **Côtes du Roussillon** Altaïr★★★ £D

MAS DES BAUX Côtes du Roussillon

Owner: Serge et Marie-Pierre Baux Chemin du Mas Durand, 66140 Canet-en-Roussillon

Small Roussillon property producing a comprehensive range of *vin de pays* red, white and rosé as well as a fine, pure and complex Côtes du Roussillon red. There are just over 12 ha under vine and output is around 2,500 cases a year, with the objective being to reach 4,000 cases. The first *vendange* was only in 1999. There is a minimalist approach here in the best sense: all vineyard work is carried out as naturally as possible and handling is kept to a minimum in the cellar. Growing conditions are ideal, with sunny days, just sufficient rainfall and superbly drained soils with a layer of *galets roulés* helping to check yields on average at 25 to 35 hl/ha. Fermentation is traditional and the reds are fully destemmed. The white Baux Blond, from Muscat à Petit Grains, is cool-fermented and aged for four months in *inox* with *bâtonnage*. Like the rosé Rouge à Levres it should be drunk young and fresh. The red Velours Rouge is the softest and most immediately accessible of the reds. A blend of Grenache and Syrah, it gets a short ageing in *inox* and because of this is bottled after a light fining and earth filtration. Rouge Gorge blends Syrah and Mourvèdre with some old Grenache (over 35 years) and is aged in old oak for 12 months. The top *vin de pays* Rouge Baux is a rich and opulent blend which adds Cabernet Sauvignon to the Rhône red varietals and gets 12 months in new oak. The Côtes du Roussillon Soleil Rouge is tighter, more restrained and elegant. Low-yielding younger Syrah and Mourvèdre are blended with some of the oldest Grenache. It is aged in a combination of *inox* and older oak. The top reds will comfortably improve for five years or more. (DM)

● **Côtes du Roussillon** Soleil★★★ £C
● **Vin de Pays des Côtes Catalanes** Velours Rouge★★ £B Rouge Gorge★★★ £B Rouge Baux★★★ £C
◉ **Vin de Pays des Côtes Catalanes** Rouge à lèvres★★ £B
○ **Vin de Pays des Côtes Catalanes** Baux Blond★★ £B

DOM. DU MAS BLANC Banyuls & Collioure   A:VTr, C&R

Owner: Jean-Michel Parcé 9 Avenue du Général-de-Gaulle, 66650 Banyuls-sur-Mer
Splendid 21-ha Banyuls and Collioure property developed by the late Dr André Parcé and now run by his son Jean-Michel. There are four Collioures. La Llose is the regular bottling while there are three very fine single-vineyard wines: the Cosprons Levant is an old-vine blend of Mourvèdre, Syrah and Counoise, Clos du Moulin is produced from Mourvèdre and Counoise and Les Junquets is from Syrah with a hint of Roussanne and Marsanne for fragrance. Production of these three is small but they are very impressive, refined reds. Some of the very best Banyuls is also created here. There are two Rimage bottlings that have spent less time in cask, the sumptuous Cuvée de la Saint-Martin, which has intense, nutty, *rancio* notes and the Hors d'Age de Solera, resembling a great old Oloroso. These are expensive. (DM)

● **Collioure** La Llose★★ £B Clos du Moulin★★★ £C Cosprons Levant★★★ £C Les Junquets★★★★ £D
● **Banyuls** Rimage★★★★ £E La Coume★★★★ £F

MAS DE LA DEVÈZE Côtes du Roussillon-Villages   A: L&S

Owner: Anne-Lise & Olivier Bernstein 66720 Tautavel
This is a recently established property in the Roussillon village of Tautavel producing both red and white. A premium red Le Mas will be available in 2005. The Bernsteins originate from Burgundy but like others have realised the great potential of the Agly Valley for making light rather than fortified wines of considerable flair and intensity. At their old restored Mas they have installed a brand new winery. The vineyards are planted in a mix of limestone, clay and schistous marl, providing excellent drainage to optimise the intensity of the fruit and provide adequate mineral nourishment. The 66 is a soft, forward brambly red dominated by Grenache. Matured in tank there is just a small portion of Syrah in the blend. The Mas red is Grenache and Syrah, aged in oak. The very characterful, barrel-fermented nutty Mas white blends Maccabeu and Grenache Gris in equal amounts. These are well priced wines to watch. (DM)

● **Côtes du Roussillon-Villages** 66★★ £B
○ **Vin de Pays des Pyrénées Orientales**★★★ £B

DOM. MATASSA Vin de Pays des Côtes Catalanes   A:Adm

Owner: Tom Lubbe & Sam Harrop 66600 Calce
Just over 300 cases are made a year at this excellent high altitude property near the village of Calce in the Agly Valley. A white and red are produced. Tom Lubbe is also a partner at The OBSERVATORY in South Africa with his sister Catherine. Much care is lavished on the vineyards and teas are used to treat the soil

helping guard against fungal disease and aid full early ripening. The Matassa wines like those at the Observatory are marked by their surprisingly firm, gripping acidity and should develop well in bottle. The white is dominated by Grenache Gris and is barrel-fermented and aged for around nine months but without *batonnage*. The red is currently just classified as Vin de Table because of the tedious bureaucracy of the area and is dominated by highly characterful very old vine Carignan, full of dark pepper and herbal spices. Unusually there is around 5 per cent of Grenache Noir, Blanc and Gris interspersed in the vineyard. Reserved and youthfully tight the red particularly requires three or four years at a minimum. (DM)

● **Vin de Table** Matassa★★★★ £E

O **Vin de Pays des Côtes Catalanes** Matassa★★★ £D

DOM. PIÉTRI-GÉRAUD   Banyuls & Collioure   A: M&V

Owner: Piétri-Géraud Family   66190 Collioure

This is a very fine mother-and-daughter domaine producing benchmark Collioure and Banyuls. As well as an excellent Collioure – one of the best in the appellation – a white Banyuls and dense Cuvée Joseph Geraud are produced. The vineyards are planted on steep terraced, schistous slopes, to a combination of old Grenache and Carignan (the vines are generally above 50 years of age) and younger Syrah and Mourvèdre. Yields are naturally low, barely 30 hl/ha, and the wines are generally marked by their style and refinement. In the Collioure, a blend of Grenache (60%) with Syrah and Mourvèdre, filtration is avoided. The Banyuls Blanc gets a year in large vats, while the Cuvée Joseph Geraud sees an extended ageing period of seven years to bring out more complex,smoky *rancio* characters. The red Collioure will benefit from four or five years' cellaring. (DM)

● **Collioure★★★** £C

DOM. POUDEROUX   Maury   A: THt

Owner: Robert Pouderoux   2 Rue Emile Zola, 66460 Maury

Splendid producer, with a range of not only excellent Côtes du Roussillon reds but some very fine fortified wines as well. Although among the finest of the new wave of red wine producers in the Roussillon, the Poudereaux domaine is no flash in the pan. The family have been involved in Maury viticulture since 1826. Indeed it is this continuity across the last century in particular that is responsible for the splendid raw material available to Robert Poudereaux. His vineyards are planted to Grenache, Syrah, Mourvèdre and Carignan grown on finely drained soils of black and white schist and limestone. There is a first-class barrel-fermented white of real density produced from Grenache Blanc, even in a marginal vintage like 2002 on the edge of three stars. Among the dry reds Latour de Grès is dense and powerful, marked by the characteristic dark berry and spice complexity of old-vine Carignan. Terre Brune blends Grenache, Syrah and Mourvèdre and gets an extra week of vatting to add depth. Like Latour de Grès it is aged in older barrels. The premium, richly opulent and complex Mouriane also blends Grenache, Syrah and Mourvèdre. Macerated on its skins for a month or more and aged in new oak for a year, it demands five years' patience. There is a splendid range of Maury all produced solely from Grenache Noir. Vendange is aged in a combination of *cuve* and bottle until release, The Mise Tardive gets three years in barrel, which adds complexity and more tertiary aromas. The top two wines are a serious step up. The Hors d'Age gets twelve years in small oak, the Grande Reserve four years in a combination of *foudres* and *bonbonnes*. There is also an excellent fortified Muscat, grown on schistous soils. Rich and opulent it is in complete contrast to the Maury reds with ripe, fresh grapey character. (DM)

● **Côtes du Roussillon-Villages** Latour de Grès★★★ £B Terre Brune★★★ £C Mouriane★★★★ £E

● **Maury** Vendange★★★ £C Mise Tardive★★★ £C Hors d'Age★★★★ £D Grande Reserve★★★★ £E

O **Côtes du Roussillon-Villages★★** £C

O **Muscat de Rivesaltes★★★** £D

DOM. PUIG-PARAHŸ   Côtes du Roussillon

Owner: Georges Puig-Parahÿ   Le Fort de Saint-Pierre, 66300 Passa

Georges Puig-Parahÿ's domaine is sizeable in comparison to those of his like-minded, quality-conscious neighbours. This however is relative, certainly in comparison to the New World because Georges produces a vast total of some 8,000 to 9,000 cases a year! The Puig family have been involved in Roussillon viticulture since the phylloxera crisis in France in 1878 and as a result own some remarkable old-vine holdings. Grenache is up to 80 years old, Carignan as much as 130. Syrah and Mourvèdre are also now planted to produce modern-style wines. There is a good, clean and fresh, impressively grapey Muscat Vin de Pays but more serious are the Sant Lluc and Miserys whites blended from Grenache Blanc and Gris. The former is vinified *en cuve;* the latter in a combination of tank and new oak. With low yields in well-drained argilo-calcaire soils the three Côtes du Roussillon reds are of good to very good quality. Mes Amis is mainly Carignan and Grenache but has marvellous old-vine character – not complex but exciting. Georges is similarly aged in *cuve* but is more serious and structured, containing Grenache, Syrah and Mourvèdre as well as Carignan. The top two *cuvées*, Le Fort de Saint-Pierre and Ballides, are both ageworthy. The former is aged in *cuve,* the latter in *barrique.* The Saint-Pierre is the better balanced, its beguiling fruit offering great class and purity. A range of exciting fortifieds are available to taste at the domaine. (DM)

● **Côtes du Roussillon** Le Fort Saint-Pierre★★★ £C Ballides★★★ £D
● **Côtes du Roussillon** Mes Amis★★ £B Georges★★★ £B
O **Vin de Pays d'Oc** Sant Lluc★★ £B Miserys★★ £B
O **Vin de Pays d'Oc** Muscat Sec★ £B

DOM. DE LA RECTORIE   Banyuls & Collioure   larectorie@wanadoo.fr   A: A&B,Bal,Cam

Owner: Parcé Frères   54 Avenue du Puig-Delmas, 66650 Banyuls-sur-Mer

One of the finest producers of Collioure and Banyuls. There are three *cuvées* of red Collioure and a presentable rosé. Of the reds Col de Bast is the lightest and made from 100% Grenache, whereas the denser and more structured La Coume Pascole is a blend of Grenache, Syrah and Carignan. The sturdiest of the three, Le Seris, is produced from very old Carignan and Grenache vines. Even the latter two are not in any way overblown; they are more wines of refinement and elegance. These are complemented by a white *vin de pays,* L'Argile, a powerfully oaked Grenache Gris. Very good Banyuls includes two regular *cuvées* – the best is Cuvée Léon Parcé, which is aged for around a year in cask and an altogether different, less evolved style to that found at MAS BLANC – and an aged wine, L'Oublée, which is understandably pricey. (DM)

● **Collioure** Col de Bast★★ £B La Coume Pascole★★★ £D Le Seris★★★ £C
● **Banyuls** Cuvée Léon Parcé★★★ £C
O **Vin de Pays de la Côte Vermeille** L'Argile★★★ £C

DOM. DES SCHISTES   Côtes du Roussillon-Villages   A:M&V,P&S,ACh

Owner: Jacques Sire   1 Avenue Jean-Lurçat, 66310 Estagel

A small, first-class range of both table and fortified wines is produced at this 44-ha property. The reds are characterised by the old-vine quality of the fruit, which adds an extra dimension. Indeed some of the oldest vines are approaching 80 years. Tradition is a forward, fruit-driven style blended from Syrah, Grenache and Carignan and vinified both traditionally and with some carbonic maceration. Les Terrasses is produced from the same varieties but with a higher proportion of Syrah aged in one-year-old oak, the balance in *cuve.* Stylish and intense, there is a real mineral quality running through the wine. La Coumeille, the top red, is 100 per cent Syrah, aged in oak of which only a small portion is new and the wine is very fine with a really spicy, dark, intense fruit quality. There's a lovely nutty and raisiny Maury and a very good floral yet powerful and concentrated Muscat de Rivesaltes. (DM)

● **Côtes du Roussillon-Villages** Tradition★★ £B Les Terrasses★★★ £C La Coumeille★★★ £C
● **Maury** Cerisaie★★★ £C
O **Muscat de Rivesaltes**★★★ £B

DOM. SEGUELA Côtes du Roussillon-Villages   A:GVF,May

Owner: Trinidad & Jean-Pierre Seguela 12 Avenue de Caramany, 66720 Rasiguères
Production is small at this dedicated Roussillon producer, with a total of less than 3,000 cases made annually. Yields are kept very low, fruit is carefully sorted prior to vinification and in the cellar filtration is avoided. What marks these wines out is the depth and purity of their fruit. Increasingly they are matching the structure of the very best. Les Condalies is a blend mainly of Carignan but with some Syrah and Grenache also. Soft easy tannins and spicy brambly fruit mark the style of the wine, which is excellent value. Cuvée Jean-Julien is a dense old-vine blend of Syrah and Carignan partly aged in new oak (but this is seamlessly handled), while the Planète-Seguela is an astonishingly low-yielding (as low as 12 hl/ha) *assemblage* of Carignan, Syrah, Grenache and Cinsault and is refined, long and well-structured. (DM)
● **Côtes du Roussillon-Villages** Les Condalies★★★£B Cuvée Jean-Julien★★★ £C Planète-Seguela★★★★ £E

DOM. DE LA SERRE Maury

Owner: Jean-Louis Vera & Yves Blanc 66460 Maury
Among the larger of the new wave of domaines in the Agly Valley. There are 20 ha planted at Maury and a further 10 ha of Syrah around the village of Cassagnes. The vines range from 25 to 120 years of age and the complex old-vine character of the Grenache and Carignan at Maury is reflected in the wines. Quality is key here. Consultant Bordeaux winemaker Daniel Bonnet (who advises various domaines in the region) ensures that all the grapes are sorted prior to fermentation and 100% new oak is being used for ageing all three wines. Each is blended from Grenache, Carignan and Syrah. The 2002 Serre Longue came in at a whopping 16% alcohol but such is the ripeness and firm mineral structure that the wine remains balanced. Hypogée posseses that extra depth and dimension. Firmly, structured and very complex. Most expensive is the tiny production Cuvée Pierre Levée. Expect the wines to develop well in bottle over at least five to seven years. (DM)
● **Côtes du Roussillon-Villages** Serre Longue★★★★ £C Hypogee★★★★ £D

DOM. SERRELONGUE Maury

Owner: Julien Fournier 149 Avenue Jean Jaurès, 66460 Maury
Tiny domaine producing exquisite wines from a small holding of just 5 ha. The vineyards are planted to a combination of Mourvèdre, Syrah, Carignan and Grenache and vine age ranges from 20 to 120 years. This combined with high-altitude vineyards and a committed approach to reducing yields results in wines of remarkable depth and purity. Do not expect fruit bombs, the overriding character here is minerality, with subtle deeply spicy black fruits and an intensity rarely found in the Midi. The Extrait de Passion blends Grenache with Mourvèdre and is aged in *demi-muids.* The Esprit de Vin also has a proportion of Syrah and seems to have that small extra dimension on the palate. These are beguiling wines, full-bodied and rampantly alcoholic but balanced too. (DM)
● **Côtes du Roussillon-Villages** Extrait de Passion★★★★ £D Esprit de Vin★★★★★ £E

DOM. DES SOULANES Vin de Pays des Côtes Catalanes

Owner: Cathy & Daniel Laffite Mas de Las Fredas, 66720 Tautavel
This is another recently established operation in the vineyards of the Roussillon. Based at Tautavel in the heart of Côtes du Roussillon, two of the the the wines here take the Vin de Pays des Côtes Catalanes classification. They will also be producing Côtes du Roussillon-Villages and Maury fortifieds. The Laffites have 17 hectares spread across 18 diverse parcels with their Grenache and Carignan planted in a mix of schistous soils. The red Jean Pull is a soft, ripe and brambly style with 35 per cent Carignan as well as Grenache. A rich opulent character to the fruit is ensured low yields and old vines. The Cuvee Bastoul-Laffite is sturdier, firmer and will develop extremely well in bottle. Dominated by Grenache, yields are barely 20 hl/ha and the wine is aged in barriques for 12 months and bottled unfiltered. A domaine to watch.(DM)
● **Vin de Pays des Côtes Catalanes** Cuvee Jean Pull★★★ £B Cuvee Bastoul-Laffite★★★ ★ £C

DOM. DU TRAGINER Banyuls & Collioure

Owner: Jean-François Deu   56 Avenue du Puig del Mas, 66650 Banyuls-sur-Mer

A fine range of Banyuls and improving Collioures are produced at this small 9 ha property. Red varieties Mourvèdre, Syrah, Grenache and Carignan are planted along with Grenache Blanc and Gris as well as Muscat. The vineyards are planted on schistous soils and since 1997 have been farmed organically. Jean-François Deu is the only remaining Banyuls grower to plough his vineyards by mule; indeed his name means mule driver in Catalan. There is a very good white Collioure which is fermented relatively cool and aged in *cuve*, with piercing spicy, citrus fruit. The red Collioures are traditionally vinified with a maceration on the skins of 25 days. The Traditionelle is aged in *foudre*, Al Riberal in one- to five-year-old *barriques* and the Octobre and the top label Cuvée de Capitas in new and one-year-old barrels. The wines took a real step up in the 2001 vintage. Full of dark spicy fruit the Octobre and Cuvée de Capitas are impressively structured and ageworthy. Like PIÉTRI-GÉRAUD, Traginer is one of the few remaining producers of a Banyuls Blanc. Blended from Grenache Blanc, Grenache Gris and Muscat à Petit Blancs, the wine has a marked floral as well as grapey character with considerably more intensity than you would generally find in white Port. Of the red Banyuls the Rimage is marked by its fresh berry fruit and is bottled after seven months. Mise Tardive is aged in *foudre* for two and a half years and has a notably evolved nutty character. Best of all though, the Grand Cru Hors d'Age is aged for at least 10 years in *demi-muid*. It is rich and toffeed with real depth and intensity. (DM)

● **Collioure** Traditionelle★★ £B Al Riberal★★ £B Octobre★★★ £C Cuvée de Capitas★★★ £C
● **Banyuls** Mise Tardive★★★ £C Rimage★★★ £C Grand Cru Hors d'Age★★★★ £E
O **Collioure**★★ £B O **Banyuls** Mise Tardive★★ £C

Also see the following Rhône *négociants* with an entry in the section *Rhône Valley:*
M CHAPOUTIER
JEAN-LUC COLOMBO
TARDIEU-LAURENT

ROUSSILLON OTHER WINES OF NOTE

CH. PLANÈRES ● **Côtes du Roussillon** £B
DOM. FERRER-RIBIÈRE ● **Côtes du Roussillon** Cana★★★ £D Sélénae★★★ £E
DOM. FORÇA-REAL ● **Côtes du Roussillon-Villages** £B ● **Rivesaltes** Hors d'Age £B
DOM. LAPORTE ● **Côtes du Roussillon** Domitia £B
LA PRÉCEPTORIE DE CENTERNACH ● **Vin de Pays des Côtes de Catalanes** Terre Promise £B
● **Côtes du Roussillon-Villages** ● **Bandol** Cuvée des Bartavelles £D
L'ETOILE ● **Banyuls** Extra Vieux £D
DOM. L'HÉRITIER ● **Côtes du Roussillon** Romani £C
DOM MARCEVOL ● **Côtes du Roussillon** £B Prestige £C
MAS CRÉMAT ● **Côtes du Roussillon** £B Fût de Chêne £C
DOM. OLIVIER PITHON ● **Côtes du Roussillon** £B Vignes de Saturne £C
DOM. SARDA-MALET ● **Côtes du Roussillon** Réserve £C Terroir Mailloles £D
DOM. VAQUER ● **Vin de Pays des Côtes de Catalanes** L'Exception £D
DOM. VIAL-MAGNÈRES ● **Banyuls** Vintage £B

Work in progress!!

Wines from the following producers under consideration for the next edition
DOM. D'ARFEUILLE (VIN DE PAYS DES CÔTEAUX DES FENOUILLÈDES)
CLOS DEL REY (VIN DE PAYS D'OC)
DOM. GRAIN D'ORIENT (VIN DE PAYS DES CÔTEAUX DES FENOUILLÈDES)
MAS JANEIL (MAURY)

DOM. DE LA PERTUISANE (MAURY)
DOM. TERRE ROUSSE (MAURY)

Author's choice (DM)

Dry and fortifieds from the Roussillon

CELLIER DES TEMPLIERS ● **Banyuls Grand Cru** Henri Vidal

DOM. DE CASENOVE ● **Côtes du Roussillon** Commandant François Jaubert

DOM. DES CHÊNES ● **Côtes du Roussillon-Villages** Tautavel

DOM. DU CLOS DES FÉES ● **Côtes du Roussillon-Villages** La Petite Sibérie

DOM. FONTANEL ● **Côtes du Roussillon-Villages** Prieuré

DOM. GARDIES ● **Côtes du Roussillon-Villages** La Torre

DOM. GAUBY ○ **Vin de Pays de Côtes Catalanes** Coume Gineste

DOM. LA TOUR VIEILLE ● **Collioure** Puig Oriol

MAS AMIEL ● **Maury** Charles Dupuy

DOM. DU MAS BLANC ● **Banyuls** La Coume

DOM. DE LA RECTORIE ● **Collioure** La Coume Pascole

DOM. DES SCHISTES ○ **Muscat de Rivesaltes**

Provence & Eastern France

This section of the guide covers Provence and Corsica along with the alpine vineyards of the Jura and Savoie. The latter are steeped in tradition and relatively unknown but some fine and very diverse styles are produced. Provence has emerged in recent years with a number of exciting high quality small domaines from most of her appellations. The change has been less dramatic than in the Midi, but here too many quality-minded individuals are bringing a new focus to viticulture and expressing the potential of their terroirs. The role of Provence as a purveyor of easy-drinking pink plonk to sun-seeking tourists is gradually changing and indeed many of the examples are much improved. However the overall importance of moderate quality rosé in the region's wine production is still depressingly high.

Provence and Corsica

While rosé remains the mainstay of Provençal wine production, exciting reds and some very well-made whites have emerged over the last fifteen years or so. In the foothills of the Alpes-Maritimes inland of Nice the tiny appellation of **Bellet,** with a total of a mere 39 ha under vine, offers some unusual albeit pricey, well-structured reds and lightly floral nutty whites and fruity rosés. The proximity of neighbouring Italy shows itself with the Braquet (Brachetto) among the varieties that make up the permitted red blend, along with Folle Noir and the more usual Grenache and Cinsault. The vineyards are planted at altitude of some 300 m, moderating the climate. This provides an unusual opportunity in ripening Chardonnay in such a southerly maritime climate, which in the whites is blended with Rolle.

The vast bulk of central Provence is covered by the appellations of **Côtes de Provence** and **Coteaux Varois.** While both produce vast amounts of glugging rosé, some very impressive reds are being produced from blends of Rhône varieties, some with the addition of Cabernet Sauvignon. The **Coteaux d'Aix en Provence** and the spectacularly sited vineyards of **Les Baux de Provence** produce similar wines. Domaine de Trevallon, now forced to label its wine as Vin de Pays des Bouches du Rhône, set the trend with a stunning blend of Cabernet and Syrah. There are a number of other such blends now; some like Trevallon use more traditional ageing in large vats while others are seduced by new oak. Whatever the approach an exciting array of different styles is emerging.

Palette is another tiny AC of just 40 ha for both red and white and with only two established producers, although others are emerging. Château Crémade has yet to challenge Château Simone, thus far the only producer of wines of real quality. An extensive number of varieties can be planted but increasingly replanting is concentrated on Syrah, Grenache and Mourvèdre.

The two coastal appellations of **Cassis** and **Bandol** between Marseilles and Toulon are sources of red, white and rosé. Generally Cassis tends to be pretty dull fare but there is the odd impressive white. The best whites and rosés from Bandol are good but it is the reds that you should look out for. The appellation is situated in the foothills just inland of the port of Bandol in a natural coastal amphitheatre. The vineyards stretch from La Ciotat in the east to Sanary-sur-Mer in the west and enjoy a unique warm, dry maritime climate. The style of the wine itself varies surprisingly due to differing calcareous, gravel and clay soils and varying levels of Mourvèdre, the main grape variety. Established Bandol leaders Domaine Tempier and Château Pibarnon are now being joined by a new wave of small, high-quality growers. This is an exciting area to follow. Remember, though, that these wines need cellaring, often for up to a decade.

There are three main appellations on the island of Corsica; **Vin de Corse, Patrimonio** and **Ajaccio.** Almost all viticulture is carried out around the coast. The forested, mountainous interior is far too extreme for viticulture. There are also a number of *crus* within the Vin de Corse appellation: **Calvi, Sartène, Figari, Porto-Vecchio** and **Coteaux du Cap Corse.** Both Coteaux du Cap Corse and Patrimonio are entitled to the Muscat du Cap Corse appellation and it is some of these good to very good rich fortified Muscats which offer the greatest excitement here. Some good reds, albeit somewhat rustic, are also produced from the native Nielluccio along with Grenache, Carignan and Cinsault.

Jura

Located to the west of Burgundy's Côte d'Or, the vineyard area is situated at altitude on the western slopes of the Jura mountains. There are a number of appellations here. The **Côte du Jura** AC encompasses the whole region and produces red, rosé and white wine. Reds and rosés are produced from the local Poulsard and Trousseau as well as Pinot Noir. Those produced from Pinot are the best bets. Among the whites, Chardonnay is good but of more interest are the nutty, characterful Savagnin-based wines. Some oak is used but it tends to be subtle and restrained. The speciality of the region is *vin jaune*. This is not dissimilar to fino sherry in character as it is aged under a yeast film, yet it remains unfortified. The wine is remarkably ageworthy. *Vin jaune* can also be found under the **Arbois**, **Château Chalon** and **L'Étoile** AC's. At Arbois good red and white (from the same varieties as in the Côte du Jura), *vin de paille* and sparkling wines are also produced. Château-Chalon and L'Étoile are much smaller appellations. The former is solely for the production of *vin jaune*. In L'Étoile dry whites from Chardonnay and Savagnin and some moderate sparkling wine are produced as well as *vin jaune*. The rare *vin de paille* is, like those in the northern Rhône, a late-harvested sweet white with a hint of nutty oxidation. Most sparkling wine is made by the traditional method and is labelled as **Crémant de Jura**. There is the odd decent example.

Savoie

This high alpine vineyard area is located just to the south-west of Geneva. The regional AC is **Vin de Savoie**. There are some good whites from the Altesse grape which are fresh and floral and reds from Pinot Noir and Mondeuse. The latter particularly are worth considering. Good light, fresh, dry whites from Altesse and sparkling wines from Molette (with some Altesse) are produced under the **Seyssel AC**. The Chasselas-based whites at **Crepy AC** are generally unexciting.

A-Z of producers by appellation

Provence

1 Les Baux de Provence
2 Coteaux d'Aix en Provence
3 Palette
4 Côtes de Provence
5 Coteaux Varois
6 Cassis
7 Bandol
8 Bellet

Provence & Eastern France vintages

It is extremely difficult in a large region such as Provence to make specific vintage assessments. However, there have been significant changes in vintage conditions from one year to another throughout the region. These variations are more pronounced as you move further inland. Bandol, particularly, has a very benign maritime climate and is reasonably consistent.

The more established Provençal red appellations have consistently produced wines that develop well with age. Bandol, particularly, with its high percentage of the structured and noble Mourvèdre, is a very ageworthy red. Among the top older years for premium Provençal reds (mainly Bandol) are 1989, 1988, 1985, 1982, 1978, 1975 and 1970.

The whites throughout the area are generally intended for drinking young, although the best traditional examples from the likes of Château Simone in Palette will keep for a decade.

In general most red and white from Jura and Savoie should be drunk young. However, in the Jura, *vin jaune* is remarkably long-lived; it is typically released with 10 years age. Other Savagnin-based white also develops well for a decade or so. Top years in the Jura have been 2000, 1999, 1996, 1995, 1990, 1989, 1988 and 1985.

Provence vintage chart

	Bandol	Côtes de Provence Top Reds	Les Baux de Provence Top Reds
2003	★★★★ A	★★★/★★★★ A	★★★/★★★★ A
2002	★★★ A	★★★ A	★★★ A
2001	★★★★ A	★★★★ A	★★★★ A
2000	★★★★/★★★★★★ A	★★★★/★★★★★★ A	★★★★/★★★★★★ A
1999	★★★★ A	★★★★ B	★★★★ B
1998	★★★★/★★★★★★ A	★★★★/★★★★★★ B	★★★★/★★★★★★ B
1997	★★★/★★★★ B	★★★ C	★★★C
1996	★★★/★★★★ B	★★★/★★★★ C	★★★/★★★★ B
1995	★★★/★★★★ B	★★★/★★★★ C	★★★/★★★★ C
1994	★★★ C	★★★ D	★★★ C
1993	★★★/★★★★ C	★★/★★★ D	★★/★★★ D
1991	★★★/★★★★ C	★★★ D	★★★ D
1990	★★★★★ B	★★★★★ D	★★★★★ C

Provence

DOM. DES BÉATES   Coteaux d'Aix-en-Provence   www.chapoutier.com   A: Men

Owner: M Chapoutier/Pierre-Francois Terrat   Route de Caireval, 13410 Lambesc

Biodynamic operation that attracted the interest of Michel CHAPOUTIER of the Rhône Valley in the late 1990s. Four labels are now produced here. The soft, fruity Les Béatines red, white and rosé are easygoing, drink-me-now styles. The Domaine Saint-Estève red and white are more serious, the former now characteristic of the Chapoutier style, providing a typically forward supple, rounded red. These should be drunk young although the red will benefit from keeping for a year or two. The superior Domaines des Béates and Terra d'Or labels are blends of Cabernet Sauvignon, Syrah and Grenache. The Domaine label is structured, dense and powerful but with supple, well-rounded, ripe tannin. It will develop well in the medium term. The fruit from the oldest vines, which are around 45 years old, is reserved for the top *cru*, Terra d'Or, which is a serious step up. Vinified and aged in new oak, it is surprisingly approachable but rich and concentrated with a velvety texture. Complex dark berry fruit, herbal spice and subtle oak are all seamlessly integrated. (DM)

● **Coteaux d'Aix-en-Provence** Béates★★★ £C Terra d'Or★★★★ £E
● **Coteaux d'Aix-en-Provence** Domaine Saint-Estève★ £B Les Béatines★ £B

DOMAINES BUNAN   Bandol   www.bunan.com   A:Yap

Owner: Bunan Family   83740 La Cadière-d'Azur

One of the longest-established producers in the appellation, the Bunan family arrived in Bandol in 1961. The family business is run to this day by Paul Bunan and his son Laurent, who has gained an international perspective having worked in California. The focal point of production here is Bandol from three estates. Along with the reds, both white and rosé are produced at all three estates and these are sound examples of the appellation, the whites fermented cool in stainless steel to emphasise their fruit. In addition to this there is a Côtes de Provence property, Domaine Belouve, producing solid red, white and rosé. Three generic Bandols are produced under the Domaines Bunan label but it is the estate reds that are the real excitement. The Mas de La Rouvière and Moulin des Costes regular bottling are the lighter wines. Moulin des Costes gets a slightly longer vatting and has Grenache as well as Mourvèdre, Cinsault and Syrah, which comprise the Mas de La Rouvière blend. The Moulin des Costes offers slightly more spicy, peppery characters but both will develop well with five years' ageing. The Chateau de la Rouvière is richer, more complete, sourced from a single plot of just over 2.5 ha. Dense, spicy dark fruit and truffles are defined in its impressive fruit. Firmly tannic in its youth, it demands six or seven years' patience. The top wine, Cuvée Charriage, is the richest and lushest of the wines. Vinified with cold maceration and extended maceration of up to a month, it is structured but supple and should be very fine with 8 to 10 years' cellaring. (DM)

Château de La Rouvière
● **Bandol**★★★★ £D

Moulin des Costes
● **Bandol**★★★ £C Cuvée Charriage★★★★ £E

Mas de la Rouvière
● **Bandol**★★★ £C

CH. BAS   Coteaux d'Aix-en-Provence

Owner: Georges de Blanquet   13116 Vernègues

Sizeable property producing sound to very good red, white and rosé under the Coteaux d'Aix-en-Provence appellation. There are 72 ha of vines on the estate with 64 ha planted to reds and production is now over 30,000 cases a year. Three separate ranges, L'Alvernègue, Pierre du Sud and Cuvée du Temple, all include a red, a white and a rosé. The L'Alvernègue wines are soft, forward and fruit-driven. The red offers a little structure and grip, although it should be drunk young. The Pierre du Sud wines are a step up in quality, with well-defined fruit character, and are also for drinking young – although the red will stand short ageing. The Cuvée du Temple wines are of a different order. The rosé is part barrel-fermented and has surprising depth and structure for the style. The red, a blend of Syrah, Cabernet Sauvignon and Grenache, has impressive depth. Richly texured with subtle spicy undertones, it should be aged for three or four years at least. Perhaps the standout wine here is the barrel-fermented white, blended from Sauvignon Blanc, Rolle and Grenache Blanc. Subtle use of oak and very pure citrus and herb spice fruit are supported by a rich creamy finish. While the wine drinks very well young it will also stand a little age. (DM)

● **Coteaux d'Aix-en-Provence** L'Alvernègue★ £B Pierre du Sud★ £B Cuvée du Temple★★★ £B
O **Coteaux d'Aix-en-Provence** Pierre du Sud★ £B Cuvée du Temple★★★ £B
◉ **Coteaux d'Aix-en-Provence** Pierre du Sud★ £B Cuvée du Temple★★ £B

CH. DE BELLET   Bellet   chateaudebellet@aol.com

Owner: Ghislain de Charnacé   Quartier Saint-Roman, 440 Route de Saquier, 06200 Nice
One of a handful of properties in the tiny appellation of Bellet in the Provençal hills inland of Nice. As at neighbouring CHATEAU DE CRÉMAT, a red, white and rosé are produced. Because the vineyards are in a protected *mesoclimate* and planted at altitude, they are cooler than their southerly location would suggest. This enables Chardonnay to ripen successfully as well as the local Rolle that completes the white blend. The red and rosé are produced from Folle Noire, Bracquet, Cinsault and Grenache. The Bracquet variety can also be found further east in Piedmont in Italy, where it is known as Brachetto. The wines are good; the red perfumed, supple and approachable and the white lightly floral and aromatic with an underlying nutty character. They may be approached young but will benefit from a year or two in the cellar. The rosé should be drunk young. (DM)

● **Bellet★★★ £D** O **Bellet★★ £D** ◉ **Bellet★** £C

CH. LES VALENTINES   Côtes de Provence   gilles@lesvalentines.com

Owner: Gilles Pons   83250 La Londe-les-Maures
From just over 20 ha of biodynamically farmed vineyards, Les Valentines, like a number of other Côtes de Provence properties, is showing what this appellation is capable of achieving. As well as the Côtes de Provence bottlings, soft, easy-drinking red, white and rosé are produced under the Caprice de Clementine label. The rosé Les Valentines blends Cinsault with Grenache, Syrah, Mourvèdre and Tibouren. It has better definition and intensity than most Provençale examples. Les Valentines Blanc is dominated by very old Ugni Blanc and is vinified from a combination of fruit picked early for freshness and late for increased richness, which adds both weight and complexity. Of the two reds, Les Valentines is vibrant, pure and accessible young, a blend of Grenache, Syrah and a little Cabernet Sauvignon and Mourvèdre. Particularly impressive is the small-production Cuvée Bagnard, which is sourced from the best parcels of Syrah, Mourvèdre and Cabernet Sauvignon and aged for 12 months in *demi-muids*. Richly textured, with hints of dark berry fruit, oriental spice and mocha, it will add further complexity with five or so years of cellaring. (DM)

● **Côtes de Provence★★** £B Bagnard★★★★ £D
◉ **Côtes de Provence★★** £B

CH. DE PIBARNON   Bandol   pibarnon@wanadoo.fr   A: Bal, ABy, N&P, P&S

Owner: Eric de Saint-Victor   410, Chemin de la Croix-des-Signaux, 83740 La Cadière d'Azur
One of the two best and most established properties in the appellation, the other being Domaine TEMPIER. The style of wine is quite different, though. The red here is powerful and structured, very backward in its youth, requiring up to a decade to fully develop. A very large proportion of Mourvèdre (90 to 95 per cent) accounts for the dark, brambly and mineral style of its wine, dense but very refined as well. The site is ideal for ripening the variety: well-drained limestone-based soils and vineyards that are cooled by elevation as well as being very sunny ensure fruit loaded with intense flavour and fine, well-ripened but

sturdy tannins. The 2001 looks to be quite exceptional. While the red excels, the white and rosé are a touch less exciting but good nonetheless. (DM)

● Bandol★★★★ £D   O Bandol★★ £C
◉ Bandol★ £C

CH. PRADEAUX   Bandol   A: HHB,Lay

Owner: Cyrille Portallis   676 Chemin des Pradeaux, 83270 Saint-Cyr-sur-Mer
Just over 4,000 cases of red are made here from 20 ha of prime Bandol vineyard that is permanently being encroached upon by urban planners. A small amount of rosé is also produced. The blend is almost exclusively Mourvèdre with a little Grenache. Traditionally vinified, the fruit is not destemmed, and the wine is aged in large wooden *foudres* for over three years which helps in softening its raw youthful tannic edge. It is a wine that demands a minimum of six to seven years in the cellar. Anything less would be to miss the point of it. (DM)

● Bandol★★★★ £D

CH. REVELETTE   Coteaux d'Aix-en-Provence   A:N&P

Owner: Peter Fischer   13490 Jouques
This 25 ha domaine produces a very good *vin de pays* Chardonnay, Le Grand Blanc, as well as one of the very best reds in the region. The vineyards, located inland of the Mont Saint-Victoire, are some of the highest in the Coteaux d'Aix-en-Provence at around 400 metres. This is reflected in the style and elegance of the wines. The regular red, white and rosé Coteaux d'Aix-en-Provence are well-priced although relatively simple by comparison. The red Grand Rouge is a blend dominated by Syrah and Cabernet Sauvignon. It is given a long vatting and aged in small oak. Very finely crafted and with great purity of fruit, it requires a minimum of five to six years to reveal its full complexity and rich intensity. (DM)

● Coteaux d'Aix-en-Provence Le Grand Rouge★★★★ £E

CH. ROMANIN   Coteaux d'Aix-en-Provence   www.romanin.com   A:Wgg

Owner: Jean-Pierre Peyraud   13210 Saint-Remy-de-Provence
Sizeable, biodynamically farmed property of 250 ha. Currently 58 ha are planted to vines with the older vines in sandy, loamy, calcareous soils whereas the newer plantings are in calcareous, stony soils. The climate is not only warm, dry and sunny but during the growing season there is sufficient wind to help rather than hinder balanced growth. Production is gradually increasing and is currently just under 17,000 cases a year, 80 per cent of which is red. The rosé Les Baux is soft and easy drinking, the white more serious with pronounced fresh, lightly herbal fruit character and good intensity, in part achieved through blocking the malolactic. It is a blend of Rolle, Ugni Blanc and Bourboulenc. Jean le Troubador is a light, easy-drinking red made from the youngest vines, which are just over 10 years old. La Chapelle de Romanin is in effect the second wine of the property, made from an extensive blend of young-vine Syrah, Grenache, Cabernet Sauvignon and Mourvèdre along with older Carignan, Cinsault and Counoise. Lightly spicy and herbal with ripe berry fruit, the wine is aged for around a year in *inox* and cement. The Romanin red blends Grenache, Syrah, Cabernet Sauvignon and Mourvèdre. As yet although good it lacks the weight and depth of the best examples of the region, in part because the Syrah and Mourvèdre are still young. The top wine, the Coeur Tertius is sourced from Syrah, Mourvèdre, Cabernet Sauvignon and Grenache from the best site on the property. Vine age ranges from 8 to 40 years so the best should be yet to come. Finely structured with medium weight, it has a nice balance of dark fruits, cedar and herb spice, with subtle and well-judged oak. The 2000, which was an excellent year here, is right on the edge of four stars. (DM)

● Les Baux-de-Provence★★ £C Coeur Tertius★★★ £E
● Les Baux-de-Provence La Chapelle de Romanin★ £B
O Les Baux-de-Provence★★ £B

CH. DE ROQUEFORT Côtes de Provence   A:Vex

Owner: Raimond de Villeneuve 13830 Roquefort-la-Bedoule

Raimond de Villeneuve now runs one of the most exciting domaines in Provence, with a firm emphasis on high quality. The property is just inland of the Bandol appellation and benefits from vineyards planted at an altitude of over 300 metres. The first vintage to be bottled here was as recent as 1995; prior to this the fruit was sold off in bulk. The estate is farmed on biodynamic principles, not because its trendy but because de Villeneuve believes this approach will provide the best balance for his vineyard. Of the whites a straightforward *vin de pays* produced from Clairette is joined by the more serious, minerally Genêts, which also has Rolle in the blend and is partially barrel-fermented. The Corail rosé is soft and easygoing. It is, though, the three reds that stand out here. The very well-priced Mûres blends Grenache, Syrah, Carignan, Cinsault and Cabernet Sauvignon. Pure, elegant and intense, it will keep well. The Rubrum Obscurum is rich, dense and powerful. Loaded with dark old-vine character, it blends Grenache, Mourvèdre and Carignan. It was very good indeed in 1999, 2000 and 01, and 03 may well be of similar calibre. In exceptional years Raimond also produces a similarly dense blend of Syrah and Carignan called La Pourpre. The top reds here should be given five to seven years. (DM)

● **Côtes de Provence** Corail★ £B Mûres★★★ £B Rubrum Obscurum★★★★ £E
○ **Côtes de Provence** Genêts★★ £B

CH. ROUTAS Coteaux Varois www.routas.com   A: Col,BBR

Owner: Philippe Bieler Chateauvert, 83149 Bras

Established for upwards of a decade, Routas is located in the wild inland Provençale hills of the Coteaux Varois and has vineyards that are just that bit cooler than its neighbours'. Philippe Bieler has invested considerably in both the vineyard and the cellar, with state-of-the-art vinification equipment. Winemaking is now handled by Jean-Louis Bavay although previously Bob Lindquist of QUPE in California provided consultancy advice. Production runs at around 20,000 cases and the wines, particularly the top reds and the white Coquelicot, are good to very good. The reds, fashioned in a full but approachable style, will nevertheless improve with some cellar time. Le Trou de Infernet is a blend of Grenache, Syrah and Cabernet Sauvignon whereas Agrippa d'Aubigne is just Syrah and Cabernet Sauvignon. There is an easy-drinking white blend of southern French grapes, the Wild Boar white. The two best wines truly stand out: Cyrano, a spicy, smoky 100 per cent Syrah, and Coquelicot, a nutty, subtly oaked, herb-scented blend of Viognier and Chardonnay. (DM)

● **Coteaux Varois** Carignane★★ £B Wild Boar Cabernet Sauvignon★★ £B
● **Coteaux Varois** Cuvée Le Trou de Infernet★★★ £C Cuvée Agrippa d'Aubigne★★★ £C
● **Vin de Pays du Var** Cuvée Cyrano★★★ £C
○ **Vin de Pays du Var** Cuvée Coquelicot★★★ £C

CH. SIMONE Palette   A:Yap

Owner: Rougier family 13590 Meyreuil

This is the benchmark property in the tiny appellation of Palette just outside Aix-en-Provence. The property has around 17 ha of vineyard and there are a bewildering number of permitted red varieties under the appellation regulations. Small quantities of some of the rarer ones are still planted but the emphasis is increasingly on Grenache, Mourvèdre and Syrah. White varieties are dominated by Clairette and it is the white which is the most exciting of the wines. Full, rich and decidedly old fashioned, it nevertheless possesses some marvellous nutty, spicy and honeyed notes which increase with age. The red is good but can be somewhat rustic and four-square. There's a small amount of decent but pricy rosé. (DM)

● **Palette**★★★ £E ○ **Palette**★★★★ £E

CH. VANNIÈRES Bandol www.chateauvannieres.com   A: C&O

Owner: Colette & Eric Boisseaux 83740 La Cadière d'Azur

One of the best of the current generation of Bandol producers. Along with the likes of CHATEAU PRADEAUX and Domaine du GROS NORÉ this is a property that's knocking on the door of PIBARNON and TEMPIER. The wine is a powerful but stylish example of the appellation. All its intense, dark-berry Mourvèdre character and intense herbal, garrigue scents will shine through when the tannin has had time to soften and the wine achieves real balance and harmony. Good floral white Bandol is produced along with a good rosé and recently a red Côtes de Provence, an increasingly impressive junior version of the *grand vin*. (DM)

● **Bandol★★★★** £E

DOM. DE LA COURTADE Côtes de Provence   A:GBa

Owner: Henri Vidal 83400 Ile-de-Porquerolles

The Ile-de-Porquerolles is best known as a secluded destination for holidaying Mediterranean yachtsmen. The island lies off the coast of Provence between Bandol and Saint-Tropez. There are some 30 ha of vines, 13 ha of them the white Rolle. This is used exclusively to vinify the white Côtes de Provence, which is lightly oaked and displays some ripe tropical notes as well as a more typically southern nutty character. It will stand a little age as will the red Alycastre, which is the second wine here, produced to ensure the integrity of the top red. The *grand vin* is a rich, brambly, spicy blend of Mourvèdre, Grenache and Syrah and is impressive, concentrated and worth seeking out. (DM)

● **Côtes de Provence★★★** £D Alycastre★★ £B
O **Côtes de Provence★★** £D

DOM. DU GRAND CROS Côtes de Provence www.grandcros.fr

Owner: Faulkner Family 83660 Carnoules

A fairly extensive range of red, white and rosé is made at this 22-ha property situated in the foothills of the Massif des Maures in the centre of the Var. Vineyard development here is ongoing and new planting is at a density of 4,000 to 5,000 vines per hectare with a cover crop of grass to stress the vines sufficiently to optimise fruit ripening. Farming is as natural as possible with minimal use of pesticides and fungicides. Fruit-driven, forward wines are released under the Domaine label. Of more interest are a cool-fermented Chardonnay and a Carignan that are both *vin de pays*. The Carignan gets some pre-fermentation maceration to highlight its dark blackberry, spicy, peppery fruit. The regular Côtes de Provence wines are labelled L'Esprit de Provence and include a red blended from Cabernet Sauvignon and Syrah and a soft, forward rosé produced from Grenache and Cinsault along with a little Syrah and Rolle to add depth. Just 5 per cent of the 8,000-case production is accounted for by the two Nectar wines. The white is a barrel-fermented Chardonnay, whereas the red is a rich, powerful and impressively concentrated Cabernet Sauvignon, with just a touch of Syrah and Grenache, produced from yields of just 20 hl/ha. A 48-hour cold soak is undertaken prior to a temperature-controlled vinification which emphasises the dark, cedary fruit. Ageing is for 12 months in small oak with micro-oxygenation rather than conventional racking. In general the wines should be drunk young but the Nectar red will develop very well in bottle for five years or more. (DM)

● **Côtes de Provence** L'Esprit de Provence★★ £B Nectar★★★ £C
● **Vin de Pays des Maures** Carignan★★ £B
O **Vin de Pays des Maures** Chardonnay★★ £B
◉ **Côtes de Provence** L'Esprit de Provence★ £B

DOM. DU GROS NORÉ Bandol www.gros-nore.com   A:Han

Owner: Alain Pascal 675 Chemin de l'Argile, 83740 La Cadière d'Azur

The first vintage at this newly established Bandol producer was as recent as 1997, but it was still one of real class and style. Almost all of the 11.5 ha are planted to red varieties but a small amount of white is also produced – a typically fat wine with broad, warm, nutty fruit – as well as a reasonable rosé. The improtant wine is the red Bandol, a big, brooding unfiltered blend of Mourvèdre, Grenache and Cinsault full of dark, savoury, roasted aromas with real intensity and purity. A complex, spicy, herbal undercurrent adds interest to the beefy fruit. Backward in its youth it needs time. Very characterful and likely to improve in bottle for up to a decade or more. (DM)

● Bandol★★★★ £C O Bandol★★ £C

DOM. HAUVETTE   Les Baux   A:CdP

Owner: Dominique Hauvette   13210 Saint-Rémy-de-Provence
Dominique Hauvette's small 13-ha property is fast emerging as one of the finest, not only in Les Baux but in Provence. A small range of three reds and one white of uniformly excellent quality is produced. The white Blanc de Blancs – a blend of Marsanne, Roussanne and Clairette, and as such labelled as *vin de pays* – is part barrel-fermented and aged on lees with *bâtonnage*. There is a piercing, nutty, citrus intensity here with finely judged oak and a rich creamy texture. It should develop very nicely in the medium term. The red Amethyste is based unusually around Cinsault, with varying amounts of Carignan, Grenache, Syrah and occasionally Cabernet Sauvignon. It is the softest, lushest of the Hauvette reds but there is sufficient structure, elegance and refinement to enable short-term development. The Cornaline is bigger, with a raw almost *sauvage* character from a blend driven by Carignan (60 per cent) with equal proportions of Cinsault and Grenache. The top red, the Domaine Hauvette, blends 50 per cent Grenache with 30 per cent Syrah and a balance of Cabernet Sauvignon. Two years in *foudres* and small oak are comfortably absorbed. The wine is rich, powerful and seriously structured. Expect to age it for at least five to seven years to get the best out of it. (DM)

● Coteaux d'Aix-en-Provence Améthyste★★★ £D Cornaline★★★ £D
● Les Baux-de-Provence★★★★ £D
O Vin de Pays des Bouches du Rhone Blanc de Blancs★★★ £D

DOM. LA BASTIDE BLANCHE   Bandol   bastide.blanche@libertysurf.fr   A:BRW

Owner: EARL Bronzo   367 Route des Oratoires, 83330 Sainte-Anne-du-Castellet
Red, white and rosé are produced under the Bandol AC at this 28 ha property, established by the Bronzo family over 30 years ago. The vineyards are cultivated largely organically and great care is taken at harvest to select the best fruit. The three reds here inevitably stand out. The sturdy Longue Garde is around three-quarters Grenache with the balance Mourvèdre. Both the Fontanieu and Estagnol are Mourvèdre bottlings. These last two wines are produced from vines grown on different soils. The reds will all develop very well for a decade or longer and require cellaring for at least four to five years. (DM)

● Bandol Longue Garde★★★ £C Fontanieu★★★★£D Estagnol★★★★ £D

DOM. LAFRAN VEYROLLES   Bandol   A: PBW

Owner: Mme Jouve-Férec   2115 Route de l'Aigle, 83740 La Cadière-d'Azur
Very impressive red Bandol is now being made at this 10-ha property, with production small at less than 4,000 cases per year. Mourvèdre dominates the red plantings, while the whites are a mix of Clairette and Ugni Blanc. The vineyards are farmed organically and the argilo-calcareous soils provide an excellent base for growing fruit of the highest quality. The white is one of the better examples produced in the appellation, as is the softly strawberry-scented rosé. The two reds with their sizeable Mourvèdre component stand out. Both are dense, powerful and finely structured. Firm youthful tannin will be seamlessly integrated with five or six years' ageing. The 2001 reds were quite exceptional, effortlessly of five star quality. (DM)

● Bandol Tradition★★★★ £D Spéciale★★★★ £D
◉ Bandol ★ £C

DOM. DE LA LAIDIÈRE Bandol

Owner: Freddy Estienne   426 Chemin du Font-Vive, Sainte-Anne-d'Evenos, 83330 Evenos
Well-crafted and good-value red, white and rosé are produced at this Bandol property of some 24 ha. The bulk of the vineyard is planted to red varieties, with 60 per cent Mourvèdre and 20 per cent each of Cinsault and Grenache. The rosé is ripe and forward, while the white, from a blend of Clairette and Ugni Blanc, has a light nutty elegance and a hint of herb spice. The red, as is the case at most Bandol properties, is the key wine. Firmly structured in its youth with a savoury, almost meaty character to its fruit it will gain an extra dimension with five years' age.(DM)
● Bandol★★★ £C

DOM. LA SUFFRENE Bandol

Owner: Cédric Gravier   1066 Chemin du Cuges, 83740 La Cadière d'Azur
Up until the 1996 vintage Cédric Gravier sold his harvest to the co-op. His welcome decision to vinify under his own label has resulted in some of the best wines to emerge from what is arguably the top Provençale appellation. A fresh *vin de pays* red and soft, easy rosé are produced but it is the Bandols that stand out. There is a sound rosé produced from Mourvèdre, Cinsault, Grenache and Carignan. The white blends 75 per cent Clairette with the balance Ugni Blanc. Vinified and aged in *inox* it has impressive depth and intensity, with a mix of floral, spice and citrus aromas. The regular Bandol is a blend of Mourvèdre, Grenache, Cinsault and just a little Carignan. Sturdy and structured with traditional, dark berry fruit and meaty characters, it shows all the potential to improve with five or six years' cellaring. The very rich, supple and concentrated top wine, Cuvée des Lauves, is dominated by Mourvèdre with just 5 per cent of old Carignan adding dark pepper notes to the sumptuous dark fruit. (DM)
● Bandol★★★ £C Cuvée des Lauves★★★★★ £E
O Bandol★★ £C

DOM. DE LAUZIÈRES Les Baux

Owner: Jean-Daniekl Schlaepfer & Gérard Pitton   Le Destet, 13890 Mouriès
Jean-Daniel Schlaepfer discovered this superbly located property at the heart of the Baux-de-Provence appellation in 1992. The vineyards are planted to a varied mix of Grenache, Syrah, Mourvèdre, Carignan, Cinsault and Petit Verdot among the reds and Grenache Blanc with a tiny amount of Clairette for the whites. Two very fair reds are produced as Baux-de-Provence, the lighter Equinoxe and the denser and more structured Solstice, but the owners believe that the conventional varieties authorised by the appellation authorities here are not capable of expressing the greatest potential of the estate and the top wines are labelled as *vin de table*. The white Astérie is a pure and very intense barrel-fermented varietal Grenache Blanc. The oak is superbly handled with the piercing citrus and creamy, nutty fruit dominating the wine. The red Sine Nomine very unusually blends 75 per cent Petit Verdot with the balance Grenache. Rich, powerful and very concentrated, this muscular red needs at least five or six years. (DM)
● Les Baux-de-Provence Solstice★★ £C Sine Nomine Vin de Table★★★★ £E
O Astérie Vin de Table★★★★ £D

MAS DE LA DAME Les Baux   www.masdeladame.com   A: L&W, HHB, AVn

Owner: Anne Ponitowski & Caroline Missoffe   13520 Les Baux-de-Provence
Good-quality producer from Les Baux-de-Provence with 57 ha of vineyards. The property was immortalised by Vincent Van Gogh when he painted it in 1889. As one would expect the great majority of vines are red varieties but there are 5 ha of whites including some Sémillon. Very good olive oils are also produced from the estate's 25 ha of olive groves. A relatively extensive range of wines is made here with consultancy provided by Jean-Luc COLOMBO. The red Réserve and white Cuvée de la Stèle offer reasonable value and straightforward drinking. The Coin Caché white is very stylish, floral, nutty and

perfumed, the Cuvée de la Stèle red rich and chunky with hints of garrigue and smoke. The Coin Caché red is a supple, smoky, powerful, old-vine blend of Grenache and Syrah. (DM)

● **Les Baux-de-Provence** Réserve★★ £B Cuvée de la Stèle★★★ £C Coin Caché★★★ £D
O **Les Baux-de-Provence** Coin Caché★★★ £D
◉ **Côtes de Provence★** £B   ◉ **Coteaux d'Aix-en-Provence** Cuvée de la Stèle★★ £B
◉ **Les Baux-de-Provence** Rosé Mas★ £B

DOM. RABIEGA Côtes de Provence www.rabiega.com A: L&S

Owner: Vin & Spirit AB Sweden Clos d'Ière Méridional, 83300 Draguinan
Owned by the Swedish Vin & Spirit operation since 1988, this property, produces good to very good red and white under both the Domaine Rabiega label and Rabiega Vin, the recently established negociant label for a range of very good well priced reds and whites. Of these the low yielding Carignan, Carbase aged in a mix of new and used oak and the elegant brambly Mourbase, produced from Mourvedre and aged in new French, Slovenian and Hungarian oak stand out among the reds. Whites are not ignored either. The Roussanne, Rouxanne is elegant and aromatic, the Svala produced from Rolle is barrel-fermented and aged on lees for up to nine months, it offers weight, extract and subtle nut and citrus character. It has the structure to develop for a few years. The Domaine Rabiega vineyards are planted on limestone and clay soils near Draguignan. The property is farmed organically and there are some 9 ha under vine, with productiona mere 1,600 to 1,700 cases a year. A fine ripe, tropically scented, barrel-fermented white, Clos d'Ière Blanc, produced from Sauvignon Blanc, Chardonnay and Viognier, is impressive, as is the Clos d'Ière I, a powerful, dense, oak-aged Syrah. The Clos d'Ière II was produced for the last time in the 2001 vintage. The wine blended Carignan, Grenache and Cabernet Sauvignon. (DM)

● **Côtes de Provence** Carbase★★ £C Mourbase★★ £C Clos d'Ière I★★★★ £E
O **Vin de Pays du Var** Clos d'Ière★★★ £E
O **Côtes de Provence** Rouxanne★★ £C Svala★★ £C

DOM. RICHEAUME Côtes de Provence A: BGL

Owner: Henning Hoesch 13114 Puyloubier
Very good estate that has been producing consistently excellent wine under the Côtes de Provence appellation for years. The property consists of some 25 ha planted largely to Cabernet Sauvignon, Syrah, Grenache and Merlot. There is also a little Viognier, from which a decent white is made. The Tradition includes all four red varieties, complemented by fine varietal Cabernet and Syrah bottlings and a splendid *grand vin,* Cuvée Columelle. This massive, dense and very concentrated wine is one of the best reds in Provence. (DM)

● **Côtes de Provence** Tradition★★★ £C Cuvée Columelle★★★★ £E

DOM. RIMAURESQ Côtes de Provence www.rimauresq.fr A:May

Owner: Wemyss Family 83970 Pignans
This fine 36-ha Scottish-owned property is notable for making some of the best examples of rosé in the Côtes de Provence. They are fine and pure with subtle, elegant red berry fruit and like all the wines here have a persistent mineral character which lends a tight, firm structure. This is particularly notable in the reds and in part may be attributable to the soils which are crystalline rock with sandstone and gravel. Average vine age is now 40 years and some are up to 70 years. Replacement planting is now ensuring an increased vine density of up to 5,000 vines per hectare in an ongoing drive to improve quality. A superior range labelled Cuvée R has been introduced for red, white and rosé. The red R blends solely Syrah and Cabernet Savignon, whereas the regular red is mainly Cabernet with much smaller proportions of Syrah, Mourvèdre and Carignan. Both whites are blended from Ugni Blanc and Rolle and ageing is in *demi-muids.* The Cuvée R rosé is produced from older plantings of Cinsault, Grenache and Mourvèdre, which gives it extra depth and that piercing mineral and red berry fruit intensity. Both the reds are firmly structured with a herb spice

character, the Cuvée R being fuller and deeper but with a background touch of austerity in its youth. Give it five years or so to soften. (DM)

● **Côtes de Provence★★** £B Cuvée R★★★ £D
◉ **Côtes de Provence★** £B Cuvée R★★ £C

DOM. SAINT-ANDRÉ DE FIGUIÈRE Côtes de Provence A:

Owner: Alain & Francois Combard 83250 La Londe-les-Maures

This 19-ha property located just inland between Toulon and Saint-Tropez, with the Massif des Maures immediately to the north, benefits from a benign, sunny maritime climate. As a result the Combards tend to enjoy better growing conditions than other Provençale properties in difficult years like 2002. Quality is characterised here by a range of excellent old-vine and reserve *cuvées*. As well as the premium wines there are both a red and white released as Vin du Pays du Var and a regular bottling of red, white and rosé, respectively labelled *cuvées* François, Magali and Valérie, all of which offer good everyday drinking. The three Côtes de Provence wines are a step up. The rosé Vieilles Vignes is blended from 30- to 35-year-old Mourvèdre, Cinsault and Grenache, a wine of impressive intensity for the style. The white Vieilles Vignes is a cool-fermented blend of Ugni Blanc, Rolle and Sémillon, whereas the splendidly pure and intense Cuvée Delphine is barrel-fermented and aged on lees. It is 100 per cent Rolle. The two top reds are impressively structured with real depth and concentration. The Vieilles Vignes is blended from Mourvèdre, 100-year-old Carignan (unusually vinified together) and Syrah. The Reserve is 90 per cent Mourvèdre with the balance Syrah. Both get an extended maceration of one month before ageing for up to a year in used oak. Cellaring for five years or so will bring added complexity in both wines. (DM)

● **Côtes de Provence** Vieilles Vignes★★★ £C Grande Cuvée Vieilles Vignes Réserve★★★ £D
○ **Côtes de Provence** Vieilles Vignes★★ £D Grande Cuvée Delphine Réserve★★★ £D
◉ **Côtes de Provence** Vieilles Vignes★★ £D

DOM. TEMPIER Bandol A: Sav, SVS

Owner: Peyraud family Le Plan du Castellet, 83330 Le Castellet

This is one of the great Bandol producers and has remained so for the past two decades despite the emergence of newer names such as PIBARNON and more recently GROS NORÉ. More than anything these wines are characterised by their elegance and refinement as opposed to the sheer power and density often achieved elsewhere. There are around 28 ha planted to red varieties but a mere 1 ha to white. Along with the five reds there is also a very decent rosé. The regular *cuvée* produced from the youngest vines on the property is somewhat light in comparison to the other wines. Cuvée Spéciale is denser and richer, with altogether greater concentration. It is, though, the three single vineyard wines, La Tourtine, Migoua and Cabassou, that stand out. The latter, with the highest proportion of Mourvèdre, is the sturdiest of the trio, the Migoua the most stylish and elegant. All will age gracefully for well over a decade. (DM)

● **Bandol** Cuvée Classique★★ £C Cuvée Spéciale★★★ £D
● **Bandol** La Tourtine★★★★ £E Migoua★★★★ £E Cabassou★★★★★ £E
◉ **Bandol★★** £C

DOM. DE TERREBRUNE Bandol

Owner: Georges Delille 724 Chemin de la Tourelle, 83190 Ollioulles

The red Bandol produced by Georges Delille from his 25-ha vineyard is a massive, muscular and brooding example of the appellation. The vineyards have an ideal aspect with finely drained calcareous soils and the average vine age is now moving towards 30 years, adding intensity, depth and character to the fruit. This is a true *vin de garde*: a dense smoky, spicy Mourvèdre requiring seven or eight years at a minimum to achieve true balance and harmony. The small amount of rosé and white produced is of a reasonable quality, the latter capable of some age. (DM)

● **Bandol★★★★** £D
◉ **Bandol★★** £C ○ **Bandol★★** £C

DOM. DE LA TOUR DU BON   Bandol

Owner: Claude Hocquard   714 Chemin des Olivettes, 83330 Le Brûlat-du-Castellet
A small property with just 12 ha planted to vines. Production is small at some 3,500 cases but the quality of the red Bandols is very good indeed. These are stylish, supple and very well crafted and the Saint-Ferréol is finely structured, refined and very long-lived – a wine of not only weight and concentration but wonderful herbal intensity. As with so many properties in the appellation, though, the rosé and white are decent and well enough made but lack the interest of the reds. (DM)

● **Bandol★★★** £D Saint-Ferréol★★★★ £E
O **Bandol★★** £C

DOM. DE TREVALLON   Les Baux-de-Provence   www.trevallon.fr   A: Yap, Har

Owner: Eloi Dürrbach   13103 Saint-Étienne-du-Grès
It remains one of the ludicrous features of the *appellation contrôlée* regulations that this benchmark Provençale red is now only entitled to *vin de pays* status. Theoretically there should be some Grenache planted but the vineyard with north-facing calcareous slopes will not ripen the variety adequately. The *mesoclimate* here is remarkably cool, much more so than one would imagine. The resulting red blend of Cabernet and Syrah and the tiny amount of white produced (barely more than a couple of barrels) are very impressive and remarkably refined wines. Cask-aging of the red is in large older wood and it needs at least five years to unfurl. The wine is a classic Provençale example of the blend with floral *garrigue* scents underpinning the concentrated, dark, cedary fruit. The white is a barrel-fermented blend of Marsanne, Roussanne and Chardonnay, very fine and intense with concentrated, lightly floral, nutty fruit. (DM)

● **Vin de Pays des Bouches-du-Rhône★★★★★** £F
O **Vin de Pays des Bouches-du-Rhône★★★★★** £G

Also see the following Rhône *négociant* with an entry in the section *Rhône Valley:*
JEAN-LUC COLOMBO

Jura

DOM. BERTHET-BONDET   Château-Chalon

Owner: Jean Berthet-Bondet   39210 Château-Chalon
First-class traditional Jura producer, making top-quality whites from Chardonnay and the local white Savagnin. Of the two Côtes du Jura dry whites, Alliance is produced from Chardonnay, the more complex and structured Tradition from a blend of Savagnin and Chardonnay. Both wines offer marvellously pure and intense mineral and light citrus fruit characters. In the Tradition an almost salty tang underpins the wine. The Château-Chalon, a *vin jaune*, is not dissimilar to a top level Fino sherry and has an earthy, salty character derived from the layer of *flor* yeast under which it is aged in cask. Unlike Fino, these wines have a piercing acidity, lending them the structure for very long ageing. The wines require time to show at their best. (DM)

O **Côtes du Jura** Alliance★★★ £B Tradition★★★★ £C
O **Château-Chalon★★★★** £E

OTHER WINES OF NOTE

Provence

DOM. DES ALYSSES ● Coteaux Varois £C

DOM. DE LA BÉGUDE ● Bandol £C

CH. BARBANAU ● Côtes de Provence £B

CH. DE BEAUPRÉ ● Coteaux d'Aix-en-Provence Clos Victoire £D

CH. CALISSANNE ● Coteaux d'Aix-en-Provence Clos Victoire £D

CH. DU GALOUPET ● Côtes de Provence £B   O Côtes de Provence £B

CH. LA CALISSE ● Coteaux Varois Patricia Ortelli £C

CH. LA MOUTÈTE ● Côtes de Provence Vieilles Vignes £C

CH. MINUTY ● Côtes de Provence Prestige £C   ◉ Côtes de Provence Prestige £C

CH. REAL MARTIN ● Côtes de Provence £C Optimum £D

CH. SAINTE-ROSELINE ● Côtes de Provence Prieuré £D

CH. SALETTES ● Bandol £D

CH. DES SARRINS ● Côtes de Provence £B

CH. VIGNELAURE ● Coteaux d'Aix-en-Provence £C

CLOS SAINTE-MAGDELEINE O Cassis £C

COMMANDERIE DE PEYRASSOL ● Côtes de Provence Cuvée Marie-Estelle £C O Côtes de Provence Cuvée Marie-Estelle £C

DOM. DU DEFFENDS ● Coteaux Varois Marie Liesse £B Clos de La Truffière £B

DOM. DE LA FRÉGATE ● Bandol £B

DOM. DE L'HERMITAGE ● Bandol £C

DOM. DE JALE ● Côtes de Provence La Bouisse £C La Nible £C O Côtes de Provence La Garde £C ◉ Côtes de Provence La Garde £C

LA FERME BLANCHE O Cassis £C

DOM. LA GALANTIN ● Bandol £C

DOM. GAVOTY ● Côtes de Provence Cuvée Clarendon £C

MAÎTRES VIGNERONNES DE SAINT-TROPEZ ● Bandol La Roque £C

MAS DE CADENET ● Côtes de Provence Mas Négrel Cadenet £C

MAS DE GOURGONNIER ● Les Baux-de-Provence Réserve £D

MAS SAINTE-BERTHE ● Les Baux-de-Provence Louis David £B

DOMAINES OTT - CLOS MIREILLE O Côtes de Provence Blanc de Côte £C L'Insolent £E

DOMAINES OTT - CH. ROMASSAN ● Côtes de Provence Longue Garde £E O Côtes de Provence £D

DOMAINES OTT - CH. DE SELLE ● Bandol £E

DOM. SORIN ● Côtes de Provence Cuvée Privée £C   ● Bandol £C

DOM. DE TRIENNES ● Vin de Pays des Var Les Auréliens £B

Corsica

ANTOINE ARENA ● Patrimonio Carco di Sole £B Carco £C O Muscat du Cap Corse £C

DOM. CULOMBU O Calvi £B

CLOS CANARELLI ● Vin de Corse-Figari £C O Vin de Corse-Figari £C

CLOS CULOMBU O Vin de Corse-Calvi £B

DOM. LECCIA ● Patrimonio £B Petra Bianca £C O Patrimonio £B

ORENGA DE GAFFORY ● Patrimonio £B O Muscat de Cap Corse £C

DOM. DE TORRACCIA ● Vin de Corse Porto-Vecchio Oriu £C

Jura & Savoie

CH. DE RIPAILLE O Vin de Savoie £B

DOM. DURAND-PERRON O Château-Chalon £E

DOM. LABET O Côtes du Jura Chardonnay/Savagnin £B Fleur de Chardonnay £B Les Varrons £C

DOM. JEAN MACLE O Cotes du Jura £B O Château-Chalon £E

DOM. LOUIS MAGNIN ○ Roussette de Savoie £B ● Vin de Savoie Mondeuse Vieilles Vignes £B
DOM. JACQUES PUFFENEY ○ Arbois Chardonnay £B
ANDRÉ ET MICHEL QUÉNARD ○ Roussette de Savoie Altesse £B
● Vin de Savoie Mondeuse Vieilles Vignes £B Pinot Noir £B
DOM. ROLET ○ Côtes du Jura Chardonnay/Savagnin £C ○ Arbois Tradition £C Vin Jaune £E

Work in progress!!
Wines from the following producers under consideration for the next edition
CH D'ARLAY (CÔTES DU JURA)
CH. ROCHE REDONNE (BANDOL)
DOM. DU CLOS D'ALARI (CÔTES DE PROVENCE)
DUPÉRÉ-BARRERA (CÔTES DE PROVENCE)
JEAN-PIERRE GAUSSEN (BANDOL)
DOM. GENTILE (PATRIMONIO)
CAVESW DE LA REINE JEANNE (ARBOIS)
DOM RIJCKAERT (ARBOIS)
RAYMOND QUÉNARD (VINB DE SAVOIE)

Author's choice (DM)
Emerging classics from Provence
DOM. DES BÉATES ● Coteaux d'Aix-en-Provence Terra d'Or
CH. DE PIBARNON ● Bandol
CH. PRADEAUX ● Bandol
CH. ROUTAS ○ Vin de Pays du Var Cuvée Coquelicot
CH. SIMONE ○ Palette
DOM. DE LA COURTADE ● Côtes de Provence
DOM. DU GROS NORÉ ● Bandol
DOM. LAFRAN-VEYROLLES ● Bandol Tradition
DOM. RABIEGA ● Côtes de Provence Clos d'Ière I
DOM. RICHEAUME ● Côtes de Provence Cuvée Columelle
DOM. TEMPIER ● Bandol Cabassou
DOM. DE TREVALLON ● Vin de Pays des Bouches-du-Rhône

South-West France

This section of the guide covers south-western France. A number of the regions in the south-west are close neighbours of Bordeaux: and the style inevitably mirrors that of the Bordelais. Further south, both in the Lot Valley at Cahors and south towards the Pyrenees at Madiran and Jurançon, first-class dry and sweet whites and rich, stylish reds are becoming justifiably known to a wider audience.

South-West France

Immediately to the east of Bordeaux on the river Dordogne is Bergerac . There are a number of ACs north and south of the river, but the large, generic **Bergerac AC** encompasses all the smaller sub-regions. Red, white and rosé are produced from the Bordeaux varieties. Quality is fairly pedestrian with high yields and widespread mechanical harvesting. The number of good reds and whites being produced here is, however, increasing. Lees-enrichment and *bâtonnage* are now being used for whites and new oak is increasingly common for both reds and whites. The **Côtes de Bergerac** and **Pécharmant** are immediately to the north of the town of Bergerac. The former is a source of some good reds and sweet whites (labelled as Côtes de Bergerac Moelleux). Pécharmant should do better than it does with its well-drained sandy, limestone soils. To the south of the river are the sweet-white ACs of **Monbazillac** and **Saussignac**. The former is worth considering as an alternative to Sauternes. The wines can be remarkably rich and complex with heady levels of botrytis. Be aware though that they are becoming more established and prices are rising. Both ACs are a blend of Sémillon and Sauvignon Blanc. Some good red and dry white is made at **Montravel** in vineyards bordering the Côtes de Castillon in Bordeaux. Sweet styles are also produced here and in the small ACs of **Côtes de Montravel** and **Haut-Montravel**. Thus far they lack the richness and depth found in Monbazillac.

South of Bergerac are the appellations of the **Côtes de Duras**, **Côtes du Marmandais** and **Buzet**. Both red and white are produced in the vineyards around Duras, with an occasional late-harvest white. As at Bergerac, Bordeaux varieties are planted. The reds tend towards a vegetal character and the whites are at best fresh and grassy. More new oak is being used, with varying success. Marmandais and Buzet appellations are red only, with more interest in the Côtes du Marmandais, where as well as Bordeaux grapes some indigenous south-western varieties are also permitted.

To the south-east of Bergerac along a 30-mile stretch of the river Lot are the vineyards of **Cahors**. Some of the finest red wines of the south-west are now produced here. Auxerrois (Malbec) dominates plantings, with some Merlot and Tannat. Expect anything from light, plummy, easy-drinking wines (occasionally with a green vegetal note) to serious and very structured ageworthy reds. Prices of the best examples seem to be surging upwards. West of Cahors the AC of **Marcillac** produces spicy reds from Fer-Servadou, while to the south the VDQS of the **Coteaux du Quercy** produces reds of some potential. further south, towards Toulouse, are the VDQS of both the **Côtes du Brulhois** and **Lavilledieu**; and the **Côtes du Frontonnais** AC. The latter has turned out a number of interesting reds based on the Negrette grape. The wines are both perfumed and spicy, the best impressively structured. To the north-east of Toulouse, **Gaillac** AC offers some unusual and diverse styles; Mauzac is the key white variety, although Muscadelle is also important. Good dry and sweet wines are produced along with *perlé* (a lightly sparkling white) and Gaillac Mousseux, produced by the *méthode rural*. The majority of the red is light and generally disappointing.

To the south are the great red and white wines of Gascony. This is also bulk-white **Vin de Pays des Côtes de Gascogne** country. The **Madiran** and **Pacherenc du Vic-Bilh** ACs share the same geographical area and many growers produce both. Pacherenc can be dry or sweet and is produced from Gros and Petit Manseng, Petit Courbu and Arrufiac, with the odd touch of Sémillon and Sauvignon Blanc (for *moelleux*) blended in. The best are very good. Madiran itself produces powerful, dense and ageworthy reds based on Tannat and often blended with a bit of Cabernets Franc and Sauvignon and Fer-Servadou. It was here that the technique of micro-oxygenation was developed to harness and soften the Tannat's often aggressive and sturdy tannins. Some of the wines are world-class and provide very good value. **Jurançon** is without doubt the finest white-wine appellation of the south-west. Gros and Petit Manseng as well as Petit Courbu are planted. The wines can be sublime, particularly the sweet styles. Yields are low and inevitably prices are rising. The reds of nearby **Béarn** are generally light and insubstantial. To the south-west of Jurançon, nestled into the foothills of the

Pyrenees, **Irouléguy** provides some good reds and whites from the same varieties as at Madiran and Jurançon.

South-West France vintages

In general most red and white should be drunk young and only a number of appellations provide wines with the substance for real ageing. Top Cahors needs several years in bottle and evolves well. Jurançon, both dry and sweet, will improve over half a decade or more and keep much longer. Top Madiran, more approachable than in the past, needs five years at least, particularly the top cuvées. Throughout the south-west 2003, 2002, 2001, 2000, 1999, 1998, 1996 and 1995 were good. 1993, 1990 and 1988 are worth considering for top Jurançon and the trio of 1990, 1989 and 1988 for top Madiran.

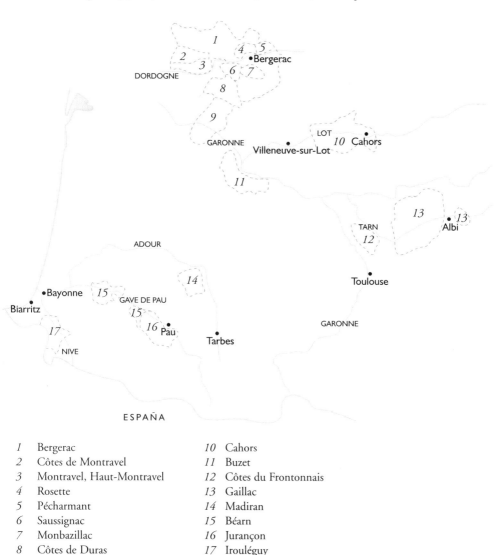

1 Bergerac	*10* Cahors
2 Côtes de Montravel	*11* Buzet
3 Montravel, Haut-Montravel	*12* Côtes du Frontonnais
4 Rosette	*13* Gaillac
5 Pécharmant	*14* Madiran
6 Saussignac	*15* Béarn
7 Monbazillac	*16* Jurançon
8 Côtes de Duras	*17* Irouléguy
9 Côtes du Marmandais	

DOM. BERTHOUMIEU Madiran barre.didier@wanadoo.fr A: CdP, AVn

Owner: Didier Barré Dutour, 32400 Viella

Impressive 25-ha Madiran property producing around 15,000 cases a year. The main focus of the property and, it has to be said, the best wines are the two Madiran *cuvées*. Vinification is traditional and the wines have considerable extract and youthful tannin after a maceration of three weeks or so. The Tradition is spicy, dense and structured with an earthy, mineral core. A blend of Tannat, Cabernet Sauvignon, Cabernet Franc and Fer-Servadou, it is aged partly in wood and partly in *cuve*. The old-vine Charles de Batz is a rich, brooding wine with sweet, chocolaty notes. It sees a large portion of new oak. The wines here are extensively racked as opposed to using micro-oxygenation to minimise those burly, aggressive Tannat tannins. The result is uniformly ripe and supple. The Pacherenc Sec is crisp and fresh, while the sweet Symphonie d'Automne is weighty, rich and more aromatic. (DM)

● **Madiran** Tradition★★ £B Charles de Batz★★★★ £C
O **Pacherenc de Vic-Bilh** Sec★ £B Cuvée Symphonie d'Automne Doux★★ £C

ALAIN BRUMONT Madiran www.montus-madiran.com A: THt, CdP, HHB, N&P

Owner: Alain Brumont Château Bouscassé, 32400 Maumusson

With a large vineyard holding of some 140 ha and a total production of 65,000 to 70,000 cases, Alain Brumont makes impressively structured, rich and very concentrated Madiran under the Montus and Bouscassé labels as well as a softer, more immediately appealing example labelled Torus. He also produces good dry Pacherenc de Vic Bilh under the Montus label. Mainly Petit Courbu, the wine is barrel-fermented and aged and is rich, nutty and intensely honeyed in character. There is also a Bouscassé white that is not vinified in oak and is understandably more aromatic in nature. A number of very good late-harvest Pacherencs are produced as well. Bouscassé is the secondary property, producing a well-priced regular Madiran and a dense and powerful Vieilles Vignes. The approach to vinification emphasises power and extraction. Maceration lasts for over four weeks and no micro-oxygentation is employed during maturation. The regular Château Montus is full of firm, dark-fruited Tannat character. The Cuvée Prestige is pricey but a serious step up. Very, powerful and structured, it demands seven or eight years' ageing to achieve a harmonious balance of fruit and tannin. It will show great refinement with time. Three special *cuvées* have now been introduced, Argile, Les Menhirs and La Tyre. All offer real weight, power and structure. La Tyre, undoubtedly the finest, offers extraordinary depth and richness but at a very heavy price.(DM)

Alain Brumont
● **Madiran** Torus★★ £B

Château Montus
● **Madiran**★★★ £C Cuvée Prestige★★★★ £F La Tyre★★★★ £F La Tyre★★★★★ £G
O **Pacherenc de Vic-Bilh**★★★ £C

Château Bouscassé
● **Madiran**★★ £B Vieilles Vignes★★★★ £D Argile★★★★ £D
O **Pacherenc de Vic-Bilh**★★ £B

DOM. CAUHAPÉ Jurançon domainecauhape@wanadoo.fr A: SsG, M&V, N&P

Owner: Henri Ramonteu Quartier Castet, 64360 Monein

Henri Ramonteu's domaine is sizeable for the region at some 40 ha but he is arguably the finest exponent of the appellation. He makes an extensive range with two dry and four sweet wines from very low-yielding vineyards. The sweet wines are classified according the harvesting date of the grapes. The dry styles are produced mainly from Gros Manseng and vinified with some skin contact, with the Sève d'Automne being barrel-fermented, and all the wines are kept on their lees. The sweet wines, with a high proportion of Petit Manseng are increasingly luscious and richly concentrated but with a fine, fresh backbone of acidity. They are structured and very ageworthy. Rare and only produced when conditions favour it from Petit Manseng fruit harvested close to the year's end, Quintessence is among the great wines not only of Jurançon but of France as well. (DM)

O **Jurançon** Chant des Vignes★★ £B Sève d'Automne★★★ £C
O **Jurançon** Ballet d'Octobre★★★ £C Symphonie de Novembre★★★★ £C Noblesse du Temps★★★★ £E

CHAPELLE LENCLOS Madiran
A:THt, CdP

Owner: Patrick Ducournau 32400 Maumusson Laguian
Patrick Ducournau has 18 ha of vineyards of which a mere 2.5 ha are planted to white varieties, from which he produces decent, lightly honeyed and intense Pacherenc de Vic-Bilh, occasionally as a *moelleux*. The main focus is on the Madiran reds. There are two wines here. The Domaine Mouréou is supple and surprisingly approachable for the appellation. The wine is mainly aged in tank and requires a little time to take the hard edge off its tannins. La Chapelle Lenclos is denser and more structured; it will be better with four or five years' ageing. The wine is partly aged in *cuve* and partly in large 400-litre barrels. Winemaker Damiens Sartori is trying to emphasise fruit and underplay the oak influence that is increasingly evident in some of his neighbours' wines. Much of the style is achieved by the process of micro-oxygenation, which was developed by Ducournau. (DM)

● **Madiran** Domaine Mouréou★★ £B la Chapelle Lenclos★★★ £C
O **Pacherenc de Vic-Bilh** Moelleux★★ £B

CH. D'AYDIE Madiran
A:GBa, AVn

Owner: Laplace family 64330 Aydie
A small but fine range of Madirans and Pacherenc de Vic-Bilhs is produced at this sizeable property. There are 45 ha of vineyards of which 35 ha are devoted to producing Madiran. Decent, straightforward red Madiran is released as Fleury-Laplace, which is produced from bought-in fruit and offers a soft, accessible example of the appellation. Odé d'Aydie is the second label and is reasonably dense and powerful. The Château d'Aydie is a serious step up, full of dark fruit, well-judged oak and firm, youthful tannin. Five or six years' ageing is needed. The wine is kept on its lees in barrel and micro-oxygenation is employed. Pacherenc is produced in a dry style under the Frédéric Laplace label, which is both aromatic and intense, with piercing green, nettly fruit. Rich and impressively concentrated *moelleux* is also made. (DM)

● **Madiran** Odé d'Aydie★★ £B Château d'Aydie★★★ £C
O **Pacherenc de Vic-Bilh** Frédéric Laplace★★ £B

CH. BARRÉJAT Madiran

Owner: Denis Capmartin 32400 Maumusson
Good to very good Madiran is made by Denis Capmartin at his 22-ha domaine. One of the important keys to quality here is the impressive age of some of the vineyards, which are farmed along organic principles. For the remarkable top label, Vieux Ceps, some of the vines are an astounding 200 years of age. The regular Madiran Tradition is as forward as Madiran manages to be but it still needs a year or two to soften its hard youthful edge, which is promoted by a lengthy 21-day *cuvaison* and ageing in *cuve*. Richer and lusher in texture is the Séduction, a blend of 60 per cent Tannat and 40 per cent Cabernets Sauvignon and Franc. Aged in small oak *barriques*, a small proportion new, it is ripe and full of deep, dark, cedary fruit and subtle spicy oak. The Vieux Ceps has just 20 per cent of the Cabernets blended with Tannat. It is both rich and understandably very complex. The top two wines will benefit from at leasts five years, ageing. (DM)

● **Madiran** Tradition★★ £B Séduction★★★ £C Vieux Ceps★★★★ £C

CH. BEAULIEU Côtes du Marmandais

Owner: Robert Schulte 32400 Maumusson
Robert Schulte is among a small handful of producers independently striving for fine quality in this

lesser-known appellation. Most of his neighbours choose to sell to the local co-op. Beaulieu's 26.5 ha of vineyards have great potential and are planted on a mix of gravel and calcareous soils. The vineyard is also being replanted to achieve a density of up to 6,000 vines per hectare, which will improve quality further. Three reds are made here and the style is traditional, particularly for the Côtes du Marmandais and top Cuvée de l'Oratoire. You need to give them at least four or five years' ageing to soften their firm youthful edge. These latter two wines are about structure rather than fruit. The Galapian de Beaulieu, produced from young vines, is softer and more obviously fruit-driven. The Cuvée de l'Oratoire comes from vines up to 40 years old and is produced from a yield of just 18 to 20 hl/ha. It is impressively dense, rich and concentrated. (DM).

● **Côtes du Marmandais**★★ £B l'Oratoire★★★ £C Galapian de Beaulieu★ £B

CH. DU CÈDRE Cahors chateauducedre@wanadoo.fr A: CdP, GWW

Owner: Pascal et Jean-Marc Verhaeghe 46700 Vire-sur-Lot
The Verhaegue family possess some 25 ha of vineyards and produce three good to very good reds. The regular Cahors is made from the youngest vines. It is a ripe, brambly, forward style for drinking young. The Prestige *cuvée* is altogether sturdier and denser. The top wine, Le Cèdre, is now fairly pricey, particularly for the appellation. Produced entirely from old Malbec vines and aged in 100 per cent new oak, it is powerful, structured and very ageworthy – best with five years in the cellar or more. There are also ongoing experiments here with lees-ageing for reds and the use of micro-oxygenation. (DM)

● **Cahors**★ £B Prestige★★ £C Le Cèdre★★★★ £E

CH. LAFFITTE-TESTON Madiran A: CdP, GWW

Owner: Jean-Marc Laffitte 32400 Maumusson
Jean-Marc Laffitte producers not only good Madiran but also some of the most striking examples of Pacherenc du Vic-Bilh. His output of over 20,000 cases is not inconsiderable for the region but fine quality is maintained throughout. He has just over 34 ha of red varieties, 70 per cent of which are Tannat, as well 5.5 ha of white Petit and Gros Manseng and a smattering of Courbu. The stylish Ericka is barrel-fermented, with a fair proportion of new wood being used, and offers impressively piercing floral, nutty, spicy fruit. The Moelleux is opulent and richly textured. Both will evolve well in the short term. The Madiran Tradition is good if a touch angular in its youth, while the Vieilles Vignes is altogether rounder and fuller and is capable of adding real complexity with six or seven years' ageing. (DM)

● **Madiran** Tradition★★ £B Vieilles Vignes★★★ £C
O **Pacherenc du Vic-Bilh** Ericka★★★ £B Moelleux★★★ £C

CH. LAGREZETTE Cahors www.chateau-lagrezette.tm.fr A:CCC

Owner: Alain-Dominique Perrin 46140 Caillac
Another recent top-quality performer in Cahors, Alain-Dominique Perrin is a wealthy entrepreneur whose portfolio includes prestige jewellery operation Cartier. No expense is spared at this 65-ha property and roving consultant Michel Rolland provides guidance over vinification. Classic Rolland techniques are all evident including pre-fermentation maceration, extended vatting, malolactic in barrel and judicious use of new oak. A number a soft fruity Cahors are made under the *négociant* Domaine de Lagrezette label: Grezette, Expression de Grezette and Chevalier-Lagrezette. Grezette is a straightforward commune wine, while Expression and Chevalier get a touch of used oak for ageing. The rich and impressively concentrated Château Lagrezette is a regular Cahors given an extended maceration of up to four weeks. The two prestige *cuvées*, Dame Honneur and the very pricey Pigeonnier, are a step up, particularly the deep and saturated Pigeonnier, which is nudging five stars. It is 100 per cent Malbec sourced from the property's oldest vines and produced from a yield of barely more than 15 hl/ha. The Dame Honneur will benefit from five years or so, the Pigeonnier a year or two longer. (DM)

● **Cahors**★★★ £C Chevaliers★★ £C Lagrezette Dame Honneur★★★★ £E Pigeonnier★★★★★ £G

CH. TIRECUL-LA-GRAVIÈRE Monbazillac A:L&S

Owner: Claudie et Bruno Billancini 24240 Monbazillac

Arguably the top property for sweet Monbazillac. The Billancinis have just 9 ha or so planted and produce a tiny amount – some 1,500 cases in total every year. The style is radically different from their neighbours' with intensely honeyed wines full of rich fruit, quince, toast and very marked botrytis. They achieve this by controlling yields and conducting a succession of *tris* as extensive as any top Sauternes property. The regular bottling is very impressive with rich fruit and spicy, vanilla notes from new oak. There is also a tiny volume of the special and very pricey Cuvée Madame. The wines may be enjoyed young but will keep very well. (DM)

● **Monbazillac**★★★★ £E Cuvée Madame★★★★★ £F

CH. TOUR DES GENDRES Bergerac A:CdP,GWW,HHB

Owner: De Conti family Les Gendres, 24240 Ribagnac

Very impressive Bergerac property with a range of reds and whites produced as Bergerac as well as a red Côtes de Bergerac, the stylish and concentrated Gloire de Mon Père. There is a total of some 43 ha of vineyards with more than half planted to red varieties. Production is now over 25,000 cases a year, which is in no way detrimental to quality. White planting is typically Bordelais, mainly Sémillon with Sauvignon Blanc and around 10 per cent Muscadelle; reds are dominated by Merlot and full of rich, plummy fruit. In addition to the regular range, Casanova des Conti wines – a simple fruit-driven white blend of Sémillon, Sauvignon and Muscadelle and a red comprising mainly Merlot with some Cabernet Sauvignon – are produced exclusively for the UK market. The top *cuvées* have real dimension and class. The Anthologia bottlings are as impressive as anything yet produced from the region, the red adding a round, supple character through partial barrel-fermentation. The white is marvellously intense and pure with beautifully balanced oak. It has only been released in 1996 and 2001. Some of the vineyards are now being farmed biodynamically. (DM)

● **Bergerac**★ £B Moulin des Dames★★★ £D Cuvée Anthologia★★★★ £E
● **Côtes de Bergerac** Gloire de Mon Père★★★ £B
○ **Bergerac** Cuvée des Conti★★ £B Moulin des Dames★★★ £C Cuvée Anthologia★★★★ £E
◉ **Bergerac**★ £B

CH. VIELLA Madiran A: Ben

Owner: Alain Bortolussi Les Gendres, 24240 Ribagnac

The Bortolussi family is in the course of renovating the splendid old château at this property. They make a simple, very straightforward Bearn rosé but of more importance is a good barrel-fermented dry Pacherenc du Vic-Bilh from mainly Arrufiac, as well as a little Gros and Petit Manseng, and a very fine late-harvest Pacherenc which is 100 per cent Petit Manseng. The latter is luscious but very finely structured, with a glorious ripe citrus and mineral character. The good regular Madiran is aged in *cuve* with 40 per cent Cabernets Franc and Sauvignon blended with Tannat. It needs a year or two to add some flesh. The Cuvée Prestige is rich, dense and powerfully structured. It is 100 per cent Tannat and aged in new wood. A minimum of four to five years is needed to achieve an equilibrium of fruit and oak. The wines are all very fairly priced. (DM)

● **Madiran**★★ £B Cuvée Prestige★★★ £C
○ **Pacherenc du Vic-Bilh**★★ £B Moelleux★★★ £C

CLOS LAPEYRE Jurançon jean-bernard.larrieu@wanadoo.fr A: HHB

Owner: Jean-Bernard Larrieu La Chapelle de Rousse, 64110 Jurançon

There are 12 ha under vine here and both dry and sweet styles are produced. The regular Jurançon Sec is fermented in stainless steel and kept on its lees for added depth. The old-vine Vitatge Vielh is barrel-fermented, which gives greater weight. Three sweet wines are made. The regular Moelleux is full and spicy with nicely balanced acidity; the barrel-fermented Sélection is richer and more intensely citrusy with subtle oak in the background. The top late-harvested wine, Vent Balaguer, is produced solely from Petit Manseng grapes that are marked by *passerillage*. Remarkably rich and concentrated, it is only produced in the most exceptional years. (DM)

O Jurançon Sec★ £B Vitatge Vielh★★ £B Moelleux★★ £B Sélection Petit Manseng★★★ £C

CLOS TRIGUEDINA   Cahors   www.clos-triguedina.com   A: CdP, HHB

Owner: Jean-Luc Baldés   46700 Puy l'Evêque
The Baldés family have been in the region for nearly two centuries and in the Prince Probus *cuvée* they established one of the benchmark wines of the appellation long before some of the more recently famous names. To this they have added a massive, dark new *cuvée*, New Black Wine, named after the fabled Cahors of old. There are 57 ha of reds and just 2 ha of whites. From the latter they produce a good barrel-fermented *vin de pays* white blended from Chardonnay and Viognier and a small amount of late-harvest Chenin Blanc. Some rosé is also produced but it is the red Cahors which defines quality here. In order to maintain the standard of the top wines, two forward and fruit-driven secondary labels are also released. Of these, Domaine Labrande comes from a separate property, while Balmont de Cahors is produced at Clos Triguedina. The estate red is a structured and impressively ageworthy example of the appellation. Aged in used oak, it is full of spicy tobacco and red berry fruit. Prince Probus is fuller and darker with a marked vanilla undercurrent from new wood. (DM)

● Cahors★★ £C Prince Probus★★★ £D New Black Wine★★★★ £E

CLOS UROULAT   Jurançon   A: HHB

Owner: Charles Hours   Quartier Trouilh, 64360 Monein
Charles Hours possesses a small holding of some 7 ha with the bulk planted to Petit Manseng and the balancing 25 per cent Gros Manseng with a bit of Courbu. Just two wines are produced here and very good and attractively priced they are too. Both wines are barrel-fermented. The dry Cuvée Marie is full of intense, citrus character and subtle, vanilla oak. The sweet Clos Uroulat is unctuous and rich with a few years in bottle but has marvellously fresh acidity cutting through it. Both will develop well with time. (DM)

● Jurançon Cuvée Marie★★ £B Clos Uroulat★★★ £C

PRIMO PALATUM   Vin de Pays d'Oc   xavier.copel@primo-palatum.fr   A: N&P

Owner: Xavier Copel   1 Cirette, 33190 Morizes
Xavier Copel has now established himself as a very successful small-scale merchant and *négociant*, specialising in limited-production bottlings from the important South-West appellations as well as as in Languedoc and Roussillon. He sources fruit from some of the best growers in each of the appellations he works in. Overall production is less than 6,000 cases a year and some wines are barely more than *micro-cuvées*. Apart from the wines rated below, his considerable range includes bottlings from Bordeaux, Graves, Sauternes and in the Midi, Minervois and the Côtes du Roussillon. The regular or lesser bottlings are labelled Classica and the top *cuvées* within an appellation are usually labelled Mythologia. The wines are very impressive: modern and stylish, with an emphasis on *terroir*, and always impeccably made in the various growers' own cellars. (DM)

● Cahors Classica★★★ £C Mythologia★★★★ £D
● Vin de Pays d'Oc Classica★★ £C Mythologia★★★ £C
O Limoux Anthologie★★★ £D Jurançon Classica★★★ £D Mythologia★★★★ £E

DOM. ROTIER   Gaillac   A: GWW

Owner: Alain Rotier & Francis Marre   32400 Maumusson
Good-quality small Gaillac grower with an output of around 14,000 cases a year. Alain Rotier has been

vinifying his own wines since 1985 and has now been joined by his brother-in-law Francis Marre. They farm 31 ha of vines, 70 per cent of which are red. The vines are now approaching an average age of 30 years and in an ongoing drive to improve quality vine density is being increased from 4,000 to over 6,000 vines per hectare. Regular red, white and rosé are labelled Initiales and a *perlé* is included in the range. More significant wines appear under the Gravels and Renaissance labels and the reds both stand out. The Renaissance is structured and dense and shows impressive dark fruit and cedary complexity. The dry whites don't have quite the same depth but are good examples nonetheless. The sweet white Renaissance Doux shows good, rich peachy fruit with a fine, piercing citrus structure. Most of the wines are forward and approachable but expect the Renaissance wines to develop well in the medium term, particularly the sweet white and the red. (DM)

● **Gaillac** Gravels★★ £B Renaissance★★★ £B
O **Gaillac** Gravels★ £B Renaissance★★ £B Renaissance Doux★★★ £C

OTHER WINES OF NOTE

DOM. ABOTIA ● **Irouléguy** £B
DOM. DE L'ANCIENNE CURE ● **Bergerac** Abbaye £B L'Extrase £D
O **Monbazillac** £B Cuvée de l'Abbaye £E
DOM. ARRETXIA ● **Irouléguy** £B Haitza £C
DOM. BELLEGARDE O **Jurançon** £B Cuvée Thibaut £C
DOM. BRANA ● **Irouléguy** £B
DOM. BRU-BACHÉ O **Jurançon** Casterrasses £B Quintessence £C
DOM. GUY CAPMARTIN ● **Madiran** Tradition £B Cuvée de Couvent £B
DOM. CASTERA O **Jurançon** £B
DOM. DE CAUSSE-MARINES O **Gaillac** Greilles £B Délires d'Automne £D
CH. BAUDARE ● **Côtes du Frontonnais** Tradition £B
CH. BEAUPORTAIL ● **Pécharmant** Fûts de Chêne £B
CH. BÉLINGARD O **Bergerac** Blanche de Bosredon £B O **Monbazillac** Blanche de Bosredon £D
CH. BELLEVUE-LA-FORÊT ● **Côtes du Frontonnais** £B Préstige £B Optimum £B
CH. BOUISSEL ● **Côtes du Frontonnais** £B Cuvée d'Or £B Cuvée Sélection £B
CH. LA CAMINADE ● **Cahors** £B
CH. LES MIADOUX O **Bergerac** £B
CH. LAMARTINE ● **Cahors** £B Cuvée Particulière £C Expression £D
CH. LA MOULIÈRE ● **Côtes de Duras** £B O **Côtes de Duras** £B
CH. LE ROC ● **Côtes du Frontonnais** £B Cuvée Reservée £B Cuvée Don Quichotte £B
CH. MASBUREL O **Montravel** £B ● **Côtes de Bergerac** £C
CH. MIAUDOUX ● **Côtes de Bergerac** £B O **Saussignac** £D
CH. MOULIN CARESSE ● **Bergerac** £B O **Montravel** Fûts de Chêne £B
CH. PEYROS ● **Madiran** £B Greenwich 43 N £C
CH. PLAISANCE ● **Côtes du Frontonnais** £B Cuvée Thibaut £B
CH. LES RIGALETS ● **Cahors** Cuvée Prestige £B Cuvée Quintessence £D
CH. THEULET ● **Bergerac** £B O **Monbazillac** £C
CH. DE TIREGAND ● **Pécharmant** £C
CLOS DE GAMOT ● **Cahors** £B
CLOS LA COUTALE ● **Cahors** £B
CLOS THOU O **Jurançon** Guilhouret Sec £C
CAVE DE COCUMONT ● **Côtes du Marmandais** Béroy £B
DOM. DU CRAMPILH ● **Madiran** Vieilles vignes £B Cuvée Baron £B
CAVE DE CROUSEILLES ● **Madiran** £B
DOM. DURAND-PERRON O **Château-Chalon** £E
DOM. ETXEGARAYA ● **Irouléguy** £B
DOM. DE GINESTE O **Gaillac** Grande Cuvée £B ● **Gaillac** Grande Cuvée £B
DOM. DU HAUT-MONTLONG ● **Côtes de Bergerac** Vents d'Anges £C

DOM. ILARRIA ● **Irouléguy** £B
DOM. LABRANCHE-LAFFONT ● **Madiran** Tradition £B Vieilles Vignes £B
DOM. LAFFONT ● **Madiran** Cuvée Hecaté £D
DOM. LARREDYA ○ **Jurançon** Sec £B Sélections des Terrasses £C
DOM. DE LAULAN ○ **Côtes de Duras** £B
LES VERDOTS ○ **Bergerac** Clos des Verdots £B Grand Vin Les Verdots £D
● **Côtes de Bergerac** Clos des Verdots £B Grand Vin Les Verdots £E
DOM. MONTAURIOL ● **Côtes du Frontonnais** Tradition £B Mons Aureolus £B
DOM. PINERAIE ● **Cahors** Château Pineraie £B
DOM. DE LA MÉTAIRIE ● **Pécharmant** £B
ROBERT PLAGEOLES ○ **Gaillac** Mauzac Vert £B Vin d'Autan £F
PRODUCTEURS PLAIMONT ● **Côtes de Saint-Mont** Château de Sabazan £B
DOM. ELIAN DA ROS ● **Côtes du Marmandais** Le Vin est Une Fête £B Chante Coucou £C

Author's choice (DM)
Cellarworthy South West reds
DOM. BERTHOUMIEU ● **Madiran** Charles de Batz
ALAIN BRUMONT ● **Madiran** Château Montus Cuvée Prestige
CHAPELLE LENCLOS ● **Madiran** la Chapelle Lenclos
CH. D'AYDIE ● **Madiran** Château d'Aydie
CH. BARREJAT ● **Madiran** Vieux ceps
CH. BEAULIEU ● **Côtes du Marmandais** L'Oratoire
CH. DU CÈDRE ● **Cahors** Le Cèdre
CH. LAGREZETTE ● **Cahors** Pigeonnier
CH. TOUR DES GENDRES ● **Bergerac** Moulin des Dames
CH. VIELLA ● **Madiran** Cuvée Prestige
CLOS TRIGUEDINA ● **Cahors** Prince Probus
PRIMO PALATUM ● **Cahors** Mythologia

Six diverse regional whites

DOM. CAUHAPÉ ○ **Jurançon** Noblesse du Temps
CH. TIRECUL-LA-GRAVIÈRE ○ **Monbazillac** Cuvée Madame
CH. TOUR DES GENDRES ○ **Bergerac** Cuvée Anthologia
CH. VIELLA ○ **Pacherenc du Vic-Bilh** Moelleux
CLOS UROULAT ○ **Jurançon** Clos Uroulat
CH. LAFFITTE-TESTON ○ **Pacherenc du Vic-Bilh** Ericka

In order to give some coherence to Italy's plethora of wine regions and appellations we have divided it into five major sections: Piedmont & North-West Italy, North-East Italy, Tuscany, Central Italy, and Southern Italy & Islands. As an aid to orientation, all of Italy's 20 regions are included within one of the sections below and all of the most important DOCs and DOCGs are summarised. They are covered in greater detail in the individual chapters that follow.

Piedmont & North-West Italy

The wines of North-West Italy are numerous and diverse. Most of the top reds are produced in small quantities.

Valle d'Aosta

A wide range of wines from diverse (mostly French) grape varieties come from a handful of good producers, most if not all under the **Valle d'Aosta** DOC. The wines are little seen beyond the borders of this mountain enclave.

Piedmont (Piemonte)

Noble Nebbiolo provides majestic **Barolo** and **Barbaresco** but also fine reds in **Roero** and, rarely, in **Ghemme** and **Gattinara**. All are DOCG, including Roero from 2004. Numerous fine examples of Barbera – albeit in diverse styles – emanate from the DOCs of **Barbera d'Alba** and **Barbera d'Asti**. Blended Barbera and Nebbiolo appear as **Langhe** or **Monferrato** DOC sometimes blended with a proportion of French varieties. Intense Dolcetto appears under the DOCs of **Dolcetto di Dogliani** and **Dolcetto di Diano d'Alba**, and of more varied style and in greater quantities in **Dolcetto d'Alba** DOC. Among the many other wines, Arneis appears as dry white **Roero Arneis**, **Gavi** is another dry white, made from the Cortese grape, and **Moscato d'Asti is a** fine sweet Muscat.

Lombardy (Lombardia)

While there's no fine wine to be had from anywhere close to Milan there is fine sparkling DOCG **Franciacorta** from the edge of Lake Iseo. Elegant reds based on Chiavennasca (Nebbiolo) come from close to Switzerland in the Alps as DOCG **Valtellina Superiore**. An intense, powerful version produced from dried grapes, **Valtellina Sforzato**, is also DOCG. In the south of Lombardy in an extension to the Colli Piacentini (see Emilia-Romagna) diverse everyday reds and whites are produced under the **Oltrepò Pavese** and **Valcalepio** DOCs. (For Lugana whites see Veneto)

Liguria

Liguria is known for some occasionally well-made if not widely exported wines, mostly lighter-style reds and whites. DOCs include **Cinqueterre** (white only), **Colli di Luni, Riviera Ligure di Ponente** and **Rossese di Dolceaqua** (red only).

North-East Italy

This region is at last beginning to receive greater international recognition for both quality and diversity in both colours and from native grapes as well as international varieties.

Trentino-Alto Adige

The few excellent producers in Trentino make both varietal and blended reds and whites from international varieties, some as **Trentino** DOC, others IGT. Native varieties include the white Nosiola and the potentially exciting smoky, black-fruited red, Teroldego (as **Teroldego Rotaliano**). Decent sparkling wine appears as **Trento**. Much of the quality from the German-speaking South Tirol takes the form of familiar varietals under the **Alto Adige** DOC, including Chardonnay, Sauvignon, Gewürztraminer, Pinot Bianco, Pinot Grigio, Pinot Nero, Cabernet Sauvignon and Merlot, but the recent blaze of quality comes from the native Lagrein.

Veneto

Valpolicella and **Amarone/Recioto di Valpolicella** are the stars of the Veneto, with very good examples now proliferating. **Soave** (now DOCG for Superiore) from a top producer is of a different order too, whether dry or sweet (**Recioto di Soave** DOCG). If **Bardolino** was always overrated (despite being DOCG for Superiore) there are outcrops of good quality, red and white, in **Breganze, Colli Berici** and **Colli Euganei** DOCs as well as some attractive fizz in **Prosecco**. White **Lugana** and decent red and white **Garda** DOC wines come from vineyards close by Lake Garda.

Friuli-Venezia Giulia

More of Italy's fine whites come from Friuli than anywhere else but there are increasing amounts of fine reds too. Whether varietal or blended most quality wines will bear one of three DOCs: **Collio, Colli Orientali del Friuli** or **Friuli Isonzo**. Of the international varieties, Chardonnay, Sauvignon, Pinot Grigio, Pinot Bianco, Cabernet Sauvignon and Merlot predominate. Native whites, Tocai Friulano, Ribolla Gialla, Malvasia can be very good while the best native reds, Schioppettino and Pignolo, must be tasted. Wines from the DOCs of **Friuli Grave, Friuli Latisana** or **Friuli Aquileia** are typically more everyday.

Tuscany (Toscana)

The sheer volume of fine wine from Tuscany is remarkable. Much of it derives from Sangiovese, though the extent of its Tuscan character can sometimes be enhanced by the inclusion of other natives such as Canaiolo or Colorino or (in some instances only) compromised by Merlot, Cabernet Sauvignon, Syrah and other interlopers. These international varieties are very successful in their own right, often as varietal examples.

The classic appellations (all DOCG) include **Carmignano, Chianti** (often appended with a sub-zone name such as **Colli Fiorentini** or **Colli Senesi** – the best being **Rufina**), **Chianti Classico** (Tuscany's heart), **Brunello di Montalcino** (for the biggest, most powerful pure Sangiovese) and **Vino Nobile di Montepulciano**. The best-known white appellation is **Vernaccia di San Gimignano**.

DOCs or sub-zones close to the Tuscan coast and southern Maremma include **Montecarlo, Colline Lucchesi, Colline Pisane, Montescudaio, Bolgheri, Val di Cornia** and **Morellino di Scansano** but here, as in the classic appellations, many fine wines are sold as simply IGT Toscana.

Central Italy

Too often ignored by the wine drinker only familiar with Tuscany and Piedmont. Shame! because there's a mushrooming number of good producers and some real originals.

Emilia-Romagna

Viticulturally, there are two halves to this region too. By far the best reds are Romagna's **Sangiovese di Romagna** DOC – a very serious alternative to Sangiovese from Tuscany – or IGT equivalents from the best producers. To be sure, Emilia has fabulous ham, cheese and other food products but generally only adequate whites and reds from hillside slopes (*colli*), most notably in the **Colli Piacentini** and **Colli Bolognesi** DOCs.

Marche

Marche is for dry white Verdicchio (either **Verdicchio dei Castelli di Jesi** or **Verdicchio di Matelica** DOCs), some of it very good, but also for other more everyday dry whites such as **Falerio dei Colli Ascolani** DOC. The best reds are based on Montepulciano, especially **Rosso Conero** DOC. From a good producer, **Rosso Piceno** DOC as well as IGT reds based on Sangiovese or imported varieties can offer both quality and value.

Umbria

There are lots of interesting reds and whites to be found in Umbria. Good **Montefalco Rosso** should be tried as should the more demanding **Montefalco Sagrantino** DOCG. A raft of other excellent reds, sold as IGT Umbria, are usually based on Cabernet Sauvignon, Merlot or Sangiovese. **Orvieto** (a DOC which also covers part of Lazio) when made by a good producer offers personality without heaviness.

Lazio

Lazio has football and **Frascati**. I'd argue that more of the latter is now clean and characterful. Some other good dry whites are made too as are much-improved reds, even if most come from Merlot, Cabernet or Syrah.

Abruzzo & Molise

Source of many of the best examples of the Montepulciano grape, especially as **Montepulciano d'Abruzzo** DOC (DOCG in the Colline Teramane). The best are powerful, fleshy, flavoursome and ageworthy. The main white appellation is **Trebbiano d'Abruzzo** DOC even if most examples from the Trebbiano grape are unexciting. Some adequate examples of Chardonnay are produced as IGTs.

Southern Italy & Islands

Increasingly a cornucopia of vinous delights, especially for reds and whites but also for sweet and fortified wines.

Campania

Aglianico is the star, as **Taurasi DOCG** but also in **Aglianico del Taburno, Falerno del Massico, Sannio** DOCs and various IGTs. Excellent, mostly dry whites come from native grapes Greco, Fiano and Falanghina as **Greco di Tufo, Fiano di Avellino** (both DOCG) and **Sannio** and **Taburno** DOCs for Falanghina.

Basilicata and Calabria

Basilicata has more fine Aglianico, nearly all of it labelled **Aglianico del Vulture** DOC. Calabria has a few exciting reds; most derive much of their character and quality from the native Gaioppo grape.

Puglia

Negroamaro and Primitivo provide many of the best Puglian reds, many of them sold as IGTs but **Salice Salentino, Brindisi** and **Primitivo di Manduria** are leading DOCs. Further reds come from Montepulciano and Uva di Troia, some under **Castel del Monte** DOC, and there's some unexpectedly good Chardonnay, again much is sold as IGT.

Sicily (Sicilia)

Ever-burgeoning quantities of quality reds and whites are nearly all sold as IGT Sicilia, as there are few DOCs of note. Leading native varieties Nero d'Avola and Nerello Mascalese compete with imports such as Cabernet Sauvignon, Merlot and Syrah. Most significant of the DOCs are **Cerasuolo di Vittoria** and **Etna** for reds, and **Moscato di Pantelleria** and **Passito di Pantelleria** for often delicious sweet Muscat.

Sardinia (Sardegna)

The true potential of Sardinia remains largely untapped but there are already good dry whites from Vermentino, as **Vermentino di Sardegna** DOC and **Vermentino di Gallura** DOCG. Increasingly fine reds are from Cannonau or Carignano, as **Cannonau di Sardegna** and **Carignano del Sulcis** DOCs respectively or from several IGTs.

1   Valle d'Aosta
2   Piedmont (Piemonte)
3   Lombardy (Lombardia)
4   Liguria
5   Trentino-Alto Adige
6   Veneto
7   Friuli-Venezia Giulia
8   Tuscany (Toscana)
9   Emilia-Romagna
10 Marche
11 Umbria
12 Lazio
13 Abruzzo
14 Molise
15 Campania
16 Puglia
17 Basilicata
18 Calabria
19 Sicily (Sicilia)
20 Sardinia (Sardegna)

Piedmont & North-West Italy

Piedmont has made progress like almost no other wine region over the past 20 years. There is both outstanding quality and considerable diversity. What is really wonderful about Piedmont is man's connection with the land and the importance of the link between fine wine, the physical environment and the human endeavour therein. It is illustrated as well here as in any wine region in the world.

Red wines

At the heart of Piedmont viticulture are the Langhe hills. The finest grape is Nebbiolo. The two great wines are **Barolo** and **Barbaresco**, both DOCG, though some of the best wines from these zones are now sold under the **Langhe** DOC. One of the region's greatest strengths derives from its peasant landholding heritage. While *commerciante* or large *négociant* houses flogged the grapes of any number of small growers under generic labels in the 1950s and 60s, the subsequent success and leadership of Angelo Gaja and others paved the way for small growers to do likewise – a trend that really gained momentum in the 80s and 90s. Outside money tends to be the exception in Piedmont yet some producers have been highly receptive to new ideas. Both Barolo (a little over 1,500 ha) and Barbaresco (just over 600 ha) are fairly small wine regions and it is common for growers here to have just one or two hectares of this or that *cru*.

Barolo is spread for the most part over five communes: La Morra, Barolo, Castiglione Falletto, Monforte d'Alba and Serralunga. Verduno is the most significant of six other communes that encroach on the DOCG. The southern part of Monforte and Serralunga (in the east) have mostly the older Helvetian soils, said to favour strength and structure. La Morra soils are predominantly on younger Tortonian soils, a chalky marl giving greater perfume and a less rigorous structure. Between the two there tends to be a mix of the two with varying amounts of sand and clay. More clay can help in very hot years but a higher sand component can improve drainage in cool, wet years.

Barbaresco is almost exclusively restricted to just three communes. Almost half of it comes from the commune of Barbaresco, where 60 per cent of the vineyard area is is given over to Barbaresco production, compared to only a little over 20 per cent of the vineyard area in neighbouring Neive and Treiso. Barbaresco generally is slightly less powerful than Barolo, more perfumed and ready to drink a little sooner, but producer and site are the real determinants of style and character. The wines are required to have a minimum of nine months' wood-ageing and are released a year earlier than Barolo (which must have two years in wood).

In both zones much is made of a modern versus traditional approach to winemaking yet the reality is less distinct, with a range of different approaches to vinification and winemaking. The important differences centre around the length of maceration; the type and use of oak (size, age and origin); temperature and style of fermentation; and the type of fermentation vessel – we have tried to highlight some of these differences within the individual producer profiles. Of course these differences apply as much in Burgundy but in this relatively isolated, conservative area the differences of opinion have taken on an extra intensity. There are many outstanding wines across the spectrum.

Nebbiolo under other guises includes **Carema**, **Gattinara**, **Ghemme** and **Roero** in Piedmont, and **Valtellina Superiore** in Lombardy. In the latter the wines may also be identified by one of four subzones: Grumello, Inferno, Sassella or Valgella. But nowhere is the combination of soils, elevation and mesoclimate as predisposing as in the Langhe hills. The majority of other good examples currently come from Roero and Valtellina.

Piedmont's second great grape is Barbera, which can take on a number of guises. The leading two appellations are **Barbera d'Alba** and **Barbera d'Asti**. The Superiore version of the latter is now redefined by three subzones: Colli Astiani, Nizza and Tinella. Barbera has a great affinity with new oak and many of the top examples have spent around 12 months in *barriques*. Barbera also combines well with Nebbiolo and there are many good oak-aged, deeply fruity, lush examples (typically **Langhe** DOC) that can be drunk quite young or kept. The more northerly hills of the Asti and Alessandria provinces include similar interesting blends under the **Monferrato** DOC.

Dolcetto doesn't quite make the cut in fine wine terms. It does, however, make both wonderfully fruity everyday wine or something more intense and concentrated and often better with a year or two of bottle-age, depending on its maker. There are three leading manifestations: **Dolcetto d'Alba**, the small **Dolcetto di Diano d'Alba** and **Dolcetto di Dogliani**. Dolcetto is also included in the Monferrato DOC, while **Dolcetto di Ovada** is mostly of the fruity, juicy type.

What else is there? Other natives varieties include Freisa and Grignolino, both sold under most of the regional DOCs, but exciting examples are few. There's also sparkling red fizz, actually DOCG in **Brachetto d'Acqui** (from Brachetto) and **Malvasia di Castelnuovo Don Bosco** from Malvasia Nera. How significant are the French imports? Not very, but Cabernet Sauvignon features in many a Langhe or Monferrato blend (see above), Merlot to a lesser extent. Pinot Nero (Pinot Noir) has yet to really impress, while only a very small amount of Syrah is planted.

Beyond Piedmont, in Lombardy, Pinot Nero, Bonarda and Barbera figure in the rarely other than ordinary **Oltrepò Pavese**. Cabernet Franc (or, as likely, Carmenère), Merlot, Cabernet Sauvignon and Pinot Nero are also used for sometimes very good **Terre di Franciacorta** reds.

White and sparkling wines

The perfumed and characterful Arneis (frequently as **Roero Arneis**) and relatively high acid Cortese (the best examples sold as **Gavi del Comune di Gavi** – those at the heart of a wider zone) are the leading native whites. Other natives include Favorita, a distinctive herb-scented wine, and Erbaluce as **Erbaluce di Caluso** or the better sweet version from dried grapes, **Caluso Passito**. Pigato and Vermentino are important in Liguria as **Rivera Ligure di Ponente** varietals, but the latter also in **Colli di Luni** and **Cinqueterre**. In the east of Lombardy some attractive dry white **Lugana** is made from Trebbiano di Lugana (*see* North-East Italy).

Yet the most important white grape in North-West Italy is Moscato Bianco. This, the 'good' Muscat (Muscat Blanc à Petits Grains), is very widely planted in the Asti and Alba hills in Piedmont. Good **Asti** is a well-made, sweet party fizz and much better than some of the nasty acidic and green branded stuff made in Germany, France and elsewhere. But **Moscato d'Asti**, made on a different scale, can be incomparably better. Delightfully perfumed and low in alcohol, it is excellent with fresh fruit. A very small amount of *passito*-style Muscat is made in an Asti enclave called **Loazzolo**. Chambave Moscato is another sweet example from the Valle d'Aosta.

The closest Italy has to top Champagne in quality is **Franciacorta**. Here, near Lake Iseo in Lombardy, Chardonnay, Pinot Bianco and Pinot Nero grapes are combined in serious *metodo classico* sparkling wines. Satèn is a softer, creamier, low-pressure version.

Of imports, Chardonnay is the leading variety, usually appearing as **Langhe** Chardonnay but occasionally under the regionwide **Piemonte** DOC. Really top examples are relatively few but there is potential here. It is also increasingly important in Oltrepò Pavese and Terre di Franciacorta whites. There are small amounts of Sauvignon and even less Riesling, Viognier and other Rhône varietals.

Leading Barolo crus

La Morra

Arborina, Brunate, Cerequio, Conca di Annunziata, Fossati, Gattera, Giachini, La Serra, Rocche di Annunziata

Barolo

Brunate, Cerequio, Fossati (all three are shared with La Morra) Bricco Viole, Cannubi, Cannubi Boschis, Le Coste, Sarmassa

Castiglione Falletto

Bricco Boschis, Fiasco, Monprivato, Villero, Rocche

Monforte d'Alba

Bussia Soprana, Bricco Cicala, Colonello, Gavarini, Ginestra, Mosconi, Pianpolvere

Serralunga d'Alba

Cerretta, Falletto, Francia, Lazzarito, Marenca-Rivette, Parafada, Prapò, Vigna Rionda

Leading Barbaresco crus:

Barbaresco

Asili, Martinenga, Montefico, Montestefano, Ovello, Pajé, Pora, Rabajà, Rio Sordo, Roncagliette, Secondine

Neive

Bricco, Gallina, Marcorino, Messoirano, Santo Stefano, Serraboella and Starderi

Treiso

Pajoré, Valeirano

A-Z of producers by appellation

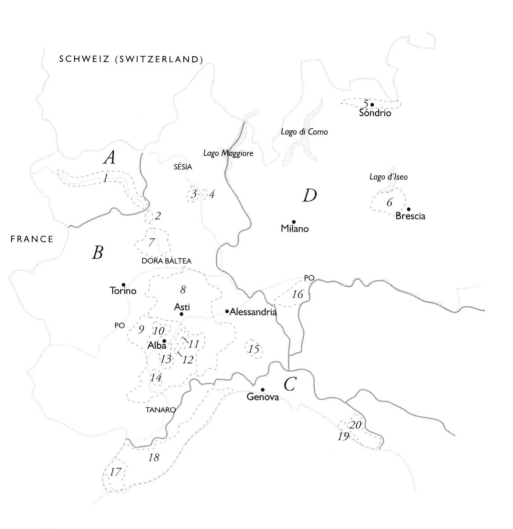

Regions:

A	Valle d'Aosta
B	Piedmont (Piemonte)
C	Liguria
D	Lombardy (Lombardia)

Appellations:

1	Valle d'Aosta
2	Carema
3	Gattinara
4	Ghemme
5	Valtellina Superiore
6	Franciacorta
7	Erbaluce di Caluso, Caluso Passito
8	Barbera d'Asti, Moscato d'Asti
9	Langhe
10	Roero, Roero Arneis
11	Barbaresco
12	Dolcetto di Diano d'Alba
13	Barolo
14	Dolcetto di Dogliani
15	Gavi
16	Oltrepò Pavese
17	Rossese di Dolceaqua
18	Riviera Ligure di Ponente
19	Cinqueterre
20	Colli di Luni

Piedmont vintages

There's never been a better time to add a selection of the best Piedmont wines to a wine cellar. Not just great Barolo and Barbaresco for the medium- and long-term (8 to 30 years) but much excellent Langhe and Barbera for the short- and medium-term (4 to 12 years). When to drink depends on a producer's own style but also on your own preference, whether for the fruit intensity and boldness of youth or the more mellow complexity that comes with age.

2003: After too much rain in 2002, it was too hot and dry with some vines suffering heat stress. Very promising Dolcetto, and some top Barbera, but much more difficult for Nebbiolo.

2002: There's not much enthusiasm for this vintage given the poor summer which was atypically wet and cool with rot problems. Added to this some prize vineyards were devastated by hail, severely denting production as well as quality. Worse for Dolcetto and Barbera, not bad Nebbiolo as the sun eventually emerged; dedication and rigorous selection has produced good, if not great wine.

2001: A very promising vintage and the last in a long string of fine vintages in Piedmont that began with 1995. A hot summer followed a wet spring and hopes were very high. But from September intermittent rain and hail had a negative effect on quality for some.

2000: There's exceptional quality Barolo and Barbaresco from a select few but also less inspired examples. A very hot August followed a cool July and in some instances the consequent rapid ripening apes 1997 in wines of over-ripe fruit and under-ripe tannins. Generally better in Serralunga than La Morra. A below par year for Dolcetto.

1999: This vintage seems to combine the fruit richness and ripeness of 97 with more of the structure of 96. Good for Barbera, Dolcetto and Nebbiolo, with many ageworthy exciting wines.

1998: A smallish crop from a hot dry summer that concluded with some rain. Colours are more evolved, more typical for the Nebbiolo-based wines; many are full, ripe and balanced. Another very fine vintage for medium- to long-term cellaring.

1997: Two words characterise this vintage: hot and dry. The very ripe, occasionally overripe fruit has resulted in wines with a sweet, lush fruit character and relatively low acidities. Generally the tannins are good and ripe but in some instances are quite marked (a lack of physiological ripeness due to the heat) and this will only become more apparent as the primary fruit evolves. Some won't keep but many will, given the chance.

1996: Cool and classic, with gradual even ripening. Many growers picked very late to produce wines that are fully ripe but powerfully structured. One to cellar for at least 10 to 15 years particularly from the so-called traditional producers. Pretty consistent too, though a few of the newer names were still finding their way. Hail hit some badly and reduced quantities overall.

1995: The first of an unprecedented run of good to great vintages. Though not at the same level as 1996 - 2001, attractive, well-structured if slightly leaner Barolo and Barbaresco. The best are now showing well.

1994: If generally weak, with a lack of real fruit concentration, there are some attractive, forward Nebbiolo-based wines. Go for a specific recommendation or expect to be disappointed.

1993: The best vintage between 90 and 95. Worth a punt from a grower with a good track record but some are too firm for the fruit levels. Some good if not great Riservas were also made.

1992: Wet, depressing – the poorest vintage of the 90s. No longer one to take a chance on (if you ever could) – even for the best Barolos – but there were rare successes.

1991: A lack of balance was typical of 91, the first weak vintage in a gloomy spell for Piedmont. Generally poorly balanced wines emerged from a wet vintage.

1990: The last outstanding vintage prior to 1996. Sustained hot weather gave rise to rich, ripe wines. The first wave of exciting new producers (Clerico, Sandrone, R Voerzio *et al*) became well-established stars. A good vintage to discover how great Barolo/Barbaresco begins to evolve.

1989: Another classic year with powerful, structured wines. Most can still be kept but it depends on the signature of the grower or producer.

1988: Some Nebbiolo was compromised by rain but the best are dense sturdy wines that have aged well. Many will still keep.

Earlier years: Few 1987s★★ ever achieved real harmony but 1986★★★ provided some very attractive Barolo and Barbaresco – but stick with the top wines now, others are past it. 1985★★★ and 1982 ★★★★ were excellent vintages but there were nothing like the number of top examples now being made. Beware of many of the *négociant* labels; seek out a classic from a small grower instead. 1979★★★ provided some refined wines but most of the rare remaining bottles are past their best. Though long-lived, both 1978★★★ and 1974★★★ can be rather tough and old-fashioned – taste before buying any quantity and be sure of its provenance. Well-stored examples from 1971 can still be classic while 1970, 67, 64 and 61 might tempt the intrepid.

Piedmont vintage chart

	Barolo	Barbaresco	Barbera (premium)
2003	NYR	NYR	NYR
2002	NYR	★/★★★ B	★/★★ C
2001	★★★★/★★★★★ A	★★★★/★★★★★ A	★★★★ B
2000	★★★/★★★★★ A	★★★/★★★★★ A	★★★★/★★★★★ B
1999	★★★★/★★★★★ A	★★★★/★★★★★ A	★★★/★★★★ C
1998	★★★★ B	★★★★ B	★★★★ C
1997	★★★★/★★★★★ B	★★★★/★★★★★ B	★★★★ /★★★★★ C
1996	★★★★/★★★★★ B	★★★★/★★★★★ B	★★★ C
1995	★★★/★★★★ C	★★★/★★★★ B	★★★/★★★★ C
1994	★★/★★★ C	★★/★★★ C	★★/★★★ D
1993	★★★ C	★★★ C	★★★ C
1992	★/★★ C	★/★★ C	★/★★ D
1991	★★/★★★ C	★★ C	★★★ D
1990	★★★★/★★★★★ C	★★★★/★★★★★ C	★★★★/★★★★★ D
1989	★★★★/★★★★★ C	★★★★/★★★★★ C	★★★★/★★★★★ D
1988	★★★/★★★★ C	★★★/★★★★ C	★★★/★★★★ D

Piedmont & North-West Italy/A-Z of producers

ANNA MARIA ABBONA Dolcetto di Dogliani www.amabbona.com A: **Mgi**, L&W

Owner: Anna Maria Abbona & Franco Schellino Fraz. Moncucco 21, 12060 Farigliano (CN)
The historic zone of Dogliani has undergone a considerable resurgence in the past decade. It's easy to be dismissive about a zone dedicated to Dolcetto, but the best are very good indeed. Anna Maria's Maioli is made from vines planted in 1935; rich, almost velvety with lovely fruit, but powerful too with a refined structure. An oak-aged Superiore adds smoke and spice and is equally good, though it benefits from an extra year or two's age. An attractive fleshy Barbera, Cadò, which doesn't qualify as Barbera d'Alba due to the location, includes 10 per cent Dolcetto. (PW)

● **Dolcetto di Dogliani** Sorì dij But★★ £B Maioli★★★ £C Superiore★★★ £C
● **Langhe** Cadò★★ £D ● **Langhe** Dolcetto★ £B

M & E ABBONA Dolcetto di Dogliani www.abbona.com A: **LoW**

Owner: Marziano Abbona Via Torino 242, 12063 Dogliani (CN)
Marziano Abbona is one of the stars of Dogliani, but with ever expanding vineyard holdings alsoproduces fine Barolo and Barbaresco. All three *crus* are aged partly in *barrique* and partly in large oak casks and combine strength with a certain finesse. Of the two Barolos, the Terlo Ravera is from Novello, the more powerful Pressenda from Monforte d'Alba. Some Nebbiolo d'Alba is also produced from the latter. In the Dogliani zone, where half the vineyards are, old vines in Doriolo are source for (unoaked) Dolcetto Papà Celso which shows a breadth uncommon to most examples of the variety. A further special selection was first bottled as a *Superiore* version in 2001. I Due Ricu combines Barbera, Nebbiolo and Cabernet. Also made is a white, Cinerino Bianco, from Viognier. (PW)

● **Dolcetto di Dogliani** Papà Celso★★★ £B Vigna Dariolo★★ £B Vigneto Muntâ★★ £B
● **Barbaresco** Faset★★★ £E ● **Barolo** Terlo Ravera★★★ £E Pressenda★★★★ £E
● **Barbera d'Alba** Rinaldi★★ £C ● **Langhe** I Due Ricu★★ £D

CLAUDIO ALARIO Dolcetto di Diano d'Alba A: **WTs**, Bib, Sav, Hrd

Owner: Claudio Alario Via Santa Croce 23, 12055 Diano d'Alba (CN)
This estate and BRICCO MAIOLICA are champions of the small Dolcetto zone that lies between Barolo and Barbaresco yet both are as notable for their Nebbiolo as for Dolcetto. Here both the Nebbiolo d'Alba and Barolo are perfumed, balanced and ageworthy. Consistently well-made Barolo Riva from the commune of Verduno has excellent texture, breadth and length. Of the Dolcetto, Costa Fiore is the more concentrated but backward version and is best with an extra year or two. Claudio Alario is also a good reasonably priced source of Barbera d'Alba and Nebbiolo d'Alba. (PW)

● **Dolcetto di Diano d'Alba** Costa Fiore★★★ £B Montegrillo★★ £B
● **Barbera d'Alba** Valletta★★ £C ● **Nebbiolo d'Alba** Cascinotto★★ £C
● **Barolo** Riva★★★ £E

GIANFRANCO ALESSANDRIA Barolo A: **Win**, Fal, F&R

Owner: Gianfranco Alessandria Loc. Manzoni 12, 12065 Monforte d'Alba (CN)
Gianfranco Alessandria is an inspired young grower with a range of ripe, full and stylish reds. The top wines all show a measure of new oak but it is never obvious or allowed to dominate. An intense Barbera Vittoria from 65-year-old vines, and beautifully balanced Barolo San Giovanni (a special selection rather than vineyard-specific) are particularly worthy but all of the wines deliver good fruit in a modern accessible style. Gianfranco's version of Insieme (see ALTARE), 40 per cent Nebbiolo with the balance 'Vittoria' Barbera and Cabernet, is one of the best. (PW)

● **Barolo**★★★ £E San Giovanni★★★★ £F
● **Barbera d'Alba**★★ £B Vittoria★★★★ £C ● **Dolcetto d'Alba**★ £B
● **Insieme**★★★★ £F

ELIO ALTARE Barolo   A: Fal, F&R

Owner: Elio Altare Fraz. Annunziata 51, 12064 La Morra (CN)

Elio Altare is La Morra's and Barolo's great moderniser as well as mentor to a group of other small growers – ALESSANDRIA, CORINO, Silvio GRASSO, MOLINO, REVELLO and VEGLIO. Radically low yields, short maceration times and rows of *barriques* are now common to all but nobody else quite manages to get the extra depth and concentration of Altare. It is not a purist's Barolo that emerges yet one of terrific concentration and balance that still conveys something of its origins. Super-Langhes Arborina (Nebbiolo), Larigi (Barbera) and La Villa (Nebbiolo/Barbera) take the new oak theme to its logical (or illogical, depending on your viewpoint) conclusion. Altare was also the proponent behind Insieme. The band of seven producers share winemaking resources and expertise to produce delicious, concentrated modern oak-aged blends – variations on a Nebbiolo, Barbera, Cabernet and/or Merlot theme – a percentage of the proceeds go to local cultural and artisanal causes. 1997 Barolos and 98 Langhe reds were withheld due to cork contamination problems but excellent 99s across the board are a testament to Elio Altare's resolve and the maintenance of his very high standards. (PW)

- ● **Barolo★★★** £E Arborina★★★★ £F Brunate★★★★ £F
- ● **Langhe** Arborina★★★ £F Larigi★★★★ £F La Villa★★★★ £F
- ● **Barbera d'Alba★★** £C ● **Dolcetto d'Alba★★** £B
- ● **Insieme★★★★** £F

ANTICHI VIGNETI DI CANTALUPO Ghemme www.cantalupovigneti.it   A: AIF

Owner: Arlunno family Via Michelangelo Buonarroti 5, 28074 Montelupo Albese (NO)

Ghemme's one producer that gives real credibility to the zone's DOCG status. Input from top enologist Donato Lanati helps even if in the main the wines follow a fairly traditional, unadventurous vinification. Typically rather austere and firm when young, the wines mellow with age and their already enticing perfumes become ever more complex. While the regular Ghemme includes a little Vespolina and Uva Rara, special bottlings are pure Nebbiolo. Carellae and Breclemae are vineyard-specific, while Signore di Bayard is a special selection which is aged in French *barriques* (a third new). The latter is often the most flattering when young but also has the greatest dimension, intensity and sheer style. Colline Novaresi wines, Agamium (Nebbiolo) and Primigenia (Nebbiolo/Uva Rara/Vespolina), are characterful but not at the same level. Unoaked white Carolus combines Arneis, Greco and Chardonnay. There is much quality Ghemme from recent good vintages though there is no Collis Carellae in 1998 or 2001 and no Ghemme at all is likely from the 2002 vintage! (PW)

- ● **Ghemme★** £D Collis Carellae★★ £E Collis Breclamae★★★ £E Signore di Bayard★★★ £E

ARALDICA VINI PIEMONTESI Barbera d'Asti www.araldicavini.com   A: Mer, AAA

Owner: 'Cooperative' Viale Laudano 2, 14040 Castel Boglione (AT)

Araldica is a large co-op with 300 members and 900 ha of vineyard. Under the direction of Claudio Manera it has become synonymous with approachable soundly made Piemontese reds and whites. Recent acquisitions, including Il Cascinone in the Monferrato hills (where the vineyards are being restored) and La Battistina in Gavi, will provide grapes of superior origins from which to fashion some high-quality wines too. Widely seen are the Alasia varietals which include bright, clean fruity Barbera, Dolcetto, Chardonnay and Cortese. Promising are Barbaresco (Corsini) and Barolo (Revello). Under the Poderi Alasia label are a series of premium wines based on individual vineyards including Barbera d'Asti Rive, Roero Arneis Solaria, Langhe Nebbiolo Castellero and Sauvignon Camillona. An increasingly good Monferrato blend, Luce Monaca combines Barbera with Merlot and Cabernet Sauvignon. *Barrique*-fermented Chardonnay (Roleto) and oak-aged Pinot Nero (Re Nero) are also produced. (PW)

Araldica:
- ● **Barbera d'Asti** Ceppi Storici★ £B Vigneti Croja★★ £B
- ○ **Gavi** Madonnina★ £B

Poderi Alasia:
● **Barbera d'Asti** Rive★★ £C   ● **Monferrato** Luce Monaca★★ £D
● **Nebbiolo d'Alba** Poderi Alasia Castellero★ £C
O **Roero Arneis** Podere Alasia Sorilaria★★ £C   O **Monferrato** Camillona★★ £C

ASCHERI Barolo www.ascherivini.it   A: **Eno**, Bat, Swg

Owner: Ascheri family   Via G. Piumati 23, 12042 Bra (CN)
Matteo Ascheri has an energy to match his bear-like stature. A list of his accomplishments includes planting Viognier and Syrah at Bra (outside the Barolo zone), creating the Osteria Murivecchi in the family's old cellars, promoting the Langhe at home and abroad – yet all the while maintaining realistic prices and good quality. Matteo believes strongly in natural winemaking, and recent vintages show improvement from the regeneration of the family's vineyards, with wines of bright, pure varietal character. Of two *cru* Barolos, Vigna dei Pola comes from the Pisapolla *cru* in the Verduno vineyards that lie south of Ascheri's base in Bra. The more traditional (moderately long fermentation, ageing in mostly old wood) Sorano comes from Serralunga and has more depth, grip and class. From 1999 fruit from the best vines within Sorano was vinified separately to produce Coste & Bricco and the first wines offer yet more style and expression. (PW)
● **Barolo** Vigna dei Pola★★★ £E Sorano★★★ £E Sorano Coste & Bricco★★★★ £F
● **Nebbiolo d'Alba** Bricco San Giacomo★★ £C   ● **Barbera d'Alba** Vigna Fontanelle★★ £C
● **Dolcetto d'Alba** Vigna Nirane★★ £B   ● **Montalupa Syrah**★★ £D
O **Montalupa Viognier**★★ £D   O **Roero Arneis** Cristina Ascheri★ £C

AZELIA Barolo   A: **J&B**

Owner: Luigi Scavino   Via Alba-Barolo 27, 12060 Castiglione Falletto (CN)
Less well-known than Enrico Scavino, Luigi similarly owns a decent chunk of the excellently positioned Fiasco vineyard, which has certain similarities to the nearby Monprivato and Villero *crus*. The regular Barolo, made from younger vines, sees mostly large wood (*botte grande*) but the two *crus* Bricco Fiasco and San Rocco (the latter from Serralunga) both receive 50 per cent new oak. There is evident structure but the wines are balanced with good weight, depth and dimension and definite class. Barolos are consistently fine in successive top vintages from 95 onwards. All need at least six to eight years' age. Barbera d'Alba which also sees some new oak is toasty, spicy and deep-fruited and best with at least three to four years' age. (PW)
● **Barolo**★★★ £E Bricco Fiasco★★★★ £F San Rocco★★★★ £F
● **Barbera d'Alba** Vigneto Punta★★★ £D   ● **Dolcetto d'Alba** Bricco dell'Oriolo★ £C

PRODUTTORI DEL BARBARESCO www.produttori-barbaresco.it   A: **V&C**

Owner: 'Cooperative'   Via Torino 52, 12050 Barbaresco (CN)
This super co-op manages around a sixth (100 ha) of Barbaresco's relatively tiny vineyard area. It is democratically run and winemaker Gianni Testa adheres to traditional lines with lengthy maceration and ageing in large *botti*. But what perfume, grace and charm they achieve in the top *crus* in a good vintage! These wines are a purist's delight, capturing much of the essence of Nebbiolo and a splendid expression of the grape in some of the most hallowed patches of soil in Barbaresco. What's more, the single-vineyard Riservas sell for less than many other producers' regular Barbaresco. All will keep for, and sometimes need, a decade or more. For the uninitiated, try the lovely 1997s, which have great vinosity and lowish acidity. Though the *crus* were not made in 1998 other recent vintages are also proving very promising although older bottles from more difficult years are likely to be more variable. (PW)
● **Barbaresco Riserva** Asili★★★★ £E Moccagatta★★★★ £E Montefico★★★★ £E
● **Barbaresco Riserva** Montestefano★★★★ £E Rabajà★★★★ £E Ovello★★★ £E
● **Barbaresco Riserva** Pajé★★★ £E Pora★★★ £E Rio Sordo★★★ £E
● **Barbaresco**★★ £D   ● **Langhe Nebbiolo**★ £B

LUIGI BAUDANA Barolo   A: THt

Owner: Luigi Baudana Fraz. Baudana 43, 12050 Serralunga d'Alba (CN)
With barely 5 ha of vineyards, Luigi Baudana's small output nonetheless encompasses most of the main styles common to Langhe producers. Full ripeness and a particular intensity are common to all. A solid regular Barolo (if slightly weaker in 1998) is surpassed by Cerretta Piani, which has the extract and power associated with Serralunga but also a certain elegance that vintages such as 96 or 99 seem certain to accentuate with a decade's age. A Baudana *cru* from 99, more meaty but balanced, shows promise too. Barbera (with some *barrique*-influence) and Dolcetto are of a good standard, while Lorenso Rosso is a satisfactory example of the oak-influenced Nebbiolo/Barbera/Merlot blend. Any charm the white Lorenzo, from Sauvignon and Chardonnay, might have, however, is masked by oak. A varietal Chardonnay, on the other hand, delivers good fruit and intensity for the price. (PW)
● **Barolo★★★** £E Cerretta Piani★★★★ £E
● **Barbera d'Alba** Donatella★★ £C ● **Dolcetto d'Alba** Sorì Baudana★★ £B
● **Langhe** Lorenso★★★ £C ○ **Langhe Chardonnay★★** £B

BAVA Barbera d'Asti www.bava.com   A: BBR

Owner: Bava family Strada Monferrato 2, 14023 Cocconato d'Asti (AT)
Advertising and marketing have given this medium-sized producer a higher profile than many in Piedmont, despite its being closer to Torino than any of the leading wine towns. Barbera is the leading variety and usually impressive if not that cheap in the two top examples, Pianalto and Stradivario. Other wines, including Moscato d'Asti, are less exciting if typically sound, safe bets, although the sweet, fragrant, *frizzante* red Malvasia di Castelnuovo Don Bosco is fun if drunk very young. (PW)
● **Barbera d'Asti** Libera★ £C Arbest★ £C
● **Barbera d'Asti** Superiore Pianalto★★ £D Superiore Stradivario★★ £D
● **Malvasia di Castelnuovo Don Bosco★** £B ○ **Monferrato** Alteserre★ £C

BELLAVISTA Franciacorta www.bellavistasrl.it   A: Alv

Owner: Vittorio Moretti Via Bellavista 5, 25030 Erbusco (BS)
Under the direction of Vittorio Moretti and winemaker Mattia Vezzola, Bellavista make brilliant, refined yet full-flavoured sparkling wines that deservedly sell for the same prices as good non-vintage Champagne. Most include at least a component of barrel-fermentation to add further complexity. The non-vintage Brut Cuvée (predominantly Chardonnay with a little Pinot Noir and Pinot Blanc) is the most affordable, and made in by far the greatest quantities, of the DOCG Franciacorta. Gran Cuvée Brut is a step up, three parts Chardonnay to one of Pinot Noir. The Rosé is a sheer delight (60/40 Pinot Noir and Chardonnay) while the soft, creamy and delicately sparkling non-vintage Satèn is a lovely example of this low-pressure style. Pas Operé has no final addition of sugar, making it the driest of the range. A Riserva named after the owner has extended ageing on its lees (around six years). The still wines are sold under the Terre di Franciacorta DOC. The best of these is the rich, complex Chardonnay and Pinot Bianco blend, Convento della Santissima Annunciata. Varietal Chardonnay Uccellanda is rich and oaky while a Pinot Noir, Casotte, has good texture but is not among the best Italian examples (see North-East Italy). A powerful Cabernet/Merlot blend, Solesine, can show well with 5 to 10 years' age when from a warm vintage. None of the still wines offers particularly good value for money but try the very classy fizz at least. (PW)
○ **Franciacorta** Brut Cuvée★★ £D Gran Cuvée Brut★★★ £E
○ **Franciacorta** Gran Cuvée Pas Operé★★★ £E Gran Cuvée Satèn★★★ £E
◉ **Franciacorta** Gran Cuvée Brut Rosé★★★
○ **Terre di Franciacorta** Convento della Santissima Annunciata★★★ £E
○ **Terre di Franciacorta** Uccellanda★★ £E ● **Terre di Franciacorta** Rosso★ £C
● **Casotte★★** £E ● **Solesine★★** £E

BERTELLI Barbera d'Asti

Owner: Aldo & Alberto Bertelli   Fraz. San Carlo 38, 14055 Costiglione d'Asti (AT)
Aldo and his son Alberto make only a few barrels of this and that, but what there is can be very very good even if it isn't always so. Barbera aside, it's as if France (her grape varieties and a few oaks too) has come to Piedmont. Deep, rich and characterful Chardonnay is very powerful if sometimes slightly at the expense of better definition and expression. The Barberas are often rich, very ripe and always oaky, but in San Antonio Vieilles Vignes the marvellous old vine fruit depth easily contains the oak with a resultant complexity, seamless structure and a very long finish. Red I Fossaretti is a big, extracted Cabernet that usually works with plenty of age, while the white Fossaretti from Sauvignon Blanc is similarly in an outsized Bordeaux mould. St. Marsan is the label for a Rhône pair, the red a very intense Hermitage-like Syrah of marginal balance. The white, a Roussanne/Marsanne blend was produced in a one-off moderately sweet, rich (but balanced) style in 2000 from late-harvested grapes. Mon Mayor is usually a well-oaked but fruit-intense Nebbiolo/Cabernet but is not convincing in 99 (though better in 2000). Such occasional blips in the wines' technical soundness however, has done nothing to dampen the prices they command. Also made is Plissé from Gewürztraminer. (PW)
- **Barbera d'Asti** Giarone★★★ £E Montetusa★★★ £E San Antonio Vieilles Vignes★★★★ £E
- **Monferrato** I Fossaretti★★★ £E Mon Mayor★★★ £E
- ○ **Piemonte Chardonnay** Giarone★★★★ £E   ○ **Monferrato** I Fossaretti★★ £E
- **St Marsan**★★★ £E   ○ **St Marsan**★★★ £E

ENZO BOGLIETTI Barolo   A: **L&W**

Owner: Enzo & Gianni Boglietti   Via Roma 37, 12064 La Morra (CN)
A young grower with only a modest patchwork of vines but those sites include Brunate, Case Nere and Fossati (noted for Barbera as much as Nebbiolo). Full of fruit, oak-enriched, and with relatively soft but abundant tannin, these are good examples of the modern style – perhaps why the old-vine Barbera Vigna dei Romani (from Fossati) can impress almost as much as the Barolos. Fossati and Case Nere see a lot of new oak (50 and 80 per cent respectively) and the structure can suffer a little from the treatment, though there is better harmony with age. The classy Brunate, subject to only a small percentage of new oak but a longer maceration, is intense and compact when young but the most expressive and stylish of the three. All need 8 to 10 years' age. Ripe, potent Dolcetto Tiglineri oozes delicious old-vine fruit but needs a couple of years' age. Langhe Buio, Nebbiolo with some Barbera (80/20), spends 18 months in mostly new *barriques* but has considerable charm and style, especially with three or four years' age. (PW)
- **Barolo** Brunate★★★★★ £F Case Nere★★★★ £F Fossati★★★★ £F
- **Barbera d'Alba**★★ £B Vigna dei Romani★★★ £E Roscaleto★★★ £E
- **Dolcetto d'Alba**★ £B Tiglineri★★ £C   ● **Langhe Nebbiolo**★ £B   ● **Langhe** Buio★★★ £D

BONGIOVANNI Barolo   A: CeB, F&R

Owner: Davide Mozzoni   Via Alba-Barolo 4, 12060 Castiglione Falletto (CN)
Davide Mozzoni is not afraid to experiment and takes diverse approaches to making each of his Barolos. The regular version (from three different plots), subject to cold maceration and a short fermentation, is relatively light but modern with some charm. With Pernanno the total maceration is longer and the temperature allowed to rise to the mid-30s as the fermentation reaches completion. The extract, weight and richness evident on the palate is reinforced by ageing in (60 per cent) new *barriques*. Micro-oxygenation is employed for the two fruity Dolcettos; the more compact, structured Diano d'Alba deserves to be drunk with an extra year or two's age. Faletto (Cabernet, Merlot and Barbera) is fruit-rich and oaky. While these moderately priced wines are good rather than exciting, it will be interesting to see how the styles evolve. (PW)
- **Barolo**★★★ £E Pernanno★★★★ £E
- **Langhe** Faletto★★★ £D   ● **Barbera d'Alba**★★ £C
- **Dolcetto d'Alba**★★ £B   ● **Dolcetto di Diano d'Alba**★★ £B

BRAIDA Barbera d'Asti www.braida.it   A: **GFy, Bal**, Gau, L&W, BBR, N&P

Owner: Anna Bologna Via Roma 94, 14030 Rocchetta Tanaro (CN)
Plenty has been written about Giacomo Bologna, who was one of Piedmont's great characters as well as innovators. Bricco dell'Uccellone, first made in 1982, is the original oak-aged Barbera of outsized proportions. Bricco della Bigotta can often match it, while Ai Suma, which incorporates late-harvested grapes, can be even richer and more powerful. All should but don't always improve for a decade and my feeling is they are often best after six to eight years. There seems to be a real return to form from the late nineties but stick to the top vintages. Il Bacialé adds Pinot Nero to Barbera. Braida is also one of the Hastae six. Working with BERTA, CHIARLO, COPPO, PRUNOTTO and VIETTI, this is an Asti/Alba axis to promote Barbera. A single wine, Quorum, is made by Riccardo Cotarella. Rich, oaky and flattering, only with the 2001 vintage is it beginning to show the depth and style of the very best. The serious stuff aside, Barbera La Monella, Brachetto and Moscato are great examples of their effervescent type but the latter two (as ever with these styles) are best within six months of the vintage. (PW)

Braida:
● **Barbera d'Asti** Bricco della Bigotta★★★ £E Bricco dell' Uccellone★★★ £E Ai Suma★★★★ £F
● **Barbera del Monferrato** La Monella★ £B ● **Monferrato** Rosso Il Bacialé★★ £C
● **Brachetto d'Acqui**★★ £B O **Moscato d'Asti** Vigna Senza Nome★ £B
Hastae:
● **Barbera d'Asti** Quorum★★★★ £G

BRICCO MAIOLICA Dolcetto di Diano d'Alba www.briccomaiolica.it   A: **L&S**

Owner: Angelo Accomo Fraz. Ricca, Via Bolangino 7, 12055 Diano d'Alba (CN)
Beppe Accomo's 20-ha estate is arguably the best in this zone, rivalled only by that of Claudio ALARIO. Nebbiolo, like CORREGGIA'S or CASCINA CHICCO'S (both in Roero), is one of the few in the Langhe outside Barolo and Barbaresco to be taken seriously. Then there are really good examples of Barbera and Dolcetto too. The oak in the best wines is taken up by decent ripe, intense fruit and consistently so. The Briccolero Barbera in fact doesn't see any wood, while the Vigna Vigia receives 50 per cent new, 50 per cent used and Il Cumot Nebbiolo is put in 'second use' *barriques*. There is splendid fruit in both Dolcettos; the *cru* has a little more amplitude and some gentle spice from six months in used wood. The oak-influenced white Langhe combines Chardonnay and Sauvignon, wile the red Langhe Lorié is one of the best Piedmont Pinots made. First made in 2001 is a new varietal Merlot, Filius – a rare Piemontese example of the grape. (PW)

● **Nebbiolo d'Alba** Il Cumot★★★ £D
● **Barbera d'Alba** Briccolero★★ £B Vigna Vigia★★★ £D
● **Dolcetto di Diano d'Alba**★ £B Sorì Bricco Maiolica★★ £C
● **Langhe** Lorié★★ £D O **Langhe** Rolando★★ £C

BROVIA Barolo www.brovia.net   A: **VDu**, Gau, Bat

Owner: Brovia family Via Alba-Barolo 54, 12060 Castiglione Falletto (CN)
Sisters Elena and Cristina Brovia, aided by their father Giacinto, regularly produce full, muscular but ageworthy Barolo from local plots and another (Cà Mia) in Serralunga, all without the aid of small new oak barrels. Instead, large 3,000-litre French oak is used following a relatively long maceration of around 20 days. The elegance of Rocche (di Castiglione) may be contrasted with the intensity of Villero or the build of Ca' Mia. *Barriques* are reserved for Dolcetto, especially the remarkable Solatio. Late-harvested, this purple, high-ethanol monster is typically deep, smooth and balanced. Scarce it is, but like those from other champions of intense Dolcetto (CA' VIOLA, MARCARINI, G MASCARELLO, VAJRA *et al*) it deserves to be tasted. Barberas are good too. Through the efforts of Elena's husband, Alex Sanchez, who hails from Cataluña, this fine range should become more widely seen. (PW)
● **Barolo** Ca' Mia★★★★ £F Rocche dei Brovia★★★★ £F Villero★★★★ £F

● **Barbera d'Alba** Brea★★★ £E Sorì del Drago★★ £D
● **Dolcetto d'Alba** Vignavillej★★ £C Solatio★★★ £E

BUSSIA SOPRANA Barolo

Owner: S Casiraghi & G Rossi Loc. Bussia 81, 12065 Monforte d'Alba (CN)
Silvano Casiraghi has a minority stake in some of the *crus* made famous by ALDO CONTERNO. Excellent Barolos are produced from part of 22 ha of vineyards. The wines have been particularly good since the mid-nineties; the 99s the best of the most recent vintages. Lesser-known Mosconi, from the south of the commune, is in a more rugged, powerful style that provides an interesting contrast with the more mellow Bussia and refined Colonello. (PW)
● **Barolo** Bussia★★★ £F Mosconi★★★ £F Vigna Colonello★★★★ £F
● **Barbera d'Alba**★ £C Vin del Ross★★ £D ● **Dolcetto d'Alba**★ £C

PIERO BUSSO Barbaresco   A: Goe

Owner: Piero Busso Via Albesani 8, 12057 Neive (CN)
Piero Busso controls 8 ha from the heart of the Neive commune and believes in a natural expression of each variety and the importance of place (or *tipicità*). He has little time for technology but does use *barriques* (50 per cent new) for Barbaresco Bricco Mondino. While the oak does show in this *cru*, all the wines have classic perfumes and structure typical to their variety and add richness and complexity with age. At least six to eight years' is needed for the Barbarescos. New from 1999 is a third *cru*, Gallina. Dolcetto and Barbera sometimes struggle for full ripeness and usually need a year or two to soften. The Langhe white is a blend of Chardonnay and Sauvignon Blanc, the Chardonnay component fermented and aged in *barrique*, while not special it will keep at least three to four years. New from 2000 vintage is another promising Barbaresco, San Stefanetto. (PW)
● **Barbaresco** Bricco Mondino★★ £E Vigna Borgese★★★ £E
● **Barbera d'Alba** Vigna Majano★★ £C ● **Dolcetto d'Alba**Vigna Majano★ £B
O **Langhe** Bianco di Busso★ £C

CA' DEL BOSCO Franciacorta www.cadelbosco.com   A: Eno, N&P

Owner: Santa Margherita group Via Case Sparse 20, 25030 Erbusco (BS)
Maurizio Zanella was one of Italy's modern pioneers for quality wine and was already receiving wide acclaim by the early 1980s. Now one of two outstanding, prestigious Franciacorta sparkling wine producers, Maurizio continues to direct and inspire. While BELLAVISTA sparkling wines are at least as good, the still wines here remain a good notch or two higher. Pinèro (Pinot Nero or Pinot Noir), the Bordeaux blend, Maurizio Zanella, and Chardonnay have more competition than a decade ago but remain among the best Italian examples. The most recent innovation is Carmenero, a varietal Carmenère and a first for Italy (though it seems likely that, as in Chile, there could be a good deal of this variety planted, particularly in the North-East). Red and white Curtefranca (previously Terre di Franciacorta) are also good. All the grapes are estate-grown from some 140 ha of vineyard. For the sparklers, fermentation of the base wine is finished in *barrique* following by some ageing before the second fermentation. The regular Brut combines Chardonnay, Pinot Blanc and a little Pinot Noir, while the Rosé is more Pinot Noir-based. As at BELLAVISTA there's a very fine Satèn but the finest sparkler is the rich, complex, mouthfilling Cuvée Annamaria Clementi. Only the regular Brut is non-vintage. Prices have always been high. (PW)
O **Franciacorta** Brut Non-Vintage★★ £D Brut Vintage★★ £E
O **Franciacorta** Dosage Zero★★★ £E Cuvée Annamaria Clementi★★★★ £F
O **Franciacorta** Satèn★★★ £F ◉ **Franciacorta** Rosé★★ £E
O **Terre di Franciacorta Chardonnay**★★★★ £F
O **Curtefranca Bianco**★ £C ● **Curtefranca Rosso**★★ £C
● **Carmenero**★★★ £F ● **Maurizio Zanella**★★★★ £F ● **Pinero**★★★ £F

CASCINA CHICCO Roero www.cascinachicco.com

Owner: Enrico & Marco Faccenda Via Roma 80, 12043 Canale (CN)
The Faccenda brothers, Enrico and Marco, have 20 ha from which a broad range of good-quality Langhe wines are produced. An excellent Barbera is usually better than anything else – a suave, spicy and scented Bric Loira that is aged in *barriques*. However in the best years for Nebbiolo this is rivalled by a fine Roero Valmaggiore that once again shows the refinement and expression possible from this appellation. Nebbiolo d'Alba Mompissano can show similar flair when the conditions are right. Roero Arneis can be good too while Arcass is an attractive, aromatic sweet version of Arneis. (PW)

● **Barbera d'Alba★** £B Granera Alta★★ £C Bric Loira★★★ £D
● **Roero** Mulino della Costa★★ £C Valmaggiore★★★ £D
○ **Roero Arneis** Anterisio★ £B
● **Nebbiolo d'Alba** Mompissano★★ £C

CASCINA VAL DEL PRETE Roero

Owner: Mario Roagna Strada Santuario 2, 12040 Priocca (CN)
Mario Roagna has transformed the grapes from 8 ha of family vineyards into a small fine range of wines in recent years, maximising the potential from a natural amphitheatre of vines first worked, then purchased back in 1977, by his late father, Lino (Bartolomeo). A delightful fruit-driven, unoaked regular Barbera contrasts with Carolina (named for his mother) which comes from a single parcel of vines and is aged for 16 months in new *barriques*. The oak is evident but there is fabulous style to its smoke and plum richness too. A small amount of Roero has been made since 1998 though its oak/fruit balance is more marginal. Better is the Nebbiolo expression in Vigna di Lino; vintages such as 2000 and 01 should be super with five years' age or more. Arneis has more weight and structure than usual and will keep a year or two. Quantities are small, even the bigger-volume Arneis and Barbera *normale* don't much exceed 1,000 cases each. (PW)

● **Barbera d'Alba★★** £B Superiore Carolina★★★ £C ● **Roero★★** £C
● **Nebbiolo d'Alba** Vigna di Lino★★★ £C ○ **Roero Arneis** Luèt★★ £B

CA' VIOLA Dolcetto d'Alba www.caviola.com   A: **HHB**, NYg, Sel

Owner: Giuseppe Caviola Borgata San Luigi 11, 12063 Dogliani (CN)
Beppe Caviola has given many a small *Piemontesi* grower the technical help to produce wines of the standard to ensure they are in demand both in Italy and abroad. More recently his expertise has also been sought throughout Italy including by UMANI RONCHI in the Marche. Though a modernist, he earns respect particularly because he doesn't impose a formula but adapts his expertise to the philosophy of the individual producer. Ca' Viola is his own range of wines. Though now based in Dogliani most of his grapes are sourced from Montelupo Albese (between Barolo and Barbaresco). The wines are ripe, lush and fruit-rich, very easy to drink but with good structure. Foremost is the excellent Bric du Luv, a consistently fine *barrique*-aged Barbera, but fine Dolcetto is also made in two versions. Barturot is the best selection from old vines, subtly enhanced by oak, and shows great depth and intensity, while Vilot is in a fruity, quaffing style. Rangone was produced from Pinot Nero but the fruit now (from 2000) goes into a version of L'Insieme which includes Barbera and Nebbiolo. (PW)

● **Dolcetto d'Alba★** £B Barturot★★ £C Vilot★ £C
● **Langhe** Bric du Luv★★★ £E Rangone★★ £E

CASTELLO DI CALOSSO Barbera d'Asti www.castellodicalosso.it   A: **Orb**

Owner: (an association of producers) Piazza del Castello 7, 14052 Calosso (AT)
What do you do if you have at most a few hectares and produce high quality Barbera d'Asti but need a stronger identity while still making your wine? The 10 growers of the Castello di Calosso all have a small parcel of old-vine Barbera (ranging from 40 to 70 years old) but share the same label under which they

promote their own bottlings. The standard is high but not uniform and stylistically there are important differences too. While one or two struggle for balance nearly all are concentrated with a measure of oak and have a rich, ripe fruit intensity as well as impressive breadth and length. The growers (or estates) followed by their single-vineyard Barberas are: Livio Sorin and Giorgio Pavia's Due Colline (Rodotiglia), Maurizio Domanda (Crevacuore), Fabio Fidanza (Sterlino), Giorgio Fogliati (La Cascinetta), Mauro Grasso (Sant' Anna), Renzo Grasso (Camp Màina), Aldo and Giuseppe Bussi's La Badia (Belletta), Ignazio Giovine's L'ARMANGIA (Vignali), Roberto Paschina (Musiano) and TENUTA DEI FIORI (Rusticardi). Some of these make other wines of a standard to be worthy of a separate entry in the future. (PW)

- **Barbera d'Asti** Musiano Roberto Paschina★★★ £E Sant'Anna Mauro Grasso★★★ £E
- **Barbera d'Asti** Camp Màina Renzo Grasso★★★ £E Rodotiglia Due Colline★★★ £E
- **Barbera d'Asti** Sterlino Fidanza★★★ £E Crevacuore Domanda★★★ £E
- **Barbera d'Asti** Belletta La Badia★★★ £E La Cascinetta Giorgio Fogliati★★★★ £E
- **Barbera d'Asti** Vignali L'Armangia★★★ £D Rusticardi Tenuta dei Fiori★★★ £E

CAUDRINA Moscato d'Asti www.caudrina.it

Owner: Romano Dogliotti Strada Brosia 20, 12053 Castiglione Tinella (CN)
Moscato d'Asti may not age but Romano Dogliotti has been making some of the finest examples for over 20 years. He applied new technologies to grapes (off steep slopes to the east of Barbaresco) first vinified by his father. Wonderfully fragrant with apple, citrus, grape and musk scents, the intense, tangy La Galeisa is exquisite when drunk with just a few months' bottle-age. Barbera d'Asti is increasingly good too (in both versions), while oaked Chardonnay and a very good fully sparkling Asti are also made. (PW)

- **Barbera d'Asti** La Solista★ £C Superiore Montevenere★★ £D
- O **Moscato d'Asti** La Caudrina★★ £B La Galeisa★★★ £C
- O **Asti** La Selvatica★★ £C
- O **Piemonte Chardonnay** Mej★ £C

CAVALLOTTO Barolo www.cavallotto.com   A: **Goe**

Owner: Olivio & Gildo Cavalotto Loc. Bricco Boschis, 12060 Castiglione Falletto (CN)
Cavallotto's 23 ha of vineyard constitute the Bricco Boschis estate. In the past Cavallotto's wines have tended to lack excitement but the input of a new generation, Olivio Cavallotto's two sons and daughter, are having an impact and the most recent releases have made the most of nature's beneficence. A traditionally minded producer, Cavallotto ages the wines in large Slavonian oak casks. The money saved by not buying new oak seems to have been invested instead in more care in the vineyard (which includes the 2.5 ha solely owned Vigna San Giuseppe) and winery. Barolos recommended from 1997. (PW)

- **Barolo** Bricco Boschis★★ £E Riserva Vignolo★★ £F
- **Barolo** Riserva Bricco Boschis Vigna San Giuseppe★★★ £F
- **Dolcetto d'Alba** Vigna Melera★ £B Vigna Scot★ £B   ● **Langhe Freisa★** £C

CERETTO Barolo www.ceretto.com   A: **AWW**, Maj, N&P

Owner: Bruno & Marcello Ceretto Loc. San Cassiano 34, 12051 Alba (CN)
In the 1970s Ceretto evolved from an old-style merchant house into a modern one owning most of its grape sources. Of the many fabulous sites, the most famous perhaps is the Bricco Asili *cru*, (confusingly nearly all the Barbarescos produced carry this name) but it is in Barolo's Bricco Rocche (which adjoins Villero in Castiglione Falletto), Prapò and Brunate that the brothers Ceretto usually have their top wines. Each property is overseen from the impressive headquarters at the La Bernadina estate where Riesling (Arbarei), and also Cabernet, Merlot and Pinot Nero (the three combined in Monsordo Rosso with a little Nebbiolo) are vinified. New oak is used in all the top wines, which when on form are sleek and concentrated but veer towards being hard and lean when not. 1997 and 1999 Barolos are the most recommended of recent releases. (PW)

● **Barolo** Zonchera★★ £F Brunate★★★★ £F Prapò★★★★ £F Bricco Rocche★★★★ £H
● **Barbaresco** Asij★★ £G Bernadot★★ £G Fasêt★★ £F Bricco Asili★★★ £H
● **Langhe** Monsordo★★ £E O **Langhe Arneis** Blangé★ £C
● **Barbera d'Alba** Piana★ £D ● **Dolcetto d'Alba** Rossana★ £B
● **Nebbiolo d'Alba** Lantasco★ £D O **Piemonte** Brut La Bernardina★ £D

MICHELE CHIARLO Barolo www.chiarlo.it A: **Hal**, Odd

Owner: Michele Chiarlo Stada Nizza-Canelli 99, 14042 Calamandrana (AT)
With 110 ha, Chiarlo is one of the most substantial vineyard owners in Piedmont. A major part of this is
for Barbera d'Asti production but it also includes some top *crus* for Nebbiolo and a chunk of Gavi. While
the wines are competently made it is often the Barberas (particularly the consistently fine La Court) and
Monferrato reds that impress as much as the Barbaresco and Barolos. The latter despite their origins, can
seem a little inelegant when tasted alongside their peers. Of recent releases such as the 99s the Cerequio
shows the most purity and style, as well as balance. Barbaresco Asili shows fine quality too but is deceptive
in its accessibility, and like the Barolos needs time for the tannic backbone to soften. Often encountered are
the Monferrato reds, the seductive Countacc! from Cabernet Sauvignon, Nebbiolo and Barbera, and
moderately priced Airone from Barbera, Cabernet and Shiraz. (PW)
● **Barolo** Cannubi★★★ £F Brunate★★★ £F Cerequio★★★★ £F
● **Barbaresco** Asili★★★ £F ● **Barbera d'Asti Nizza** Superiore La Court★★★ £D
● **Barbera d'Asti** Superiore Le Orme★★ £B Cipressi della Court★★ £B
● **Monferrato** Montemareto Countacc!★★★ £D Airone★★ £B
O **Gavi del Comune del Gavi** Fornaci di Tassarolo★ £C
O **Moscato d'Asti** Rocca dell'Uccellette★★ £C Nivole★★ £C

QUINTO CHIONETTI Dolcetto di Dogliani www.chionettiquinto.com

Owner: Quinto Chionetti Fraz. San Luigi, 12063 Dogliani (CN)
The benchmark producer in Dogliani now has plenty of competition (Anna Maria ABBONA, M&E
ABBONA, Luigi EINAUDI, PECCHENINO and others). Of some 14 ha, six are designated Briccolero, but
these are often given a close run by the rest, sold as San Luigi. Both are delicious, perfumed, full of fruit and
best with one to two years' age. (PW)
● **Dolcetto di Dogliani** Briccolero★★★ £C San Luigi★★★ £C

FRATELLI CIGLIUTI Barbaresco A: **M&V, BBR**, PWa, The, P&S

Owner: Renato Cigliuti Via Serraboella 17, 12057 Neive (CN)
The *cru* of Serraboella occupies slopes south-east of, and across from the town of Neive. It is shared between
Cigliuti and PAITIN. Of Renato Cigliuti's six hectares, 2.5 with a south-west aspect are planted to Nebbiolo.
The resultant Barbaresco shows the craft of a dedicated grower. Concentrated, it shows some oak influence
and quite powerful but ripe tannnins which enable it to improve for a decade or more. Briccoserra (a
Barbera/Nebbiolo blend sourced mostly from the nearby Bricco vineyards), Dolcetto and Barbera rarely
disappoint. A small part of Serraboella's Barbera fruit has been bottled as Campass since 2000 while new
from the 1999 vintage is another very promising Barbaresco, Vigna Erte. (PW)
● **Barbaresco** Serraboella★★★★ £E
● **Barbera d'Alba** Serraboella★★ £C Campass★★★ £C
● **Langhe** Briccoserra★★★ £E ● **Dolcetto d'Alba** Serraboella★ £C

DOMENICO CLERICO Barolo A: **J&B**, P&S, NYg, F&R

Owner: Domenico Clerico Loc. Manzoni 67, 12065 Monforte d'Alba (CN)
Domenico Clerico shot to prominence in the 1980s and has been one of Barolo's most consistent superstars
ever since. Even from the miserable early 90s, the wines stand out. Maceration times are relatively short and

most of the small oak is new but the wines don't lack for stuffing or structure. Clerico has built up 19 ha, more than 40 per cent of it for three fabulous Barolos. The Ginestra *cru* provides both classy Ciabot Mentin Ginestra and more international Pajana; Mosconi, a stone's throw to the south, the rich, fleshy Per Cristina. Also very worthy, in descending order of value for money, are Barbera, Dolcetto and Arte (*barrique*-aged, 90 per cent Nebbiolo topped up with Barbera and, since 99, Cabernet too). (PW)

● **Barolo** Ciabot Mentin Ginestra★★★★★ £F   Pajana★★★★★ £F   Riserva Per Cristina★★★★★ £F
● **Langhe** Arte★★★ £E   ● **Langhe Dolcetto** Visadì★★ £B
● **Barbera d'Alba** Trevigne★★★ £C

ELVIO COGNO   Barolo   www.elviocogno.com   A: PaV

Owner: Nadia Cogno & Valter Fissore   Loc. Ravera 2, 12060 Novello (CN)
Wedged against the Monforte and Barolo communes in the south-west of the Barolo zone is a decent chunk of the Novello commune. Its sole significant and historic *cru*, Ravera, is given expression by both Cogno and M&E ABBONA. From their 9 ha of vineyard, Nadia Cogno's husband, Walter Fissore, makes robustly flavoured wines with an extra intensity to the fruit than most. All are deep, well-balanced and benefit from a little extra bottle-age. Ravera, with a muted *barrique* influence, assumes an earthy, truffly, savoury complexity with even a little age. Rich, powerful Barolo Vigna Elena, first made in 1997, is unusual in being produced solely from the Rosé clone of Nebbiolo. Montegrilli is a *barrique*-aged blend, half Nebbiolo and half Barbera. Nas-cetta is from the obscure local grape Nascetta, a portion of the grapes *barrique*-fermented and aged; it is attractively perfumed and gently creamy. (PW)

● **Barolo** Ravera★★★ £E   Vigna Elena★★★★ £E
● **Barbera d'Alba** Bricco dei Merli★★ £C
● **Dolcetto d'Alba** Vigna del Mandorlo★ £B   ● **Langhe** Montegrilli★★ £D
O **Nas-cetta**★★ £B

ALDO CONTERNO   www.poderialdoconterno.com   A: Lib, ACh, Maj, Vne, V&C, F&M

Owner: Aldo Conterno   Loc. Bussia 48, 12065 Monforte d'Alba (CN)
It is now 35 years since Aldo Conterno set out on his own (leaving the family estate of Giacomo Conterno to his brother Giovanni) but even by the late 1980s he had already established a house of formidable reputation (and inspiration). The style of Barolo is considered traditional because they are aged in large Slavonian oak but aspects of their vinification are more modern. The wines from 25 ha of estate vineyards are made by sons Franco and Stefano. All, but particularly Cicala, Colonello and Granbussia (a Riserva selection of all plots), show lovely style and dimension on the palate, and the ensuing complexity and nuance most other examples miss. *Barriques* come into play for Barbera, Chardonnay Bussiador and Langhe blends Il Favot (Nebbiolo) and Quartetto (Nebbiolo, Barbera, Cabernet and Merlot). Printanié (a second Chardonnay) and Dolcetto are unoaked. (PW)

● **Barolo** Bussia★★★★ £F   Cicala❂❂❂❂❂ £G
● **Barolo** Colonello❂❂❂❂❂ £G   Riserva Granbussia❂❂❂❂❂ £H
● **Langhe** Il Favot★★★ £E   Quartetto★★★ £E
O **Langhe** Bussiador★★★ £D   Printanié★ £C
● **Barbera d'Alba** Conca Tre Pile★★★ £D   ● **Dolcetto d'Alba**★ £B

GIACOMO CONTERNO   Barolo   A: JAr

Owner: G Conterno family   Loc. Ornati 2, 12065 Monforte d'Alba (CN)
Giovanni Conterno, whose signature was the legendary Monfortino Barolo Riserva, died early in 2004. Younger son Roberto now continues the 'traditional' work made famous by his father. Long maceration times (five to six weeks) and extended ageing (six to seven years) in large, old oak barrels are two essential elements, producing a wine of sometimes unequalled intensity, power and longevity. Cascina Francia, a little easier to obtain, is also a great wine. Though there has been some moderation in the winemaking, the wines still show great breadth, intensity and persistence in a robust and tannic style: macho Barolo. Gutsy

Dolcetto and Barbera are true to the house style. (PW)

● **Barolo** Cascina Francia★★★★★ £G Riserva Monfortino✪✪✪✪✪ £H
● **Barbera d'Alba**★★ £D ● **Dolcetto d'Alba**★★ £C

CONTERNO-FANTINO Barolo www.conternofantino.it A: **Eno**, N&P, NYg

Owner: G Fantino & C Conterno Via Ginestra 1, 12065 Monforte d'Alba (CN)
A partnership that serves as a beacon to others determined to producer flawless, modern-style Barolos. The rich and complete Sorì Ginestra is a great wine if not quite among Barolo's élite. Vigna del Gris is almost at the same level and can show a more floral, exquisite perfume but just misses the extra depth and structure of Sorì Ginestra. Parussi is new from 1997. Monprà (Nebbiolo/Barbera Cabernet) is a usually a good example of the *barrique*-aged Langhe blend, while the Chardonnay is one of the better Piedmont examples. (PW)

● **Barolo** Sorì Ginestra★★★★★ £F Vigna del Gris★★★★ £F Vigna Parussi★★★ £E
● **Langhe** Monprà★★★ £E O **Langhe Chardonnay** Bastia★★★ £D
● **Barbera d'Alba** Vignota★★ £C ● **Dolcetto d'Alba** Bricco Bastia★★ £B

CONTRATTO Asti www.contratto.it A: **Vex**

Owner: C & A Micca-Bocchino Via G B Giuliani 56, 14053 Canelli (AT)
A producer of Asti in the 19th century Contratto has been rejuvenated following its purchase in 1994 by the Bocchino Grappa house. Winemaker Giancarlo Scaglione (FORTETO DELLA LUJA) has revived the production of a vineyard-specific Asti (De Miranda) made by a variation on the traditional or Champagne method. This elegant, wonderfully perfumed sparkler will actually keep a year or two. A number of other *metodo classico* wines are made from Pinot Nero and Chardonnay. Barolo Cerequio and Barbera Solus Ad are modern and well-made and if previously lacking a little individuality show greater depth and more character in the most recent releases. (PW)

● **Barolo** Cerequio Secolo★★★★ £F
● **Barbera d'Asti** Panta Rei★ £B Solus Ad★★★ £D
O **Piemonte** Chardonnay Sabauda★ £C
O **Asti** De Miranda★★★ £C O **Brut Riserva Giuseppe Contratto**★★ £D

LUIGI COPPO & FIGLI Barbera d'Asti www.coppo.it A: **Res**

Owner: Coppo family Via Alba 68, 14053 Canelli (AT)
Brilliant Barberas have been made here for a number of years. Pomorosso is a deep, rich and complex example and often among the best made, it shows what a match good Barbera fruit is for new oak. Other Barbera can be good but are not of the same order but Alterego (Cabernet/Barbera) adds more richness in late 90s vintages and Mondaccione is one of the few serious still, dry Freisas (see also VAJRA). Also notable are one of the best oak-fermented and aged Piedmont Chardonnays (Monteriolo) and ripe fizz. Pricey but impressive Riserva della Famiglia Barbera d'Asti is released with a little more age (as is a Chardonnay equivalent). (PW)

● **Barbera d'Asti** Pomorosso★★★★ £E Camp du Rouss★★ £C L'Avvocata★ £B
● **Langhe** Mondaccione★★ £C ● **Monferrato** Alterego★★★ £D
O **Piemonte Chardonnay** Costebianche★ £B Monteriolo★★★ £D
O **Riserva Brut** Coppo★★ £C

CORDERO DI MONTEZEMOLO Barolo www.corderodimontezemolo.com A: **Eur**

Owner: G & E Cordero di Montezemolo Fraz. Annunziata 67, 12064 La Morra (CN)
Well-directed estate with modern, pristine cellars, drawing on 29 ha of vineyard (much of it owned) centred on the spur of Monfalletto in Annunziata. The property has been transformed over two decades and the wines since 1995 are impressive. Maceration times are now very short and there is much experimentation

with different types of new oak but the approach remains flexible. It remains to be seen how well the current crop of fine vintages will age. Enrico VI shows the class of the Villero *cru* in Castiglione Falletto, while a promising Bricco Gattera from the Lebanese cedar-topped knoll of Monfalletto has been made since 1997. Barbera Funtanì is very good *barrique*-aged example while Curdè is an estate blended red from Pinot Nero, Barbera and Nebbiolo. New is a Barolo Riserva Gorette. (PW)

● **Barolo** Monfalletto★★★ £E Bricco Gattera★★★★ £F Enrico VI★★★★ £F
● **Barbera d'Alba★** £C Superiore Funtanì★★★ £D
● **Dolcetto d'Alba★** £B
○ **Langhe Arneis★** £B ○ **Langhe Chardonnay** Elioro★ £C

GIOVANNI CORINO Barolo   A: J&B, F&R

Owner: Giovanni Corino Fraz. Annunziata 24, 12064 La Morra (CN)
Another producer of the Annunziata sub-zone in La Morra making modern-styled, fruit-rich Barolo. Since the mid-1980s brothers Renato and Giuliano have highlighted the quality inherent in Giachini, a small 3.5-ha *cru*, immediately east of Rocche dell'Annunziata. Raspberry, coffee and earth are typical aromas, the tannins tight but ripe. As well as several other Barolo *crus* made in small quantities, Vecchie Vigne is a superior selection made since 1997 and is deep and powerful with great cellaring potential. New since 99 is another Barolo, Roncaglie. Many of the modern vanguard produce excellent Barbera and Corino is no exception. Insieme is pretty good here too (see ALTARE), this one mostly Nebbiolo and Barbera with a little Cabernet and Merlot. (PW)

● **Barolo★★** £E Arborina★★★ £F Giachini★★★ £F Rocche★★★★ £F Vecchie Vigne★★★★ £H
● **Barbera d'Alba★** £B Pozzo★★★ £E ● **Dolcetto d'Alba★** £B ● **Insieme★★★** £F

MATTEO CORREGGIA Roero www.matteocorreggia.com   A: J&B, Sav

Owner: Ornella Correggia Cascina Garbinetto 124, 12043 Canale (CN)
Roero's inspirational grower died tragically in June 2001. His legacy from 14 years of undinting effort is Nebbiolo and Barbera of unprecedented quality from the 'other' (northern) side of the River Tanaro. Ornella Correggia is now assisted by Luca Rostagnano in her efforts to maintain quality. Both Nebbiolo and Barbera undergo a relatively short maceration before being aged in new oak. Like others of modernist leanings who have really succeeded, there is a density and quality to the fruit that ensure the wines have real character, structure and aroma. The dense, powerful *cru* Roero red, made since 1996, is consistently very impressive while a new Langhe blend, Le Marne Grigie was released from the 2000 vintage. It combines Nebbiolo and Barbera with Cabernet Sauvignon, Cabernet Franc and Merlot. Also made is Anthos, a dry version of Brachetto, and Langhe Bianco, an oak-aged Sauvignon. (PW)

● **Roero★** £B Ròche d'Ampsèj★★★ £E ○ **Roero Arneis★** £B
● **Nebbiolo d'Alba** La Val di Preti★★★ £D
● **Barbera d'Alba** Marun★★★ £D

LUIGI EINAUDI Dolcetto di Dogliani www.podereieinaudi.com   A: L&S, Bal

Owner: P & R Einaudi Borgata Gombe 31, 12063 Dogliani (CN)
This estate was made famous by the first president of the Italian republic, but has been recently reinvigorated by Paola Einaudi and her husband Giorgio Ruffo. Though Dogliani-based, with 30 ha of Dolcetto vineyards, other plots provide grapes for top-flight Barolo. Costa Grimaldi from 1997, 98 or 99 is a very complete and harmonious Barolo with great intensity and a match for that from the recently acquired Cannubi vines. Both show real class and have excellent cellaring potential. Dense, intense Dolcetto needs a year or two but the *crus* are consistently among the best of the zone. The fruit-rich, oak-aged Langhe Luigi Einaudi blends Cabernet, Nebbiolo, Barbera and Merlot. (PW)

● **Barolo★★★** £E Costa Grimaldi★★★★ £E Nei Cannubi★★★★ £F
● **Langhe Nebbiolo★★** £C ● **Langhe** Luigi Einaudi★★★ £E ● **Piemonte Barbera★★★** £C
● **Dolcetto di Dogliani★** £B I Filari★★★ £C Vigna Tecc★★★ £C

FONTANAFREDDA Barolo www.fontanafredda.it A: **Eno**, JNi, NYg, V&C, Hrd

Owner: Monte dei Paschi di Siena Bank Via Alba 15, 12050 Serralunga d'Alba (CN)
Directed by Giovanni Minetti, Fontanafredda is one of the heavyweights of the Barolo region. Tenementi Fontanafredda refers specifically to the premium wines, now being bottled with new labels in heavy bottles. Many vineyards are owned, particularly in Serralunga where the massive winery complex is found, but much is bought in too. Some poor past performances seem to have been put behind them as the whole range of wines has been recently much improved. From 1997, 98 and 99 the Barolos are significantly different, much more modern and expressive in style. The most perfumed, La Villa, is from the Barolo commune, while deeper La Rosa and more structured Lazzarito are from Serralunga. The latter has been combined with La Delizia from 99. Barbera Papagena and Dolcetto di Diano d'Alba are the best-value wines, but Barolo Serralunga is reasonably priced too. Decent *metodo classico* sparklers are rather better than the ubiquitous Asti. New Moscato d'Asti, Moncucco is also very good, with classic intensity and exotic grapiness. (PW)

● **Barolo** Serralunga d'Alba★★★ £D Vigna La Villa★★★ £F Vigna La Rosa★★★★ £F
● **Barolo** Vigna La Delizia★★★ £F Vigna Lazzarito★★★★ £F ● **Barbaresco** Coste Rubin★★★ £D
● **Barbera d'Alba** Papagena★★ £C ● **Langhe** Eremo★ £B
● **Dolcetto di Diano d'Alba** Vigna La Lepre★★ £B O **Moscato d'Asti** Moncucco★★ £B

FORTETO DELLA LUJA Loazzolo A: **Vim**

Owner: Giancarlo Scaglione Regione Bricco, Borgata Rosso, 14050 Loazzolo (AT)
Giancarlo Scaglione has put more than a few producers on the map. One wine, a late-harvest (Vendemmia Tardiva) Muscat (with its distinctive 'wound ribbon' label) was until recently what both this tiny DOC and its producer were all about. Production is now in the hands of son Gianni. Half the grapes are dried and half are late-harvested and botrytis-affected. A slow, very extended fermentation adds an oxidative component and honey, nuts and dried figs complement a rich fruit core. Other unusual but good-quality wines include a late-harvest Brachetto and a partly *barrique*-aged blend of Barbera and Pinot Nero, Le Grive. (PW)

O **Loazzolo** Piasa Rischei★★★ £E
O **Moscato d'Asti** Piasa San Maurizio★ £C
● **Monferrato** Le Grive★★ £D ● **Piemonte Brachetto** Forteto Pian dei Sogni★★ £E

GAJA Barbaresco A: **L&W**, JAr, Maj, P&S, NYg, V&C, Hrd, F&M

Owner: Angelo Gaja Via Torino 36 A, 12050 Barbaresco (CN)
Piedmont's *numero uno*, Gaja has been a veritable phenomenon in the pursuit of quality and the promotion of his native region. Consumption of the the the often stupendous single-vineyard wines, especially the trio from Barbaresco vineyards but also Sperss, is pretty much restricted to the wealthy. The first to be made (from 1967) was Sorì San Lorenzo; the most austere in its youth, it is based on the Secondine *cru*. Both Sorì Tildin (made from 1970, the year winemaker Giudo Rivella arrived), often the richest and deepest, and the more forward Costa Russi (1978) derive from the Roncagliette *cru*. Sperss, the ex-Barolo, is sourced from the Marenca and Rivette *crus* in Serralunga. All these former Barbaresco and Barolo *crus* may now include a very small percentage of Barbera. The most notable other wine for me is the Gaia e Rey Chardonnay, rich and expressive without mimicking the classic Burgundian style. Interestingly it is fermented in stainless steel before being aged for six to eight months in oak *barriques* of mixed European origin. Darmagi is pure Cabernet while Sito Rey is from Barbera. Sito Moresco combines Nebbiolo, Merlot and Barbera. This trio of reds are also of good quality if missing the hallmarks of greatness. Gaja, it would seem, only needs time before reaching the peak of whichever vinous summit he attempts. Brunello (PIEVE SANTA RESTITUTA) is now (since 1995) showing the Gaja stamp of elegance together with characteristic breadth and structure. CA' MARCANDA will shift the spotlight to Bolgheri. Quantities of the top wines remains small and the prices necessarily high. (PW)

● **Barbaresco**✪✪✪✪✪ £H
● **Langhe Nebbiolo** Costa Russi★★★★★ £H Sorì San Lorenzo✪✪✪✪✪ £H Sorì Tildin✪✪✪✪ £H
● **Langhe Nebbiolo** Sperss✪✪✪✪✪ £H Conteisa★★★★★ £H
● **Langhe Rosso** Darmagi★★★ £H Sito Moresco★★★ £D Sito Rey★★★ £F
O **Langhe Chardonnay** Gaia e Rey★★★★ £G Rossj-Bass★★★ £E

FILIPPO GALLINO Roero   A: Gau

Owner: Gianni Gallino   Valle del Pozzo 63, 12043 Canale d'Alba (CN)
Production here is confined to red and white Roero and Barbera but quality has shot up and like
CORREGGIA, CASCINA CHICCO or MALVIRÀ shows what's possible from the best of Roero's soils. The
Gallino family now have 12 ha of vineyards and production of around 5,000 cases has increased a little from
2003. Both Barbera and Nebbiolo are strengths, the Superiore versions, in particular, are increasingly full
but well-structured with fine tannins. (PW)
● **Barbera d'Alba**★ £B ● **Barbera d'Alba** Superiore★★★ £C
● **Roero**★ £B Superiore★★★ £C
O **Roero Arneis**★ £B

ETTORE GERMANO Barolo www.germanoettore.com   A: Ast, P&S

Owner: Sergio Germano   Loc. Cerretta 1, 12050 Serralunga d'Alba (CN)
Compared to La Morra, Serralunga is somewhat bereft of top-flight small growers but Sergio Germano,
who has relatively recently assumed control and ownership from his father Ettore, is certainly one.
Renovation and expansion have aided the emergence of dense but well-structured Barolos. Of the two *crus*
Prapò shows more refinement and style than the regular example, while Cerretta, which has up to two years
in *barriques* (around a quarter new), is more powerful and complex. Small oak is also used for an intense
Barbera, Vigne della Madre, and Langhe Balau, an unusual blend of (mostly) Dolcetto and Barbera. Langhe
Nebbiolo shows good character while a Langhe Bianco, Binel, is also unusual in combining Chardonnay
and Riesling. Both Prapò and Cerretta should be drunk with at least 8 to 10 years' age. (PW)
● **Barolo**★★★ £E Prapò★★★ £F Cerretta★★★★ £F
● **Barbera d'Alba** Vigna della Madre★★★ £D
● **Langhe** Balau★★ £D O **Langhe** Binel★★ £D
● **Dolcetto d'Alba** Lorenzino★ £B Pra di Pò★★ £C

ATTILIO GHISOLFI Barolo   A: Ock

Owner: Gian Marco Ghisolfi   Fraz. Bussia 27, 12065 Monforte d'Alba (CN)
Gian Marco is one of a number of talented young Piedmont winemakers able to harness the fruit potential
that results from his father's viticultural expertise. The Barolo vines are located in the lesser known Visette
cru (a sub-*cru* of Bussia) and the wine shows lovely weight and richness with deep, intense fruit. Though it
can be drunk reasonably young, it should improve for a decade. *Barriques* are used for two Langhe red
blends. The rich, expansive Alta Bussia is 80 per cent Barbera, 20 Nebbiolo, while a very individual, if firm,
Carlin adds Freisa to Nebbiolo. Barbera Vigna Lisi comes from old vines, receives 50 per cent new oak and
is sleek and stylish with three or four years' age. All show a similarly deft winemaking touch and fine fruit.
Pinay is a Pinot Nero of some promise, though the vines are still young. A new Barolo *cru*, Fantini, will
appear from the 2000 vintage. (PW)
● **Barolo** Bricco Visette★★★★ £E
● **Barbera d'Alba**★ £B Vigna Lisi★★★ £C
● **Langhe Rosso** Alta Bussia★★★ £E Carlin★★ £C Pinay★★ £C

BRUNO GIACOSA Barbaresco www.brunogiacosa.it   A: JAr, Sel, N&P, F&R

Owner: Bruno Giacosa Via XX Settembre 52, 12057 Neive (CN)
Bruno Giacosa has made many of the great bottles of Barolo and Barbaresco over the last 40 years. Much of his reputation rests on buying the best grapes from an intimate knowledge of the best vineyards. The renown of Barbaresco *crus* Asili, Rabajà, Santo Stefano and Barolo *crus* Vigna Rionda, Falletto and Villero owes much to Giacosa's supremely complex and harmonious renditions of Nebbiolo. With so many growers now making their own wines, Giacosa has also acquired vineyards of his own – some 15 ha includes some of the best sites, namely Asili in Barbaresco and Falletto in Serralunga. Riservas made from both sites in 1996 were only released in 2001 (Riserva bottles have a red label rather than the usual white). Winemaker Dante Scaglione still employs a fairly traditional winemaking practice but the maceration times are now only moderately long and he uses large French oak rather than the once much-favoured Slavonian casks. These are not wines for drinking young, though they might show well with six or seven years. Keep all the *cru* Barbaresco and Barolo for a decade from the vintage date – only then will it be possible to see if current releases stack up against some of the legendary older bottlings. The prices they obtain tends to reflect their sought-after status. Barbera, Dolcetto and Roero Arneis are consistently good among several other wines made. (PW)

● **Barbaresco** Rabajà★★★★ £G Asili★★★★★ £G Santo Stefano di Neive★★★★★ £G
● **Barolo** Falletto di Serralunga★★★★★ £H Rocche del Falletto di Serralunga✪✪✪✪✪ £H
● **Nebbiolo d'Alba** Valmaggiore★★ £C   ● **Barbera d'Alba** Falletto di Serralunga★★★ £C
● **Dolcetto d Alba** Falletto di Serralunga★ £B   O **Roero Arneis★★** £C

ELIO GRASSO Barolo   A: Mgi, L&W, Fal, F&R

Owner: Elio Grasso Loc. Ginestra 40, 12065 Monforte d Alba (CN)
Elio Grasso has 14 ha of prized steep hillside vineyards in the east of the Monforte commune. He has spent more than 20 years working his historic family vineyards and has recently relinquished the winemaking responsibility to his son Gianluca. An exisiting pair of refined, scented Barolos have been complemented by a *barrique*-aged Barolo from the replanted Runcot, a superior plot within Gavarini. As with other top *barrique*-aged examples from this area (CLERICO or CONTERNO-FANTINO) there is an inherent richness and structure from the fruit to marry with that from the oak. Maceration times are longer than for his neighbours' wines and Runcot, already impressive, seems certain to achieve greatness as the vines age. Barbera, Dolcetto and a little Chardonnay are very worthy too. (PW)

● **Barolo** Gavarini Vigna Chiniera★★★★ £E Runcot★★★★ £E Ginestra Casa Matè★★★★★ £E
● **Barbera d'Alba** Vigna Martina★★★ £C   ● **Dolcetto d'Alba** Vigna dei Grassi★★ £B
O **Langhe Chardonnay** Educato★ £B

SILVIO GRASSO Barolo   A: Fal, N&P, F&R

Owner: Alessio Grasso Cascina Luciani 112, 12064 La Morra (CN)
This modern 10-ha estate run by Federico Grasso can be relied on for very well-made Barolos. Both the Luciani and Manzoni *crus* lie near the eastern periphery of La Morra at slightly lower altitudes than some of the more celebrated *crus* in the zone. Though of the modern type, both show full, ripe fruit and excellent balance with well-integrated oak on the palate. Of the two, Ciabot Manzoni sometimes has the edge but it depends on the vintage. Both are best with 5 to 10 years' age. Federico's Insieme (see ALTARE) is a blend of almost half Nebbiolo with roughly equal parts of Barbera, Cabernet and Merlot – aged entirely in new oak. From the 99 vintage there are two new Barolos, Giachini and Pì Vigne. (PW)

● **Barolo★★★** £E Bricco Luciani★★★★ £F Ciabot Manzoni★★★★ £F
● **Barbera d'Alba★** £B Vigna Fontanile★★ £C   ● **Dolcetto d'Alba★** £B
● **Insieme★★★** £F

ICARDI Barbera d'Asti   A: **Ast**, Odd, But, VKg

Owner: Pierino Icardi Via Balbi 30, 12053 Castiglione Tinella (CN)
This sizeable 65-ha estate to the east of Barbaresco is run by Claudio and Ornella Icardi and makes an extraordinary plethora of pleasurable wines, most in small quantities. The wines often combine remarkable drinkability and good varietal character with a succulent fruit richness, though occasionally at the cost of character. Yet quality is high and the wines' opulence and vinosity could be suited to palates that find most Piemonte wines too demanding. Barolo Parej shows increasing depth and structure, particularly in the 1999. A new Barbaresco Montubert (from 2000) is a fine fruit-rich expression of Nebbiolo as is Langhe Pafoj. Bricco del Sole combines Barbera, Nebbiolo and Cabernet. Langhe Nej is 100 per cent Pinot Nero, while the white Pafoj is partially *barriqued* Chardonnay/Sauvignon. Moscato and Brachetto are light and moderately sweet – fresh and splendidly scented if drunk young. Grignolino (Bric du Su) and Cortese (Balera) are also produced. (PW)
- ● **Barolo** Parej★★★★ £F
- ● **Barbera d'Alba** Surì di Mù★★ £C   ● **Barbera d'Asti** Tabarin★★ £B Nuj Suj★★★ £D
- ● **Langhe** Nej★★ £D Pafoj★★★ £E   ● **Dolcetto d'Alba** Rousori★★ £B
- ● **Monferrato** Cascina Bricco del Sole★★★ £E
- O **Monferrato** Pafoj★ £D   O **Piemonte** Chardonnay Surissara★ £D
- O **Moscato d'Asti** La Rosa Selvatica★★ £B   ● **Piemonte Brachetto** Surì Vigin★★ £B

LA BARBATELLA Barbera d'Asti

Owner: Sonvico family Strada Annunziata 55, 14049 Nizza Monferrato (AT)
Giuliano Noè, a top consultant enologist, is the winemaker here. What he has done with Angelo Sonvico's few well-situated hectares showcases his skills. One of the most celebrated Barbera d'Asti together with Sonvico, the Barbera/Cabernet blend for long known as La Vigna di Sonvico, have earned this estate an enviable celebrity in the heart of Asti's hills. The wines have proven ageing potential and possess power and concentration but without excess. Newish Mystère, made since 1999, is another pricey but increasingly fine red that adds Pinot Nero to Barbera and Cabernet Sauvignon. Whites Noè and new Non è combine Cortese with Sauvignon. (PW)
- ● **Barbera d'Asti Nizza** Superiore Vigna dell'Angelo★★★ £E
- ● **Barbera d'Asti★★** £C   ● **Monferrato** Sonvico★★★★ £F Mystère★★★ £E
- O **Monferrato** Noè★★ £C Non è★★ £C

LA GIUSTINIANA Gavi   A: **Lib**, Vne

Owner: Lombardini family Fraz. Rovereto 5, 15066 Gavi (AL)
Few Gavi producers are worth making a fuss about. La Giustiniana is one of the few exceptions. Enrico Tomalino with help from Donato Lanati is now producing consistently full, concentrated unwooded Gavi from this 30-ha estate. Lugarara is the mainstay; better, though, is slightly minerally, appley Montessora, with more intensity and persistence. A special selection, Just (sold outside the DOCG), in which a relatively small percentage of the wine goes into *barrique*, is full, creamy and that much better again. Made since 1998 is a red version of Just – *barrique*-aged, ripe and balanced, and predominantly from Barbera. Whites are best within a couple of years of the vintage. New from the 2001 vintage is a lees-enriched version of Gavi called 'IL'. For immediate drinking there's some very good fizzy Brachetto d'Acqui and Moscato d'Asti from the 11-ha Contero estate at Strevi that is also owned by the Lombardini family. (PW)
La Giustiniana:
- O **Gavi del Comune di Gavi** Lugarara★★ £C Montessora★★★ £C   O **Just★★★** £E
- ● **Monferrato** Rosso Just★★ £D
Contero:
- ● **Brachetto d'Acqui★★** £B   O **Moscato d'Asti di Strevi★★** £B

LA SCOLCA Gavi www.scolca.it   A: **Alv, Sel**

Owner: Giorgio Soldati   Fraz. Rovereto 170/R, 15066 Gavi (AL)
La Scolca has long been Gavi's most widely admired estate but others (Gian Piero Broglia, Castellari Bergaglio, LA GIUSTINIANA and Villa Sparina) have, with expert help, surpassed it for quality. Regular and Villa Scolca versions lack personality and concentration and even the Etichetta Nera (Black Label) can be found wanting. More interesting are the sparkling Gavi Spumante which are well-balanced and attractively toasty with a fine bead. Soldati La Scolca, released around eight years after the vintage is refined and complex. (PW)

O **Gavi** Etichetta Nera★ £D
O **Gavi Spumante** Brut Soldati★★ £C Pas Dosé★ £C
O **Soldati La Scolca Brut Millesimato★★** £C

LA SPINETTA Barbaresco   A: **Eno, WTs,** Wtr, Bal, Res, JNi, NYg, Unc, P&S, Han, Hrd

Owner: Rivetti family   Via Annunziata 17, 14054 Castagnole Lanze (AT)
Giorgio Rivetti has become one of Italy's most talked-about winemakers. Being based just north of the Barbaresco zone, he, with brothers Carlo and Bruno, first made his mark with excellent Moscato, Barbera and a blend called Pin (Nebbiolo, Barbera and Cabernet). But the creation of new Barbaresco wines from the *crus* Gallina and Starderi (in Neive) and Valeirano (in Treiso) has rocketed the Rivetti name to fame. The wines are unequivocally modern. Moscato apart, nearly all the wines see the inside of a *barrique*, but they are profound with super fruit. Of the Barbarescos, Starderi is the most structured of the three, Valeirano perhaps most concentrated, while Gallina is a touch softer and more expressive. Yet I'd as happily drink the smoky, old-vine Barbera d'Asti Superiore or the consistently brilliant Pin. Other whites include a Sauvignon sold under the Langhe DOC, *barrique*-aged Chardonnay and new sweet Moscato from dried grapes (La Spinetta Oro). Also new is an extremely promising new Barolo Campe' (from 2000 vintage) from 7 ha of established vines. In the coastal hills of Tuscany Giorgio Rivetti is also developing his own interpretation of Sangiovese (see CASANOVA DELLA SPINETTA). (PW)

● **Barbaresco** Vigneto Gallina★★★★★ £G Vigneto Starderi★★★★★ £G Vigneto Valeirano★★★★★ £G
● **Barbera d'Asti** Ca' di Pian★★★ £D Superiore★★★★ £E
● **Barbera d'Alba** Vigneto Gallina★★★★ £E ● **Monferrato** Pin★★★★ £E
O **Langhe** Bianco★★ £E O **Piemonte** Chardonnay Lidia★ £C
O **Moscato d'Asti** Biancospino★★ £B Bricco Quaglia★★ £B
O **Moscato d'Asti** Passito★★ £E

TENUTA LA TENAGLIA Barbera d'Asti www.latenaglia.com

Owner: A & E Ehrmann   Via Sanctuario di Crea 6, 15020 Serralunga di Crea (AL)
La Tenaglia rose to prominence in the 1980s on the basis of very good Barbera, championing the Monferrato hills not far south of the River Po. 18 ha of a 33-ha estate are planted to vines at an altitude of 450 m. The pursuit of quality is reinforced with the use of outside expertise, including the services of eminent Tuscan enologist Attilio Pagli. Barbera is still the top wine, particularly the sumptuous, complex *barrique*-aged Emozioni from a single vineyard of 70-year-old vines. Giorgio Tenaglia comes from a selection of the best vines and is leaner but stylish, needing a year or two to soften. A third, the Monferrato Barbera, is firmly textured (and a little overoaked in 2000). Crea is a simpler, unoaked Barbera d'Asti. Half a hectare is dedicated to Syrah and the resulting Paradiso is peppery and black-fruited. Chardonnay (Oltre) is not unlike a good Pouilly-Fuissé but only a little is made. Regular unoaked Piemonte Chardonnay is adequate but no more, as is Grignolino. (PW)

● **Barbera d'Asti** Giorgio Tenaglia★★ £C Emozioni★★★ £D
● **Barbera del Monferrato** Superiore Tenaglia è★★ £C
● **Paradiso★★** £D O **Piemonte Chardonnay** Oltre★★ £E

MALVIRÀ   Roero   www.malvira.com

A: **Tri**, V&C

Owner: R & M Damonte   Via Carse Sparse-Loc. Canova 144, 12043 Canale (CN)
Brothers Roberto and Massimo consistently produce Arneis that is as good as any. Renesio is an unwooded version, while Trinità sees some oak and Saglietto is oak-fermented and aged. All three can show real personality and style. Reds too, are of a very good standard, making the most of the recent string of fine vintages. The Roero Superiore has been bottled as two separate *crus* from the 1999 vintage and both combine intensity with real elegance and should be drunk with five years' age. The remaining Nebbiolo is sold as Langhe Nebbiolo. San Guglielmo is an unwooded, perfumed and reasonably priced example of the Langhe Barbera/Nebbiolo blend. The oak-aged Treuve combines Sauvignon and Chardonnay with Arneis. (PW)

- **Roero Superiore** Mombeltramo★★★ £D Trinità★★★ £D
- **Langhe Nebbiolo**★ £B   ● **Langhe Nebbiolo** San Guglielmo★★ £D
- **Barbera d'Alba**★ £C San Michele★★ £C
- O **Roero Arneis** Renesio★★ £B Trinità★★ £B Saglietto★★ £C   O **Langhe** Treuve★★ £C

GIOVANNI MANZONE   Barolo

Owner: Giovanni Manzone   Via Castelletto 9, 12065 Monforte d'Alba (CN)
Giovanni Manzone's 7.6 ha centre on the *cru* Gramolere in the Castelletto part of the Monforte commune. A special part of it is bottled as Bricat and a Riserva is also made in the best years. A tiny amount of elegant, floral Barolo from nearby Santo Stefano (Perno) has been recently added. There is partial use of French *tonneaux* (new and used) but maceration times are moderately long and Giovanni is avowedly not in the modern camp. A distinctive wild mint and woodsmoke character seems typical of Gramolere (rather than a lack of ripeness as some have suggested), with extra intensity and dimension in Bricat. A concentrated old-vine Barbera La Serra is the pick of the rest. Tris unusually combines the Piedmont trio of Nebbiolo, Barbera and Dolcetto. A very interesting white, Rosserto, is made from Rossese Bianco and is unique in Piedmont. (PW)

- **Barolo** Gramolere★★ £D Perno Santo Stefano★★★ £E Bricat★★★★ £E Riserva★★★★ £F
- **Barbera d'Alba**★ £B La Serra★★★ £C   ● **Dolcetto d'Alba** La Serra★★ £B
- **Langhe** Tris★★ £C   O **Rosserto**★★ £C

MARCARINI   Barolo   www.marcarini.it

A: **RsW**, Rae, BBR, UnC, F&R

Owner: L & M Marchetti   Piazza Martiri 2, 12064 La Morra (CN)
The Barolo here is traditionally styled, with no new oak. Though a little firm and unexpressive when young, the wines can often age impressively from a good vintage. Though the inherent quality of the *crus* is apparent, these very structured if fruit-intense versions contrast with the likes of those from VOERZIO. Much attention is also paid to the Dolcettos, especially the rich Boschi di Berri made from vines over a 100 years old grown on their own roots – a factor which may account for the distinctive almondy, slightly earthy streak running through the intense berry fruit flavours. One to try at least once. Langhe Nebbiolo and Moscato d'Asti are also made. (PW)

- **Barolo** Brunate★★★★ £E La Serra★★★★ £E
- **Barbera d'Alba** Ciabot Camerano★★ £C
- **Dolcetto d'Alba** Fontanazza★ £B Boschi di Berri★★★ £C

MARCHESI DI GRÉSY   Barbaresco   www.marchesidigresy.com

A: **Mer**, Amp, ACh

Owner: Marchesi di Grésy   Via Rabajà 43, 12050 Barbaresco (CN)
The Tenute Cisa Asinari actually comprises three estates but the centrepiece is the famous Martinenga *cru*. Though not ultra-consistent, the tight, dense, compact impression that the individual plots – Camp Gros (adjoining Rabajà) and Gaiun (an extension of Asili) – give when young can lead to splendid graceful and complex drinking after a decade or more. There is some use of *barriques*, though more for Virtus

(Barbera/Cabernet) and Villa Martis (Nebbiolo/Barbera) than for the Barbarescos. Other wines, sourced from Monte Aribaldo at Treiso, include two Chardonnays and one of Piedmont's best Sauvignons. Both a Moscato d'Asti and a Moscato Passito (L'Altro) are produced from the third estate, La Serra. (PW)

● **Barbaresco** Martinenga★★ £F Camp Gros★★★★ £F Gaiun★★★★ £F
● **Langhe** Virtus★★ £E Villa Martis★★ £E ● **Dolcetto d'Alba** Monte Aribaldo★ £B
○ **Langhe Chardonnay**★ £C Grésy★ £E ○ **Langhe Sauvignon**★★ £C

FRANCO M MARTINETTI Barbera d'Asti   A: **VDu**, F&R

Owner: Franco Martinetti Via San Francesco da Paola 18, 10123 Torino
Martinetti employs the father-and-daughter team of Giuliano and Elena Noè (see LA BARBATELLA) to make top quality wines from leased vineyards. A string of good vintages of Barbera (Montruc) and Barbera/Cabernet (Sul Bric) have been made. These are powerful, concentrated reds with breadth and refinement. They are characterised by the seamless quality of their tannins whilst capable of ageing for a decade or more from top vintages. Whites are impressive too. Minaia, once again being sold as Gavi, is very classy for this generally overrated appellation; Martin, from the obscure local variety Timorasso, offers ripe pear, quince, citrus peel and exotic fruits – both are *barrique*-aged, ripe, concentrated and sophisticated. Marasco (named for the Marasco cherry), a Barolo blended from the sites in the Barolo commune, has been made since 1997 and is very modern and seductive yet not superficial, albeit without the dimension or expression of the best. The appealing fruity Banditi Barbera is one for everyday. (PW)

● **Barbera d'Asti** Bric dei Banditi★ £B Superiore Montruc★★★★ £E
● **Monferrato** Sulbric★★★★ £E ● **Barolo** Marasco★★★ £F
○ **Gavi** Minaia★★★ £D ○ **Colli Tortonesi** Martin★★★ £E

BARTOLO MASCARELLO Barolo   A :Fal

Owner: Bartolo Mascarello Via Roma 15, 12060 Barolo (CN)
Classic traditionally styled Barolo, made without concession to the modernists. Not for wimps, these are always powerful, broad and firmly tannic yet harmonious and superbly expressive wines with age. Don't even think about drinking it young or indeed at all if those from the likes of REVELLO are your ideal Barolo. 10 to 15 years' age is usually a minimum. Barbera and Dolcetto are also sturdy but balanced and *terroir*-derived. Bartolo's 1996 Barolo featured the controversial 'No Barrique No Berlusconi' label that is now a collector's item worldwide. 97 and 98 appear the most successful of recent vintages but time may provide other contenders. (PW)

● **Barolo**★★★★★ £F
● **Barbera d'Alba** Vigna San Lorenzo★★ £C ● **Dolcetto d'Alba** Monrobiolo e Rué★★ £C

GIUSEPPE MASCARELLO & FIGLIO www.mascarello1881.com   A: **Wtr**, BBR, UnC

Owner: Mauro Mascarello Via Borgonuovo 108, 12060 Monchiero (CN)
Monprivato is one of the great *crus* of Castiglione Falletto and the entire Barolo zone. Superbly situated, its 6 ha face south-west at around 280 m. The wines in the best years combine superb fruit quality with an effortless structure and balance. A Riserva Ca' d' Morissio, first produced in 1993, is made only from the Michet subvariety of Nebbiolo and undergoes longer ageing in large oak. Mauro, now aided by his son Giuseppe (first names are passed from grandfather to grandson in Piedmont) also makes very small amounts of Barolo from nearby Bricco and Villero as well as Santo Stefano di Perno. Barbera and Dolcetto show great character and extract and benefit from bottle-age. Barbera Codana (which adjoins Monprivato) is from old vines, as is Scudetto, a selection from Santo Stefano di Perno. Langhe Status is Nebbiolo with a little Barbera and Freisa added in. Langhe Freisa can show all the style and intensity possible from this variety if braced by abundant fine tannin. (PW)

● **Barolo** Monprivato★★★★★ £F Riserva Ca' d' Morissio★★★★★ £F
● **Barolo** Bricco★★★ £E Santo Stefano di Perno★★★ £ Villero★★★★ £F

● **Langhe Nebbiolo**★ £B ● **Langhe** Status★★ £C ● **Langhe Freisa** Toetto★★ £C
● **Barbera d'Alba** Santo Stefano di Perno★★ £C Scudetto★★★ £D Codana★★★ £D
● **Dolcetto d'Alba** Bricco★★ £C Santo Stefano di Perno★★ £C

MOCCAGATTA Barbaresco

Owner: Franco & Sergio Minuto Via Rabajà 24, 12050 Barbaresco (CN)
The Minuto brothers are a reliable source for good modern-style wines. From 12 ha of vineyards, Barbarescos are ripe and intense but with a certain style and elegance too. Cole shows the most structure and dimension, while Balin is the most supple but there is little to choose between them. All deserve to be kept for 5 to 10 years. The Basarin Barbera adds a breadth and lushness to the perfumed regular version of this grape. Dolcetto is more of a quaffing wine but the *barrique*-fermented and aged version of Chardonnay is increasingly good and will keep a year or two. (PW)
● **Barbaresco** Basarin★★★ £E Bric Balin★★★ £E Cole★★★ £E
● **Barbera d'Alba**★ £C Basarin★★ £D ● **Dolcetto d'Alba**★ £B
○ **Langhe Chardonnay**★ £B Buschet★★ £D

MAURO MOLINO Barolo   A: F&R

Owner: Mauro Molino Fraz. Annunziata 111, 12064 La Morra (CN)
Though based in the Annunziata part of La Morra, Mauro Molino, recently assisted by his son, Matteo, also has a few rows of vines in Monforte. As with other Altare disciples, short maceration times and *barrique*-aging are employed but the fruit quality he gets after 10 years of being at it full-time makes for good Barolo. Of two *crus*, it is considered that the higher calcareous content of Gancia gives rise to its firmer tannic structure but both show real weight and complexity in addition to fine aromatic character. Mauro's Insieme is a fairly typical blend, 40 per cent Nebbiolo with the balance equal parts Barbera, Cabernet and Merlot. He is also not alone in planting Chardonnay where the Piedmontese red grapes simply don't work. Accanzio is mostly Barbera and Nebbiolo. (PW)
● **Barolo**★★★ £E Vigna Conca★★★★ £F Gancia★★★★ £F
● **Barbera d'Alba**★ £B Gattere★★★ £D ● **Dolcetto d'Alba**★ £B
● **Langhe** Accanzio★★ £D ● **Insieme**★★★ £F
○ **Langhe Chardonnay** Livrot★★ £C

FIORENZO NADA Barbaresco www.nada.it

Owner: Fiorenzo Nada Loc. Rombone, 12050 Treiso (CN)
Bruno Nada (Fiorenzo's son) runs a small operation from just 7 ha. The fruit quality and intensity resulting from much diligence in the vineyard is, with some assistance from Giuseppe Caviola (CA' VIOLA), harnessed into fine, elegant yet structured reds that add richness with age. Rombone, a potentially great *cru*, faces south-west; the Nadas' superior selection from these slopes is aged in *barriques* but evolves into a very refined classy example with 5 to 10 years' age. Seifile, a Barbera/ Nebbiolo blend also gets the small oak treatment and is characterised by its complexity and fruit intensity. Dolcetto and Barbera, the latter of which sees some oak, are ripe-fruited but could sometimes use a little more weight. An estate that deserves to be better known. (PW)
● **Barbaresco**★★★ £E Rombone★★★★ £F
● **Langhe** Seifile★★★ £F ● **Dolcetto d'Alba**★ £C **Barbera d'Alba**★ £C

NINO NEGRI Valtellina Superiore www.giv.it   A: **Eno**, Res, Sel, NYg

Owner: GIV Via Ghebellini 3, 23030 Chiuro (SO)
Nino Negri is owned by Italy's largest wine group – GIV or Gruppo Italiano Vini – and is directed by the respected enologist Casimiro Maule. There are good examples of all four Valtellina Superiore DOCG sub-zones: Grumello, Inferno, Sassella and Valgella. Though traditionally vinified, most are partly aged in

barrique, of light to medium body, at their best they are intense, perfumed and elegant. Sfursat or Sforzato is a high-alcohol version (typically 14.5°) made from semi-dried grapes; in the top wine, Sfursat 5 Stelle, the grapes spend three-and-a-half weeks on their skins prior to ageing exclusively in new *barriques*. Drunk young it can be a bit overwhelming, with its sweet, intense fruit and evident tannin and acidity, yet it is enticingly perfumed with floral and preserved raspberry and cherry aromas. The oak-aged, perfumed white Ca' Brione is based on Nebbiolo vinified as a white wine and can show unusual structure and weight. (PW)

● **Valtellina Sfursat★★★** £E 5 Stelle★★★★ £F
● **Valtellina Superiore** Grumello Vigna Sassorosso★★ £C Inferno Mazér★★ £C
● **Valtellina Superiore** Sassella Le Tense★★ £C Vigneto Fracia★★★ £E
○ **Ca' Brione★★** £C

ANGELO NEGRO & FIGLI Roero www.negroangelo.it A: GWW

Owner: Giovanni Negro Fraz. Sant'Anna 1, 12040 Monteu Roero (CN)
Giovanni Negro's Roero estate is one of the appellation's leaders. While half of the 50-odd ha are planted to Arneis, it is the Barbera and Nebbiolo that have really forged a reputation for this family. The top wine, Sudisfà, is deep and powerful with ripe, smooth tannins but there is good quality throughout the reds. Good examples of Arneis are also produced, a fresh slightly spicy regular version contrasts with fuller more characterful single-vineyard Gianat and Perdaudin examples. A small amount of grapes for the latter are dried for a sweet version. In addition to those below, Birbet (Brachetto), and Favorita are also made. Bric Millon is a promising new red based on Croatina but includes some Barbera and Cabernet Sauvignon. (PW)

● **Roero★★** £B Prachiosso★★ £C Sudisfà★★★ £D
● **Barbera d'Alba** Nicolon★★ £B Bric Bertu★★★ £C
○ **Roero Arneis★★** £B Gianat★★ £C Perdaudin★★ £C ○ **Perdaudin Passito** £D

ANDREA OBERTO Barolo A: Alv, V&C

Owner: Andrea Oberto Borgata Simane 11, 12064 La Morra (CN)
The father and son team of Andrea and Fabio Oberto make excellent examples of Barbera, Dolcetto and Barolo. Previously operating from rather cramped cellars they have recently moved into new winery premises. Rotofermenters have been used since 2000 but maceration times are moderate rather than short. Andrea Oberto initially made his name with Barbera, especially for the very rich, ripe *barrique*-aged Giada (from 60- to 70-year-old vines), though even the regular version is based on relatively old vines and is decidedly good value. New oak is used for all the Barolos as well as the 60/40 Nebbiolo/Barbera blend, Fabio Rocche, from a parcel directly below SCAVINO's, is a lovely example of the *cru*, with its unique perfumed, floral character around a deep fruit core. Delicious *cru* Dolcetto will keep a year or two. (PW)

● **Barolo★★★** £E Vigneto Albarella★★★★ £F Rocche★★★★ £F
● **Langhe** Rosso Fabio★★★ £D
● **Barbera d'Alba★★** £B Giada★★★ £D
● **Dolcetto d'Alba★** £B Vantrino Albarella★★ £C San Francesco★★ £C

FRATELLI ODDERO Barolo www.odderofratelli.it A: Alv, Sel

Owner: Giacomo & Luigi Oddero Via Santa Maria, 28, 12064 La Morra (CN)
The Odderos are long-time vineyard owners, now with a very significant 60 ha, a proportion of it in some of Barolo's most notable *crus*. Some examples of these, such as (Mondoca di) Bussia Soprana (from Monforte) or Vigna Rionda (Serralunga) are now starting to realise their true potential – they had a tendency to be rather rustic and rugged in the past. Some input from leading consultant Donato Lanati has helped. Vineyards less suited to Nebbiolo have been planted to Barbera, Dolcetto and even Cabernet (Furesté is 100 per cent Cabernet from La Morra vineyards) and Chardonnay (Collaretto). If the wines remain reasonably priced, this promises to be a good label for characterful, structured, and widely available, Barolo – but stick to the *crus* as regular bottlings are a bit dull. (PW)

● **Barolo** Mondoca di Bussia Soprana★★★ £E   Rocche di Castiglione★★★ £E
● **Barolo** Rocche dei Rivera★★★ £E   Vigna Rionda★★★ £E
● **Langhe** Furesté★★ £D   **O Langhe Chardonnay** Collaretto★ £C

ORSOLANI   Erbaluce di Caluso   www.orsolani.it   **A: Mgi**

Owner: G-F Orsolani   Via Michele Chiesa 12, 10090 San Giorgio Canavese (TO)
Orsolani has become the main proponent of the Erbaluce grape and the small zone created for it north of
Torino. Around half of 15 ha on glacial morraine are owned and in recent vintages the wines have shown
greater consistency and quality. La Rustìa is now the name for a tangy dry version with a lightly herbal spice
and dried peach character. Vignot Sant'Antonio is more concentrated with some *barrique* influence. The
top wine though is Sulé (since 1995; previously sold as La Rustìa), a rich, sweet, honeyed version of Erbaluce
made from dried grapes and fermented in *barriques* before spending three years in barrels. Carema (from
Nebbiolo), while relatively light, shows some promise. There's also vintage-dated sparkling wine from
Erbaluce, Orsolani Brut Cuvée Storica. (PW)
O Erbaluce di Caluso La Rustìa★★ £B Vignot Sant' Antonio★★ £C
O Caluso Passito Sulé★★★ £E   ● **Carema** Le Tabbie★ £D

PAITIN   Barbaresco   www.paitin.it   **A: HSA, Win, BBR**

Owner: Secondo Pasquero-Elia   Via Serra Boella 20, 12057 Neive (CN)
The Pasquero-Elia have 17 ha of vineyards incorporating part of the *cru* of Serraboella (next to CIGLIUTI).
There was acclaim for their Barbaresco back in the 1980s and after the difficult early 90s, quality has taken
another step forward. Dense and firm when young, though increasingly accessible too, it promises a lovely
style and complexity with 8 to 10 years' age. Other wines are made to high standards too: in the Langhe
red, Paitin, a little Cabernet and Syrah are now added to Barbera and Nebbiolo in a sleek *barrique*-aged
blend. Barbera, especially Campolive, and Dolcetto show a touch of class too. A white Campolive is from
Sauvignon and Chardonnay while Roero Arneis (Vigna Elisa) is also made. (PW)
● **Barbaresco** Sorì Paitin★★★ £E   ● **Langhe** Paitin★★★ £D
● **Barbera d'Alba** Campolive★★★ £C   Serra Boella★★ £C
● **Dolcetto d'Alba** Sorì Paitin★★ £B   ● **Nebbiolo d'Alba** Ca'Veja★ £C

PARUSSO   Barolo   www.parusso.com   **A: Eno, NYg, N&P**

Owner: Marco & Tiziano Parusso   Loc. Bussia 55, 12065 Monforte d'Alba (CN)
From 20 ha of vineyards Marco Parusso fashions a high-quality range of wines that continues to improve.
Vinification and ageing are modern: 24 months in new French *barriques* for the Barolos, though oak rarely
dominates the top examples (plots within Bussia), Vigna Munie, Vigna Rocche and since 1998, Vigna
Fiurin. There is a weight and depth to go with their evident style, complexity and length on the palate. They
are a step up from the less expensive but perfumed, occasionally oaky but classy Mariondino and supple,
very attractive fruit-filled Piccole Vigne which comes from young vines. Other wines include excellent
Barberas (the superior Superiore is from old vines) and Langhe Bricco Rovella, a Nebbiolo, Barbera and
Cabernet blend, especially good in 99. Langhe Nebbiolo is also made, usually one of the very best examples
of elegant, accessible Nebbiolo. For white, two versions of Sauvignon are produced, a nettly unoaked
example and the riper, richer Bricco Rovella which is *barrique*-aged. (PW)
● **Barolo** Bussia Vigne Rocche★★★★★ £F Bussia Vigne Munie★★★★ £F
● **Barolo** Piccole Vigne★★★ £E Mariondino★★★★ £E Bussia Vigna Fiurin★★★★ £F
● **Barbera d'Alba** Ornati★★★ £C   ● **Barbera d'Alba** Superiore★★★★ £E
● **Dolcetto d'Alba** Piani Noce★★ £B   ● **Langhe Nebbiolo**★★ £C
● **Langhe** Bricco Rovella★★ £D   **O Langhe Bianco**★★ £C Bricco Rovella★★ £D

PECCHENINO Dolcetto di Dogliani www.pecchenino.com A: Odd

Owner: Orlando & Attilio Pecchenino Borgata Valdiberti 59, 12063 Dogliani (CN)
Brothers Orlando and Attilio go to great lengths in order to make making better and better Dolcetto at this 25-ha estate. This means not just powerful concentrated examples but increasingly, with the aid of micro-oxygenation, Dolcetto with finer textures and less obtrusive structures. Of the dense yet succulent Dolcettos, San Luigi is unoaked, the classy Sirì d'Jermu sees some used oak and half the Bricco Botti is aged in new oak. The barrique-aged Langhe red, La Castella is based on Barbera but includes 30 per cent Nebbiolo. New are Quass, a lush, fleshy but well-balanced varietal Barbera, and Langhe Nebbiolo, Vigna Botti - both first made from the 2001 vintage. A solitary white, Vigna Maestro is Chardonnay-based. Prices are proportionate to quality. (PW)
● **Dolcetto di Dogliani** San Luigi★★ £B Siri d'Jermu★★★ £C
● **Dolcetto di Dogliani** Superiore Bricco Botti★★★ £D
● **Langhe** La Castella★★★ £D O **Langhe** Vigna Maestro★ £C

PELISSERO Barbaresco www.pelissero.com A: **Alv**, Odd, Sel

Owner: Giorgio Pelissero Via Ferrere 19, 12050 Treiso (CN)
Under Giorgio Pelissero, quality at this 20-ha estate has soared dramatically in recent years. At its heart is Vanotu, a vineyard at the intersection of Barbaresco's three main communes and the source of an increasingly complex and stylish Barbaresco. It spends 18 months in mostly new oak but this is increasingly well-integrated into a rich, ripe fruit core. The regular Barbaresco is attractive with good substance and reasonable depth. The 99s show slightly better definition and depth than the 2000s but will require more time. There's plenty of fruit in Dolcetto too, especially Augenta – a vibrant, perfumed and expressive example of the grape. Barbera is ripe and long while Langhe Nebbiolo shows a fine preserved raspberry fruit intensity. Barbera and Nebbiolo are harmoniously combined in 'Long Now' – named for the Long Now Foundation clock (www.longnow.org) – a modern, oaky example of this blend. Freisa (a lightly fizzy style), Grignolino and Favorita are also made. (PW)
● **Barbaresco**★★★ £E Vanotu★★★★ £F
● **Langhe Nebbiolo**★★ £C ● **Langhe** Long Now★★★ £D
● **Dolcetto d'Alba** Munfrina★★ £B Augenta★★ £C ● **Barbera d'Alba** Piani★★ £C

VIGNAIOLI ELVIO PERTINACE Barbaresco

Owner: 'Cooperative' Loc. Pertinace 2, 12050 Treiso (CN)
Named for a Roman emperor (Pertinax) of very brief reign, this co-op established in the 1970s controls some 80 ha of vineyards. Cesare Barbero supervises the making of a very reasonably priced Barbaresco and three relatively inexpensive *crus*. The use of some new oak complements the natural density and structure in the wines, and all show good *tipicità*. This being a Treiso-based operation, Dolcetto also features prominently in wines that are firm but with good fruit. Also produced are adequate examples of Langhe Nebbiolo and Langhe Chardonnay. A typical Langhe blend, Pertinace comes from Nebbiolo, Barbera and Cabernet Sauvignon. (PW)
● **Barbaresco**★★ £D Vigneto Castellizzano★★★ £E Vigneto Marcarini★★★ £E Vigneto Nervo★★★ £E
● **Dolcetto d'Alba**★ £B Vigneto Castellizzano★ £B Vigneto Nervo★★ £B

PIO CESARE Barolo www.piocesare.it A: **Cib**, Fal, F&R

Owner: Pio Boffa Via Cesare Balbo 6, 12051 Alba (CN)
Cesare Pio established this house in the 19th century and its success as a *commerciante* or *négociant* make it a well-known name. Direction now comes from Pio Boffa whose recent vineyard acquisitions bring the estate holdings to over 40 ha but has long included the prized Il Bricco and Ornato *crus*. The two wines produced from these sites, Barbaresco and Barolo respectively, can show real depth and a certain stylishness

together with the propensity to age. Recent releases, particularly the 97s,98s and 99s show better richness and expression than previously. Regular Barbaresco is increasingly good too. Barbera Fides and Chardonnay Piodilei absorb a good measure of oak but consistently show depth and character too. On the downside Dolcetto, regular Barbera, Nebbiolo and Arneis, and even the house Barolo could still be more. (PW)

● **Barbaresco★★★** £E Il Bricco★★★★ £F
● **Barolo★★** £F Ornato★★★★ £G
● **Barbera d'Alba** Fides★★ £D
○ **Langhe Chardonnay** Piodilei★★ £D ○ **Piemonte Chardonnay** L'Altro★ £C

E PIRA & FIGLI Barolo   A: Eno, JNi, N&P, F&R

Owner: Chiara Boschis Via Vittorio Veneto 1, 12060 Barolo (CN)
Chiara Boschis has only recently assumed control of this old Barolo producer. The prize here is 2.5 ha of Cannubi and recent efforts display tremendous class. There is impressive complexity and considerable elegance and purity that reflect its origins. The wines build in richness and depth with age and despite the use of new oak there is an underlying structure that demands cellaring. Recent vintages have been very good and suggest an even higher rating in the future. From a further 0.5 ha is a second Barolo, Via Nuova (also in the Barolo commune) which shows similar dimension if not the class or complexity of Cannubi. Barbera shows increasing style and purity from 2001 and is best with three years' age or more. Dolcetto is less exciting. (PW)

● **Barolo** Cannubi★★★★★ £F Via Nuova★★★★ £F
● **Barbera d'Alba★★** £C ● **Dolcetto d'Alba★** £C

LUIGI PIRA Barolo   A: Bal, JNi, N&P, F&R

Owner: Luigi Pira Via XX Septembre 9, 12050 Serralunga d'Alba (CN)
Giampaolo Pira is rightly considered the hottest young winemaker in Serralunga and with his brother, Romolo, and father, Luigi, is forging one of Barolo's most exciting new estates (albeit from less than 10 ha of vineyard). Since 1995 he has further underlined the potential of Serralunga with excellent wines from the Marenca, Margheria and (since 1997) Vigna Rionda *crus*. Having cut yields and modified the vinification, he is now producing dense, structured Barolos that are extremely concentrated and powerful with great cellaring potential. A mix of *barriques, tonneaux* (both new and used) and large wood is used; Vigneto Margheria sees 60 per cent new oak, while the minute quantities of Vigna Rionda receive 100 per cent new oak. Both deserve 10 years' cellaring. A tiny amount of Langhe Nebbiolo is also made, with a seductive fruit and texture that more examples should show. Unoaked Dolcetto is good too. (PW)

● **Barolo** Margheria★★★★ £F Vigna Rionda★★★★★ £G
● **Barolo★★★** £E Marenca★★★★ £F
● **Nebbiolo d'Alba** Le Ombre★★★ £F ● **Dolcetto d'Alba★★** £C

FERDINANDO PRINCIPIANO Barolo   A: HSA

Owner: Americo Principiano Via Alba 19, 12065 Monforte d'Alba (CN)
Thanks to his dad, young Ferdinando has 10 ha of well-tended, mostly old vines in the south-eastern corner of the Barolo zone to work with. With some help from Giuseppe Caviola, the wines from the most recent vintages are really starting to shine. The main Barolo is the Boscareto *cru*, adjacent to Cascina Francia of GIACOMO CONTERNO in the south of the Serralunga commune. This can be a wine of great character, complexity (including woodsmoke and truffles) and structure too as is apparent in the 1999 version. The same *cru* also provides half the Barbera for La Romualda – the rest coming from the celebrated Barbera vineyard Pian Romualdo (see PRUNOTTO). Rich, ripe and lush with old-vine blackberry fruit, it is best with at least two or three years' age. A small amount of another Barolo, Le Coste (from Monforte d'Alba) though less powerful than Boscareto show good balance and intensity. (PW)

● **Barolo** Boscareto★★★★ £E Le Coste★★★ £E
● **Barbera d'Alba** La Romualda★★★ £D ● **Dolcetto d'Alba** Sant'Anna★ £B

PRUNOTTO Barolo www.prunotto.it   A: **BWC,** Vts, FWC, Cam, Sel, N&P, F&R

Owner: Antinori   Loc. San Cassiano 4/G, 12051 Alba (CN)
One of the best known names from the Langhe – and that was before ANTINORI (see Tuscany) took over. Once a traditional *commerciante*, Prunotto now owns an increasing percentage of the vineyard sources and there is some use of 500-litre French oak. Yet stylistically Antinori seem to be building on the legacy of the celebrated Beppe Colla rather than imposing a new order. A consistent and not excessively priced range is headed by the *cru* Barolo Bussia. At least something of the harmony and balance, if not the concentration or size of this Barolo can be seen in nearly all the wines. Noted Barbera d'Alba Pian Romualdo has recently been surpassed by the super Barbera d'Asti Costamiole, albeit with a considerable price differential. (PW)
- **Barbaresco★★** £E   Bric Turot★★★ £F
- **Barolo★★★** £E   Bussia★★★★ £F
- **Nebbiolo d'Alba** Occhetti★★ £B   ● **Barbera d'Alba★** £B   Pian Romualdo★★★ £C
- **Barbera d'Asti** Fiulot★★ £B   Costamiole★★★★ £E
- **Dolcetto d'Alba★** £B   Mosesco★★ £B   O **Moscato d'Asti★** £B   O **Roero Arneis★** £B

ALDO RAINOLDI Valtellina Superiore www.rainoldi.com   A: **VDu,** May

Owner: Giuseppe Rainoldi   Via Stelvio 128, 23030 Chiuro (SO)
The wines have been improved and modernised here to the extent that this narrow alpine valley might yet receive more attention. The length and flavour intensity in the top wines is striking. The *barrique*-aged Il Crespino (from 100 per cent Nebbiolo) is but one of several Valtellina Superiore. As well as an Inferno Barrique (aged in the same) there are versions of Grumello and Sassella; the Sasella Riserva delivers a lovely savoury complexity with age. As at NINO NEGRI it is the Sfursat (Valtellina Sforzato DOCG) that shows the most power and concentration. The Fruttaio Ca' Rizzieri is similarly aged in *barriques* and is dense and powerful with excellent depth and intensity. More unusual is a very attractive white, Ghibellino made from Nebbiolo (vinified as a white) and 30 per cent Sauvignon. Though of only moderate structure the Sauvignon isn't allowed to dominate and it shows enticing ripe fruit.(PW)
- **Vatellina Sforzato★★** £D   Fruttaio Ca' Rizzieri★★★★ £E
- **Valtellina Superiore** Il Crespino★★ £C   Inferno Riserva Barrique★★★ £D   Sassella Riserva★★★ £C
- O **Ghibellino★★** £C

RENATO RATTI Barolo www.renatoratti.com   A: **ViV**

Owner: Pietro Ratti & Massimo Martinelli   Fraz. Annunziata 7, 12064 La Morra (CN)
Renato Ratti was one of the key modernisers in Barolo in the 80s. Now under the direction of Pietro Ratti a new cellar has been built and some outside consultancy sought to give a renewed boost to quality. There are now 35 ha of vines which as well as the 'Marcenasco' vineyards in La Morra includes vineyards in the Asti and Monferrato hills. Barolos can at times lack a little weight and richness yet have an understated charm and personality. Production of Conca was only resumed in 98, after replanting. Villa Pattono, a blend of Barbera (at least half) with Cabernet and Merlot is much more showy, with a succulent, almost creamy, ripe red and black fruit character. Barbera d'Alba and other wines show good intense fruit and sound structure. (PW)
- **Barolo** Marcenasco★★ £E   Conca Marcenasco★★★ £F   Rocche Marcenasco★★★ £F
- **Monferrato** Villa Pattono★★★ £D
- **Barbera d'Alba** Torriglione★★ £C   ● **Dolcetto d'Alba** Colombè★★ £B

FRATELLI REVELLO Barolo www.revellofratelli.com   A: Fal, NYg, F&R

Owner: Fratelli Revello   Fraz. Annunziata 103, 12064 La Morra (CN)
Fruit-bomb Barolo? Revello, with 11 ha of vineyards, represents a softer face to Barolo with almost unbelievably short maceration times (albeit in rotofermenters) and plenty of new oak. There's no denying the wines' accessibility and upfront fruit appeal when very young but there's not the depth or structure of

the very best despite some firm tannins beneath the fruit. It is possible that they will age quite well but I doubt much of it will get the chance given the fruit charm and lush immediacy of the wines. It does feel slightly as if we've been given the icing minus the cake yet despite these reservations the wines broaden Nebbiolo's appeal. Regular Barbera and Dolcetto are aged in stainless steel but the small quantities of an explosively fruity Barbera d'Alba Ciabot du Re (from 25-year-old vines) spend 16 months in *barrique*. The Revellos' Insieme (see ALTARE) now includes a little Petit Verdot along with the Nebbiolo, Barbera and Cabernet Sauvignon. A further Barolo, from the Gattera *cru*, was first produced in 1999. (PW)

● **Barolo**★★ £E Vigna Conca★★★ £F Vigna Giachini★★★ £F Rocche★★★ £F
● **Barbera d'Alba**★ £C Ciabot du Re★★★ £D ● **Dolcetto d'Alba**★ £B
● **Insieme**★★★ £F

ALBINO ROCCA Barbaresco   A: J&B, NYg, F&R

Owner: Albino Rocca   Via Rabajà 15, 12050 Barbaresco (CN)
Albino Rocca and his son Angelo now have 13 ha (2 ha leased) and make two contrasting and very good Barbarescos. The richer, more lush but also more structured Brich Ronchi, made in greater quantities, receives the new *barrique* treatment, while Loreto, aged only in large oak, is a more pure, elegant expression of Nebbiolo. Barbera is also first class here; in the modern barrique-aged mould it shows better depth and balance than most. The white Langhe, La Rocca is a *barrique*-aged Cortese and is better than most Gavi while a Chardonnay shows the gently spicy ripe fruit characteristic of many Piedmont Chardonnay if not much more. All are reasonably priced. (PW)

● **Barbaresco** Vigneto Brich Ronchi★★★★ £E Vigneto Loreto★★★★ £E
● **Barbera d'Alba** Gèpin★★★ £D ● **Dolcetto d'Alba** Vignalunga★★ £B
○ **Langhe** La Rocca★★ £C ○ **Langhe Chardonnay** Da Bertù★ £B

BRUNO ROCCA Barbaresco www.brunorocca.it   A: Lib, HHB, N&P, C&R

Owner: Bruno Rocca   Via Rabajà 29, 12050 Barbaresco (CN)
The name Rabajà, one of Barbaresco's leading *crus,* derives from Bruno Rocca's original family estate and accounts for five of a total of 8 ha of vineyards. From it Bruno Rocca makes an excellent modern interpretation. His Barbaresco Rabajà is ripe, concentrated with impressive breadth as well as a more restrained oak character and better depth since 1998. A second Barbaresco, called Coparossa and made since 1995, includes grapes from the Fausoni and Pajorè *crus* and is increasingly good too if not quite at the level of Rabajà. There's fine quality from both the 1999 and 2000 vintages for the Barolos, already anticipated in the more fruit-driven Langhe red Rabajolo (from Cabernet, Barbera and Nebbiolo). Barbera, Dolcetto and a Chardonnay are also very competently made. (PW)

● **Barbaresco** Coparossa★★★★ £F Rabajà★★★★★ £F
● **Barbera d'Alba**★★★ £C ● **Dolcetto d'Alba** Vigna Trifolè★ £B
● **Langhe** Rabajolo★★★ £E ○ **Langhe Chardonnay** Cadet★★ £C

ROCCHE DEI MANZONI Barolo www.rocchedeimanzoni.it   A: Alv

Owner: Valentino & Iolanda Migliorini   Loc. Manzoni Soprani 3, 12065 Monforte d'Alba (CN)
Production here, from in excess of 40 ha spread over four separate estates, is quite substantial by the usual standard for a Piedmont grower. The imposing and well-financed cellar turns out modern, bold and oaky wines that are good examples of their type. Of an ever-expanding range of Barolos, Cappella di Santo Stefano (made since 1996) is emerging with the most class and depth. The relatively forward Bricco Manzoni combines Nebbiolo with Barbera while Quatr Nas is composed of Nebbiolo, Cabernet Sauvignon, Merlot and Pinot Nero. While the latter has been a little over-hyped in the past, the 99, with its complex black fruits character and deceptively supple texture, has plenty of underlying substance. Pinònero is pure Pinot Nero. Chardonnay is oaky but distinctly Piemontese, while the sparkling wine is creamy, toasty and yeasty. (PW)

● **Barolo** Vigna Big★★★ £F Vigna d'la Roul★★★ £F Bussia Pianpolvere Soprano★★★ £F
● **Barolo** Cappella di Santo Stefano★★★★ £F
● **Barbera d'Alba** Sorito Mosconi★★ £C
● **Langhe** Bricco Manzoni★★ £E Quatr Nas★★★ £E Pinònero★ £E
O **Langhe Chardonnay** L'Angelica★★ £E O **Valentino Brut** Riserva Elena★ £E

SANDRONE www.sandroneluciano.com A: RsW, WTs, P&S, UnC, Rae, BBR, NYg, V&C, Hrd

Owner: Luciano Sandrone Via Pugnane 4, 12060 Barolo (CN)
Luciano Sandrone remains as progressive and open-minded as ever yet continues to bring out greatness of both place and grape. The vines are tended by Luciano's brother Luca. Barolos are always super with splendid complexity and terrific breadth on the palate but also balanced and harmonious, with great length and a fine tannic backbone. Maceration times are quite lengthy and 600-litre oak is favoured. More or less equal amounts are made of both the famous *cru* Cannubi Boschis and sometimes equally fine Le Vigne (blended from the Brunate, Bussia, Cerretta and Vignane *crus*). The wines generally are also expressive of the vintage, unlike others that are forced into the same mould each year. Sandrone's 16 ha also provide good fruit-rich expressions of Barbera and Dolcetto while Nebbiolo d'Alba is one of a relatively few decent examples of this appellation. Since 1999, Pe Mol, a Langhe blend of Barbera and Nebbiolo (60/40) has also been made. (PW)
● **Barolo** Cannubi Boschis⓿⓿⓿⓿⓿ £H Le Vigne★★★★★ £G
● **Barbera d'Alba**★★★ £D ● **Dolcetto d'Alba**★★ £C
● **Langhe** Pe Mol★★ £E ● **Nebbiolo d'Alba** Valmaggiore★★ £C

SAN FEREOLO Dolcetto di Dogliani www.sanfereolo.com

Owner: Nicoletta Bocca & Francesco Stralla Borgata Valdibà 59, 12063 Dogliani (CN)
As with most Dogliani producers the focus here is Dolcetto. The estate's 10 ha covers several different sites within the Valdibà subzone which is the name given to what has become the regular Dolcetto. The most important Dolcetto is the San Fereolo version now designated *superiore*. This consistently deep, dense Dolcetto, among the best of the zone or anywhere for that matter, seems to improve with every vintage. A small part of it is aged in new oak the rest in large Slavonian casks. Also made is a little of '1593' which see 50 per cent new oak - an attempt at producing a long-lived style. The vineyards also provide a rich, intense Barbera that is aged partly in new oak and sold under the Langhe DOC as Brumaio. Both *barriques* and the larger *tonneaux* are used. A few hundred bottles of a new white from Gewürztraminer and Riesling (sold as Langhe Bianco) were first produced in 2001. (PW)
● **Dolcetto di Dogliani** Valdibà★★ £C Superiore San Fereolo★★★ £C
● **Langhe** Brumaio★★★ £C

SARACCO Moscato d'Asti www.paolosaracco.com

Owner: Paolo & Roberto Saracco Via Circonvallazione 6, 12053 Castiglione Tinella (CN)
No reds here, just one of several producers making exquisite Moscato d'Asti (CAUDRINA, LA MORANDINA and Elio PERRONE are others) that deserves to be better known in English-speaking countries. The superior bottling is the Moscato d'Autunno, a sweet concentrated example with delightful fusion of floral and fruity scents, reflected to some extent in the lighter yet intense regular version. Saracco also make good Chardonnay, both an unoaked Prasuè and a stylishly oaked Bianch del Luv with attractive peach, spice and melon notes. A perfumed, herbal white, Graffagno combines Riesling with Sauvignon and Chardonnay. (PW)
O **Moscato d'Asti**★★ £B O **Piemonte** Moscato d'Autunno★★★ £B
O **Langhe Chardonnay** Prasuè★ £B Bianch del Luv★★ £C
O **Langhe** Graffagno★ £C

PAOLO SCAVINO   Barolo   A: J&B, N&P, F&R

Owner: Enrico Scavino   Via Alba-Barolo 59, 12060 Castiglione Falletto (CN)
Enrico Scavino, like CLERICO, SANDRONE and others who shot to prominence in the 1980s, has proved to be very successful and the premium prices are a reflection of the continued high demand for his wines. He makes arguably the definitive example of Barolo Rocche dell'Annunziata, adding power and breadth to the *cru's* classic perfume. Also often superb, Cannubi and Bric del Fiasc show a little more of the structure indicative of their origins. Scavino, who works with his daughter Enrica, has been a keen proponent of the use of new oak for ageing Nebbiolo though this includes both *barriques* and larger wood. Occasionally the wines have suffered from an excess of oak but recently there has been good balance. The Barbera now has many rivals but still rewards cellaring of at least five to six years. Corale is a *barrique*-aged blend of mostly Nebbiolo and Barbera topped up with Cabernet Sauvignon. The white equivalent is Sorriso, from Chardonnay and Sauvignon. Recent vineyard acquisitions on the slopes of Roddi in the very north of the Barolo zone promise to highlight a previously unrealised potential. (PW)
● **Barolo**★★★ £F   Carobric★★★★ £G   Cannubi★★★★ £G   Bric del Fiasc★★★★★ £G
● **Barolo Riserva** Rocche dell'Annunziata★★★★★ £G
● **Barbera d'Alba** Affinato in Carati★★★ £E   ● **Dolcetto d'Alba**★ £B
● **Langhe** Corale★★★ £E

ALDO & RICCARDO SEGHESIO   Barolo   A: Fal, N&P, F&R

Owner: Aldo & Riccardo Seghesio   Fraz. Castelletto 19, 12065 Monforte d'Alba (CN)
Brothers Aldo and Riccardo make seductive, showy and accessible Barolo in the modern style, which somewhat belies their location in the Castelletto sub-zone of Monforte where the wines more often are noted for their structure and rigour. I feel there could be more in terms of stuffing yet apart from the slightly excessive oak it does have obvious appeal. An oaky but rich, deep Barbera works better and is similarly remarkably approachable. Bouquet, a blend of Nebbiolo, Cabernet and Merlot, is much in the same mould while ripe, fruity unoaked Barbera and Dolcetto are also made. (PW)
● **Barolo** Vigneto La Villa★★★ £E
● **Barbera d'Alba**★★ £C Vigneto della Chiesa★★★ £D
● **Langhe** Bouquet★★ £D   ● **Dolcetto d'Alba** Vigneto della Chiesa★★ £B

SOTTIMANO   Barbaresco

Owner: Sottimano family   Loc. Cottà 21, 12057 Neive (CN)
Sottimano is a still expanding estate with additional recent vineyard acquisitions of Barbaresco vineyards. Direction comes from Rino Sottimano but he is assisted by his son Andrea and the rest of his family. Significant improvements in quality continue to accrue from the recent run of top vintages. Small amounts (only a few thousand bottles of each) of ripe *barrique*-aged Barbaresco are made from the Cottà, Currà, Fausoni and Pajoré *crus*. All are well-structured with generally well-balanced tannins and alcohol and show good complexity with five or six years' age or more. The 99s and 2000s are arguably the best to date. Barbera and Dolcetto also reflect the new standards being attained here. Maté is a dry, fruity Brachetto. (PW)
● **Barbaresco** Cottà★★★ £E   Fausoni★★★ £E   Currà★★★★ £E   Pajoré★★★★ £E
● **Barbera d'Alba** Pairolero★★★ £C
● **Dolcetto d'Alba** Bric del Salto★★ £B   Cottà★★ £B

TRIACCA   Valtellina Superiore   www.triacca.com   A: Col

Owner: Triacca brothers   Via Nazionale 121, 23030 Villa di Tirano (SO)
Domenico Triacca is one of a few who show what Valtellina is capable of (NINO NEGRI, Mamete PREVOSTINI, RAINOLDI and Conti SERTOLI SALIS are others worth a try). As much work is going into improving the vineyards as the cellar, reducing yields and improving the canopy to obtain better light penetration and subsequently better, riper Nebbiolo fruit. Typically it is the Sfursat/Sforzato that is one of

the best wines, but the *barrique*-aged Prestigio is of comparable quality. Del Frate, a herbal, minerally Sauvignon, shows there's potential for this grape here too. (PW)

● **Valtellina Sforzato** San Domenico★★★ £E
● **Valtellina Superiore** Prestigio★★★ £E Riserva La Gatta★★ £C
○ **Del Frate★★** £C

G D VAJRA Barolo   A: **Lib**, ACh, Vne, P&S, V&C, Hrd

Owner: Aldo Vaira   Via delle Viole 25, 12060 Barolo (CN)
Based in the Vergne sub-zone of the Barolo commune, those of Aldo Vaira's vines grown locally are at an altitude atypically high for Barolo. The protected, south-facing Bricco delle Viole ripens Nebbiolo with a distinctive floral, plum and cherry fruit character but equally a *superiore* Barbera of great vigour and intensity. This altitude suits Dolcetto too and the best grapes from two nearby plots, Coste di Vergne and Fossati, have long produced a magnificent spicy, earthy Dolcetto with intense black plum fruit. Wait at least five years for this or keep as long again – it will outlive many Barberas and a few Barolos too. Aldo's Langhe Bianco is a very pure perfumed Riesling, tinged with lime, while Kyé is a wonderfully expressive and increasingly refined, powerful dry Freisa. Wood is used for ageing most wines, but almost exclusively large Slavonian oak. As a result the wines are not lush or soft but have both a varietal fruit intensity and a *terroir*-derived character. Great care goes into all wines and regular Dolcetto, Barbera and Nebbiolo are also a delight to drink. (PW)

● **Barolo★★★** £E Bricco delle Viole★★★★ £F
● **Barbera d'Alba★★** £C Superiore★★★ £D
● **Dolcetto d'Alba★** £B Coste & Fossati★★★★ £C
● **Langhe Freisa** Kyé★★★ £C ● **Langhe Nebbiolo★★** £C
○ **Langhe Bianco★★** £D

MAURO VEGLIO Barolo   A: Fal, N&P, F&R

Owner: Mauro & Daniela Veglio   Fraz. Annunziata 50, 12064 La Morra (CN)
ELIO ALTARE'S neighbour, the serious, dedicated Mauro Veglio might just be his truest disciple. The 10 ha combine plots from both Mauro's and his wife Daniela's families. Barolos have relatively short maceration in rotofermenters prior to ageing in 225-litre *barriques* (60 per cent new). Castelletto, from Monforte vineyards, is the most fleshy and perhaps most characterful. Arborina is sourced from outside the winery doors. These are made in the greatest quantities. Gattera is a relatively forward, attractive, poised example, while a tiny amount of floral, elegant and cherry-flavoured Rocche is also made. In general they have been very good over the recent string of good vintages. Cascina Nuova Barbera is aged only in *barriques* and is best with at least three to four years' age. Good regular Barbera and Dolcetto can be drunk very young. Insieme is Nebbiolo, Barbera and Cabernet. (PW)

● **Barolo** Arborina★★★ £F Castelletto★★★ £E Gattera★★★ £E Rocche★★★ £E
● **Barbera d'Alba★** £B Cascina Nuova★★ £D
● **Dolcetto d'Alba★** £B ● **Insieme★★★** £F

VIETTI Barolo www.vietti.com   A: **Vim**, N&P, F&R

Owner: Currado-Vietti & Cordero family   Piazza V Veneto 5, 12060 Castiglione Falletto (CN)
Established for more than a century this house came to prominence under the direction of Alfredo Currado. 32 ha of vineyards have gradually been acquired and the majority of the wines are now produced from estate vineyards. Single-vineyard Barolos are sourced from top *crus*. While traditionally vinified, most are now partly *barrique*-aged and Lazzarito in particular can show more than a hint of oak when young. Yet there is a big difference between these and some of the more forward, easy, modern examples from other producers. They add real weight and richness with cellaring. Rocche is the most traditionally styled and often the most classic but it is worth waiting at least seven years before drinking any of them. Often superb, Barbera d'Alba Scarrone Vigna Vecchia usually repays similar ageing. Barbera d'Asti La Crena is a notable single-vineyard

example while other wines are soundly made. (PW)

- **Barolo** Castiglione★★ £E Brunate★★★ £F Lazzarito★★★★ £F Rocche★★★★ £F
- **Barbaresco** Masseria★★ £E
- **Barbera d'Alba** Scarrone★★ £D Scarrone Vigna Vecchia★★★ £E
- **Barbera d'Asti** Tre Vigne★ £C La Crena★★★ £E
- **Dolcetto d'Alba** Tre Vigne★ £B Sant'Anna★ £B
- O **Roero Arneis**★ £B O **Moscato d'Asti** Cascinetta★★ £B

VIGNA RIONDA – MASSOLINO Barolo   A: Lib, Vne, F&M

Owner: Massolino brothers Piazza Cappellano 8, 12050 Serralunga d'Alba (CN)
One of Langhe's best traditional producers, based around one of her top *crus* – Vigna Rionda. Barolos tend to show a more typical Nebbiolo colour than from those who use lots of new oak and can be deceptive and difficult to assess in their youth. Plump and flattering they are not, but the breadth and length is apparent even when young and the tight, intense core builds with age to give fullness and a marvellous complexity after a decade or so. Margheria is intense and tannic, with a certain elegance. Parafada, a more modern style with a short but high-temperature maceration and partial *barrique*-ageing, adds more breadth and weight allied to great length. Vigna Rionda Riserva, subject to a three-week maceration, can show still more fullness, depth and complexity. *Barriques* are also used for Barbera, Chardonnay and Langhe blend Piria (Barbera/Nebbiolo). All are good examples of their type, particularly the Barbera d'Alba Gisep. (PW)

- **Barolo**★★★★ £E Margheria★★★★★ £F Parafada★★★★★ £F
- **Barolo Riserva** Vigna Rionda❂❂❂❂❂ £F
- **Barbera d'Alba** Gisep★★★ £D ● **Dolcetto d'Alba** Barilot★★ £B
- **Langhe** Nebbiolo★ £C ● **Langhe** Piria★★ £E
- O **Langhe** Chardonnay★★ £C

GIANNI VOERZIO Barolo   A: JAr, P&S, PWa, F&R

Owner: Gianni Voerzio Strada Loreto 1, 12064 La Morra (CN)
Gianni Voerzio doesn't make the blockbuster, super-concentrated wines of his brother, ROBERTO VOERZIO, but from 12.5ha he does produce a consistent and diverse range of very fine, even elegant wines. All have great vigour, deep fruit and good balance. Arneis and Dolcetto are excellent examples, both alive and intense, the Dolcetto with splendid definition and uncommon style for this grape. Barbera and the Nebbiolo/Barbera blend, Serrapiù, show the most marked oak influence but this melts into the the rich pure fruit with a little age. Barolo La Serra is dense and intriguing when young, inviting at least 8 to 10 years' cellaring. Prices are on the high side but not out of step with quality. (PW)

- **Barolo** La Serra★★★★★ £G ● **Langhe** Serrapiù★★★ £E
- **Barbera d'Alba** Ciabot della Luna★★★ £D ● **Dolcetto d'Alba** Rochettevino★★★ £C
- **Langhe Freisa** Sotto I Bastioni★★ £C ● **Langhe Nebbiolo** Ciabot della Luna★★ £D
- O **Roero Arneis** Bricco Cappellina★★ £C O **Moscato d'Asti** Vignasergente★ £C

ROBERTO VOERZIO Barolo   A: Eno, WTs, JNi, Hrd, N&P, F&R

Owner: Roberto Voerzio Loc. Cerreto 1, 12064 La Morra (CN)
Voerzio's prices have inevitably risen in line with his seeming unending ascent of the Piedmont hierarchy. In fact he took a little longer to achieve greatness in his wines than other stars. Relentless in his pusuit of low yields and very concentrated fruit and unwavering in his use of new oak, he now achieves balance and harmony in all wines that earlier vintages sometimes lacked. New, from 1998, is a bottling of the *cru* Sarmassa, which lies immediately below Cerequio and therefore in the Barolo commune. Also new is another Barolo based in part on Rocche dell'Annunziata, while a tiny amount of an outstanding Riserva, Vecchie Viti dei Capalot e delle Brunate, is bottled only in magnums. Voerzio's mega-Barbera is the most powerful and concentrated made anywhere. Vignaserra is Nebbiolo with Cabernet Sauvignon (and/or Barbera) and has regularly among the best of its type but was produced for the last time in 2000. Some of

the fruit will now go into a new Nebbiolo-based blend. (PW)

● **Barolo** Brunate✪✪✪✪✪ £H   Cerequio✪✪✪✪ £H
● **Barolo** La Serra★★★★★ £H   Sarmassa★★★★★ £H
● **Barbera d'Alba Riserva** Vigneto Pozzo dell Annunziata✪✪✪✪✪ £F
● **Dolcetto d'Alba** Priavino★★ £B   ● **Langhe** Vignaserra★★★ £D

OTHER WINES OF NOTE

GIOVANNI ABRIGO ● **Barbera d'Alba** Marminela £B   ● **Dolcetto Diano d'Alba** Garabei £B
ORLANDO ABRIGO ● **Barbera d'Alba** Vigna Roreto £B   ● **Dolcetto d'Alba** Vigna dell' Erto £B
● **Barbaresco** £D Vigna Montersino £E
G ACCORNERO & FIGLI ● **Barbera del Monferrato** Superiore Bricco Bastista £E Cima £E
● **Monferrato** Centenario (Cabernet Sauvignon/Barbera) £E
GIOVANNI ALMONDO ● **Roero** Bric Valdiana £C   ● **Barbera d'Alba** Valbianchera £C
FAMIGLIA ANSELMA ● **Barolo** £E Adasi £F
BATASIOLO ● **Barolo** Bofani £F Boscareto £F Cerequio £F Corda della Briccolina £F
CARLO BENOTTO ● **Barbera d'Asti** Superiore Balau £B Vigneto Casot £B Rupestris £C
NICOLA BERGAGLIO ● **Gavi del Comune di Gavi** La Minaia £C
BERSANO ● **Barbera d'Asti** Superiore Nizza £C Superiore Generala £D
GUIDO BERTA ● **Barbera d'Asti** Superiore Canto di Luna £C
FRANCO BOASSO GABUTTI ● **Barolo** Gabutti £E
S & E BOROLI ● **Barolo** Bussia £E Villero £E   ● **Barbera d'Alba** Bricco dei Fagiani £C
● **Dolcetto d'Alba** Madonna di Como £B   ○ **Moscato d'Asti** Aureum £B
FRANCESCO BOSCHIS ● **Dolcetto di Dogliani** Sorì San Martino £B Vigna dei Prey £B
BOVIO ● **Barolo** Arborina £F Gattera £F Rocchettevino £E   ● **Barbera d'Alba** Regia Veja £C
GIACOMO BREZZA ● **Barolo** Bricco Sarmassa £F Cannubi £F
BRICCO MONDALINO ● **Barbera del Monferrato** Gaudium Magnum £D
● **Barbera d'Asti** Il Bergantino £B
GIAN PIERO BROGLIA - LA MEIRANO ○ **Gavi** Bruno Broglia £C
● **Monferrato** Bruno Broglia (Barbera/Merlot/Cabernet Sauvignon) £C
BRUNA ○ **Riviera Ligure di Ponente** Pigato U Bacan £C Le Russeghine £B
CABUTTO - TENUTA LA VOLTA ● **Barolo** Vigna La Volta £E
● **Langhe** Vendemmiaio (Nebbiolo/Barbera) £C
CAPPELLANO ● **Barolo** Gabutti £E Gabutti Franco £E
TENUTA CARRETTA ● **Barbaresco** Cascina Bordino £E   ● **Barolo** Cannubi £E
CA' ROSSA ● **Roero** Audinaggio £C Mompissano £C   ● **Barbera d'Alba** Mulassa £C
CASCINA CASTLÈT ● **Barbera d'Asti** Superiore Litina £C Passum £D
● **Monferrato** Policalpo (Barbera/Cabernet Sauvignon) £C   ○ **Piemonte Moscato Passito** Avié £E
CASCINA CUCCO ● **Barolo** Vigna Cucco £E
CASCINA FONDA ○ **Moscato d'Asti** £B   ○ **Driveri Moscato Spumante** £C
○ **Vendemmia Tardiva** (Moscato) £C
CASCINA GARITINA ● **Barbera d'Asti** Bricco Garitta £B
CASCINA LA GHERSA ● **Barbera d'Asti** Superiore Camparò £B La Vignassa £D
● **Monferrato** La Ghersa (Barbera/Cabernet Sauvignon/Merlot) £E
CASCINA MONREALE ● **Barbera d'Asti** Superiore Valentina £C
CASTELLARI BERGAGLIO ○ **Gavi** Fornaci £B Rolona £B Rovereto V Vecchia £C   ○ **Pilìn** £D
CAVALLERI ○ **Franciacorta** Brut Collezione Eslusiva £D Satèn £C
PODERI COLLA ● **Barolo** Bussia Dardi Le Rose £F   ● **Barbaresco** Roncaglia £F
PAOLO CONTERNO ● **Barolo** Ginestra £F   ● **Barolo Riserva** Ginestra £G
● **Barbera d'Alba** Ginestra £D   ● **Dolcetto d'Alba** Ginestra £B
GIUSEPPE CORTESE ● **Barbaresco** Rabajà £E
DAMILANO ● **Barolo** Cannubi £E   ● **Barbera d'Alba** £C   ● **Dolcetto d'Alba** £B
WALTER DE BATTÉ ○ **Cinque Terre** £C   ○ **Cinque Terre Sciacchetrà** £D
DELTETTO ● **Roero** Braja £C   ● **Barbera d'Alba** Bramé £C   ○ **Roero Arneis** San Michele £C
ALESSANDRO & GIAN NATALE FANTINO ● **Barolo** Vigna dei Dardi £E

BENITO FAVARO ○ **Erbaluce di Caluso** Le Chiusure £C

FERRANDO ● **Carema** Etichetta Nera £E   ○ **Erbaluce di Caluso** Cariola Etichetta Nera £C
○ **Caluso Passito** Vigneto Cariola £F

FONTANABIANCA ● **Barbaresco** Sorì Burdin £E

TENUTA GARETTO ● **Barbera d'Asti Superiore** In Pectore £B   Favà £C

GASTALDI ● **Barbaresco** £E   ● **Langhe** Castlè (Nebbiolo) £F   ○ **Langhe Chardonnay** £C
○ **Langhe** Gastaldi (Chardonnay/Sauvignon) £D

FRATELLI GIACOSA ● **Barbaresco** Rio Sordo £E   ● **Barolo** Vigna Mandorlo £E
● **Barbera d'Alba** Maria Gioana £B

GILLARDI ● **Dolcetto di Dogliani** Cursalet £B   Vigneto Maestra £B
● **Langhe** Yeta (Dolcetto/Cabernet Sauvignon) £D   ● **Harys** (Syrah/Cabernet Sauvignon) £E

TENUTA GIUNCHEO ● **Rossese di Dolceaqua** Pian del Vescovo £D

FRATELLI GRASSO ● **Barbaresco** Bricco Spessa £D   Sorì Valgrande £D

GIACOMO GRIMALDI ● **Barolo** Le Coste £E

HILBERG - PASQUERO ● **Barbera d'Alba** Superiore £C   ● **Nebbiolo d'Alba** £C

HOHLER ● **Barbera d'Asti** Pian Bosco £C   Pian Bosco Barrique £D

I PAGLIERI - ROAGNA ● **Barbaresco** Crichet Pajé £E

ISABELLA ● **Barbera d'Asti** Superiore Bric Stupui £C

OTTAVIANO LAMBRUSCHI ○ **Colli di Luna Vermentino** Colle Marina £C   Sarticola £C

LA MORANDINA ● **Barbera d'Asti** Varmat £C   ○ **Moscato d'Asti** £B

GIANLUIGI LANO ● **Barbaresco** £E   ● **Barbera d'Alba** Fondo Prà £C

L'ARMANGIA (also see Castello di Calosso) ○ **Piemonte Chardonnay** Robi e Robi £C

LES CRÊTES ● **Valle d'Aosta Fumin** Vigne La Tour £C   ● **Valle d'Aosta Syrah** Coteau La Tour £C;
○ **Valle d'Aosta Chardonnay** Frissonnière Cuvée Bois £C

MARCHESI ALFIERI ● **Barbera d'Asti** La Tota £B   ● **Barbera d'Asti** Superiore Alfiera £D
● **Monferrato Rosso** San Germano (Pinot Nero) £D   Rosso dei Marchesi (Barbera/Pinot Nero) £B

MARCHESI DI BAROLO ● **Barolo** Cannubi £E   Sarmassa £E   ● **Langhe** Picit £D

MARIO MARENGO ● **Barolo** Bricco Viole £E   Brunate £E

LUIGI MINUTO - CASCINA LUISIN ● **Barbaresco** Rabajà £F   Sorì Paolin £F
● **Barbera d'Alba** Maggiur £B   Asili £D

MONCHIERO CARBONE ● **Roero** Printi £C   Srü £C   ● **Barbera d'Alba** Mon Birone £B
○ **Roero Arneis** Re Cit £B

MONTARIBALDI ● **Barbaresco** Sorì Montaribaldi £E   ● **Barbera d'Alba** dü Gir £B
● **Dolcetto d'Alba** Niccolini £B

MONTE ROSSA ○ **Franciacorta** Brut Cabochon £E   Brut Satèn £D
⊙ **Franciacorta** Brut Cabochon Rosé £E

MONTI ● **Barbera d'Alba** £C   ● **Langhe** (Cabernet Sauvignon/Merlot/Nebbiolo) Dossi Rossi £D
○ **Langhe** (Chardonnay/Riesling) L'Aura £C

MORGASSI SUPERIORE ● **Sarastro** (Barbera/Cabernet Sauvignon) £C   ● **Tamino** (Syrah) £D

FRATELLI MOSSIO ● **Dolcetto d'Alba** Bricco Caramelli £B   Piano delli Perdoni £B

TENUTE NEIRANO ● **Barbera d'Asti** Superiore Le Croci £C

PALLADINO ● **Barolo** San Bernardo £E   Vigna Broglio £E

ELIO PERRONE ○ **Moscato d'Asti** Clarté £B   Sourgal £B   ● **Barbera d'Asti** Grivò £C

PIRA ● **Dolcetto di Dogliani** Vigna Bricco dei Botti £B   Vigna Landes £B
● **Dolcetto d'Alba** Vigna Fornaci £B   ● **Piemonte** Barbera Briccobotti £C

MAMETE PREVOSTINI ● **Valtellina Superiore** Corte di Cama £E   Sassella Sommarovina £D
● **Valtellina** Sforzato Albareda £E

PUNSET ● **Barbaresco** Campo Quadro £E

RICCHINO ● **Dolcetto Diano d'Alba** Rizieri £B

RICCI CURBASTRO ○ **Franciacorta** Satèn Brut £C   Extra Brut £C

GIUSEPPE RINALDI ● **Barolo** Brunate - Le Coste £F   Cannubi - San Lorenzo - Ravera £F

ROCCHE COSTAMAGNA ● **Barolo** Rocche dell'Annunziata Bricco Francesco £F
● **Barbera d'Alba** Annunziata £B   Rocche delle Rocche £D   ● **Dolcetto d'Alba** Rubis £B

SAN ROMANO ● **Dolcetto di Dogliani** £B   Vigna del Pilone £B   Superiore Dolianum £C

CANTINE SANT' AGATA ● **Barbera d'Asti** Superiore Cavalé £C

CANTINE SANT' EVASIO ● **Barbera d'Asti** Superiore Nizza £C
SCAGLIOLA ● **Barbera d'Asti** SanSì £C Selezione £C O **Moscato d'Asti** Volo di Farfalle £B
GIORGIO SCARZELLO E FIGLI ● **Barolo** Vigna Merenda £F ● **Barbera d'Alba Sup.** £C
F & M SCRIMAGLIO ● **Barbera d'Asti Superiore** Acsé £D Crutin £C Bricco Sant'Ippolito £B
● **Monferrato** Tantra (Barbera/Cabernet Sauvignon) £D
MAURO SEBASTE ● **Barolo** Monvigliero £E Prapò £E
SYLLA SEBASTE ● **Barolo** Bussia £E
SERTOLIS SALIS ● **Valtellina Superiore** Inferno £C Sassella £C Corte della Meridiana £D
● **Valtellina** Sforzato Canua £F
MICHELE TALIANO ● **Barbaresco** Ad Altiora £E ● **Barbera d'Alba** Laboriosa £B
TENUTA DEI FIORI ● **Monferrato Rosso** Cinquefile (Barbera/Cabernet Sauvignon) £C
TERRE DA VINO ● **Barolo** Paesi Tuoi £D Poderi Parussi £E
● **Barbera d'Asti** La Luna e i Falò £B
TERRE ROSSE O **Rivera delle Ligure Ponente** Pigato £B Pigato Apogèo £C Vermentino £B
● **Solitario** (Rossese/Grenache/Barbera) £E
GIANCARLO TRAVAGLINI ● **Gattinara** £D Riserva £E Tre Vigne £E
UBERTI O **Franciacorta** Brut Francesco I £C Brut Magnificentia £E Extra Brut Comarì del Salem £E
RINO VARALDO ● **Barbaresco** Bricco Libero £E Sorì Loreto £E ● **Barbera d'Alba** £C
ERALDO VIBERTI ● **Barolo** £E ● **Barbera d'Alba** Vigna Clara £C
VILLA SPARINA O **Gavi** Monte Rotondo £D ● **Dolcetto d'Acqui** d'Giusep £B
● **Monferrato** Rivalta (Barbera) £D

Author's choice (PW)

Two dozen outstanding Barolo
AZELIA ● **Barolo** San Rocco
ENZO BOGLIETTI ● **Barolo** Brunate
BROVIA ● **Barolo** Rocche dei Brovia
ELVIO COGNO ● **Barolo** Vigna Elena
DOMENICO CLERICO ● **Barolo** Ciabot Mentin Ginestra
ALDO CONTERNO ● **Barolo** Colonello
GIACOMO CONTERNO ● **Barolo** Riserva Monfortino
CONTERNO-FANTINO ● **Barolo** Sorì Ginestra
CORDERO DI MONTEZEMOLO ● **Barolo** Bricco Gattera
LUIGI EINAUDI ● **Barolo** Nei Cannubi
ETTORE GERMANO ● **Barolo** Cerretta
ATTILIO GHISOLFI ● **Barolo** Bricco Visette
BRUNO GIACOSA ● **Barolo** Rocche del Falletto di Serralunga
ELIO GRASSO ● **Barolo** Ginestra Casa Matè
BARTOLO MASCARELLO ● **Barolo**
GIUSEPPE MASCARELLO & FIGLIO ● **Barolo** Monprivato
ARMANDO PARUSSO ● **Barolo** Bussia Vigne Rocche
E PIRA & FIGLI ● **Barolo** Cannubi
LUIGI PIRA ● **Barolo** Margheria
LUCIANO SANDRONE ● **Barolo** Le Vigne
PAOLO SCAVINO ● **Barolo** Bric del Fiasc
VIGNA RIONDA - MASSOLINO ● **Barolo** Parafada
GIANNI VOERZIO ● **Barolo** La Serra
ROBERTO VOERZIO ● **Barolo** Brunate

12 exciting Barbaresco

PRODUTTORI DEL BARBARESCO ● **Barbaresco** Riserva Montefico

PIERO BUSSO ● **Barbaresco** Vigna Borghese

CERETTO ● **Barbaresco** Bricco Asili

GAJA ● **Barbaresco**

BRUNO GIACOSA ● **Barbaresco** Santo Stefano di Neive

LA SPINETTA ● **Barbaresco** Vigneto Starderi

MARCHESI DI GRESY ● **Barbaresco** Martinenga Camp Gros

MOCCAGATTA ● **Barbaresco** Bric Balin

PAITIN ● **Barbaresco** Sorì Paitin

PELISSERO ● **Barbaresco** Vanotu

ALBINO ROCCA ● **Barbaresco** Brich Ronchi

BRUNO ROCCA ● **Barbaresco** Rabajà

10 other special North-West reds

ANTICHI VIGNETI DI CANTALUPO ● **Ghemme** Signore di Bayard

MATTEO CORREGGIA ● **Nebbiolo d'Alba** La Val di Preti

ELIO ALTARE ● **Insieme**

BRICCO MAIOLICA ● **Nebbiolo d'Alba** Il Cumot

CA' DEL BOSCO ● **Maurizio Zanella**

LA SPINETTA ● **Monferrato Rosso** Pin

MALVIRÀ ● **Roero Superiore** Mombeltramo

NINO NEGRI ● **Valtellina** Sfursat 5 Stelle

ANGELO NEGRO & FIGLI ● **Roero** Sudisfà

ALDO RAINOLDI ● **Valtellina** Sfursat Fruttaio Ca' Rizzieri

15 super Barbera

GIANFRANCO ALESSANDRIA ● **Barbera d'Alba** Vittoria

BERTELLI ● **Barbera d'Asti** San Antonio Vieilles Vignes

BRAIDA ● **Barbera d'Asti** Ai Suma

CASCINA VAL DEL PRETE ● **Barbera d'Alba** Superiore Carolina

CASTELLO DI CALOSSO/MAURO GRASSO ● **Barbera d'Asti** Rodotiglia

LUIGI COPPO & FIGLI ● **Barbera d'Asti** Pomorosso

HASTAE ● **Barbera d'Asti** Quorum

LA BARBATELLA ● **Barbera d'Asti** Superiore Vigna dell'Angelo

LA SPINETTA ● **Barbera d'Asti** Superiore

TENUTA LA TENAGLIA ● **Barbera d'Asti** Emozioni

FRANCO M MARTINETTI ● **Barbera d'Asti** Superiore Montruc

ANDREA OBERTO ● **Barbera d'Alba** Giada

FERDINANDO PRINCIPIANO ● **Barbera d'Alba** La Romualda

VIETTI ● **Barbera d'Alba** Scarrone Vigna Vecchia

ROBERTO VOERZIO ● **Barbera d'Alba** Riserva Vigneto Pozzo dell'Annunziata

10 diverse Dolcetto

ANNA MARIA ABBONA ● **Dolcetto di Dogliani** Maioli

CLAUDIO ALARIO ● **Dolcetto di Diano d'Alba** Costa Fiore

ENZO BOGLIETTI ● **Dolcetto d'Alba** Tiglineri

BROVIA ● **Dolcetto d'Alba** Solatio

CA' VIOLA ● **Dolcetto d'Alba** Barturot

LUIGI EINAUDI ● **Dolcetto di Dogliani** I Filari

MARCARINI ● **Dolcetto d'Alba** Boschi di Berri

SAN FEREOLO ● **Dolcetto di Dogliani** San Fereolo

G D VAJRA ● **Dolcetto d'Alba** Coste & Fossati

GIANNI VOERZIO ● **Dolcetto d'Alba** Rochettevino

If Italy contained only the viticultural resources of Piedmont and Tuscany, that would be wealth enough, but there is much, much more even if a large part of it is too often ignored by an increasingly homogenised wider world. In North-East Italy fine, elegant whites are produced in the Alto Adige and fuller, more concentrated examples in Friuli-Venezia-Giulia, from a mix of both local and international varieties. Some of Italy's finest sweet wines also come from the North-East while all three provinces now also provide high-quality reds. While some come from the like of Cabernet Sauvignon or Merlot, more and more outstanding original reds result from a realisation of the true potential of the native grapes: not just Corvina in the Veneto for Valpolicella and powerful Amarone but also Lagrein and Teroldego in Trentino-Alto Adige and even the previously obscure Pignolo and Schiopettino in Friuli.

Trentino-Alto Adige

The German-speaking South Tyrol (Südtirol) is becoming an increasingly reliable source of elegant, perfumed dry white wines. Most of the wines are are labelled as **Alto Adige** DOC with a varietal name and many of the grapes are familar to wine drinkers. The best examples of Chardonnay, Sauvignon, Gewürztraminer, Pinot Bianco and Pinot Grigio are both concentrated and elegant and are complemented by some ripe reds from Cabernet Sauvignon and Merlot as well as one or two genuinely good examples of Pinot Nero. The native Lagrein has emerged over the past decade as a superior grape variety and most of the top producers now offer a premium oak-aged version, often in addition to simpler, supple, spicy, brambly examples. Lago di Caldaro (or Kalterersee) which now comes under the Alto Adige DOC can be a light but attractive perfumed red from the Schiava grape. *Scelto* (or Auslese) indicates a higher degree of ripeness. The quality of the co-operative wines tended to be consistent if unexciting in the past but many have taken a big leap forward in the last decade, adding to the supply of quality wines forged by Lageder and Hofstätter.

As in the Alto Adige, the regional **Trentino** DOC covers a wide range of varietals and though the standard is generally lower than in the Alto Adige several small producers signal the quality possible. The greatest originality comes in the shape of an excellent red in **Teroldego Rotaliano** (from the Teroldego grape). Regrettably there are not that many examples yet but the superb wines of Foradori show what is possible with higher-density planting and low yields. The potential of another native variety, Marzemino, remains unrealised but some attractively floral, plummy examples do exist. Though Trentino is a major producer of sparkling wine, few examples of **Trento** have the quality to compete with the best fizz from around the world.

Veneto

The Adige river swings out of Trentino-Alto Adige and turns more easterly as it runs through Verona. On the lowest reaches of the Lessini Mountains to the north are the hills of Valpolicella, merging with Soave to the east. A number of producers have turned their backs on these classic appellations (using instead a regional IGT) as they believe they have failed to shed an image of cheap, simple plonk. In terms of quality wine the international reputation of this noble Italian province has come to depend chiefly on **Amarone della Valpolicella**. From a still relatively small number of producers, top examples of this powerful red, made from partially-dried grapes, are among Italy's finest reds. When not fully fermented to dryness this results in the sweeter **Recioto della Valpolicella,** while *amandorlato* is sometimes used to describe an in-between style. The biggest challenge for producers of Amarone is to retain some of the typicity of the style while losing the rusticity that has plagued its image. The excessively raisiny character and high levels of volatile acidity have become less apparent as cellar hygiene has improved and more care has gone into eliminating grapes affected by rot. Many are now aged in new oak but whether more modern or traditional in style, Amarone's strength and character don't give it the greatest versatility. Fortunately, despite the trend to increased quantities of Amarone, a few producers have radically improved the quality of **Valpolicella.** Modern producers have thrown out the lesser of the traditional grapes, concentrating on Corvina, but are also introducing small percentages of other grapes – such as Syrah in the case of Allegrini. Most of the best examples have benefited from some sort of enrichment. The technique known as *ripasso* (the name is exclusive to Masi) involves passing the finished wine over fermented Amarone skins, improving both the texture and character of the wine. Many a producer's premium version of Valpolicella (sometimes from a single vineyard and usually as Valpolicella Classico Superiore) benefits from it but not all – others directly incorporate a percentage of dried grapes at some point during the fermentation, producing a sort of hybrid Valpolicella/Amarone. The best Amarone need at least five to six years' age and will keep for 10 to 15. Recioto is often better drunk younger but top examples will keep as long. Top examples of Valpolicella generally drink well with three to five years' age but exceptionally will keep for more than a decade. The best recent vintages are 2000, 97, 95, 93, 90, 88 and 85 but from a top producer wines from most other years are also very good, including recently 98 and even the more difficult 99.

Soave at its best is much more than an anonymous dry white – instead it can be a concentrated and stylish medium-bodied white, capable of some age in the best examples, which are produced either solely from Garganega or with a small amount of Chardonnay. Wine from dried grapes, as **Recioto di Soave**, can be an excellent sweet white. **Bianco di Custoza** and **Bardolino** to the west, on the eastern and southern fringes of Lake Garda, are sometimes cited as substitutes for Soave and Valpolicella but usually only compare with basic examples of each. From the western shores of Lake Garda one or two producers make quite concentrated, stylish **Lugana** as well as other blends (that incorporate Chardonnay and Sauvignon in the case of Ca' dei Frati). North of historic Vicenza is **Breganze**, which owes its reputation to one producer, Maculan. As well as splendid sweet whites from the native white Vespaiolo, good quality has been realised from Cabernet Sauvignon and Merlot. Vignalta in the **Colli Euganei**, found south of Padova (Padua), has also been successful with both Merlot and Cabernet but makes good dry whites too. **Prosecco** is the region's fizz and from a good producer can be fresh and attractive if drunk young.

Friuli-Venezia Giulia

Friuli's production (like that of Trentino-Alto Adige) is dwarfed by that of the Veneto but in terms of the number of top-quality producers the two are equals. French varieties have been planted for many years in the hilly **Collio** and **Colli Orientali del Friuli** DOCs, but despite the quality of the wines produced from them they fail to give the region a distinctive stamp. Yet beyond Chardonnay, Sauvignon Blanc, Pinot Grigio and Pinot Bianco there are ever-better examples of Tocai Friulano, Ribolla Gialla and Malvasia Istriana: wines of distinctive character – and high quality from a top producer. The flatter **Friuli Isonzo** has emerged over the past decade as the third major quality zone, led by a young generation of growers making some of the most concentrated and structured whites anywhere in the region. While a good number of the wines are made in the prevalent unoaked fashion, an increasing number of the best wines have added structure from some use of oak. Fine light, sweet whites are made by several producers from the native grapes Picolit and Verduzzo. Red wines are increasingly important and with better training, higher-density planting and lower yields the grassy character once common to so many of the reds from Cabernet Sauvignon, Cabernet Franc and Merlot has been replaced by a lush, ripe berry fruit richness in best examples. Also showing much promise in the most recent vintages are some intense and concentrated examples of native varieties, Pignolo, Refosco and Schioppettino. Soundly made but rarely exciting whites and reds are produced in the large, mostly flat zone of **Friuli Grave** or even the smaller southern zones of **Friuli Aquileia** or **Friuli Latisana**.

A-Z of producers by region

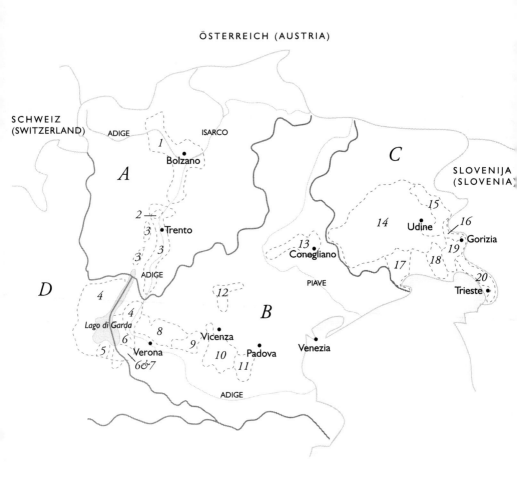

Regions:

A Trentino – Alto Adige
B Veneto
C Friuli-Venezia Giulia
D Lombardy (Lombardia)

Appellations:

1 Alto Adige
2 Teroldego Rotaliano
3 Trentino
4 Garda
5 Lugana
6 Bardolino
7 Bianco di Custoza
8 Valpolicella
9 Soave
10 Colli Berici
11 Colli Euganei
12 Breganze
13 Prosecco di Conegliano-Valdobbiadene
14 Friuli Grave
15 Colli Orientali del Friuli
16 Collio
17 Friuli Latisana
18 Friuli Aquileia
19 Friuli Isonzo
20 Carso

ALLEGRINI Veneto www.allegrini.it **A: Lib**, ACh, Vne, UnC, Con, P&S, BBR, F&M, Sel, Hrd

Owner: Franco & Marilisa Allegrini Corte Giara, 37022 Fumane di Valpolicella (VR)

The 70-ha Allegrini estate is Valpolicella's leading producer of modern-style reds. The wines have excellent fruit, balance, depth and intensity and develop marvellously smooth velvety textures with age. While a good regular Valpolicella is based on the three traditional grapes, two single-vineyard reds, previously Valpolicella *crus* but now sold as Veronese IGT, continue to evolve. Both are based on Corvina (70 percent) and Rondinella, but La Grola also includes 10 per cent Syrah and 5 per cent Sangiovese since 1998. Palazzo della Torre, a *ripasso*-style version (but enriched by dried grapes rather than Amarone lees) also includes a Sangiovese component. Oak is also a feature of the best wines, including the Amarone, which shows marvellous richness and concentration in the most recent releases. La Poja is a pure Corvina made from late-harvested grapes grown on the top of the La Grola hill and is a wine of striking intensity and depth, now with a long-established record of production. Villa Giona is separate property in the Classico zone but with 5 ha planted exclusively to Cabernet Sauvignon, Merlot and Syrah. The 2000 vintage (50/40/10) is intense and very ripe, even raisiny, but not without promise. The sweet Recioto, Giovanni Allegrini, is dedicated to the memory of the Allegrinis' father, who founded the company. Amarone, La Grola and Palazzo della Torre are all made in significant quantities and should be easy to obtain. (PW)

● **Amarone della Valpolicella Classico**★★★★★ £F ● **La Poja**★★★★★ £F
● **La Grola**★★★ £D ● **Palazzo della Torre**★★★ £D
● **Recioto della Valpolicella Classico** Giovanni Allegrini★★★ £F

ANSELMI Veneto **A: Eno**, NYg, N&P, FWC, Sel, V&C

Owner: Roberto Anselmi Via San Carlo 46, 37032 Monteforte d'Alpone (VR)

Roberto Anselmi used to make Soave. 'Used to' because all the wines are now Veneto IGT as one of the Veneto's, indeed Italy's pioneers for quality continues the pursuit of excellence beyond the restraints of the appellation. Only the regular bottling of San Vicenzo is made in substantial quantities but quality is consistently high. Two former *crus* offer a marked contrast in style with two or three years' age: Capitel Foscarino offers a lovely pure citrus and yellow plum fruit, while Capitel Croce divides opinion somewhat with its slightly exaggerated oak-influenced style with some spice, even coconut character. Foscarino and San Vicenzo include a little Chardonnay. The star, though, is the wonderfully elegant, pure-fruited and classy sweet wine, I Capitelli. A red from Cabernet Sauvignon, Realda, shows concentrated blackcurrant fruit and a leafy influence. (PW)

○ **Capitel Foscarino**★★★ £C ○ **Capitel Croce**★★ £C
○ **San Vicenzo**★ £B ○ **I Capitelli**★★★ £D
● **Cabernet Sauvignon Realda**★★ £C

BORGO DEL TIGLIO Friuli-Venezia Giulia **A: Ast**, P&S, F&M, UnC, But

Owner: Nicola Manferrari Loc. Brazzano, Via San Giorgio 71, 34070 Cormóns (GO)

Nicola Manferrari has 9 ha spread across three distinct vineyard sites. The cooler sites are planted to Riesling, Sauvignon and Chardonnay while those warmed by the Adriatic include the red grape varieties. Whites in particular are made to a high standard with good ripeness and intensity as well as the capacity to age. In addition to regular varietal examples of good varietal character, superior versions are also made. Tocai, for instance, in Ronco della Chiesa shows more oak-influence and much better structure, while Chardonnay Selezione adds more depth, complexity and richness, over the standard bottling. In Studio di Bianco, Tocai, Sauvignon and Riesling are deftly combined in a stylish, ripe white with both depth and intensity. Reds are more variable, sometimes not quite achieving full ripeness in both fruit and tannins yet when they do there is good supple plummy, berry fruit depth. Rosso della Centa is a pure Merlot while Collio Rosso Riserva adds 25 to 30 per cent Cabernet Sauvignon to Merlot. (PW)

○ **Collio** Chardonnay★★ £D Chardonnay Selezione★★★ £E
○ **Collio** Tocai★★ £C Tocai Ronco della Chiesa★★★ £E

O **Collio** Malvasia Selezione★★ £C   O **Collio Bianco** Studio di Bianco★★★ £E
● **Collio** Rosso della Centa★★ £E   ● **Collio Rosso** Riserva★★ £E

BORGO SAN DANIELE   Friuli-Venezia Giulia   www.borgosandaniele.it   A: **Ast,** UnC

Owner: Mauro Mauri   Via San Daniele 16, 34071 Cormòns (GO)
Mauro Mauri and his sister Alessandra make a small but uniformly high-quality range of wines from 19 ha
of vineyards. They undertake staggered picking to produce whites that impress both for their individuality
and structure. Most singular is a smoky, scented Tocai fermented and aged in *botti grandi* that combines
citrus with exotic flavours. Both Pinot Grigio and Arbis Blanc (Chardonnay, Sauvignon, Pinot Bianco and
Tocai) have a measure of *barrique* influence and show a little more breadth. Arbis Blanc in particular
impresses for its fruit richness and texture. A little red, Arbis Ròs, is also made from the two Cabernets and
Pignolo. With very cool but intense redcurrant, red cherry fruit and a hint of carob, it will turn chocolaty
but can be let down by a slightly green edge. (PW)
O **Fruili Isonzo** Tocai★★★ £C   Pinot Grigio★★ £C
O **Friuli Isonzo Bianco** Arbis Blanc★★★ £D   ● **Arbis Ròs**★★ £D

TOMMASO BUSSOLA   Veneto   A: **Bal,** L&W,The, P&S,Vts, NYg, Res, Hrd

Owner: Tommaso Bussola   Loc. San Peretto, Via Molino Turri 30, 37024 Negrar (VR)
A brilliant and dedicated young grower with 9.5 ha of vineyards, Tommaso Bussola only started on his own
in the early 1990s yet is now one of the stars of Valpolicella. As well as a regular bottling (BG – named for
his uncle, Giuseppe Bussola with whom he started out) of each wine, there are premium wines labelled TB
made from the finest fruit and aged in new oak. Amarone Vigneto Alto vies with the moderately sweet
Recioto TB as the best of the lot. The wines are wonderfully perfumed with ever more depth and
concentration in the most recent releases. While production is small and prices very high for the TB wines,
the BG versions (with more average prices) show fine fruit and intensity and are better than many
bigger-volume examples. The purchase of a second estate with 15.5 ha of elevated vineyards should ensure
that demand for his wines is better satisfied. Older vintages, while good, are not at the same level as that
seen since 1997. (PW)
● **Amarone della Valpolicella Classico** BG★★★ £E TB★★★★★ £G TB Vigneto Alto★★★★★ £G
● **Valpolicella Classico** BG★★ £B Superiore TB★★★ £C
● **Recioto della Valpolicella Classico** BG★★★ £E TB★★★★★ £F

CA' DEI FRATI   Lombardia   www.cadeifrati.it   A: **Lib,** Con,Vne, Res, P&S, F&M, Sel, NYg

Owner: Dal Cero family   Fraz. Lugana, Via Frati 22, 25010 Sirmione (BS)
Ca' dei Frati have set high standards for Lugana in the same way that Anselmi and Pieropan have done for
Soave. Wines range from a consistently stylish and characterful Lugana I Frati through Brolettino, which is
distinguished by its elegance and texture, to Pratto, an IGT white blend of Lugana, Chardonnay and
Sauvignon, which is lush and exotic with great length of flavour. The sweet Tre Filer is made from the same
varieties as Pratto but the grapes are dried for three months prior to being fermented and aged in *barriques*.
A small amount of a concentrated Grande Annata Brolettino is also produced, the 1999 the most successful
to date. Aside from the excellent whites the quality of a red, Ronchedone, is also improving. First produced
from the two Cabernets and Merlot, it now includes increasing amounts of Groppello, Marzemino,
Sangiovese and Barbera. Rosé (Chiaretto) and a sparkling Lugana are also made. (PW)
O **Lugana** I Frati★★ £B Brolettino★★★ £C Brolettino Grande Annata★★★ £D
O **Pratto**★★★ £D   O **Tre Filer**★★ £E

CESCONI   Trentino   A: **Lib,** Gau,Vne, SVS

Owner: Paolo Cesconi   Loc. Pressano, Via Marconi 39, 38015 Lavis (TN)
The Cesconi family have been grape growers for generations but it is the current generation of four young

brothers, Alessandro, Franco, Lorenzo and Roberto, that have transformed this small 12-ha estate. Having switched the vines to Guyot training they produce wines of an atypical ripeness and richness, and have risen quickly to be one of Trentino-Alto Adige's best estates. All the wines show good depth and intensity with good varietal definition, if not yet the extra finesse or flair to compete with the very best from Friuli. Oak is employed with restraint in an aromatic Sauvignon, weighty Chardonnay and full, creamy Pinot Grigio. An unoaked Traminer is at least the equal of any of these. Olivar, a blend of Pinot Bianco, Pinot Grigio and Chardonnay can be the most complete and complex while a Merlot with cool fruit but good depth has been made since the 1998 vintage. Pivier, sold as an IGT, is effectively a Riserva Merlot and is oakier but with plenty of style as well as more depth and richness. (PW)

O **Olivar**★★★ £D   O **Trentino** Chardonnay★★★ £C   O **Trentino** Traminer Aromatico★★★ £C
O **Trentino** Pinot Grigio★★ £C   O **Trentino** Sauvignon★★ £C   O **Trentino** Nosiola★ £C
● **Trentino** Merlot★★ £C   ● **Pivier**★★★ £D

COLTERENZIO   Alto Adige   www.colterenzio.com   A: **Eno**

Owner: 'Co-operative' Loc. Cornaiano / Girlan, Strada del Vino 8, 39050 Appiano/Eppan (BZ)
The Cantina Produttori Colterenzio, a co-op formed by 28 grape growers, is amongst the finest of the Alto Adige's many good co-ops, though has rivals in the like of SAN MICHELE APPIANO and TERLANO. Under the direction of Luis Raifer the image and profile of Colterenzio has been transformed and investment has been realised. The improved fruit from the 320 ha of vineyards is now utilised by his son Wolfgang who oversees the winemaking. There is sound quality at a regular 'classic' varietal level, though the wines can be a little simple and sometimes lacking concentration. A step up are the 'vineyard series' Praedium-labelled wines which bridge the gap between the 'classic' wines and the premium Cornell label. Cornell wines, though more pricey, are consistently impressive and show the influence of expert enologist Donato Lanati. Chardonnay Cornell in particular stands out for its excellent concentration, depth and balance over a string of recent vintages. Sauvignon Lafoa is partially *barrique*-fermented and aged and can show excellent intensity and complexity but is occasionally a little overdone. Also good are the top reds, both the blended Cornelius (Cabernet/Merlot) and a powerful but less harmonious Cabernet Sauvignon Lafoa. Lagrein Cornell has arguably the most character, showing off the smoky, earthy, roasted qualities this grape can produce. In fact even the 'classic' Lagrein is most attractive. Other Cornell wines are Pinot Nero (Schwarzhaus) and Moscato Rosa. Varietal Merlot (Riserva Siebeneich) is also made. (PW)

O **Alto Adige** Chardonnay Cornell★★★ £E   Pinot Grigio Cornell★★ £D
O **Alto Adige** Sauvignon Prail★★ £C   Sauvignon Lafoa★★★ £E   Pinot Bianco Weisshaus★★ £C
O **Alto Adige** Gewürztraminer★ £C   Gewürztraminer Cornell★★ £D
● **Alto Adige** Cornelius Cornell★★★ £E   Cabernet Sauvignon Lafoa★★★ £F
● **Alto Adige** Lagrein Grieser★★ £C   Lagrein Cornell★★★ £E

CORTE SANT'ALDA   Veneto   www.cortesantalda.it   A: **Wtr**, DWS, BBR, UnC, Fal, F&M

Owner: Marinella Camerani Loc. Fioi, Via Capovilla 28, 37030 Mezzane di Sotto (VR)
For those who insist that only a handful of really good producers make Valpolicella and Amarone, Corte Sant'Alda is likely to be one of several they have missed. Much of the 15 ha of vineyard has been newly replanted employing single-Guyot training (rather than the traditional pergola system) for better-quality fruit. In addition oak vats are now being used for fermentation in a multi-faceted approach to further improving quality. Since the late 1990s these sleek, elegant wines have been of indisputably good quality, with excellent expression but no lack of intensity or concentration either. In fact for composed, balanced examples of Valpolicella, Amarone and Recioto this is as good a producer as any. Even the regular Valpolicella, Ca' Fiui is good – one of the best non-*ripasso* examples made. Minute quantities of Amarone were also produced in a Mithas version in 1997. A dry white, Retratto, is made from Sauvignon complemented by Chardonnay and Garganega, while some Soave (Partenio) is also made from an additional 2 ha. (PW)

● **Amarone della Valpolicella**★★★★ £E   ● **Recioto della Valpolicella**★★★★ £E
● **Valpolicella** Superiore Mithas★★★ £C   ● **Valpolicella** Superiore Ripasso★★★ £C
● **Valpolicella** Ca' Fiui★★ £B

ROMANO DAL FORNO   Veneto   A: JAr, Far, BBR, Fal

Owner: Romano Dal Forno   Fraz. Cellore, Via Lodoletta 4, 37030 Illasi (VR)
Valpolicella's most sought-after producer doesn't even hail from the Classico hills north-west of Verona but from slopes further to the east. It is not yet clear how his own site compares to the best slopes in the Classico zone but a radical retraining of the vines (trained low at very high densities) in order to obtain fully ripe, concentrated fruit and the use of new oak set his wines apart from the rest. The Valpolicella shows an extract and concentration missing in most Amarone and bears no resemblance to much of what shares the name. The quality is stunning and not simply showy and fruit-rich but deep and structured, with remarkable character and complexity. Most recently it has been produced only from grapes with a short amount of drying. Extraordinary Amarone and Recioto of unprecedented breadth and depth set the standard for others to emulate (Tomasso BUSSOLA comes closest). Quantities are very small, reflected in their 'cult status' prices. (PW)
● **Amarone della Valpolicella** Vigneto di Monte Lodoletta❍❍❍❍❍ £H
● **Recioto della Valpolicella** Vigneto di Monte Lodoletta❍❍❍❍❍ £H
● **Valpolicella Superiore** Vigneto di Monte Lodoletta★★★★ £F

GIROLAMO DORIGO   Friuli-Venezia Giulia   www.montsclapade.com   A: Rec

Owner: Girolamo Dorigo   Via del Pozzo 5, 33042 Buttrio (UD)
All of Dorigo's excellent wines are labelled for either one of two hillside sources, both acquired in 1966: Montsclapade and Ronc di Juri. Girolamo's son Alessio is now assuming greater responsibility for a range encompassing international as well as several local varieties. Chardonnay has a definite oak accent but delicious fruit, balance and refinement and there's a good Bordeaux-style Sauvignon. Yet it is for reds as much as whites that these wines should be tried. Successful examples of Refosco and Tazzelenghe have great fruit expression and relatively harmonious structures for these difficult grapes and if you can't afford MOSCHIONI's Schioppettino, Dorigo's appealing example shows a lovely peppery varietal expression. A little powerful, extracted Pignolo is also made. The top red, however, is the Bordeaux blend labelled simply Montsclapade, a very composed example with cedary crushed berry fruit that oozes style. Brilliant in 1999, it could be drunk now or kept another five years. Dorigo's Picolit is one of the best examples of this elegant sweet white, though the honeyed Verduzzo isn't far behind. Sparkling wine from Chardonnay and Pinot Nero is also made. (PW)
○ **Colli Orientali del Friuli** Chardonnay Vigneto Ronc di Juri★★★ £D
○ **Colli Orientali del Friuli** Sauvignon Ronc di Juri★★ £D
○ **Colli Orientali del Friuli** Picolit Vigneto Montsclapade★★★ £E Verduzzo Vigneto Ronc di Juri★★ £E
● **Colli Orientali del Friuli Rosso** Montsclapade★★★ £E
● **Colli Orientali del Friuli** Schioppettino Vigneto Montsclapade★★ £C
● **Colli Orientali del Friuli** Refosco Vigneto Montsclapade★★ £C Tazzelenghe Vigneto Ronc di Juri★★ £D

LIVIO FELLUGA   Friuli-Venezia Giulia   www.liviofelluga.it   A: Lib,Vne, P&S, F&M, Hrd

Owner: Livio Felluga   Fraz. Brazzano, Via Risorgimento 1, 34071 Cormòns (GO)
This is one of the grand estates of Friuli, having been established by Livio Felluga in the 1950s. It is now being taken to new heights by his offspring, who have 135 ha to manage but with the expertise of consultant Stefano Chioccioli to assist them. The most widely acclaimed white, Terre Alte, is a blend of Tocai, Pinot Bianco and Sauvignon Blanc, a wine of exquisite balance and elegance rather than concentration. Previously unoaked, a portion of the wine now receives some time in *barriques* and the most recent vintages (2001, 00) seem a little overdone and less good than previously. An otherwise stylish and intense Illivio, an oak-aged Pinot Bianco, could also use a little more restraint. At a lower level is a well-concentrated, aromatic

and characterful blend of Chardonnay and Ribolla Gialla, Shàrjs. Unoaked varietals are also of a high standard. The Picolit is an exceptionally fine if pricey, example of the grape. It is medium-sweet with honeyed vanilla, wild flowers and dried fruit characters – both long and refined and not in the least bit coarse or heavy. Reds include an attractive Merlot/Cabernet Sauvignon, Vertigo, and a deep, polished, lushly berry-fruited Merlot, Sossò. More characterful but less refined in flavour is an excellent example of Refosco. (PW)

○ **Colli Orientali del Friuli Rosazzo Bianco** Terre Alte★★★ £E   ○ **Sharjs**★★ £C
○ **Colli Orientali del Friuli** Pinot Grigio★★ £C   Sauvignon★★ £C   Tocai★★ £C
○ **Colli Orientali del Friuli** Pinot Bianco Illivio★★★ £C   Picolit Riserva★★★★ £G
● **Colli Orientali del Friuli** Merlot Riserva Sossò★★★ £F   Refosco dal Peduncolo Rosso★★★ £F
● **Vertigo**★★ £C

FORADORI   Trentino   A: JAr, N&P

Owner: Elisabetta Foradori   Via Damiano Chiesa 1, 38017 Mezzolombardo (TN)
Foradori is one of the top estates in all of Italy yet comes from a zone that is little known outside the country. Elisabetta Foradori is something of a celebrity in Italy for her renditions of Teroldego Rotaliano. Previously two single-vineyard versions (Vigneto Sgarzon, Vigneto Morei) were made, surpassed only by Granato, the top selection, but since 1997 only the regular version and Granato have been retained. The regular version now shows real poise and persistence allied to a deep, smoky, bramble and mineral character (especially good in 2001). In Granato, a wine of great style and class, are added tobacco, spice and cedar, beautifully harmonised oak, and dense but fine, ripe tannins that ensure long ageing. An increasingly fine white is also made. Myrto contains 40 per cent each of Chardonnay and Sauvignon Blanc, complemented by 20 per cent of Pinot Bianco; it is well-defined with attractive floral and fruit characters. Under the Vigneti delle Dolomiti IGT come very small quantities of very good Ailanpa, from Syrah, and Karanar, a blend of Cabernet Sauvignon, Syrah, Petit Verdot and Merlot. Prices are very reasonable for the quality. (PW)

● **Teroldego Rotaliano**★★ £C   Granato★★★★ £E
● **Ailanpa**★★★ £E   ● **Karanar**★★★ £E   ○ **Myrto**★★ £C

FRANZ HAAS   Alto Adige   www.franz-haas.it   A: Lib, Vne, P&S, F&M, V&C

Owner: Franz Haas   Via Villa 6, 39040 Montagna (BZ)
This 40-ha estate has become one of the most consistent in the Alto Adige, producing good reds as well as whites nearly every year. The quality of the fruit and the harmony in the wines give them an extra edge over other good examples. Wines labelled Schweizer or Cru indicate a superior bottling. The excellent Manna, a beautifully composed blend of Riesling, Chardonnay, Traminer Aromatico (or Gewürztraminer) and Sauvignon, shows a marvellous aromatic fruit quality with a Chardonnay-like weight in the mouth yet is intense and vibrant (if a little coarse and exaggerated in 2001). There's good depth and flavour in the varietals too. Istante is a structured but distinctive red from Cabernet Franc, Cabernet Sauvignon and Merlot, ripe and stylish in recent vintages, with enticing ripe Cabernet Franc aromatics. Adequate sappy Pinot Nero is also made, but much better is a more concentrated and complex Schweizer version. The moderately sweet Moscato Rosa is a fine, perfumed, delicious and generally well-balanced example of its type. Lagrein Scuro (or Dunkel) can also be good. (PW)

○ **Alto Adige** Pinot Bianco★ £B   Traminer Aromatico★★ £C   ○ **Manna** Schweizer★★★ £D
◉ **Alto Adige** Moscato Rosa★★★ £F   ● **Istante**★★★ £D
● **Alto Adige** Merlot Schweizer★★ £D   Pinot Nero★ £C   Pinot Nero Schweizer★★ £D

HOFSTÄTTER   Alto Adige   www.hofstatter.com   A: Mgi, N&P

Owner: Foradori Hofstätter family   Piazza Municipio 5, 39040 Termeno (BZ)
Hofstätter produces both the best Pinot Noir and one of the best Gewürztraminers in Italy. Though not a world-beater, the top Pinot Noir, from Vigna Sant'Urbano on high slopes at Mazon, shows a depth and

texture uncommon to Italian examples and is increasingly successful even in more difficult vintages. Martin Foradori, who has assumed the direction of the estate from his father, has the fortune to have one or two particularly favoured sites among the estate's 45 ha of vineyards and the training is gradually being switched from pergola to the Guyot system. The stunningly sited 3.5-ha Crozzol vineyards, acquired in 1995, are organically cultivated and now the source of another Pinot Nero. Other site-specific reds include Yngram, at its best a concentrated expressive blend from mostly Cabernet Sauvignon and Petit Verdot with a little Syrah (70/25/5 in the fine 2000), and the *barrique*-aged Lagrein, Steinraffler. For whites, the Kolbenhof Gewürztraminer from the village of Söll shows a depth and richness not found in many Alto Adige examples (the poorest of which are based on ordinary Traminer). Bianco Vigna San Michele, a blend of Pinot Bianco, Chardonnay and Riesling partly aged in *barriques*, shows similar weight and style and a subtle oak influence. New is a late-harvested Gewürztraminer, Joseph. (PW)

● **Alto Adige** Pinot Nero Riserva★ £C Pinot Nero Barthenau Vigna Sant'Urbano★★★ £E
● **Alto Adige** Lagrein Steinraffler★★★ £E ● **Yngram**★★★ £E
O **Alto Adige** Gewürztraminer★★ £C Gewürztraminer Kolbenhof Söll★★★ £D
O **Alto Adige** Pinot Bianco★★ £C O **Alto Adige Bianco** Barthenau Vigna San Michele★★ £C

IL CARPINO Friuli-Venezia Giulia www.ilcarpino.com

Owner: Silvano Cibini & Franco Sosol Loc. Sovenza 14/A, 34070 San Floriano del Collio (GO)
Il Carpino was established in 1987 but has only become one of the best estates in Friuli in the past four or five years. Excellent white and red wines, predominantly varietal, show a combination of superb fruit and fine balance. A fine gentle, stylish Chardonnay is complemented by a partially oaked Sauvignon which has excellent definition, rich, ripe fruit and a lingering finish. Bianco Carpino is an equal blend of both with good harmony. A fine citrusy, herbal Ribolla Gialla is also produced as is some Malvasia. Red wines are based on Merlot. A plush brambly Rosso Carpino includes 20 per cent Cabernet Sauvignon and shows lots of promise. Even better is Rubrum (potentially four stars), a sumptuous, black plum-fruited Merlot that tastes not unlike a young Pomerol. Both reds show good ageing potential. While all the Il Carpino wines see some French oak, Vigna Runc, a promising second label, is for unoaked varietals. Whites include Chardonnay, Pinot Grigio, Ribolla Gialla and an aromatic, floral, gooseberryish and concentrated Sauvignon Blanc. Merlot is also produced under this label. Occasionally the wines show some reduction. (PW)

Il Carpino:
O **Collio** Sauvignon★★★ £C Chardonnay★★★ £C Pinot Grigio★★ £C Ribolla Gialla★★ £C
O **Bianco Carpino**★★ £C ● **Rosso Carpino**★★ £C ● **Rubrum**★★★ £D
Vigna Runc:
O **Collio** Sauvignon★★ £B O **Collio** Pinot Grigio★ £B O **Collio** Ribolla Gialla★ £B

INAMA Veneto www.inamaaziendaagricola.it   A: **Wtr, JAr**, Rae, F&M, UnC, AoW, F&R

Owner: Inama family Loc. Biacche 50, 37047 San Bonifacio (VR)
Stefano Inama assumed control of the winemaking here in the early 1990s and the wines have attracted plenty of attention ever since. Two single-vineyard Soaves are *barrique*-fermented and aged while an unoaked regular (Vin Soave) Superiore version can be very good, with citrusy, grapefruit notes, fine balance and subtle leesy and minerally hints. The championing of Chardonnay and Sauvignon in the Soave district has attracted a fair amount of controversy. Both are produced in oaked and unoaked versions. Stefano Inama also makes Bradisismo, a blend of 70 per cent Cabernet Sauvignon and 30 per cent Carmenère from the Colli Berici. It displays intense wild plum and bramble fruit but also a touch of austerity and leafy herbaceousness, though this is less pronounced with age. Also from the Colli Berici estate is Oracolo, a new single-vineyard varietal Cabernet Sauvignon, first made in 2000. Vulcaia Après is a late-harvested version of Sauvignon, while BINOMIO Montepulciano d'Abruzzo is produced in conjunction with La Valentina (see Central Italy). (PW)

O **Soave Classico Superiore** Vin Soave★★ £B Vigneti di Foscarino★★★ £C Vigneto du Lot★★★ £D

O **Vulcaia Sauvignon**★★ £C   O **Vulcaia Fumé**★★ £D
O **Chardonnay**★★ £C   Campo dei Tovi★★ £D
● **Bradisismo**★★★ £E

VINNAIOLI JERMANN   www.jermannvinnaioli.it   A: **Eno,** Vne, Sel, Hrd, UnC, V&C, NYg

Owner: Silvio Jermann   Loc. Villanova, Via Monte Fortino 21, 34070 Farra d'Isonzo
Silvio Jermann is the long-time champion of Friuli, having produced excellent whites for an age. These are not just wines of good concentration and ripe fruit but ones with good definition and character and with an added elegance and refinement in the top examples that other powerful examples lack. The prices have always been a little ahead of others but when Jermann is on form, which is most of the time, they deserve to be. Vinnae, the least expensive of the blended whites, combines Ribolla Gialla, Malvasia and Riesling and is balanced and characterful. Capo Martino, which adds a lot more richness, is a blend of Pinot Bianco and Tocai with a little Malvasia and Picolit. Better though and often the top wine is Vintage Tunina (Sauvignon, Chardonnay, Ribolla Gialla, Malvasia and Picolit), which shows intense stylish fruit, wonderful elegance and refinement, and superb length of flavour. Though it might be drunk young it is best with five years' age. Dreams ('Were Dreams, now it is just wine!' – to give it its full name – and originally sold as 'Where the Dreams have no end', in homage to U2's Bono) is a Chardonnay with rich oak spice and ripe fruit that can show real precision and lovely harmony on the palate and is a rare Italian example that can stand comparison with a fine Burgundian white. As well as those varietals below, other whites include Müller-Thurgau and Sauvignon. For red, a little intense Pinot Nero (Red Angel on the Moonlight) and Pignolo (Pignacolusse) are produced. In the latter, 2000 is better balanced than the 99, with a seductive fullness to match the extract, and is long with fine tannins. New from 2001 is Blau & Blau – a blend of Pinot Nero (Blauburgunder) and Blaufrankisch. (PW)

O **Vintage Tunina**★★★★ £E   O **Dreams**★★★★ £E
O **Capo Martino**★★★ £E   O **Pinot Bianco**★★ £C   O **Pinot Grigio**★★★ £C
O **Vinnae**★★ £C   O **Traminer Aromatico**★★ £C   O **Riesling Afix**★ £C
● **Pignacolusse**★★★ £E   ● **Red Angel on the Moonlight**★★ £C

ALOIS LAGEDER   Alto Adige   www.lageder.com   A: **Bib,** Hrd, NYg

Owner: Lageder family   Tenuta Löwengang, Via dei Conti 9, 39040 Magre' (BZ)
Lageder is the Alto Adige's leading private estate, driven on to exacting standards by the dynamic 'current' Alois Lageder (fifth generation). Though owning a relatively small percentage of their own vineyards, through close links with growers they are converting from pergola-trained vines to *spalliera* training on an increasingly organic basis. While the wines can be a little simple and dilute at the 'classic' varietal level, there are some fine examples of single-vineyard wines (especially the Sauvignon Lehenhof, Pinot Bianco Haberlehof and Pinot Grigio Benefizium Porer) and the estate premium varietals and blends. The elegant, perfumed whites show real style with three years' bottle age or more. Cor Römingberg is the top red from a high-density, Guyot-trained vineyard – a rich, ripe and concentrated Cabernet Sauvignon (with three per cent Petit Verdot) with a fine minerally depth and class that has few rivals in North-East Italy. Though from older vines and of some style and intensity, the Cabernet Sauvignon blend, Löwengang (including 15 per cent each of Cabernet Franc and Merlot) rather pales beside it. Much better is the white equivalent, a marvellously rich, deep, tightly structured and ageworthy Chardonnay. Also emerging with some promise are Pinot Noir, especially Krafuss, Lagrein (Lindenburg) and a rich Chardonnay and Sauvignon blend, Tannhammer. New is a premium varietal Merlot (labelled with the vintage in Roman numerals). Casòn Hirschprunn is a separate single estate of 32 ha purchased in 1991. The blended whites and reds, especially the 'reserves' Contest (Pinot Grigio, Chardonnay, Sauvignon and a little Viognier and other Rhône varietals) and Casòn (Merlot, both Cabernets, Lagrein and others), show lovely fruit and real style and composure. The estate white Etelle and red Corolle are similar blends but see less oak. Varietal Chardonnay and Pinot Grigio have also been added. All are sold under the Mitterberg IGT. (PW)

Alois Lageder:
O **Alto Adige** Sauvignon Terlaner★ £B Sauvignon Lehenhof★★★ £C
O **Alto Adige** Chardonnay Buchholz★ £B Chardonnay Löwengang★★★ £D
O **Alto Adige** Gewürztraminer★ £B Gewürztraminer Am Sand★★ £C
O **Alto Adige** Pinot Bianco Haberlehof★★ £B Pinot Grigio Benefizium Porer★★ £C
● **Alto Adige** Cabernet Löwengang★★ £E Cabernet Sauvignon Cor Römigberg★★★★ £E
● **Alto Adige** Lagrein Lindenburg★★ £D

Casòn Hirschprunn:
● **Corolle**★ £C ● **Casòn**★★★ £D
O **Etelle**★★ £C O **Contest**★★★ £D

LE SALETTE   Veneto   A: **Ast**

Owner: F Scamperle & M Grisi   Via Pio Brugnoli 11/C, 37022 Fumane di Valpolicella (VR)
Franco Scamperle makes consistent, stylish and very drinkable Valpolicella and Amarone. Apart from
regular Valpolicella Classico all the wines are vineyard-specific. Of two single-vineyard Valpolicellas, Ca'
Carnocchio is produced solely from dried grapes and combines the supple texture of a good Valpolicella
with more of the flavour depth associated with Amarone. There are also two versions of both Amarone and
Recioto. The intense but only moderately concentrated La Marega Amarone is aged only partly in *barrique*
while the Pergole Vece version (made only in the best years) is aged entirely in *barriques*. Both Amarone and
Recioto wines have significantly more depth and complexity in the Pergole Vece versions. A sweet white,
Cesare Passito, is made from dried Garganega, Malvasia and Moscato grapes. (PW)
● **Amarone della Valpolicella Classico** La Marega★★★ £E Pergole Vece★★★★ £F
● **Valpolicella Classico Superiore** I Progni★★ £C Ca' Carnocchio★★★ £C
● **Recioto della Valpolicella Classico** Le Traversagne★★ £E Pergole Vece★★★ £F

MACULAN   Veneto   A: **BWC**, Odd, Vts, Sel

Owner: Fausto & Franca Maculan   Via Castelletto 3, 36042 Breganze (VI)
A brother-and-sister partnership runs the well-known 35-ha Maculan estate, the only producer of real note
in the Breganze zone some way north of Vicenza. Famed for their production of some of Italy's finest sweet
wines, they also make very good reds, initially as Cabernet Sauvignon Ferrata but more recently as simply
Fratta, the premium blend of Cabernet Sauvignon and Merlot. Other reds include Brentino, a fruit-driven
Merlot/Cabernet blend, a varietal Merlot, Crosara, and a Pinot Nero, Altura. Dry whites are improving
with more subtle oak treatment. Ferrata now combines Chardonnay with Sauvignon. Pino & Toi is an
unoaked blend of Pinot Bianco, Pinot Grigio and Tocai. Sweet whites include the grapy, aromatic
Dindarella from a strain of Moscato, Fior d'Arancio, while Torcolato is made from dried Vespaiola,
Garganega and Tocai grapes. Only the botrytis-affected grapes are selected for Acininobili which is aged (but
not fermented) in new French oak *barriques*. There is an extra intensity to its sweet dried-fruit richness, well
checked by acidity, but it is made in much smaller quantities than the sometimes equally impressive
Torcolato. (PW)
● **Fratta**★★★ £F ● **Breganze Rosso** Crosara★★ £D
● **Breganze** Cabernet Sauvignon Palazzotto★★ £C ● **Brentino**★ £B
O **Ferrata**★★ £D O **Breganze Bianco** Breganze di Breganze★ £B
O **Acininobili**★★★★ £G O **Breganze** Torcolato★★★★ £E O **Dindarello**★★★ £D

MASI   Veneto   www.masi.it   A: **BWC**, Odd, Vts, Sel

Owner: Boscaini family   Fraz. Gargagnago, Via Monteleone, 37020 Sant'Ambrogio della Valpolicella
This large family firm is synonymous with Valpolicella and Amarone and has been a leader in
experimentation and innovation in the Valpolicella zone. Firsts include the bottling of single-vineyard
Amarone and Recioto (Campolongo di Torbe, Mazzano and Mezzanella), the re-introduction of the *ripasso*
method in Campofiorin (and for which they have the registered trademark) and the revised dried-grape

variation for enrichment (a refermentation) in Brolo di Campofiorin from a special parcel of the same vineyard. Then there are the new wines from 'rescued' grape varieties, the best of which is Osar, based on Oseleta (80 per cent – though complemented by the main Valpolicella grape, Corvina). Toar from Corvina and Rondinella also includes some Oseleta. Both wines show some new-oak influence. However, as impressive as early releases of many of the wines have been, down the years there has been a tendency for quality to gradually slip away and at times the wines have also been characterised by a somewhat high-toned character, leading sometimes to excessive levels of volatile acidity as the wines have aged. At a lower level there is better value to be had elsewhere and on occasion some of the well-established premium wines can lack depth and richness when tasted against some of the zone's leading wines. Production is large from a total of 360 ha of vineyards; as well as 160 ha in the Veneto, there are significant holdings in western Friuli. Grandarella, a newish red from dried grapes, is of Friuli origins; a blend of Refosco (75 per cent) complemented by Carmenère and Corvina, it has powerful, intense fruit if not the concentration or dimension of top Amarone. The range also includes the wines of the Serègo Alighieri estate. Best is the Amarone, Vaio Armaron, while recently introduced Possessioni red and white are modest. Two wines have also been produced from Argentina's Tupungato Valley in Mendoza. Corbec Appassimento from semi-dried Corvina and Malbec grapes (70/30) and Passo Doble, essentially reverse proportions using a dried-grape component for enrichment. (PW)

Masi:
● **Amarone della Valpolicella** Campolongo di Torbe★★ £E Costasera★★★ £E Mazzano★★★ £F
● **Recioto della Valpolicella Classico** Amandorlato Mezzanella★★ £E
● **Campofiorin★** £B ● **Brolo di Campofiorin★★** £C ● **Toar★★** £B ● **Osar★★★** £E
● **Grandarella★★★** £D O **Soave Classico** Colbaraca★★ £B
Serègo Alighieri:
● **Amarone della Valpolicella** Vaio Armaron★★★ £E ● **Recioto della Valpolicella** Casal dei Ronchi★★ £E

MIANI Friuli-Venezia Giulia   A: **Ast**, BBR, UnC

Owner: Enzo Pontoni   Via Peruzzi 10, 33042 Buttrio (UD)
Enzo Pontoni' s meagre output is some of the most-sought after wine in northern Italy. His vineyards total 18 ha, and while most, but not all, of the vines are in production, quantities are extremely modest due to low yields and severe selection. The wines are beautifully crafted, expressive, detailed and very classy, nearly perfectly balanced. The Sauvignon is barrel-fermented but far finer and more complex than most made in this style – intense and elegant even in the difficult 2002 vintage. Concentrated Tocai Friulano captures the essence of the grape, while Merlot, a combination of two different parcels, comes in part from 40-year-old vines. It is aged in new oak but is pure with the enticing berries and plum expression too rarely seen in Merlot from around the world and manages to avoid underripeness even in cooler vintages – a fine, elegant 2000 is lighter but 2001 promises the more usual concentration. Also made are Ribolla Gialla, Chardonnay and a few hundred bottles of an exceptional and sought-after Refosco (Calvari). Taste them if you get the chance. (PW)
O **Colli Orientali del Friuli** Tocai Friulano★★★ £E Sauvignon★★★ £E
● **Colli Orientali del Friuli** Merlot★★★★ £E

MOSCHIONI Friuli-Venezia Giulia

Owner: Michele Moschioni   Loc. Gagliano, Via Doria 30, 33043 Cividale del Friuli (UD)
To see just what is possible without compromise and by producing wine as naturally as possible try the wines from Michele Moschioni. Also seek them out to discover the potential of hitherto obscure local red varieties in Fruili. From 11 ha of vines grapes are late-harvested or in some instances the fruit is partially dried (for 10 days) for added concentration (though now less so than in the first blockbuster releases of these wines). The top wines (all potentially rating five stars) see 100 per cent new oak for anything up to two years but this is easily absorbed by the concentrated fruit. The basic Rosso is from young-vine Merlot and Cabernet with a little of the native varieties. Refosco, aged in 50 per cent new oak has excellent

concentration and texture and the wild plum and brambly fruit of the variety. Celtico Rosso (around half-and-half Cabernet Sauvignon and Merlot) has terrific intensity and concentration, with dried fruits and fig aromas giving way to blackberry and black plum flavours. Despite the extract and richness, this is much more approachable than most Amarone but deserves 10 years' age or more. Of at least comparable quality are Moschioni's two brilliant creations from local varieties. There is a marvellous contrast between the pure, seductive elegance of the Schiopettino with floral and spicy sweet cherry-fruited intensity and the wildness, mineral, carob and black-fruited muscularity of Pignolo. The extract and tannin in the latter needs 8 to 10 years to mellow, while Schiopettino, though concentrated and powerful, could be drunk much sooner. The 2001s are the most expressive yet. (PW)

● **Colli Orientali del Friuli** Schioppettino★★★★ £E Pignolo★★★★★ £F
● **Colli Orientali del Friuli** Refosco dal Peduncolo Rosso★★★ £D
● **Colli Orientali del Friuli** Celtico Rosso★★★★ £E Rosso Moschioni★★ £C

JOSEF NIEDERMAYR Alto Adige www.niedermayr.it

Owner: Josef Niedermayr Via Casa di Gesù 15, Cornaiano 39050 Appiano/Eppan (BZ)
This long-established producer achieves quality across a large range, from top reds to simple but soundly made basic varietals with good flavour intensity. The leading whites are the premium examples of Gewürztraminer and Sauvignon with excellent structures and distinctive, penetrating aromas. Less successful are Terlano Hof Zu Pramol and Perelle (Pinot Grigio and Chardonnay) which though flavoursome and characterful show a touch of coarseness too and seem a bit overdone (though they may appeal to some palates). Better is a very well-made sparkling Talento Comitissa Brut Riserva (Pinot Bianco and Chardonnay) made by Niedermayr's enologist Lorenz Martini. Here the flavours are kept more in check, while the structure and length underscore its quality. An intense *passito*-style Aureus, a blend of mostly Chardonnay and Sauvignon, shows delicious ripe fruit and good balance. All of Niedermayr's versions of Lagrein are good. A very good Lagrein Riserva is complemented by Euforius, which adds Merlot and Cabernet Sauvignon; this works a lot better than might be expected and is typically complex and composed. As well as a simple but flavoursome regular Pinot Nero, also made is a more structured Pinot Nero Riserva. (PW)

Josef Niedermayr:
O **Alto Adige** Gewürztraminer Doss★★★ £C O **Alto Adige** Sylvaner★ £B
O **Alto Adige** Sauvignon Naun★★ £C Sauvignon Allure★★★ £C
O **Alto Adige Terlano** Hof Zu Pramol★ £C O **Perelle**★★ £C O **Aureus**★★★ £F
● **Alto Adige** Lagrein Aus Gries★ £B Lagrein Aus Gries Blacedelle★★ £C
● **Alto Adige** Lagrein Aus Gries Riserva★★★ £D ● **Euforius**★★★ £D
Lorenz Martini:
O **Alto Adige Talento** Comitissa Brut Riserva Vintage★★ £C

PIEROPAN Veneto www.pieropan.it   A: **Lib**, Vne, BBR, ACh, Res, P&S, Hrd, NYg, V&C

Owner: Leonildo Pieropan Via Camuzzoni 3, 37038 Soave (VR)
The Pieropan Soaves are made in the vineyard, in the sense that the greatest efforts have gone into producing ever better-quality grapes from this 30-ha estate. Both a reliably good Soave Classico and single-vineyard Calvarino are unoaked and based on Garganega complemented by a superior type of Trebbiano, Trebbiano di Soave. In recent years La Rocca, made solely from Garganega from a 5.5 ha slope, has been fermented and aged in double-sized *barriques* and has added more richness to its pure-fruited expression. Both this and Calvarino may be drunk young but typically keep for at least five years. The range of dry whites is complemented by a fine Recioto di Soave Le Colombare, for which the ripest Garganega grapes are dried for several months to produce a rich, ripe and delicately nutty sweet wine after two years in large wood. Passito della Rocca, in contrast, is based on Sauvignon and Riesling grapes (with smaller percentages of Trebbiano di Soave and Garganega) and aged in *barriques* to produce a more intense, exotic fruit and honeyed richness. A little of another sweet wine, Santa Lucia, is made when conditions allow for late-

harvested botrytis-affected Garganega grapes. (PW)

O **Soave Classico** Superiore★★ £B Vigneto Calvarino★★★ £C Vigneto La Rocca★★★ £D
O **Recioto di Soave** Le Colombare★★★ £E O **Passito della Rocca**★★★ £F

POJER & SANDRI Trentino   A: Ast

Owner: M Pojer & F Sandri Loc. Molini 4-6, 38010 Faedo (TN)
Mario Pojer and Fiorentino Sandri make wines as refined as any in North-East Italy and have been quietly maintaining high standards for close on three decades. For something unusual, the attractive unoaked varietals include a floral and herb-scented Nosiola but even Müller Thurgau is good in the context of the variety. Whites culminate in Faye, Chardonnay with 10 per cent Pinot Bianco. It is elegant and classy with a lovely fruit expression, building gently in texture and complexity with age. The red version of Faye is not a blockbuster but a very stylish, beautifully textured wine from Cabernet Sauvignon, Cabernet Franc, Merlot and Lagrein. Maso Besler is a new project in the Cembra Valley where production is focused on just a single white blend and a single red blend from what will be 4.5 ha of vineyards. The *barrique*-aged white is very promising with fine perfume, weight and intensity from a mix of Pinot Bianco, Sauvignon, Riesling, Incrocio Manzoni and Kerner. Pojer & Sandri's long-established, often exquisite sweet wine, Essenzia, typically includes Chardonnay, Sauvignon, Riesling, Gewürztraminer and Kerner. A sparkling Brut Cuvée is also made, from Chardonnay and Pinot Nero. Most of the wines are sold under the Vigneti delle Dolomiti IGT. (PW)

Pojer & Sandri:
O **Chardonnay**★★ £B O **Faye**★★★★ £D
O **Trentino** Traminer Aromatico★★ £C
O **Sauvignon**★★ £C O **Nosiola**★★ £B O **Müller Thurgau** Palai★ £B
O **Essenzia**★★★ £E ● **Rosso Faye**★★★ £D
Maso Besler:
O **Besler Bianck**★★★ £D

QUINTARELLI Veneto   A: Wtr, Fal

Owner: Giuseppe Quintarelli Via Cerè 1, 37024 Negrar (VR)
Already a legend, Giuseppe Quintarelli is Valpolicella's greatest advocate of artisanal winemaking. The wines, still bottled and labelled by hand, are based on the three classic grapes of Valpolicella but with a few interlopers. They have great power, extract and intensity, needing long barrel-ageing to evolve into something complex yet demanding. Good (sometimes great) as the wines have been in the past, the ratings reflect their current quality – which has been surpassed by those showing greater winemaking sophistication. Nonetheless, the wines will always attract those in search of sheer intensity and extract even if the balance and texture are sometimes found wanting. Alzero is made from partially dried Cabernet Franc grapes while a very small amount of a white from dried grapes is also made. Prices reflect the wines' cult status. (PW)

● **Amarone della Valpolicella Classico** Monte Ca' Paletta★★★★ £H
● **Recioto della Valpolicella Classico** Monte Ca' Paletta★★★ £H
● **Valpolicella Classico** Superiore Monte Ca' Paletta★★★ £E ● **Alzero**★★★ £H

ROCCOLO GRASSI Veneto

Owner: Bruno & Marco Sartori Via San Giovanni di Dio 21, 37030 Mezzane di Sotto (VR)
Marco Sartori is a rapidly rising star of Valpolicella even if his 8 ha of Valpolicella vineyard, Roccolo Grassi (not all of it yet in production) lie well to the east of the Classico zone (and north-east of Verona – DAL FORNO is in the adjacent valley to the east). There is a real focus on quality in the vineyard, in pursuing low yields per vine and in obtaining fully ripe fruit. A rigorous selection is apparent in the wines which are clean, modern and very fruit-driven yet with classic flavours. The tannins are ripe and there is good balancing acidity. In Amarone there is real richness and depth and it is almost overwhelming in its intensity

if drunk young. The sheer impact of the fruit to some extent obscures any elegance the wines might otherwise show but the real test will be to see how recent releases mature. Marco also has 4 ha of Vigneto La Broia for the production of Soave and Recioto di Soave. The latter is almost decadent in its ripe and overripe exotic fruit characters. There is guava, quince, overripe apple and pear, preserved citrus and muscovado sugar but it avoids being raisiny. The wines previously appeared under the name Bruno Sartori, which could easily have been confused with the large commercial operation of Sartori. (PW)

● **Amarone della Valpolicella**★★★ £E ● **Recioto della Valpolicella**★★★ £E
● **Valpolicella** Superiore Roccolo Grassi★★★ £C
O **Soave** Superiore La Broia★ £B   O **Recioto di Soave** La Broia★★★ £E

RONCHI DI MANZANO   Friuli-Venezia Giulia   www.ronchidimanzano.com   **A: Vim**

Owner: Roberta Borghese Via Orsaria 42, 33044 Manzano (UD)
This 60-ha estate in the Colli Orientali del Friuli zone produces a wide range of whites and reds, for the most part reasonably priced and well-defined examples of their type. Varietal whites are most impressive: vigorous, expressive and fruit-centred. All are aged intelligently (whether in stainless steel, large wood or *barrique* or some combination of these) according to the grape's character. The Ronc di Rosazzo white blends Sauvignon, Chardonnay, Tocai and Picolit in a ripe, stylish, vibrant, harmonious whole that can be drunk young or kept for three or four years. Among the reds, regular varietal examples of Cabernet Sauvignon, Cabernet Franc and Merlot could use more richness and ripeness. However, a very promising young-vine Ronc di Subule from new vineyards planted at much higher densities (8,000 vines/ha) shows opulent pure fruit, well-integrated with new oak. Le Zuccule, a blend of Cabernet Sauvignon and Merlot, and the Ronc di Rosazzo red, which adds Refosco to the blend, show good fruit intensity and lush textures but are not overwhelmed by oak. A varietal Refosco is more robust and earthy but also more characterful than the blends. Two Ronc di Rosazzo sweet whites are good examples of Verduzzo and Picolit respectively, the former slightly more perfumed and refined, the latter more raisiny. (PW)

O **Colli Orientali del Friuli Rosazzo Bianco** Ronc di Rosazzo★★★ £C
O **Colli Orientali del Friuli** Tocai Superiore★★ £B Pinot Grigio★★ £B Chardonnay★★ £B Sauvignon★★£B
O **Colli Orientali del Friuli Rosazzo** Picolit Ronc di Rosazzo★★★ £E Verduzzo Ronc di Rosazzo★★★ £E
● **Colli Orientali del Friuli** Refosco dal Peduncolo Rosso★★ £B Merlot Ronc di Subule★★★ £D
● **Colli Orientali del Friuli Rosazzo Rosso** Ronc di Rosazzo★★ £C ● **Le Zuccule**★★ £D

RONCO DEL GELSO   Friuli-Venezia Giulia   **A: Ock, The**

Owner: Giorgio Badin Via Isonzo 117, 34071 Cormòns (GO)
Giorgio Badin has done much down the years to improve quality on his family's estate. He makes mostly unoaked whites with good purity and intensity from 20 ha of vines. Most of the varietals can be a little reticent when first bottled and need at least two years' age to show at their best. The Pinot Bianco and Latimis, a blend of Tocai, Pinot Bianco and Riesling, can be drunk soonest. Giorgio Badin believes Pinot Grigio can lack for aromatic complexity and as a consequence his Sot Lis Rivis benefits from small oak and shows real weight and a stylish complexity. The one red, a Merlot, also benefits from oak-ageing and though it can start out a little cool and angular, it is usually soft and plummy with a little age. A new winery should give quality a further boost. (PW)

O **Friuli Isonzo Bianco** Latimis★ £B   O **Friuli Isonzo** Pinot Bianco★★ £B
O **Friuli Isonzo** Sauvignon★★ £C Tocai Friulano★★ £C Riesling★★ £C
O **Friuli Isonzo** Pinot Grigio Sot Lis Rivis★★ £C   ● **Friuli Isonzo** Merlot★★ £C

RUSSIZ SUPERIORE   Friuli-Venezia Giulia   www.marcofelluga.it   **A: BWC**

Owner: Marco Felluga & family Via Russiz 7, 34070 Capriva del Friuli (GO)
Russiz Superiore is the leading estate of the Marco Felluga family. Like his older brother (Livio FELLUGA), Marco Felluga has Friulian viticulture in his blood and has similarly made an important contribution to establishing the region as Italy's leading area for white wines. His son Roberto and daughter Alessandra

continue to expand the family's influence and holdings (and another daughter, Patrizia, is behind the promising estate of ZUANI). The wine that has done the most for the reputation of Russiz Superiore is the red Riserva degli Orzoni, Cabernet Sauvignon complemented by Cabernet Franc and Merlot. Rich and structured, it has good depth and ripeness but impresses most in top vintages like 1997. As well as some consistently fine varietals, a blended white, Russiz Disôre, is made from from Pinot Bianco, Tocai, Sauvignon and Ribolla Gialla. The leading wines from the 130-ha Marco Felluga estate are Carantan, a stylish plummy red from Cabernet Franc, Cabernet Sauvignon and Merlot, and Molamotta, a blend of Pinot Bianco, Tocai and Ribolla Gialla. Good varietals include Chardonnay, Sauvignon, Tocai, Refosco and unusually (for Friuli), Moscato Rosa. Since 1994, the historic Castello di Buttrio, with 20 ha of vineyards, has been developed to become the source of a single red (Marburg, from Pignolo and Refosco) and white (Overstein, from Tocai and Ribolla Gialla). The family has also acquired an estate on the western fringe of Chianti Classico, San Niccolò a Pisignano, which is the source of a new red, Sorripa, from Sangiovese, Cabernet Sauvignon and Merlot. (PW)

Russiz Superiore:
O **Collio** Pinot Grigio★★ £C Sauvignon★★ £C
O **Collio Bianco** Russiz Disôre★★★ £D ● **Collio Rosso** Riserva degli Orzoni★★★ £E
● **Collio** Cabernet Franc★★ £D Merlot★★ £D

Marco Felluga:
● **Carantan★★★** £E ● **Refosco★★** £C O **Collio Bianco** Molamotta★★ £C
O **Collio** Tocai★★ £C Sauvignon★★ £C Chardonnay★★ £C

SAN LEONARDO Trentino www.sanleonardo.it A: JAr, Res, P&S
Owner: Marchese Carlo Guerrieri Gonzaga Loc. Borghetto, 38060 Avio (TN)
There are only 18 ha of vineyards but this large estate of 300 ha dates back to the Middle Ages, being originally the site of a monastery. It is held in high regard for a single red wine that has been developed by the current owner with help from the enologist Giacomo Tachis. Improvements to both the vineyard and vinification have been ongoing and in a good year (such as 1997) can result in a complex, refined yet rich, full expression of a cooler-climate blend of Cabernet Sauvignon, Cabernet Franc and Merlot (60/30/10). With deep blackcurrant, spice, plum and subtle herbal character it adds further complexity and fullness with another three or four years' cellaring after its release (six to eight years total). In some years it is not made at all and it has occasionally been disappointing, but good 1990s vintages (and 2000) have been of a generally very high standard. A varietal Merlot is effectively a second wine and though lighter, typically shows good style with attractive berry fruit and soft, supple tannins. Another red, the *barrique*-aged Villa Gresti is Merlot-based but also includes 10 per cent Carmenère. (PW)
● **San Leonardo★★★★** £E ● **Merlot di San Leonardo★★** £C

PRODUTTORI SAN MICHELE APPIANO Alto Adige www.stmichael.it A: Eur, Hrd
Owner: 'Cooperative' Via Circonvallazione 17/19, 39057 Appiano (BZ)
The wines of St Michael Eppan, the more usually seen form of the name, are made under the direction of one of Italy's great white winemakers, Hans Terzer. Drawing on 300 ha of vineyards, all the whites show good fruit and the mid-range varietals are defined by the vineyard area from which they are sourced. At the premium level the wines from the prized Sanct Valentin vineyards show greater aromatic complexity as well as an extra precision and refinement that put them ahead of most other Alto Adige examples. Gewürztraminer and Sauvignon are particularly stylish but quality of all the varietals is exemplary. An exquisite sweet white, Passito Comtess', from dried Gewürztraminer, Riesling, Sauvignon and Pinot Bianco grapes, is wonderfully perfumed but finely balanced and concentrated too. Reds can be very good as well, ripe with good expression and supple textures after at least two or three years' ageing. Most exciting of the reds is a very promising Sanct Valentin Lagrein, made since 2000. (PW)
O **Alto Adige** Chardonnay Merol★★ £D Chardonnay Sanct Valentin★★★ £D
O **Alto Adige** Sauvignon Lahn★★ £C Sauvignon Sanct Valentin★★★ £D

O **Alto Adige** Pinot Bianco Schulthauser★★ £C Pinot Grigio Sanct Valentin★★ £D
O **Alto Adige** Riesling Montiggl★★ £C Gewürztraminer Sanct Valentin★★★ £D
O **Alto Adige Bianco** Passito Comtess' Sanct Valentin★★★★ £E
● **Alto Adige** Pinot Nero Riserva★★ £C Pinot Nero Sanct Valentin★★ £E
● **Alto Adige** Cabernet Sanct Valentin★★ £E Lagrein Sanct Valentin★★★ £E

SCHIOPETTO Friuli-Venezia Giulia www.schiopetto.it A: **L&S**, Hrd, NYg, N&P

Owner: Mario Schiopetto Via Palazzo Arcivescovile 1, 34070 Capriva del Friuli (GO)
Mario Schiopetto was one of the great figures of Friulian viticulture. Up until his recent death in 2003 he continued to work with his family and winemaker Stefano Menotti to make some of Friuli's best unoaked white varietals, something he had done since the 1970s. Pinot Bianco, Pinot Grigio, Malvasia, Sauvignon and Tocai Friulano in particular show the intense, clear-fruited expressions that have earned such respect. The small estate of Podere dei Blumeri was added in 1996, to make a total of 30 ha of vineyards. Here Sauvignon, Chardonnay and Pinot Grigio have been made with a similar intensity, excellent concentration and individual expression. Wary of the flavours of new oak, Mario Schiopetto has only recently made any use of oak. Large Slavonian casks are now used for a series of wood-fermented and aged varietals. Amrità (Pinot Bianco), Pardes (Tocai) and Tarsia (Sauvignon) are richer, creamier and fuller; less pure perhaps but more complex and likely to last for up to a decade. Also made is an impressive, harmonious, unoaked blended white, Blanc des Rosis, from Pinot Bianco, Tocai, Sauvignon and Malvasia, while the red Rivarossa is a blend of Merlot, Cabernet Sauvignon and Cabernet Franc. First made in 2002 is a refined but concentrated blend (partly oak fermented and aged) of Chardonnay and Tocai called simply Mario Schiopetto. A new red, Blumeri Rosso is Merlot-based but includes Cabernet Sauvignon and Refosco. (PW)
O **Collio** Pinot Bianco★★★ £C Pinot Bianco Amrità★★★ £E
O **Collio** Tocai Friulano★★ £C Tocai Friulano Pardes★★★ £E
O **Collio** Sauvignon★★ £C Sauvignon Tarsia★★★ £E
O **Collio** Pinot Grigio★★ £C O **Blanc des Rosis**★★★ £E ● **Rivarossa**★★ £C

SERAFINI & VIDOTTO Veneto A: **Ast**, AoW

Owner: Francesco Serafini & Antonello Vidotto Via Arditi 1, 31040 Nervesa della Battaglia (TV)
From close to the River Piave north of Treviso, this estate would seem to be well off the beaten track for quality yet the wines from Francesco Serafini and Antonello Vidotto suggest otherwise. These reds perhaps owe more to dedicated work in the vineyards (some 18 ha) and careful selection rather than to site but are of commendable quality. The top wine, Rosso dell'Abbazia, is a blend of the two Cabernets (80 per cent) with 10 per cent each of Merlot and Pinot Nero in 2000 and is aged in new *barriques*. Cool but ripe-fruited with real intensity and extract, it also shows considerable complexity and a Bordeaux-like refinement. The struggle for ripeness is more evident in lesser vintages like 99 yet the wines can still show well with age (seven or eight years). Pinot Nero can also be most enchanting with smoke, floral, herb, berry, cherry, even redcurrant aromas, if missing the texture or breadth of fine Burgundy. More moderately priced is the medium-bodied Phigaia After the Red, based on Cabernet Franc and Merlot. Though more likely to show a hint of greeness, it is sound, flavoursome and can be drunk quite young. A white, Il Bianco dell'Abazia, is a Sauvignon/Chardonnay blend but it has not been tasted. (PW)
● **Rosso dell' Abazia**★★★★ £E
● **Pinot Nero**★★★ £E ● **Phigaia After The Red**★★ £C

TEDESCHI Veneto www.tedeschiwines.com A: **Hal**, Maj, N&P, Sel, V&C

Owner: Tedeschi family Fraz. Pedemonte, Via Verdi 4, 37020 San Pietro in Cariano (VR)
The fifth generation of Tedeschis to be involved in making wine here in the heart of the Valpolicella zone is now in charge. They control 67 ha of vineyards, 22 ha of which are owned. Of a substantial range, the best wines are the premium Amarone and Recioto which show classic vigour, flavour intensity and power. More occasionally made is a Fabriseria Amarone Classico, effectively a Riserva. The modern, *barrique*-aged

Rosso La Fabriseria adds a small amount of Cabernet Sauvignon to Corvina, Corvinone, Rondinella and Dindarella. Also made are a sweet white from Garganega and Soarin grapes, Vin de la Fabriseria, a *ripasso* red, Capitel San Rocco, of variable quality and basic generics of Valpolicella, Bardolino, Soave, etc. (PW)

● **Amarone della Valpolicella Classico★★** £D Capitel Monte Olmi★★★★ £E La Fabriseria★★★★ £E
● **Recioto della Valpolicella Classico** Capitel Monte Fontana★★★ £E
● **Valpolicella Classico** Superiore Capitel dei Nicolò★★ £C ● **Rosso La Fabriseria★★★** £D

MATIJAZ TERCIC Friuli-Venezia Giulia A: **Mgi**, L&W

Owner: Matijaz Tercic Loc. Bucuie 9, 34070 San Floriano del Collio (GO)
This is an increasingly good and reasonably priced source of Fruili wines with a perceptible increase in quality year on year. To impressive intensity and concentration have been added more expression and better balance. The best wine is the Collio Bianco Planta, Chardonnay with 10 per cent Pinot Bianco. This combines a gently creamy texture with good complexity and has the structure to improve for at least four or five years. Vino degli Orti is produced from Tocai, Malvasia and Riesling and manages to be delightfully aromatic but concentrated too. This, like all the ripe, intense and stylish, white varietals is vinified and aged in stainless steel. Merlot is usually cool with a touch of herbaceous green pepper character to its smoky, plummy fruit yet is characterful and well made. A varietal Ribolla Gialla is also made. (PW)

O **Collio Bianco** Planta★★★ £C O **Vino degli Orti★★** £C
O **Collio** Pinot Grigio★★ £C Sauvignon★★ £C Chardonnay★★ £C ● **Collio** Merlot★★ £C

CANTINA TERLANO Alto Adige www.cantina-terlano.com A: **Ast**, But, P&S, F&M

Owner: 'Cooperative' Via Silberleiten 7, 39018 Terlano (BZ)
The Terlan or Terlano cooperative is another of the Alto Adige's dynamic co-ops. The wines are made by Hartmann Donà in a bold and flavoursome mould in contrast to the refinement and subtlety sought by others in the region. Above a regular (Classico) series of varietals are an extensive range of vineyard designated varietals and four premium releases with prices to match. While oak can be a little too intrusive in these top *cuvées*, it does further enhance their structure, and one-off releases of Terlano and Sauvignon with more than a decade's age give an indication of their sometimes exceptional ageing potential. Both the Terlano Classico and the premium Nova Domus achieve good harmony between Pinot Bianco, Sauvignon and Chardonnay. The best of the reds are two versions of Lagrein both which need a minimum three to five years age open up fully, especially Porphyr which comes from 70 year old vines. Also made are Merlot (Riserva Siebeneich), Pinot Nero (Riserva Montigl), Cabernet (Riserva Siemegg) and other native varieties. (PW)

O **Alto Adige** Pinot Bianco Vorberg★★ £C Sauvignon Quarz★★★ £D Gewürztraminer Lunare★★ £D
O **Alto Adige Terlano** Classico★★ £B Nova Domus★★★ £D
● **Alto Adige** Lagrein Riserva Gries★★ £C Lagrein Riserva Porphyr★★★ £D

VIE DI ROMANS Friuli-Venezia Giulia A: **Lib**,Vne, Hrd

Owner: Gianfranco Gallo Loc. Vie di Romans 1, 34070 Mariano del Friuli (GO)
Those who dismiss the quality of Chardonnay and Sauvignon produced in Friuli need to taste the wines of Gianfranco Gallo. From 30 ha of vines the grapes are turned into wines with a richness, intensity – but even more importantly a breadth and a structure – that few other examples approach. There are two Chardonnays: Ciampagnis Vieris is the unoaked version, with a tangy, pure fruit intensity; the richer, more complex and structured Vie di Romans spends 12 months in French oak. Piere is the unoaked Sauvignon, concentrated and intense with good grip if less flattering than the delicately creamy, ripe and harmonious Vieris. Flor di Uis is a very flavoursome and characterful blend of Malvasia, Tocai, Riesling and Chardonnay (each vinified separately). A *barrique*-aged and fermented Pinot Grigio, Dessimis, is rich and creamy with a lot of depth but is arguably the least refined of the whites. The Merlot-based red Voos dai Ciamps (not made in 2000) also shows real depth and intensity and an almost velvety texture with several years' age. (PW)

O **Friuli Isonzo** Chardonnay Ciampagnis Vieris★★★ £D   Chardonnay Vie di Romans★★★★ £E
O **Friuli Isonzo** Sauvignon Piere★★★ £E   Sauvignon Vieris★★★ £E   Pinot Grigio Dessimis★★★ £E
O **Friuli Isonzo Bianco** Flor di Uis★★★ £E   ● **Friuli Isonzo Rosso** Voos dai Ciamps★★★ £E

VIGNALTA   Veneto   A: **Ast**

Owner: L Gomiero, F Zanovello & G Cardin   Fraz. Luvigliano, Via dei Vescovi 5, 35038 Torreglia
Many wine lovers would have trouble locating Valpolicella in the Veneto so what chance has Colli Euganei?
The hills south-west of Padova don't in fact have much of a reputation yet for more than a decade Vignalta
has produced fine reds and interesting whites. The top red is Gemola, 70 per cent Merlot complemented
by Cabernet Franc, a cool but ripe, elegant Bordeaux-like red that ages gracefully. A Rosso Riserva from a
similar blend hasn't the same depth or concentration but is typically supple and expressive. A small volume
of an unusual blend of Petite Sirah, Primitivo and Barbera called Agno Tinto was first made in 1998. As
the list of varieties might suggest, this is a deep-coloured, robust, earthy but characterful red; just a little
more concentration and it could be very good indeed. Of the whites the Chardonnay comes from a
30-year-old vineyard and is *barrique*-fermented and aged, but the best is the refined sweet Moscato, Fior
d'Arancio Alpinae. (PW)
● **Colli Euganei Rosso** Rosso Riserva★★ £C   Gemola★★★ £D
● **Agno Tinto**★★ £D
O **Colli Euganei** Pinot Bianco★★ £C   Pinot Bianco Agno Casto★★ £C   Chardonnay★★ £C
O **Colli Euganei** Fior d'Arancio Alpinae★★★ £E   O **Moscato Sirio**★ £B

VILLA RUSSIZ   Friuli-Venezia Giulia   www.villarussiz.it   A: **Bib**, NYg

Owner: Instituto Adele Cerruti   Via Russiz 6, 34070 Capriva del Friuli (GO)
The dynamic Gianni Menotti directs this very professionally run estate and winery for the charitable
institute Adele Cerruti. Whilst there is excellent intensity and varietal expression in the regular
bottlings, it is only in the special versions that an extra depth and structure is truly evident. All the varietal-
labelled whites are vinified in stainless steel and don't see any oak. Regular Sauvignon is
particularly good – long and tangy, intense and aromatic – while Sauvignon de la Tour adds more breadth
and structure from 10 months on its lees. Oak is employed for a very small production of Gräfin de la Tour,
a Chardonnay which spends 12 months in *barriques*. Similarly small quantities are made of the red Graf de
la Tour from 100 per cent Merlot. With two years in *barrique* it typically shows a richness and ripeness that
can be missing in the regular Merlot and Cabernet, which are aged in a mix of small and large oak, the
Cabernet being a blend of both Cabernet Sauvignon and Cabernet Franc. Other varietals usually made to
a high standard are Riesling, Malvasia and Ribolla Gialla. (PW)
O **Collio** Tocai Friulano★★ £C   Pinot Bianco★★ £C   Pinot Grigio★★ £C
O **Collio** Sauvignon★★ £C   Sauvignon de la Tour★★★ £D
O **Collio** Chardonnay Gräfin de la Tour★★★ £D   ● **Collio** Merlot Graf de la Tour★★ £E

LE VIGNE DI ZAMÒ   Friuli-Venezia Giulia   www.levignedizamo.com   A: **HSA**

Owner: Zamò family   Loc. Rosazzo, Via Abate Corrado 4, 33044 Manzano (GO)
The Zamò family commenced wine production in the late 1970s but their roots in the Friuli hills stretch
back to 1924. Their now sizeable operation has undergone many changes over the past decade, with a
transformation in vineyard resources that now total 55 ha, either owned or leased, from the zones around
Rocca Bernarda, Buttrio and Rosazzo. A modern winery with a battery of stainless steel tanks underpins the
cleanliness and freshness of regular varietals, while oak is employed for the premium Pinot Bianco, Tullio
Zamò (named after the family patriarch), and Ronco delle Acacie, from Tocai, Chardonnay and Pinot
Bianco. Both can show impressive texture and complexity if missing the balance and elegance for more.
Tocai is nearly always good, whether in the regular version or the old-vine Cinquant'Anni. Forty per cent
of the vineyard is planted to red grapes and the quality of the special bottlings no doubt owes something to
consultancy from top enologist Franco Bernabei, better known for his Tuscan endeavours. The characterful

Ronco dei Roseti is mostly from Merlot and the two Cabernets. The best red is usually the richly textured and concentrated Merlot Cinquant' Anni, which has the structure to improve for 5 to 10 years. Tiny amounts of Pignolo and Schioppettino are also made. (PW)

O **Colli Orientali del Friuli** Tocai Friulano★★ £C Tocai Friulano Vigne Cinquant' Anni★★★ £C
O **Colli Orientali del Friuli** Sauvignon★★ £C Pinot Bianco Tullio Zamò★★ £C
O **Colli Orientali del Friuli Bianco** Ronco delle Acacie★★★ £C
● **Colli Orientali del Friuli** Merlot Vigne Cinquant' Anni★★★ £E
● **Colli Orientali del Friuli Rosso** Ronco dei Roseti★★★ £D

ZENATO Veneto www.zenato.it   A: **Eur,** Hrd

Owner: Sergio Zenato   Via San Benedetto 8, 337019 Peschiera del Garda (VR)

Sergio Zenato established this well-known house in 1960 which though Lugana-based also includes a significant production from Valpolicella. Whilst the regular *cuvées* only rarely offer much excitement, the special bottlings can be very good indeed. As well as vibrant, chewy Valpolicella Ripassa there are the 'signature' Riserva wines – powerful Amarone and a concentrated Lugana. New is a *barrique*-fermented and aged Chardonnay Riserva. Good Lugana (Vigneto Massoni) is also made from the Santa Cristina estate, where production also includes Cabernet Sauvignon (blended with a little Merlot and Corvina in Alberto), Chardonnay and sweet white, Rigoletto, made from dried Lugana grapes. La Sansonina is an estate owned by Carla Prospero, the wife of Sergio Zenato. The existing Merlot vines were supplemented by further plantings and, while the inaugural 1997 vintage (sold in magnums) was 100 per cent Merlot, the 98 adds in Cabernet Sauvignon. This stylish red is fully ripe and shows a chocolaty, cedary complexity with five years' age or more. (PW)

Zenato:
O **Lugana** Vigneto Massoni★★ £C Riserva Sergio Zenato★★ £C
● **Valpolicella Classico** Superiore★ £B   ● **Valpolicella** Superiore Ripassa★★ £C
● **Amarone della Valpolicella Classico**★ £E Riserva Sergio Zenato★★★ £F
La Sansonina:
● **Sansonina**★★★ £D

ZUANI Friuli-Venezia Giulia   A: **Bal,** UnC

Owner: Patrizia Felluga   Loc. Giasbana 12, 34070 San Floriano del Collio (GO)

Patrizia Felluga, one of the daughters of Marco Felluga (RUSSIZ SUPERIORE), and her son Antonio Zanon produce two marvellous white wines. Their stated goal is to make whites that are a typical expression of a specific vineyard site rather than producing varietals or a blend of varietals from different sites (as most do in Friuli). Both wines are a blend of Tocai Friulano, Pinot Grigio, Chardonnay and Sauvignon Blanc. Zuani Vigne is an unoaked version that is full, ripe and concentrated with excellent flavour, freshness and depth. The wine labelled simply Zuani Collio Bianco is from fruit that is harvested a little later and is a more ambitious oak-aged version, spending eight to nine months in *barrique*. This has greater breadth and complexity, the citrus and mineral fruit meshed with leesy and oak-given characters, but successive releases show great style and balance (try from 2002 or 03). While this 7 ha estate is expanding, volumes are currently small. (PW)

O **Collio Bianco**★★★★ £D Zuani Vigne★★★ £C

OTHER WINES OF NOTE

ABBAZIA DI NOVACELLA O **Alto Adige** Kerner £B Kerner Praepositus £C
O **Alto Adige** Sylvaner £B O **Weiss Praepositus** (Sylvaner/Pinot Grigio/Chardonnay) £C
● **Alto Adige** Blauburgunder Praepositus (Pinot Nero) £E ◉ **Alto Adige** Rosenmuskateller £E
IGINO ACCORDINI ● **Amarone della Valpolicella Classico** Le Bessole £E
STEFANO ACCORDINI ● **Amarone della Valpolicella** Acinatico £E
● **Recioto della Valpolicella** Acinatico £E
ADAMI O **Prosecco** Bosco di Gica Brut £B O **Prosecco** Vigneto Giardino £C
BASTANICH O **Colli Orientali del Friuli** Pinot Plus (Pinot Grigio/Pinot Bianco) £C Tocai Plus £C
O **Vespa Bianco** (Chardonnay/Sauvignon/Picolit) £C
● **Calabrone** (Refosco/Pignolo/Cabernet Franc/Merlot) £C
BERTANI ● **Amarone della Valpolicella** Classico £F
CARLO BOGONI O **Soave Classico** Superiore La Ponsara £B
BRIGALDARA ● **Amarone della Valpolicella** Classico £D
CA' RUGATE O **Soave Classico** Superiore Montealto £C Superiore Monte Fiorentine £C
O **Montealto** (Garganega) £C
VITICOLTORI CALDARO O **Alto Adige** Gewürztraminer Campaner £C
CANTINA DEL CASTELLO O **Soave Classico Superiore** £B Pressoni £C
O **Soave Classico Superiore** Acini Soavi (late-harvested, dry) £D
MICHELE CASTELLANI & FIGLI ● **Amarone della Valpolicella** I Castei Campo Casalin £E
● **Recioto della Valpolicella** I Castei Campo Casalin £D
CORTEFORTE ● **Amarone della Valpolicella** £E ● **Recioto della Valpolicella** Amandorlato £E
COSTARIPA ● **Maim** (Groppello) £C
DAMIJAN O **Collio Bianco** Kaplja (Chardonnay/Tocai Friulano/Malvasia Istriana) £C
O **Collio** Ribolla Gialla £C ● **Collio Rosso** Prelit (Cabernet Sauvignon/Merlot) £C
DI LENARDO O **Fruili Grave** Toh! (Tocai Friulano) £B O **Fruili Grave** Chardonnay £B
● **Pass the Cookies** (sweet - Verduzzo) £D ● **Friuli Grave** Refosco £B ● **Friuli Grave** Cabernet £B
PETER DIPOLI O **Alto Adige** Sauvignon Voglar £D
MAURO DRIUS O **Collio** Pinot Bianco £C Sauvignon £C Tocai Friulano £C
O **Collio Bianco** Vignis di Siris (Sauvignon/Tocai/Pinot Bianco) £C
ERSTE & NEUE – PRIMA & NUOVA O **Alto Adige** Gewürztraminer Puntay £C
FERRARI O **Trento** Brut Giulio Ferrari Riserva del Fondatore £F O **Trento** Brut Perlé £D
WALTER FILIPUTTI O **Colli Orientali del Friuli** Picolit Monastrium Rosarium £E
NINO FRANCO O **Prosecco** Brut £C O **Prosecco** Rive di San Floriano £C
GINI O **Soave Classico** Superiore £B La Froscà £B Contrada Salvarenza Vecchie Vigne £C
O **Recioto di Soave** Col Foscarin £E Renobilis £E
JOSKO GRAVNER O **Collio** Ribolla £F
O **Collio Bianco** Breg (Sauvignon/Chardonnay/Pinot Grigio/Ribolla) £F
GUERRIERI RIZZARDI ● **Amarone della Valpolicella** £E
EDI KANTE O **Carso** Malvasia £C Chardonnay £C Sauvignon £C
LA CAPPUCINA O **Soave** Superiore Fontégo £B Superiore San Brizio £C
LA CASTELLADA O **Collio** Chardonnay £C Ribolla Gialla £C
O **Collio Bianco** Bianco della Castellada (Sauvignon/Tocai/Pinot Grigio/Ribolla Gialla) £D
LA TUNELLA O **Colli Orientali del Friuli** Campo Marzio £C
● **Colli Orientali del Friuli** Cabernet Franc £C
● **Colli Orientali del Friuli Rosso** L'Arcione (Cabernet Sauvignon/Merlot/Schioppettino) £D
LE RAGOSE ● **Valpolicella Classico** Superiore Le Sassine £B ● **Amarone della Valpolicella** £E
LE VIGNE DI SAN PIETRO ● **Cabernet Sauvignon Refolà** £E
O **Bianco di Custoza** San Pietro £C O **Due Cuori** (sweet – Moscato Giallo) £F
LIS NERIS O **Friuli Isonzo** Chardonnay Sant' Jurosa £D Pinot Grigio Gris £C Sauvignon Picol £C
O **Lis** (Pinot Grigio/Chardonnay/Sauvignon) £C
O **Confini** (Pinot Grigio/Riesling/Malvasia/Traminer) £D O **Tal Lùc** (sweet – Verduzzo) £F
LIVON O **Collio** Chardonnay Braide Mate £C Pinot Grigio Braide Grande £C

O **Braide Alte** (Chardonnay/Sauvignon/Moscato Giallo/Picolit) £C

LOREDAN GASPARINI ● **Capo di Stato** (Cabernets/Merlot/Malbec) £E

LORENZON/I FEUDI DI ROMANS O **Friuli Isonzo** Sauvignon Blanc £B Pinot Grigio £B
● **Friuli Isonzo** Merlot £B

MARION ● **Valpolicella Superiore** £D ● **Teroldego** £D ● **Amarone della Valpolicella** £F

ORNELLA MOLON TRAVERSO O **Sauvignon** £C O **Traminer** £C ● **Piave** Merlot £C
● **Vite Rossa** (Merlot/Cabernets) £C ● **Riserva Rosso di Villa** (Merlot/Cabernet Sauvignon) £D

MURI-GRIES O **Alto Adige** Lagrein Riserva Abtei £D

NICOLIS ● **Valpolicella Classico** Superiore Seccal £C
● **Amarone della Valpolicella** £E ● **Recioto della Valpolicella** £E

PIERPAOLO PECORARI ● **Merlot Baolar** £D
O **Chardonnay Soris** £C O **Sauvignon Kolaus** £C O **Sauvignon Altis** £C

PRÀ O **Soave Classico** Superiore £B Vigneto Monte Grande £B Colle Sant'Antonio £C

PUIATTI O **Collio** Sauvignon I Ruttars £C O **Collio** Pinot Grigio I Ruttars £C
● **Collio** Pinot Nero I Ruttars £D

DARIO RACCARO O **Collio** Tocai Friulano £C

RONCO DEL GNEMIZ O **Colli Orientali del Friuli** Chardonnay £D

RONCO DELLE BETULLE O **Colli Orientali del Friuli** Sauvignon £B Tocai Friulano £B
● **Colli Orientali del Friuli** Cabernet Franc £C Franconia £C

RONCUS O **Roncús Bianco Vecchie Vigne** (Malvasia/Tocai/Ribolla Gialla) £D
O **Pinot Bianco** £C O **Collio** Tocai Friulano £C

RUGGERI O **Prosecco** Riserva Giustino Bisol £C

RUSSOLO O **Malvasia Istriana** £B O **Doi Raps** (Pinot Grigio/Sauvignon/Moscato Giallo) £C
O **Pinot Grigio** Ronco Calaj £B O **Tocai Friulano** Ronco Calaj £B O **Müller Thurgau** Musignaz £B
● **Pinot Nero** Grifo Nero £C ● **Borgo di Peuma** (Merlot/Cabernet Franc/Refosco) £C

TENUTA SANT' ANTONIO ● **Amarone della Valpolicella** Campo dei Gigli £E
● **Valpolicella Superiore** La Bandina £C

GIORDANO SIRCH/FORNALIS O **Sirch** (Tocai Friulano/Ribolla Gialla/Sauvignon) £B

SPECOGNA O **Colli** Orientali del Friuli Tocai £C O **Pinot Grigio** £C

SPERI ● **Amarone della Valpolicella** Vigneto Monte Sant'Urbano £E
● **Recioto della Valpolicella** I Communai £E

SUAVIA O **Soave Classico** Superiore Monte Carbonare £C Superiore Le Rive £D
O **Recioto di Soave Classico** Acinatum £F

TAMELLINI O **Soave** Superiore £B O **Soave Classico** Anguane £B Le Bine £C

CANTINA PRODUTTORI TERMENO ● **Alto Adige** Lagrein Urban £D
O **Alto Adige** Gewürztraminer Maratsch £C Gewürztraminer Nussbaumer £D
O **Alto Adige** Pinot Grigio Unterebner £C Sauvignon £C

TERPIN O **Collio Bianco** £D

TIEFENBRUNNER O **Feldmarschall Von Fenner** (Müller Thurgau) £D
● **Linticlarus Cuvée** (Lagrein/Cabernet Sauvignon/Merlot) £D

TRABUCCHI ● **Valpolicella Superiore** Terre del Cereolo £C ● **Amarone della Valpolicella** £E
● **Recioto della Valpolicella** £E

VALLAROM O **Trentino** Chardonnay Riserva Vigna di Brioni £C

CANTINA VALPANTENA/FALASCO ● **Valpolicella** Valpantena Ripasso £B
● **Amarone della Valpolicella** £D ● **Recioto della Valpolicella** Tesauro £D

C. S. VALPOLICELLA ● **Amarone della Valpolicella** Domini Veneti £D Vigneti di Jago £E
● **Recioto della Valpolicella** Domini Veneti £D Vigneti di Moron £E

VILLA MONTELEONE ● **Amarone della Valpolicella Classico** £E

ELENA WALCH O **Alto Adige** Gewürztraminer Kastelaz £D Pinot Bianco Kastelaz £C
O **Alto Adige** Pinot Grigio Castel Ringberg £C Riesling Castel Ringberg £C

VISTORTA ● **Merlot** £C

VIVIANI ● **Valpolicella Classico** Superiore Campo Monar £C
● **Amarone della Valpolicella** Casa dei Bepi £F ● **Recioto della Valpolicella** £E

Author's Choice (PW)

12 premium reds

ALLEGRINI ● La Poja

GIROLAMO DORIGO ● Colli Orientali del Friuli Rosso Montscalapade

LIVIO FELLUGA ● Colli Orientali del Fruili Merlot Riserva Sossò

FORADORI ● Teroldego Rotaliano Granato

HOFSTÄTTER ● Alto Adige Pinot Nero Barthenau Vigna Sant'Urbano

ALOIS LAGEDER ● Alto Adige Cabernet Sauvignon Cor Römigberg

MIANI ● Colli Orientali del Friuli Merlot

MOSCHIONI ● Colli Orientali del Friuli Celtico Rosso

JOSEF NIEDERMAYR ● Alto Adige Lagrein Aus Gries Riserva

RUSSIZ SUPERIORE ● Collio Rosso Riserva degli Orzoni

SAN LEONARDO ● San Leonardo

VIGNALTA ● Gemola

10 superior Valpolicella (or equivalent)

ALLEGRINI ● La Grola

TOMMASO BUSSOLA ● Valpolicella Classico Superiore TB

CORTE SANT'ALDA ● Valpolicella Superiore Mithas

ROMANO DAL FORNO ● Valpolicella Superiore Vigneto di Monte Lodoletta

LE SALETTE ● Valpolicella Classico Superiore Ca' Carnocchio

MARION ● Valpolicella Superiore

QUINTARELLI ● Valpolicella Classico Superiore Monte Ca' Paletta

ROCCOLO GRASSI ● Valpolicella Superiore Roccolo Grassi

TRABUCCHI ● Valpolicella Superiore Terre di Cereolo

ZENATO ● Valpolicella Superiore Ripassa

10 reds for meditation

ALLEGRINI ● Amarone della Valpolicella Classico

TOMMASO BUSSOLA ● Recioto della Valpolicella Classico TB

CORTE SANT'ALDA ● Recioto della Valpolicella

LE SALETTE ● Amarone della Valpolicella Classico Pergole Vece

MOSCHIONI ● Colli Orientali del Friuli Pignolo

QUINTARELLI ● Amarone della Valpolicella Classico Monte Ca' Paletta

SPERI ● Amarone della Valpolicella Classico Vigneto Monte Sant' Urbano

TENUTA SANT' ANTONIO ● Amarone della Valpolicella Campo dei Gigli

TEDESCHI ● Amarone della Valpolicella Classico Capitel Monte Olmi

ZENATO ● Amarone della Valpolicella Classico Riserva Sergio Zenato

20 first class whites

BORGO DEL TIGLIO ○ Collio Bianco Studio di Bianco

CA' DEI FRATI ○ Pratto

CESCONI ○ Trentino Chardonnay

COLTERENZIO ○ Alto Adige Chardonnay Cornell

LIVIO FELLUGA ○ Colli Orientali del Fruili Rosazzo Bianco Terre Alte

FRANZ HAAS ○ Manna

HOFSTÄTTER ○ Alto Adige Gewürztraminer Kolbenhof Söll

IL CARPINO ○ Collio Chardonnay

VINNAIOLI JERMANN ○ Vintage Tunina

PIEROPAN ○ Soave Classico Superiore La Rocca

POJER & SANDRI ○ Faye

RONCHI DI MANZANO ○ Colli Orientali del Friuli Rosazzo Bianco Ronc di Rosazzo

RUSSIZ SUPERIORE O Collio Bianco Russiz Disôre
PRODUTTORI SAN MICHELE APPIANO O Alto Adige Gewürztraminer Sanct Valentin
SCHIOPETTO O Collio Pinot Bianco Amrità
CANTINA TERLANO O Alto Adige Sauvignon Quarz
VIE DI ROMANS O Friuli Isonzo Chardonnay Vie di Romans
VILLA RUSSIZ O Collio Sauvignon de la Tour
LE VIGNE DI ZAMÒ O Colli Orientali del Friuli Tocai Friulano Vigne Cinquant'Anni
ZUANI O Collio Bianco

...and some fine sweet whites

ANSELMI O I Capitelli
GIROLAMO DORIGO O Colli Orientali del Friuli Picolit Vigneto Montscalapade
MACULAN O Breganze Torcolato
PIEROPAN O Passito della Rocca
POJER & SANDRI O Essenzia
RONCHI DI MANZANO O Colli Orientali del Friuli Rosazzo Verduzzo Ronc di Rosazzo
PRODUTTORI SAN MICHELE APPIANO O Alto Adige Bianco Passito Comtess' Sanct Valentin

Rinascimento

Appropriately Tuscany's wine renaissance or rinascimento *could be said to have its beginnings in Florence, thanks to the firm of Antinori. Its artists include individual producers but of as much importance are the highly trained and experienced enologists that are consulted by the majority of producers to a greater or lesser degree. Over the past three decades Tuscany has also attracted a fair amount of outside investment and talent, including Swiss and English winemakers and entrepreneurs. In the new millennium, with winemaking of a generally high standard, increasing emphasis is placed on style, including the appropriateness of international varieties and the importance of expressing something of the wine's origins or* tipicità *(typicality). As well as unprecedented quality from Sangiovese, and very good Cabernet Sauvignon, Merlot and Syrah, more effort is being spent on achieving not just good varietal expression but also maximising the different manifestations possible from permutations of place, soil and climate. While the best wines show richness and concentration it is not at the expense of finesse and elegance.*

Red wines

Central Tuscany and the classic appellations

The heart of Tuscany is **Chianti Classico**, its most historic and still its most important wine zone. The blunder of massive replanting in the 1960s with productive but poor-quality clones has started to be atoned for by recent replantings that have benefited from the research project known as Chianti Classico 2000. While the Chianti Classico DOCG now permits increasing amounts of other, foreign, varieties (usually at the expense of natives such as Canaiolo and Colorino), it is still based for the most part on Sangiovese (with pure examples possible since 1996). The leading communes are Greve in Chianti, Barberino Val d'Elsa, Castellina in Chianti, Radda in Chianti, Gaiole in Chianti and Castelnuovo Berardenga. Part of the communes of Tavarnelle Val di Pesa and San Casciano Val di Pesa are also included. While there are some discernible differences between each, as important are elevation, specific mesoclimates and soil types (there is much variation within each commune), better identified in sub-zones such as Monti (Gaiole) and Panzano (Greve). Interestingly, in a 'Chianti Classico 2000' tasting demonstrating the characteristics of different trialled clones there was as much affinity between wines from different clones grown in the same location, as those from the same clones but different sites. But arguably still more important is the style of winemaking. The use of new oak and variations in fermentation length, type, temperature, etc. all play a significant part in emphasising or smothering differences in *terroir*. Regular or *normale* Chianti Classico can be sold with a year's age, whereas Riservas, which are more likely to have been *barrique*-aged, are only released from the beginning of the third year after the vintage (i.e. the 2002s from January 2005). While a few high-profile estates have re-established Chianti Classico as their leading wine, others promote a so-called Super-Tuscan, first created as a *vino da tavola* when the laws were more restrictive and now often sold under the Toscana IGT. These include varietal Cabernet Sauvignon and Merlot, blends of the two together and blends of each with Sangiovese. There is also varietal Syrah and even Pinot Nero. This profusion of wine types is repeated in almost every important wine zone in Tuscany.

Chianti Classico is surrounded by several viticultural zones of differing size and importance. Immediately north in the hills closest to Florence, is **Chianti Colli Fiorentini**. North-east of Florence, from hills on either side of the river Sieve (but pressing up against the Apennines) is the small zone of **Chianti Rufina** where a small number of producers make a soaring, elegant expression of Sangiovese. Intruding into Rufina's eastern flank is the high-altitude **Pomino**, notable for its historical inclusion of French varieties and its domination by Frescobaldi. From the other side of Florence are another minor Chianti zone, **Chianti Montalbano**, and the small but high-quality zone of **Carmignano**. Though revived only since the 1970s there are historical references both to its quality and to the planting of Cabernet Sauvignon, of which 20 per cent may be added to Sangiovese. South of Carmignano and west of Colli Fiorentini is a further small Chianti zone, **Chianti Montespertoli**. West of Chianti Classico are the medieval towers of San Gimignano. Limited success with the white Vernaccia (see below) has resulted in increased planting of red varieties. Some fine blends, mostly

Sangiovese, Cabernet Sauvignon or Merlot, or a combination of these are sold mainly as Toscana IGT in preference to a newish **San Gimignano** DOC. Lesser examples of Sangiovese tend to be sold as **Chianti Colli Senesi**. This zone extends from here south around the lower reaches of Chianti Classico and also surrounds the Brunello and Vino Nobile zones – often giving the fullest and most meaty non-Classico Chianti.

Brunello di Montalcino DOCG is a wine like no other in Tuscany. Here it is hotter and drier than in any other major zone and the bigger, more muscular wines, offered by an ever growing number of producers, have maintained high prices thanks in part to a more singular, focused image that has been effectively promoted both locally and on foreign markets. Yet the quality of these pure Sangiovese (locally called Brunello) wines varies greatly. Excessive wood-ageing requirements were blamed for the wines drying out, especially in lighter years when there is insufficient fruit to support it. However, though the wines are only available from the fifth year after the vintage (the 2000s in 2005) there is now much greater flexibility about the type of wood used to age the wines and some styles are characterised by their use of new oak. The introduction of **Rosso di Montalcino** DOC, effectively a second wine, has helped cash flow. Its more accessible, fruit-driven style also means these wines can be drunk much younger, though some examples have better structure and depth than lighter, more forward Brunello and need at least three to five years' age. The most structured and ageworthy Brunello tends to come from the higher ridges and many individual sub-zones are beginning to emerge. **Sant'Antimo** DOC covers examples of blends of Sangiovese and other (foreign) varieties as well as varietal examples from other grapes grown in the zone.

Vino Nobile di Montepulciano DOCG lies to the east of Montalcino around its own small historic town. Unlike Brunello, pure Sangiovese (here called Prugnolo Gentile) was not permitted until very recently and many examples contain a percentage of Canaiolo and sometimes Mammolo. Vino Nobile has had difficulty reclaiming its historic status but is currently good value from a leading producer. Lesser vineyards are assigned as **Rosso di Montepulciano** which is not the same concept as Rosso di Montalcino and most examples are much more modestly structured and for drinking within a couple of years of the vintage. Further east in the Val di Chiana a new **Cortona** DOC has been created with provision for varietal Merlot and Syrah (and Chardonnay – see below) among other varieties, and is already being utilised by Antinori, Avignonesi and Tenementi D'Alessandro. Further north in the Valdarno (and east of Chianti Classico) is another minor Chianti zone, **Chianti Colli Aretini**, currently being rescued from its former obscurity by Petrolo and others, though the best wines are sold as Toscana IGT.

Many of Tuscany's new stars come from within the areas discussed above but increasingly important are the mostly unexploited western and southern areas of viticulture first highlighted by Sassicaia but developed at an accelerating pace over the past couple of decades.

The Tuscan coast and the new Tuscany

The most northern of the Tuscan coastal zones is the **Colline Lucchesi** for wines from slopes on either side of the historic and beautiful town of Lucca. As in the east at Rufina, the vineyards lie close to the Apennines and there is a growing number of progressive producers. Plantings in the more restrictive zone around the town of **Montecarlo** include several French varieties and many of the best wines from both DOCs are sold as Toscana IGT. Some way south and east of Pisa the hills are demarcated as **Colline Pisane** for another of the minor Chianti zones but Sangiovese, Cabernet Sauvignon and Merlot blends of high quality are made. Similarly promising wines are being produced from within the **Montescudaio** DOC, though again both these and the Pisane wines tend to be sold as Toscana IGT. From Castello del Terriccio, located on the periphery of these zones but one of the most high-profile producers in the area, it is but a short distance south to the famous zone of Bolgheri.

Bolgheri (and the commune of Castagneto Carducci) is where the narrow strip of the coastal Maremma might be said to start properly. Cabernet Sauvignon and Merlot dominate but Sangiovese is not completely ignored and the DOC (which includes a single-wine sub-zone for Sassicaia) covers blends that include any (or all) of the three varieties. There is a mix of both smaller producers, such as Michele Satta,

Grattamacco and Le Macchiole, and big powerful names including Antinori (Guado al Tasso), Gaja (Ca' Marcanda), Mondavi (Ornellaia) and A & G Folonari (Campo del Mare). There is still more potential to the south of Bolgheri. One such hotspot is **Suvereto**, where Cabernet and Merlot again are favoured and the wines of Tua Rita, Montepeloso and Gualdo del Re have incited others such as Vittorio Moretti of Bellavista (Petra) to join the action. The wider, encompassing DOC of **Val di Cornia** adjoins Bolgheri in the north but also contains a southern outcrop north of Piombino on the coast.

The next step south on an emerging coastal patchwork is Massa Marittima which opens out into the southern Maremma. Of emerging importance, it has its own extensive DOC: **Monteregio di Massa Marittima**. South of Grosseto is **Morellino di Scansano** DOC, the most important appellation in the southern Maremma for Sangiovese-based reds (led by Le Pupille). Cabernet Sauvignon and Merlot are also important here, though only given IGT status. The area between these two DOCs is also demarcated, as **Montecucco**, and connects up with Brunello. Other southern appellations include **Parrina**, overlooking the coast at Orbetello and centred on the vineyards of a single producer, La Parrina. **Sovana** DOC extends to the Lazio border and makes provision not only for Sangiovese-based reds but also varietal Sangiovese, Cabernet Sauvignon and Merlot. One further zone, to the east of Sovana near the Umbria border, is Sarteano, notable for the wines of Tenuta di Trinoro.

White wines

Most of Italy's best as well as most original dry whites can be found under the North-East, Central and Southern Italy sections. In Tuscany there is generally less excitement even if there are reasonable quantities of attractive everyday whites. The problem for long has been the dominance of the humdrum Trebbiano grape. Deciding what to replace it with is rarely a priority for producers in this very 'red' region. Many have worked with Chardonnay (and the new **Cortona** DOC embraces it) but while a small number of examples are very good, most lack the elegance or class that might inspire greater dedication and even better results. Equally only a handful of examples have emerged with the structure that would guarantee greater longevity. Best known is **Vernaccia di San Gimignano** which can be reasonably characterful if most examples lack the depth or style that it's DOCG status implies. Several of the coastal appellations offer whites, including Colline Lucchesi and Montecarlo whose grapes include Semillon and Roussanne. From Montescudaio, Trebbiano is complemented by Sauvignon Blanc and Vermentino, the latter two also showing good style in Bolgheri. Val di Cornia sanctions Vermentino with Trebbiano and from further south in the Maremma good Vermentino can also be found. **Bianco di Pitigliano,** which overlaps with the most southern red DOC, Sovana, is a dedicated white wine zone for occasionally characterful Procanico/Greco/Malvasia blends.

Tuscany's best and most individual wine from white grapes has to be **Vin Santo** though it varies enormously in quality, style and sweetness. Made from dried grapes, usually hung from rafters, the best examples tend to be predominantly Malvasia rather than Trebbiano. They range from dry to rich, concentrated and sweet, and from the gently oxidised and fruit-rich (preserved fruits and citrus peel) to more old-fashioned, more overtly nutty oxidised examples. Like the best extra virgin olive oils, few taste alike. As exciting as it can be, price and quality are often a reflection of the efforts that have gone into its production. The one or two good examples of the sweet wine **Moscadello di Montalcino** (from Moscato Bianco grapes grown in the Brunello zone) are also worth a try.

A-Z of producers by appellation

1 Colline Lucchesi
2 Montecarlo
3 Chianti
4 Carmignano
5 Colli Fiorentini
6 Chianti Rufina
7 Pomino
8 Chianti Montespertoli
9 Chianti Classico
10 Colli Aretini
11 Colline Pisane
12 San Gimignano
13 Chianti Colli Senesi

14 Montescudaio
15 Bolgheri
16 Val di Cornia
17 Monteregio di Massa Marittima
18 Montecucco
19 Brunello di Montalcino
20 Vino Nobile di Montepulciano
21 Morellino di Scansano
22 Parrina
23 Sovana

Tuscany vintages

Tuscany produces plenty of red wine for short and medium-term cellaring but to date not that much that has provided real pleasure for a 15- or 20-year celebration. Many of the best reds, be it Chianti Classico Riserva, the best Vino Nobile, reds from the Tuscan coast or other blends including Cabernet or Merlot, are at or near their best with 5 to 10 years' age, the very best after 10 to 15 years. Certainly some of the most sought-after labels will last longer but how much they will continue to improve is more debatable. Brunello from 1990, 93, 95 and 97 should go the distance of two decades though most also have the balance to be ready to drink at half that age. A good Rosso di Montalcino will age better than a weaker, more forward Brunello and give a lot more satisfaction. The style of any producer's wines is as important as location or the primary grape variety so where possible the comments should be considered together.

2003: In Tuscany as elsewhere, Europe's scorching summer meant extreme heat. Yields are down, not helped by April frost but it's all about coping with the blistering conditions. From the earliest vintage in half a century, well-established vineyards and those that normally struggle for ripeness should produce rich, ripe or very ripe Sangiovese. Fruit from less good vineyards and other grapes, particularly Merlot is often raisined and many of the faults of the poorer 2000s look likely to be repeated. So variable quality once again but expect highs as well as lows.

2002: As for most but not all of Italy this was a difficult vintage in Tuscany. However, despite being plagued by rain and cool temperatures it's a mixed picture with some pockets of quality – especially the Maremma and southern zones. Top producers have made good wine though many of the region's top reds neither should nor will appear. In some instances this translates to good value at lower levels as the best fruit cascades down but *caveat emptor* for, as in 92, a little good fruit can too easily be wasted if blended into vats of poor, dilute and unripe wine.

2001: Like 2000 this was another vintage affected by heat stress due to a very hot, dry summer. Late rains were, in some instances, detrimental rather than beneficial to the quality of the fruit. Quantities are down on average and quality while generally very good, does range from the dilute and out of balance to fully ripe, very concentrated reds. A vintage that will highlight those producers who have their vineyards in the best shape.

2000: Not of the order of 99 or 97, with the characteristics typical of lack of full physiological ripeness resulting in part from a very hot August. Many Chianti Classico *normale* show an over-ripe fruit character with less intensity than usual and a slight hollowness and high alcohol levels. There is also a lack of complete ripeness in their tannins. Those from a recommended producer however are less likely to show these defects and will have good richness and ripeness. Many very ripe Vino Nobile were compromised by a slightly coarse structure, it is hoped Brunello will reach the level of 98.

1999: A very fine vintage if not quite of the standard of 1997. If the fruit is less immediately seductive there is excellent drinking now at the lower levels and excellent ageing potential from good acidities, ripe tannins and ample fruit densities in more serious examples. A vintage to buy before the wines disappear, like the 97s. Fine Rosso di Montalcino prefigured some excellent Brunello, not as rich as 1997 but nonetheless full yet elegant and ageworthy.

1998: Another highly successful but much more variable vintage. Some weakness and a slightly hard edge to some Vino Nobile but generally pretty good from the best producers; if anything more uneven in Chianti Classico. Already seems likely to be characterised as a vintage of greater elegance than is typical with real style and complexity where there was full ripeness. 98 Brunello is generally very good and, though not all will keep, much richer and more consistent than 96.

1997: An outstanding vintage, and the best of the 20th century in terms of the amount of high quality red wine produced. Though most of the best Chianti Classico *normale* have been consumed with gusto there remains much that should be cellared including both regular and Riserva Brunello (very rich, powerful and tannic) but also other premium examples from all over Tuscany. The top wines have excellent ageing potential and a fair number will be at or near their best with 10 years.

1996: A good if generally overrated Tuscan vintage with some surprisingly weak, relatively forward wines in most zones. The best producers, however, did very well, the greatest consistency coming from Bolgheri. The greatest disappointments are in Brunello, where apart from Siro Pacenti and a handful of others, this is a decidedly poor vintage. The majority are fast-evolving wines that lack substance and balance and will need to be drunk soon.

1995: A poor growing season but saved by fine October weather. Elegant, stylish Chianti Classico and fine quality in the premium blends or Super-Tuscans. Many Chianti Classico Riserva or their equivalents are now emerging with considerable charm and style where they previously appeared a bit slight. Brunello, if occasionally too structured, has classic keeping qualities and has yet to approach its peak.

1994: Rain-affected growing season, though picked in mostly dry conditions; the reds are generally lighter than 1993 though there is often more elegance. Never the most concentrated, most wines from Chianti Classico and the surrounding areas are already at or near their best. A reasonable vintage in Brunello, too, with more weight and richness than the 96s but a lack of complete ripeness in fruit and tannins takes the edge off some. Not one to pay over the odds for.

1993: Though poorly received, 1993 has proved to be the source of rich, gutsy if slightly rough-hewn reds. The best have good richness and are capable of further development. Some solid powerful Brunello, too, the best examples still need more time to soften and add further complexity.

1992: The worst vintage of the last decade or so in Tuscany though some of the lesser wines were better than expected as some producers opted not to produce their Super-Tuscan blends. A vintage for drinking up, if at all.

1991: An uneven vintage and although some wines showed good intensity, a lack of balance characterised many. Only the best have aged with style, most should have been drunk up.

1990: A great year – but only in the context of the period. There are many more fine wines from 1997, the next great year, due to more widespread winemaking know-how and viticultural improvements. Nonetheless many of the celebrated properties produced marvellous wines with fabulous ripeness and balance. All the top wines may be drunk now but some bottles ought to be kept in order to see what is possible with further age.

1989: A surprisingly light and forward vintage in Tuscany (best for Brunello), not matching the generally high quality seen in other leading European wine regions in 89. The best provided attractive early drinking but little was worth keeping.

1988: Always a firm, relatively austere vintage and there are still a fair number of top wines that have mellowed with age, allowing an intense ripe fruit to emerge more fully with age. Some fine Super-Tuscans and Brunello, in particular, to drink now and in some cases, keep a little longer.

Earlier years: For earlier vintages the picture is decidedly bleak. Much of what was very good is now past its best. This is true of 1986 which with a decade's age provided some excellent Chianti Classico Riservas and Super-Tuscan blends. 1985 was a generally outstanding vintage with very ripe, flamboyant wines but only a handful of classics are likely to drink well or improve further. 1983 and 1982 were also very good vintages yet, other than the occasional Brunello, few had the stuffing or structure for two decades' ageing. Of still older vintages only 75, 71 or 70 are worth taking a chance on.

Tuscany vintage chart

	Chianti Classico (Riserva)	Vino Nobile di Montepulciano	Brunello di Montalcino	Bolgheri/Suvereto
2003	NYR	NYR	NYR	NYR
2002	★★ A	★/★★ A	NYR	★/★★★ A
2001	★★★★ A	★★★/★★★★ A	NYR	★★★★ A
2000	★★★/★★★★ B	★★★/★★★★ B	★★★/★★★★ A	★★★★ A
1999	★★★★/★★★★★★ B	★★★★/★★★★★★ A	★★★★/★★★★★★ A	★★★★/★★★★★★ B
1998	★★★ B	★★★/★★★★ B	★★★/★★★★ B	★★★/★★★★ B
1997	★★★★★ B	★★★★★ B	★★★★★ B	★★★★/★★★★★ B
1996	★★★ C	★★★ C	★★ C	★★★★ B
1995	★★★★ B	★★★/★★★★ C	★★★★ B	★★★/★★★★ C
1994	★★★ C	★★★ C	★★★ C	★★★ C
1993	★★★/★★★★ C	★★★ C	★★★★ B	★★★/★★★★ C
1992	★★ D	★/★★ D	★/★★ C	★★ C
1991	★★★ C	★★★ C	★★★/★★★★ C	★★★ C
1990	★★★★/★★★★★★ C	★★★★/★★★★★ C	★★★★/★★★★★★ B	★★★★/★★★★★ C
1989	★★/★★★ D	★★/★★★ D	★★★/★★★★ C	★★★ C
1988	★★★★ C	★★★★ C	★★★★ C	★★★★ C

ALTESINO Brunello di Montalcino   A: **PFx**, N&P

Owner: Elisabetta Angelini Gnudi   Fraz. Torrenieri, Loc. Altesino, 53028 Montalcino (SI)
Altesino is a well-established and well-respected source of Brunello. A recent change of ownership has brought it under the same ownership as CAPARZO but it continues to be directed by Claudio Basla. As well as Sangiovese, Cabernet Sauvignon and Merlot also form part of the estate's 30 ha but, though the resulting wines are often attractive and well made, they rarely challenge a *barrique*-aged Sangiovese, Palazzo d'Altesi, a wine devised when the mandatory ageing for Brunello was too long. Alte di Altesi is a blend of Sangiovese and Cabernet (70/30), Borgo d'Altesi 100 per cent Cabernet, while Quarto d'Altesi is based on Merlot. Of recent Brunellos, after an adequate 1994, a superior 95 and 97 and stylish 98 are typical of what is possible here: full, ripe and meaty, approachable soon after release but best with 7 to 10 years' age. In certain years both a powerful Riserva and Montosoli have been produced. The latter comes from a particularly favoured sub-zone in the northern part of Brunello. Made only in top years it adds both concentration, depth and finesse. Rosso di Altesino, an inexpensive blend of Sangiovese and Cabernet, should not be confused with the (mostly dependable) fruit-driven Rosso di Montalcino. (PW)
- **Brunello di Montalcino★★★** £E Riserva★★★★ £F Montosoli★★★★ £F
- **Palazzo d'Altesi★★★** £D ● Alte d'Altesi★★★ £D ● Borgo d'Altesi★★ £E ● Quarto d'Altesi★★ £E
- **Rosso di Montalcino★** £C O Vin Santo★★ £E

ANTINORI www.antinori.it   A: **BWC**, AAA

Owner: Piero Antinori   Piazza degli Antinori 3, 50123 Firenze
It's been said many times that no one has done more for Tuscan wine than Piero Antinori and this is well borne out in the radical innovation and experimentation as well as expansion he has brought about. He and his daughters continue to promote quality and to enlarge the empire which spans some 1,400 ha of vineyards. The Tuscan estates are covered below but see also PRUNOTTO (Piedmont & NW Italy), CASTELLO DELLA SALA (Central Italy) and TORMARESCA (Southern Italy). In common with many large producers, quality at the lower levels is not very exciting. Most famous are the wines of the Santa Cristina estate, Tignanello and Solaia. Tignanello, for many the original Super-Tuscan, was first made in 1971 and has been a blend of Sangiovese and Cabernet Sauvignon since 1975 (typically 80/20 but 5 per cent of the 20 is sometimes Cabernet Franc). Not every vintage has qualified as great but it's still a very good wine, as the 1999 shows. Solaia is Antinori's flagship and usually a very worthy one at that with added breadth and class; it is primarily Cabernet Sauvignon with support from Sangiovese and Cabernet Franc. Syrah is now produced from Antinori's Cortona vineyards, and the impressive Bramasole (made since 2000) confirms the grape's potential in this part of Tuscany (see Luigi D'ALESSANDRO). Vino Nobile di Montepulciano comes from the large La Braccesca estate and is consistently a good, full example of the DOCG. More promising however is a new example (2001) from the Santa Pia sub-zone which shows greater expression and style. Antinori's 60-ha Brunello estate, Pian delle Vigne, was only purchased in 1995. The wine is sophisticated, modern but not classically Brunello, if atypically good in 1996 and very good in 97, 98 and 99 too. Guado al Tasso is Antinori's vast estate in Bolgheri and from 300 ha of vineyards is produces a consistently excellent red from Cabernet Sauvignon and Merlot. There are also other properties scattered about Tuscany for whites and lesser reds including vineyards in the fashionable Maremma. Antinori's interests also extend abroad, into Hungary, California and most recently Chile, where it is undertaking a joint venture with Haras de Pirque. (PW)
Antinori:
- **Solaia○○○○○** £H ● **Tignanello★★★★** £G
- **Chianti Classico** Riserva Badia a Passignano★★ £C Riserva Marchese Antinori★★ £D
- O **Vin Santo del Chianti Classico** Marchese Antinori★★ £E
La Braccesca:
- **Vino Nobile di Montepulciano★★** £C ● **Merlot★★** £E
- **Cortona Syrah** Bramasole★★★★ £E

Pian delle Vigne:
● **Brunello di Montalcino**★★★ £E
Guado al Tasso:
● **Bolgheri Rosso**★★★★ £G ○ **Bolgheri** Vermentino★★ £B ◉ **Bolgheri** Scalabrone★ £B

ARGIANO Brunello di Montalcino www.argiano.net A: **Lib**, P&S, F&M, Sel

Owner: Contessa Noemi Marone Cinzano Loc. Argiano, 53024 Montalcino (SI)
It is now more than a decade since this historic estate with 48 ha of vineyards came under new ownership and direction but the improvements from changes overseen by Giacomo Tachis (instrumental in the success of SASSICAIA) during the 1990s continue to accrue. The Brunello is structured and powerful, with considerably more depth and dimension than most, especially evident in the 1995, a backward, tannic but exciting 97 and very good 98 and 99. The *barrique*-aged Solengo, a blend of Cabernet Sauvignon, Syrah and Merlot (and previously Sangiovese), has been consistently rich and stylish since first created from the 1995 vintage. With the help of Hans Vinding-Diers, 3,000 bottles of a special *barrique*-aged *cuvée* of the oldest vines of Sangiovese, Suolo, were produced in the 2000 vintage. It is refined, intense and classy though less characterful than Solengo. This property, the Tenuta di Argiano with its own 16th-century villa, should not be confused with the neighbouring SESTI/CASTELLO DI ARGIANO. (PW)
● **Brunello di Montalcino**★★★★ £F
● **Solengo**★★★★ £F ● **Rosso di Montalcino**★★ £C

AVIGNONESI www.avignonesi.it A: **Lib**, P&S, N&P, F&M, V&C

Owner: Falvo brothers Via Gracciano nel Corso 91, 53040 Montepulciano (SI)
With 109 ha spread over four estates, Avignonesi continue to be the most important producer in Montepulciano. At one point it was as well known for production of non-indigenous varieties as for Vino Nobile but in recent years it has been experimenting with local varieties and gradually improving the quality of the Prugnolo (Sangiovese) in its vineyards. The other varieties in the classic Vino Nobile blend have also been retained. The result is a regular Vino Nobile of increasing consistency, purity and real class. Some of the austerity of past vintages has gone but there is still a structure that ensures fine drinking with five years' age or more. Riserva Grandi Annate applies only to the best years and usually adds considerable depth and dimension. Though one of the estates is planted to international varieties they are now given less prominence in the range of wines. Grifi, a famous Sangiovese/Cabernet blend, was discontinued after the 1996 vintage though the '50 & 50' Merlot/Sangiovese produced jointly with CAPANNELLE continues. International and native varieties are also combined in a more everyday Avignonesi Rosso (Sangiovese/Cabernet Sauvignon/Merlot). Desiderio, previously a varietal Merlot, now includes up to 15 per cent Cabernet, while Il Marzocco is a bold, powerful, toasty Chardonnay. Production of Vin Santo, one from Malvasia, Trebbiano and Grechetto grapes and Occhio di Pernice from Prugnolo (Sangiovese), is tiny (around 3,000 half-bottles of the first, 1,000 of the latter), but the richness, texture and complexity in these wines is incomparable. They ferment and age over eight and 10 years respectively so the latest releases are from vintages more than a decade ago. Light, fresh cherryish Rosso di Montepulciano is also made. (PW)
● **Vino Nobile di Montepulciano**★★★ £C Riserva Grandi Annate★★★★★ £E
● **Cortona** Merlot Desiderio★★★ £F ● **Avignonesi Rosso**★ £B
○ **Cortona** Chardonnay Il Marzocco★★★ £C
○ **Vin Santo**✪✪✪✪✪ £H ● **Vin Santo** Occhio di Pernice✪✪✪✪✪£H

BANFI Brunello di Montalcino www.castellobanfi.com A: **Vim**, Hrd, Maj

Owner: Mariani family Loc. Sant'Angelo Scalo, 53020 Montalcino (SI)
No one has made an impact on Montalcino and Tuscan viticulture like Banfi. Millions of American dollars have been poured in to reshape the entire south-western corner of the Brunello zone. There are 800 ha planted to vines and superb facilities for making great wine. However the inherent potential (or lack of it) of some of these vineyards and the varieties to which they have been planted has caused the greatest

contention. What does work with increasing consistency is Sangiovese for Brunello, which despite the volumes – more than 40,000 cases of the regular example – is rich, ripe and well-balanced if missing the extra depth and breadth of the best examples. The excellent Riserva Poggio all'Oro is more complex, structured and elegant, while another single-vineyard example, Poggio alle Mura, has also been made since the 1997 vintage. Rosso di Montalcino can show good Brunello-like breadth and depth in the best years, while Florus is a flavoursome, well-balanced example of Moscadello di Montalcino. Of the international wines, the premium blends are the most successful. Summus combines Sangiovese, Cabernet Sauvignon and Syrah, while Excelsus is composed of Cabernet and Merlot in equal measure. As varietals, Cabernet Sauvignon Tavernelle shows good richness, Syrah Colvecchio shows the most promise but Merlot Mandrielle is less convincing. A Pinot Nero, Belnero, is also made. Chardonnay Fontanelle can show real richness and depth but seems most successful (with better strucure) in the less good years for reds. Lesser whites and reds are well-made but only occasionally have sufficient quality to their fruit. Centine is an adequate blend of Sangiovese (60 per cent), Cabernet Sauvignon and Merlot, Col di Sasso just Sangiovese and Cabernet. New is a mid-priced blend, Cum Laude comprised of Sangiovese, Cabernet Sauvignon, Merlot and Syrah. (PW)

● **Brunello di Montalcino**★★★ £E Poggio alle Mura★★★★ £F Riserva Poggio all'Oro★★★★ £G
● **Rosso di Montalcino**★★ £C ● **Summus**★★★★ £E ● **Excelsus**★★★★ £F
● **Sant'Antimo** Cabernet Sauvignon Tavernelle★★ £D Syrah Colvecchio★★ £D Merlot Mandrielle★ £D
○ **Sant'Antimo** Chardonnay Fontanelle★★ £C ○ **Moscadello di Montalcino** Florus★★ £D

ERIK BANTI Morellino di Scansano www.erikbanti.com

Owner: Erik Banti Loc. Fosso dei Molini, 58054 Scansano (GR)
Erik Banti, a pioneer of viticulture in the southern Maremma, makes good Morellino di Scansano from 55 ha of vineyards. Moderately long maceration, 15 days for the Riserva, and the use of Slavonian oak are favoured. Carato, previously IGT, is particularly good value and includes 15 per cent of other varieties to complement the Sangiovese. The Riserva, a pure Sangiovese, comes from the Ciabatta vineyard and is intense and extracted, with the herb scents and fruit quality typical of the Maremma. Poggio Maestrino, from a vineyard of the same name, was previously named only for the successive year of its production (2000 is the fourth, Annoquarto). Well-oaked (in French *barriques*) and including 10 per cent Merlot, it misses the character of Ciabatta. Banti also makes the range of food products, Italia & Gusto. (PW)

● **Morellino di Scansano**★★ £B Carato★★★ £C Riserva Ciabatta★★★ £D
● **Poggio Maestrino**★★★ £E

FATTORIA DI BASCIANO Chianti Rufina   A: Bib

Owner: Renzo Masi Viale Duca della Vittoria 159, 50068 Rufina (FI)
Paolo Masi (son of Renzo) made major improvements to the estate's viticulture and winemaking from the early 1990s and the quality is evident in the good vintages of the late 90s. High-quality fruit and careful handling as well as long macerations and malolactic fermentation in *barrique* for the top wines are key components. While the major part of 30 ha is planted to Sangiovese, there is also some Cabernet Sauvignon, and Merlot and Syrah coming on stream. The regular Chianti Rufina shows ripe, lively fruit with a couple of years' age, without being overly austere, and is a good example of the zone. Chianti Rufina Riserva and two special *cuvées* are better still, with added richness and style; Vigna Il Corto and I Pini are currently blends of Sangiovese and Cabernet (90/10 and 50/50 respectively). Perhaps reflecting the predisposition of these soils (and climate) for Sangiovese, I Pini is the least vibrant and individual of the three top wines. While not yet challenging the supremacy of SELVAPIANA or Nipozzano's best (see FRESCOBALDI), Basciano delivers both fine quality and value. A good source for Vin Santo too. Wines sold under the Renzo Masi label are made from bought-in grapes and if not generally of the same standard can provide good-value drinking, particularly the Sangiovese/Cabernet blend, Erta & China. (PW)

● **Chianti Rufina**★★ £B Riserva★★★ £C

● **Vigna Il Corto**★★★ £C ● **I Pini**★★★ £C
● **Erta e China**★★ £B ○ **Vin Santo**★★ £C

BIONDI-SANTI Brunello di Montalcino www.biondisanti.it A: Alv

Owner: Franco Biondi-Santi Loc. Greppo, 53024 Montalcino (SI)
This is still Montalcino's most famous estate, even if the wines are no longer the most expensive (see SOLDERA). Franco Biondi-Santi continues to make the wines with a traditional, non-interventionist approach and without any outside assistance. The wines don't lack for power or depth or indeed complexity but can be quite forbidding when young, with a structure that makes you wonder if there's enough stuffing to match. Certainly in top vintages it would seem that there is but patience is required. Rosso di Montalcino comes in two bottlings, a white label from young-vine fruit, and a red stripe from fruit not used for Brunello. Franco's son Jacopo handles the wines' distribution along with those of Pierluigi Tagliabue, which he has helped to make at the estate of his wife's family, Villa Poggio Salvi. Here, with input from Vittorio Fiore, a more forward, approachable but flavousome Brunello is made but it is also where two very good *barrique*-aged reds were first created. They are now produced from Jacopo's own estate in the Maremma, Castello di Montepò. Schidione is Sangiovese with some Cabernet Sauvignon and Merlot, while Sassoalloro, produced in much greater quantities, is pure Sangiovese. Rich and oak-influenced, the best examples of both also have considerable structure and ageing potential. (PW)

Tenuta Greppo:
● **Brunello di Montalcino**★★★ £H Riserva★★★★ £H

Villa Poggio Salvi:
● **Brunello di Montalcino**★★★ £F

Castello di Montepò:
● **Schidione**★★★ £E ● **Sassoalloro**★★★ £D

BOSCARELLI Vino Nobile di Montepulciano www.poderiboscarelli.com A: Bal, BBR

Owner: Paola De Ferrari Corradi Loc. Cervognano, Via di Montenero 28, 53045 Montepulciano (SI)
Luca and Niccolò work with their mother and long-time consultant Maurizio Castelli to keep this small estate (just 13 ha of vineyards) at the top of the Montepulciano hierarchy. They are rivalled only by POLIZIANO and AVIGNONESI, though there is an increasing number of good estates (among others also see DEI). The wines here provide not only extra richness and depth but also better proportions and greater refinement, while the regular bottling has no equal at this level. There is an ongoing commitment to quality, with increased planting densities and improvements to vinification. 'Boscarelli', like the Vino Nobile and single-vineyard Vigna del Nocio, is based on Sangiovese but is the only wine to see *barriques*. There is great consistency in vintages of the mid- to late 1990s and if prices are at a slight premium over some producers, the wines are good value both in a Tuscan and a wider sense. Rosso de Ferrari is the more everyday wine but better than most Rosso di Montepulciano. (PW)
● **Vino Nobile di Montepulciano**★★★ £C Vigna del Nocio★★★★ £D
● **Boscarelli**★★★★ £E ● **Rosso de Ferrari**★ £B

FATTORIA DEL BUONAMICO Montecarlo www.buonamico.it A: Rec

Owner: Gruppo Concerto Hotels Via Provinciale di Montecarlo 43, 55015 Montecarlo (LU)
Directed by Vasco Grassi and Francesco Berti, Buonamico is one of the leaders of the relatively unsung DOC of Montecarlo, which has been growing both Tuscan and French grape varieties for several hundred years. 24 ha of the 37 ha estate are planted to vines which include Semillon, Sauvignon Blanc, Pinot Bianco, Cabernet Sauvignon, Syrah and Merlot as well as Sangiovese, Canaiolo and Trebbiano. The Montecarlo red and white are the well-made basic wines, while Il Fortino is produced from 80-year-old Syrah vines and shows marvellous fruit intensity in a medium-bodied style that will keep for up to a decade. Cercatoja Rosso combines Sangiovese, Cabernet Sauvignon, Merlot and Syrah and is aged in small French oak; if missing

some richness at first, it opens out with a little age. Vasario Bianco, based on Pinot Bianco, is *barrique-*fermented and aged. It also shows plenty of flavour intensity and has the structure to improve for at least two or three years. Oro di Re, a late-harvested blend of mostly Sauvignon Blanc and Semillon with a little Pinot Bianco, was first made in 1997 and again in 99. It is a light- to medium-bodied, individual, complex and very fine sweet wine (with the finest honeycomb and dried exotic fruit flavours). It is made in just a few hundred half-bottles – quite delightful if you should come across it. A little Cercatoja Rosato, based on Sangiovese, is also made. (PW)

● **Il Fortino**★★ £D   ● **Cercatoja Rosso**★★ £D
○ **Vasario Bianco**★★ £C   ○ **Oro di Re**★★★ £E

CA' MARCANDA Bolgheri   A: JAr, F&M, Maj, IVV, FWC

Owner: Angelo Gaja   Loc. Santa Teresa 272, 57022 Castagneto Carducci (SI)
The style and shape of the wines from Angelo Gaja's lavish new Bolgheri estate are beginning to emerge. Young vines it would seem might limit the potential here for a bit but given the Gaja pedigree fabulous wines can't be too far off. This is even illustrated by Promis, the most affordable wine thus far. It is a blend of Merlot, Syrah and Sangiovese and in the difficult 2002 vintage, though lacking richness and depth, is surprisingly complex and classy. Magari, the estate's second wine is produced from Merlot, Cabernet Sauvigon and Cabernet Franc. It was better in 2000 than 01 but it could be that in 01 more emphasis went into the top wine, labelled simply Ca' Marcanda. Made from the same grapes, the latter looks very impressive and will be rated with further vintages. We have been promised much greater quantities and more moderate prices than seen from Gaja's other operations but don't hold your breath waiting for a bargain. (PW)

● **Magari**★★★ £E   ● **Promis**★★★ £D

CAPANNELLE Chianti Classico   A: N&P

Owner: James Sherwood   Loc. Capannelle, 53013 Gaiole in Chianti (SI)
This estate with 15 ha of vineyards achieved a high profile under Raffaele Rossetti during Tuscany's wine revolution. Under the ownership of American James Sherwood since 1997, the wines continue to be very good but Capannelle, one of the most prominent *vini da tavola*, is no longer made. The grapes now form part of a Chianti Classico Riserva thus marking a return to the once (and arguably rightly) vilified DOCG. The style has always been for very ripe fruit and lots of oak, at times to excess. However all the wines have terrific flavour complexity and style particularly when given the 8 to 10 years' age they deserve. The best wine is the rich, complex '50 & 50', a collaboration with AVIGNONESI, which provides the Merlot component to complement Capannelle's Sangiovese. Solare is a bold innovation, containing as it does a significant percentage of Malvasia Nera. Chardonnay is also made. (PW)

● **Chianti Classico** Riserva★★★ £E   ● **50 & 50**★★★★ £E
● **Solare**★★★ £F

TENUTA CAPARZO Brunello di Montalcino www.caparzo.com   A: Ast, P&S, UnC, N&P

Owner: Elisabetta Angelini Gnudi   Strada Provinciale del Brunello, 53024 Montalcino (SI)
Almost half of this 180-ha estate is planted to vines, making Caparzo one of Brunello's more significant producers. It is directed by Nuccio Turone with ongoing consultancy from Vittorio Fiore. Quality is high, sometimes very high indeed, as in certain vintages of Vigna La Casa. With the exception of the 1996s which, though adequate, are not of the standard at which the wines are rated below, the vintages of the mid and late-1990s at least maintain their considerable reputation. Occasionally there is a question mark over the balance and stability but there is also remarkable concentration, depth and power with very ripe, fine tannins in the best years. Formerly *vini da tavola*, now Sant'Antimo DOC red and white, Ca' del Pazzo (Sangiovese/Cabernet Sauvignon) and Le Grance (mostly Chardonnay but also Sauvignon and Gewürztraminer) still show good fruit and the intelligent use of new oak. Caparzo also owns the Chianti

Classico estate of Borgo Scopeto (a large estate but with only 37 ha of vines) in Castelnuovo Berardenga. The most recent releases reflect a new winemaking direction and, as well as Chianti Classico and Riserva, from 1998 there is a new single-vineyard Riserva, Misciano, and Super-Tuscan, Borgonero, from Sangiovese, Syrah and Cabernet Sauvignon. (PW)

Tenuta Caparzo:
● **Brunello di Montalcino**★★★ £E Riserva★★★★★ £F Vigna La Casa✪✪✪✪✪ £F
● **Rosso di Montalcino**★★ £C Vigna La Caduta★★★ £C ● **Rosso Caparzo Sangiovese**★★ £B
● **Sant'Antimo** Ca' del Pazzo★★★ £D ○ **Sant'Antimo** Le Grance★★ £C
○ **Moscadello di Montalcino** Vendemmia Tardiva★ £E

Borgo Scopeto:
● **Chianti Classico** Riserva Misciano★★ £D

CAPEZZANA Carmignano www.capezzana.it   A: **Lib**, ACh, Res, N&P, P&S, Hrd, Sel, V&C

Owner: Contini Bonacossi family Loc. Seano, Via Capezzana 100, 59015 Carmignano (PO)
Thanks to the direction of Count Ugo Contini Bonacossi, Capezzana has long been the foremost estate in the small Carmignano zone west of Florence. There's now a younger generation taking charge and Stefano Chioccioli has been recruited as a consultant. While there's no longer a Riserva, the Carmignano (around 20 per cent Cabernet Sauvignon and 10 per cent Canaiolo in addition to Sangiovese) has a refined structure, lovely depth and a touch of class missing in many other Tuscan reds. It achieved a new level of excellence with the 1999 vintage (four stars). Ghiaie della Furba, originally a sort of Tuscan Bordeaux blend, now adds a little Syrah to Cabernet Sauvignon and Merlot and is a wine of persuasive style. Both benefit from five years' ageing or more but were disappointing in 2000. Barco Reale, a lighter style based on Sangiovese and pioneered by Capezzana, can have delicious forward fruit but is best with just a couple of years' age. Capezzana's Vin Santo is elegant and refined with a classic, aged, gently oxidised character, though not the richness of some. Vin Ruspo is a relatively rare Rosato from this part of Italy and Chardonnay is also made. Non-wine products include impressive grappa and extra virgin olive oil. No Carmignano was made in 2002 to the benefit of the Barco Reale. (PW)
● **Carmignano** Villa di Capezzana★★★ £D ● **Ghiaie della Furba**★★★ £E
● **Barco Reale di Carmignano**★ £B ○ **Carmignano Vin Santo**★★★ £E

CARPINETO Chianti Classico www.carpineto.com   A: **Hal**, Nid, TPg

Owner: G C Sacchet & A M Zaccheo Loc. Dudda 17/B, 50020 Greve in Chianti (FI)
Established in 1967, Carpineto is based at Dudda in the northern part of Greve. However, while Chianti Classico production is important it is better known for two IGT reds as much of 121 ha of vineyards are located further afield, including 70 ha in the Montepulciano area. Dogajolo from Sangiovese and Cabernet Sauvignon is made in bigger quantities than Chianti Classico *normale* and is typically supple and scented with reasonable intensity and depth. The premium Farnito is a cedary, intensely blackcurrant Cabernet Sauvignon that is deep and chewy but cellarworthy, needing 10 years' ageing from a good vintage like 1999 (it was less good in 2000). Vino Nobile Riserva and Rosso di Montepulciano are also produced. Regular Chianti Classico is usually sound if unexciting but a ripe, intense Riserva gives much more, albeit in an oaky style. Oak, intensity and extract also feature prominently in a series of new 'Appodiati' single-vineyard wines first made in 1999. Poggio Sant'Enrico is 100 per cent Sangiovese and Sillano incorporates Cabernet Sauvignon (60/40 in 1999), while Molin Vecchio includes Syrah (20 per cent) as well as Cabernet Sauvignon (10 per cent). All three are quite backward and extracted even with more than four years' age. Poggio Sant'Enrico is the most dominated by oak, Molin Vecchio perhaps the most individual and balanced but it needs a little more ripeness in its tannins. All need at least 8 to 10 years' age. With a slightly lighter touch, more refined structures and greater expression, these wines could be very good indeed. Chardonnay and Vin Santo are also made but haven't been tasted. In 2003 Carpineto bought a large estate in a part of the Maremma covered by the Monteregio di Massa Marittima DOC with the intention of establishing vineyards there. (PW)

● **Chianti Classico★** £C Riserva★★★ £D ● **Farnito★★★** £E
● **Vino Nobile di Montepulciano** Riserva★★ £D ● **Dogajolo★** £B

CASANOVA DELLA SPINETTA Colline Pisane

A: **Eno**, NYg

Owner: Rivetti family Loc. Casanova, 56030 Terricciola (PI)
Angelo Gaja (CA' MARCANDA) is not the only celebrated *Piemontesi* working his magic in Tuscany. Giorgio
Rivetti (LA SPINETTA) has a small 8.5 ha estate at Terriciola in the Pisa hills (not far to the north and east
of CASTELLO DEL TERRICCIO) but unlike Gaja has chosen to apply his artistry to Sangiovese. The first
commercial release of Sezzana was 2001 (though it was also made to a high standard in 2000) and it is a
beautifully crafted wine with a splendid purity to its crushed cherry fruit. Finely underpinned by oak with
real depth and intensity, it also includes a little Colorino. The quality and style already augur well for the
future. One to follow. (PW)
● **Sezzana★★★★** £E

CASALOSTE Chianti Classico www.casaloste.it

A: **RsW**, Rae, SVS

Owner: Giovanni Battista & Emilia d'Orsi Via Montagliari 32, 50020 Panzano (FI)
A small 10.5-ha estate in Panzano that has recently turned out a string of fine Chianti with greater depth,
weight and interest than many better-known estates. The efforts and commitment of Giovanni Battista and
the results of his collaboration with consultant Gabriella Tani (whose efforts have produced fine Chianti at
nearby CAROBBIO as well) deserve a wider reputation. Chianti Classico *normale* benefits from a little age
and has the potential to improve for five years or so from a vintage like 1999. Two Riservas are even better
but must be given at least three to five years' ageing. (PW)
● **Chianti Classico★★** £C Riserva★★★ £D Riserva Don VincEnzo★★★ £E

CASANOVA DI NERI Brunello di Montalcino

A: **Eur**, Far, JAr, Tur

Owner: Giacomo Neri Podere Casanova, Loc. Torrenieri, 53028 Montalcino (SI)
Another of Brunello's relatively new stars and not a one-vintage wonder. Giacomo Neri works with the
widely consulted Carlo Ferrini to produce increasingly rich, stylish meaty Brunello even in more difficult
vintages like 1994 and 96. There is some use of new wood as well as the traditional large *botti* but this only
enhances the structure not the flavours. The 27 ha are not confined to one site, which makes it possible to
produce both Tenuta Nuova and Riserva Cerretalto as well as a regular Brunello. The 1997s were superb,
both Tenuta Nuova and Reserva, but the 99s are very fine too. Rosso is full and stylish, better than much
commercial Brunello, and should be drunk with three to five years' age. Pietradomice is a deep, brash,
Brunello-like Cabernet Sauvignon that wants for a little more refinement. (PW)
● **Brunello di Montalcino★★★** £E Tenuta Nuova★★★★ £F Riserva Cerretalto★★★★★ £F
● **Rosso di Montalcino★★** £C ● **Pietradomice★★★** £E

CASTELLARE DI CASTELLINA Chianti Classico

A: **Bal**

Owner: Nettuno srl Loc. Castellare, 53011 Castellina in Chianti (SI)
Directed by Paolo Panerai, Castellare first became well known for one of Tuscany's most innovative Super-
Tuscans, I Sodi di San Niccolò, and for the elegant labels that feature a different bird with each
vintage. The 25 ha of vineyards are well sited and both renewed investment and the retention of Maurizio
Castelli as consultant should ensure continued success. However the wines can be a bit uneven, even if very
satisfying with considerable finesse and elegance when they are on song. Regular Chianti Classico is typically
bright and attractive but has been a little lean of late, despite some excellent vintages. The regular Riserva
has only been at the level of a decent *normale*, though a single-vineyard version, Il Poggiale, is considerably
better. It is the distinctive, perfumed and complex I Sodi that still provides the greatest interest; its balance,
depth and style make it a worthy flagship wine. Versions of international varieties are also made but only in
very small quantities. These include Sauvignon Blanc (Spartito di Castellare), Chardonnay (Canonico di

Castellare) and Cabernet Sauvignon (Coniale di Castellare) but only the latter is regularly convincing. The best wines are no longer cheap, particularly I Sodi and a newish Merlot, Poggio ai Merli (made since 1999). (PW)

● **Chianti Classico Riserva★** £D   Riserva Vigna Il Poggiale★★★ £E
● **I Sodi di San Niccolò★★★** £F   ● **Coniale di Castellare★★** £E

CASTELLO DEI RAMPOLLA Chianti Classico   A: **Bal, Wgg**, UnC

Owner: Di Napoli Rampolla family Via Santa Lucia in Faulle, 50020 Panzano (FI)
The Conca d'Oro south of the town of Panzano has long been considered one of Chianti Classico's finest sub-zones. Principe Alceo Di Napoli Rampolla favoured Cabernet Sauvignon over Sangiovese and more than half the current 42 ha of vineyard are planted to it. Sammarco was the wine that made the estate famous and only includes 20 per cent Sangiovese with the Cabernet. It continues to be a firm, powerful and aristocratic red with great dimension and fine blackcurrant, herb and small-berried fruit. The estate is now run along biodynamic lines by son Luca and daughter Maurizia (with continued guidance from Giacomo Tachis), who have brought to fruition a project started by their father, La Vigna d'Alceo. Of particular interest is the high density (8 to 10,000 vines per hectare; twice that of many Tuscan vineyards) and low spur-training. The wine is a blend of 85 per cent Cabernet and 15 per cent Petit Verdot. It has been sensational since its first vintage in 1996. Vigna d'Alceo spends less time in wood than Sammarco and has quite a contrasting texture and profile, but there is terrific purity, depth and intensity in a superb 99. Chianti Classico Riserva, which included a little Cabernet, has been phased out but it would be wrong to overlook the regular Chianti Classico, which usually shows how well Sangiovese does in these soils. With lots of class and intensity within a sturdy frame, it needs to be kept for at least five years from a good vintage. (PW)

● **Vigna d'Alceo❋❋❋❋❋** £G   ● **Sammarco★★★★★** £F
● **Chianti Classico★★★** £C

CASTELLO DEL TERRICCIO www.terriccio.it   A: **L&S**, F&M

Owner: G A Rossi de Medelana e Serrafini Ferri Via Bagnoli 56040 Castellina Marittima (PI)
Castello del Terriccio lies not far to the north of Bolgheri and was one of the first of the many other fine estates that now dot the Tuscan coastline. Thanks to considerable investment and a determination to produce wines of the highest order, the estate, with 50 ha of vines, is now well known in fine wine circles. Winemaking expertise has come from Carlo Ferrini and Terriccio's fame has been spearheaded by two fine reds. Lupicaia is the high-priced flagship red (Cabernet Sauvignon with 10 per cent Merlot) and is intended to compete with Bordeaux's best. It is powerful, intense and oaky with deep lush blackcurrant and black cherry fruit but plenty of structure too, and though of high quality gives only a hint of its origins. The considerably cheaper Tassinaia, from roughly equal parts Cabernet Sauvignon, Merlot and Sangiovese, is similarly flattering, developing delicious chocolate and plum flavours with a little age. There is similar ambition to produce great whites. Early vintages showed some lovely ripe fruit but lacked structure or depth. Recently help has come from Hans Terzer who makes the excellent whites of SAN MICHELE APPIANO co-op in Alto Adige. There's already a marked improvement in Con Vento which is 100 per cent Sauvignon Blanc. Saluccio was a barrel-fermented and aged Chardonnay but it is a stainless steel-aged version, Rondinaia, that is being pursued. From 2000 a tiny amount (just 6,000 bottles) of an exciting new blend was produced. Called Castello del Terriccio it blends Syrah with Mourvèdre and Petit Verdot (50/25/25) but could also include Tannat in the future. Also made is an unwooded pure Sangiovese, Capannino. (PW)

● **Lupicaia★★★★** £G   ● **Tassinaia★★★** £D
O **Rondinaia★★** £D   O **Con Vento★★** £C

CASTELLO DELLA PANERETTA · Chianti Classico · A: **Vim,** V&C

Owner: Maria Carla Musso · Strada della Paneretta 35, Barberino Val d'Elsa (FI)
Located in the very west of Chianti Classico, this historic estate produces a range of wines often notable for the quality of the old-vine fruit. The vines are planted on fine *galestro-alberese* soils, pockets of which are found in other estates in Barberino Val d'Elsa. All the wines have good concentration and ripe, intense fruit, though can lack a little for structure, especially in weaker vintages – a problem likely to be solved by the recent recruitment of consultant Niccolò d'Aflitto. Chianti Classico Riservas include both a regular Riserva and a single-vineyard wine, Torre a Destra, both which typically show plump, rich fruit. Terrine is unusual in consisting of equal parts Canaiolo and Sangiovese and shows a fine fusion of floral, black fruit and oak-given characters. Quattrocentenario by contrast is 100 per cent Sangiovese from the estate's best old-vine fruit. Vin Santo is also made. (PW)
● **Chianti Classico**★★ £C Riserva★★ £C Riserva Torre a Destra★★★ £D
● **Terrine**★★★ £D ● **Quattrocentenario**★★★★ £E

CASTELLO DI AMA · Chianti Classico · www.castellodiama.com · A: **WTs,** JAr, F&M, P&S

Owner: Lorenza Sebasti (& others) · Loc. Ama, Fraz. Lecchi in Chianti, 53010 Gaiole in Chianti (SI)
During the explosion of Super-Tuscans in the 1980s, Castello di Ama instead chose to emphasise Chianti Classico, producing four single-vineyard versions that were the equal of the best *vini da tavola*. Winemaker Marco Pallanti, who has been involved with Ama for 20 years and is married to director Lorenza Sebasti, still makes two single-vineyard versions but now only in small quantities and only in the best years. Both Bellavista (which includes a percentage of Malvasia Nera) and La Casuccia (Merlot complements the Sangiovese) combine intensity with nuance and elegance but the latter is the richer of the two. As at a number of top estates attention is now focused on a single bottling of Chianti Classico, more in the manner of a Bordeaux château. Ama's Chianti Classico starts out quite firm but with good intensity and depth as well as a certain class others lack. Given the vineyards' elevation (450 to 480 m), more difficult vintages such as 1998 can be a little lean but the wines gain richness with age and a top vintage such as 97 or 99 will improve for at least five years. Tuscany's first great Merlot, L'Apparita, was produced here and it continues to be one of the very best. Relatively high fermentation temperatures and a long maceration precede ageing in 100 per cent new Allier oak. This now sizeable (90-ha) estate also provides an attractive, well-balanced Chardonnay, Al Poggio, capable of a little age, and some Pinot Nero, Il Chiuso. (PW)
● **Chianti Classico**★★ £C Vigneto Bellavista★★★★ £E Vigneto La Casuccia★★★★ £E
● **L'Apparita** ★★★★ £F **O Al Poggio**★★ £B

CASTELLO DI FONTERUTOLI · www.fonterutoli.it · A: **Eno,** JNi, F&M, Hrd, P&S, Vne

Owner: Mazzei family · Loc. Fonterutoli, 53011 Castellina in Chianti (SI)
The Fonterutoli estate, one of Chianti Classico's finest, dates from 1435. In recent times (from the 1995 vintage) it has taken the lead in attempting to restore the reputation of Chianti Classico, sacrificing a well-established Super-Tuscan, Concerto (a Sangiovese/Cabernet blend) and a previously made Riserva Ser Lapo to this end. The focus of production from 62 ha of vines, under the direction of brothers Filippo and Francesco and the continued winemaking expertise of the respected Carlo Ferrini, is the Castello di Fonterutoli estate wine, a premium selection of the two best plots of Sangiovese (dubbed by some a super-Chianti Classico). It is *barrique*-aged and is a rich, ripe modern example with excellent intensity and depth that put it on a different level from most Chianti Classico (including Riservas). A second selection is labelled simply Fonterutoli but is of similar quality to much good Chianti Classico. One Super-Tuscan still made is Siepi (from a vineyard of this name) – a wonderfully rich, enticing blend of equal parts of Sangiovese and Merlot. The same direction is employed at the 30-ha Belguardo estate in the southern Maremma where ever better Morellino di Scansano is made. In addition from the 2000 vintage a major new Cabernet Sauvignon-based estate wine (Tenuta di Belguardo) shows great promise, as does a well-priced, scented and characterful Serrata di Belguardo (Merlot/Sangiovese/Cabernet Sauvignon). The Mazzei family also have

close links with the neighbouring estate of LA BRANCAIA as well as GHIZZANO in the Pisa hills. (PW)

Castello di Fonterutoli:
● **Chianti Classico** Castello di Fonterutoli★★★★ £E
● **Chianti Classico** Fonterutoli★★ £C
● **Siepi**★★★★ £F ● **Poggio alla Badiola**★★ £B
Tenuta Belguardo:
● **Morellino di Scansano** Poggio Bronzone★★★ £C
● **Tenuta di Belguardo**★★★★ £F ● **Serrata di Belguardo**★★ £C

CASTELLO DI MONSANTO Chianti Classico www.castellodimonsanto.it **A: Cib**, CKr

Owner: Fabrizio Bianchi   Via Monsanto 8, 50021 Barberino Val d'Elsa (FI)

Fabrizio Bianchi bought this estate in 1961 and the focus on producing a great Chianti Classico in the years that followed created an illustrious reputation. That wine, Il Poggio, is still very good but is not of the lush, new-oak style favoured by some (less than half the wine goes into second-use *barriques*, the rest into large Slavonian oak) and the resulting lighter, more evolved colour precedes a palate of good breadth and excellent flavour depth. Based on a 5.5-ha vineyard, it is also a true Chianti Classico in the sense that it is mostly Sangiovese with some Canaiolo and a little Colorino and it will evolve slowly for many years. There is no doubt that this style of Chianti Classico is not in vogue and it could be that denser planting and winemaking changes could better express its potential. From the rest of the estate's 70 ha come a regular Riserva and three other premium reds. Fabrizio Bianchi lends his name to both a pure Sangiovese and a Chardonnay. Tinscvil is a blend of Sangiovese and Cabernet Sauvignon but can display an earthy, herbal aspect, while Nemo can be a very distinctive cedary, but also Tuscan-scented, Cabernet Sauvignon with intense sweet fruit within a muscular frame. (PW)

● **Chianti Classico** Riserva★ £D Riserva Il Poggio★★★ £E
● **Fabrizio Bianchi**★★ £E ● **Tinscvil**★ £D ● **Nemo**★★★ £E
○ **Fabrizio Bianchi Chardonnay**★ £C

CASTELLO DI POPPIANO Colli Fiorentini www.conteguicciardini.com **A: GWW**

Owner: Conte Ferdinando Guicciardini   Via di Fezzana 43, 50025 Montespertoli (FI)

This Colli Fiorentini estate has belonged to the Guicciardini from the mid-12th century and the current count Ferdinando can claim an ancestor who corresponded regularly with Machiavelli, who lived nearby. In wine terms this location is too often associated with something less impressive but the 120 ha of vines here produce some of the best wines of the Colli Fiorentini. The traditional wines include some Canaiolo and Colorino along with the Sangiovese. Il Cortile is a fine example of Chianti from these hills. A denser Riserva must be given at least five years' age, yet misses a little of the style of the *normale*. Of the new-style reds two in particular stand out. In Tricorno, Sangiovese combines with Cabernet Sauvignon and Merlot; well-oaked, concentrated and powerful, it is quite individual for this blend. Increasingly impressive Syrah, with a dash of blueberry and white pepper, includes 10 per cent Sangiovese. In Tosco Forte the proportions are reversed. Vin Santo, produced from Malvasia, is of the old-fashioned style; very biscuity and nutty yet with good concentration. Ancient as Poppiano is, it sustains new life in a seven-year-old property with 35 ha of vines in the Maremma. Adding to a regular Morellino di Scansano, the first Riserva was produced from the 2001 vintage. (PW)

Castello di Poppiano:
● **Chianti Colli Fiorentini** Il Cortile★★ £B ● **Chianti Colli Fiorentini** Riserva★★ £C
● **Tricorno**★★★★ £D ● **Syrah**★★★ £C ● **Tosco Forte**★★ £C
○ **Vernaccia**★ £B ○ **Vin Santo** della Torre Grande★★ £E
Massi di Mandorlaia:
● **Morellino di Scansano**★★ £B

CASTELLO DI VOLPAIA Chianti Classico www.volpaia.com A: **Adm**, L&W, Odd, V&C

Owner: Giovanella Stianti Loc. Volpaia, Piazza della Cisterna 1, 53017 Radda in Chianti (SI)
While much is made of sub-zones like Panzano and Monti, there are many other good small areas within the Chianti Classico zone, such as the cluster of fine small estates in the hills north-east of Radda. Giovanella Stianti and her husband Carlo Mascheroni, have long made elegant, stylish wines, assisted in the 1980s and 90s by Maurizio Castelli. This includes Super-Tuscans Coltassala (redesignated a Chianti Classico Riserva since the 1998 vintage), from Sangiovese and a little Mammolo, and Balifico, which is Sangiovese complementd by Cabernet Sauvignon. Coltassala in particular has shown the elegance, refinement and grace that Sangiovese can attain. The downside is that some of the wines struggle for ripeness and adequate richness in poorer vintages and there is not the consistency that some critics have suggested. Changes have taken place recently. The wines are now made by Lorenzo Regoli with consultancy from Riccardo Cotarella and from a top recent vintage such as 1997 or 99 there is delightful drinking at all levels. Regular Chianti Classico is now labelled simply Volpaia. Some Vin Santo and a little white are also made. (PW)
● **Chianti Classico★** £B Riserva★★ £C Riserva Coltassala★★★ £E
● **Balifico★★★** £E

CASTELLO VICCHIOMAGGIO Chianti Classico www.vicchiomaggio.it A: **Hal**, Vts

Owner: John Matta Via Vicchiomaggio 4, 50022 Greve in Chianti (FI)
John Matta's well-sited estate, topped by an impressive Renaissance castle, has been transformed since it was bought by his family in 1966. It now runs to 33 ha and with help from Giorgio Marone, produces three very good Sangiovese-based reds. Arguably the best of these is the Chianti Classico Riserva La Prima which comes from the estate's oldest vines. The wine consistently shows good richness, depth and a preserved black fruits character. Made in greater quantities is the Riserva Petri, which complements Sangiovese with a small percentage of Cabernet rather than the native Canaiolo and Colorino used in La Prima. While good, it hasn't quite the extra intensity or structure of La Prima. Both are aged partly in *barrique*, while Ripa delle More (almost pure Sangiovese) is entirely so. Ripa delle Mandorle is a less inspiring but cheaper blend of Sangiovese and Cabernet Sauvignon, while Chianti Classico San Jacopo can provide adequate everyday drinking. New from 2001 is Semifonte di Semifonte, a premium red from Cabernet Sauvignon, Sangiovese and Merlot grapes. (PW)
● **Chianti Classico** Riserva Petri★★ £D Riserva La Prima★★★ £E
● **Ripa delle Mandorle★** £C ● **Ripa delle More★★★** £E

CERBAIONA Brunello di Montalcino A: **Bal**

Owner: Diego Molinari Loc. Cerbaiona, 53024 Montalcino (SI)
Diego Molinara's 7-ha estate can be one of Brunello's greats. The concentration, depth and power combined with a thrilling aromatic and flavour complexity make it a superb cellaring investment even at the price. However, of those vintages tasted there is marked variation and the wines can lack for balance and cleanliness. The rating therefore only applies to certifiable great vintages such as 1997 and 90. Though the estate now seems to be hitting its stride (with a very good 98 too), other older vintages should only be bought in any quantity (not that there's much to be had) once tasted. A second wine labelled simply Cerbaiona adds Cabernet Sauvignon, Merlot, Syrah and Malvasia Nera to Sangiovese, and can also be variable. (PW)
● **Brunello di Montalcino★★★★★** £F ● **Cerbaiona★★★** £E

CIACCI PICCOLOMINI D'ARAGONA www.ciaccipiccolomini.com A: **Bal**, Vts, F&R

Owner: Giuseppe Bianchini Via Borgo di Mezzo, Loc. Castelnuovo dell'Abate, 53020 Montalcino (SI)
This substantial estate with a fine 17th-century *palazzo* and 35 ha of vineyards is in the favoured south-east corner of the Brunello zone. After making waves with the 1988 and 90 vintages it has continued, first under

Roberto Cipresso and now Paolo Vagaggini, to make fine modern-styled Brunello and Rosso. Brunello is ripe and full-textured, with good breadth and depth, relatively approachable when released but generally better with 10 years' age. Good examples were made in 1994, 95, 97, 98 and 99, but 96 is not of the usual standard and is faster evolving. Riservas from 95 and 97 add more extract and weight over the regular example. The ripe, smoky, meaty Rosso is high in alcohol but typically has good richness and depth and with three to five years' age makes a better bet than many a poor Brunello. The estate also has plantings of French varieties. Ateo is a Sangiovese/Merlot/Cabernet Sauvignon blend which wants for a little more depth while Fabius, which is based on Syrah is intense and very ripe, not classic but with a wild Tuscan quality to it. A new estate, Santo Stefano, has been acquired in the Montecucco DOC and is run by Giuseppe's son Paolo. (PW)

● **Brunello di Montalcino** Vigna di Pianrosso★★★ £E Riserva★★★★ £F
● **Rosso di Montalcino** Vigna della Fonte★★ £C
● **Sant'Antimo** Ateo★★ £E Fabius★★★ £E

COL D'ORCIA Brunello di Montalcino A: Alv

Owner: Francesco Marone Cinzano Fraz. Sant'Angelo in Colle, 53020 Montalcino (SI)
Col d'Orcia is one of the best known and most respected names in Montalcino. The large estate includes 130 ha of vines but the wines are made to a high standard. Ex-BANFI winemaker Pablo Harri now directs winemaking and there is consultancy from Maurizio Castelli. The vintages of regular Brunello in the mid-1990s shows plenty of fruit, slightly more evolved in 1994, 96 and 98, more tannic but richer in 95, 97 and 99. A tendency to firm, slightly drying tannins can detract and structure can be too dominant in the regular Riserva. The Riserva Poggio al Vento comes from 5.5 ha of south-facing slopes and can develop a marvellous complexity with a decade's ageing. As well as Brunello there is a consistent and gutsy, characterful Rosso di Montalcino, while Rosso degli Spezieri is a bright, fruity blend of Sangiovese, Ciliegiolo and Merlot for early consumption. Olmaia is the major concession to foreign varieties and is a very powerful, rich, oaky Cabernet Sauvignon, although it still wants for a little more refinement both in its structure and flavours. Moscadello di Montalcino is very honeyed with intense, very ripe fruit yet is not in the least heavy. Some Chardonnay (Ghiaie) and Pinot Grigio are also made. (PW)

● **Brunello di Montalcino**★★★ £E Riserva Poggio al Vento★★★★ £F
● **Rosso di Montalcino**★★ £C ● **Rosso degli Spezieri**★ £B ● **Olmaia**★★★ £F
○ **Moscadello di Montalcino** Pascena★★★ £D

COLOMBAIO DI CENCIO Chianti Classico www.wilhelm-chianti.com A: L&S

Owner: Werner Wilhelm Loc. Cornia, 53013 Gaiole in Chianti (SI)
It is not every day that interesting new estates join the established order of Chianti Classico's hillsides. The focus here is on just two reds, a Chianti Classico (originally a Riserva but no longer given this designation) from Sangiovese (and a little Merlot) and a Cabernet Sauvignon, Sangiovese and Merlot blend, Il Futuro. Winemaking is directed by Jacopo Morganti with input from established enologist Paolo Vagaggini (FULIGNI and others). There's no mistaking the oak in Il Futuro but there's also powerful, ripe, deep, lush berry richness and a sleek texture. The length, intensity and promise is there but time is needed to see how much expression and finesse will be apparent with five years' age or more. Chianti Classico is good but not of the previous standard in 2001. (PW)

● **Chianti Classico** I Massi★★★ £D ● **Il Futuro**★★★★ £E

CORZANO & PATERNO Chianti A: THt, Han, UnC

Owner: Gelpke family Fraz. San Pancrazio, Via Paterno 8, 50020 San Casciano Val di Pesa (FI)
For sleek, pure Tuscan reds, Corzano & Paterno is a label to seek out. From 15 ha of vineyard on the outer rim of the Classico zone, Alijoscha Goldschmidt produces a small but fine range of wines. Il Corzano, the premium red, is the finest expression and, though international in its composition and modern vinification,

it is far removed from the many bland examples of this genre. A wine of splendid texture and complexity, it is a blend of mostly Sangiovese and Cabernet Sauvignon but including a little Merlot (40/45/15 in the 2000). Oak is also present in stylish Chianti and Chianti Riserva but again it is set against pure fruit and good depth. The quality possible from Malvasia and Trebbiano grapes can be seen in a very fine and intense sweet white, Passito di Corzano (or in older vintages, Vin Santo). For dry whites there are two *barrique*-aged Chardonnays, Aglaia and Il Corzanello. (PW)

● **Il Corzano**★★★★ £E
● **Chianti** Terre di Corzano★★ £B Riserva Tre Borri★★★ £D
O **Aglaia**★★ £E O **Passito di Corzano**★★★ £E

COSTANTI Brunello di Montalcino   A: **Lib, P&S**

Owner: Andrea Costanti Loc. Colle al Matrichese, 53024 Montalcino (SI)
Costanti was one of the first recorded producers of Brunello. Andrea Costanti, who has run this estate for close on two decades, now oversees both the high-altitude 7-ha vineyard area of Colle al Matrichese, east of Montalcino itself, and a further 4 ha in the Calbello vineyard at Montosoli, purchased in 1997. He works with Vittorio Fiore to produce elegant but long-lasting Brunello that starts out a little forbidding but shows considerable finesse and style with 10 years' age or more. There is richer fruit and less austerity than previously but similar ageing capacity in recent vintages. A Riserva is only produced in really exceptional years. Rosso di Montalcino shows both more breadth and refinement than is usual but needs at least five years' age. From the Calbello property are produced a second very good Rosso di Montalcino and a Merlot/Cabernet Sauvignon blend, Ardingo. The latter shows excellent ripe black fruit and a fine structure and promises to be at its best with 6 to 10 years' age. Vermiglio is a partly *barrique*-aged Sangiovese with the emphasis on the fruit character. (PW)

● **Brunello di Montalcino**★★★ £E Riserva★★★★ £F
● **Rosso di Montalcino**★★ £D Calbello★★ £E
● **Ardingo**★★★ £E

LUIGI D'ALESSANDRO Cortona   A: **L&S**

Owner: D'Alessandro family Loc. Camucia, Via Manzano 15, 52042 Cortona (AR)
It must have taken not only money but also plenty of courage to establish a new wine estate in the relative viticultural wilderness of eastern Tuscany. Chardonnay, Viognier and Syrah and even some Gamay were planted at high densities for Tuscany (7,000 vines per hectare), but the range has gradually evolved to focus on Fontarca, a rich, blended white from Chardonnay and Viognier, and Il Bosco, pure Syrah. The Chardonnay component (60 to 85 per cent) of Fontarca is *barrique*-fermented and the wine is ripe and aromatic, powerful and high in alcohol. It is not made for long cellaring but provides marvellous exotic, peachy fruit within a couple of years of the vintage. The red offers similarly impressive fruit of the black plum, herb, spice and floral spectrum. It has a lovely intensity and richness but, importantly, framed within a more complete structure that suggests as much pleasure with five years' age or more. Il Vescovo was made from Gamay but Il Vescovo II is intended as a second wine for Il Bosco and is similarly 100 per cent Syrah, but mostly from younger vines. It provides an alternative to a good Côtes du Rhône Syrah. The wines now come under the new Cortona DOC. Traditional wine also gets a look-in in the form of a little Vin Santo (from the classic Trebbiano and Malvasia). Production is relatively modest and prices proportionate to quality. (PW)

● **Cortona Syrah** Il Bosco★★★★ £D Il Vescovo II★★ £B
O **Fontarca**★★★ £C

DEI Vino Nobile di Montepulciano   A: **L&S, JNi**

Owner: Dei family Via di Martiena 35, 53045 Montepulciano (SI)
Catherina Dei has 37 ha over which she lavishes much attention and the fruit intensity she procures is of a

different order to run-of-the-mill Vino Nobile. Consultancy comes from one of Tuscany's best, Niccolò D'Afflitto, and the regular Vino Nobile has been supremely consistent since the mid-1990s. There is ripe, stylish, concentrated fruit but also an initial firmness that makes for better drinking with three to five years' age, when it has developed a spicy, savoury complexity. A Riserva (called Bossona since 1999) adds more weight and structure and shows a little *barrique* influence but the new oak is mostly reserved for an unusual premium blend from a single vineyard of Sangiovese, Syrah, Cabernet Sauvignon and Petit Verdot, Sancta Catharina. If more variable this has generally been a lush, ripe characterful wine since its inception in 1994. Rosso di Montepulciano is also made and is light (if with a little more richness in the best years), round and fresh if drunk with a couple of years' age. Prices are very reasonable by any reckoning. (PW)

● **Vino Nobile di Montepulciano**★★★ £C Riserva Bossona★★★ £D
● **Sancta Catharina**★★★ £D

FATTORIA DI FELSINA Chianti Classico A: **Lib**, ACh, N&P, Vne, P&S

Owner: Poggiali family Strada Chiantigiana 484, 53019 Castelnuovo Berardenga (SI)
Under Giuseppe Mazzocolin (whose wife's family also own CASTELLO DI FARNETELLA) and consultant Franco Bernabei this now substantial property (82 ha) has become one of Chianti Classico's quality heavyweights. Felsina always shows off the best of this southern commune, where the wines are more earthy, gutsy and fleshy (hinting at Brunello) than the more elevated, more northerly zones. The best wines, Riserva Rancia, the premium oak-aged Sangiovese, Fontalloro, and increasingly the rich Cabernet Sauvignon, Maestro Raro, all show greater complexity and add a touch of refinement but there are no wimps here. A Chardonnay, I Sistri, has never lacked for flavour either. Recent releases have been a little uneven, occasionally wanting for more finesse in their structures (very ripe 2000s, Fontalloro and Rancia, are good in the context of the vintage). Regular Chianti Classico is best with at least three years' age, others with five or more. Renown has also brought higher prices and the value for money of old is no longer there. (PW)

● **Chianti Classico**★★ £C Riserva★★ £D Riserva Rancia★★★ £E
● **Fontalloro**★★★★ £F ● **Maestro Raro**★★★ £F
○ **Chardonnay** I Sistri★★ £C

TENUTE AMBROGIO E GIOVANNI FOLONARI www.tenutefolonari.com A: **AWW**

Owner: Ambrogio & Giovanni Folonari Via De Bardi 28, 50125 Firenze (FI)
This is the new project of the Folonari family members who were formerly part of RUFFINO. As well as taking possession of the Cabreo and Nozzole estates, the father-and-son team of Ambrogio and Giovanni Folonari have moved quickly to embellish their holdings. New Vino Nobile estate Gracciano Svetoni and Brunello producer La Fuga are complemented by an estate being developed in Bolgheri, Campo del Mare. The most outstanding of the ex-Ruffino wines is the Cabernet Sauvignon, Il Pareto, from the Nozzole estate but a Sangiovese/Cabernet Sauvignon blend (70/30), Cabreo Il Borgo, is just as well known and can show similar intensity and depth of fruit in top vintages. Both need five years' age but will keep for much longer. Cabreo La Pietra is a *barrique*-fermented and aged Chardonnay of long-standing and is typically rich and creamy with ripe fruit and plenty of depth and good length, but can be a little ungainly. The Spalletti estate in Chianti Rufina also forms part of the holdings. (PW)

Tenuta di Nozzole:
● **Chianti Classico** Riserva La Forra★★ £C ● **Il Pareto**★★★★ £F
Tenute del Cabreo:
● **Cabreo Il Borgo**★★★ £E ○ **Cabreo La Pietra**★★★ £D
Tenuta La Fuga:
● **Brunello di Montalcino**★★★ £E

FONTODI Chianti Classico www.fontodi.com   A: **Lib**, ACh, Res, BBR, P&S, Hrd, V&C, Vne

Owner: Manetti family   Via San Leolino 89, 50020 Panzano (FI)
Fontodi Chianti Classico is a benchmark example that most other producers, except a few makers of super-Chianti Classico, should be aiming to emulate. At its price position it is rarely (if ever) matched and shows marvellous vigour, intensity and style. Fontodi, with 67 ha of vineyards, is fortunate to have not only a great location (Panzano's Conca d'Oro) but also the dedication of Giovanni Manetti in the vineyards and long-term winemaking direction from Franco Bernabei. Chianti Classico Riserva Vigna del Sorbo includes 10 per cent Cabernet Sauvignon and shows great refinement and style. Flaccianello della Pieve was one of the first great pure-Sangiovese Tuscan wines and still shows lovely dimension and evident class (very good in 2000 and 99 if slightly overripe in the latter). Syrah has also been made for several years and is beginning really to hit its stride (since 1998) with an intense fruit core, though it still lacks the refinement and style to compete with similarly priced examples from around the world. Pinot Nero has also improved but is less suited to the soils (and climate) than the Syrah. A white, Meriggio, is made from barrel-fermented Pinot Bianco and some Sauvignon Blanc. (PW)
● **Chianti Classico**★★★ £C Riserva Vigna del Sorbo★★★★ £E
● **Flaccianello**★★★★ £F ● **Syrah Case Via**★★★ £E ● **Pinot Nero**★ £E

FRESCOBALDI www.frescobaldi.it   A: **Hal**, AAA

Owner: Marchesi de' Frescobaldi   Via Santo Spirito 11, 50125 Firenze
The Frescobaldi empire is one of Tuscany's most historic and important. The 1,000 ha of vineyards spread over nine estates include some prime sites. Subject to the expertise of Lamberto Frescobaldi and Niccolò d'Afflitto many of the wines are richer and riper than they were in the 1980s and early 90s. The best wine is unquestionably the very fine Montesodi (from 20 ha of vineyards) from the Chianti Rufina estate, Nipozzano. Of long-standing reputation, it is a wine of real class with great length and structure; a wine to drink with a decade's age or more. The much bigger-volume Nipozzano Riserva can also show a certain style and, with age, charm. Mormoreto, an intense Cabernet Sauvignon that includes some Cabernet Franc is also produced on this estate. From more elevated vineyards in the enclave of Pomino the whites in particular show recent improvement; Il Benefizio is a *barrique*-aged blend of predominantly Chardonnay. The other major outpost of quality is the Castelgiocondo estate in Montalcino. However, even if recently improved (the rating applies since 1997), earlier vintages of Brunello have been very disappointing and the Rosso di Montalcino, Campo ai Sassi, is rarely of a quality worthy of its appellation. Lamaione is a varietal Merlot of good fruit and consistency. The initially over-hyped Luce della Vite, also has its source in Montalcino. A joint venture with Robert Mondavi, it is a blend of Sangiovese and Merlot in equal measure and recently impresses for extract and density but is now a little overdone and lacks the refinement that its price would suggest. Lucente, more Sangiovese than Merlot, is the second wine and has improved yet doesn't represent good value for money. A range of modest varietals is also being produced under the Danzante label. A promising new premium wine, Giramonte, made since 1999, comes from the Castiglioni estate in the Colli Fiorentini, where Chianti and Cabernet Sauvignon are also produced. Seductive, stylish aromas precede a palate structure of slightly less sophistication but of wide appeal. Basic Frescobaldi brands, including Rèmole Chianti, are just that: basic. A 2002 Morellino di Scansano, Santa Maria is decent given the vintage. Frescobaldi has also recently ventured into Friuli in North-East Italy, taking a controlling interest in Collio producer Attems. (PW)

Marchesi de' Frescobaldi:
● **Chianti Rufina** Riserva Nipozzano★★ £C Montesodi★★★★★ £E
● **Mormoreto**★★★ £E ● **Pomino**★ £C
O **Pomino**★ £B Il Benefizio★★ £C
Tenuta di Castelgiocondo:
● **Brunello di Montalcino**★★★ £E Riserva★★★★ £F
● **Lamaione**★★★ £E

Tenuta di Castiglioni:
● **Giramonte★★★** £F ● **Chianti★** £C
Frescobaldi/Mondavi:
● **Luce della Vite★★★** £G ● **Lucente la Vite★★** £D

FULIGNI Brunello di Montalcino   A: **L&S**, N&P

Owner: Eredi Fuligni Via Soccorso Saloni 33, 53024 Montalcino (SI)
At just 8 ha, this is one of the many small Brunello estates and one of the few that are really worth hunting down. The erudite Roberto Guerrini makes wine to contemplate and savour and while there is the classic Brunello muscle and size there is also more elegance than is typical. Despite a modest 1996 quality has been consistently first-rate even in less good vintages, when many others are disappointing. After a very good regular 1998, 97 and 95 both the 99 and Riserva 97 are outstanding, the culmination of the collaboration between Guerrini and his consultant Paolo Vagaggini. The SJ or San Jacopo, with a Merlot component, is lush with a seductive immediacy, while the Rosso shows terrific intensity and vibrancy of fruit. Brunello is reasonably priced vis-à-vis the competition. (PW)
● **Brunello di Montalcino** Vigneti dei Cottimelli★★★★★ £E Riserva★★★★★ £F
● **Rosso di Montalcino** Ginestreto★★★ £C ● **San Jacopo★★** £C

GAGLIOLE www.gagliole.com

Owner: Thomas & Monika Bär-Bettschart Loc. Gagiole 42, 53011 Castellina in Chianti (SI)
Swiss banker Thomas Bär has a passionate commitment to making fine wine. Seven of 9 ha of vines on slopes in Castellina, not far from LA BRANCAIA, are currently in production. Luca D'Attoma is the consultant of choice. Sangiovese-based Gagliole includes around 10 per cent Cabernet Sauvignonm and fermentation is in conical oak vats with a total maceration of three to four weeks. The result is a very complete modern, sophisticated red with a lush, creamy texture and rich blackberry fruit but it is also a wine of some style and individuality. Of the most recent vintages, 2001 improves on an 00 that avoids the defects of that vintage. More original and even better than Gagliole is Pecchia, so far only made in 1999 and from 30-year-old vines, but a candidate for a five-star rating. (PW)
● **Gagliole Rosso★★★★** £E

TENUTA DI GHIZZANO Colline Pisane www.tenutadighizzano.com   A: **L&S**, Eno

Owner: Pierfrancesco Venerosi Pesciolini Via della Chiesa 13, 56030 Ghizzano di Peccioli (PI)
Ghizzano is the leading property in the Colline Pisane, an increasingly good source of rich, ripe reds further up the coast from the famous Bolgheri zone. The large estate (350 ha) has belonged to this noble family since the 14th century and the relatively small vineyard of 16 ha is currently being expanded to 25 ha. The estate is managed by the owner's daughter, Ginevra, and two wines fashioned by enologist Carlo Ferrini have established the family's reputation as wine producers. Veneroso is primarily a blend of Sangiovese and Cabernet Sauvignon (but with 5 per cent Merlot in 1999) while Nambrot, originally a varietal Merlot, now includes an increasing amount of Cabernet. Both are aged in new oak and made in a rich, lush modern style. Nambrot is a little fuller and more succulent but Veneroso has the greater class. Chianti Colline Pisane is fruity and stylish while a tiny quantity of Vin Santo, San Germano, is also made. (PW)
● **Nambrot★★★★** £E ● **Veneroso★★★★** £E
● **Chianti Colline Pisane★** £B

BIBI GRAETZ   A: F&R

Owner: Bibi Graetz Via di Vincigliata 19, 50014 Fiesole (FI)
Bibi Graetz has 10 ha at Fiesole just outside Florence. If this seems an unlikely place for making fine wines then try his one and only wine, Testamatta. Just 23,000 bottles of 2001 were produced, with an

eye-catching label that is also his own work. Consultancy comes from the highly regarded Alberto Antonini team. The blend is very Tuscan with 70 per cent Sangiovese balanced by mostly Colorino and Canaiolo but also a little Malvasia Nera and Moscato Nero. The fruit comes from vines that are 30 to 60 years old and vinification is in open fermenters. The result is an inky-black red of marvellous intensity and originality. Powerful and extracted, it should be cellared rather than used to impress your friends. The wine is rated on the basis of just two vintages (2001 and 00) but this is very promising – if you can find it. (PW)

● **Testamatta**★★★★ £E

GRATTAMACCO/COLLE MASSARI   Bolgheri   www.collemassari.it   A: Sec

Owner: P Meletti Cavallari/Claudio Tipa   Loc. Grattamacco, 57022 Castagneto Carducci (LI)
Grattamacco was only the second estate to commercialise wine production from the now-famous zone of Bolgheri. Piermario Meletti Cavallari worked steadily to refine a great red wine of his own but in 2002 leased his estate to Claudia Tipa of Colle Massari (a 300-ha estate in the southern Maremma with young plantings) for 10 years. The red Grattamacco, a blend now dominated by Cabernet Sauvignon with the balance from Sangiovese and Merlot comes from 10 of the 11 ha of gently sloping vineyards on a 30-ha estate. Over recent years the wine has become increasingly refined and harmonious but without losing its individuality, its fine perfume of spice, floral and herb scents and dark berried fruit. There is good depth and a certain rigour to the structure but great length of flavour. Older vintages (pre-1992) contain Malvasia Nera rather than Merlot. Future vintages, following investment and input from Tipa, should be interesting. The perfumed white is from Vermentino, a small portion of it *barrique*-fermented, and is ripe and full if not that complex. (PW)

● **Bolgheri** Superiore★★★ £E   ○ **Bolgheri** Bianco★★ £B

GUALDO DEL RE   Val di Cornia   A: L&S, N&P

Owner: N Rossi & M T Cabella   Loc. Notri 77, 57028 Suvereto (LI)
Under Barbara Tamburini's consultancy both the composition and the quality of several wines here have had a serious makeover. Generally there is successively better depth, concentration and intensity in the three premium reds going from 1999 to 00 to 01. The wines also have better textures and fruit expression. I Rennero is now pure Merlot but included Pinot Nero in the first two vintages (98 and 99). It is more varietal, with a mineral streak to its deep, ripe, black fruit character in 2001. Federico Primo is 100 per cent Cabernet Sauvignon from 2000, having previously included Merlot, while Gualdo del Re is from Sangiovese. Of the whites, Strale, 100 per cent *barrique*-femented and aged Pinot Bianco, used to be known as Lumen but is a good spicy, creamy, Tuscan example of the variety. Vermentino is very attractive if drunk very young, while basic Eliseo red and white have good character if only moderate structure and substance. A sweet Aleatico, Amansio, is also made. (PW)

● **Val di Cornia Suvereto** Gualdo del Re★★★ £D   Federico Primo★★★ £D   I Rennero★★★ £D
○ **Strale**★★ £C   ○ **Valentina Vermentino**★★ £B
○ **Val di Cornia Bianco** Eliseo★ £B   ● **Val di Cornia Rosso** Eliseo★ £B

IL PALAZZINO   Chianti Classico   A: J&B

Owner: Alessandro & Andrea Sderci   Loc. Monti, 53010 Gaiole in Chianti (SI)
Relatively few estates are as committed to the pursuit of a classic expression of Chianti Classico as Il Palazzino. Alessandro Sderci distinguishes between four different sites and achieves a quite different expression and level of quality from each. While technical assistance is sought, he is determined to avoid any style imposition from an outside consultant. The Sderci's finest plot of vines is Grosso Sanese, planted over 30 years ago. 100 per cent Sangiovese and sold as a *vino da tavola* from 1981 till 1993, it is now among the top flight of Chianti Classico. A small part of Grosso Sanese may be set aside as Riserva and given slightly longer ageing in *barriques*. These are 10-year wines but currently the excellent 1997 or 98 might be broached. La Pieve comes from four parcels around a church, is *barrique*-aged (a third new) and has

impressive depth, although also some of the austerity of the other wines if drunk too young. More fruit-driven but with less structure is Argenina, while La Cascina Girasole (sold as an IGT) is simpler and reflects its cooler origins. (PW)

● **Chianti Classico** Grosso Sanese★★★★ £C Riserva Grosso Sanese★★★★ £D
● **Chianti Classico** Argenina★★ £C La Pieve★★★ £C
● **La Cascina Girasole**★ £B

IL POGGIONE Brunello di Montalcino www.tenutailpoggione.it A: **Eno**, N&P

Owner: Leopoldo & Livia Franceschi Fraz. Sant'Angelo in Colle, 53020 Montalcino (SI)

Il Poggione has made some excellent Brunello for 40-odd years, in fact during all the time that Pierluigi Talenti (see TALENTI) was winemaker here – from 1958 until his death in 1999. The large estate with just over 100 ha of vines is now under the direction of Pierluigi's protégé – Fabrizio Bindocci. The wines have been slightly old-fashioned: full and structured, always with a fair amount of tannin but balanced and capable of long ageing, although already exhibiting a deep, savoury complexity and richness soon after their release; in fact everything that lighter, more superficial examples lack. The balance can be more marginal in a lighter vintage but not in recent vintages such as 1995, 97, 98 or 99. There is even more power, structure and breadth in the long-lived Riserva (especially an exceptional 1997). The Rosso, too, rarely lacks for depth or intensity but shows more obvious plummy black fruits and plenty of grip. Future vintages look likely to maintain the fine tradition if perhaps tending to a more overt fruit richness that can also be seen in San Leopoldo, a Sangiovese/Cabernet Sauvignon/Cabernet Franc blend. The wines are very reasonably priced for the quality and there's very good olive oil too. (PW)

● **Brunello di Montalcino**★★★★ £D Riserva★★★★★ £E
● **Rosso di Montalcino**★★ £B ● **San Leopoldo**★★★ £C

ISOLE E OLENA Chianti Classico A: **Lib**, Vne, ACh, Res, F&M, Hrd, Sel, P&S, V&C

Owner: De Marchi family Loc. Isole 1, 50021 Barberino Val d'Elsa (FI)

Paolo De Marchi is perhaps Tuscany's finest ambassador, effortlessly combining dynamism and humility in a tireless pursuit of quality. A *vignaiolo* first and winemaker second, over more than two and a half decades he has poured a massive amount of energy (and intelligence) into reshaping an estate (now with 48 ha of vineyards) bought by his family in the 1960s. The wines have been very good for a long time but only now that he has developed his own clones of Sangiovese and reclaimed the most taxing vineyards are the best fruits of his labours being transformed into ever better wines. From the great Cepparello (from Sangiovese) through powerful, long-lived Cabernet Sauvignon and stylish Syrah to vibrant Chianti Classico the wines are intense, complete and expressive with both depth and elegance. A vertical tasting of any of the wines will show how they also manage to reflect something of the vintage character yet without the defects (for example an elegant yet full Chianti in the difficult 2002 vintage). Whites as well as reds are made and, though the Chardonnay has had its ups and downs, it is usually one of Tuscany's best examples, while the Vin Santo is consistently brilliant. (PW)

● **Cepparello**★★★★★ £F ● **Chianti Classico**★★ £C
● **Cabernet Sauvignon** Collezione De Marchi★★★★ £F ● **Syrah** Collezione De Marchi★★★★ £E
O **Chardonnay** Collezione De Marchi★★★ £D O **Vin Santo**★★★★ £F

LA BRANCAIA Chianti Classico www.brancaia.com A: **Eno**, JNi, NYg, Hrd, V&C, Vne

Owner: Bruno & Brigette Widmer Loc. Poppi 42b, 53017 Radda in Chianti (SI)

Up until 1997 the La Brancaia wines were made at FONTERUTOLI and there are still close links between the two properties. Since 1999 the estate has been under the direction of Barbara Widmer, daughter of the Swiss owners, who has recently been joined by her husband, Martin Kronenberg. The 19 ha comprise two estates, 9-ha Brancaia (in Castellina) and 10-ha Poppi (in Radda). The Chianti Classico is pure Sangiovese, while Brancaia Il Blu (with a blue label) includes 40 per cent Merlot and 5 per cent Cabernet. Both see some new wood and this is evident in the finished wines but both also show ripe stylish fruit and good depth. The more structured Brancaia is better with five years' age or more, while the Chianti Classico can be drunk a little sooner. A third wine, Tre, usually shows good fruit in a supple style. While quality has increased, so have the prices. 'Brancaia in Maremma' is a new estate being developed in the southern Maremma which will eventually extend to 35 ha of vineyards. The first release of Ilatraia (from 2002) is exceptionally good; based on Cabernet Sauvignon, it also contains 30 per cent Sangiovese and 10 per cent Petit Verdot. (PW)

● **Chianti Classico**★★★ £D   ● **Brancaia Il Blu**★★★★ £E
● **Tre**★★ £C

LA MASSA Chianti Classico   A: JAr, Dec

Owner: Giampaolo Motta Via Case Sparse 9, 50020 Panzano (FI)
Neapolitan Giampaolo Motta and enologist Carlo Ferrini make two very good modern-styled Chianti Classicos from 27 ha of vines. The experienced Motta now has almost a decade of vintages behind him from these prime vineyards in the much vaunted Panzano sub-zone. Both wines are aged in *barriques* and are always full of ripe, intense fruit. While predominantly Sangiovese (85 to 90 per cent), both also include some Cabernet Sauvignon and/or Merlot. If less individual than some, they do deliver consistently high quality. The regular version is best with three to five years' age, while the greater depth and structure of Giorgio Primo deserves five or more. The 2000s, while good, miss the balance and fruit succulence of the 99s. Unfortunately prices are high, even given the quality. In 2001 the regular Chianti Classico was replaced by a new wine, La Massa, with a notably reduced percentage of Sangiovese (and therefore not qualifying as Chianti Classico) but a significant step up in quality. (PW)

● **Chianti Classico**★★ £D Giorgio Primo★★★★ £F

MAURIZIO LAMBARDI Brunello di Montalcino

Owner: Maurizio Lambardi Podere Canalicchio di Sotto 8, 53024 Montalcino (SI)
Committed grower Maurizio Lambardi's Canalicchio di Sotto, like a number of Brunello's small estates, doesn't produce that much wine but what there is can be very good. His wines have a depth and fullness that show off the quality of his fruit. Their lushness and richness make a vintage like 1995 or 98 both accessible now but capable of another 10 years' ageing. Though not all are of the same standard, there is generally good quality across recent vintages. From the best vintages, an intense vibrant Rosso needs three to five years to show at its best. (PW)

● **Brunello di Montalcino**★★★ £E ● **Rosso di Montalcino**★★ £C

LANCIOLA Chianti Classico www.lanciola.net   A: HSA, Wat, The, UnC

Owner: Guarnieri family Via Imprunetana 210, 50023 Impruneta (FI)
The 80-ha estate of Lanciola, nearly half of it planted to vines, lies at the top of the Classico zone. By rights the wines ought not be anything special here but in recent vintages they have certainly offered plenty of substance and vibrancy. At the level of Chianti Classico Riserva and the premium red, Terricci (Sangiovese with 15 per cent Cabernet Sauvignon and 5 per cent Cabernet Franc), this translates as broad, muscular wines that can be slightly overdone in terms of oak and extract. Both shouldn't be drunk with less than five years' age. Within their context, regular Chiantis, both Classico and Fiorentini, are, however, more successful, with a vigour and intensity well matched by a stylish fruit expression. In short, don't expect great finesse here but you will get plenty of wine for your money. Chardonnay (Ricciobianco), Pinot Nero (Riccineri) and Vin Santo are also made. (PW)

● **Terricci**★★★ £D ● **Chianti Classico** Le Masse di Greve★★ £B Riserva★★ £C
● **Chianti Colli Fiorentini**★★ £B

LE CORTI/PRINCIPE CORSINI Chianti Classico www.principecorsini.com A: Ast

Owner: Principe Corsini Via Bolgherese 189/A, 57020 Castagneto Carducci (LI)
As recently as 1992 Duccio Corsini, the son of the Principe Corsini, set out to produce high-quality wine with view to restoring the historic Villa di Corsini. The estate, in the family since Renaissance times, covers 250 ha with 49 ha of vineyards. Duccio Corsini is assisted by one of Tuscany's best consultant winemakers, Carlo Ferrini. There are three fine Chianti Classicos, a good *normale* (Le Corti), a more structured Riserva (Cortevecchia) and the premium bottling, Don Tommaso. The wines are ripe, intense and modern but typically Chianti Classico, with particularly good structure and depth in Don Tommaso. The latter was not produced in 2002, to the benefit of a surprisingly good *normale*. The family also have a holding in the Maremma, Tenuta Marsiliana, producing a deep, penetrating and characterful IGT primarily from Cabernet Sauvignon and Merlot but also including Syrah and other varieties. A floral and herb-scented second wine is also produced from this estate. Also under the ownership of the Principe Corsini is the Titignano estate in Umbria where the SALVIANO wines (see Central Italy) are made. (PW)

Le Corti:
● **Chianti Classico** Le Corti★★ £B Riserva Cortevecchia★★ £C Don Tommaso★★★ £D
Tenuta Marsiliana:
● **Marsiliana★★★** £E

LE FILIGARE Chianti Classico A: M&V, HHB, P&S

Owner: Del Conte srl Via Sicelle 37, Loc. San Donato in Poggio, 50020 Barberino Val d'Elsa (FI)
This attractive estate is at a relatively high altitude on lean, stony soils and shows increasing promise with its wines. Carlo Burchi has doubled the original vineyard area to 12 ha and now works with his son Filippo and enologist Dr Luciano Bandini. Though the wines can be a little tight and compact if tasted very young, there is usually an underlying fruit richness which makes for sleek, elegant, stylish and fruity Chianti with a little age. In the regular version the Sangiovese is complemented by Canaiolo and Colorino, while the Riserva includes Colorino and Merlot and spends longer in oak. Podere Le Rocce is a blend of Cabernet Sauvignon and Sangiovese (65/35) that is quite sturdy but with the potential to add richness with age. Newish Pietro is a more ambitious premium blend of Merlot, Sangiovese and Syrah that is more powerful and extracted but will be rated with further vintages. In terms of keeping, Chianti Classico *normale* is best with two or three years, Riserva with three to five, while even more time is needed for the Podere Le Rocce. A small amount of Vin Santo is also made. (PW)
● **Chianti Classico★★** £C Riserva Maria Vittoria★★★ £D
● **Podere Le Rocce★★★** £D

FATTORIA LE FONTI Chianti Classico A: May

Owner: Imberti family Loc. San Giorgio, 53036 Poggibonsi (SI)
Tuscany needs more producers like this – small estates that are maximising the potential of a small but coherent range of wines. Le Fonti's success seems to owe much to Lorenzo Bernini, who is responsible for the 22 ha of vineyards, and consultant Paolo Caciorgna, who makes the wines. Vito Arturo is named for the Imberti brothers' father, who bought the estate in 1956. The single-vineyard, 100 per cent Sangiovese wine struggled a little for balance in the difficult 2000 vintage but the quality and intensity of the fruit that promise a four-star rating in the near future. Only a notch or two lower is the Chianti Classico Riserva, also pure Sangiovese. The *normale* (with 5 per cent Canaiolo) starts out a little lean but will fill out if given three years' age. Rather traditionally styled and of moderate sweetness, Vin Santo has a roasted nuts, date and walnut character but also dried citrus and a honeyed intensity. These wines shouldn't be confused with those of Azienda Agricola LE FONTI. (PW)
● **Chianti Classico★** £B Riserva★★★ £C
● **Vito Arturo★★★** £D ○ **Vin Santo del Chianti Classico★★** £E

427

LE MACCHIOLE Bolgheri www.lemacchiole.it A: **L&S,** F&R

Owner: Cinzia Campolmi Via Bolgherese 189/A, 57020 Castagneto Carducci (LI)
Le Macchiole is as outstanding a producer of Bolgheri as its neighbours ORNELLAIA or SASSICAIA.
Eugenio Campolmi transformed both the 18-ha estate and the way the wines were made before his recent
early death. His success owes much to enologist Luca D'Attoma, responsible for several of Tuscany's most
exciting creations. Made in the greatest quantities, the estate red, Macchiole, is Sangiovese-based but with
5 per cent Cabernet Sauvignon in 1999 and 10 per cent each of Merlot and Cabernet Franc in 2000. The
latter in particular seems to add character; sleek and compact, it opens out with age. Three other reds are
made in small quantities, each less than 1,000 cases in the 2001 vintage. Paléo Rosso was originally a
Cabernet Sauvignon-based wine complemented by Sangiovese and Cabernet Franc. However the Cabernet
Franc increased from15 per cent in 1999 to 30 in 2000, while the 2001 is entirely from Cabernet Franc.
Despite this evolution, it has sustained a characteristic mineral-imbued, intense, small berry fruit character
within a structured frame. At least five years' age is recommended, as it is for two reds that fully deserve their
cult status. The quality of the tremendously rich, classically varietal Merlot, Messorio, and deep, structured,
minerally Syrah, Scrio, is quite spellbinding. Paléo Bianco, from Chardonnay and Sauvignon, is ripe and
stylish. (PW)
● **Bolgheri** Rosso Superiore Paléo★★★★ £E ● **Macchiole Rosso★★★** £D
● **Messorio★★★★★** £H ● **Scrio★★★★★** £H
O **Paléo Bianco★★** £D

LE PUPILLE Morellino di Scansano A: **Lib,** Res,Vne, P&S, NYg

Owner: Elisabetta Geppetti Piagge del Maiano 92/A, 58040 Istia d'Ombrone (GR)
For long the one outstanding producer from the heart of the southern Maremma, Le Pupille was well
established before a recent wave of newcomers from other parts of Tuscany rushed to join in. Quality
(already good) soared in the 1990s under a string of top-flight consultants, the latest being ex-technical
director of Bordeaux's Château LAFITE, Christian Le Sommer. Regular Morellino di Scansano has always
shown off the character of Sangiovese in this zone with its wild herb and delightful berry fruit character. A
fine Riserva with extra weight and structure was produced until 1998 but efforts are now going into making
an even better regular example and further improving the quality of the excellent single-vineyard Poggio
Valente, introduced in 1997. There is marvellous style and complexity in this wine that newer producers in
Morellino will take some time to emulate. Even better and now a marvellously rich, concentrated wine is
Saffredi, a blend of Cabernet Sauvignon and Merlot (70/30). All three reds need a little age: three years for
the regular Morellino, five or more for Poggio Valente and Saffredi. Solalto, a delicious sweet wine with
gently spicy dried peach and apricot fruit, is a late-harvested blend of Sauvignon, Traminer and Semillon. (PW)
● **Morellino di Scansano★★** £C Poggio Valente★★★ £D
● **Saffredi★★★★** £F O **Solalto★★★** £E

LISINI Brunello di Montalcino www.lisini.com A: N&P, RsW, Rae, UnC

Owner: Lisini family Fraz. Sant'Angelo in Colle, 53020 Montalcino (SI)
Franco Bernabei is the consultant of choice for the Lisinis. From 12 ha of vineyards he ensures good
consistency and attractive wines even in lesser vintages. Though there is real Brunello complexity and weight
the wines are generally more for the medium than long term. The exception is the single-vineyard wine
Ugolaia. Potentially very exciting, it can be just a little overdone in terms of structure, though the necessary
balance for long keeping is usually there. The regular Brunello was very good in 1997, but in 98 struggles
for balance and is developing prematurely. The 95 and 97 Ugolaia however show great depth and
dimension. The Rosso can also impress with its forward, lush and vibrant black fruit character. (PW)
● **Brunello di Montalcino★★★** £F Ugolaia★★★★ £F
● **Rosso di Montalcino★★** £C

LIVERNANO   Radda in Chianti   www.livernano.it   A: **L&S**

Owner: Marco Montanari   Loc. Livernano, 53017 Radda in Chianti (SI)
Livernano is a restored medieval hamlet that, like a number of others, was abandoned in the post-war migration to the cities. Marco Montanari is Swiss, one of several making an impression on the Tuscan wine scene. He has just 12.5 ha of vines which have been replanted at higher densities under the guidance of eminent agronomist Remigio Bordini. Winemaking expertise comes from the highly respected Stefano Chioccioli. The Livernano blend (Cabernet/Merlot/Sangiovese) shows good intensity and structure as well as increasing depth and concentration, though for me more exciting (and aptly named) is Puro Sangue, a very pure, powerful expression of Sangiovese which promises much with five to seven years' age. Small amounts of Anima, a *barrique*-aged white from Chardonnay, Sauvignon and Traminer, are also made. (PW)
● **Purosangue★★★★** £E   ● **Livernano★★★** £E

MASTROJANNI   Brunello di Montalcino   A: **Col**, F&R

Owner: Mastrojanni family   Podere Loreto, Fraz. Castelnuovo dell' Abate, 53020 Montalcino (SI)
One of the few really great Brunello producers, Mastrojanni commands almost 19 ha of steep stony slopes in the south-eastern confines of the DOCG. Both large and small wood are used for ageing but it's not obvious in these deep, dark monsters. Structured, with dense but ripe tannins, the wines always show an expansive quality in the mouth that few of the more modern, oak-influenced styles even approach. Sometimes the balance is not quite there or the wine is a bit deficient, as in 1996, or relatively advanced though good (98), but the depth, class and complexity from vintages like 90, 93, 95 97 or 99 make this an excellent investment for keeping for 10 to 15 years (i.e. 5 to 10 more after release). Very small quantities of a rich, complex Riserva are made in the best years and occasionally produced is a special selection, Schiena d'Asino (which may need closer to two decades). San Pio (Sangiovese/Cabernet Sauvignon) is more accessible in the short-term as is a Rosso which can be excellent in good vintages, with Brunello-like fullness but always needing another two or three years after its release (at two years). Botrys is a late-harvested blend of Moscato and Malvasia. (PW)
● **Brunello di Montalcino★★★★** £F   Riserva★★★★ £F   Schiena d'Asino★★★★ £F
● **Rosso di Montalcino★★** £D   ● **San Pio★★★** £D

MONTE BERNARDI   Chianti Classico   www.montebernardi.com   A: **RsW**, Rae, UnC

Owner: Schmelzer family, Stak Aivaliotis & Sharon Firth   Via Chiantigiana, 50020 Panzano (FI)
Stak Aivaliotis is passionate about wine and has developed Monte Bernardi since the late 1980s with the aim of producing the best wine in the region. Though the 53-ha estate (with 6 ha of vines) is now run by the Schmelzer family (since 2004), winemaking direction continues to come from Giorgio Marone. The intention has always been to produce pure wines with minimal interference. A rigorous selection and – relatively unusual for Tuscany – a prolonged pre-fermentation maceration are employed as well as the use of a basket press. High-quality French oak, some of it new, is used in the ageing of all the wines and this is evident in their structures and flavours. The wines are increasingly rich and intense but could still use a little more sophistication. Sa'etta is ripe, oaky, intense and vibrant, the 99 the most promising to date. It is produced from 100 per cent Sangiovese while the Chianti Classico Paris now includes a little Canaiolo. Tzingana is a blend of Merlot and Cabernet Sauvignon but also includes Cabernet Franc and Petit Verdot. Prices are high but there is promise in the wines that suggests quality may soon gain parity. (PW)
● **Chianti Classico** Paris★★ £D
● **Sa'etta★★★** £E   ● **Tzingana★★★** £F

MONTEPELOSO   Val di Cornia   A: **Bal**, UnC

Owner: Fabio Chiarelotto   Loc. Montepeloso 82, 57020 Suvereto (LI)
This estate is one of Suvereto's stars, making wines of extraordinary concentration from well-sited vineyards.

The wines from 8 ha of vines are made by consultant Fabrizio Moltard. Low yields and *barrique*-ageing make for wines with deep, rich, powerful fruit and fine, ripe tannins. Gabbro is from Cabernet Sauvignon and Cabernet Franc while Nardo is predominantly Sangiovese but with a little Cabernet Sauvignon and Montepulciano. Both are made in very small quantities and highly sought after, so are not cheap. Eneo, predominantly Sangiovese but also including a little Canaiolo and Ciliegiolo, is made in greater quantities. This is increasingly fine and good value (labelled Val di Cornia Rosso prior to 2000). The quality of the 2002s, if not quite at the level of 01, is very good indeed. Very promising new varietal examples of Syrah and Sangiovese were also made in 02, both show great concentration, purity and length of flavour. (PW)

● Gabbro★★★★★ £F   ● Nardo★★★★★ £F
● Eneo★★★★ £C

MONTEVERTINE   www.montevertine.it   A: **Eur**, N&P, Res

Owner: Martino Manetti   Loc. Montevertine, 53017 Radda in Chianti (SI)
Sergio Manetti became one of the legends of the modern Tuscan wine renaissance after creating the pure-Sangiovese, single-vineyard Super-Tuscan Le Pergole Torte. The striking labels are the work of artist Alberto Manfredi. The small estate now has 10 ha of vineyards at high altitude, though not all are fully in production. Le Pergole Torte is subject to a lengthy maceration (25 to 30 days) before ageing, only initially in *barriques*. Besides Le Pergole Torte there are two other top reds – Il Sodaccio, which is also from a single vineyard, and Montevertine (previously designated Riserva), which approximates to a regular traditional Chianti Classico, albeit a very good one. Both include a little Canaiolo. All three can show marvellous quality, at once very stylish and harmonious, complex with excellent dimension on the palate, gaining in richness with age and with great length of flavour. It can be easy to underestimate quality when the wines are very young but usually with five to eight years' age the full potential becomes apparent. Quality is not entirely consistent but tends to follow the best vintages. Pian del Ciampolo is a recently introduced cheaper red with a bright, more forward, floral fruit character. Following his father's death in 2000, it will be interesting to see where Martino Manetti takes this fine estate as he continues to be assisted by the venerable Giulio Gambelli. A very small amount of white wine is also produced. (PW)

● Le Pergole Torte★★★★★ £F   ● Il Sodaccio★★★★ £E
● Montevertine★★★ £E   ● Pian del Ciampolo★ £B

MORIS FARMS   Monteregio di Massa Marittima   www.morisfarms.it   A: **Bal**, C&B, Vts, But

Owner: Moris family   Loc. Curanuova, 58024 Massa Marittima (GR)
The Moris family's substantial landholding in the Maremma includes 70 ha of vineyards. 40 ha of these fall under the Monteregio di Massa Marittima DOC and 30 ha qualify as Morellino di Scansano. Generally sound if robust examples of both are produced, particularly an intense, extracted Riserva of the latter. The Monteregio has a bit more substance than the standard Morellino due to lower yields. The real star however is Avvoltore, a powerhouse Sangiovese-based wine of great vigour and depth. Cabernet Sauvignon and Syrah (20 and 5 per cent respectively) play an important part in its consistently rich, floral and crushed berry fruit complexity. It is balanced with great length and usually best with six to eight years' age. (PW)

● Avvoltore★★★★ £E
● Morellino di Scansano★ £C Riserva★★ £D   ● Monteregio di Massa Marittima★★ £C

TENUTA DELL' ORNELLAIA   Bolgheri   www.ornellaia.it   A: **JAr**, F&M, UnC, BBR, F&R

Owner: Robert Mondavi & Frescobaldi   Via Bolgherese 191, 57020 Bolgheri (LI)
Now under the ownership of Mondavi and Frescobaldi, Ornellaia has seen continued changes to winemaking personnel since its inception. Lodovico, Piero ANTINORI's younger brother, was able to set up on his own in the 1980s due to his inheritance from his mother's family. No expense was spared transforming 70 ha of mostly scrubby countryside into a model wine estate. Currently responsibility falls to Thomas Duroux and the main focus of production continues to be the estate blend, Ornellaia, from

Cabernet Sauvignon, Merlot and Cabernet Franc (now made in excess of 12,000 cases a year). Le Serre Nuove, positioned as a second wine, has been made since 1997. Large volumes are made of Le Volte, the least expensive wine and a blend of Cabernet Sauvignon, Sangiovese, and Merlot; it has been somewhat irregular in terms of quality, rarely providing value for money. Made in more modest quantities, if not quite as scarce as it once was, is the pure Merlot, Masseto – the estate's most sought-after wine. The sheer opulence of the fruit in Masseto has no equal for some of its more impassioned fans. There's little doubt about the quality of this or of Ornellaia, though the ratings below only apply to the best vintages. The more classically structured Ornellaia requires the greater patience. Poggio alle Gazze, a ripe and zesty Sauvignon-based white, was last made in 2001. (PW)

● **Bolgheri** Rosso Superiore Ornellaia★★★★★ £G ● **Masseto★★★★★** £H
● **Bolgheri** Rosso Le Serre Nuove★★★ £E ● **Le Volte★** £B

SIRO PACENTI Brunello di Montalcino A: **JAr**, Lay, BBR, Far

Owner: Giancarlo Pacenti Loc. Pelagrilli 1, 53024 Montalcino (SI)
Giancarlo Pacenti has turned a good estate into an outstanding one in just a few short years. In recent vintages quality has been exemplary, in fact arguably it has become the best regular Brunello available since 1995, including an excellent 96 and an outstanding 97, 98 and 99. Some new oak is used but this does not overwhelm the marvellous quality of the fruit and extract. Not only is there superb richness, breadth and power but the wine possesses great length, really fine tannins and impeccable balance. Pacenti also makes a rich, concentrated Brunello-like Rosso di Montalcino, with the weight if not the dimension of a really decent example at that. Unfortunately some wine brokers are only too aware of the quality and its speculative potential but prices are not crazy when a merchant or retailer has bought first-hand. At least these wines can be bought in the confidence of finding out what great Brunello tastes like, whether drunk now or with another 10 to 15 years' age. A little Riserva is sometimes made but has not been tasted from recent vintages. (PW)

● **Brunello di Montalcino**✪✪✪✪✪ £F
● **Rosso di Montalcino★★★** £D

PERTIMALI/LIVIO SASSETTI Brunello di Montalcino A: **J&B**, F&R, Fal

Owner: Livio Sassetti Loc. Pertimali, 53024 Montalcino (SI)
Pertimali is a 9-ha estate producing slightly old-fashioned Brunello of great richness and depth within a sturdy frame. A meaty Rosso di Montalcino too can be full, ripe and savoury with a little age, showing the true character of Sangiovese in this zone. Vigna dei Fili di Seta, a blend of Sangiovese and Cabernet Sauvignon, is the only wine likely to have seen any small wood and is more modern, with rich, dense fruit to the fore. However, a note of caution, particularly for the Brunello – despite some really fine examples (for which the rating is given) such as the 1995, quality can be uneven with sometimes questionable balance (a slightly bruising, monolithic 98) and stability: an otherwise very promising 99 is slightly high-toned. Individual vintages should be tasted before buying by the case (the 96 is best avoided). A very small amount of Riserva is also made but can be superb as in 97. (PW)

● **Brunello di Montalcino★★★★** £F Riserva★★★★★ £F
● **Rosso di Montalcino★★** £C ● **Vigna dei Fili di Seta★★★** £D

PETROLO Colli Aretini www.petrolo.it A: **Lib**, Vne, But, P&S

Owner: L. Bazzocchi Sanjust & L. Sanjust Fraz. Mercatale Valdarno, 52020 Montevarchi (AR)
From the Colli Aretini (east, over the Monti del Chianti from Gaiole in Chianti Classico) comes one of Tuscany's finest pure Merlots. Made in very small quantities, Galatrona has not only remarkable richness and concentration but a depth, spice and individuality that compares with the very best Pomerol. But while the Merlot joins the spiral of cult wines, Luca Sanjust and his mother, with expert help, have tried to ensure that the entire production (from a total of 31 ha) bears little relation to the humble status of the Colli Aretini

zone in which they are based. Torrione is for Sangiovese what Galatrona is for Merlot. Made in much greater quantities it has been very impressive since 1997, if not of the same concentration or proportions as Galatrona. Terre di Galatrona is the regular wine and combines Sangiovese (70 per cent) with Merlot as well as a little Cabernet Sauvignon but is always likely to be at its ripest and fullest in the best vintages. Vin Santo and olive oil are also produced. (PW)

● Galatrona★★★★ £F
● Torrione★★★ £D   ● Terre di Galatrona★ £B

PIEVE SANTA RESTITUTA   Brunello di Montalcino   A: JAr, L&W, F&R

Owner: Gaja family   Loc. Chiesa Santa Restituta, 53024 Montalcino (SI)
Angelo GAJA's first venture into Tuscany was this small, wonderfully sited Brunello estate. While all eyes are now on what comes out of his major undertaking in Bolgheri, CA' MARCANDA, the wines here are beginning to show the impact of his winemaker, Guido Rivella. Two Brunellos are made – Rennina, a superior selection from the best vines, and Sugarille, from a single-vineyard site. The original 11 ha have been expanded and will eventually total 35 ha, still small by comparison with the zone's biggest producers. The wines already command high prices, whether by design or demand, but show an elegance and structure that since 1995 have set them apart from most other Brunello. The first vintages formulated with the Gaja magic are only beginning to be ready for drinking as both wines need at least 10 to 12 years' age (and should keep for considerably longer). (PW)

● Brunello di Montalcino Rennina★★★★★ £G Sugarille★★★★★ £G

POGGERINO   Chianti Classico   www.poggerino.com   A: L&S

Owner: Piero & Benedetta Lanza   Via Poggerino 6, 53017 Radda in Chianti (SI)
This fine 11-ha estate is in some of Chianti Classico's highest hills (between 400 and 500 m) north-east of Radda. After a remarkable Riserva made in 1990, the wines have maintained a high standard under the continued efforts and winemaking skill of Piero Lanza. A small amount of Merlot supplements the plantings of Sangiovese and is used in both a minor supporting role in the Chianti Classico and as an equal partner in the premium *cuvée*, Primamateria. While new oak and concentrated ripe fruit are much in evidence, there is also an elegance and stylishness to the wines derived at least in part from the elevation, aspect and soil of the vineyards. The Chianti Classico shows the fine spice, cherry and herb notes characteristic of Sangiovese and deserves two or three years' age. A small amount of a fine Riserva from a single vineyard, Bugialla, is made in good years – recently in 2000, 99 and 97 – and deserves five years' age. Primamateria (first made in 1997) shows intense sweet berry fruit depth, great length and superfine tannins and is very approachable but best with five years' ageing or more. For everyday drinking, Il Labirinto is made from young vines of Sangiovese and intended as a second selection for the Chianti Classico. (PW)

● Chianti Classico★★ £B Riserva Bugialla★★★ £E
● Primamateria★★★★ £E   ● Il Labirinto★ £B

POGGIO AL SOLE   Chianti Classico   A: THt, Res, UnC, P&S

Owner: Giovanni Davaz   Fraz. Sambuca, Loc. Badia a Passignano, 50020 Tavarnelle Val di Pesa (FI)
Giovanni Davaz is one of a special group of Tuscan winemakers whose dedication in the vineyard and great care in maximising the potential of the grapes from a favoured site results in wines a breed apart from the increasing amounts of well-made wine in Tuscany. The 14 ha are in the vicinity of ANTINORI'S most famous vineyards. The majority of production is Chianti Classico, both a splendid, sleek, intense and stylish *normale* and a poised, elegant but graceful and beautifully defined Casasilia. There are also two concessions to international varieties: Selvasera is a Merlot/Cabernet Sauvignon blend but with similar refinement to Casasilia, while a Syrah, although lacking the concentration of a top Côte-Rôtie, has fine fruit and intensity and the length of flavour that characterises all the wines. Don't expect blockbusters or immediate gratification in these wines; instead, elegance triumphs over power. At least three years is needed for the

regular Chianti Classico and five or more for the other wines. (PW)

● **Chianti Classico★★★** £C Casasilia★★★★ £E
● **Seraselva★★★** £E ● **Syrah★★★** £E

POGGIO SCALETTE   A: **Mgi**, L&W

Owner: Adriana Assjé Di Marcorà-Fiore   Loc. Ruffoli, Via Barbiano 7, 50022 Greve in Chianti (FI)
Only one wine is made here by top enologist Vittorio Fiore, who put together this small 12.5-ha estate close
to QUERCIABELLA in the 1990s. Resurrecting an old vineyard with some very old vines he was able to
expand the estate and keeps only the best grapes for Il Carbonaione. The wine has always been 100 per cent
Sangiovese and is a very fine example, with pure fruit, ample breadth and depth and lovely harmony. It has
been consistently good since its first vintage in the difficult 1992 vintage and it was very impressive in the
somewhat uneven 98 vintage. 99 arguably shows the most promise of the recent fine trio of 01, 00 and 99.
Vittorio's son Jurij is now responsible for the vineyards and the day-to-day running of the estate. Though
the wine now qualifies as Chianti Classico, it retains IGT status as Alta Valle delle Greve, giving it some
regional definition in the absence of Chianti Classico sub-zones. (PW)
● **Il Carbonaione★★★★★** £F

POGGIOPIANO Chianti Classico   A: **Mer**, Con, Fal

Owner: Bartoli family   Via di Pisignano 29, 50025 San Casciano Val di Pesa (FI)
Not to be confused with Fattoria di Poggiopiano, this small property (Azienda Agricola Poggiopiano) is
found in San Casciano Val di Pesa in the north-west of the Chianti Classico zone and is run by Stefano
Bartoli and his brother Alessandro. Consultancy for the two wines comes from Luca D'Attoma. Most
remarkable is the premium red, Rosso di Sera, which combines a high 15 per cent of Colorino (an exciting
grape but seldom used in a significant percentage) with Sangiovese. The wine has a delicious spicy,
black-fruited depth and a lush texture but with a floral, cherry character that distinguishes it from less
interesting efforts that include Merlot instead. A second vineyard now supplements the estate vineyards of
only 9 ha but production of Rosso di Sera is limited to around 1,000 cases a year. If you manage to acquire
some, particularly from the most recent vintages (2001 is particularly recommended), it is worth waiting at
least five years before drinking it. In the interim there's 01 or 99 Chianti Classico, both with excellent
breadth, intensity and depth. (PW)
● **Chianti Classico★★** £C ● **Rosso di Sera★★★** £E

POLIZIANO www.carlettipoliziano.com   A: **Eno**, JNi, Res, N&P, F&M, Vne, V&C

Owner: Federico Carletti   Via Fontago 1, Loc. Montepulciano Stazione, 53040 Montepulciano (SI)
In the past two decades Poliziano (named for the Renaissance poet, Politian) has been propelled to the top
echelon of producers, not just in Montepulciano but in all of Tuscany, by its owner Federico Carletti.
Assisted for the past eight years by the brilliant Carlo Ferrini, he has given the wine range greater focus and
taken the quality consistently higher. Most encouraging has been the quality of the regular Vino Nobile,
with its atypical intensity and weight, which has continued to improve despite being made in increased
quantities (in excess of 10,000 cases). However, it is the top two wines that are most exciting. Asinone, from
a 9-ha vineyard, adds more breadth, complexity and sheer style over the regular version but with similar
preserved cherry fruit intensity. Le Stanze is an outstanding Tuscan Cabernet Sauvignon (close to five stars)
with wonderful depth and intensity but also shows increasing elegance and style. Other wines include a
Rosso di Montepulciano that is fuller and fleshier than any other versions and most resembles a good
Chianti Classico *normale*. Elegia, was a fine oak-aged Sangiovese made until 1995. Poliziano's 120 ha of
vineyard includes the Lohsa estate in the Maremma from which is produced very good Morellino di
Scansano. It includes 10 per cent Ciliegiolo and has a spicy, vibrant, pure fruit character and is adding more
depth as new vines come on stream. Also from Lohsa is the new Mandrone di Lohsa (from 2001), a
Cabernet Sauvignon-based wine that also includes Alicante and Petit Verdot. (PW)

Poliziano:
● **Vino Nobile di Montepulciano★★★** £C Asinone★★★★ £E
● **Le Stanze★★★★** £E ● **Rosso di Montepulciano★** £B
Azienda Agricola Lohsa:
● **Morellino di Scansano★★★** £C

QUERCIABELLA Chianti Classico www.querciabella.com A: **Pol**, Cam, Res, Han, F&R

Owner: Sebastiano Cossia Castiglioni Via di Barbiano 17, 50022 Greve in Chianti (FI)
One of Chianti Classico's grand estates, Querciabella is run by Sebastiano (son of its founder Giuseppe) Castiglioni, who is gently guided by winemaker Guido De Santi. The range from 26 ha of vineyards was until recently restricted to just four wines: Chianti Classico, a Riserva and red and white Super-Tuscans. All the wines have a certain strength as well as individuality – the structure amply supports a considerable richness of fine intense fruit (from low yields). Chianti Classico Riserva is no longer produced (last vintage 1999) but both this and *normale* include a little Cabernet Sauvignon and Merlot yet retain a distinctive Tuscan character. New from 2000 is Palafreno, a rich, refined blend of approximately equal parts Merlot and Sangiovese. This has been made to a similar standard to the deservedly acclaimed red Camartina, a wine of great class and intensity currently from Sangiovese and Cabernet Sauvignon as well as some Merlot and a little Syrah. It is not made when the quality is not up to scratch (no 1998, 92 or 89). Batàr, from Chardonnay and Pinot Bianco (65/35 in 2001), is a rich, powerful, complex white with an almost exotic fruit character. Earlier vintages were sometimes a little overblown but there has been less oak and more elegance since 1998. Of the reds, even the *normale* Chianti needs three years' ageing or more, Camartina a minimum of six or seven; Palafreno is a little more approachable. Look out for new wines from 36 ha of vineyards at Alberese in the Maremma. (PW)
● **Camartina★★★★★** £F ● **Palafreno★★★★** £E O **Batàr★★★** £E
● **Chianti Classico★★** £C Riserva★★★ £D

BARONE RICASOLI/CASTELLO DI BROLIO A: **Eno**, Cam, NYg, FWC, ThP, F&R

Owner: Ricasoli family Loc. Cantine del Castello di Brolio, 53013 Gaiole in Chianti (SI)
This noble property had a rough ride under corporate ownership for a couple of decades until it was re-acquired in 1993 by the Ricasoli family, led by Francesco Ricasoli. Brolio's importance in the modern era (Baron Bettino Ricasoli set out the parameters for Chianti Classico in the 1870s) added more clout to a decision taken four years later to establish a flagship Chianti Classico in a move to try to restore the pre-eminence of its name in the zone. The wine is made from 100 per cent Sangiovese from a selection of the best vineyards and aged in predominantly new French oak. Successive vintages, if quite oaky, are increasingly expansive and stylish. As the vineyards (the vast estate includes 227 ha of vines) continue to improve, so should the wine. That labelled simply Brolio is a 'second' wine. A classic nutty, biscuity Vin Santo is also made under the Castello di Brolio label. The Barone Ricasoli label, which also includes wine from bought-in grapes, includes Casalferro (recently a blend of Sangiovese with some Merlot), a consistently impressive red which shows typical concentration, intensity and ageing potential in the 1999 vintage. Torricella is a *barrique*-aged Chardonnay of increasing refinement while other wines of improving quality include the inexpensive Formulae, based on Sangiovese. New is Campo Ceni, a lightly oaked varietal Sangiovese. (PW)

Castello di Brolio:
● **Chianti Classico** Brolio★★ £C Castello di Brolio★★★★ £E
O **Vin Santo★★★** £D

Barone Ricasoli:
● **Chianti Classico** Riserva Rocca Guicciarda★ £C
● **Casalferro★★★** £E O **Torricella★★** £C

RIECINE Chianti Classico www.riecine.com A: **THt**, Dec, Han, UnC, F&M

Owner: Gary Baumann & Sean O'Callaghan Loc. Riecine, 53013 Gaiole in Chianti (SI)
Owned for more than two decades by Englishman John Dunkley, this small jewel already had a considerable reputation before coming under the control of American Gary Baumann in 1996/7. Dunkley had the good fortune, in 1971, to buy a vineyard already planted to a remarkably high-quality clone of Sangiovese and further small increases in vineyard area from sites scattered around the Gaiole commune have brought in more good fruit. The wines have always shown great concentration, intensity and a purity and elegance that have set them apart from most examples. More recently they have shed some of the austerity that some tasters found overwhelming, though they were never intended to be drunk in their youth. The wines will still age very well but now have a richer texture and greater suppleness. Chianti Classico is still best with three to five years' ageing, Riserva and La Gioia (also Sangiovese) with 6 to 10, sometimes more. No Riserva or La Gioia was made from the 2002 vintage but the regular Chianti Classico will be even better as a result. The stampede to the Maremma has even seduced Riecine, so expect new wines from new vineyards in Montecucco DOC in the future. Though not cheap, Riecine prices have always been a fair reflection of quality. (PW)
● **Chianti Classico**★★★ £D Riserva★★★★ £E
● **La Gioia**★★★★ £F

ROCCA DI MONTEGROSSI Chianti Classico A: **HSA**, UnC, P&S

Owner: Ricasoli-Firidolfi family & Marco Ricasoli Loc. Monti in Chianti 53010 Gaiole in Chianti (SI)
Marco Ricasoli's 18 ha have been cleaved from those of CASTELLO DI CACCHIANO, which is now under the control of his brother Giovanni. They are related to the Ricasoli family of the area's most famous estate, Castello di Brolio (see RICASOLI). Ever finer Chianti Classico (Sangiovese with 10 per cent Canaiolo, and the only wine produced in 2000) and Riserva (entirely Sangiovese from 1999) are becoming classic pure Tuscan wines. Geremia, 100 per cent Sangiovese up to and including 98, included 7 per cent Merlot in a transitional 99 but from the 01 vintage will be a Cabernet Sauvignon and Merlot blend. This emphasis on establishing the purity and typicity of Chianti Classico is to be admired and will hopefully set an example that others will follow. There is real distinction to the bright, vibrant fruit character in these composed, refined wines, as well as a depth and structure that ensure they age well. Regular Chianti Classico needs two to three years' ageing, the Riserva five and most vintages of Geremia need closer to 10. Marvellously rich Vin Santo is made in very small quantities. This is now a first-division estate and one to follow. (PW)
● **Chianti Classico**★★★ £C Riserva San Marcellino★★★★ £D
● **Geremia**★★★★ £E ○ **Vin Santo**★★★★ £E

RUFFINO www.ruffino.com A: **Alv**

Owner: Marco & Paolo Folonari Via Aretina 42/44, 50065 Pontassieve (FI)
One of the most famous Tuscan houses, Ruffino was divided in 2000 (see Ambrogio e Giovanni FOLONARI) and some of its prized vineyards, including those of the Nozzole estate, have been lost. Yet there are still great swathes of vineyard scattered around the leading wine zones. Vino Nobile di Montepulciano Lodola Nuova is not overly concentrated but shows some of the character of the appellation, while Brunello from Il Greppone Mazzi can be an attractive, savoury example in a good vintage. The real excitement comes from the Chianti Classico zone, which produces a wine of great class and breadth in top vintages, Riserva Ducale Oro. Slightly old-fashioned in style, it needs at least five to eight years' age but can last considerably longer. That without the gold (Oro) label is not of the same standard. Better still is Romitorio di Santedame (Colorino/Sangiovese), a highly original wine of great character and superb fruit but needing similar age to the Oro. Following the loss of the Cabreo wines, a new Chardonnay, Il Solatio, has been added. Modus is a relatively new red combining Sangiovese, Cabernet Sauvignon and Merlot with good balance and increasing style. Ruffino also makes an attractive white, Libaio (Chardonnay with a little Pinot Grigio) and the large-volume Chianti Classico Aziano. (PW)

Tenimenti Ruffino:
● **Chianti Classico** Santedame★★ £C Riserva Ducale★★ £C Riserva Ducale Oro★★★★ £E
● **Romitorio di Santedame★★★★★** £G ● **Modus★★★** £F

Il Greppone Mazzi:
● **Brunello di Montalcino★★** £E

Lodola Nuova:
● **Vino Nobile di Montepulciano★★** £E

SALVIONI/LA CERBAIOLA Brunello di Montalcino A: JAr, Lay, F&R

Owner: Giulio Salvioni Piazza Cavour 20, 53024 Montalcino (SI)
This classic handmade Brunello of great elegance and complexity is made in small quantities but such is its quality and expression of Montalcino-grown Sangiovese that it deserves to be tasted at least once. Given the dedication of its makers, Giulio Salvioni and his son Davide, there is no need to track down the most raved-about vintage either, as the quality of the wines from the mid-1990s (including an atypically fine 96 and beautifully balanced 98) seems certain to be maintained. Traditionally produced without any new oak, the wine undergoes a long maceration followed by around two years in large Slavonian oak casks. The wine is rich, deep and powerful with superb texture and definition and great expression both in aroma and flavour. The elevated 2.26-ha site of Cerbaiola usually yields little more than 5,000 bottles a year but quantities are vintage-dependent as the production of a little Rosso is used to help maintain the very high standards. (PW)
● **Brunello di Montalcino**✪✪✪✪✪ £G ● **Rosso di Montalcino★★★** £E

SAN FABIANO CALCINAIA Chianti Classico www.sanfabianocalcinaia.com A: GID

Owner: Guido Serio Loc. Cellole, 53011 Castellina in Chianti (SI)
Cellole is one of two estates that make up 34 ha of vineyard; the second, San Fabiano, is at lower altitude and 10 km from Castellina. Top consultant Carlo Ferrini has helped raise the quality of the reds. His hand is most evident in Cerviolo Rosso, a very worthy flagship wine. Seemingly somewhat unimaginative in its make-up of Sangiovese mixed with large helpings of Cabernet Sauvignon and Merlot (50/25/25 in 2000), it is nevertheless a very distinguished red of excellent concentration and density. Old vine fruit, earth and mineral notes add class and complexity. Regular Chianti Classico, aged only in one- and two-year oak is typically supple and stylish. The Riserva is potentially a lush, flattering red but is marked by too much oak in both 1999 and 00. A Chardonnay is also made but the balance isn't quite right yet in this either. (PW)
● **Cerviolo Rosso★★★★** £E
● **Chianti Classico★★** £B Riserva★★ £D

SAN FELICE Chianti Classico www.agricolasanfelice.com A: Cib, Fal, F&R

Owner: RAS SpA Loc. San Felice, 53019 Castelnuovo Berardenga (SI)
The property of insurance company Reunione Adriatica Sicurtà, this grand estate with 200 ha of vines is noted for its experiments with Sangiovese and other grapes (especially native varieties). During a long period of development under Enzo Morganti, both Vigorello, a Sangiovese/Cabernet Sauvignon blend, and a single-vineyard Chianti Classico Riserva Poggio Rosso (containing 10 per cent of Colorino) were created. Both wines can be long-lived, intense and stylish, but though richer, Vigorello can be dominated by its Cabernet component. A second Chianti Classico Riserva, Il Grigio, made in much greater quantities, is not of comparable quality but can offer a dense, chewy mouthful. The regular Chianti Classico, though a big-volume wine (50,000 cases), can show good fruit and perfume, especially in good vintages. Two whites are also made: a Chardonnay, Ancherona, and a Vermentino/Sauvignon Blanc blend, Belcaro. Also included in San Felice's production are 14 ha of vineyards of the Campogiovanni estate in Montalcino from which some fine Brunello has been produced, including an excellent 1995 (but below par 97 and 98), as well as a little Riserva Il Quercione. (PW)

San Felice:
● **Chianti Classico** Riserva Poggio Rosso★★ £C   ● **Vigorello**★★ £E
Campogiovanni:
● **Brunello di Montalcino**★★★★ £E

SAN FILIPPO - FANTI   Brunello di Montalcino

Owner: Filippo Baldassare Fanti   Loc. San Filippo, 53020 Montalcino (SI)
The Tenuta San Filippo includes 14 ha of vineyards in the south-east corner of the Montalcino zone. Owner Filippo Fanti is now in his third term as president of the Brunello *consorzio* and with the assistance of enologist Stefano Chioccioli has recently ensured that his own wines are up there amongst the best (other rising stars in Montalcino include FOSSACOLLE, LA FIORITA and LA TOGATA and SAN POLO). The depth, drive and structure in 1997, 98 and 99 are most impressive. Deep colour and an oak influence are characteristic but there is also good balance and harmony between fruit and oak. There's also the promise of marvellous complexity and texture with 10 years' age or more. Rosso di Montalcino is good too but in an internationally-styled Sant'Antimo Rosso (*barrique*-aged Sangiovese) the Sangiovese character has been somewhat snuffed out. Vin Santo is also made. (PW)
● **Brunello di Montalcino**★★★★ £E   ● **Rosso di Montalcino**★★ £C
● **Sant'Antimo Rosso**★ £B

SANGERVASIO   Colline Pisane   www.sangervasio.com   A: L&W

Owner: Tommasini family   Loc. San Gervasio, 56036 Palaia (SI)
Sangervasio is just one of several estates in the Pisa hills earning credibility for this zone relatively close to the Tuscan coast. Part of a large estate, 22 ha of vineyards are cultivated organically (biodynamic from 2003) and planting densities are being radically increased. The great potential here seems certain to be realised by Luca Tomassini, who currently employs top consultant Luca D'Attoma (who works at LE MACCHIOLE among others) to produce two intense, tightly structured reds. A Sirio is Sangiovese-based but including 5 per cent Cabernet Sauvignon while I Renai is oaky, powerful Merlot with a lot of extract but good ageing potential. Both wines need at least five years to show at their best. A second wine, Sangervasio (from Sangiovese, Merlot and Cabernet not used for the top reds) has been made since 2002. Also produced are Vin Santo, Recinaio, a dry white, Marna (Chardonnay, Vermentino and Sauvignon), and rosé, Aprico. (PW)
● **A Sirio**★★★ £E   ● **I Renai**★★★ £E
● **Sangervasio**★ £B

SAN GIUSTO A RENTENNANO   Chianti Classico   A: **Bal**, UnC, NYg, JAr

Owner: Martini di Cigala family   Loc. Monti, 53013 Gaiole in Chianti (SI)
This is a much venerated estate run by brothers Francesco and Luca Martini di Cigala and all the wines are made to a very high standard. The focus is very much on Sangiovese and as natural as possible an expression of it. The wines are particularly notable for strength allied to an intense preserved fruits quality which makes for complex, classy wines with the necessary age. In top years even the Chianti Classico *normale* shows these attributes and easily surpasses some of the more expensive offerings. The Riserva (with 5 per cent Canaiolo) is more muscular but shows exquisite fruit and great length and is only bettered by the premium Sangiovese, Percarlo, made from 5.5 ha of the estate's 30 ha of vineyards. This big, structured wine is made from very ripe fruit and subject to long ageing in *barrique* (more than 50 per cent new). It more closely resembles a top Brunello in style than most wines from the Classico zone and has a great track record. There's also an outstanding, wonderfully complex example of Vin Santo (based primarily on Malvasia) and from recent vintages a varietal blockbuster Merlot, La Ricolma, aged in 100 per cent new oak, but quantities of both are minuscule. Regular Chianti Classico excepted, don't drink any of the wines with less than six years' age; 10 or more is often better. In the 2000 vintage a new bottling of Chianti Classico, Le Baroncole, was produced instead of a Riserva. Prices are very fair. (PW)

● **Chianti Classico**★★ £C Riserva★★★ £D
● **Percarlo**★★★★ £E ● **La Ricolma**★★★★ £F
O **Vin Santo**★★★★ £F

ENRICO SANTINI Bolgheri A: **C&B,** F&R

Owner: Enrico Santini Loc. Campo alla Casa 74, 57022 Castagneto Carducci (LI)
Enrico Santini has 10 ha in Bolgheri and is its most interesting new star. His first vintage was as recent as 2000 and the vines are young but the leading wine, Montepergoli, is worth contrasting with the zone's heavyweights. Advice from near neighbour Michele SATTA and consultancy from Attilio Pagli have helped in producing a profound red of real vigour and intensity and lovely berry fruit aroma and flavour. The blend is mostly Cabernet Sauvignon, Merlot and Syrah with some Sangiovese. The latter contributes more to an attractive, spicy, perfumed second wine, Poggio al Moro, that represents much better value than equivalent wines from other Bolgheri producers. Both reds also show a refinement that Satta's can lack. Santini's white has good weight but could be more focused; from Sauvignon and Vermentino, the latter seems to contribute more to its character. (PW)
● **Bolgheri Rosso** Poggio al Moro★★ £C Montepergoli★★★★ £E
● **Bolgheri Bianco** Campo alla Casa★ £C

SASSICAIA/TENUTA SAN GUIDO www.sassicaia.com A: **Lib, JAr,** BBR, P&S, F&M,Vne

Owner: Marchese Nicolò Incisa della Rocchetta Loc. Capanne 27, 57020 Bolgheri (LI)
Much has been written about what is arguably Italy's single most famous wine, including a book by Marco Fini. Its production has been much expanded from the original elevated Castiglioncello vineyard that provided the first commercial and much celebrated vintage, 1968. The vast San Guido estate now has about 60 ha of vineyards spread over four main plots, resulting in a production in excess of 12,000 cases a year. The wine, for long sold as a *vino da tavola*, has since 1994 had its own special zone in the Bolgheri DOC, which the Marchese has done much to promote. It is now a blend of 85 per cent Cabernet Sauvignon and 15 per cent Cabernet Franc and is aged for up to two years in French *barriques* (a third new). The five-star rating applies only to outstanding vintages and, while efforts in the 1990s generally don't match exceptional vintages like 1985, most years still reveal a beautifully composed wine with a delicious sweet black fruits intensity and elegant complexity that is sustained on a very long finish. Five years' ageing is a minimum, the best will improve for 20 or more. A new wine called Guidalberto, more modestly priced and from different vineyards, was first made in the 2000 vintage. Composed of Merlot, Cabernet Sauvignon and Sangiovese (50/30/20), it is aged for 12 months in *barriques* and shows cool fruit and some sophistication. (PW)
● **Bolgheri Sassicaia**★★★★★ £G
● **Guidalberto**★★★ £E

MICHELE SATTA Bolgheri A: SCh, F&R

Owner: Michele Satta Loc. Vigna al Cavaliere 61, 57022 Castagneto Carducci (LI)
Michele Satta isn't one of Bolgheri's big names but makes some good wines from 30 ha of vineyards. Piastraia is the top wine, a blend of Sangiovese, Cabernet Sauvignon, Merlot and Syrah. It doesn't lack for extract or depth but sometimes wants for more refined tannins. Nonetheless it is usually full, complex and characterful. Cavaliere (previously Vigna al Cavaliere) is unusual in the zone in being pure Sangiovese and, if again characterful, it can be more angular than Piastraia. Whites have always been important: Costa di Guilia, from Vermentino and Sauvignon, is aromatic and attractive if no more; Giovin Re, a varietal Viognier, is very ripe and oak-influenced but lacks the structure and definition of good Condrieu. Basic Bolgheri Rosato and Bianco are also produced. (PW)
● **Bolgheri Rosso** Piastraia★★★ £E ● **Cavaliere**★★ £D
● **Giovin Re**★★ £C ● **Costa di Giulia**★ £B

FATTORIA SELVAPIANA   Chianti Rufina   A: **Lib**, Vne, ACh, Sel

Owner: Francesco Giuntini Antinori   Via Selvapiana 3, 50068 Rufina (FI)
For years this noble estate, in the Giuntini family since 1827, was the only rival to FRESCOBALDI's Nipozzano estate in the small but exciting zone of Chianti Rufina. The combination of energy and austerity in the wines when young can seem daunting to wine drinkers used to soft, oak-rich reds but there is both a purity to the fruit and refinement in the wines that sets them apart from all but the best Chianti Classico. From 25 ha of vineyards, Federico Masseti and consultant Franco Bernabei have been producing very good wines for a number of years, especially a single-vineyard Riserva Bucerchiale. It shows great intensity and depth but always deserves to be kept for at least six or seven years and will keep for as long again. A second single-vineyard wine, Fornace (previously sold as Chianti Rufina Riserva), contains an increasing amount of Cabernet Sauvignon and is more obvious and fleshy but with good complexity. A regular Riserva was last made in 1997 and was particularly good in the absence of Bucerchiale in that year due to frost. This wine now enriches a good *normale* that always requires a couple of years' age before drinking. Vin Santo is very good too with rich ripe fruit and a refined nutty complexity. (PW)
● **Chianti Rufina**★★ £B   Riserva Bucerchiale★★★★ £E
● **Fornace**★★★ £E   O **Vin Santo**★★★ £E

SETTE PONTI   www.tenutasetteponti.com   A: C&C, Res, Vts, Hfx

Owner: Moretti family   Loc. Oreno, Fraz. San Giustino Valdarno, 52020 Terranuova Bracciolini (AR)
This is a very slick and professional operation which has produced fabulous wines from the eastern side of the Valdarno in a very short space of time. Some 64 ha of vineyards are a mix of new and well-established plantings. The estimable Carlo Ferrini is the consultant winemaker. Oreno (3,000 cases) is from Sangiovese, Cabernet Sauvignon and Merlot (50/25/25). Crognolo, produced in slightly greater quantity (almost 4,000 cases), is 90 per cent Sangiovese with the balance partly from Merlot. Both are rich yet gently textured wines with a beautifully detailed fruit intensity. Oreno, as might be expected, is the more international of the two but is concentrated and very harmonious; Crognolo expresses more of its origins in a sweet-fruited expression of Sangiovese. It will be interesting to see if quality can be at least maintained as volume grows. It is worth noting that the wines are closer in quality than the price disparity suggests. Watch out for the estate blended red from Poggio al Lupo in the Maremma. (PW)
● **Oreno**★★★★ £F   ● **Crognolo**★★★ £D

SOLDERA   Brunello di Montalcino   www.soldera.it   A: **Bal**, Fal, Sec, F&R, Rae, UnC

Owner: Gianfranco Soldera   Case Basse, Loc. Villa Santa Restituta, 53024 Montalcino (SI)
Gianfranco Soldera's estate of just 8 ha is Brunello's most controversial. Sourced from some of Montalcino's best slopes (next to Gaja's PIEVE SANTA RESTITUTA), the grapes are grown organically with great effort going into not only maximising the fruit quality but also enriching the ecosystem. The winemaking is natural, with no temperature control, and a long and rigorous maceration precedes a stay of (often) more than five years in large oak *botti*. The resulting wines of, at times, extraordinary breadth and complexity can make most modern-styled efforts seem rather simplistic and one-dimensional. In certain vintages (such as 1995) Riservas are now produced from the two different vineyards of Intistieti and Case Basse but these are not released until six to seven years after the vintage. In other years a single Brunello is produced (designated Riserva if considered worthy). The best recent vintages are 1997, 95 and 90 (all five stars). Problems of stability due to high levels of volatility have occasionally been an issue in the past, but the greatest dilemma for most would-be drinkers is which car to sell in order to buy a case or two. (Prices are always £H). (PW)

TALENTI Brunello di Montalcino   A: **Bib,** Hfx

Owner: Riccardo Talenti   Loc. Pian di Conte, Fraz. Sant'Angelo in Colle, 53020 Montalcino (SI)
Riccardo Talenti's father was one of those instrumental in creating a worldwide reputation for Brunello. The 13-ha estate created by Pierluigi Talenti after receiving great acclaim for the Brunello of IL POGGIONE has been a reliable source of fine Brunello for nearly two decades. Enologist Carlo Ferrini now works with Riccardo and it will take some time to see how the style evolves. In the meantime, recent vintages show classic character, breadth and style with nicely covered tannins and will maintain the reputation for ageing very well. 1996 was a little weaker but by no means poor, 98 good for the vintage, 99 very promising, while both regular and Riserva versions in 95 and 97 can be drunk reasonably soon or kept for another 10 years. Talenti Rosso is a fruit-centred blend of Sangiovese, Syrah, Canaiolo and Colorino. (PW)
● **Brunello di Montalcino★★★★** £E Riserva★★★★ £F
● **Rosso di Montalcino★★** £C ● **Talenti★★** £C

TENUTA DI TRINORO www.trinoro.com   A: Sec, C&B, F&R

Owner: Andrea Franchetti Via Ribattola 2, 53047 Sarteano (SI)
From high up in the hills, a little way south of Montepulciano, come some of Tuscany's currently most talked-about wines. Andrea Franchetti is the creator of this estate established from virgin wine territory in 1992. Passing over Sangiovese, Bordeaux varieties, particularly Cabernet Franc, Merlot and Petit Verdot were chosen to be planted at high densities. At around 600 m altitude the 16 ha of vineyards would be too high further north in Tuscany, but the cool nights counter the summer heat experienced near the Umbrian and Lazio borders. Trinoro is the main wine and based primarily on Cabernet Franc (70 per cent) with about 20 per cent Merlot and the balance Cabernet Sauvignon and Petit Verdot. Clearly the terroir is something special, given not only the richness but also the originality of the wine. While the vines are still young, yields are very low and there is marvellously pure, concentrated black fruit and a hint of wild herbs in a refined structure. A new second wine, Le Cupole di Trinoro, has been introduced and a tiny amount of Cincinnato is also made from the local variety Cesanese d'Affile. Palazzi, a blend of roughly equal parts Merlot and Cabernet Franc, was made until 1999. Franchetti has also invested in establishing a new vineyard on the northern slopes of Mount Etna in Sicily. Passopisciaro is old-vine Nerello Mascalese from an existing leased vineyard. (PW)
● **Tenuta di Trinoro★★★★** £G

TUA RITA Val di Cornia   A: **L&S, JAr,** Fal, F&R

Owner: Rita Tua Loc. Notri 81, 57028 Suvereto (LI)
Tua Rita and more recently Montepeloso have set the standards for Suvereto, one of Tuscany's brightest new zones since the mid-90s. The Merlot, Redigaffi, is among Tuscany's half-dozen top Merlots but continues to be made in tiny quantities that mean it is of somewhat academic interest to most wine drinkers. Rather more of the Cabernet/Merlot blend (roughly two parts Cabernet to one of Merlot), Giusto di Notri, is produced, but in an equally powerful, dense, expansive style and with similarly excellent texture and balance. While some patience is needed, both wines promise to keep for at least a decade. The wine currently made in the greatest quantity and often overlooked in all the hype is the red Perlato del Bosco. Produced from Sangiovese, it is also considerably more affordable and has seductive, forward fruit but good depth and style too. Whites, too, are worthy; the oak-fermented and aged Lodano (previously known as Sileno) is an aromatic, creamy blend of Chardonnay, Gewürztraminer and Riesling. Production is being increased but much of the 30 ha of vineyards are young vines and it will be some time before more significant quantities of the top wines (with their demand-inflated prices) are available. (PW)
● **Redigaffi★★★★★** £H ● **Giusto di Notri★★★★★** £F
● **Perlato del Bosco★★★** £D O **Lodano★★** £C

VALDICAVA Brunello di Montalcino   A: **VDu**, Tur, F&R

Owner: Vincenzo Abbruzzese Fraz. Valdicava, 53024 Montalcino (SI)
One of Brunello's small growers, this estate has come to the fore under the direction of Vincenzo Abbruzzese (though it has belonged to his family for half a century) and the winemaking skills of Attilio Pagli. The style is for Brunello of real weight, power and richness without recourse to new oak and there is excellent complexity and dimension. The wines don't usually lack for depth and the 1999 now puts Valdicava up amongst the best going. There is usually the structure to improve for at least a decade, and longer in the Riserva Madonna del Piano (from 1998, 97, 95 or 90). Regular Brunello was very good in 95 and 97, and super in 99. Though savoury and flavoursome, 96 and to a lesser extent 98 are much more advanced. Both 97 and 98 Riservas are very good but need at least another five years. 2002 Rosso di Montalcino is particularly good and is in the mini-Brunello mould as no Brunello will be offered in this vintage. (PW)
● **Brunello di Montalcino**★★★★ £F Riserva Madonna del Piano★★★★★ £G
● **Rosso di Montalcino**★★★ £C

TENUTA DI VALGIANO Colline Lucchesi www.valgiano.it   A: Sec

Owner: Moreno Petrini Via di Valgiano 7, Loc. Valgiano, 55010 Capannori (LU)
The Lucchese hills are the northernmost of several pockets of viticulture gaining prominence on the western coast of Tuscany. Valgiano is arguably the leading estate but it is only one of several of emerging importance in the area. The 16 ha of vineyards are on poor gravelly soils at around 250 m altitude, between the coast and the Apennines. Much importance is placed on ensuring that the wines express their origins and a sense of place; organic practices are employed to this end. The estate red is 60 per cent Sangiovese with the balance from Syrah and Merlot, and is rich and succulent with good depth and balance. Palistorti is a similar blend but from younger vines; effectively a second wine, it is lighter and more perfumed but has good depth and intensity too. The most stylish red, however, is the racy Scasso dei Cesari, a pure Sangiovese from 40-year-old vines from two contrasting soil types. A cooling Apennine influence favours the retention of acidity and the production of a characterful white, Giallo dei Muri. A blend of mostly Vermentino, Trebbiano and Malvasia but also including a little Chardonnay, it was less successful in 2002. The top two reds are on good form in both 2000 and 01 vintages. All the wines are now sold under the Colline Lucchesi DOC. (PW)
● **Colline Lucchesi** Tenuta di Valgiano★★★ £E Scasso dei Cesari★★★ £E
● **Colline Lucchesi** Rosso dei Palistorti★★ £C ○ **Colline Lucchesi** Giallo dei Muri★ £B

FATTORIA VALTELLINA Chianti Classico www.fattoria-valtellina.com   A: Hfx

Owner: Fattoria Valtellina srl Loc. Rietine, 53013 Gaiole in Chianti (SI)
Valtellina is a small estate whose wines have commanded a premium ever since acquiring an enviable reputation under Giorgio Regni. In recent years the wines have been made by Andreas Stössel with some input from the much-consulted Vittorio Fiore. They are not of the easy-going, quaffing type but rather firm, dense, powerful wines with lots of extract that can require some patience. There is a tendency to overripeness in the top wines in the best years but this doesn't compromise their ageing potential. If the wines could occasionally use a little more harmony and finesse they don't want for flavour, complexity or power. Convivio is three parts Sangiovese to one part Cabernet Sauvignon while the newer Il Duca (di Montechioccioli) swells the ranks of varietal Tuscan Merlots. A note of caution – recent tastings of both Chiantis show questionable levels of volatility. (PW)
● **Chianti Classico**★★ £C Riserva★★★ £E
● **Convivio**★★★ £E ● **Il Duca**★★★ £G

VECCHIE TERRE DI MONTEFILI Chianti Classico   A: **RsW**, Rae, N&P

Owner: Roccaldo Acuti Via San Cresci 47, 50022 Greve in Chianti (FI)
The reputation of this estate, the property of the Acuti family since 1979, rests primarily with two very fine

Super-Tuscans. The quality and symmetry of the wines was recognised in the 1980s and has been maintained due to the skill of Vittorio Fiore. Bruno di Rocca is a Cabernet Sauvignon/Sangiovese blend and usually a stylish but concentrated fusion of berryish fruit and elegant oak after some ageing. More distinctive, with a lovely complexity and acquiring an increasingly rich and smooth texture with age, is a pure Sangiovese, Anfiteatro. Regular Chianti Classico also shows a stylish complexity but evolves more quickly than some *normale*. A white, Villa Regis, is a *barrique*-aged blend of Chardonnay that includes some Sauvignon Blanc and Traminer; while attractive and well-made, it is not for long-keeping. (PW)

● **Bruno di Rocca★★★★** £F   ● **Anfiteatro★★★★** £F
● **Chianti Classico★** £C   O **Vigna Regis★** £D

VILLA CAFAGGIO   Chianti Classico   www.villacafaggio.it   A: BBR, Amp, N&P, Vne

Owner: Basilica Cafaggio (Casa Girelli) Via San Martino in Cecione 5, 50022 Panzano (FI)
A very professionally directed estate, Villa Cafaggio is a dependable name for high-quality Chianti Classico and Tuscan blends. Stefano Farkas produces ripe, vibrant, almost chewy wines with lovely perfume and sweet fruit on the palate. There are 30 ha of vineyards in Panzano's Conca d'Oro as well as a further 10 ha that are leased; they are planted mostly to Sangiovese but also to some Cabernet Sauvignon and Merlot. Efforts to maximise fruit quality include the selection of, and replanting with, superior clones as well as the adoption of green harvesting. In the winery, the use of concentrated must adds richness in lighter years, while micro-oxygenation has also been employed since the 1999 vintage. New oak is important to the style of the wines, enhancing both structure and flavour – 100 per cent is used in the top two wines. San Martino, from a single vineyard, is now pure Sangiovese (older vintages include a little Cabernet), while Cortaccio is 100 per cent Cabernet Sauvignon but used to include a little Sangiovese. Both add a little more concentration and style over a very good Chianti Classico Riserva. A single-vineyard Riserva Solatio Basilica (from 4 ha) is even better but has not been made in the most recent vintages due to replanting. All the wines benefit from a little extra age, Chianti Classico *normale* is best with three years, Riserva with four or five and Cortaccio and San Martino with at least five years. Prices are reasonable for the quality. (PW)

● **Chianti Classico★★** £C   Riserva★★★ £D   Riserva Solatio Basilica★★★ £D
● **Cortaccio★★★** £E   ● **San Martino★★★** £E

VILLA PILLO   www.villapillo.com   A: L&S

Owner: John & Kathe Dyson Via Volterrana 24, 50050 Gambassi Terme (FI)
Villa Pillo is one of a number of estates to show that good wine is not restricted to the well-established areas or even the much vaunted newer regions of the coastal or southern Maremma. Being off the beaten track, north of San Gimignano, and with reds from non-native varieties may not endear the estate to everyone but the wines are both interesting and of good quality. Marco Chellini now makes the wines but 90s vintages were made by Paolo di Marchi of ISOLE E OLENA. Syrah has been the star wine, with some lovely pepper, berry and mineral character as well as a fleshy succulence. Merlot too shows good fruit intensity, while Vivaldaia from Cabernet Franc has an overly herbaceous, green component yet can also show good depth and texture. Vin Santo, only released with five years' age has good dried fruit, brazils and walnut complexity but promises more fruit richness than previously in the 1997 version. Borgoforte is a simple, fruity red of variable composition. (PW)

● **Syrah★★★** £E   ● **Merlot** Sant'Adele★★★ £E
● **Vivaldaia★** £E   O **Vin Santo del Chianti★★★** £E

OTHER WINES OF NOTE

FATTORIA AMBRA ● **Carmignano** Vigna Santa Cristina in Pilli £B Riserva Le Vigne Alte Montalbiolo £C
● **Carmignano** Riserva Elzana £C
BADIA A COLTIBUONO ● **Chianti Classico** Riserva £D   ● **Sangioveto** (Sangiovese) £F
BADIA DI MORRONA ● **Vigna Alta** (Sangiovese) £D
● **N'Antia** (Sangiovese/Cabernet Sauvignon/Merlot) £D
FATTORIA DEI BARBI ● **Brunello di Montalcino** Riserva Vigna del Fiore £E
BARICCI ● **Brunello di Montalcino** £E
BINDELLA ● **Vino Nobile di Montepulciano** £C   ● **Vallocaia** (Sangiovese/Cabernet Sauvignon) £D
BORGO SALCETINO ● **Chianti Classico** Riserva Lucarello £D   ● **Rossole** (Sangiovese/Merlot) £D
BRUNELLI ● **Brunello di Montalcino** £E
CAMPOSILIO ● **Camposilio** (Sangiovese/Merlot/Cabernet Sauvignon) £D
CANALICCHIO DI SOPRA ● **Brunello di Montalcino** £E   ● **Rosso di Montalcino** £C
PODERE CAPACCIA ● **Chianti Classico** £C Riserva £D   ● **Querciagrande** (Sangiovese) £E
G FUSO CARMIGNANI ● **For Duke** (Syrah/Sangiovese) £D   ○ **Vin Santo** £E
CAROBBIO ● **Chianti Classico** £C Riserva £D   ● **Leone** (Sangiovese) £D
● **Pietraforte** (Cabernet Sauvignon) £D
CASA EMMA ● **Chianti Classico** £C Riserva £E   ● **Soloio** (Merlot) £F
CASAFRASSI ● **Chianti Classico** £C
CASALE-FALCHINI ○ **Vernaccia di San Gimignano** Ab Vinea Doni £B
● **Campora** (Cabernet Sauvignon) £C
CASTEL RUGGERO ● **Chianti Classico** £C
CASTELLO D'ALBOLA (Zonin) ● **Chianti Classico** Riserva £D
● **Acciaiolo** (Sangiovese/Cabernet Sauvignon) £E
CASTELLO DEL TREBBIO ● **Chianti Rufina** Riserva Lastricato £C
● **Pazzesco** (Merlot/Syrah/Sangiovese) £C
CASTELLO DI BOSSI ● **Chianti Classico** £B Riserva Berardo £D   ● **Girolamo** (Merlot) £E
● **Corbaia** (Sangiovese/Cabernet Sauvignon) £F
CASTELLO DI CACCHIANO ● **Chianti Classico** Millennio £D
CASTELLO DI FARNETELLA ● **Chianti Colli Senesi** £B   ● **Lucilla** (Sangiovese/Merlot) £B
● **Poggio Granoni** (Sangiovese/Cabernet Sauvignon/Syrah) £F
CASTELLO DI MELETO ● **Fiore** (Sangiovese) £D
CASTELLO DI QUERCETO ● **Cignale** (Cabernet Sauvignon/Merlot) £E
● **Il Querciolaia** (Sangiovese/Cabernet Sauvignon) £E   ● **La Corte** (Sangiovese) £E
CECCHI ● **Spargolo** (Sangiovese) £E   ● **Morellino di Scansano** Riserva Val delle Rose £C
CENNATOIO ● **Chianti Classico Riserva** £D Riserva O'Leandro £D   ● **Etrusco** (Sangiovese) £E
CENTOLANI ● **Brunello di Montalcino** Tenuta Friggiali £E Pietranera £E
CERRO DEL MASSO ● **Chianti** £B
CESANI ● **Luenzo** (Sangiovese/Colorino) £C   ○ **Vernaccia di San Gimignano** Sanice £B
GIOVANNI CHIAPPINI ● **Guado de' Gemoli** (Cabernet Sauvignon/Merlot) £E
CIMA ○ **Vermentino** £C   ○ **Candia dei Colli Apuani** Vigneto Candia Alto £C
● **Anchigi** (Sangiovese) £C   ● **Romalbo** (Sangiovese/Massaretta) £D   ● **Montervo** (Merlot) £D
DONATELLA CINELLI COLOMBINI ● **Brunello di Montalcino** £E Riserva £F
● **Brunello di Montalcino** Progetto Prime Donne £E   ● **Rosso di Montalcino** £C
COLIBERTO ● **Monteregio di Massa Marittima** Riserva Thesan (Sangiovese/Cabernet Sauvignon) £C
COLLE SANTA MUSTIOLA ● **Poggio Ai Chiari** (Sangiovese/Colorino) £D
COLLELUNGO ● **Chianti Classico** £C Riserva £D Roveto £E
COLLEMATTONI ● **Brunello di Montalcino** £D
COLLESORBO ● **Brunello di Montalcino** £E Riserva £F   ● **Rosso di Montalcino** £C
CONTUCCI ● **Vino Nobile di Montepulciano** £C
DEL CERRO (Saiagricola) ● **Vino Nobile di Montepulciano** £C Antica Chiusina £E
● **Manero** (Sangiovese) £E   ● **Poggio Golo** (Merlot) £E
FASSATI (Fazi Battaglia) ● **Vino Nobile di Montepulciano** Pasiteo £C Riserva Salarco £D
FATTORIA DI FIANO/UGO BING ● **Chianti Colli Fiorentini** £B

● **Fianesco** (Sangiovese & others) £D
FOSSACOLLE ● **Brunello di Montalcino** £E
GUALDO AL MELO ● **Bolgheri** £C
GUICCIARDINI STROZZI/FATTORIA CUSONA ● **Sòdole** (Sangiovese) £D
● **Millanni** (Sangiovese/Cabernet Sauvignon/Merlot) £E ● **Selvascura** (Merlot) £C
I BALZINI/FILIPUTTI & D'ISANTO ● **I Balzini** (Sangiovese/Cabernet Sauvignon) £E
I GIUSTI & ZANZA ● **Dulcamara** (Cabernet/Merlot) £E ● **Belcore** (Sangiovese/Merlot) £C
IL BORRO ● **Il Borro** (Merlot/Cabernet Sauvignon/Syrah/Petit Verdot) £F
IL BRUSCELLO ● **Val di Cornia** Loco dei Frati £D
IL CARNASCIALE ● **Caberlot** £F
IL CORNO ● **Colorino dell' Corno** (Colorino) £E
IL MACCHIONE ● **Vino Nobile di Montepulciano** Riserva Caggiole £C
INCONTRI (Martelli & Busdraghi) ● **Val di Cornia** Lago Bruno £D
LA CIARLIANA ● **Vino Nobile di Montepulciano** £C Riserva £D
LA COMANDINA ● **Vintore** (Sangiovese/Colorino) £D
LA FIORITA ● **Brunello di Montalcino** £F ● **Laurus** (Sangiovese/Merlot) £C
LA GERLA ● **Brunello di Montalcino** £E Riserva £F
LA NOVELLA ● **Chianti Classico** £B Riserva £D
IL PARADISO DI FRASSINO ● **Brunello di Montalcino** Montosoli £E
● **Do - 12 Uve** (Sangiovese/Cabernet Sauvignon/Petit Verdot/Syrah) £C
LA PARRINA ● **Parrina Rosso** Muraccio £B Riserva £C
LA PODERINA (Saiagricola) ● **Brunello di Montalcino** £E Poggio Banale £F
● **Rosso di Montalcino** £C
LA QUERCE ● **Chianti Colli Fiorentini** La Torretta £C ● **La Querce** (Sangiovese/Colorino) £D
LA RAMPA DI FUGNANO ● **Bombereto** (Sangiovese) £C ● **Gisèle** (Merlot) £E
LA REGOLA ● **Montescudaio** La Regola (Sangiovese/Merlot/Cabernet Sauvignon) £C
LA RENDOLA ● **L'Incanto** (Sangiovese/Merlot) £C ● **La Pineta** (Sangiovese) £C
LA SELVA ● **Prima Causa** (Cabernet Sauvignon/Merlot) £D
LA TOGATA/TENUTA CARLINA ● **Brunello di Montalcino** £F
PODERE LA VIGNA ● **Brunello di Montalcino** £E ● **Rosso di Montalcino** £C
LAVACCHIO ● **Chianti Rufina** £B Riserva £C
● **Cortigiano** (Cabernet Sauvignon/Merlot/Sangiovese) £D
PODERE LE BONCIE/LE TRAME ● **Chianti Classico** Le Trame £C
LE CALCINAIE O **Vernaccia di San Gimignano** Vigna ai Sassi £C
● **Teodoro** (Sangiovese/Merlot/Cabernet Sauvignon) £C
LE CALVANE ● **Chianti Colli Fiorentini** Riserva Il Trecione £C
● **Borro del Boscone** (Cabernet Sauvignon) £D
LE CASALTE ● **Vino Nobile di Montepulciano** £C Riserva £C
LE CINCIOLE ● **Chianti Classico** £B Riserva Petresco £D
LE FONTI ● **Chianti Classico** Riserva £C ● **Fontissimo** (Sangiovese/Cabernet) £D
LE SORGENTI ● **Chianti Colli Fiorentini** £B ● **Scirus** (Merlot/Cabernet) £D
CANTINE LEONARDO DA VINCI ● **Chianti** £B Poggio de' Sassiduri £B Riserva £C
● **San Zio** (Sangiovese) £D ● **Sant' Ippolito** (Merlot/Syrah) £D O **Ser Piero** (Chardonnay) £B
COSTANZA MALFATTI ● **Morellino di Scansano** £D
MANNUCCI DROANDI ● **Chianti Classico** Riserva Ceppeto £C ● **Campolucci** (Sangiovese) £D
MANTELLASSI ● **Morellino di Scansano** Riserva £C Riserva Le Sentinelle £C
● **Querciolaia** (Alicante) £C
MARCHESI PANCRAZI/TENUTA DI BAGNOLO ● **Pinot Nero Villa di Bagnolo** £D
MASSIA VECCHIA ● **Terziere** (Alicante) £D ● **La Fonte di Pietrarsa** (Cabernet Sauvignon/Merlot) £E
MELINI ● **Chianti Classico** Riserva Vigneti La Selvanella £D
MERLINI ● **Guadi Piani** (Sangiovese/Cabernet Sauvignon) £C
CANTINA DI MONTALCINO ● **Brunello di Montalcino** £E
MONTECALVI ● **Montecalvi** (Sangiovese & other) £E
MONTELLORI ● **Salamartano** (Cabernet Sauvignon/Merlot) £D ● **Dicatum** (Sangiovese) £D
SILVIO NARDI ● **Brunello di Montalcino** Vigneto Manachiara £F
NITTARDI ● **Chianti Classico** Riserva £D

NOTTOLA ● **Vino Nobile di Montepulciano** Vigna del Fattore £C
OLIVETO ● **Brunello di Montalcino** £F ● **Rosso di Montalcino** Il Roccolo £B
PALAZZO VECCHIO ● **Vino Nobile di Montepulciano** £B
PANIZZI ○ **Vernaccia di San Gimignano** £C Riserva £D
● **San Gimignano** Folgóre (Sangiovese/Merlot/Cabernet Sauvignon) £E
PANZANELLO ● **Chianti Classico** £B Riserva £C
PARADISO ● **Paterno II** (Sangiovese) £D ● **Saxa Calida** (Cabernet Sauvignon/Merlot) £E
PETRA ● **Val di Cornia** £C
FATTORIA DI PETROIO ● **Chianti Classico** £B Riserva £D
PIAGGIA/MAURO VANNUCCI ● **Carmignano** Riserva £D
PIANCORNELLO ● **Brunello di Montalcino** £E
PIAZZANO ● **Chianti** Riserva Rio Camerata £C
ENRICO PIERAZZUOLI ● **Carmignano** Riserva Le Farnete £E ● **Chianti Montalbano** Riserva £C
● **Chianti Classico** Matroneo £C
AGOSTINA PIERI ● **Brunello di Montalcino** £E ● **Rosso di Montalcino** £C
POGGIO ANTICO ● **Brunello di Montalcino** £E Altero £E Riserva £F
POGGIO ARGENTIERA ● **Morellino di Scansano** Bellamarsilia £C Capatosta £D
POGGIO GAGLIARDO ○ **Montescudaio** Linaglia (Vermentino based) £B Vignalontana (Chardonnay) £B
● **Montescudaio** Rosso (Sangiovese/Ciliegiolo/Canaiolo) £B Malemacchie (Sangiovese based) £B
● **Montescudaio** Gobbo ai Pianacci (Merlot/Cabernet Sauvignon/Sangiovese) £D
● **Montescudaio** Ultimosole (Cabernet Sauvignon/Cabernet Franc) £C Rovo (Sangiovese) £D
POGGIOLUNGO ● **Morellino di Scansano** Riserva £C
POGGIO DI SOTTO ● **Brunello di Montalcino** £G
POGGIO SAN POLO ● **Brunello di Montalcino** £F ● **Rosso di Montalcino** £D
● **Mezzo Pane** (Sangiovese/Cabernet Sauvignon) £E
PRATESI ● **Carmignano** £D
QUERCIA AL POGGIO ● **Chianti Classico** £C Riserva £D
RISECCOLI ● **Chianti Classico** Riserva £D ● **Saeculum** (Sangiovese/Cabernet Sauvignon/Merlot) £F
○ **Vin Santo del Chianti Classico** £D
ROCCA DELLE MACÌE ● **Roccato** (Sangiovese/Cabernet Sauvignon) £E
● **Ser Gioveto** (Sangiovese) £E
ROCCA DI CASTAGNOLI ● **Chianti Classico** £B Riserva Capraia £C
● **Buriano** (Cabernet Sauvignon) £F ● **Stielle** (Sangiovese/Cabernet Sauvignon) £E
ROCCACCIA ● **Fontenova** (Sangiovese/Ciliegiolo) £C ● **Poggio Cavalluccio** (Ciliegiolo) £D
RUSSO ● **Val di Cornia** Ceppitaio £B Riserva Barbicone (Sangiovese) £D
● **Sassobucato** (Merlot/Cabernet Sauvignon) £D
PODERE SALICUTTI ● **Brunello di Montalcino** £F ● **Rosso di Montalcino** £C
● **Dopoteatro** (Cabernet Sauvignon/Sangiovese/Canaiolo) £D
SAN FILIPPO – ROSI ● **Brunello di Montalcino** £F
SASSOTONDO ● **Sovana** Superiore Franze (Sangiovese) £C ● **San Lorenzo** (Ciliegiolo) £D
SCOPETONE ● **Brunello di Montalcino** £E ● **Rosso di Montalcino** £C
SERRAIOLA ○ **Monteregio di Massa Marittima** Violina (Vermentino) £C
● **Monteregio di Massa Marittima** Lentisco (Sangiovese) £C
● **Campo Montecristo** (Sangiovese/Merlot/Syrah) £D
SESTI/CASTELLO DI ARGIANO ● **Brunello di Montalcino** £F ● **Rosso di Montalcino** £D
● **Sant'Antimo** Terra di Siena (Cabernet Sauvignon/Merlot) £E
SOLARIA - PATRIZIA CENCIONI ● **Brunello di Montalcino** £F ● **Rosso di Montalcino** £C
SORBAIANO ○ **Montescudaio** Lucestraia (Sauvignon/Vermentino/Trebbiano) £C
● **Pian di Conte** (Sangiovese) £C ● **Montescudaio** Rosso delle Miniere £D
SUVERAIA ● **Monteregio di Massa Marittima** Bacucco di Suveraia £D
TERRABIANCA ● **Chianti Classico** Riserva Croce £C ● **Piano del Cipresso** (Sangiovese) £C
● **Ceppate** (Cabernet Sauvignon/Merlot) £E ● **Campaccio Riserva** (Sangiovese/Cabernet Sauvignon) £E
TERRE DEL SILLABO ● **Niffo** (Cabernets/Sangiovese/Merlot) £E
TERUZZI E PUTHOD ○ **Terre di Tufi** (Vernaccia/Malvasia/Vermentino) £C
○ **Carmen** (Sangiovese – vinified as a white) £C
GIULIANO TIBERI ● **Le Vespe** (Sangiovese based) £C

TORRACCIA DI PRESURA ● **Chianti Classico** Il Tarocco £B Riserva Il Tarocco £C
TREROSE (Tenementi Angelini) ● **Vino Nobile di Montepulciano** La Villa £D Simposio £E
FATTORIA UCCELLIERA ● **Castellaccio** (Sangiovese/Cabernet Sauvignon) £D
VAL DI SUGA (Tenementi Angelini) ●　　**Brunello di Montalcino** £E
VALDIPIATTA ● **Vino Nobile di Montepulciano** Riserva £E
● **Tre Fonti** (Cabernet Sauvignon/Sangiovese/Canaiolo) £D
FATTORIA VARRAMISTA ● **Varramista** (Syrah/Merlot/Sangiovese) £D
VIGNAMAGGIO ● **Chianti Classico** Riserva Monna Lisa £C
● **Obsession** (Cabernet Sauvignon/Merlot) £E O **Vin Santo** £E
VILLA ARCENO ● **Chianti Classico** Riserva £C
● **Arguzzio** (Merlot/Cabernet Sauvignon/Sangiovese) £E
VILLA MONTE RICO ● **Val di Cornia** £C
VILLA SANT' ANNA ● **Vino Nobile di Montepulciano** £C
● **I Valloni** (Sangiovese/Cabernet Sauvignon) £D
WANDANNA ● **Montecarlo Rosso** Terre dei Cascinieri £C
● **Virente** (Syrah/Merlot/Cabernet Sauvignon) £D

Author's Choice (PW)

20 classic Tuscans reds
ANTINORI ● **Solaia**
AVIGNONESI ● **Vino Nobile di Montepulciano** Riserva Grandi Annate
BOSCARELLI ● **Vino Nobile di Montepulciano** Vigna del Nocio
CAPANNELLE ● **50 & 50**
CASTELLO DI RAMPOLLA ● **Vigna d'Alceo**
CORZANO & PATERNO ● **Il Corzano**
GAGLIOLE ● **Gagliole Rosso**
ISOLE E OLENA ● **Cepparello**
LE PUPILLE ● **Saffredi**
MONTEVERTINE ● **Le Pergole Torte**
PETROLO ● **Galatrona**
POGGIOPIANO ● **Rosso di Sera**
POLIZIANO ● **Vino Nobile di Montepulciano** Asinone
RIECINE ● **La Gioia**
RUFFINO ● **Romitorio di Santedame**
QUERCIABELLA ● **Camartina**
SAN GIUSTO A RENTENNANO ● **Percarlo**
SETTE PONTI ● **Crognolo**
TENUTA DI TRINORO ● **Tenuta di Trinoro**
VECCHIE TERRE DI MONTEFILI ● **Anfiteatro**

12 outstanding Chianti
CASTELLO DI AMA ● **Chianti Classico** Vigneto Bellavista
CASTELLO DI FONTERUTOLI ● **Chianti Classico** Castello di Fonterutoli
CASTELLO DI VOLPAIA ● **Chianti Classico** Riserva Coltassala
CASTELLO VICCHIOMAGGIO ● **Chianti Classico** Riserva La Prima
FATTORIA DI FELSINA ● **Chianti Classico** Riserva Vigneto Rancia
FONTODI ● **Chianti Classico**
FRESCOBALDI ● **Chianti Rufina** Montesodi
IL PALAZZINO ● **Chianti Classico** Grosso Sanese
LA MASSA ● **Chianti Classico** Giorgio Primo
POGGIO AL SOLE ● **Chianti Classico** Casasilia
FATTORIA SELVAPIANA ● **Chianti Rufina** Riserva Bucerchiale
ROCCA DI MONTEGROSSI ● **Chianti Classico** Riserva San Marcellino

12 diverse top quality Brunello

BANFI ● Brunello di Montalcino Riserva Poggio all'Oro

TENUTA CAPARZO ● Brunello di Montalcino Vigna La Casa

CASANOVA DI NERI ● Brunello di Montalcino Tenuta Nuova

COL D'ORCIA ● Brunello di Montalcino Riserva Poggio al Vento

COSTANTI ● Brunello di Montalcino Riserva

FULIGNI ● Brunello di Montalcino Vigneti dei Cottimelli

MASTROJANNI ● Brunello di Montalcino Schiena d'Asino

SIRO PACENTI ● Brunello di Montalcino

PERTIMALI/LIVIO SASSETTI ● Brunello di Montalcino Riserva

PIEVE SANTA RESTITUTA ● Brunello di Montalcino Sugarille

SALVIONI/LA CERBAIOLA ● Brunello di Montalcino

SAN FILIPPO - FANTI ● Brunello di Montalcino

12 coastal marvels

ANTINORI/GUADO AL TASSO ● Bolgheri Rosso

CASTELLO DEL TERRICCIO ● Lupicaia

TENUTA DI GHIZZANO ● Veneroso

GRATTAMACCO/COLLE MASSARI ● Bolgheri Rosso Superiore

LE MACCHIOLE ● Scrio

MONTEPELOSO ● Nardo

TENUTA DELL'ORNELLAIA ● Bolgheri Rosso Superiore Ornellaia

SANGERVASIO ● A Sirio

ENRICO SANTINI ● Bolgheri Rosso Montepergoli

SASSICAIA/TENUTA SAN GUIDO ● Bolgheri Sassicaia

TUA RITA ● Redigaffi

TENUTA DI VALGIANO ● Tenuta di Valgiano

Central Italy

Just as culturally there is so much to be discovered just beyond the bounds of Tuscany so it is when it comes to viticulturally derived masterpieces. This is not a section of also-rans but includes exciting top-quality producers – some working in a Tuscan vein but with much more to offer besides. Away from those famous appellations can be found an increasing number of fine reds from not only from the likes of Sangiovese, Sagrantino and Montepulciano, native in these diverse regions, but also Cabernet Sauvignon and Merlot, as well as stylish whites from Verdicchio.

Emilia-Romagna

Emilia has, besides **Lambrusco** (with four DOC zones of its own), two significant DOCs for hillsides to the south of the cities of Piacenza and Bologna. Both the **Colli Piacentini** (contiguous with Lombardy's Oltrepò Pavese) and **Colli Bolognesi** can produce decent Cabernet Sauvignon and Barbera as well as Chardonnay, Sauvignon and Malvasia. **Gutturnio** is a speciality of the former, a blend of Barbera and Bonarda of good character and quality from a handful of producers. Much more exciting in viticulture terms is Romagna, where the best Sangioveses outside Tuscany are now produced. Though much **Sangiovese di Romagna** is pretty basic, the best examples have depth, intensity and excellent texture and concentration where there is denser planting and lower yields. Several of the best producers (including Drei Donà, San Patrignano and Zerbina) have formed an association, Convito di Romagna aiming to better promote Romagna and Sangiovese. Most also make good wines from Chardonnay, Cabernet Sauvignon and other imports. Both a slightly nutty, dry and a sweet version of **Albana di Romagna** are made; the latter, as *passito*, made from dried grapes, is usually far superior.

Marche

This region is best-known for **Verdicchio dei Castelli di Jesi** and both the wines from this zone and the more inland **Verdicchio di Matelica** show increasing concentration, structure and style from a top producer. Late-harvested, *passito* (from dried grapes) and sparkling versions highlight the grape's versatility, although most of the best are dry and subtly oaked. With odd exceptions, **Falerio** (dei Colli Ascolani) tends to be much more ordinary, its blend usually dominated by the boring Trebbiano. The Marche's best red is **Rosso Conero**, an often spicy, sturdy red based on the Montepulciano grape - top examples include those from Garofoli and Le Terrazze. As Conero it is now a brand new DOCG but top Montepulciano-based wines (from Dezi, Oasi degli Angeli, Contrada Castelletta or Velenosi) are also sold as IGT Marche. The latter also covers some exciting reds from foreign varieties or unusual blends (see Boccadigabbia, Dezi, Le Terrazze). **Rosso Piceno**, which incorporates a greater percentage of Sangiovese is produced from a wide zone, though Superiore is more restricted, and there are fewer good examples. **Colli Pesaresi** covers several of the diverse but interesting wines of Mancini.

Umbria

Sangiovese is the leading red variety in Umbria and the regular red from the region's most important zone, Montefalco is based on it. **Montefalco Rosso** also includes a small percentage of Sagrantino and in the very best examples offers a characterful alternative to similarly priced Chianti or other Tuscan equivalents. Other Sangiovese-based appellations include **Colli Amerini** and **Colli del Trasimeno**, though both are becoming better known for rich, ripe, modern reds based on Cabernet Sauvignon and/or Merlot. The best wine from Montefalco is **Sagrantino di Montefalco**, from a grape that gives remarkable colour, extract, acid and alcohol. It needs careful vinification but at best produces an intense, concentrated, powerful yet original Italian red and the small plantings are on the increase. Sweet versions from dried grapes are labelled *passito*. **Colli Martani**, a much more extensive zone lying mostly to the west of Montefalco, can provide attractive whites from Grechetto. South of Perugia is the small zone of **Torgiano** (DOCG for a Riserva version) for reds based on Sangiovese but also including Canaiolo and Ciliegiolo. The Lungarotti reds responsible for its status are not currently making the most of their potential though there are at last signs of a sustained revival.

Lazio

The most important appellation in Lazio is now the regional IGT. Whether from the border with Umbria and Tuscany, the coast (Cerveteri) or the Colli Albani (Alban hills) many new wines are appearing. The majority are reds made from Cabernet Sauvignon and/or Merlot, though Sangiovese occasionally forms the main component. The established DOCs of **Est! Est!! Est!!!**, **Orvieto** (shared with Umbria) and **Frascati** are for the most part all based on the Trebbiano grape and offer little in terms of serious quality, but there are some reasonable examples of each and some good, late-harvested sweet styles. Frascati based on Malvasia tends to be much better.

Abruzzo & Molise

Abruzzo has two region-wide DOCs and most wines are either **Montepulciano d'Abruzzo**, if red, or **Trebbiano d'Abruzzo**, if white. There are an increasing number of good examples of the red; characterful, peppery and good value if well-made and so much more when the fruit is top-notch. There is an increasing number of ambitious examples but though not many approach the refinement or complexity of Valentini or the power and richness of Masciarelli. Montepulciano d'Abruzzo Colline Teramane is DOCG but it remains to be seen whether top producers will adopt it. The rosato version of Montepulciano, Cerasuolo is variable - both from producer to producer and vintage to vintage. Decent examples of other varietals and blends can appear under the **Controguerra** DOC. In Molise, **Biferno** was until recently its one important DOC. Like the reds of Abruzzo it is based on Montepulciano but additionally includes some Aglianico. The white is similar to Trebbiano d'Abruzzo. Newly created is a region-wide **Molise** DOC including essentially varietal examples of Aglianico, Montepulciano, Falanghina, Greco and Moscato.

A-Z of producers by region

Regions:
A Emilia-Romagna
B Marche
C Umbria
D Lazio
E Abruzzo
F Molise

Appellations:
1   Colli Bolognesi
2   Albana di Romagna
3   Sangiovese di Romagna
4   Colli Pesaresi
5   Falerio dei Colli Ascolani
6   Verdicchio dei Castelli di Jesi
7   Verdicchio di Matelica
8   Rosso Conero
9   Rosso Piceno
10 Rosso Piceno Superiore
11 Colli del Trasimeno
12 Torgiano Rosso Riserva
13 Montefalco Sagrantino
14 Colli Martani
15 Orvieto
16 Est! Est!! Est!!!
17 Colli Amerini
18 Frascati
19 Montepulciano d'Abruzzo
20 Biferno

STEFANO BERTI Romagna

Owner: Stefano Berti Loc. Ravaldino in Monte, Via La Scagna 18, 47100 Forlì
Stefano Berti has only been making his own wine since 2000 but with the 01 Calisto he has made a Sangiovese di Romagna of such character and intensity as to add further proof of the quality possible from this zone. Winemaking help is provided by Leonardo Conti of the Attilio Pagli/Alberto Antonini consultancy team. Fruit comes from both older vines and newer plantings but easily absorbs 12 months in new oak. The wine has drive, intensity and a stylish mineral, herb and black fruits complexity. If there is not yet the extra breadth of the very best examples, future vintages should add it. Quantities are small if increasing, but it was not made in 2002. A second red, Ravaldo, which is only partially barrique-aged benefitted from the grapes instead. This too, has plenty of style and appeal. (PW)
● **Sangiovese di Romagna Superiore** Ravaldo★★ £C Calisto★★★ £D

BOCCADIGABBIA Marche www.boccadigabbia.com   A: **L&S**

Owner: Elvidio Alessandri Contrada Castelletta 56, Fontespina, 62012 Civitanova Marche (MC)
Boccadigabbia, one of the leading red wine producers of the Marche comprises 28 ha from home vineyards and the more recently acquired 18-ha Villamagna estate. Under the extremely competent winemaking of Fabrizio Ciufoli, this includes some of the best Rosso Piceno going. The single-vineyard Saltapicchio (previously sold as Rosso Piceno) now, like most of the other wines, appears under the Marche IGT. It shows some herbs, smoke and cherry fruit together with good acidity and well-balanced tannin. An attractive, herb scented Mont'Anello white is based on Maceratino and Verdicchio. French varieties have been planted at Boccadigabbia since the early 19th century (introduced when the region was under Napoleonic rule), so non-native varietals are no recent sell-out. Their quality is of a high standard, too – all the wines show ripe fruit and some oak influence but with good balance. Pinot Grigio, with ripe citrus, pear and spicy notes, is a rare good example outside North-East Italy. but the best wine is a stylish, powerful but elegant, pure blackcurrant-fruited Cabernet Sauvignon that has few rivals outside Tuscany. Newish Merlot, Pix is promising, at once powerfully structured and finely textured. (PW)
● **Akronte★★★★** £E ● **Pix★★★** £E ● **Pinot Nero Il Girone★** £D
● **Rosso Piceno★★** £C ● **Sangiovese Saltapicchio★★** £C
O **Chardonnay Montalperti★★** £C O **Pinot Grigio La Castelletta★★** £B
O **Colli Maceratesi Ribona** Mont'Anello★ £B

ARNALDO CAPRAI Umbria www.arnaldocaprai.it   A: **L&S, Bal,** JAr, P&S, Hrd

Owner: Arnaldo Caprai Val di Maggio, Loc. Torre, 06036 Montefalco (PG)
This modern powerhouse operation has brought the small Montefalco zone and its Sagrantino grape wide recognition both within Italy and on foreign markets. Since the late 1980s the winery, vineyards (90 ha in production) and the wines have been transformed under Marco Caprai (Arnaldo's son) and his winemaking consultant Attilio Pagli. The leading Sagrantino wines are extremely concentrated, powerful and structured. These are not wines for early drinking but are complex and demanding, needing at least seven to ten years' age. The Sagrantino 25 Anni is an Italian classic, utterly compelling with terrific aromatic complexity and superb texture and dimension in the mouth. An unusual sweet (*passito*) version is very intense, with much of the wild berry character of Sagrantino but a certain finesse too. Montefalco Rosso Riserva, in contrast, is based on Sangiovese (70 per cent) with the balance from Sagrantino and Merlot. A long maceration shows in the wine's breadth and rich texture. Lesser wines are also very good, including a stylish, intense regular Montefalco Rosso and a fresh, citrusy white from Grechetto. Montefalco Bianco combines Chardonnay, Trebbiano and Sauvignon with Grechetto. There are ongoing experiments with other varieties including international ones such as Syrah and Malbec. New is Outsider (from 2000), a plush, concentrated red from Merlot and Cabernet Sauvignon. Most accessible of all the reds is Poggio Belvedere, an unoaked blend of Sangiovese and Ciliegiolo (80/20). (PW)
● **Sagrantino di Montefalco** Colle Piano★★★★ £E 25 Anni❂❂❂❂❂ £F Passito★★★ £F

● **Montefalco Rosso**★★ £C Riserva★★★ £D ● **Poggio Belvedere**★★ £B
O **Grechetto dei Colli Martani** Grecante★★ £B

CASTELLO DELLA SALA Umbria www.antinori.it A: **BWC**, UnC, Sel

Owner: Antinori Loc. Sala, 05016 Ficulle (TR)
The Castello della Sala is a major outpost of the ANTINORI family, with 160 ha in the vicinity of the 14th-century castle after which the estate is named. It was acquired by Niccolò Antinori (father of Piero) in 1940. The principal wine, Cervaro della Sala, has an established track record as one of Italy's best Chardonnays, with a refinement and gentle minerality missing from most of the bigger, more concentrated examples. As much as 20 per cent of the wine is Grechetto but its relative propensity to age also sets it apart from others. A second Chardonnay shows good richness and depth and decent value for money. Conte della Vipera is Sauvignon with a small addition of Chardonnay while Muffato della Sala is an oak-aged botrytised sweet wine of moderate richness and sweetness made from varying percentages of Sauvignon, Grechetto, Gewürztraminer and Riesling. Orvieto is made in three versions: Superiore, Campogrande and an *amabile* (medium-dry) version, Casasole. (PW)

O **Cervaro della Sala**★★★★ £E
O **Chardonnay**★★ £C O **Conte della Vipera**★★ £C ● **Pinot Nero**★★ £E
O **Muffato della Sala**★★ £E O **Orvieto** Classico Superiore★ £B

CASTELLUCCIO Romagna www.ronchidicastelluccio.it A: **Mgi**, Bal

Owner: Vittorio, Ermanno & Gian Michele Fiore Via Tramonto 15, 47015 Modigliana (FC)
This was the first estate in Romagna to set out to prove that Sangiovese from Romagna could compete with top examples from Tuscany. Renowned Tuscan consultant Vittorio Fiore (POGGIO SCALETTE), already involved with making the wines to a standard not previously associated with Romagna, bought into the 16-ha estate in 1999. The wines, made by Vittorio's son Claudio, used to be sold as *vino da tavola* in order to distance them from the lowly perception of the Sangiovese di Romagna DOC but most are now sold under the Forlì IGT. As well as the revamping of winemaking efforts, single *crus* – Ronco delle Ciliegi and Ronco delle Ginestre – were planted as long ago as 1975 to high-quality clones at a higher density and continue to be improved by the viticulturalist, Remigio Bordini. A third *cru*, Ronco della Simia, was also made until very recently but there are now just the two original sites. Ciliegi shows more class and elegance than an increasingly rich-fruited and good-value Sangiovese di Romagna, Le More. Ginestre, the top wine, comes from a 2-ha site and adds more weight, power and complexity. Sauvignon Blanc is the other variety of choice. Lunaria is a very distinctive mineral and very ripe citrus example that is partially barrel-fermented, resulting in a gentle leesy influence. Though not classically varietal, it can be more convincing than the richer, more ' *barriqued* Ronco del Re. All the reds need at least two or three years to get going; the *crus* are best with five or more. Whites can be drunk young or kept for a year or two. New Massicone, a blend of Cabernet Sauvignon and Sangiovese is promising, ripe and intense (if oaky in 2000 with some slightly green oak tannins on the finish). (PW)

● **Ronco dei Ciliegi**★★★ £C ● **Ronco delle Ginestre**★★★★ £D
● **Sangiovese di Romagna** Le More★★ £B O **Lunaria**★★£B O **Ronco del Re**★★ £D

PODERE CASTORANI Abruzzo A: **Eno**

Owner: B Cavuto, L Cavuto, L Petricelli & E Trulli Contrada Oratorio 1, 65020 Alanno (PE)
First-rate Montepulciano d'Abruzzo is a relatively rare beast but this new partnership promises something special. The name has a ring of motor racing about it and the owners include Formula One racing driver Jarno Trulli's father and his manager. Also on board is expert viticulturalist Bruno Cavuto who oversees the estate's 30 ha of well-established vines. The wines are made by the fourth partner, Luca Petricelli, whose experience includes winemaking in Bordeaux and Spain. A very good 2000, beautifully made with concentrated black cherry and spice, has been followed by an even more convincing 01. Rich and deep with

lots of Montepulciano flesh and individuality, it shows just what is possible with a good site and the right know-how in Abruzzo. One to follow. (PW)

● **Montepulciano d'Abruzzo**★★★ £E

CATALDI MADONNA Abruzzo www.cataldimadonna.it

A: **Ast**, P&S

Owner: Luigi Cataldi Madonna Loc. Piano, 67025 Ofena (AQ)
Montepulciano d'Abruzzo producer Luigi Cataldi Madonna is just beginning to realise the full potential of the fruit from his elevated vineyards beneath the Gran Sasso (the highest peak of the Appenines). The style is for bold, full-flavoured reds with soft, ripe tannins. Not subtle, they still lack a little sophistication but have broad appeal. A regular example offers reasonable value but there is much more in the two top bottlings. Maladrino sees one-third new oak while in Tonì it is two-thirds. The power, flavour and concentration are all givens and there is added complexity and length in Tonì, though both wines can want for a little more definition. Cataldi Madonna's two Cerasuolos are among the better examples, made with good freshness and lively floral fruit if drunk young. A further red, Occhiorosso is Cabernet Sauvignon with a little Montepulciano. (PW)

● **Montepulciano d'Abruzzo**★★ £B Maladrino★★ £C Tonì★★★ £D
○ **Trebbiano d'Abruzzo**★ £B

CORONCINO Marche

A: **Mgi**, L&W

Owner: Lucio Canestrari & Fiorella De Nardo Contrada Coroncino 7, 60039 Staffolo (AN)
A better Verdicchio than Coroncino's Gaiospino is hard to find. The husband-and-wife team started out in 1982 and have just 7 ha of vineyards. Gaiospino is sourced from the best vineyard, Spescia – a steep 2.7-ha site – and part is fermented and aged in double-sized *barriques*. Though high in alcohol, the wine has a gentle pear and quince fruit intensity, with definition and style that belie its body. A Fumé version was also made in 1998. A second Verdicchio, Il Coroncino, comes from vineyards around the winery and if less refined has good fruit richness. New from 2000 is a pricey new premium Verdicchio, Stracacio. (PW)

○ **Verdicchio dei Castelli di Jesi Classico** Superiore Il Coroncino★★ £B Gaiospino★★★ £C
○ **Verdicchio dei Castelli di Jesi Classico** Bacco★ £B

DEZI Marche

A: **Ast**

Owner: Romolo & Remo Dezi Contrada Fontemaggio 14, 63029 Servigliano (AP)
The Dezi family have 20 ha of vineyard over which much care is lavished. Production is organic and the quality of the fruit can be seen in all the wines. The top wines are a much praised Sangiovese called Solo and a less trumpeted pure Montepulciano, Regina del Bosco. Solo has finely detailed fruit and an elegance quite unexpected for the Marche. It is moderately concentrated and when young the effect of up to two years in new French oak is evident, but its class shows through. Regina del Bosco shows lots of style too. It is more structured, with the soft flesh and black-fruited complexity of Montepulciano. Dezio is a much more affordable Montepulciano that can include some Sangiovese and is aged in large oak *botte*. It is supple and expressive with good length. The perfumed white Le Solagne is a ripe, flavoursome blend of Malvasia and Verdicchio. All are sold as Marche IGT. (PW)

● **Solo**★★★★ £E ● **Regina del Bosco**★★★ £E
● **Dezio**★★ £C ○ **Le Solagne**★ £B

DI MAJO NORANTE Molise www.dimajonorante.com

A: **L&S**

Owner: Di Majo Norante family Contrada Ramitello 4, 86042 Campomarino (CB)
Alessio Di Majo's 60-ha estate is essentially organic and has been Molise's one really notable producer for more than a decade. Yet only more recently, with the input of consultant Riccardo Cotarella, has there been real consistency and a further increase in quality across the range. Reds are now led by a premium example of greater breadth and intensity than previously seen. This Don Luigi comes from 90 per cent

Montepulciano with the balance from Tintilia and is a rich, oaky *cuvée* – just occasionally a little overdone. The long-established blend Ramitello Rosso is produced from Sangiovese and Aglianico and is ripe, balanced and characterful. Contado shows plenty of Aglianico fruit and style if not yet the depth and structure synonymous with the best examples of this grape, while a varietal Sangiovese needs a little more refinement. Whites are ripe and clean with plenty of fruit. A Greco has dried peach, apricot and spice if modest structure while the partially oaked, lightly creamy Biblos from Falanghina and Greco (70/30) remedies this deficiency. Don Luigi excepted, the wines continue to be well-priced for the fruit and character they deliver. (PW)

● **Molise** Don Luigi★★★ £E Aglianico Contado★★ £B   ● **Biferno Rosso** Ramitello★★ £B
● **Sangiovese**★ £B   O **Biblos**★★ £B   O **Molise** Greco★★ £B Falanghina★★ £B

DREI DONÀ - LA PALAZZA Romagna www.dreidona.it

Owner: Claudio Drei Donà   Loc. Massa di Vecchiazzano, Via del Tesoro 23, 47100 Forlì
Claudio Drei Donà, together with his son Enrico and Tuscan consultant Franco Bernabei, makes a small but very competent range of wines from 27 ha of vineyards. Pruno, the best if not the most expensive wine, is made from the oldest part of a single vineyard. Notturno, Sangiovese from younger vines, is effectively the second wine and reveals plenty of very attractive plum and cherry fruit. Magnificat is varietal Cabernet Sauvignon with plenty of substance and style and a chocolaty-coffee complexity from a vineyard planted in the late 1980s. Graf Noir is a rich, characterful blend of Sangiovese, Cabernet Sauvignon, Cabernet Franc and Negretto Longanesi. Il Tornese is Chardonnay aged in double-sized *barriques* and large wood with good intensity and evident lees-driven character, while Varenne is an unoaked version. (PW)

● **Sangiovese di Romagna** Superiore Riserva Pruno★★★ £D   ● **Notturno Sangiovese**★★ £B
● **Magnificat**★★★ £E   ● **Graf Noir**★★★ £F   O **Il Tornese**★ £C

FALESCO Lazio   A: **BWC**, Res, N&P, Blx

Owner: Renzo & Riccardo Cotarella   S S Cassia Km 94, 155, 01027 Montefiascone (VT)
This substantial 250-ha estate on the Lazio/Umbria border belongs to two of Italy's most famous winemaker brothers – Renzo Cotarella, ANTINORI's winemaker, and the widely consulted enologist Riccardo Cotarella. The local appellation is the normally nondescript Est! Est!! Est!!! but Poggio dei Gelsi is a bright, perfumed and fruity white of some style. It is also made in a late-harvest version. A good, characterful if oaky, dry white, Ferentano, is made from one of the local grapes, Roscetto, and there is also an attractive Grechetto. But it is the reds have caused the most interest. Montiano is a high-quality, lush, showy Merlot, not classic but with lots of extract, complexity and excellent flavour length. Marciliano (produced only since 1999) is at least as impressive with slightly roasted intense blackcurrant and blackberry fruit from Cabernet Sauvignon and Cabernet Franc, arguably with the greater depth of the two. Both need 8 to 10 years' age. At a more affordable level is a 'second' fruity Merlot (dell'Umbria) and Vitiano, a supple, forward, aromatic blend of Cabernet Sauvignon, Merlot and Sangiovese made in large quantities. Pomele, first made in 2001, is from Aleatico. (PW)

● **Montiano**★★★★★ £E   ● **Marciliano**★★★★★ £E
● **Merlot**★★ £C   ● **Vitiano**★★ £B   O **Ferentano**★★ £C
O **Est! Est!! Est!!!** Poggio dei Gelsi★★ £B Poggio dei Gelsi Vendemmia Tardiva★★ £D

GAROFOLI Marche www.garofolivini.it   A: **Hal**

Owner: Garofoli family   Via Arno 9, 60025 Loreto (AN)
Fourth-generation Carlo and Gianfranco Garofoli now head this large family firm which was founded in 1871 and has been making wines for over a century. They focus on producing top-quality Verdicchio from low yields. Serra Fiorese is a Riserva aged in oak and can show considerable richness and depth with three or four years' age, but the best Verdicchio is the unoaked Podium, with lovely breadth, weight and a refinement only seen in a handful of examples. Also made are a *passito* version from dried grapes, Brumato,

and a sparkling wine from Verdicchio. Two Rosso Conero are both 100 per cent Montepulciano. The premium version, Grosso Agontano, aged in *barriques* for 12 months, has ample breadth and complexity and should be drunk with five years' age or more. All the wines, but particularly the whites, are very well priced for the quality. (PW)

O **Verdicchio dei Castelli di Jesi Classico** Superiore Macrina★★ £B   Podium★★★ £B
O **Verdicchio dei Castelli di Jesi Classico** Riserva Serra Fiorese★★★ £C
● **Rosso Conero** Vigna Piancarda★★ £B   Riserva Grosso Agontano★★★ £D
● **Rosso Piceno** Colle Ambro★ £B

LA FIORITA LAMBORGHINI   Umbria   www.lamborghinionline.it   A: SCh, JAr, F&R, Far, Las

Owner: Patrizia Lamborghini   Loc. Soderi 1, 06064 Panicale (PG)
Two very good reds are made at this beautiful estate at the southern end of Lago Trasimeno purchased by Ferruccio Lamborghini (Patrizia's father) in 1971. Riccardo Cotarella (see FALESCO) has made the wines in recent vintages and the 1999s and 2000s are a further improvement on his highly acclaimed but overhyped 97s. Campoleone, an equal blend of Sangiovese and Merlot, is the more international of the wines, but shows terrific intensity, powerful new oak and crushed small berry fruit within a vibrant structure. It is a wine of great potential if not originality. The second wine, Trescone, is a sleek and intense blend of Sangiovese, Ciliegiolo and Merlot (50/30/20) with distinctive plum and cherry fruit. Both reds are subject to a long maceration. Trescone is aged in large wood as against the one year's ageing in new *barriques* that the Campoleone receives. Trescone needs at least three years' ageing in bottle, Campoleone twice that. Both are sold under the Umbria IGT. (PW)

● **Campoleone★★★★★** £F   ● **Trescone★★** £C

LA MONACESCA   Marche   www.monacesca.it   A: **Wtr**, Add, UnC

Owner: Casimiro Cifola   Contrada Monacesca, 62012 Matelica (MC)
La Monacesca, named for a settlement of Benedictine monks, is located in Matelica, the smaller, lesser known of Marche's two Verdicchio zones. Ripe and concentrated unoaked Verdicchio with good depth and character are produced from 27 ha of vineyards at 400 m altitude. The superior bottling, gently nutty and buttery with spice, citrus and a minerally quality, shows greater refinement and definition than a well-made regular version. The top white, Mirum, is produced from late-harvested grapes, giving added richness and complexity. All three can be drunk young but keep well. Also made is a varietal Chardonnay, Ecclesia, and an increasingly good red, Camerte (Sangiovese/Merlot). (PW)

O **Verdicchio di Matelica★** £B   La Monacesca★★ £B   Riserva Mirum ★★★ £C
● **Camerte★★★** £D

LE TERRAZZE   Marche   A: **Fie, BBR**

Owner: Antonio Terni   Via Musone 4, 60026 Numana (AN)
To rhythms of Bob Dylan, the laid-back Antonio Terni is steadily building production towards 10,000 cases of wine a year. Under the winemaking expertise of Attilio Pagli, Rosso Conero (from 100 per cent Montepulciano) shows better ripeness and richness than most examples. The Sassi Neri, in particular, with an extended maceration (three weeks) and a year in *barriques* (a third new) shows real depth, succulence and elegance with three years' age or more. Chaos is a lush, black-fruited blend of Montepulciano (50 per cent), Syrah and Merlot aged in new oak. Visions of J, which rapidly sold out from the 1997 vintage, is made when conditions are exceptional. A little unoaked Chardonnay, Le Cave, is also made. (PW)

● **Rosso Conero★** £B   Sassi Neri★★★ £D
● **Chaos★★★** £E   O **Le Cave★** £B

FATTORIA MANCINI Marche www.fattoriamancini.com A: **BWC**, P&S, Vts

Owner: Mancini family Strada dei Colli 35, 61100 Pesaro (MC)
Luigi Mancini has got all sorts of weird ideas, but the intent and results deserve to be taken seriously. From slopes high above the rim of the Adriatic, Pinot Nero, which came with Napoleon's troops nearly 200 years ago, is the grape of choice. From it is made a white wine, Impero Bianco, of an exotic, almost decadent fruit character, vaguely similar to an over-the-top Alsace Pinot Gris. In a second white, the unoaked Roncaglia, Pinot Nero is again vinified as a white wine where it complements Albanella, a little-known variety said to have Albariño as a parent – though of modest structure, the wine is full of ripe nectarine and exotic fruits. The best Pinot however is kept for three reds. Impero Rosso has rather old-fashioned Burgundian flavours albeit without the finesse of which Pinot is capable, but there's no disputing the character and complexity of these ripe, meaty but well-balanced examples. A 2001 Riserva shows more oak as well as a lot of extract and intensity and should be put aside for at least five more years. Blu, previously half Pinot Nero and half Ancellotto, now includes a little Montepulciano. This powerful black-fruited wine also needs time but shows great promise. Sangiovese is also made. (PW)
● **Blu**★★★ £D ● **Colli Pesaresi Focara** Pinot Nero Impero★★★ £D
O **Colli Pesaresi** Roncaglia★★ £B O **Impero Bianco**★★ £B

MASCIARELLI Abruzzo www.masciarelli.it A: P&S, N&P

Owner: Gianni Masciarelli & Marina Cvetic Via Gamberale 1, 66010 San Martino sulla Marrucina
In Gianni Masciarelli, the Abruzzo has another great star. Together with Marina Cvetic he has constantly improved quality to the point where this estate has become a flag-bearer for Montepulciano d'Abruzzo. Villa Gemma is the top wine and impresses for its texture, depth and richness of fruit that owes something to both fruit quality and a prolonged maceration in wood. Also increasingly good (and less expensive) is the Marina Cvetic version. Following the successful 2000 vintage, 01 and 02 were very good years for Montepulciano, so there is promise of even better things to come. Other reds include a less successful but improving Cabernet Sauvignon, now showing a more refined structure than previously. Masciarelli's top white is a wine of increasing stature too – the barrel-fermented Trebbiano d'Abruzzo has good depth and breadth with a fine herbal, mineral complexity. Cerasuolo is also made while Villa Gemma Bianco is a stainless steel-fermented Trebbiano with 10 per cent Cococciola (a variety not previously encountered). (PW)
● **Montepulciano d'Abruzzo** Villa Gemma★★★★ £F Marina Cvetic San Martino Rosso★★★ £D
● **Cabernet Sauvignon** Marina Cvetic★★ £E
O **Trebbiano d'Abruzzo** Marina Cvetic★★★ £E O **Chardonnay** Marina Cvetic★★ £D

ANTONIO & ELIO MONTI Abruzzo www.vinimonti.it

Owner: Antonio & Elio Monti Contrada Pignotto 62, 64010 Controguerra (TE)
This small operation draws from 15 ha of vineyards to make around 7,000 cases of wine each year. Its reputation is for powerful, structured if somewhat rustic reds, although recently there has been input from Riccardo Cotarella and the wines show more oak influence but also more vigour and fruit purity without sacrificing their marvellous complexity and flavour expression. The single-vineyard Pignotto, of which only 11,000 bottles are made, is potentially an outstanding wine. Following a very long maceration, it is aged in French *barriques*. Wonderfully complex with earth, coffee, wild herbs, oak spice, plum and other black fruits, it also powerful and extracted. There is good integration between fruit and structure but it does demand 10 years' ageing from all but the most masochistic of drinkers of such big reds. A little white is also made. Beyond a decent Trebbiano d'Abruzzo, Dorato del Sole, there's Raggio di Luna, a characterful white in which Chardonnay is added to Trebbiano and some local varieties. Cerasuolo (Montepulciano vinified as a white) has more the colour of a light red rather than a rosé and has pretty fruit. (PW)
● **Montepulciano d'Abruzzo**★★★ £C Pignotto★★★★ £E
O **Controguerra** Raggio di Luna★ £B

OASI DEGLI ANGELI   Marche   www.kurni.it   A: **Wtr**, PaV, BBR, F&R

Owner: Eleonora Rossi   Contrada Sant' Egidio 50, 63012 Cupra Marittima (AP)
Marco Casolanetti and Eleonora Rossi produce just one very sought-after wine. Kurni was first made in 1997 (a white from Trebbiano, Esedra, was also made in the first two vintages) and is a powerful, very ripe, complex expression of the Montepulciano grape. Winemaker Giovanni Basso takes a rigorous approach to quality both in the vineyard and cellar which along with the tiny production has fuelled the wine's cult status. Despite some variability in limited tastings, the wine usually achieves balance if teetering on the brink. The fruit verges on the over-ripe but the richness and extract is balanced by fine tannins. Production, currently less than 5,000 bottles, is slowly increasing, though seems unlikely to ever satisfy demand even at its relatively high price. (PW)
● **Kurni★★★★** £F

PIEVE DEL VESCOVO   Umbria   www.pievedelvescovo.it

Owner: Pieve del Vescovo srl   Via Giacomo Leopardi 82, 06068 Corciano (PG)
Two very good wines are now made on this estate named for the 14th century Castello di Pieve di Vescovo. Much of the vineyard area (22 ha of a 120-ha estate) has recently been replanted, particularly that used to make the premium red, Lucciaio. A blend of roughly equal parts Merlot and Cabernet Sauvignon with 15 per cent Sangiovese, it is aged for 12 months in *barrique*, a third new. It shows both substance and style with good *terroir* expression but needs time to harmonise its structure. Piovano by contrast is based on Sangiovese complemented by Canaiolo and Ciliegiolo and shows excellent, stylish fruit character. It promises to be very appealing with three to four years' age. Tezio (not tasted) is an equal blend of Merlot and Cabernet Sauvignon. (PW)
● **Colli del Trasimeno** Piovano★★ £B   ● **Lucciaio★★★** £D

SALADINI PILASTRI   Marche   www.saladinipilastri.it   A: **Lib**, ACh

Owner: Conte Saladino Saladini Pilastri   Via Saladini 5, 63030 Spinetoli (AP)
The name Saladini Pilastri denotes an ancient lineage and an estate hundreds of years old but its wine production is only just getting into its stride. Since the arrival of Domenico D'Angelo in the mid-nineties viticulture has been switched to an organic basis. The fruits of these efforts are now being more fully realised thanks to consultancy from Alberto Antonini. The wines are better balanced and more expressive than previously, with plenty of extract but not the hardness of old. The top wine is Vigna Montiprandone (70 per cent Montepulciano), a concentrated red with truffle, plum, blackberry and spice, but intense fruit is seen in all examples of Rosso Piceno including an increasingly good basic. In Pregio del Conte, Aglianico instead of Sangiovese complements the Montepulciano, adding style though still wanting for better harmony. Of the other Saladini Pilastri wines a decent, simple, herbal Falerio is made but much better is Vigna Palazzi which adds in a little Sauvignon and Chardonnay and gains extra style and depth without becoming boring. Domenico D'Angelo also benefits from the collaboration with the Antonini team for his own wine, Vespro, a Montepulciano/Syrah (70/30) blend from the small estate of CONTRADA CASTELLETTA. Though the vines are young, yields are low and the promise of 2001 has been surpassed by the 02 with splendid black plum, spice, licorice and carob fruit in a modern style. (PW)
● **Rosso Piceno Superiore★★** £B   Vigna Montetinello★★ £B   Vigna Monteprandone★★★ £C
● **Rosso Piceno★** £B   Vigna Piediprato★★ £B   ● **Pregio del Conte★★** £C
○ **Falerio** Vigna Palazzi★★ £B

SAN PATRIGNANO   Romagna   www.sanpatrignano.org

Owner: Cooperativa San Patrignano   Loc. Ospedaletto, Via San Patrignano 53, 47852 Coriano (RN)
This remarkable community, founded by Vincenzo Muccioli and now run by his son, Andrea, is a centre of drug and social rehabilitation near Rimini. Part of the international Rainbow network, it is financed

through private donations and activities such as wine production, in which it is fortunate to have the services of Riccardo Cotarella (see FALESCO). The wines are very good indeed, from mostly older vineyards, but new vineyards are coming on stream and a total of 100 ha is planned, half of which will be planted to Sangiovese. The top wine, Sangiovese di Romagna Riserva Avi, made in very small quantities, is bottled with a different label every year. Since 1999 it comes from new vineyards that are more densely planted to higher-quality clones. It is very concentrated, dense and structured but with a sleek and elegant texture. Also impressive is a second Riserva, Zarricante, which is aged in a mixture of old and new oak. A regular version, Aulente, spends eight months in large wood and exhibits lovely pure cherry fruit and good depth. All three wines need time: three years for Aulente, at least five for the Riservas. Montepirolo is a classy Bordeaux blend that combines Cabernet Sauvignon with Merlot, Cabernet Franc and sometimes a little Petit Verdot. Structured, concentrated with great length, it requires five to eight years' ageing. New (from 2001) is Noi, a blend of Sangiovese, Cabernet Sauvignon and Merlot (60/20/20). A varietal stainless steel-vinified Sauvignon Blanc, Vintàn is also made. (PW)

● **Sangiovese di Romagna** Aulente★★ £C Riserva Zarricante★★★ £D Riserva Avi★★★★ £E
● **Montepirolo★★★** £E

SAN VALENTINO Romagna www.vinisanvalentino.com A: **Eno**

Owner: Mascarin family Fraz. San Martino in Venti, Via Tomasetta 11, 47900 Rimini
A 14-ha estate on hills near Rimini on the Adriatic coast purchased by Giovanni Mascarin in 1990. Progressive changes and improvements over the last decade and a half are now resulting in some very impressive wines. His son Roberto took over in 1997, hired consultant Fabrizio Moltard in 2000 and will oversee a new gravity-fed winery from 2005. Though most of the vines average around 10 years' age, high densities combined with leaf-plucking and green-harvesting result in low yields. The reds are now very good indeed. There are two fine Sangiovese di Romagna, pure ripe-fruited Scabi and classy intense Riserva Terra di Covignano, that also benefits from some old-vine fruit. A powerful Cabernet Sauvignon, Luna Nuova has the blackberry, mineral and earth of good Romagna Cabernet. Also made but not tasted is Eclissi di Sole, Sangiovese with 10 per cent Cabernet Sauvignon and whites which include Fiore, a *barrique*-aged Chardonnay, and Alta Marea from Pagadebit and Chardonnay. Also a member of the Convito di Romagna. (PW)

● **Sangiovese di Romagna Superiore** Scabi★★ £B Riserva Terra di Covignano★★★★ £D
● **Luna Nuova★★★** £E

SARTARELLI Marche www.sartarelli.it A: **Ast**, P&S, UnC, F&M

Owner: D. Sartarelli & C. Pozzi Via Coste del Mulino 24, 60030 Poggio San Marcello (AN)
This 51-ha estate is one of the best sources in the Marche for ripe, flavoursome Verdicchio. The regular example is typically bright, fresh and fruit-driven with ripe apple, floral and yellow plum flavours. Tralivio is partially *barrique*-aged, resulting in a richer texture but more of a leesy influence and less refinement and fruit purity. It is better with at least three years' age. The Contrada Balciana, which has a year in *barrique*, can start out a little awkwardly too but has good intensity and lots of depth and character, though still seems to miss a little refinement that would ensure a higher rating. (PW)

O **Verdicchio dei Castelli di Jesi Classico★★** £B Tralivio★★ £C Contrada Balciana★★ £D

SPORTOLETTI Umbria www.sportoletti.com A: **L&S**

Owner: Ernesto & Remo Sportoletti Via Lombardia 1, Capitanloreto, 06038 Spello (PG)
One of the best of a new wave of producers in Umbria and Lazio, many of whom have been helped by Riccardo Cotarella in producing high-quality reds. Brothers Ernesto and Remo have 20 ha of vines at around 400 m on the hills of Spello and Assisi north of Montefalco and within a new Assisi DOC. The top red, Villa Fidelia, is an oak-aged blend of Merlot with Cabernet Sauvignon and Cabernet Franc (usually 70/20/10) from 4 ha of vineyards. It has typical 'Cotarella' richness, depth and concentrated fruit but also

a splendid smoke, sweet spice and mineral individuality and is potentially a classic. A second red, Assisi Rosso (Merlot/Sangiovese) is ripe and plummy with a lush, supple mouthfeel and is quite stylish for what can often be a rather boring blend. Villa Fidelia Bianco is an increasingly good white, an oak-aged blend of Chardonnay and Grechetto, while the texture of a varietal Grechetto has been subtly enhanced by oak. (PW)

● **Villa Fidelia Rosso**★★★★★ £E   ● **Assisi** Rosso★★ £B
O **Villa Fidelia Bianco**★★ £C   O **Assisi** Grechetto★ £B

UMANI RONCHI Marche www.umanironchi.it   A: **Eno**, JNi, Vne, Vts, Hrd, Sel

Owner: Bianchi Bernetti family   S.S 16 Km 310+400, 60027 Osimo (AN)
Despite being a big volume producer in its more basic brands, in its best wines Umani Ronchi offers a good quality introduction to the wines from the central Adriatic coast. These include good Verdicchio in both stainless steel fermented-examples (Villa Bianchi and single-vineyard Casal di Serra) and the partially oak-aged and fermented Riserva Plenio. Verdicchio is also combined with Chardonnay in the oak-aged Le Busche. Reds from the Montepulciano grape show good character too, especially in Rosso Conero San Lorenzo and Cúmaro. In Pelago, the richer, oakier red flagship wine, Montepulciano has been successfully combined with Cabernet Sauvignon and Merlot (typically 50/40/10). Yet despite a pretty good record for consistency and flavour there's not quite the value for money of old. The wines can also sometimes lack for balance and definition. As well made as they can be, it seems there should be more life and intensity to most of the range. A new Vecchie Vigne version of Casal di Serra shows more intensity and vigour. Among other wines made are a varietal Sangiovese, Medoro, and a sweet white from botrytised Sauvignon grapes, Maximo. (PW)

O **Verdicchio dei Castelli di Jesi** Casal di Serra★ £B Riserva Plenio★★ £C   O **Le Busche**★ £C
● **Rosso Conero** San Lorenzo★ £B Cúmaro★★ £C   ● **Pelago**★★★ £E
● **Montepulciano d'Abruzzo** Jorio★ £B

VALENTINI Abruzzo   A: **Wtr**, BBR

Owner: Edoardo & Francesco Paolo Valentini   Via del Baio 2, 65014 Loreto Aprutino (PE)
The Valentinis, father and son, offer one of the great alternatives to the modern school of winemaking. The greatest care goes into producing high-quality fruit from *tendone*-trained vines planted at low densities. From a total of 64 ha of vines, only a small quantity is released under Valentini's distinctive label. Much of the wine is sold off in bulk and if it is not up to standard then no wine is produced at all. There is no temperature control, only large old wood, and no fining or filtration. After the wine is bottled it is kept until it is considered ready to drink. At it's best, the red (100 per cent Montepulciano) is a wine of great power and dimension that slowly releases it's complex aromas and flavours that include dried flowers, cedar, coffee, spice, pepper and berry fruit. It is best with at least a decade's age and the best recent vintages are 1995, 92, 90, 88 and 85. On its present showing the 97 is not up with these. The white from Trebbiano shows a subtle range of floral, herbal and fruit-derived scents but is more notable for its texture than its depth or richness. Some pink Cerasuolo is also made. (PW)

● **Montepulciano d'Abruzzo**★★★★ £F   O **Trebbiano d'Abruzzo**★★★ £F

ZERBINA Romagna www.zerbina.com

Owner: Germiniani family   Loc. Marzeno, Via Vicchio 11, 48010 Faenza (RA)
This 40-ha estate is brilliantly run by Cristina Geminiani whose wines have maintained or bettered consistent high standards over the past decade or more. Viticultural improvements, particularly planting at higher densities, continue to underpin quality. The top wine, Pietramora, from a single vineyard of old vines, shows an extra level of richness and dimension since 1997. Torre di Ceparano comes from more densely planted *alberello* (bush-trained) vines and has gained in texture and concentration as the vines have aged. The greatest part of the Sangiovese production comes in the shape of the unoaked Ceregio, a supple, fruity, earlier-drinking example. A special selection of Ceregio, Vigna Querce, is made in exceptional years

such as 2001 and 1997 and offers much more depth and intensity. For Marzieno a little Cabernet Sauvignon and Merlot are added to Sangiovese; lush, powerful and oaky, it misses the class and personality of Pietramora. Scacco Matto is an excellent rich, concentrated botrytised sweet wine from Albana grapes, while a lighter version, Arrocco, is made from second-choice fruit or in lesser vintages. An attractive, partly oak-fermented and aged dry white, Tergeno, is made from (mostly) Chardonnay with a little late-harvested Albana. (PW)

● **Sangiovese di Romagna Superiore** Ceregio★ £B Vigna Querce★★ £B Torre di Ceparano★★ £C
● **Sangiovese di Romagna Superiore** Riserva Pietramora★★★★ £E ● **Marzieno★★★** £E
O **Tergeno★★** £C O **Albana di Romagna** Passito Arrocco★ £D Scacco Matto★★★ £F

OTHER WINES OF NOTE

ADANTI ● Montefalco Sagrantino £C Passito £D
AGRIVERDE ● Montepulciano d'Abruzzo Riseis £B Plateo £D
ANTONELLI ● Montefalco Rosso Riserva £D ● Montefalco Sagrantino £E
AURORA ● Barricadiero (Montepulciano/Cabernet Sauvignon/Merlot) £C ● Rosso Piceno Superiore £B
FRATELLI BARBA ● Montepulciano d'Abruzzo Colle Morino £B
BARBERANI O Orvieto Classico Superiore Calcaia Muffa Nobile £E
● Lago di Corbara Foresco (Sangiovese/Cabernets)
BELISARIO O Verdicchio di Matelica Vigneti Belisario £B Vigneti del Cerro £B
O Verdicchio di Matelica Riserva Cambrugiano £C
BINOMIO (INAMA & LA VALENTINA) ● Montepulciano d'Abruzzo Binomio £E
BISCI O Verdicchio di Matelica Vigneto Fogliano £B
MARIO & GIORGIO BRUNORI O Verdicchio dei Castelli di Jesi Classico Superiore San Niccolò £B
BUCCI O Verdicchio dei Castelli di Jesi Classico Riserva Villa Bucci £C
TENUTA CARACCIOLO ● Montepulciano d'Abruzzo Duchi di Castelluccio £B
CARMINUCCI ● Rosso Piceno Superiore Naumachos £C
CASTEL DE PAOLIS O Frascati Superiore Vigna Adriana (Malvasia/Viognier) £C
● Quattro Mori (Syrah/Merlot/Cabernet Sauvignon/Petit Verdot) £D
CANTINA COLLI AMERINI ● Torraccio (Sangiovese) £B
CLETO CHIARLI ● Lambrusco Grasparossa di Castelvetro Pruno Nero £B Enrico Cialdini £B
COLPETRONE (Saiagricola) ● Montefalco Rosso £B ● Montefalco Sagrantino £E
LEONE CONTI O Albana di Romagna Passito Non Ti Scordar di Me £D
CONTRADA CASTELLETTA (see Saladini Pilastri) ● Vespro (Montepulciano/Syrah) £C
BARONE CORNACCHIA ● Montepulciano d'Abruzzo £B
PIERO COSTANTINI/VILLA SIMONE O Frascati Superiore Villa dei Preti £B Vigneto Filonardi £C
TENUTA DE ANGELIS ● Anghelos (Montepulciano/Sangiovese/Cabernet Sauvignon) £D
DECUGNANO DEI BARBI O Orvieto Classico Superiore IL £B
● IL (Sangiovese/Montepulciano/Canaiolo) £C
PAOLA DI MAURO-COLLE PICCHIONI O Le Vignole (Malvasia/Trebbiano/Sauvignon) £B
● Colle Picchioni Vigna del Vassallo (Merlot/Cabernets) £D
FAZI BATTAGLIA ● Rosso Conero Riserva Passo del Lupo £C
O Verdicchio dei Castelli di Jesi Classico Superiore Le Moie £B Riserva San Sisto £C
FONTANA CANDIDA O Frascati Superiore Terre dei Grifi £B Superiore Vigneto Santa Teresa £B
● Kron (Merlot/Sangiovese) £C
ILLUMINATI ● Montepulciano d'Abruzzo Zanna £C ● Controguerra Rosso Riserva Lumen £E
CANTINE INTESI ● I Calanchi - Numi (Cabernet Sauvignon) £C
LA BERTA ● Sangiovese di Romagna Superiore Solano £B Riserva Olmatello £C
● Almante (Alicante) £C
LA CARRAIA O Orvieto Classico Poggio Calvelli £B
● Sangiovese £B ● Fobiano (Merlot/Cabernet Sauvignon) £D
LA PALAZZOLA ● Merlot £D ● Rubino (Cabernet Sauvignon/Merlot) £D
LA TOSA ● Colli Piacentini Cabernet Sauvignon Luna Selvatica £C
● Colli Piacentini Gutturnio Vignamorello £C

LA VALENTINA ● **Montepulciano d'Abruzzo** Spelt £C Bellovedere £F
TENUTA LA VIOLA ● **Sangiovese di Romagna** Superiore II Colombarone £C
FATTORIA LAILA ● **Rosso Piceno** £B ● **Lailum** (Montepulciano) £D
LANARI ● **Rosso Conero** Fibbio £C
LAURENTINA ● **Rosso Piceno** Talliano £C
LE CANIETTE ● **Rosso Piceno** Morellone £C ● **Rosso Piceno** Nero di Vite £E
LE VELETTE ● **Calanco** (Sangiovese/Cabernet Sauvignon) £C ● **Gaudio** (Merlot) £C
LEOPARDI DITTAJUTI ● **Rosso Conero** Vigneti del Coppo £B Pigmento £D
● **Casirano** (Montepulciano/Cabernet Sauvignon/Syrah) £C
LUNGAROTTI ● **Giubilante** (Cabernets/Sangiovese/Canaiolo/Montepulciano) £D
● **San Giorgio** (Cabernet Sauvignon/Sangiovese/Canaiolo) £E
● **Torgiano Riserva** Rubesco Vigna Monticchio £E O **Chardonnay** Aurente £C
LURETTA O **Colli Piacentini** Malvasia Dolce Le Rane £E
GIOVANNA MADONIA ● **Sangiovese di Romagna** Superiore Riserva Ombroso £C
MARCHETTI ● **Rosso Conero** Riserva Villa Bonomi £C
MARRAMIERO ● **Montepulciano d'Abruzzo** Incanto £B Inferi £C
ERMETE MEDICI & FIGLI ● **Lambrusco Reggiano** Secco Arte e Concerto £B
MONTE SCHIAVO ● **Rosso Conero** Adeodato £D
● **Esio** (Cabernet Sauvignon/Montepulciano/Merlot) £C
MORODER ● **Rosso Conero** Dorico £D
PALAZZONE O **Orvieto Classico** Terre Vineate £B Campo del Guardiano £C
O **Muffa Nobile** (Sauvignon) £E ● **Armaleo** (Cabernet Sauvignon) £D
PARADISO ● **Mito** (Cabernet Sauvignon/Merlot/Syrah) £E ● **Barbarossa** £D
FRANCO PASETTI O **Pecorino** £C
POGGIO BERTAIO ● **Sangiovese** Cimbolo £C
ROCCA DI FABRI ● **Sagrantino di Montefalco** £E ● **Faroaldo** (Sagrantino/Cabernet Sauvignon) £E
O **Grechetto dei Colli Martani** £C
CASA VINICOLA ROXAN ● **Montepulciano d'Abruzzo** Taverna Nova £B Galelle £C
SALVIANO/TITIGNANO ● **Lago di Corbara** Turlò £B (Sangiovese/Cabernet Sauvignon)
SAN SAVINO ● **Rosso Piceno** Superiore Picus £D ● **Versacrum** (Montepulciano) £E
● **Fedus** (Sangiovese) £E
SANTA BARBARA O **Verdicchio dei Castelli di Jesi Classico** Le Vaglie £B Stefano Antonucci £C
● **Stefano Antonucci** (Merlot/Cabernet Sauvignon/Montepulciano/Syrah) £C
● **Pathos** (Merlot/Cabernet Sauvignon/Syrah) £E
SPOLETODUCALE ● **Montefalco Rosso** Casale Triocco £B ● **Montefalco Sagrantino** Casale Triocco £D
LUCANGELI AYMERICH DI LACONI/TAVIGNANO O **Verdicchio dei Castelli di Jesi** Misco £C
TERRA D'ALIGI/SPINELLI ● **Montepulciano d'Abruzzo** Tatone £C
TERRAGENS ● **Romio** (IGT Forlì Sangiovese) £C
TERRE CORTESI MONCARO O **Verdicchio dei Castelli di Jesi Classico** Verde di Cà Ruptae £B
O **Verdicchio dei Castelli di Jesi** Riserva Vigna Novali £C Passito Tordiruta £D
● **Rosso Conero** Riserva Vigneto del Parco £C ● **Barocco** (Montepulciano/Cabernet Sauvignon) £C
VIGNETO DELLE TERRE ROSSE ● **Colli Bolognesi** Cabernet Sauvignon Enrico Vallania £D
O **Colli Bolognesi** Chardonnay Giovanni Vallania £C
TRAPPOLINI ● **Sangiovese** Paterno £D
TRE MONTI ● **Sangiovese di Romagna Superiore** Thea £C Riserva £C
TRERE' ● **Sangiovese di Romagna** Riserva Amarcord d'un Ross £C
VALLONA ● **Colli Bolognesi** Cabernet Sauvignon Selezione £C ● **Afederico** (Merlot) £C
VALORI ● **Montepulciano d'Abruzzo** £B Vigna Sant'Angelo £C
ERCOLE VELENOSI O **Falerio dei Colli Ascolani** Vigna Solaria £B
● **Ludi** (Montepulciano/Cabernet Sauvignon/Merlot) £D ● **Rosso Piceno** Superiore Roggio del Filare £C
ZACCAGNINI & C. O **Verdicchio dei Castelli di Jesi Classico** Salmàgina £B Pier delle Vigne £C
CICCIO ZACCAGNINI ● **Montepulciano d'Abruzzo** Castello di Salle £B
● **Montepulciano d'Abruzzo** Cuvée dell'Abate £C San Clemente £C

Author's Choice (PW)

10 excellent Sangiovese di Romagna

STEFANO BERTI ● Sangiovese di Romagna Superiore Calisto

CASTELLUCCIO ● Ronco dei Ciliegi

CASTELLUCCIO ● Ronco delle Ginestre

DREI DONÀ - LA PALAZZA ● Sangiovese di Romagna Superiore Riserva Pruno

LA BERTA ● Sangiovese di Romagna Superiore Riserva Olmatello

LA VIOLA ● Sangiovese di Romagna Superiore Il Colombarone

GIOVANNA MADONIA ● Sangiovese di Romagna Superiore Riserva Ombroso

SAN PATRIGNANO ● Sangiovese di Romagna Riserva Avi

SAN VALENTINO ● Sangiovese di Romagna Riserva Terra di Covignano

ZERBINA ● Sangiovese di Romagna Riserva Pietramora

10 Montepulciano based reds

PODERE CASTORANI ● Montepulciano d'Abruzzo

CATALDI MADONNA ● Montepulciano d'Abruzzo Tonì

DI MAJO NORANTE ● Molise Don Luigi

GAROFOLI ● Rosso Conero Riserva Grosso Agontano

LANARI ● Rosso Conero Fibbio

LE TERRAZZE ● Rosso Conero Sassi Neri

MASCIARELLI ● Montepulciano d'Abruzzo Villa Gemma

ANTONIO & ELIO MONTI ● Montepulciano d'Abruzzo Pignotto

OASI DEGLI ANGELI ● Kurni

VALENTINI ● Montepulciano d'Abruzzo

10 individual stars

BOCCADIGABBIA ● Akronte Cabernet Sauvignon

CAPRAI ● Sagrantino di Montefalco 25 Anni

CASTELLO DELLA SALA ○ Cervaro della Sala

FALESCO ● Montiano

LA FIORITA LAMBORGHINI ● Campoleone

LE TERRAZZE ● Chaos

FATTORIA MANCINI ● Blu

PIEVE DEL VESCOVO ● Lucciaio

SPORTOLETTI ● Villa Fidelia Rosso

ZERBINA ● Marzieno

10 alternatives to Chardonnay

CASTEL DE PAOLIS ○ Vigna Adriana

CORONCINO ○ Verdicchio dei Castelli di Jesi Classico Superiore Gaiospino

FALESCO ○ Est! Est!! Est!!! Poggio dei Gelsi

GAROFOLI ○ Verdicchio dei Castelli di Jesi Classico Superiore Podium

LA MONACESCA ○ Verdicchio di Matelica La Monacesca

FATTORIA MANCINI ○ Pinot Nero Impero Bianco

PALAZZONE ○ Orvieto Classico Campo del Guardiano

SARTARELLI ○ Verdicchio dei Castelli di Jesi Classico Superiore Contrada Balciana

UMANI RONCHI ○ Verdicchio dei Castelli di Jesi Classico Riserva Plenio

VALENTINI ○ Trebbiano d'Abruzzo

Southern Italy & Islands

For years fans of Italian wine have glimpsed the quality and originality of the south but have been frustrated by a lack of consistently fine examples. Since the mid- to late nineties, the once-isolated pockets of quality have been growing and spreading and there are now many excellent producers in the Mezzogiorno. As in much of Italy the general standard of winemaking is at an unprecedented level. Add this to some high-quality vineyard sources, both new and old, and a rich hoard of native grape varieties and you begin to see what is possible. Campania vies with Puglia and Sicily as the south's most important quality wine producing area but there are now both good-value bottles and world-class wines, often with prices to match, to be had in all regions.

Campania

Taurasi is Campania's leading appellation based on its most important grape, Aglianico. Its DOCG status may have once wanted for endorsement but now there are many good examples and a few outstanding wines which show the depth, structure and class of the grape that result when winemaking expertise is employed and the fruit quality has been maximised. Increasing amounts of good **Greco di Tufo** and **Fiano di Avellino** (both DOCG since 2003) are also produced in the Avellino hills but several of the best wines from this exciting area appear under the Irpinia IGT, the ancient name for the zone. Avellino's leaders are Mastroberardino and Feudi di San Gregorio but good examples come from several others. To the north in the neighbouring province of Benevento another white, Falanghina, is starting to show real promise under the DOCs of **Sannio**, **Sant'Agata dei Goti**, **Solopaca** and **Taburno**. More good Aglianico also appears under each, especially the **Aglianico del Taburno**. Production is being led by the co-op, Cantina del Taburno. From vineyards in the Caserta province (nearer to Lazio), Aglianico is complemented by Piedirosso in increasingly good **Falerno del Massico** though it is the reds from Aglianico vines from the slopes of the Roccamonfina volcano that send the senses into overdrive (see Galardi). The **Lacryma Christi del Vesuvio** red from the slopes of Vesuvius is also based on Piedirosso. Whites from the island of **Ischia** (such as those from D'Ambra) and the wines of the **Costa d'Amalfi** show potential too. Others new stars such as Montevetrano and Luigi Maffini are located in the south of Campania.

Basilicata

In Basilicata, as in Campania, the great red grape is Aglianico and at last there are now several good sources of high quality examples of **Aglianico del Vulture** from the elevated slopes of Monte Vulture. Recent vintages of the top wines from Le Querce or Cantine del Notaio, amongst others, may now be compared with those from Paternoster or D'Angelo, who are invariably the only sources of older wines of quality. Good inexpensive examples also come from Cantine Sasso, and the Vulture and Venosa co-ops.

Puglia

More than anything else, Puglia provides value for money. **Salice Salentino** is the best-known of the many DOCs on the Salento peninsula based on the Negroamaro grape, but topped up with some Malvasia Nera. They range from simple gutsy, baked, raisiny examples to more complex, lush and sweet-fruited versions. Alezio, Copertino, Leverano and Squinzano offer similar reds if fewer good examples. The best Negroamaro comes from *alberello* (bush-trained) vines and the reds of **Brindisi** are also based on it. Those who have long proven its potential such as Cosimo Taurino and Vallone are being joined by newer exponents including Conti Zecca, La Corte, Li Veli, Tormaresca and Vetrere, accounting for a profusion of varietal examples (many excellent value) as well as blends based on Negroamaro but complemented by Montepulciano or Cabernet Sauvignon. **Primitivo di Manduria** is the most important DOC on the peninsula for Primitivo (a grape said to be identical to California's Zinfandel if of discernably different character according to some winemakers). Primitivo also appears under broader IGTs such as Tarantino and several of the Salento peninsula's best wines are sold as Salento IGT. There are now many good examples, several extremely good value for money (from some of those already mentioned plus Apollonio, Pervini and other producers in the Accademia dei Racemi). On the high plateau of central Puglia, Primitivo is also DOC in **Gioia del Colle**.

To the north lies **Castel del Monte** and here Uva di Troia, Montepulciano and Aglianico feature. All three grapes have excellent potential as is becoming increasingly apparent from the likes of Torrevento, Rivera or Tormaresca. The last, Antinori's southern outpost, is also using Cabernet Sauvignon.

Calabria

Calabria continues to be the weakest of the southern Italian regions for good quality wine. The most important DOC is **Cirò**, for a characterful red based almost exlusively on Gaglioppo, and a more ordinary white from Greco Bianco. There are only a handful of significant producers including Librandi, the region's leading estate. Two other DOCs, **Savuto** and **Scavigna**, used by Odoardi, include a substantial proportion of Gaglioppo in the blend. Scavigna can also include significant percentages of Aglianico, Cabernet Sauvignon and Merlot.

Sicily (Sicilia)

The sea of vines in the west of Sicily is why the island vies with Puglia as Italy's most productive region. For long most of it has been pretty simple, dilute stuff but both here in the DOC zones of **Marsala** and **Alcamo**, and in pockets all over the island, many excellent new producers have recently come to the fore. Cabernet Sauvignon, Merlot, Syrah and Chardonnay are the foreign stars while Nero d'Avola and Nerello Mascalese are increasingly important native red grapes. The latter two are combined in a small zone near Messina called **Faro** but the majority of the new wave of fine Sicilian reds are sold as Sicilia IGT. Other DOCs include **Cerasuolo di Vittoria**, where Frappato is usually combined with Nero d'Avola in a characterful, concentrated and perfumed red, and **Contessa Entellina** DOC, which covers a wide range of reds and whites of the producer Donnafugata. The vineyards on the lower slopes of Mount Etna are **Etna** DOC. While some producers focus on the international varieties, others are more committed to promoting the native varieties and what is most exciting about Sicily is this very mix of quality-minded producers – to be certain it needs them all. Success and acclaim with international varieties at worst serves as a kind of Trojan horse facilitating a more sustained assault of native varieties in foreign markets. From off-shore come **Malvasia delle Lipari** from this volcanic island group to the north and **Moscato di Pantelleria** from an especially windswept volcanic island that lies closer to Tunisia than Sicily. The richer, sweeter **Passito di Pantelleria** versions from dried grapes are the most exciting.

Sardinia (Sardegna)

Several of Sardinia's DOCs are region-wide and typically account for everyday reds and whites of reasonable value if from a good source. These include **Cannonau di Sardegna**, **Monica di Sardegna** and **Vermentino di Sardegna**. The best wines containing Cannonau (a clone of Grenache), from Argiolas or Dettori, do not come under the regional DOC but are wines of much greater depth and complexity. **Vermentino di Gallura**, from a more restricted northern zone, is the island's only DOCG but examples of both Vermentinos can be wonderfully fresh and aromatic. Most of Sella & Mosca's red wines fall under **Alghero** DOC, named for the town on the north-west coast. **Carignano del Sulcis** is also a more defined zone (in the south-west corner) where the best of Sardinia's many co-ops is based and makes some remarkably good Carignano-based reds that bear little resemblance to basic Carignan from the Languedoc-Roussillon. Another pocket of exceptional Carignano is at Arzachena in the far north (see Capichera). Cagnulari is another Sardinian red variety of some potential if Giovanni Cherchi's results can be emulated. **Vernaccia di Oristano** is a small zone producing oxidised, sherry-like wines – those from Attilio Contini are of high quality.

A-Z of producers by region

Regions:
A   Campania
B   Basilicata
C   Puglia
D   Calabria

Appellations:
1   Falerno del Massico
2   Greco di Tufo
3   Fiano di Avellino
4   Taurasi
5   Aglianico del Vulture
6   Castel del Monte
7   Gioia del Colle
8   Primitivo di Manduria
9   Brindisi
10   Salice Salentino
11   Cirò

12   Savuto
13   Faro
14   Etna
15   Cerasuolo di Vittoria
16   Contea di Sclafani
17   Marsala
18   Alcamo
19   Contessa Entellina
20   Vermentino di Gallura
21   Alghero
22   Vernaccia di Oristano
23   Carignano del Sulcis
24   Vermentino di Sardegna, Cannonau di Sardegna

ABBAZIA SANTA ANASTASIA Sicilia www.abbaziasantanastasia.it A: **L&S**

Owner: Francesco Lena Contrada Santa Anastasia, 90013 Castelbuono (PA)
This superbly sited estate high above the sea on the north coast of Sicily emerged as one of the island's brightest new stars in the 1990s. It wines first grabbed attention after help from the Tuscan enologist Giacomo Tachis and are now made under guidance from Riccardo Cotarella (see FALESCO). Most impressive is the top wine, Litra, made from 100 per cent Cabernet Sauvignon since 1999 but previously including Nero d'Avola. It is intense and ripe, with blackcurrant, black plum, mineral and a hint of herbs within a full, structured but balanced frame. Still-improving Passomaggio is Nero d'Avola with 20 per cent Merlot. Given the vineyard altitude of 400–500 m above sea level, whites also have potential here. Baccante is a late-harvested Chardonnay fermented in new oak and fairly rich from some residual sugar, while Gemelli, first made in 2000, is Chardonnnay with a little Sauvignon Blanc. Bianco di Passamaggio (previously called Zurrica) is an unoaked blend of Inzolia with a percentage of Chardonnay and Pinot Bianco. Least expensive are a basic but well-made trio of red (varietal Nero d'Avola), white (varietal Inzolia) and rosé (varietal Nerello Mascalese). Drink Litra with five years' age or more, others wines can be drunk young. (PW)

● Litra★★★★ £E ● Montenero★★ £C ● Passomaggio★★ £B
O Baccante★★ £C O Gemelli★★ £C O Bianco di Passamaggio★ £B

ACCADEMIA DEI RACEMI Puglia www.accademiadeiracemi.it A: **Mer**, Wtr, UnC

Owner: (an association of producers) Via Santo Stasi Primo, ZI, 74024 Manduria (TA)
The idea of an umbrella organisation for a network of growers in Puglia's Salento peninsula was conceived and then realised by Gregory (Gregorio) Perrucci of Pervini. Launched as recently as 1999 it has done much to promote the good-value reds of this area, particularly from old Primitivo vines. Pervini itself is fired by the younger generation of the Perrucci family. Fabrizio Perrucci is the winemaker and has worked closely with highy regarded consultant Roberto Cipresso since 1996 on the wines of the family's own 45-ha estate, Felline, as well as making the wines for the rest of the association. Typically all the wines have good fruit, balance and real character. Pervini's Bizantino Rosso is a blend of Negroamaro and Primitivo as is Felline's Alberello, while the new L'Evangelista is Primitivo with a little Montepulciano (90/10). Felline's Vigna del Feudo, previously a blend of Primitivo, Montepulciano and a little Cabernet and Merlot, is now Primitivo, Malvasia Nera and Ottavianello in equal proportions. Primo Amore is a sweet version of Primitivo. La Quadratura del Cerchio has been developed by Roberto Cipresso – a blend of Primitivo and Sangiovese (70/30), it is now in its third incarnation (*terze viaggio*). The wines from Masseria Pepe, Sinfarosa, and Casale Bevagna should not be overlooked, epecially the Primitivos – Sinfarosa's excellent 'Zinfandel' or Pepe's complex Dunico. Newer wines from Tenuta Pozzopalo and Torre Guaceto (Sum, from the Susumaniello grape, and Dedalo from Ottavianello) are promising. (PW)

Pervini
● Primitivo di Manduria Archidamo★★ £B Primo Amore★★ £C
● Bizantino Rosso★★ £B ● Squinzano L'Evangelista★★ £B
Felline
● Primitivo di Manduria★★★ £B ● Vigna del Feudo★★ £B
● Alberello★ £B ● La Quadratura del Cerchio★★ £C
Masseria Pepe
● Primitivo di Manduria Dunico★★ £C ● Primitivo del Tarantino Portile★★ £B
Sinfarosa
● Primitivo di Manduria Zinfandel★★★ £C ● Primitivo★★ £B
Casale Bevagna
● Salice Salentino Te Deum Laudamus★★ £B

Tenuta Pozzopalo
● **Primitivo di Manduria** Giravolta★★ £C
Torre Guaceto
● **Sum**★★ £D ● **Dedalo**★★ £B

ARGIOLAS Sardegna www.cantine-argiolas.it   A: **Eur**, F&R

Owner: Antonio Argiolas Via Roma 56-58, 09040 Serdiana (CA)
Argiolas is one of Sardinia's two leading producers (the other is SANTADI). It is run by Franco and Giuseppe Argiolas, sons of Antonio Argiolas, but with assistance from leading enologist Giacomo Tachis. Since 1985 the 230-ha estate has been completely replanted with the emphasis on local Sardinian varieties. There are good examples of some of the island's more widely seen DOCs including Costamolino (Vermentino di Sardegna); Costera (Cannonau di Sardegna); Perdera (Monica di Sardegna); and S'elegas (Nuragus di Cagliari), a crisp dry white. The best wines, however, are sold under the IGT Isola dei Nuraghi. Argiolas is mostly Vermentino, while Angialis, a fine light sweet wine, is made from (mostly) Nasco and Malvasia. Newish Cerdeña is a (pricey) *barrique*-fermented and aged Vermentino. The top red is the deep but structured Turriga, based on Cannonau but with 5 per cent of each of Carignano, Malvasia Nera and the Sardinian variety Bovale. Similarly structured is Korem, from Bovale, Carignano and a little Cannonau. Most wines should be drunk young but Korem and Turriga (subject to a delayed release) usually need more bottle-age after release; the Turriga is best with 10 years' age. SerraLori is a rosé made from a mix of grapes. (PW)
● **Turriga**★★★★ £F ● **Korem**★★ £D
● **Monica di Sardegna** Perdera★ £B ● **Cannonau di Sardegna** Costera★★ £C
O **Angialis**★★★ £D O **Argiolas**★★ £B O **Vermentino di Sardegna** Costamolino★★ £B
O **Nuragas di Cagliari** S'elegas★ £B

BENANTI Sicilia www.vinicolabenanti.it

Owner: Giuseppe Benanti Via Garibaldi 475, 95029 Viagrande (CT)
The Benanti family have had vines on the lower slopes of Mount Etna since the late 19th century. Since 1988 Giuseppe Benanti has identified some of the best densely planted old-vine vineyards from the northern, southern and eastern slopes of Etna and experimented with, primarily, the local varieties in order to produce wines of great character and individuality. Some new single-varietal reds, with at times too firm and ungiving a structure, are not so convincing. Nero d'Avola is the most composed, while both Nerello Mascalese and Nerello Cappuccio are difficult to enjoy despite a delightful complexity. If these and other wines need more supple textures and tannins Benanti deserve space here on the basis of the excellent Lamorèmio red alone. From equal parts Nerello Mascalese, Nero d'Avola and Cabernet Sauvignon, it has a fascinating black fruits, mineral and herbs complexity and is also much more profound and better balanced than the varietals. Rosso di Verzella, Rovittello and Serra della Contessa all combine Nerello Mascalese and Nerello Cappuccio but come from quite diverse locations and altitudes, the last having perhaps the most agreeable structure. Whites are generally soundly made and individual, including a varietal Carricante, the scented and intense Pietramarina; a Carricante/Chardonnay blend in the flavoursome if unsubtle Edèlmio; and the only known example of the obscure Minnella grape, made from vines growing amongst the Nerello Mascalese. Better, though, is the sweet Passito di Pantelleria that combines intensity and refinement in its spiced, honeyed apricot fruit and is one of the best going. (PW)
● **Lamorèmio**★★★★ £E ● **Etna Rosso** Serra della Contessa★★ £D Rovittello★★ £C
● **Nero d'Avola**★★ £D ● **Nerello Cappuccio**★★ £D
O **Etna Bianco** Superiore Pietramarina★★ £C O **Edèlmio**★★ £C O **Minnella**★ £C
O **Passito di Pantelleria** Coste di Mueggen★★★ £E

ANTONIO CAGGIANO Campania www.cantinecaggiano.it   A: J&B

Owner: Antonio Caggiano   Contrada Sala, 83030 Taurasi (AV)
Antonio Caggiano is one of the stars of Taurasi yet only turned his attention to making fine wines in 1990. Now he makes a range of reds and whites, all to a consistently high standard. Foremost is the single-vineyard Taurasi Vigna Macchia dei Goti, from Aglianico which is then aged in one- and two-year-old wood. It shows some classic tar, earth, smoke and black plum fruit characters, with no lack of depth or character and fine tannins. Also from a single vineyard comes Salae Domini, which spends 10 to 12 months in *barrique* and is sold under the IGT Aglianico dell' Irpinia. Though oak is apparent it integrates well with a fine, ripe fruit character. Taurì, an inexpensive version of Aglianico displaying some of the grape's classic character, is also sold under the IGT. Béchar is a fruit-intense Fiano di Avellino that is not too structured – as wines from this appellation sometimes can be. FiaGre is a *barrique*-aged blend of 70 per cent Fiano and 30 per cent Greco. Fresh when young, it will also keep a couple of years. A potent Greco di Tufo, Devon, was made in 2002. Also produced is a lovely, elegant sweet white, Mel, from dried Fiano and Greco grapes, with lightly spicy pear and quince among its delicious flavours. (PW)
● **Taurasi** Vigna Macchia dei Goti★★★ £E
● **Salae Dominii★★★** £D   ● **Taurì★★** £C
O **Fiano di Avellino** Béchar★★ £C   O **FiaGre★** £B   O **Mel★★★** £E

CANTINE DEL NOTAIO Basilcata www.cantinedelnotaio.com   A: BBR

Owner: G Giuratrabochetti   Via Roma 159, 85028 Rionero in Vulture (PZ)
This a very new operation but one already making exciting Aglianico del Vulture. The owner is one of several producers working with Aglianico to profit from the expertise of Luigi Moio, a professor of oenology in Naples. The premium example La Firma is subject to a lengthy maceration and has 12 months in new French oak which adds complexity to a splendid expression of Aglianico fruit. The wine hasn't yet quite the same sophistication in structure as some of its rivals but is very promising in both the 2000 and 01 vintages. Both deserve at least five or six years' age. A second example, Il Repetorio, has less depth but is more immediate and fruit-accented with attractive pepper, spice and berry notes, though still benefits from a little bottle age. A sweet wine, L'Autentica, comes from Moscato and Malvasia grapes and is very apricotty and fruit-intense if relatively straightforward. (PW)
● **Aglianico del Vulture** Il Repetorio★★ £C   La Firma★★★★ £D
O **L'Autentica★★** £E

CAPICHERA Sardegna www.capichera.it   A: Bal

Owner: Ragnedda family   07021 Arzachena (SS)
Brothers Fabrizio and Mario Ragnedda only began to produce their own wines from their family estate in the far north of Sardinia in the 1980s. There are now 60 ha of vines and quality from Vermentino (for whites) and Carignano (for reds) is very good indeed, although the wines do come with a price to match. 'Capichera' is the estate white, an intense, perfumed Vermentino. Vigna'ngena is a slightly more affordable version. Vendemmia Tardiva, late-harvested (but dry) and *barrique*-aged, is a splendid wine with refined, pure fruit and great length. Both Carignanos are ripe and classy; Assajé is stainless steel-fermented and aged. The powerful *barrique*-aged Mantènghja has added depth and concentration but should be drunk only with eight years' age or more. If only the wines were a bit cheaper! (PW)
● **Mantènghja★★★★** £F   ● **Assajé★★★** £D   O **Capichera Vendemmia Tardiva★★★** £F
O **Capichera★★** £D   O **Vermentino di Gallura** Vigna 'Ngena★★ £C

CEUSO Sicilia www.ceuso.it

Owner: Antonino, Giuseppe & Vincenzo Melia   Via Enea 18, 91011 Alcamo (TP)
Though based in the Alcamo zone in western Sicily, best known for its dilute whites, thus far Ceuso has

concentrated on high-quality reds. With 25.5 ha of the estate planted to vines, they combine the best of the traditional and modern. In Custera, a wonderfully characterful, concentrated and powerful red with deep smoky, earthy aromas, the native Nero d'Avola grape is combined with Cabernet Sauvignon and Merlot (50/30/20). Though given 12 months in *barrique*, it is freshened up in vats before 18 months' bottle-age prior to release. As the vine age for Custera increases (now 13 years old from 8.5 ha) so does the wine's richness, although the 2000 is a little disappointing. Fastaia, added in 2000, is effectively a second wine, with relatively small contributions from Merlot and Cabernet Franc. It shows a deep smoky and powerful southern character as well as polished tannins. Both wines may be drunk young but will keep, Custera perhaps 10 years. More wines are promised and new from 2002 is Scurati, a reasonably priced varietal Nero d'Avola. (PW)

● Custera★★★ £D   ● Fastaia★★ £C

GIOVANNI CHERCHI   Sardegna

Owner: Giovanni Cherchi   Loc. Sa pala e sa chessa, 07049 Usini (SS)
This small Sardinian operation is worth tracking down for the quality of its Vermentinos alone but the soft, appealing, scented reds have a similar intensity and the same ability to evoke something of the essence of the island. The sage, pear, citrus and spice character Cherchi achieves in his Vermentino makes for delightful whites for relatively early drinking. The *barrique*-aged Boghes, also from Vermentino shows a deft use of oak and lovely complexity with a couple of years' age. Most intriguing of the reds, a varietal Cagnulari is not a wine of great depth or structure but its delightful fruit character is now inspiring other growers to plant it. Luzzana is a blend of equal parts Cannonau and Cagnulari; scented and oak-influenced with preserved berry-fruit character, it is deserving of at least three to four years' age. The non-DOC wines are sold under the Isola dei Nuraghi IGT. (PW)

● Cannonau di Sardegna★★ £C   ● Cagnulari★★ £C   ● Luzzana★★★ £C
O Vermentino di Sardegna Pigalva★★ £B Tuvaoes★★★ £C   O Boghes★★★ £C

COTTANERA   Sicilia www.cottanera.it   A: **Ast**, Res, L&W

Owner: Guglielmo & Vincenzo Cambria   Contrada Iannazzo, 95030 Castiglione di Sicilia (CT)
An exciting new operation on the northern side of Mount Etna at 700 m altitude. Since 1995 the Cambria brothers have begun to transform the 43 ha of vines bought by their father some 40 years ago. Consultancy comes from Leonardo Valenti and the first vintage was as recent as 1999. The wines at the top level – including Grammonte, a varietal Merlot; Nume, Cabernet Sauvignon; Sole di Sesta, varietal Syrah; and L'Ardenza, varietal Mondeuse (surely Sicily's if not Italy's only example) – show remarkable fruit intensity, concentration and definition. All are aged in new French oak for 18 months. They are powerful and vibrant with great potential, but it is still early days and it remains to be seen how well the wines age and how much finesse time will add, but all should be given at least five years from the vintage. Grammonte and Nume betray a cooler, herbal aspect in 2001. Considerably less expensive is Fatagione, a blend of Nerello Mascalese and Nero d'Avola (90/10), which shows very intense fruit and much of the potential complexity of Nerello Mascalese. The moderately priced Barbazzale red is a similar blend to Fatagione but more open and immediate, while the promising unoaked white version comes from old vineyards of Inzolia. (PW)

● Grammonte★★★ £E   ● L'Ardenza★★★ £E   ● Sole di Sesta★★★ £E
● Nume★★★ £E   ● Fatagione★★★ £D
● Barbazzale Rosso★★ £B   O Barbazzale Bianco★★ £B

CUSUMANO   Sicilia www.cusumano.it   A: **Eur**, WTs, Odd, Hrd

Owner: Alberto Cusumano & Diego Cusumano   S.S. 113, Contrada San Carlo, 90047 Partinico (PA)
Alberto and Diego Cusumano control 140 ha of vineyards and with the help of consultant Mario Ronco are proving to be another of Sicily's new revelations. Two premium reds are based on Nero d'Avola, though the French varieties are also successful here. Sàgana is a varietal Nero d'Avola fermented and aged in

2,000-litre barrels and shows ripe, intense fruit. By contrast, Noà, which adds Cabernet Sauvignon and Merlot to Nero d'Avola, is aged in French *barriques*. It is even better, with more depth and complexity in a seamless harmonious blend. A *barrique*-fermented Chardonnay, Jalé, and varietal Inzolia, Cubìa, show fine fruit and each spends six months on its lees, though this works less well in the latter. Produced without any wood but good value are a brambly, spicy, blackberry Benuara, which adds Syrah to Nero d'Avola, and a fresh, stylish white from Inzolia and Chardonnay, called Angimbé. Inexpensive varietal examples of Nero d'Avola, Merlot and Syrah produced under the Nadarìa label are more everyday but could use a little more ripeness and richness. Inzolia under the same label is more appealing. (PW)

● Sàgana★★★ £D   ● Noà★★★ £D   ● Benuara★★ £B
○ Cubìa★★ £C   ○ Jalé★★ £C   ○ Angimbé★★ £C
○ Alcamo Nadarìa★ £B   ○ Nadarìa Inzolia★ £B

D'ANGELO   Basilicata   A: **Alv**, Sel

Owner: Donato & Lucio D'Angelo   Via Provinciale 8, 85028 Rionero in Vulture
The secret to appreciating D'Angelo wines is patience for although the Aglianico del Vulture reds show impressive fruit and complexity when young they add greater richness, harmony and a deep, savoury complexity with long ageing. An increasing percentage of production comes from estate fruit, including the single-vineyard Riserva, Caselle, from a 5-ha site. Canneto is a selection of Aglianico from old vines and is aged in *barriques* but has a similarly profound structure and good ageing potential. Another estate vineyard, Serra delle Querce (6.2 ha), is the source of an increasingly persuasive *barrique*-aged blend of Aglianico and Merlot. Intense and minerally with smoke, pepper and berry fruit character despite the oak influence, this too deserves at least five years' age. New Donato d'Angelo is expansive and very long in the 2000 vintage but will need time to fill in. Vigna dei Pini is a fresh attractive white if drunk young. (PW)

● Aglianico del Vulture★★ £B   Riserva Vigna Caselle★★★ £C
● Canneto★★★★ £C   ● Serra delle Querce★★★★ £D

MARCO DE BARTOLI   Sicilia   A: **Cib**

Owner: Marco de Bartoli   Contrada Fornara 292, 91025 Marsala (TP)
A crusader for the original unfortified Marsala, for five years between 1995 and 2000 Marco de Bartoli was prevented by the authorities from making any wine. He now continues with his sons Renato (a trained winemaker) and Sebastiano and currently produces Vigna La Miccia, the youngest and freshest style fortified with a little *mistella*, and a Marsala Superiore (also fortified) from wines aged for around 10 years in a sort of *solera* system. Small amounts of extraordinary old wines are used for blending with younger wines, as in Vecchio Samperi Ventennale, an unsweetened and unfortified blend of older and younger vintages but with an average age of 20 years. This is the best expression of what very ripe Grillo grapes can achieve with considerable age and is full of rich, toffeed dry fruits, candied peel, dates, nuts and other nuances of flavour. Other wines include some from the island of Pantelleria (the production of which was the source of the controversy), the very good Passito di Pantelleria Bukkuram, and a fine dry version of Zibibbo (Muscat of Alexandria) called Pietranera. New are a dry white from Grillo, Grappoli del Grillo, and a Merlot, Rosso di Marco. (PW)

○ Vigna La Miccia★★ £C   ○ Marsala Superiore★★★ £D   ○ Vecchio Samperi Ventennale★★★★ £D
○ Passito di Pantelleria Bukkuram★★★ £D   ○ Pietranera★★ £B

DETTORI   Sardegna   www.tenutedettori.it

Owner: Dettori family   Loc. Badde Nigolosu, 07036 Sénnori (SS)
To appreciate these fabulous wines be prepared to take some time and leave your preconceptions behind. Alessandro Dettori is uncompromising in the making of his wine. His 13 ha of very low-yielding *alberello* (bush-trained) vines lie close to the sea (but at 250 m altitude) in Sénnori in north-west Sardinia. There is no oak whatsoever, no filtration, no fining, no additions or adjustments and Alessandro accepts it might

not always work but is undeterred. Vermentino from 2002, if lacking typical Vermentino freshness, shows uncommon weight, texture and pure, cool fruit. Three single-vineyard Cannonau from 2001 show diverse character. Tuderi, from 40-year-old vines is full and powerful yet mellow with deep fruit. An intense, licoricy Tenores (from 40- to 60-year-old vines) is the most extracted and discernably tannic, and highest in alcohol with highish acidity too, needing at least five years' age. Dettori (from 60- to 120-year-old vines) has fabulous red fruit and lightly mineral, floral complexity. There is lovely breadth and purity – a wine to savour and savour (in a decent glass) before trying to procure another bottle. The Moscadeddu (2002), from a local variant of Moscato, has a gorgeous nose of purest honeycomb, delicate apricot and allspice. Medium-dry, it is not as concentrated as might be expected. 2002 was a particularly difficult vintage and more vintages need to be tasted in order to be able to rate the wines (which are not cheap - whites £D, Tuderi and Tenores £E, Dettori £F) but don't expect the greatest consistency given the approach. It also remains to be seen how the wines will age, suffice to say they could be very special indeed. (PW)

DONNAFUGATA Sicilia www.donnafugata.it   A: **Vim**, Hrd, F&M

Owner: Rallo family Via Sebastiano Lipari 18, 91025 Marsala (TP)

The Rallo family left only their name in Marsala production and have devoted themselves to making table wines in the last decade. They even have what is effectively their own DOC for the top reds and whites grown at altitude in western Sicily. The best reds had a tendency to over-extraction but input from Carlo Ferrini, one of Tuscany's very best consultants, should continue the trend to richer, softer examples with finer tannins. This augurs particularly well for the already complex and classy Mille e Una Notte, based on Nero d'Avola, while Tancredi (Nero d'Avola with some Cabernet Sauvignon) shows more refinement with the 2000 and 01. Angheli adds Merlot to Nero d'Avola and seems fullest and ripest when the Merlot is most successful. Whites include the scented Vigna di Gabri from 100 per cent Ansonica (Inzolia), which has real style and length, while the Chardonnay Chiarandà del Merlo shows a southern richness but also has more structure and better balance than some. The usually fresh and aromatic Anthìlia is produced from Ansonica and Cataratto. From the family's vineyards in Pantelleria, Ben Ryé is very much in the dried fruit, apricot spectrum of these sweet wines but has excellent intensity and balance. (PW)

● **Contessa Entellina** Tancredi★★★ £D   Mille e Una Notte★★★★ £F   ● **Angheli**★★ £C
○ **Contessa Entellina** Vigna di Gabri★★ £C   Chiarandà del Merlo★★ £E   ○ **Anthìlia**★ £B
○ **Moscato di Pantelleria** Kabir★★ £D   ○ **Passito di Pantelleria** Ben Ryé★★★ £E

FEUDI DI SAN GREGORIO Campania www.feudi.it   A: **Alv**, Odd, P&S, F&R

Owner: Capaldo & Ercolino families Loc. Cerza Grossa, 83050 Sorbo Serpico (AV)

In a short space of time this winery based in the Avellino hills of Campania has risen to be the region's leading producer and one of the most exciting in Italy. Viticultural help has come from the esteemed Attilio Scienza, while the wines are made by Mario Ercolino. Plenty of oak is used and the reds are modern but with fabulous fruit, concentration and depth. Two single-vineyard versions of Taurasi are particularly fine, while Serpico is arguably southern Italy's finest red, a wine of majestic depth and length of flavour. Pàtrimo, only made since 1999, is a prodigious varietal Merlot, with marvellous fruit and depth, if not quite the breadth of Serpico. The range of whites, which used to include late-harvested versions of Fiano di Avellino (Pietracalda) and Greco di Tufo (Cutizzi), has been simplified. Falanghina, Greco and, in particular, Fiano grapes are used here to make some remarkable whites and are a much better bet than many an overpriced, poorly structured Viognier. Campanaro is late-harvested Fiano that has been fermented to dryness and partially *barrique*-aged, producing a rich, exotic but balanced wine. A sweet version from partly botrytised grapes, Privilegio, reveals intense ripe fruit and moderate sweetness. Idem is also sweet but includes Moscato, Greco, Falanghina and Coda di Volpe as well as Fiano. Merlot excepted, it is remarkable that the quality of all these wines is based on the native local varieties. While the top wines are no longer cheap there's both quality and value in the more moderately priced Rubrato, an Aglianico that is sold, along with many of the more unusual wines, under the Irpinia IGT. More is to come as operations in Basilicata, Puglia and Molise reach fruition but already includes excellent Aglianico del Vulture and Primitivo di Manduria. (PW)

● **Taurasi**★★★ £C Piano di Montevergine★★★★ £E Selve di Luoti★★★★ £E
● **Serpico**★★★★★ £F ● **Pàtrimo**★★★★ £F ● **Rubrato**★★ £B
● **Primitivo di Manduria** Ognisole★★★ £C ● **Aglianico del Vulture** Efesto★★★★ £E
○ **Fiano di Avellino**★★★ £C ○ **Greco di Tufo**★★ £C ○ **Sannio Falanghina**★★ £C
○ **Campanaro**★★★ £D ○ **Idem**★★★ £E ○ **Privilegio**★★★ £E

GALARDI Campania   A: F&R

Owner: F Catello, D Catello & M L Murena S P Sessa Mignano, 81030 Sessa Aurunca (CE)
In the north of Campania, between the volcano of Roccamonfina and the sea, Galardi produces tiny quantities of just one wine, Terra di Lavoro, from Aglianico (80 per cent) and Piedirosso. Only now do the plots of vines wedged between groves of chestnut trees at 400 m total 9 ha. Eventually there will be 40,000 bottles of this new classic but just 9,000 were made in 2001. With help from Riccardo Cotarella, Terra di Lavoro (Roccamonfina IGT) is now a superb, fabulously complex red of great depth and stunning length, with a wealth of black fruits, mineral and earth, spice and herbs. It has improved in nearly every vintage since it was first made in 1994 and shows, along with some of the other stunning wines of this region, what tremendous potential there is here. Cult status means high prices. Try the 99 if you can first find it and then afford it. (PW)

● **Terra di Lavoro**★★★★★ £F

LA CORTE Puglia www.renideo.com   A: Ast, JNi, Res, F&M

*Owner: **Renideo** Via Trepuzzi, 73051 Novoli (LE)*
Chris Ringland of the cult Barossa winery Three Rivers has been recruited to work with La Corte's winemaker Giuseppe Caragnulo. Their aim is to produce great wines from Primitivo and Negroamaro. Primitivo is labelled as Zinfandel to the irritation of some Californian winemakers but the quality at least does their name no harm. Grapes are both bought-in and sourced from leased vineyards. The superior bottlings are labelled simply La Corte and come from old-vine fruit that has 12 months in oak. Both show very ripe fruit, considerable intensity and extract and while needing more age are a significant step up from the more affordable Zinfandel Anfora and Negroamaro Solyss. The top wine is Ré (first made 2001), a selection of the best Negroamaro and Primitivo, that shows greater complexity and style. The Renideo group also comprises La Rendola in Tuscany but these wines still want for both consistency and excitement. (PW)

● **Ré**★★★ £D ● **Zinfandel La Corte**★★★ £C ● **Negroamaro La Corte**★★★ £C
● **Zinfandel Anfora**★★ £B ● **Negroamaro Solyss**★★ £B

TENUTA LE QUERCE Basilicata www.tenutalequerce.com   A: Ast, But, VKg

Owner: Pietrafesa family Contrada Le Querce, 85100 Barile (PZ)
Le Querce is a major new star and part of the wider wine revolution in Basilicata. 60 ha of a 100-ha estate are planted to vines averaging 35 years of age at an elevation of 450 m. The regular example, Il Viola, is produced in ample quantities (10,000 cases) yet has good fruit intensity and some style. Rosso di Costanza adds more density and shows impressive length as well as an oak influence from 12 months in *barrique* and needs five years' age. The crowning glory, however, is Vigna della Corona, of which just 7,000 bottles are produced from a single plot of vines. This is a marvellously expansive wine but with a structure that demands at least six to eight years' age following a very long maceration and 18 months in French oak. Much of the complexity, expression and nobility of Aglianico is ensnared here. The Pietrafesa family also produce the wines of Cantina Sasso, a source of reasonably priced, soundly made Aglianico del Vulture. (PW)

Tenuta Le Querce
● **Aglianico del Vulture** Il Viola★★ £B Rosso di Costanza★★★ £D Vigna Corona★★★★★ £F

Cantine Sasso
● **Aglianico del Vulture★★** £B

LEONE DE CASTRIS   Puglia   www.leonedecastris.com   A: Alv

Owner: Leone de Castris family   Via Senatore de Castris 26, 73015 Salice Salentino (LE)
Leone de Castris represent the more traditional face of Puglia, dating back to the 17th century. The large volume winery draws on around 400 ha of vineyards on the Salento peninsula. Among an extensive range of inexpensive wines basic Salice Salentino Maiana offers warm sun-ripened fruit but not much else. However a Riserva, subject to ageing in large oak casks, is a big step up and shows a classic dark raisiny character with black plum, black cherry and chocolate fruit. Better again is the Donna Lisa Riserva. In fact until recently this was a Salice like no other, with a significant oak contribution to its complex character. If sometimes a little overdone, it is very complete when successful (as in 1999) and deserves 8 to 10 years' age. The white equivalent is, somewhat surprisingly, a *barrique*-fermented and aged Chardonnay. More interesting is the characterful unoaked Messapia from the native Verdeca. Other reds include an intense if slightly one-dimensional Primitivo, Santera, and Ilemos, a combination of Primitivo, Montepulciano, Merlot and Negroamaro. The latter, though awkward and disjointed in 1998, was much better in 99. Five Roses is the widely seen rosé, also made in an Anniversario version. Both should be drunk very young. New from 2000 is Messere Andrea, a *barrique*-aged blend of Negroamaro and Cabernet Sauvignon (85/15). Other wines include Elo Veni, a varietal Negroamaro, and La Rena, a second varietal Primitivo. (PW)
● **Salice Salentino** Riserva★★ £B Riserva Donna Lisa★★★ £C
● **Primitivo di Manduria** Santera★★ £B ● **Illemos★★** £C
O **Salice Salentino** Riserva Donna Lisa★★ £C O **Messapia★★** £B

MASSERIA LI VELI   Puglia   www.liveli.it   A: Lib

Owner: Falvo, Guercia Sammarco & Maci families   72020 Cellino San Marco (BR)
This new undertaking between Angelo Maci and Tuscan heavyweight Avignonesi has already produced some excellent examples of varietal Negroamaro. Passamante, sold as Salento IGT, is the least expensive with just six months' ageing in wood and stainless steel before bottling. It shows plenty of extract, fruit and soft, ripe tannins. Deep, powerful and more structured is Salice Salentino Pezzo Morgana, which promises to peak with five to six years' age, becoming richer and more chocolaty. The longest ageing is given to a Salice Salentino Riserva, Morgana Alta (18 months before a further 12 months in bottle). The 2000 shows a marvellous complexity and a suggestion of old-vine fruit with great depth and length of flavour. This single vintage suggests a four-star wine in the making. Prices are not typical of Salice Salentino but then neither is the quality. (PW)
● **Salice Salentino** Pezzo Morgana★★★ £C ● **Passamante★★★** £B

LIBRANDI   Calabria   www.librandi.it   A: Eno, F&M

Owner: Librandi family   Contrada San Gennaro, S S 106, 88811 Cirò Marina (KR)
Librandi is the leading producer of Calabria from a base near Cirò Marina on the Ionian coast. A long-established enterprise, the family gradually moved from being growers into production of bulk wines before bottling their own wines. Vineyards have slowly been expanded to the present 230 ha and, building on the early involvement of enologist Severino Garofano, expertise since 1998 has come from top Piedmontese enologist, Donato Lanati. After initially planting international varieties which resulted in their top red, Gravello (Gaglioppo/Cabernet Sauvignon), much thought (with advice from Attilio Scienza) has gone into the planting of a 160-ha site at Rosaneti, where many Calabrian varieties are being revived. The first great success of this strategy is Magno Megonio, a *barrique*-aged varietal Magliocco. It is becoming increasingly persuasive with a more refined structure in the 2001, showing a floral aspect to a preserved red and black fruit character that becomes carob-tinged with age. Best value is the Cirò Riserva Duca San Felice, a characterful red with gamey, earthy, black plum and herb characters and intense chocolaty flavours;

slightly rustic but good. The non-DOC wines are sold under the Val di Neto IGT. Critone is a fresh, well-made blend of Chardonnay and Sauvignon Blanc, while Le Passule is a light yet intense honeyed and refined sweet wine from Mantonico. First produced in 2001 is a rich dry and oaky version of Mantonico called Efeso. Librandi also produced good rosé in the Terre Lontane *rosato* from Gaglioppo and Cabernet Franc. Simple Cirò Bianco, Rosso and Rosato are also made. (PW)

● **Gravello**★★★ £D   ● **Magno Megonio**★★★ £E
● **Cirò Rosso** Riserva Duca San Felice★★ £B
○ **Le Passule**★★★ £D   ◉ **Terre Lontane**★ £B

LUIGI MAFFINI   Campania.   A: **Bib**

Owner: Luigi Maffini   Frazione San Marco, Loc. Cenito, 84071 Castellabate (SA)

From just 6 ha Luigi Maffini makes around 2,500 cases each of a very creditable red and white as well as 6,000 bottles of a premium red. The intense, fruit-driven white Kràtos (pure Fiano) has inviting scents of spice, herb, dried peach and apricot. While it doesn't have the structure for long keeping it is delightful when young. The marginally cheaper red Klèos, from Aglianico, Piedirosso and Sangiovese, is relatively forward but again provides lots of attractive fruit. However it is Cenito, an oak-aged blend of Aglianico and Piedirosso that shows the greatest promise. Despite a tendency to an excess of oak, there is also a depth and fullness that suggests the wine's considerable character will emerge with around 8 to 10 years' age. If these wines have yet to fully profit from the fruit that is obtained, this is nonetheless a name to follow. (PW)

● **Cenito**★★★ £D   ● **Klèos**★★ £B   ○ **Kràtos**★★ £C

MASTROBERARDINO   Campania   www.mastroberardino.com   A: **BWC, Cib**, Sel

Owner: Mastroberardino family   Via Manfredi 75-81, 83042 Atripalda (AV)

For decades Mastroberardino was Campania's one producer of note and the first to promote the wines of Taurasi, Fiano di Avellino and Greco di Tufo. Having rebuilt following a devastating earthquake in 1980, the family now control 350 ha of vineyards and produce around 200,000 cases of wine a year. The estate is run by the tenth-generation Carlo and Piero Mastroberardino but winemaking is still overseen by their father, Antonio. A split between brothers Antonio and Walter Mastroberardino in 1994 led to Walter and his family establishing TERREDORA. The leading wine here is the Taurasi Radici, which is aged in a mixture of large and small oak. Complex and refined with impressive dimension and power, it only shows at its best with around a decade's age. This is now complemented by a new wine, Naturalis Historia (after Pliny the Elder's great work), which adds 15 per cent Piedirosso to Aglianico. It spends two years in small oak and is richer and more modern in style. A varietal Aglianico, Avellanio, also shows good fruit. The best versions of Greco di Tufo (Nova Serra) and Fiano di Avellino (Radici) are intense, ripe and varietal. The More Maiorum version of the latter is unusual in being oak-fermented and aged before a long bottle refinement (two-and-a-half years) prior to release. From 1996 Mastroberardino was given responsibility for replanting historic vineyard sites (totally about 1 ha) among the ruins of ancient Pompeii. The culmination of these efforts is Villa dei Misteri, a *barrique*-aged blend of Piedirosso and Sciascinoso (90/10), first produced in 2001. With intense red fruits, especially cherry and cranberry, it is an intriguing wine though its modest structure and depth maybe due to young vines. Also produced under the Pompeiano IGT are an oak-fermented white from Coda di Volpe, and oak-aged red from Piedirosso (with 10 per cent Aglianico) under the Avalon label. Relatively large volumes of Lacryma Christi del Vesuvio are also produced, the white from Coda di Volpe, the red from Piedirosso. (PW)

● **Taurasi** Radici★★★★ £E   ● **Naturalis Historia**★★★ £F
● **Avellanio Aglianico**★ £B   ● **Avalon**★ £C   ○ **Avalon**★ £C
○ **Fiano di Avellino** Radici★★ £C   More Maiorum★★ £D
○ **Greco di Tufo** Vignadangelo★ £B   Nova Serra★★ £C

MONTEVETRANO Campania www.montevetrano.com A: **Wtr**, UnC, F&M, NYg, Las, F&R

Owner: Silvia Imparato Via Montevetrano, 84099 San Cipriano Picentino (SA)
Production of Montevetrano is only slightly higher (at 28,000 bottles a year) than GALARDI's Terra di Lavoro, another of the super-Campanian wines made by Riccardo Cotarella. Silvia Imparato's few hectares are at San Cipriano Picentino in hills behind the bustling coastal city of Salerno. Here Cabernet Sauvignon (60 per cent of the blend) and Merlot (30 per cent) hold sway, while Aglianico makes up the balance. The wine sold under the Colli di Salerno IGT has great structure and depth with considerable complexity and elegance and is not simply another internationally styled red. If this wine and others like it have little connection with commercial realities, they do provide the inspiration for others, while the rise and rise of FEUDI DI SAN GREGORIO, for example, shows that quality and quantity can be combined. (PW)
● Montevetrano★★★★★ £F

MORGANTE Sicilia www.morgante-vini.it A: **Lib**, NYg, But, N&P

Owner: Morgante family Contrada Racalmare, 92020 Grotte (AG)
Former growers and suppliers of wine for blending, the Morgante family have been producing their own wine since 1998 under the winemaking expertise of Riccardo Cotarella. From part of more than 200 ha of vines Nero d'Avola is made in two versions: a regular version (15,000 cases a year) has four months of oak-ageing, while Don Antonio (3,000 cases) is a superior selection which spends 12 months in new French oak. The oak is quite prominent in the latter but there is depth and intensity too in a sleek and stylish structure. The regular example, with good character and intensity, can be drunk quite young; Don Antonio is better with three to five years' age and will keep for longer. (PW)
● Nero d'Avola★★ £B ● Don Antonio★★★ £D

SALVATORE MURANA Sicilia A: **Eno**

Owner: Salvatore Murana Contrada Kamma 276, 91017 Pantelleria (TP)
Salvatore Murana is the top producer of Passito di Pantelleria, a delicious sweet wine made from Zibibbo grapes on the windswept volcanic island of Pantelleria between Sicily and Tunisia. The wines, especially at the top level, show greater refinement than others now being exported in increasing numbers. Murana's wines are named for the sub-zones from which they are produced. Martingana is the most concentrated and raisiny, a very powerful but stylish example. Khamma is also an excellent example with classic dried apricot and date aromas and flavours. Moscato di Pantelleria is a lighter style with lower alcohol and from grapes subjected to a shorter drying period. Mueggen has good intensity and a spicy, dried fruit character; Turbè is the least expensive version. New is a dry version of Zibibbo called Gadì. (PW)
O Passito di Pantelleria Khamma★★★ £F Martingana★★★★ £F
O Moscato di Pantelleria Mueggen★★ £E

PALARI Sicilia A: **Wtr**

Owner: Salvatore Geraci Loc. Santo Stefano Briga, 98137 Messina
In the premium wine from the Palari estate we are witnessing the revival of a wine name famous in the 14th century: Faro. From steep slopes high above the Straits of Messina, Salvatore Geraci undertook to breath life back into a DOC that had almost ceased to exist. Working with his brother, Giampiero, he also enlisted the winemaking expertise of Donato Lanati. Only local grapes have been used – Nerello Mascalese and Nerello Cappuccio as well as smaller amounts of other obscure varieties – though vinification and maturation are modern with ageing in French *barriques*. The wine impresses most with its nuanced complexity, which includes red fruits, coffee, herb and dried flowers, and its dimension and length. But this is also a wine of refined, discreet structure: don't come seeking colour, extract or incredible fruit richness – this is from a different part of the quality spectrum. Rosso del Soprano is a stylish second wine that can be drunk young or kept. (PW)
● Rosso del Soprano★★ £C ● Faro★★★★ £E

PATERNOSTER Basilicata www.paternostervini1925.com   **A: Eno**, Hfx

Owner: Giuseppe Paternoster & family   Via Nazionale 23, 85022 Barile (PZ)
In the rush for the new wave of quality wines now coming out of Basilicata this venerable producer should not be overlooked. This is still very much a family winemaking enterprise, dating back to 1925. Vinification and ageing is relatively traditional and in the top example, Don Anselmo, produces a deep, powerful wine, classically tight and closed in youth but rich and mesmerising with age. Almost as good but in a different, more modern style is Rotondo, which is subject to a shorter maceration and spends 14 months in *barriques*. The wine is richer and more immediate but stylish and sophisticated too. The bigger-volume Synthesi (aged mostly in large Slavonian casks) is ripe and supple, not a big wine but with good structure and needing just a couple of years' age. Also made are a partially *barrique*-fermented white from Fiano, Bianco di Corte, and a sweet white from Moscato grapes, Clivus. (PW)
● **Aglianico del Vulture** Synthesi★★ £C   Rotondo★★★★ £E   Don Anselmo★★★★ £E

PLANETA Sicilia www.planeta.it   **A: Eno**, JNi, Vne, P&S, Vts, Hrd, F&M, Res

Owner: Alessio, Francesca & Santi Planeta   Contrada Dispensa, 92013 Menfi (AG)
Planeta is a seemingly unstoppable engine that is producing marvellously consistent quality and doing wonders for Sicily's image in foreign markets. Building on an early reputation for international grapes some of the finest wines now also come from native varieties and more are being developed. The dynamic young Planetas have a wise and gifted winemaker in Carlo Corino. Total holdings now consist of four estates/wineries and 350 ha of vineyards: the Ulmo winery (near Sambuca) and the newer Dispensa winery (near Menfi) are in the west of Sicily but wines are also produced in Vittoria in the south and Noto in the south-east corner of the island (for new Moscato di Noto and Eloro DOC Nero d'Avola). The top wines are relatively expensive; the Santa Cecilia, from Nero d'Avola, and a pure Syrah are often the best with excellent fruit and length. Cabernet Sauvignon is very good too and a rich, intense Merlot shows more class since 2001. Cerasuolo di Vittoria, made since 2001 (and especially good value in 03) is a classic blend of Nero d'Avola and Frappato (60/40) with distinctive perfume, spice and very ripe red fruits. Rich, ripe Chardonnay is complex and powerful and a very good example of this style, showing more refinement in cooler vintages such as 2002. La Segreta Rosso and Bianco are much cheaper yet made to a high standard and represent the best value for money. The red is a blend of Nero d'Avola, Merlot and Syrah (60/20/20) and is consistenly good. The white is based on Grecanico but includes significant percentages of Chardonnay, Viognier and Sauvignon Blanc and the combination of citrus and more exotic fruit really sings out. Another white, Alastro, combines Grecanico and Chardonnay but a *barrique*-fermented component of the latter overwhelms the fruit somewhat. Cometa is an impressive powerful, concentrated, partly barrel-fermented and oak-aged white from Fiano grapes – not subtle but rich in exotic and dried stone fruits aromas and flavours. (PW)
● **Santa Cecilia**★★★ £D   ● **Syrah**★★★ £D
● **Burdese Cabernet Sauvignon**★★★ £D   ● **Merlot**★★★ £D   ○ **Chardonnay**★★★ £D
● **Cerasuolo di Vittoria**★★★ £C   ● **La Segreta**★★ £B   ○ **La Segreta**★★ £B
○ **Cometa**★★★ £C   ○ **Alastro**★ £B

RIVERA Puglia www.rivera.it   **A: Mdl**

*Owner: De Corato family & **Gancia**   Contrada Rivera, 70031 Andria (BA)*
Rivera is the leading advocate of the Castel del Monte DOC, which is relatively little known outside Italy, and has for years produced a characterful well-priced red in its Il Falcone. A considerably extended range now includes a flagship red ‚Pier Apuliae, from Nero di Troia (Uva di Troia). Made since the 2000 vintage, it shows much of the personality and class of this grape as well as a fine structure. In neither this nor in the more moderately priced Il Falcone (with 30 per cent Montepulciano) is oak allowed to dominate. Both wines, but particularly the deeper, more concentrated Pier Apuliae need time to show their true complexity. Cappellaccio, a 100 per cent Aglianico, is increasingly fine, while Triusco is straight Primitivo, soundly made

and reasonably priced. Rupicolo is an inexpensive red from the same grapes as Il Falcone but with the proportions reversed. Whites are more than adequate too, with an existing Chardonnay Preludio No.1 now complemented (from 2002) by a new, small-volume version, Lama di Corvo. Sauvignon and a rosé are also made. (PW)

● **Castel del Monte** Puer Apuliae★★★ £E Riserva Il Falcone★★ £B
● **Castel del Monte** Aglianico Riserva Cappellaccio★★ £B Rupicolo★ £B ● **Triusco**★★ £B
O **Castel del Monte** Chardonnay Preludio No.I★★ £B

SANTADI Sardegna www.cantinadisantadi.it   A: **Eno**,Vne, Hrd, P&S

Owner: 'Co-operative' Via Su Pranu 12, 09010 Santadi (CA)
The success and renown of the Santadi co-op is based around the Carignano grape (France's humble Carignan). The key here, as with a few top examples in the Languedoc, is that it ripens fully. Santadi has a deserved following for its combination of quantity and quality. The top wine is Terre Brune which also includes a tiny amount of Bovaleddu and is aged for 16 to 18 months in new French *barriques*. It is rich, powerful and structured, southern in its warmth and flavours and usually needs another three to five years' ageing after it is released (so is best with eight years' age or more). Rocca Rubia is made in much greater quantities (more than 12,000 cases) and has less weight and structure but plenty of style and can be drunk a little sooner. Baie Rosse (produced in 1997 and 98) was a herb-scented and ripe black fruited example of Carignano made in collaboration with the co-op on the island of Calasetta. Araja is an unoaked Carignano that includes 15 per cent Sangiovese. A basic yet stylish Carignano Grotta Rossa can be a good quaffing wine. Several good whites are also made. The Cala Silente has some lees contact for added complexity; citrusy, herbal Pedraia from Nuragus grapes is very fresh and appealing if drunk young; and Villa di Chiesa is a barrel-fermented blend of Vermentino and Chardonnay. The best white, however, is the sweet Latinia based on Nasco (as is the ARGIOLAS sweet wine), with lovely ripe fruit, real intensity, style and balance. (PW)

● **Carignano del Sulcis** Grotta Rossa★ £B Riserva Rocca Rubia★★★ £C Superiore Terre Brune★★★★ £E
● **Baie Rosse**★★★ £C ● **Araja**★ £B
O **Vermentino di Sardegna** Villa Solais★ £B Cala Silente★★ £B O **Nuragus di Cagliari** Pedraia★ £B
O **Villa di Chiesa**★ £C O **Latinia**★★★ £E

SELLA & MOSCA Sardegna www.sellaemosca.com   A: **Alv**, P&S, Sel

*Owner: **Campari group** Loc. I Piani, 07041 Alghero (SS)*
Owned by the makers of Cinzano and Riccadonna, Sella & Mosca makes a diverse range of wines from around 500 ha of vineyards in the north-west of Sardinia. Operations are directed by Mario Consorte, who combines the traditional and modern to produce an unusual range of wines. Most intriguing (but not recently tasted) is Riserva Anghelu Ruju, a fortified wine produced from Cannonau grapes dried in the sun for 15 days before spending eight years in large oak casks. As well as developing complex tertiary flavours, it reveals powerful spice and dried fruit characters too. Other reds include the firmly structured Tanca Farrà from Cannonau and Cabernet Sauvignon and Marchese di Villamarina, a varietal Cabernet. Terrerare is a red from Carignano del Sulcis but in common with most of Sella & Mosca's reds, it could use a little more refinement. Good examples of Vermentino are made while Le Arenarie is from Sauvignon Blanc. Terre Bianche is from the Torbato grape, only grown in the Alghero zone on Sardinia. (PW)

● **Alghero** Tanca Farrà★★ £C Marchese di Villamarina★★ £E
O **Vermentino di Gallura** Monteoro★ £B O **Vermentino di Sardegna** La Cala★ £B

CANTINA DEL TABURNO Campania www.cantinadeltaburno.it   A: **Eno**, Han, NYg,Vts

Owner: 'Co-operative' Via Sala, 82030 Foglianise (BN)
It is always a good sign when a region's co-ops start turning out high-quality wines. The decision to do so by the agrarian co-op of the Benevento province, with a winery close to the foot of Monte Taburno, is a recent one – helped by input from the University of Naples. Whites are a speciality with excellent examples

of Falanghina, Fiano and hitherto obscure Coda di Volpe. The quality of regular Falanghina and Fiano has improved immeasurably in successive vintages and the 2003s are the best yet. Small amounts of Falanghina are bottled as Cesco dell' Eremo and Folius, both with some *barrique* influence. Wood is also used for the varietal Coda di Volpe, subtly cradling its ripe, intense preserved fruit character. The spice, earth, smoke and plum of fine Aglianico are well expressed in Delius, especially with four or five years' age, but a better-value Fidelius is a decent introduction too. The crowning achievement is the Bue Apis from vineyards on the slopes of Monte Taburno, an Aglianico of great breadth and structure that sees 18 months in new oak following a long maceration. Its price reflects both its quality and limited production of just a few thousand bottles. A *passito* Falanghina, Ruscolo, is also produced. (PW)

● **Bue Apis**★★★★ £F ● **Delius**★★★ £D ● **Aglianico del Taburno** Fidelis★★ £B
○ **Serra Docile** Coda di Volpe★★ £C ○ **Taburno Falanghina**★★ £C ○ **Taburno Greco**★★ £C

TASCA D'ALMERITA Sicilia www.tascadalmerita.it A: **BWC**, Vts

Owner: Tasca d'Almerita family Contrada Regaleali, 90020 Sclafani Bagni (PA)
This large estate was acquired as long ago as 1830 and though much reduced by land reform in the 1950s currently has around 400 ha of high-altitude vineyards. Direction comes from the current Count, Lucio Tasca d'Almerita, who is dedicated not just to continuing, but to improving on the standards that set the estate apart when wine from Sicily meant nothing more than plonk. Winemaker Luigi Guzzo has recently had consultant input from Carlo Ferrini and there is ongoing research into grape varieties. Rosso del Conte (Nero d'Avola with a little Perricone) and Cabernet Sauvignon are the two leading reds, made to a consistently high standard. The Rosso del Conte, full of bramble, plum and spice fruit, is fleshy and ripe, adding chocolate and coffee flavours with age – composed yet characterful. The Cabernet is both powerful and remarkably refined. Nero d'Avola has been combined with Cabernet in Cygnus and with Merlot in Camastra, while Lamùri is a new varietal version. Whites are led by a rich, powerful Chardonnay which has good depth and well-integrated oak. Unwooded whites include the flavoursome Nozze d'Oro, from Inzolia and unidentified varieties (called Tasca), and characterful Leone d'Almerita which combines Cataratto with Chardonnay and Sauvignon. All wines used to appear under the Sicilia IGT, but the top wines now have their own DOC, Contea di Sclafani. Basic Regaleali red, white and rosé are made in big quantities and are excellent quaffing wines. (PW)

● **Contea di Sclafani** Rosso del Conte★★★★ £D Cabernet Sauvignon★★★★ £E
○ **Contea di Sclafani** Chardonnay★★★ £D Nozze d'Oro★★ £C
● **Camastra**★★ £C ● **Cygnus**★★ £C ○ **Leone d'Almerita**★★ £B

COSIMO TAURINO Puglia www.taurinovini.it A: **Hal**, Maj

Owner: Taurino family SS 605, 73010 Guagnano (LE)
Francesco Taurino works with the estate's long-serving consultant, Severino Garofano, who helped to produce most of Puglia's few memorable wines before its recent awakening. Rich, robust yet harmonious reds rely on the principles of picking very ripe fruit at low yields and the intelligent use of new oak. It is now a 165-ha estate but the top wine Patriglione comes from just 20 ha of vines, with a high average vine age. It is a wonderfully rich, complex and beautifully structured expression of southern Italy and its quality is surely the best argument in favour of the Negroamaro grape (though the wine also includes 10 per cent Malvasia Nera). The modestly priced Notarpanaro, a similar blend, is also produced from old vines and is dense and flavoursome. Both wines qualify for the DOC Brindisi but are sold as Salento IGT. The popular Salice Salentino Riserva, produced in fair quantity (60,000 cases), typically shows good intensity of flavour. A white, I Sierri, is from Chardonnay and Malvasia while Scaloti is a decent rosé. (PW)

● **Patriglione**★★★★ £E ● **Notarpanaro**★★ £B ● **Salice Salentino** Riserva★ £B

479

TELARO/LAVORO & SALUTE Campania www.vinitelaro.it

Owner: Telaro family Via Cinque Pietre, 81045 Galluccio (CE)
The three Telaro brothers produce a distinctive range of reasonably priced wines from Campania's leading grape varieties. The 40 ha of vines on their 85-ha estate on the lower slopes of the Roccamonfina volcano in northern Campania are farmed organically. Aglianico forms the basis of the reds and Falanghina, Fiano and Greco the whites. The top two reds are the Riservas, Ara Mundi from 100 per cent Aglianico and Calivierno, which includes some 10 to 15 per cent Piedirosso. Both show deep earth, mineral, herb and ripe fruit complexity, good density and ripe tannins as well as a proven ability to age well. Of similar style and character but more immediate and fruit-driven is Montecaruso, which also includes a little Piedirosso. Whites from Fiano and Greco are well made with good fruit. Falanghina shows extra style when made in a late-harvested Vendemmia Tardiva version. Unusual is a sweet Aglianico-based red made from dried grapes, Passito delle Cinque Pietre. Concentrated and intense, it shows reasonable balance if some astringency, avoids being too raisiny and releases a fusion of red fruit flavours and spice. (PW)
- **Galluccio Riserva** Ara Mundi★★★ £D Calivierno★★★ £D
- **Galluccio** Montecaruso★★ £B ● **Passito delle Cinque Pietre**★★ £D
- O **Galluccio** Ripabianca Falanghina★ £B O **Falanghina Vendemmia Tardiva**★★ £B
- O **Greco Le Cinque Pietre**★★ £B O **Fiano Le Cinque Pietre**★★ £B

TORMARESCA Puglia www.tormaresca.it   A: **BWC**,Vts, Cam

Owner: Vigneti del Sud (Antinori) Via Matenità ed Infanzia 21, 72027 San Pietro Vernotico (BR)
I wouldn't expect anything less than an unqualified success from an ANTINORI venture into Puglia and so it's proving. A total of 350 ha of vineyards are split between two estates, which give their names to the top two reds. Both the Masseria Maime (100 per cent Negroamaro), and Bocca di Lupo (90 per cent Aglianico, 10 per cent Cabernet Sauvignon) show great fruit definition, excellent texture and balance. Modern, yes, but characterful too. The deep spice and berry fruit of the Maime is one to contrast with other top examples of Negroamaro. At least as good is a deep, blackberry, earth and spice-rich Torcicorda, a varietal Primitivo from old vines. On a simpler level, there's good intensity (if also a slightly underripe aspect in the 2001) in the regular and relatively inexpensive Tormaresca Rosso, a blend of Negroamaro with Cabernet Sauvignon. Beyond a sound, attractive regular Chardonnay is the impressively rich if only moderately complex Pietrabianca. (PW)
- **Masseria Maime**★★★ £D ● **Castel del Monte** Bocca di Lupo★★★ £C
- **Torcicoda**★★★ £C ● **Tormaresca Rosso**★ £B
- O **Castel del Monte** Pietrabianca★★★ £C O **Tormaresca Chardonnay**★ £B

TORREVENTO Puglia www.torrevento.it   A: **Tri**

Owner: Azienda Vinicola Torrevento Srl Loc. Castel del Monte, 70033 Corato (BA)
Torrevento doesn't make the best wines in Puglia but quality has been steadily improved while prices remain low and although there's now lots of good value from any number of producers, few maintain it throughout the range so successfully. Located in the elevated Alta Murgia part of Puglia, Torrevento also provides an insight into the potential of the Uva di Troia grape as well as the more usual suspects, Negroamaro and Primitivo. Regular Castel del Monte red adds 20 per cent Aglianico to Uva di Troia while Vigna Pedale is 100 per cent Uva di Troia. In Torre del Falco the two Cabernets are complemented by Uva di Troia. The reds in particular show better balance and better expression than in the 90s. Winemaker Pasquale Carparelli also makes the I Pastini wines under his own label. In addition to stylish Primitivo and somewhat Viognier-like Locorotondo (from Verdecca, Fiano and Bianco d'Alessano) is an Aleatico, Elogia della Lentezza. A new Torrevento wine, Kebir, *barrique*-aged Cabernet Sauvignon and Uva di Troia, is the only wine priced at significant premium. Dulcis in Fundo is an attractive and aromatic, light but intense sweet wine. (PW)
Torrevento:
- **Castel del Monte Rosso**★ £A Riserva Vigna Pedale★★★ £B ● **Salice Salentino**★★ £B

● **Torre del Falco**★ £B   ◉ **Castel del Monte Rosato**★ £A
○ **Castel del Monte Bianco**★ £A   ○ **Moscato di Trani** Dulcis in Fundo★★ £B
Carparelli:
● **Primitivo** I Pastini★★ £B   ○ **Locorotondo**★★ £B

VALLONE Puglia   www.agricolevallone.com   A: **Mer**, L&W

Owner: Vallone family   Via XXV Luglio 5, 73100 Lecce
Vallone is comprised of three estates that include 170 ha of vines among other crops. As at some other top Puglian outfits, enologist Severino Garofano helps produce wines to a consistently high standard. The outstanding wine, Graticciaia, is a partially *barrique*-aged red made from (mostly) Negroamaro grapes that have been dried for around three weeks on mats (*graticci*) in the warm autumn sun. The resulting wine has powerful aromas of spice, very ripe berry, dried fruit and tobacco. There is rich, concentrated sweet fruit, depth and power but good balance and it may be drunk soon after release or kept. Other wines include Brindisi Rosso Vigna Flaminio (also made as a *rosato*), which shows very ripe fruit in a very supple structure while intensely flavoured Salice Salentino is one of the best made. Some Sauvignon Blanc is grown for both a dry white, Corte Valesio and a *passito* (dried grapes) version, Passo delle Viscarde, that also includes some Malvasia. (PW)

● **Graticciaia**★★★ £E   ● **Brindisi** Vigna Flaminio★★ £B
● **Salice Salentino** Vereto★ £B

CONTI ZECCA Puglia   www.contizecca.it   A: **HHB**, Hfx

Owner: Alcibiade Zecca   Via Cesarea, 73045 Leverano (LE)
From across the Salento peninsula in Puglia, Conti Zecca pumps out some fairly serious volume across the basic range, Donna Marzia but this also affords enologist Dr Fernando Antonio Romano the opportunity to make more modest quantities of progressively better wines from the DOCs of Salice Salentino and Leverano at slightly higher prices. From a fine wine point of view it also makes possible a premium red of very impressive fruit richness and complexity that is simply called Nero. Only 25,000 bottles are made. Based on Negroamaro it also includes 30 per cent Cabernet Sauvignon. Slightly less rich, more oaky yet very stylish Terra substitutes Aglianico for the Cabernet component. Both deserve five years' age. Also of commendable quality (and similarly striking labels) are a soft yet concentrated and characterful Primitivo and Cantalupi Riserva, a Salice Salentino of quite serious quality for the appellation (80 per cent Negroamaro and 20 per cent Malvasia Nera). The latter is particularly good value. (PW)

● **Nero**★★★ £D   ● **Leverano Riserva** Terra★★★ £C
● **Primitivo**★★ £B   ● **Salice Salentino Riserva** Cantalupi★★ £B
● **Leverano** Vigna del Saraceno★ £B   ○ **Leverano** Vigna del Saraceno★ £B

OTHER WINES OF NOTE

A MANO ● **Prima Mano** (Primitivo) £C
ANTICA MASSERIA DEL SIGILLO ● **Primitivo Sigillo Primo** £B
● **Terre del Guiscardo** (Primitivo/Merlot/Cabernet Sauvignon) £B
ANTICHI PODERI JERZU ● **Cannonau di Sardegna** Marghìa £B
● **Radames** (Cannonau/Cabernet Sauvignon/Carignano) £D
APOLLONIO ● **Copertino Rosso Riserva** Divoto £B   ● **Primitivo Terragnolo** £B
● **Valle Cupa** (Negroamaro /Primitivo) £B
BASILISCO ● **Aglianico del Vulture** £D
BOTROMAGNO ○ **Gravina** (Greco/Malvasia Bianca) £B   ○ **Gravisano** Passito di Malvasia £E
● **Pier delle Vigne** (Aglianico/Montepulciano) £B   ● **Primitivo** £B
CALATRASI ● **D'Istinto Magnifico** (Sangiovese/Cabernet Sauvignon/Syrah/Merlot) £C
CANDIDO ● **Cappello di Prete** (Negroamaro) £B
● **Duca di Aragona** (Negroamaro/Montepulciano) £C

● **Immensum** (Negroamaro/Cabernet Sauvignon) £C
CANTELE ● **Amativo** (Negroamaro/Primitivo) £C
● **Varius** (Negroamaro/Cabernet Sauvignon/Montepulciano) £B
CASTELLO MONACI ● **Salice Salentino** £B
CANTINE COLOSI O **Malvasia delle Lipari** Naturale di Salina £C Passito di Salina £D
O **Moscato di Pantelleria** £C O **Passito di Pantelleria** £D
COLLI DI LAPIO/CLELIA ROMANO O **Fiano di Avellino** £D
ATTILIO CONTINI O **Vernaccia di Oristano** Riserva £C Antico Gregori £E
COS ● **Cerasuolo di Vittoria** £B ● **Scyri** (Nero d'Avola) £C O **Ramí** (Inzolia/Grecanico) £B
D'ALFONSO DEL SORDO ● **Guado San Leo** (Uva di Troia) £D
● **Contrada del Santo** (Uva di Troia/Merlot) £C
DE CONCILIIS ● **Donnaluna Aglianico** £B ● **Naima** (Aglianico) £D
DUCA DI SALAPARUTA ● **Duca Enrico** (Nero d'Avola) £F
● **Triskelè** (Nero d'Avola/Cabernet Sauvignon/Merlot) £D O **Bianco di Valguarnera** (Inzolia) £E
FEOTTO DELLO JATO ● **Rosso di Turi** (Merlot) £C ● **Syrae** (Syrah) £C
O **Zabbya** (Cataratto - mod. sweet) £D
BENITO FERRARA O **Greco di Tufo** £C Vigna Cicogna £D
FEUDO PRINCIPI DI BUTERA (Zonin) ● **Nero d'Avola Deliella** £E
● **Merlot Calat** £E ● **Cabernet Sauvignon San Rocco** £E
FIRRIATO ● **Harmonium** (Nero d'Avola) £D ● **Camelot** (Cabernet Sauvignon/Merlot) £C
CANTINE FLORIO O **Marsala** Vergine Oro Terre Arse £C Vergine Oro Baglio Florio £C
O **Marsala Superiore** Riserva Vecchioflorio £C
O **Vino Liquoroso di Pantelleria** Morsi di Luce £C
CANTINA SOCIALE GALLURA O **Vermentino di Gallura** Canayli £B
GROTTA DEL SOLE ● **Campo Flegrei Piedirosso** £B ● **Lacryma Christi del Vesuvio** £B
● **Quarto di Sole** (Piedirosso/Aglianico) £C O **Campo Flegrei Falanghina** £B O **Greco di Tufo** £B
GULFI ● **Nerojbleo** (Nero d'Avola) £B
HAUNER O **Malvasia delle Lipari** Passito £E
LA RIVOLTA ● **Aglianico del Taburno** £B
SALVATORE MOLETTIERI ● **Taurasi** Vigna Cinque Querce £C
ODOARDI ● **Savuto** £B ● **Scavigna** Garrone £C
PALA O **Vermentino di Sardegna** Crabilis £B O **Entemari** (Vermentino/Chardonnay/Malvasia) £C
● **Cannonau di Sardegna** Triente £B ● **S'Arai** (Cannonau/Carignano/Bovale) £D
PAOLO PETRILLI ● **Cacc'e mmitte di Lucera** Agramonte £C ● **Ferraù** (Uva di Troia/Sangiovese) £C
ROSA DEL GOLFO ◉ **Rosato Rosa del Golfo** £B
● **Quarantale Riserva Mino Calò** (Negroamaro/Primitivo) £D
ALFONSO ROTOLO O **Valentina Paestrum** (Fiano) £B
TENUTE RUBINO ● **Marmorelle Rosso** (Negroamaro/Malvasia Nera) £B ● **Visellio** (Primitivo) £C
● **Jaddico** (Negroamaro/Montepulciano/Malvasia Nera) £C ● **Torre Testa** (Susumaniello) £D
O **Marmorelle Bianco** (Chardonnay/Malvasia Bianca) £B
FATTORIA SAN FRANCESCO ● **Cirò Rosso** Rondo dei Quattro Venti £C
SETTESOLI ● **Mandrarossa Bonera** (Nero d'Avola/Cabernet Sauvignon) £B
SOLIDEA O **Moscato di Pantelleria** £C O **Passito di Pantelleria** £D
SPADAFORA ● **Don Pietro** (Nero d'Avola/Cabernet Sauvignon/Merlot) £C
● **Virzì Rosso** (Nero d'Avola/Syrah) £C ● **Schietto** (Cabernet Sauvignon) £D
TERRE DEGLI SVEVI ● **Aglianico del Vulture** Re Manfredi £B
TERREDORA ● **Taurasi** Fatica Contadina £D O **Irpinia Falanghina** £B
O **Fiano di Avellino** Terre di Dora £C Campore £C O **Greco di Tufo** Loggia della Serra £C
TORRE QUARTO ● **Tarabuso** (Primitivo) £C ● **Bottaccia** (Uva di Troia) £C
● **Quarto Ducale** (Primitivo/Uva di Troia) £C
VALLE DELL' ACATE ● **Cerasuolo di Vittoria** £C ● **Il Moro** (Nero d'Avola) £C
VALLE DELL' ASSO O **Galatina Rosso** £B ● **Galatina Negroamaro** £B
CANTINA SOCIALE VERMENTINO O **Vermentino di Gallura** Funtanaliras £B
● **Cannonau di Sardegna** Tàmara £C ● **Galana** (Cabernet Sauvignon/Carignano/Cannonau/Cagnulari) £D
VESTINI CAMPAGNANO O **Palagrello Bianco** £D ● **Palagrello Nero** £E

VETRERE ○ Finis Terrae (Chardonnay/Fiano) £B ● **Tempio di Giano** (Negroamaro) £B
● **Livruni** (Primitivo) £B ● **Lago della Pergola** (Negroamaro) £C ● **Barone Pazzo** (Primitivo) £C
VILLA MATILDE ○ Falerno del Massico Vigna Caracci £B
● Falerno del Massico £B ● **Vigna Camarato** (Aglianico) £D
CONSORZIO VITICOLTORI ASSOCIATI DEL VULTURE ● Aglianico del Vulture Carpe Diem £B
● **Aglianico del Vulture** Vetusto £C

Author's choice (PW)

15 southern red stars

ABBAZIA SANTA ANASTASIA ● **Litra**
ARGIOLAS ● **Turriga**
BENANTI ● **Lamorèmio**
CEUSO ● **Custera**
DETTORI ● **Cannonau Dettori**
DONNAFUGATA ● **Contessa Entellina Mille e Una Notte**
LIBRANDI ● **Gravello**
MONTEVETRANO ● **Montevetrano**
MORGANTE ● **Don Antonio**
PALARI ● **Faro**
SANTADI ● **Carignano del Sulcis** Superiore Terre Brune
TASCA D'ALMERITA ● **Contea di Sclafani** Rosso del Conte
COSIMO TAURINO ● **Patriglione**
VALLONE ● **Graticciaia**
CONTI ZECCA ● **Nero**

10 superior expressions of Aglianico

BASILISCO ● **Aglianico del Vulture**
ANTONIO CAGGIANO ● **Taurasi** Vigna Macchia dei Goti
CANTINE DEL NOTAIO ● **Aglianico del Vulture** La Firma
D'ANGELO ● **Canneto**
FEUDI DI SAN GREGORIO ● **Taurasi** Selve di Luoti
GALARDI ● **Terra di Lavoro**
TENUTA LE QUERCE ● **Aglianico del Vulture** Vigna Corona
SALVATORE MOLETTIERI ● **Taurasi** Vigna Cinque Querce
PATERNOSTER ● **Aglianico del Vulture** Rotondo
TELARO/LAVORO & SALUTE ● **Galluccio** Riserva Ara Mundi

15 brilliant inexpensive reds

ACCADEMIA DEI RACEMI/FELLINE ● **Vigna del Feudo**
ACCADEMIA DEI RACEMI/SINFAROSA ● **Primitivo di Mandura** Zinfandel
APOLLONIO ● **Vale Cupa**
TENUTA LE QUERCE ● **Aglianico del Vulture** Il Viola
LEONE DE CASTRIS ● **Salice Salentino** Riserva
MORGANTE ● **Nero d'Avola**
PLANETA ● **La Segreta Rosso**
COSIMO TAURINO ● **Notarpanaro**
TELARO/LAVORO & SALUTE ● **Galluccio** Montecaruso
CANTINA DEL TABURNO ● **Aglianico del Taburno** Fidelis
TORREVENTO ● **Castel del Monte** Riserva Vigna Pedale
VALLE DELL'ACATE ● **Cerasuolo di Vittoria**
VALLONE ● **Salice Salentino** Vereto
VETRERE ● **Tempio di Giano**
CONTI ZECCA ● **Salice Salentino** Riserva Cantalupi

10 captivating whites

BENANTI ○ **Etna Bianco** Superiore Pietramarina
ANTONIO CAGGIANO ○ **Fiano di Avellino** Béchar
GIOVANNI CHERCHI ○ **Vermentino di Sardegna** Tuvaoes
COS ○ **Ramì**
CUSUMANO ○ **Cubìa**
FEUDI DI SAN GREGORIO ○ **Sannio** Falanghina
PLANETA ○ **Cometa**
SANTADI ○ **Vermentino di Sardegna** Cala Silente
TASCA D'ALMERITA ○ **Contea di Sclafani** Nozze d'Oro
TORMARESCA ○ **Castel del Monte** Pietrabianca

10 delicious sweet whites

ARGIOLAS ○ **Angialis**
BENANTI ○ **Passito di Pantelleria** Coste di Mueggen
BOTROMAGNO ○ **Gravisano** Passito di Malvasia
ANTONIO CAGGIANO ○ **Mel**
DE BARTOLI ○ **Passito di Pantelleria** Bukkuram
DONNAFUGATA ○ **Passito di Pantelleria** Ben Ryé
FEUDI DI SAN GREGORIO ○ **Privilegio**
LIBRANDI ○ **Le Passule**
SALVATORE MURANA ○ **Passito di Pantelleria** Martingana
SANTADI ○ **Latinia**

While for years the quality of Spanish wine in the more established regions and DOs had been acceptable it could also have fairly been said that the real potential in the country remained untapped. However, the past half-decade or so has seen dramatic change both in fine-wine production and in lesser regions. There are new-wave Riojas and an abundance of great reds from Castilla y Leon, but other, smaller regions like Priorat have also been providing some remarkable and striking wines in recent years. Further south, in the great centre of the country, relaxation of the regulations governing irrigation and a desire to harness the potential of some fine, old bush-vine plantings of regional varieties has brought small but commendable change. It remains depressing, however that with all this there is still a sizeable amount of very mediocre wine being produced in almost all the established regions.

The North-East

País Vasco is the Spanish Basque country and home to two tiny DOs with barely 125 ha between them. Both are close to the coast between Bilbao and San Sebastien. **Getariako Txakolina** is the more western of the two and slightly larger than **Bizkaiko Txakolina**. The best are dry, quite steely whites based on Hondarribi Zuri. The north-western sector of the **Rioja** DO stretches into País Vasco and includes some of the best of the region's sites in the Rioja Alavesa. The Rioja wine zone spreads out of the administrative region of Rioja, its borders stretching into Navarra to its north-east and Castilla y León to the west. The wine area is split into three sub-regions: Alavesa, Alta and Baja. Tempranillo performs well in the limestone soils of the Alavesa, which is moderated by cooling breezes, as is the Alta. The latter, though, has heavier clay soils more suitable for Garnacha, which dominates the plantings in the hotter Baja sub-region. Graciano is also planted and makes an important impact on many blends as well as providing the odd varietal. Most wines are a blend of the regions and, while generally the fruit of the Alavesa is the finest, there are outposts of quality in all three. Whites are dominated by Viura with some Garnacha Blanca and Malvasia but few are of anything like the quality of the reds. Of equal importance is the approach of the bodegas. The area has some very substantial producers but quality remains variable. The original ageing classifications of Crianza, Reserva and Gran Reserva are still in place but varietal labels are becoming far more commonplace and many fine new-wave premium wines are being produced, which are generally vinified with French rather than American oak. Some, it has to be said, are very pricey.

Navarra shares the native Tempranillo, Garnacha and Viura with Rioja but also has considerable plantings of the international varieties; Cabernet Sauvignon, Merlot and Chardonnay are all found in abundance here. Some impressive wines are produced but one often feels price is a key in the producer's approach and there should be more excitement than there is. To the east and stretching far towards the south of Navarra are the arid plains of Aragón. Bulk wine is generally the order of the day but there are two DOs worth considering: **Campo de Borja** and **Somontano**. There is nothing spectacular but some good reds and the occasional Chardonnay stand out.

Running south from the Pyrenees and along the Mediterranean coast on the Costa Brava is Cataluña, home to a number of diverse wine regions. Right up close to the French border a few fine, traditional reds are made in the **Empordà-Costa Brava** DO. Some good red and white is produced from the **Costers del Segre** DO and a vast array of indigenous and international grapes are planted. To the immediate east are the vineyards of **Conca de Barberá**, cooled by altitude and source of good Chardonnay and Pinot Noir, but most of the fruit is sold on. Just inland from the coast and south-west of Barcelona are the vineyards of **Penedès**, established in a global sense by the efforts of Miguel Torres. Some fine reds and whites are produced, again from a mix of local and international varieties but much of the output is relatively pedestrian. Interestingly the odd low-volume, garage-style red is appearing too. Penedès is also the centre of the vast **Cava** DO. These sparkling wines are made by the traditional method from a combination of local Macabeo, Parellada and Xarel-lo as well as Chardonnay and Pinot Noir. Some well-crafted vintage bottlings are produced but generally the quality is sound at best. Many operations are very substantial and automation in the cellars is common. Cava at the lower levels can often display a marked rubbery character.

Immediately to the west of Penedès are the vineyards of **Tarragona**, which has a superior new sub-region, **Monsant** DO, and the small, very high-quality region of **Priorat**. Tarragona is planted to a range of varieties and fortified wines are still produced here. It is the reds, though, that excel and none more so than the suberb old-vine plantings of Garnacha. The best can rival top-quality Châteauneuf-du-Pape. The reds in Priorat are the wines with the greatest potential. They include a fascinatingly variable blend comprising Garnacha, Cariñena, Cabernet Sauvignon, Syrah, Merlot and Pinot Noir. The vineyards are ideally planted in finely drained, stony soils and the climate is warm but not excessively so.

The North-West

The wines of north-western Spain are produced in Castilla y León and Galicia. Immediately to the west of Rioja is **Ribera del Duero** which, along with exceptional examples in Rioja and Priorat, produces the finest reds in the country. The historic Vega Sicilia bodega is based here and top reds are produced in and around the region as *vino de mesa* as well as DO. While the greatest Ribera del Duero wines are both magnificent and pricey, a vast number remain depressingly mediocre. The wines are based on Tinto Fino (Tempranillo) but may also include Cabernet Sauvignon, Merlot and Malbec in the blend.

To the north-west is the small DO of **Cigales**, where some improving, structured reds are made, and to the west the white-wine DO of **Rueda**. Interesting barrel-fermented wines from both Sauvignon Blanc and the local Verdejo are produced. The latter can be responsible for some very striking and potentially ageworthy whites. Immediately west of Rueda and also centred on the Duero river towards Zamora and Portugal is the warm red-wine area of **Toro**. The vineyard area here has always promised much but it is only recently that wines of real depth have begun to emerge, some world-class. A local strain of Tempranillo, Tinto de Toro, is the mainstay of blends but Garnacha is also permitted. In the far west of the Castilla y León region is the small DO of **Bierzo** which now produces both easy-drinking and exciting reds and a little white.

Next to Bierzo but in fact in Galicia is **Valdeorras**. Reds are produced, like those in Bierzo, from Mencía but of particular note are the whites produced from the unusual, indigenous Godello. The best are floral, ripe and respond well to handling in oak. Some attractive, fruity whites are also produced in **Ribeiro** but the greatest interest lies in the coastal vineyards of **Rías Baixas**. Their strikingly aromatic whites are generally best enjoyed young but the odd example is successfully barrel-fermented and will keep in the short to medium term, not dissimilar in this respect to Condrieu.

Central Spain

The vast central plains and particularly **La Mancha** are not generally associated with wines of any substance. Things are beginning to change, though, and new and interesting wines are emerging. Identifying cooler mesoclimates and harnessing the sheer quality of some of the old bush vines and outcrops of well-drained soils are some of the keys. The introduction of irrigation over the last decade has also given this arid area greater scope. It would appear so far that the best potential for reds is to the east of the area nearer the coast in **Valencia**, in the DOs of **Utiel-Requena** and **Jumilla**. The indigenous Bobal and Monastrell are both proving very successful. Some good fortified wine is produced from Monastrell at **Alicante**, as are some fine, sweet Moscatels. Cabernet Sauvignon, Merlot and Syrah are also grown with the aid of irrigation to the north of La Mancha. **Valdepeñas** used to be considered a beacon amongst the other wine regions of the area but nothing of real consequence has emerged recently.

The South

The south is fortified-wine country, most specifically the sherries of **Jerez y Manzanilla**. Andalucía is also home to the fortified wines of **Montilla-Moriles** and **Málaga**. Most of the former are decidedly ordinary but there are some exceptional wines from old *soleras*. The wines of Málaga are very rare, a blend of sweet wine and grape juice, some of which is fortified. The sherry industry is centred around the towns of Jerez and Sanlúcar de Barrameda to the north of Cádiz. The wines are all raised in a *solera* system which is maintained by fresh young wines. Fino sherry in Jerez is very similar to Manzanilla at Sanlúcar. Both are best drunk on release for their fresh, salty character imbued by a period under *flor* yeast. Manzanilla Pasada is a nutty, aged wine, having been exposed to *flor* influence, as is Amontillado. Oloroso will have no *flor* character at all, having been immediately fortified above 18 degrees alcohol. Palo Cortado is halfway in style between Fino and Amontillado. Rich and concentrated fortified Moscatel is also produced in the area as well as Pedro Ximènez.

A-Z of producers by region

Rueda

BOD. DE CRIANZA CASTILLA LA VIEJA	492
HERMANOS DEL VILLAR	509

Tarragona

CELLER DE CAPÇANES	493

Toro

MAURODOS	502
REJADORADA	505

Utiel Requena

MUSTIGUILLO	503

1	Rías Baixas	*13*	Campo de Borja
2	Ribeiro	*14*	Somontano
3	Valdeorras	*15*	Costers del Segre
4	Bierzo	*16*	Empordà-Costa Brava
5	Toro	*17*	Conca de Barberá
6	Cigales	*18*	Penedès
7	Rueda	*19*	Tarragona
8	Ribera del Duero	*20*	Priorat
9	Bizkaiko Txakolina	*21*	Montsant
10	Getariako Txakolina	*22*	Terra Alta
11	Rioja	*23*	Utiel-Requena
12	Navarra	*24*	Valencia

25	Alicante
26	Yecla
27	Jumilla
28	Almansa
29	Valdepeñas
30	La Mancha
31	Vinos de Madrid
32	Montilla-Moriles
33	Málaga
34	Jerez-Xérès-Sherry, Manzanilla
	Sanlúcar de Barrameda

Spanish vintages

Although there is a reasonably uniform climate in most of Spain's more southerly regions, the chart below should provide a good guide as to what to expect with the premium red-wine areas. The maturity guide applies to top wines. Spains fine reds are increasingly ageworthy and this as well as a move towards earlier releases requires the top crus to be cellared after release despite highly sophisticated modern winemaking in the best examples. Dry whites generally should be drunk on or shortly after release. The great fortified wines will be ready to drink on release.

Spanish vintage chart

	Rioja	Ribera del Duero	Priorat
2003	★★★★ A	★★★★/★★★★★★ A	★★★★ A
2002	★★★/★★★★ A	★★★/★★★★ A	★★★/★★★★ A
2001	★★★★/★★★★★★ A	★★★★/★★★★★ A	★★★★ A
2000	★★★ B	★★★ A	★★★/★★★★ A
1999	★★★/★★★★ B	★★★/★★★★ A	★★★/★★★★ A
1998	★★★ B	★★★/★★★★ A	★★★★/★★★★★★ A
1997	★★★ B	★★★ B	★★★ B
1996	★★★ B	★★★★ B	★★★★ B
1995	★★★★ B	★★★★ B	★★★★ B
1994	★★★★/★★★★★★ B	★★★★ B	★★★★/★★★★★★ B
1993	★★★ C	★★/★★★ C	★★★/★★★★ B
1990	★★★/★★★★ C	★★★★ C	★★★★ C

Spain/A-Z of producers

AALTO Ribera del Duero www.aalto.es A: F&R,N&P

Owner: Aalto Bodegas y Vinedos SA Roa de Duero, 09300 Burgos
Very impressive new estate producing a richly concentrated, dense, modern style Ribera del Duero. The operation is relatively small with production of between 8,000 and 9,000 cases a year from 82 ha of vineyards. Aalto owns 32 ha and lease a further 50 ha and both are effectively farmed organically. All the vines are over 40 years old and yields can easily be kept to a minimum. Among the small group of partners Mariano Garcia looks after winemaking; formerly he spent 30 years as the enologist at VEGA SICILIA. His regime ensures careful sorting and ageing in 70 per cent new French oak. The wine is powerful, supple and very complex, full of dark fruits and oriental spices. The PS bottling adds an extra dimension and will only be released in the best vintages. (DM)
● **Ribera del Duero** Aalto★★★★ £E Aalto PS★★★★★ £F

ABADÍA RETUERTA Castilla y León www.abadia-retuerta.com A: C&D,JAr

Owner: Novartis Group Sardon de Duero, 47540 Valladolid
Ambitious but very impressive project based just outside the boundaries of Ribera del Duero. There are now over 200 ha of vineyards and although the range is extensive, quality is uniformly impressive. Considerable investment has been put into the operation, which includes a state-of-the-art, gravity-fed winery. The Bordeaux red varieties are planted as well as Tempranillo and Syrah. Viña Arnaldo, Primicia and Rivola offer attractive early drinking, while the Abadía Retuerta Especial red is fuller, more structured and with more oak. El Campanario Reserva is produced from Tempranillo, El Palomar from Tempranillo and Cabernet Sauvignon. Limited amounts of three special top *cuvées* represent the pinnacle here: Pago Valdebellón from Cabernet Sauvignon, Pago Negrallada from Tempranillo and PV produced from Petit Verdot. These top reds are very ageworthy. (DM)
● **El Palomar** Vino de Mesa★★★★ £F ● **Pago Negrallada** Vino de Mesa★★★★★ £G
● **Selección Especial** Vino de Mesa★★★ £D ● **Cuvée El Campanario** Vino de Mesa★★★ £E
● **Primicia** Vino de Mesa★ £B ● **Viña Arnoldo** Vino de Mesa★★ £B ● **Rivola** Vino de Mesa★★ £C

BODEGAS AGNUSDEI Rías Baixas A:Msp

Owner: David Castro Axis Seames, 36968 Meaño, Pontevedra
This small operation was established just three years ago and there are 18 ha of vineyards in the heart of the Rías Baixas region in the Valle do Salnés. Investment continues in new winery equipment and some fruit is still bought in while the estate vineyards gradually come on stream. The sole wine here is 100 per cent Albariño, tank-fermented and full of enticing minerally, steely floral fruit. Both fresh and intense, it is best drunk young for its perfume – say within its first 12 to 18 months. This is undoubtedly a winery to watch in the region as its vineyards age. (DM)
○ **Rías Baixas** Albariño★★★ £C

AGRO DE BAZÁN Rías Baixas

Owner: Agro de Bazan S.A. Tromoedo 46, Villanueva de Arosa, 36628 Pontevedra
Small, first-class producer in this potentially high-quality appellation in Galicia, with a mere 13 ha under vine. Many Albariño-based whites are produced for early consumption and can lack grip and structure, as is the case with the approachable, but attractively aromatic Granbazán Verde. However, the Granbazán Ambar is richer and more concentrated, resembling a good Condrieu. It has a pure mineral structure and the depth to develop well over two or three years – not long-lived but richly harmonious with a little bottle-development. (DM)
○ **Rías Baixas** Granbazán Verde★★ £B Granbazán Ambar★★★ £C

ALEMANY I CORRIO   Penedès   A: **Vne**

Owner: Laurent Corrio & Joan & Irene Alemany   Melió, 78, 08720 Vilafranca del Penedès
In comparison to many other premium Penedès operations this is veritably tiny, a warehouse winery with
an output of less than 500 cases a year of the brilliant red Sot Lefriec. Now a very passable second wine, Pas
Curtei, has been added to help ensure the integrity and quality of the top wine. Both Laurent Corrio and
Irene Alemany studied enology in Burgundy and the partners now have 8 ha of their own vineyards planted
to old-vine Cariñena (60 years) and 20-year-old Merlot and Cabernet Sauvignon. Both wines are blends of
the three varieties, with Merlot dominating. The wines are handled as naturally as possible by gravity and
inert gas and bottled unfined and unfiltered. The Sot Lefriec will develop very well with six or seven years'
age. (DM)
● **Penedès** Pas Curtei★★ £C Sot Lefriec★★★★ £F

FINCA ALLENDE   Rioja   fallende@fer.es   A: **M&V**

Owner: Miguel Angel de Gregorio   Pl. Ibarra 1, Briones, 26330 La Rioja
One of the very best producers in Rioja. The first wine was actually only produced here in 1995. Most of
the fruit comes from their own vineyards in the Rioja Alta although some other growers are used also.
Impressive Rioja Blanco, blended from Viura and Malvasia is fermented and aged for a year in French oak.
The Rioja Tinto gets just over a year in a combination of French and American wood. There are two other
very concentrated and complex reds. Calvario is Tempranillo with a bit of Garnacha and Graciano and
comes from a single vineyard planted in 1945. The top wine, the pricey Aurus from 60-year-old vines, is
equally impressive – unfiltered and vinified with some whole bunches as well as being given a lengthy
conventional maceration of around four weeks, thus adding weight and a supple texture. Both very complex
and harmonious, it will age gracefully. (DM)
● **Rioja**★★ £B Calvario★★★★ £F Aurus★★★★★ £G
O **Rioja** Blanco★★ £B

ISMAEL ARROYO   Ribera del Duero   www.valsotillo.com   A: **N&P, NYg**

Owner: Arroyo family   Los Lagares 71, Sotillo de la Ribera, 09441 Burgos
Fine, quality producer of dense, powerful and tannic Ribera del Duero. The wines can be among the best
in the DO. Top wines from the small 16-ha estate vineyard holding go under the Val Sotillo label and
include Crianza, Reserva and Gran Reserva. Even the Crianza is very structured while the Gran Reserva has
formidable extract with concentrated, dark fruit, subtle, spicy oak and real refinement. These are wines that
demand to be cellared. (DM)
● **Ribera de Duero** Val Sotillo★★ £B Val Sotillo Crianza★★★ £C Val Sotillo Reserva★★★ £E
● **Ribera de Duero** Val Sotillo Gran Reserva★★★★ £F

ARTADI   Rioja   A: **BBR, GVWV, NYg, Bal, F&M**

Owner: Cosecheros Alaveses S.A.   Ctra. Logroño, Laguardia, 01300 Alava
This is the brand name of the Cosecheros Alaveses bodega and an impressive range of new-wave Rioja is
produced here from 75 ha of vineyards. The range includes well-crafted regular white and red; the former
is barrel-fermented while the latter sees no oak. A level up are the Viñas de Gain Crianza and the more
expensive Pagos Viejos Reserva. Both are rich, ripe and concentrated reds in marked contrast to the many
other disappointing examples emanating from the region in recent years. There are also two other very
impressive Reservas: Viña El Pisón comes from a single vineyard whereas the Grandes Añadas is a very
limited special bottling. It is only released in the greatest years and is very pricey. A fine modern source of
Rioja, the company also now has an investment in the newly established Navarra property Artazu and in
particular the old-vine Grenache Santa Cruz de Artazu. (DM)
● **Rioja** Viñas de Gain★ £B Viñas de Gain Crianza★★ £C Pagos Viejos Reserva★★★ £E

● **Rioja** Viña El Pisón Reserva★★★★ £F
O **Rioja** Viñas de Gain★ £B

BODEGA BALCONA   Bullas   www.paralelo40.org/partal/

Owner: Josefa Fernández   C/ Democrazia 7, 30180 Bullas, Murcia
The Fernández family made their first vintage as recently as 1998, having been inspired by José Luis Pérez Verdú of MAS MARTINET in Priorat. They have been grape growers for generations and as such have a tremendous resource in extensive plantings of old-vine Monastrell, many plots approaching 50 years of age. The climate here is benign with warm summer days contrasting with cool nights as a result of the altitude of the vineyards (around 825 m). The soils are a combination of clay and limestone, which provides an excellent base for high-quality vine growth. Investment has been extensive in the winery with stainless steel tanks, temperature control and French and American oak for maturation. Two wines are currently being produced. The Seleccion is mainly Monastrell and can be a bit four-square and rustic. The Crianza by contrast is vibrant and intense with piercing dark, spicy berry fruit and supple, well-rounded tannins. It will develop well over four or five years. (DM)

● **Bullas** Partal Seleccion★ £B Partal Crianza★★★ £C

BARBADILLO   Jerez y Manzanilla   www.barbadillo.com   A: JEF

Owner: Antonio Barbadillo S.A.   Luis de Eguilaz 11, Sanlúcar de Barrameda, 11540 Cádiz
This producer is based in Sanlúcar de Barrameda and the key focus is the production of good and often exceptional Manzanilla. There are two lighter styles, Solear and En Rama, which resemble Jerez Fino. The En Rama is very intense with a real salty, yeasty depth and a piercing background citrus character. In addition there is an excellent, nutty, aged style of Amontillado de Sanlúcar – bone-dry, almost austere but marvellously intense – a Manzanilla Pasada and the rich, powerful and heady Cuco Oloroso. A number of remarkable old wines from venerable soleras are available and labelled as Relics, including Amontillado, Oloroso, Palo Cortado and Pedro Ximénez. They are understandably very pricey but are surely at the pinnacle of great sherries. (DM)

O **Solear** Manzanilla★★ £B O **En Rama** Manzanilla★★ £B O **Principe** Amontillado★★★ £C
O **Cuco** Oloroso Seco★★★ £C O **Amontillado de Sanlúcar**★★★ £C O **Manzanilla Pasada**★★★ £C
O **Obispo Gascón** Palo Cortado★★ £C O **La Cilla** Pedro Ximénez★★ £C

BODEGAS BORSAO   Campo de Borja   www.bodegasborsao.com   A:Bur

Owner: Co-operative   Capuchinos, 10, Borja, 50540 Zaragoza
Long-established operation with over 400 members who between them control 1,450 ha of vineyards. It has long been regarded as a source of well-made and well-priced regional Spanish reds. However, over recent vintages quality seems to be improving and the wines, particularly at the top end, are more sophisticated and exciting. The Viña Borgia (labelled as such in the UK) is a good, straightforward, fruit-driven style of 100 per cent Garnacha. It is also labelled Primizia in other markets. The Borsao blends Garnacha with Tempranillo and Cabernet Sauvignon as do the more seriously structured Crianza and Reserva Seleccion labels. The Crianza is aged in French and American oak for 8 months, the Reserva solely in French barrels for over a year. The most exciting wine, though ,is the 100 per cent Garnacha, Tres Picos, sourced from vineyards of 35 to 40 years of age. A wine of classical structure and depth, offering complex dark berry fruit and herbal spices. The top reds will develop well in the short term. (DM)

● **Campo de Borja** Crianza Selección★★ £B Reserva Selección★★★ £B Tres Picos★★★ £C
● **Campo de Borja** Vina Borgia★ £B Borsao★★ £B

BODEGAS DE CRIANZA CASTILLA LA VIEJA   www.palaciodebornas.com   A: Res

Owner: Sanz family   Ctra. Madrid-A Coruña, Rueda, 47490 Valladolid
This is one of the best modern producers of Rueda. As well as white-wine interests in Rueda it also produces

impressive Toro at the Bodegas Toresanas, including the Toro Amant Barrica – a supple, modern, fruit-driven style with some depth and substance. Among a fine line-up of Rueda whites under the Palacio de Bornos label there are a grassy, fresh Sauvignon Blanc that should be drunk young and three wines based on Verdejo. The Superior, which has a touch of Viura, is similarly fresh, grassy and herbaceous in style. Other wines are handled in oak. The Fermentado en Barrica is rich, toasty and buttery, while the Vendimia Seleccionada is more structured, with the pure green Verdejo fruit always making itself felt. (DM)

O **Rueda** Bornos Sauvignon Blanc★★ £B Superior Palacio de Bornos★★ £B
O **Rueda** Palacio de Bornos Fermentado en Barrica★★ £B Palacio de Bornos Vendimia Selecionnada★★★ £C
Bodegas Toresanas
● **Toro** Amant Barrica★★ £B

CELLER DE CAPÇANES Tarragona capsanes@retemail.es A: Vni

Owner: Co-operatve Llabería, Capçanes, 43776 Tarragona

Arguably Spain's finest co-operative, established way back in 1933, it must also be regarded as among the very best in Europe. It was really only in 1995 that high quality was achieved as a result of the production of a remakable Kosher wine, Flor de Primavera. This initiative was promoted by the Jewish community of Barcelona who wished to produce a high-quality wine under strict *Lo mebushal* conditions, with everything carried out by a rabbi (with guidance) and no pasteurisation of the wine. It has evolved into a splendid blend of Cabernet Sauvignon, Garnacha, Tempranillo and Cariñena. With the resulting new investment that this development brought the range of reds here is now extensive and generally very impressive. The 120-strong membership provides some splendid old-vine Garnacha, Tempranillo and Cariñena as well as Merlot, Syrah and Cabernet Sauvignon, drawing on close to 250 ha of vineyards. The top-labelled reds are now classified under the recently established Monsant DO. Among the best wines are two ripe, berry-fruited styles – Mas Collet and Lasendal – which have a big dollop of Garnacha. Lasendal has some Syrah adding firm, tannic depth. Costers del Gravet is fuller and more structured – a blend of Cabernet Sauvignon, Garnacha, Cariñena and Tempranillo – but the tannin can be a touch raw in its youth. The Vall de Calàs, a blend of Merlot, Garnacha and Tempranillo is suppler and rounder with dark plum fruit. The top two wines, Mas Turtò and Cabrida, are both massively extracted, dense and powerful reds. The former is dominated by old-vine Garnacha, with Cabernet Sauvignon and Syrah lending structure and perfume. Cabrida, 100 per cent very old-vine Garnacha (some close to 100 years), is macerated on skins for four to five weeks and has a modern touch with malolactic in barrel, most of the oak being French. It is immensely concentrated, just lacking that element of extra refinement for true greatness but very impressive and ageworthy nonetheless. All of the wines offer excellent value for money. (DM)

● **Monsant** Mas Collet★★ £B Lasendal★ £B Costers del Gravet★★★ £B Vall de Calàs★★ £B
● **Monsant** Mas Turtò★★★ £C Flor de Primavera★★★ £D Cabrida★★★★ £E

CASA CASTILLO Jumilla A: M&V

Owner: Sánchez-Cerezo Roch family Ctra. Jumilla-Hellín, Jumilla, Murcia

Among a number of rising stars from Spain's lesser-known southern regions. Despite the hot, arid climate of the area the vineyards here are planted at an altitude of over 700 m and this elevation and the limestone soils provide old bush-vine Monastrell (Mourvèdre) of exceptional quality. Vendimia, a blend of Tempranillo as well as Monastrell, is full of vibrant juicy fruit; the varietal Monastrell is richer, fuller but equally approachable young. The top two wines are impressively concentrated and structured. Las Gravas has 40 per cent Cabernet Sauvignon and 10 per cent Syrah in the blend to lend grip to the dark, brambly old-vine fruit. It is aged in French oak. Pie Franco is 100 per cent Monastrell from ungrafted vines that are over 60 years old. Rich, dense and spicy, the wine is aged in mainly American oak. So far these all offer very good value. (DM)

● **Jumilla** Vendimia★ £B Monastrell★★ £B Las Gravas★★★★ £C Pie Franco★★★★ £D

CASTELL DEL REMEI Costers de Segre www.castelldelremei.com A: Mor, His

Owner: Cusiné family 25333 Lleida

Apart from RAIMAT, this is the only major quality producer in this DO and arguably the best. Good to very good reds are made here along with Blanc Panell, a tank-fermented blend of Macabeo, Sauvignon Blanc and Chardonnay, and Oda Blanc, which is vinified and aged on lees for six months in American oak. The reds really stand out. Gotim Bru is a ripe, forward blend of Tempranillo, Merlot and Cabernet Sauvignon with a spicy hint of cinnamon from 10 months' ageing in American wood, which is used for all the reds here. Oda is denser and more structured, a blend of Merlot, Cabernet Sauvignon and Tempranillo. The top label, 1780, is a firmly structured blend of Cabernet Sauvignon, Tempranillo and Merlot. The top two reds will benefit from two or three years' cellaring after release. (DM)

● **Costers del Segre** Gotim Bru★★ £B Oda★★ £C 1780★★★ £D

CELLER DEL PONT Priorat www.cellerdelpont.com A: Vni

Owner: Francisco Fernández & Montse Nadal C/ del Riu No1, 43374 La Vilella Baixa

Recently established small Priorat property producing less than 400 cases a year of a sturdy, powerful and richly mineral-laden red, Lo Givot. The wine is a blend of Garnacha, Cariñena, Cabernet Sauvignon and Syrah. At present the vineyard area stretches over around 5 ha, and half of the vines are over 50 years old, planted on free-draining shale hillside slopes. All of the varieties are vinified separately in stainless steel and maturation takes place in mainly French and some American oak for 12 to 14 months. The wine is full of dark, spicy Grenache varietal character and is less austerely mineral and *sauvage* in style and character than some others from the appellation. It deserves five or six years' ageing to show at its best. (DM)

● **Priorat** Lo Givot★★★★ £F

CIMS DE PORRERA Priorat cims@arrakis.es A: JAr

Owner: Cims de Porerra SL Ctra. Torroja, s.n. Porrera, 43739 Valladolid

One of an increasing number of top-quality performers from this small but great appellation. There are 55 ha of vines here, producing a firmly structured, rich and concentrated Priorat Classic dominated by Cariñena blended with Garnacha and just a touch of Cabernet Sauvignon. It is dark, spicy and beguiling in its fiery complexity. Two small-scale single-vineyard bottlings, Finca Pigat and Finca La Tena are both 100 per cent Cariñena. There is a good, much more forward second wine, Solanes. Produced from younger vines, it will provide an exciting example of what the DO has to offer at a relatively affordable price. (DM)

● **Priorat** Classic★★★★ £F Solanes★★★ £D

CLOS DEL LLOPS Priorat closmogador@sendanet.es A: GBa

Owner: Luc Van Isegem Camí Manyetes, Gratallops, 43737 Tarragona

This is another property with valuable input from winemaker René Barbier Ferrer, the owner of CLOS MOGADOR and consultant to Daphne Glorian at CLOS I TERASSES. Output is relatively small, barely 1,000 cases a year, so the wine, Clos Manyetes, is inevitably scarce. It is dark and almost impenetrable in its youth, with a very marked, deep, spicy character from Cariñena, which dominates a blend also comprising Garnacha. The Cariñena is grown in slate soils and, while this variety may not be being heavily replanted in the region, examples like this demonstrate the real personality that it can give. The wine deserves cellaring for at least five years to better integrate its fierce, fiery nature. (DM)

● **Priorat** Clos Manyetes★★★★★ £E

CLOS FIGUERAS Priorat europvin@infonegocio.com

Owner: Charlotte & Christopher Cannan Camí Manyetes, Gratallops, 43737 Tarragona

This is the home estate of Bordeaux-based wine broker Christopher Cannan, who also owns the excellent Montsant operation, EUROPVIN-FALSET. Not yet among the leaders of the appellation, the top wine here,

Clos Figueras, is nevertheless an excellent example of old-vine Garnacha and Cariñena, which account for around 80 per cent of its blend. The Cannans acquired the estate in 1997 on advice from René Barbier and 10 ha out of a total of 17 ha are planted on the famous *licorella* schistous soils. A second label, Font de la Figuera, is softer, rounder and much more approachable. It has less Garnacha and Cariñena in the blend and includes more Syrah, Mourvèdre and Cabernet Sauvignon. Produced from younger vines, it nevertheless gives an idea of the character of the main wine. There are also some Viognier vines and these contribute to the recently established CLOS NELIN. (DM)

● **Priorat** Font de la Figuera★★★ £D Clos Figueras★★★★ £F

CLOS I TERASSES Priorat closeramus@terra.es A: **JAr**, F&R

Owner: Daphne Glorian Valls 24, Gratallops, 43737 Tarragona
Very small but very impressive 10-ha Priorat property established in 1989 and one of a number of emerging operations that have transformed this small DO from rustic backwater to an important wine region. Two wines are made here: the top wine, Clos Eramus, is a super-rich blend of Garnacha, Cabernet Sauvignon and Cariñena; the well-priced second wine, Laurel, is produced from Cabernet Sauvignon. Clos Erasmus is given extended ageing in new oak and is a massively dense, powerful and exotic style of red. It is both very concentrated and complex, but very firm when young and requires six to seven years' ageing. (DM)
● **Priorat** Clos Erasmus★★★★★ £F

CLOS MOGADOR Priorat closmogador@sendanet.es A: **GBa**,Bal

Owner: René Barbier Ferrer Camí Manyetes, Gratallops, 43737 Tarragona
Talented owner and winemaker René Barbier Ferrer advises at a number of other wineries, including Daphne Glorian's CLOS I TERASSES, as well as producing wine here at his own 20-ha property. Clos Mogador is yet another super-rich, extracted, deep and dense example of this exciting appellation. The blend is Garnacha, Cabernet Sauvignon, Syrah and, unusually, Pinot Noir, which just adds a piercingly fragrant note. A big, structured wine, it will develop very well with age. Barbier is also involved at CLOS DEL LLOPS and works with Christopher Cannan in producing the stylish white Priorat CLOS NELIN. (DM)
● **Priorat** Clos Mogador★★★★★ £F

CLOS NELIN Priorat closmogador@sendanet.es A: **GBa**

Owner: René Barbier Ferrer Camí Manyetes, Gratallops, 43737 Tarragona
As well as producing his brilliant CLOS MOGADOR red, René Barbier Ferrer has long been interested in making a benchmark white Priorat. The final blend for the wine is a fascinating mix of Garnacha Blanca, Viognier, Pinot Noir (vinified as a white) and a little Roussanne, Marsanne and Maccabeo. The Barbier plots are located at high altitude on the hill of Ermita, one of the great sites of the appellation. Viognier is also supplied by Christopher Cannan of CLOS FIGUERAS, who mistakenly planted it instead of Syrah. Output in 2001 was tiny, but the 2002 vintage sees the release of a little over 200 cases. The wine is part vinified in oak and part in stainless steel and has great style and intensity. Nutty and already showing impressive complexity, it is immediately accessible and is best enjoyed in its relative youth. (DM)
○ **Priorat** Clos Nelin★★★★ £E

CONTINO Rioja www.contini-sa.com A: **L&W**,Frt,Sel

Owner: Viñedos del Contino S.A. Finca San Gregorio, Laserna, 01321 Alava
This traditional Rioja property is part-owned by CVNE and the wines are made by them. There is a total of some 60 ha of vineyards, 4 ha of which are Graciano. There were some cellar problems in the late 1980s but these have now been eradicated. There are now straightforward Crianza and Reservas which have reasonable depth and are supple and velvety in texture. As well as these, there is a varietal Graciano which is firmer and less approachable along with the single-vineyard Viña del Olivo. Both of these will develop

well in the medium-term. (DM)

● **Rioja** Crianza★ £B Reserva★★ £D Graciano★★ £E Viña del Olivo★★★ £E

COSTERS DEL SIURANA Priorat   A: **LyS**, NYg, Vne, F&M

Owner: Carlos Pastrana Manyetes, s/n Gratallops, 43737 Tarragona
Sizeable operation by Priorat standards with 40 ha of estate vineyards. Carlos Pastrana was one of the earlier pioneers of the appellation, establishing his estate in the 1980s. Of the wines the dense and powerful Clos de l'Obac is a dark, fiery and impressively structured blend of Garnacha and Cabernet Sauvignon in equal parts, with a little Merlot, Syrah and Cariñena. Dolç de l'Obac is an unusual sweet red blended from Syrah, Garnacha and Cabernet Sauvignon. The Miserere bottling is a blend of Cabernet Sauvignon, Garnacha, Tempranillo and Merlot as well as Cariñena. It is lighter with reasonable depth and a soft rounded structure but, while good, has a leaner edge than others and I feel there should be more. (DM)
● **Priorat** Miserere★★★ £E Clos de l'Obac★★★★ £F Dolç de l'Obac★★★★ £G

HERMANOS CUADRADO Ribera del Duero   A: N&P

Owner: Cuadrado family Finca Villacreces, Ctra. de Soria, Quintanilla de Onésimo, 47350 Valladolid
This new Ribera del Duero property is producing some of the best wine in the DO. The vineyard is planted to Tinto Fino (Tempranillo), Merlot and Cabernet Sauvignon but thus far the wine has been produced solely from Tinto Fino. Just 2,000 cases are made and the Finca Villacreces is a powerful, firm, ageworthy example of the appellation. A new and very pricey *super-cuvée*, Nebro, is also made in tiny quantities. (DM)
● **Ribera del Duero** Finca Villacreces★★★★ £E

DOMINIO DE PINGUS Ribera del Duero   A: C&B, BBR, Sel, F&M

Owner: Peter Sisseck Hospital, Quintanilla de Onésimo, 47350 Valladolid
Now a cult wine among the top Ribera del Duero reds and rivalled for price only by VEGA SICILIA and the top limited *cuvées* from Priorat. Pingus was in fact only established as recently as 1995. Very modern in style and approach, the wine is massively extracted but has remarkably intense, pure, dark and spicy fruit. Malolactic fermentation in barrel provides a supple, velvety texture resulting in a wine which is not only approachable but very ageworthy. The second label, Fleur de Pingus, is also impressive. Sisseck is also the consultant overseeing the production of the wines of Mas Gil in Catalunya. (DM)
● **Ribera del Duero** Pingus❂❂❂❂❂ £H

PEDRO DOMECQ Jerez y Manzanilla   A: **ADo**, AAA

*Owner: **Allied Domecq** San Ildefonso 3, Jerez de la Frontera, 11404 Cádiz*
Among the largest companies in Jerez de la Frontera with 1,100 ha of vineyards and a huge commercial range of sherry. The Fino La Ina is very well known and is a good example of the style: light and fresh with an attractive salty, almost nutty tang. Better though are the rich, dry and austere Amontillado 51-1A, the Palo Cortado Capuchino, the Oloroso Sibarita and the Venerable Pedro Ximénez. All of these are now classified as VORS. Some pretty average Rioja is made under the Marqués de Arienzo label and the company has interests as far afield as Mexico. (DM)
○ **La Ina** Fino★ £B ○ **Amontillado 51-1A**★★★ £D ○ **Sibarita** Oloroso★★★ £D

BODEGAS ESTEFANIA Bierzo   A: **Ala**

Owner: José Luis González Ctra. de Dehesas a Posada del Bierzo, 24390 Ponferrada (León)
Like Cigales, Bierzo is beginning to emerge as a serious supplier of good to very good reds alongside the more established appellations of Ribera del Duero and Toro. This is undoutedly the case here with two reds of striking depth, character and quality under the Tilenus label as well as a good value budget wine called simply Tilenus. The property was established as recently as 1999 and the first vintage was in 2000. There

are just 5 ha under vine. As is the case elsewhere, old bush vines make a significant contribution to the quality and here they are between 70 and 105 years old. The wines are produced solely from the local Mencia grape and excitingly offer an original array of flavours not found elsewhere. The variety has generally been cropped to high levels in the region and consequently light, simple wines have resulted. However the dark, spicy depths achieved in the Pagos de Posada give an indication of just what is possible. Both the top reds will develop very well in the medium term with five or six years' age. (DM)

● **Bierzo** Tilenus Crianza★★★ £C Tilenus Pagos de Posada★★★★ £E

EUROPVIN FALSET Montsant   A:GBa

Owner: Christopher Cannan & Rene Barbier Ferrer Ctra. de Bellmunt, P21 - Sort de Capellans
One of the three great red producers in Tarragona, along with the co-operative of Capçanes and Joan d'Anguera. Owned by Christopher Cannan, who also owns the Priorat property CLOS FIGUERAS, and Rene Barbier of CLOS MOGADOR, this joint venture was established in 1999. The objective is to provide similarly exciting wine to those of neighbouring Priorat and Europvin is working closely with the Falset co-operative to harness the best fruit from the co-op's member growers. There are two wines, both rich and concentrated. Laurona is blended from a mix of Garnacha, Cariñena, Syrah, Cabernet Sauvignon and Merlot, while the Seleccio de 6 Vinyes comes from a more conventional 80 per cent Garnacha and 20 per cent Cariñena. A fair proportion of new oak is used for ageing but it is the larger 500-litre casks; the Seleccio is also fermented in new oak after a long maceration. Malolactic is in barrel and the wines are kept on their lees during maturation. Expect both wines to develop well in the medium term; the Seleccio will add further complexity for up to a decade. (DM)

● **Montsant** Laurona★★★ £C Selecció de 6 Vinyes★★★★ £E

CELLERS J.M. FUENTES Priorat granclos@airtel.net   A:Bal

Owner: Cellers Fuentes Hernandez Monsant 2, Bellmont del Priorat, Tarragona
Small Priorat producer established in 1995, making an impressively structured and concentrated Gran Clos *cuvée* as well as a decent second wine, El Puig, and a straightforward nutty white Vinya Llisarda. There are 11 ha under vine planted in schistous soils and much of the production is sold internationally. Gran Clos is blended from mainly Garnacha with Cariñena and a touch of Cabernet Sauvignon. A wine of formidable extract but with beguiling dark, spicy berry fruit, it will develop well with five to seven years' ageing. (DM)

● **Priorat** Gran Clos Joset Maria Fuentes★★★★ £E

ALEJANDRO FERNÁNDEZ Ribera del Duero   A:JAr,May,Sel

Owner: Alejandro Fernández Real 2, Pesquera de Duero, 47315 Valladolid
VEGA SICILIA may be the most famous property in this potentially great DO but Alejandro Fernández isn't far behind. His two wineries, Pesquera and Condado de Haza, produce some of the best examples here at all quality levels. The Pesquera Crianza is stylish and concentrated whereas the Reserva and Gran Reserva are real benchmarks – very dark, powerful and marked by subtle, cedary oak and, in the case of the Gran Reserva, a formidable structure. The Cuvée Janus is made only in great years and is not only massive in extract but remarkably fine. Sadly it is made in tiny quantities. The Condado de Haza wines don't quite match their stablemates but are impressive nonetheless. The Crianza is surprisingly forward in style, the Alenza more extracted and inevitably rich and heady. The Reservas and Gran Reservas demand to be cellared. Two interesting new projects are DEJHESA LA GRANJA and EL VINICULO. The former is in the region of Zamora, where Fernández is producing a 100 per cent Tempranillo that is aged for 24 months in American oak. At El Viniculo in La Mancha he produces two further Tempranillo varietals, one a Crianza aged for six months, the other a Reserva which sees 12 months in cask. In both cases American oak is used to complement the rich, and ripe warm-grown fruit. (DM)

Pesquera
● **Ribera del Duero** Crianza★★★ £C Reserva★★★★ £E Gran Reserva❍❍❍❍❍ £G
Condado de Haza
● **Ribera del Duero** Crianza★★ £C Alenza★★★★ £G

BODEGAS EMETERIO FERNÁNDEZ Cigales www.lalegua.com A: **Msp**, Ben

Owner: Emeterio Fernández Ctra. Cigales No1, 47194 Valladolid
Winemaking was established here only in 1997. The wines are marketed under the La Legua label in Spain and elsewhere but in the UK they appear under the Aleno label. There are 80 ha of potentially great vineyards planted in alluvial soils with finely drained topsoils which are a mix of stones and pebbles. The vineyard currently comprises 72 ha of Tinta Fina (Tempranillo) and 4 ha each of Garnacha and Cabernet Sauvignon. Two entry-level fruit-driven reds are produced, Joven and Criado en Barrica. There is no doubting the impressive quality and depth of the fruit here and the 1999 Reserva is edging towards three stars. However, early releases of both the Crianza and Reserva have shown a slightly rustic character. As young winemaker Adolfo Gonzalez Lazaro continues to refine the winemaking a new special *cuvée* Capricho has also now been released. Like that other great red of Castilla y Leon, Pingus, this is hand destemmed grape by grape. (DM)
● **Cigales** La Legua Crianza★ £C La Legua Reserva★★ £C

FERNÁNDEZ DE PIÉROLA Rioja www.pierola.com A: **Msp**,Ben

Owner: Carlos Bujanda Fernández de Piérola Ctra. Logroño s/n Finca El Somo, 01322 Moreda
Three fine reds and a relatively light barrel-fermented wild yeast white are made at this newly established Rioja estate located in the north of the region in the Rioja Alavesa. While the majority of the region's output is still blended from different sites, these wines are all *terroir*-driven. The Moreda, a tributary of the Ebro, helps moderate the climate and provides nourishment for the deep-rooted, low-yielding vines. High altitude, protection provided by the Sierra de Cantabria mountains and finely drained soils high in minerals also contribute to the style and quality. The reds are marked by their purity of fruit and elegant intensity. The red Litium Reserva is richer and fuller with more obvious creamy oak character than the more piercingly fruit-driven Crianza and Reserva. Both Reservas will evolve well in the medium term. (DM)
● **Rioja** Crianza★★ £C Reserva★★★ £D Litium Reserva★★★ £E
○ **Rioja** Oak Fermented★ £B

GONZÁLEZ BYASS Jerez y Manzanilla www.gonzalezbyass.com A:AAA

Owner: González Byass S.A. Manuel MªGonzález 12, Jerez de la Frontera, 11403 Cádiz
One of the most famous names in sherry production with a large volume of regular Fino and Amontillado that is sound but somewhat unexciting. However, the Tio Pepe brand, while produced in very large quantity, is nonetheless an impressive Fino – salty and intense with piercing citrus notes. Of a different order are a number of super-rich Amontillados and Olorosos. These include the refined Oloroso Añada, as well as the full, rich Alfonso, Apóstoles, and most notably Matusalem. Two other very impressive, full-bodied styles are made. The Amontillado Del Duque is dry, very intense and almost overwhelms one with its full, rich and toffeed *rancio* character. The Noé Pedro Ximénez is unctuously sweet, very rich and heady but refined too. The Rioja firm BODEGA BRETÓN is also run by González Byass. The wines, with the exception of the Alba de Bretón, are fairly uninspiring, though. (DM)
○ **Tio Pepe** Fino★★ £B
○ **Alfonso** Oloroso★★ £C **Añada** Oloroso★★★ £E ○ **Apóstoles** Oloroso★★★★ £E
○ **Matusalem** Oloroso★★★★★ £F ○ **Del Duque** Amontillado❍❍❍❍❍ £F
○ **Noé Pedro** Pedro Ximénez★★★★ £E

GRAMONA Penedès

Owner: Gramona family Industria 36, 08770 Sant Sadurni d'Anoia
Well-established Penedès producer founded in 1921, with an extensive range of both still wines and fine Cavas. The Gramona family have 29 ha of their own vineyards and also buy in fruit to cover their requirements. The range of Cavas includes dry and medium styles and focuses heavily on the indigenous varieties of the area with generally very good results. The Imperial Gran Reserva has some 10 per cent of Chardonnay in support of Xarel-lo and Maccabeo. The III Lustros is solely indigenous varieties, Xarel-lo (70 per cent) and Maccabeo. It gets an extended period of five to six years on its lees. The wines offer reasonable value and are interesting alternatives to lesser Champagnes. A premium Celler Battle Grand Brut gets up to eight years on its yeast lees, while Argent has a much higher proportion of Chardonnay. Of the still wines the Gessami is a fresh, vibrant, fruit-driven blend of Muscat and Sauvignon Blanc with impressive depth and intensity. The Sauvignon Blanc is barrel-fermented on its lees for three to six months and offers a subtle melange of citrus, green apple and nutmeg flavours. A Chardonnay is also produced and there is an Ice Wine, Collecio, from Gewürztraminer and another from Riesling. The grapes are artificially frozen in the winery, in a form of cryo-extraction. A Merlot, Merlot & Co, which is blended with a little Syrah, and Pinot Noir Bru de Gramona are both matured in wood, some new. (DM)

O **Penedès** Gessami★★ £B Sauvignon Blanc★★★ £C Collecion★★★ £C
O **Cava** Imperial Gran Reserva★★ £C III lustros★★★ £D

HERETAT VALL-VENTÓS Penedès www.raventosrosell.com A:Msp

Owner: Joan Raventós Rosell Ctra, San Sadurni-d'Anoia, 08783 Masquerna, Barcelona
Joan Raventos Rosell set up this 60-ha property in the Mid to Upper Penedès in 1987 and he now vinifies his wines in a state-of-the-art winery. No expense is spared on stainless steel tanks, temperature control or barrels for maturation. Still wines are released under the Heretat Vall-Ventós label, the range of Cavas as Joan Raventós Rosell. Of these the Brut Reserva Heretat vintage is particularly striking. A blend of Macabeo, Chardonnay and Parellada, it gets extended time on lees as does the Brut Gran Heretat. The Heretat Vall-Ventós whites are marked by banana-like, estery cool-fermentation aromas and are aged in tank not in wood. The reds are a soft, fruity Merlot, an altogether more serious Cabernet Sauvignon with good grip and structure and best of all a classy Reserva. This is a blend of Cabernet Sauvignon, Merlot and Syrah. Tight, restrained and well-structured with hints of mint, spice and black pepper, this is more refined than many of the often alarmingly over-extracted reds from Penedès. It will be all the better for five or six years' ageing. (DM)

● **Penedès** Merlot★ £B Cabernet Sauvignon★★ £C Reserva★★★ £C
O **Penedès** Chardonnay★ £B
O **Cava** Brut Reserva Heretat★★ £C

HIDALGO Jerez y Manzanilla www.lagitana.es A:AAA

Owner: Hidalgo family Banda de la Playa 42, Sanlúcar de Barrameda, 11540 Cádiz
Large Sanlúcar-based operation with some impressive sherry brands. Best-known is La Gitana Manzanilla, which provides consistently good value with fresh, tangy, lightly salty fruit. It particularly needs to be drunk young. There are two volume ranges and the better wines go under the Napoleon label. The Amontillado is slightly toffeed and nutty but dry, and there is a fresh Fino Superior and an evolved and nutty Oloroso Abocado. Generic sherry styles are produced simply under the Hidalgo label. Jerez Cortado is a soft, round style but from a very old *solera*. There are also two single-vineyard wines: Amontillado and Manzanilla Pastrana. The Manzanilla is an aged Pasada, with an evolved, nutty character as well as an underlying hint of citrus. The Amontillado is a wine that originally started life as a Manzanilla. The former is now VOS. The range is completed by the impressive collection of rare Viejo wines. The Amontillado and Oloroso are now classified as VORS. The latter is almost bone dry but full of evolved *rancio* notes. Impressively complex. (DM)

○ **La Gitana** Manzanilla★ £B   ○ **Napoleon** Amontillado★★ £B **Napoleon** Fino Superior★★ £B
○ **Amontillado Pastrana**★★★★ £E   ○ **Manzanilla Pastrana**★★★ £B   ○ **Jerez Cortado**★★★ £C
○ **Amontillado Viejo**★★★★ £E   ○ **Palo Cortado Viejo**★★★ £D   ○ **Oloroso Viejo**★★★★ £E

IJALBA   Rioja   www.ijalba.com   A: HHB,VRt

Owner: Dionisio Ruiz Ijalba Ctra. Pamplona, Logroño, 26006 La Rioja
Three reds and a decent fruity white, Genoli, are produced at this 70-ha property. The Múrice Tinto
Crianza is a good modern, fruit-driven style. The Graciano Tinto is precisely that, an unusual, varietal
Graciano which is full of dark brambly fruit. It is structured and will age well and is quite unlike most Rioja
in style. Continuing the unusual approach is a new varietal Maturana Tinto, Dionisio Ruiz Ijalba. A level
up, the Reserva is 90 per cent Tempranillo, while the small-production Reserva Especial is an equal blend
of Tempranillo and Graciano. Both are full, deep and extracted styles with surprising weight and depth.
Better with four or five years' ageing. (DM)
● **Rioja** Múrice Tinto Crianza★ £B   Graciano★★ £B   Reserva★★★ £D

BODEGA NIÑO JESÚS   Calatayud   A: **Msp**,Ben

Owner: Co-operative Las Tablas, s/n, 50313 Aniñón
The output of this co-op used to be sold off in bulk but recently the members have decided to make a range
of their own from some excellent old Garnacha and Tempranillo bush vines ranging from 60 to 80 years of
age. The local Xirac has also recently been introduced and there is a little white Maccabeo. A new state-of-
the-art winery was completed for the 2000 vintage and the new range of wines is now marketed under the
Estecillo label. Quality is aided by high-altitude vineyards planted at between 650 and 880 m. The reds are
produced using gentle basket presses and the quality of the vibrant Joven and Viña Viejas in particular is
very striking. The Crianza bottling is a touch more rustic. Drink the wines relatively young to enjoy their
vibrant fruit, although they will stand a little age. (DM)
● **Calatayud** Estecillo Joven★★ £B   Estecillo Viña Viejas★★★ £B   Estecillo Crianza★★ £C

LEDA VIÑAS VIEJAS   Castilla y Leon   A: F&M ,N&P

Owner: Leda Viñas Viejas SL 47320 Tudela de Duero, Valladolid
This is an exciting new project along the lines of MAURO and ABADIA RETUERTA, producing first-class
red wine not just from within the boundaries of the Ribera del Duero DO. Winemaker César Munoz, who
is also responsible for the up-and-coming Ribera wines at Bodegas MONTEBACO is one of the partners
here. Currently some of the 100 per cent Tinto Fino fruit is sourced from Ribera and some from the Cigales
DO; the average age of the vines is 50 years. The resulting wine is deep, dark and formidably extracted but
with a fine balance and supple structure. It will age very well for a decade or so. (DM)
● **Viña Leda**★★★★ £E

BODEGA LÓPEZ HERMANOS   Málaga   www.lopezhermanos.com   A: **Mps**,Vts

Owner: Hermanos Burgos López. C/ Canadá, 10, 29006 Málaga
This large, family-owned operation has been making the wines of Málaga since before the arrival of the
phylloxera vine louse. Throughout the last century production of these wines based on Pedro Ximénez and
Moscatel has declined dramatically. The bulk of the 400,000-case output here is sourced from the family's
180 ha of vineyards and the wines are produced using sun-dried grapes aged on mats. Best of the PX range
is the Reserva de Familia which has a lightly nutty and raisiny character and reasonable depth. Most exciting
are two splendid Transañejo bottlings which are aged in solera and average around 50 years of age. Dark
and extraordinarily rich, the Moscatel in particular has remarkable depth and a piercing intensity. Truly
among Spain's vinous gems. (DM)
○ **Málaga** PX Reserva de Familia★★ £C   Transañejo PX Don Juan★★★★★ £F
○ **Málaga** Transañejo Moscatel Don Salvador★★★★★ £F

EMILIO LUSTAU Jerez y Manzanilla www.emilio-lustau.com A: M&V,F&M

Owner: Emilio Lustau S.A. Pl. del Cubo,4 Jerez de la Frontera, 11403 Cádiz
Sizeable sherry operation supplying a considerable international own-label market. It also has a splendid range of high-quality sherries sold under its own label. A good Solera Reserva range includes salty, good-value Puerto Fino, Palo Cortado Peninsula and Amontillado Escuadrilla. The Almacenista label offers very impressive, nutty Manzanilla Amontillado, a beautifully evolved, very lightly salty Manzanilla Pasada and the richly concentrated Amontillado del Puerto. The Emperatriz Eugenia Oloroso is more developed and shows greater *rancio* character. The Old East India Solera is full of nutty, burnt toffee aromas. Very unusual and very rich, almost overly so, is the Moscatel Superior Emilin. A considerable range of very fine old wines are also offered from the company's oldest *soleras* under the Very Old, Very Old Rare and Single Cask labels. (DM)

O **Puerto Fino** Solera Reserva★★ £B   O **Palo Cortado Peninsula** Solera Reserva★★ £B
O **Almacenista** Manzanilla Pasada★★★ £D   O **Almacenista** Manzanilla Amontillado★★★ £D
O **Empertriz Eugenia** Oloroso★★★ £D   O **Old East India Solera** Oloroso★★★★ £D
O **Moscatel Superior** Emilin★★★ £D

MARQUÉS DE GRIÑÓN Castilla la Mancha www.marquesdegrinon.com A: Maj,CeB,Sel

Owner: Marqués de Griñón S.A. Avenida del Ebro, 26540 Alfaro, La Rioja
Based in Rioja and part-owned by the giant Arco Bodegas Unidas group (whose brands include Berberana and Marqués de Monistrol). The main focus of interest are the Dominio de Valdepusa wines produced on the Marqués's private 30-ha estate to the south of Madrid. These are very well crafted and stylish reds in one of Spain's large, arid and far from fancied wine regions. The key here is the use of irrigation and a commitment to viticulture with sophisticated modern trellising. Four good to very good reds are produced: Cabernet Sauvignon, Petit Verdot, Syrah and a blend of all three, Eméritus.The Syrah is rich and smoky and the Petit Verdot scented yet firm – it needs more time than the others, five or six years. The Cabernet, surprisingly, has quite a green note which can show through in the Eméritus as well. The Marqués de Griñón label is also used for the straightforward Durius brands; red and white are produced and the white from Rueda fruit can be good. Marqués de Griñón Rioja is also well established: the Alea Crianza is simple but a bit one-dimensional, while Reserva is good, with depth and some concentration. (DM)

Dominio de Valdepusa
● **Cabernet Sauvignon** Montes de Toledo★★ £C   ● **Petit Verdot** Montes de Toledo★★★ £C
● **Syrah** Montes de Toledo★★★ £C   ● **Émeritus** Montes de Toledo★★★★ £E

Marqués de Griñón Rioja
● **Rioja** Reserva Colección Personal★★ £D

MARQUÉS DE MURRIETA Rioja A: MMD,Sel,F&M

Owner: Creixell family Ctra. Zaragoza, Km.5 Logroño, 26006 La Rioja
This most conservative of the Rioja bodegas produces traditional reds and whites which are exposed to considerable periods of oak-ageing. There are some 300 ha of vineyards and production is sizeable at 250,000 cases or so a year. Gran Reservas are now all released under the Castillo d'Ygay label and Reservas are now simply Murrieta. The white Reserva El Dorado is citrusy with very marked vanilla essence – oaky but good. The Castillo d'Ygay white is more evolved but very intense. The red Reserva and Gran Reserva can be more variable with occasionally very high volatile acidity. At their best they are splendidly rich, particularly the Castillo d'Ygay Especial which can be of a different order. In a concession to new-wave Rioja styles a premium red, Dalmau, is now produced. It is firm, structured and above all elegant and it should develop well with five or six years' cellaring. A less oaked, straightforward white Misela is also produced in Rioja, and in Rías Baixas a peachy, lightly exotic white Pazo de Barrantes, which should be drunk young. (DM)

● **Rioja** Reserva★★ £C Gran Reserva Especial Castillo d'Ygay★★★ £E Dalmau Reserva★★★★ £F
O **Rioja** Reserva El Dorado★★ £B

MARQUÉS DE RISCAL   Rioja   www.marquesderiscal.com   A: L-P, His

Owner: Herederos del Marqués de Riscal   Torrea 1, Elciego, 01340 Alava
Much development and expense has been put into this noble old bodega in recent years. Paul Pontallier of Château MARGAUX in Bordeaux has provided additional guidance in the winery. Some of the releases in the early 1990s were variable to say the least, but things seem to be taking a welcome turn for the better. The Riojas under the Marqués de Riscal label can still disappoint but the Barón de Chirel Reserva is very impressive: rich but structured and firm in its youth. It will make excellent drinking with five or six years' bottle-development. Riscal's Rueda has been consistently good in recent years. The fresh Superior and Sauvignon should both be enjoyed young; the Limousin is lightly oaky and leesy and will benefit from keeping for two or three years. (DM)

● **Rioja** Gran Reseva★ £D Reserva Baron de Chirel★★★ £F
O **Rueda** Sauvignon Blanc★ £B Superior★ £B Limousin★★ £B

MAS MARTINET   Priorat   martinet@arrakis.es   A:N&P, Rae

Owner: Pérez Overjero family   Ctra, Falset-Gratallops, Falset, 43730 Tarragona
Small family-run operation producing some excellent results in this high-quality DO. The Perez Ovejero family possess some 7 ha of vineyards which yield a marvellously complex, structured wine. In Clos Martinet they handcraft a wine with more elegance and less raw power than some of the wines of their neighbours but rarely with less intensity or finesse. It is a blend of Garnacha, Syrah, Cabernet Sauvignon and Cariñena. One of the winemakers here, José Luis Perez, was also involved with CIMS DE PORRERA. The second wine, Martinet Bru, like the Clos Martinet itself, is very well priced and relatively soft and accessible, if lacking the depth and quality of some of the other secondary labels now emerging. (DM)

● **Priorat** Martinet Bru★★ £C Clos Martinet★★★★ £F

MAURO   Castilla y León   www.bodegasmauro.com   A: JAr,Sel,F&M

Owner: Bodegas Mauro S.A.   Cervantes 12, Tudela de Duero, 47320 Valladolid
Like that other top-quality Castilla y León producer ABADIA RETUERTA, this property also specialises in fine-quality reds under the *vino de mesa* classification. A total of slightly more than 15,000 cases are made from 35 ha. The vineyards are planted mainly to Tempranillo but also to Syrah and Garnacha and soils are well drained and stony. Three reds are produced: a supple, opulent, forward style simply labelled Mauro; a Vendimia Seleccionada, which is richer and firmer; and a single-vineyard *cuvée*, Terreus, which is produced in limited volumes and only when the vintage conditions are particularly fine. It comes from very old vines and requires medium-term cellaring. There is also a new Toro property, Bodega MAURODÓS, established by Mariano Garcia, one of the partners as well as the winemaker here. The red Viña San Román shows great potential. (DM)

● **Mauro** Vino de Mesa★★★ £D Vendimia Seleccionada Vino de Mesa★★★★ £F Terreus★★★★★ £F

MAURODOS   Toro

Owner: Garcia family   Carretera N-122, Villaester, Valladolid
As well as the excellent wines he has been involved in developing at MAURO, enologist Mariano Garcia established this benchmark Toro property in the mid 1990s. Just one wine is made, Vina San Roman, a varietal Tinta de Toro. Production is still small at just over 4,000 cases a year. It is a marvellously dense, opulent and richly textured red, full of dark berry fruit and supple tannin. The considerable structure and initially firm grip from both the tannins and oak will necessitate a little patience. Given five or six years' ageing the wine should provide ample reward. (DM)

● **Toro** Viña San Román★★★★ £F

BODEGA ABEL MENDOZA   Rioja

Owner: Abel Mendoza Monge   Ctra, Penacerrada, 7, 26338 San Vicente de la Sonsierra, La Rioja
One of an emerging number of high-quality small bodegas. Three reds and a white Rioja are made here. The white is barrel-fermented and comes from Malvasia. The reds are solely from Tempranillo and aged in French rather than American oak. The 18 ha of vineyards in the shadow of the Sierra Cantabria mountains are planted in clay/limestone and stony, sandy soils, which provide an excellent *terroir*. The entry-level red is a vibrant, fruit-filled, exuberant wine produced by carbonic maceration for drinking young. The Jarrarte is a stylish, well-structured barrel-aged (older barrels are used) Rioja, with rich fruit and supple, well-rounded tannins. It will develop well over four to five years. The top wine, the Selección Personal, is aged in new oak. Powerful, dense and impeccably balanced it has the depth and structure to develop very well over 8 to 10 years. 2001 and 02 have been very good, on the edge of five stars. (DM)
● **Rioja** Jarrarte Maceracion Carbonica★★ £B Jarrarte★★★ £C Seleccion Personal★★★★ £E

MUGA   Rioja   www.bodegasmuga.com   A: **C&D**,Res,N&P

Owner: Muga family   Barrio de la Estación, Haro, 26200 La Rioja
This family-owned bodega is small by Rioja standards. The approach is fiercely traditional for most of the range and at best the wines can be very good. There can also be infuriating variations in quality with oxidation and high volatile acidity being regularly encountered. Fermentation is in wooden vats and ageing in oak. Nevertheless the Reserva and Gran Reserva can display classically mellow, rounded Tempranillo character with vanilla and coconut notes infused from extended time in cask. Tempranillo is blended with Garnacha, Mazuelo and Graciano in the Reserva and Prado Enea; with Mazuelo and Graciano in the impressive and expensive new, modern-style Torre Muga, which is loaded with vibrant blackberry fruit and velvety tannin. Good white Fermentado en Barrica shows some depth and some decent, fruity rosé completes the range. (DM)
● **Rioja** Reserva★★ £C Gran Reserva Prado Enea★★★ £D Torre Muga★★★★ £F
○ **Rioja** Bianco★ £B

MUSTIGUILLO   Valencia   mustiguillo@inicia.es   A: **Lib**,NYg

Owner: Sarríon family   Chera 20, Requena, 46340 Valencia
Recently established but very impressive new producer with some 80 ha of vineyards in unheralded Valencia. Much of the vineyard is planted to very old, unirrigated Bobal, which provides potentially exceptional raw material. Currently production is less than 2,000 cases but this will rise. Tempranillo, which is by no means young at 30 years, and Cabernet Sauvignon are also planted. Two wines are produced. Finca Terrerazo is the suppler and more forward of the two; it is a blend of Bobal, Tempranillo and Cabernet and is aged for 16 months in a mix of mainly French and American oak. The pricier Quincha Corral is more structured and firm, a blend of both Bobal and Tempranillo. Winemaking is distinctly modern, with fermentation completed in barrel followed by the malolactic. These are rich, concentrated wines full of dark fruit and cedar. They are likely to improve in bottle for five years or more. (DM)
● **Finca Terrerazo** ★★★ £D ● **Quincha Corral**★★★ £F

PALACIOS REMONDO   Rioja   www.ddnet.esvinhos/herenciaremondo   A: **M&V**

Owner: Palacios Remondo family   Avenida Zargosa 8, Alfaro, 26540 La Rioja
As well as producing his own range in Priorat, Alvaro PALACIOS has also had a significant recent contribution to the family property in the Rioja Baja. The 150 ha of vineyards are covered with large pebbles and provide a formidable resource for intensely flavoured fruit. There is a relatively simple, lightly oaked white Plácet, but it is the reds here which impress. La Vendimia is partly vinified by carbonic maceration, which provides a wine of immediate appeal. Dark and spicy La Montesa Crianza spends a year in oak. Propriedad is fermented in large wooden casks and then transferred to *barrique* for malolactic. It is supple

and richly extracted. Dos Viñedos is a blend of varieties – Tempranillo with some Garnacha and Graciano sourced from two higher-altitude vineyards. Rich and concentrated, it is aged in both French and, for a shorter time, American oak. It will benefit from three or four years' cellaring. (DM)

● **Rioja** Herencia Remondo La Vendimia★ £B   Herencia Remondo La Montesa Crianza★★ £B
● **Rioja** Propriedad H Remondo★★★ £C   Dos Viñedos★★★★ £F
O **Rioja** Plácet★ £B

ALVARO PALACIOS   Priorat   alvaropalacios@ctv.es   A: C&B, BBR,Sel

Owner: Alvaro Palacios   Finca El Colomé, Gratallops, 43737 Tarragona
Alvaro Palacios established this excellent small property in the late 1980s and he produces some very good to quite exceptional examples of the Priorat DO from his 10 ha of vineyards. Experience gained in the Napa Valley has enabled him to produce modern, very finely crafted examples from this small but great region. Les Terasses is produced from fruit sourced throughout the area. The result is always harmonious and impressive, the wine displaying supple tannin and an exotic, dark fruit quality. The magnificently concentrated L'Ermita, produced from very old vines, is dominated by Garnacha with a hint of Garnacha Blanco, Cabernet Sauvignon and Cariñena. Finca Dofi has less Garnacha, although that is still the main variety, with a firm structure provided by the inclusion of Cabernet Sauvignon, Syrah, Merlot and Cariñena. It is very complex, with an almost floral, cedary character as well as the rich, dark fruit of the Garnacha. Finca Dofi and L'Ermita are both refined and very ageworthy, improving effortlessly for a decade or more. (DM)

● **Priorat** Les Terasses★★★ £C   Finca Dofi★★★★★ £F   L'Ermita**OOOOO** £H

PARÉS BALTÁ   Penedès   www.paresbalta.com

Owner: Joan Cusiné   Masis Can Baltá s/n, 08739 Pacs del Penedès
This sizeable and ancient Penedes producer, established in 1790, has an extensive range which includes both still wines and Cava. There are 174 ha under vine and the total output is now approaching 70,000 cases a year. The regular Cavas and still wines offer decent value for money and the Mas Elena red stands out, a soft, lightly herbal, forward blend of Cabernet Sauvignon, Merlot and Cabernet Franc. The Special Selection wines, produced in small volume and from the lowest yielding sites, are of greater interest and some impressive results are being achieved. Long maceration and new oak are the order of the day for the reds, with barrel-fermentation on lees for the two premium whites, Mas de Carol and Electio, both vinified from Chardonnay. There is a new juicy, fruity Shiraz, Radix, as well as two sturdy premium reds. Mas Irene blends Cabernet Franc and Merlot, whereas Absis is a mix of the Bordeaux varieties. The Mas Irene is medium-full with some elegance, the Absis bigger and firmer, almost overly so. It requires a minimum of six to seven years to shed its burly tannins. The winery also produces the very limited-production Dominio Cusiné 1790. (DM)

● **Penedès** Mas Elena★ £B   Mas Irene★★ £C   Absis★★★★ £H
O **Penedès** Mas de Carol Fermentato en Barrica★★ £C   Electio★★★ £E

PAZO DE SEÑORÁNS   Rías Baixas   www.pazodesenorans.com   A: Vni

Owner: Marisol Bueno & Javier Mareque   Vilanoviña, 36637 Meis
This is one of the most consistent properties in the Rías Baixas appellation, founded in 1989. Output remains small at barely 4,000 cases a year. The regular bottling is supported by a limited-release Seleccion de Añadas which unlike the regular wine is held in tank and matured for over two years before bottling. The Rías Baixas label is bottled early and displays some of the best peachy, tropical, mineral and grassy characters to be be found in the aromatic Albariño grape. Both wines should be drunk soon after release. (DM)

O **Rias Baixas**★★★ £C

PÉREZ PASCUAS Ribera del Duero   A: **RsW**, BBR

Owner: Perez Pascuas family   Ctra. Roa, Pedrosa de Duero, 09314 Burgos
One of a regrettably still small number of top-quality producers in this great north-western appellation. The operations was established in 1980 and has some 100 ha of vineyards planted mainly to Tempranillo but also some Cabernet Sauvignon and Merlot. The wines are powerful and quite extracted and are now aged in a mix of French and American oak. Under the Viña Pedrosa label there are fine, structured Crianza and Reserva, as well as a denser, richer Gran Reserva with considerable tannin – a wine that demands patience. Pérez Pascuas, from a single vineyard, is very refined and complex as well as powerful and firmly tannic when young. A silky, velvety texture will emerge with age, though. Gran Reservas particularly should be cellared for at least seven or eight years. A very small amount of a Pérez Pascuas Gran Seleccion is also made. (DM)
● **Ribera del Duero** Viña Pedrosa★★ £C Viña Pedrosa Crianza★★★ £D Viña Pedrosa Reserva★★★ £E
● **Ribera del Duero** Viña Pedrosa Gran Reserva★★★★ £G
● **Ribera del Duero** Pérez Pascuas Gran Reserva★★★★ £G

REJADORADA Toro www.rejadorada.com   A:**Msp**,Ben

Owner: Luis & Agustin Remesal   Rejadorada, 11, 49800 Toro (Zamora)
This is one of a number of impressive, newly emerging properties in this exciting region. Much press has been given to Numanthia-Termes, Pintia and MAURODOS but other exciting, less visible estates are equally worth considering, particularly during a period of spiralling prices for cult wines in Spain. Rejadorada itself is very new and was founded only in 1999, although their vineyards are some of the oldest in the region and include a number of plots that date back to pre-phylloxera times. Of the three wines the Roble is typically forward and vibrant. The Crianza by contrast is more seriously structured as a result of 12 months' ageing in oak. The Sango Reserva is rich, dense and powerful, full of dark spicy fruit and underpinned by toasty vanilla oak. Surprisingly approachable, this should develop well over five or six years. (DM)
● **Toro** Tinto Roble★★ £C Crianza★★★ £C Sango Reserva★★★ £E

REMELLURI Rioja remelluri@sea.es   A:**Adm**

Owner: Rodríguez family   Ctra. Rivas de Tereso, s/n Labastida, 01330 Alava
This has now been established as one of the best of the new-wave Rioja producers for more than a decade. Telmo RODRIGUEZ, responsible for building the reputation of the bodega, has a number of other projects as well, producing wines in many of Spain's major appellations. There are 90 ha planted in the Rioja Alavesa and the vineyards are tended organically. French rather than American oak is used during the wine's *élevage* and the style provides greater fruit than is normally the case in the region. The Reserva and Gran Reserva, particularly, are structured and will stand some ageing – the latter will be all the better for five or six years in your cellar. The Crianza is supple and approachable. (DM)
● **Rioja** Crianza★★ £C Reserva★★★ £D Gran Reserva★★★ £E

REMÍREZ DE GANUZA Rioja www.remirezdeganuza.com   A:**Vni**

Owner: Fernando Remírez de Ganuza   Constitución 1, 01307 Samaniego
Top-quality Rioja bodega based in the Rioja Alavesa with 57 ha under vine. Three good to exceptional reds of real distinction are produced and the Trasnocho is one of the region's great wines. In addition an easy-drinking, forward wine, Erre Punto R, is mainly produced by carbonic maceration. The richly textured Fincas de Ganuza Reserva is an immediately appealing blend dominated by Tempranillo. The tannin is supple and round and it will drink well young. The Reserva is more classically structured. Tight and restrained in its youth, it is a wine marked more by its elegance than its weight or concentration. Give it four five years at least. By contrast, the opulent and exotic Trasnocho is a massive, highly extracted but marvellously balanced Tempranillo: pricey but one of the very best of the new wave of Rioja reds. The remarkable 2001 is surprisingly open; however, this a wine that will add complexity with age. (DM)

● **Rioja** Remirez de Ganuza Reserva★★★★ £E Trasnocho★★★★★ £F
● **Rioja** Fincas de Ganuza Reserva★★★ £D

LA RIOJA ALTA   Rioja   www.riojaalta.com   A:**LyS**,NYg,BBR,Sel,F&M

Owner: La Rioja Alta Group S.A.   Avda de Vizcaya, s/n 26200, Haro-La Rioja
This is one of the most fiercely traditional of the old Rioja bodegas. It is a moderately sizeable
operation with a production of around 40,000 cases a year. It was originally founded in 1890 and some
founding families still have a share in the company. It is renowned for some of the very best traditional
Reservas and Gran Reservas. Interests include the Bodega Torre de Oña, also in Rioja, where a modern,
fruit-driven Baron de Oña is made and the Rías Baixas property Lagar de Fornelos, where a straightforward,
peachy, fruit-driven white is produced. At the La Rioja Alta winery the wines are given considerable
cask-ageing. The Viña Alberdi Reserva is the most modern with a mere two years in oak, a high proportion
of it new. The Gran Reservas 904 and 890 spend respectively five and eight years in cask. There is no doubt
that the sheer quality of the fruit and the wines' intensity is exemplary but releases tasted throughout the last
five years have been patchy. A new state-of-the-art winery has also been completed in the Ribera del Duero
and the first wines from the 76-ha vineyard there are yet to be released. Two vintages have now been vinified.
Prior to this the fruit from the first seven harvests was sold to other producers. (DM)

La Rioja Alta
● **Rioja** Viña Alberdi Reserva★★ £D Viña Arana Reserva★★ £D Viña Ardanza Reserva★★★ £E
● **Rioja** 904 Gran Reserva★★★ £F 890 Gran Reserva★★★★ £G

Bodega Torre de Oña
● Rioja Barón de Oña Reserva★★ £D

CELLERS RIPOLL SANS   Priorat   www.closabatllet.com   A: **Vni**

Owner: Marc Ripoll   C/ Baixada, Consolació, 4, Gratallops, 43737 Tarragona
This is a very good recently established small Priorat estate. Both red and white examples are made in artisan
style and quantity. Marc Ripoll has some excellent terraced vineyards and vines up to 90 years of age which
contribute significantly to the dense, black-fruited, mineral-laden red. Firmly structured and ageworthy, it
is a blend of Cariñena (65 per cent), Garnacha (21 per cent) and Cabernet Sauvignon (8 per cent) with the
balance Syrah. The wine is aged in a mix of French and American oak for just over a year. The white is
produced solely from the local Escanyavella and is a fruit-driven style for early drinking. (DM)
● **Priorat** Closa Batllet★★★★ £E

RODA   Rioja   A: Odd,N&P,F&R,Tur

Owner: Rottlan-Daurella family   Av. Vizcaya, 5 Haro, 26200 La Rioja
Impressive 50-ha Rioja property producing two Reservas and a new-wave Rioja *super-cuvée*, the very pricey
Cirsion. The property was established in 1986 but much of the vineyard is over 30 years old. Current
plantings comprise mainly Tempranillo with a smattering of Graciano and Garnacha. Roda I is the flagship
of the two Reservas, powerful and concentrated but with the characteristic underlying spicy, berry fruit
character of Tempranillo. Roda II is lighter but still much more than a second wine. Cirsion is rich,
structured and cedary – a wine of great finesse and breeding. (DM)
● **Rioja** Roda I Reserva★★★★ £E Roda II Reserva★★★★ £E Cirsion★★★★★ £G

BODEGA RODERO   Ribera del Duero   www.bodegasrodero.com   A: **Msp**,Ben

Owner: Carmelo Rodero   Carretera de Boada s/n, 09314 Pedrosa de Duero, Burgos
This bodaga belongs to a long-established family of growers in the Duero Valley who until 1990 sold their
fruit to VEGA SICILIA. They now focus on producing a fine traditional range of appellation wines. There
are a total of just over 80 ha of vineyards, mostly planted at altitude on well-drained sites that are naturally
low in rainfall. This well-stressed environment provides grapes of great flavour intensity. The average age of

the vineyard is now over 35 years and as well as the local Tinta del Pais (Tempranillo), a small amount of Cabernet Sauvignon and Merlot are also planted. Barrel maturation is in a mix of French and American oak. The top wines are impressively ageworthy and the Gran Reserva offers real depth and power. Backward and restrained in its youth, it demands six or seven years' patience. (DM)

● **Ribera del Duero** Crianza★★★ £C Reserva★★★★ £E Gran Reserva★★★★ £G
● **Ribera del Duero** Joven★ £C Roble★★ £C

TELMO RODRÍGUEZ Rioja A: **Adm**

Owner: Telmo Rodríguez Siete Infantes de Lara, 5, 26006 Logroño
Telmo Rodriguez is one of Spain's great winemaking stars. From his base in Logroño he produces an extensive range of wines from throughout the country in highly diverse styles. A good, fresh, fruit-driven Rueda, Basa Blanco, is vinified from mainly Viura. Three good to very good examples of Ribera del Duero are produced including the exceptional Matellana which is rich, dense and full of dark fruit and smoky spices. It will improve for a decade or more. The Rioja Lanzaga is medium weight with typical light berry Tempranillo fruit, whereas the Altos de Lanzaga is rich, stylish and impressively structured with well-integrated oak and very good depth. Toro is increasingly a source of some of Spain's most exciting up-and-coming reds and the well-priced Dehesa Gago and opulent, spicy Pago La Jara are no exception. Expect the La Jara to develop well with 7 to 10 years' ageing. Some fine reds are also produced from lesser areas. From Cigales comes the leafy, light berry-fruited Viña 105. There are two *vino de la tierra* bottlings. Pegaso comes from Castilla y Leon and is tight and well crafted, less obviously extracted than some of Rodriguez's wines but very classy. The recently added Montazo is sourced from 50-year-old vines near Madrid. It is rich and forward, almost jammy. Of particular interest here is the splendid Moscatel-based Málaga, Molino Real, which like the top wines from LOPEZ HERMANOS has remarkable richness and intensity. All the top reds will develop very well with age. (DM)

● **Ribera del Duero** Gazur★★★ £E M2★★★ £E Matellana★★★★★ £G
● **Rioja** Lanzaga★★ £C Altos de Lanzaga★★★★ £F
● **Toro** Dehesa Gago★★★ £C Pago La Jara★★★ £E ● **Cigales** Vina 105★★ £C
● **Vino de la Tierra** Pegaso★★★ £D Montazo★★★ £D
○ **Málaga** MR Moscatel★★ £B Molino Real★★★★ £E

ROTLLÁN I TORRA Priorat www.closabattlet.com A: **Mor,F&R,Tur**

Owner: Rotllán family Balandra, 8, Torroja del Priorat, 43737 Tarragona
Jordi Rotllan's family estate of 24 ha was founded in 1984 and now offers some excitingly dark, spicy and fiery examples of this appellation, arguably the greatest now for reds. As well as the three bottlings rated below, the firm has also now released a Gran Reserva from both the 1995 and 96 vintages. The Balandra is 50 per cent Garnacha, 25 per cent Cariñena and 25 per cent Cabernet Sauvignon and is aged for 10 months in American oak. The more sophisticated Amadis also has some Syrah and Merlot blended in and is aged in finer French oak. The Tirant is a similar blend but includes very old (up to 100 years) Garnacha and Cariñena. Aged in new French oak with malolactic fermentation in barrel, this is the richest and finest of the trio and will improve in bottle for up to 15 years. (DM)

● **Priorat** Balandra★★★ £D Amadís★★★ £E Tirant★★★★ £E

BODEGAS SAN ALEJANDRO Calatayud www.san-alejandro.com A:**Msp**

Owner: Co-operative Ctra. Calatayud-Cariñena, 50330 Miedes de Aragón (Zaragoza)
This sizeable Aragon co-op was established in 1962 and now numbers around 300 growers who between them control around 1,100 ha of vineyards. As a result of this a range of wines is offered but one in particular stands out. Expresión is produced from some of the best and oldest vineyard blocks owned by the members. The wine is blended from a combination of just over 50 per cent 75- to 80-year-old Garnacha and younger Tempranillo and Syrah. Aged in a combination of French and American oak with malolactic fermentation in barrel, the wine is full of spicy, dark berry fruit and just the merest hint of vanilla. It has a firm enough

structure with sufficiently supple tannin to drink well young and to continue to develop over five or six years. (DM)

● **Expresión** Calatayud★★★£C

TERRAS GAUDA Rías Baixas www.terrasgauda.com A:P&S

Owner: Bodegas Terras Gauda S.A. Ctra. Tui-AGuarda, Rosal, 36760 Pontevedra
Founded in 1990, this is one the best properties in Rías Baixas. The vineyards in the Rosal Valley are close to the River Miño, which provides a benevolent mesoclimate. All of the wines are based on the aromatic Albariño, with a small amount of Loureiro and Caiño Blanco. The Abadía de San Campio is marked by its piercing, almost peachy, aromatic fruit, while the Terras Gauda label offers more depth and concentration. Both are cool-fermented to emphasise their fruit. The Terras Gauda Black Label is vinified in oak, a portion new, with *bâtonnage*. The wine has a weighty oak character but loses some of its exuberant fruit in the process. (DM)

O **Rias Baixas** Abadía de San Campio★★ £B Terras Gauda★★★£C Terras Gauda Black Label★ £C

TORRES Penedès www.torres.es A:JFe,Sel

Owner: Torres family Comercio 20, Vilafranca del Penedès, 08720 Barcelona
Very important producer, now making wines from grapes sourced throughout Cataluña. The Penedès firm of Jean León has been added to the operation and its wines are now of a uniformly much higher quality than they were before the acquisition by Torres. Overseas interests have been established in Chile with the MIGUEL TORRES brand but for many years now these have continued to disappoint. By contrast Miguel Torres' sister MARIMAR TORRES produces well-made and well-priced, cool-climate Chardonnay and Pinot Noir in California's Sonoma Green Valley. The Torres range is extensive and the regular wines are often less exhilarating than they might be. You have to look for the mid-range and top-flight labels to find real excitement. Among the reds, Atrium is a plummy, ripe Merlot, and Gran Coronas a blend of mainly Cabernet Sauvignon and Tempranillo. New to the range is Nerola, mainly Syrah with some Monastrell. The top reds include the Mas Borrás Pinot Noir which has still to show the quality achieved elsewhere with this tricky variety. The Mas la Plana Cabernet Sauvignon is structured and cedary, and the Grans Muralles is of real interest – a very local blend of Monastrell, Garnacha Tinta, Cariñena, Garró and Samsó, full of exotic dark fruit. Reserva Real is a very impressive blend of Cabernet Sauvignon, Merlot and Cabernet Franc. Of the whites, the commercial Viña Esmeralda is a blend of Moscatel and Gewürztraminer and has a dollop of residual sugar. More serious is Fransola, a lightly-oaked blend of mainly Sauvignon Blanc with some local Parellada. Milmanda is the pricey top Chardonnay from Conca de Barberá and Waltraud is a fine lime- and mineral-scented Riesling. Top reds are undoubtedly ageworthy; Reserva Real requires considerable patience. (DM)

Torres
● **Gran Coronas** Penedès★ £B ● **Atrium Merlot** Penedès★ £B
● **Mas la Plana** Penedès★★★ £E ● **Reserva Real** Penedès★★★★ £H
● **Grans Muralles** Conca de Barberá★★★ £E
O **Gran Viña Sol** Penedès★ £B O **Waltraud** Penedès★★★ £C O **Fransola** Penedès★★★ £D
O **Milmanda** Conca de Barberá★★★ £E

Jean León
O **Chardonnay** Penedès★★ £C

VALDESPINO Jerez y Manzanilla A: HWC

Owner: A.R. Valdespino S.A. Pozo del Olivar 16, Jerez de la Frontera, 11480 Cádiz
Marvellous, old-fashioned sherry producer with an impressive holding of old *soleras* to provide some of the best examples to be found in Jerez. The salty and intense Fino Inocente has a marked *flor* yeast character but should be drunk as soon after purchase as possible to enjoy its fresh, pungent, citrus character. There is a

very rich and toffee-like Pedro Ximénez Solera Superior which can only really be sipped. The Palo Cortado Cardenal is one of the very best examples of this unusual style. There are a number of rich and dry Amontillados. Tio Diego has an almost austere, tangy finish; Don Tomás has greater depth and concentration. By far the most interesting of the three is the remarkable, intense, nutty and fragrant Coliseo, one of the greatest sherries. This along with the Palo Cortado Cardenal and the rich and concentrated Oloroso su Majestad are now VORS. (DM)

O **Inocente** Fino★★ £B   O **Cardenal** Palo Cortado★★★ £C   O **Solera Superior** Pedro Ximénez★★★ £C
O **Tio Diego** Amontillado★★ £B   O **Don Tomás** Amontillado★★★ £C   O **Coliseo** Amontillado❍❍❍❍❍£E
O **Su Majestad** Oloroso★★★★ £D

CELLER VALL LLACH   Priorat   www.fm2.com/vallllach   A: F&R

Owner: Luis Llach   43739 Porrera, Tarragona
Singer Luis Llach founded this first-class Priorat property in the early 1990s. He also has an interest in CIMS DE PORRERA. The first vintage bottled at Vall Llach was 1998. An important key to quality here has been the acquisition of some very old vineyards, varying from 60 to 90 years of age and sited on slatey slopes. Viticulture is generally organic and chemicals are avoided. New plantings of Garnacha, Cabernet Sauvignon, Merlot and Syrah have been undertaken and these generally make up the bulk of the second wine, Embruix. They also contribute texture and complexity to the main wine. Vall Llach itself is dominated by old-vine Cariñena, with Garnacha and Cabernet Sauvignon blended in. It is a dark, spicy, brooding beast, full of fiery *sauvage* character. It will require four or five years' cellaring to soften its raw youthful edge. (DM)

● **Priorat**★★★★★ £F Embruix★★★ £C

VEGA SICILIA   Ribera del Duero   www.vega-sicilia.com   A: M&V,BBR,F&M

Owner: Alvarez family   Ctra. N-122, Valbuena de Duero, 47359 Valladolid
Spain's most famous red wine producer. The quality of its wines in Ribera del Duero in recent years has been challenged by the likes of ALEJANDRO FERNANDEZ and DOMINIO DE PINGUS but Vega Sicilia remains quite distinct in style and approach. The top wine, Unico, which is a blend of Tinto Fino with Cabernet Sauvignon, Malbec and Merlot, is still given extended cask-maturation, although this has been reduced to help preserve the wine's fruit character. A non-vintaged Reserva Especial is also produced – very expensive and evolved in style. The second wine, Valbuena, produced from Tinto Fino and Merlot, has more obvious fruit character. In a move to provide a more contemporary approach but to retain the style of Vega Sicilia, a new winery, Alión, was established in 1991. These are impressive, structured and dense modern examples of the DO produced solely from Tinto Fino and full of dark, spicy fruit, supple tannin and cedary oak. Alión will benefit from at least five years' cellaring. Both Unico and Valbuena are accessible on release but will develop very well in bottle. The Alvarez family have also invested in Hungary in the Tokaji operation OREMUS. (DM)

Bodegas Vega Sicilia
● **Ribera del Duero** Valbuena★★★★ £F Unico❍❍❍❍❍ £H Reserva Especial★★★★★ £H
Bodegas y Viñedos Alión
● **Ribera del Duero** Alión★★★★★ £E

HERMANOS DEL VILLAR   Rueda   A: Msp

Owner: Del Villar family   Zarcillo, s/n, 47490 Rueda (Valladolid)
Striking producer of Verdejo-based whites in the Rueda region of Castilla y Leon. Owner and winemaker Pablo de Villar has some 70 ha of Verdejo planted in a number of sites in stony alluvial soils. There are also 15 ha planted to Sauvignon Blanc and a further 20 ha to Tempranillo. The Sauvignon Blanc is sound enough but it is the two Verdejo whites that offer the most interest. The regular bottling is cool-fermented in tank and Villar has isolated his own wild yeast strain. While the regular bottling has some straightforward grassy flavours and just a hint of tropical fruit, the Fermentado en Barrica is of a different order. Finely

structured with subtle oak tones and rich almost honeyed peachy fruit, this is one of the leading examples of the style. It should develop well in bottle for two or three years. (DM)

O **Rueda** Oro de Castilla Verdejo★ £B   O **Rueda** Oro de Castilla Verdejo Fermentado en Barrica★★★ £C

OTHER WINES OF NOTE

ALBET I NOYA O **Chardonnay** Collecció £B   ● **Penedès** Reserva Marti £C
CELLERS ALTA O **Alella** Lanius £C   ● **Alella** Orbus Crianza £C
ALVEAR O **Montilla-Moriles** Alvear CB £C
ALZANIA ● **Navarra** Crianza £C
ANTAÑO O **Rueda** Viña Mocén £B
BODEGAS ARZUAGA ● **Ribera del Duero** Crianza £C
HEREDEROS DE ARGÜESO O **San León** Manzanilla £B
BELLMUNT DEL PRIORAT ● **Priorat** Primitiu de Bellmunt £E
BELONDRADE Y LURTON O **Rueda** £B Oak Aged £B
BODEGAS BILBAINAS ● **Rioja** la Vicalanda Reseva £B
RAMÓN BILBAO ● **Rioja** Reserva £C Gran Reserva £D
BODEGAS BRETÓN ● **Rioja** Alba de Bretón £F
CAMPILLO ● **Rioja** Reserva £C Gran Reserva £D
CAMPO VIEJO ● **Rioja** Gran Reserva Marqués de Villamanga £D
CAN FEIXES O **Chardonnay** Penedès £C
CAN RÀFOLS DELS CAUS ● **Penedès** Gran Caus £D Caus Lubis £D
CASA DE LA ERMITA ● **Jumilla** £B
CASTAÑO ● Yecla Coleccion £B Monastrell Dulce £B
CELLER DE CANTONELLA ● **Costers del Segre** Cérvoles £B
CHIVITE O **Navarra** Colección Reserva Blanco £E
CILLAR DE SILOS ● **Ribera del Duero** Crianza £D
CODORNÍU O **Cava** Jaume Brut Non-Vintage £C
CUEVAS DE CASTILLA O **Rueda** £B
CVNE ● **Rioja Viña** Real Reserva £D Imperial Reserva £D Gran Reserva £E
DELGADO ZULETA O **La Goya** Manzanilla £B
BODEGA DOS VICTORIAS ● **Toro** Elias Mora Crianza £C Gran Elias Mora £E
O **Rueda** José Pariente £B
ENATE ● **Somontano** Reserva £E Reserva Especial £F
CELLER DE L'ENCASTELL ● **Priorat** Roquers de Porrera £E
BODEGAS FARINA ● **Toro** Reserva £B Campus £C
BARARA FORÈS O **Terra Alta** El Quinta £C   ● **Terra Alta** Coma d'En Pou £C
FREIXENET O **Cava** Reserva Vintage £C
BODEGAS GODEVAL O **Valdeorras** Viña Godeval £B
GRAND RECOSIND ● **Ampurdan Costa Brava** Crianza £B Gran Reserva £C
GRANJA FILLABOA O **Rias Baixas** Albariño £C
GUELBENZU ● **Navarra** Evo £C Lautus £E
GUETA-LUPIA ● **Priorat** £F
GUTIÉRREZ DE LA VEGA ● **Viña Ulises** £C   O **Casta Diva** £D
HACIENDA MONASTERIO ● **Ribera del Duero** Crianza £D Reserva £E
JUAN DE LA BARREDA ● **Torre de Barreda** Vino de la Tierra £B
CELLERS JOAN D'ANGUERA ● **Monsant** La Planella £B Finca l'Argata £C El Bugador £E
LAGAR DE CERVERA O **Rías Baixas** £C
LA PERLA DEL PRIORAT ● **Priorat** Clos les Fites £D Comte Pirene £E Comte Pirene Seleccion £E
BODEGAS LA TAPADA ● **Valdeorras** Guitián Fermentado en Barrica £C
LÓPEZ DE HEREDIA/VIÑA TONDONIA ● **Rioja** Crianza Viña Gravonia £B Reserva Viña Bosconia £E
● **Rioja** Reserva Viña Tondonia £D
LUSCO DO MIÑO O **Rías Baixas** £C
MAGAÑA ● **Navarra** Dignus Crianza £B
MARQUÉS DE ALELLA O **Alella** Crianza £B

MARQUÉS DE CÁCERES ● **Rioja** Gaudium £C
MARQUES DE VARGAS ● **Rioja** Reserva £D
MARTÍNEZ BUJANDA ● **Rioja** Conde de Valdemar Reserva £B Reserva £C Gran Reserva £D
MAS D'EN COMPTE ● **Priorat** Cal Pla £C Negre £E
O **Priorat** Cal Pla Bianca £C Garnacha Blanca £E
MAS D'EN GIL ● **Priorat** Coma Vella £D Clos Fontà £E O **Priorat** Coma Blanca £D
MAS IGNEUS ● **Priorat** Fa 112 £E
MATARROMERA ● **Ribera del Duero** Crianza £C Reserva £E
MIGUEL MERINO ● **Rioja** Reserva £E
BODEGAS MONTEBACO ● **Ribera del Duero** Crianza £E
BODEGAS EMILIO MORO ● **Ribera del Duero** £C Malleolus £E
MONTICELLO ● **Rioja** Viña Cumbrero £B Reserva £C
OSBORNE O **Solera India** Oloroso £E O **Alonso el Sabia** Oloroso £G
OTAZU ● **Navarra** Crianza £B Reserva £C O **Chardonnay** Navarra £B
PAGO DE CARRAOVEJAS ● **Ribera del Duero** Crianza £C Reserva £F
BODEGAS PALACIO ● **Rioja** Cosme Palacio y Hermanos £D
PINTIA ● **Toro** £E
PIRINEOS ● **Somomontano** Moristel £B Merlot-Cabernet £B
BODEGAS PRIMICIA ● **Rioja** Crianza £B Reserva £C
BODEGAS PROTOS ● **Ribera del Duero** Crianza £C Reserva £E
CELLERS PUIG & ROCA ● **Penedes** Augustus Trajanus £C O **Penedes** Augustus Chardonnay £C
RAÏMAT ● **Costers del Segre** Mas Castell £D Vallcorba £D
REAL SITIO DE VENTOSILLA ● **Ribera del Duero** PradoRey Crianza £C PradoRey Reserva £D
TEÓFILO REYES ● **Ribera del Duero** Crianza £C
BODEGAS RIOJANAS ● **Rioja Gran** Albina £C
SANCHEZ ROMATE O **Amontillado** NPU £C
BODEGAS HERMANOS SASTRE ● **Ribera del Duero** Viña Sastre Crianza £C Pago de Santa Cruz £E
● **Ribera del Duero** Regina Vides £F
SCALA DEI ● **Priorat** Negre Garnacha £C
SEÑORÍO DE SAN VICENTE ● **Rioja** San Vicente £E Sierra Cantabria Coleccion Privada £E
TARSUS ● **Ribera del Duero** Quinta de Tarsus £B Tarsus £D
TORO ALBALÁ O **Montilla-Moriles** Pedro Ximénez Don PX £C
VALPICULATA ● **Toro** £D
JANE VENTURA ● **Penedes** Margalló £C Finca Els Camps £D Mas Vilella £D
VIÑA BAJOZ ● **Toro** Crianza £B Reserva £C
VIÑAS DEL VERO ● **Somontano** Gran Vos £C
VIÑA MEIN O **Ribeiro** £B
VIÑA SOLORCA ● **Ribera del Duero** Crianza £C
VINICOLA DEL PRIORAT ● **Priorat** Onix £C
WILLIAMS & HUMBERT O **Dos Cortados** Palo Cortado £C **Dry Sack Solera Especial** £D

Work in progress!!

Wines from the following producers under consideration for the next edition

ARTAZU (NAVARRA)
BIENVENIDA DE VINOS (TORO)
BODEGAS JUAN-MAUNUEL BURGOS (RIBERA DEL DUERO)
CAVAS DEL CASTILLO DE PERELADA (EMPORDÀ-COSTA-BRAVA)
CAMPO ELISEO (TORO)
CESAR PRINCIPE (CIGALES)
DESCENDIENTES DE J PALACIOS (BIERZO)
DITS DEL TERRA (PRIORAT)
DOMINIO DE ATAUTA (RIBERA DEL DUERO)
FINCA EL BOSQUE (RIOJA)
HEREDAD GUZMAN ALDAZABAL (RIOJA)

CELLER JOAN SIMÓ (PRIORAT)
BODEGAS LOS ASTRALES (RIBERA DEL DUERO)
FINCA LUZON (JUMILLA)
CELLER MARTI FABRA CARRERAS (EMPORDÀ-COSTA-BRAVA)
MAS DOIX (PRIORAT)
MAS GIL (CATALUNYA)
BODEGAS MASIA SERRA (EMPORDÀ-COSTA-BRAVA)
BODEGAS GERARDO MÉNDEZ (RIAS BAIXAS)
NUMANTHIA-TERMES (TORO)
PAGO DEL AMA (CASTILLA LA MANCHA)
PASANAU GERMANS (PRIORAT)
PAZO SAN MAURO (RIAS BAIXAS)
QUINTA LA QUIETUD (TORO)
QUINTA SARDONIA (CASTILLA Y LEÓN)
BENJAMIN ROMEO (RIOJA)
FINCA SANDOVAL (MANCHUELA)
SIERRA CANTABRIA (RIOJA)
SIERRA SALINAS (YECLA)
UVAGUILERA (RIBERA DEL DUERO)
BODEGAS VALSACRA (RIOJA)
VENUS LA UNIVERSAL (MONTSANT)
VIÑA SILA (RUEDA)
VIÑA VILLABUENA (RIOJA)
VIZCARRA RAMOS (RIBERA DEL DUERO)

Author's choice (DM)

The Spanish new wave

AALTO ● **Ribera del Duero** Aalto PS
ABADÍA RETUERTA ● **Pago Valdellón** Vino de Mesa
AGRO DE BAZÁN ○ **Rías Baixas** Granbazán Ambar
CELLER DE CAPÇANES ● **Monsant** Flor de Primavera
CASA CASTILLO ● **Jumilla** Pie Franco
CLOS I TERASSES ● **Priorat** Clos Erasmus
CLOS MOGADOR ● **Priorat** Clos Mogador
LEDA VINAS VIEJAS ● **Vina Leda**
DOMINIO DE VALDEPUSA ● **Émeritus** Montes de Toledo
MAURO ● **Mauro** Terreus
MAURODOS ● **Toro** Viña San Román
CELLER VALL LLACH ● **Priorat**

Established and emerging classics

FINCA ALLENDE ● **Rioja** Aurus
ISMAEL ARROYO ● **Ribera de Duero** Val Sotillo Gran Reserva
ARTADI ● **Rioja** Viña El Pisón Reserva
DOMINIO DE PINGUS ● **Ribera del Duero** Pingus
ALEJANDRO FERNÁNDEZ - PESQUERA ● **Ribera del Duero** Gran Reserva
MARQUÉS DE MURRIETA ● **Rioja** Gran Reserva Especial Castillo d'Ygay
MARQUÉS DE RISCAL ● **Rioja** Reserva Baron de Chirel
ALVARO PALACIOS ● **Priorat** L'Ermita
PÉREZ PASCUAS ● **Ribera del Duero** Pérez Pascuas Gran Reserva
LA RIOJA ALTA ● **Rioja** 890 Gran Reserva
RODA ● **Rioja** Cirsion
VEGA SICILIA ● **Ribera del Duero** Unico

Portugal, including Port & Madeira

The fantastic revolution taking place in the quality of Portuguese wines continues. At the cutting edge are some brilliant winemakers making both everyday wines of great value and character and also exciting new wines of unprecedented quality for this ancient wine-producing country. The Douro, followed by Alentejo, provides the greatest riches but there are exciting wines from nearly all the major regions. There is still much poor wine at lower levels and even moderately ambitious efforts can show winemaking faults or a lack of balance – but the best wines from leading producers can be tried with confidence. Portugal's burgeoning middle classes consume for the lion's share of the best wines and have pushed up prices but small quantities are exported and many new wines are being introduced every year.

Port & the Douro

The five leading varieties in this spectacular region were identified in the 1970s as Touriga Nacional, Tinta Roriz, Touriga Franca (previously called Touriga Francesa), Tinta Barroca and Tinto Cão. Some consider a sixth, Tinta Amarela, to be equally important. Though all were often planted as field blends that might include any number of other varieties, there has been an increasing trend towards planting by single variety. Where it is feasible on the steep schistous slopes, quality-conscious producers now favour vertical plantings (as used in the Mosel) with a resultant increase in density. But these vineyards co-exist with old-fashioned (occasionally single-row) terracing (*socalcos*) and the bulldozed terracing (*patamares*) that was introduced in the 1970s and allowed for greater mechanization.

In the west of the region the Serra do Marão range of mountains has a significant effect on the climate. There is a successive drop-off in average rainfall in stages from relatively rain-soaked Porto to Régua (Baixo Corgo – the westernmost of three sections), to Pinhão (Cima Corgo), to the dry, flatter lands of the Douro Superior (close to Spain) where there is some use of irrigation. Producers have shown it is possible to get grapes fully ripe in the Baixo Corgo around Régua, though they are likely to be hardest hit in rain-affected vintages. Cima Corgo is the classic port country with the greatest concentration of 'A' classified vineyards (vines are classified A to F) and most of the famous *quintas*. A quinta defines a farm or estate which may be composed of vineyards of more than one grade. The quintas overlooking the Douro are important but so are those found on several small tributaries, especially those from the valleys of the Rio Pinhão and the Rio Torto. Here the greatest differences in character, structure and style are discernible from individual *terroirs*. Although many of the classic Vintage Ports are sourced from here fine port is also made in the Douro Superior.

Port has traditionally been stored at the port lodges in Vila Nova da Gaia (opposite Porto), but since 1986 it has been permitted to make, store and ship port at its source in the Douro. Quinta do Noval and Quinta de la Rosa were two of the first to take advantage of this but it is necessary to have cool cellars if the wines are not to take on a distinctive baked character known as Douro bake. Although autovinification is common for most ports, the best Vintage Ports are made by fermenting in *lagares*. Traditionally this involves treading by foot (though this is now being closely imitated by robotic devices) which allows the rapid but gentle extraction of colour, tannin and extract in the 48 hours or so before the fermentation is arrested by the addition of port brandy. Temperature control of *lagares* and the chilling of brandy are also used to harmonise this addition and avoid a spirity component in the resulting port.

Most table reds were previously made from inferior grapes or sites, but in the past decade leading producers have established potentially high-quality sites (or harnessed the potential of existing sites) specifically for Douro reds, resulting in a remarkable revolution in both the quality and quantity of premium examples. The best wines impress not only with splendid fruit, depth and structure but also the stylish minerality that the Douro's soils can bring. As with port, some of it is coarse, baked or unattractively earthy but the best are rich, complex and characterful.

Other regions

Good **Vinho Verde**, made in the Rios do Minho region, is rare. Despite changes to viticulture, the damp climate makes it difficult to get Alvarinho (the best grape), Loureiro, Trajadura or other grapes fully ripe for the white version that is widely exported. **Beiras**, a large region to the south of the Douro, includes both the Bairrada and Dão DOCs. Labels showing simply Beiras Vinho Regional can be wines that fall outside the regulations for these DOCs as well as wines from the wider region. Excellent vintages can be few and far between in **Bairrada**. The biggest problem is rain and the diseases which can result from it. The clay soils are largely planted to the Baga grape which is high in both tannin and acidity and it can be difficult to achieve full ripeness in its tannins. Nonetheless wines of great depth and character, if idiosyncratic style and flavour, are possible and much progress has been made in recent years. The **Dão** has granitic sandy soils and is less exposed to the coast than Bairrada. Though once associated with tough, tannic reds that only occasionally showed well with considerable age, the last six or seven years have seen a dramatic improvement in quality and there has been increased planting of Touriga Nacional and Tinta Roriz on well-sited hillsides. Both grapes have been produced varietally as have Jaen, Alfrocheiro Preto and even some Tinta Cão, though these grapes generally perform better as part of a blend. The best estates now offer rich, ripe, modern but characterful reds. Fine quality whites have also been made from Malvasia Fina and Encruzado, the latter particularly promising in gently oaked varietal examples.

Estremadura covers undulating hillsides north of Lisbon but despite its proximity to the coast it avoids much of the cloud cover and rain of more northerly maritime-influenced areas such as Bairrada and Vinho Verde. It has long produced more wine than any other region, much of it from large co-ops. But here, too, things have improved and a handful of individual estates are emerging with some creditable wines. **Alenquer** is the most important sub-regional DOC. In the **Ribatejo**, despite many high-yielding vineyards, there is some good value to be had where a top winemaker has been contracted to make the wines. Both regions have a smattering of foreign varieties, including Cabernet Sauvignon and Syrah, but premium, sometimes varietal, examples of Portugal's best grapes are far more important.

One grape, Castelão (Periquita), brought to the region by José Maria da Fonseca in 1830, dominates production in **Terras do Sado** and nowhere else does it work varietally quite so well. The best smoky, minerally, earthy examples are sold as **Palmela** (a more defined area of mostly sandy soils on the Setúbal peninsula) or Terras do Sado. Based on Muscat of Alexandria variants, **Setúbal** and **Moscatel de Setúbal** (predominantly Moscatel) are famous fortified wines of good quality, particularly from José Maria da Fonseca. The still relatively small, scattered vineyards of **Alentejo** lie close to the Spanish border and are drier and less maritime-influenced. Most of the top Alentejo reds are blends based on Trincadeira and Aragonês (Tinta Roriz), with Castelão, Alicante Bouschet or even Cabernet Sauvignon as minor components. Syrah has been made varietally and shows promise in a rich, powerful if slightly earthy, robust way. Ripe, sound, attractive whites are on the increase from the Alentejo (grapes include Roupeiro and Arinto) but only a handful show sufficient depth or structure to improve beyond a couple of years' age.

Madeira

Madeira is made by a small number of shippers who for the most part buy grapes from the island's many small growers. Tinta Negra Mole dominates their vineyards but the best Madeira comes from the slowly increasing amounts of the traditional varieties. The wine needs to be made from at least 85 per cent of either Malvasia (Malmsey), Bual (Boal), Verdelho or Sercial to be labelled as such. As well as being fortified, fundamental to Madeira's style are a high level of acidity and a degree of caramelisation due to heating. Most Madeira, especially the stuff used for cooking, undergoes the *estufagem* process which involves a period in a hot store (*estufa*). The best wines, however, are made by the *canteiro* system, whereby the wine is only subjected to natural heating in cask over a period of three years or more. As a result the wines are less coarse and have less of a burnt-sugar flavour.

Each of the traditional varieties is associated with a certain degree of sweetness. The greater the sweetness, the higher the percentage of spirit in the wine as the fermentation is arrested at an earlier stage to retain a higher sugar level. The richest and sweetest, Malmsey – often pungent, full and toffeed – is usually the most easily appreciated but most examples miss the elegance and definition associated with the smoky, spicy, dried-fruits Bual (Boal), which is less sweet but still a dessert-style wine. The best Verdelho (of moderate sweetness) is often tangy yet lightly honeyed with dried citrus fruits and a certain delicacy of flavour and aroma. The dry Sercial, often with daunting acidity, can show a fine citrusy (orangey), nutty and dried-fruit complexity with age.

The best commercial styles are the 10-year-old and 15-year-old wines. The age indicated will be an average as the wines are blended to maintain a consistent style. Even from the best shippers, 3-year-old Madeira will almost invariably be made from Tinta Negra Mole and is likely to involve the addition of caramel and the use of concentrated must. Vintage Madeira will have spent at least 20 years in cask but many of the very best have spent 50 years or even 100 years in wood. Once bottled it continues to age but at a very slow rate. As they are only made in tiny quantities it is imperative to consult a specialist before parting with the considerable sums needed to secure a bottle. Rare examples of two other traditional grapes, Moscatel and Terrantez, are also occasionally encountered.

Port styles

There are two basic styles of port: those matured in bottle and those aged in wood. Of the first, **Vintage Port** applies to any port that meets the requirements of the IVP (Instituto do Vinho do Porto or Port Wine Institute) and is usually bottled before the summer of the second year after the harvest. While the title implies the 'declared' vintages bearing a house name, it applies equally to single-quinta ports and 'off-vintage' ports (or 'second label' – a shipper's port from a non-declared year, increasingly made as a true single-quinta example). These wines, which may be bought through a wine merchant or agent prior to being shipped, will always require decanting. Late Bottled Vintage Port (or **LBV**) spends four to six years in large vats and the majority are fined and filtered to avoid any sediment forming in the bottle and are ready to be consumed when released. 'Traditional' examples, however, more closely resemble Vintage Ports in character and depth and, though they must be aged for a further three years in bottle before release, are not necessarily ready to drink when released. Some, having only the minimum bottle-age, will improve for a further five or six years. **Crusted Port**, like Traditional LBVs and Vintage Port, will throw a sediment but is a blend of two or three vintages rather than one and the year given is that of its bottling.

Of the wood-matured styles the most credible are those tawnies with an indication of age. Though extensively blended to maintain a house style, these gently oxidised styles can show considerable complexity and refinement. The quality of **10-year-old Tawny Port** is, however, extremely variable and in many instances the quality doesn't match the price. At worst they are simple, coarse and tired but better, fresher, balanced examples can show a date, nut, fig and toasty complexity that is seen more often in examples of the more pricey **20-year-old Tawny Port**. **30-and 40-year-old** examples are variable (sometimes excessively volatile) and expensive but at their best have an intense, nutty *rancio* character and complexity not dissimilar to an aged sherry. **Colheita Port** is effectively a tawny port of a single vintage and is labelled with both the year of the *colheita* (harvest) and bottling year. They have a minimum of seven years in cask and can have all the qualities of the best tawnies with an indication of age but don't always have the fruit to further improve with extended bottle age. The most commercially important port is the relatively inexpensive **Vintage Character** or **Premium Ruby**. The best offer good fruit intensity in an easy-drinking style and their brand names are more familiar to many consumers than the name of the style. Regular **Ruby Port** is very young, fruity port (at best) while some basic Tawny Port is simply a poor Ruby cut with some **White Port**. The latter, from white grapes but turning amber with age, is usually best avoided as many taste sweet and doctored. A few are dry and nutty with some refinement.

A-Z of producers by region

1   Vinho Verde
2   Douro, Port
3   Bairrada
4   Dão
5   Alenquer
6   Palmela, Setúbal

RIOS DO MINHO

TRÁS-OS-MONTES
TUA
DOURO

1

Pinhão
2

Porto DOURO   Peso da Régua

Viseu

3   *4*

Coimbra

BEIRAS

ESTREMADURA

RIBATEJO
TEJO

5

Portalegre

ALENTEJO

Estremoz

Lisboa   *6*

Évora

Setúbal

TERRAS DO SADO

Reguengos de Monsaraz

Vidigueira

Moura

GUADIANA

ALGARVE

Faro

Port vintages

It used to be so simple. Vintage Port was made when the port shippers 'declared' a particular vintage was of sufficient quality to justify the bottling of a house port from that year. In other years, the same wine would be bottled under the name of a leading estate or quinta. But in a swing towards estate-based ports, some true single quintas make a port more in the mould of a Bordeaux château, that is to say in almost every year. Nonetheless general declarations are still important and still tend to highlight the very best years, though examples from a top source – whether a true single quinta or that of an 'off-vintage' quinta name – can surpass weaker efforts from a declared year. As the declarations are made 15 months to two years after the harvest there is always a second vintage coming under consideration, leading sometimes to a so-called 'split declaration' as some shippers decide to wait and declare the younger wine instead. For a true guide to longevity both the vintage assessment and that of the individual producer's style and reputation must be taken together. **Those years underlined denote a wide declaration.**

2003: In the year of Europe's extreme heat Portugal's Douro fared better than most, in most cases the vines being able to draw on sufficient ground water to avoid stress or raisining from spells of extreme heat in June and August. Expect a vintage declaration but as elsewhere in Europe don't expect a universal success.

2002: This is a year the rains fell to spoil a potentially fine vintage. September's 'Friday the 13th' was lucky for only a few (mostly in the Douro Superior) in the sense that they had picked most of the grapes already before the start of a more than a month of miserable weather. Nonetheless, some good, forward, fruit-emphasised single-quinta ports were made by those who care about quality.

2001: The winter preceding this growing season was incredibly wet resulting in the widely televised tragic bridge collapse over the river on March 4. Despite the reasonably dry growing season and good harvest conditions, the moisture absorbed in the early part of the year has dampened quality to some extent, though volumes are up.

2000: Rain in the early part of the growing season and a poor flowering were compensated for by a hot, dry ripening period. Yields were very low but the best wines have an incredible intensity of fruit and fine ripe tannins. There is not perhaps quite the size or power of certain other excellent vintages but the wines promise to be long-lived with great expression and classic character in the top names.

1999: Though characterised by irregular, low rainfall much of it fell at harvest as the rain set in from mid-September. Top quality was hard to achieve and while most small estates made Vintage Port, the shippers opted for their single-quinta ports. Good quality but it will be overshadowed by 2000.

1998: Due to an irregular growing season with intermittent heavy rain at harvest, and despite very low yields, this year is one of good rather than great quality. The best single-quinta ports are reasonably concentrated and intense but more modestly structured and lack real stuffing. Nonetheless some will be attractive in the medium term where there is good winemaking.

1997: The season had something of a hole in the middle, with a cool, wet midsummer. The return of the sun and real heat more than saved the vintage. The wines have quite firm but ripe structures and the best are well-concentrated too. Less successful than 1994 or 2000 yet still a very promising vintage with many excellent wines. The very best may come from Fonseca, Niepoort and Noval (Nacional) as well as Dow, Graham, Taylor and Vesúvio.

1995: A very hot August ensured a vintage of good concentration to follow 1994. The wines are often very ripe and there are more raisiny characters and a lack of flavour finesse in some. At least half a dozen shippers declared, though most of the top names opted for single-quinta port instead.

1994: The most outstanding port vintage in recent times. Universally declared, the wines initially showed a remarkably seductive fruit but a deep, tannic back bone that suggests classic wines with 20, 30 or more years' age. Now is not the time to drink them, especially when many older vintages, that are drinking so well, often cost less.

1992: A very high-quality vintage declared by a few who preferred this to 1991. The cynical dismissed Taylor-Fonseca motives in the Tricentenary year of Taylor's founding yet, as at Vesúvio and Niepoort, port of real class and concentration was made.

1991: Given the mixed form of the 80s, 1991 is emerging as something of a turning point in vintage fortunes. It was also the start of a much brighter era for port's commercial prospects. The wines are full and firm, not a seductive or elegant vintage but with plenty of power in the best examples. Despite more than a decade's age the best examples such as Dow, Graham and Warre deserve considerably longer.

1987: Few declarations but whether Vintage or single-quinta, one for drinking up.

1985: A much-touted vintage on the basis of extremely favourable vintage conditions but while exceptional for a few, generally it is very patchy. The heat at vintage time precipitated winemaking problems which, though remedied in subsequent vintages, led to washed-out, sometimes volatile wines. Generally a success for the well-equipped Symington group (Graham is superb); only a few others, including Fonseca capitalised on nature's benevolence.

1983: Muscle and structure typified many of the wines from this vintage but the best have added flesh and richness with age. Another Symington year and while Taylor and Niepoort are also very good, bottles from Cockburn and Ramos Pinto can be more variable.

1982: The more hasty chose to declare this instead of the superior 1983 and got it badly wrong. A few, including Sandeman and Niepoort, did rather better but these and the best single-quinta should now be drunk up.

1980: A year unjustly overlooked and for a time considered second-rate but those from the Symington stable in particular have done much to restore its reputation. To those in the know, Dow, Graham and Warre have long provided a remarkably good and well-priced source of port.

1977: A classic year but with many examples now near their best, it doesn't seem to have quite the staying power of 1966 or 63. Variation has been noted in Taylor and more recently in Dow. Fonseca has been consistently brilliant and Graham, Niepoort and Smith Woodhouse seem to have got better and better while Warre too has proven its worth down the years.

1975: There were few exceptions to what turned out to be a relatively light and fast-maturing vintage.

1970: Up until and including 1970 much Vintage Port was bottled in the UK rather than at source and this fine vintage does sometimes show the variations in quality this can bring. Nonetheless a very good vintage with most wines showing excellent balance and fine tannins, often displaying the particular style of a shipper's port to good effect. The likes of Dow, Graham, Fonseca, Noval's Nacional, Niepoort and Taylor will continue to improve.

1966: An excellent vintage of very powerful ports, the best of which are likely to last even longer than the classic 1963. However there are slightly fewer really great wines and of those most do not possess the extra finesse or harmony of its predecessor. Nonetheless very fine examples from Cálem, Delaforce, Dow, Fonseca, Graham, Noval's Nacional and Taylor. Drink now or keep.

1963: The finest proven vintage of the second half of the 20th century, and remarkably consistent too. Cockburn, Croft, Delaforce, Dow, Fonseca, Graham, Noval's Nacional, Taylor and Warre provide the evidence. Of recent declarations only 1994 poses any sort of threat to its supremacy. As well as continued ageworthiness, it is the balance and marvellous refinement in the wines that set them apart from other top years. Drink now or keep.

Earlier Years: Great port years extend back the length of the entire 20th century but those still truly alive and great become increasingly scarce with the years (as well as hard to find and prohibitively expensive). 1960 is a fully mature vintage but good bottles exist from a number of shippers; Cockburn's seems the most likely to keep a lot longer. 1955 has always had more vigour and richness and while many are tiring, well-sourced bottles of Dow, Graham, Fonseca and the regular Noval will live on. Older vintages (48, 45, 35, 34, 31, 27 and others) should only be be bought where the wines have been impeccably stored and from a reliable bottler (see 1970).

Portuguese red wine vintages

While not covered in the vintage commentary above, the best Portuguese table wines have considerable ageing potential. In general, the best reds, whatever their origins, will keep for five to ten years but the majority of such wines have been made in the last few years and do not come from earlier vintages. Therefore while the vintage chart needs to be considered in conjunction with comments in the specific producer entry, in most instances buy from a recent good vintage whether for drinking young or to cellar for a substantial period.

Port vintage chart   Portuguese red vintage chart

				Douro	Dão	Alentejo
2003	NYR		2003	★★★★/★★★★★ A	★★★/★★★★★ A	★★★/★★★★★ A
2000	★★★★/★★★★★ A		2002	★★/★★★★ B	★★/★★★ B	★★★/★★★★ B
1997	★★★/★★★★ A		2001	★★★★/★★★★★ A	★★★★ A	★★★★ B
1995	★★★ B		2000	★★★★/★★★★★ A	★★★★ B	★★★★ B
1994	★★★★★ A		1999	★★★/★★★★ B	★★★ B	★★★/★★★★ B
1992	★★★★ B		1998	★★/★★★ B	★★ C	★★/★★★ B
1991	★★★/★★★★ B		1997	★★★★ B	★★★★/★★★★★ B	★★★★ C
1987	★★/★★★ C		1996	★★/★★★ B	★★★★ B	★★/★★★ C
1985	★★/★★★★ A		1995	★★★/★★★★ B	★★★★/★★★★ C	★★★★ C
1983	★★★★ C		1994	★★★★/★★★★★ C	★★★/★★★★ C	★★★ C
1980	★★★ C		1992	★★★★ C	★★★/★★★★ C	★★/★★★ D
1977	★★★★/★★★★★ C		1991	★★★★ C	★★★/★★★★ C	★★★/★★★★ C
1970	★★★★ C		1990	★★★ D	★★/★★★ D	★★★★ D
1966	★★★★/★★★★★ C					
1963	★★★★★ C					

DOMINGOS ALVES DE SOUSA Douro

Owner: Domingos Alves de Sousa Qta. da Gaivosa, Apartado 15, 5031 Santa Marta de Penaguião
Quinta da Gaivosa is one of two leading estates of Domingos Alves de Sousa located in the Lower Douro north of Régua. The Gaivosa wine is one of the most stylish and refined reds of the Douro; there is not the weight or richness of other examples but it is long and distinguished and drinks well with three years' age or more. The smaller Quinta do Vale da Raposa is the source of several reds, including a round, fruity, regular Douro, two good varietal expressions and a deep, powerful Grande Escolha, which has excellent ageing potential. Like Gaivosa it is based on Touriga Nacional, Tinta Cão and Tinta Roriz. Three other estates, Estação, Caldas and Aveleira provide mostly inexpensive but generally well-made reds (Estação Colheita Seleccionada shows extra vigour and intensity). New and very promising is Alves de Sousa Pessoal from the Gaivosa vineyards; a 1999 shows more powerful, earthy character than Gaivosa if less refinement and composure. No Gaivosa was made in 2001 or 2002 but 2003 will be worth looking out for. White wine is also made if of more variable quality. Cume is a new inexpensive red with a smart modern label; simple but supple and berryish. (PW)

Quinta da Gaivosa:
● **Douro★★★** £C

Quinta da Estaçao:
● **Douro** Colheita Seleccionada★★ £C

Quinta do Vale da Raposa:
● **Douro★** £B Tinta Roriz★★ £B Touriga Nacional★★ £B Grande Escolha★★★ £C

BARBEITO Madeira   A: **RyR**, BBR, Res, F&M, P&S, Hfx, RGr, F&R

*Owner: De Freitas family & **Kinoshita Shoji** Estrada Monumental 145, 9000-098 Funchal, Madeira*
Barbeito has a interesting range of commercial Madeiras as well as small stock of very old vintage examples. Operations are directed by Riccardo de Freitas, who has been involved in the winemaking since 1991. All the grapes are bought in and all the wines are *canteiro* wines, subject only to natural heating. The wines are generally drier and with higher acidities than some due to a policy of not de-acidifying. Nor are the wines caramelised as is more usually the case. Single Harvest, made only from Tinta Negra Mole, and with dried fruits, nut, fig and date flavours, shows what is possible from this variety. The Boal (Bual) Veramar averages five years' age and has excellent fruit and intensity for this level. For more classic fire power, the range of 10-year-old wines should be tried. Again the Boal is fine, while a Special Reserve 20-year-old adds still more power, intensity and length. The breadth and potency of both of these contrast with the elegance and purity in a very small-production single cask example, 1993 Malvasia Colheita Cask 3a, followed by 1994 Cask 18a. New 1981 Verdelho (£F, replacing the 1980 version) is a fine example of the elegance and style of good Verdelho. These and other treasures besides deserve a wider audience. (PW)

O **Single Harvest★★★** £D   O **Madeira** Boal Veramar★★★ £C
O **Madeira** 10-year-old Boal Reserve★★★ £E 10-year-old Sercial Reserve★★★ £E
O **Madeira** 20-year-old Special Reserve Malvasia★★★★ £F

CAVES ALIANÇA Beiras www.caves-alianca.com   A: **Mer**, ACh

Owner: DãoS.A Apartado 6, 3781-908 Sangalhos
Once associated with the mediocrity of much Portuguese table wine, Caves Aliança has undergone a major transformation in the past decade and now provides much-improved quality at all levels. The company owns large estates in the Douro Superior, Beiras Interior, Dão and Alentejo. The basics are simple but increasingly well made, but much more interesting are the reasonably priced Bairrada Garrafeira, Douro Foral Grande Escolha, Palmela Particular and Dão Particular. From a good vintage these all show regional character and gain a savoury intensity with three to five years' age. New premium wines see winemaker Francisco Antunes working with Michel Rolland to produce flagship reds from three estates: Quinta das

Baceladas (Bairrada), Quinta dos Quatro Ventos (Douro) and Quinta da Terrugem in Alentejo. The latter, a blend of Aragonês (Tinta Roriz) and Trincadeira (70:30), is very fine, with smoke, earth and black plum, good breadth and an excellent expression of the Alentejo. T da Terrugem (90 per cent Aragonês) was first made in 1999. It is very classy, combining power and finesse, and promises to be a new classic Portuguese red. Quatro Ventos, primarily Touriga Franca and Tinta Barocca, shows real potential while a new Reserva (mostly Tinta Roriz and Touriga Franca) made in 2001 is even more promising. The Baceladas Merlot/Cabernet Sauvignon/Baga blend is individual but with true Bairrada character. New Dão red Quinta da Garrida shows a classic Dão personality imbued with floral and mineral notes. (PW)

Aliança:
- ● **Douro** Foral Grande Escolha★★ £B ● **Bairrada** Garrafeira★★ £B
- ● **Dão** Particular★★ £B ● **Palmela** Particular★★ £B

Quinta da Terrugem:
- ● **Alentejo** Quinta da Terrugem★★★ £C T da Terrugem★★★★★ £F

Quinta dos Quatro Ventos:
- ● **Douro**★★★ £C

Quinta da Garrida:
- ● **Dão**★★★ £B

CHURCHILL Port www.churchills-port.com **A: EdV**, HHB, CPp, L&S, Tan, P&S, Res, FWC

Owner: Churchill Graham Lda Rua da Fonte Nova 5, 4400 Vila Nova de Gaia
The port house established by Johnny Graham and his brothers has come a long way in just over 20 years. In the early days port was made in rented, cramped quarters and solely from bought-in grapes but now the company has expanded and it acquired two important quintas of its own in 1999: Quinta da Gricha and Quinta do Rio. The ports have always been made to a high standard, for a time drawing on grapes from the Fojo and Manuela quintas, and generally show rich, ripe fruit and good balance, avoiding overripeness or an excessive spirity character. The Vintage Port, in particular, has got better with successive declarations. Best recent years are 2000, 97, 94 and 91. Other ports are competitively priced and often better value than the equivalents from the biggest names. Served slightly chilled, the amber-coloured dry white port is a rare good example. The single-quinta Quinta da Gricha port (from 1999, 00 and 01) and Quinta do Rio (01) now complement the fine Agua Alta made in 1998, 96, 95 and 92. Douro reds are now also being made. (PW)

- ● **Vintage Port**★★★★ £F Quinta da Gricha★★★ £E ● **Crusted Port**★★★ £C
- ● **Late Bottled Vintage Port** Traditional★★ £C ● **10-year-old Tawny Port**★★ £C
- ● **Finest Vintage Character Port**★★ £B O **White Port** Dry Aperitif★ £B

COCKBURN Port www.cockburns-usa.com **A: ADo**, AAA

Owner: Cockburn Smithes Ca (Allied Domecq) Rua das Coradas 13, 4400 Vila Nova de Gaia
Established in 1815, Cockburn is one of the best-known port names. Much of its recent popularity is down to the success of the simple, sweet Special Reserve, a Vintage Character port. Quinta do Tua and, since 1989, Quinta dos Canais are two excellent quintas that form part of a substantial vineyard resource. The Vintage Port, for many years of only moderate quality or worse, has returned to form – good in 1991 and 97, excellent in 94 and 00. Mature vintages such as 1963, 60 and 55 or even older bottles can be superb (the rating only applies to the best vintages). The single-quinta Quinta dos Canais shows a lovely fruit purity and intensity and if it is less long-lived than the Vintage it still shows the quality of fruit that it brings to the blend. LBV is modest but tawnies show good intensity and length of flavour. (PW)

- ● **Vintage Port**★★★★ £F Quinta dos Canais★★★ £E
- ● **10-year-old Tawny Port**★ £C ● **20-year-old Tawny Port**★★ £E

CORTES DE CIMA Alentejo www.cortesdecima.pt A: Adm, JNi, Maj

Owner: Hans Kristian Jørgensen & family Cortes de Cima, 7960-999 Vidigueira

For ripe, modern-styled reds, Cortes de Cima continue to be one of the Alentejo's leaders. It is located in Vidigueira, the southernmost of the Alentejo's subzones, and the wines are made by the owner, Dane Hans Kristian Jørgensen. There are now from 95 ha of vineyards many which have been converted to the Smart Dyson training system, thanks to input from viticultural expert Richard Smart. Since 1997 the wines have been consistently fine; fruit-driven with excellent varietal expression, particularly from the Portuguese grapes. The ripe, fleshy Cortes de Cima varies in composition but always includes Syrah, Aragonês and Trincadeira. A dark, dense Reserva (Syrah and Aragonês in 2001) marries new oak to a splendidly complex fruit character and is usually the top wine. A powerful varietal Syrah, Incógnito, is concentrated and adequately balanced despite being high in alcohol. It has lots of character but is at the very ripe end of the spectrum and lacks the finesse of a top Rhône example. From the 2002 vintage an enticingly aromatic Touriga Nacional and a second varietal Syrah have been made. Varietal Aragonês (labelled Aragonez) is usually impressive too but then there are no poor wines here. The more forward, soft, fruity Chaminé is good value, while Courela is the basic red. In 2003 the first white was produced, a varietal Antão Vaz. (PW)

● Cortes de Cima★★ £C Reserva★★★★ £E
● Incógnito★★★ £E ● Aragonez★★★ £E
● Chaminé★ £B

CROFT Port www.croftport.com A: Men, AAA

Owner: Fladgate partnership Apartado 5, 4401 Vila Nova de Gaia

What later became known as Croft had its beginnings in 1678 and its leading quinta, Quinta da Roêda, has provided the backbone of all its best Vintage Ports in the 20th century. Prior to the 1990s it is necessary to go back to 1977, 70, 66, 63, 60 or 55 for a really great Croft port but improvements in the 90s did make a difference. Yet despite making better ports recently (1991, 94 and 00 for Vintage Port and 95 and 97 for Roêda) there still seems to be some variability in the wines and Croft's real salvation seems likely to come from its recent purchase by the estimable Taylor-Fonseca group. Croft's Vintage has often been characterised by a certain muscularity stemming from its Roêda base. Of the other ports, a decent 10-year-old Tawny is made while the LBV with some upfront fruit is of the filtered type. 'Distinction' is the Vintage Character port and this along with Fine White, Fine Ruby and Fine Tawny are the big-volume basic ports. (PW)

● Vintage Port★★★ £F Quinta da Roêda★★ £E
● 10-year-old Tawny Port★★ £E

DELAFORCE Port A: Men, AAA

Owner: Fladgate partnership Largo Joaquim Magalhaes, 4401-501 Vila Nova de Gaia

Delaforce, like Croft became part of the Taylor-Fonseca group in 2001. Up till then the Delaforce family had continued to be involved with the winemaking, despite having relinquished ownership in 1968 at what was a very difficult time for the port trade. The wines are noted for being fruit-rich, stylish and refined at their best. That 'best' vanished after 1977 but the 92, 94 and 00 made by Nick Delaforce show some lovely fruit, although they are not in the blockbuster mould. Older vintages still very much alive are 1966, 63, 60 and 55. The sculptured terraces of Quinta da Corte (adjoining Ramos Pinto's Bom-Retiro) are a key component of fruit quality and have been the source of a delicious if relatively forward, medium-weight single-quinta port when a vintage isn't declared. Recent vintages are 2001, 97, 95 and 91. Late Bottled Vintage, if more superficial, can also reveal good fruit, while the tawnies show more finesse than most yet have good intensity too. There seems little doubt that the wines will get even better under the new regime. (PW)

● Vintage Port★★★ £E Quinta da Corte★★ £E
● 20-year-old Tawny Port Curious and Ancient★★★ £E
● 10-year-old Tawny Port His Eminence's Choice★★ £C ● Late Bottled Vintage Port★ £C

DOW Port www.dows-port.com   A: **JEF**,AAA

Owner: Symington group   Travesso Barão de Forrester, Apartado 10, 4401-997 Vila Nova de Gaia
Though a part of the Symington empire, as Silva & Cosens, the Dow port brand has a very distinct profile. There is a weight and dimension to the top years that, combined with an elegance and poise, puts them among the best, as recently seen in 1994, 97 and 00. Other vintages to try include 1985, 83, 80, 77, 70, 66, 63, 55 and 45. Even older vintages can still have some life, as does a fully-mature 1960 – although the 77 is now showing some variability. It is quite a structured port but its fine tannins are covered in layers of ripe fruit. In lesser years the wine can appear more muscular and occasionally a hint of spirit can also show through. However, Quinta do Bomfim, from slopes close to Pinhão in the heart of the Douro, was until recently the most important quinta in the region and some fine ports have been made under this name in non-declared years including 1998, 95, 92, 90, 87, 86 and 84. Dow also includes the exciting Quinta Senhora da Ribeira, which lies across the Douro from Quinta da Vesúvio in the Douro Superior. Once owned by Silva & Cosens and still part of its grape resources in recent years, its acquisition by the Symingtons in 1998 has resulted in excellent single-quinta ports from 98 through 2001. Winemaking facilities have been boosted by the high-tech Quinta do Sol, where many of the ports are made. Crusted Port shows something of the Dow style at a moderate price and Late Bottled Vintage, though of the filtered type, can have good fruit richness and some depth. Tawnies tend to be quite vigorous but with good complexity at the 20-and 30-year level, while Trademark is an acceptable Vintage Character port. (PW)

● **Vintage Port❂❂❂❂❂** £F   Quinta do Bomfim★★★★ £E   Quinta Senhora da Ribeira★★★★ £F
● **30-year-old Tawny Port★★★** £F   ● **20-year-old Tawny Port★★** £D
● **10-year-old Tawny Port★** £C   ● **Crusted Port★★★** £C   ● **Late Bottled Vintage Port★★** £C

ESPORÃO Alentejo www.esporao.com   A: **JEF**, Hrd

Owner: Finagra   Apartado 31, 7200-999 Reguengos de Monsaraz
Herdade do Esporão represents a massive investment and real faith in the potential of the Alentejo region and the Roquette family (behind QUINTA DO CRASTO) has been very successful in developing what is now 600 ha of vineyards spread across five different sites. Despite the size, winemaker David Baverstock (a leading influence in the development of modern, quality Portuguese wines) has set a high standard in both red and white wines. The Esporão-labelled and varietal wines are bold, powerful, ripe, intense, fruit-driven and oak-influenced. The Esporão Reserva is currently a blend of Trincadeira, Aragonês and Cabernet Sauvignon aged in American oak for 12 months and shows good richness and depth with three to four years' age. Newish Private Selection/Garrafeira is powerful with lots of oak, extract and breadth and needs a decade to show at its best. The pick of a series of varietal examples are Alicante Bouschet, Aragonês, Syrah and Touriga Nacional. Vinha da Defesa includes red, white and rosé. The red is based on Aragonês while the white, with good tangy, citrusy fruit, is produced from Antão Vaz, Arinto and Roupeiro. The same white varieties are oak-aged to give a ripe, spicy, creamy and peachy if unsubtle Esporão Reserva with moderate ageing potential. Private Selection white is Sémillon with Marsanne (90/10) and could easily be mistaken for a concentrated Barossa example. At an everday level the best vintages of Monte Velho red can provide decent value. Least expensive are the Alandra red and white. Sparkling wine, a sweet wine and a range of olive oils and cheeses are also produced. (PW)

● **Alentejo** Esporão Reserva★★ £B   Esporão Private Selection★★★★ £E
● **Alicante Bouschet★★★** £C   ● **Aragonês★★★** £C   ● **Syrah★★★** £C
● **Touriga Nacional★★** £C   ● **Trincadeira★★** £C
● **Vinha da Defesa★** £B   ● **Monte Velho★** £A
O **Alentejo** Esporão Reserva★★ £B   Esporão Private Selection★★ £C
O **Roupeiro★** £B   O **Vinha da Defesa★** £B

FERREIRA Port   A: **BWC**, Sel, F&R

*Owner: **Sogrape** Rua da Carvalhosa 19, 4400 Vila Nova de Gaia*
Ferreira was built up by one of the legends of the Douro, Dona Antónia Adelaide Ferreira (whose diminutive name 'Ferreirinha' is used for the company's table-wine production). Ferreira makes the most gutsy, earthy example among the leading Vintage Ports; it is often very ripe and raisiny but with plenty of raw intensity and can age impressively. It is declared more frequently than most, including good years that were not generally declared (recently 1999 and 95) as well as 2000, 97, 94 and 91. Late Bottled Vintage with character and depth is not shy, while the tawnies maintain fruit intensity; spice and dried fruits in the Quinta do Porto, with additional refined, nutty complexity in the Duque de Bragança. Four important quintas are included in the Ferreira holdings: Quinta do Porto, Quinta do Seixo, Quinta do Caedo and Quinta da Leda. The last is the centre of production for table wines including Barca Velha, first produced in 1952 and for long Portugal's most famous red. Now aged in new French oak (previously Portuguese), it is based on Tinta Roriz but also includes Touriga Nacional, Touriga Franca, Tinta Barroca and Tinta Amarela and is only blended and subsequently released when deemed ready (with 5 to 10 years' age). The fruit sources have changed but the current signs suggest that future vintages of the Leda reds will be at least as good as the best to date. The current vintage for Barca Velha is 1995 but in addition good (rather than great) years are released as Casa Ferreirinha Reserva (previously Reserva Especial), although some vintages of this have had finesse at the expense of richness. Of the new reds, Quinta da Leda and Callabriga are based on Touriga Nacional but complemented by varying percentages of Tinta Roriz and Touriga Franca. Together with a varietal Touriga Nacional these wines show more power and greater depth and structure than many of the new wave of Douro reds but need 7 to 10 years to develop fully. (PW)

Ferreira:
● **Vintage Port**★★★ £E ● **Late Bottled Vintage Port**★★ £C
● **Tawny Port** 10-year-old Quinta do Porto★★ £D
● **20-year-old Tawny Port** Duque de Bragança★★★ £E

Casa Ferreirinha:
● **Douro** Casa Ferreirinha Reserva★★ £E Barca Velha★★★★ £F
● **Douro** Quinta da Leda★★★ £C Quinta da Leda Touriga Nacional★★★ £C
● **Douro** Callabriga★★ £C Vinha Grande★★ £B

FOJO Douro   A: ARe, Vne

Owner: Maria Doroteia Serôdio Borges Fermentoes, 5060 Sabrosa
A small property in the heart of the Douro already with an excellent reputation established around an estate red produced in the 1996 vintage. Jorge and his sister Margarida Serôdio Borges actually manage two quintas, Fojo and Manuela. Fojo was intended to be made in only the best vintages and there has been no rush to follow the initial release, the grapes instead going into a supple, characterful second wine, Vinha do Fojo. Grapes from very old vines of Touriga Franca and Tinta Roriz are foot-trodden in *lagares* before being finished in open fermenters. Fojo, produced again in 2000 has power, depth and complexity, and is particularly striking in the quality and intensity of its fruit – best with a decade's age. The more accessible Vinha do Fojo can be drunk sooner but will also keep. (PW)
● **Douro** Vinha do Fojo★★ £C Fojo★★★★ £F

FONSECA Port www.fonseca.pt   A: **Men**, AAA

*Owner: **Fonseca Guimaraens** Rua Barão de Forrester 404, 4400 Vila Nova de Gaia*
Fonseca is one of the truly great Vintage Ports and a name most serious port drinkers know well. Though under the same ownership as Taylor it has a very distinct identity of its own. Fruit comes from the Cruzeiro, Santo António (both in the Pinhão Valley) and Panascal quintas and the wines have recently been fashioned by David Guimaraens, following the successful tenure by his father (Bruce Guimaraens) before him. Fonseca has a rich and expansive style with often explosive fruit intensity and marvellous depth of flavour,

yet doesn't lack for structure. Great vintages include 2000, 97, 94, 92, 85, 77, 70, 66, 63 and 55. Fonseca Guimaraens is the name of the consistently very fine 'off-vintage' port, made in good years when there isn't a declaration; it can generally be bought with confidence at a somewhat more affordable price. A single-quinta, Quinta do Panascal (which may be visited), is also sometimes made in these years. The standard is generally high in the other ports, too, with good vigour and intensity in the tawnies and usually good fruit in a filtered-type LBV. Bin 27 is one of the best of the big-brand Vintage Character ports. A dry White Port, Siroco, is also made. (PW)

● **Vintage Port**✪✪✪✪✪ £G Fonseca Guimaraens★★★★ £E Quinta do Panascal★★★ £E
● **10-year-old Tawny Port**★★ £C ● **20-year-old Tawny Port**★★★ £E
● **Late Bottled Vintage Port**★ £C ● **Bin No. 27**★ £B

JOSÉ MARIA DA FONSECA Terras do Sado www.jmf.pt A: HMW

Owner: Soares Franco family Apartado 8, Vila Nogueira de Azeitão, 2925 Azeitão
This long-established family producer has 850 ha of vines at its disposal between the two regions of Terras do Sado and Alentejo. These include the large Algeruz vineyard purchased in 1989 and subsequently used to develop better clones of local Portuguese varieties but also trialling Syrah, Tannat, Viognier and Sauvignon Blanc. The wines are made by seventh-generation Domingos Soares Franco. Some of the big-volume brands can show attractive fruit if lacking the structure and concentration for more. Whites including Quinta de Camarate and Primum are generally sound but like the reds want for more intensity and excitement. Periquita (Castelão) and red Primum (from Touriga Nacional and Touriga Franca) could use a little more richness. Periquita Clássico, released with some age, shows more of the classic spicy, berry, savoury and chocolaty Castelão character. Better still are the Garrafeira wines, RA, CO (both from Castelão), TE (Castelão/Cabernet) and more recently FSF (Shiraz, Trincadeira and Tannat in 2001), which show excellent complexity, depth and intensity; all are best with 6 to 10 years' age. New in 2000 is Hexagon, produced from the grape varieties of FSF plus Touriga Nacional, Tinta Cão and Touriga Franca. Like FSF it is foot-trodden in *lagares* and aged in new French and American oak. Also new are promising Colecção Privada Domingos Soares Franco varietals that include Touriga Nacional, Touriga Franca, Trincadeira, Tannat and Syrah. From the Douro come the Domini wines, a joint venture with Cristiano van Zeller (QUINTA DO VALE DOÑA MARIA). Domini Plus shows classic Douro character and intensity in a modern style; better in 2001 than 00. The other great strength is Setúbal (fortified sweet Moscatel and other varieties), ranging from a youngish vintage-dated Alambre that is grapey and fresh with citrus peel, ripest peach and apricot character, to a deep-coloured, honeyed Moscatel Roxo with an orange peel aroma, through to a rich, gently oxidised Superior (recent vintages are 1962, 64, 65 and 66) with a sweet intensity of dates and nuts. Most extraordinary, however, is a limited-release bottling called Trilogia (a blend of 1900, 34 and 65). Very intense yet not excessively sweet, it has marvellous finesse to its honeyed, citrus peel and nutty aromas and flavours. (PW)

José Maria da Fonseca:
● **Periquita** Clássico★★ £C
● **Garrafeira** CO★★ £C RA★★ £C FSF★★★ £C
○ **Setúbal** Superior★★ £E Moscatel Roxo 20-year-old★★ £E
○ **Moscatel de Setúbal** Alambre★ £B

Domingos Soares Franco & Cristiano Van Zeller:
● **Douro** Domini★ £B Domini Plus★★★ £E

GRAHAM Port www.grahams-port.com A: JEF, AAA

Owner: Symington group Travesso Barão de Forrester, Apartado 19, 4401-997 Vila Nova de Gaia
In terms of quality if not quantity, Graham's reputation is anchored by its brilliant Vintage Port. If not quite as sought after as Taylor or Fonseca in the last decade, it nonetheless has proven itself to be one of the top ports in almost every widely declared vintage, perhaps the most consistently fine of all. The wines are big,

rich and sweet-fruited with a lush opulence that conceals ripe, compact tannins. The same intensity of fruit holds up magnificently over 20, 30, 40 years or more. Excellent vintages include 2000, 97, 94, 91, 85, 83, 80, 77, 70, 66, 63, 55 and 45. In non-declared years the wine has long been produced as the often excellent Malvedos Vintage Port, named for Quinta dos Malvedos (at Tua, upriver from Pinhão) where 70 ha of vineyards were replanted in the 1980s. Other important components of the Vintage Ports are Quinta das Lages and Quinta da Vila Velha in the Rio Torto, south of Pinhão. Graham's aged tawnies are adequate with quite an evolved character in the 20-year-old version. Small amounts of 30- and 40-year-old versions are also made. The LBV (of the filtered type) is fruity, round and agreeable if lacking real depth. An intense, grapey Six Grapes is one of the better examples of the Premium Ruby or Vintage Character style. A Crusted Port is now also made. (PW)

● **Vintage Port**❍❍❍❍❍ £F Malvedos★★★★ £E
● **10-year-old Tawny Port**★ £D ● **20-year-old Tawny Port**★★ £E
● **Late Bottled Vintage Port**★ £C ● **Six Grapes**★ £B

HENRIQUES & HENRIQUES Madeira A: **HWC**, F&M, Evg

Owner: Henriques & Henriques SA PO Box 4296, 9053 Funchal, Madeira
A leading Madeira producer equipped with a modern winery and making excellent, consistent commercial Madeiras, especially the 10-year-old and 15-year-old versions of the noble varieties, Sercial, Verdelho, Malmsey and Bual. The historic family firm was started in 1850 but the family have been landowners on Madeira for centuries. Most impressive is their ability to produce high quality in all styles (some shippers manage only one or two) across vibrant citrusy Sercial, elegant honeyed Verdelho, rich nutty Bual and still richer, sweeter but less refined Malmsey. The 15-year-old versions generally add that bit more intensity and richness which better balances the assertive acidities. Very small amounts of outstanding Vintage Madeira (at very high prices) are available from specialist stockists, some vintage-dated from the late 19th century and other even more venerable examples without a specific vintage date. (PW)

○ **Madeira** 15-year-old Sercial★★★ £E 15-year-old Verdelho★★★ £E
○ **Madeira** 15-year-old Bual★★★ £E 15-year-old Malmsey★★★ £E
○ **Madeira** 10-year-old Sercial★★ £D 10-year-old Verdelho★★★ £D 5-year-old Verdelho★ £C
○ **Madeira** 10-year-old Bual★★★ £D 5-year-old Bual★★ £C 10-year-old Malmsey★★ £D

HERDADE GRANDE Alentejo www.herdadegrande.pt A: **Ock**, The

Owner: António Manuel Lança Adega da Herdade Grande, 7960 Vidigueira
António Lança is a qualified viticulturalist who has been producing his own wines since 1996 from 60 ha of vines in a 350-ha estate that also includes olives and other crops. The winemaking facilities have been considerably expanded in the last three or four years and more of the grapes are now turned into Herdade Grande wines (rather than being sold to Esporão). Production is planned to peak at around 40,000 cases. There has been a corresponding rise in quality. A soundly structured estate white made from Antão Vaz sees negligible oak and shows a subtle mineral quality. The red estate wine comes from Aragonês and Trincadeira (plus 10 per cent Cabernet and Syrah) and is a good, intense, berryish wine of adequate breadth and structure. Altogether more exciting is a premium red from 50-year-old vines (90 per cent Aragonês) that spends 12 months in (mostly) American oak. Made in 1999 and 2001 it is rich, concentrated and powerful with lots of oak and extract but with the fruit to match, displaying a licorice, chocolate, carob and berry succulence. It is likely to be best with 8 to 10 years' age. Second label Condado das Vinhas red and white are soundly made but don't show the same fruit quality as the Herdade Grande wines. (PW)

○ **Alentejo** Herdade Grande Colheita Seleccionada★★ £B
● **Alentejo** Herdade Grande★★ £C Herdade Grande Colheita Seleccionada★★★★ £D

J P VINHOS Terras do Sado www.jpvinhos.com A: Ehr

Owner: J P Vinhos SA Apartado 54, Vila Norgueira de Azeitão, 2925-901 Azeitão

J P Vinhos is a significant and sizeable producer in the Terras do Sado with some 500 to 600 ha of vineyards, some in the neighbouring regions of Alentejo and Estremadura. Though there are no outstanding wines, the best have good flavour and intensity. Tinto da Ânfora is a good, occasionally variable, gutsy example of Alentejo fruit and personality – mostly Aragonês (Tinta Roriz) with a little Trincadeira, Castelão and Alfrocheiro Preto, oak-aged in wood of mixed origins. Much better but at a price is a Grande Escolha version made in the best years. Full and concentrated with deep spice, cedar and savoury notes, it is aged in 100 per cent new Allier oak for eight months. Quinta do Bacalhôa is a single-estate wine, mostly Cabernet Sauvignon but with 10 per cent Merlot, that tastes not unlike a slightly rustic, earthy Graves – a ripe, meaty, characterful example with ample earthy blackcurrant fruit and depth. Má Partilha, a varietal Merlot, can be slightly raisiny if savoury, while Meia Pipa is an equal blend of Cabernet and Castelão. Whites, too, are not without character. Cova da Ursa is a barrel-fermented Chardonnay that is flavoursome but better balanced and more restrained than in early efforts. Other well-known brands include a light, dry Catarina based on Fernão Pires with a barrel-fermented Chardonnay component, and adequate fruity Monte das Ânforas red and white. J P Tinto and Branco are the basic red and white. Sparkling wine, both Loridos Bruto, (from Castelão and Fernão Pires), and Loridos Chardonnay are produced from grapes grown in Estremadura. New varietals under the Só label ('Só' meaning 'only') are Syrah (from 99) and Touriga Nacional (2001). The Syrah has character and some intensity if still needing a little more refinement both in flavour and structure. (PW)

● **Tinto da Ânfora★** £B Grande Escolha★★★ £D
● **Quinta do Bacalhôa★★** £C ● **Má Partilha★** £C ● **Só Syrah★★** £C
O **Cova da Ursa★** £B O **Moscatel de Setúbal★★** £C

MADEIRA WINE COMPANY Madeira www.madeirawinecompany.com A: JEF, AAA

Owner: Symington group Old Blandy Wine Lodge, Avenida Arriaga 32, Funchal, Madeira

This is the leading producer of Madeira and includes the well-known brand names of Blandy's, Cossart Gordon and Leacocks. Some marvellous Vintage Madeiras are made but only in small quantities, usually only a few thousand bottles at best. The bigger-volume, so-called commercial Madeiras with an indication of age can show plenty of style too, if not the same concentration or complexity. Wines labelled with one of the noble varieties (most are almost 100 per cent rather than the required minimum of 85 per cent) are now only made using the *canteiro* system and used American oak casks are employed for ageing. Blandy's wines are generally richer and sweeter than those of Cossart Gordon but the wines are similarly made. Cossart Gordon's 10-year-old Verdelho and Bual are particularly fine for this level, the delicacy and harmony of the Verdelho contrasting with the tangy, orangey, peel-and-spice fruit intensity of the richer Bual. Blandy's 15-year-old Malmsey is both concentrated and elegant and is a significant step up from the 10-year-old version. For the many fine Vintage Madeiras consult a specialist; both Cossart Gordon and Blandy's include rare vintages of Terrantez. (PW)

Blandy's:
O **Madeira** 15-year-old Malmsey★★★ £E 10-year-old Malmsey★★ £D 5-year-old Malmsey★★ £C
O **Madeira** Dry Duke of Sussex★ £C

Cossart Gordon:
O **Madeira** 15-year-old Bual★★★ £E 10-year-old Bual★★★ £D 5-year-old Bual★★ £C
O **Madeira** 10-year-old Verdelho★★★ £D

Leacocks:
O **Madeira** 10-year-old Bual★★ £D

NIEPOORT Port   A: **RyR**, Bib, Rae, Res, P&S, OxW, BBR, F&M, FWC

Owner: Niepoort family   Rua Infante D. Henrique 39, 4050 Porto

Dirk Niepoort, fifth generation of this Dutch-owned shipper, is obsessed with wine to the benefit of wine lovers everywhere. Working with winemakers Jorge Serôdio Borges and Nick Delaforce he produces both outstanding Douro table wines and an extraordinary array of fine ports in almost every style imaginable. The Vintage Port is marked by its raw power and vigour in youth but with almost unequalled intensity and length of flavour. Niepoort has two quintas of its own (Quinta de Nápoles and Quinta do Carril) as well as control of an expanding Quinta do Passadouro and from the latter produces a single-quinta port in good years. Secundum (2001, 00 and 99) is effectively a second selection to the Vintage Port and in a lighter style, though it should be richer if a Vintage Port isn't made and is likely to add richness with age. Much of Niepoort's early reputation was for tawnies and *colheitas* of great refinement. An extremely fine 10-year-old Tawny Port shows great subtlety and complexity in a class of port that is too often overpriced for the quality. The very fine *colheitas* are from a string of vintages that run from 1994 back to the early part of the 20th century. Dirk Niepoort also makes the best White Port going, with atypical elegance and freshness. Then there are the red wines produced from old, low-yielding vines which have excellent structure and weight. Redoma has been produced for a decade and while its price has crept up with the quality there is marvellous fruit and a rugged Douro complexity but a certain elegance too. The Redoma white (also produced as a Reserva in 2000) is quite remarkable for Portugal: from grapes grown at altitude, it is a barrel-fermented and aged white of real depth and structure, capable of ageing for at least three to four years. When on form (as in 2001) Redoma Rosé, given a little wood ageing, remains fresh and characterful for several years. A pricey new flagship red, Batuta (like Redoma sourced from north-facing slopes), was first produced in 1999; deep, intense and powerful but already splendidly complex, it is already one of the Douro's (and Portugal's) greatest reds. More affordable is Vertente, which combines accessibility and fine fruit with good richness and texture. Another new premium wine, Charme, was first made in 2000. Here the emphasis is on elegance from old vine Tinta Franca and Tinta Roriz that is not destemmed. Amazingly a 2002 is quite burgundian in style with seductive red fruits, spice and some, but not excessive, oak influence. Red is also made from Quinta de Nápoles and has been produced from Passadouro (from Tinta Roriz and Touriga Franca grapes foot-trodden in *lagares*). Jorge Serôdio Borges and his wife, winemaker Sandra Tavares, have also been making their own red, PINTAS, since 2001. (PW)

● **Vintage Port**✪✪✪✪✪ £F Quinta do Passadouro★★★★ £F Secundum★★★ £E
● **Colheita Port**★★★★ £E ● **10-year-old Tawny Port**★★★ £E ● **30-year-old Tawny Port**★★★★ £F
● **Late Bottled Vintage Port**★★★ £C ○ **White Port**★★ £C
● **Douro** Passadouro★★★ £D Vertente★★★ £C Redoma★★★★ £E Batuta★★★★★ £F
◉ **Douro** Redoma★★ £B ○ **Douro** Redoma★★★ £C

LUIS PATO Bairrada   A: **LyS**, Vne, Hrd, Sel

Owner: Luis Pato   Óis do Bairro, 3780 Amoreira da Gândara

Luis Pato has been Bairrada' great moderniser, introducing green harvesting, complete destemming, temperature control and *barrique*-ageing to fashion the region's and some of Portugal's top wines. The flavours of Baga are not to everyone's taste but these are excellent, ageworthy examples of what is possible. A combination of new and one-year-old Allier *barriques* are used for the top single-vineyard wines. The best of these, from 70-year-old vines in a 0.7-ha vineyard, is Vinha Barrosa, with terrific intensity and dimension and a remarkable earthy, truffly, old-vine richness. Vinha Pan and Vinha Barrio are almost as good, the Pan perhaps more tannic and intense than the more mineral Barrio. Moinho from younger vines is arguably the least of these wines yet doesn't lack for intensity, breadth or style. A very small amount of wine is produced from ungrafted vines and fermented in new oak and bottled as Baga Pé Franco. Though very structured it has extraordinary aromas and flavour including earth, truffles, smoke, coffee, black plum; it probably needs to be kept for a minimum of a decade before drinking. As might be expected the wine is bottled without fining or filtration. A regular Baga has more forward, spicy, black-plum fruit and is lightly structured. A premium white has also been made since 1998. Again vineyard-specific, Vinha Formal is made from 100-per-cent Bical that is fermented and aged in oak. The oak is not allowed to dominate and the wine reveals subtle yet intense, ripe fruit with excellent breadth and structure to improve for at least three or four years. In recent vintages the wines have been labelled as Vinho Regional Beiras. (PW)

● Quinta do Ribeirinho Baga Pé Franco★★★★ £F ● Baga★ £B
● Vinha Barrosa★★★★ £D ● Vinha Pan★★★ £D ● Vinha Moinho★★★ £D
● Vinha Barrio★★★ £D ○ Vinha Formal★★★ £C ○ Maria Gomes★★ £B

PINTAS   Douro/Port   A: C&B

Owner: J S Borges & S Tavares   Avenida Júlio de Freitas 6, Vale de Mendiz, 5085-101 Pinhão
From a 1.8-ha south-facing vineyard previously used for port production comes another profound Douro red. The small property belongs to Jorge Serôdio Borges (NIEPOORT's winemaker) and his wife, Sandra Tavares (QUINTA DO VALE DOÑA MARIA). Grapes from a field blend of mixed planting (more than 30 different grape varieties of 80-year-old vines) are fermented and foot-trodden in *lagares*. The malolactic fermentation is completed in *barriques* in which the wine is aged for 15 months. 2001 shows fabulous fruit and depth though a mere 5,000 bottles were made. In 2002 a combination of some early picking and a rigorous selection have produced a lovely wine if not of quite the same depth as the 2001 (4,500 bottles). (PW)

● Douro★★★★ £E

QUINTA DA CORTEZIA   Estremadura

Owner: José Miguel Clímaco Reis Catarino   2580-101 Aldeia Gavinha (Alenquer)
Miguel Catarino is a trained viticulturalist and winemaker who works as a consultant in the Alentejo but also has a 70-ha estate of his own in Estremadura. Here his obsession with light and soils has resulted in remarkable fruit quality from family vineyards that have been replanted in stages since 1991. Only a percentage is currently produced under the Cortezia label, led initially by three varietals (made since 1997). The wines are dense and compact when young but with a pure varietal intensity and fine, ripe tannins. The wines perhaps lack flair but deserve to be drunk with at least five years' age. More impressive than the varietal examples is the Reserva from Touriga Nacional, Tinta Roriz and Merlot (20/50/30 in the 1999 but mostly Touriga in 2001). There is more complexity, extract and structure as well as depth and richness particularly in the more harmonious 2001. Making use of a new gravity-fed winery from 2004, white wines will be produced for the first time from Chardonnay, Fernão Pires and Arinto grapes that were previously sold to other producers. New Vinha Conchas red is good value, light, berryish and supple for early drinking. (PW)

● Quinta da Cortezia Reserva★★★★ £E
● Merlot★★★ £C ● Touriga Nacional★★★ £C ● Tinta Roriz★★★ £C

QUINTA DAS HEREDIAS   Port   A: Gau

Owner: Mauricette Mordant   Quinta do Convento, Távora, 5120 Tabuaço
This emerging port house has already produced some very fine ports despite being only recently established. Mauricette Mordant, who helped found Champagne house Vranken, bought the historic monastery of Quinta do Convento (San Pedro das Aguias) on the Rio Távora outright from Vranken in 1996. It also includes the quintas of Espinhos and Calcado as well as Heredias – comprising 82 ha in the Cima Corgo. All the ports will eventually be entirely estate produced, most of the grapes having been sold off until 1999. Winemaker Jean Hugues Gros makes well-defined, balanced ports with expressive fruit across a range of styles. Though some wines necessarily include older bought-in wines, all are impressive including a marvellously complex 40-year-old Tawny. Ruby has excellent fruit for this level while Vintage Port from 2001 shows both elegance and depth. A traditional Late Bottled Vintage also shows good style while a dry White Port from 100 per cent Malvasia Fina has good balance between spiced fruit characters and more

nutty tertiary flavours. Some Douro red is also made but the emphasis is on port. (PW)

● **Late Bottled Vintage Port**★★ £D ● **40-year-old Tawny Port**★★★★★ £G
● **10-year-old Tawny Port**★★★ £D ● **20-year-old Tawny Port**★★★★ £E
● **Ruby Port**★★ £B ○ **White Port** Meio Seco★★ £C

QUINTA DE CABRIZ / DÃO SUL Dão A: FWW

Owner: Dão Sul Apartado 28, 3430-909 Carregal do Sal
The Dão Sul partnership is based on the Quinta de Cabriz with a dynamic winemaking team that has seen them branch out into the Douro and Bairrada and even Estremadura and Alentejo. Having benefited from input from the winemaking expertise of the highly esteemed Professor Virgílio Loureiro, the winemaking is now overseen by Carlos Moura. There is considerable diversity not only in source but from the everyday to much more serious. From Cabriz itself comes a decent fruity, regular Dão, a better Reserva and good varietal examples – particularly the Touriga Nacional (a 2000 is ageing impressively). Also made in 1999 was a premium blended version, Escolha Virgílio Loureiro, with great depth, style and complexity. A ripe and concentrated white equivalent, fermented and aged in oak for six month, was a blend of Encruzado, Malvasia Fina and Borrado das Moscas. An affordable supple savoury Dão is produced from Quinta do Ribeiro Santo. As Encostas do Douro, Dão Sul also has two estates in the Douro: Quinta do Brasileiro (Quinta Sá de Baixo) and Quinta das Tecedeiras. Quinta Sá de Baixo Grande Escolha, first made in 2000 and from old vines, shows lots of Douro character and richness. Tecedeiras Reserva (from Touriga Nacional, Tinta Roriz and Touriga Franca) shows a lovely amalgam of floral, mineral and black fruits and excellent intensity. Dourat is a cross-border collaboration adding Touriga Nacional from Tecedeiras to an equal amount of Grenache from Priorat, sourced from Josep Puig (Cellers Puig & Roca and Vinedos Ithaca) – one that will probably excite EU bureaucrats. Wines from Bairrada include those from the 10-ha Quinta do Encontro. As well as a very good Superior estate wine, a good richly fruity varietal Touriga Nacional has been produced. Also made in 2000 was Homenagem, a collaboration between Cabriz and Luis PATO. It is a blend of 50 per cent Touriga Nacional and 50 per cent Baga and a wine of formidable structure but marvellous fruit, depth and character. There's good potential too in a port-like wine, Vinho Fino (from Touriga Nacional), which shows lovely sweet, black-plum fruit if not the dimension or depth of a top Vintage Port. (PW)

Quinta de Cabriz :
● **Dão** Reserva★★ £D Touriga Nacional★★★ £C
○ **Dão** Encruzado★★ £B
Quinta do Brasileiro:
● **Douro** Quinta do Brasileiro★★ £B Quinta Sá de Baixo Grande Escholha★★★ £E
Quinta das Tecedeiras:
● **Douro** Reserva★★★ £D
Quinta do Encontro:
● **Bairrada** Superior★★★ £C ●**Touriga Nacional**★★ £C

QUINTA DE CHOCAPALHA Estremadura A: C&B

Owner: Alice & Paulo Tavares da Silva Casa Agrícola das Mimosas, 2580 Aldeia Galega da Merceana
Quinta de Chocapalha is the family estate of talented winemaker Sandra Tavares da Silva (also see QUINTA DO VALE DOÑA MARIA). It comprises 40 ha of vineyards in a particularly blessed part of Estremadura. Quinta de Chocapalha adjoins QUINTA DA CORTEZIA but the wines are made in a contrasting way. For the red wines the grapes are foot-trodden in stone *lagares* (in robotic *lagares* from 2003) and femented in French oak vats. All are then aged in French *barriques*, and in the case of the top wine, called simply Chocapalha, in new oak for 15 months. Chocapalha (not made in 2002) is a blend of mostly Touriga Nacional and Tinta Roriz; it shows excellent fruit and extract but also a depth and texture not encountered in other good Estremadura reds. The regular Quinta de Chocapalha includes Castelão and Alicante in the blend with Touriga Nacional and Tinta Roriz. Also made is a distinctive Cabernet Sauvignon with a mint

and mineral quality to its berry and blackcurrant fruit. In cooler vintages (like 2002) there is a struggle for ripeness in fruit and tannins although it is still soundly made. Such is the potential of 2003 a special reserve is also being considered from the Chocapalha fruit. Also showing great promise and new from 2003 is a Chocapalha white from Chardonnay and Arinto (60/40) with the Chardonnay component fermented and aged in *barriques*. (PW)

● **Chocapalha★★★** £C ● **Quinta de Chocapalha★★** £B
● **Cabernet Sauvignon** Quinta de Chocapalha★★ £B

QUINTA DE LA ROSA Douro/Port www.quintadelarosa.com A: **M&V,** JNi, Hrd, Sel, OxW

Owner: Bergqvist family Quinta de la Rosa, 5085-215 Pinhão
The Bergqvist family took back control of its vineyards in the 1980s, producing their own port for the first time in 1988. Quinta de la Rosa has in fact demonstrated how successful a more estate-centred approach can be (given sufficiently cool storage) and makes a Vintage Port in every vintage (1993 excepted) in the manner of a Bordeaux château. Tim Bergqvist, with help from David Baverstock, has steadily improved quality as the extensive winery buildings have been renovated and vineyards upgraded and in some instances replanted. The medium-weight Vintage Port shows the balance but excellent fruit intensity that characterises these ports and the 2000 promises to be the best yet. In 1999 an excellent single-vineyard example was made from old vines in Vale do Inferno. Other good vintages include 1997, 96 (as Vinha Velha), 95, 94 and 92. Finest Reserve is essentially a Vintage Character port but far better than the norm, with real elegance and intensity, while a traditional Late Bottled Vintage shows more depth than filtered examples. Quinta de la Rosa table wines are just as important as the ports and both a partially oaked regular example (from Tinta Roriz, Touriga Franca and Tinta Barocca) and more oaky Reserva (needing at least three to five years' age) are excellent, well-priced Douro reds. A very fine varietal Tinta Roriz was made in 1998. Also made are a perfumed white, a rosé and a cheaper (unwooded) second red, Vale da Clara. (PW)

● **Vintage Port★★★★** £E
● **10-year-old Tawny Port** Tonel No. 12★★ £C ● **Late Bottled Vintage Port★★★** £C
● **Finest Reserve★★** £B ● **Ruby Port** Lote 601★ £B
● **Douro★★** £B Reserva★★★ £D ● **Douro** Vale di Clara★ £B O **Douro★** £B

QUINTA DE MACEDOS Douro www.quintamacedos.com A: **RyR**

Owner: Paul & Raymond Reynolds Sarzedinho, 5130 Ervedosa do Douro
This very promising small property on the Rio Torto has been sympathetically revived by Paul Reynolds and his brother Raymond, a UK wine shipper. It runs to just 6.8 ha but much of it is planted to old vines. Viticulture is organic and old terraces of varying aspect have a mixed planting of Douro varieties (but led by Touriga Franca). Replanting has been undertaken where necessary and buildings have been restored including the stone *lagares*. A vertical basket press has also been installed for further extraction. The leading wine, Quinta de Macedos (first made in 2000) is produced from the oldest vines (60 to 80 years old) and spends 20 months in new French oak. The result is a deep, very rich, very ripe concentrated red with classic Douro complexity. It avoids over-ripeness, over-extraction or excess oak but has a structure and density that deserves at least 10 years' ageing. Lagar de Macelos (also from 2000) with more Tinta Roriz comes from slightly younger vines and spends less time in oak. Although it is soft and approachable the abundant fine tannins suggest more time is needed. A third, more accessible wine, Pinga do Torto from younger vines of Tinta Roriz, Touriga Nacional and Touriga Franca, only part of which sees some oak, is due for release in the latter half of 2004. All three wines will be rated with further vintages. (PW)

QUINTA DE RORIZ Douro/Port www.quintaderoriz.com A: **JEF,** Hrd, BBR, F&R

Owner: João van Zeller Quinta de Roriz, Ervedosa do Douro, 5130-113 S. João da Pesqueira
Quinta de Roriz was famous as an individual-quinta port in the 19th century but has only recently been re-established as an independent operation by the van Zeller family – the Vintage Port was made by

others for most of the 20th century. There are currently 42 ha within a sheltered amphitheatre some distance up-river from Pinhão but still within the Cima Corgo. Its revival is being achieved with help from the SYMINGTON family – the wines are made at their Quinta do Sol facility. The Vintage Port was particularly exciting in the 2000 vintage (one of the very best going) but was also made in 2001 and 2002. What marks it out is its sheer class, with a dimension, definition and complexity seen only among the top names. Two Douro table wines have made a good initial impression too. The stylish Reserva (Touriga Nacional/Touriga Franca/Tinta Roriz) is aged in new French *barriques* and has lots of depth and extract; better balanced in 2001 than 2000 but the latter should show better harmony with six or seven years' age. (PW)

● **Vintage Port**★★★★★ £E
● **Douro** Prazo de Roriz★★ £B Quinta de Roriz Reserva★★★ £C

QUINTA DO CÔTTO Douro/Port   A: **LyS**, BBR

Owner: Montez Champalimaud Lda   Cidadelhe, 5040 Mesão Frio
Owner and winemaker Miguel Champalimaud has made Douro reds from the early 1980s, long before the recent explosion in their production. The Côtto wines are concentrated and muscular but with much greater refinement in recent years than the slightly tough, brawny, if characterful efforts from the 1980s and early 1990s. The Grande Escolha does in fact mean what are considered by their maker to be the great years, when a selection of Touriga Nacional, Tinta Roriz and Touriga Franca grapes undergo an extended maceration prior to ageing in new Portuguese oak. Still rather forbidding in its youth, there is good dimension as well as increasing complexity with age; it shouldn't be drunk with less than six to eight years' cellaring. The regular Côtto needs time too, often five years. As well as a flavoursome white Douro, decent Vinho Verde (from a mix of varietals subject to some oak influence) has good fruit and ripeness but more elegant are varietal Loureiro and Avesso sold as Vinho Regional Minho. Good Vintage Port is also made occasionally. (PW)

Quinta do Côtto:
● **Douro**★★ £C Grande Escolha★★★ £E
● **Vintage Port**★★★ £E
○ **Douro**★ £B

Paço de Teixeiró:
○ **Vinho Verde**★ £B   ○ **Loureiro**★★ £B   ○ **Avesso**★★ £B

QUINTA DO CRASTO Douro/Port   A: **Adm, Eno**, NYg, Hrd, ARe, Vts

Owner: Roquette family   Gouvinhas Ferrão, 5060 Sabrosa
With a superbly sited winery and 60 ha of vineyards, Crasto has built an enviable reputation for both splendid table wines and fruit-rich ports. Winemaking is currently overseen by Susana Esteban and Tomás Roquette. The regular Douro red was an exceptional buy in the first vintages but if it has lost a little weight and intensity it still offers good Douro character within a modern structure. A somewhat oaky Reserva adds extra intensity but a varietal Tinta Roriz (foot-trodden prior to continuing its fermentation in open fermenters) shows marvellous fruit, oak, smoke and spice and just manages to match its 100 per cent new oak treatment. Varietal versions of Tinta Cão and Touriga Nacional were made in 1999 while two small-volume premium reds were first produced from the 1998 vintage, Vinha da Ponte and Doña Maria Teresa. Both show a structure, depth and dimension that put them among the Douro's very best. Vintage Port (made in 1994, 95, 97, 99, 00 and 01) is a consistently excellent, medium-weight and medium-term example with a stylish, ripe fruit intensity. A traditional Late Bottled Vintage Port is more forward but with an attractive, moderately sweet fruit character. Wines from a new property in the Douro Superior will also be made at Crasto. (PW)

● **Douro**★ £B Reserva★★ £C Tinta Roriz★★★ £D Vinha da Ponte★★★★ £E
● **Vintage Port**★★★ £E ● **Late Bottled Vintage Port**★★ £C

QUINTA DO INFANTADO   Port

A: **Lib, ACh**

Owner: Roseira family   5085-217 Covas de Douro
The Roseira family have been making their own wines since 1978 from 45 ha of vineyards on a small northern tributary of the Douro downstream from Pinhão. João Roseira works with the talented Luís Soares Duarte and all the wines, even a Ruby, are made in *lagares* and are richly extracted. The incremental addition of spirit results in less being added and an avoidance of the spirity character seen in some Vintage Ports. Infantado's Vintage Port is powerful, intense and extracted, with more finesse in vintages since 1997. Also made is a traditional (i.e. throwing a sediment) Late Bottled Vintage of great extract and intensity. Needless to say a 10-year-old Tawny is vigorous and refined, unlike some of the rather tired, relatively simple examples that exist. João Roseira is also producing the table wines of Bago de Touriga, again in collaboration with Luís Soares Duarte. (PW)

● **Vintage Port★★★★** £E   **Late Bottled Vintage Port★★★** £D
● **10-year-old Tawny Port★★★** £E   ● **Douro★★** £B

QUINTA DO NOVAL   Douro/Port   www.quintadonoval.com

A: **Par, AAA**

Owner: AXA-Millésimes   Avenida Diogo Leite 256, 4400-111 Vila Nova de Gaia
Today direction at Noval comes from Christian Seely of AXA-Millésimes (the corporate owner of CH. PICHON-LONGUEVILLE and other prestigious properties) while the wines are made by António Agrellos. But it got its start in modern times from António José da Silva, who first isolated the famous 2.5 ha of ungrafted vines that produce Nacional, the most sought-after of all ports. A port of great breadth, power and dimension, with a distinctive earthy, spicy dark plum character, it adds flesh and richness with age to become an often riveting port after 20, 30 or more years. 2000, 97, 94, 70, 66, 63 and 62 are great vintages and, if price is any guide, so is 1931. A 2001 also shows much promise. Production from the low-yielding vines that average 35 to 40 years' age is tiny (200 to 300 cases) and bottles are hard to secure. The regular Quinta do Noval Vintage (which benefits from Nacional fruit when that wine is not made) has been a very exciting port in recent vintages (2000, 97, 95, 94, 91) after a lean spell prior to the 90s. It, too, is structured but profound and very ageworthy. Silval, though named after one of Noval's own vineyards, is essentially a second selection but still a high-quality, medium-full style. Noval for a time made the ports from the excellent QUINTA DO RORIZ but the property's owners are now making their own wines in collaboration with the Symingtons. Noval's Late Bottled Vintage is in the traditional sediment-throwing style and is a fine, concentrated example, particularly in top vintages. There is also a fine range of aged tawnies and vintage-dated *colheitas* with dates ranging from 1987 back half a century. Other commercial styles are adequate if not more. Raven is a new, distinctly packaged Premium Ruby. (PW)

● **Vintage Port★★★★★** £F   Nacional●●●●● £H   Silval★★★★ £E
● **40-year-old Tawny Port★★★** £G   ● **20-year-old Tawny Port★★★** £F
● **10-year-old Tawny Port★★** £D   ● **Colheita Port★★★** £E
● **Late-Bottled Vintage Port★★** £C   ● **LB★** £B

QUINTA DO PORTAL   Douro/Port   www.quintadoportal.com

A: **CHk, GWW, Vne**

Owner: Mansilha family   E. N. 323 Celeirós do Douro, 5060 Sabrosa
Quinta do Portal is not one quinta but four. Portal itself was once known as Quinta do Casal de Celeirós while the estates also include the Quinta do Confradeiro at Celeirós in the Pinhão Valley. Money and expertise have not been spared and the most recent vintages show that it is now all starting to come together. The style is for oaky wines but recently this has been matched by a ripe, intense fruit expression. Previous wood-taint problems have been addressed with help from one of the leading experts in this field, Pascal Chatonnet. Though they are reasonably pricey, varietal expressions of Tinta Roriz and Touriga Nacional are very attractive (varietal Touriga Franca was also made in 2001) while the Grande Reserva (from 2001 and 2000) is oaky but shows a convincing fruit depth and richness that should harmonise with 8 to 10 years' age. Vintage Port, from Quinta dos Muros grapes, shows good promise from

the 2000 vintage. This is the vintage to buy from, when all the wines show greater richness and better balance and appear to be free of any taint problems. (PW)

● **Douro**★ £B Reserva★★ £B Grande Reserva★★★ £E
● **Douro** Tinta Roriz★★ £D Touriga Nacional★★★ £D

QUINTA DO VALE DOÑA MARIA Douro/Port A: Bib, L&S, C&B

Owner: Joana Lemos & Cristiano van Zeller Sarzedinho, 5130 S. João da Pesqueira
Cristiano van Zeller's family once owned QUINTA DO NOVAL but now he is involved in some capacity in the production, direction or distribution of several Douro estates as well as one or two from further afield. The 10-ha vineyard of Vale Doña Maria (in his wife's family for generations) on the Rio Torto is an old-fashioned, mixed planting, with many of the vines 50 to 60 years old. Grapes are foot-trodden in *lagares*, for a rich, fleshy, characterful and seductive red. The rating applies to top vintages such as 2000 and 01, though a softer, more perfumed 02 is also very good. Also produced in most vintages is an increasingly fine Vintage Port. Both are made by Sandra Tavares da Silva with some input from Francisco Olazabal of QUINTA DO VALE MEÃO. Cristiano van Zeller also has a joint venture with Domingos Soares Franco (see José Maria da FONSECA), producing both a Vintage Port and a new table wine called Domini from properties in the Douro Superior (Alto Douro). Also located in this harsh, dry area is the large estate of Quinta da Portela da Vilariça (property of the Morais Vaz family), where the small vineyard among ancient village ruins is being expanded with input in the winemaking and direction from van Zeller. A fine Vilariça estate red from Touriga Franca, Touriga Nacional and Tinta Cão is complemented by a varietal Touriga Nacional; both show splendid perfume, depth and intensity albeit at the very ripe end of the spectrum. Sandra Tavares, as well as making the wines of another Douro property since 1999 (Casal de Loivos), also makes a fine estate red for her own family in Estremadura, QUINTA DE CHOCAPALHA. (PW)

Quinta do Vale Doña Maria:
● **Douro**★★★★ £C ● **Vintage Port**★★★★ £E
Quinta da Portela da Vilariça:
● **Douro**★★ £B Touriga Nacional★★★ £C

QUINTA DO VALE MEÃO Douro/Port A: RyR, N&P, C&R

Owner: Francisco Javier de Olazabal Vila Nova de Foz Côa
Francisco Javier de Olazabal was president of FERREIRA until 1998 and his 62 ha of vineyards (part of a 270-ha estate established by Olazabal's ancestor, Dona António Adelaide Ferreira) used to provide the basis of Barca Velha. The best grapes from this estate in a bend in the Douro only 30 km or so from the Spanish border are now made into an outstanding estate red by his son Francisco, a trained winemaker. Comprising Touriga Nacional (60 per cent), Touriga Franca (20), Tinta Roriz (10) and 5 per cent each of Tinto Cão and Tinta Barroca, the wine is initially foot-trodden and spends two years in new Allier oak. There is a depth and breadth, as well as elegance and class, to this potentially five-star wine that sets it apart from all but the best top Douro reds – the same qualities (not surprisingly) that distinguish the best vintages of Barca Velha. An excellent second wine, Meandro, aged in used oak, is medium-bodied but shows great style too, displaying intense, juicy, plummy fruit and an excellent finish. A complex, aromatic Vintage Port was made in 2001 and 2000, the latter with very ripe, sweet fruit, shows lots of promise. (PW)

● **Douro** Quinta do Vale Meão★★★★★ £E Meandro★★★ £C

QUINTA DO VALLADO Douro/Port A: Bib, NYg

Owner: Jorge Viterbo Ferreira & Herdeiros Vilarinho dos Freires, 5050 Peso da Régua
Vallado is a revitalised estate in the Lower Douro (Baixo Corgo) on the Rio Corgo run by Francisco Ferreira and his uncle, Guilherme Alvares Ribeiro. A new winery was completed in the late 1990s to handle the fruit from new and restructured vineyards totalling 64 ha. An unwooded, regular estate red (from a field blend of varieties) shows the earthy, smoky, dark, plum fruit of the Douro in a well-balanced,

concentrated (and affordable) form. The wines are made by QUINTA DO VALE MEÃO's Francisco Olazabal and commercialised by Cristiano van Zeller of QUINTA DO VALE DOÑA MARIA. A Reserva, aged in new French oak, has been made since 1999 and shows more sophistication as well as extra depth and concentration in the 2000 vintage. Some Douro white is also made. (PW)

● Douro★★ £B Reserva★★★ £C

QUINTA DO VESUVIO Port www.quinta-do-vesuvio.com   A: JEF, AAA

Owner: Symington group Travessa Barão de Forrester, Apartado 26, 4401-997 Vila Nova de Gaia
This estate of 400-odd ha spread over seven hills was one of the grand properties of the 19th century. In 1989 it was bought by the Symington family and turned into one of the new breed of true (château-like) quintas. The wine from the expanding vineyard (currently 100 ha of vines) is made and matured on the estate. Its massive *lagares* and winery buildings are being renovated but there has been a wine of high quality made in almost every vintage since 1989 (not 93) and these have been outstanding in the top years, including 2001, 00 (which could be the most intense, compressed, tight, densely-fruited example yet), 95, 94 and 92. Other years, including 1997, 96, 91 and 90, can be very good too, there being much less vintage variation in the dry Douro Superior than further downstream. At its best the extraordinary ripeness in the tannins, as well as the fruit from low-yielding vines, can make the wine tempting when quite young but it will also be very interesting to see how well it might show with 20 or 30 years' age. High percentages of Tinta Roriz and Tinta Barroca (along with Touriga Nacional and Touriga Franca) contribute to its unique character. (PW)

●Vintage Port✪✪✪✪✪ £F

QUINTA DOS ROQUES Dão   A: RyR, Han, C&R, P&S, F&M, Evg

Owner: Manuel Lopes de Oliveira Abrunhosa do Mato, 3530 Mangualde
In the space of just a few years, Quinta dos Roques has emerged as arguably the Dão's leading estate, producing modern, accessible wines from ongoing experimentation with different varieties, blends and refinements to vinification. Vineyards now total 40 ha and the winemaking still benefits from the expertise of Professor Virgílio Loureiro, now widely recognised as one of Portugal's finest winemakers. The characterful, medium-weight regular dos Roques red is based on Touriga Nacional but also includes Alfrocheiro Preto and Tinta Roriz. All three grapes have also been vinified varietally (since the 1996 vintage but not in 98), giving excellent fruit expression and good concentration and structure. The Touriga Nacional has additional breadth and a deep plum and violet character with a hint of pine and white pepper, and is the best of these. Better still is a Reserva made from an old vineyard of mixed plantings that includes Tinta Roriz and Touriga Nacional. Wine from the nearby estate of Quinta das Maias is also made here, the reds reflecting the importance of the local Jaen in the 12 ha of vineyards at 700 m. Both the regular Maias red and varietal Jaen can show a slightly smoky, spicy, wild berry fruit; the varietal example adds more flesh, intensity and structure. A new 'black label' premium Maias red, Rótulo Preto, was made in 2000 from very old vines and is very exciting. A herb-scented Malvasia is a rare good Dão white but a subtly oaked Encruzado with refined peach and exotic notes is even better. Some sparkling rosé is also made. (PW)

Quinta dos Roques:
● Dão Tinto★★ £B Reserva★★★★ £D
● Dão Tinto Cão★★ £C Alfrocheiro Preto★★ £C Touriga Nacional★★★ £D
○ Dão Encruzado★★ £C

Quinta das Maias:
● Dão Tinto★ £B Jaen★★ £C
○ Dão Malvasia Fina★ £B

JOÃO PORTUGAL RAMOS   Alentejo   www.jportugalramos.com   A: **Oak**, ARe

Owner: João Portugal Ramos   Monte da Caldeira, 7100-149 Estremoz

For more than 20 years, João Ramos has been the leading consultant enologist in the south of Portugal, working for some of Alentejo's best co-operatives. His own project has gained increasing momentum in the past decade, producing wines under his own label on his estate near Estremoz but also working for others as a consultancy. The top wine is the Marqués de Borba Reserva (2000, 99 and 97 are all very good), a powerful but composed blend of Aragonês (Tinta Roriz), Trincadeira and some Alicante Bouschet and Cabernet Sauvignon, with excellent dimension and weight, needing 5 to 10 years to show at its best. Vila Santa, with the same varieties (if more based on Trincadeira), shows style and harmony, even elegance and continues to be excellent value for money. Varietal examples of Trincadeira and Aragonês show good fruit definition and supple structures. A varietal Syrah of considerable black fruit intensity if more marginal balance has been made since 2000. More unusual, if not unique, is a supple, perfumed varietal Tinta Caiada. A simple Marqués de Borba white and varietal Antão Vaz are good, clean whites for early consumption. Of the other wines, very promising is the very ripe and powerful Quinta de Viçosa Syrah/Trincadeira, also from the Alentejo. The wines from Falua co-op in Ribatejo include Conde de Vimioso Reserva, a characterful, extracted red from Touriga Nacional, Tinta Roriz and Cabernet Sauvignon. Of interest too are the wines of Quinta de Foz de Arouce in the Beiras, owned by João's father-in-law. A new 100 per cent Baga single-vineyard wine, Vinha de Santa Marta, was produced in 2001. It shows a classic rugged, black-fruited Baga character but will require patience. Production of a white was resumed in 2004. From the Beira Interior, the blended red (Touriga Nacional, Tinta Roriz and Tinta Barocca) of Almeida Garrett is a big step up from two value-for-money varietals. Pegos Claros, a good example of Palmela, has shown greater consistency and stability since being made by João Ramos. (PW)

João Portugal Ramos:
● **Alentejo** Marqués de Borba★ £B Marqués de Borba Reserva★★★★ £E
●**Vila Santa★★★** £B   ● **Trincadeira★★** £B   ● **Aragonês★★** £B
● **Syrah★★** £B   ● **Tinta Caiada★★** £B   O **Antão Vaz★** £B

Quinta da Viçosa:
● **Syrah/Trincadeira★★★** £C

Quinta de Vimioso:
● **Conde de Vimioso** Reserva★★ £C

Quinta de Foz de Arouce:
● **Quinta de Foz de Arouce★★** £B

Almeida Garrett:
● **Almeida Garrett★★** £C   ● **Touriga Nacional★** £B   ● **Tinta Roriz★** £B

Quinta da Ponte Pedrinho:
● **Dão** Reserva★★ £C

Pegos Claros:
● **Palmela** Reserva★★ £B

RAMOS PINTO   Douro/Port   A: **MMD**, JNi, BBR, L&W, Hfx, FWC

Owner: Adriano Ramos Pinto SA   Avenida Ramos Pinto 380, 4401-997 Vila Nova de Gaia

It was the father of Ramos Pinto's director and winemaker, João Nicolau de Almeida, who created Barca Velha (see FERREIRA), the Douro's first great red wine, and Ramos Pinto has been one of the leading proponents in the recent revival of table wines (last made in any quantity before port evolved into a fortified style). Duas Quintas wines are named for the high vineyards (600 m) of Bon Ares and the lower Ervamoira (both deep in the Douro Superior). Quality of the regular red has been variable but from the best years a Reserva (from at least 50 per cent Touriga Nacional) has shown good style, fruit intensity and more refinement than is typical, although it is poor value for money. A deep, vigorous and classy Reserva Especial from a field blend of old vines (actually from Bom-Retiro, the company's leading estate on the Rio Torto) was made in 1999 and 2000. A little white table wine is also made. Most consistent and refined of the ports is a 20-year-old Tawny from Bom-Retiro. It has depth and intensity (sometimes missing in this category) as well as complexity and refinement. Vintage Port has been better in recent vintages (1997 and 94 at least) but although it has a certain individuality, it wants for more depth and richness. Late Bottled Vintage can be remarkably full and powerful while a modest Vintage Character port is named for a fourth quinta, Urtiga. (PW)

Ramos Pinto:
- **Vintage Port★★★** £E ● **Late Bottled Vintage Port★★** £C
- **20-year-old Tawny Port** Quinta do Bom-Retiro★★★ £E
- **10-year-old Tawny Port** Quinta da Ervamoira★ £D

Duas Quintas:
- **Douro★** £B Reserva★★ £E Reserva Especial★★★★ £F

REAL COMPANHIA VELHA   Douro/Port   www.realcompanhiavelha.pt   A: **FEM, PLB**

Owner: Real Companhia Velha   Rua Azevedo Magalhães 314, 4430 Vila Nova de Gaia
The Douro's largest landowner and biggest maker of port enjoys wide distribution around the globe. Its Royal Oporto brand is familiar to most consumers even if they haven't drunk it. Its inclusion here, however, is for its revitalised production of Douro table wines, one or two of which are worthy of more than passing mention. The Evel red offers plenty of fruit while the Porca de Murça Riserva adds more structure and complexity. But for those interested in premium Douro reds it is a Grande Escolha version of Evel (from Touriga Nacional, Touriga Franca and Tinta Cão) and the revived Grantom label (which adds Cabernet Sauvignon to the two Touras) that should be tasted. Both these reds have quite a forbidding structure but the Evel Grande Escolha in particular shows a capitivating complexity and intensity that suggest a four-star rating if quality is maintained. Unusual for the Douro is a Chardonnay from low-yielding vines on the Quinta do Cidrô that delivers good flavour and texture. (PW)
- **Douro** Quinta dos Aciprestes★ £B Porca de Murça Reserva★★ £B
- **Douro** Evel★ £B Evel Grande Escolha★★★ £D Grantom★★★ £E
- O **Quinta do Cidrô Chardonnay★** £B

RIBEIRA D'ERVIDEIRA   www.ervideira.com   A: **RyR**, Cam, But, Hfx, Han, Amp, F&M, P&S

Owner: Duarte Leal da Costa   Ribeira d'Ervideira, Herdadinha, 7200-042 Vendinha
Wines have been made here since 1998 from re-established family vineyards. Fruit sourced only from these 160 ha is transformed into around 60,000 cases of consistent and characterful wine. Least expensive are the Terras d'Ervideira red and white which are well-made with ripe fruit and good structures. Both are typical Alentejo blends, the herbal, citrusy white from Antão Vaz, Roupeiro and Arinto, and the bright red fruited red from Trincadeira, Aragonês and Castelão. In the Vinha d'Ervideira red the Castelão component is replaced by Alicante Bouschet and Cabernet Sauvignon (together making 30 per cent) and has more depth and extract. The most ambitious of the reds is the Conde d'Ervideira Reserva from a similar blend but subject to eight months in new oak. This needs a minimum of five to six years' age in order to show its full potential. A white equivalent is 100 per cent Antão Vaz fermented and aged in oak, its mealy, spicy character is slightly overdone but it has good fruit and structure and won't fall apart. (PW)
- **Terras d'Ervideira★★** £B ● **Vinha d'Ervideira★★** £B ● **Conde d'Ervideira Reserva★★★** £C
- O **Terras d'Ervideira★★** £B O **Conde d'Ervideira Reserva★★** £B

SANDEMAN   Port   www.sandeman.com   A: **PRc**, L&S, F&R

Owner: Sogrape   Largo Miguel Bombarda 3, 4400 Vila Nova de Gaia
Like Graham's, Sandeman is of Scottish origins and its familiarity to occasional port drinkers has been reinforced by the famous brand logo of the Sandeman 'Don'. In the 50 years since the company went public

it has had a torrid time quality-wise under changing ownership. A revival has been started in the past decade following the purchase, and subsequent replanting, of Quinta do Vau since 1988. Its newest owners perhaps offer the best chance of a sustained revival given the example of Ferreira's form under the same ownership. Since 1994, there has been good richness if not the greatest depth in both the Vintage Port and Vau (made when the Vintage Port isn't declared). Of older vintages, some very good ports were made in the 50s and 60s, although most of these are tiring now and are not as good as the top examples. Tawnies are a strength, however, with particular elegance and finesse in the 20-year-old Tawny. Recently in very good form has been the Vintage Character port, Signature (known as Founders Reserve outside the UK). (PW)

● **Vintage Port Vau ★★★** £E
● **Signature★★** £B
● **Imperial Aged Tawny Port★★** £C ● **20-year-old Tawny Port★★★** £E

SIDÓNIO DE SOUSA Bairrada   A: Amp, But, Evg

Owner: Sousa family Largo da Vila, 3780-120 Sangalhos
This small estate of 12 ha has some very old vines (up to 100 years) and the wines are made very traditionally. Winemaker Rui Moura Alves, who also makes the wines at Casa de Saima, Quinta de Baixo and Quinta das Bágeiras, uses natural yeasts, favours the retention of stems, uses concrete *lagares* and wooden plungers, and ages the wine where appropriate in large, old Portuguese wood. This approach, even more than at the other properties, really works here – perhaps because of the quality of the fruit. A Reserva shows good intensity, a silky mouthfeel and a stylish, savoury complexity. The remarkable, powerful Garrafeira, with deep savoury fruit, great depth and intensity and enveloping but refined tannins, is only made in exceptional vintages (just a few thousand bottles of 1995 and 97 were made). The most recent releases (1999 Reserva, 2000 Reserva and Garrafeira) haven't been tasted. There's also a sparkling red made from 100 per cent Baga. (PW)

● **Bairrada** Reserva★★ £C Garrafeira★★★ £E

SMITH WOODHOUSE Port www.smithwoodhouse.com   A: JEF, AAA

Owner: Symington group Travessa Barão de Forrester, Apartado 19, 4401-997 Vila Nova de Gaia
It is to be hoped that the going prices for the ports from this excellent, consistent house continue at the recent level. The Vintage Port, based on the Madalena quinta in the Rio Torto valley, has a certain spicy individuality and is typically succulent, intense and well-balanced. Top recent vintages include 2000, 97, 94, 92, 91, 85, 83, 80 and 77. A good Madalena port has been made in certain non-declared years (such as 1988 and 82) but with more distinction as a true single-quinta port in 1995 and 99. A traditional (i.e. it leaves a sediment) Late Bottled Vintage maintains the house style and integrity. Other wines include Lodge Reserve, which is a decent Vintage Character port, and a 10-year-old Tawny. (PW)

● **Vintage Port★★★★★** £E Madalena★★★ £D
● **Late Bottled Vintage Port★★★** £C ● **Lodge Reserve★** £B

SOGRAPE www.sogrape.pt   A: SsG, Hrd, Con, Maj

Owner: Sogrape Vinhos de Portugal SA Rua 5 de Outubro 558, Aldeia Nova, 4430-761 Avintes
Portugal's largest producer includes the port companies of Ferreira, Offley and Sandeman but the focus of table-wine production is in Dão, where the flagship estate of Quinta dos Carvalhais has been developed. Varietal wines from here have been quite impressive but the vines are still relatively young and, though both Touriga Nacional and Tinta Roriz have been reasonably full with good breadth, they have lacked a little richness. Powerful Carvalhais Reserva (Touriga Nacional/Tinta Roriz/Alfrocheiro Preto) is profound and complex with excellent dimension and length but needs 8 to 10 years' age. A varietal Encruzado, fermented and aged in French oak for six months, adds a little richness with a couple of years' age. Sogrape's 'regional' Reservas can be very good value when on form, as they currently are; softly textured with good flavour intensity and a regional stamp. Also very impressive and reasonably priced is the Herdade do Peso Aragonês

(made in 1997 and 2000) showing the classic character of Tinta Roriz in the Alentejo. Brands such as Terra Franca, Vila Régia and Duque de Viseu, while inexpensive and very successful, at best show a simple, agreeable fruit character. Adequate Vinho Verde is made at Quinta de Azevedo. (PW)

Sogrape:
● **Douro** Reserva★★ £B   ● **Dão** Reserva★★ £B   ● **Alentejo** Reserva★★ £B
● **Herdade do Peso Aragonês**★★★ £C   O **Bairrada** Reserva★★ £B

Quinta dos Carvalhais:
● **Dão** Tinta Roriz★★★ £C   Touriga Nacional★★★ £C   Reserva★★★★ £E
O **Dão** Encruzado★★★ £C

SYMINGTON   www.symington.com   A: JEF, NYg, Hrd, BBR, F&R

Owner: Symington family   Travessa Barão de Forrester 86, 4401-997 Vila Nova de Gaia
The Symington family runs the Douro's leading port shippers, owning DOW, GRAHAM, QUINTA DO VESÚVIO, SMITH WOODHOUSE and WARRE, and, through the MADEIRA WINE COMPANY, is also the leading producer of Madeira. Gould Campbell is one of two lesser labels made in widely declared years. While it has lacked real weight and richness in recent vintages it was very good (three stars) in 1980, 83 and 85. The other minor port brand, Quarles Harris, has been the better of the two in recent declarations (1997 and 2000) and is an attractive, short- to medium-term port for drinking with 10 years' age. The Symingtons are also helping to further realise the potential from QUINTA DE RORIZ. Though late in joining the revival in table-wine production, a basic (inexpensive but disappointing) table red, Altano, has been made since 1999. A Reserva is better but should have more oomph at the price. Chryseia is a new premium table wine made in collaboration with Bruno Prats (the former owner of CH. COS D'ESTOURNEL); 2001 is a big improvement on 2000, the first vintage. Time will be needed to see how it stacks up against the increasingly formidable competition. Post Scriptum is the quite striking, well-balanced second wine, not unlike a good Haut-Médoc. (PW)

Gould Campbell:
● **Vintage Port**★★ £E   ● **Late Bottled Vintage Port**★ £C

Quarles Harris:
● **Vintage Port**★★★ £E

Silva & Cosens:
● **Douro** Altano Reserva★ £B

Prats & Symington:
● **Douro** Chryseia★★★★ £E   Post Scriptum★★★ £C

TAYLOR'S   Port   www.taylor.pt   A: Men, AAA

Owner: Taylor Fladgate & Yeatman SA   Rua do Choupelo 250, 4401-501 Vila Nova de Gaia
An exemplary port producer, and with FONSECA, part of an expanding group that now includes CROFT and DELAFORCE. Vintage Port is based on the famous Quinta de Vargellas in the Douro Superior and the larger Terra Feita quinta in the Rio Pinhão valley, but new vineyards have recently been purchased in both of these sectors of the Douro. Fruit from the Pinhão provides the greater structure while the Douro Superior gives a more floral perfume and great intensity of fruit. Taylor's structure, marvellous depth and class set it apart from most other ports and occasionally it is unrivalled for its completeness. The classic Taylor's style can best be seen in 2000, 97, 94, 92, 85, 83, 80, 77 (though there is variation in this vintage), 70, 66 and 63. The 1960 and 55 can still be lively and impressive, while the 75 is an excellent example in this lighter vintage and 1948, 45 and 27 are classic older vintages. In good non-declared years, Quinta de Vargellas is made (with a high percentage of very old vines it has recently been made in a Vinha Velha version) and can be a stunning port in its own right, while Terra Feita has also been produced as a single-quinta port. Other ports are generally less exciting, 10-year-old Tawny is disappointing against the best examples, though the 20-year-old is better and 30 and 40-year-old versions are also made in small quantities. Late Bottled Vintage

(a style created by Taylor's) is a spicy, fruity and characterful filtered example while First Estate (Vintage Character) is similarly good of its type. A White Port called Chip Dry is also made. (PW)

- **Vintage Port**✪✪✪✪✪ £F   Quinta de Vargellas★★★★ £E   Quinta de Terra Feita★★★ £D
- **10-year-old Tawny Port**★ £C   ● **20-year-old Tawny Port**★★ £E
- **Late Bottled Vintage Port**★★ £B   ● **First Estate**★ £B

WARRE   Port   www.warre.com   A: **JEF**,AAA

Owner: Symington group   Travessa Barão de Forrester, Apartado 26, 4401-997 Vila Nova de Gaia
Last but not least in the Symington portfolio of great port houses, Warre makes a consistently fine Vintage Port. It is perfumed, with a rich, spice, fig and black fruit intensity and a lushness that together form part of a distinctive character that alone makes it worth cellaring. In certain top vintages it will age for 40 years or more. The best include 2000, 97, 94, 91, 85, 83, 80, 77, 70, 66, 63, 60 and 55, though the last three of these are tiring. Quinta da Cavadinha in the Rio Pinhão valley, not far from either QUINTA DO NOVAL or TAYLOR's Terra Feita, forms the main component of the Vintage Port and can be excellent when released in non-declared years. The traditional Late Bottled Vintage is rightly considered one of the best made and the current release usually has around 10 years' age yet can still be kept. Tawnies include a fine, complex, 20-year-old, and the mould-breaking Otima (with a clear-glass bottle), now made in both 10-year-old and 20-year-old versions. Warrior, a Vintage Character port, though of modest structure, actually tastes something like the Vintage Port and is one of the best in its category. (PW)

- **Vintage Port**★★★★★ £F   Quinta da Cavadinha★★★ £E
- **Late Bottled Vintage Port**★★★ £C
- **20-year-old Tawny Port**★★★ £E   ● **10-year-old Tawny Port** Otima★ £C   Sir William★ £C
- **Warrior Special Reserve**★ £B

OTHER WINES OF NOTE

BOAS QUINTAS ● **Dão** Quinta da Fonte do Ouro (Touriga Nacional/Tinta Roriz/Jaen) £B
● **Dão** Quinta da Fonte do Ouro Touriga Nacional £D
H M BORGES O **Madeira** 10-year-old Sercial Reserve £D   10-year-old Boal Reserve £D
O **Madeira** 10-year-old Malmsey Reserve £D
BRIGHT BROTHERS ● **Douro** TFN (Touriga Franca/Touriga Nacional) £B
● **Palmela** Reserva (Castelão) £B
BURMESTER ● **Vintage Port** £E   Quinta de Nossa Senhora do Carmo £E
● **Late-Bottled Vintage Port** £C
CÁLEM ● **Vintage Port** £E   ● **Colheita Port** £D   ● **20-year-old Tawny Port** £E
● **40-year-old Tawny Port** £G
C.A.R.M (Casa Agricola Rui Madeira) ● **Douro** Reserva £C   Praemium £D
● **Quinta da Urze** Touriga Nacional £B   Tinta Roriz £B   Touriga Franca £B
C.A.R.M.I.M. (Reguengos de Monsaraz co-op) ● **Alentejo** Reguengos Garrafeiras dos Sócios £C
CASA CADAVAL (Ribatejo) ● **Padre Pedro** (Castelão/Trincadeira/Pinot Noir/Cabernet Sauvignon) £A
● **Herdade de Muge** (Trincadeira/Castelão/Merlot) £B   ● **Trincadeira** £B
● **Cabernet Sauvignon** £B   ● **Merlot** £B
CASA DE SAIMA ● **Bairrada** Reserva £C   Garrafeira £C
CASA SANTOS LIMA (Estremadura) ● **Touriga Nacional** £B   ● **Tinta Roriz** £B   ● **Trincadeira** £B
● **Quinta dos Bons Ventos** (Castelão/Camarate/Tinta Roriz) £B   ● **Quinta das Setencostas** £B
● **Touriz** (Touriga Nacional/Tinta Roriz) £C
CASAL BRANCO ● **Ribatejo** Falcoaria (Castelão/Trincadeira/Alicante) £B
O **Ribatejo** Falcoaria (Fernão Pires) £B
D'OLIVEIRA O **Madeira** 10-year-old Verdelho £E   10-year-old Boal £E
DFJ VINHOS ● **Grand' Arte** Alicante Bouschet £B   Trincadeira £B   Touriga Franca £B
● **Manta Preta** (Touriga Nacional/Tinta Roriz) £B

FUNDAÇÂO EUGÉNIO DE ALMEIDA (Alentejo) ● **Pera Manca** (Aragonês/Trincadeira) £F
● **Cartuxa** (Aragonês/Trincadeira/Castelão) £C Reserva £D
O **Pera Manca** (Arinto/Antão Vaz Perrum) £D
HERDADE DOS COELHEIROS ● **Tapada de Coelheiros** (Trincadeira/Aragonês/Cabernet S.) £C
MARTINEZ ● **Vintage Port** £E Quinta da Eira Velha £E ● **10-year-old Tawny Port** £C
HERDADE DO MOUCHÃO (Alentejo) ● **Herdade do Mouchão** £D
POÇAS ● **Vintage Port** £E ● **Late Bottled Vintage Port** £C
● **Douro** Reserva (Touriga Naciona/Touriga Franca/Tinta Roriz/Tinta Barroca) £D
QUINTA DA CARVALHOSA (Douro) ● **Campo Ardosa** (Tinta Roriz/Touriga Franca/Touriga Nacional) £E
QUINTA DA LAGOALVA (Ribatejo) ● **Reserva** (Cabernet Sauvignon/Castelão) £B
● **Alfrocheiro** £B ● **Syrah** £B
QUINTA DA PELLADA ● **Dão** Touriga Nacional £D
QUINTA DAS BÁGEIRAS ● **Bairrada** Reserva £C
QUINTA DE ABRIGADA ● **Alenquer** (Castelão/Alicante Bouschet) £B
● **Alenquer** Vinha Nobre (Castelão/Camarate/Tinta Miúda) £B
QUINTA DE BAIXO ● **Bairrada** Reserva £C Garrafeira £C
QUINTA DE PAÇOS O **Vinho Verde** Casa do Capitão £B O **Casa de Paços** Arinto £B
QUINTA DE PANCAS (Estremadura) ● **Cabernet Sauvignon** Special Selection £D
● **Touriga Nacional** Special Selection £D
QUINTA DE SAES ● **Dão** Reserva £B
QUINTA DO CARMO (Alentejo) ● **Quinta do Carmo** (Aragonês/Trincadeira/Alicante B/Cabernet) £C
QUINTA DO COVELA (Minho) O **Escolha** (Chardonnay/Avesso/Gewürztraminer) £B
● **Escolha** (Touriga Nacional/Cabernet Franc/Merlot/Syrah) £C
QUINTA DO MOURO (Alentejo) ● **Quinta do Mouro** £C
QUINTA DO MOINHO (Algarve) ● **Vida Nova** (Shiraz/Aragonês/Trincadeira/Mourvèdre) £B
CAVES SÃO JOÃO ● **Dão** Reserva Seleccionada Porta dos Cavalheiros £B

Author's choice (PW)

15 classic Vintage Ports
COCKBURN ● **Vintage Port**
CHURCHILL ● **Vintage Port**
DOW'S ● **Vintage Port**
FONSECA ● **Vintage Port**
GRAHAM'S ● **Vintage Port**
NIEPOORT ● **Vintage Port**
POÇAS ● **Vintage Port**
QUINTA DO INFANTADO ● **Vintage Port**
QUINTA DE RORIZ ● **Vintage Port**
QUINTA DO NOVAL ● **Vintage Port**
QUINTA DO NOVAL ● **Vintage Port Nacional**
QUINTA DO VESUVIO ● **Vintage Port**
SMITH WOODHOUSE ● **Vintage Port**
TAYLOR'S ● **Vintage Port**
WARRE'S ● **Vintage Port**

15 alternative 'single Quinta' type ports
COCKBURN ● **Vintage Port** Quinta dos Canais
CROFT ● **Vintage Port** Quinta da Roêda
DELAFORCE ● **Vintage Port** Quinta da Corte
DOW ● **Vintage Port** Quinta do Bomfim
DOW ● **Vintage Port** Senhora da Ribeira

FONSECA ● **Vintage Port** Guimaraens
GRAHAM ● **Vintage Port** Malvedos
NIEPOORT ● **Vintage Port** Quinta do Passadouro
QUINTA DE LA ROSA ● **Vintage Port**
QUINTA DO NOVAL ● **Vintage Port** Silval
QUINTA DO VALE DOÑA MARIA ● **Vintage Port**
SANDEMAN ● **Vintage Port** Vau
SMITH WOODHOUSE ● **Vintage Port** Madalena
TAYLOR'S ● **Vintage Port** Quinta de Vargellas
WARRE ● **Vintage Port** Quinta da Cavadinha

15 new order Portuguese reds

ALVES DE SOUSA ● **Douro** Quinta da Gaivosa
CAVES ALIANÇA ● **Alentejo** Quinta da Terrugem
CORTES DE CIMA ● **Reserva**
FERREIRA ● **Douro** Quinta da Leda
FOJO ● **Douro** Fojo
NIEPOORT ● **Douro** Redoma
NIEPOORT ● **Douro** Batuta
LUIS PATO ● **Vinha Barrosa**
PINTAS ● **Douro**
QUINTA DE CABRIZ ● **Dão** Escholha Virgilio Loureiro
QUINTA DO CRASTO ● **Douro** Vinha da Ponte
QUINTA DO VALE DOÑA MARIA ● **Douro**
QUINTA DO VALE MEÃO ● **Douro**
QUINTA DOS ROQUES ● **Dão** Reserva
JOÃO PORTUGAL RAMOS ● **Alentejo** Marqués de Borba Reserva

15 Good Value Portuguese reds

ALVES DE SOUSA ● **Douro** Quinta do Vale da Raposa Tinta Roriz
CASA SANTOS LIMA ● **Touriz**
CASAL BRANCO ● **Ribatejo** Falcoaria
CAVES ALIANÇA ● **Palmela** Particular
CORTES DE CIMA ● **Chaminé**
DFJ VINHOS ● **Manta Preta**
ESPORÃO ● **Alentejo** Reserva
QUINTA DA PORTELA DA VILARIÇA ● **Douro**
QUINTA DE LA ROSA ● **Douro**
QUINTA DE RORIZ ● **Douro** Prazo de Roriz
QUINTA DO CÔTTO ● **Douro**
QUINTA DO VALLADO ● **Douro**
JOÃO PORTUGAL RAMOS ● **Vila Santa**
SOGRAPE ● **Douro** Reserva
VINHA D'ERVIDEIRA ● **Vinha d'Ervideira**

Germany

Germany's often exquisite white wines deserve wider recognition and support. However the difficulty for the consumer in understanding her wine styles and wine names, combined with a depressing amount of poor wine has proved an insurmountable barrier, at least until recently. At a lower level the wines are now riper and cleaner and are increasingly marketed in a direct modern way. While there is still too much that is underripe or dilute, often with harsh, aggressive acidity and typically with a high level of sulphur or dirty sulphides character (most acute when the wines are drunk young, as they usually are) there also a growing number of inexpensive and consistently well made dry or off-dry Rieslings. The same success is also being achieved with Weissburgunder (Pinot Blanc), Silvaner and other grapes but it is with Riesling, one of the world's finest grapes, that the momentum must be maintained. More clarity in terms of what degree of sweetness to expect would also help the wine drinker. From such a base it is hoped more consumers will then discover some of the many outstanding producers profiled below. Those with an established reputation have recently been joined by increasing numbers of fine, often small, newer operations. Apart from the sweet wines, which are expensive to produce and made in tiny quantities, many of the wines are very reasonably priced for the quality.

Making sense of German wine styles

There are two basic quality levels, QbA (*Qualitätswein bestimmter Anbaugebiete*) and QmP (*Qualitätswein mit Prädikat*). It is the Prädikat wines that we are concerned with. There are six Prädikat (or classifications) of ripeness included under QmP and for each a minimum must weight (sugar level in the grape) must be obtained. **Kabinett** is the lowest level and should mean a light, dry white but too much Kabinett wine isn't up to scratch – not just from the more marginal Mosel but also the many underperforming estates in the Rheingau and elsewhere. **Spätlese** (meaning late-harvest) wines are riper but critical to quality in all the styles is the balance between residual sugar and acidity. Most Spätlese that are dry will be labelled Trocken or alternatively Halb-Trocken for an off-dry style. From the same producer a straight Spätlese might then be expected to be at least partially sweet. Auslese wines are made from riper grapes again and are usually sweeter in style, though some producers have made quite dry wines from **Auslese** levels of ripeness. Wines from many sites made this way will finish up lacking balance yet some examples maintain it and have an individual style and complexity. While Auslese wines only sometimes show some botrytis influence, the still riper and sweeter categories of **Beerenauslese** and the rare **Trockenbeerenauslese** are made only from handpicked, shrivelled grapes, almost invariably enriched by noble rot. Eiswein is dependent on freezing conditions (rather than botrytis) for concentrating grapes that are high in both sugar and acidity.

In addition to the different levels of ripeness, most Prädikat wines also come from a single site. In fact almost any German wine of real quality comes from an individual vineyard or site (an *Einzellagen* name) usually suffixed with a village name, though this is now being downplayed in the Pfalz. These names are emphasised in bold throughout the German section. Certain sites lend themselves to favour the production of one style but not necessarily another. Some top growers also distinguish between different parcels within a top site. The Gold Capsule (*Goldkapsel*) represents what a grower considers higher quality within a specific category of ripeness and it usually indicates a greater degree of botrytis character. It is most common with Auslese wines of which there might be three or four different bottlings only distinguished one from another by the inclusion of small stars on the label. Only where these are being made on a fairly regular basis have they been included within producer entries. They are indicated (to avoid confusion with the wine's rating) as either '1 Stern', '2 Sterne', etc., or simply 'Gold Capsule' (*Goldkapsel*) or even 'Long Gold Capsule' (*Lange Goldkapsel*).

Many of Germany's top estates belong to a consortium usually referred to as the VDP (*Verband Deutsches Prädikatsweingüter*) and their labels carry its emblem of an eagle. Many of the best and rarest sweet wines are set aside for sale at the VDP auction (as *Versteigerungswein*). Some wine merchants who specialise in German wines will additionally stock some of these wines following a successful bid. The VDP has also been important in promoting the establishment of a vineyard classification system. Since 1999 an increasing number of producers have labelled some or all of their wines from the best vineyards under the top level of the classification. All must be a minimum of Spätlese must weight. Those from the Rheingau are designated *Erstes Gewächs* (here it is also legally approved) with three Roman arches at the bottom of the label. In the Mosel it is *Erste Lage* while in the Pfalz and other regions the designation is *Grosses Gewächs*. From the 2002 vintage, many of these have started appearing in a special bottle with an embossed symbol: a figure '1' next to a bunch of grapes. In 2000, two new categories were introduced for dry wines. Both basic Classic level and premium Selection wines are varietal but the latter also come from a single vineyard.

When looking for good-quality wines from Germany, it is very important to be aware that village names have also been used in conjunction with a *Grosslage* name (looking much like the name of a specific site but actually referring to a broader sweep of inferior vineyards). Infamous wines such as Piesporter Michelsberg or Niersteiner Gutes Domtal wines have thus been allowed to demean the reputation of a fine village and mislead the consumer.

Germany's wine regions

Mosel-Saar-Ruwer

Riesling is king in the Mosel and the top wines are almost exclusively from this grape. The vines are planted individually on often perilously steep slopes above the exaggerated twists and turns of the river below. The River Mosel flows along the Luxembourg border before turning towards Trier and it is almost immediately joined by the important tributary, the Saar. Viticulture is very marginal and only in the best years, and only then in the best sites, are sublime steely, minerally wines made, sometimes with piercing acidity but developing a marvellous, vibrant, honeyed intensity with age. Farthest from the Mosel are the vineyards of **Serrig**, most notably **Schloss Saarstein**; downstream **Saarburg** is distinguished by the **Rausch** vineyard. These, like most of the top vineyards, lie obliquely to the river. Further downstream are **Ockfener Bockstein**, the **Kupp** vineyard from behind **Ayl**, and **Scharzhofberg** from one of Germany's great names, Egon Müller. The village of **Oberemmel** and its fine vineyards, including **Hütte**, lie in a recess away from the Saar and are often overlooked. **Braune Kupp** by contrast is on the river itself, north of **Wiltingen**, as is **Altenberg**, another great site, opposite the village of **Kanzem**. The Ruwer is a trickle by contrast with the Mosel but boasts some exceptional sites that produce exquisite, elegant wines in exceptional vintages. In the village of **Kasel** are the fine **Kehrnagel** and **Nies'chen** sites but the greatest vineyards are those of **Eitelsbach**, with **Karthäuserhofberg** and the **Abtsberg** vineyard of Maximim Grünhaus/von Schubert.

Obtaining full ripeness (and thus potential greatness) on the Mosel proper is a problem and only in its middle section, the Mittel Mosel, are the great gems of Mosel viticulture consistently superb. Travelling downstream from Trier, opposite the village of **Leiwen**, the very steep **Laurentiuslay** is the first fine site, from which several good interpretations are made. **Trittenheim's** best vineyards are **Leiterchen** and **Apotheke**, which can show a cool, delicate minerality, but the really outstanding sites in this section of the river are the south-facing vineyards either side of **Piesport**, **Goldtröpfchen** and **Domherr**, which can show a marvellous intensity of blackcurrant, peach and citrus fruit. **Kesten** marks another fine stretch of vineyard beginning with **Paulinshofberg** and culminating in the **Juffer** and, especially, the **Juffer-Sonnenuhr** sites opposite the village of **Brauneberg**. These wines show a marvellous mineral intensity from a number of top growers. Between here and Bernkastel are some good vineyards around **Lieser** (**Niederberg Helden**) and **Mülheim** (**Helenenkloster**) but the most impressive are on the dramatic steep slopes that run northwards along the Mosel from behind **Bernkastel**. These begin with the small celebrated **Doctor** vineyard, **Graben** and **Lay**, but stretch on to **Domprobst**, the great site of **Graach**, flanked on either side by the fine **Himmelreich** and **Josephshof** vineyards. The same great slope then continues with the **Sonnenuhr** vineyard opposite **Wehlen**, which extends as far as **Zeltingen**. Many of the Mosel's finest producers are located in this section and wines from the likes of Willi Schaefer, Dr Loosen, Markus Molitor, Joh Jos Prum, Max Ferd Richter and Selbach-Oster offer high quality but differing interpretations. The Bernkastel wines can tend either to be very expensive without always showing their full potential or, as this is a much misused name, have little to do with the great vineyards behind the village. Two *Grosslage* names to be aware of are Badstube (often fine as it is restricted to the best sites) and the much wider Kurfürstlay. Just downstream of Zeltingen is arguably the last brilliantly exposed segment of the Mittel Mosel. The last two great village names are Ürzig, with its famous **Würzgarten** ('spice garden') vineyard, and **Erden**, which lies opposite the almost sheer **Prälat** and similarly south-facing **Treppchen** vineyard.

The last stretch of the Mosel before it reaches the Rhine at Koblenz is known as the Terrassenmosel for its narrow terraces. Though not held in the same esteem as those vineyards in the Mittel Mosel there is undoubted potential here beginning to be realised by a number of small growers. In particular, quite powerful, minerally examples have been realised from the **Röttgen** and **Uhlen** vineyards of **Winningen**.

Mittelrhein

The scattered vineyards on the picturesque north-running stretch of the Rhine constitute the small region of Mittelrhein. They can be seen both north and south of Koblenz but the best wines come from a handful of producers around **Bacharach** which has several good sites with slatey soils. As in the Mosel, Riesling is king and good examples have a distinctive floral, mineral intensity.

Nahe

The Nahe has more land planted to vineyards than the Rheingau but much less Riesling, yet its best examples can combine the best qualities of both the Mosel and Rheingau. The greatest stretch of vineyards lies south of the spa town of **Bad Kreuznach**. The town itself has potentially outstanding sites in **Kahlenberg**, **Krötenpfuhl** and **Brückes** but, though improving, quality has not been maximised. Most famous are the vineyards of **Niederhausen**, especially **Hermannshöhle**. Dönnhoff is a brilliant producer which has also underscored the quality of **Brücke** (associated with **Oberhausen**, across the river) and **Kupfergrube**, which along with **Felsenberg** is one of the great vineyards of **Schlossböckelheim**. The village of **Norheim** has good south-facing sites in **Dellchen**, **Kafels** and **Kirschneck** while **Traisen** has **Bastei** and **Rotenfels** but this section of the Nahe needs others besides Dönnhoff to make more of its inherent potential. Much further upstream, refined Rieslings are produced at **Monzingen** by Emrich-Schönleber from the **Halenberg** and **Frühlingsplätzchen** vineyards. Downstream from Bad Kreuznach, and nearer to the Rhine, is **Dorsheim**, where the top sites of **Burgberg**, **Goldloch** and **Pittermännchen** show good richness from Schlossgut Diel. The **Pittersberg**, **Dautenpflänzer** and **Rheinberg** sites of **Munster-Sarmsheim** can also be a source of good-quality Riesling.

Rheingau

One glance at a map of German wine regions makes it obvious why this particular region has been held in high regard for so long. Tight contours above the Rhine, as it swings west south-west for 30 km, indicate an ideal swathe of vineyards, some of which have long belonged to some of Germany's most aristocratic estates. Despite the potential, quality remains mixed and is as likely to come from an emerging smaller grower with less well-known sites as from a more famous name. As the river starts to swing north again, Spätburgunder is planted in the **Höllenberg** vineyard above **Assmannshausen** but Riesling otherwise dominates these vineyards as in no other German region. In the main section, where some of the leading villages are to be found, the vines stretch well back from the river. The best wines show a riper, richer fruit intensity that contrasts with the generally lighter, more elegant examples from the Mosel. The citrus, apple and white peach flavours more prevalent in the Mosel are replaced more often by peach, nectarine and apricot, even at Kabinett and Spätlese levels of ripeness.

Rudesheim's best vineyards lie opposite Bingen almost directly above the river, **Berg Schlossberg** and **Berg Rottland** on the steepest slopes are the finest but several others can also produce high quality. Moving east, Geisenheim, famous for its wine school, includes the vineyards of Kläuserweg and Rothenberg, while perched high above it is the historic estate of **Schloss Johannisberg** with its own separate *Einzellage* identity. Behind the neighbouring village of Winkel, **Schloss Vollrads** too is an *Einzellage* in its own right and efforts are being made to restore its flagging reputation. **Winkel** also has two fine vineyards in **Jesuitengarten** and **Hasensprung**. Further east, **Oestrich** deserves to be better known as both the **Doosberg** and **Lenchen** sites can provide top-quality Riesling in the right hands. The village of Hallgarten lies high above Oestrich but it is only with Hattenheim and Erbach, from vineyards close to the river, that better sites are found. **Hattenheim** includes **Wisselbrunnen**, **Nussbrunnen** and, in Mannberg, has the extension of **Erbacher Marcobrunn**, from which some of the Rheingau's most powerful, flavoursome Rieslings can be made. Erbach also includes fine sites in Siegelsberg, Schlossberg and Hohenrain.

Kiedrich lies a long way back from the river but has steep slopes in **Grafenberg** and a high-profile producer in Robert Weil. The vineyard of **Wasseros** also has the potential for top quality. To the east of Kiedrich is **Rauenthal**, a village from which stylish, spicy, minerally Riesling can be made from several outstanding sites. Currently the potential of **Baiken** and **Gehrn** is not being realised but fine examples of **Nonnenberg** and **Rothenberg** do exist. Neighbouring Martinsthal (Langenberg) and other villages closer to Wiesbaden also contain fine if lesser-known vineyards such as **Wallufer Walkenberg**. At its eastern end, the Rheingau vineyards are not on the Rhine at all but on the river Main as it flows west into the Rhine. **Hochheim** includes several top sites from a relatively narrow wedge of vineyard, including **Domdechaney**, **Kirchenstück** and **Hölle**.

Rheinhessen

Germany's most extensively planted and productive region is also the source of a significant amount of its poorest wine. The leading grapes are Müller-Thurgau and Silvaner, much of it destined for oceans of bland semi-sweet blends. It is yet again Riesling grown at the Rhine's edge that produces the best wines. **Bingen**, in the region's north-west corner, at the juncture of the Nahe and the Rhine rivers, has one important vineyard, the **Scharlachberg**, but it is a famous stretch of vineyards from around Oppenheim and up to Nackenheim that produces the great Rieslings. The steep east- and south-east-facing escarpment of the Roter Hang hill that runs from behind Nierstein towards Nackenheim includes most of the top sites, particularly those on the sweep of the Rhine itself. Fine **Niersteiner** vineyards include the **Orbel**, **Heiligenbaum**, **Ölberg**, **Hipping**, **Brudersberg** and **Pettenthal**, while **Rothenberg** (whose top producer is Gunderloch) comes under **Nackenheim**. Behind **Oppenheim** (like Nierstein, sullied by a *Grosslage* name), lie **Herrenberg** and **Sackträger**, two more potentially outstanding sites. At Flörsheim-Dalsheim, in the southern hinterland, Weingut Keller has highlighted the potential of this area and established the reputation of the **Dalsheimer Hubacker** vineyard, while a short distance to the north the Wittmann family are forging a reputation for the best vineyards of Westhofen.

Pfalz

Riesling is the most planted variety in the Pfalz but occupies only 21 per cent of the vineyard, so there are many other grapes that assume an important role here as well. There is very fine Rieslaner and excellent Scheurebe and the wines are noted for a lush richness checked by a vibrant acidity. Good examples of the 'Pinots' – Grauburgunder, Weissburgunder and Spätburgunder – are made too. The Pfalz is effectively a continuation of Alsace, and the Haardt mountains offer similar protection to the Vosges, often ensuring a sunny, dry autumn. The region's best producers are no longer confined to the Mittelhaardt, a rich vein of sites made famous by Bassermann-Jordan, Bürklin-Wolf and von Buhl.

On hillside slopes on the western edge of the villages (running northwards) of Ruppertsberg, Deidesheim and Forst are some of the finest sites. The best from **Ruppertsberg** include **Gaisböhl**, **Hoheburg** and **Reiterpfad**, while those from **Deidesheim** include **Hohenmorgen**, **Leinhöhle**, **Kieselberg**, **Kalkofen** and **Grainhübel**. **Forst** has two outstanding sites in **Jesuitengarten** and **Kirchenstück** but also **Freundstück**, **Pechstein** and **Ungeheuer**. The last fine sites in this stretch are clustered together just south of **Wachenheim** and includes **Gerümpel**, **Goldbächel** and **Rechbächel**. From here the vineyards continue virtually unbroken and north of the spa town Bad Dürkheim, from close to **Ungstein** (Herrenberg) and **Kallstadt** (**Saumagen**), there is still more potential for outstanding wines. Many producers now make a Riesling Spätlese Trocken from a top site and label it as *Grosses Gewächs* (in the manner of an Alsace Grand Cru). A growing number of good producers make fine Rieslings from outside this particularly well-protected belt. The most high-profile of these, Müller-Catoir, is as successful with Rieslaner, Scheurebe and Muskateller as with Riesling.

Baden

This fast-growing, resurgent region (now Germany's third most important in terms of quantity), lies directly across the Rhine, here forming the border with France, from Alsace. Production is dominated by large co-operatives but exciting small, private producers are more responsible for its growing reputation for quality. Though a quarter of the planting is Müller-Thurgau, the leading variety is red. Spätburgunder (Pinot Noir) accounts for almost a third of the vineyard area. Grauburgunder (or Ruländer as it is also called here) and Weissburgunder in both oaked and unoaked styles are also important, as is Traminer. From this elongated stretch of vineyards, those from the areas of Kaiserstuhl and Ortenau produce some of the finest wines. In Kaiserstuhl's volcanic soils all three 'Pinots' do particularly well from around the towns of **Achkarren, Burkheim, Ihringen** and **Oberrotweil**. Further north, Riesling (as Klingelberger) assumes some significance in **Durbach** (especially from the **Plauelrain** vineyard) and in the Ortenau, where the quality obtained by Laible suggests its true potential is only just beginning to be realised.

Franken

In Franken, as in the Rheinhessen, the variety that dominates production is Müller-Thurgau, though not from a quality perspective. Silvaner is the most important quality grape and Franken is where this grape shows the greatest interest and complexity. Riesling hardly figures at all, in part because the more continental growing season isn't always long enough to achieve full ripeness. Yet from certain locations, usually close to the broad, snaking Main river, it shows a style and complexity that owes something to the soils (often limestone-rich) as well as the grape. **Escherndorf** has one outstanding site, **Lump**, where brilliant wines from Horst Sauer, including Riesling and Silvaner, deserve the widest recognition. **Iphofen** to the south is blessed with excellent vineyards in **Julius-Echter-Berg** and **Kronsberg**. Other locations with good sites include Würzburg (the famous **Würzburger Stein**) and those of **Randersacker**. Top grower Paul Fürst (Weingut Rudolf Fürst) showcases the quality of **Bürgstadter Centgrafenberg** Riesling and Spätburgunder. If the squat *Bocksbeutel* bottle comes as a surprise, and is more difficult to pour from, don't be dissuaded from trying the quality inside.

Other regions

Good Spätburgunder is made in the very small region of Ahr, named for a northerly tributary of the Rhine, while the modest amounts of wine produced in Hessische Bergstrasse is mostly Riesling. There are substantial vineyards areas in Württemberg where reds are as important as whites, and increasingly good quality, if from a select number of producers. Wine quality from the small Saale-Unstrut and Sachsen regions, at the extreme northern latitudes of continental European viticulture, has improved since Germany's reunification but there are no stars yet.

A-Z of producers by region

RHEIN

• Bonn

1 *2*

AHR

• Koblenz

2

Bacharach   Wiesbaden   • Frankfurt

MOSEL   *7* *7*

3   •Mainz

Bernkastel-Kues •   • Nackenheim

MAIN   *11*

6   *11*   *11*

Trier •   Bad Kreuznach

Saarburg •   *4*   NAHE   *8*   *10*   • Würzburg

5   RUWER   *13*

SAAR   Bad Dürkheim •

Deidesheim •   Heidelberg

9   RHEIN

1   Ahr   *13*

2   Mittelrhein   Karlsruhe •

3   Mosel   FRANCE   *12*   NECKAR

4   Ruwer

5   Saar   Stuttgart

6   Nahe

7   Rheingau

8   Rheinhessen

9   Pfalz

10 Hessische Bergstrasse   *13*

11 Franken   • Freiburg

12 Württemberg

13 Baden   *13*   *13*

13   Bodensee *12*

SCHWEIZ

German vintages

What is produced each year from German vineyards is dependent on the climatic conditions – especially during the months of October and November. Top years provide greater ripeness and plentiful Spätlese and Auslese and, if the conditions are right, botrytis enrichment for Beerenauslese and Trockenbeerenauslese styles. In a poor year only Kabinett and a little Spätlese might be made. When to drink wines and potential longevity are very producer-dependent but the generalised guide in the table below is based on Spätlese and Auslese levels of ripeness. An example from the Mosel is likely to need a little more time than one from the warmer Rhine but the producer will be of much greater significance. While well-made Kabinett can be drunk within a year or two of the vintage, most Spätlese or Auslese needs three or four years' age to start to show well. Whether they will keep for another couple of years or a further five or 10 or 15 (or more) depends on the specific wine and vintage quality. Eiswein from a great vintage like 1998 can age very impressively but even when well-balanced from the outset it usually retains its penetrating acidity. Recent vintages are very exciting, the outstanding 2001 followed by some exceptional ageworthy wines in 2002 (if very little of the very sweet styles) and the super-rich, ripe 2003s which are exceptional when the balance is right.

German vintage chart

	Mosel Riesling	Rhine Riesling	Pfalz Riesling
2003	★★★★/★★★★★★ A	★★★★/★★★★★★ A	★★★★/★★★★★★ A
2002	★★★★/★★★★★★ A	★★★★/★★★★★ A	★★★★/★★★★★ A
2001	★★★★★ B	★★★★★ B	★★★★★ B
2000	★★★/★★★★ B	★★★ B	★★/★★★ B
1999	★★★/★★★★ B	★★★/★★★★ B	★★★★ B
1998	★★★★ B	★★★★ B	★★★★/★★★★★★ B
1997	★★★★ B	★★★/★★★★ C	★★★/★★★★ C
1996	★★★/★★★★ C	★★★★ C	★★★★/★★★★★★ B
1995	★★★★/★★★★★★ B	★★★/★★★★ B	★★/★★★ C
1994	★★★★ C	★★★★ C	★★★/★★★★ C
1993	★★★★ C	★★★★ C	★★★★ C
1992	★★★/★★★★ C	★★★/★★★★ C	★★★/★★★★ C
1991	★★★/★★★★ C	★★/★★★ D	★★/★★★ D
1990	★★★★★ C	★★★★★ C	★★★★★ C

BASSERMANN-JORDAN Pfalz www.bassermann-jordan.com A: **WBn**

Owner: Margrit & Gabriele von Bassermann-Jordan Kirchgasse 10, D-67142 Deidesheim

This famous Pfalz estate (Weingut Geheimer Rat Dr von Bassermann-Jordan is its full name) has been revitalised since the mid-1990s. With 42 ha, the estate is large but includes vineyards in some of the best sites of Forst and Deidesheim. Under the winemaking direction of Ulrich Mell come intense, ripe Rieslings (at the Spätlese level and higher) with good balanced acidities. *Grosses Gewächs* versions are particularly impressive in 2001 and 2002. The wines below are only a selection of what is made, but almost anything of Spätlese level or above made since 1997 is worth trying. (PW)

O **Forster Jesuitengarten** Riesling Spätlese Trocken★★ £C
O **Forster Pechstein** Riesling Kabinett Trocken★ £B
O **Forster Kirchenstück** Riesling Auslese★★★ £D
O **Deidesheimer Hohenmorgen** Riesling Spätlese Trocken Grosses Gewächs★★★ £E
O **Deidesheimer Hohenmorgen** Riesling Auslese★★★ £E Riesling Eiswein★★★ £F
O **Deidesheimer Kalkofen** Riesling Spätlese Trocken Grosses Gewächs★★★ £E

WGT. BERCHER Baden www.germanwine.de/weingut/bercher A: **WBn**

Owner: Eckhardt & Rainer Bercher Mittelstadt 13, D-79235 Vogtsburg

Bercher has 24 ha of vines in southern Baden and plantings are dominated by the three Pinots. More than 70 per cent of production comes from Spätburgunder, Weissburgunder or Grauburgunder. Burkheimer Feuerberg wines qualify as *Grosses Gewächs* and those labelled 'SE' are particularly good, with real richness and depth. Weissburgunder is stylish, intense and long, while the Spätburgunder shows splendid flavour complexity. Some very good, well-balanced Eiswein is also made when conditions allow; it is intense and tangy, full of ripe nectarine and dried peach fruit. The dry whites should be drunk within three to four years of the vintage. (PW)

O **Burkheimer Feuerberg** Weissburgunder Spätlese Trocken SE★★★ £C
O **Burkheimer Feuerberg** Grauburgunder Spätlese Trocken SE★★ £C
O **Chardonnay** Spätlese Trocken SE★★ £C
● **Burkheimer Feuerberg** Spätburgunder Spätlese Trocken SE★★★ £E

JOSEF BIFFAR Pfalz www.biffar.com

Owner: Gerhard & Annette Biffar Niederkirchener Strasse 13, D-67146 Deidesheim

Gerhard Biffar has 12 ha of vineyards in the heart of the Pfalz, three-quarters of which are planted to Riesling. Some excellent wines were produced from the late 1980s onwards as the cellars were gradually modernised until a hiccup in the late 90s in part due to successive changes in winemaking personnel. Recent wines show a crystalline purity, poise and intensity since 2001. Both Wachenheimer Gerümpel and Deidesheimer Grainhübel Rieslings give full justification to the sites' *Grosses Gewächs* status. There is excellent definition too in the racy sweeter styles. (PW)

O **Wachenheimer Gerümpel** Riesling Grosses Gewächs★★★ £C
O **Deidesheimer Grainhübel** Riesling Grosses Gewächs★★★ £C
O **Deidesheimer Kieselberg** Riesling Auslese★★★ £E
O **Deidesheimer Kalkofen** Riesling Eiswein★★★★ £G

GEORG BREUER Rheingau www.georg-breuer.com A: **NYg**, N&P

Owner: Bernhard Breuer family & Heinrich Breuer Grabenstrasse 8, D-65385 Rüdesheim

Bernhard Breuer was passionate about Rheingau Riesling and was one of its leading advocates until his death in 2004. His legacy is not only an estate of some 26 ha but also joint ventures in South Africa (MONT DU TOIT) and Portugal's Douro (QUINTA DA CARVALHOSA). The Rheingau vineyards include 2.6 ha in the highly rated Rüdesheimer Berg Schlossberg, 1 ha in Berg Rottland and the entire 5 ha of Rauenthaler Nonnenberg. All three sites are classified as *Erstes Gewächs,* giving ample scope for making fine Rheingau

Rieslings. The wines improved considerably in the 1990s and in recent vintages have been particularly good. Sweeter styles generally show good botrytis richness, with good intensity and length of flavour in the Gold Capsule Auslese wines; the Rauenthal Nonnenberg is most stylish and distinctive. Just a little more focus and refinement would put the wines among the very best from the Rheingau. They can be a little reduced if drunk very young. Some Grauburgunder and Spätburgunder are also made. Prices are high for the quality. Old varieties Orleans and Heunisch are also being replanted here. (PW)

O **Rüdesheim Berg Rottland** Riesling Trocken★★ £D Riesling Auslese Gold Capsule★★★★ £F
O **Rüdesheim Bischofsberg** Riesling Auslese Gold Capsule★★★ £F
O **Rüdesheim Berg Schlossberg** Riesling Trocken★★ £D Riesling Auslese Gold Capsule★★★ £G
O **Rauenthal Nonnenberg** Riesling Trocken★★ £D Riesling Auslese Gold Capsule★★★★ £F
O **Riesling** Trocken Montosa★ £B

REICHSRAT VON BUHL   Pfalz   www.reichsrat-von-buhl.de   A: FEM, JNi, SVS

Owner: Reichsrat von Buhl GmbH   Weinstrasse 16, D-67146 Deidesheim
It has taken some time but Japanese investment has put this once famous estate established in 1849 back on the map of the Pfalz's best (it is leased to a consortium of Japanese wine merchants).With 50 ha of vineyards spread across some enviable sites it would be a shame if the wines were not special and, the Yen having been spent, the wines have been back on form since 1994. It is difficult to separate the top Rieslings for quality, coming as they do from some out-and-out top Pfalz vineyards, yet no two are alike. The very classy, mineral-imbued Forster Pechstein is hard to better in a top vintage like 2002 but the initially more austere Ruppertsberger Reiterpfad has underlying concentration, a white peach fruit intensity and a touch of spice. Others are scarcely less good. As is the trend in the Pfalz there is now much emphasis on the production of *Grosses Gewächs* but some fine sweet wines are made too, including Riesling from Forster Ungeheuer and Scheurebe from Ruppertsberger Reiterpfad. (PW)

O **Forster Pechstein** Riesling Grosses Gewächs★★★★ £C
O **Forster Kirchenstück** Riesling Grosses Gewächs★★★ £C
O **Deidesheimer Paradiesgarten** Riesling Grosses Gewächs★★★ £C
O **Ruppertsberger Reiterpfad** Riesling Grosses Gewächs★★★ £C
O **Forster Jesuitengarten** Riesling Spätlese★★★ £C

BÜRKLIN-WOLF   Pfalz   www.buerklin-wolf.de   A: AWs, CPp, Lay, Tan, N&P

Owner: B Bürklin-von Guradze & C von Guradze   Weinstrasse 65, D-67157 Wachenheim
Since the mid-1990s Christian von Guradze has restored the reputation of this large and historic estate. Its 85.5 ha of vineyards include several of the Pfalz's top sites which under the new classification system have been designated *Grosses Gewächs*. The focus has been to produce a top full-bodied dry Riesling in each and these wines, all Spätlese Trocken, much more closely resemble top Alsace wines than anything from other areas in Germany. Forster Jesuitengarten is rich and minerally with real weight and an Alsace-like oiliness; the Kirschenstück is a brilliant wine with terrific minerality, great intensity, concentration and excellent ageing potential; Deidesheimer Hohenmorgen shows an unusual, spicy character and deep, pure fruit; while Ruppertsberger Gaisböhl is broader but long and classy. Less expensive, the 'B'-rated Wachenheimer Rechbächel and Ruppertsberger Hoheburg are a little lighter but have good length and intensity. Cheaper again is a Bürklin Estate Riesling, which offers good fruit character. Other good wines include a very sweet Scheurebe Beerenauslese that is just rescued by its acidity and a very intense sweet Muskateller Trockenbeerenauslese with rich, vibrant, apricotty fruit that also teeters on the brink. Some Chardonnay and Spätburgunder are also made. (PW)

O **Forster Kirchenstück** Riesling Grosses Gewächs★★★★★ £E
O **Forster Ungeheuer** Riesling Grosses Gewächs★★★★ £E
O **Forster Jesuitengarten** Riesling Grosses Gewächs★★★ £D
O **Forster Pechstein** Riesling Grosses Gewächs★★★ £D
O **Deidesheimer Hohenmorgen** Riesling Grosses Gewächs★★★ £D

O **Ruppertsberger Gaisböhl** Riesling Grosses Gewächs★★★ £D
O **Ruppertsberger Hoheburg** Riesling Grosses Gewächs★★★ £C
O **Wachenheimer Rechbächel** Riesling Grosses Gewächs★★★ £C Riesling Trockenbeerenauslese★★★★ £H
O **Bürklin Estate** Riesling★★ £B O **Scheurebe** Beerenauslese★★ £F
O **Muskateller** Trockenbeerenauslese★★★★ £H

A CHRISTMANN Pfalz www.weingut-christmann.de A: F&R

Owner: Steffen Christmann Peter-Koch-Strasse 43, D-67435 Gimmeldingen
Steffen Christmann's 14 ha of vineyards include four leading Pfalz vineyard sites (Deidesheimer Hohenmorgen, Gimmeldinger Mandelgarten, Königsbacher Idig and Ruppertsberger Reiterpfad), each designated *Grosses Gewächs*. The wines show intense, ripe fruit and a full, lush, almost creamy character yet with good intensity and acidity. Though they are made in a Trocken style there is also a little sweetness, similar to many of the Alsace *grands crus* in recent vintages. Christmann's own sweet wines are very sweet, intense and succulent but generally well-balanced, with the richness underpinned by a vibrant structure. Small amounts of Trockenbeerenauslese and Eiswein are also made as is a Spätburgunder (Pinot Noir) from Königsbacher Idig. (PW)
O **Königsbacher Idig** Riesling Trocken Grosses Gewächs★★★ £C Riesling Auslese★★★ £E
O **Gimmeldinger Mandelgarten** Riesling Trocken Grosses Gewächs★★★ £C
O **Ruppertsberger Reiterpfad** Riesling Trocken Grosses Gewächs★★★ £C
O **Deidesheimer Hohenmorgen** Riesling Trocken Grosses Gewächs★★★ £C

J J CHRISTOFFEL Mittel Mosel www.moenchhof.de A: RsW, HRp

Owner: Hans Leo Christoffel Schanzstrasse 2, D-54539 Ürzig
The recently retired Hans Leo Christoffel has leased his minute holding of Riesling vines to neighbour Robert Eymael (MÖNCHHOF/ROBERT EYMAEL), who has taken full responsibility for the wines' production and sale. However a separate identity has been maintained for the wines, over which Christoffel still has some influence. The Ürziger Würzgarten wines are excellent with lovely spice, citrus (and riper peach and nectarine in the riper styles), and penetrating intensity and depth, particularly in reasonably priced special selections. Fine Rieslings are also produced from Erdener Treppchen. (PW)
O **Ürziger Würzgarten** Riesling Kabinett★★ £B Riesling Spätlese★★ £C
O **Ürziger Würzgarten** Riesling Auslese 1 Stern★★★ £C Riesling Auslese 3 Sterne★★★★ £D
O **Ürziger Würzgarten** Riesling Eiswein★★★★★ £G

DOMDECHANT WERNER'SCHES Rheingau www.domdechantwerner.com A: LWT

Owner: Dr Franz Werner Michel Rathausstrasse 30, D-65234 Hochheim
This estate of 12.5 ha dates back to 1780 when it was acquired by the dean (Domdechant) of the cathedral at Mainz. The current Dr Franz Werner Michel provides a solid range of wines particularly from the Domdechaney and Kirchenstück sites. There is plenty of intensity together with spice, citrus and riper fruit flavours and good balance, though in most there is not yet the style, richness or persistence for really fine quality. In 2001 a superior Riesling Spätlese Trocken Long Gold Cap was made from Domdechaney. Eiswein is made from both Kirchenstück and Domdechaney when conditions permit. (PW)
O **Hochheimer Kirchenstück** Riesling Spätlese★★★ £C Riesling Erstes Gewächs★★★ £D
O **Hochheimer Domdechaney** Riesling Spätlese Trocken★★ £C Riesling Erstes Gewächs★★★ £D
O **Hochheimer Domdechaney** Riesling Spätlese★★★ £C Riesling Auslese★★★ £D

DÖNNHOFF Nahe www.doennhoff.com A: WSS, HRp, Tan, L&W, L&S, JNi, SVS, P&S

Owner: Helmut Dönnhoff Bahnhofstrasse 11, D-55585 Oberhausen
Helmut Dönnhoff is quite rightly regarded as one of Germany's most celebrated winemakers. He makes prodigious Rieslings from 14.5 ha of vineyards, mostly from sites in Schlossböckelheim, Niederhausen and Oberhäusen, where the Brücke vineyard is *Alleinbesitz* (solely owned). Even QbA can be distinctive if more

modest in cooler years, while excellent examples of Riesling Kabinett include an Oberhäuser Leistenberg that shows both terroir and ripe fruit. Spätlese and Auslese wines show splendid concentration, a fine minerally intensity and considerable elegance. The range of vividly expressed flavours, from cool blackcurrant, apple and citrus to ripe peach, is matched by a lingering intensity of fruit. Schlossböckelheimer Kupfergrube Spätlese is intense and long and adds a dash of spice to a delicious ripe peach and blackcurrant character. Particularly concentrated and very classy, if initially less expressive, are Spätlese and Auslese from Oberhäuser Brücke that can appear with a Gold Capsule designation. The Eiswein from the same vineyard is quite exquisite, very sweet and intense and pure but beautifully balanced with honeyed, spicy, dried stone-fruit flavours that go on and on. Those named for a day of the week add a slight premium. Some Weissburgunder and Grauburgunder are also made. Brilliant wines in 2001, 02 and 03. (PW)

O **Riesling QbA**★★ £B   O **Norheimer Dellchen** Riesling Kabinett★★ £B
O **Oberhäuser Leistenberg** Riesling Kabinett★★★ £C
O **Schlossböckelheimer Felsenberg** Riesling Spätlese★★★ £D
O **Schlossböckelheimer Kupfergrube** Riesling Spätlese★★★ £D
O **Niederhäusen Hermannshöhle** Riesling Spätlese★★★ £D   Riesling Auslese★★★★★ £F
O **Oberhäuser Brücke** Riesling Spätlese★★★★ £E   Riesling Auslese★★★★★ £F   Riesling Eiswein✪✪✪✪✪ £H

EMRICH-SCHÖNLEBER   Nahe   www.emrich-schoenleber.com   A: CTy, HRp

Owner: H & W Schönleber   Naheweinstrasse 10A, D-55569 Monzingen
This is now arguably the second great estate of the Nahe (after Dönnhoff). Though still small (at 14 ha), it has been improved and much enlarged by Werner Schönleber. Through careful selection and attentive winemaking he produces tight, sleek, intense Rieslings with lovely balance and great length of flavour from the previously unsung village of Monzingen. Riesling Kabinett from Frühlingsplätzchen shows a lovely elegant, gently spicy, minerally intensity, while a contrasting vigorous Halbtrocken version from a different part of the same vineyard needs a little age. The estate also includes 4 ha of the steep Halenberg vineyard, a source of wines with minerally, refined flavours. A regular Spätlese from this site is medium-dry but both Halbtrocken and Trocken versions are also produced, while energised Auslese also come in a super 3 Sterne Gold Capsule version. Halenberg Eiswein is beautifully delineated and is one of those where citrus flavours, especially grapefruit and lime, often prevail over riper peach or apricot. A little Eiswein is also produced from the Frühlingsplätzchen vineyard. A ripe Grauburgunder emphasises fruit. (PW)

O **Monzinger Frühlingsplätzchen** Riesling Kabinett★★ £B   Riesling Spätlese★★★ £C
O **Monzinger Halenberg** Riesling Spätlese★★★ £C   Riesling Auslese★★★★ £D
O **Monzinger Halenberg** Riesling Auslese 3 Sterne★★★★★ £F   Riesling Eiswein★★★★★ £H
O **Monzinger** Grauburgunder Spätlese Trocken★ £C

WGT. GÖTTELMANN   Nahe

Owner: Ruth Göttelmann Blessing & Götz Blessing   Rheinstrasse 77, D-55424 Münster-Sarmsheim
Götz Blessing and his wife Ruth Göttelmann-Blessing are both trained enologists and have worked very hard to improve both the quality of their grapes and the resulting wines. There are now 12.5 ha of vineyards (10 of them owned) of classic steep slate-covered slopes, 70 per cent of which are planted to Riesling. A long, cool, natural fermentation is favoured resulting in wines of often piercing minerally citrus and blackcurrant fruit. The acidity can be a little too sharp in some of the drier styles but a reduction in yields seems to contribute to good flavour length. The Dautenpflänzer Riesling Spätlese shows a Mosel-like elegance. All the Rieslings need age and promise to be very lively even with five to ten years' age at Spätlese level or higher. A pure lemony, minerally Weissburgunder Spätlese Trocken also opens out with time. (PW)

O **Münsterer** Riesling Kabinett Trocken★ £B   O **Münsterer Dautenpflänzer** Riesling Spätlese★★ £B
O **Münsterer Kapellenberg** Riesling Spätlese Trocken★★★ £B
O **Münsterer Rheinberg** Riesling Spätlese★★ £B   Riesling Beerenauslese★★★ £F
O **Münsterer** Weissburgunder Spätlese Trocken★ £B

GRANS-FASSIAN   Mittel Mosel   www.grans-fassian.de

Owner: Gerhard Grans   Römerstrasse 28, D-54340 Leiwen
Gerhard Grans is credited with generating increased acclaim for Leiwen and its leading site, Laurentiuslay, following a series of impressive wines in the late 1980s. The estate dates back to 1624 and is located in the tight horseshoe bend of the Mosel between Leiwen and Trittenheim. Just over 9 ha of vineyards include the top sites of Trittenheimer Apotheke and Piesporter Goldtröpfchen. The wines have ample ripe fruit and excellent structure too, the exotic richness in the sweeter styles well checked by balancing acidity. Grans' efforts received further endorsement in 2001 with membership of the VDP. Some slightly weaker 2000s excepted, recent vintages have been very good. (PW)

O **Leiwener Laurentiuslay** Riesling Spätlese★★ 'S' £C Riesling Eiswein★★★★ £H
O **Piesporter Goldtröpfchen** Riesling Spätlese★★ £D Riesling Auslese★★★ £D
O **Trittenheimer Apotheke** Riesling Spätlese★★ £D Riesling Auslese★★★ £D
O **Trittenheimer Apotheke** Riesling Beerenauslese★★★★ £D

GUNDERLOCH   Rheinhessen   www.gunderloch.de   A: **WSS**, JNi, BBR, ACh, C&R, Hrd, Has

Owner: Agnes Hasselbach-Usinger   Carl-Gunderloch-Platz 1, D-55299 Nackenheim
Fritz and Agnes Hasselbach's 12.5 ha of vineyards are steeply sloping and well protected. The famed Rothenberg site with its distinctive red slatey soils is as steep as some of those on the Mosel and produces some of the richest, most intense Rieslings in Germany. There is an explosive richness of fruit at Spätlese level with ever-increasing intensity, power and structure at higher levels of ripeness. The wines are also generally very well balanced, enabling them to be drunk fairly young, though most should be kept for five years or considerably longer. A little wine is also made from the Niersteiner Oelberg and Niersteiner Pettenthal sites. Drei Sterne Auslese is a good example of characterful Trocken style Auslese, while Jean-Baptiste is an off-dry Kabinett estate wine. Newish Red Stone Riesling is a light, racy, commercial example. (PW)

O **Red Stone** Riesling QbA★ £B   O **Jean Baptiste** Riesling Kabinett★★ £C
O **Nackenheimer Rothenberg** Riesling Kabinett★★ £C Riesling Spätlese★★★ £D
O **Nackenheimer Rothenberg** Riesling Auslese★★★★ £E Riesling Auslese Drei Sterne★★★ £E
O **Nackenheimer Rothenberg** Riesling Auslese Gold Cap★★★★★ £F Riesling Beerenauslese✪✪✪✪✪ £H

WGT. FRITZ HAAG   www.weingut-fritz-haag.de   A: **J&B, Rae**, JAr, HRp, L&W

Owner: Wilhelm Haag   Dusemonder Hof, Dusemonder Strasse 44, D-54472 Brauneberg
This estate of 7.5 ha produces some of the finest, most elegant Rieslings in the Mosel from one of its greatest sites, Brauneberger Juffer-Sonnenuhr. Wilhelm Haag is not only one of the region's leading winemakers but also a leader in promoting quality throughout the region. The wines start out very taut and concentrated with a remarkably fine, minerally intensity and gradually open out with age. There is increasing weight and richness in Spätlese level and higher, culminating in a small amount of Beerenauslese. Bottlings of Spätlese wines and higher from individual numbered casks are also made and prices vary according to the considered quality of each. As extremely fine and elegant as the wines can be, sulphur or reductive characters can be intrusive when the wines are young. (PW)

O **Brauneberger Juffer-Sonnenuhr** Riesling Kabinett★ £B Riesling Spätlese★★★ £C
O **Brauneberger Juffer-Sonnenuhr** Riesling Auslese★★★★ £D   Riesling Auslese Gold Capsule★★★★★ £E

WGT. REINHOLD HAART   Mittel Mosel   www.haart.de   A: RsW

Owner: Theo Haart   Ausoniusufer 18, D-54498 Piesport
This small 6-ha estate is centred on Piesporter Goldtröpfchen, one of the great sites of the Mittel Mosel. Piesport, a name shamelessly debased by commercial exploitation in the latter half of the 20th century, actually played an important part in the propagation of Riesling in preference to lesser varieties in the 18th

century. Theo Haart's wines are made naturally without any overarching style imposition, maximising quality in the context of the vintage and by reducing yields. The intensely blackcurrant fruit is characteristic, so too is a profusion of peach, apricot and citrus in many Spätlese and Auslese wines as well as exotic fruits in the sweetest styles. It is this flavour and intensity that marks out the wines' quality, supported by a subtle minerality and perfectly balanced acidity. Other sites such as Dronhofberger give cooler green apple and citrus flavours but share this intensity. Wintrich Ohligsberg (which like Goldtröpfchen qualifies as *Erste Lage*) offers spice and ripe peach at the Auslese level. The true potential of these wines is only revealed with age. Some Gold Capsule bottlings are made as are a little Beerenauslese or Trockenbeerenauslese, though the last can be difficult to obtain as they are usually set aside as *Versteigerungswein* (wines for auction). (PW)

O **Dhron Hofberger** Riesling Spätlese★★ £C
O **Piesporter Domherr** Riesling Spätlese★★★ £C Auslese★★★★ £D
O **Piesporter Goldtröpfchen** Riesling Kabinett★★ £B Spätlese★★★ £C Auslese★★★★ £D
O **Wintrich Ohligsberg** Riesling Auslese★★★ £C

PRINZ VON HESSEN Rheingau www.prinz-von-hessen.com A: OW**L**

Owner: Prinz & Landgraf von Hessen Grund 1, D-65366 Johannisberg
One of several improving domaines in the Rheingau. Following much investment in renewing the cellars, and direction from Markus Sieben, much more is being made of the potential of 45 ha of vineyards. Sweet styles are now very good indeed and progress can also be seen in several of the drier styles, with better richness and texture in the *Erstes Gewächs*. The wines are increasingly showing both the texture and structure and the ripe fruit that are sadly rarer than they should be in the Rheingau. The gentle spice and concentrated very ripe fruit in the sweeter styles of Johannisberger Klaus is particularly captivating. A little red Frühburgunder (a strain of Pinot Noir) is also made. (PW)

O **Johannisberger Klaus** Riesling Auslese★★★ £D Riesling Beerenauslese★★★★ £D
O **Johannisberger Klaus** Riesling Kabinett★ £B Riesling Erstes Gewächs★★★ £B
O **Winkeler Hasensprung** Riesling Erstes Gewächs★★ £C
O **Winkeler Jesuitengarten** Riesling Erstes Gewächs★★ £C

HEYL ZU HERRNSHEIM Rheinhessen www.heyl-zu-herrnsheim.de A: W**B**n

Owner: Ahr family foundation Mathildenhof, Langgasse 3, D-55283 Nierstein
Nierstein has few estates of real quality but the Rieslings produced here in recent vintages under the direction of Markus Ahr and the winemaking of Michael Burgdorf give a real lead to others in the area. The 24 ha of vineyards encompass all the top sites between Nierstein and Nackenheim, including sole ownership of the small Brudersberg site. All the wines are much improved but riper styles of the vineyard-designated examples (Brudersberg, Oelberg and Pettenthal) show the most emphatic progress, with greater depth and intensity. These are sweet, intense and concentrated wines with ripe fruit in the finish. In contrast Niersteiner Pettenthal Grosses Gewächs is minerally, dry and rather austere. Above the basic estate bottlings of Riesling, Weisser Burgunder and Silvaner are Rotschiefer versions that come only from the red slate soils. A little Beerenauslese and Trockenbeerenauslese from the Pettenthal and Brudersberg sites are also made. (PW)

O **Niersteiner Pettenthal** Riesling Trocken Grosses Gewächs★★ £D Riesling Auslese★★★ £E
O **Niersteiner Oelberg** Riesling Auslese Gold Capsule★★★★ £F
O **Niesteiner Brudersberg** Riesling Auslese★★★ £F
O **Riesling** Trocken Rotschiefer★★ £C O **Weisser Burgunder** Trocken Rotschiefer★★ £C

HEYMANN-LÖWENSTEIN www.heymann-loewenstein.com A: M&V, Sel, ACh

Owner: R. Löwenstein & C. Heymann-Löwenstein Bahnhofstrasse 10, D-56333 Winningen
Reinhard Löwenstein's 12 ha of vineyard cling to extremely steep terraces in the Terrassenmosel, only a short distance from Koblenz and the juncture of the Mosel with the Rhine. He makes some magnificent dry wines from stone walled slopes perfectly angled to the low sun. The atypically warm

mesoclimate combines with a long ripening season and low yields to produce excellent fruit. The slate soils are distinct from those in the Mittel Mosel and the resulting wines are a very different expression of the Mosel too. They tend to be either fermented to dryness or made in more fully sweet styles (Auslese and above), though the winemaking approach is very 'hands-off'. Sweet wines show exquisite fruit and definition. The *Erste Lage* wines from parcels of vines within Winninger Uhlen were very successful in 2001 and 02, delivering intense, mineral elegance in the Laubach, more depth and weight in Roth Lay and cooler promise in Blaufüsser Lay. The length of flavour and complexity in all three is most impressive. Of other names used that don't refer to a vineyard site, Schieferterrassen indicates a vineyard blend while a vom Blauem Schiefer Riesling comes from a different 'blue' type of slate within Uhlen. (PW)

O **Winninger Uhlen** Riesling 'Blaufüsser Lay' Erste Lage★★★ £C Riesling 'Laubach' Erste Lage★★★ £D
O **Winninger Uhlen** Riesling 'Roth Lay' Erste Lage★★★ £D Riesling 'Roth Lay' Auslese★★★★ £F
O **Winninger Rottgen** Riesling★★★ £D Riesling Auslese★★★ £F
O **Hatzenporter Kirchberg** Riesling★★ £C
O **Schieferterrassen** Riesling★ £C Eiswein★★★★★ £H   O **Vom Blauem Schiefer** Riesling★★ £C

WGT. TONI JOST Mittelrhein A: HRp, F&R

Owner: Peter Jost Oberstrasse 14, D-55422 Bacharach am Rhein
Peter Jost, the Mittelrhein's one grower of real renown, has 8.5 ha of vineyards and the majority of the wines come from Bacharacher Hahn, the region's the leading site. The wines are typically perfumed, citrus and zingy, adding riper peach and apricot flavours in the sweet styles. A basic Riesling Trocken can be a little lean; the Kabinett is usually riper and with better intensity and a little sweetness. Spätlese and Auslese show intense, mineral and floral characters, with increased sweetness though not the extra depth and concentration expected at these levels of ripeness. A Beerenauslese, however, is typically very ripe, with an accentuated botrytis character and good balance between intense, sweet fruit and a vibrant acidity that ensures long ageing. A little wine is also made from the Rheingau as is some Spätburgunder. Recent vintages lack the poise and definition that were once the hallmarks of these wines. (PW)

O **Bacharacher Hahn** Riesling Kabinett★ £B Riesling Spätlese★★ £C
O **Bacharacher Hahn** Riesling Auslese★★★ £D Riesling Beerenauslese★★★★ £H

JULIUSSPITAL Franken www.juliusspital.de

Owner: Juliusspital Foundation Klinikstrasse 1, D-97070 Würzburg
Founded in 1576, the hospice of Juliusspital has a long history of wine production as well as care for the needy. With 168 ha of vines, production is not insubstantial. Of the most interest are the top Spätlese wines from some of Franken's best sites. These are elegant and refined, with good definition that lets the fruit sing out with a little bottle-age. The Silvaner and Riesling are bottled in the distinctive dark green *Bocksbeutel* bottles. Volkacher Karthäuser Weisser Burgunder is bottled in a Burgundy-type bottle and the light touch employed in the winemaking shows just how well this grape (Pinot Blanc) can perform here. As well as those rated below, good wines are made from other top sites such as Randersackerer Pfülben and Escherndorfer Lump. (PW)

O **Würzburger Stein** Riesling Spätlese Trocken★★★ £D Rieslaner Auslese★★★ £D
O **Würzburger Stein** Silvaner Spätlese Trocken★★ £C
O **Würzburger Innere Leiste** Silvaner Spätlese Trocken★★ £C
O **Iphöfer Julius-Echter-Berg** Riesling Spätlese Trocken★★ £D Silvaner Spätlese Trocken★★ £C
O **Volkacher Karthäuser** Weisser Burgunder Spätlese Trocken★★ £D

KARLSMÜHLE Ruwer www.karlsmuehle.com A: HRp, F&R

Owner: Peter Geiben Im Mühlengrund 1, D-54318 Mertesdorf
Peter Geiben's 12 ha of vineyards are spread over some excellent Ruwer sites, namely those in Lorenshöf (Felsay and Mäuerchen) and Kasel (Nies'chen and Kehrnagel). The wine quality since the late 1990s puts him among the best growers in the Mosel-Saar-Ruwer. The wines have excellent ripeness (in a cool, mineral,

citrus/apple vein) and intensity, ranging from the light, stylish and fruit-intense Mäuerchen Kabinett to sweet, concentrated and elegant Nies'chen Auslese. An incredibly sweet and tangy Eiswein, the Kehrnagel, has smoky, spicy, mineral and honeyed aromas and dried fruit flavours, deserving plenty of age. All the wines are extremely well priced for the quality. (PW)

O **Lorenzhöfer Mäuerchen** Riesling Kabinett★★ £B
O **Lorenzhöfer** Riesling Spätlese★★ £B Riesling Auslese Gold Capsule★★★ £D Eiswein★★★★ £F
O **Kaseler Nies'chen** Riesling Spätlese★★★ £B Riesling Auslese Long Gold Capsule★★★★ £E
O **Kaseler Kehrnagel** Eiswein★★★★★ £G

WGT. KARTHÄUSERHOF www.karthaeuserhof.com A: OWL, CTy, F&R, SVS, Has, Sel

Owner: Christoph Tyrell Weingut Karthäuserhof, D-54292 Trier-Eitelsbach
Christoph Tyrell's historic Ruwer estate is one the great names of the Mosel-Saar-Ruwer. The 19 ha of vineyards are based on the famous Eitelsbacher Karthäuserhofberg site, which produces vivid, intense, elegant expressions of Riesling. Ludwig Breiling has made the wines in recent vintages and a very high quality standard has been set. Flavours range from apple, white peach, blackcurrant, citrus and mineral in Kabinett and Spätlese (usually produced in a Trocken or Feinherb version as well) to nectarine, peach and exotic fruits in Auslese and Eiswein. The latter show marvellous richness as well as the same vibrant acidity and long finish seen in all the wines. In any given vintage bottlings of Auslese from individual numbered casks can be superb (the Nr 24 in 2003 for instance); their purity and class are apparent even when starting out intense and closed. QbA Riesling has decent weight and flavour and a dry Weissburgunder is also made. (PW)

O **Eitelsbacher Karthäuserhofberg** Riesling QbA★ £B Riesling Kabinett★★ £B
O **Eitelsbacher Karthäuserhofberg** Riesling Spätlese Trocken★★★ £C Riesling Spätlese★★★ £C
O **Eitelsbacher Karthäuserhofberg** Riesling Riesling Auslese★★★★ £D Eiswein❍❍❍❍❍ £H

WGT. KELLER Rheinhessen www.weingut-keller.de A: HRp, F&R

Owner: Klaus Keller Bahnhofstrasse 1, D-67592 Flörsheim-Dalsheim
Away from the Rheinterrassen (the steep slopes between Oppenheim and Nackenheim), the Rheinhessen doesn't have that much to offer, yet Klaus Keller and his son Klaus-Peter are showing that outstanding wines are possible in the hilly countryside around Flörsheim-Dalsheim, where they have 12.5 ha, almost half planted to Riesling but a quarter to Weissburgunder and Grauburgunder. They produce some fine dry wines but better still are the marvellously exuberant sweeter styles with scintillating fruit richness and excellent balance and length of flavour. There is not perhaps the sheer class or elegance that more northern sites can bring but the rich, exotic fruit intensity is hard to resist. As well as very small amounts of outstanding Trockenbeerenauslese, some Spatburgunder is made. All the better wines deserve some age and will keep for a decade. (PW)

O **Dalsheimer Hubacker** Riesling Kabinett Trocken★ £B
O **Dalsheimer Hubacker** Riesling Spätlese★★ £C Riesling Spätlese Trocken★★ £C
O **Dalsheimer Hubacker** Riesling Auslese★★★ £F Riesling Auslese 3 Sterne★★★★ £G

VON KESSELSTATT Mosel www.kesselstatt.com A: Lay, ABy, BBR, Cam, Odd, JNi

Owner: Günther Reh family Schlossgut Marienlay, D-54317 Morscheid
The Günter Reh family possess 38 ha of vineyard land in the Mosel, all of it planted to Riesling and much of it in leading sites. Yields are moderate and the aim is for natural, unmanipulated wines. Fermentation is in stainless steel with extended ageing on the fine lees. Typically the wines are properly ripe and clean with fruit emphasised and good acid balance, though sulphur levels can detract from the wines. At their best they also reflect something of their origins if not necessarily competing with the top examples from a given site. Those rated below include wines from most but not all the famous sites that are regularly made. There are several more good wines besides, though 'RK' Riesling and new dry Palais Kesselstatt Riesling are not amongst them. (PW)

O Josephöfer Riesling Kabinett★ £B Riesling Spätlese★★ £C
O Graacher Domprobst Riesling Spätlese★★ £C
O Kaseler Nies'chen Riesling Kabinett★ £B Riesling Spätlese★★ £C Riesling Eiswein★★★★ £G
O Piesporter Goldtröpfchen Riesling Spätlese★★★ £C Riesling Auslese★★★ £D
O Scharzhofberger Riesling Spätlese Long Gold Capsule★★★ £D Riesling Eiswein★★★★ £G

KOEHLER-RUPRECHT Pfalz   A: Win

Owner: Bernd Philippi Weinstrasse 84, D-67169 Kallstadt
The predisposition here is for dry wines with good structure. With only a little more than half the 12.5-ha estate planted to Riesling there are also examples of Pinot Blanc, Pinot Gris, Chardonnay and Pinot Noir. Barrel-fermented versions of the whites are labelled 'Philippi'. All show good ripeness, usually with integrated lees and oak character. Pinot Noir can be particularly good in the warmest vintages. Some Gewürztraminer and Scheurebe are also made but Riesling is once again the main attraction. It comes from the very good Kallstadter Saumagen site where limestone soils give vigorous, ripe fruited and minerally examples. 'R' bottlings are particularly good with added concentration and character, usually with a spicy botrytis influence. After a delayed release 'R' wines will continue to age superbly. Generally speaking, all the Rieslings age very well (losing any youthful reductive aromas) though there have been occasional exceptions. Bernd Philippi is also a partner in the Douro estate QUINTA DA CARVALHOSA. (PW)
O Kallstadter Saumagen Riesling Spätlese Trocken★★ £C Auslese Trocken★★★ £D
O Kallstadter Saumagen Riesling Auslese 'R'★★★★ £D Riesling Eiswein★★★★★ £G
O Pinot Blanc Philippi★★ £C   **O Chardonnay** Philippi★★ £C   ● **Pinot Noir** Philippi★★ £D

PETER JAKOB KÜHN Rheingau www.weingutpjkuehn.de   A: CTy, Tan

Owner: Peter & Angela Jakob Kühn Mühlstrasse 70, D-65375 Oestrich im Rheingau
Quality has been on the up and up here in the past decade and Peter Jakob Kühn now makes exemplary Rheingau Rieslings from his long-established family estate with 13 ha of organically tended vineyards. Kühn's Oestrich Lenchen wines combine the richness of the Rheingau with the elegance of the Mosel. Off-dry Riesling Kabinett is one of the very best in Germany at this level, with beautifully defined fruit and bright but not harsh acidity. The Spätlese has exquisite sweet fruit and lovely balance, while the Auslese is very pure, concentrated, wonderfully poised and complex (more like a Beerenauslese in style in 2003). Outstanding Beerenauslese (stunning in 2003) with a waxy, honeyed quality and superb preserved-fruit and botrytis richness contrasts with a vibrant, very sweet, but less rich or complex Eiswein. Doosberg provides complex, expressive dry wines. All the wines deserve some age and the sweeter styles should have at least five years. Some Spätburgunder is also made. The debate surrounding closures is also having an impact in Germany. While the Stelvin cap is now increasingly widely used Peter Jakob Kühn has bottled some of his wines under a 'crown seal' in order to eliminate taint of any kind. (PW)
O Oestricher Doosberg Riesling Zwei Trauben QbA★★ £C Riesling Erstes Gewächs★★★ £D
O Oestricher Lenchen Riesling Kabinett★★★ £C Riesling Spätlese★★★ £C
O Oestricher Lenchen Riesling Auslese★★★★ £F Riesling Beerenauslese★★★★★ £H
O Oestricher Lenchen Riesling Eiswein★★★★ £H

FRANZ KÜNSTLER Rheingau www.weingut-kuenstler.de   A: RsW, HRp, DWS, NYg, Has

Owner: Gunter Künstler Freiherr-vom-Stein-Ring 3/Kirchstrasse 38, D-65239 Hochheim
Since the mid-1990s Gunter Künstler has been able to draw upon extensive vineyards spread over the Hochheim slopes, having added those of the Aschrott estate to an existing estate first established by his father in 1965. The 26 ha include the top sites of Hochheimer Hölle, Kirchenstück and Domdechaney. The more traditionally made wines, such as a fine Kirchenstück Spätlese, show wonderful peach and nectarine richness, well checked by good acidity. Gunter Künstler has also made a feature of producing completely dry wines from an Auslese level of ripeness, with a powerful honeyed Kirchenstück and a splendidly complex, ripe and distinctive Hölle version. A characterful, weighty example from the Stielweg

vineyard shows a coarser, botrytised influence and is not as convincing. Non-dry examples of Auslese, such as that from Domdechaney (or a very good Hölle Gold Capsule in 2003) show lovely fruit richness and depth. There's also very sweet, deep, rich Beerenauslese and Trockenbeerenauslese. Other wines include a stylish, elegant if oaky cherry-fruited Pinot Noir (Spätburgunder) Auslese, its price presumably pushed up by local demand, and an attractive sparkling wine, Non Plus Cuvée M (Pinot Noir/Chardonnay), in which the strawberry, cherry notes of Pinot dominate. (PW)

O **Hochheimer Hölle** Riesling Spätlese Trocken★★ £D Riesling Auslese Trocken★★★ £E
O **Hochheimer Hölle** Riesling Beerenauslese★★★★ £H Riesling Trockenbeerenauslese★★★★★ £H
O **Hochheimer Kirchenstück** Riesling Spätlese★★★ £D Riesling Auslese Trocken★★★ £E
O **Hochheimer Kirchenstück** Riesling Trockenbeerenauslese★★★★★ £H
O **Hochheimer Domdechaney** Riesling Auslese★★★ £E
O **Hochheimer Stielweg** Riesling Auslese Trocken★★ £E
O **Hochheimer Reichstal** Riesling Kabinett★★ £B ● **Pinot Noir** Auslese★★ £F

___

ANDREAS LAIBLE Baden www.weingut-laible.de

Owner: Andreas & Ingrid Laible Am Bühl 6, D-77770 Durbach
This relatively little-known (outside of Germany at any rate) producer makes wines of a quality unprecedented in the Ortenau area of Baden. From just 6 ha of vineyards there is consistently high quality, not just in Riesling (Klingelberger as it is called here) but also in Gewürztraminer and Scheurebe. All the wines come from the Durbacher Plauelrain site and the top examples have lovely concentrated, fruit, with depth, body and good acidity. The top wine is the Riesling Auslese Trocken, a rich, honeyed yet dry, concentrated and complex example with great length of flavour. A richer Achat bottling of Riesling Spätlese Trocken contrasts with a racier regular version that offers a cooler spectrum of fruit flavours. Gewürztraminer is lush, ripe and intense and there is a cocktail of fruit in a rich but well-balanced Scheurebe. Chardonnay, Grauburgunder and Spätburgunder are also made to a high standard. (PW)

O **Durbacher Plauelrain** Riesling Auslese Trocken★★★★ £D
O **Durbacher Plauelrain** Riesling Spätlese Trocken★★ £C Riesling Spätlese Trocken Achat★★★ £C
O **Durbacher Plauelrain** Gewürztraminer Auslese★★★ £C Scheurebe Auslese★★★ £C

___

WGT JOSEF LEITZ Rheingau www.leitz-wein.de   A: **WSS**, L&W, JNi

Owner: Johannes Leitz Theodor Heuss-Strasse 5, D-65385 Rudesheim
With 10 ha of vines in some of Rudesheim's best vineyards, Johannes Leitz is one of the Rheingau's rising stars. The results of improved vineyard health and more natural winemaking shine through in the wine quality. Vineyards such as Berg Schlossberg particularly lend themselves to the elegant, intense style of Rheingau Riesling he is making. Quality runs throughout the many different bottlings produced from ripe, attractive QbA or Kabinett examples to richer yet elegant, ripe mineral, peach and apricot fruited Spätlese, Auslese and Beerenauslese. Eiswein, such as that from Klosterberg, is tight, intense and long. Prädikat styles produced from each site vary from year to year. (PW)

O **Rudesheimer Berg Roseneck** Riesling Kabinett★★ £B Riesling Spätlese★★★ £D
O **Rudesheimer Berg Schlossberg** Riesling Spätlese★★★ £D
O **Rudesheimer Drachenstein** Riesling Beerenauslese★★★★ £H
O **Rudesheimer Magdalenenkreuz** Riesling Spätlese★★ £C
O **Rudesheimer Klosterberg** Riesling Eiswein★★★★ £H
O **Rudesheimer Kirchenpfad** Riesling Auslese★★★★ £F

___

CARL LOEWEN Mittel Mosel www.weingut-loewen.de   A: **HRp**, JAr

Owner: Karl-Josef Loewen Matthiasstrasse 30, D-54340 Leiwen
Karl-Josef Loewen has been a champion of the very good Laurentiuslay vineyard which lies at the heart of his 7-ha estate. Here he produces Rieslings with lovely finesse and expression: minerally and spicy with a suggestion of elderflower. They are also characterised by excellent balance and length of flavour. Bottlings

from individually numbered casks can be exceptionally good – for example the Nr 21 Auslese made in 2003. Varidor is a dry generic Riesling while an Alte Reben (old vine) version is also dry, if full and more New World-like. There is also a bright intense fruit in the wines from the under-rated Thörnicher Ritsch. When conditions permit he produces a splendid classy Leiwener Klostergarten Eiswein, with an interplay of preserved citrus and tropical fruit flavours. This, like all the wines, is very fairly priced. The ripe peachy 2003s are super, contrasting with cooler, more appley and restrained 2002s. (PW)

O **Leiwener Klostergarten** Riesling Kabinett★★ £B Riesling Eiswein★★★★★ £F
O **Thörnicher Ritsch** Riesling Spätlese★★★ £B Riesling Auslese★★★★ £C
O **Leiwener Laurentiuslay** Spätlese★★★ £B Riesling Auslese★★★ £C

DR LOOSEN   www.drloosen.com   A: WSS, GWW, JNi, HRp, Tan, NYg, L&S, SVS, Hrd

Owner: Ernst Loosen St Johannishof, D-54470 Bernkastel-Kues
Probably the best-known quality producer from the Mosel today, Ernst Loosen has achieved a remarkable transformation in both the quality and image of a 12-ha estate with some choice Mittel Mosel plots. The wines have lovely depth and intensity but also real elegance and a distinctive expression of their origins. Whether the splendid succulent fruit richness of Wehlener Sonnenuhr, the spice-lined finesse of Ürziger Würzgarten or the more exotic class of Erdener Prälat, there is excellent ripeness, definition and concentration that owes much to old vines and low yields. Wines are also made from the Erdener Treppchen and Graacher Himmelreich sites. The approach is organic and non-interventionist, though the wines (if drunk young) have sometimes shown a little too heavy a use of sulphur, something less apparent in the most recent vintages. All the wines should be kept for at least three to four years, except perhaps the widely seen Dr L, which can have good intensity and attractive fruit. A little Beerenauslese and Trockenbeerenauslese is also made. Ernst Loosen also produces excellent dry Rieslings at the J L WOLF estate, and another in Washington State in conjunction with CH. STE MICHELLE. (PW)

O **Ürziger Würzgarten** Riesling Spätlese★★★ £D Riesling Auslese★★★★ £E
O **Wehlener Sonnenuhr** Riesling Kabinett★★ £C Riesling Spätlese★★★ £D
O **Wehlener Sonnenuhr** Riesling Auslese★★★★ £E Riesling Auslese Gold Capsule★★★★★ £F
O **Erdener Prälat** Riesling Auslese★★★★ £F Riesling Auslese Gold Capsule★★★★★ £F
O **Erdener Treppchen** Riesling Kabinett★★ £C Riesling Spätlese★★★ £D Riesling Auslese★★★★ £E
O **Bernkasteler Lay** Riesling Kabinett★★ £C Riesling Eiswein★★★★★ £H
O **Riesling Dr 'L'** ★ £B

MAXIMIN GRÜNHAUS/VON SCHUBERT   www.vonschubert.com A: Rae, OWL, HRp

Owner: Dr Carl-Ferdinand von Schubert Maximin Grünhaus, D-54318 Mertesdorf
The most famous estate of the Ruwer Valley is based on the Maximin Grünhaus vineyards which, like those of Karthäuserhof on the other side of the river, face south-east on slopes running obliquely to the small Ruwer river. The estate has for the past two decades been in the capable hands of Dr Carl-Ferdinand von Schubert and his winemaker Alfons Heinrich. The heart of the solely owned site of 34 ha is the Abtsberg vineyard, which produces sublime Rieslings of outstanding expression and definition. Class and finesse are paramount to the style of the wines; overwhelming power and concentration are not sought. Apart from the ripest styles, delicious lime, mineral, floral, apple and white peach flavours prevail, but there is also the structure and intensity to age for years. Most splendid are the numbered Ausleses of varying richness (and price, £E to £F) but almost always of at least four-star quality. Some Beerenauslese is also sometimes made. Eiswein shows great finesse and lots of concentration and rich, ripe fruit in the best years but with cooler flavours and less concentration in less successful years. All the wines need at least three to four years' ageing for the fruit to emerge and any lingering fermentation odours to disappear. (PW)

O **Maximim Grünhauser Abtsberg** Riesling Kabinett★★ £C Riesling Spätlese★★★ £C
O **Maximim Grünhauser Abtsberg** Riesling Auslese★★★ £D Riesling Eiswein★★★★ £H
O **Maximim Grünhauser Herrenberg** Riesling Spätlese★★ £C

MARKUS MOLITOR   Mittel Mosel   www.wein-markus-molitor.de   A: BBR, F&R

Owner: Markus Molitor   Haus Klosterberg, D-54470 Bernkastel-Wehlen
Markus Molitor has 35 ha of vineyards from which he produces ripe and sweet styles of Riesling. The best of these are from the excellent Zeltinger Sonnenuhr in the heart of the Mittel Mosel. The wines are extraordinarily rich, concentrated, intense and ripe for the Mosel but they succeed in retaining sufficient acidity and balance to allow them to be either drunk young or kept (at least in the medium term). While a Riesling Kabinett can be disappointing, there is a honeyed, ripe, peach richness in versions of Riesling Spätlese and the best Auslese and a Beerenauslese show a deep marmalady botrytis character and a luscious richness. Eiswein has vibrant preserved citrus and grapefruit flavours but lacks the complexity of the very best. Sadly prices are very high and the Trockenbeerenauslese are reserved to be sold as *Versteigerungswein* (at auction). (PW)
O **Zeltinger Sonnenuhr** Riesling Spätlese★★★ £C
O **Zeltinger Sonnenuhr** Riesling Auslese★★★ £E Riesling Auslese 3 Sterne★★★★ £H
O **Zeltinger Sonnenuhr** Riesling Beerenauslese★★★★ £H
O **Bernkasteler Badstube** Riesling Eiswein★★★ £H

MÖNCHHOF/ROBERT EYMAEL   Mittel Mosel   www.moenchhof.de   A: RsW, Rae

Owner: Robert Eymael   Mönchhof, D-54539 Ürzig
Robert Eymael has been running the ancient Mönchhof estate since 1994. His 10 ha of vineyards are planted only to Riesling and concentrated on three of the finest sites of the Mittel Mosel: Ürziger Würzgarten, Erdener Treppchen and the great Erdener Prälat. The wines show classic delicacy, intensity and refined fruit flavours, especially at Spätlese and Auslese levels of ripeness. Wines from the Würzgarten (spice garden) of Urzig are famed for their spicy character. The Mönchhof examples show this characteristic spiciness, as well as hints of mineral, ripe peach and nectarine fruit. While there's currently not the concentration or length of flavour seen in the very best examples from these sites, prices aren't excessive for the quality. Also under Robert Eymael's direction (and an interesting contrast) are the wines of the small estate of J J CHRISTOFFEL. (PW)
O **Ürziger Würzgarten** Riesling Spätlese £C Riesling Auslese★★★★ £D
O **Erdener Prälat** Riesling Auslese★★★ £D
O **Erdener Treppchen** Riesling Kabinett★★ £B Riesling Spätlese Trocken★★ £C Riesling Auslese★★★ £D

GEORG MOSBACHER   Pfalz   www.georg-mosbacher.de   A: HRp

Owner: Mosbacher family   Weinstrasse 27, D-67147 Forst
The lion's share of the Mosbacher family's 15 ha is planted to Riesling. Richard Mosbacher works with his daughter Sabine and her husband Jürgen Düringer to give excellent expression to plots of vines in some of the leading Pfalz vineyards. The *Grosses Gewächs* wines possess fresh, ripe intense fruit and good flavour depth yet there is real differentiation between each site. The striking mineral intensity and depth in the powerful Forster Ungeheuer (grown on mid-slope sandstone soils) contrasts with the open, expressive Deidesheimer Kieselberg (from stoney sandy soils), which includes some exotic fruit flavours. Vines from the small Forster Freundstück site also provide *Grosses Gewächs* Riesling as well as favouring Eiswein production. Good Rieslings are also made from lesser-known sites around Deidesheim and Forst. There is also some Weissburgunder and Gewürtraminer. More wines will be rated in future editions. (PW)
O **Forster Ungeheuer** Riesling Spätlese Trocken Grosses Gewächs★★★ £D
O **Forster Freundstück** Riesling Spätlese Trocken Grosses Gewächs★★★ £D
O **Deidesheimer Kieselberg** Riesling Spätlese Trocken Grosses Gewächs★★★ £D

MÜLLER-CATOIR   Pfalz   A: HRp, N&P, F&R

Owner: Jakob Heinrich Catoir   Mandelring 25, D-67433 Haardt
A wine estate made great through the efforts of winemaker Hans-Günther Schwarz. The 20 ha of vineyards

are not on the Pfalz's most famous sites but very intense, fine wines are produced across a range of lesser-known vineyards. The wines provide a real contrast to the exquisite balance and finesse seen in the top Mosel wines as, although well-balanced and fine, they are characterised more by their power and thrilling intensity, which have earned them an almost fanatical following. Those from Rieslaner are the most individual and characterful of all, with remarkable sweetness and power at Auslese level and higher. Riesling, though intense, doesn't always have quite the depth or concentration seen in other top Pfalz examples. Sweet, exotic Scheurebe and good dry examples of Grauburgunder, Weissburgunder and Muskateller are also made. (PW)

O **Gimmeldinger Mandelgarten** Riesling Auslese★★★ £F
O **Gimmeldinger Schlössel** Rieslaner Spätlese Trocken★★ £C
O **Mussbacher Eselshaut** Rieslaner Spätlese★★ £D   Rieslaner Auslese★★★ £E
O **Mussbacher Eselshaut** Rieslaner Trockenbeerenauslese❂❂❂❂❂ £H
O **Haardter Bürgergarten** Riesling Spätlese Trocken★ £C   Rieslaner Beerenauslese★★★★ £G
O **Haardter Bürgergarten** Muskateller Trocken★★ £C
O **Haardter Herrenletten** Riesling Spätlese Trocken★ £C
O **Haardter Mandelring** Scheurebe Spätlese★★ £C   Scheurebe Auslese★★★ £F

EGON MÜLLER/SCHARZHOF   Saar   www.scharzhof.de   A: **J&B, DAy, OWL**, HRp

Owner: Egon Müller Scharzhof, D-54459 Wiltingen

Egon Müller IV now runs an estate with a reputation like no other in Germany. The fame of the Scharzhofberg site and the prices that the top sweet wines command align it with the most prestigious domaines in the world. The closest village to the south-east-facing slopes is Wiltingen but this is not included in the wines' names. As well as the wines from 8 ha of estate vineyards the wines from the 4-ha Le Gallais estate are produced here. The latter come from Braune Kupp north of Wiltingen, which, unlike those of Scharzhofberg (in a side valley), lies above the river Saar itself. The top sweet wines start out firm, intense and taut but have tremendous underlying concentration with the potential to last for decades. Small amounts of Trockenbeerenauslese and Eiswein (both of five-star quality) are made when conditions permit. As well as regular versions of Spätlese and Auslese, several superior, numbered versions are also released. All need at least ten years' age. Almost all the wines are sold at auction (so prices can vary considerably). Only a basic Schwarhof Riesling, a Kabinett and a Spätlese are reasonably affordable, if not great value. (PW)

O **Scharzhofberger** Riesling Auslese★★★★ £G   Riesling Beerenauslese❂❂❂❂❂ £H
O **Scharzhofberger** Riesling Kabinett★★ £C   Riesling Spätlese★★★ £E
Le Gallais
O **Wiltinger Braune Kupp** Riesling Spätlese★★ £D   Riesling Auslese Gold Capsule★★★★ £H

DR PAULY-BERGWEILER   Mittel Mosel   www.pauly-bergweiler.com   A: **OWL**

Owner: Dr Peter Pauly   Gestade 15, D-54470 Bernkastel-Kues

This producer comprises two estates. In addition to the Pauly-Bergweiler estate are the vineyards of Peter Nicolay that have come from Dr Pauly's wife's family. Lighter, simpler styles of Riesling are better made than most, while there is lovely definition and refinement in the Prädikat wines. The family is fortunate to have nearly 2 ha of vineyards in the Bernkasteler Badstube am Doctorberg; wines from here retain a minerally elegance whilst building in richness with age. Riesling Spätlese (and sometimes higher ripeness levels) is also made from Graacher Himmelreich and Wehlener Sonnenuhr. Wines from the Peter Nicolay estate include Riesling Spätlese and Auslese from Ürziger Goldwingert and Erdener Prälat. (PW)

Dr Pauly-Bergweiler
O **Riesling** Dr Pauly Classic★ £B   O **Riesling** Dr Pauly Noble House★ £B
O **Erdener Treppchen** Riesling Selection★★ £B
O **Bernkasteler Badstube am Doctorberg** Riesling Spätlese★★★ £C   Riesling Auslese★★★ £D

JOH JOS PRÜM Mittel Mosel   A: J&B, OWL, JAr, HRp

Owner: Dr Manfred & Wolfgang Prüm Uferallee 19, D-54470 Bernkastel-Wehlen
The famed 14.5-ha estate of Dr Manfred Prüm is centred on the great Wehlener Sonnenuhr site but also includes Zeltinger Sonnenuhr, Graacher Himmelreich and Bernkasteler Lay. The wines are justly renowned for their longevity and the refinement that ageing brings. In fact, a wonderful, racy intensity and minerally elegance used only to become apparent with several years' age but the most recent vintages can be drunk quite young. After a decade or more a Spätlese can show a delicate toastiness and subtle, honeyed perfume preceding a beautifully delineated, fruit-filled palate. The Auslese-level wines retain a finesse and delicacy seen in Kabinett and Spätlese wines but add more depth and intensity to riper fruit flavours, including peach and apricot, rather than white peach and apple. Five-star Beerenauslese and Trockenbeerenauslese wines are sold at auction and can be difficult to obtain. Late bottling means the wines are usually a year behind most other producers, becoming available only in the second year after the vintage. (PW)
O **Wehlener Sonnenuhr** Riesling Kabinett★★ £C Riesling Spätlese★★★ £C
O **Wehlener Sonnenuhr** Riesling Auslese★★★★ £E Riesling Auslese Gold Capsule✪✪✪✪✪ £H
O **Graacher Himmelreich** Riesling Kabinett★★ £C Riesling Spätlese★★★ £C

ÖKONOMIERAT REBHOLZ Pfalz www.oekonomierat-rebholz.de

Owner: Hansjörg Rebholz Weinstrasse 54, D-76833 Siebeldingen
Although he is based in the less-celebrated southern part of Pfalz, Hansjörg Rebholz manages to make some of the region's best wines. Don't expect the power or weight of the likes of BÜRKLIN-WOLF, rather a very fine, intense, *terroir*-derived expression of Riesling. The cool, pure mineral intensity of the Kastanienbusch from red slate soils contrasts with the minerally warmth derived from the gravel and sandstone of the Im Sonnenschein site. Good as these are, only a little over a third of the estate's 14 ha of vineyard are planted to Riesling. Fifty per cent is comprised of the Pinots (Blanc, Gris and Noir) and Chardonnay. The Siebeldingen Im Sonnenschein Weisser Burgunder is a superb example of this grape. It comes from a more fossil-rich part of the vineyard than the Riesling and is very composed and complex, on an altogether different quality level from most German examples. Spätburgunder is also made to exacting standards from the same site but we have yet to taste it. The wines rated below are but a few of those produced. (PW)
O **Birkweiler Kastanienbusch** Riesling Spätlese Trocken Grosses Gewächs★★★★ £E
O **Siebeldingen im Sonnenschein** Riesling Spätlese Trocken Grosses Gewächs★★★ £D
O **Siebeldingen im Sonnenschein** Weisser Burgunder Spätlese Trocken Grosses Gewächs★★★ £D

BALTHASAR RESS Rheingau www.ress-wine.com   A: May

Owner: Stefan & Christian Ress Rheinallee 7, D-65347 Hattenheim
The Ress wines have a slightly chequered past in terms of quality, at times lacking a little definition or depth depending on the wine and vintage, and occasionally ageing a little quickly. Father (Stefan) and son manage a substantial 33 ha of vineyards that includes parcels in some of the best sites around Hattenheim. The recent trio of excellent vintages has made for a more consistent showing with many of the Rieslings typified by an attractive and elegant expression of citrus and nectarine fruit (and a mineral influence in some) backed by fine acidity. There's still not the extra intensity, depth or concentration of the Rheingau's best but their accessiblity and refined, pleasing style will deservedly attract more wine drinkers to German Riesling. Flavoursome, gently creamy Weissburgunder is also made. The wines listed below are but a few from an extensive range. (PW)
O **Hattenheimer Nussbrunnen** Riesling Erstes Gewächs★★★ £D Riesling Auslese★★★ £D
O **Rüdesheimer Berg Schlossberg** Riesling Erstes Gewächs★★★ £D
O **Rüdesheimer Berg Rottland** Riesling Erstes Gewächs★★★ £D
O **Hochheimer Steilweg** Riesling Spätlese Trocken★★ £B
O **Hattenheimer Schutzenhaus** Riesling Kabinett Trocken★★ £B O **Weissburgunder** Trocken★ £B

MAX FERD. RICHTER Mosel www.maxferdrichter.com   A: **CTy**, Tan, Res, BBR, SVS, F&M

Owner: Richter family Hauptstrasse 37/85, D-54486, Mülheim-Mosel

Dr Dirk Richter is the current director of this family estate, established over 300 years ago. The 15 ha of vineyards are in some of the Mittel Mosel's best sites. There is a characteristic ripeness and intensity, and the fine acidity and the class of the top vineyards comes through. No two wines are quite the same: a complex, intense, apricotty Juffer-Sonnenuhr Spätlese, for instance, contrasts with the more citrus elegance of Graacher Himmelreich Spätlese. The small *Alleinbesitz* (solely owned vineyard) of Mülheimer Helenenkloster consistently produces an outstanding Eiswein – a sweet and tangy potion of citrus peel, dried peach, spice and more exotic flavours that lingers long in the mouth. The Veldenzer Elisenberg vineyard is also under the sole ownership of the family and the source of fine Rieslings (including an excellent Cask 60 Auslese in 2003). Prices are fair, a good Richter Estate QbA included. (PW)

O **Graacher Domprobst** Riesling Spätlese Halbtrocken★★ £B Riesling Auslese★★★ £C
O **Graacher Himmelreich** Riesling Kabinett★★ £B Riesling Spätlese★★★ £B
O **Oehlener Sonnenuhr** Riesling Kabinett★★ £B Riesling Spätlese★★★ £C
O **Brauneberger Juffer** Riesling Kabinett★★ £C Riesling Spätlese★★★ £C
O **Brauneberger Juffer-Sonnenuhr** Riesling Spätlese★★★ £C Riesling Auslese★★★★ £D
O **Mülheimer Helenenkloster** Riesling Eiswein★★★★★ £H

ST. URBANS-HOF Mittel Mosel www.urbans-hof.de   A: **FEM**, SVS

Owner: Nik Weis Urbanusstrasse 16, D-54340, Leiwen

For fine Mosel wines that are fully ripe with extra intensity yet without sacrificing their elegance or individuality, this estate is hard to beat. Young Nik Weis is making the most of his family's considerable viticultural resource of 38 ha planted mostly to Riesling and his winemaker Rudolf Hoffmann is clearly able to harness the potential of fruit that is riper and more concentrated than most. Piesporter Goldtröpfchen wines, from a particularly steep part of the vineyard just above the river's edge, show rich, intense blackcurrant, citrus and peach fruit, yet elegance too. The Ockfener Bockstein wines are splendidly individual with a smokey and mineral, very ripe citrus character at Auslese level. The wines from Leiwener Laurentiuslay are of similar quality. Highish sulphur levels can detract at Kabinett level but these wines too will age and will then taste immeasurably cleaner. A small amount wine is usually designated Gold Capsule and Eiswein is also produced from Leiwener Klostergarten. (PW)

O **Piesporter Goldtröpfchen** Riesling Kabinett★★ £B Riesling Spätlese★★★ £C Riesling Auslese★★★★ £E
O **Leiwener Laurentiuslay** Riesling Spätlese★★ £C
O **Ockfener Bockstein** Riesling Kabinett★ £B Riesling Spätlese★★★ £C Riesling Auslese★★★★ £E
O **Wiltinger Schlangengraben** Riesling Auslese Gold Capsule★★★★ £E

HORST SAUER Franken www.weingut-horst-sauer.de   A: **NYg**, J&B

Owner: Horst Sauer Bocksbeutelstrasse 14, D-97332 Escherndorf

In the space of a few vintages, Horst Sauer has emerged as the best producer in Franken and one of the new stars of Germany. There is both complexity and individuality in all the better wines, while elegance and well-detailed fruit are evident even in Riesling Kabinett. From a total of almost 10 ha of vineyards in one of Franken's most prized vineyard sites, Escherndorfer Lump, there is Silvaner of similar quality to Riesling and both have excellent balance and composure in dry and sweeter styles. Quite superb Riesling Beerenauslese and Riesling and Silvaner Trockenbeerenauslese all combine richness and expression; intense spice, mineral and dried fruit flavours linger long on the finish. A Scheurebe Spätlese is an excellent example of this variety too and even Müller-Thurgau has good intensity and shows a light minerally elegance. Partially *barriqued* Sennsucht Silvaner is a successful diversion in a more international style. Some Pinot Noir rosé is also made. (PW)

O **Escherndorfer Lump** Riesling Kabinett Trocken★★ £B Riesling Spätlese Trocken★★★ £C
O **Escherndorfer Lump** Riesling Beerenauslese★★★★★ £F Riesling Eiswein★★★★★ £G

O **Escherndorfer Lump** Riesling Trockenbeerenauslese❍❍❍❍❍ £G
O **Escherndorfer Lump** Silvaner Trockenbeerenauslese❍❍❍❍❍ £G
O **Escherndorfer Lump** Silvaner Spätlese Trocken★★★ £C Silvaner Auslese★★★★ £E
O **Eschendorfer Lump** Scheurebe Spätlese★★★ £C O **Müller-Thurgau**★ £B
O **Sehnsucht** Silvaner Spätlese Trocken★★ £C

WILLI SCHAEFER Mittel Mosel   A: Rae, HRp, Tan, F&R

Owner: Willi Schaefer Hauptstrasse 130, D-54470 Graach
There are arguably no finer examples of Rieslings from the village of Graach than those from Willi Schaefer's extremely modest 3.2 ha. These pure, intense wines are not in the least overpowering but are wonderfully expressive and long with more richness at Auslese level. Those from Domprobst are superior to those from Himmelreich, being consistently finer, riper and fuller. That said, even the Himmelreich Kabinett can show fine apple, grapefruit and lemon that contrast with the peachier, mineral intensity in Domprobst Kabinett and Spätlese. A perfect balance of acidity and concentrated, riper fruit is typical in the Domprobst Auslese. Some individually numbered casks of Auslese from both Domprobst and Himmelreich are also made, as is a little Beerenauslese. (PW)
O **Graacher Domprobst** Riesling Kabinett★★ £B Riesling Spätlese★★★ £C Riesling Auslese★★★★ £D
O **Graacher Himmelreich** Riesling Kabinett★ £B Riesling Spätlese★★ £C

SCHLOSS LIESER Mittel Mosel www.weingut-schloss-lieser.de   A: J&B, HRp, Tan, F&R

Owner: Thomas Haag Am Markt 1, D-54470 Lieser
Thomas Haag, who is the son of Wilhelm Haag of the Fritz HAAG estate, has been responsible for the much-improved quality that has revitalised this once-famous 7.5-ha estate centred on the Lieser Niederberg Helden site. His taut, intense and ripe Rieslings add richness and complexity in the higher Prädikat styles and with age. Auslese wines (there is typically more than one bottling) in particular attain the exquisite combination of finesse and richness that exemplifies the best sites of the Mittel Mosel. The only negative point about some recent releases has been the tendency to an excessive sulphur or sulphides taint, however most should lose this with additional bottle age. A little 3 Sterne Auslese and some Beerenauslese are also made. The wines are reasonably priced. (PW)
O **Lieser Niederberg Helden** Riesling Auslese 1 Stern★★★ £C Riesling Auslese 2 Sterne★★★★ £E
O **Lieser Niederberg Helden** Riesling Spätlese★★ £B O **Riesling** Kabinett★★ £B

SCHLOSS SAARSTEIN Saar www.saarstein.de   A: CTy, Has, SVS, C&R

Owner: Christian Ebert Schloss Saarstein, D-54455 Serrig
Christian Ebert runs this 10-ha estate bought by his father in 1956. It is based, for the most part, on the wholly-owned Serriger Schloss Saarsteiner vineyard, where steep slopes on forest-topped hillside afford the best protection in what is otherwise at the margins for successful viticulture. The grapes struggle to get fully ripe, resulting in a very cool green fruits character, especially in cooler vintages. The best acid/sugar balance is usually seen in Auslese level wines; below this the sweetness can initially mask the fruit purity underneath (*Süssreserve* sometimes being added to check the high acidity levels). Patience is needed but the crushed blackcurrant leaf, green apple, citrus and mineral complexity becomes increasingly enticing with age. Alcohol levels are always low, even by Mosel standards. As well as a little Beerenauslese and Eiswein, some Weissburgunder is also produced. (PW)
O **Serriger Schloss Saarsteiner** Riesling Kabinett★ £B Riesling Spätlese★★ £C
O **Serriger Schloss Saarsteiner** Riesling Auslese★★★ £D Riesling Auslese Gold Capsule★★★★ £E

SCHLOSS SCHÖNBORN Rheingau www.schoenborn.de   A: Lwt, C&B

Owner: Graf von Schönborn Hauptstrasse 53, D-65347 Hattenheim
Schloss Schönborn has a collection of 50ha of the very best vineyard land in the Rheingau, including

Erbacher Marcobrunn, that must be the envy of many a small grower. Despite some quality ups and downs there are indications of a more sustained revival over recent vintages. As well as improvement in the sweeter styles there is increasing depth and texture in *Erstes Gewächs* bottlings. Most wines show a little sulphur when young but this is less marked with age and the best vintages will age very well indeed. (PW)

O **Erbacher Marcobrunn** Riesling Kabinett★ £C Riesling Spätlese★★ £C Riesling Erstes Gewächs★★ £C
O **Hattenheimer Pfaffenberg** Riesling Spätlese★★ £C Riesling Erstes Gewächs★★ £C
O **Rüdesheimer Berg Schlossberg** Riesling Auslese★★★ £E
O **Rüdesheimer Berg Rottland** Riesling Auslese★★★ £E

SCHLOSS VOLLRADS Rheingau www.schlossvollrads.com A: **Lib**, FSt, Sel

Owner: Nassauische Sparkasse Schloss Vollrads, D-65375 Oestrich-Winkel
This celebrated Rheingau estate with a history stretching back to the 14th century has been put on a new footing since come under the ownership of a bank. Since 1999 the estate and winemaking direction has come from Dr Rowald Hepp and quality from a massive 58 ha of vineyards, planted entirely to Riesling, is seeing a slow but steady return. The 2002 vintage seems a significant leap forward with good minerality and depth even at Kabinett level but there is still the potential for even better wines. Intense ripe peach and citrus fruit at Spätlese level (and apricot at higher ripeness levels) combined with good balanced acidity promises wines of good concentration, definition and ripeness. Some Beerenauslese and Trockenbeerenauslese were also made in 2002. (PW)

O **Schloss Vollrads** Riesling QbA★ £B Riesling Kabinett★★ £C
O **Schloss Vollrads** Riesling Spätlese★★★ £D Riesling Auslese★★★ £E

SCHLOSSGUT DIEL Nahe www.schlossgut-diel.com A: **Win, OWL**, HRp, F&R

Owner: Armin Diel Schlossgut Diel, D-55452 Burg Layen
Armin Diel, a leading expert on German wines and a German television celebrity, finds time to make some very good wines from 16 ha centred on Dorsheim's top sites. His Rieslings are rich and intense but usually well-balanced. Even Kabinett from the Dorsheimer Pittermännchen is ripe, full and delicious while Spätlese from 2001, 02 and 03 make for a fascinating contrast. All share a floral, herbal, mineral, blackcurrant and nectarine profile but the more citrus, elegant 01 contrasts with thearomatic, complex 02 and the rich, very ripe, exuberant 03 (four stars). Diel also makes barrique-fermented Pinot Gris, Pinot Blanc (Cuvée Victor is a blend of the two) and Pinot Noir. 2002 Cuvée Caroline is plump, with good depth of ripe red fruits and oak if missing the dimension and class of fine Burgundy. Diel de Diel is a characterful basic blend of the three white varieties. (PW)

O **Dorsheimer Pittermännchen** Riesling Kabinett★★ £B Riesling Spätlese★★★ £D Riesling Auslese★★★★ £E
O **Dorsheimer Goldloch** Riesling Kabinett★★ £B Riesling Spätlese★★ £C Riesling Auslese★★★ £E
O **Dorsheimer Burgberg** Riesling Kabinett★★ £B Riesling Auslese★★★★ £E Riesling Eiswein★★★★ £H
O **Grauburgunder★★** £C O **Weissburgunder★★** £C O **Cuvée Victor★★** £E

SELBACH-OSTER Mittel Mosel www.selbach-oster.de A: **BBR**, JNi, Rae, JAr, HRp, L&W

Owner: Hans & Johannes Selbach Uferallee 23, D-54492 Zeltingen
This 13.8-ha estate has been in the family since 1661 and is now run by Johannes Selbach and his wife. Some fine Mosel wines are made, with depth, elegance and fine, cool, apple, citrus and white peach flavours. Particularly stylish is a classy Zeltinger Sonnenuhr Riesling Auslese, though this and other wines can sometimes suffer from a excessive level of sulphur. Though this is usually only detected in the wines when young, sometimes with age a more fixed sulphides character detracts from what are otherwise lovely wines. A little Beerenauslese and Trockenbeerenauslese are also made from Zeltinger Sonnenuhr. Wines labelled J&H Selbach are produced from bought-in grapes as part of a *négociant* business. (PW)

O **Wehlener Sonnenuhr** Riesling Kabinett★★ £B O **Zeltinger Schlossberg** Riesling Spätlese★★ £C
O **Zeltinger Sonnenuhr** Riesling Spätlese★★★ £C Riesling Auslese★★★ £C Auslese I stern★★★★ £D
O **Graacher Domprobst** Riesling Spätlese★★ £C Riesling Auslese★★ £D

TESCH   Nahe   www.weingut-tesch.de   A: HRp

Owner: Tesch family   Naheweinstrasse 99, D-55450 Langenlonsheim

Dr Martin Tesch, a biochemist, has been uncompromising in taking his family estate forward since 1996. He has focused mostly on dry wines, and from 2003 exclusively so. Almost 19 ha are planted predominantly to Riesling and a contrasting range of full, expressive examples are produced. Clean uncomplicated labels indicate only the vineyard (as many Pfalz producers now do). Karthäuser, Krone and St Remigiusberg are from Laubenheim; Königsschild and Löhrer Berg from Langenlonsheim. Karthäuser is at once fruit-driven and vigorous but has a certain subtlety as well, Königsschild impresses with size and ripeness of spiced citrus fruit and Krone (from mixed soils) is more mineral and herbal, but all are fine. The least expensive Riesling Unplugged is a good example of the new image, a quality dry Riesling certain to attract more consumers to German wines. Tastings of St Remigiusberg, potentially the top example, are insufficient for a rating. Good examples of riper, sweeter styles have also been made. (PW)

O **Karthäuser** Riesling Spätlese Trocken★★★ £B   O **Königsschild** Riesling Spätlese Trocken★★★ £B
O **Löhrer Berg** Riesling Spätlese Trocken★★ £B   O **Krone** Riesling Spätlese Trocken★★★ £B

GEHEIMRAT J WEGELER   Rheingau, Mosel & Pfalz   www.wegeler.com

Owner: Rolf Wegeler family   Friedensplatz 9-11, D-65375 Oestrich-Winkel

The Wegeler family have some outstanding vineyard sites totalling some 80 ha, the majority in the Rheingau but with significant holdings in the Mosel and Pfalz too. Oliver Haag, son of Wilhelm Haag (of FRITZ HAAG) directs the winemaking for some very good Rheingau wines. There is refinement and lovely definition in Winkeler Jesuitengarten, more weight and power in Berg Schlossberg. Other examples come from Berg Rottland, Oestricher Lenchen and Geisenheimer Rothenberg. From the Mosel there's a range of fine Spätlese and higher ripeness level wines from the Wehlener Sonnenuhr and Bernkasteler Doctor sites that show depth, richness and ripeness. More wines will be rated with further tastings. (PW)

Gutshaus Oestrich:
O **Winkeler Jesuitengarten** Riesling Grosses Gewächs★★★ £C
O **Rüdesheimer Berg Schlossberg** Riesling Grosses Gewächs★★★ £C
Gutshaus Bernkastel:
O **Bernkasteler Doctor** Riesling Spätlese★★★ £D   Riesling Auslese★★★★ £E
O **Wehlener Sonnenuhr** Riesling Auslese★★★ £E

ROBERT WEIL   Rheingau   www.weingut-robert-weil.com   A: HBJ, DWS, N&P, F&M

Owner: Suntory   Mühlberg 5, D-65399 Kiedrich

Wilhelm Weil continues the revitalisation of this large Rheingau estate with 65 ha of vineyards planted almost exclusively to Riesling. Since the 1990s the wines have shown remarkable intensity and richness, especially in the sweeter styles. At the top level the wines really excel but also sell for very high prices, at least partly fuelled by an almost cult following. At the heart of the domaine is one of the finest vineyards in the Rheingau, Kiedricher Gräfenberg, a site of historical significance and reputation. Everything possible is done to ensure that grapes are as rich, ripe and concentrated as possible and this is particularly apparent at the Auslese level and higher. The rich, sweet, apricot and dried-peach fruit, braced by tangy acidity, becomes more honeyed and magnificent with age. It is a shame to drink these wines too young. Wines from other vineyards, sold as Weil Estate Riesling, though reasonably lush and concentrated, don't show the elegance or lingering fruit intensity of the Kiedricher Gräfenberg wines. An *Erstes Gewächs* bottling from the Grafenberg site is now a cut above other Rheingau examples. Spätburgunder and tiny amounts of Trockenbeerenauslese are also made. (PW)

O **Kiedricher Gräfenberg** Riesling Spätlese★★★ £D   Riesling Erstes Gewächs★★★★ £E
O **Kiedricher Gräfenberg** Riesling Auslese★★★★ £F   Riesling Auslese Gold Capsule★★★★★ £H
O **Kiedricher Gräfenberg** Riesling Beerenauslese Gold Capsule❂❂❂❂ £H   Riesling Eiswein❂❂❂❂ £H

WGT. WITTMANN Rheinhessen www.wittmannweingut.com   A: **WBn,** Bal

Owner: Philipp Wittmann   Mainzer Strasse 19, D-67593 Westhofen
Quality from the 25-ha Wittmann estate has risen steadily over recent years and like Weingut KELLER it is breathing new life into the Rheinhessen. It is very much a family enterprise with tireless effort going into improving the health of the vineyard, which is certified as organic. Around half the plantings are Riesling, the best examples of which, both dry and sweet, are now really first class and stand comparison with top examples from other regions. 'S' selection wines have an extra intensity and rich fruit on the finish as well as the vibrant acidity that is common to all the range. The Auslese 'S' from Westhofer Morstein pulsates with honey, botrytis and ripe fruit. Patience is required for the powerful but austere *Grosses Gewächs* bottling from the top three vineyards, Aulerde, Kirschspiel and Morstein. The Aulerde starts out the tightest but has excellent potential, Kirschspiel shows excellent fruit and length of flavour and the stylish Morstein has a subtle spice, mineral and fruit complexity. In addition to good Silvaner and Weisser Burgunder (Pinot Blanc) some Chardonnay is also produced. More esoteric wines include sweet versions of Huxelrebe and Albalonga (a Rieslaner-Silvaner crossing). (PW)

O **Westhofener Kirschspiel** Riesling Grosses Gewächs★★★ £D
O **Westhofener Morstein** Riesling Grosses Gewächs★★★ £D   O **Westhofener** Riesling Trocken 'S'★★ £D
O **Westhofener Morstein** Riesling Spätlese £D   Riesling Auslese 'S'★★★★ £E
O **Westhofener Aulerde** Riesling Grosses Gewächs★★★ £D   Riesling Trockenbeerenauslese★★★★ £H
O **Silvaner** Trocken 'S'★★ £C   O **Weisser Burgunder** Trocken 'S'★★ £C

J L WOLF Pfalz www.jlwolf.com   A: **WSS,GWW,** Has,CPp, P&S

Owner: Ernst Loosen & Sturm family   Weinstrasse 1, D-67157 Wachenheim
Expertise and investment from Ernst Loosen quickly realised the potential from 10 ha of vineyards belonging to the country estate of Villa Wolf. The majority of the vines are Riesling planted in some of the Pfalz's most vaunted sites. Applying the same organic approach used for the DR LOOSEN wines in the Mosel, as well as reducing yields and improving vinification, has resulted in a high quality but contrasting range of wines. They are naturally broader and more powerful than Mosel styles but also very complex and classy at what is called 'grand cru' level, which includes Pechstein, Ungeheuer and Jesuitengarten from Forst, and Leinhöhle from Deidesheim. So called 'premier crus' from Wachenheim are also fine: Wachenheimer Belz is dry, intense and gently refined. There's good character too in 'village' wines, especially Wachenheimer Riesling. Least expensive are the 'estate' varietal wines sold under the Villa Wolf label; most widely seen is the Grauburgunder, exported as Pinot Gris. More pricey 'J L' labelled Spätburgunder and Grauburgunder are also made. (PW)

O **Forster Pechstein** Riesling Spätlese Trocken★★★★ £D
O **Deidesheimer Leinhöhle** Riesling Spätlese Trocken★★★ £D
O **Wachenheimer Belz** Riesling Spätlese Trocken★★★ £C
O **Wachenheimer** Riesling★★ £B   O **Forster** Riesling★★ £B

OTHER WINES OF NOTE

ACHAM-MAGIN (Pfalz) O **Forster Kirchenstück** Riesling Trocken Grosses Gewächs £D
O **Ruppertsberger Reiterpfad** Riesling Trocken Grosses Gewächs £D
ALDINGER (Württemberg) O **Fellbacher Lämmler** Riesling Spätlese Trocken Grosses Gewächs £D
BASTIAN (Mittelrhein) O **Bacharacher Posten** Riesling Grosses Gewächs £D   Riesling Auslese £D
J B BECKER (Rheingau) O **Wallufer Walkenberg** Riesling Spätlese Trocken £D   Auslese Trocken £C
BERGDOLT (Pfalz) O **Kirrweiler Mandelberg** Weissburgunder Spatlese Trocken £B   Grosses Gewächs £C
CASTELL'SCHES DOMÄNENAMT (Franken) O **Casteller Schlossberg** Riesling Spätlese Gr. Gewächs £D
O **Casteller Schlossberg** Silvaner Grosses Gewächs £D   Rieslaner Auslese £F

CRUSIUS (Nahe) O Schlossböckelheimer Felsenberg Riesling Spätlese £C
O Traiser Rotenfels Riesling Spatlese £C
DIEFENHARD (Rheingau) O Martinsthaler Langenberg Riesling Erstes Gewächs £C
RUDOLF FÜRST (Franken) O Bürgstadter Centgrafenberg Riesling Spätlese £C Riesling Eiswein £H
O Bürgstadter Centgrafenberg Weissburgunder Trocken £D ● Spätburgunder 'R' £F
KURT HAIN (Mosel) O Piesporter Goldtröpfchen Riesling Spätlese £B Riesling Auslese £C
FREIHERR VON HEDDESDORFF (Mosel) O Winninger Röttgen Riesling Spätlese £B Auslese £D
DR. HEGER (Baden) O Ihringer Winklerberg Weissburgunder Spätlese 3 sterne £D
O Ihringer Winklerberg Muskateller Spätlese 3 Sterne £D
● Ihringer Winklerberg Spätburgunder 3 Sterne £E
VON HÖVEL (Saar) O Oberemmeler Hütte Riesling Spätlese £B Riesling Auslese £C
WEINGUT JOHANNISHOF (Rheingau) O Johannisberger Klaus Riesling Spätlese £C
O Rüdesheimer Berg Rottland Riesling Auslese £E
KARL-HEINZ JOHNER (Baden) O Weisser Burgunder 'SJ' £E O Grauer Burgunder 'SJ' £E
● Spätburgunder 'SJ' £E
HERIBERT KERPEN (Mosel) O Wehlener Sonnenuhr Riesling Spätlese £B
AUGUST KESSELER (Rheingau) O Rüdesheimer Berg Schlossberg Riesling Spätlese Trocken £D
O Rüdesheimer Berg Roseneck Riesling Spätlese Gold Capsule £D
KNIPSER (Pfalz) O Dirmsteiner 'Himmelsrech' Mandelpfad Riesling Spätlese Trocken Gr. Gewächs £D
O Laumersheimer 'Steinbuckel' Mandelberg Riesling Spätlese Trocken Grosses Gewächs £D
KRUGER-RUMPF (Nahe) O Münsterer Kapellenberg Riesling Kabinett £B
O Münsterer Dautenpflänzer Riesling Spätlese £B Riesling Spätlese Trocken £B
O Münsterer Pittersberg Riesling Auslese £E
SYBILLE KUNTZ (Mosel) O Lieser Niederberg Helden Riesling Dreistern Spätlese £C
O Lieser Niederberg Helden Riesling Beerenauslese £H
LANGWERTH VON SIMMERN (Rheingau) O Erbacher Marcobrunn Riesling Kabinett £B
O Hattenheimer Wisselbrunnen Riesling Spätlese £C Riesling Beerenauslese £E
LINGENFELDER (Pfalz) O Freinsheimer Goldberg Riesling Spätlese Trocken £B
O Grosskarlbacher Osterberg Riesling Spätlese Halbtrocken £B
O Grosskarlbacher Burweg Scheurebe Kabinett Trocken £B
FÜRST LÖWENSTEIN (Rheingau) O Hallgarten Schönhell Riesling Erstes Gewächs £D
O Homburg Kallmuth Riesling Spätlese Trocken Grosses Gewächs £D
O Homburg Kallmuth Silvaner Spätlese Trocken Grosses Gewächs £D
ALFRED MERKELBACH (Mosel) O Ürziger Würzgarten Riesling Spätlese £B
MEULENHOF (Mosel) O Erdener Treppchen Riesling Spätlese £B Riesling Auslese £B
O Erdener Prälat Riesling Auslese £C
MEYER-NÄKEL (Ahr) ● Spätburgunder Trocken 'S' £E
WEINGUT PAULINSHOF (Mosel) O Brauneberger Juffer-Sonnenuhr Riesling Spätlese Trocken £C
O Brauneberger Juffer Riesling Spätlese £C O Brauneberger Kammer Riesling Spätlese Halbtrocken £C
O Kestener Paulinshofberger Riesling Auslese £D
WEINGUT PFEFFINGEN (Pfalz) O Ungsteiner Herrenberg Riesling Spätlese Trocken £B
S A PRÜM (Mosel) O Wehlener Sonnenuhr Riesling Spätlese £C Riesling Auslese Gold Capsule £H
O Graacher Himmelreich Riesling Eiswein £H
QUERBACH (Rheingau) O Oestrich Lenchen Riesling Trocken No.1 £B Riesling Trocken No.2 £B
O Oestrich Doosberg Riesling Erstes Gewächs £C
JOHANN PETER REINERT (Saar) O Kanzemer Altenberg Riesling Spätlese £B Riesling Auslese £C
O Schloss Reichartshausen Riesling Spätlese £C O Hattenheimer Schützenhaus Riesling Kabinett £B
WEINGUT SALWEY (Baden) O Chardonnay Kabinett £C
O Oberrotweiler Kirchberg Weissburgunder Spätlese Trocken Grosses Gewächs £D
O Oberrotweiler Kirchberg Spätburgunder Spätlese Trocken Grosses Gewächs £E
O Oberrotweiler Eichberg Ruländer Trockenbeerenauslese £G Ruländer Eiswein £H
SCHÄFER-FRÖHLICH (Nahe) O Monzinger Frühlingsplätzchen Riesling Grosses Gewächs £C
O Bockenauer Felseneck Riesling Auslese £E
SCHLOSS JOHANNISBERG O Riesling Spätlese £C Auslese £F Beerenauslese £H Eiswein £H
SCHLOSS REINHARTSHAUSEN (Rheingau) O Erbacher Marcobrunn Riesling Erstes Gewächs £D

SCHMITT'S KINDER (Franken) O Randersacker Pfülben Riesling Spätlese Grosses Gewächs £C
WEINGUT AM STEIN (Franken) O Würzburger Innere Leiste Riesling Grosses Gewächs £D
O Stettener Stein Riesling Eiswein £H
DR H THANISCH (ERBEN THANISCH) (Mosel) O Bernkasteler Lay Riesling Spätlese £C
O Bernkasteler Badstube Riesling Auslese £F O Bernkasteler Doctor Riesling Auslese £F
DR HEINZ WAGNER (Saar) O Ockfener Bockstein Riesling Spätlese £B Riesling Auslese £C
O Saarburger Rausch Riesling Spätlese £C
DR WEHRHEIM (Pfalz) O Birkweiler Kastanienbusch Riesling Spätlese Trocken Grosses Gewächs £D
O Birkweiler Mandelberg Weisser Burgunder Trocken Grosses Gewächs £D
HANS WIRSCHING (Franken) O Iphöfer Julius-Echter-Berg Riesling Spätlese Trocken Gr. Gewächs £D
O Iphöfer Julius-Echter-Berg Silvaner Spätlese Trocken Grosses Gewächs £D
O Iphöfer Kronsberg Weisser Burgunder Spätlese Trocken Grosses Gewächs £D
O Iphöfer Julius-Echter-Berg Rieslaner Beerenauslese £G
WÖHRWAG (Württemberg) O Untertürkheim Herzogenberg Riesling Spätlese Trocken Gr. Gewächs £D
ZILLIKEN (Saar) O Saarburger Rausch Riesling Spätlese £C Riesling Auslese £E

Author's choice (PW)

10 classic dry or off-dry Mosel Riesling

GRANS-FASSIAN O Leiwener Laurentiuslay Riesling Spätlese 'S'
WGT. FRITZ HAAG O Brauneberger Juffer-Sonnenuhr Riesling Spätlese
WGT. REINHOLD HAART O Piesporter Goldtröpfchen Riesling Spätlese
HEYMANN-LÖWENSTEIN O Winninger Uhlen Riesling 'Roth Lay' Erste Lage
KARLSMÜHLE O Kaseler Nies'chen Riesling Spätlese
WGT. KARTHÄUSERHOF O Eitelsbacher Karthäuserhofberg Riesling Spätlese Trocken
DR LOOSEN O Wehlener Sonnenuhr Riesling Spätlese
ST. URBANS-HOF O Ockfener Bockstein Riesling Spätlese
WILLI SCHAEFER O Graacher Domprobst Riesling Spätlese
SCHLOSS LIESER O Lieser Niederberg Helden Riesling Spätlese

15 more superior dry or off-dry Riesling

BASSERMANN-JORDAN O Deidesheimer Hohenmorgen Riesling Spätlese Trocken Grosses Gewächs
REICHSRAT VON BUHL O Forster Pechstein Riesling Grosses Gewächs
BÜRKLIN-WOLF O Forster Kirchenstück Riesling Grosses Gewächs
CHRISTMANN O Gimmeldingen Mandelgarten Riesling Trocken Grosses Gewächs
DÖNNHOFF O Niederhäusen Hermannshöhle Riesling Spätlese
EMRICH-SCHÖNLEBER O Monzinger Frühlingsplätzchen Riesling Spätlese
PETER JAKOB KÜHN O Oestricher Lenchen Riesling Kabinett
PRINZ VON HESSEN O Johannisberger Klaus Riesling Erstes Gewächs
WGT. KELLER O Dalsheimer Hubacker Riesling Spätlese Trocken
FRANZ KÜNSTLER O Hochheimer Hölle Riesling Auslese Trocken
ANDREAS LAIBLE O Durbacher Plauelrain Riesling Auslese Trocken
WEINGUT JOSEPH LEITZ O Rudesheimer Berg Schlossberg Riesling Spätlese
ÖKONOMIERAT REBHOLZ O Birkweiler Kastanienbusch Riesling Spätlese Trocken Grosses Gewächs
SCHLOSSGUT DIEL Dorsheimer Pittermännchen Riesling Spätlese
WGT. WITTMANN O Westhofener Kirchspiel Riesling Grosses Gewächs

10 stupendous German sweet wines

GEORG BREUER O Rauenthal Nonnenberg Riesling Auslese Gold Capsule

DÖNNHOFF O Oberhäuser Brücke Riesling Eiswein

GUNDERLOCH O Nackenheimer Rothenberg Riesling Beerenauslese

DR LOOSEN O Bernkasteler Lay Riesling Eiswein

MARKUS MOLITOR O Zeltinger Sonnenuhr Riesling Beerenauslese

MÜLLER-CATOIR O Mussbacher Eselshaut Rieslaner Trockenbeerenauslese

JOH JOS PRÜM O Wehlener Sonnenuhr Riesling Auslese Gold Capsule

MAX FERD. RICHTER O Mülheimer Helenenkloster Riesling Eiswein

HORST SAUER O Escherndorfer Lump Riesling Trockenbeerenauslese

ROBERT WEIL O Kiedricher Gräfenberg Riesling Auslese Gold Capsule

10 fine German whites not from Riesling

WGT. BERCHER O Burkheimer Feuerberg Weissburgunder Spätlese Trocken SE

EMRICH-SCHÖNLEBER O Monzinger Grauburgunder Spätlese Trocken

DR HEGER O Ihringer Winklerberg Muskateller Spätlese 3 sterne

ANDREAS LAIBLE O Durbacher Plauelrain Gewürztraminer Auslese

MÜLLER-CATOIR O Haardter Mandelring Scheurebe Auslese

HORST SAUER O Escherndorfer Lump Silvaner Auslese

JULUISSPITAL O Würzburger Stein Silvaner Spätlese Trocken

ÖKONOMIERAT REBHOLZ O Siebeldingen im Sonnenschein Weisser Burgunder Spätlese Trocken Grosses Gewächs

WEINGUT SALWEY O Oberrotweiler Kirchberg Weissburgunder Spätlese Trocken Grosses Gewächs

HANS WIRSCHING O Iphofer Julius-Echter-Berg Rieslaner Beerenauslese

Austria & Switzerland

From a growing band of small producers, Austria provides the world with outstanding dry whites, superb sweet wines and ever more interesting, good quality reds. Yet international recognition and appreciation of the great strides made has been slow in coming. From the steep hillside vineyards above the Danube (Donau) come the great Rieslings and Grüner Veltliners of the Wachau, as well as from the neighbouring regions of Kremstal and Kamptal. Around the Neusiedlersee, a broad shallow lake in the east that extends into Hungary, are spread the vineyards providing the grapes for the outstanding sweet wines as well as much of the raw materials for the current revolution in red wine production. Switzerland too has its quality regions and more producers deserving of an international reputation seem certain to emerge.

Austria

Wachau & Kremstal

The Wachau is the leading wine region of Niederösterreich (Lower Austria) and together with Kremstal and Kamptal produces the majority of Austria's top dry Rieslings and Grüner Veltliner. Wachau's Rieslings are generally much closer in style to Alsace than Germany; full and powerful, with a marvellous concentration and purity of fruit within a vibrant structure. The very best have great class and age impressively. The more traditional grape of Grüner Veltliner also excels, with great depth and power to its peppery fruit character. There are three levels within the Wachau's system of ripeness: Steinfeder, Federspiel and Smaragd. The relatively low-alcohol style of Steinfeder is for early drinking but the best Federspiel are more structured and concentrated and will keep for at least three or four years. The best quality however always comes from the Smaragd examples, named after a little green lizard. German classifications of ripeness are used for sweeter styles (Auslese, Beerenauslese, etc.), made in small quantities by some growers when conditions permit. Wines from the leading vineyards are sometimes labelled with only the vineyard, or *Ried*, name (*Ried* Klaus for example) and not the associated village.

Behind Spitz are the top sites of **Hochrain** and **Singerriedel**, given brilliant expression by Hirtzberger, while Weissenkirchen includes the **Steinriegl**, **Achleiten** and **Klaus** sites close to the village. Further downstream are the particularly favoured steep terraces running from Dürnstein around past Oberloiben and Unterloiben; top vineyards include **Kellerberg**, **Loibner Berg** (or Loibner Loibenberg), **Schütt** and **Steinertal** but fine examples are also made from several other sites. Wachau merges seamlessly into Kremstal, though there are not the same number of outstanding vineyards or producers here. In order to avoid much of what is in fact decidedly ordinary, look for wines from Nigl or Salomon, the latter highlighting the splendour of the **Kögl** vineyard.

Kamptal

Kamptal in the valley of the Kamp is away from the Danube but the potential of vineyards around the wine town of Langenlois is increasingly being realised. Until recently only one producer, Bründlmayer, stood out but there are now several good sources. The top vineyards are Zöbinger **Heiligenstein** and Strasser **Gaisberg** from which several producers make good wines. As other excellent producers such as Fred Loimer or Schloss Gobelsburg come to the fore so does a recognition of other great vineyard sites including Langenloiser **Steinmassl** or Kammerner **Lamm**.

Traisental

Traisental, east of the Wachau and centred on another Danube tributary, the Traisen, was only officially recognised as a distinct wine region in 1995. Though it lacks the imposing terraces of the Wachau and it can be more of a struggle to get fully ripe fruit, it does boast at least one good producer in Neumayer.

Burgenland

Formerly part of Hungary, the edge of Burgenland forms all of Austria's border with its eastern neighbour. The best wines are the sweet whites made around the shores of the Neusiedlersee. On its western shore in Neusiedlersee-Hügelland, around the town of Rust, the traditional **Ausbruch** style is made, now generally a full, sweet white with higher alcohol than wines made in the Germanic style (but with a must weight between those of Beerenauslese and Trockenbeerenauslese). The leading wine town for sweet whites on the eastern shore of the Neusiedlersee is Illmitz and the low-lying vineyards produce Austria's most stunning examples, led by those of Kracher. In both regions Welschriesling, Muskat Ottonel, Pinot Blanc, Pinot Gris and Chardonnay are the most important white grapes; Chardonnay, unusually, in both sweet and dry styles.

Reds are also increasingly important in Burgenland, both from Neusiedlersee (especially around Gols and Mönchhof) and Neusiedlersee-Hügelland but also from southern Burgenland. Grapes include Zweigelt, St-Laurent, Pinot Noir, Blaufränkisch and also Cabernet Sauvignon and Merlot, all of which can be made either varietally or as a blend of some combination of these, often aged in new oak. Previously rather robust, earthy and brambly, Blaufränkisch-based reds are showing increasing refinement. For the sceptical or those already hooked on great Grüner or Riesling do try the diverse but top quality reds from the likes of Kollwentz, Feiler-Artinger, Triebaumer or Juris.

Other regions

In Steiermark (Styria), especially Südsteiermark close to the Slovenian border, some aromatic, lively Sauvignon Blanc and Chardonnay (here called Morillon) are made. Lighter, unoaked examples sold as *Steirische Klassik* are often best as more serious efforts can be high in alcohol and overoaked. Vienna has a lot of land planted to vines for everyday dry whites. South of the capital is the Thermenregion, once famous for the sweet whites of Gumpoldskirchen from Zierfandler and Rotgipfler grapes but now making mostly dry whites and reds. North of Vienna is Weinviertel, where again there's little of real excitement, though producers such as Pfaffl and Graf Hardegg show there is potential for good dry whites.

Switzerland

Despite high altitudes, Switzerland has several sheltered, sometimes terraced vineyard regions that owe their existence to the moderating influence of lakes or rivers. In the **Valais**, centred on the River Rhône in its upper reaches, south-facing vineyards provide some interesting reds from unusual native grapes such as Cornalin and Humagne but also Pinot Noir and Syrah. The **Vaud** region arches around Lac Léman (Lake Geneva) and the white Chasselas grape dominates production. Beyond the lake's eastern end is Chablais (with the villages of Aigle and Yvorne) and the north-western shore is known as La Côte, but it is between the two, in Lavaux, where some really intense, minerally examples have been produced. Villages include Chardonne, Cully, Epesses and Saint-Saphorin and extremely good Chasselas from Louis Bovard shows why **Dézaley** and **Calamin**, designated Grands Crus, enjoy such a good reputation. North of Zürich, close to the German border, some Pinot Noir and Chardonnay is made in isolated pockets. Some good examples of Merlot are made in **Ticino** (a wedge of Switzerland in the Italian lakes) but quality is very uneven, due in part to often difficult vintage conditions; even the better examples can age prematurely. The best rich, ripe examples come from Christian Zündel and a handful of others. When they include a little Cabernet Sauvigon they are sold as **Rosso del Malcantone**.

A-Z of producers by region

Austria

Wachau

Kremstal

Kamptal

Traisental

Neusiedlersee-Hügelland

Neusiedlersee

Switzerland

Lauvaux

1 Wachau
2 Kremstal
3 Kamptal
4 Traisental
5 Donauland
6 Weinviertel
7 Wien
8 Thermenregion
9 Carnuntum
10 Neusiedlersee-Hügelland
11 Neusiedlersee
12 Mittelburgenland
13 Südburgenland
14 Süd-Oststeiermark
15 Südsteiermark
16 Weststeiermark

Austrian vintages

In Austria vintages are of considerable importance, particularly in the Wachau for its leading Rieslings and Grüner Veltliners. More difficult vintages can not only result in a lack of richness and ripeness but can fail to provide the balance essential for ageing. The ratings given to Wachau Riesling in the chart should be considered for the best Smaragd examples but might also be applied to equivalent examples from Kremstal or Kamptal regions where vintage conditions are usually similar. Good examples are better with three or four years' age but will keep for a decade, sometimes longer from a top vintage. The rarer sweet styles, Auslese and Beerenauslese, made in the Wachau will also prove ageworthy. The dramatic flooding in 2002 ruined grapes from vines on the flat ground but quality appears very promising from terraced vineyards. 2003 was the hottest vintage ever and the wines have more alcohol and less acidity and quality is very good indeed from a good producer.

The sweet wines of Neusiedlersee and Neusiedlersee-Hügelland, while producer-dependent, will nearly always benefit from at least five years' age and will keep for a decade or more.

Austrian vintage chart

	Wachau/Kremstal/Kamptal Riesling	Wachau/Kremstal/Kamptal Grüner Veltliner	Neusiedlersee/N-Hügelland Sweet whites
2003	★★★★/★★★★★★ A	★★★★/★★★★★★ A	★★★★/★★★★★★ A
2002	★★★★ A	★★★★ A	★★★★ A
2001	★★★★ B	★★★★/★★★★★★ B	★★★/★★★★ A
2000	★★★★ B	★★★★ B	★★★★/★★★★★ B
1999	★★★★/★★★★★ B	★★★★/★★★★★ B	★★★★ B
1998	★★★/★★★★ B	★★★/★★★★ C	★★★★ B
1997	★★★★/★★★★★★ B	★★★★/★★★★★★ C	★★★★ B*
1996	★★ C	★★ D	★★★ C
1995	★★★★ B	★★★★ C	★★★★★ B
1994	★★★ C	★★★ D	★★/★★★ C
1993	★★★/★★★★ C	★★★/★★★★ C	★★★★ C
1992	★★★ C	★★★ D	★★/★★★ D
1991	★★/★★★ D	★★★ C	★★★★ C
1990	★★★★/★★★★★★ C	★★★★/★★★★★ C	

* little produced

LEO ALZINGER Wachau www.alzinger.at A: **NDb**

Owner: Leo Alzinger Unterloiben 11, A-3601, Austria

The wines of this small 8-ha estate are difficult to obtain but are some of the best of the Wachau. Leo Alzinger now works with his son (also called Leo) to produce slightly more Grüner Veltliner than Riesling from top sites including Loibenberg and Steinertal. These wines are typically intense, taut and steely when young but with an underlying richness and concentration. As they evolve, their true class, minerality and considerable complexity become apparent. At least five years' age is required. More accessible if slightly less classy are Riesling and Grüner Veltliner from Liebenberg while there's a fine concentrated example of Grüner (especially the Smaragd version) from the Mühlpoint site below Steinertal. As well as Riesling and Grüner Veltliner from other sites, a little of a Reserve Grüner Veltliner and a Chardonnay are also made but have not been tasted. (PW)

O **Loibner Loibenberg** Riesling Smaragd★★★★ £D
O **Loibner Steinertal** Riesling Smaragd★★★★ £D Grüner Veltliner Smaragd★★★ £D
O **Dürnsteiner Liebenberg** Riesling Smaragd★★★ £D Grüner Veltliner Smaragd★★★ £D
O **Loibner Mühlpoint** Grüner Veltliner Federspiel★★ £C Grüner Veltliner Smaragd★★★ £D

DOMAINE LOUIS BOVARD Lavaux www.domainebovard.com A: Tan

Owner: Louis Bovard SA La Maison Rose, Place d'Armes 2, 1096 Cully, Switzerland

The wines of Louis Bovard serve as an inspiration to other Swiss growers. Based in Cully on pretty terraced slopes above Lac Léman, brothers Antoine and Louis-Philippe Bovard produce Chasselas-based wines without equal. The wines are remarkably stylish and finely balanced with mineral, citrus, apple and a delicately nutty character. In the Dézaley Grand Cru Médinette there is added depth, structure and intensity and the wines can easily age for five years or more. From Saint-Saphorin, both a varietal Chasselas, L'Archevesque, and a blend of Chasselas and Chenin Blanc are made. The two grapes work surprisingly well together in the latter, another elegant white with an intense long finish. This too is better with a little age and should keep for five years or more. As well as some Sauvignon, some red is made from Merlot, Pinot Noir and Syrah, and sold as Dézaley Grand Cru. (PW)

O **Dézaley** Grand Cru Médinette★★★ £C O **Calamin** Cuvée Speciale★★ £C
O **Saint-Saphorin** L'Archevesque★★ £C Chasselas/Chenin★★ £C
O **Aigle** Cuvée Noe★★ £C O **Epesses** Terre à Boire★★ £B

BRÜNDLMAYER Kamptal www.bruendlmayer.com A: **RsW**, NYg, N&P, Rae, SVS

Owner: Willi Bründlmayer Zwettlerstrasse 23 A-3550 Langenlois, Austria

Willi Bründlmayer's organically run estate is the best dry white wine producer in Austria outside the Wachau and it rivals the best of those. About 60 ha of lyre-trained vineyards occupy sites around the town of Langenlois. The most outstanding of these is Zöbinger Heiligenstein, producing superb Rieslings with depth, power and vibrant ripe fruit; still fuller and more complex is an Alte Reben (old vines) example. A fine mineral-edged Steinmassel Riesling is also produced but Grüner Veltliner is at least as important, with full, flavoursome examples with green peppercorn and yellow plum fruit, particularly lush and ripe in the Ried Lamm bottling. Top examples of each deserve to be drunk with four to five years' age, while regular Kamptaler Terrassen examples (from a blend of sites), which show good fruit if not the same style or concentration, can be drunk young. Though Grüner Veltliner (Ried Loiser Berg and Ried Kaferberg are two more fine examples) and Riesling account for more than half of what is produced, a well-balanced, ripe, medium-weight Chardonnay that avoids being too oaky or leesy is also good. Traditional-method sparkling wine and some Pinot Noir (Cécile) are also made, as are occasional sweet but superb Beerenauslese (1998) or Trockenbeerenauslese (2000) from both Grüner Veltliner and Riesling. (PW)

O **Riesling** Alte Reben★★★★★ £D O **Zöbinger Heiligenstein** Riesling★★★★ £C
O **Langenloiser Steinmassel** Riesling★★★ £C O **Riesling Kamptaler Terrassen**★★ £B
O **Grüner Veltliner** Alte Reben★★★★ £C O **Kammerner Lamm** Grüner Veltliner★★★ £D

O **Langenloiser Berg Vogelsang** Grüner Veltliner★★ £B   O **Grüner Veltliner Kamptaler Terrassen**★★ £B
O **Chardonnay**★★ £C

BIRGIT EICHINGER   Kamptal   www.weingut-eichinger.at

Owner: Eichinger family   Langenloiser Strasse 365, A-3491 Strass im Strassertal, Austria
In Austria, as elsewhere, female winemakers tend to be a small minority but as is often the case the amount
of quality wine they produce is not commensurate with their numbers. Birgit Eichinger is one of the
emerging stars of Kamptal where her 8 ha of vines include the two top sites, Heiligenstein and Gaisberg.
Both Grüner Veltliner and Riesling from Gaisberg are fine, with a touch of minerality in the first and a pure
classy, citrus depth to the latter. Riesling from Heiligenstein is bigger yet structured with great style and
depth. Grüner Veltliner from Wechselberg also highlights the potential of this site. The ripest Grüner grapes
from Gaisberg and Heiligenstein go into a partially oaked wine called Goliath that has good richness, length
and complexity, if struggling a little for balance. Also made is a very good example of unoaked Chardonnay
(from Strasser Gaisberg), while a second Chardonnay, Strasser Stangl, is oaked and more international, yet
still with good fruit purity. Prices are estimates and may be less than indicated. (PW)
O **Zöbinger Heiligenstein** Riesling★★★★ £D   O **Grüner Veltliner Goliath**★★★ £D
O **Strasser Gaisberg** Riesling★★★ £C   Grüner Veltliner★★★ £C   Chardonnay★★ £C
O **Strasser Wechselberg** Grüner Veltliner★★ £B   O **Strasser Strangl** Chardonnay★★ £C

FEILER-ARTINGER   Neusiedlersee-Hügelland   www.feiler-artinger.at   A: **FWW**, SVS

Owner: Hans Feiler   Hauptstrasse 3, A-7071 Rust, Austria
Kurt Feiler works with his father to make fine, elegant sweet whites plus some dry whites and reds on his
family's estate. Ruster Ausbruch, the traditional sweet wine of Rust, is based on Pinot Blanc
(Weissburgunder) and Welschriesling while a Pinot Cuvée version (as the name suggests) adds Pinot Gris
(Ruländer) to Pinot Blanc. True to the style, the wines are more fully fermented than sweet German wines
and have an alcohol level (13.5 per cent) similar to Sauternes. The wines are honeyed and refined with lots
of ripe botrytised fruit intensity but vary in richness and style according to the vintage. The partially barrel-
fermented Pinot Cuvée shows a lovely balance between sweetness and acidity. Very good Beerenauslese
(from Weissburgunder, Chardonnay and Welschriesling) and a Traminer Beerenauslese were made in 2002.
Also made are well-balanced examples of the intense gutsy reds with which Burgenland is increasingly
associated. The characterful, smoky Solitaire, a blend of Blaufränkisch, Zweigelt, Merlot and Cabernet
Sauvignon, has peppery, sweet brambly fruit and ripe tannins, becoming increasingly complex with five
years' age or more. A very convincing example of an Austrian Cabernet Sauvignon/Merlot blend is also
made (numbered with successive vintages: the 2001 vintage is 1007) though it is pricey in an international
context. Other reds include Zweigelt and Pinot Noir. Several dry varietal whites are made too, including a
pretty, grapy, off-dry Muscat Ottonel with better concentration than most examples of this grape. The
barrel-fermented Cuvée Gustav (from Pinot Gris, Chardonnay and Neuburger) emphasises the oak but has
creamy pear, quince and melon fruit. (PW)
O **Ruster Ausbruch**★★★★ £E   Pinot Cuvée★★★★★ £F
O **Muscat Ottonel** Halbtrocken★★ £B   O **Cuvée Gustav**★★ £C
● **Solitaire**★★★ £E   ● **Cabernet Sauvignon/Merlot**★★ £E   ● **Blaufränkisch Umriss**★★ £B

FREIE WEINGÄRTNER WACHAU   Wachau   www.fww.at   A: **FWW**, Wvr

Owner: 'Cooperative'   Freie Weingärtner Wachau, A-3601 Dürnstein, Austria
This Wachau co-op with around 600 growers produces some of the most readily available and
affordable examples of Grüner Veltliner and Riesling from the Wachau. While the wines are not at the same
level as the very best private estates, standards are nonetheless quite impressive. They
generally show good definition and intensity though have tended to lack a little zip when tasted young.
However 2002 and 03 wines promise to be the best yet produced. From 01 the Domäne Wachau label was

introduced for wines from individual vineyard sites. As well as the leading wines listed below, individual bottlings from other sites such as Singerriedel and 1000-Eimer-Berg are also produced. Dry wines are generally best with between two and five years' age, though will keep longer in top vintages. A sweet Beerenauslese shows good botrytris character if missing the extra style and balance of a top example. (PW)

O **BA** Beerenauslese★★ £D

Domäne Wachau
O **Terrassen** Grüner Veltliner Federspiel★★ £B Riesling Smaragd★★ £C
O **Dürnsteiner Kellerberg** Grüner Veltliner Smaragd★★ £C Riesling Smaragd★★★ £C
O **Loibener Loibenberg** Riesling Smaragd★★★ £C O **Riesling Exceptional**★★★ £C
O **Weissenkirchener Achleiten** Grüner Veltliner Smaragd★★★ £C Riesling Smaragd★★★ £C

HIEDLER Kamptal www.hiedler.at   A: **BBR**, FWC

Owner: Ludwig Hiedler & María Angeles Hiedler-Bustos Am Rosenhügel 13, A-3550 Langenlois
An Austrian-Spanish husband-and-wife team, the Hiedlers make a wide range of styles including sweet wines, reds, and Chardonnay and Weissburgunder/Pinot Blanc from 20 ha of vineyards around Langenlois. But the real focus is of course Grüner Veltliner, accounting for over half the vineyard area, and Riesling. With the emphasis on fruit intensity the wines are in marked contrast to many other producers. There is also impressive depth and minerality to the top wines if not the extra class or expression of some. Grüner Veltliner Thal Novemberlese, harvested in November, adds much more depth over a soundly made Spiegel version. Rieslings Steinhaus and Heiligenstein show atypically rich fruit while Riesling Maximum is a big, rich, powerful, somewhat Alsace-like offering but develops well. Riesling is also made from Gaisberg and Loiserberg and there are further examples of Grüner Veltliner. A cool, minerally Sauvignon Blanc shows some potential too. (PW)

O **Riesling Maximum**★★★★ £E O **Heiligenstein** Riesling★★★ £D
O **Steinhaus** Riesling★★★ £C Sauvignon Blanc★★ £B
O **Spiegel** Grüner Veltliner★★ £B O **Thal** Grüner Veltliner Novemberlese★★★ £C

HIRSCH Kamptal www.weingut-hirsch.at

Owner: Hirsch family Hautptstrasse 76, A-3493 Kammern-Langenlois, Austria
Hirsch, with 20 ha of vineyards in production, are one of Austria's rising stars. Great care is taken to achieve full physiological ripeness while natural yeasts and whole-bunch pressing are employed in order to enhance a natural expression of terroir. This is best seen in two contrasting premium Rieslings. The Gaisberg from mica-schist soils shows a mineral, citrus and subtle spice character, while the sandstone of Heilingenstein imparts very ripe fruit, spice as well as a certain minerality. Johannes Hirsch believes in delaying bottling as long as possible and from 2002 Grüner Veltliner Lamm and Rieslings Gaisberg and Heiligenstein are labelled either April or September. Grüner Veltliner Lamm is also made in an Alte Reben version. All wines are bottled with screwcaps. (PW)

O **Zöbinger Heiligenstein** Riesling★★★ £D O **Zöbinger Gaisberg** Riesling★★★ £D
O **Zöbinger** Riesling★★★ £C O **Kammerner Lamm** Grüner Veltliner★★★ £D

FRANZ HIRTZBERGER Wachau   A: **FWW**, NYg, P&S, SVS, N&P, F&M

Owner: Franz Hirtzberger Kremserstrasse 8, A-3620 Spitz an der Donau, Austria
The differences between the Wachau's élite (also see KNOLL, F-X PICHLER and PRAGER) are more stylistic than qualitative and it is common to find that one producer pleases more one year or on one particular occasion and another at a different time. From 12 ha of rocky soils there is a pure pristine fruit intensity to Hirtzberger's examples of Grüner Veltliner and Riesling. The wines are structured examples, taut and concentrated, but beautifully balanced. Of the top Rieslings in the (ripest) Smaragd style, Hochrain is a classic Wachau example with great length of flavour, while the splendid minerally Singerriedel has superb structure underpinning the fruit richness. There is an underlying strength and intensity to Honivogl Grüner

Veltliner that like the Rieslings deserves five years' ageing before drinking. Smaragd Grüner from Axpoint and Rotes Tor are also classic, Federspiel from the latter an excellent, more affordable example of balanced Grüner Veltliner. In addition some Weissburgunder and Grauburgunder are also produced. (PW)

O **Hochrain** Riesling Smaragd★★★★ £F   O **Singerriedel** Riesling Smaragd★★★★★ £F
O **Setzberg** Riesling Smaragd★★★★ £E   O **Steinterrassen** Riesling Federspiel★★★ £C
O **Axpoint** Grüner Veltliner Smaragd★★★★ £D   O **Honivogl** Grüner Veltliner Smaragd★★★★ £E
O **Rotes Tor** Grüner Veltliner Federspiel★★★ £C   Grüner Veltliner Smaragd★★★★ £D

JOSEF JAMEK   Wachau   www.jamekweingut.at   A: NDb

Owner: Jamek family Joching 45, A-3610 Weissenkirchen, Austria
Josef Jamek was one of the pioneers of the dry styles of Riesling and Grüner Veltliner that have re-established Austria's winemaking reputation. The 25-ha estate is now run by one of his daughters, Jutta and her husband, Hans Altmann. Low yields contribute to an intense varietal expression as well as something of the individual terroir. The wines are pure, intense and very classy in the case of the Ried Klaus Riesling, with a floral, mineral aspect and citrus and nectarine fruit. Concentrated but firm when young they generally need time to soften and become easier to drink. Chardonnay is also made while reds include Zweigelt and Spätburgunder. More wines will be rated with further tastings. (PW)

O **Ried Klaus** Riesling Smaragd★★★★ £E
O **Ried Achleiten** Grüner Veltliner Federspiel★★ £C   Grüner Veltliner Smaragd★★★ £D

JURTSCHITSCH SONNHOF   Kamptal   www.jurtschitsch.com   A: VDu, Odd

Owner: Jurtschitsch family Rudolfstrasse 39, A-3550 Langenlois, Austria
This traditional family estate, run along ecological principles and with parcels in some of Kamptal's top sites, is making excellent progress, now producing wines of a quality close to the top tier of Wachau/Kamptal dry whites. Edwin Jurtschitsch, one of three brothers, is responsible for the vineyards and pays particular attention to reducing yields, a dedication reflected in the both the intensity and length of flavour achieved with Grüner Veltliner and the particularly fine fruit and gentle minerality in the best Rieslings. Most wines drink well with just two or three years' age. While the selection of wines varies somewhat from year to year it usually includes those listed below. Small quantities of sweet wines (Trockenbeerenauslese and even Eiswein) from Riesling, Grüner Veltliner and Chardonnay are made when conditions favour it. (PW)

O **Zöbinger Heiligenstein** Riesling★★★ £C   Riesling Auslese★★★ £D   Riesling Reserve★★★★ £E
O **Riesling Alte Reben**★★★ £D   O **Grüner Veltliner Trockenbeerenauslese**★★★★ £F
O **Grüner Veltliner Alte Reben**★★★ £C   O **Grüner Veltliner Reserve**★★★ £D
O **Ried Schkenbickl** Grüner Veltliner★★★ £C   O **Ried Steinhaus** Grüner Veltliner★★ £C

KOLLWENTZ-RÖMERHOF   Neusiedlersee-Hügelland   www.kollwentz.at

Owner: Anton Kollwentz family Hauptstrasse 120, A-7051 Grosshöflein, Austria
One of Burgenland's leading estates, well-known in Austria and its German-speaking neighbours, but deserving of wider recognition particularly for its deep, complex and original reds. Grapes have been adapted to a range of different soil types in 20 ha of vineyard. Selective picking and much work in the vineyard results in moderate yields of high quality grapes. The Steinzeiler from Blaufränkisch, Cabernet Sauvignon and Zweigelt (60/20/20) has marvellous complexity, with earth, truffle, plum, tobacco and coffee hints, if not the dimension of a world-class red. Cabernet Sauvignon is very good in a cooler style with round, plump berry fruit and well-integrated oak after a little bottle age, though it can sometimes struggle for fully ripe tannins. Relatively high levels of volatility can sometimes impede their otherwise undoubted ageing potential. Varietal Blaufränkisch and Zweigelt are also produced as is Eichkogel, an equal blend of the two varieties. Single vineyard Chardonnays including Tatschler and Gloria are made from different parts of the Leithagebirge, which has calcareous soils, but while the potential is there they don't currently have the depth or fruit intensity to match their powerful, oaky frames. Better balanced is a vibrant

unoaked Sauvignon Blanc, Steinmühle. Very ripe, intense honeyed sweet wines are also made, not of the explosive concentration of Kracher yet very sweet, richly botrytised and well-balanced. Prices are high due to local demand. (PW)

● **Steinzeiler**★★★ £E ● **Cabernet Sauvignon**★★ £E
○ **Welschriesling** Trockenbeerenauslese★★★ £G

EMMERICH KNOLL Wachau   A: RsW, NYg, Sec, Rae, N&P, F&M, P&S

Owner: Knoll family A-3601 Loiben, Austria
This historic family vineyard of some 12 ha, planted mostly to Grüner Veltliner and Riesling, is another that shows just how good the top Wachau whites are. Emmerich Knoll's wines can be difficult to taste when young but can become almost overwhelming in their intensity and concentration with a little age or time in the glass. Any youthful aggression also tends to dissipate as both a strong varietal character and terroir influence emerge. The Smaragd version of Loibenberg Loibner Riesling has great vigour and superb length of flavour. Both this and the elegant, refined Dürnsteiner Schütt can age for a decade or more in top vintages. Pure, ripe Riesling is also made from Ried Pfaffenberg from outside the Wachau area. Examples of Grüner Veltliner show classic peppery varietal fruit but with balanced levels of alcohol (if slightly disappointing in 2002 by their usual very high standards). Loibner Kreutles Grüner Veltliner hasn't usually the extra concentration or style of the Loibenberg Loibner or Loibner Schütt examples but nonetheless shows a lovely fruit character. A little of a special selection of the ripest (but non-botrytised fruit) is reserved for 'Vinothekfüllung' Grüner Veltliner and Riesling, while some Beerenauslese is also made when conditions permit. (PW)

○ **Loibenberg Loibner** Riesling Federspiel★★ £C Riesling Smaragd★★★★★ £E
○ **Dürnsteiner Ried Schütt** Riesling Smaragd★★★★★ £E ○ **Pfaffenberg Steiner** Riesling Kabinett★★★ £C
○ **Loibenberg Loibner** Grüner Veltliner Smaragd★★★ £D Grüner Veltliner Vinothekfüllung★★★★ £E
○ **Loibner Schütt** Grüner Veltliner Smaragd★★★ £D
○ **Loibner Ried Kreutles** Grüner Veltliner Federspiel★★ £B Grüner Veltliner Smaragd★★ £C

KRACHER Neusiedlersee www.kracher.at   A: NYg, P&S, Fal, Bal, N&P, SVS, Tan

Owner: Alois Kracher Weinlaubenhof, Apetlonerstrasse 37, A-7142 Illmitz, Austria
The sweet wines of Alois Kracher are some of the finest going, not just Austria's best but among the top examples made anywhere. If propelled ever onward by 'Luis', in fact three generations of Kracher work together to produce consistently outstanding wines, making the most of the favourable conditions for botrytis enrichment afforded by Lake Neusiedl and surrounding small lakes (known as Seewinkel). Those labelled Zwischen den Seen ('between the lakes') are unoaked examples, usually from naturally spicy, aromatic indigenous varieties, while the Nouvelle Vague wines are oaked. The pick of several very sweet, very intense Trockenbeerenauslese are Grande Cuvée (No.6, usually Chardonnay dominated but with a significant percentage of Welschriesling), Nouvelle Vague Chardonnay (No.7, of sublime sweetness and impeccable balance), and Zwischen den Seen Welschriesling (of varying sweetness depending on the bottling and vintage but always refined). Perfumed, honeyed, grapy Muskat Ottonel (No.2 in 2000 and 01) is also delicious. A reasonably affordable introduction is the Cuvée Beerenauslese (typically Chardonnay and Welschriesling), a good, rich, not excessively sweet example with concentrated botytrised fruit and the finely balanced acidity so characteristic of these wines. Barrique-aged reds, Blend I and Blend II, from Zweigelt and Blaufränkisch, are also made. Though all sweet wines are numbered they are listed below without any as the numbers sometimes change with a new vintage. Also there can be a second (or even third) version, of greater sweetness, of certain varietals. (PW)

○ **Grande Cuvée** Trockenbeerenauslese✪✪✪✪ £G
○ **Chardonnay Nouvelle Vague** Trockenbeerenauslese✪✪✪✪ £G
○ **Welschriesling Zwischen den Seen** Trockenbeerenauslese★★★★★ £E
○ **Scheurebe Zwischen den Seen** Trockenbeerenauslese★★★★ £E
○ **Muskat Ottonel Zwischen den Seen** Trockenbeerenauslese★★★★ £E
○ **Traminer Nouvelle Vague** Trockenbeerenauslese★★★ £E ○ **Cuvée Beerenauslese**★★★ £D

LOIMER Kamptal www.loimer.at   A: Lib, ACh, Res

Owner: Fred Loimer Kamptalstrasse, A-3550 Langenlois, Austria
Like most in Kamptal, Fred Loimer has more than half of his estate planted to Grüner Veltliner but a quarter of his 25 ha is also planted to Riesling. He excels at producing both. The wines are precise but pure and expressive with real depth and length. On current form Loimer looks set to join the established Wachau/Kamptal superstars of BRÜNDLMAYER, HIRTZBERGER, KNOLL, F-X PICHLER and PRAGER. There is excellent Grüner Veltliner, a classic full Käferberg and more elegant and expressive Spiegel. Two *cru* Rieslings are beautifully made, a spicy, citrus and mineral Seeberg and Steinmassl with breadth, concentration and a white peach fruit purity. LOIS is a light but expressive introductory Grüner Veltliner. For more depth and intensity try the regular Langenlois varietals which are excellent value for money. Also made are Chardonnay, a Chardonnay/Grauburguner blend called simply 'Fred Loimer', and Pinot Noir. For a new joint venture, 'Loimer and friends', grapes are sourced from Gumpoldskirchen in the Thermenregion region. (PW)

O **LOIS★** £B O **Grüner Veltliner Langenlois★★** £B
O **Spiegel** Grüner Veltliner★★★ £C O **Käferberg** Grüner Veltliner★★★ £C
O **Riesling Langenlois★★★** £B O **Seeberg** Riesling★★★★ £C O **Steinmassl** Riesling★★★★ £D

NEUMAYER Traisental

Owner: Ludwig Neumayer Inzerdorf 22, A-3130 Inzerdorf ob der Traisen, Austria
Due east of the Wachau region, on the Traisen, a tributary of the Danube, Ludwig Neumayer has 8 ha of scattered parcels of vineyard. Despite the relative obscurity he makes better wines than some of those with parcels in the Wachau's highly rated sites. Similarly his best wines are derived from Grüner Veltliner and Riesling though Weissburgunder, Chardonnay and Sauvignon are also important. While it is apparent that the wines sometimes struggle for full ripeness and the flavours are cool and citrusy, there is nonetheless good intensity and length to the wines. The Wein vom Stein wines in particular, from a selection of the best parcels, show fine fruit expression, purity and length of flavour, even if they are slightly austere in their. Both Grüner Veltliner and Riesling are best with at least two or three years' age. (PW)

O **Rafasetzen** Grüner Veltliner★ £B O **Berg** Riesling★★ £C
O **Der Wein vom Stein** Grüner Veltliner★★ £C Riesling★★★ £C
O **Chardonnay★** £B

NIGL Kremstal www.weingutnigl.at   A: Gau

Owner: Martin Nigl Priel 7, A-3541 Senftenberg, Austria
The wines have been good here for some time but seem to have moved up a further notch in quality in recent vintages. A wide range of Grüner Veltliner and Riesling from top sites in Kremstal are made and the best are now very good indeed. Contrasting Rieslings range from the racy, minerally, elegant Piri to the taut, intense and concentrated Hochäcker or the deep, pure and stylish Privat (a selection from Piri and old vines). The Privat version of Grüner Veltliner is full-bodied and powerful with very ripe fruit, yet remains balanced; an Alte Reben version is atypically rich and profound for this variety. All have good ageing potential; Rieslings in particular show at their best with at least three to five years' age or more. As well as those below, other wines include Grüner Veltliner from Ried Zwelt, and Riesling from Kremser Kremsleiten. (PW)

O **Kremser Freiheit** Grüner Veltliner★★ £C O **Senftenberger Hochäcker** Riesling★★★ £E
O **Senftenberger Piri** Grüner Veltliner★★★ £D Riesling★★★ £D
O **Grüner Veltliner Privat★★★★** £D O **Riesling Privat★★★** £E
O **Grüner Veltliner Alte Reben★★★★** £D

NIKOLAIHOF Wachau www.nikolaihof.at

A: **RsW**, Rae, SVS, P&S

Owner: Saahs family   Nikolaigasse 3, A-3512 Mautern, Austria
Nikolaus and Christine Saahs make fine biodynamically produced Riesling and Grüner Veltliner from 20 ha of vineyards that have been a source of wine for more than a thousand years. The vines have a high average age and recent vintages have added a little extra intensity to wines that have good definition and style. Riesling is particularly long-lived, whether the restrained, minerally vom Stein or intense, refined Im Weingebirge (both from the Wachau) or steely, elegant Steiner Hund from just outside the area, in Kremstal. Even the fine Federspiel version of vom Stein will improve for five years or more. The Saahs' characterful Im Weingebirge Grüner Veltliner shows a smoky, earthy influence in a quite full, fat Smaragd version and good ripeness in a Federspiel version. Both can be drunk young and the Smaragd version with up to five years' age. Of other varieties grown, Weissburgunder shows good depth and structure. (PW)

O **vom Stein** Riesling Federspiel★★ £C Riesling Smaragd★★★ £E
O **Steiner Hund** Riesling Reserve★★★★ £E   O **Im Weingebirge** Riesling Smaragd★★★ £E
O **Im Weingebirge** Grüner Veltliner Federspiel★★ £C Grüner Veltliner Smaragd★★★ £D
O **Hefeabzug** Grüner Veltliner★★ £C   O **Baumgarten** Weissburgunder★★ £C

F-X PICHLER   Wachau

A: **RsW**, NYg, Rae, F&R, N&P, Sec, P&S

Owner: Franz Xaver Pichler   Oberloiben 27, A-6301 Dürnstein, Austria
Franz Xaver Pichler is acclaimed by many to be the Wachau's finest producer and it's hard to dispute given the extremely high quality in his top Smaragd Riesling and Grüner Veltliner of great extraction and concentration. Certainly no effort is spared in maximising the quality potential from 7.5 ha of vineyards. The Loibner Berg is consistently the most classy and concentrated of the Rieslings but that from the steep Dürnsteiner Kellerberg vineyard has great refinement, purity and length of flavour, while the von den Terrassen shows terrific richness and intensity in outstanding vintages. If more youthfully austere, Steinertal has a beauty and definition that becomes increasingly apparent after five years or more. The Grüner Veltliners are marvellous too; a deep, dense and structured Loibner Berg is perhaps the finest of several made but a full, vibrant Kellerberg and intense, long Von den Terrassen are also top wines. More forward Federspiel examples are produced from the Loibner Klostersatz and Frauenweingarten sites. Of great potential if somewhat less typical are the special supercharged selections of Riesling (Unendlich – endless or never-ending) and Grüner Veltliner ('M'), both highly concentrated old-vine versions that are high in alcohol. (PW)

O **Loibner Berg** Riesling Smaragd⊙⊙⊙⊙⊙ £E Grüner Veltliner Smaragd★★★★ £E
O **Dürnsteiner Kellerberg** Riesling Smaragd★★★★★ £E Grüner Veltliner Smaragd★★★★ £E
O **Von den Terrassen** Riesling Smaragd★★★★ £E Grüner Veltliner Smaragd★★★ £E
O **Steinertal** Riesling Smaragd★★★★ £E

RUDI PICHLER   Wachau

A: **Gau**, NYg

Owner: Rudi Pichler   Wösendorf 38, A-3610 Weissenkirchen, Austria
Rudi Pichler's wines are meant to be different, aiming for greater concentration and structure as well as ripe, intense fruit flavours. The use of indigenous yeast and higher fermentation temperatures can add an almost exotic quality to the riper styles. Yet the balance is excellent with good definition and and minerality. There is real strength and depth in the top *crus* at Smaragd level, not the austerity of some but still requiring at least five years' ageing to show at their best. Of the single vineyard (Ried) wines, both Kollmütz and Hochrain Grüner Veltliner illustrate his style very well. An intensely mineral Steinriegl, and an Achleiten with great length and class, do the same for Riesling. Blended Terrassen Smaragd Riesling and Grüner Veltliner are very good too and even Wachauer Federspiel wines, with cooler citrus flavours but no under-ripeness, show plenty of vigour and intensity. If less well-known than other Wachau producers, this is now a name to track down. Some but not all of the wines are rated below. (PW)

O **Weissenkirchner Achleiten** Riesling Smaragd★★★★★ £E
O **Weissenkirchner Steinriegl** Riesling Smaragd★★★★ £E
O **Wösendorfer Hochrain** Grüner Veltliner Smaragd★★★★ £D
O **Wösendorfer Kollmütz** Grüner Veltliner Smaragd★★★★ £D
O **Terrassen** Grüner Veltliner Smaragd★★★★ £D   Riesling Smaragd★★★★ £D
O **Wachauer** Grüner Veltliner Federspiel★★ £C   Riesling Federspiel★★★ £C

PRAGER Wachau   www.weingutprager.at   A: **M&V**, NYg, Fal, P&S, F&M

Owner: Ilse Prager & Toni Bodenstein   A-3610 Weissenkirchen, Austria
Franz Prager did much to establish the pre-eminence of top dry whites from the Wachau. His daughter Ilse and her winemaker husband Toni Bodenstein have sought to produce dry wines of ever greater harmony and longevity as well as making some fine sweet wines when conditions permit. From the village of Weissenkirchen come several fine Smaragd Rieslings, including a superb minerally, peachy Steinriegl that is firm when young but with great depth and length, adding richness and complexity with age. Both Riesling and Grüner Veltliner from the Achleiten site are also very fine and can show a little spice as well as an intense fruit depth. Fine Auslese and occasional Trockenbeerenauslese examples are also made from this site. Of the other fine Rieslings, a very refined Wachstum Bodenstein Riesling (from the highest vineyard at 460m) contrasts with a bolder, more forward Kaiserberg example and a distinctive, minerally, cool-fruited Klaus. All wines benefit from even more age than is typical for the best Wachau whites; Rieslings need five years but will keep for a decade. An intense, fruit-rich Chardonnay Smaragd is also made and has good structure and depth. (PW)

O **Weissenkirchen Steinriegl** Riesling Federspiel★★ £C   Riesling Smaragd★★★★ £E
O **Weissenkirchen Achleiten** Riesling Smaragd★★★★ £E   Grüner Veltliner Smaragd★★★ £D
O **Weissenkirchen Wachstum Bodenstein** Riesling Smaragd★★★★ £E
O **Weissenkirchen Klaus** Riesling Smaragd★★★★ £E
O **Dürnsteiner Kaiserberg** Riesling Smaragd★★★ £D   O **Dürnsteiner Hollerin** Riesling Smaragd★★★ £D
O **Weissenkirchen Weitenberg** Grüner Veltliner Smaragd★★★ £D

SALOMON-UNDHOF Kremstal   www.undhof.at   A: **L&S**

Owner: Salomon family   Undstrasse 10, A-3504 Krems-Stein, Austria
An estate that has remained in the same family since 1792. Bertold Salomon has recently returned to take up the mantle from his older brother Erich. Recent releases are particularly good. Von Stein Grüner Veltliner comes from two small plots of eroded rocky soils producing a wine of lovely minerality and intensity that starts out quite austere. Another fine Grüner comes from old vines in Lindberg, the lower part of Wachtberg. The terraces of Kögl provide fine Riesling with extra depth and concentration in a Reserve that is in essence a very pure, elegant style. While the Salomon's 20ha of vineyards are almost exclusively Grüner Veltliner or Riesling, a little Gelber Traminer is also made. A very attractive wine, it combines good fruit intensity with a mix of spice, floral and lychee characters. (PW)

O **Gelber Traminer** Reserve★★ £D   O **Grüner Veltliner Hochterrassen**★ £B
O **Undhof Wieden** Grüner Veltliner★★ £C   O **Von Stein** Grüner Veltliner Reserve★★★ £D
O **Pfaffenberg** Riesling★★ £C   O **Kremser Kögl** Riesling★★★ £C   Riesling Reserve★★★★ £D

SCHLOSS GOBELSBURG Kamptal   www.gobelsburg.at   A: **FWW**, NYg, P&S, SVS, Hrd

Owner: 'Stift Zwettl'   Schlossstrasse 16, A-3550 Gobelsburg, Austria
This ancient estate still belongs to a Cistercian monastery and the castle itself was built in the early 18th century. Under the winemaking direction of Michael Moosbrugger, with consultancy from Willi BRÜNDLMAYER since 1996, the wines have made amazing progress over recent vintages. 35 ha of vineyards give both Grüner Veltliner and Riesling that are fully ripe and intense but of superb definition and concentration too. There is great style and refinement in a rich yet poised Alte Reben Riesling (from Gaisberg) with a sublime pure fruit character, while a composed, concentrated and classy Heiligenstein is

also marvellous. Regular Gobelsburger Riesling and Renner Grüner Veltliner are good value. Sparkling wine, reds (Zweigelt, Merlot, Pinot Noir), and *Messwein* (altar wine) are also made. (PW)

O **Zöbinger Heiligenstein** Riesling★★★★★ £C   O **Gaisberg** Riesling★★★★ £C
O **Riesling Alte Reben**★★★★★ £D   O **Riesling Gobelsburger**★★ £B
O **Kammerner Lamm** Grüner Veltliner★★★★ £D   O **Kammerner Grub** Grüner Veltliner★★★ £C
O **Kammerner Renner** Grüner Veltliner★★★ £C   ● **Pinot Noir**★★ £D

ERNST TRIEBAUMER Neusiedlersee-Hügelland   www.triebaumer.com   **A: GWW**

Owner: Triebaumer family   Raiffeisenstrasse 9, A-7071 Rust, Austria
Ernst Triebaumer (or ET) is one of the best known names of Burgenland. From a total of 16 ha of vineyard, son Herbert Triebaumer is now responsible for a wide range of styles. Some 5 ha are his own vineyards which he bottles under his own label. What is made in a given vintage depends to some extent on the climatic conditions. Ernst Triebaumer whites include Neuburger, Welschriesling, Weissburgunder, Chardonnay and Sauvignon Blanc. An unusual Chardonnay Spätlese was made in 2002 from botrytis-free grapes. Under Herbert's label are a light, elegant aromatic Gelber Muskateller and Grüner Veltliner. But the best grape is Blaufränkisch and up to four versions are made: Aus den Rieden, Gmärk, Oberer Wald and Ried Marienthal. The latter comes from a vineyard of fossilised limestone soils and sees 70 per cent new oak but is only made in exceptional years. All Blaufränkisch develop well over five years or more; tasted too young they can seem a little harsh or lean but with age the wines soften and become increasingly complex. Maulwurf (not tasted) is a pricey blend of Blaufränkisch with Cabernet Sauvignon and Merlot. Herbert's own blend of Cabernet Sauvignon with Blaufränkisch wants for a little more ripeness. Also made in the hot summer of 2000 was a barrique-aged Cabernet Sauvignon/Merlot (an ET wine) which though stylish and promising, shows a slight lack of physiological ripeness. St-Laurent is also made. For sweet wines there's fine Ruster Ausbruch made from Chardonnay, Weissburgunder and Welschriesling. Varietal versions are also produced. (PW)

Ernst Triebaumer
● **Blaufränkisch** Aus den Rieden★★ £B   Ried Marienthal★★★ £E
O **Chardonnay Ried Pandkräftn**★★ £C   O **Ruster Ausbruch**★★★★ £F

Herbert Triebaumer
● **Cabernet Sauvignon/Blaufränkisch**★ £C
O **Grüner Veltliner**★★ £B   O **Gelber Muskateller**★ £B

VELICH Neusiedlersee   www.velich.at   **A: Fie, BBR, SVS**

Owner: Velich family   Seeufergasse 12, A-7143 Apetlon, Austria
From Apetlon in the Neusiedlersee, a short distance from the Hungarian border, the Velich brothers make Austria's finest Chardonnay. Tiglat is a single-vineyard example that combines depth and richness with real poise and elegance. It is neither too ripe nor too oaky or leesy as some Austrian examples are. A second Chardonnay, Darscho, hasn't the same depth or style but is balanced and has good fruit intensity. Cuvée OT (Ohne Titel – without title) is a relatively inexpensive blend of Chardonnay with 20 per cent Welschriesling and a little Muscat Ottonel – a perfumed, peachy white for early drinking. Neusiedlersee is of course more famous for its sweet wine production and Velich make some fine examples. Seewinkel Beerenauslese is based on Chardonnay (with Neuburger and Bouvier) and shows good botrytis richness if not the greatest finesse but a Welschriesling Trockenbeerenauslese is both sweet, intense and very refined in vintages like 1999, 98 and 95. Richer and more powerful if less scintillating is a Trockenbeerenauslese from the Tiglat vineyard. (PW)

O **Apetlon Chardonnay Darscho**★★ £C   **Chardonnay Tiglat**★★★ £E
O **Cuvée OT**★ £B   O **Seewinkel** Beerenauslese★★★ £D
O **Welschriesling** Trockenbeerenauslese★★★★ £F   O **Tiglat** Trockenbeerenauslese★★★ £F

OTHER WINES OF NOTE

Austria

PAUL ACHS (Neusiedlersee) ● Pinot Noir £E

JOHANN DONABAUM (Wachau) O Loibner Garten Grüner Veltliner Smaragd £C

FELSNER (Kremstal) O Grüner Veltliner Alte Reben £C

ALOIS GROSS (Südsteiermark) O Ratscher Nussberg (Chardonnay/Grauburgunder) £C
O Gelber Muskateller £B   O Grauburgunder £B

GRAF HARDEGG (Weinviertel) O Pinot MAX (Pinot Blanc/Chardonnay) £B   O Viognier V £C

HEINRICH (Neusiedlersee) ● Gabarinza (Zweigelt/Blaufränkisch/St. Laurent/Cabernet S./Syrah) £E

JURIS (Neusiedlersee) ● Pinot Noir Selection £C   Reserve £D   ● St. Laurent Reserve £D
● Wolfjäger (Blaufränkisch/Zweigelt) £B   ● Blaufränkisch Reserve £D   O Chardonnay Altenberg £B

KRUTZLER (Süd Burgenland) ● Blaufränkisch Reserve £D   ● Perwolff (Blaufränkisch) £E

LACKNER-TINNACHER (Südsteiermark) O Steinbach Morillon (Chardonnay) £C

HELMUT LANG (Neusiedlersee) O Sauvignon Trockenbeerenauslese £E
O Eiswein Cuvée (Scheurebe) £E

HANS & ANITA NITTNAUS (Neusiedlersee) ● Commondor (Merlot/Cabernet Sauvignon/Zweigelt) £E
● Pannobile (Zweigelt/Blaufränkisch) £C   O Heideboden (Chardonnay/Pinot Blanc) £B
● Heideboden (Zweigelt/Blaufränkisch/Cabernet Sauvignon/Merlot/Syrah) £B
O Trockenbeerenauslese (Chardonnay/Sauvignon Blanc/Neuburger) £F

WILLI OPITZ   O Eiswein (Welschriesling) £G
O Weisser Schilfmandl Muskat Ottonel Trockenbeerenauslese £G

PFAFFL (Weinviertel) O Hundsleiten Sandtal Grüner Veltliner £C   O Goldjoch Grüner Veltliner £C

PITTNAUER (Burgenland) O Altenberg Chardonnay £C
● Pinot Noir £C   ● St. Laurent Alte Reben £C

JOSEF PÖCKL (Neusiedlersee) ● Zweigelt Classique £B

ERICH & WALTER POLZ (Südsteiermark) O Morillon Hochgrassnitzberg £C
O Weissburgunder Grassnitzberg £B

PRETTEREBNER (Neusiedlersee) ● Blaufränkisch £B   ● St. Laurent £C

PRIELER (Neusiedlersee-Hügelland) ● Blaufränkisch Ried Goldberg £D

HEIDI SCHRÖCK (Neusiedlersee-Hügelland) O Ruster Ausbruch (mostly Furmint) £F

STÖLZERHOF (Neusiedlersee) O Trockenbeerenauslese Samling 88 (Scheurebe) £F
● Trockenbeerenauslese Zweigelt £F

MANFRED TEMENT (Steiermark) O Sauvignon Steirische Klassik £B
O Morillon Steirische Klassik £B

TINHOF (Neusiedlersee-Hügelland) O Fuchsenriegl (Neuburger/Weissburgunder) £C
● Feuersteig (Blaufränkisch/Zweigelt/St. Laurent) £C   ● Gloriette (Blaufränkisch) £D
O Trockenbeerenauslese (Weissburgunder) £F

UMATHUM (Neusiedlersee) ● Frauenkirchener Haideboden (Zweigelt/Blaufränkisch/Cabernet) £C
● Frauenkirchener Ried Hallebühl (Zweigelt/Blaufränkisch) £F

DR. UNGER (Kremstal / Wachau) O Ried Silberbügel Riesling Reserve £C
O Ried Oberfeld Grüner Veltliner Alte Reben £C   O Ried Innausen Pinot Gris Reserve £C

Switzerland

GANTENBEIN (Graubünden) ● Pinot Noir £F   O Chardonnay £E

GIALDI (Ticino) ● Sassi Grossi (Merlot) £E

DANIELE HUBER (Ticino) ● Montagna Magica (Merlot/Cabernet Franc/Cabernet Sauvignon) £E

IMESCH VINS (Valais) O Valais Pinot Noir Loquette £C

DOM. DU MONT D'OR (Valais) O Johannisberg du Valais £C

CAVES ORSAT (Valais) ● Cornalin du Valais Primus Classicus £D

ROUVINEZ (Valais) ● Le Tourmentin (Pinot Noir/Cornalin/Humagne/Syrah) £C

CHRISTIAN ZÜNDEL (Ticino) ● Rosso del Malcantone Orrizonte £E

Author's choice (PW)

12 superior Austrian Riesling

LEO ALZINGER O Loibner Steinertal Riesling Smaragd
BRÜNDLMAYER O Zöbinger Heiligenstein Riesling Alte Reben
FRANZ HIRTZBERGER O Singerriedel Riesling Smaragd
FREIE WEINGÄRTNER WACHAU/DOMÄNE WACHAU O Loibener Loibenberg Riesling Smaragd
JURTSCHITSCH SONNHOF O Zöbinger Heiligenstein Riesling Alte Reben
EMMERICH KNOLL O Dürnsteiner Ried Schütt Riesling Smaragd
LOIMER O Langenloiser Steinmassl Riesling
NIGL O Riesling Privat
NIKOLAIHOF O vom Stein Riesling Smaragd
F-X PICHLER O Dürnsteiner Kellerberg Riesling Smaragd
RUDI PICHLER O Weissenkirchener Achleiten Riesling Smaragd
PRAGER O Weissenkirchen Achleiten Riesling Smaragd

12 superb Grüner Veltliner

BRÜNDLMAYER O Kammerner Lamm Grüner Veltliner
BIRGIT EICHINGER O Strasser Gaisberg Grüner Veltliner
HIEDLER O Thal Grüner Veltliner Novemberlese
FRANZ HIRTZBERGER O Honivogl Grüner Veltliner Smaragd
JOSEF JAMEK O Ried Achleiten Grüner Veltliner Smaragd
EMMERICH KNOLL O Loibenberg Loibner Grüner Veltliner Smaragd
LOIMER O Langenloiser Spiegel Grüner Veltliner
NIGL O Grüner Veltliner Alte Reben
NIKOLAIHOF O Im Weingebirge Grüner Veltliner Smaragd
F-X PICHLER O Loibner Berg Grüner Veltliner Smaragd
PRAGER O Weissenkirchen Achleiten Grüner Veltliner Smaragd
SCHLOSS GOBELSBURG O Kammerner Lamm Grüner Veltliner

7 sweet whites

BRÜNDLMAYER O Zöbinger Heiligenstein Riesling Trockenbeerenauslese
FEILER-ARTINGER O Ruster Ausbruch Pinot Cuvée
KRACHER O Grande Cuvée Trockenbeerenauslese
HANS & ANITA NITTNAUS ● Trockenbeerenauslese
HEIDI SCHROCK O Ruster Ausbruch
ERNST TRIEBAUMER ● Ruster Ausbruch
VELICH O Welschriesling Trockenbeerenauslese

8 leading reds

FEILER-ARTINGER ● Solitaire
HEINRICH ● Gabarinza
JURIS ● St. Laurent Reserve
KOLLWENTZ-RÖMERHOF ● Steinzeiler
KRUTZLER ● Perwolff
HANS & ANITA NITTNAUS ● Pannobile
PRETTEREBNER ● Blaufränkisch
ERNST TRIEBAUMER ● Ried Marienthal Blaufränkisch

This may seem a somewhat diverse geographical section, but in wine terms the countries covered here are either small and developing, or large, but as yet happy, it would appear, to service the bulk and own-label market places rather than seek to establish any quality reputation of their own. In England the future of fine wine production may very well be in sparkling winemaking. In countries like Greece, Israel, Lebanon and now also Algeria and Morocco there is clear potential thanks to their Mediterrannean climates. Isolated viticultural outposts in Eastern Europe too suggest there is undoubted scope for the future. The sweet wines now being produced at Tokaji in Hungary are an example of just what investment, technology and a commitment to excellence can achieve.

In **England** growers continue to face the annual challenge of bringing in an adequate quality grape harvest. For several decades the industry has struggled with modest varieties and crossings of mostly German origin. The problem is that there is a scarcity of reasonable grapes that will ripen adequately in such a cool and damp northerly climate. One variety that has proved to work particularly well here, producing the occasional wine of depth and character, is the **Seyval Blanc**, although, due to the bizarre machinations of the European quality regulations, it is entitled only to table wine (rather than quality wine) status, the reason being that the variety is a hybrid. The real key, though, has been planting and sourcing fruit from existing vineyards on the southern English downland chalk soils in order to produce some first-class sparkling wines. It is worth considering that less than half the Champagne *vignoble* is planted in the same fabled chalk. Chardonnay and Pinot Noir too are being successfully grown and contributing to some very impressive recent results. It may be that the hot summer of 2003 produces wines of a different dimension here.

In Eastern Europe the **Czech** and **Slovak Republics** both produce some decent dry whites. In the Czech Republic whites from the likes of Grüner Veltliner and Gewürztraminer are produced in **Bohemia** and **Moravia** and in the Slovak Republic some well-made commercial reds originate from the **Nitra** region, as well as good stylish whites from **Pezinok** just north of Bratislava. Further east, nothing of real note has yet emerged from the **Ukraine** or **Moldova** despite there being some modern winemaking input in the latter. In **Romania** the best potential would appear to rest with the sweet botrytised wines of **Cotnari** and **Murfatlar** but some outside investment would be an immense advantage.

In **Hungary**, apart from Tokaji, few wines of real quality have been produced. Again, investment has been centred on the bottom of the market. There is potential, particularly with the reds from the southern **Villány-Siklós** region. **Tokaji**, though, is a different matter. Investment aplenty has flooded into the region and some of the results are stunning. The wines are now altogether fresher, more intense and with some truly splendid botrytis character in the best examples. Among the great recent years to look out for are 2000, 99, 96, 95, 93 and 88. It's a shame that the same technology has failed to reach that part of the appellation in the Slovak Republic.

In South-Eastern Europe **Slovenia** produces some crisp dry whites and a few reasonable sweet wines close to the Austrian border, but has struggled to shake off its 'Laski Rizling' image. **Croatia** produces a few gutsy reds, while **Bulgaria** ought to produce much more in the way of quality than it does. **Greece** has real potential and an increasing number of stylish modern whites and rich plummy reds are now being made as well as a few established classics like the sweet **Muscats** from the island of **Samos**. As wine producers begin to exploit more high-potential viticultural sites this may become a very exciting country for wine. The industry in **Israel** is still largely focused on the production of kosher wines, many from the **Golan Heights**, but an increasing number of stylish reds and whites are being produced there as well. In **Lebanon**, after decades of war and strife, new producers are joining the long-established Chateau Musar in producing dense, powerful wines of heady character. Fine reds are also emerging from **Algeria** and **Morocco** from old bush vines.

BIBLIA CHORA ESTATE Greece   A:Ecl

Owner: Vasilis Tsaksarlis & Vangelis Gerovasileiou Kokkinohori, 64008 Kavala
The two owners of this recently established operation are both enologists and their wines are marked by
impressive pure fruit character. The 150 ha of vineyards are planted in the sparse flinty soils of Mount
Pangeon in the north of the country. This location combines with cooling breezes from the nearby
Strymonic Gulf to provide ideal growing conditions. Greek varieties Assyrtiko and Agiorgitiko have both
been planted as well as Sauvignon Blanc, Chardonnay, Semillon, Syrah, Merlot and Cabernet Sauvignon.
Four wines are currently released: the Estate Red and White, a ripe, spicy Syrah rosé and a barrel-fermented
Chardonnay. The Estate White blend of Sauvignon Blanc with Assyrtiko has well-judged oak and good
peachy, citrus fruit. The Estate Red is currently a classic Bordeaux blend of Merlot and Cabernet Sauvignon.
Twelve months in new oak provide a rich, characterful wine with marked dark berry fruit. The red will
develop well over four or five years; the other wines should be broached young, particularly the rosé. (DM)
● **Estate Biblia Chora Red** Pangeon★★★ £C
O **Estate Biblia Chora White** Pangeon★★★ £C
O **Estate Biblia Chora Rosé** Pangeon★ £B

DISZNÓKÖ Tokaji   A: PFx

Owner: AXA Millésimes PF 10, 3910 Tokaj
Disznókö was created in 1992 and, as with a number of Tokaji producers, considerable investment has been
put into this operation, including major new cellars. The estate spreads over 150 ha of which 100 ha on
volcanic clay soils are farmed. Of these 60 ha contain very old vines. Although newly established in its latest
manifestation, the estate has a history stretching back over 300 years and was classified as a First Growth by
royal decree in 1772. A full range of Tokaji styles is produced and the top sweet wines have marvellous
botrytis complexity. With as much care being lavished on the base wine as the *aszu*, the wines are very
opulent and exotic but have comfortably enough acidity for balance. (DM)
O **Tokaji** Aszú 5 Puttonyos★★★★ £E Aszú 6 Puttonyos★★★★ £F

DENBIES England www.denbiesvineyard.co.uk

Owner: Denbies Wine Estate London Rd, Dorking, Surrey RH5 6AA
Very substantial operation with more than 100 ha planted on limestone soils near Dorking. In selecting the
site the potential ripening of the grapes was carefully evaluated. At their best these wines are indeed among
the finest the country offers, but the range is extensive and production sizeable, approaching 40,000 cases
a year, and some wines are fairly ordinary. As elsewhere, sparkling wines have good potential and there have
been some impressive sweet whites over the past few vintages. (DM)
O **Classic Brut** Vintage★ £B

EVHARIS ESTATE Greece www.evharis.gr   A: Ecl,Han,NYg

Owner: Eva-Maria Boehme & Harris Antoniou 24 Lagoumitzi str. 176 71, Athens
Small 30-ha Greek estate located between Athens and Corinth with vineyards planted in the foothills of the
Gerania Mountains. Indigenous white Assyrtiko, Roditis and Athiri along with red Agiorgitiko are joined
by international varieties Chardonnay, Sauvignon Blanc, Syrah, Merlot and Grenache. A good
floral and intense tank-fermented Estate White blends Assyrtiko with Chardonnay and Sauvignon and is
marked by the herbal character of the Assyrtiko. The Estate Red blends Syrah, Merlot and Grenache and
displays fine, rich berry fruit, with an undercurrent of herbs and thyme and impressive intensity. It is aged
in French oak for 12 months, lending it depth and structure. Estate bottlings of Syrah, Merlot and
Chardonnay are also produced and a red Bordeaux blend, Melapus, has also been added. The Syrah is
particularly striking with impressive depth and a firm structure provided by grapes grown at altitude. The
wines are now bottled without filtration. An impressive varietal Assyrtiko white is also produced, fermented

and aged in French oak for six months with very subtle oak tones and aromas of citrus and summer fruits. The budget Ilaros red and white are decent fruit-driven and immediately appealing wines. The top reds should be aged for at least a couple of years in bottle. (DM)

● **Estate Red** Gerania★★★ £C   ● **Syrah Estate** Gerania★★★ £C
● **Merlot Estate** Gerania★★ £C   ● **Ilaros Red** Gerania★ £B
O **Estate White** Gerania★★ £B   O **Asyrtiko Estate** Gerania★★ £B
O **Ilaros White** Gerania★ £B

GAIA ESTATE   Greece   www.gaia-wines.gr   A: Odd

Owner: Leon Karatsalos & Yannis Paraskevopoulos   22 Themistokleous str. 151 22, Athens
Founded in 1994, this is one of the finest producers in Greece. The company run two separate wine estates. It established the Thalassitis property on the volcanic island of Santorini in 1994 and followed this up in 1996 with a property at Koutsi in Nemea. Production in Nemea is focused around three reds all made from the indigenous Agiorgitiko. The Notios red is soft, brambly and forward; a varietal Agiorgitiko is fuller and better structured. Very impressive is the dense and concentrated top red, Gaia Estate, with a firm structure and real depth. A juicy rosé is also produced from a variety known as 14-18h. The Koutsi range is completed by Notios white, a blend Moschofilero and Roditis, and a benchmark for retsinas, Ritinitis Nobilis, vinified from Roditis grown in a cool climate at high altitude. Two intense, piercing, mineral-scented whites are produced from Santorini: Thalassitis and Thalassitis Oak. The key to quality here lies in the 70- to 80-year-old very low-yielding ungrafted Assyrtiko vines. The regular Thalassitis is cool-fermented but not to the detriment of the naturally intense mineral and honeysuckle aromas. The Thalassitis Oak is fermented in new oak and aged on lees for five to six months. The oak is very well integrated, lending increased structure rather than flavour, and the wine will develop well in the short term. Gaia Estate is capable of further development for up to 10 years. Enjoy the other wines young. (DM)

● **Notios** Nemea★ £B   ● **Agiorgitiko** Nemea★★ £B   ● **Gaia Estate** Nemea★★★★ £D
O **Thalassitis** Santorini★★★ £C   O **Thalassitis Oak** Santorini★★★ £C
O **Notios** Nemea★ £B   O **Ritinitis Nobilis** Retsina★ £B
◉ **14-18h** Nemea★ £B

HATZIDAKIS   Greece   www.hatzidakiswines.gr   A: Ecl,

Owner: Haridimos Hatzidaki   Pyrgos Kallistis. GR-84701, Santorini
The barren landscape of the island of Santorini in the heart of the Cyclades is home to another first-class producer of top whites. This small family venture was established in 1997 and Haridimos Hatzidaki makes some of the most piercing and mineral examples from the island in his underground cellars. Indeed, these are such some of the most exciting dry whites to have emerged from Greece in recent years. There are two very good citrus and mineral unoaked dry whites: Santorini blends Assyrtiko, Aidani and Athiri, while Aidani-Assyrtiko is dominated by Aidani and is the more citrusy of the two. Santorini Barrel is 100 per cent Assyrtiko vinified and aged in partly new wood, with rich nutty, citrus and mineral characters dominating the oak. Nykteri Santorini is produced from some of the oldest vines on the property. Aged in wood, it is richer and more opulent than the other whites, more honeyed than mineral. Mavrotragano is a reasonably good red made from the grape of the same name, but it lacks the intensity and excitement of the whites. Haridimos also makes a very good, piercingly intense Vin Santo from dried grapes. Aged in cask for three years, it is marked by complex dried fruits and honey and has excellent balance and a firm acidic backbone. (DM)

● **Mavrotragano** Santorini★ £C
O **Santorini**★★ £B   O **Aidani-Assyrtiko** Santorini★★ £B
O **Santorini Barrel**★★★ £C   O **Nykteri** Santorini★★★ £C
O **Vin Santo** Santorini★★★★ £E

LUMIÈRE   Morocco

Owner: Gérard Depardieu c/o Terroirs d'Exception, 33330 Saint-Christophe des Bardes, France
Gérard Depardieu's 6-ha estate at Meknes, based within the appellation of Guerrouane, produces a remarkable old-vine blend of Grenache, Carignan and Syrah. The actor also owns the fine Domaine de SAINT AUGUSTIN in Algeria and has established new benchmarks for what can be achieved in these unheralded regions. The varieties here are planted in near equal amounts and the average age of the vineyard is now over 70 years. Despite the warm climate, the vineyard benefits from its 600 m altitude and yields are restricted to less than 20 hl/ha. Both leaf plucking and green harvesting are carried out to help ensure fruit of the highest quality. In the winery there is minimal interference. *Pigeage* is employed and cellar operations are handled by gravity. The wine is aged in new French oak. It is perhaps the finest expression of richly concentrated old-vine red produced in North Africa. Ripe, heady, dark, spicy fruit with layers of blackberry, herb and black pepper is finely balanced with a supple, youthfully firm structure. Attractive young, the wine will benefit from four or five years' ageing. (DM)
O **Guerrouane** Cuvée Lumière★★★★ £E

MASSAYA   Lebanon   www.massaya.com   A:THt

Owner: Massaya partnership   24 Lagoumitzi str. 176 71, Athens
With some of the ups and downs in quality in recent releases from CHÂTEAU MUSAR, Massaya is arguably now the finest producer in the Lebanese Bekaa Valley, although the style is very different. The Massaya range of wines is produced at the Ghosn family's restored Tanaïl property which includes an Arak distillery, boutique and barbecue facilities as well as the Massaya winery. In 1998 the family formed a partnership with the Bruniers of VIEUX-TÉLÉGRAPHE in Châteauneuf-du-Pape, Hubert de Boüard of Laforest of Château ANGELUS and Daniel Hebrard of Château TRIANON in Saint-Emilion to provide the expertise to make top-quality wine from the Bekaa. Three reds are now made as well as a couple of whites and a soft fruity rosé, a blend of Cinsault, Syrah and Cabernet Sauvignon. The classic white is soft, nutty and approachable, a blend of Sauvignon Blanc, Chardonnay, Clairette and Ugni Blanc. The Selection is a step up; it is dominated by Chardonnay and has no Ugni. Both are cool-fermented to emphasise their fruit. The three reds that are the key wines here. The Classic is a forward and fruit-driven blend of Cinsault, Cabernet Sauvignon and Mourvèdre. The Selection is bigger and sturdier with firm tannins and some depth. It blends Cinsault and Syrah with a little Cabernet. The top Reserve red is dense, powerful and concentrated, a blend dominated by Cabernet Sauvignon with some Mourvèdre and Syrah. It will benefit from at least five years' ageing. The quality of the wines here is improving vintage by vintage so expect more to come. (DM)
● **Classic** Bekaa Valley★★ £B   ● **Selection** Bekaa Valley★★★ £C   ● **Selection** Bekaa Valley★★★★ £D
O **Classic** Bekaa Valley★ £B

NYETIMBER   England

Owner: Nichola and Andy Hill   Gay Street, West Chiltington, Pulborough, West Sussex RH20 2HH
The ancient Nyetimber Manor, which dates back to before Domesday Book was compiled, is now the base for one of the very best wine producers in England. The Hills purchased the property in 2001 and quality continues to move forwards under winemaker Dermot Sugrue. The close-spaced vineyards were established in the mid-1980s and are planted on ideally exposed south-facing slopes of greensand over limestone soils. The first vintage was in 1992. Pinot Noir, Pinot Meunier and Chardonnay are all now planted. Two excellent sparkling wines are produced solely from first press juice and are aged on their lees for five years or so before disgorging. The Classic Cuvée blends mainly Chardonnay with lesser amounts of the Pinots; the current release is the 1995. The Blanc de Blancs is leaner, more intense and piercing and will add more with a little age after release. Given the regular problems of the English climate, it is interesting to consider the potential of warmer years. The quality of the 2003 base wine tasted in 2004 would suggest that some exceptional bottles will emerge, sadly not before 2009. (DM)
O **Classic Cuvée** Vintage★★★ £D   **Première Cuvée** Blanc de Blancs Vintage★★★ £D

OREMUS Tokaji   A:M&V,F&M

Owner: Alvarez family   Damjanich.u.7, H-3950 Sarospatek

Oremus was created in 1993 as a joint venture between Tokaji Kereskedöhóz (the former state-run commercial house) and Bodegas VEGA SICILIA (see Spain). It is named after the vineyard where the original Tokaji was produced in 1650. A full range of styles is produced, from basic dry Furmint to exceptional and heady Essencia, and modern technology is taken advantage of: rotofermenters, for example, are used to macerate the *aszu* berries. The Essencia wine (and it is on the borderline of not being classified as such – in 1995 it had only 3% of alcohol) is astonishing: residual sugar is in excess of 400 g/l but fierce acidity provides an extraordinary balance. All the sweet wines are impressive. (DM)

O **Tokaji** Aszú 5 Puttonyos★★★ £E Essencia✪✪✪✪✪ £H

DOM. DE SAINT AUGUSTIN Algeria

Owner: Gérard Depardieu   c/o Terroirs d'Exception, 33330 Saint-Christophe des Bardes, France

Gérard Depardieu produces two impressive reds here and these along with his LUMIÈRE wine from Morocco are North African benchmarks. The vineyards are planted at between 400 and 500 m altitude and this helps to moderate the high summer temperatures. The yields are kept low, particularly for the Cuvée Monica (16 hl/ha in 2002), and green harvesting is practised during the growing season. The age of the vineyards, at an average of 40 years, also helps. The harvest is conducted by hand and brought into the winery (a converted chapel) in refrigerated trucks to preserve the fruit's freshness. The regular bottling La Confession blends Grenache, Carignan and Syrah, whereas the Cuvée Monica more unusually comprises Grenache, Carignan and Alicante. Dense, very rich and loaded with dark berry fruit, it is almost raisiny but the concentration on the palate is impressive. These are exciting and characterful wines. (DM)

O **Coteaux de Tlemcen** Cuvée Monica★★★ £E

ISTVAN SZEPSY Tokaji   A:RsW,F&M

Owner: Istvan Szepsy

Istvan Szepsy was originally a director of the co-operative in Mád. In recent years he has been establishing his own small vineyard holding with some of the best sites in the region. He has reverted his vineyards to traditional bush-vine pruning and keeps yields under tight control. The quality is reflected in wines which are unusually fresh for the region. Indeed there has been a general move throughout the region to produce wines with less oxidative character and these perhaps more than any others really reflect this new approach. The Aszú 6 Puttonyos is remarkably intense. Szepsy is also involved with American financier Anthony Hwang in a new venture, Kiralyudvar, where similarly impressive fresh Tokaji styles are being produced. They have also recently taken a controlling interest in the top Vouvray estate HUET L'ECHANSONNE. (DM)

O **Tokaji** Noble Late Harvest★★★ £D Aszú 6 Puttonyos✪✪✪✪✪ £G

ROYAL TOKAJI WINE COMPANY Tokaji   A RTo, BBR

Owner: Royal Tokay Wine Co   Rakoczi Ut 35, H-3909 Mád

This was the first of the foreign investments in the Tokay region in 1989. A consortium including Danish winemaker Peter Vinding-Diers and wine writer Hugh Johnson formed the company in partnership with 63 growers, providing a formidable resource of top vineyard sites. The attention in the vineyard is undoubtedly paying off and yields have been almost halved to an average of around 40 hl/ha. The wines are rich and intense, without a hint of oxidation, and have a more overtly orange peel and nutty character than other examples. (DM)

O **Tokaji** Blue Label 5 Puttonyos★★ £E Aszú Nyulaszo 6 Puttonyos★★★★ £G Essencia✪✪✪✪✪ £H

SAMOS CO-OPERATIVE Greece www.greekwinemakers.com   **A:Ecl**

Owner: Co-Operative Malagari, Samos

Fine, long-established producer of sweet Muscat. The total scope of the operation is vast with 4,000 members and production approaching 800,000 cases a year. Vines are planted right across the island with some at altitudes of up to 800 m. This contributes to the quality of the top wines – indeed, all of the Muscats are sourced from mountain-grown grapes. The Vin Doux, Grand Cru and Anthemis are fortified in a similar manner to other Muscats in France and elsewhere. Vin Doux offers simple, straightforward grapey fruit, while the Grand Cru is sourced from higher-altitude vineyards and has more developed and complex flavours. Anthemis is aged in cask for five years and has impressive depth and structure. The Nectar differs in that it is vinified from dried grapes and is not fortified. The wine has significantly less oxidative character than the Anthemis along with a quite marked high-toast oak character and a real piercing intensity. A limited number of library releases are being held by the winery: a 1975 Nectar has a strong, developed *rancio* character but maintains sufficient freshness to offer a wine with lots of interest. (DM)

O **Samos** Vin Doux★ £B Grand Cru★★ £B Anthemis★★ £B Nectar★★★ £C

THREE CHOIRS Gloucestershire www.three-choirs-vineyards.co.uk

Owner: Three Choirs Vineyards Ltd Newent, Gloucestershire GL18 1LS

Top-quality English property with 28 ha of vineyards. Dry and sweet whites are made as well as sparkling non-vintage and vintage bottlings. Considerable effort goes into grape crossing and hybrid research here because of the vagaries of the English climate and the results are generally fairly successful. (DM)

O **Bacchus** Reserve★★ £B

OTHER WINES OF NOTE

England

BREAKY BOTTOM O **Seyval Blanc** East Sussex £B
CHAPEL DOWN O **Epoch** Vintage Brut Kent £C
RIDGEVIEW O **Bloomsbury** Vintage East Sussex £C
VALLEY VINEYARDS O **Ascot Brut** Non-Vintage Berkshire £B

Greece

ANTONOPOULOS ● **Cabernet Nea Dris** Patras £C
GENTILINI O **Robola** Cephalonia £B
DOMAINE GEROVASSILIOU ● **Syrah** Epanomi £C O **Malagousia** Epanomi £B
HARLAFTIS ● **Argilos** Attika £B ● **Chateau Harlaftis** Attika £B O **Chardonnay** £B
KIR-YIANNI ● **Yianakohori** Imathia £D O **Sauvignon Blanc** Florina £C
DOMAINE MERCOURI ● **Domaine Mercouri** Red £C O **Foloi** £B
DOMAINE VASSILIOU ● **Erythros** Attica £C O **Ambelones** Koropi £B

Hungary

CHÂTEAU MEGYER O **Tokaji** Aszú 5 Puttonyos £E
CHÂTEAU PAJZOS O **Tokaji** Aszú 5 Puttonyos £E
CROWN ESTATES O **Tokaji** Aszú 5 Puttonyos £D

Lebanon

CHÂTEAU KEFRAYA ● **Château Kefraya** Red £C
CHÂTEAU MUSAR ● **Château Musar** Red £C

oDynamic pace among small, high-quality wine producers is evident throughout California, and this is as much the case here as elsewhere in the state. As well as the more established cooler areas like the Russian River, new vineyards are now being developed on the Sonoma Coast with great success. Wine prices have been and remain buoyant – a wealthy local market combined with scarcity among the top wines ensures this. There are great Cabernets here but this is generally Chardonnay and Pinot Noir territory, with some exceptional Zinfandel in warmer sites. Some magnificent wines, yes, but without the stratospheric prices of the Napa Valley collectors' Cabernets.

Geography

The North Coast of California is a vast area. It takes in Mendocino and Lake Counties, over 100 miles to the north of San Francisco, as well as Sonoma County, which runs southwards west of the Mayacamas Mountains and then takes in the western end of Carneros, at the head of San Pablo Bay. The whole viticultural area is encompassed under the **North Coast** AVA. What enables such diverse vinegrowing is cool coastal breezes and sea fogs that drift in through coastal gaps. The most significant of these – the Petaluma gap – provides an effective cooling fan for the vast Sonoma vineyard, north and south of the town of Santa Rosa. It is only thanks to these cooling breezes and sea fogs, which dominate the summer months along the state's coastline all the way south towards Santa Barbara, that fine wine production is possible in California at all.

Mendocino and Lake Counties

Mendocino is a large, sprawling vinegrowing area, mostly cool and particularly suitable for Pinot Noir and Chardonnay. The **Anderson Valley**, which opens up to the ocean, in particular produces a number of restrained, stylish examples and is also an excellent source of sparkling wine. To the north-east of the sector are the warmer AVAs of **Redwood Valley** and **Potter Valley**. Some increasingly impressive Syrah, Zinfandel and Cabernet are grown here. Lake County and the **Clear Lake** AVA, **Guenoc** and **Benmore Valley** sub-AVAs are located to the east, across the Mayacamas Mountains. Clear Lake and Guenoc are best-suited to growing reds – Cabernet Sauvignon and Zinfandel – as well as a ripe style of Chardonnay and Sauvignon Blanc. Benmore Valley by contrast is significantly cooled by elevation and provides tighter, more restrained Chardonnay.

Northern Sonoma

This is really the heartland of North Coast vinegrowing and it includes the warm red-grape areas of **Dry Creek Valley** and **Alexander Valley** to the north-east. These are located to the west and east respectively of the meandering northern sections of the Russian River which runs through the towns of Asti, Geyserville and Healdsburg. Tremendous Zinfandel and Syrah can be found in both AVAs. Excellent restrained Chardonnay, structured Cabernet and meritage styles are all sourced from the higher mountain slopes of the Alexander Valley. To the immediate east of here is the **Knights Valley**, source of some first-class Chardonnay and Cabernet Sauvignon. **Chalk Hill** AVA is just to the south and is dominated by the winery of the same name. South of Healdsburg the considerable expanse of the **Russian River Valley** AVA opens out. To the far west on the Sonoma Coast some very impressive Chardonnay and Pinot Noir is now being produced and takes the **Sonoma Coast** AVA. The Russian River area is now very well established as a source of exemplary Pinot Noir and Chardonnay and, in the warmer eastern sites, very good Syrah and Zinfandel. To the south-west is the distinctly cool.

Sonoma Green Valley AVA, a source of top-quality sparkling wines and restrained styles of Chardonnay and Pinot Noir.

Sonoma Valley

The **Sonoma Valley** AVA itself is located to the south of Santa Rosa and is home to some of the largest producers on the North Coast. The valley is bordered by the Mayacamas range to the east and the Sonoma

Mountains to the west. The appellation runs from north to south-east through the towns of Oakmount, Kenwood, Glen Ellen and Sonoma itself. The western range has its own AVA, **Sonoma Mountain**, and provides impressive examples of restrained Chardonnay, Pinot Noir and Cabernet Sauvignon. In general the better reds are planted in the warmer northern sections of the AVA while the southern sector that borders Carneros produces stylish whites but also good Pinot Noir. Some of the best and sturdiest Cabernet blends and Zinfandels are sourced from the higher slopes leading into the Mayacamas Mountains.

A-Z of producers by region

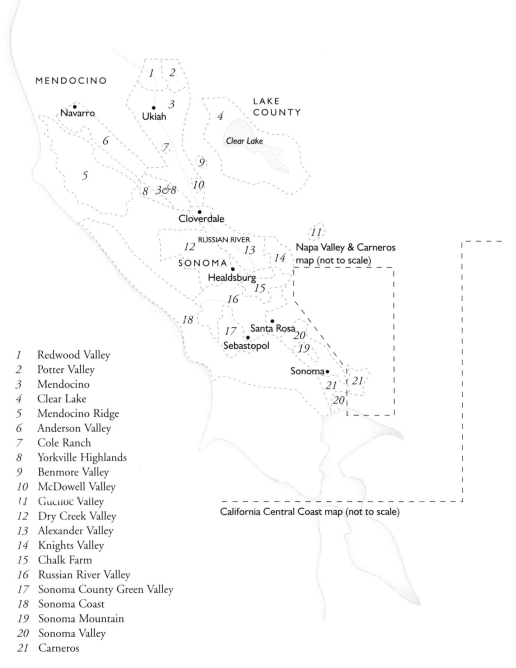

1   Redwood Valley
2   Potter Valley
3   Mendocino
4   Clear Lake
5   Mendocino Ridge
6   Anderson Valley
7   Cole Ranch
8   Yorkville Highlands
9   Benmore Valley
10 McDowell Valley
11 Guenoc Valley
12 Dry Creek Valley
13 Alexander Valley
14 Knights Valley
15 Chalk Farm
16 Russian River Valley
17 Sonoma County Green Valley
18 Sonoma Coast
19 Sonoma Mountain
20 Sonoma Valley
21 Carneros

California North Coast vintages

As is the case elsewhere in California, there can be significant variation between mesoclimates within regions with inevitably Cabernet, Zinfandel and other late ripening varieties working best in the warmer sites and early-ripening Chardonnay and Pinot Noir performing best in the cooler parts of the Russian River, Sonoma Coast and Sonoma Green Valley. However the charts below will give you a good general idea of what to expect from recent vintages. With regard to earlier years, the occasional 1987, 1985, 1984 and 1980 Cabernet and perhaps really top-flight Zinfandel might be worth a punt. 1978 and 1970 were also classic Cabernet years.

California North Coast vintage chart

	Pinot Noir	Chardonnay	Zinfandel	Cabernet Sauvignon
2003	★★★★ A	★★★★ B	★★★★/★★★★★ A	★★★★/★★★★★ A
2002	★★★★ A	★★★★ B	★★★★ A	★★★★A
2001	★★★★ A	★★★★ B	★★★★ A	★★★★/★★★★★ A
2000	★★★/★★★★B	★★★ B	★★/★★★ B	★★★ A
1999	★★★★ B	★★★/★★★★ B	★★★★ B	★★★/★★★★ A
1998	★★★/★★★★ B	★★★/★★★★ C	★★/★★★ C	★★★ B
1997	★★★★ C	★★★★ C	★★★/★★★★ C	★★★★ B
1996	★★★/★★★★ C	★★★ C	★★★/★★★★ C	★★★/★★★★ B
1995	★★★/★★★★ C	★★★★ C	★★★/★★★★ C	★★★★ B
1994	★★★★ D	★★★/★★★★ D	★★★★ C	★★★★ B
1993	★★★/★★★★ D	★★★★ D	★★★/★★★★ C	★★★/★★★★ B
1992	★★★/★★★★ D	★★★★ D	★★★/★★★★ C	★★★★ B
1991	★★★/★★★★ D	–	★★★★ C	★★★★ C
1990	–	–	★★★★ D	★★★★ C

ARROWOOD Sonoma Valley www.arrowoodvineyards.com   A: **RMi**

Owner: Robert Mondavi 14347 Sonoma Highway, Glen Ellen, CA 95442
Dick Arrowood sold his interest in this medium-sized operation in 2000 but will remain as winemaker and direct the style and focus of the winery. There is no doubt that his immense experience, gained not only at Arrowood but also previously as winemaker at CHATEAU ST JEAN, will continue to maintain and drive quality here. The wines themselves are all sourced from Sonoma Valley fruit. There are two ranges: the premium Arrowood wines and those under the Grand Archer label. The latter can offer very good value and are vinified with just a hint of oak, the objective being to emphasise varietal character. There is a fairly extensive range of premium Arrowood bottlings: classy citrusy Chardonnay from Sonoma County as well as Chardonnay, Cabernet and Merlot under the Réserve Spéciale label. Alary Ranch Chardonnay was added with the 2000 vintage and Alta Vista Vineyard with the 2001. Malbec and Rhône styles are of equal importance, the best of which are from Saralee's Vineyard and most recently Syrah from the Kuljian Vineyard in Dry Creek. Newly added are red and white Rhône blends Côte de Lune, the latter again sourced from Saralee. The Arrowood range is completed by Gewürztraminer, fine Pinot Blanc and two luscious late-harvest Rieslings. (DM)

● **Cabernet Sauvignon** Réserve Spéciale★★★★ £G Sonoma County★★★ £F
● **Syrah** Sonoma Valley★★★ £F
O **Chardonnay** Sonoma County★★★ £E   O **Viognier** Saralee's Vineyard★★★ £D

BEHRENS AND HITCHCOCK Mendocino County   A: **THt,F&M**

Owner: Les Behrens & Bob Hitchcock PO Box 1127, Calistoga, CA 94515
Very impressive small producer specialising in tiny lots (often barely more than 100 cases of a *cuvée*) of startling, massive, super-rich reds from a number of varieties sourced throughout the North Coast. The range includes top Syrah from the Alder Springs Vineyard and Petite Sirah from York Creek, along with some concentrated, powerful blends. Ode to Picasso is a fat, forward combination of Syrah, Cabernet Sauvignon, Merlot and Cabernet Franc. Chien Lunatic is virtually all Syrah with a touch of Cabernet Sauvignon. Cuvée Lola is a meritage blend based on Cabernet Franc; the Heavyweight by contrast is dominated by Syrah. The whole range is marked by a style that emphasises full, sumptuous fruit with formidable depth and extract. Although there is a greater structure and grip in the Cabernet-based *cuvées*, these are wines that offer supple tannins, rich fruit and not inconsiderable alcohol. (DM)

● **Cabernet Sauvignon** Kenefick Ranch★★★★★ £F ● **Merlot** Fortuna Vineyard★★★★ £E

BENZIGER Sonoma Mountain www.benziger.com   A: **N&P**

Owner: Mike Benziger 1883 London Ranch Road, Glen Ellen, CA 95442
Large, family-run operation producing an extensive range of wines. The best are very good and by comparison with many other California examples good value. The family also owns the Imagery Estate winery, which sells a good-quality range from lesser varieties at the cellar door only. Sonoma County wines are straightforward and good value whereas the Reserves are blended from the winery's best lots. Numerous limited-production, vineyard-designated wines are made, with some of the vineyards farmed biodynamically. (DM)

● **Cabernet Sauvignon** Reserve Sonoma County★★ £E ● **Merlot** Reserve Sonoma County★★ £E
O **Chardonnay** Reserve Carneros★★★ £D   O **Fume Blanc** Sonoma County★ £C

CHALK HILL WINERY Chalk Hill www.chalkhill.com   A: **J&B**

Owner: Fred Furth 10300 Chalk Hill Road, Healdsburg, Sonoma County, CA 95448
This producer unusually possesses its own AVA and has been for many years committed to maximising the quality of the fruit from estate vineyards. The whites are made in a full, ripe style with judicious use of new oak for both Sauvignon and Chardonnay. Vineyard Selection bottlings of both Pinot Gris and Chardonnay

have now been added to the range. The reds are leaner than some, with the odd green hint entering the equation, but at best express attractive, berry fruit character. Library Releases are also offered, along with a very small amount of the expensive Vineyard Selection Adele's Merlot. An equally small production of rich and luscious botrytised Semillon Vineyard Selection is produced when vintage conditions permit. (DM)

● **Cabernet Sauvignon** Estate★★★ £E ● **Merlot** Estate★★ £E
○ **Chardonnay** Estate★★★ £E ○ **Sauvignon Blanc** Estate★★ £D
○ **Pinot Gris** Estate★★ £D

CHATEAU ST JEAN Sonoma Valley www.chateaustjean.com

Owner: Beringer Wine Estates 8555 Sonoma Highway, Kenwood, CA 95452
The original and striking 'Chateau' here was built in 1920, pre-Prohibition. The current winery was founded in 1973 and the estate comprises some 100 ha (250 acres), of which 32 ha (80 acres) are planted to vines. These, along with three additional vineyards, Robert Young, Belle Terre and La Petite Etoile, provide the foundation for the good and pricey Reserve and vineyard-designated wines. Sonoma County wines are well-priced and regularly offer good-value drinking. A number of speciality and limited-release wines are sold exclusively at the tasting room. (DM)

● **Pinot Noir** Sonoma County★★ £C ● **Merlot** Sonoma County★★ £C
○ **Chardonnay** Sonoma County★★ £B Belle Terre Vineyard★★★ £C
○ **Fume Blanc** Sonoma County★★ £B La Petite Etoile★★★ £C
○ **Gewürztraminer** Sonoma County★★ £B

CLOS DU BOIS Alexander Valley www.closdubois.com   A: ADo

Owner: Allied Domecq 19410 Geyserville Avenue, Geyserville, CA 95441
Large-volume winery producing close to half a million cases annually. The straightforward Sonoma County Classic range is the mainstay of the winery but can be impressive on occasion. Appellation Reserve wines are a step up, but it is the vineyard-designated and Winemakers Reserve *cuvées* which are the benchmarks here. Winemakers Reserve Cabernet and Marlstone in particular are dense, concentrated and well structured, the latter a blend of Cabernet Sauvignon, Merlot, Cabernet Franc, Malbec and Petit Verdot from the vineyard of the same name. For value and style the two top Chardonnays are subtly oaked, with good citrusy, leesy depth and a certain finesse. (DM)

● **Merlot** Reserve★ £C ● **Tempranillo** Reserve★ £C
● **Cabernet Sauvignon** Briarcrest Vineyard★★ £E Winemakers Reserve★★★ £F
● **Marlstone** Alexander Valley★★★ £E
○ **Chardonnay** Reserve★ £B Flintwood★★ £D Calcaire★★ £D

DEHLINGER Russian River Valley

Owner: Tom Dehlinger 6300 Guerneville Road., Sebastopol, CA 95472
Dehlinger remains among the very top echelon in the Russian River, continually crafting outstanding unfiltered Pinot Noir, Syrah and Chardonnay. Cabernet Sauvignon does not quite hit the same heady heights, although it is rich, structured and impressive in top years. The quantities of single-vineyard Pinot Noir from the Octagon and Goldridge sites are tiny but well worth seeking out, as is the Goldridge Syrah. The reds are not only powerful and structured but very refined as well, and will drink well in the medium term. (DM)

● **Cabernet Sauvignon** Estate★★★ £E ● **Syrah** Estate★★★★ £E
● **Pinot Noir** Estate★★★★ £E Octagon Vineyard★★★★ £E
○ **Chardonnay** Estate★★★★ £D

DRY CREEK VINEYARDS Dry Creek www.drycreekvineyard.com   A: Bal

Owner: David Stare 3770 Lambert Bridge Road, Healdsburg, CA 95448
Medium-sized winery notable for good, well-priced Fumé Blanc in a very much more herbaceous style than many and a number of rich and impressive Zinfandels. The latter have been produced consistently over a number of vintages and while full and vibrant they are rarely overblown. With old-vine Zinfandel fruit increasingly in demand throughout the state, Dry Creek has established its own 'Heritage' clone, propagated from old-vine cuttings on phylloxera-resistant rootstock. From the 1997 vintage on, a small quantity – some 500 cases – of a new super-premium Cabernet Endeavour has also been released along with single-vineyard Zinfandel from the Beeson and Somers Ranches. (DM)

● **Syrah** Dry Creek★ £C   ● **Merlot** Reserve★★ £D   ● **Cabernet Sauvignon** Reserve★★ £D
● **Zinfandel** Heritage Clone★★ £C   Old Vines★★★ £C   Reserve★★★ £D
○ **Fume Blanc** DCV3★ £B   ○ **Chardonnay** Reserve★ £C

EDMEADES Anderson Valley www.kjsales.com/brands/edmeades   A: KJn, WTs

Owner: Kendall-Jackson 5500 Highway 128, Philo, CA 95403
Mendocino-based winery, producing an extensive range of full, brambly Zinfandels and well-structured Petite Sirah and Syrah. The Mendocino vineyards for the Zinfandel and Petite Sirah are above the coastal fog line and the warm sunny days are complemented by cool nights, providing good acidity for structured wines. They are typically big and brawny, offering weight and power rather than finesse. They are vinified using wild yeast fermentation and, as in all the best Jackson family wines, handling is kept to a minimum and fining and filtration eschewed. Top *cuvées* can be very impressive. Cool Anderson Valley vineyards provide the source for Pinot Noir and Chardonnay. These are good although they can on occasion lack a little balance and refinement. (DM)

● **Pinot Noir** Anderson Valley★★ £C   ● **Syrah** Eaglepoint Vineyard★★ £D
● **Petite Sirah** Eaglepoint Vineyard★★★ £D   ● **Zinfandel** Mendocino★ £C   Ciapusci★★★ £C
● **Zinfandel** Eaglepoint Vineyard★★★ £D   Mendocino Ridge★★★ £D
○ **Chardonnay** Anderson Valley★★ £C
○ **Gewürztraminer** Anderson Valley★★ £B

GARY FARRELL Russian River Valley www.garyfarrell.com   A: Vin

Owner: Allied Domecq 10701 Westside Road, Healdsburg, CA 95448
Formerly the winemaker at ROCHIOLI and DAVIS BYNUM, Gary Farrell has more recently become notable for stylish, elegant Chardonnay and Pinot Noir under his own label. The Rochioli vineyard remains an important source of fruit for him, along with Starr Ridge and Olivet Lane vineyards. A more recent addition is Central Coast Chatdonnay and Pinot Noir from the famed Bien Nacido vineyard. Chardonnay is made in a rich, tropical style but with well-judged oak, while Pinot is ripe, full and packed with dark plum and berry fruit. Zinfandel is good but can at times lack the quality of the other two varietals. Good too are Encounter, a meritage red blend of Cabernet Savignon, Merlot and Cabernet Franc, and Hillside Select Merlot. (DM)

● **Pinot Noir**★★★ £E   Starr Ridge Vineyard★★★ £E   Rochioli Vineyard★★★★ £F
● **Zinfandel** Dry Creek★★ £C   Bradford Mountain★★★ £E
○ **Chardonnay**★★★ £E   Bien Nacido★★★ £E   Rochioli Vineyard★★★★ £F

FETZER VINEYARDS Redwood Valley www.fetzer.com   A: BFW

Owner: Brown Forman 13601 Eastside Road, Hopland, CA 95449
Large-scale Mendocino County producer with an extensive range and one that champions organic wine production. The Barrel Select and Private Collection bottlings are the best bets and generally represent pretty decent value for money. The style is for rich and ripe wines with evident, sometimes unsubtle oak handling. Big and full, they can also be marked by high alcohol. One feels a touch more refinement would provide a

better balance. Fetzer also owns the Bonterra winery which itself produces a fairly large range, particularly among the Rhône varietals as well as Zinfandel, Cabernet Sauvignon and Sangiovese, the latter only available outside the US. (DM)

Fetzer
● **Zinfandel** Valley Oaks★ £B Barrel Select★★ £B   ● **Merlot** Barrel Select★ £B
● **Cabernet Sauvignon** Barrel Select★ £B   Napa Valley Reserve★ £C
● **Pinot Noir** Bien Nacido Limited Release Reserve★★ £C
O **Chardonnay** Sundial★ £B Barrel Select★ £B   O **Gewürztraminer** Echo Ridge★ £B
O **Sauvignon Blanc** Echo Ridge★ £B

Bonterra
● **Syrah** Bonterra★★ £C
O **Chardonnay** Bonterra★★★£C   O **Roussanne** Bonterra★★ £C   O **Viognier** Bonterra★★ £C

FLOWERS   Sonoma Coast   www.flowerswinery.com   A: Vin

Owner: Flowers family   28500 Seaview Road, Cazadero, CA95421
Very good Sonoma coastal property with vineyards planted in volcanic soils and moderated by cooling maritime breezes making for an ideal environment for cultivating Chardonnay and Pinot Noir. Vinification follows age-old Burgundian techniques for both varieties. As well as the wines rated here Chardonnay has also come from the Porter Bass Vineyard in western Sonoma, while Pinot Noir has emerged from the Keefer Ranch in the Sonoma Green Valley AVA. The Andreen-Gale bottlings are a special vineyard selection from within the family's estate property, the Chardonnay being a selection of the oldest Wente clones. Chardonnay is restrained and minerally with a fine balance of citrus fruit and subtle, lightly toasty oak. The Andreen-Gale is more structured and intense. Pinot is full of bright berry fruit and hints of smoky cherries. The depth and intensity of the Andreen-Gale *cuvée* suggests three or four years' ageing will be rewarded. (DM)
● **Pinot Noir** Sonoma Coast★★★£E Estate Camp Meeting Ridge★★★★ £E Andreen-Gale★★★★ £F
O **Chardonnay** Sonoma Coast★★★£E Estate Camp Meeting Ridge★★★★ £E Andreen-Gale★★★★ £E

FOPPIANO   Russian River Valley   www.foppiano.com   A: WTs

Owner: Foppiano family   12707 Old Redwood Highway, Healdsburg, CA95448
The Foppiano family own some 80 ha (around 200 acres) of prime Russian River vineyards. There are good solid, earthy reds here: the Sangiovese is one of the better Californian examples but the real stars are the two Petite Sirah *cuvées*. Both are dense, powerful but supple examples of this sometimes raw and tannic variety. The Russian River bottling, with concentrated dark berry fruit and spicy black pepper undercurrents, represents particularly good value. (DM)
● **Sangiovese** Alexander Valley★★ £C   ● **Zinfandel** Dry Creek Valley★ £B Reserve★★ £C
● **Merlot** Sonoma County★ £C Reserve★★ £D   ● **Cabernet Sauvignon** Russian River★★ £C
● **Petite Sirah** Russian River★★★ £C Reserve★★★ £E

FRICK   Dry Creek Valley   www.frickwinery.com

Owner: Bill & Judy Frick   23072 Walling Road, Geyserville, CA 95441
Small Rhône specialist with some Merlot as well. Frick produces just 2,500 cases a year from 2 ha (5 acres) of vines on a small property established in 1976 in a cooler sector of the Dry Creek Valley. Key to the style here is a naturally stressed vineyard planted on steep, well-drained slopes. The result is vines which struggle just sufficiently in order to achieve fruit with real intensity. The wines are not huge blockbusters but nevertheless show rich and concentrated fruit with balance and finesse. A Cinsault rosé is also produced and new is C Squared, a Rhône-style blend of Cinsault and old-vine Carignan from Mendocino. All offer good value. (DM)
● **Syrah** Owl Hill★★★ £C   ● **Cinsault** Dry Creek★★ £C   ● **Merlot** Dry Creek★★ £C
O **Viognier** Gannon Vineyard★★ £C

FRITZ WINERY Dry Creek Valley www.fritzwinery.com

Owner: Fritz family 24691 Dutcher Creek Road, Cloverdale, CA 95425
Fritz was established as long ago as 1979 and production is still small at some 12,000 cases a year. Grapes come from both the Dry Creek Valley and the cooler Russian River, which provides an excellent source for Chardonnay, particularly the famed Dutton Ranch. Helen Turley of MARCASSIN spent a couple of years consulting here and the quality shines through. Minimalist practices such as native yeast fermentation are employed. The Zins are vibrant and full of rich fruit, the Chardonnay broad, nutty and toasty and Sauvignon fresh and grassy for drinking young. The range is completed by a well-priced Carignane and two restrained cedary Cabernet Sauvignons from Sonoma County and the high-altitude Rockpile Vineyard. (DM)
● **Zinfandel** Old Vine★★ £C Rogers Reserve★★★ £E
○ **Sauvignon Blanc** Sonoma County★★ £B
○ **Chardonnay** Dutton Ranch★★★ £C Dutton Ranch Shop Block★★★ £E

GALLO OF SONOMA Dry Creek Valley www.gallosonoma.com　　　　A: EJG

Owner: Gallo family 3387 Dry Creek Road, Healdsburg, CA 95448
One of the world's largest wine companies, E & J Gallo, is known the world over for its Gallo and Turning Leaf volume labels – the former hugely successful but largely unexciting. There is also a Coastal range from the giant facility at Modesto in California's Central Valley, but it is the wines now produced from the vast Sonoma Valley vineyard holdings which provide the real interest. Seven vineyards are owned, spread throughout Sonoma from Barelli Creek in the north to Two Rock in the south. A sound range produced under the Sonoma label is blended from separate lots and offers reasonable value. Better, though, are the selected single-vineyard wines, particularly the rich and powerful, spicy, berry-fruited Zinfandel and the Estate Vineyard Chardonnay and Cabernet Sauvignon. While the latter is not quite up there with the major super-premium Napa examples, it is an impressive wine and in the context of top-quality California Cabernet and meritage blends is moderately priced. (DM)
● **Cabernet Sauvignon** Estate★★★★ £F Barelli Creek★★ £D Frei Ranch★★ £D Stefani Vineyard★★ £D
● **Zinfandel** Barelli Creek★★★ £D Frei Ranch★★★ £D
○ **Chardonnay** Estate★★★ £E Laguna Vineyard★★ £D Two Rock★★ £D Stefani Vineyard★★ £E

GEYSER PEAK Alexander Valley www.geyserpeakwinery.com　　　　A: Max

Owner: Henry Trione 22281 Chianti Road, Geyserville CA 95441
This is a substantial operation with production now running at 600,000 cases annually. Unusually the winemaking team is Australian, led by Daryl Groom who was recruited from PENFOLDS in 1989. The Sonoma County wines are generally sound and tend to emphasise straightforward fruit characters. The numerous Block Collection wines are sourced from single vineyards and include Chardonnay, Merlot, Zinfandel, Cabernet Sauvignon and Viognier. The Reserve wines differ in that they are produced from blending a number of the winery's best lots. At the top of the range is the limited-release Bin Series, including Shiraz and Sangiovese. Throughout the range expect big, ripe fruit characters with the top-label reds providing wines with weight and structure and medium-term cellaring potential. (DM)
● **Shiraz** Sonoma County★ £B Reserve★★ £D
● **Alexandre** Meritage Reserve★★ £E Zinfandel Sonoma County★★ £B
● **Cabernet Sauvignon** Block Collection Vallerga Vineyard★★ £D Reserve★★ £D
○ **Sauvignon Blanc** Sonoma County★ £B ○ **Chardonnay** Sonoma County★ £B
○ **Viognier** Block Collection Sonoma Preston Vineyard★★ £C

HANZELL Sonoma Valley www.hanzell.com　　　　A: Vin

Owner: De Brye Estate Trust 18596 Lomita Avenue, Sonoma, CA 95476
Small producer located high up in the Mayacamas Mountains. Hanzell was established way back in 1953 and has long been a pioneer of first-class Chardonnay and Pinot Noir from its hillside estate vineyard. The

operation is built on the quality of this mountain *terroir*. The Chardonnay is a tight, structured example in its youth with well-judged oak and subtle citrus notes, altogether different from many fuller, fatter examples produced by its neighbours. The Pinot is rich and vibrant, with concentrated dark berry flavours and just a hint of game. Both wines will age well and will benefit from four or five years' ageing. (DM)

● **Pinot Noir** Estate★★★ £F
○ **Chardonnay** Estate★★★★ £F

HARTFORD FAMILY WINERY   Sonoma Green Valley   www.hartfordcourt.com   **A: May**

Owner: Hartford family   8075 Martinelli Road, Forestville, CA 95436
Founded in 1993 by Don Hartford and his wife Jennifer Jackson-Hartford, of the KENDALL-JACKSON clan, this operation is dedicated to producing Pinot Noir, Zinfandel and Chardonnay. Winemaker Mike Sullivan purposely crafts very Burgundian styles of Chardonnay and Pinot – tighter, more structured wines than many of their neighbours'. Both are good medium-term cellar propositions. Zinfandel is produced in a ripe, full style but retains real finesse. The Hartford label encompasses Chardonnay and Pinot Noir from the Sonoma Coast as well as a range of Russian River Zinfandels from the Hartford, Dina's, Fanucchi-Wood Road and Highwire vineyards. In addition to this an extensive range of single-vineyard *cuvées* is made under the Hartford Court label. Pinot Noir comes from a number of sources: there is a Marin County bottling, as well as wines from Velvet Sisters Vineyard in Anderson Valley, the Sevens Bench Vineyard in Carneros and Jennifer's Vineyard on the Sonoma Coast. Russian River Pinot is produced from the Arrendell and Dutton-Sanchietti vineyards. Some impressive Chardonnay is produced from the Stone Côte, Laura's and Seascape vineyards on the Sonoma Coast as well as the Three Jacks Vineyard bottling from the Russian River. All stand out. (DM)

Hartford
● **Pinot Noir** Sonoma Coast★★★ £C   ● **Zinfandel** Russian River Valley★★★★ £D
○ **Chardonnay** Sonoma Coast★★★ £C
Hartford Court
○ **Chardonnay** Three Jacks Vineyard★★★★ £E
● **Pinot Noir** Marin County★★★ £E Velvet Sisters Vineyard★★★ £E Dutton Sanchietti★★★★ £E

PAUL HOBBS   Sonoma County   www.paulhobbs.com

Owner: Paul Hobbs   3355 Gravenstein Highway North, Sebastopol, CA 95472
Winemaker Paul Hobbs spends the northern-hemisphere spring months vinifying wines in South America, where he has helped in shaping the style at VALDIVIESO and CATENA. Indeed he has produced his own premium Argentine Malbec, Cobos, from high altitude vineyards in the Upper Mendoza with partners Andrea Marchiori and Luis Barraud. Equally important, he also produces benchmark wines in California from Cabernet Sauvignon, Merlot, Pinot Noir and Chardonnay. His main focus is on single-vineyard wines, particularly an extensive number from Chardonnay, produced in very small quantities. Handling is minimal and the wines are vinified with wild yeasts. Oak is carefully integrated and the primary objective is to provide wines of balance and finesse. Top selections for Chardonnay and Pinot Noir, labelled Cuvée Agustina, are unquestionably very impressive and both very pricey and in short supply. (DM)

● **Cabernet Sauvignon** Napa Valley★★★ £F   ● **Pinot Noir** Hyde Vineyard★★★★ £F
○ **Chardonnay** Russian River★★★ £E

KENDALL-JACKSON   Sonoma County   www.kj.com   **A: KJn**

Owner: Jackson family   5007 Fulton Road, Fulton, CA 95439
Vast, private wine company, founded by Jess Jackson, producing an extensive range under its own label and also owning or part-owning a considerable number of wine operations in the premium-wine sector throughout California. Leading brands include Camelot (good value from the Central Coast), EDMEADES, LA CREMA and Pepi, and the company also has interests in Italy (VILLA ARCENO), Chile (CALINA),

Argentina (Tapiz) and Australia. Jess Jackson and his wife Barbara Banke have connections with the HARTFORD FAMILY WINERY and MATANZAS CREEK, as well as owning CAMBRIA, STONESTREET and VÉRITÉ, and a number of independently run estates have been set up to produce top-quality reds. The LOKOYA wines emanate from single-vineyard, benchland and mountain-vineyard sites, while the ATALON labels are drawn from varied sources. The super-premium CARDINALE is blended from Napa and Sonoma fruit sources. Under the Kendall-Jackson logo, more affordable wines include the Collage reds and Vintners Reserve red and whites. The Grand Reserve label is a step up, producing cool-climate wines from coastal vineyards, while the Vineyard Series wines are sourced from select sites that show good potential at a moderate price. The top wines under the K-J label are the Great Estates and the Stature series. At the top end, the wines are good to very good but, with the reds in particular, you feel more finesse and less overt muscle would take them a step further. (DM)

Kendall-Jackson
● **Cabernet Sauvignon** Buckeye Vineyard★★ £E Great Estates Alexander Valley★★★ £F Stature★★★★ £G
● **Pinot Noir** Great Estates Monterey★★ £E
● **Zinfandel/Shiraz** Collage California★ £B ● **Zinfandel** Great Estates Dry Creek Valley★ £E
O **Chardonnay** Grand Reserve★★ £C Great Estates Sonoma Coast★★★ £E
O **Chardonnay** Great Estates Arroyo Seco★★★ £E Stature★★★★ £F

KISTLER   Russian River Valley   A: WTs
Owner: Steve Kistler   4707 Vine Hill Road, Sebastopol, CA 95472
This has long been a name associated with some of the greatest California Chardonnay. More recently Steve Kistler has been producing some marvellous, rich and vibrant Pinot Noirs as well. Both varieties are made in very small lots from a number of different sites throughout Sonoma as well as the Russian River Valley. The Kistler Vineyard, Durrell Vineyard, Dutton Ranch, Hudson Vineyard, McCrea Vineyard, Vine Hill, Hirsch and Camp Meeting Ridge have all been sources of wines that are invariably of at least four-star quality. Cuvée Cathleen is the top Chardonnay, while the ultimate expressions of Pinot Noir here are Cuvée Elizabeth from the Occidental Vineyard and Cuvée Catherine. The Chardonnays are characterised by full, rich, honeyed notes along with an elegant, mineral core; the Pinots can be explosive with youthful, weighty tannins, suggesting real cellaring potential. (DM)

● **Pinot Noir** Sonoma County★★★ £E Kistler Vineyard✪✪✪✪✪ £G
O **Chardonnay** Sonoma County★★★ £E Les Noisetiers Sonoma Coast★★★★ £F Dutton Ranch★★★★★ £F
O **Chardonnay** Hudson Vineyard✪✪✪✪✪ £G Kistler Vineyard✪✪✪✪✪ £G

LA CREMA   Russian River Valley   www.lacrema.com   A: KJn
Owner: Kendall-Jackson 3690 Laughlin Road, Windsor, CA 95492
A smaller winery in the Kendall-Jackson empire, La Crema, originally established in 1979, is owned and run by sisters Laura Jackson-Giron and Jennifer Jackson. It produces good, well-crafted and reasonably priced Pinot Noir and Chardonnay, along with Viognier, Zinfandel and now Syrah as well. These are good value, if not wines to set the world alight. The Chardonnay is typically ripe and exotic with tropical notes and evident oak, the reds are marked by forward, ripe berry fruit. Russian River and Carneros bottlings are a step up. (DM)

● **Pinot Noir** Sonoma Coast★★ £C Russian River★★ £D Carneros★★★ £D
● **Zinfandel** Sonoma County★★ £C
O **Chardonnay** Sonoma Coast★★ £C Russian River★★★ £C O **Viognier** Sonoma Valley★★ £C

LANDMARK   Sonoma Valley   www.landmarkwine.com   A: Lay
Owner: Colhoun family   101 Adobe Canyon Road, Kenwood, CA 95452
Very fine and stylish Chardonnays and Pinot Noirs are made on this property by winemaker Eric Stern. During the mid-1990s roving wine consultant Helen Turley of MARCASSIN provided additional input and direction. There is a commitment here to producing wines from the ripest fruit from low-yielding,

meticulously-tended vineyards and with minimal intervention. Chardonnay is the main focus, the Overlook label providing great value. Two straightforward budget label Chardonnays are also now offered, Adobe Canyon and Courtyard. The wines are in the rich, lightly tropical vein with nutty oak but impressive grip and structure as well. The Grand Detour Pinot Noir is sourced from the high-altitude Van der Kamp vineyards of Sonoma Mountain and the wine is structured and concentrated with a gamey undercurrent. In addition a small amount of equally impressive, ripe and forward Pinot Noir is produced from the Kastania Vineyard, to which has now been added a low-yielding Syrah Steel Plow, sourced from the Sonoma Mountain El Farolito Vineyard. (DM)

● **Pinot Noir** Sonoma County★★★ £E Grand Detour★★★★ £E
O **Chardonnay** Overlook Vineyard★★★ £D Damaris Reserve★★★★ £E Lorenzo Vineyard★★★★ £E

LAUREL GLEN Sonoma Mountain www.laurelglen.com A: AWM

Owner: Patrick Campbell Box 1419, Glen Ellen, CA 95442
Small operation with some 16 ha (40 acres) of prime vineyards planted to Cabernet Sauvignon, Merlot and Cabernet Franc. Cabernet Sauvignon is very much the dominant variety. The property has thin, rocky and superbly drained soils which provide an excellent base for producing around 3,000 cases a year of explosive Cabernet Sauvignon and a second wine Counterpoint. Patrick Campbell also produces three excellent youthful gluggers. Reds is sourced from old bush vines at Lodi and is based on Zinfandel, Petite Sirah and Carignane, while Terra Rosa is a Cabernet Sauvignon from Chile's Central Valley. More serious are Za Zin, produced from ancient vines planted in California's Central Valley at Lodi, and Quintana, a dark vibrant Cabernet Sauvignon from a number of North Coast vineyard sources. Patrick Campbell is also involved with ACHAVAL-FERRER in Argentina, producing a new premium Malbec, Vale La Pena, from an exceptional 80-year-old vineyard at La Consulta to the south of Mendoza. (DM)

● **Cabernet Sauvignon** Sonoma Mountain★★★★ £E ● **Counterpoint** Sonoma Mountain★★ £D
● **Za Zin** Lodi★★ £B ● **Reds** Lodi★ £B

LYNMAR WINERY Russian River Valley www.lynmarwinery.com A: Vin

Owner: Lyn and Mara Fritz 3909 Frei Road, Sebastopol, CA 95472
Very good newly established Russian River winery with vineyards at their own Quail Hill Ranch. The first vintage released was 1996. Production is solely concentrated on hand-crafted Chardonnay and Pinot Noir. The regular estate bottlings are labelled Quail Vineyard and offer very good value for money. Reserves of both varieties are produced as well as limited-bottling Quail Cuvées, which are more restrained in style. The top wines are the Five Sisters bottlings which are a significant step up in both quality and price. The Chardonnay, particularly, is marked by super-ripe opulent fruit and layer upon layer of flavour. The Pinot Noirs are full of of rich dark berry fruit and spicy oak, varying from around 30 per cent for the regular estate wine to 80 per cent for the Five Sisters. A very limited production Pinot Noir, Requiem, was also produced in 1999. (DM)

● **Pinot Noir** Quail★★★ £D Reserve★★★★ £E Five Sisters★★★★★ £F
O **Chardonnay** Estate★★★★ £D Quail Cuvée★★★★ £E Five Sisters★★★★★ £F

MARCASSIN Sonoma Coast

Owner: Helen Turley & John Wetlaufer PO Box 332, Calistoga, CA 94515
Helen Turley has achieved a cult reputation among California winemakers, consulting to some of the top producers throughout the North Coast. In 1990 she and her husband John Wetlaufer established the Marcassin winery and have developed their own vineyard, planted to Pinot Noir and Chardonnay. Other Chardonnay *cuvées* are also produced from the Lorenzo Vineyard, Three Sisters and Upper Barn, with Pinot Noir from Blue Slide Ridge and the Three Sisters Vineyard. The wines are produced in tiny amounts, only a couple of hundred cases per bottling, and will be nigh on impossible to find. Their reputation is formidable and you can expect the wines invariably to be of at least four-star quality, often five. They are very expensive. (DM)

MARIMAR TORRES   Sonoma Green Valley   www.marimarestate.com   A: JEF

Owner: Marimar Torres   11400 Graton Road, Sebastopol, CA 95472
Based in the cool Sonoma Green Valley sub-appellation, Miguel TORRES' sister Marimar established this operation in 1986, planting the small 33-ha (81-acre) Don Miguel vineyard equally between Chardonnay and Pinot Noir. A new property in the Freestone Valley on the Sonoma Coast is also being planted to Pinot Noir. There is a European approach to viticulture with high vine density helping to ensure low-yielding, piercing fruit. The vineyards have been tended entirely organically since 2003 and cover crops are planted to control vigour and provide a better balance. Vinification is typically Burgundian. The Chardonnay is barrel fermented and aged on lees with 100 per cent malolactic and the Pinot Noir is by separate parcel and clone with a small proportion of whole bunches adding complexity. The wines are always restrained and well balanced with good medium-term cellaring potential. (DM)

● **Pinot Noir** Don Miguel Vineyard★★★★ £E
O **Chardonnay** Don Miguel Vineyard★★★ £E

MARTINELLI   Russian River Valley   www.martinelliwinery.com   A: AWM, Vin

Owner: Steve Martinelli   3360 River Road, Windsor, CA 95492
Steve Martinelli and winemaker Helen Turley produce brilliant Zinfandel, some of the very best in the state; the Jackass Hill is a benchmark for all. You can also find very classy Chardonnay and Pinot Noir here sourced from a number of sites. These are wines of real complexity and style. Pinot is produced in very small quantities, barely 300 cases per bottling, but you can invariably expect wines of at least three stars, often four. The Chardonnay is honeyed and toasty but with an intense, mineral complexity. There are a number of bottlings of this too, with Gold Ridge and Woolsey Road again numbering barely 300 to 400 cases each. (DM)

● **Zinfandel** Giuseppe & Luisa★★★★ £E   Jackass Hill✪✪✪✪✪ £E
● **Pinot Noir** Blue Slide Ridge★★★★ £F   Bondi Home Ranch★★★★ £F   Reserve★★★★ £F
O **Chardonnay** Charles Ranch★★★★ £E   Martinelli Road★★★★ £E
O **Gewürztraminer** Martinelli Vineyard★★★ £C   O **Sauvignon Blanc** Martinelli Vineyard★★★ £D

MATANZAS CREEK   Sonoma County   www.matanzascreek.com   A: May

Owner: Jess Jackson & Barbara Banke   6097 Bennett Valley Road, Santa Rosa, CA 95404
Medium-sized operation producing mainly Chardonnay, Sauvignon Blanc, Merlot and an increasing amount of impressive Syrah, with total volume around 40,000 cases annually. The winery produced some stunning wines during the late 1980s and early 90s, but more recent offerings have been disappointing. Indeed, prior to the involvement of Jess Jackson the wines were better known for their lofty prices than their quality, but with the Jackson influence this winery looks to be back in the top division. Small amounts of a powerful Reserve Merlot, very pricey Journey meritage blend, a Sonoma Valley Syrah and a promising Mendocino Viognier are also now being made. (DM)

● **Merlot** Sonoma Valley★★★ £E
O **Sauvignon Blanc** Sonoma Valley★★★ £C   O **Chardonnay** Sonoma Valley★★★★ £E

PETER MICHAEL   Knights Valley   www.petermichaelwinery.com   A: Vin

Owner: Peter Michael   12400 Ida Clayton Road, Knights Valley, Calistoga, CA 94515
Sir Peter Michael's Knights Valley winery has, for well over a decade, been producing very fine cool- climate wines, with mountain vineyard sources a key element. The Chardonnay *cuvées* are all very impressive with a combination of rich, ripe, honeyed fruit and deftly handled oak. The combination of different clones, native yeast fermentation and careful selection in the vineyard and cellar all contribute and the wines have been increasing in both subtlety and complexity. Sauvignon Blanc is stylish and not dissimilar to top white Graves – it is barrel-fermented with lees-ageing and *bâtonnage* but is tight and structured with a mineral

restraint. The Moulin Rouge Pinot is a more recent addition from the famed Pisoni Vineyard in the Santa Lucia Highlands. The top red, Les Pavots, is from the vineyard of the same name and is a dark, brooding blend of Cabernet Sauvignon, Merlot and Cabernet Franc. It is among the finest Bordeaux blends in California and requires a minimum of six to seven years' age to show at its best. (DM)

● **Pinot Noir** Le Moulin Rouge★★★ £F ● **Les Pavots** Knights Valley❂❂❂❂❂ £G
○ **Sauvignon Blanc** Les Après-Midi★★★★ £F
○ **Chardonnay** La Carrière★★★★ £F Belle Côte★★★★★ £F Mon Plaisir★★★★★ £G
○ **Chardonnay** Cuvee Indigene❂❂❂❂❂ £G

MOON MOUNTAIN VINEYARD Sonoma Valley

Owner: Chalone Wine Group 1700 Moon Mountain Drive, Sonoma, CA 95476
In late 2002 the CARMENET winery, where the Moon Mountain Cabernet had been produced, was sold to BERINGER BLASS estates. Included in the sale were the ripe and exuberant Zinfandel Evangelo Vineyard and stylish Sauvignon/Semillon Reserve. Time will tell how the wines fare under new ownership. Chalone retained ownership of the original estate vineyard and winery, as well as DYNAMITE VINEYARDS label which is now run as a separate operation under the Chalone umbrella. The Cabernet Reserve is a classically ripe, full, almost chocolaty style. Powerful certainly, but there could be more finesse. Cabernet Franc is also now produced from the estate vineyard, while Zinfandel comes from the Monte Rosso Vineyard and a Semillon/Sauvignon Blanc from the Paragon Vineyard in the Edna Valley. (DM)

● **Cabernet Sauvignon** Moon Mountain Reserve★★★£F

ROBERT MUELLER Russian River Valley   A: Vin

Owner: Robert & Lori Mueller 120 Foss Creek Circle, Healdsburg, CA 95448
The Muellers established their small family winery in the centre of Healdsburg in 1991. Since then production has gradually risen to 3,500 cases a year of good, rich and stylish Pinot Noir and Chardonnay. Chardonnay is in a ripe, classically forward California style and should be approached in its youth. The Pinots show impressive deep berry fruit, with some gamey elements and supple, well-balanced tannins. As well as Emily's Cuvée, tiny quantities of pricey Pinot have also been produced from the Summa Vineyard on the Sonoma Coast. (DM)

● **Pinot Noir** Emily's Cuvée★★★★ £E
○ **Chardonnay** LB★★★ £E

PAPAPIETRO PERRY Russian River Valley www.papapietro-perry.com   A: WTs

Owner: Ben Papapietro & Bruce Perry 4441 Westside Road, Healdsburg, CA 95448
The first commercial vintage waas as recent as 1998 at this very new, small but high-quality warehouse winery with two very good Pinot Noirs and a tiny amount of Chardonnay. Production of the Pinots is a mere 650 cases each. A number of classic Pinot techniques are used. The wines get a three day cold soak and are fermented by vineyard lot in small containers. The wines are regularly hand plunged to aid extraction and to keep the temperature of the fermenting must under control. The dark and richly concentrated wines are aged in 60 per cent new oak which is seamlessly integrated. Both are bottled unfined and unfiltered. The Peters Vineyard, from the Sonoma Coast offers just a little more depth and intensity. (DM)

● **Pinot Noir** Russian River★★★★ £E Peters Vineyard★★★★ £E

A RAFANELLI Dry Creek Valley

Owner: Dave Rafanelli 4685 West Dry Creek Road, Healdsburg, CA 95448
Dave Rafanelli has some excellent hillside vineyard sites in the Dry Creek Valley from which he ensures top quality fruit for his own estate wines. He not only produces superlative old-vine, highly complex and characterful Zinfandel, but some impressive Cabernet Sauvignon as well. The estate vineyards are dry-farmed (i.e. without recourse to irrigation) and yields are always kept to a minimum. (DM)

● **Zinfandel** Dry Creek★★★★ £C
● **Cabernet Sauvignon** Dry Creek★★★ £D

RAVENSWOOD Sonoma Valley www.ravenswood-wine.com A: JAr

Owner: Canandaigua 18701 Gehricke Road, Sonoma, CA 95476
No longer small, with production now at some 400,000 cases a year, this Sonoma winery has a major focus on good to very good Zinfandel. The winery was founded in 1976 by winemaker Joel Peterson and partner Reed Foster, who have now sold a controlling interest to Constellation Brands, a part of Canandaigua. Vintners Blend is a good budget label, including Zinfandel, Merlot and Chardonnay. In the second tier are the County Series wines, sourced from vineyards throughout the state, including several Zinfandels. The top wines are in the vineyard-designated series. Along with the many Zinfandels offered there are two meritage reds, Ranch Salina and Pickberry, plus Icon, a blend of Syrah, Grenache and Mourvèdre. Chardonnay comes from the Sangiacomo Vineyard. Top reds are fine cellar prospects. It will be interesting to see whether quality is maintained under the new ownership. (DM)
● **Cabernet Sauvignon** Sonoma County★★ £D ● **Merlot** Sonoma County★★ £C
● **Rancho Salina** Moon Mountain★★★ £E
● **Zinfandel** Monte Bello ★★★★ £E Old Hill Ranch★★★★ £E
● **Zinfandel** Amador County★★ £C Napa Valley★★ £C Sonoma County Old Vines★★★ £C
O **Chardonnay** Sangiacomo Vineyard★★ £D

J ROCHIOLI Russian River Valley A: RsW

Owner: Tom Rochioli 6192 Westside Road, Healdsburg, CA 95448
The Rochioli family have been grape growers for far longer than they have been wine producers. They do however produce some of the best Pinot Noir and Chardonnay from the Russian River, along with impressive Sauvignon Blanc and big, full, very rich Zinfandel, of which there is a striking Sodini Vineyard bottling. As well as the estate Pinot Noir and Chardonnay, there are a number of single-vineyard bottlings of each produced in very small quantities, almost invariably rating three stars or more. (DM)
● **Pinot Noir** Estate★★★★ £E ● **Zinfandel** Estate★★★ £D
O **Chardonnay** Estate★★★★ £E O **Sauvignon Blanc** Estate★★★ £C

ROEDERER ESTATE Anderson Valley www.roederer-estate.com A: MMD,F&M

Owner: Louis Roederer SA 4501 Highway 128, Philo, CA 95466
Champagne house LOUIS ROEDERER has set up its California outpost in the cool Anderson Valley. Unlike a number of their competitors they concentrate on producing just three wines. The regular Brut NV, made from all three Champagne grapes, and Rosé, from Pinot Noir, provide reasonable value and a riper, fuller style than their French counterparts. The Brut L'Ermitage is altogether more serious, a very well structured blend of Pinot Noir and Chardonnay that is both long and complex. (DM)
O **Brut** L'Ermitage★★★★ £E O **Brut** NV★★ £D
◉ **Brut** Rosé BV★★ £E

SAUSAL Alexander Valley www.sausalwinery.com

Owner: Sausal family 7370 Highway 128, Healdsburg, CA 95448
The Sausal family produce around 10,000 cases a year from their 50 ha (125 acres) of estate vineyards. As the top Zinfandel label suggests, some of the vines here are over 100 years of age and it shows in the quality of the reds. Both the Private Reserve and Century Vines are barrel-aged in top-class French oak to add complexity and depth. The resulting wines are supple but finely structured. A straight-forward red and white are also offered as well as a good Sangiovese. (DM)
● **Cabernet Sauvignon** Estate★★★ £D
● **Zinfandel** Family★★ £C Private Reserve★★★ £D Century Vines★★★★ £D

SEGHESIO Dry Creek Valley www.seghesio.com **A: Lib**,Sel

Owner: Seghesio family 14730 Grove Street, Healdsburg, CA 95448
The Seghesio family have been based in the Sonoma Valley since 1895, although they only decided to bottle their own fruit as recently as 1983. Today there are 162 ha (400 acres) of prime vineyard sites which are producing some of the best Zinfandel and Italian-style wines in California. The Zins all have marvellous depth and purity – full of ripe fruit but complex and very intense. There's good to very good Sangiovese, with the newly added Venom from Rattlesnake Hill produced from yields of just 2.5 tons to the acre. The wine stands out among California examples of the variety. Ommagio (meaning 'homage'), like many top *cuvées* produced by winegrowers around the world, celebrates earlier generations. It is a stylish blend of Sangiovese and Cabernet Sauvignon. The top reds will develop well in the medium term. (DM)
- **Pinot Noir** Keyhole Ranch★★★ £E ● **Barbera** California★★ £D
- **Sangiovese** Alexander Valley★★ £D Old Vine "Chianti Station"★★★ £E 'Venom'★★★★ £E
- **Omaggio** Alexander Valley★★★★ £E
- **Zinfandel** Sonoma Valley★★★ £C Home Ranch★★★★ £E Cortina★★★★ £E Old Vine★★★★ £E
- O **Pinot Grigio** Russian River★★ £B O **Arneis** Russian River★★ £C

SIDURI Russian River Valley www.siduri.com **A: Vin**

Owner: Diana & Adam Lee 980 Airway Court, Suite C, Santa Rosa, CA 95403
An extensive range of fine and stylish Pinot Noirs, as well as impressive Syrah from the Novy Vineyard among others, have been made by this small warehouse operation on the outskirts of Santa Rosa since its first vintage in 1994. The Lees practise an absolutely minimalist approach to winemaking and to date no wine they have bottled has been either fined or filtered. The objective is to produce wines that are expressive of the region or individual *terroir* from which they have been sourced. A range of single-vineyard bottlings number the Hirsch and high-profile Pisoni vineyards among them. Pinot is now sourced all the way from the Willamette Valley in Oregon down to the new Santa Rita AVA in Santa Barbara County – the only problem being that there's not very much about. (DM)
- **Pinot Noir** Sonoma County★★★ £E Santa Lucia★★★★ £F Van der Kamp Vineyard★★★★ £F
- **Syrah** Novy Vineyard★★★ £D

WH SMITH Sonoma County **A: Vin**

Owner: Bill Smith 13719 Dog Bar Road, Grass Valley, CA 95492
Bill Smith established his reputation for making great California reds when he ran the LA JOTA winery on Howell Mountain, creating massive and powerful Cabernet Sauvignon and Petite Sirah – some of legendary proportions. The Smiths have sold their interest in La Jota in order to pursue their most recent venture, vinifying stylish Pinot Noir on the Sonoma Coast. As well as the intense and complex Hellenthal Vineyard, a Sonoma Coast bottling is also offered. The style is one of elegance rather than power, with an attractive undercurrent of piercing, red berry fruit and well-judged oak. (DM)
- **Pinot Noir** Hellenthal Vineyard★★★ £E

SONOMA-CUTRER Russian River Valley www.sonomacutrer.com **A: BFW**,L&S

Owner: Brown Forman 4401 Slusser Road, Windsor, CA 95492
Originally established as a top-notch producer of Chardonnay in 1973 by Brice Cutrer Jones, the Sonoma-Cutrer star has waned a little. The wines are nevertheless consistent, particularly the two leading *cuvées*. With the exception of Les Pierres, which is just to the north of Carneros, the vineyard plots are all Russian River. The Russian River Ranches bottling is a blend of all the winery's vineyards throughout the region, while the two single-vineyard wines are classified as its Grand Cru program. The tiny-production top wine is the Founders Reserve, selected from the five best barrels of the vintage and bottled without filtration. This is not a vineyard selection but purely the very best barrels from the three vineyards. (DM)
- O **Chardonnay** Russian River Ranches★★ £C The Cutrer★★★ £E Les Pierres★★★ £E

ST FRANCIS VINEYARDS   Sonoma Valley   www.stfranciswine.com   A: HMA

Owner: Joe Canton, Lloyd Martin, Kopf family   100 Pythian Road, Santa Rosa, CA 95409
Impressive, medium-sized Sonoma winery founded in 1971. An extensive range is produced, solely from
Sonoma County fruit and at the top end the quality is striking. Zinfandels, both Old Vines and Pagani
Ranch, are huge, brooding, super-ripe examples of the variety. Perhaps just a little more elegance and
refinement would take these Zins to a higher level. Nuns Canyon bottlings of both Merlot and Cabernet
are impressive and very stylish. The Cabernet Kings Ridge Reserve, the top label, is powerful, refined and
very well crafted. It will age gracefully and needs a minimum of six years. A fairly extensive range of reserve
reds are also available solely from the winery. (DM)

● **Zinfandel** Old Vines★★★ £D   Reserve Pagani Vineyard★★★★ £E
● **Merlot** Sonoma County★ £C   Reserve Nuns Canyon Vineyard★★★ £E
● **Cabernet Sauvignon** Sonoma County★★ £C   Reserve Nuns Canyon Vineyard★★★ £E
● **Cabernet Sauvignon** Kings Ridge Vineyard Reserve★★★★ £G
○ **Chardonnay** Sonoma County★ £C   Reserve Behler Vineyard★★ £D

STEELE   Lake County   www.steelewines.com   A: Vin

Owner: Jed Steele   4350 Thomas Drive at Highway 29, Kelseyville, CA 95451
Jed Steele has enormous experience of the wine business in California, having previously been the founding
winemaker at KENDALL-JACKSON. He established his own label in 1991 and he now produces an
extensive range of reds and whites, with the top-of-the-line examples coming from an almost bewildering
array of single-vineyard sources. These are not only impressive and stylish but represent very good value for
money. Chardonnay is on the one hand rich and opulent, on the other balanced by a fine mineral
undercurrent, and there are two unusual late-harvest examples from the Dupratt and Sangiacomo vineyards.
The reds are supple, well-structured and accessible at a young age. They will however develop well in bottle.
Shooting Star is the winery's second label, providing good fruit-driven wines at very fair prices. Often these
will be one-, sometimes two-star wines. (DM)

● **Pinot Noir** Carneros★★★ £D   Sangiacomo Vineyard★★★ £D   Bien Nacido★★★ £E
● **Cabernet Franc** Lake County★★ £C   Merlot Lake County★★★ £D
● **Zinfandel** California★★★ £C   Catfish Vineyard★★★ £D
● **Syrah** Lake County★★ £C   Parmalee-Hill★★★ £D
○ **Chardonnay** Cuvée California★★★ £C   Lolonis Vineyard★★★ £D   Dupratt Vineyard★★★ £D
○ **Chardonnay** Bien Nacido★★★★ £D   Durrell Vineyard★★★★ £E
○ **Pinot Blanc** Santa Barbara County★★ £C

STONESTREET   Alexander Valley   www.stonestreetwines.com   A: KJn, WTs

Owner: Kendall-Jackson   7111 Highway 128, Healdsburg, CA 95448
One of a number of high-quality, medium-sized wineries in the Jackson family empire. Merlot, Chardonnay
and the meritage red Legacy, a blend dominated by Cabernet Sauvignon, are all impressive. Chardonnay is
in a rich, tropical style, with the top bottlings showing both refinement and the structure for mid-term
cellaring. The reds are big, powerful and brooding, marked by high alcohol. They are rich almost chocolaty,
with just the occasional green note in lesser vintages. A fruit-driven Sauvignon Blanc from the Upper Barn
Vineyard has also been added to the range. (DM)

● **Merlot** Alexander Valley★★★ £C   ● **Legacy** Alexander Valley★★★★ £F
● **Cabernet Sauvignon** Alexander Valley★★ £D   Christopher's Vineyard★★★ £G
○ **Chardonnay** Sonoma County★★★ £C   Block Sixty-Six★★★★ £D   Upper Barn★★★★ £E

VÉRITÉ   Sonoma Valley   www.veritewines.com   A: May

Owner: Kendall-Jackson   4611 Thomas Road Healdsburg CA 95448
Recently established Jackson family premium operation specialising in Bordeaux red styles. The wines are

all hand-crafted from various sites throughout Sonoma County. The vineyard sources are classic mountain *terroirs* and winemaker Pierre Seillan is able to source what the winery refers to as *micro-crus*, producing wines from the very best blocks of a number of estates. Fruit comes from the Alexander, Bennett and Knights Valleys as well as Carneros and Atlas Peak. La Joie emulates the Left Bank of Bordeaux and is a blend of roughly two-thirds Cabernet Sauvignon with the balance Merlot. Youthfully backward and firmly structured, it is nevertheless very concentrated with fine, intense, very ripe dark berry fruit. La Muse, 90 per cent Merlot and 10 Cabernet Sauvignon, is more forward and opulent. Full of dark plum and spicy oak, the wine is richly textured, supple but finely structured. Undoubtedly the option of being able to source superb fruit from a number of sites adds complexity. Very impressive, the wines need just an extra dimension to take them into the absolute top division. The third wine in the portfolio is Le Désir, a Saint-Emilion style blend of Cabernet Franc and Merlot with a touch of Cabernet Sauvignon which was released for the first time in the second half of 2003. (DM)

● **La Joie** Sonoma County★★★★★ £G **La Muse** Sonoma County★★★★★ £G
● **Le Désir** Sonoma County★★★★★ £G

WILLIAMS SELYEM   Russian River Valley   A: Vin

Owner: John & Kathe Dyson   1861 Lewis Street, Ballard CA 93463
The Dysons purchased this classic Sonoma property from founders Burt Williams and Ed Selyem in 1998. Winemaker Bob Cabral has stayed on and continues to make the same artisan styles of Chardonnay and Pinot Noir as Williams and Selyem. The Pinots are rich and concentrated, marked by their powerful, earthy tannins, while the Chardonnay can be lusciously rich but with none of the overt tropical notes found in neighbouring wines. A plethora of single-vineyard labels are produced every vintage and rarely are these less than four stars. Ferrington and Rochioli Pinot is now very pricey as is Heintz Chardonnay. These are Sonoma wines for the longer haul. There are two very interesting, rich and intense sweet wines from Gewürztraminer and Muscat. Both are opulent in style but well-structured with a fine mineral-fresh acid balance. (DM)

● **Pinot Noir** Sonoma County★★★★ £E Russian River★★★★★ £F Hirsch Vineyard★★★★★ £F
● **Zinfandel** Russian River★★★★ £E Bacigalupi Vineyard★★★★ £E
O **Chardonnay** North Coast★★★★ £F Allen Vineyard★★★★ £F Hirsch Vineyard★★★★ £F
O **Gewürztraminer** Late Harvest San Benito County★★★★★ £G
O **Muscat Canelli** Late Harvest Russian River Valley★★★★£G

OTHER WINES OF NOTE

ALDERBROOK ● **Zinfandel** Russian River Reserve £E O **Sauvignon Blanc** Dry Creek £B
ANCIEN ● **Pinot Noir** Carneros £E O **Chardonnay** Carneros £E
BANNISTER ● **Pinot Noir** Floodgate Mountain £D ● **Zinfandel** Dry Creek £C
BELVEDERE ● **Pinot Noir** Russian River £D O **Chardonnay** Russian River £C
BOEGER ● **Cabernet Sauvignon** Eldorado £C ● **Barbera** Eldorado £C
● **Tempranillo** Reserve £C ● **Zinfandel** Old Vine £C
BOGLE VINEYARDS ● **Zinfandel** Walker Vineyard £B ● **Petite Sirah** California £B
O **Chardonnay** California £B O **Chenin Blanc** California £B
AUGUST BRIGGS ● **Pinot Noir** Russian River £D O **Chardonnay** Russian River £D
CANEPA CELLARS O **Chardonnay** Gauer Ranch Adobe III £E
SEAN CAPIAUX ● **Pinot Noir** Widdoes Vineyard £E Pisoni Vineyard £F
CARLISLE ● **Syrah** Sonoma County £E ● **Zinfandel** Dry Creek £D Two Acres Russian River £E
CARMENET ● **Zinfandel** Evangelo Vineyard £D O **Sauvignon Semillon** Reserve £C
CÈAGO ● **Merlot** Mendocino £E
CHATEAU SOUVERAIN ● **Cabernet Sauvignon** Winemakers Reserve £E
CHRISTOPHER CREEK ● **Petite Sirah** Russian River £D ● **Syrah** Russian River £C
DAVID COFFARO ● **Zinfandel** Dry Creek Valley £C Estate Old Vines £C
BR COHN ● **Cabernet Sauvignon** Olive Hill Special Selection £F O **Chardonnay** Joseph Herman £D

COTURRI ● **Zinfandel** Sonoma Valley P Coturri Family Vineyards £C
DAVIS BYNUM ● **Pinot Noir** Le Pinot Rochioli Vineyard £F
DE LOACH ● **Zinfandel** Russian River OFS £D ○ **Chardonnay** Russian River OFS £D
DUMOL ● **Pinot Noir** Russian River £F ○ **Chardonnay** Russian River £E
DUXOUP WINE WORKS ● **Syrah** Dry Creek Valley £C ● **Charbono** Napa Valley £B
DYNAMITE VINEYARDS ● **Cabernet Sauvignon** Sonoma County £C
MERRY EDWARDS ● **Pinot Noir** Russian River £D Olivet Lane £E Klopp Ranch £E
FAILLA JORDAN ● **Syrah** Que Syrah Vineyard £E
FERRARI CARANO ● **Cabernet Sauvignon** Tre Monte £E ○ **Chardonnay** Tre Monte £E
FISHER ● **Cabernet Sauvignon** Coach Insignia £F Wedding Vineyard £G
○ **Chardonnay** Coach Insignia £D
ADRIAN FOG ● **Pinot Noir** Floodgate £F C23 Russian River £F Hawkeye Vineyard £F
GREENWOOD RIDGE VINEYARDS ● **Zinfandel** Scherrer Vineyards £C
GUENOC ● **Cabernet Sauvignon** Beckstoffer IV Reserve £E ● **Petite Sirah** Estate £E
○ **Chardonnay** Genevieve Magoon Reserve £E
GUNDLACH-BUNDSCHU ● **Zinfandel** Rhinefarm Vineyards £D
● **Cabernet Sauvignon** Rhinefarm Vineyards £D
HANDLEY ● **Pinot Noir** Reserve £E ○ Brut Anderson Valley Vintage £D
HANNA ● **Cabernet Sauvignon** £E Bismarck Ranch £F ● **Zinfandel** Bismarck Ranch £E
HAYWOOD ● **Zinfandel** Los Chamizal Vineyard £C
HIDDEN CELLARS ● **Petite Sirah** Heritage Eaglepoint Ranch £D ● **Sorcery** £D
HOP KILN ● **Zinfandel** Primitivo Vineyard £C ● **Marty Griffin's Big Red** California £B
IRON HORSE VINEYARDS ○ **Classic Vintage Brut** Sonoma Green Valley £D
○ **Blanc de Blancs** Sonoma Green Valley £E
J WINE COMPANY ○ **Chardonnay** Russian River £E ○ **Pinot Gris** Russian River £C ○ **Vintage Brut** £D
JORDAN ○ **Chardonnay** Estate £D ● **Cabernet Sauvignon** Estate £E
KENWOOD VINEYARDS ● **Zinfandel** Jack London £C
● **Cabernet Sauvignon** Jack London £E Artist Series £F
KUNDE ESTATE ● **Cabernet Sauvignon** Reserve £D ○ **Sauvignon Blanc** Magnolia Lane £C
LAMBERT BRIDGE ● **Zinfandel** Dry Creek £C Crane Creek Cuvee £E
LANCASTER ESTATE ● **Lancaster** Alexander Valley £F
LAZY CREEK ○ **Gewürztraminer** Anderson Valley £C
LIMERICK LANE ● **Zinfandel** Collins Vineyard £D
MARIETTA CELLARS ● **Syrah** California £C
MAYO FAMILY ○ **Chardonnay** Barrel Select £D
McCRAY RIDGE ● **Merlot** Two Moon Vineyard £F
McDOWELL ● **Syrah** Reserve £C ○ **Viognier** Reserve £C
MICHEL-SCHLUMBERGER ● **Cabernet Sauvignon** Reserve Dry Creek Valley £D
MURPHY-GOODE ● **Cabernet Sauvignon** Brenda Block £E ○ **Chardonnay** Sonoma County £C
NALLE WINERY ● **Zinfandel** Dry Creek Valley £C
NAVARRO VINEYARDS ● **Pinot Noir** Méthode a l'Ancienne £C ○ **Gewürztraminer** Anderson Valley £B
OPTIMA ● **Cabernet Sauvignon** Alexander Valley £E ● **Pinot Noir** Russian River Valley £E
PACIFIC ECHO ○ **Brut** Non Vintage £C Vintage Blanc de Blancs £D Vintage Private Reserve £E
◉ **Brut** Vintage Rose £D
PEZZI KING ● **Zinfandel** Maple Vineyard £D
RANDOM RIDGE ● **Cabernets** Mount Veeder £D ● **Zinfandel** Old Wave £D
QUIVIRA ● **Zinfandel** Dry Creek £D ○ **Sauvignon Blanc** Fig Tree Vineyard £B
RUTZ CELLARS ● **Pinot Noir** Weir Vineyards £E ○ **Chardonnay** Dutton Ranch £D
SCHERRER VINEYARD ● **Cabernet Sauvignon** Alexander Valley £F ● **Pinot Noir** Russian River £E
● **Zinfandel** Old and Mature Vines £E
SEBASTIANI ● **Cabernet Sauvignon** Cherry Block £F ● **Mourvèdre** Domenici Vineyard £D
SEBASTOPOL ● **Pinot Noir** Dutton Ranch £D ● **Syrah** Dutton Ranch £E
○ **Chardonnay** Dutton Ranch £D
SIMI ● **Cabernet Sauvignon** Reserve £G ○ **Sendal** Reserve £C
SKEWIS ● **Pinot Noir** Floodgate Vineyard £F Montgomery Vineyard £F

SOLITUDE ● **Pinot Noir** Sangiacomo Vineyard £D   O **Chardonnay** Sangiacomo Vineyard £D
STUHLMULLER ● **Cabernet Sauvignon** Alexander Valley £E   O **Chardonnay** Alexander Valley £C
JOSEPH SWAN ● **Pinot Noir** Steiner Vineyard £D   ● **Zinfandel** Frati Ranch £D   Stellwagen Vineyard £D
TARIUS ● **Pinot Noir** Russian River £E   ● **Zinfandel** Aldine Vineyard £D
TRENTADUE ● **Petite Sirah** Alexander Valley £C   Old Patch Red £C   ● **Zinfandel** Alexander Valley £C
TRIA ● **Zinfandel** Dry Creek £C
WELLINGTON VINEYARDS ● **Zinfandel** Russian River Valley £C   ● **Syrah** Sonoma County £C

Work in progress!!

Wines from the following producers under consideration for the next edition

ACORN WINERY
ANAKOTA
ANCIEN WINES
BELLA VINEYARDS
BLACKFORD
COPAIN WINES
DUNAH
EDGEHILL
GAMBA VINEYARDS
HUNDRED ACRE VINEYARD
NOVY FAMILY
PAX WINE CELLARS
RENARD
WALTER HANSEL
WHETSTONE

Author's choice (DM)

A selection of Sonoma blockbuster reds

BEHRENS AND HITCHCOCK ● **Cabernet Sauvignon** Kenefick Ranch
DEHLINGER ● **Syrah** Estate
FOPPIANO ● **Petite Sirah** Russian River Reserve
GALLO OF SONOMA ● **Cabernet Sauvignon** Estate
HARTFORD ● **Zinfandel** Russian River Valley
KENDALL JACKSON ● **Cabernet Sauvignon** Stature
MARTINELLI ● **Zinfandel** Jackass Hill
PETER MICHAEL ● **Les Pavots** Knights Valley
SEGHESIO ● **Omaggio** Alexander Valley
VÉRITÉ ● **La Joie** Sonoma County

Benchmark Pinot Noirs

GARY FARRELL ● **Pinot Noir** Rochioli Vineyard
HANZELL ● **Pinot Noir** Estate
HARTFORD COURT ● **Pinot Noir** Dutton Sanchietti Vineyard
PAUL HOBBS ● **Pinot Noir** Cuvée Agustina
KISTLER ● **Pinot Noir** Kistler Vineyard Vineyard
LYNMAR WINERY ● **Pinot Noir** Five Sisters Vineyard
PAPAPIETRO PERRY ● **Pinot Noir** Peters Vineyard
J ROCHIOLI ● **Pinot Noir** Estate
SIDURI ● **Pinot Noir** Van der Kamp Vineyard
WILLIAMS SELYEM ● **Pinot Noir** Hirsch Vineyard

A selection of cool climate Sonoma whites

ARROWOOD O **Viognier** Saralee's Vineyard
KISTLER O **Chardonnay** Hudson Vineyard
LA CREMA O **Chardonnay** Russian River Valley
LANDMARK O **Chardonnay** Damaris Reserve
LYNMAR WINERY O **Chardonnay** Five Sisters Vineyard
MARCASSIN O **Chardonnay** Marcassin Vineyard
MARTINELLI O **Chardonnay** Charles Ranch
PETER MICHAEL O **Chardonnay** Cuvee Indigene
ROEDERER ESTATE O **Brut** L'Ermitage
STEELE O **Chardonnay** Durrell Vineyard

California/Napa & Carneros

The Napa Valley has now been producing high-quality wine for over three decades and indeed many properties go back to pre-Prohibition times. As in the other major viticultural regions of California, dynamic change is continuous and new operations, particularly boutique and very small scale premium red producers, are emerging all the time. Of one thing there is no doubt: winemakers here and particularly those working with classic Bordeaux varieties, are able to charge super-premium prices. These days the top Bordeaux reds can seem relative bargains in comparison to some of their Napa counterparts. There is no question that an increasing number of truly world-class wines continue to emerge from Napa but also that there are as many that are priced too highly and quite simply struggle to justify their lofty tags. If you are looking for some very serious bottles they're certainly here, but some care and research is needed before purchasing

Geography

The **Napa Valley** AVA runs along an extensive river valley stretching from north of Calistoga along the Napa River to south of the town of Napa itself and just edging towards San Pablo Bay at the northern end of San Francisco Bay. South-west of Napa, the Carneros AVA is located south of the Mayacamas Mountains and effectively divides the Sonoma and Napa Counties viticultural regions. In Napa, like Sonoma and Mendocino, the climate is moderated by cool marine breezes and coastal fog.

Northern Napa

Calistoga's benchland vineyards are the warmest in the Napa Valley, because little of the moderating sea breeze drifts this far. The topography becomes semi-mountainous to the west with the **Spring Mountain District** AVA and to the east the **Howell Mountain** AVA, which is an extension of the Coastal Ranges. There are a number of exceptional Cabernet Sauvignons, Merlots and meritage blends, produced from vineyards within these mountain AVAs. Equally impressive wines are also emerging from sites similarly cooled by altitude but on the lower slopes, both to the west, and east of the valley. These sites are characterised by excellent aspects and soil drainage, both of which are hallmarks in the production of great wine. The key to these wines is their structure; their mountain origin gives them a unique stamp. They can be the least approachable when young but among the longest-lived and most refined of Napa's great reds. This is essentially Cabernet country but there are some good Chardonnays, one or two stylish Syrahs and Viogniers and some very good Zinfandel.

Central Napa

The central section of the Napa Valley is the heart of its best benchland vineyards for Cabernet Sauvignon and Bordeaux-style red blends. This takes in an area that runs from **St Helena** in the north to cooler **Yountville** in the south and encompasses the AVAs of **Rutherford** and **Oakville**. It is difficult to generalise as wine quality is by no means determined by the traditional Rutherford Bench yardstick: the bench is a narrow strip of vineyard stretching north of the town of Rutherford with gravel and sandy-clay soils producing potentially great wines, but in recent years a whole host of other small vineyard sites have proven to have excellent growing conditions, many of them taking the Napa Valley AVA. However, in general the wines to the north at St Helena are the ripest and most opulent, while those from Yountville have the tightest structure. These generalisations are offset by exceptional producers outperforming their neighbours and by many sites which are influenced by the sloping hills of Howell Mountain to the east and Spring Mountain and the Mayacamas to the west. As well as the Bordeaux styles, good Zinfandel and Syrah are grown throughout this stretch of vineyards.

Southern Napa

To the east of Yountville are the AVAs of **Stags Leap District** and **Atlas Peak**. To the west **Mount Veeder** provides sturdy reds with Zinfandel and Syrah increasingly successful; some fine, tightly structured Chardonnay and peachy Viognier are also produced. Stags Leap is somewhat of a conundrum. There are some very fine wines produced in these gravel soils but also a number of underperformers. Atlas Peak has so far disappointed. The winery of the same name has experimented with only moderate success with Sangiovese, Cabernet Sauvignon and Chardonnay. To the west of Napa, towards the Wild Horse Valley, the Bordeaux varieties and Chardonnay have all been successful.

Carneros

Part-Sonoma County and part-Napa County, Carneros AVA is just inland to the north of San Pablo Bay and directly affected by those cool, marine breezes. This is key for the production of sparkling base wine and it is no surprise that a number of sparkling-wine operations are based here, including California offshoots of some of the big European names. Pinot Noir and Chardonnay are successful and, more surprisingly, in warmer mesoclimates so is spicy, black pepper-styled Syrah, notably from the Hudson Vineyard.

A-Z of producers by region

1   Napa Valley
2   Howell Mountain
3   Diamond Mountain
4   Spring Mountain
5   St Helena
6   Rutherford
7   Oakville
8   Yountville
9   Mount Veeder
10 Stag's Leap District
11 Atlas Peak
12 Carneros

California Napa & Carneros vintages

As elsewhere in California, it is difficult to provide a locally specific guide but there is a reasonable consistency through the region and the charts below give a fair indication of what you should expect, both in terms of quality and ageability. If you have cellared or are considering purchasing some older top Cabernet then earlier vintages that are looking particularly good are 1987, 1986 and more speculatively 1978, 1974 and 1970.

California Napa & Carneros vintage chart

	Cabernet and Meritage Blends	Zinfandel	Pinot Noir	Chardonnay
2003	★★★★/★★★★★ A	★★★★/★★★★★ A	★★★★ A	★★★★ B
2002	★★★★ A	★★★★ A	★★★★ A	★★★★ A
2001	★★★★/★★★★★ A	★★★★ A	★★★★ A	★★★★ B
2000	★★/★★★ A	★★/★★★ B	★★★/★★★★ B	★★★/★★★★ B
1999	★★★/★★★★ A	★★★★ B	★★★★ B	★★★/★★★★ C
1998	★★★ B	★★/★★★ C	★★★/★★★★ C	★★★ C
1997	★★★★ A	★★★/★★★★ B	★★★★ C	★★★★ C
1996	★★★/★★★★ B	★★★/★★★★ C	★★★/★★★★ C	★★★ C
1995	★★★★ B	★★★/★★★★ C	★★★/★★★★ C	★★★★ D
1994	★★★★/★★★★★ B	★★★★ C	★★★★ C	★★★/★★★★ D
1993	★★★★ B	★★★/★★★★ C	★★★ D	★★★★ D
1992	★★★★ B	★★★/★★★★ C	★★★/★★★★ D	★★★★ D
1991	★★★★ C	★★★★ C	★★★/★★★★ D	–

Napa Valley & Carneros/A-Z of producers

ABREU Napa Valley   A: **THt**

Owner: David Abreu   2366 Madrona Avenue, St Helena, CA 94574
David Abreu is best-known among his fellow winegrowers as a superlative viticulturalist. Numbered among his distinguished clientele are GRACE FAMILY, VIADER and PAHLMEYER. As well as his many vineyard-management commitments, he fashions a massive, super-ripe Cabernet with a hint of Merlot and Cabernet Franc from this first-class vineyard. The wine is one of the most 'collectable' in California and as such is very pricey and almost impossible to find. (DM)
● **Cabernet Sauvignon** Madrona Ranch❶❶❶❶❶ £H

ACACIA Carneros www.acaciawinery.com

Owner: Chalone Group   2750 Las Amigas Road, Napa, CA 94552
Acacia has always produced wines that are soundly made and represent reasonable value for money if sometimes lacking a touch of character or sense of place. The wines are particularly marked by their ripe fruit and for opulent reds and tropically styled whites at competitive prices they are all good bets. Chardonnay is forward, oaky and richly textured. The Marsh label is aged on lees from other bottlings. The generic Carneros is the volume wine; it has a very sizeable output with 36,000 cases made in the 2002 vintage and gets nine months ageing in one third new French oak. The Sangiacomo Vineyard output is tiny in comparison: just 300 cases. Aged in 80 per cent new French and American oak it is a clear step up in quality. Pinot Noir in its various guises offers bright berry fruit with greater depth and power in the Beckstoffer Vineyard and smaller-production, premium Field Blend (produced from four young-vine Dijon clones) and St Clair Vineyard examples. The range is completed by a good regular sparkling Brut. (DM)
● **Pinot Noir** Carneros★★ £D Beckstoffer Vineyard★★★ £D
○ **Chardonnay** Marsh★★ £C Carneros★★ £C
○ **Brut Vintage**★★ £E

ARAUJO Napa Valley www.araujoestatewines.com   A: **THt**

Owner: Bart Araujo   2155 Pickett Road, Calistoga, CA 94515
These formidable wines are all produced from the Eisele Vineyard, originally owned by JOSEPH PHELPS, in the north-eastern part of the Napa Valley. As well as the Cabernet Sauvignon there is a first class Syrah and most recently Altagracia, a Bordeaux red blend of Cabernet Sauvignon, Petit Verdot and Merlot. Both are sadly produced in tiny quantities. Even scarcer is the occasional bottling of Viognier. The variety is mainly planted to blend with the Sauvignon Blanc and to provide fragrance for the Syrah. Since its purchase by the Araujos in 1990, a considerable effort has been put into the vineyard with its superbly drained stony soils and mountain-moderated climate. Winemaker Françoise Peschon is aided by roving international wine consultant Michel Rolland. The approach is as one would expect, delivering wines with rich, immensely concentrated fruit and supple and rounded tannins. The Cabernet is blended with a little Cabernet Franc, Petit Verdot and Merlot. The Sauvignon Blanc has a hint of Viognier and is part barrel- and part tank-fermented and then aged on lees for six months. With a total of just 16.6 ha (41 acres) under vine there is an inevitable scarcity here. Release prices are very fair but the auction market quickly gets a hold. All the reds are immensely ageworthy, however you might consider broaching them with five or six years' age, particularly if you're lucky enough to have a case or two. (DM)
● **Cabernet Sauvignon** Eisele Vineyard❶❶❶❶❶ £H
○ **Sauvignon Blanc** Eisele Vineyard★★★ £C

ARIETTA Napa Valley www.arietta.com   A: **Vin**

Owner: John Kongsgaard/Fritz Hatton   PO Box 349, Oakville, CA 94562
John Kongsgaard consults widely for other wineries as well as producing some superb Rhône styles under

his own label. Here he has established a partnership with Fritz Hatton to produce very small-scale, high-quality reds modelled mainly on the wines of Bordeaux. The Merlot is 100 per cent varietal, dark, cedary, exceptionally balanced and very long and complex. The Hudson H Block is more Saint-Emilion than Pomerol in style; it blends 60 per cent Cabernet Franc with the balance Merlot. It is the firmest of the trio. The Variation One is dominated by Syrah and blended unusually with Merlot. Opulent, exotic and loaded with smoky, dark fruit it is the most approachable of the wines. Given some of the stratospheric prices elsewhere, the wines look like pretty good value. All will benefit from at least four to five years' cellaring and will keep very well. (DM)

● **Merlot** Napa Valley★★★★★ £G   ● **H Block One Red** Napa Valley★★★★★ £G
● **Variation One Red** Napa Valley★★★★★ £G

ATALON   Napa Valley   www.atalon.com   **A: May**
Owner: Kendall-Jackson   7600 St. Helena Highway, Oakville, CA 94562
Recently established super-premium winery owned by Jess Jackson, producing wines which are intended to complement his LOKOYA and CARDINALE brands. A wide range of Napa vineyard sources are being called on. Some vineyard-specific wines are only available at the winery, such as the seriously pricey Cabernet Sauvignon Beckstoffer Vineyard bottling. These are very impressive, dense and powerful wines although, as with so many premium California reds, the top labels are very expensive. The Cabernets stand out from the Merlots. (DM)

● **Merlot** Napa Valley★★★ £F   Napa Mountain Estates★★★★ £F
● **Cabernet Sauvignon** Napa Valley★★★★ £F   Napa Mountain Estates★★★★★ £G

BACIO DIVINO   Rutherford   www.baciodivino.com   **A: WTs**
Owner: Claus Janzen   P.O. Box 131, Rutherford, CA 94573
With a total output of just 2,500 cases a year, Claus Janzen's operation is small even by California cult-winery standards. The Bacio Divino red is a very stylish, impressive and unusual blend of Cabernet Sauvignon, Sangiovese and Petite Sirah. Part of Claus Janzen's inspiration was tasting the red at Domaine de TREVALLON in Provence, itself a blend of unconventional varieties. The Bacio Divino is a rich, smoky and succulent wine, accessible and ripe with velvety tannins and great depth. Second label Bacio Angelico has been replaced by Pazzo. This is now a blend of Sangiovese, Cabernet Sauvignon and Petite Sirah and is produced in a lush, forward style to be enjoyed sooner rather than later. (DM)

● **Bacio Divino** Napa Valley★★★★★ £G

BEAULIEU VINEYARD   Rutherford   www.beaulieuvineyards.com   **A: PFx,AAA**
Owner: Diageo Chateau and Estates Wine Co   1960 St Helena Highway, Rutherford, CA 94573
Historic Napa winery founded in 1900 and, like STERLING, now a part of the Diageo group. The Beaulieu reputation was established by the legendary André Tchelistcheff. While quality was distinctly variable during the 1980s, the late 90s saw a marked improvement. An enormous range of wine is offered under Coastal, Appellation, Reserve and Speciality labels and some good quality can be found at the lower price levels. The Signet Collection wines are a clear step up in quality and often offer excellent quality as well as value. Beauzeaux is a juicy blend of Zinfandel, Valdiguié, Charbono, Petite Sirah and Grenache. Ensemble is an attractive, spicy, Southern Rhône-style blend, while the top-end Cabernets are particularly impressive. The premium Tapestry is a typical Bordeaux-style blend. (DM)

● **Syrah** California★★ £C   North Coast Signet Collection★★★ £D
● **Beauzeaux** Napa Valley★★ £C   ● **Ensemble** California★★ £C
● **Zinfandel** Napa Valley★ £C   Napa Valley Signet Collection★★★ £D
● **Pinot Noir** Carneros★ £C   Carneros Reserve★ £E   ● **Merlot** Napa Valley ★★ £D
● **Cabernet Sauvignon** Coastal★★ £C   Georges de Latour★★★★ £G   Clone 4★★★★ £H   Clone 6★★★★ £H
● **Tapestry** Reserve Napa Valley★★ £E
O **Chardonnay** Carneros Reserve★★ £D

BERINGER   St Helena   www.beringer.com   A: BWC,AAA

Owner: Beringer Blass   2000 Main Street, St Helena, CA 94574
Now a part of the global BERINGER BLASS group, this winery was established 125 years ago and has always produced wines of good to very good quality at all price levels. Much of this success must be attributed to the skills of winemaking chief Ed Sbragia whose top *cuvées* remain some of the very best in California. Estate vineyards continue to be developed and for a number of the premium labels the home St Helena vineyard, planted on well-drained soils in the Spring Mountain foothills, remains a key to quality. The two entry-level ranges provide sound, everyday wines, if, it has to be said, a touch unexciting. Stone Cellars emphasises the classic varieties whereas the California series focuses on the more unusual including white Zinfandel, Merlot and the gluggable Beringer Nouveau. The Founders Estate range is a level up and generally some oak, new and old, is used to lend structure and an added dimension to the wines. Appellation series wines are produced with more of an emphasis on *terroir*. Some new French oak is used for ageing and some good bottles can be found. A further step up, the Alluvium wines are red and white meritage blends, the red dominated by Merlot and, like the white, approachable in its youth. At the pinnacle are the Private Reserve and Limited Release labels. A number of top Cabernets come from a range of single vineyards. An increasing amount of very good Cabernet Franc from Howell Mountain is also being produced along with North Coast Sangiovese and a fine botrytised dessert Semillon/Sauvignon blend, Nightingale. (DM)
- ● **Alluvium Red** Knights Valley★★★ £E
- ● **Cabernet Sauvignon** Knights Valley Reserve★★★ £E Private Reserve★★★★★ £G
- ● **Merlot** Napa Valley★★ £D Reserve Bancroft Ranch Howell Mountain★★★★ £F
- ● **Pinot Noir** North Coast★ £C Reserve Stanly Ranch Carneros★★ £D
- ● **Zinfandel** Clear Lake★ £B
- O **Alluvium** Knights Valley★★★ £D
- O **Chardonnay** Napa Valley★★ £C Private Reserve★★★★ £E Sbragia Limited Release★★★★ £E
- O **Sauvignon Blanc** Napa Valley★★ £B
- O **Viognier** Napa Valley★★ £D

ROBERT BIALE   Napa Valley   www.robertbialevineyards.com   A: OWL

Owner: Robert Biale   2040 Brown Street, Napa, CA 94559
The Biale family have owned vineyards in the Napa Valley for decades but more recently they have established themselves as a very impressive small producer of mainly old-vine Zinfandel from a range of sources including their home vineyard, along with Petite Sirah and a little Syrah, Barbera and Sangiovese. The key to quality here is tight control of yields both in their own vineyards and through working closely with the small growers who also supply grapes. With so much California Zin now massively extracted and overblown, these examples show remarkable refinement and balance. This is artisan California winegrowing at its best. The Zins will drink very well young as well as aging gracefully. (DM)
- ● **Zinfandel** Estate★★★★ £E Spenker Vineyard★★★ £D Monte Rosso Vineyard★★★★ £E
- ● **Petite Sirah** Estate★★★ £E

BLOCKHEADIA RINGNOSII   Napa Valley   A: WTs

Owner: Michael Ouellette   Lorenza Lake Winery, 1764 Scott Street, St Helena, CA 94574
Michael Ouellette founded Blockheadia in 1992. Around 11,000 cases of well-priced, characterful Zinfandel, Petite Sirah (recently added) and Sauvignon Blanc are now produced. Fruit comes from a number of sources and is always hand-picked. The wines are very much in the fruit-driven mould with minimal oak influence. The Zins are marked by spicy, dark fruits and they are medium weight rather than blockbusters. The Sauvignon Blancs are vinified without oak and offer a mix of lightly tropical fruit with a soft mineral undercurrent. They are also well-balanced and tend to avoid some of the excessively alcohol levels found elsewhere. The wines are all approachable on release. (DM)
- ● **Zinfandel**★★ California £C Mendocino County★★ £D Napa Valley★★★ £E
- O **Sauvignon Blanc** California★★ £C Napa Valley★★ £C

BRYANT FAMILY   Napa Valley

Owner: Bryant family   1567 Sage Canyon Road, St Helena, CA94574
With production of just over a 1,000 cases the Bryant Cabernet has become one of a handful of blue-chip California examples of the variety alongside such illustrious names as ARAUJO, COLGIN, GRACE FAMILY, HARLAN and SCREAMING EAGLE. The property is located in the Pritchard Hill sector of the Napa, close to CHAPPELLET and the Bryants evidently achieve much more from the area than their neighbours. The vineyards benefit from cooling breezes channelled directly from Lake Hennessey on the eastern slopes of the valley. While the wine has immense depth and power, consultant Helen Turley has created a style that is also supple and rounded, approachable at five or six years. In part this is achieved with a five-day cold soak prior to fermentation. The wine is bottled without filtration. Philip Melka has now replaced Turley in overseeing the winemaking. Expect the wine to age gracefully and be prepared to pay a very high price for it.(DM)

● **Cabernet Sauvignon**✪✪✪✪✪ £H

CAFARO   Napa Valley   www.cafaro.com   A: **Lib**

Owner: Joe Cafaro   1550 Allyn Avenue, St Helena, CA 94574
Joe Cafaro is a successful consultant winemaker who has made wine for the likes of ACACIA and DALLA VALLE. He also owns a small winery where he produces stylish, supple and complex Cabernet, Merlot and most recently a small amount of Syrah from the Cafaro Family Vineyard. His property is on slopes just to the south of Stags Leap. The wines are all marked by their purity of fruit and fine, elegant structure, without some of the aggressive tannin found elsewhere from mountain-grown reds. Ripe, intense berry fruit is well balanced with lightly spicy oak. Just over 300 cases of a Cabernet Sauvignon Reserva have been released from the excellent 1999 vintage, which Cafaro believes adds an extra dimension. Compared with much of the competition these wines are great value. (DM)

● **Merlot** Napa Valley★★★★ £F ● **Cabernet Sauvignon** Napa Valley★★★★ £F
● **Syrah** Cararo Family Vineyard★★★★ £E

CAIN CELLARS   Spring Mountain   www.cainfive.com   A: **J&B**,N&P

Owner: Jim and Nancy Meadlock   3800 Langtry Road, St. Helena   CA 94574
This is a spectacularly sited Spring Mountain estate with some 34 ha (84 acres) planted to Cabernet Sauvignon, Merlot, Malbec, Cabernet Franc and Petit Verdot, which make up the flagship Cain Five – a medium-full, ripe, chocolaty and lightly cedary blend. The Concept, another meritage blend dominated by Cabernet Sauvignon but with a hint of Syrah for perfume, is sourced from benchland as well as hillside vineyards. This is softer and more approachable than its mountain-grown big brother. Cain Cuvée is a non-vintage Bordeaux blend in a soft, forward style. The range is completed by Musque – a fresh, lightly herbal Sauvignon Blanc. (DM)

● **Cain Five** Napa Valley★★★★ £G ● **Cain Concept** Napa Valley★★ £E ● **Cain Cuvee** Napa Valley★ £C
○ **Cain Musque** Ventana Vineyard★★ £C

CAKEBREAD CELLARS   Rutherford   www.cakebread.com   A:**C&B**

Owner: Cakebread family   8300 St Helena Highway, Rutherford, CA 94573
Now a fairly substantial operation which the Cakebread family have been running for well over two decades. Production is approaching 100,000 cases, including an extensive premium range. Chardonnay and Sauvignon are both rich and oaky in style, with the Reserve and Rutherford bottlings adding an extra element of depth and texture. Regular Merlot and Cabernet are well crafted and both are big, powerful and quite alcoholic reds. Pinot Noir and Syrah have both been made from Carneros fruit and recently released is a blend of the two called Rubaiyat, a tank-fermented forward, fruit-driven, easy-drinking red. The top *cuvées* are the three super-premium Cabernets. As well as the Benchland Select, very small quantities of Vine

Hill Ranch and Three Sisters are made.(DM)

● **Merlot** Napa Valley★★ £E **Cabernet Sauvignon** Napa Valley★★★★ £F Benchland Select★★★★ £G
O **Chardonnay** Napa Valley★★ £E Reserve★★★ £F
O **Sauvignon Blanc** Napa Valley★★ £C Rutherford★★★ £D

CARDINALE Napa County www.cardinale.com A:WTs,KJn

Owner: Kendall-Jackson 7600 St Helena Highway, Oakville, CA 94562

This very pricey red is the jewel in the crown of the KENDALL-JACKSON empire. It is actually vinified in the same facility as the single-vineyard wines of the LOKOYA label. It is a blend of Cabernet Sauvignon and Merlot sourced from prime vineyards in Oakville as well as mountain plots on Mount Veeder, Atlas Peak and Howell Mountain in Napa and the Alexander and Knights Valleys in Sonoma, which explains the generic California appellation. A massively powerful and concentrated red with copious quantities of super-ripe cassis and hints of cedar underpinned by high-toast oak, in the best vintages the wine convincingly earns five stars. Yet you do feel that just a hint more refinement would add that final dimension. (DM)

● **Cardinale Proprietary Red** California★★★★★ £H

CAYMUS Rutherford www.caymus.com A: Vin

Owner: Chuck Wagner PO Box 268, Rutherford, CA 94573

Two good to very good Cabernet Sauvignons are vinified here. Chuck Wagner also produces very stylish Chardonnay at his Central Coast winery MER SOLEIL as well as a late-harvest Viognier. Conundrum is a classy white, blended from an unusual mix of Sauvignon Blanc, Semillon, Chardonnay, Viognier and Muscat Canelli. It is ripe and aromatic with a hint of new oak. It is planned that the wine will have its own facility based in Monterey County, as it stands alone as a separate brand rather than being a subsidiary Caymus label. The Special Selection, one of California's great reds, needs cellaring and will improve in bottle for 5 to 10 years. The grapes are harvested lot by lot and vinified with extended maceration on skins and ageing in new French oak. The 1999 was particularly impressive; 2000 is also seriously worth noting for your cellar. (DM)

● **Cabernet Sauvignon** Napa Valley★★★ £F Special Selection Napa Valley★★★★★ £H
O **Conundrum** California★★★ £C

CHAPPELLET Napa Valley www.chappellet.com

Owner: Chappellet family 1581 Sage Canyon Road, St. Helena, CA 94574

This winery, located on Pritchard Hill close to BRYANT, has had a variable record in recent years. Most interesting is the impressive Chenin Blanc. Vinified from old vines with just a hint of oak this is a striking and unusual example of the variety for California. On occasion a late-harvest version is produced, which can be remarkably rich and intense. Signature Cabernet and Chardonnay have both shown recent form as should be expected from first-class vineyards with meagre, well-drained stony soils. The Mountain Cuvée, a meritage blend, is effectively the third Cabernet-based wine here. Sangiovese and Zinfandel are also produced as well as an extraordinarily expensive Pritchard Hill Estate Vineyards Cabernet Sauvignon and the Pritchard Hill Estate Vineyards Cabernet Franc which is blended with a little Merlot, Cabernet Sauvignon and Cabernet Franc. (DM)

● **Merlot** Napa Valley★★ £D
● **Cabernet Sauvignon** Signature★★★ £E
O **Chardonnay** Napa Valley★★ £C Signature★★★ £E
O **Chenin Blanc**★★ £B Old Vine Cuvée★★★ £B

CHATEAU MONTELENA Napa Valley www.montelena.com A: **Vin**

Owner: Jim Barrett 1429 Tubbs Lane, Calistoga, CA 94515
One of a few genuinely historic Napa wineries dating back to the 1880s. Nowadays the winery is best- known for one of the greatest Cabernet-based reds from the US. Even in lesser years the Montelena Estate red has a reputation for real quality. It is a backward and powerfully structured wine that stands in marked contrast to the many ripe and supple, opulent styles that have emerged more recently. A minimum of 10 years is required to enjoy it at its best; often opening a bottle early will cause great disappointment as with some of the great wines of France. A varietal Zinfandel has now replaced the St Vincent which blended Zinfandel and Sangiovese. It is a typically fine, elegant and structured example of the grape in keeping with the winemaking approach here. The Chardonnay is a particularly restrained, tight and mineral-laden example, stylish and impeccably balanced. Unlike many examples from California it will develop well with age. (DM)

● **Zinfandel** Montelena Estate★★★ £D
● **Cabernet Sauvignon** Napa Valley★★★ £E Montelena Estate★★★★★ £H
O **Chardonnay** Napa Valley★★★ £E

CHATEAU POTELLE Mount Veeder www.chateaupotelle.com A: **CKr,J&B**

Owner: Marketta & Jean-Noël Fourmeaux 3875 Mt Veeder Road, Napa, CA 94558
The Fourmeaux family origins are in the French wine trade but Marketta and Jean-Noël have made a very good job of producing classically original, stylish Californian wines. The VGS labels are particularly impressive, none more so than the Zinfandel and Cabernet Sauvignon vinified from estate-grown mountain fruit. These are big, structured wines which need time, five years or so, to soften their youthfully aggressive, at times angular tannins. Chardonnay is barrel-fermented with nicely judged oak, Sauvignon Blanc is fresh and floral but further complexity is added with a small amount of Semillon and a portion of the fruit barrel-fermented on lees. (DM)

● **Zinfandel** VGS★★★ £F **Cabernet Sauvignon** VGS★★★ £F
O **Chardonnay** VGS★★★ £E O **Sauvignon Blanc** Napa Valley★★ £B

CLINE CELLARS Carneros www.clinecellars.com A: **WTs**

Owner: Fred Cline 24737 Highway 121, Sonoma, CA 95476
Along with Randall Grahm of BONNY DOON, Fred Cline was one of the original Rhône Rangers. From his 142-ha (350-acre) Carneros property he produces a plethora of Zins and some first-class Rhône styles. The family have some of the most extensive plantings of Rhône varieties in the state and account for no less than 85 per cent of all Mourvèdre plantings, although fruit is also sourced elsewhere. Some solid whites are also produced but they lack the same excitement as the reds, with their vibrant, spicy, berry fruit character. At the top end they posses not only rich, concentrated fruit but marvellously honed, supple tannins – wines of weight and finesse. The fact that they represent great value is another major plus. (DM)

● **Syrah** Carneros★★★ £C
● **Red Truck Red** Vin Rouge California★ £B ● **Carignane** Ancient Vines Contra Costa County★★ £C
● **Mourvèdre** Ancient Vines Contra Costa County★★★ £D Small Berry Vineyard★★★★ £D
● **Syrah** California★★ £C Sonoma County★★★ £D
● **Zinfandel** California★★ £B Ancient Vines California★★★ £C Big Break Vineyard★★ £D
● **Zinfandel** Bridgehead Vineyard★★★ £D Jacuzzi Family Vineyard★★★ £D Fulton Road★★★ £E
● **Zinfandel** Live Oak Vineyard★★★ £D
O **Cotes d'Oakley** Vin Blanc California★ £B O **Marsanne** Carneros★ £C O **Viognier** Carneros★★ £C
O **Roussanne** Carneros★★ £C

COLGIN CELLARS Napa Valley www.colgincellars.com

Owner: Ann Colgin PO Box 254, St Helena, CA 94574
Colgin now offers three super-premium bottlings. All are extremely expensive (the $175-plus winery release prices can rapidly be dwarfed by trading prices at auction) and all are based on Cabernet Sauvignon, although the Cariad red is 55 per cent Cabernet Sauvignon, 35 per cent Merlot and 5 per cent Cabernet Franc (all sourced from the Madrona Vineyard) as well as 5 per cent Petit Verdot. Unblended Cabernet Sauvignon in two guises is produced from the Herb Lamb and Tychson Hill vineyards. Total production is barely 1,000 cases annually. The wines are neither fined nor filtered and spend around two years in new French oak. All undoubtedly offer considerable weight, depth and rich textures. Helen Turley of MARCASSIN was the guiding force behind the winemaking here up to 1998, when the mantle was taken on by Max Aubert – formerly of another benchmark producer, PETER MICHAEL – who is also making top-quality Chardonnay under his own Aubert label. Expect the wines to be of at least four- to five-star quality if you can obtain any through the mailing list. (DM)

CORISON Napa Valley www.corison.com   A:DDr

Owner: Cathy Corison 987 St Helena Hwy, St Helena, CA 94574
Cathy Corison produces a small amount of Napa Cabernet Sauvignon sourced from a variety of top quality benchland vineyard sites. Unlike many wines produced by her Napa neighbours, the Corison Cabernet is not overblown and has considerable depth and finesse. Aged in around 50 per cent new French oak the wine shows remarkably well young but will evolve impressively with cellaring. A very limited amount of a special *cuvée* from the Kronos Vineyard is also produced, which requires more patience and a deeper pocket. (DM)
● **Cabernet Sauvignon**★★★★ £F

ROBERT CRAIG Napa Valley www.robertcraigwine.com   A:THt,MyC

Owner: Robert Craig 830 School Street, Suite 14, Napa, CA 94558
Small, high-quality Napa operation established in 1992 and sourcing fruit from a number of locations. Affinity is a typical Bordeaux-style blend of Cabernet Sauvignon, Merlot and Cabernet Franc. Ripe, supple and surprisingly elegant it can be approached relatively young. The two Cabernets are equally stylish but require more time to tame their mountain tannins. The Syrah is in a rich, vibrant, dark-fruit style as might be expected from warm-climate Paso Robles but has gained increased elegance from blending a portion of fruit from Los Olivos in Santa Barbara. Zinfandel from Amador County was added with the 2000 vintage and looks promising. The Chardonnays are a little less impressive than the reds but have reasonable depth with ripe citrus fruit and a marked tropical character and should be broached young. Drink the reds over the short to medium term. (DM)
● **Cabernet Sauvignon** Mount Veeder★★★★ £E Howell Mountain★★★★ £E
● **Affinity** Napa Valley★★★★ £E ● **Syrah** Central Coast★★★ £D
○ **Chardonnay** Carneros★★ £C Sonoma County★ £C

CUVAISON Napa Valley www.cuvaison.com   A: THt,Sel

Owner: Schmidheiny family 4550 Silverado Trail, Calistoga, CA 94515
Medium-sized operation producing over 60,000 cases a year of which 65 per cent is Chardonnay. Fruit is sourced from its own vineyards, including a 162-ha (400-acre) property in Carneros, as well as from elsewhere; the recently acquired Brandlin Ranch on Mount Veeder will provide further resources of estate fruit for vintages to come. The wines are well-crafted, well-priced and always reliable but never really set the world alight. Nonetheless they are very well priced in a California context. Most impressive is the Estate Selection Chardonnay which gets 15 months in mainly new high-quality French oak. Syrah from the Carneros estate and Napa Valley fruit and Zinfandel from Napa sources have been added to the the range with the 2000 vintage. Expect both to have reasonable potential. (DM)
● **Cabernet Sauvignon** Napa Valley★★ £D ● **Merlot** Napa Valley/Carneros★★ £D

● **Pinot Noir** Napa Valley Carneros ★★ £D
○ **Chardonnay** Napa Valley/Carneros★★ £C Estate Selection Carneros★★★ £E

DALLA VALLE   Oakville   www.dallavallevineyards.com   A: THt

Owner: Naoko Dalla Vale   7766 Silverado Trail, Napa, CA 95448
One of Napa's small-volume, super-premium wineries with a first-class hillside site to the east of Oakville. The vines are planted in sparse red clay and volcanic soils which forces them to struggle for excellence. Also crucial to quality here is the extra sunshine the vineyard receives compared with those of the valley floor 120 m (400 ft) below, which results in grapes of exquisite flavour and concentration. Three wines are produced under the guidance of Mia Klein of SELENE. The main focus of production is Cabernet Sauvignon plus a small amount of the even more impressive Maya, from the vineyard of the same name. Both are dominated by Caberenet Sauvignon with a small proportion of Cabernet Franc blended in. A stylish, dark cherry-laden Sangiovese, Pietre Rosse, is also made. The Cabernet Sauvignon and Maya are dense, massive and hugely extracted wines requiring a minimum of six to seven years' ageing; the Pietre Rosse can be approached much sooner. (DM)
● **Cabernet Sauvignon** Estate★★★★★ £H

DARIOUSH   Napa Valley   www.darioush.com

Owner: Darioush Khaledi   4240 Silverado Trail, Napa, CA 94558
Darioush Khaledi established this winery as recently as 1997 but the results are already impressive. He owns 13 ha (33 acres) of vineyards around the site of the new winery building, which is in the course of construction, along with 10 ha (25 acres) in the Mount Veeder and Atlas Peak AVAs. The top wines are released under the Signature label while there is a secondary Estate label for Chardonnay and Cabernet Sauvignon. The Signature reds are rich, vibrant and impressively dense and powerful. Cabernet Sauvignon is blended with Merlot, Cabernet Franc and Petit Verdot. A Signature meritage red which is markedly cheaper than the Signature Cabernet Sauvignon has now been added to the range. The wines have minimal handling in the cellar and the Cabernet and Shiraz are bottled without filtration. Expect them to age well over the medium term. (DM)
● **Cabernet Sauvignon** Signature★★★ £F ● **Merlot** Signature★★★ £E ● **Shiraz** Signature★★★ £F
○ **Chardonnay** Signature★★ £E ○ **Viognier** Signature★★ £D

DIAMOND CREEK   Diamond Mountain   www.diamondcreekvineyards.com   A: L&W

Owner: Al Brounstein   1500 Diamond Mountain Road, Calistoga, CA 94515
Supreme Cabernet Sauvignon has been made here for a great deal longer than most of the new generation of *super-cuvées*. These are not just wines of massive extract and weight, sourced from prime mountain sites and each individually stating its own *terroir*, they are wines of grace, power and above all immense refinement. Volcanic Hill is the fullest and longest lived. Red Rock Terrace, like Volcanic Hill, comes from a warm site and is the most accessible of the trio whereas Gravelly Meadow – from the coolest of the three sites – is tight and restrained. You would be well-advised to cellar for at least 10 years to enjoy one of these bottles at its best. A fourth vineyard, Lake, is the coolest and smallest of the five plots on the property. Occasionally it produces extraordinary wines; there have only been eight vintages of it since 1972 and it almost always fetches a small fortune at auction. The fifth plot, called Petit Verdot and planted entirely to the variety, has now come on stream and provides additional blending resources for all the wines. (DM)
● **Cabernet Sauvignon** Gravelly Meadow❍❍❍❍❍ £H   Volcanic Hill❍❍❍❍❍ £H
● **Cabernet Sauvignon** Red Rock Terrace❍❍❍❍❍ £H

DOMAINE CARNEROS   Carneros   www.domaine.com   A: HMA

Owner: Champagne Taittinger   1240 Duhig Rd., Napa, CA 94559
California outpost of the Champagne house TAITTINGER. As well as the sparklers it has recently been producing some stylish and reasonably impressive Pinot Noirs, available only from the winery. These are in a ripe and full berry fruit style. Famous Gate is aged for 10 months in one half new oak and has a little structure; the Domaine bottle is softer and more immediately accessible. Avante-Garde, an entry-level example, has now been added. The Le Rêve Blanc de Blancs is the pinnacle of the sparkling range. A wine of some considerable style, it is almost exclusively Chardonnay with a tiny proportion of Pinot Blanc. Real complexity is gained from the five years spent on lees. (DM)
O **Brut Non-Vintage**★ £C   Vintage Cuvée★★ £D   Blanc de Blancs Le Rêve★★★ £E

DOMAINE CHANDON   Yountville   www.chandon.com

Owner: LVMH   1 California Drive, Yountville, CA 94599
Probably the best-known among the California sparkling wine producers and established way back in 1973, Chandon is also producing a limited amount of Carneros-sourced still wine from the traditional Champagne varieties bottled as varietals. Of the sparkling wines, l'Étoile is refined and reasonably intense; the Vintage is bigger and fuller with marked toasty, bready notes; while the small amount of the rare Mount Veeder *cuvée*, a Blanc de Blancs which spends four years on lees, is tight, well-structured and stylish. Riche, an extra dry style has also now been added to the range. (DM)
O **Brut** Classic★ £B   Reserve★★ £C
O **Blanc de Noirs** ★★ £B   O **l'Étoile**★★ £E   O **Vintage**★★ £F
◉ **l'Étoile**★★ £E

DOMINUS ESTATE   Yountville   www.dominusestate.com   A: C&B,M&V

Owner: Christian Moueix   2570 Napanook Road, Yountville, CA 94599
Christian Moueix is a member of the Bordeaux dynasty responsible for Château PETRUS. Some of the exotic but firm youthful elements of that great wine are reflected in Dominus despite it being a blend dominated by Cabernet Sauvignon. The key is in the winemaking and while the ripe fruit character of the Napanook Vineyard shows through it still possesses a classically powerful tannic structure. It requires up to a decade or more of ageing to show at its best, providing a wine of balance, subtlety and refinement. The Napanook is an impressive second label first produced in 1996. It is considerably more forward than the *grand vin* and can be approached easily with three or fours years' development. (DM)
● **Dominus**✪✪✪✪ £H   Napanook★★★ £E

DUCKHORN   St Helena   www.duckhorn.com   A: L&W

Owner: Dan & Margaret Duckhorn   1000 Lodi Lane, St Helena, CA 94574
This has evolved into a mid-sized operation since it was founded in 1978. Around 1,000 tons of fruit are crushed and production is now around 60,000 cases. The main focus of the operation is Merlot. A good regular Napa Valley bottling is joined by top-end examples from estate fruit as well as two other premium labels from Howell Mountain and the Three Palms vineyard. Cabernet Sauvignon is also good. As well as the Napa bottling, an Estate and two single-vineyard wines, Monitor Ledge and Patzimaro, are also produced. The style was of an iron fist but is tamer these days, with suppler tannin. The wines will still benefit from four or five years' cellaring and the top wines will keep very well. The Paraduxx is an unusual blend of Zinfandel with a touch of Merlot and Cabernet, while the Decoy maintains the integrity of the top wines. A new winery facility for the Paraduxx is due to be completed in 2005. The Duckhorns have also purchased vineyards and a winery in the cool Anderson Valley to produce stylish Pinot Noir under the Goldeneye label. (DM)
● **Cabernet Sauvignon** Napa Valley★★★ £F

● **Merlot** Decoy Migration★★ £D Napa Valley★★★ £E
● **Merlot** Howell Mountain★★★★ £F Three Palms★★★★ £F
● **Paraduxx** Napa Valley★★★ £E
○ **Sauvignon Blanc** Napa Valley★★ £C

DUNN VINEYARDS Howell Mountain   A: AWM

Owner: Randy Dunn 805 White Cottage Road, Angwin, CA 94508
Randy Dunn was one of the pioneers of great mountain-grown Cabernet. He established his own operation in 1979 during the time he was winemaker at CAYMUS. Output is now capped at around 4,000 cases a year. The estate bottling, Howell Mountain, is a massive wine almost always offering formidable concentration and depth with real finesse as well. Ageing is for two and a half years in half new and half used oak. The Napa Valley Cabernet is in a marginally softer style but is nevertheless a considerable and seriously structured wine. Both wines get a light filtration which Dunn believes adds stability but are not fined; retaining tannin is key to their longevity. Both understandably require cellaring, the Estate Howell Mountain for a minimum of a decade. Also noteworthy is the value offered by both wines in these days of extraordinarily high prices for Napa reds. (DM)
● **Cabernet Sauvignon** Napa Valley★★★★ £F Estate Howell Mountain✪✪✪✪✪ £F

FAR NIENTE Oakville www.farniente.com   A: Hal, T&W

Owner: Gil Nickel 1350 Acacia Drive, Oakville, CA 94562
There are just two main wines at this well-established (first vintage 1979) estate in the heart of Napa. The original winery here dates back to 1885 and was created from gold-rush money. Fruit quality is maintained through ownership of vineyards in five sites and covering no less than 101 ha (250 acres). The Cabernet is a typically powerful Napa expression requiring several years' cellaring to be enjoyed at its best. The Chardonnay has been fine-tuned over recent vintages and is an unusually elegant and refined style with a well-honed, tight oak influence and the balance to offer real promise with age. Its taut mineral style is in marked contrast to other Napa examples of the variety. (DM)
● **Cabernet Sauvignon**★★★★ £G
○ **Chardonnay**★★★★ £F

FLORA SPRINGS St Helena www.florasprings.com   A: Vin, Win

Owner: Komes family 1978 West Zinfandel Lane, St Helena, CA 94574
Sizeable family-owned and run operation with a broad selection of wines. The Komes' now own nearly 200 ha (500 acres) of Napa vineyards, providing a considerable resource for their range. The two flagships are the Cabernet Sauvignon Hillside Reserve and the proprietary red Trilogy, a blend of Cabernet Sauvignon, Merlot, Cabernet Franc and Malbec. Both are ageworthy and display a fine balance of ripe fruit and harmonious tannin. Both these and the Wild Boar Vineyard Cabernet require five years' ageing. Two further single-vineyard varietal Cabernets have now been added to the range from the Holy Smoke Vineyard at Oakville and the Out of Sight Vineyard in the southern Napa. The Merlot bottlings are more accessible. Italian styles feature prominently in the range, both red and white. Poggio del Papa, the top Italian red, is a Tuscan-influenced blend of Sangiovese, Merlot and Cabernet Sauvignon and there is well-priced Pinot Grigio as well.(DM)
● **Cabernet Sauvignon** Napa Valley★★★ £D Wild Boar Vineyard★★★ £F Hillside Reserve★★★★ £G
● **Merlot** Estate★★★ £D Windfall Vineyard★★★ £E ● **Sangiovese** Napa Valley★★ £B
● **Trilogy** Napa Valley★★★★ £F
○ **Chardonnay** Barrel Fermented Reserve★★★ £D ○ **Soliloquy** Oakville★★★ £D

FORMAN   St Helena   A: AWM

Owner: Ric Forman   1501 Big Rock Road, St Helena, CA 94574
Ric Forman makes impressive examples of both Chardonnay and Cabernet Sauvignon as well as a little Merlot. Vineyards established in the early 1980s are the source of his excellent raw material. Planted mainly in volcanic gravel and sand, they are sparse and provide naturally low-yielding fruit. The Chardonnay is rich and lightly tropical with a pure mineral edge and well-integrated oak. It has unusually good grip and structure for a Napa example, being fermented and aged in oak but without the malolactic fermentation. The Cabernet Sauvignon is rich, concentrated and cedary, with subtle cassis notes in the background. The wine is firmly structured and possesses the depth and fruit quality to develop well in bottle for five or more years and keep considerably longer. The wines are notable for their excellent value.(DM)
● **Cabernet Sauvignon** Napa Valley★★★★ £E
O **Chardonnay** Napa Valley★★★★ £D

FRANCISCAN   Oakville   www.franciscan.com   A:PWa

*Owner: **Canandaigua**   1178 Galleron Road, Highway 29 at Galleron Road, St Helena, CA 94574*
Agustin Huneeus sold Franciscan to Canandaigua in 1999 along with the two sister wineries ESTANCIA and MOUNT VEEDER WINERY, although he retained his prestige QUINTESSA operation. The wines here are good rather than inspired but in most cases offer reasonable value for money. They are very much in a rich California vein, being very ripe, upfront and fruit-driven. They will show well young. Cuvée Sauvage is in a very rich, high-toast oak style. The Magnificat red will develop well with five years' ageing or so. Small amounts of premium ageworthy reds are released and have included Merlot Reserve which is blended with 20 per cent Cabernet Sauvignon and more recently a very pricey Clos Vineyard Reserve which is 50 per cent Cabernet Franc with the balance Merlot and Cabernet Sauvignon. (DM)
● **Cabernet Sauvignon** Napa Valley★★ £D   ● **Merlot** Napa Valley★★ £C   ● **Magnificat**★★★ £F
O **Chardonnay** Napa Valley★★ £C   Cuvée Sauvage★★★ £E

PETER FRANUS   Rutherford   www.franuswine.com   A: THt

Owner: Peter Franus   P.O. Box 10575, Napa, CA 94581
Impressive small producer with a range sourced from a number of committed grape growers. Total production is now some 7,500 cases. The style is very much one of minimal intervention and the wines are impressive without being overdone. Cabernet comes from a number of Napa sources. A single-vineyard bottling from the Rancho Chimiles vineyard was added with the 1999 vintage but only 250 are made each year. Zinfandel is always stylish and vibrant: Napa-sourced Rancho Chimiles and the Planchon Vineyard label from 100-year-old Contra Costa vines are both impressive but the the best of the three is the stylish and complex Mount Veeder wine from Brandlin Vineyard. Sauvignon comes in two guises: Farella-Park is barrel-fermented; the Stewart Vineyard bottling from Carneros sees no wood. (DM)
● **Cabernet Sauvignon** Napa Valley★★★ £E
● **Zinfandel** Planchon Vineyard★★★ £C   Rancho Chimiles★★ £C   Brandlin Vineyard★★★ £D
O **Sauvignon Blanc** Farella-Park Vineyard★★ £C   Stewart Vineyard★ £C

FROG'S LEAP   Rutherford   www.frogsleap.com   A: L&W, M&V,F&M

Owner: John Williams   8815 Conn Creek Road, Rutherford, CA 94573
John Williams established Frogs Leap with Larry Turley, who went on to make superstar Zins at TURLEY CELLARS. The emphasis of the marketing here is on fun, reflected in the labelling. Pull a cork and you'll see what I mean. However, the wine is serious and can be very impressive. The style is for forward, ripe, fleshy reds with sufficient structure to age nicely in the medium term and for rich, fruity whites. The Rutherford red, a blend of Cabernet Sauvignon and Cabernet Franc sourced from a number of dry-farmed vineyards, is serious and powerful. A small amount of Syrah is now produced from Carneros and there is a fun,

everyday white Leapfrögmilch made from Riesling and Chardonnay plus a few hundred cases of juicy rosé labelled Pink made from old-vine Valdiguié. (DM)

● **Cabernet Sauvignon** Napa Valley★★★ £E ● **Rutherford** Napa Valley★★★ £F
● **Merlot** Napa Valley★★★ £D ● **Zinfandel** Napa Valley★★★ £C
○ **Chardonnay** Napa Valley★★ £C ○ **Sauvignon Blanc** Napa Valley★★★ £C

GLORIA FERRER Carneros www.gloriaferrer.com

Owner: Freixenet 23555 Highway 121, Sonoma, CA 95476
The style here is for rich, ripe sparkling wines sourced mainly from estate vineyards in Carneros. While the wines are typically Californian, the impressive winery and cellar, referred to by the Ferrer family as 'Champagne Caves', is designed in an unusual hacienda style. The Chardonnay is a style that should be enjoyed young. The Pinot Noir and Merlot, which also come from Carneros, will stand just a little age. The sparkling wines, which all benefit from sufficiently lengthy lees-ageing, are ready on release. The Royal Cuvée spends an extended six years on its yeast, while the flagship Carneros Cuvée has a high proportion of reserve wine and seven years on its lees. A tiny amount of the Late-Disgorged ETS can also be obtained direct from the winery. At the time of writing the vintage available was 1987, so expect a wine with a very evolved character. (DM)

○ **Chardonnay** Carneros★★ £C
○ **Sonoma Brut** Sonoma County★ £C ○ **Blanc de Noirs** Carneros★★ £C
○ **Royal Cuvée** Carneros★★ £C ○ **Carneros Cuvée** Carneros★★★ £E
◉ **Brut Rosé** Carneros★★ £C

GRACE FAMILY VINEYARDS St Helena www.gracefamilyvineyards.com

Owner: Dick Grace 1210 Rockland Drive, St Helena, CA 94574
This tiny operation was the first of the now numerous Calfornia cult wineries and the Grace Family is one of the most exalted premium Cabernets in California. It commenced production in 1978 and barely 400 cases are made annually from the family vineyard. This was one of the first vineyards to be planted with close-spaced vines, avoiding the need for herbicides or pesticides, and biodynamic farming is being evaluated at present. Part of the production is auctioned for charity so the remainder is extremely rare. Big, richly textured and immensely powerful, it is a wine respected for its balance and finesse as much as its sheer concentration. If you can find any, expect to pay a very high price. Some very decent olive oil is also made. (DM)

GREEN AND RED VINEYARD Napa Valley www.greenandred.com   A:AWM,Win

Owner: Jay Hemingway 3208 Chiles Valley Road, St Helena, CA 94574
Small estate in the Chiles Valley on the eastern side of the Napa Valley whose main focus is Zinfandel. Consultancy input from Helen Turley of MARCASSIN has provided the stimulus for well-crafted ripe and supple examples of the variety. The Chiles Mill is an estate-vineyard bottling and is a level up on the Chiles Valley Zin sourced from a number of neighbouring sites. The California label is the lightest of the three and comes from vineyards in Lake County, Lodi, Paso Robles and Napa County. Chardonnay is barrel-fermented using native yeasts and spends nine months in oak. The range also now includes Sobrante, a blend of Zinfandel and Syrah, as well as Sauvignon Blanc. Sobrante is aged in a combination of French and American oak. The Sauvignon Blanc sees a touch of oak during fermentation and malolactic is blocked to preserve freshness. The wines are all reasonably priced. (DM)

● **Zinfandel** California★★ £C Chiles Valley Vineyards★★★ £C Chiles Mill Vineyard★★★ £C
○ **Chardonnay** Napa Valley★ £C

GRGICH HILLS   Rutherford   www.grgich.com   A: Fol

Owner: Mike Grgich   1829 St Helena Highway, Rutherford, CA 94573
Mike Grgich made his reputation at CHATEAU MONTELENA before going on to establish a formidable track record under his own label. His Chardonnay is big, full and typically opulent in a classic ripe and forward tropical Napa style. It is aged for 10 months in French oak and should be enjoyed in its first two or three years. The ripe and lightly grassy Fumé Blanc has its malolactic blocked for freshness and should be drunk young. Two powerful and firmly tannic Cabernets, including a pricey limited-release Yountville Selection, are joined by a Zinfandel that is rich and heavily extracted with vibrant dark berry fruit, full of depth but a touch short on refinement. A late-harvest white is also produced from Chardonnay and Johannisberg Riesling. (DM)

● **Cabernet Sauvignon** Napa Valley★★ £F   ● **Merlot** Napa Valley★★ £E
● **Zinfandel** Napa and Sonoma Counties★★ £D
O **Chardonnay** Napa Valley★★ £E   O **Fumé Blanc** Napa Valley★ £C

HARLAN ESTATE   Oakville   www.harlanestate.com   A: THt

Owner: Bill Harlan   PO Box 352, Oakville, CA 94562
Small, very high-quality producer dedicated solely to super-premium Bordeaux-style reds. The property is located in the western foothills of Oakville and around 15 per cent of the estate's 100 ha (240 acres) are under vine. Yields are restricted to an absolute minimum and output rarely gets close to 2,000 cases a year. The Harlan Estate Red meritage is a blend of Cabernet Sauvignon, Merlot, Cabernet Franc and Petit Verdot. In the winery vatting time is extensive and the wine may stay in contact with its skins for up to two months. Winemaker Bob Levy gets additional consultancy from Michel Rolland and between them they produce a wine of immense dimension and of great richness. Bill Harlan's intention is to craft the California equivalent of one of Bordeaux's First Growths and it must be said this is one of the state's great reds. It is regularly over 14 per cent alcohol, significantly higher than top Bordeaux, and the biggest difference is the ripeness and sheer opulent concentration of the wine's fruit. The Maiden is a very impressive second label. (DM)

● **Estate Red** Napa Valley✪✪✪✪✪ £H

HARRISON VINEYARDS   Napa Valley   www.harrisonvineyards.com

Owner: Lyndsey Harrison   1527 Sage Canyon Road, St Helena, CA 94574
Small, family-run producer with an output of just 3,000 cases a year located on Pritchard Hill in the eastern Napa. Lyndsey Harrison herself is the winemaker, gaining valuable consultancy input from John Kongsgaard of KONGSGAARD and ARIETTA. The full gamut of modern winemaking techniques is brought to bear, native yeasts are used for fermentation and fining and filtration eschewed. An impressive range now includes Syrah, Merlot, Merlot Reserve and a meritage blend of Merlot, Cabernets Sauvignon and Franc and, unusually, some Syrah. Chardonnay is barrel-fermented with lees-stirring and also bottled unfined and without filtration. The reserve reds are aged in top-quality French oak. They are finely structured and will develop well in bottle over five to seven years. (DM)

● **Cabernet Sauvignon** Estate★★★ £F   Reserve★★★★ £G   ● **Zebra Zinfandel**★★ £C
O **Chardonnay** Napa Valley★★★ £E   Reserve★★★ £F

HAVENS   Carneros   www.havenswine.com   A: All

Owner: Havens & Scot families   2055 Hoffman Lane, Napa, CA 94558
A good, small range of wines with Merlot a key element in the portfolio. Certainly rich and impressive when at their plummy best, the wines can be marked by oak. As well as the two Merlot *cuvées*, Bourriquot is a Bordeaux-style blend, but Right Bank rather than Left, being a stylish blend of Cabernet Franc and Merlot. Syrah is sourced from the Hudson Vineyard in Carneros, the estate Napa vineyard and the Trubody Ranch

in northern Napa; the oak here is reined in and the style is ripe and forward. Its also worth looking out for the limited-production Syrah sourced from the Hudson Vineyard, the best wine in the range. The wines will develop well in the medium term and the Bourriquot and Hudson Syrah are real cellaring propositions. (DM)

● **Bourriquot** Napa Valley★★★★ £E ● **Merlot** Napa Valley★★ £D Reserve Carneros★★★ £E
● **Syrah** Napa Valley★★★ £E Hudson Vineyard★★★★ £E

HEITZ CELLARS St Helena www.heitzcellar.com   A: J&B

Owner: Heitz family 500 Taplin Road, St Helena, CA 94574
One of the original benchmark producers of premium Napa reds, particularly the great Martha's Vineyard Cabernets. Quality has been up and down during the 1980s and 1990s but the wines are now sounder and they seem generally to be improving. The Bella Oaks and Trailside bottlings are a touch lighter than Martha's Vineyard but impressive nevertheless. Chardonnay is in a tighter style than some of its neighbours and is only lightly oaked. There are a total of 142 ha (350 acres) of estate vineyards spread throughout Napa and as well as Cabernet and Chardonnay some Grignolino and Zinfandel are produced. (DM)

● **Cabernet Sauvignon** Napa Valley★★★ £E Bella Oaks Vineyard★★★ £F Trailside Vineyard★★★ £F
● **Cabernet Sauvignon** Martha's Vineyard★★★★ £H
○ **Chardonnay** Napa Valley★★ £C Cellar Selection★★★ £D

HESS COLLECTION Mount Veeder www.hesscollection.com   A: BWC

Owner: Donald Hess 4411 Redwood Road, Napa, CA 94558
Unusual operation in that Donald Hess also provides visitors with access to his extensive art collection. The wines here are impressive, particularly the Cabernet Sauvignon and Chardonnay, produced under the Hess Collection label and vinified from estate Mount Veeder fruit. There are now three ranges. In addition to the Hess Collection wines there is the Hess Estate Cabernet Sauvignon blended from a range of Napa sources in a style that is round and approachable. Cabernet Sauvignon, Merlot, Syrah and Chardonnay under the Hess Select label are produced from a 142-ha (350-acre) estate-owned vineyard in the Pinnacles area of Monterey. Donald Hess also owns or has an interest in GLEN CARLOU in South Africa, Peter LEHMANN in Australia's Barossa Valley, Bodega NORTON in Argentina and, closer to home, the BLOCKHEADIA winery. (DM)

● **Cabernet Sauvignon** Napa Valley Collection★★★ £E Collection Reserve★★★★ £F
● **Cabernet Sauvignon** California Select★ £B Napa Valley Hess Estate★★ £C
○ **Chardonnay** Napa Valley Collection★★★ £C California Select★ £B

JADE MOUNTAIN Napa Valley www.chalonewinegroup.com   A: M&V

Owner: Chalone Wine Group 621 Airpark Road, Napa, CA 94558
Jade Mountain was founded by Jim Paras in 1984. Now part of the Chalone group this exceptional winery has been producing very impressive Rhône styles along with fine Merlot for more than a decade. Winemaking was originally in the highly capable hands of Doug Danielak and now under consulting winemaker Alison Green Doran. Paras Vineyard with its easterly exposure and steep rocky terraces is not dissimilar to the slopes of the northern Rhône and provides much of the fruit. These are not the blockbuster, super-extracted ripe fruit offerings which abound elsewhere throughout the state. La Provençale blends Mourvèdre, Syrah and Grenache; Les Jumeaux Cabernet, Syrah and Mourvèdre. Côte du Soleil is a lighter style with a little Merlot added to Mourvèdre and Syrah. The varietal Syrah itself is powerful but restrained. The two single-vineyard wines in particular need time. Merlot is not only rich and concentrated, but finely structured with impeccable balance. The sheer quality here is often misunderstood: these are wines that need time to fully unfurl and show at their best. (DM)

● **La Provençale California** ★★★ £C ● **Merlot** Caldwell Vineyard★★★★ £E Paras Vineyard★★★★ £E
● **Mourvèdre** Contra Costa County★★★★ £C

● **Syrah** Napa Valley★★★★ £D   Paras Vineyard★★★★★ £F   Hudson Vineyard★★★★★ £F
○ **Viognier** Paras Vineyard★★★★ £D

KONGSGAARD   Napa Valley   A: Vin

Owner: John Kongsgaard PO Box 349, Oakville, CA 94562
John Kongsgaard produces wines of formidable weight and concentration. The approach is one of minimal intervention in the cellar allied to wild yeast fermentation and the wines are neither fined nor filtered. The Chardonnay is a very impressive example of the variety, combining the best subtle elements of great Burgundy with a richly textured, almost explosive dose of honeyed Napa fruit. The finish is very long and complex. While the Chardonnay is not exactly made in abundance (less than 1,000 cases), there is only a tiny amount of two Rhône styles – a Roussanne/Viognier blend, rich in texture with a fine, intense nutty complexity, and a very powerful and impressive Syrah produced from Carneros fruit. This will comfortably stand alongside the finest examples of the variety from the northern Rhône and is of undoubted super five-star quality and may in time be compared with the greats such as GUIGAL's La Mouline and Jean-Louis CHAVE's Hermitage. (DM)
● **Syrah** Napa Valley✪✪✪✪✪ £H
○ **Chardonnay** Napa Valley★★★★★ £G   ○ **Roussanne/Viognier** Napa Valley★★★★★ £G

LAGIER MEREDITH   Mount Veeder   www.lagiermeredith.com   A: AMW

Owner: Carole Meredith & Steve Lagier   4967 Dry Creek Road, Napa, CA 94558
This property high up on Mount Veeder was purchased by Lagier and Meredith in 1986. Remote and seemingly far away from the humdrum of Napa Valley grape growing, the redwood forests nearby are home to mountain lions and coyotes. One wine is made here, a richly textured, very pure and intense Syrah. The first vines were planted in 1986 and the first wine released from the 1996 vintage. The total area under vine is very small at less than 2 ha (4 acres), of which the tiniest proportion is planted to Viognier. The site is above the night time valley fog resulting in more even daily temperatures. This allied to finely drained, volcanic soils means the fruit gets a naturally lengthy hang time producing grapes of impressive flavour intensity and fine tannins. Bottled without filtration, expect this Syrah to develop very well over five to seven years. The only problem is there's very little available. (DM)
● **Syrah** Mount Veeder★★★★ £F

LAIL VINEYARDS   Rutherford   www.lailvineyards.com   A: Vin

Owner: Robin Daniel Lail   PO Box 249, Rutherford, CA 94573
Although this is a newly established small-scale winery, owner Robin Daniel Lail's family history goes back to the beginnings of viticulture in Napa itself. One of her ancestors, Gustav Niebaum, established the original Inglenook winery in 1879. Just the one wine is made here, a Bordeaux blend of two-thirds Cabernet Sauvignon and one-third Merlot. Sourced from a mere 2.3 ha (5.6 acres) annual production is between 1,200 and 1,500 cases. Winemaker Philippe Melka continues to produce an increasingly stylish, elegant and very finely structured meritage red. (DM)
● **J Daniel Cuvée** Napa Valley★★★★ £F

LA JOTA   Howell Mountain   www.lajotavineyardco.com

Owner: Markham Vineyards   1102 Las Posadas Road, Angwin, CA 94508
Throughout the 1980s and 90s La Jota has been a source of some of the most powerful and impressive examples produced in the Howell Mountain AVA. The winery has become famed for massive dense and tannic reds that need considerable cellaring but develop very well in bottle. Ownership has passed from Bill Smith (now vinifying Sonoma Valley Pinot Noir under his own W H SMITH label) to MARKHAM vineyards. Winemaker Kimberlee Nicholls continues to maximise the potential of the 11 ha (28 acres) of prime mountain vineyards. The Anniversary Release is 100 per cent Cabernet Sauvignon; the Howell

Mountain has some Merlot blended in and is softer and rounder in its youth. As well as the Cabernet Sauvignons, a few hundred cases of Cabernet Franc and Petite Sirah are also produced. (DM)

● **Cabernet Sauvignon** Howell Mountain★★★ £E Anniversary Release★★★★ £F

LEWIS CELLARS Napa Valley www.lewiscellars.com   A: Win

Owner: Randy Lewis 524 El Cerrito Avenue, Hillsborough, CA 94010
If like me you're a motor racing fan you'll be delighted by the quality of the powerful, dense Cabernet-based reds hand-crafted by former Indy 500 star Randy Lewis and his wife Debbie. This small, bespoke range (production is still kept at around 8,500 cases) is marked by rich fruit and in the top reds power and structure. They are quintessential California wines but serious and very impressive. For the Cabernet Reserve you need to wait for the tannins to subside but it will be worth it. Good Chardonnay, including excellent Reserve and Bacaglia Lane bottlings, is also produced and Syrah and Pinot Noir have been added to the range of reds. The range is completed by Alec's Blend, an unusual fruit-driven combination of Syrah and Merlot. (DM)

● **Cabernet Sauvignon** Napa Valley★★★★ £F Reserve★★★★ £G
● **Merlot** Napa Valley★★★ £E

LITTORAI St Helena www.littorai.com   A: Vin

Owner: Ted and Heidi Lemon PO Box 180, St Helena, CA 94574
Before establishing his own St Helena-based winery, Ted Lemon gained considerable winemaking experience in Burgundy as well as California. This is reflected in a range of Chardonnays and Pinot Noirs which are distinctly Burgundian in style. The winery name derives from the Latin *litor* and means 'the coasts'; Lemon's objective is to make the best examples he can of the Burgundy varieties from North Coast vineyard sources. Chardonnay is subtle, structured and only lightly tropical. Pinot Noir shows intense, subtle berry fruits and is always well meshed by firm but supple tannin. As well as the Charles Heitz and Theriot bottlings, Chardonnay comes from Mays Canyon in the Russian River, while Pinot also emerges from the One Acre and Cerise vineyards in the cool Anderson Valley. That classic cool-climate red berry character is particularly apparent in the Savoy Vineyard Pinot; the Theriot has more dark fruit and plum than the other wines, being fuller and richer in texture. Expect the Chardonnays to develop well over five to seven years. The Pinots and particularly the Savoy Vineyard will keep a little longer. (DM)

● **Pinot Noir** Hirsch Vineyard★★★★ £E Savoy Vineyard★★★★★ £F Theriot Vineyard★★★★ £F
O **Chardonnay** Charles Heintz Vineyard★★★★ £F Theriot Vineyard★★★★ £F

LIVINGSTON MOFFETT Rutherford www.livingstonwines.com   A: Vin

Owner: Livingston family 1895 Cabernet Lane, St Helena, CA 94574
Originally known as Livingston, the name has been changed because of confusion with the volume label owned by E & J GALLO. These are hand-crafted premium wines made under the direction of John Kongsgaard who produces exceptional wines under his own KONGSGAARD label. Two very good Cabernets are produced: the Moffett is from the family estate vineyard; the Stanley's Selection is sourced from a number of first-class vineyards planted on stony, free-draining hillsides. Both wines are refined and harmonious. Gemstone is the flagship from the vineyard of the same name in Yountville and is a typical Bordeaux blend of Cabernet Sauvignon, Cabernet Franc, Merlot and, unusually for California, a hint of Petit Verdot, all of which are vinified separately. The range is completed by a small amount of Genny's Vineyard Chardonnay, vinified with wild yeasts, and Syrah from the Mitchell Vineyard, with a little Viognier blended in. Top Cabernets are ageworthy and require four or five years' patience – a little more for Moffett and Gemstone. (DM)

● **Cabernet Sauvignon** Moffett Vineyard★★★★ £F Stanley's Selection★★★★ £E
● **Gemstone★★★★** £F ● **Syrah** Mitchell Vineyard★★★ £E

LOKOYA Oakville www.lokoya.com   A: WTs

Owner: Kendall-Jackson 7600 St Helena Highway, Oakville, CA 94562
This is Jess Jackson's super-premium label, producing distinctive Cabernet Sauvignons that showcase the best single-vineyard characteristics of prime mountain- and benchland-grown fruit. The wines are vinified in the same facility as the flagship CARDINALE, which by contrast is a blend of Napa and Sonoma sources. While vineyard source and low yields of 2 to 3 tons per acre are key to the great fruit in the wines, vinification is aimed at maximising their potential. Long vatting times, basket-pressed grapes, 20 to 21 months in top-quality French oak all contribute and the wines are neither fined nor filtered. These are all very big, dense and powerfully structured wines, needing time to shed their early youthful austerity. The Diamond Mountain is the most opulent and has had varying small portions of Merlot and Cabernet Franc blended in depending on the year. The other *cuvées* thus far have been 100 per cent Cabernet Sauvignon. The Rutherford is more perfumed, while the Howell Mountain and Mount Veeder are the firmest of the quartet. (DM)

● **Cabernet Sauvignon** Diamond Mountain★★★★ £G Howell Mountain★★★★ £G
● **Cabernet Sauvignon** Mount Veeder★★★★ £G Rutherford★★★★ £G

LUNA Napa Valley www.lunavineyards.com   A: MyC

Owner: Michael Moone & George Vare 2921 Silverado Trail, Napa, CA 94558
Luna focuses on Italian varietals and Merlot. John KONGSGAARD provided the early winemaking direction and that role has now been taken on by Abe Schoener. Both the regular Pinot Grigio and Sangiovese are good value for money, while the pricier Canto is a proprietary Super-Tuscan-style blend of Sangiovese and Merlot with a touch of Cabernet Sauvignon for grip. Indigenous yeasts are used, the Pinot Grigio unusually gets just a hint of new barrel-fermentation with lees-enrichment and the reds are all aged in fine-grained French oak and bottled without fining or filtration. A Sangiovese Riserva is also now produced along with a little Petite Sirah/Zinfandel and a dessert wine based around Pinot Grigio, Mille Baci. In general the wines will drink well young and the Canto and Sangiovese Riserva will both benefit from short ageing. (DM)

● **Merlot** Napa Valley★★★ £E ● **Canto** Napa Valley★★★★ £F
● **Sangiovese** Napa Valley★★★ £C Riserva★★★★ £F
○ **Pinot Grigio** Napa Valley★★★ £C

MINER FAMILY VINEYARDS Oakville www.minerwines.com   A: Vin

Owner: Dave Miner 7850 Silverado Trail, Oakville, CA 94562
Recently established winery, founded in 1998. The principle source of fruit for the range is the Oakville Ranch, where Dave Miner was president. Other Napa vineyards are also used as well as Gary's and Rossella's vineyards in the Santa Lucia Highlands for striking Pinot Noir, and the Simpson Vineyard in Madera County for a floral, medium-bodied Viognier. Zinfandel is straightforward and fruit-driven and blended with a little Petite Sirah for structure. Merlot comes from both Oakville and Stagecoach Vineyard. Fine, impressively structured Cabernet Sauvignon also comes from Oakville and there is now a red meritage, The Oracle, which blends equal proportions of Cabernet Sauvignon, Merlot and Cabernet Franc. Syrah, Sangiovese and Petite Sirah are also now offered as is a small amount of Sauvignon Blanc which comes from vineyards near Yountville and is part barrel- and part stainless steel-fermented. The Chardonnays, particularly the top two labels, are very impressive. The wines are barrel-fermented with full maloctic and handled in mainly new oak. The Wild Yeast bottling is exotically tropical, rich and very concentrated. In general the wines are very approachable young, although the Cabernet needs a little time. (DM)

● **Zinfandel** Napa Valley★★ £D ● **Pinot Noir** Gary's Vineyard★★★★ £F
● **Cabernet Sauvignon** Oakville★★★ £F ● **Merlot** Oakville★★★ £F
○ **Chardonnay** Napa Valley★★ £D Oakville Ranch★★★ £E Wild Yeast★★★★ £F
○ **Viognier** Simpson Vineyard★★ £D

ROBERT MONDAVI Oakville www.robertmondavi.com A: **RMi**,BBR,F&M

Owner: Mondavi family 8575 Orcutt Road, Arroyo Grande, CA 93420
Arguably the most famous wine name in California. Robert Mondavi must take much of the credit for the positive public face of California wine when it re-emerged as a quality region in the 1970s. The company has very widespread wine interests, both in California and with overseas investments and partnerships. In addition to the large-scale premium operation at Oakville the Mondavi family also owns the Woodbridge winery facility in the Central Valley which produces pretty ordinary everyday reds and whites. At Oakville a new range of Italian varietals has been developed under the La Famiglia di Robert Mondavi label. Among the Robert Mondavi Coastal Private Selection range of varietals, the spicy, berry-laden Zinfandel stands out. The BYRON winery on the Central Coast has been a Mondavi label for some years and the prestigious ARROWOOD operation in Sonoma has also recently been acquired. OPUS ONE was the first of the Mondavi winery partnerships, established in 1979 with MOUTON-ROTHSCHILD. More recently, successful overseas forays have been made with ERRÁZURIZ in Chile to produce the premium-label Seña; with the FRESCOBALDI family in the production of the Super-Tuscan Luce; and in 2002 a controlling interest was taken in Tenuta dell' ORNELLAIA. The core of the Oakville operation, though, is the firm's premium wines and Cabernet has always been exceptional. Recently added is IO from Santa Barbara, a decent Rhône-style blend of Syrah, Grenache and Mourvèdre. These are either classified as Napa or other district bottlings as well as Reserves. A range of limited-release wines is also made and these labels are available only at the winery, some of which are undoubtedly very classy. (DM)

- **Cabernet Sauvignon** Napa Valley★★★ £E Oakville★★★★ £E Reserve Napa Valley✪✪✪✪✪ £H
- **Merlot** Napa Valley★★ £D Carneros★ £E Stag's Leap District★★★ £E
- **Pinot Noir** Napa Valley★ £C Carneros★★ £E Reserve★★★ £F
- **Zinfandel** Coastal Private Selection★★ £B Napa Valley★★★ £C
- **IO** Santa Barbara County★★ £C
- O **Chardonnay** Napa Valley★★ £C Carneros★★★ £D Reserve★★★ £E
- O **Fumé Blanc** Napa Valley★★ £C Reserve★★★ £E

MUMM NAPA Rutherford www.mummcuveenapa.com A: **ADo**,AAA

*Owner: **Champagne GH Mumm** 8445 Silverado Trail, Rutherford, CA 94573*
One of several California sparkling-wine operation with a leading Champagne house as owner. The regular Champagne from the parent can often disappoint but the California Brut Cuvée Prestige offers a very attractive, well-priced alternative. It is fresh and forward with just a touch of bready yeast character The DVX Vintage *cuvée* is of a different order, combining forward fruit with a rich, leesy character and a firm, balanced structure for short ageing on release. The range has now been extended with another premium wine, Cuvée M, which blends the Champagne grapes with a little Pinot Gris. (DM)

- O **Brut Cuvée Prestige** Napa Valley★★ £C O **Blanc de Blancs** Napa Valley★★ £C
- O **Cuvée DVX Vintage** Napa Valley★★★ £F
- ◉ **Blanc de Noirs** Napa Valley★★ £C

NEWTON Spring Mountain www.clicquot.com A: **Par**,N&P,Bal,C&R

Owner: LVMH 2555 Madrona Avenue, St Helena, CA 94574
This well-established Napa operation is now part of the expanding portfolio of Moët Hennessey premium wineries around the world along with such names as CLOUDY BAY and BOUCHARD PÈRE ET FILS, although Su Hua Newton still runs the show. The wines here have always been impressive and reasonably priced if not quite reaching the pinnacles achieved elsewhere. At the lower level the decent Red Label Chardonnay is joined by Special Cuvées from Chardonnay, Pinot Noir and Merlot. The best wines are the impressive Unfiltered bottlings produced with natural fermentation and handled by gravity in the winery. The low-volume Epic is a firm, powerfully structured Merlot sourced from the best mountainside slopes on the property, mainly with clay based soils. Recently added is a top-quality premium Cabernet Sauvignon,

Le Puzzle, which is sourced from soils with a higher chalk, gravel and loam content. Chardonnay and Pinot Noir may be approached young; the Merlot and Cabernet bottlings require longer. Epic and Le Puzzle will both benefit from four to five years' cellaring; expect Le Puzzle to be very ageworthy. (DM)

● **Cabernet Sauvignon** Unfiltered Napa Valley★★★★ £E   Le Puzzle Napa Valley★★★★★ £F
● **Merlot** Special Cuvée★★ £D   Unfiltered★★★ £E   ● **Epic** Napa Valley★★★★ £F
● **Pinot Noir** Special Cuvée★★ £D   Unfiltered Napa Valley★★★ £E
O **Chardonnay** Special Cuvée★★★ £D   Red Label★★★ £E   Unfiltered★★★★ £E

NIEBAUM-COPPOLA ESTATE   Rutherford   www.niebaum-coppola.com   **A: MyC**

Owner: Francis Ford Coppola   1991 St Helena Highway, Rutherford, CA 94573

This began as a small operation when film director Francis Ford Coppola first became involved in winegrowing, but there is now a sizeable output. The Diamond Series wines are varietals sourced throughout the North Coast and there are three wines under the Francis Coppola Presents label: Rosso, Bianco and Talia Rosé. These are straightfoward, reliable, fruit-driven wines but it is the top labels under both the Directors Reserve and Estate Wines labels that really impress. As well as the wines listed below there is a small production under the Estate label of Dolcetto, Reserve Syrah and sparkling Blanc de Blancs made in a deliberately fruit-driven style from an unusual blend of Pinot Blanc, Muscat and Sauvignon Blanc. Zinfandel Edizione Pennino is rich and powerful with dense, brambly fruit. At the pinnacle there are two Flagship wines. Blancaneaux is an unusual blend of Chardonnay, Viognier, Marsanne and Roussanne. Rubicon is a very structured, firm and powerful meritage red aged for 26 months in French oak and requires at least six to seven years' patience. (DM)

● **Cabernet Franc** Estate★★★ £E   ● **Cask Cabernet** Estate★★★ £F
● **Rubicon** Rutherford★★★★★ £G
● **Merlot** Directors Reserve★★ £D   ● **Zinfandel** Edizione Pennino★★★★ £E
O **Blancaneaux** Rutherford★★★£E   O **Chardonnay** Directors Series★★£C

OPUS ONE   Oakville   www.opusonewinery.com   **A: Par,Sel**

Owner: Robert Mondavi/Baron Philip de Rothschild SA   7900 St Helena Hwy, Oakville, CA 94562

This MONDAVI/Rothschild (MOUTON-ROTHSCHILD) joint venture was conceived in 1978, the first vintage being in 1979. At the time, super-premium Napa styles of Cabernet had not yet materialised and Opus One was uniquely highly priced among its peers. The Mondavi Reserve Cabernet Sauvignon from the great To-Kalon vineyard has, however, consistently been of a higher standard, although the Q Block part of that same vineyard contributes to Opus One. The wine, a blend of all five Bordeaux varieties, has never quite fulfilled its potential but the scale of the production means there aren't the scarcity problems found with some other top Californian reds. The wine is always given a very lengthy cuvaison of up to 40 days and is aged in 100 per cent new French oak. (DM)

● **Opus One** Napa Valley★★★★ £H

PAHLMEYER   Napa Valley   www.pahlmeyer.com   **A: RWs**

Owner: Jayson Pahlmeyer   101 South Combs, Suite 10, Napa, CA 94558

This is a top-quality, low-volume winery producing three super-premium wines, although occasional declassified lots under the Jayson label can also be very good. A committed approach to viticulture throughout Pahlmeyer's vineyard sources, with reduced yields and careful canopy management, combines with inventive winemaking by Erin Green to produce wines of depth, concentration and great finesse. In the winery the reds are partly whole-bunch fermented, helping to provide both a supple texture and a firm structure. While they should undoubtedly be cellared for at least half a decade the tannin is just a touch more balanced and harmonious than in some others. A Sonoma Coast Chardonnay has been added from the 2001 vintage. Both Chardonnays are fermented with wild yeasts in 100 per cent new oak and bottled with neither fining nor filtration. (DM)

● **Merlot** Napa Valley★★★★★ £F   ● **Proprietary Red** Napa Valley★★★★★ £F
O **Chardonnay** Napa Valley★★★★ £F

PARADIGM   Oakville   www.paradigmwinery.com   A: DDr

Owner: Ren & Marilyn Harris   683 Dwyer Road, Oakville, CA 94562
The Harris's sizeable vineyard property in the heart of Oakville underpins the admirable quality achieved at this excellent small estate. Production is very small at around 5,000 cases. Winemaking expertise is provided by Heidi Peterson Barrett and in the principal wine, the Cabernet Sauvignon (blended with Cabernet Franc and Merlot for harmony), she achieves a round supple style with richly textured blackberry fruit and a hint of vanilla and spice from ageing in high quality toasty new oak. She also handcrafts very good Merlot, a tiny amount of Zinfandel and, most recently, Cabernet Franc. (DM)
● **Cabernet Sauvignon** Estate★★★★ £E

PATZ AND HALL   Napa Valley   www.patzhall.com   A: T&W

Owner: James Hall and Donald Patz   PO Box 5479, Napa, CA 94581
The two partners here first worked for FLORA SPRINGS and during this association they determined to establish a small winemaking operation in order to produce top-quality Pinot Noir and Chardonnay. The regular bottlings of Pinot Noir (from Sonoma County as well as the Russian River) and Napa Valley Chardonnay are impressive but even more so are the small-volume runs produced from a number of single vineyards. Top Pinot Noir is now sourced from the Hyde, Burnside and Pisoni vineyards, Chardonnay and Pinot from Alder Springs in Mendocino and, most recently, Durrell Ranch. Chardonnay also comes from Dutton Ranch, Woolsey Road and recently the Tony Ranch. The wines see a high proportion of new oak and, as with so many top-quality producers now, indigenous yeasts are favoured and they are always bottled unfiltered. These are big, forward, explosive examples of both varieties. (DM)
● **Pinot Noir** Sonoma County★★★ £E Russian River★★★ £E
O **Chardonnay** Napa Valley★★★ £D Dutton Ranch★★★★ £E Woolsey Road Vineyard★★★★ £E

JOSEPH PHELPS   Napa Valley   www.jpvwines.com   A: WTs

Owner: Joe Phelps   200 Taplin Road, St Helena, CA 94574
Now a fairly large operation, originally founded in 1972, Phelps has built a reputation based on top-quality Bordeaux-style red varietals and blends. The full range encompasses those other usual suspects Chardonnay and Sauvignon Blanc, a small volume of an excellent late-harvest Scheurebe white and an extensive range of Rhône-style reds and whites. Red and white Pastiche are everyday fruit-driven wines blended mainly from a mix of Rhône varieties. The other Rhône styles include the blended Le Mistral (mainly from Syrah and Grenache and named after the fierce Mistral wind that can cause havoc in the Rhône Valley). These along with the regular Napa Valley Cabernet, Chardonnay and Sauvignon Blanc, are good but lack just a little excitement. The top label Cabernet Sauvignon from the Backus Vineyard and the magnificent Insignia are of a different order. The former is produced from 100 per cent Oakville Cabernet Sauvignon and is a massive, structured wine with very ripe, black fruit and supple tannin. The Insignia is a meritage blend of all five Bordeaux red varieties. Equally powerful and dense, this is more sumptuous and exotic than the Backus Cabernet but equally ageworthy. (DM)
● **Merlot** Napa Valley★★★ £E   ● **Insignia** Napa Valley★★★★★ £G
● **Cabernet Sauvignon** Napa Valley★★ £E Backus Vineyard★★★★★ £G
● **Le Mistral** California★★ £D   ● **Syrah** Napa Valley★★★ £E
O **Chardonnay** Ovation★★★ £E Los Carneros★★ £D
O **Sauvignon Blanc** Napa Valley★ £C   O **Viognier** Napa Valley★★ £D

PINE RIDGE   Stags Leap   www.pineridgewinery.com   A: Hal

Owner: Nancy Andrus   5901 Silverado Trail, Napa, CA 94558
Founded in 1978, this is now a relatively large property producing just mid- to premium-range wines. There are some 122 ha (300 acres) planted in 16 different vineyard locations throughout the Napa Valley. Indeed, estate-grown grapes account for some 95 per cent of the winery's production. The focus is mainly on the Bordeaux varieties, with the wines often lighter and less substantial than from some neighbouring estates. Cabernet Sauvignon now comes from Oakville and Howell Mountain as well as Rutherford and Stags Leap. A rare blend of Chenin Blanc and Viognier is cool-fermented to emphasise its fruit. Onyx, last released in the 2000 vintage, is also unusual for California, a blend of Malbec and Tannat (most commonly associated with the dark wines of Madiran). A new low-volume *cuvée*, Charmstone, was released in the 2001 vintage and blends all five Bordeaux varieties. The flagship wine is the meritage Andrus Reserve, sourced from close-planted estate vineyards in the Mayacamas. Aged in 100 per cent high-toast new oak with malolactic fermentation in barrel, this is a spicy, big, but at times austere wine. (DM)
- **Cabernet Sauvignon** Rutherford★★ £E Stags Leap District★★★ £F
- **Andrus** Reserve★★★★ £G ● **Merlot** Crimson Creek★★ £D
- **Cabernet Franc** Trois Cuvées★★★ £D
- O **Chardonnay** Stags Leap District★★ £C Dijon Clones★★★ £E
- O **Chenin Blanc-Viognier** Estate★ £B

PLUMPJACK   Oakville   www.plumpjack.com   A: Vin

Owner: Getty Family   620 Oakville Cross Road, Oakville, CA 94562
The Plumpjack winery is just a part of a leisure-based operation that specialises in food and wine and includes the luxury Squaw Valley Inn at Olympic Valley. Good to very good Cabernet Sauvignon, Merlot and Chardonnay are produced. The winery is nestled into the hills in the eastern side of the valley and surrounded by some 19.5 ha (48 acres) of estate vineyards planted in 1992. The vines are still young and so cannot be excessively restricted in terms of their yield. The best must surely be to come if the same winemaking philosophy is maintained. The Chardonnay is ripe, forward and toasty, the Cabernet powerful and structured. The very expensive Reserve offers an extra dimension at a not inconsiderable premium. New from 2001 is a Russian River Valley Syrah. (DM)
- **Merlot** Napa Valley★★ £E ● **Cabernet Sauvignon** Estate★★★ £F Reserve★★★★★ £H
- O **Chardonnay** Reserve★★★ £E

QUINTESSA   Rutherford   www.quintessa.com   A: Fie

Owner: Agustin Huneeus   1601 Silverado Trail, Rutherford, CA 94573
This winery was originally part of FRANCISCAN, itself a part of the giant Canandaigua Group. Quintessa is now solely owned by Agustin Huneeus whose other property is the Chilean winery VERAMONTE. Just one single-estate wine is produced here, a rich and powerful, very ripe Napa meritage blended from Cabernet Sauvignon, Merlot and Cabernet Franc that is loaded with oak. Certainly very good but not yet among the top flight of Napa reds. (DM)
- **Quintessa** Napa Valley★★★ £G

RAMEY   Oakville   A: M&V

Owner: David Ramey   Oakville, CA 94562
David Ramey has had a vast winemaking influence on the style of a number of leading producers, among them CHALK HILL and RUDD ESTATE, where he is still the general manager. Under his own Ramey label he produces remarkably fine Chardonnay, impressive for its finesse, intensity and sheer quality as much as for its weight and texture. While the same gamut of winery techniques may be employed here as elsewhere – natural yeast fermentation, lees-enrichment, new oak for barrel-fermentation and ageing *et al* – the key to

these wines is their sheer balance and refinement. Of the two single-vineyard bottlings the Hudson has greater weight, the Hyde a tighter, more mineral structure. Recently added to the Chardonnays are two first-class reds. The Diamond Mountain Red comes from younger vines; the Jericho Canyon is Ramey's new flagship red. Both are meritage blends and you should expect both to have exceptional potential. (DM)

O **Chardonnay** Carneros★★★★ £E Russian River★★★★ £E
O **Chardonnay** Hudson Vineyard★★★★★ £F Hyde Vineyard★★★★★ £F

RUDD ESTATE Oakville www.ruddwines.com A: Vin

Owner: Leslie Rudd 500 Oakville Crossroad, PO Box 105, Oakville, CA 94562
Leslie Rudd purchased the 22 ha (55 acres) that comprise his estate property in the heart of Oakville in 1996. His prestigious near-neighbours include SCREAMING EAGLE, HARLAN, and SILVER OAK. The high-density vineyards are planted in rocky soils on the eastern side of the Oakville benchland, almost into the foothills of the Vaca Mountains. In order to assist wine quality both during vinification and ageing, cellars with both temperature and humidity controls have been dug underneath the winery. Both the whites are barrel-fermented with natural yeasts. The Sauvignon Blanc sees just a small proportion of new wood whereas the Chardonnay is vinified in mainly new oak and gets full malolactic fermentation and 18 months ageing. Both wines are sophisticated and restrained in style, the Sauvignon marked by a fresh, grassy mineral character, the Chardonnay displaying citrus, minerals and a subtle toastiness. Both will develop well in the short term. As well as the Cabernet Sauvignon and Estate Red there is a meritage blend from the Jericho Canyon. The Cabernet has 15 per cent Cabernet Franc blended in and is tight, lean and structured in its youth but with real depth and intensity. The Estate Red is fuller and richer by contrast with dollops of oak and ripe, spicy dark fruit, yet it also has a really fine, firmly structured core that suggests great complexity with six or seven years' age. (DM)

● **Estate Red** Oakville★★★★★ £G ● **Cabernet Sauvignon** Oakville★★★★★ £F
O **Chardonnay** Bacigalupi Vineyard★★★★ £F O **Sauvignon Blanc** Napa Valley★★★ £E

SAINTSBURY Carneros www.saintsbury.com A: Adm, J&B

Owner: Richard Ward & David Graves 1500 Los Carneros Avenue, Napa, CA 94559
Long established as one of the top producers of the Burgundian varietals in Carneros. Volume has risen from 3,000 cases in 1981 to a current level of 55,000 cases of which two-thirds are Pinot Noir. The Carneros and Reserve labels of both Chardonnay and Pinot Noir are serious and refined examples of the Carneros style. The Garnet Pinot Noir offers a straightforward, fruit-laden example of the grape in the way that the best basic Burgundy should but so rarely does. A very small amount of Pinot Noir from the estate-owned, single-vineyard Brown Ranch is now bottled individually. Despite the fact that yields reach a surprisingly high 3.5 to 4 tons to the acre, the wines retain a really piercing fruit quality. The only other variety produced is a tiny amount of Pinot Gris. (DM)

● **Pinot Noir** Garnet★★ £C Carneros★★★ £D Reserve★★★★ £F Brown Ranch★★★★ £F
O **Chardonnay** Carneros★★★ £C Reserve★★★★ £E

SCHRAMSBERG Napa Valley www.schramsberg.com A: Vin

Owner: Jamie Davies 1400 Schramsberg Road, Calistoga, CA 94515
This was the first California winery to produce quality sparkling wines from the classic varieties of Champagne: Pinot Noir, Pinot Meunier and Chardonnay. All three grapes are used across the range. A straightforward non-vintage blend, Mirabelle, is vinified from Pinot Noir and Chardonnay and is a fruit-driven style intended for easy drinking. More serious are the Vintage *cuvées* of Blanc de Blancs, Blanc de Noirs, Brut Rosé and the off-dry Crémant Demi-Sec produced from Flora, a hybrid of Gewürztraminer and Semillon. Reserve is a structured and concentrated Blanc de Noirs, while the J Schram *cuvée* is part barrel-fermented and blended from the very best lots in a single vintage. (DM)

O **Blanc de Blancs**★★★ £D O **Blanc de Noirs**★★ £D O **Crémant Demi-Sec**★★ £D
O **Reserve**★★★★ £F **J Schram**★★★★ £

SCREAMING EAGLE   Oakville   www.screamingeagle.com

A: Sel,F&M,Vin

Owner: Jean Phillips   PO Box 134, Oakville, CA 94562
Perhaps first among all the recent Cabernet and meritage superstars of the Napa, certainly if rated by price achieved at auction. Jean Phillips cultivates around 20 ha (50 acres) of Cabernet Sauvignon, Merlot and Cabernet Franc around Oakville but retains just enough of her crop to produce some 500 cases of a super-concentrated, immense and profound Cabernet Sauvignon. The wine is currently sold exclusively via a mailing list and to prestigious restaurants. As such it is nigh-on impossible to find except at the major auction houses, where the prices obtained will defy belief. (DM)

SHAFER   Stags Leap   www.shafervineyards.com

A: THt

Owner: John Shafer   6154 Silverado Trail, Napa, CA 94558
The Shafer family purchased this remarkable 85-ha (210-acre) hillside property in Stags Leap District in 1972, initially establishing themselves as grape growers rather than winemakers. However, the transition to wine production has seen their status elevated to the very top echelon of vintners in the state. To support the winery's development, new estate vineyards have been established in Oak Knoll and Carneros. The winery is no longer small – it has grown from an output of 1,000 cases in 1978 to 32,000 today. There is no doubting the sheer quality of the wines, though. Red Shoulder Ranch Chardonnay comes from Carneros and is barrel-fermented in both French and American oak. Malolactic is blocked and the wine is ripe and toasty. Napa Cabernet is part-aged in American oak whereas the Merlot sees only French oak for 18 months. Of two smaller-volume *cuvées*, Firebreak is a stylish blend of Sangiovese and Cabernet Sauvignon and Relentless is a rich and powerful Syrah blended with a little Petite Sirah and aged in oak for 26 months. Most profound is the remarkable Hillside Select from the finest Stags Leap fruit – a 100 per cent Cabernet Sauvignon of power, finesse and sheer velvety harmony that is truly one of California's very great reds. (DM)
● **Cabernet Sauvignon** Napa Valley★★★★ £F   Hillside Select✪✪✪✪✪ £H   ● **Merlot** Napa Valley★★★ £E
● **Firebreak** Napa Valley★★★★ £E   ● **Relentless** Napa Valley★★★★ £F
O **Chardonnay** Red Shoulder Ranch★★★★ £E

SILVER OAK CELLARS   Napa Valley   www.silveroak.com

A: T&W

Owner: Ray Duncan   915 Oakville Cross Road, Oakville, CA 94562
Two powerful and supple Cabernets are produced at Silver Oak Cellars. The estate was established as a partnership between Ray Duncan and the late Justin Meyer, the original winemaker. Daniel Baron took over those reins and continues to produce wines of substance and quality despite production now running at around 70,000 cases a year. The style is classic northern California: the wines are rich, ripe and full but offer an accessible, rounded texture and surprisingly soft tannins; the Napa Valley label has additional finesse and depth. A new venture is a premium Merlot planted in finely drained volcanic soils at the Soda Canyon Ranch in south-eastern Napa. This is marketed under the Twomey label and promises much. (DM)
● **Cabernet Sauvignon** Alexander Valley★★★ £F   Napa Valley★★★★ £G

SPOTTSWOODE   St Helena   www.spottswoode.com

A: DDr

Owner: Mary Novak   1902 Madrona Ave, St Helena, CA 94574
This historic estate was originally established in 1882 and comprises a lavish Victorian farmhouse and a modern winery constructed in 1999. The estate has 15 ha (37 acres) planted to Cabernet Sauvignon, Cabernet Franc and Sauvignon Blanc, the latter just a single hectare (2.5 acres). The Cabernet is sourced fully from estate fruit, with a small component of Cabernet Franc in the blend. It is a deep, finely structured wine, with refined tannins and great ageing potential; in top vintages it is undoubtedly of five-star quality. The Sauvignon, sourced from estate fruit as well as vineyards in Calistoga and Carneros, is in a quintessentially California style: part barrel-fermented with lees-enrichment it is ripe, stylish and long. (DM)
● **Cabernet Sauvignon** Napa Valley★★★★★ £G
O **Sauvignon Blanc** Napa Valley★★★ £E

STAG'S LEAP WINE CELLARS Stags Leap www.cask23.com A: WTs,Sel

Owner: Warren Winiarski 5766 Silverdao Trail, Napa, CA 94558
Warren Winiarski's Stag's Leap Wine Cellars will forever be famous in wine circles as a result of the 1976 Paris tasting, when the Cask 23 outgunned the best from Bordeaux to the astonishment of the French judges on that day. The wine world has come a long way in the last 25 years and while Cask 23 remains an impressive example of hillside Napa Cabernet there is equal quality from neighbouring properties. The lower-level Fay and SLV bottlings are also good although recently prices have been creeping up. Softer and more immediately accessible examples include a Napa Valley bottling and the recently released Artemis, which uses a fair proportion of Fay vineyard fruit in its blend. The whites include some good Sauvignon Blanc, particularly the Rancho Chimiles which is barrel-fermented on lees but is not put through malolactic. The barrel-fermented Beckstoffer Ranch, a particularly stylish and balanced Chardonnay, is now joined by a tighter, fruit-driven example from the estate-owned Arcadia vineyard that is partly barrel-fermented. The top Cabernets will age very well. Reasonably priced red and white varietals are also released under the Hawk Crest brand, the best being the Vineyard Selections Cabernet Sauvignon and Merlot. (DM)

● **Cabernet Sauvignon** Napa Valley★ £E Fay Estate★★★ £F SLV★★★★ £G Cask 23★★★★ £H
● **Merlot** Napa Valley★★ £E
○ **Chardonnay** Napa Valley★ £D Arcadia★★★ £E Beckstoffer Ranch★★★ £E
○ **Sauvignon Blanc** Napa Valley★ £C Rancho Chimiles★ £D

STAGLIN FAMILY Rutherford www.staglinfamily.com A: Las

Owner: Garen and Shari Staglin 1570 Bella Oaks Lane, Rutherford, CA 94573
The Staglins founded their small winery in 1985 with 20 ha (50 acres) of vineyard which had originally been a source for André Tschelistcheff when blending his legendary vintages of the BEAULIEU VINEYARDS Private Reserve Georges de la Tour Cabernet. Production now runs at just under 10,000 cases a year, the majority Cabernet Sauvignon, with just a few hundred cases of a Sangiovese Stagliano as well as Chardonnay. The estate Chardonnay and Cabernet are both very impressive. A second label Salus is now released to ensure the integrity of the estate wines. Although the Salus wines are lighter and more obviously fruit-driven, all the wines are marked by their weight, rich texture and extract. The Rutherford bottlings achieve this with ease and the Cabernet Sauvignon in particular is very refined. Both reds and whites will age well, the Rutherford Cabernet requiring five years or so. (DM)

● **Cabernet Sauvignon** Salus★★★ £F Rutherford★★★★★ £G
○ **Chardonnay** Salus★★★ £E Rutherford★★★★ £F

DR STEPHENS ESTATE Napa Valley www.drstephenswines.com A: WTs

Owner: Don Stephens 1860 Howell Mountain Road, St Helena, CA 94574
Just Chardonnay and Cabernet are produced at this small St Helena property. Don Stephens is ably assisted by winemaker Celia Welch Masyczek who consulted for STAGLIN FAMILY among others during the 1990s. The Moose Valley Cabernet, produced from estate grapes, is richly textured with impressive concentration offering hints of cedar and mint as well as vibrant dark berry fruit. It is 100 per cent varietal and is aged in 80 per cent new oak for 22 months. An additional Rutherford Cabernet is sourced from the Walther River Block, of which just 450 cases are produced a year. The small range is completed by a rich, honeyed, almost tropical Chardonnay which is barrel-fermented in 75 per cent new oak and aged on its lees for six of its 10 months in cask. Give the reds five or six years; drink the Chardonnay young. (DM)

● **Cabernet Sauvignon** Moose Valley Vineyard★★★★ £F
○ **Chardonnay** Carneros★★★ £E

STONY HILL   Spring Mountain   www.stonyhillvineyard.com   A: Vin

Owner: Peter McCrea   3331 St Helena Highway, St Helena, CA 94574
Mountain-grown Chardonnay has been planted at this property since the 1950s – indeed 2002 marked the 50th anniversary for Stony Hill – and the McCrea family has presided over operations here since the winery was established. In California terms this is a veritable dynasty. The style for all the whites remains the same: medium-weight wines of intensity and finesse with a pure, mineral streak running through them. The vineyards are planted on meagre volcanic soils providing the necessary stress in the vines for fruit with piercing intensity. SHV is a second Chardonnay label made from younger vines and a small amount of Gewürztraminer and Tocai Friulano is also now produced; both look promising. The McCrea's also on occasion produce Semillon du Soleil, their own version of a *passito* style where the grapes are dried on mats after harvest. (DM)
O **Chardonnay** Napa Valley★★★ £D   O **Riesling** Napa Valley★★ £B

STORYBOOK MOUNTAIN   Napa Valley   www.storybookwines.com   A: AWM

Owner: Jerry Seps   3835 Highway 128, Calistoga, CA 94515
This is a Zinfandel-only winery and a very good one, located on the red clay and loam slopes of the Mayacamas. The estate vineyards surrounding the property were originally planted in the 1880s and these hillside plots continue to show the potential of the variety. Insecticides and herbicides are avoided and the wine is vinified and aged in century-old caves which provide an ideal environment with even year-round temperatures and just the right level of humidity. A combination of French, American and Hungarian oak is used to age the wines. They are full-bodied and structured, tight and firm in their youth but with the kind of cellaring potential the variety very often lacks. A top estate reserve is regularly produced with an occasional limited-production, special vintage selection Eastern Exposures which has a small amount (less than 5 per cent) of Viognier to add fragrance. The wines are excellent value. (DM)
● **Zinfandel** Atlas Peak★★★★ £C   Mayacamas Range★★★★ £C

SWANSON   Rutherford   www.swansonvineyards.com   A:L&W

Owner: W Clarke Swanson Jnr   1271 Manley Lane, Rutherford, CA 94573
Impressive and stylish wines are produced at this family-run Napa winery established in 1985. Production is now at 25,000 cases and quality has remained good to very good. As well as the three principal releases, Sangiovese, Syrah, Cabernet Sauvignon and a Late Harvest Semillon have also been produced in recent vintages. Merlot has been made since the winery was founded; it is crafted in a medium-full, supple style with an emphasis on ripe, forward, plummy fruit and well-judged oak. The premium Alexis blends mainly Cabernet Sauvignon with Syrah and also a little Cabernet Franc and Merlot from the estate Schmitt Ranch. The style is modern with an extending vatting of around four weeks and malolactic in barrel. The wine is ripe and supple with quite marked background oak spice. Give it four to five years. (DM)
● **Merlot** Napa Valley★★★ £D   **Alexis** Napa Valley★★★★ £F
O **Pinot Grigio** Napa Valley★ £C

PHILIP TOGNI   Spring Mountain   A:Vin, JAr,Rew

Owner: Philip Togni   3780 Spring Mountain Road, St Helena, CA 94574
Philip Togni is a vastly experienced winemaker, having worked at a number of major wineries during a career spanning four decades. From his own estate vineyards on Spring Mountain he produces one of the more impressive Cabernets to be found in the Napa. It is a dense, powerful wine, with considerable tannin reinforcing its mountain origins, its texture rounded by malolactic fermentation in barrel. Powerful and long-lived it requires eight to ten years in the cellar. The 2000 was right on the cusp of five stars. Togni also produces a tiny amount of a fine sweet dessert wine from Black Muscat under the Ca Togni label. (DM)
● **Cabernet Sauvignon** Spring Mountain★★★★★ £G

TURLEY CELLARS   St Helena   www.turleywinecellars.com   A: THt

Owner: Larry Turley   3358 St Helena Highway, St Helena, CA 94574

Larry Turley produces perhaps the modern benchmark for Zinfandel – massive, dark, brooding examples of the variety. The wines are increasingly made from a wide range of sources and generally bottled as single-vineyard *cuvées*. What is remarkable about these wines is that despite having alcohol levels more akin to fortified wines – 16 per cent is not uncommon – there is still a remarkable balance and purity as well as extraordinarily concentrated, ripe, berry fruit. Very good Petite Sirah is also produced from estate as well as the Napa Valley Hayne and Rattlesnake Acres vineyards. These are very powerful and long-lived wines whereas the Zins can be approachable with just two or three years. All of the wines are produced in small lots, often fewer than 200 cases, with the majority sold by mailing list. Some of the wines can offer remarkable value. (DM)

● **Zinfandel** Juvenile★★★ £C   Duarte★★★★ £D   Old Vines★★★★★ £E

VIADER   Napa Valley   www.viader.com   A: Bib,DDr

Owner: Delia Viader   1120 Deer Park Road, Deer Park, CA 94576

Very stylish and refined red wines are crafted at this small estate nestled in the foothills of Howell Mountain. Production is less than 5,000 cases a year. The vineyard is planted on well-drained volcanic soils and yields fruit of real depth and intensity. The Viader red is a blend of Cabernet Sauvignon and Cabernet Franc and is the mainstay of the winery. It is powerful, intense and supple with malolactic taking place in barrel and although there is close to 100 per cent new wood, it is seamlessly integrated, refined and harmonious. Unusually the Cabernet Franc component is aged in Russian oak. The Petit Verdot V is a rare and impressively structured example of the variety, blended with Cabernet Sauvignon and Cabernet Franc. Rich, spicy dark berry fruit is interwoven with subtle hints of cedar and finely judged oak. The wine is dense, powerful and very ageworthy. The estate Syrah comes from both Barossa Valley and Hermitage clones, which provide weight and structure. It is aged in 600-litre new oak puncheons so the oak is nicely restrained and the rich, exotic dark licorice and black pepper fruit is finely balanced by plush, supple tannins. The wine is beguiling young but expect it to add further complexity with five or six years' cellaring. A new development is the establishment of a small vineyard in the Bolgheri region of Tuscany where a wine based on Merlot with a small amount of Cabernet Franc, Cabernet Sauvignon and Sangiovese is to be produced. The first vintage is planned for 2005 or 2006. (DM)

● **Viader** Estate★★★★★ £F   ● **Viader** V Estate★★★★★ £F
● **Viader** Syrah Estate★★★★★ £F

OTHER WINES OF NOTE

ATLAS PEAK   ● **Sangiovese** Reserve Atlas Peak £D   ○ **Chardonnay** Atlas Peak £C
ALTAMURA   ● **Cabernet Sauvignon** Napa Valley £F   ● **Sangiovese** California £E
S ANDERSON   ● **Cabernet Sauvignon** SLD £D   ○ **Chardonnay** Estate £D   ○ **Brut** Napa Valley £E
ANDERSONS CONN VALLEY   ● **Pinot Noir** Valhalla Vineyard £F   ● **Eloge** Napa Valley £G
ARTESA   ● **Pinot Noir** Carneros Reserve £E   ○ **Chardonnay** Carneros Reserve £D
BARBOUR   ● **Cabernet Sauvignon** Napa Valley £G
BARNETT VINEYARDS   ● **Cabernet Sauvignon** Spring Mountain £F   ○ **Chardonnay** Napa Valley £D
BELL WINE CELLARS   ● **Cabernet Sauvignon** Napa Valley FD   Bartelle Vineyard £F
● **Syrah** Sierra Foothills Canterbury Vineyard £D
BENESSERE   ● **Zinfandel** Napa Valley £D
BLANKIET ESTATE   ● **Cabernet Sauvignon** Paradise Hills £G
BUEHLER VINEYARDS   ● **Cabernet Sauvignon** Napa Valley Estate £E   ○ **Chardonnay** Russian River£C
BURGESS CELLARS   ● **Cabernet Sauvignon** Vintage Selection Napa Valley £E
CALDWELL   ● **Cabernet Sauvignon** Napa Valley £F   ● **Caldwell Red** Napa Valley £G
CARNEROS CREEK   ● **Pinot Noir** Carneros Signature Reserve £F   ○ **Chardonnay** Palombo Vineyard£D

CARTLIDGE AND BROWNE ● **Zinfandel** California £B   O **Chardonnay** California £B
CHIMNEY ROCK ● **Cabernet Sauvignon** Stags Leap District £E   ● **Elevage** Stags Leap District £F
O Chardonnay Carneros £C
CLOS DU VAL ● **Zinfandel** Pallisade Vineyard £E   ● **Cabernet Sauvignon** Pallisade Vineyard £F
● **Cabernet Sauvignon**Vineyard Georges III £F   O **Chardonnay** Carneros £C
CLOS PEGASE ● **Cabernet Sauvignon** Napa Valley £E   O **Chardonnay** Hommage Artists Series £E
CONN CREEK ● **Cabernet Sauvignon** Limited Release £D   ● **Anthology** £F
CORNERSTONE CELLARS ● **Cabernet Sauvignon** Cornerstone Vineyard £F
COSENTINO ● **The Zin** California £D   ● **The Poet** Napa Valley £F
DEL DOTTO ● **Cabernet Sauvignon** Estate Napa Valley £F   ● **Giovanni's Tuscan Reserve** Napa Valley£F
EHLER'S GROVE ● **Cabernet Sauvignon** Napa Valley £D
EL MOLINO ● **Pinot Noir** Napa Valley £E   O **Chardonnay** Rutherford £F
ELYSE ● **Nero Misto** California £C   ● **Cabernet Sauvignon** Morisoli Vineyard £F
ETUDE ● **Cabernet Sauvignon** Napa Valley £F   ● **Pinot Noir** Carneros £E
FIFE ● **Max Cuvée** £C   ● **Zinfandel** Old Vines £C
FOLIE À DEUX ● **Zinfandel** La Grande Folie Amador County £E
FORMAN ● **Cabernet Sauvignon** Napa Valley £E   O **Chardonnay** Napa Valley £D
FREEMARK ABBEY ● **Cabernet Sauvignon** Napa Valley £E Bosché Estate £F
GIRARD ● **Petite Sirah** Napa Valley £C   O **Sauvignon Blanc** Napa Valley £C
GROTH ● **Cabernet Sauvignon** Napa Valley £E Reserve £H   O **Chardonnay** Napa Valley £C
HARTWELL VINEYARDS ● **Cabernet Sauvignon** Stags Leap District £G   O **Chardonnay** Napa Valley £E
HENDRY ● **Zinfandel** Napa Valley £D   O **Chardonnay** Napa Valley £D
JARVIS ● **Cabernet Sauvignon** Napa Valley £G   O **Chardonnay** Napa Valley £E
JONES FAMILY ● **Cabernet Sauvignon** Napa Valley £F
HL VINEYARDS ● **Cabernet Sauvignon** Herb Lamb Vineyard £H
HOWELL MOUNTAIN VINEYARD ● **Zinfandel** Old Vine £D Beatty Ranch £E
JUDD'S HILL ● **Cabernet Sauvignon** Napa Valley £D   ● **Merlot** Summers Ranch £E
ROBERT KEENAN ● **Cabernet Sauvignon** Spring Mountain £E   ● **Merlot** Napa Valley £E
KIRKLAND RANCH ● **Cabernet Sauvignon** Napa Valley £E   O **Chardonnay** Napa Valley £D
KOVES-NEWLAN ● **Zinfandel** Napa Valley £C
LAMBOURNE FAMILY ● **Zinfandel** Team Connection £D
LA SIRENA ● **Cabernet Sauvignon** Napa Valley £H   ● **Sangiovese** Napa Valley £E
LEWELLING ● **Cabernet Sauvignon** Napa Valley £E
LIPARITA ● **Merlot** Napa Valley £E   O **Sauvignon Blanc** Oakville £C
LONG MEADOW RANCH ● **Cabernet Sauvignon** Estate £E
LONG VINEYARDS ● **Cabernet Sauvignon** Estate £F   O **Chardonnay** Estate £E
MACROSTIE ● **Syrah** Blue Oaks Vineyard £C   O **Chardonnay** Carneros £C
MARKHAM VINEYARDS ● **Cabernet Sauvignon** Reserve £F   ● **Petite Sirah** Napa Valley £D
● **Zinfandel** Napa Valley £D   ● **Merlot** Napa Valley £D
LOUIS M MARTINI ● **Cabernet Sauvignon** Monte Rosso Vineyard £E
MASON CELLARS ● **Merlot** Napa Valley £D   O **Sauvignon Blanc** Napa Valley £C
MAYACAMUS O **Chardonnay** Napa Valley £E
MELKA ● **Metisse Red** Napa Valley £F   ● **Cabernet Sauvignon** Napa Valley £D
MERRYVALE ● **Merlot** Reserve Napa Valley £G   ● **Cabernet Sauvignon** Reserve Napa Valley £G
● **Profile** Napa Valley £G   O **Chardonnay** Silouette £F
MONTICELLO ● **Cabernet Sauvignon** Jefferson Cuvée £D   O **Chardonnay** Corley Reserve £D
MOUNT VEEDER WINERY ● **Cabernet Sauvignon** Napa Valley £E   ● **Reserve** Napa Valley £F
NEWLAN ● **Cabernet Sauvignon** Napa Valley £F   ● **Pinot Noir** Napa Valley £E
O **Chardonnay** Napa Valley £D
NEYERS ● **Syrah** Hudson Vineyards £F   O **Chardonnay** Napa Valley £D
NOVA ● **Merlot** Marilyn Napa Valley £C
OAKFORD ● **Cabernet Sauvignon** Estate £H
PALOMA ● **Merlot** Spring Mountain Estate £E   ● **Syrah** Spring Mountain Estate £E
PAOLETTI ● **Cabernet Sauvignon** Napa Valley Estate £E   ● **Non Plus Ultra** Napa Valley Estate £G
ROBERT PECOTA ● **Syrah** Monterey £C   O **Muscat Canelli** Moscato d'Andrea £B

PEJU ● **Cabernet Franc** Reserve £F ● **Cabernet Sauvignon** Reserve £G
○ **Chardonnay** Estate £D
PEPI ○ **Sauvignon Blanc** Two Heart £B ○ **Arneis** Central Coast £B
PRIDE MOUNTAIN ● **Cabernet Sauvignon** Napa Valley £F ● **Merlot** Napa Valley £F
○ **Chardonnay** Napa Valley £E
KENT RASMUSSEN ○ **Chardonnay** Napa Valley £D
RAYMOND ● **Cabernet Sauvignon** Reserve £E Generations £G ○ **Chardonnay** Reserve £C
REVERIE ● **Cabernet Sauvignon** Diamond Mountain £F ● **Special Reserve** Napa Valley £G
ROCKING HORSE ● **Zinfandel** Napa Valley £C ● **Cabernet Sauvignon** Garvey Family Vineyards £E
ROMBAUER ● **Zinfandel** Napa Valley £C ○ **Chardonnay** Napa Valley £C
SADDLEBACK CELLARS ● **Cabernet Sauvignon** Napa Valley £E ● **Zinfandel** Old Vines £D
ST CLEMENT ● **Merlot** Napa Valley £D ○ **Chardonnay** Abbots Vineyard £C
ST SUPÉRY ● **Merritage Red** Napa Valley £F ● **Cabernet Sauvignon** Napa Valley £E
○ **Sauvignon Blanc** Napa Valley £C ○ **Chardonnay** Dollarhide Ranch £D
SEAVEY ● **Cabernet Sauvignon** Napa Valley £F ○ **Chardonnay** Napa Valley £E
SELENE ● **Merlot** Napa Valley £E ○ **Sauvignon Blanc** Hyde Vineyard £C
SEQUOIA GROVE ● **Cabernet Sauvignon** Napa Valley £E Reserve Rutherford £F
○ **Chardonnay** Carneros £D
SHOWKET ● **Cabernet Sauvignon** Oakville £E
SIGNORELLO ● **Cabernet Sauvignon** Estate Napa Valley £E ● **Syrah** Estate Napa Valley £E
○ **Chardonnay** Carneros £D
SILVERADO VINEYARDS ● **Cabernet Sauvignon** Stags Leap District £F ● **Merlot** Napa Valley £E
ROBERT SINSKEY ● **Merlot** Reserve £E ● **Pinot Noir** Carneros £D ○ **Chardonnay** Carneros £D
SNOWDEN ● **Cabernet Sauvignon** Napa Valley £F
SPRING MOUNTAIN VINEYARD ● **Syrah** Estate £F
STERLING VINEYARDS ● **Cabernet Sauvignon** Diamond Mountain £E
● **Merlot** Three Palms Vineyard £F
SUMMERS RANCH ● **Merlot** Knights Valley £C
THE TERRACES ● **Cabernet Sauvignon** Napa Valley £F ● **Zinfandel** Napa Valley £D
TITUS ● **Cabernet Franc** Napa Valley £D ● **Petite Sirah** Mendocino County £E
TRUCHARD ● **Merlot** Carneros £D ● **Syrah** Carneros £E ○ **Chardonnay** Carneros £D
TURNBULL ● **Cabernet Sauvignon** Estate £F ○ **Chardonnay** Napa Valley £E
VINE CLIFF ● **Cabernet Sauvignon** Napa Valley £F ● **Merlot** Napa Valley £E
○ **Chardonnay** Napa Valley £E
VON STRASSER ● **Cabernet Sauvignon** Diamond Mountain £F
WHITEHALL LANE ● **Cabernet Sauvignon** Napa Valley £E Reserve £F
○ **Sauvignon Blanc** Napa Valley £B
WHITE ROCK ● **White Rock Red** Napa Valley £F ○ **Chardonnay** Napa Valley £D
ZD WINES ● **Cabernet Sauvignon** Reserve £G ○ **Chardonnay** Reserve £E

Work in progress!!

Wines from the following producers under consideration for the next edition
ARCHIPEL
AUBERT
BOND ESTATES
BROWN ESTATE
BUONCRISTIANI
CARVER-SUTRO
CROCKER AND STARR WINES
GEMSTONE VINEYARD
HOURGLASS
JUSLYN VINEYARDS
KULETO
LARKIN

LARKMEAD
LONDER VINEYARDS
MERUS
ON thEDGE WINERY
ORIGIN-NAPA
OUTPOST ESTATE
ROBERT FOLEY VINEYARDS
RUSTON FAMILY
SCHRADER CELLARS
SERDONIS
SLOAN WINE
SWITCHBACK RIDGE
TOR WINES

Author's Choice (DM)

A dozen supreme Napa reds
ABREU ● **Cabernet Sauvignon** Madrona Ranch
ARAUJO ● **Cabernet Sauvignon** Eisele Vineyard
ARIETTA ● **H Block One Red** Napa Valley
BRYANT FAMILY ● **Cabernet Sauvignon** Napa Valley
CHATEAU MONTELENA ● **Cabernet Sauvignon** Montelena Estate
DALLA VALLE ● **Cabernet Sauvignon** Estate Oakville
DIAMOND CREEK ● **Cabernet Sauvignon** Red Rock Terrace
DOMINUS ESTATE ● **Dominus** Yountville
DUNN VINEYARDS ● **Cabernet Sauvignon** Estate Howell Mountain
HARLAN ESTATE ● **Estate Red** Napa Valley
ROBERT MONDAVI ● **Cabernet Sauvignon** Reserve Napa Valley
SHAFER ● **Cabernet Sauvignon** Hillside Select

A selection of diverse Napa whites
FLORA SPRINGS ○ **Chardonnay** Barrel Fermented Reserve
FROG'S LEAP ○ **Sauvignon Blanc** Napa Valley
HESS COLLECTION ○ **Chardonnay** Napa Valley Collection
JADE MOUNTAIN ○ **Viognier** Para's Vineyard
KONGSGAARD ○ **Roussanne/Viognier** Napa Valley
LUNA ○ **Pinot Grigio** Napa Valley
MINER FAMILY ○ **Chardonnay** Wild Yeast
NIEBAUM-COPPOLA ○ **Blancaneaux** Rutherford
PAHLMEYER ○ **Chardonnay** Napa Valley
STAGLIN FAMILY ○ **Chardonnay** Rutherford

The best of Carneros
ACACIA ● **Pinot Noir** Beckstoffer Vineyard
CLINE CELLARS ● **Mourvedre** Small Berry Vineyard
CUVAISON ○ **Chardonnay** Estate Selection
DOMAINE CARNEROS ● **Pinot Noir** Famous Gate
GLORIA FERRER ○ **Carneros Cuvée** Carneros
HAVENS ● **Syrah** Napa Valley
JADE MOUNTAIN ● **Syrah** Hudson Vineyard
KONGSGAARD ● **Syrah** Napa Valley
SAINTSBURY ● **Pinot Noir** Reserve
RAMEY ○ **Chardonnay** Hudson Vineyard

California Central Coast

The coastline from around Santa Barbara to just south of San Francisco has over the last decade and a half emerged as an excellent alternative to the larger regions on the North Coast and along the Napa Valley for a number of quality wine styles. Production is more scattered but includes some very good cool-climate whites and reds and impressive Rhône styles and Zinfandels. Here, as elsewhere, new and innovative producers are emerging. Prices are high and rising although only Pinot Noir and, to a lesser extent, Syrah are getting anywhere near the stratospheric levels of the super-premium Cabernet blends on the North Coast. In order to cover the remainder of California's wine growing areas Central Valley and the Temecula region to the south of Los Angeles are also included in this section, as well as the far superior wines of Amador County, Livermore Valley and the Sierra Foothills.

Santa Barbara County

Santa Barbara County is to the north of Los Angeles and follows the coastline embracing the regional AVAs of **Santa Maria** to the north of the county, **Santa Ynez** and the recently established **Santa Rita Hills**. Santa Rita, located between the towns of Lompoc and Buellton, includes the great Sanford and Benedict Vineyard within its boundaries. This is an excellent source of top Pinot Noir and Chardonnay and is notably affected by cooling sea breezes – more so than the neighbouring Santa Ynez Valley, which is further inland. The coolest western sectors provide ripe, tropical Chardonnay, while further east some increasingly impressive Syrah, Grenache and white Rhône varieties are grown, as well as Cabernet Sauvignon and Merlot. To the north of the county the Santa Maria Valley provides some of the best Pinot Noir in the state and some excellent Chardonnay. Pinot Blanc and Syrah are also successful here.

San Luis Obispo County

The northern tip of the Santa Maria AVA lies within San Luis Obispo County, which stretches northwards along the coast and a considerable way inland to north of Paso Robles. Four AVAs are contained within its boundaries. **Arroyo Grande** and **Edna Valley** are both relatively cool. The former is a fine source of Chardonnay and Pinot Noir, whereas the Edna Valley has also provided some excellent Rhône styles and Sauvignon Blanc and Semillon. Further to the north **Paso Robles** is warmer and the wines are fuller and riper in style. This is generally red wine territory with very good Cabernet Sauvignon, Merlot, Zinfandel and Syrah. There are also white Rhône varieties planted closer to the ocean along with good Chardonnay. **York Mountain** to the west of Paso Robles is also cooled by altitude.

Monterey County

This extensive area gives its name to an AVA that stretches down from the coast at the town of Monterey along the Salinas River valley almost to Paso Robles. On the coast just to the south of Monterey are the **Carmel Valley** and, further inland, the **Santa Lucia Highlands** AVAs. The former has a surprisingly protected balmy climate and Cabernet Sauvignon and Merlot are successful; the latter is a source of some of the most impressive recent bottlings of Pinot Noir, some of it very pricey indeed. A number of top producers have sourced from the highly regarded Pisoni Vineyard. To the east of Soledad and the Salinas River is the tiny monopole appellation of **Chalone**. First-class Chardonnay, Pinot Blanc and Pinot Noir are grown here. Going south down the Salinas Valley from Soledad are the AVAs of **Arroyo Seco** and **San Lucas**.

Santa Cruz and Santa Clara Counties

Santa Cruz is the principal AVA taken for the best wines, stretching across these two counties. The area includes a whole range of mesoclimates and runs from the southern San Francisco Bay south to Santa Cruz and inland south-east almost to San Benito County, which has just one winery of note (Calera) and the tiny **Mount Harlan** AVA. Chardonnay and Pinot Noir are successful in Santa Cruz as well as warmer-grown Cabernet Sauvignon. Two of California's great reds originate here: the Ridge Monte Bello and Katherine Kennedy Cabernet Sauvignon.

Sierra Foothills, Central Valley and the South

The huge geographical area of the Sierra Foothills encompasses Amador County and stretches into the Sierra Mountains. The AVAs here are **El Dorado**, **Fiddletown** and the **Shenandoah Valley**. The area is mainly a source of top old bush vine Zinfandel but a number of Italian varieties, particularly Barbera, also enjoy some success. To the south is the giant irrigated Central Valley, heart of California's vast bulk wine industry. To the far south towards San Diego is the region of Temecula but no real wines of note have emerged.

A-Z of producers by region

Amador County
RENWOOD   662

Arroyo Grande
LAETITIA   660
TALLEY VINEYARDS   665
TESTAROSSA   666

Carmel Valley
BERNARDUS   655

Chalone
CHALONE   657

Edna Valley
ALBAN   653
EDNA VALLEY   659

Madera County
QUADY   662

Monterey County
MER SOLEIL WINERY   660
MORGAN WINERY   661
ROBERT TALBOTT   665

Paso Robles
JUSTIN   660
PEACHY CANYON WINERY   662
TABLAS CREEK   664

San Benito County
CALERA   656

Santa Cruz Mountains
BONNY DOON   655
CA DEL SOLO   656
CLOS LACHANCE   657
KATHRYN KENNEDY   660
MOUNT EDEN VINEYARDS   661
RIDGE VINEYARDS   663

Santa Maria Valley
AU BON CLIMAT   654
CAMBRIA   657
CLOS MIMI   658
COLD HEAVEN   658
IL PODERE DELL' OLIVOS   659
QUPÉ   662
LANE TANNER   665

Santa Rita Hills
BABCOCK VINEYARDS   654
BREWER CLIFTON   656

Santa Ynez Valley
ANDREW MURRAY   653
ARCADIAN   653
BECKMEN VINEYARDS   655
GAINEY   659
SANFORD WINERY   664

Shenandoah Valley
DOM. DE LA TERRE ROUGE   665

Other
EDMUNDS ST JOHN   658
ROSENBLUM CELLARS   663
OJAI   661
SINE QUA NON   664
SEAN THACKREY   666

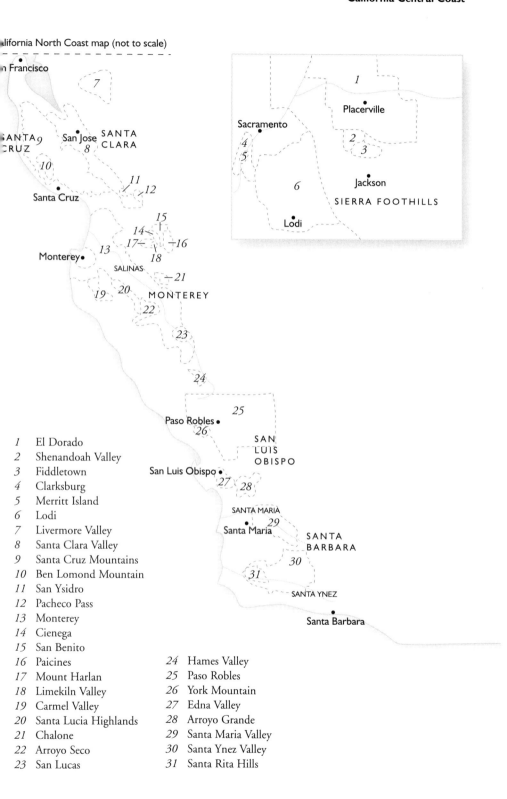

California North Coast map (not to scale)

San Francisco

7

Placerville

Sacramento

1

SANTA
CRUZ 9 San Jose SANTA
8 CLARA

4
5

2
3

10

11
12

6

Jackson

SIERRA FOOTHILLS

Santa Cruz

Lodi

15
14
17 16
13 18
16

Monterey

SALINAS

21

19 20 MONTEREY

22

23

24

25

Paso Robles

26

SAN
LUIS
OBISPO

San Luis Obispo

27 28

SANTA MARIA

29

Santa Maria

SANTA
BARBARA

30

31

SANTA YNEZ

Santa Barbara

1	El Dorado
2	Shenandoah Valley
3	Fiddletown
4	Clarksburg
5	Merritt Island
6	Lodi
7	Livermore Valley
8	Santa Clara Valley
9	Santa Cruz Mountains
10	Ben Lomond Mountain
11	San Ysidro
12	Pacheco Pass
13	Monterey
14	Cienega
15	San Benito
16	Paicines
17	Mount Harlan
18	Limekiln Valley
19	Carmel Valley
20	Santa Lucia Highlands
21	Chalone
22	Arroyo Seco
23	San Lucas

24	Hames Valley
25	Paso Robles
26	York Mountain
27	Edna Valley
28	Arroyo Grande
29	Santa Maria Valley
30	Santa Ynez Valley
31	Santa Rita Hills

California Central Coast vintages

In general the chart below should give an overall view of what to expect. The AVAs in the main are large by European standards and there can be significant variation from one mesoclimate to another within a single AVA. With the exception of the top Santa Cruz Cabernets most styles will be fading by 12 years or so.

California Central Coast vintage chart

	Pinot Noir South Central Coast	Syrah South Central Coast	Cabernet Sauvignon Santa Cruz Area	Zinfandel Amador County
2003	★★★★ A	★★★★ A	★★★★ A	★★★★ A
2002	★★★★ A	★★★★ A	★★★★ A	★★★★ A
2001	★★★/★★★★ B	★★★★ A	★★★★ A	★★★★ A
2000	★★★★ B	★★★/★★★★ B	★★★★ A	★★★★ A
1999	★★★★ B	★★★/★★★★ B	★★★/★★★★ A	★★★/★★★★ B
1998	★★★/★★★★ C	★★★/★★★★ B	★★★★ B	★★★/★★★★ B
1997	★★★★ C	★★★★ B	★★★★ B	★★★★ B
1996	★★★★ C	★★★/★★★★ C	★★★★ B	★★★/★★★★ C
1995	★★★★ C	★★★/★★★★ C	★★★/★★★★ B	★★★/★★★★ C
1994	★★★/★★★★ C	★★★/★★★★ C	★★★★ B	★★★/★★★★ C
1993	★★★/★★★★ D	★★★/★★★★ C	★★★★/★★★★★ B	★★★★ C
1992	★★★/★★★★ D	★★★★ C	★★★★ C	★★★/★★★★ D
1991	★★★★ D	★★★★ D	★★★★/★★★★★ C	★★★/★★★★ D
1990	–	★★★★ D	★★★★ C	–

ALBAN Edna Valley   A: WTs

Owner: John Alban 8575 Orcutt Road, Arroyo Grande, CA 93420

Over a period of 10 years or so John Alban has established himself as one of the finest Rhône specialists on the Central Coast. He has around 20 ha (50 acres) planted to vines in the Edna Valley from which he has been turning out increasingly fine examples. His estate vineyards are located in a cool sector of the Edna Valley, and this is reflected in the style, intensity and refinement of his wines. As well as the estate Viognier he makes a good basic example from various Central Coast sources. The estate Roussanne is one of the state's better examples, while Grenache is sourced from warmer Paso Robles. It is the remarkable Syrah bottlings, though – all of them intense and very well crafted – which stand out. Reva is the most approachable, Lorraine and the pricey Seymour sturdier and more structured. Limited-release Pandora is a cellar blend of Alban's best lots of Syrah and Grenache. (DM)

● **Syrah** Reva★★★★ £F Lorraine★★★★★ £G Seymour Vineyard★★★★★ £G
● **Grenache** Paso Robles★★★★ £F
○ **Viognier** Central Coast★★ £D Estate★★★★ £E ○ **Roussanne** Estate★★★★ £E

ANDREW MURRAY Santa Ynez Valley www.andrewmurrayvineyards.com   A: Bib

Owner: Andrew Murray 6701 Foxen Canyon Road, Los Olivos, CA 93441

Andrew Murray Vineyards is a new and very good Rhône specialist. Estate and Les Coteaux Syrah are both impressive and new from 2001 is a further bottling, South Slope, which is big, ripe and forward. A level up but still from the same variety are the marvellously dense, ageworthy and powerful Roasted Slope and the top Syrah, Hillside Reserve. Both will handle a decade in the cellar. Esperance is a stylish blend of Grenache, Syrah and Mourvèdre, full of ripe berry fruit, spices and herbs. All the components are vinified separately before final blending and ageing. The white Enchanté comprises slightly more Roussanne than Marsanne; Viognier has also featured in the wine in the past. It is held on lees but not stirred prior to bottling. Viognier is cool-fermented to emphasise its peachy, exotic character and like Enchanté it should be drunk young. These are stylish and complex wines which all show a deft handling of fruit and oak. (DM)

● **Esperance** Santa Ynez★★★ £E
● **Syrah** Estate★★★ £D Les Coteaux★★★★ £E Roasted Slope★★★★ £E Hillside Reserve★★★★ £F
○ **Enchante** Santa Ynez★★★ £D ○ **Roussanne** Estate★★★ £D
○ **Viognier** Tous Les Jours★★ £C Estate★★★ £D

ARCADIAN Santa Ynez Valley www.arcadianwinery.com

Owner: Joe Davis PO Box 1395, Santa Ynez, CA 93460

The key here is the quality of the fruit. Joe Davis wherever possible leases vineyard blocks rather than purchasing grapes, providing him with a better vineyard control. He always minimises his yields, focusing on the yield per vine rather than per hectare to optimise the balance of the vineyard. An artisan approach to winegrowing results in stylish, opulent Chardonnay and intense, finely structured Pinot Noir along with a small amount of Syrah. The latter comes from very low yields (15 hl/ha) of cool Monterey fruit and is an intense, finely crafted example with rich fruit but real finesse too. The Chardonnays possess more structure and grip than commonly found on the Central Coast while retaining an exciting level of lightly citrusy, smoky fruit. The Sleepy Hollow is the more exotic and tropical; the Bien Nacido a little tighter and more restrained. Pinot comes from a number of cool-climate sites including a pricey but magnificently rich, concentrated and piercingly intense Pisoni Vineyard bottling. Monterey is also the source of the Gary's Vineyard Pinot, a rich and gamey wine with some smoky oak. It doesn't attain quite the depth of the Pisoni but a firmly structured backbone will ensure further complexity with four or five years' age. The Fiddlestix Vineyard was added with the 2001 vintage from Kathy Joseph's (FIDDLEHEAD CELLARS) Santa Rita Hills site. It is the epitome of cool-climate Pinot in which subtle strawberry fruit is beautifully meshed with subtle oak and the wine posseses the acidity and finely honed structure to promise much with age. The Bien Nacido example is the softest and ripest of the Pinot quartet, more marked by dark berry and plum fruit and smoky oak. Vinification for all the Pinots includes whole-cluster fermentation, cold soaking and completing fermentation in barrel. The wines are bottled without fining or filtration. (DM)

● **Pinot Noir** Fiddlestix Vineyard★★★★ £F Pisoni Vineyard★★★★★ £F
● **Pinot Noir** Bien Nacido★★★★ £F Gary's Vineyard★★★★ £E
○ **Chardonnay** Bien Nacido★★★★ £E Sleepy Hollow★★★★ £E

AU BON CLIMAT Santa Maria Valley www.aubonclimat.com A:M&V,Sel,F&M

Owner: Jim Clendenen 2905 Grand Avenue, Los Olivos, CA 93441
One of the very finest exponents of Pinot Noir and Chardonnay in California. Very different to many of their peers, these are wines marked by their restrained elegance, almost Burgundian in style. This applies particularly to the Chardonnays, which are tight and surprisingly backward in their youth but with a potential and depth rarely found outside the finest examples on the Côte de Beaune. The top *cuvées* need three or four years to unfold. Jim Clendenen will often pick a small portion of the fruit early to increase the natural acidity in the wine. Pinot Noir ranges from the youthful, fruit-filled Wild Boy (blended, unusually, with Mondeuse) to the supreme Cuvée Isabelle and Knox Alexander, the vines for the latter being between 6 to 10 years old. A whole range of single-vineyard *cuvées* of both Chardonnay and Pinot are produced. The red La Bauge is generally sourced from the vast and sprawling Bien Nacido Vineyard which has been a vital source for Au Bon Climat over the last decade and a half. Both varieties have also been regularly sourced from the great Sanford and Benedict Vineyard. The Hildegard white blends Pinot Gris, Pinot Blanc and a small amount of Aligoté in a tight and restrained alternative to Chardonnay. Jim also works with his wife Morgan to produce good fruit-driven Viogniers at COLD HEAVEN, vinifies both Chardonnay and Pinot Noir in partnership at ICI/LA BAS in Oregon and makes a range of Italian-style reds and whites under the IL PODERE DELL' OLIVOS label. (DM)

● **Wild Boy** California★★ £C
● **Pinot Noir** Santa Barbara★★★ £D La Bauge au-dessus★★★★ £E Laetitia & Rincon★★★★ £E
● **Pinot Noir** Rosemary & Rincon★★★★ £E Sanford and Benedict★★★★★ £F
● **Pinot Noir** Knox Alexander★★★★★ £F Cuvée Isabelle❂❂❂❂❂ £F
○ **Hildegard** Santa Maria★★★★ £F
○ **Chardonnay** Wild Boy★★ £C Santa Barbara★★★ £D
○ **Chardonnay** Talley Vineyard★★★★ £E Santa Rita Hills★★★★ £E
○ **Chardonnay** Mt Carmel★★★★ £E Alban Vineyard★★★★ £E Talley and Rincon★★★★ £E
○ **Chardonnay** Sanford and Benedict★★★★★ £F Nuits Blanches au Bouge★★★★★ £F

BABCOCK VINEYARDS Santa Rita Hills www.babcockwinery.com A: Vin

Owner: Bryan Babcock 5175 East, Highway 246, Lompoc, CA 93436
Small to medium-sized operation producing some 20,000 cases a year across an extensive range. Located in the centre of the newly established Santa Rita AVA, the 32 ha (80 acres) of vineyards close to the ocean are cooled by regular morning mists and afternoon sea breezes. The results are generally impressive, particularly with Pinot Noir; limited bottlings come from Mount Carmel and the Cargasacchi Vineyard in Santa Barbara County. Equally impressive is the stylish and structured Syrah, Black Label. Fathom is a meritage blend and there is a more serious and pricey Cuvée Lestat. Sangiovese comes from two vineyards: Stolpman and 11 Oaks Ranch. It is partly aged in new oak. Among the whites Pinot Grigio is clean and nutty; Gewürztraminer and Sauvignon Blanc are barrel-fermented, the former with a hint of residual sugar. Chardonnay is also barrel-fermented (with a part in tank for the Santa Barbara bottling) and put through malolactic to add weight and texture. A simple, fruit-driven range labelled Troc provides affordable easy drinking. In comparison to many of their peers these wines represent particularly good value for money. (DM)

● **Pinot Noir** Santa Barbara★★ £C Grand Cuvée★★★★ £E
● **Syrah** Black Label Santa Barbara★★★ £E ● **Sangiovese** Eleven Oaks★★★ £E
● **Fathom**★★ £D
○ **Gewürztraminer** Cuvee Sublime★ £C ○ **Pinot Grigio** Santa Barbara★★ £B
○ **Sauvignon Blanc** Eleven Oaks★★ £C
○ **Chardonnay** Santa Barbara★★ £C Grand Cuvée★★★ £E

BECKMEN VINEYARDS   Santa Ynez Valley   www.beckmenvineyards.com   A: AWM

Owner: Tom Beckmen   PO Box 542, 2670 Ontiveros, Los Olivos, CA 93441
Tom Beckmen established this operation in 1994 when he bought a Santa Barbara ranch which he replanted with different rootstocks. In 1996 he added the Purisma Mountain Vineyard property which is planted at altitude and unusually on limestone-based soils. Warm summer days are complemented by cool nights which provide additional structure in the wines. As from 2003 Tom Beckmen and his son Steve, the winemaker, have begun experimenting with biodynamic farming on 12 ha (30 acres). The Cuvee Le Bec is a soft, forward blend of Grenache, Syrah, Mourvèdre and Counoise. More akin to a top Côtes du Rhône than a Châteauneuf-du-Pape this is ripe, fleshy and spicy for drinking over its first three or four years. The Purisma Grenache is altogether more serious. Dark berry and herb-spiced fruit is not impeded by new oak and the wine offers a firm enough structure to develop well for six or seven years. The original estate vineyards now also provide Sauvignon, Marsanne and some top Syrah. The Purisma Mountain Vineyard is a source not only for Grenache but also Roussanne, Syrah, Mourvèdre and a little Cabernet Sauvignon. A meritage blend Atelier (Cabernet Franc and Merlot) is also produced. An attractive source for Rhône styles, the range is also excellent value. (DM)

● **Cuvee Le Bec** Santa Barbara★★ £C
● **Grenache** Purisma Mountain Vineyard★★★ £D

BERNARDUS   Carmel Valley   www.bernardus.com   A:Goe

Owner: Ben Pon   5 West Carmel Valley Rd, Carmel Valley, CA 93924
The 20 ha (50 acres) of estate vineyards here are all planted to the Bordeaux varieties. Winemaker Mark Chesebro is committed to making traditional ageworthy reds. The Marinus, crafted from high-density plantings of Cabernet Sauvignon, Merlot, Cabernet Franc and Petit Verdot, is traditionally vinified with regular pumpovers for extraction. It spends 12 months in new oak after malolactic is completed in tank. The wine is structured and ageworthy – give it five or six years. Pinot Noir has been sourced from a number of locations including the giant Bien Nacido Vineyard. Currently it comes from both Monterey and Santa Barbara. Sauvignon Blanc and Chardonnay, both sourced from a number of Monterey County vineyards are subtly oaked with barrel-fermentation and lees-stirring. The Sauvignon has a small proportion of Semillon and is richly textured, more Graves in style than other New World herbaceous examples. Both offer good value. (DM)

● **Merlot** Carmel Valley★★ £E   ● **Marinus** Carmel Valley★★★★ £E
O **Sauvignon Blanc** Monterey County★★★ £C   O **Chardonnay** Monterey County★★★ £D

BONNY DOON   Santa Cruz Mountains   www.bonnydoonvineyard.com.   A:M&V,Sel,NYg

Owner: Randall Grahm   2 Pine Flat Road, Santa Cruz, CA 95060
Randall Grahm's Bonny Doon operation may have an eccentric and off-the-wall approach to marketing and labelling but the wines are impressive and generally very fairly priced. The Rhône varieties are the backbone of the range, indeed Grahm is often thought of as the original 'Rhône Ranger'. Le Cigare Volant (Grenache and Syrah) and Old Telegram (Mourvèdre) are both modelled on the great wines of Châteauneuf-du-Pape. Clos de Gilroy is a soft, forward Grenache which gets a cold soak to emphasise its fruit. The Cardinal Zin Zinfandel and Carignane are both well-priced examples of the varieties. Syrah is sourced from a number of vineyards, the key to making consistently elegant examples which emphasise the beguiling feminine character of the grape. The Rhône whites have included various bottles vinified from Roussanne and Viognier over the years. Roussanne is the key component of the newly labelled Le Cigare Blanc. Riesling plays an increasingly significant role. The Critique and Pacific Rim are respectively dry and steely and a touch off-dry, whereas the Heart has its Rieslings is more Auslese in style. Good Madiran and Syrah Domaine des Blagueurs from the Languedoc (most of the fruit for the latter being sourced from Michel Escande's BORIE DE MAUREL property in the Minervois) are a recent and unusual move under the Euro Doon banner, adding a further dimension to the range. Italy is also recently the source of three further

European labels. La Donna Canone is produced from Ruche in Piedmont, while Il Dormatore di Leone is Montepulciano from vineyards bordering the Marche and Abruzzo. The rare Uva di Troia grape is the source of the fragrant La Violetta. CA' DEL SOLO is Grahm's label for an Italian range produced from American vineyards. (DM)

● **Le Cigare Volant** California★★★★ £E   ● **Old Telegram** California★★★★ £E   ● **Syrah** California★★★★ £E
● **Clos de Gilroy** California★★ £B   ● **Cardinal Zin**★★ £C   ● **Carignane**★★ £C
● **Domaine des Blagueurs Syrah-Sirrah** Vin de Pays d'Oc★★ £B
● **Madiran-Heart of Darkness**★★ £C
O **Le Cigar Blanc** California★★★ £D
O **Critique of Pure Riesling**★★ £B   O **Pacific Rim Riesling**★★ £B
O **The Heart has its Rieslings**★★★ £C   O **Muscat** Vin de Glaciere★★★★ £E

BREWER CLIFTON   Santa Rita Hills   A: THt

Owner: Greg Brewer & Steve Clifton   1704 Industrial Way, Lompoc, CA 93436
Very small, recently established operation producing tiny amounts of very rich and extracted, full- blown Chardonnay and Pinot Noir from a number of vineyards in the Santa Rita Hills. Total production is barely more than 1,200 cases a year. The Pinots are fermented with whole clusters, see some new oak and are neither fined nor filtered. The oak is also reined in on the Chardonnays but they do get full malolactic, producing wines which are both richly textured and very full-bodied. As well as the wines rated here Pinot is also produced from the Ashley's, Cargasacchi and Clos Pepe vineyards, Chardonnay additionally being sourced from Ashley's, Clos Pepe and Melville. Expect similarly rich and concentrated wines. All will stand a little age but can be enjoyed young. Steve Clifton also now makes a range of very low-volume Italian varietals under the new Palomina label. It will be interesting to see how these evolve when compared with other California attempts. Greg Brewer is also the winemaker at the recently established Melville Winery outside Lompoc in the Santa Rita Hills. (DM)

● **Pinot Noir** Rozak Ranch★★★★ £E Melville★★★★ £F
O **Chardonnay** Sweeney Canyon★★★★ £E Mount Carmel★★★★★ £F

CA' DEL SOLO   Santa Cruz Mountains   www.bonnydoonvineyard.com   A:M&V,Sel

Owner: Randall Grahm   2 Pine Flat Road, Santa Cruz, CA 95060
Whereas the BONNY DOON label is based around the Rhône, Ca' del Solo is fully focused on Italy. Italian varieties have not performed with any real distinction in California and much of the reason for this is poor planting material. The Ca' del Solo range is better than most with some good, well-crafted varietal wines, both red and white, displaying attractive and abundant fruit. Big House Red is made from a variable mix of Mediterranean varieties with a touch of Cabernet Franc; Big House White is a blend of Italian and Rhône varieties along with Sauvignon Blanc. More intense and nutty and refined is the Malvasia Bianca. Both Big House wines are forward and fruit-driven for enjoying young. The varietal reds are sturdier and more structured. All are worth a punt as much for the entertaining labelling as for the wines. New is Big House Pink blended from a diverse selection of Italian grapes. (DM)

● **Big House Red**★ £B   ● **Barbera**★★ £B   ● **Sangiovese** Il Fiasco★★ £C   ● **Charbono** Farfalla★★ £C
O **Big House White**★ £ B   O **Malvasia** Bianca★★ £B
O **Pinot Grigio**★★ £C   O **Il Pescatore**★★ £C

CALERA   San Benito County   A: Bib

Owner: Josh Jensen   11300 Cienega Rd, Hollister, CA 95023
Best-known for its quartet of single-vineyard Pinot Noirs that have at times apporached cult status. Josh Jensen's objective is to handcraft wines that have more to do with classic Burgundy than with some of the more typically fruit-driven, squeaky-clean examples from his California contemporaries. On occasion the results are less than perfect but generally these are benchmarks for the state. The regular Central Coast wines are good if unspectacular and the Viognier is very good when not overly alcoholic. The winery

was the first to be completely gravity-fed. (DM)

● **Pinot Noir** Central Coast★★ £C Reed★★★ £F Selleck★★★★ £F Jensen★★★★ £F Mills★★★★ £F
○ **Chardonnay** Central Coast★★ £C Mount Harlan★★★ £E ○ **Viognier** Mount Harlan★★★ £E

CAMBRIA   Santa Maria Valley   www.cambriawine.com   A:WTs

Owner: Kendall Jackson   5475 Chardonnay Lane, Santa Maria, CA 93454
Part of the giant KENDALL JACKSON Group, Cambria is its Central Coast flagship. It is by no means small
with the total area under vine now some 565 ha (1,400 acres). Top-flight Pinot Noir is ripe and full of red-
berry fruit, and particular noteworthy are a number of Chardonnay bottlings which are barrel-fermented
with lees-ageing to add weight and complexity. Rhône varieties from the Tepusquet Vineyard also show
promise. Syrah is nicely structured with good brambly fruit intensity, more St-Joseph than Hermitage. (DM)

● **Pinot Noir** Julia's Vineyard★★ £D Bench Break★★★ £E Rae's★★★ £F
● **Syrah** Tepusquet★★ £D ● **Sangiovese** Tepusquet★ £C
○ **Chardonnay** Katherine's Vineyard★★★ £D Bench Break★★★ £E Rae's★★★ £E
○ **Viognier** Tepusquet★★ £C Late Harvest★★ £C

CHALONE   Chalone   www.chalonewinegroup.com   A: Bib

Owner: Chalone Group   Stonewall Canyon Road & Highway 146, Soledad, CA 93960
This is the original estate founded by the late Richard Graff who went on to establish the Chalone Wine
Group. The Group's interests include CANOE RIDGE and Sagelands in Washington, ACACIA, MOON
MOUNTAIN, JADE MOUNTAIN, Provenance, Orogeny Vineyards, Hewitt Vineyard, and EDNA VALLEY
VINEYARDS among others in California, Monte Xanic in the California Baja in Mexico and a partnership
with Domaines Baron Philippe de Rothschild SA in Château DUHART-MILON in Bordeaux. The Chalone
white wines are intense, subtle and slow-developing; the Chardonnay Reserve is particularly fine, the
Chenin Blanc a benchmark for the variety in California. In part this is helped by the vineyard's location 520
m (1,700 ft) above the Salinas Valley close to the Pinnacles National Monument. Indeed the estate possesses
its own AVA. The Pinot Noir by contrast with the whites has often disappointed in recent vintages. Syrah
has now been added to the Pinot and the first release was in 2002. (DM)

● **Pinot Noir** Estate★★ £E
○ **Chardonnay** Estate★★★★ £E Reserve★★★★★ £F
○ **Pinot Blanc** Estate★★★ £D Reserve★★★★ £E
○ **Chenin Blanc** Estate★★★ £D

CLOS LACHANCE   Santa Cruz Mountains   www.closlachance.com   A: Fie

Owner: Bill & Brenda Murphy   21511 Saratoga Heights Drive, Saratoga, CA 95070
This small operation founded in 1987 is producing increasingly impressive Chardonnay in three bottlings.
These are earthy, quite traditional styles with marked lees influence. The weighty and concentrated
Vanumanutagi bottling is barrel-fermented and aged in mainly new French and American oak. Pinot Noir
comes from the Santa Cruz Mountains and there is a very limited and well-made special *cuvée*, Erwin
Vineyard, which is aged in mainly new oak. The estate Cabernet is good and well-priced but it is the berry-
laden El Dorado Zinfandel that has the edge among the reds. The Murphy's now own a vineyard
development company, which they believe will help ensure a good continuity of grape supply in the fairly
unstable California vineyard fruit supply chain.(DM)

● **Zinfandel** El Dorado County★★★ £C **Cabernet Sauvignon** Santa Cruz★★ £D
● **Pinot Noir** Santa Cruz★★ £C **Merlot** Central Coast★ £C
○ **Chardonnay** Santa Cruz★★★ £C Vanumanutagi★★★ £E Napa Valley★★ £C

CLOS MIMI   Santa Maria Valley   www.closmimi.com   **A: AWM**

Owner: Tim & Mimi Spear   2717 Aviation Way, Santa Maria, CA 93455
The Spears established their small Santa Maria winery in 1996 and they make solely Syrah from a small range of sources all within the Paso Robles region. The whole approach is based on the best artisan methods employed in France and the results are impressive. They now work hand in hand with the Shell Creek, Brave Oak, White Hawk, Westerley and Core vineyards which provide small lots of low-yielding Syrah. Indeed agreements are made with the growers regarding maximum yields which will not exceed 2.5 tons to the acre, approximately 35 hl/ha. They also use a biodynamic approach to many vineyard and winemaking decisions. Vinification includes cold soaking, foot treading, *pigeage*, indigenous yeasts and naturally occuring malolactic in barrel. The wines are bottled unfined and unfiltered. The Petite Rousse is the entry-level Syrah produced from a range of sources and in the greatest volume, now approaching 2,800 cases a year. It has very good concentration at this level. The Bunny Slope is a richly dense, dark-fruited wine loaded with dark pepper and spice, aged in oak for up to three years, much in the style of Guigal. It has been the top wine up to the 2001 vintage but will be replaced with a number of other small-volume single-vineyard bottlings. Expect them to be similarly impressive. A juicy rosé Étiquette is also made. (DM)
● **Syrah** Petite Rousse★★★ £C   Bunny Slopes★★★★★ £F

COLD HEAVEN   Santa Maria Valley   **A: M&V**

Owner: Morgan Clendenen   2905 Grand Avenue, Los Olivos, CA 93441
Small, operation focused on Viognier, the brainchild of Morgan, wife of Jim Clendenen of AU BON CLIMAT. Her objective is to find the best possible cool-grown Viognier, believing that the best examples with the finest structure from Condrieu emerge from those producers who harvest with plenty of acidity. Excessive alcohol is avoided and the wines are fermented in used oak and aged until malolactic has been completed. They are cold-stabilised and lightly fined but bottled unfiltered. The Sanford and Benedict has been the best example thus far and the wine is classic cool-climate, fruit-driven Viognier with marked floral perfume and a fine, mineral undercurrent lending depth and finesse. Morgan has released an international blend in association with Yves CUILLERON, Deux C, made from part Santa Barbara and part Condrieu fruit. She also releases a little Pinot Noir from husband Jim's Le Bon Climat Vineyard and a Viognier from here is also now produced. The Viogniers may be enjoyed young but will evolve nicely for three or four years. (DM)
O **Viognier** Santa Ynez Valley★★ £C   Vogelzang Vineyard★★★ £C   Sanford and Benedict★★★ £D

EDMUNDS ST JOHN   www.edmundsstjohn.com   **A: WTs,AWM**

Owner: Steve Edmunds   1331 Walnut Street, Berkeley, CA 94709
Small warehouse winery, a benchmark among California Rhône Rangers. Very impressive Syrah, which can stand comparison with the very best of the northern Rhône, is made from a number of sources and the Wylie-Fenaughty was added with the 2000 vintage. Rocks and Gravel, originally labelled as Côtes Sauvages, is a classic southern Rhône blend of Grenache, Mourvèdre, Syrah and, most unusually for California, a hint of Counoise. Steve expects to continue working with these varieties and is now producing a more structured example, the Los Robles Viejos red, from the Rozet Vineyard with its excellent calcareous soils. With the Rhône white of the same name, a nutty and impressive blend of Viognier, Marsanne and Roussanne, he has now established an on-going relationship with the vineyard owners. Pallini Rosso, a spicy blend of mainly Zinfandel with some Grenache, is sourced from old bush vines. (DM)
● **Syrah** California★★★ £D   Parmalee Hill Vineyard★★★★ £E   Durell Vineyard★★★★ £E
● **Rocks and Gravel** California★★★ £C   ● **Los Robles Viejos** Rozet Vineyard★★★ £D
● **Pallini Rosso** Mendocino★★★ £C
O **Los Robles Viejos** Rozet Vineyard★★★ £D   O **Pinot Grigio** El Dorado County★★★ £C

EDNA VALLEY   Edna Valley   www.ednavalley.com   A: **Bib**

*Owner: Niven family/**Chalone Wine Group**   2585 Biddle Ranch Road, San Luis Obispo, CA 93401*

The Niven Family who own the Paragon Vineyard established this partnership with the CHALONE Wine Group in 1980 to produce a range of well-priced varietal wines that emphasise the cool-climate characteristics of the Edna Valley. Key here are the coastal fogs which drift inland to cool the vineyards at night during the summer growing season and the clay and volcanic rock soils. Chardonnay dominates the production of well over 100,000 cases a year and it stands out. Quality remains impressive despite the volume and the wines are good value. Chardonnay from the Paragon Vineyard is barrel-fermented and shows nicely judged lees and oak with subtle tropical and melon fruit notes. The Viognier is lighter than some others but has attractive peachy character. Both Syrah and Pinot are now also sourced from the Paragon Vineyard as are newly added Pinot Gris and Sauvignon Blanc. A small amount of Marsanne is also now made and is sourced from a number of Central Coast sites. The Syrah is bright and spicy with vibrant raspberry fruit. The Pinot is more marked by forward berry fruit than complex secondary flavours. (DM)

● **Pinot Noir** Paragon★★ £C   ● **Syrah** Paragon★★ £C
O **Chardonnay** Paragon★★★ £C   O **Viognier** Fralich Vineyard★★ £C

GAINEY   Santa Ynez Valley   www.gaineyvineyard.com

Owner: Gainey Family   3950 East Highway 246, Santa Ynez, CA 93460

Small to medium-sized operation producing around 18,000 cases a year. The Gainey Home Ranch of some 40 ha (100 acres) is planted to the red Bordeaux varieties in addition to Sauvignon Blanc. The property itself is much larger at 730 ha (1,800 acres) and the family also farm cattle. Chardonnay, Pinot Noir and Syrah have been planted at a new 48-ha (120-acre) vineyard in the cooler Santa Rita Hills. The winery facility is now gravity-fed to provide the gentlest environment possible in which to vinify the grapes. The Limited Selection Merlot, Pinot Noir, Chardonnay and Sauvignon Blanc have been impressive in recent vintages. The Merlot is bottled without filtration. Sauvignon Blanc gets some oak-ageing and the Limited Selection Chardonnay is fermented and aged in barrel on lees. The wines represent reasonable value. The 2001 vintage saw the release of a Limited Release Cabernet Franc and Triada, a Rhône-style blend of Grenache, Syrah and Viognier. (DM)

● **Merlot** Santa Ynez Valley★★ £C
O **Chardonnay** Santa Barbara★★ £C   O **Riesling** Santa Ynez Valley★★ £B
O **Sauvignon Blanc** Santa Ynez Valley★★ £B

IL PODERE DELL' OLIVOS   Santa Maria Valley   info@aubonclimat.com   A: **M&V**

Owner: Jim Clendenen   PO Box 440, Los Olivos, CA 93441

Best-known for his remarkable AU BON CLIMAT Chardonnays and Pinot Noirs, and his wife Morgan's COLD HEAVEN Viogniers, Jim Clendenen has also maintained a prolonged interest in Italian varieties. The wines have varied but the best examples are very good. Decent planting material remains a problem in California and while some vintages show real promise others are less impressive. The top red, Ragazzo Legnoso, is a richly textured blend of Nebbiolo and Barbera. This is now joined by a new premium label, Primogenito, as well as a little red Teroldego. Clendenen's commitment to established quality viticultural techniques such as mass selection may very well prove him right in the long term. (DM)

● **Barbera** Bricco Buon Natale Santa Maria★★ £B   ● **Carignan** Santa Maria★ £B
● **Nebbiolo** Bricco Buon Natale Santa Maria★★ £C
● **Ragazzo Legnoso** California★★★ £D
O **Tocai** Santa Maria★★ £B   O **Pinot Grigio** Santa Maria★★ £B

JUSTIN Paso Robles www.justinwine.com A: **Vin**

Owner: Justin Baldwin 11680 Chimney Rock Road, Paso Robles, CA 93446
Very good operation producing some of the best Bordeaux-style reds on the Central Coast. These wines may share similar grapes to their French counterparts but are altogether fuller and riper without any hint of the rusticity or jamminess often found in warm-climate Cabernet. Isosceles is a blend of Cabernet Sauvignon, Cabernet Franc and Merlot, marginally more refined than Justification, which is just over half Cabernet Sauvignon, the balance Merlot. The Halter vineyard is a full-on example of Syrah: big, powerful if less refined than a top-flight OJAI or ALBAN. A Paso Robles bottling has also now been added as has Zinfandel. Chardonnay and Sauvignon Blanc are aged in top-quality French oak and there is a limited-release reserve Chardonnay bottling which is worth considering. A number of interesting special labels can be sourced directly from the winery. Prices are very fair. (DM)
● **Justification** Paso Robles★★★★ £E ● **Isosceles** Paso Robles★★★★ £E
● **Cabernet Sauvignon** Paso Robles★★★ £D
● **Syrah** Paso Robles★★★ £D Halter Vineyard★★★★ £E
O **Chardonnay** Paso Robles★★★ £C O **Sauvignon Blanc** Paso Robles★★ £B

KATHRYN KENNEDY Santa Cruz Mountains www.kathrynkennedywinery.com

Owner: Kathryn Kennedy 13180 Pierce Road, Saratoga, CA 95070
The production here is very small with just over 3 ha (8 acres) under vine. The Estate Cabernet is highly sought after by local collectors and the most likely way of obtaining any at all is to join the mailing list. A secondary label is also produced, again in very small quantities, from selected Cabernet plots throughout the Santa Cruz AVA. A Merlot-based proprietary red, Lateral, is made from bought-in fruit and there is a small amount of Syrah from the Maridon Vineyard as well a Santa Cruz Mountains bottling. A part barrel, part tank-fermented cool-climate Sauvignon Blanc was added with the 2003 vintage. Vinification for all the reds is in small lots and the approach throughout is one of care and minimal handling. The Cabernets, particularly the Estate, will comfortably add great complexity with 10 years' age. (DM)
● **Cabernet Sauvignon** Estate★★★★★ £G

LAETITIA Arroyo Grande www.laetitiawine.com A: **JAr**

Owner: Selim Zilkha 453 Tower Grove Drive, Arroyo Grande, CA 93420
Selim Zilkha was among a number of partners who purchased Laetitia from Champagne DEUTZ in the late 1990s. As from 2001 he has acquired sole ownernership. Sound, well-priced sparklers were the foundation of production here and are still being made but the real focus of the winery now is on good-quality estate and single-vineyard Chardonnay and Pinot Noir. Around 15,000 cases a year of still wines are made, with a further 1,500 cases of sparkling. The wines are good and well made but as yet lack the depth, intensity and concentration of the best examples along the Central Coast. Estate wines are produced from Chardonnay Pinot Blanc and Pinot Noir, and there are single-vineyard Pinot Noirs from the La Colline, Les Galets and Nadia's vineyards. The estate wines are all very fairly priced; the single-vineyard Pinots will stretch the pocket a little more. (DM)
● **Pinot Noir** San Luis Obispo★★ £D Arroyo Grande Reserve★★ £E
O **Pinot Blanc** Estate★ £C O **Chardonnay** Central Coast★ £C Estate Reserve★★ £D
O **Laetitia** XD★★ £C ◉ **Brut Rose** Arroyo Grande★★★ £D

MER SOLEIL WINERY Monterey County Mersoleilwinery@aol.com A: **Vin**

Owner: Chuck Wagner PO Box 35, Rutherford, CA 94573
Several different varieties are cultivated at this small vineyard and winery near Santa Lucia. The focus is mainly on the full-on Chardonnay which is stylish and powerful and possesses an excellent balance of ripe fruit and well-judged oak. Chuck Wagner also runs CAYMUS in the Napa Valley and produces an attractive,

nutty Marsanne/Viognier blend under the Treana label in partnership with Paso Robles grape growers the Hope family. The small range is completed by Santa Barbara Pinot Noir Belle Glos and a sweet white Late Harvest Viognier which is rich and unctuous with moderate depth and intensity. (DM)

O **Chardonnay** Central Coast★★★ £D   O **Treana** Central Coast★★ £C
O **Viognier** Late Harvest Monterey★★★ £D
● **Pinot Noir** Belle Glos Santa Barbara★★ £D

MORGAN WINERY Monterey County www.morganwinery.com   A: **Bib**

Owner: Donna & Daniel Morgan Lee 590 Brunken Avenue, Suite C, Salinas, CA 93901
Small to medium-sized warehouse winery. Chardonnay, Pinot Noir and Syrah are mainly sourced from the Santa Lucia Highlands with a small amount of Chardonnay also coming from Arroyo Grande. These are first-class sources for the Burgundy varieties. Pinot Noirs come from Rosella's, Double L and Garys vineyards in the Santa Lucia Highlands and are a step up from the regular bottling. Chardonnays from three different vineyards – Double L, Metallica and Rosella's – have replaced the Reserve bottling. The Syrah is classy in a cooler, spicier style and there is a southern Rhone-style Cotes du Crow's, a blend of Syrah and Grenache. The cool-grown Monterey Sauvignon Blanc is good value, full and ripe with a hint of Alexander Valley fruit adding complexity. It is part barrel-fermented. Most of the wines will drink well young; the single-vineyard bottlings will stand a little age.(DM)

● **Pinot Noir** Santa Lucia Highlands★★ £C   ● **Syrah** Monterey★★★ £C Tierra Mar★★★ £E
O **Chardonnay** Monterey★★★ £C   O **Sauvignon Blanc** Monterey★★★ £B

MOUNT EDEN VINEYARDS Santa Cruz Mountains www.mounteden.com   A: **Vin**

Owner: Jeffrey Patterson 22020 Mt. Eden Road, Saratoga, CA 95070
The whole Mount Eden range is characteristic of the best of the Santa Cruz Mountains. The wines are deep, powerful and reserved. All will benefit from cellaring. The Pinot is a big, rich style, whereas the Cabernet Sauvignons are tight and backward in their youth with considerable structure and grip. They need time to soften the initially austere mountain tannins. Chardonnay is particularly good: restrained in style with subtle citrus fruit and fine-grained nutty, spicy oak held in the background. The wines have real depth and complexity. 2001 sees the release of the first Edna Valley Edna Ranch West Slope Chardonnay from fruit grown in an adjacent plot to the MacGregor Vineyard. The Edna Valley wines are lusher, more tropical in style than the more restrained Estate wine. (DM)

● **Cabernet Sauvignon** Estate★★★ £D Old Vine Reserve★★★★ £F   ● **Pinot Noir** Estate★★★ £E
O **Chardonnay** Estate★★★★ £E MacGregor Vineyard★★★ £D

OJAI Ventura County ojaivineyard.com   A: THt,Vin,AWM

Owner: Adam Tolmach P.O. Box 952 Oak View CA 93022
Originally involved with Jim Clendenen at AU BON CLIMAT, Adam Tolmach founded his own operation in the mid-1980s. Top Syrah has always been a focal point here and these are always classy, superbly crafted wines – subtle and restrained with real depth, and very different from the many overblown, overripe examples produced elsewhere. Chardonnay, Pinot Noir and Sauvignon are also very impressive in a bewildering number of vineyard guises, often varying from year to year. Newly established Vin du Soleil red and white Rhône blends are a change of direction for Tolmach as he seeks to maximise the potential of the southern Rhône styles and move away from what he feels is an overly varietal-dominated marketplace. (DM)

● **Pinot Noir** Bien Nacido★★★ £E Pisoni Vineyard★★★★★ £G
● **Syrah** Stolpman Vineyard★★★★ £E Thompson Vineyard★★★★★ £F
● **Syrah** Santa Barbara★★★ £D Roll Ranch★★★★ £E Bien Nacido★★★★ £E
O **Chardonnay** Talley Vineyard★★★★ £E Bien Nacido★★★★ £E Sanford and Benedict★★★★ £E
O **Sauvignon Blanc** Santa Barbara★★★ £C   O **Viognier** Roll Ranch★★★ £D

PEACHY CANYON WINERY Paso Robles www.peachycanyon.com A: **Fie**

Owner: Beckett family 4045 Peachy Canyon Road, Paso Robles, CA 93446
One of the best Zinfandel specialists on the Central Coast. These are wines that are ripe and spicy with great berry fruit, particularly the dry-farmed Benito Dusi Ranch produced from 75-year-old vines. Doug Beckett also produces a number of other impressive reds. Westside and Paso Robles are very largely Zin but have a touch of Carignane. As well as the Westside Cabernet Sauvignon there is a premium bottling, De Vine, which is a blend of the best of the estate vineyards. Para Siempre is dominated by Merlot with a little of Cabernets Sauvignon and Franc. The Incredible Red is a great-value glugger produced in 2000 from 100 per cent Zinfandel. The range now also includes Central Coast Syrah and Snow Vineyard and Old School House Zinfandels. (DM)

● **Cabernet Sauvignon** Westside★★ £D **Para Siempre** Paso Robles★★ £E
● **Paso Robles Cuvée★** £B ● **Westside** Paso Robles★★ £C
● **Zinfandel** Estate★★ £D Benito Dusi Ranch★★★ £D

QUADY Madera County A: **Hal,F&M**

Owner: Andrew Quady 13181 Road 24, Madera, CA 93639
Fortified- and sweet-wine specialist based in the arid Central Valley. Red Starboard is a port style produced from Amador County Zinfandel while the whites are produced from Muscat: Essencia from Orange Muscat and Elysium from Black Muscat. These are good, well-crafted examples if lacking the richness and finesse of the best European and Australian equivalents. (DM)

● **Starboard** Amador County★ £C
O **Essencia** Madera★★ £C O **Elysium** Madera★★ £C

QUPÉ Santa Maria Valley www.qupe.com A:**M&V**,SVS,Sel,F&M

Owner: Bob Lindquist 2531 Grand Avenue, Los Olivos, CA 93441
One of the first and still one of the finest of the California Rhône Rangers, Bob Lindquist shares winemaking facilities and a similar vision with Jim Clendenen at AU BON CLIMAT. The wines here are of a uniformly high standard; both reds and whites are subtle and elegant and very well crafted. The Bien Nacido Vineyard is the main source of fruit but Lindquist also farms the Ibarra-Young Vineyard on organic priciples. The white Bien Nacido Cuvée blends Chardonnay and Viognier and the red Los Olivos Cuvée is a classical southern Rhône style comprising Syrah, Mourvèdre and Grenache. The wine has good weight and texture with an underlying black pepper character. Perhaps the greatest contrast is between the two great Bien Nacido Syrahs, often of five-star quality, and the regular Central Coast bottling which can be a touch light and very peppery. Recent Syrah additions to the range now include bottlings from Stolpman, Alisos, Purisima Mountain and Colson Canyon vineyards. There is also now a Purisima Mountain Grenache. The whites should be broached relatively young; the top reds will evolve very well over five or six years. (DM)

● **Syrah** Central Coast★★ £C Bien Nacido Reserve★★★★ £E Bien Nacido Hillside Estate★★★★★ £E
● **Los Olivos Cuvee** Santa Barabara★★★ £E
O **Chardonnay** Bien Nacido★★★ £C Bien Nacido Reservee★★★★ £E
O **Marsanne** Ibarra Young Vineyard★★★ £C O **Viognier** Ibarra Young Vineyard★★★★ £E
O **Bien Nacido Cuvee** Santa Maria★★★ £D
O **Roussanne** Alban Vineyard★★★ £D

RENWOOD Amador County www.renwood.com A: **CHk**

Owner: Renwood Group 12225 Steiner Road, Plymouth, CA 95669
The Italian and Rhône-style wines here are all impressive but it is the great Zinfandels from old bush vines that really stand out. Renwood's vineyards are planted at altitude, generally well over 300 m (1,000 ft) above sea level, and the warm days and cool summer evenings enable good structure and acidity to be built up in the fruit. The magnificent Zinfandel D'Agostini bottling, pushing four stars regularly, is

what super-ripe, concentrated old-vine Zinfandel is all about. The good-value Sierra Series reds and Select Series whites are sourced from selected vineyards throughout the Sierra Foothills. Santino is a good-value budget label offering mainly simple Rhône styles and one of the best white Zinfandels. In general the wines should be drunk fairly young but the top Zinfandels will add further complexity with a little age. (DM)

● **Barbera** Sierra Series★★ £B Estate★★★ £C ● **Nebbiolo** Estate★★ £D
● **Sangiovese** Amador County★★ £C ● **Syrah** Sierra Series★★ £B Estate★★★ £D
● **Zinfandel** Sierra Series★★ £B Old Vine★★★ £C Fiddletown★★ £D Jack Rabbit Flat★★★ £D
● **Zinfandel** Grandpere★★★ £D Grandmere★★★ £D D'Agostini★★★ £E Amador Ice Wine★★★ £E
○ **Viognier** Select Series★★ £B Estate★★ £C

RIDGE VINEYARDS Santa Cruz Mountains www.ridgewine.com A:**M&V**,Sel,F&M

Owner: Paul Draper 17100 Monte Bello Road, Cupertino CA 95014
This is one of California's great wineries. Chardonnay, both Santa Cruz Mountains and the premium Monte Bello, is in a classically Burgundian style, intense but restrained. Some utterly superb and very complex Zinfandels are handcrafted from a range of sources. These include the Pagani Ranch, which contains some Alicante Bouschet and Petite Sirah, and York Creek, with increasing amounts of Petite Sirah. There is also one of the best examples of varietal Petite Sirah (so often hard and unyielding) and a stylish Mataro. The great Geyserville red is usually around two-thirds Zin with both Carignane and Petite Sirah in the blend. A Syrah/Grenache blend and varietal Grenache are also now produced from the Lytton Vineyard and, sticking with the southern France theme, Paul Draper also now produces a Carignane from Buchignani Ranch. There are also some well-priced varietals under the Coastal Range label. The greatest Ridge wine is the meritage Monte Bello, unquestionably one of the state's finest and longest-living Cabernet-based reds. Whether some of the newer Napa Valley super-premium examples will stand the test of time like these remains to be seen. (DM)

● **Cabernet Sauvignon** Santa Cruz Mountains★★★★ £E ● **Monte Bello**✪✪✪✪✪ £G
● **Mataro** California★★★ £E ● **Petite Sirah** York Creek★★★★ £E
● **Zinfandel** Lytton Springs★★★★ £E Pagani★★★★ £E York Creek★★★★£E ● **Geyserville**★★★★★£E
○ **Chardonnay** Santa Cruz Mountains★★★★ £E

ROSENBLUM CELLARS Santa Lucia Highlands www.rosenblumcellars.com A: **Vin**

Owner: Kent Rosenblum 2900 Main Street, Alameda, CA 94501
The Rosenblum warehouse winery is located in the San Francisco Bay area in central Alameda. Former veterinary surgeon Kent Rosenblum oversees the crushing of some 400 tons of fruit at harvest time. The main focus here is on Zinfandel and very good it is too. Even in a difficult years the wines stand out for their intensity, purity and depth and the top examples show really splendid complexity. Numerous bottlings are sourced from a diversity of regions – Contra Costa to Mount Veeder, Paso Robles to Dry Creek. Among other whies the main focus is on the Rhône Valley. There are good varietal examples of Syrah, Marsanne and Viognier and a number of fruit-filled reds are labelled Chateau La Paws. Côte du Bone Roan red is mainly Carignane with some Syrah, Mourvèdre and Grenache; the white is Viognier and Roussanne. Varietal Mourvèdre, Syrah, Petit Sirah and Zinfandel are also now released under the label. Holbrook Mitchell Trio is a meritage blend of Bordeaux varieties. There are also some impressive late-harvest bottlings including an excellent Black Muscat from the Gallagher Ranch in Madera County. Winemaker Jeff Cohn also produces a small amount of very good Syrah and Petite Sirah under his own JC CELLARS label. (DM)

● **Zinfandel** Samsel Vineyard Maggie's Reserve★★★★ £E St Peters Church Vineyard★★★★ £E
● **Zinfandel** Carla's Vineyards★★ £C Alegria Vineyard★★★ £C Eagle Point Vineyard★★★ £C
● **Zinfandel** Richard Sauret Vineyard★★★ £C
● **Syrah** England Shaw Vineyard★★★ £D Hillside Vineyard★★★ £D Fess Parker Vineyard★★★★ £E
● **Holbrook Mitchell Trio** Napa Valley★★★ £E ● **Chateau La Paws Côte du Bone Roan** California★ £B
● **Black Muscat** Gallagher Ranch★★★ £E
○ **Marsanne** Dry Creek★★★ £C ○ **Rousanne** Sanata Barbara★★★ £C
○ **Viognier** Santa Barbara★★ £C Ripkin Vineyard★★ £C

SANFORD WINERY Santa Rita Hills A:WTs

Owner: Richard Sanford 7250 Santa Rosa Road, Buellton, CA 93427

Located in the cool Santa Rita Hills AVA, Sanford produces good to very good Chardonnay, Sauvignon Blanc and Pinot Noir although quality here is not quite at the level it was a decade ago. The wines nonetheless remain very fairly priced compared to a number of their more recently arrived Central Coast equivalents. Richard Sanford is the owner of the great Sanford and Benedict Vineyard, from which a number of winemakers have crafted some of the finest examples of Pinot Noir and Chardonnay to have emerged from California. Pinot Noir, particularly La Rinconada and Sanford and Benedict, is laden with intense berry fruit and well-judged oak. Chardonnay and Sauvignon Blanc are in a ripe tropical style, with plenty of oak. (DM)

● **Pinot Noir** Santa Barbara★★ £C La Riconada★★★★ £F Sanford and Benedict★★★★ £F
O **Chardonnay** Santa Barbara★★ £C Estate Barrel Select★★★ £E Sanford and Benedict★★★★ £E
O **Sauvignon Blanc** Central Coast★ £C

SINE QUA NON Ventura County

Owner: Manfred & Elaine Krankl Ojai, CA 9

This really is the quintessential California garage winery. Warehouse style wineries have been an established feature of the industry for many years and other notable producers include Kent ROSENBLUM and Sean THACKREY. The Krankl's own no vineyards themselves and the wines can be very difficult to follow due to alarmingly regular name changes. They are though the epitome of the finest quality artisan winemaking: rich, opulent and always produced from the finest fruit. A Capella is Pinot Noir in the 2000 vintage, a wine of impressive purity and rich berry fruit sourced from the Shea Vineyard in Oregon. Previously it has been named Veiled and Left Field. The 2000 Boot is a blend of Chardonnay, Roussanne and Viognier mainly from the Central Coast. Other renditions of the blend have taken the labels Tarantella and The Boot. Pricier is a 100 per cent Roussanne, the Hussy. Syrah has variously been named Midnight Oil, Flagrante, E Raised and Imposter McCoy. The 2000 Incognito, a blend of 95 per cent Grenache and the balance Syrah, is a rival for some of the great single-vineyard and special *cuvée* bottles from Châteauneuf-du-Pape. Manfred Krankl has also regularly produced Eiswein from either Gewürztraminer or Viognier, a Vin de Paille from Semillon and occasional botrytis Viogniers. The wines are not only of the highest quality but inevitably pricey and very scarce. (DM)

● **A Capella** Pinot Noir Shea Vineyard Willamette Valley★★★★ £F
● **Incognito** Grenache/Syrah California★★★★★ £H
O **The Boot** Chardonnay/Roussane/Viognier California★★★★ £F

TABLAS CREEK Paso Robles www.tablascreek.com A: Mis

Owner: Robert Haas, Francois and Jean-Pierre Perrin 9339 Adelaida Road, Paso Robles, CA 93446

This is the first major overseas investment for the Perrin brothers of CHÂTEAU DE BEAUCASTEL in Châteauneuf-du-Pape. Along with Robert Haas they have established an important nursery for Rhône Valley planting material and are now producing increasingly impressive red and white blends as the vineyards mature. There have been changes in the range. Reserve Cuvée (originally known as Tablas Creek Rouge), a blend of Mourvèdre, Grenache, Syrah and Counoise, has confusingly now been dropped. The same fate has befallen Clos Blanc (formerly Tablas Creek Blanc), a Roussanne, Viognier, Marsanne and Grenache Blanc blend. The top red and white Esprit de Beaucastel *cuvées* remain and are blends of the same varieties. Expect similarly impressive wines. A 100 per cent Roussanne is part barrel-fermented and there are tiny amounts of Antithesis, a full-blown style of Chardonnay, as well as Panoplie, a wine based on Mourvèdre and made when vintage conditions favour. The 2000 is the most recent release. The range is completed by red and white Côtes de Tablas which are in the mould of top-quality Côtes du Rhônes. (DM)

● **Reserve Cuvée** Paso Robles★★★★ £E
O **Clos Blanc** Paso Robles★★★ £E

ROBERT TALBOTT Monterey County www.talbottvineyards.com A:Vin

Owner: Robert Talbott 53 West Carmel Valley Road, Carmel Valley, CA 93924
Small operation with vineyard resources in the Salinas Foothills and Santa Lucia Mountains. The three top Chardonnays, Kali-Hart, Sleepy Hollow and Cuvée Cynthia, are marvellously stylish cool-climate examples, delivering very fine fruit from low yields with very well judged, fine-grained oak and a rich leesy complexity. A special selection from the Diamond T Estate, bottled unfined and unfiltered, has also now been released, labelled Audrey Cuvée. These are among the very best on the Central Coast. Logan is the regular label for Chardonnay and a recently added Pinot Noir. Expect quality to match the whites. A Kali-Hart Vineyard Pinot Noir bottling has also now been released. (DM)
O **Chardonnay** Logan★★ £D Kali-Hart Vineyard★★★ £E Diamond T Estate★★★★ £E
O **Chardonnay** Sleepy Hollow Vineyard★★★★ £E Cuvée Cynthia★★★★ £E

TALLEY VINEYARDS Arroyo Grande www.talleyvineyards.com

Owner: Don and Rosemary Talley 3031 Lopez Drive, Arroyo Grande, CA 93420
First-class estate Chardonnay and Pinot Noir here. The Rosemary and Rincon vineyards have tremendous potential and as yet are still young. Both are capable at times of providing wines of five-star quality. Pinot Noir is produced from very low yields and wild yeasts and new French oak are used in the winery. Chardonnay is reared in the finest French oak and aged on lees to provide additional weight and a rich texture. The Talleys also produce the variety from their Edna Valley Olivers Vineyard site, which is planted exclusively to the variety. The Sauvignon Blanc has not reached the same stellar heights. It is blended with Semillon and part barrel-fermented. Bishops Peak is their label for a range of nicely crafted, straightforward budget wines and a Late-Harvest Riesling is also produced. The Talleys are also important suppliers to other producers such as AU BON CLIMAT. (DM)
● **Pinot Noir** Estate★★★ £D Rincon Vineyard★★★★ £E Rosemary's Vineyard★★★★ £E
O **Chardonnay** Estate★★★ £D Rincon Vineyard★★★★ £E Rosemary's Vineyard★★★★ £E
O **Sauvignon Blanc** Estate★★ £B

LANE TANNER Santa Maria Valley lanetanner@sbwines.com

Owner: Lane Tanner PO Box 286, Santa Maria, CA 93456
Lane Tanner operates a small warehouse winery in Santa Maria where she has been making first-rate Pinot Noir for a decade. As well as the Santa Maria and Bien Nacido *cuvées* there are two other small-volume examples from Melville and Julia's vineyards. She has now added a cool, peppery Syrah from the French Camp Vineyard that shows equally impressive potential. Very good and very fairly priced wines here. (DM)
● **Pinot Noir** Santa Maria★★★ £D Bien Nacido★★★ £D

DOM. DE LA TERRE ROUGE Shenandoah Valley www.terrerougewines.com A: Vin

Owner: Bill Easton PO Box 41, Fiddletown, Amador County, CA 95629
Bill Easton was one of the very first Rhône Rangers, along with the likes of Randall Grahm at BONNY DOON. Today he produces Rhône styles under the Terre Rouge label, while his Easton label supplies good fruit-driven, spicy Barbera and more serious Zinfandel. He is based in Amador County and his Shenandoah Valley vineyards are cooled due to their elevation. Syrah is the dominant red variety but in addition there is a simple fruity rosé and floral, minerally Viognier made from 20-year-old vines. Among the reds some Mourvèdre is now released from Amador County but as yet the wine is a touch lean and vegetal. The Syrahs are better. The basic *cuvée* is the Tête a Tête, which is soft and forward, as is the Côte de l'Ouest. More serious are both the Sierra Foothills and Sentinel Oak Vineyard Pyramid Block Syrahs. At its best in vintages like 2000 and 1999, the Sentinel bottling is structured and firm with good intensity, more in the style of Côte-Rôtie than Hermitage. Ascent is a fine barrel selection which sees more new oak: rich, almost opulent with impressive depth and concentration. Top reds will benefit from four or five years' ageing. (DM)

Domaine de la Terre Rouge
- **Syrah** Tête a Tête★★ £C Côte l'Ouest★★ £C
- **Syrah** Sierra Foothills★★★ £D Sentinel Oak Vineyard Pyramid Block★★★ £E
- **Syrah** Ascent★★★★ £F
- ○ **Viognier** Shenandoah Valley★★★ £E
Easton
- **Barbera** Shenandoah Valley★★ £C
- **Zinfandel** Shenandoah Valley★★★ £C

TESTAROSSA Arroyo Grande www.testarossa.com A: P&S,Por

Owner: Robert & Diana Jensen 300-A College Avenue, Los Gatos, CA 95030
The focus here is top-quality Pinot Noir and Chardonnay. Originally the wines were sourced from Monterey vineyards but the Jensens now scour the whole Central Coast to produce the best possible examples. The range covers an almost bewildering number of single-vineyard *cuvées*, which are invariably good to very good indeed, if not quite attaining the striking intensity of the top examples at AU BON CLIMAT. The Pinots are rich and gamey with no shortage of oak; the Chardonnays are riper and fuller than some of the more minerally, restrained styles elsewhere. They possess a marvellously rich weight and texture and can be enjoyed with just a year or two in bottle. (DM)
- **Pinot Noir** Santa Maria Valley★★★ £D Palazzio★★★★ £E Gary's Vineyard★★★★ £E
- **Pinot Noir** Sleepy Hollow Vineyard★★★★ £E Pisoni Vineyard★★★★ £F
- ○ **Chardonnay** Central Coast★★★ £D Castello★★★ £E Rosella's Vineyard★★★ £E
- ○ **Chardonnay** Chalone-Michaud★★★★ £E Bien Nacido★★★★ £E
- ○ **Chardonnay** Sleepy Hollow Vineyard★★★★ £E Pisoni Vineyard★★★★ £E

SEAN THACKREY Marin County www.wine-maker.net

Owner: Sean Thackrey 240 Overlook Drive, Bolina, CA 94924
Sean Thackrey originally produced a small range of top-flight Rhône-style wines from Syrah, Mourvèdre and Petite Sirah but now solely concentrates on just two wines. Orion is produced from Syrah sourced from the Rossi Vineyard in St Helena and is a massive, burly wine with tremendous potential, requiring at least five years' cellaring to shed its tannin. The Pleiades by contrast is a ripe, altogether more forward non vintage blend from a varying mix of Syrah, Grenache, Mourvèdre and Petite Sirah and may be enjoyed on release. (DM)
- **Pleiades** California★★★ £C **Orion** Rossi Vineyard★★★★★ £F

OTHER WINES OF NOTE

ADELAIDA CELLARS ● **Cabernet Sauvignon** Paso Robles £C ● **Zinfandel** Paso Robles £C
AHLGREN ● **Cabernet Sauvignon** Bates Ranch £F ● **Zinfandel** Livermore Valley £C
BLACKJACK RANCH ● **Merlot** Billy Goat Hill £E ○ **Chardonnay** Reserve £D
DAVID BRUCE ● **Pinot Noir** Santa Cruz Estate £F ● **Petite Sirah** Shell Creek Vineyard £C
BYINGTON ○ **Chardonnay** Dirk Vineyard £D
BYRON ● **Pinot Noir** Byron Vineyard £F ○ **Chardonnay** Byron Vineyard £D
CASTORO CELLARS ● **Syrah** Paso Robles £C ● **Zinfandel** Vineyard Tribute £C
○ **Viognier** Reserve £C
CONCANNON ○ **Chardonnay** Central Coast £B ○ **Viognier** Central Coast £C
CRONIN ○ **Chardonnay** Santa Cruz Mountains £C Stuhlmuller Vineyard £C
DARK STAR ● **Syrah** Meeker Vineyard £C Ricordati Paso Robles £C
DOMAINE SANTA BARBARA ○ **Chardonnay** Los Olivos £D
DOVER CANYON ● **Syrah** Paso Robles £D ● **Zinfandel** Cujo £C
EBERLE WINERY ● **Zinfandel** Sauret £C ● **Cabernet Sauvignon** Estate £D
ESTANCIA ● **Pinot Noir** Reserve £D ○ **Chardonnay** Reserve £C
FESS PARKER ● **Mélange du Rhône** Red £B ● **Syrah** ATR £D

FIDDLEHEAD CELLARS ● **Pinot Noir** Santa Maria Valley £E Willamette Valley £E
FIRESTONE ○ **Chardonnay** Santa Ynez Valley £B
THOMAS FOGARTY ● **Pinot Noir** Santa Cruz Mountains £D ○ **Chardonnay** Santa Cruz Mountains£D
FOLEY ESTATE ○ **Chardonnay** Bien Nacido Vineyard £D
FOXEN ● **Pinot Noir** Bien Nacido £D ○ **Chardonnay** Tinaquaic £D
GALANTE VINEYARDS ● **Cabernet Sauvignon** Blackjack Pasture £E ● **Merlot** Carmel £D
DANIEL GEHRS ● **Syrah** Paso Robles £C ○ **Pinot Blanc** Monterey £C
HELLER ESTATE ● **Cabernet Sauvignon** Carmel Valley Reserve £E ○ **Chardonnay** Carmel Valley £C
JAFFURS CELLARS ● **Syrah** Bien Nacido £E Thompson Vineyard £E
JC CELLARS ● **Syrah** California £D ● **Zinfandel** Rhodes Vineyard £D
KARLY ● **Syrah** Amador County £C
LOCKWOOD ○ **Chardonnay** Very Special Reserve £D
LONGORIA ● **Pinot Noir** Bien Nacido £D ○ **Chardonnay** Clos Pepé £D
MERIDIAN VINEYARDS ● **Cabernet Sauvignon** Reserve £C ○ **Chardonnay** Limited Release £C
MURRIETA'S WELL ● **Zinfandel** Livermore Valley £C ● **Vendimia Red** £E ○ **Vendimia White** £C
MORAGA ● **Cabernet Sauvignon** Bel Air £H
NICHOLS WINERY ● **Pinot Noir** Paragon Vineyard £D ○ **Chardonnay** Paragon Vineyard £D
NORMAN ● **Zinfandel** The Monster £C
PARAISO SPRINGS ○ **Chardonnay** Santa Lucia Highlands £C
STEPHEN ROSS ● **Pinot Noir** Edna Ranch £D Bien Nacido £D ○ **Chardonnay** Bien Nacido £D
SANTA BARBARA WINERY ● **Syrah** Santa Ynez £C ○ **Chardonnay** Reserve £C
SANTA CRUZ MOUNTAINS VINEYARD ● **Pinot Noir** Matteson Vineyard £D
SAUCELITO CANYON ● **Zinfandel** Arroyo Grande £B
SIERRA VISTA ● **Zinfandel** Reeves Vineyard £C
VIGIL ● **Zinfandel** Mohr Fry Ranch £C Tres Condados £B
VINO NOCETO ● **Sangiovese** Shenandoah Valley £C
WHITCRAFT ● **Pinot Noir** Bien Nacido £D ○ **Chardonnay** Bien Nacido £D
WILD HORSE WINERY ● **Merlot** Paso Robles £C ○ **Chardonnay** Central Coast £B
ZACA MESA ● **Z Cuvée** Santa Barbara £B ● **Syrah** Zaca Vineyards £C Black Bear Block £E

Work in progress!!

Wines from the following producers under consideration for the next edition
BONACCORSI
CARINA CELLARS
CARMEL ROAD WINERY
CONSILIENCE
DOMAINE ALFRED
GARRETSON WINE COMPANY
KUNIN WINES
L'AVENTURE
LINNE CALODO
MARGERUM WINE COMPANY
MELVILLE
PISONI VINEYARDS AND WINERY
RED CAR WINERY
SAXUM VINEYARDS
TANTARA WINERY

Author's Choice (DM)

A diverse selection of Central Coast reds

ALBAN ● **Syrah** Seymour Vineyard
AU BON CLIMAT ● **Pinot Noir** Cuvée Isabelle
BABCOCK VINEYARDS ● **Syrah** Black Label Santa Barbara
BONNY DOON ● **Old Telegram** California
CALERA ● **Pinot Noir** Jensen Vineyard
EDMUNDS ST JOHN ● **Rocks and Gravel** California
JUSTIN ● **Isosceles** Paso Robles
KATHRYN KENNEDY ● **Cabernet Sauvignon** Estate
OJAI ● **Syrah** Roll Ranch
RIDGE VINEYARDS ● **Monte Bello** Santa Cruz Mountains
SANFORD WINERY ● **Pinot Noir** Sanford and Benedict Vineyard
SEAN THACKREY ● **Orion** Rossi Vineyard

A selection of exciting whites

ANDREW MURRAY ○ **Enchante** Santa Ynez
BREWER CLIFTON ○ **Chardonnay** Mount Carmel
CA DEL SOLO ○ **Il Pescatore**
CHALONE ○ **Pinot Blanc** Reserve
COLD HEAVEN ○ **Viognier** Alban Vineyard
MOUNT EDEN VINEYARDS ○ **Chardonnay** Estate
QUPÉ ○ **Viognier** Ibarra Young Vineyard
ROSENBLUM CELLARS ○ **Marsanne** Dry Creek
TALBOTT ○ **Chardonnay** Diamond T Estate
TESTAROSSA ○ **Chardonnay** Sleepy Hollow Vineyar

Oregon & Washington State

The total area of vineyards in the north-west of the United States is small, certainly when compared to the sprawling expanses of California, but is nevertheless spread across a vast geographical area. Pinot Noir, Pinot Gris, Pinot Blanc and Chardonnay have now been well-established in Oregon for close to a couple of decades. A whole host of small to medium-sized wineries have emerged and new ones continue to do so. Almost all of these are to be found in the Willamette Valley. Washington State is the second largest state in terms of quality-wine production behind California, but has only recently become really well-known. New and exciting sources of top reds, from both the Bordeaux and more recently the Rhône varieties, are increasing and it seems certain that the best here is yet to come.

Oregon

As well as the **Willamette Valley** there are two other AVAs to the south, **Umpqua Valley** and **Rogue Valley**. The Umpqua Valley region sits in the river valley of the same name, with coastal ranges to the west and the Cascades range of volcanic peaks to the east. The Rogue Valley is marked by relatively high-altitude vineyards and cool-climate whites, including Gewürztraminer and Pinot Gris, are planted with some success in the westerly sectors of the AVA.

The main viticultural activity, though, is in the Willamette Valley, a vast stretch of vineyards with varied soils and an extensive array of mesoclimates running from Eugene in the south to Portland in the north. At its widest the AVA is in excess of 80 km (50 miles) and it runs north-south for 320 km (200 miles). The majority of vineyards are found in the northern half of the region between Monmouth and Portland; the greatest concentration in Yamhill County, in the centre of that area. This is mainly Pinot Noir country and the hunt for unique sites continues apace as wineries seek to establish different terroirs within the AVA. A number of white varieties are also successful, among which Pinot Gris and Pinot Blanc have the best potential. Inevitably Chardonnay is extensively planted but really striking examples are few and far between.

Washington

The vineyard area here is vast and is dominated by the giant **Columbia Valley** AVA, within which there are two sub-AVAs, the **Yakima Valley** in the west and the **Walla Walla Valley** in the east. A sizeable part of both Columbia Valley and Walla Walla in fact stretches into northern Oregon. A newly established AVA close to the coast is **Puget Sound**, yet it appears to be too cool and damp to provide wines of any substance. The Columbia Valley by contrast is dry and necessarily irrigated. Located to the east of the Cascade Mountains, it is suitable for quality wine because of its northerly latitude and consequently longer, sunnier days. Excellent Bordeaux-style reds are produced along with good Chardonnay. The Yakima Valley is also successful with these grapes and with Syrah. Perhaps the greatest potential is actually for the Rhône varieties rather than those of Bordeaux. Excellent wines of both styles have now been made in Walla Walla as well.

Oregon & Washington State vintages

With such a sprawling viticultural expanse, providing any meaningful detail on vintages is difficult. The following provide an idea of what to look for. In Oregon 2003 should be good but some wines will struggle for balance with high alcohol. 2001 was reasonable; 2002, 2000, 1999 and 1998 were good to very good. Prior to this 1996 and 1994 are reasonable bets but only top Pinot Noir will be holding up. In Washington, particularly for reds, 2003 and 2002 are very good, and only 1996 looks average over the last eight or nine years. Top reds will hold well for a decade, often longer.

A-Z of Producers by region

Oregon

Willamette Valley

Washington

Columbia Valley

Walla Walla Valley

Other

1   Puget Sound
2   Colombia Valley
3   Yakima Valley
4   Red Mountain
5   Walla Walla Valley
6   Willamette Valley
7   Umpqua Valley
8   Rogue Valley
9   Applegate Valley

Oregon

AMITY VINEYARDS Willamette Valley www.amityvineyards.com **A: PDn**

Owner: Myron Redford 18150 Amity Vineyards Road, Amity, OR 97101
Medium-sized Willamette Valley operation founded in the mid-1970s. Pinot Noir is reasonably fragrant with soft, red berry fruit but can be lacking in depth and substance. Single-vineyard bottlings have been added from the Schouten and Sunnyside vineyards as well as an Estate Vineyard bottling. These offer similar quality and value to the Winemakers Reserve. The class act and undoubted value for money here is the stylish, lightly pungent Gewürztraminer, one of the better examples in the state. (DM)
● **Pinot Noir** Willamette Valley★ £D Winemakers Reserve★★ £E
O **Riesling** Oregon★ £B O **Gewurztraminer** Oregon★★ £B O **Pinot Blanc** Willamette Valley★ £D

ARCHERY SUMMIT Willamette Valley www.archerysummit.com **A: Dis**

Owner: Pine Ridge Winery 18599 NE Archery Summit Road, Dayton, OR 97114
Small, bespoke operation producing some 10,000 cases and owned by the Andrus family, who also own the large premium PINE RIDGE operation in Napa's Stags Leap District. Very classy Pinot Noir is produced here generally and it feels as if higher standards are being achieved across the range than at the parent winery; perhaps this is down to lower volumes. The focus is on specially selected lots of Pinot Noir, providing not only style and class but individuality too. To that end over 40 ha (100 acres) of high-density vineyards have now been established. In addition to Arcus and Premier Cuvée, three other examples are produced from Renegade Ridge, Red Hills and the home Archery Summit estates. The latter is the top premium bottling and very expensive. The Vireton Blanc des Collines Rouges is a blend of the better Oregon white varieties – mainly Pinot Gris, with some Chardonnay and Pinot Blanc – and is an elegant, partly barrel-fermented style. (DM)
● **Pinot Noir** Premier Cuvée★★★★£E Arcus Estate★★★★★£F
O **Vireton** Blanc des Collines Rouges★★★£D

ARGYLE Willamette Valley www.argylewinery.com **A: LNa**

Owner: Lion Nathan PO Box 280/691, Highway 99W, Dundee, OR 97115
Now a part of the Australian PETALUMA group, this sizeable operation produces good Pinot Noir as well as top-quality sparkling wine. For both Chardonnay and Pinot Noir, the bigger-volume Willamette Valley and Reserve bottlings offer good value; limited releases under the Nuthouse and Spirithouse labels both offer a notch up in quality – again not excessively priced. Also produced are a Cabernet Franc and a Nuthouse-label Merlot. (DM)
● **Pinot Noir** Willamette Valley★★ £C Reserve★★★ £D
O **Chardonnay** Willamette Valley★ £C Reserve★★ £D
O **Riesling** Dry Reserve★ £B
O **Brut** Willamette Valley★★ £C Knudsen Vineyard★★★ £D
O **Blanc de Blancs**★★★ £E O **Extended Tirage**★★★ £E

BEAUX FRÈRES Willamette Valley www.beauxfreres.com **A: Vin**

Owner: Mike Etzel, Robert Parker, Robert Ray 15155 NE North Valley Road, Newberg, OR 97132
Undoubtedly a producer of some of the best Pinot Noir in the Willamette Valley, this operation is as well known for the involvement of wine critic Robert M Parker as for anything else. There are 10 ha (24 acres) under vine and the vineyard is still relatively young, having been planted in 1988. As with most of the current run of new vineyards, vine density is high at over 2,200 vines per acre and the latest Dijon clones are planted. Vinification occurs naturally with indigenous yeasts from the vineyard and malolactic is also allowed to occur naturally. The results are impressive. The wines are powerful and structured with greater grip and concentration than most of their contemporaries. Belles Soeurs is not a second label but an

addition to the estate wine, sourced from the excellent Shea Vineyard. (DM)

● **Pinot Noir** Beaux Frères Vineyard★★★★ £F Belles Souers Vineyard★★★★ £F

CHEHALEM Willamette Valley www.chehalemwines.com

Owner: Harry Peterson-Nedry 31190 NE Veritas Lane, Newberg OR 97132
This property was originally founded as Ridgecrest Vineyards by Harry Peterson-Nedry in 1980.
Winemaking at Chehalem did not commence until 1990. There are now three estate vineyards, Ridgecrest,
Stoller and Corral Creek, the total area under vine being some 67 ha (165 acres). Pinot Noir makes up the
bulk of the grapes at around 60 per cent, the rest being Chardonnay, Riesling, Pinot Gris and a little Gamay
Noir. As well as the three vineyard bottlings of Pinot Noir a special *cuvée* is produced, the Rion Reserve,
which is firmer and impressively structured. It should evolve well over four or five years. The wines are
generally very ripe and can have surprising alcohol levels close to 15 degrees. New oak is kept to a minimum.
The Chardonnay is barrel-fermented and gets full malolactic and lees-ageing and stirring. The limited-
production Ian's Reserve is a step up in quality. The current range is completed by a little Dry Riesling and
Pinot Gris made in both dry and late-harvest styles. (DM)

● **Pinot Noir** Ridgecrest Vineyards★★★ £E Stoller Vineyards★★★ £E Rion Reserve★★★★ £E
○ **Chardonnay** Willamette Valley★★ £D

CRISTOM Willamette Valley www.cristomwines.com   A: WTs,Sel

Owner: Gerrie family Spring Valley Road, NW Salem, OR 97304
Established in 1992, this small operation is now producing a range of excellent Pinot Noirs and some very
good whites. As well as the lightly oaked, quite restrained Chardonnay and floral Viognier there is a stylish,
mineral-scented Pinot Gris. The main focus is Pinot Noir, produced in a number of *cuvées* and from a
number of estate-owned single vineyards. As well as the impressive Louise, single-vineyard bottlings also
come from Eileen, Jessie and Marjorie. The Reserve is unusual in being sourced from eight different
vineyards and comprising five different clones. A barrel selection, it is a full, opulent style which gets
extended cask-ageing. Expect to age the Pinots successfully in the short term. (DM)

● **Pinot Noir** Mt Jefferson Cuvée★★★ £D Reserve★★★★ £E Louise Vineyard★★★★ £E
○ **Chardonnay** Celilo Vineyard★★★ £C ● **Viognier** Willamette Valley★★ £D

DOMAINE DROUHIN Willamette Valley www.domainedrouhin.com   A: M&V,Sel,F&M

Owner: Maison Joseph Drouhin PO Box 700, Dundee, OR 97115
Established in the late 1980s by Joseph DROUHIN and run by Véronique Drouhin, who controls the
winemaking. The approach to viticulture from the outset was distinctly Burgundian: at the time she was
one of the few focusing on high-density vineyard planting. The estate has some 35 ha (85 acres) under vine
in the Red Hills area, which has a climate remarkably similar to that found on the Côte d'Or. The resulting
wines are in a tight, restrained style but very pure with real depth and concentration. There is a powerful,
dark berry character to the Pinot and the Cuvée Laurène has the refined, tannic structure to promise much
with age. A very low-volume special release has also been added, the Cuvée Louise, which is a special barrel
selection of the best of the material used in the Cuvée Laurène. The Chardonnay, labelled since the 2002
as Cuvée Arthur, is elegant and understated but with a piercing, mineral and citrus undercurrent. Stylish
with well-judged oak. (DM)

● **Pinot Noir** Willamette Valley★★★★ £E Cuvée Laurene★★★★ £F
○ **Chardonnay** Cuvée Arthur★★★★ £E

PATRICIA GREEN CELLARS Willamette Valley www.patriciagreencellars.com

Owner: Patricia Green 15225 NE North Valley Road, Newberg, OR 97132
Impressive new property established by former Torii Mor winemakers Patty Green and Jim Anderson. The

focal point of the operation is the 21-ha (52-acre) Autumn Wind Vineyard in Yamhill County, which the pair purchased in 2000. The Estate bottling only accounts for a few hundred cases but they have the capacity to produce up to 6,000 cases a year and have made wines from a range of other vineyards too. These include Balcombe, Eason, Temperance Hill, Quail Hill and Four Winds. Shea Vineyard has now been added and the 2002 vintage saw the addition of a number of further labels for tiny lot productions, including grapes sourced from the Hirsch Vineyard in the Russian River. Vinification is carried out with native yeasts and lees are often added back during barrel-ageing. These are rich and concentrated, almost animal, gamey styles of Pinot with the Estate and Shea Vineyards showing impressive concentration. Well-priced Chardonnay, Sauvignon Blanc and an Oregon Pinot Noir are also produced. (DM)

● **Pinot Noir** Estate★★★★ £E Shea Vineyard★★★★ £E

KING ESTATE   Willamette Valley   www.kingestate.com   A: BBR

Owner: King family   80854 Territorial Road, Eugene, OR 97405

This is a sizeable operation – the estate is some 332 ha (820 acres) – and the largest producer of Pinot Noir in Oregon. Quality ranges from good to very good. There is a second label, Lorane, under which the winery produces soft, fruit-driven, easy-drinking Pinot Noir and Chardonnay – not complex but well made. The King Estate wines are a serious step up in quality and there a couple of classy limited-volume bottlings in the Tower series: Domaine Pinot Noir and a Pfeiffer Vineyard bottling. Low-volume speciality wines are also produced in the Collection series and include an icewine-style Pinot Gris Vin Glace, Late Harvest Riesling and Zinfandel sourced from the north of the state in the Columbia Valley and Cabernet Sauvignon from a range of warmer locations. (DM)

● **Pinot Noir** Oregon★★ £C Reserve★★★ £E
○ **Chardonnay** Oregon★ £B Reserve★★ £C ○ **Pinot Gris** Oregon★ £B Reserve★★ £C

LEMELSON VINEYARDS   Willamette Valley   www.lemelsonvineyards.com   A: JAr

Owner: Eric Lemelson   12020 Stag Hollow Road, Carlton, OR 97111

This new Willamette operation was established in 1999 with the completion of its winery facility. A small and impressive range of well priced Pinot Noirs are produced along with a good Chardonnay, dominated by melon and lightly mineral, spicy flavours rather than others which can be excessively tropical and oaky. Riesling and Pinot Gris are also made. The key though, as elsewhere throughout Willamette are the Pinots. The firm have a considerable resource in the ownership of 49 ha (120 acres) of vineyards, which they farm organically, across a range of sites and soil types and yields are always kept in check and careful attention paid to canopy management to optimise fruit ripening. The Six Vineyards bottling is soft, fruit driven and forward, a blend of all the different sources. Thea's Selection, is a rich, fruit driven style, with soft supple tannin. The Stermer Vineyard bottling and the top wine Jerome Reserve are firmer and sturdier. The Jerome Reserve is additionally aged for up to 18 months in a mix of new and used oak. Concentrated and powerful it should develop well in bottle for five years or more. (DM)

● **Pinot Noir** Stermer Vineyard★★★ £E Jerome Reserve★★★★ £E
● **Pinot Noir** Six Vineyards★★ £C Thea's Selection★★★ £D
○ **Chardonnay** Wascher Vineyard★★★ £D

PANTHER CREEK   Willamette Valley   www.panthercreekcellars.com   A: AWM

Owner: Kaplan family   455 N Irvine, McMinnville, OR 97128

Excellent producer of first-class Pinot Noir as well as Chardonnay, Pinot Gris and a bit of Melon de Bourgogne. Winemaker Michael Stevenson makes no more than 7,500 cases each year. The winery purchases fruit from 10 different vineyard sources throughout the Willamette Valley and, with long-term arrangements with growers, maintains a tight grip on viticulture. Careful sorting (*triage*) takes place prior to vinification and the practice of minimal intervention is carried through to bottling, with virtually no fining or filtration. There is a plethora of single-vineyard bottlings of Pinot Noir, of which Freedom Hill and Shea Vineyard are produced in greater volume. The Winemakers Cuvée comes from a blend of vineyards in both the Willamette and Umpqua Valleys. It is now the only blended Pinot in the range, as the last release of the Reserve was from the 1999 vintage. (DM)

● **Pinot Noir** Winemakers Cuvée★★★★ £E Reserve★★★★ £E Freedom Hill★★★★ £E

PENNER-ASH Willamette Valley www.pennerash.com

Owner: Ron & Lynn Penner-Ash PO Box 1207, Newberg, OR 97132
Ron and Lynn Penner-Ash produce some rich and concentrated Willamette Valley Pinot Noir as well as small quantities of hand-crafted Syrah and Viognier. The Syrah comes from several different Oregon growers, while the Viognier has been added with the 2002 vintage and is sourced from the Del Rio Vineyard in the south of the state. The Pinot Noir, a blend from a number of sites gets nine months in French oak, 40 per cent of the barrels being new. The wine is rich and concentrated, firmly structured with dark berry fruit and a savoury edge to the palate. It will keep well for six or seven years and drink well with a few months of release. (DM)

● **Pinot Noir** Willamette Valley★★★★ £E

PONZI Willamette Valley www.ponziwines.com

Owner: Ponzi family 14665 SW Winery Lane, Beaverton, OR 97007
Long-established Willamette Valley producer with a high reputation for its Pinot Noir. Luisa Ponzi has now taken on the winemaking mantle. Pinot Noir is certainly good if on occasion lacking the depth and substance now found in the best examples elsewhere in the valley. There is a superior Reserve bottling, as well as the tiny-production Abetina Vineyard Reserve. Of particular interest here is one of the better Pinot Gris and a good fruit-driven Arneis. These offer particularly good value. (DM)

● **Pinot Noir** Willamette Valley★★ £D Reserve★★★ £F
○ **Chardonnay** Reserve★★ £D ○ **Pinot Gris** Willamette Valley★★ £B **Arneis** Willamette Valley★ £C

REX HILL Willamette Valley www.rexhill.com   A: **Mor**

Owner: Paul Hart & Jan Jacobsen 30835 N Highway. 99W, Newberg, OR 97132
With access to 91 ha (225 acres) of top-quality vineyards this winery has consistently produced first-class Pinot Noir from a number of sites. There have been a number of stylish low-volume, single-vineyard offerings as well as a good regular Willamette Valley bottling and a consistent Reserve. The Reserve and single-vineyard *cuvées* – including Anden, Jacob-Hart, Penner-Ash, Carabella, Maresh and Seven Springs – possess that extra dimension. While reasonably pricey, they are not excessively so. Of equal interest is a very good Pinot Gris Reserve as well as a bottling from the Jacob-Hart Vineyard. The regular Pinot Gris is sound and Chardonnay(including a Maresh Vineyard bottling), Sauvignon Blanc and Viognier from the Rogue Valley are also produced. (DM)

● **Pinot Noir** Kings Ridge★ £B Willamette Valley★★ £D Reserve★★★★ £E
○ **Pinot Gris** Reserve★★★ £C

DOMAINE SERENE Willamette Valley www.domaineserene.com   A: **Vin**

Owner: Ken & Grace Evenstad 6555 NE Hilltop Lane, Dayton, OR 97114
Top-class producer of both Pinot Noir and Chardonnay. Considerable investment has gone into the estate and the results are impressive. Yields are kept to a minimum – around two tons to the acre – and the harvest is always carried out by hand. Minimal intervention in the cellars means the Pinot Noir is only racked at bottling and is neither fined nor filtered. Chardonnay, made using only the Dijon clone, is barrel-fermented and aged on its lees for up to 15 months. Tiny lots of various single-vineyard bottlings are available through the winery and there is also a flagship Pinot Noir, Grace Vineyard. The Pinot Noirs are marked by their firm structure and dark, rich and concentrated berry fruit. Time is needed to integrate the new oak in both the Evenstad Reserve and Mark Bradford. The two Chardonnays are lightly tropical, with a fine, spicy,

toasty oak character but with the firm structure that earmarks their cool-grown origins. The Clos du Soleil is the tighter, more mineral of the two. The most recent development is the Rockblock Syrah, produced from Dundee Hills fruit. It is intended that this wine will be produced in its own facility and produced in the style of top Côte-Rôtie. (DM)

● **Pinot Noir** Yamhill Cuvée★★★ £E Evenstad Reserve★★★★ £E Mark Bradford Vineyard★★★★ £F
○ **Chardonnay** Clos du Soleil★★★★ £E Cote Sud★★★★ £E

KEN WRIGHT Willamette Valley www.kenwrightcellars.com A: Vin

Owner: Ken Wright 239 North Kutch Street, Carlton, OR 97111
Ken Wright has established himself as the Willamette champion of single-vineyard Pinot Noir, seeking to show in his wines the best individual site characteristics in a single bottling, what the French refer to as *terroir*. Now working with a considerable number of vineyard owners, he produces wines from a wide range of Willamette Valley sites. Those from the Dundee Hills in the north of the valley, including Abbey Ridge Vineyard and Nysa Vineyards, tend to produce rich, forward wines with marked red berry fruit and moderate acidity; those from the Eola Hills are more structured, while the Canary Hill bottling will be easiest to find. The Guadalupe Vineyard is among the most successful bottlings here over a number of vintages. Sourced like the Shea, McCrone and Wahle Vineyard Pinots from the Yamhill foothills this is opulent, lush and forward and will drink well at a young age. A single Chardonnay, Dijon Clones, was produced from Oregon-sourced grapes, but this has been superseded by two separate vineyard bottlings from the Columbia River Celilo Vineyard site – Carabella and McCrone. A small amount of floral, subtly oaked Pinot Blanc is also produced. Because production is so limited, all these *cuvées* are incredibly hard to find. However you can expect the wines to be almost invariably of three-star quality, often four-star, and although not cheap, they are priced very fairly. (DM)

● **Pinot Noir** Guadalupe Vineyard★★★★ £E Nysa Vineyard★★★★ £E Shea Vineyard★★★★ £E
● **Pinot Noir** Canary Hill Vineyard★★★★ £E McCrone Vineyard★★★★ £E

Washington State

ANDREW WILL Washington State A: M&V,NYg,Sel

Owner: Chris Camarda 12526 SW Bank Road, Vashon, WA 98070
Very good quality throughout this range. Winemaker Chris Camarda produces elegant, very finely made reds. All the Cabernet bottlings are ripe and concentrated and display an excellent mix of black fruit and harmonious, cedary oak. The Seven Hills and Pepper Bridge are a touch lighter and more elegant than the fuller, richer Ciel du Cheval and Klipsun. The Sorella is a fine, spicy meritage blend of Cabernet Sauvignon, Cabernet Franc and Merlot, but perhaps the main interest lies in the single-vineyard Merlots. The Ciel du Cheval and the Klipsun stand out as being just that touch richer and fuller but all show impressive elegance, style and refinement. Although relatively expensive, these wines nevertheless represent good value. (DM)

● **Cabernet Sauvignon** Klipsun Vineyard★★★★ £E Ciel du Cheval★★★★ £E
● **Cabernet Sauvignon** Seven Hills★★★★ £E Pepper Bridge★★★★ £E
● **Merlot** Klipsun Vineyard★★★★★ £E Ciel du Cheval★★★★★ £E
● **Merlot** Seven Hills★★★★ £E Pepper Bridge★★★★ £E
● **Sorella**★★★★ £F

CANOE RIDGE VINEYARD Columbia Valley www.canoeridgevineyard.com

Owner: Chalone Wine Group PO Box 684, Walla Walla, WA 99362
Owned by the California-based Chalone Wine Group, which numbers among its wineries CHALONE and ACACIA in California, Canoe Ridge is a reliable rather than cutting-edge producer of good, well-made, ripe and toasty Chardonnay along with Merlot and Cabernet Sauvignon that are soft, forward reds enjoyable in

their relative youth. Merlot sees American oak; Cabernet is aged in French barrels. A stylish, more expensive Merlot Reserve is also available in more limited quantity. A straightforward blend of Cabernet and Merlot is labelled Red Table Wine and a small quantity of Gewürztraminer is produced from the Oak Ridge Vineyard. (DM)

● **Cabernet Sauvignon** Columbia Valley★★ £D   ● **Merlot** Columbia Valley★★ £D
O **Chardonnay** Columbia Valley ★★ £ D

CHATEAU STE MICHELLE Columbia Valley www.ste-michelle.com   A: PRc

Owner: Stimson Lane PO Box 1976, Woodinville, WA 98072
The largest producer in Washington State and the jewel in the Stimson Lane crown. The wines from Chateau Ste Michelle seem somehow more complete and exciting than those from sister winery COLUMBIA CREST, even at the lower levels. A considerable array of wines is produced here, including a number in overseas partnerships. The Columbia Valley is the focal point of the winery's operations and there is a new vinification facility at the Canoe Ridge Estate Vineyard, the River Ridge Winery. Other key vineyard sources are Cold Creek, Horse Heaven and Indian Wells. The regular Columbia Valley bottlings can offer very good value, particularly among the whites, with the single-vineyard series offering style, quality and diversity. There are some very good Artists Series and Reserve labels, now including Syrah sourced from a number of vineyards. The meritage red has been consistently good over the last few vintages. Of particular interest are the joint partnerships: Col Solare is a premium blend of Cabernet Sauvignon, Merlot, Syrah and Malbec produced in association with Tuscan firm ANTINORI; Eroica is a marvellously intense, opulent but crisp, mineral-scented Riesling made in partnership with Ernst LOOSEN from the Mosel-Saar-Ruwer. (DM)

● **Cabernet Sauvignon** Columbia Valley★★ £C Cold Creek★★★ £E
● **Merlot** Columbia Valley★ £C Canoe Ridge★★ £E
● **Syrah** Reserve★★★ £C
● **Col Solare** Columbia Valley★★★★ £G
O **Chardonnay** Columbia Valley★★ £C Canoe Ridge★★★ £D Cold Creek★★ £C
O **Riesling** Columbia Valley★★ £B Eroica★★★ £D
O **Sauvignon Blanc** Columbia Valley★ £B Horse Heaven★ £B
O **Semillon** Columbia Valley★ £B

COLUMBIA CREST Columbia Valley www.columbia-crest.com   A: PRc

Owner: Stimson Lane Highway 221, Columbia Crest Drive, Paterson WA 99345
Originally conceived as a junior label for CHATEAU STE MICHELLE this is now a stand-alone operation. The wines are all reasonably crafted, particularly at the top end, although there is a certain uniformity of style and you yearn for a little more character and individuality. The operation draws on extensive estate vineyards for much of its needs. An extensive line-up of varietals appear under the Columbia Valley label. The Grand Estates wines are a step up and the range is completed by some impressive Reserve reds as well as Chardonnay. The Walter Clore Private Reserve is the pinnacle here, a powerful meritage blend of Cabernet Sauvignon and Merlot in almost equal parts. New American oak is a key feature of the style. A small amount of late-harvest Semillon is produced as well as a rare icewine from the same variety. (DM)

● **Cabernet Sauvignon** Grand Estates★★ £C Reserve★★★ £D
● **Merlot** Grand Estates★★ £C   ● **Merlot** Reserve★★★ £D
● **Syrah** Reserve★★★ £D   ● **Walter Clore Private Reserve** Columbia Valley★★★ £E
O **Chardonnay** Grand Estates★ £B

COLUMBIA WINERY Washington State www.columbiawinery.com   A: For

Owner: Associated Vintners 14030 NE 145th Street, PO Box 1248, Woodinville, WA 98072
One of the pioneering wineries of Washington State under the winemaking guidance of David Lake MW, established in 1962. A considerable range is now offered. The bulk of the winery's top wines are sourced

from five prime vineyards – Red Willow, Otis, Wyckoff, Alder Ridge and Sagemoor – in both the Yakima and Columbia Valleys. The Signature series represent the best examples, bottled as single-vineyard *cuvées*. The Mainline label offers decent quality at a lower level. Columbia was one of the first Washington wineries to produce Syrah with impressive results and is now also vinifying Sangiovese, Barbera and Zinfandel. These may also prove well-suited to the climate here. (DM)

● **Cabernet Sauvignon** Otis Vineyard★★★ £D Red Willow Vineyard★★★ £D
● **Merlot** Red Willow Vineyard★★ £D ● **Syrah** Yakima Valley★ £C Red Willow Vineyard★★★ £D
O **Chardonnay** Woodburne Cuvée★★ £C Otis Vineyard★★★ £D
O **Viognier** Red Willow Vineyard★★ £C O **Pinot Gris** Yakima Valley★ £B
O **Riesling** Cellarmasters Reserve★★ £B

DELILLE CELLARS Washington State www.delillecellars.com A:**WTs**,Sel

Owner: Charles & Greg Lill, Chris Upchurch, Jay Soloff PO Box 2233, Woodinville, WA 98072
The focus here is principally on producing top-quality Bordeaux blends from a range of Yakima Valley fruit sources, the majority from the Red Mountain AVA. To this end the Lill's succeeds very well, although the wines are not perhaps quite at the pinnacle. Both the Chaleur Estate and the D2 are made in an open-knit, ripe, supple style, particularly the soft, more obviously forward D2. The Estate – Cabernet Sauvignon, Merlot and Cabernet Franc – certainly has depth and a fine tannic structure, but very much in an upfront, bold fashion with vibrant, dark chocolaty fruit. Harrison Hill differs from Chaleur in that it is a single-vineyard meritage in a tighter, more backward style. The impressive white Chaleur Estate is a blend of ripe Sauvignon Blanc and Semillon and there is also a little Syrah produced under the Doyenne label with a tiny hint of Viognier for fragrance. (DM)

● **Chaleur Estate** Red Mountain★★★★ £F ● **Harrison Hill** Red Mountain★★★★ £F
● **D2★★★** £E ● **Doyenne Syrah** Red Mountain★★★★ £F
O **Chaleur Estate** Red Mountain★★★ £E

DOMAINE STE MICHELLE Washington State www.domaine-ste-michelle.com A: PRc

Owner: Stimson Lane PO Box 1976 Woodinville, WA 98072
Stimson Lane's Washington label for sparkling wine focuses on straightforward, attractive fizz from the Columbia Valley produced at keen prices. The range comprises a Cuvée Brut, from red and white grapes, Blanc de Blancs and Blanc de Noirs. The latter two are both labelled as such, and there is an Extra Dry as well. The style is for marked fruit character rather than yeasty, bready complexity and a drink-now style. The Blanc de Blancs is a little more elegant. (DM)

O **Cuvée Brut** NV★ £C O **Blanc de Blanc** NV★★ £D

L'ECOLE NO 41 Walla Walla Valley www.lecole.com A: PDn

Owner: Martin Clubb PO Box 111, Lowden, WA 99360
Established nearly 20 years ago, L'École No 41 has consistently produced good-quality wine, both red and white. The reds are well-crafted and stylish with refined supple tannins; not blockbusters, rather good, medium-term cellar prospects. The Apogee red is sourced from the Pepper Tree vineyard and is a concentrated, cedary meritage blend of Cabernet Sauvignon and Merlot. Syrah from the Seven Hills Vineyard in Walla Walla is dark and brooding with a spicy black pepper character underpinning the fruit. The principal varieties here are Merlot and Semillon and the winery is one of the very best sources of the latter. Subtle use of oak, and a marvellously waxy, honeyed character show through in the wines. A straightforward red blend Schoolhouse Red is also produced from Merlot, both Cabernets, Carmenère and Syrah. (DM)

● **Cabernet Sauvignon** Columbia Valley★★ £D Walla Walla Valley★★★ £E
● **Merlot** Columbia Valley★★★ £D Walla Walla Valley★★★ £D Seven Hills★★★ £E
● **Syrah** Seven Hills★★★ £E ● **Apogee** Pepper Tree Bridge★★★ £E

O **Chardonnay** Columbia Valley★★ £C
O **Semillon** Columbia Valley★★ £B Seven Hills★★★ £C Fries Vineyard★★★ £C

LEONETTI CELLAR Walla Walla Valley www.leonetticellar.com

Owner: Gary Figgins 1875 Foothills Lane, Walla Walla, WA 99362
One of the very best producers of Bordeaux-style reds in Washington State with just over 77 ha (190 acres) of estate vineyards, making around 6,000 cases annually. Meritage styles are of massive proportions – powerful wines that are sturdy but refined and very long-lived – an approach that has been perpetuated here for 25 years. High quality is maintained in the vineyards, which are on fine, well-drained hillside slopes. Sustainable viticulture is practised and yields are kept down, rarely exceeding three tons to the acre. Although frowned on in some quarters, green harvesting is also practised. As well as the impressive Cabernet and Merlot, stylish Sangiovese is also produced in a softer, lighter style, displaying very good intense, dark cherry fruit. The magnificent Reserve meritage red is made in very small quantities, just 665 cases for the 2000 vintage. (DM)
● **Reserve** Walla Walla Valley✪✪✪✪✪ £G ● **Cabernet Sauvignon** Walla Walla Valley★★★★★ £F
● **Merlot** Columbia Valley★★★★★ £F ● **Sangiovese** Walla Walla Valley★★★★ £F

PEPPER BRIDGE WINERY Walla Walla Valley www.pepperbridge.com

Owner: Norm McKibben 1704 JB George Road, Walla Walla, WA 99362
This recently established estate (the winemaking facility was only completed in 2000) produces Cabernet Sauvignon and Merlot solely from the Walla Walla Valley AVA and their own Pepper Bridge and Seven Hills vineyards. These are also an important source for a number of other leading Washington wineries. The winery has been designed to be completely gravity fed from crushing to barrel-ageing. Vinification is straightforward with *pigeage* and seven to eight days on skins. Malolactic is carried out in barrel. As well as French oak, a small amount of American oak is used for ageing. Both wines have reasonable depth and concentration but have a little way to go to match the best of their neighbours. There is also a second label Amavi under which a decent, lightly peppery Cabernet Sauvignon and more impressive Syrah are produced. American as well as French and Hungarian oak are used to age the Cabernet, while just French and American is used for the Syrah, which is dark and spicy with impressive fruit. (DM)
● **Cabernet Sauvignon** Walla Walla Valley★★ £E ● **Merlot** Walla Walla Valley★★★ £E
● **Cabernet Sauvignon** Amavi Walla Walla Valley★ £C ● **Syrah** Amavi Walla Walla Valley★★ £C

QUILCEDA CREEK VINTNERS Washington State www.quilcedacreek.com A: AWM

Owner: Alex Golitzin 5226 Old Machias Road, Snohomish, WA 98290
For many, this is Washington State's greatest source of Cabernet Sauvignon and Merlot. Certainly along with LEONETTI they vie for that accolade. Originally founded in 1978 by Alex Golitzen, the nephew of the legendary André Tchelistcheff, the main focus and volume here is the Cabernet Sauvignon, now made by Alex Golitzin's son Paul. The wine is sourced from several different prime vineyards, Ciel du Cheval, Taptiel and Klipsun from Red Mountain and Champoux from Yakima Valley. If not fully Cabernet Sauvignon, it is almost so, occasionally with a tiny proportion of Merlot blended in to add some flesh. In addition to the Cabernet a very small amount of varietal Merlot and a Columbia Red are also produced. The family have now purchased the Champoux Vineyard and planted their own Golitzen Estate Vineyard in 2001 in a drive to reinforce the quality of their wines. (DM)
● **Cabernet Sauvignon** Columbia Valley★★★★★ £F

WOODWARD CANYON Walla Walla Valley woodwardcanyon.com A: Vin

Owner: Rick Small 11920 W Hwy 12, Lowden, WA 99360
In Washington State terms this fine small producer is a relative veteran. Rick Small established the winery in 1981 and production has grown from 1,200 cases to 15,000 cases today. An extensive range of

wines is produced. In addition to the medium-weight, finely structured Artists Series Cabernet Sauvignon there are additional bottlings including the soft, approachable Nelms Road and the premium Old Vines. The Charbonneau red blends Merlot and Cabernet Sauvignon, whereas the impressive, dense and firmly structured Estate Red is a blend of the best lots of Cabernet Sauvignon, Merlot and Cabernet Franc. The is a good regular Columbia Valley Chardonnay but the Celilo Vineyard is a significant step up. It is almost Burgundian in style but with a rich, toasty character. Small amounts of Barbera, Syrah and Pinot Noir are produced as well as Riesling and an Orange Muscat. The white range is completed by a meritage blend, Charbonneau Blanc, made from two-thirds Semillon and one-third Sauvignon Blanc. (DM)

● **Charbonneau Red** Walla Walla Valley★★★ £F ● **Estate Red** Walla Walla Valley★★★★ £E
● **Cabernet Sauvignon** Estate Series★★★ £F ● **Merlot** Walla Walla Valley★★★ £E
○ **Chardonnay** Columbia Valley★★★ £E Celilo Vineyard★★★★ £E

OTHER WINES OF NOTE

Oregon

ADELSHEIM ● **Pinot Noir** Elizabeth's Reserve £E
BETHEL HEIGHTS ● **Pinot Noir** Estate £D ○ **Chardonnay** Estate £D
BRICK HOUSE ● **Pinot Noir** Cuvée du Tonnellier £E
BROADLEY VINEYARDS ● **Pinot Noir** Claudia's Choice £E
CAMERON ● **Pinot Noir** Clos Electrique £E
COOPER MOUNTAIN VINEYARDS ● **Pinot Noir** Estate Reserve £E
ELK COVE ● **Pinot Noir** Reserve £F Roosevelt Vineyard £E ○ **Riesling** Willamette Valley £C
EYRIE VINEYARD ● **Pinot Gris** Willamette Valley £B
HENRY ESTATE ● **Pinot Noir** Umpqua Cuvée £E ○ **Pinot Gris** Umpqua Valley £B
MCKINLAY ● **Pinot Noir** Special Selection £E
SILVAN RIDGE ● **Pinot Noir** Willamette Valley £C ○ **Early Muscat** £B
SOKOL BLOSSER ● **Pinot Noir** Willamette Valley £D Old Vineyard Block £F
ST INNOCENT ● **Pinot Noir** Freedom Hill £E Seven Springs Vineyard £E Shea Vineyard £E
○ **Chardonnay** Seven Springs Vineyard £D
TORII MOR ● **Pinot Noir** Olson Vineyard West Block £F Olson Vineyard East Slope £F
TUALATIN ● **Pinot Noir** Willamette Valley £D ○ **Pinot Blanc** Oregon £B
WILLAKENZIE ESTATE ● **Pinot Noir** Willamette Valley £D ○ **Chardonnay** Estelle £D
WILLAMETTE VALLEY VINEYARD ● **Pinot Noir** Hoodview £E
YAMHILL VALLEY VINEYARDS ● **Pinot Noir** Willamette Valley £E

Washington State

APEX ● **Merlot** Columbia Valley £E ○ **Chardonnay** Columbia Valley £C Outlook £D
BARNARD GRIFFIN ● **Merlot** Reserve £D ○ **Fumé Blanc** Columbia Valley £B
CADENCE ● **Spring Valley Red** Walla Walla Valley £E ● **Tapteil Red** Washington £E
● **Ciel du Cheval Red** Washington £E
CAYUSE ● **Syrah** Cailloux Vineyard £E
DUNHAM CELLARS ● **Cabernet Sauvignon** Columbia Valley £E
HEDGES CELLARS ● **Red Mountain Reserve** £E
McCREA CELLARS ● **Syrah** Yakima Valley £C ○ **Viognier** Yakima Valley £C
MATTHEWS CELLARS ● **Yakima Valley Red** £E ○ **Yakima Valley White** £C
REININGER ● **Cabernet Sauvignon** Walla Walla Valley £D
SEVEN HILLS ● **Cabernet Sauvignon** Seven Hills £D Klipsun £D ● **Merlot** Seven Hills £D
SINEANN ● **Zinfandel** Old Vine £E
TAMARACK CELLARS ● **Cabernet Sauvignon** Columbia Valley £D ● **Merlot** Columbia Valley £D
WALLA WALLA VINTNERS ● **Cabernet Sauvignon** Columbia Valley £D

Work in progress!!

Wines from the following producers under consideration for the next edition

ROSS ANDREW WINERY (COLUMBIA VALLEY, WASHINGTON STATE)
BAER WINERY (COLUMBIA VALLEY, WASHINGTON STATE)
BELLE PENTE (WILLAMETTE VALLEY, OREGON)
BETZ FAMILY VINEYARDS (COLUMBIA VALLEY)
J.K. CARRIERE (WILLAMETTE VALLEY, OREGON)
COLEMAN VINEYARD (WILLAMETTE VALLEY, OREGON)
GLEN FIONA WINERY (WALLA WALLA WINERY, WASHINGTON STATE)
HAMACHER WINES (WILLAMETTE VALLEY, OREGON)
JANUIK WINERY (COLUMBIA VALLEY, WASHINGTON STATE)
NORTHSTAR (COLUMBIA VALLEY, WASHINGTON STATE)
OWEN ROE WINERY (WASHINGTON STATE)
SOOS CREEK WINE CELLARS (COLUMBIA VALLEY, WASHINGTON STATE)
SOTER VINEYARDS (WILLAMETTE VALLEY, OREGON)

Author's Choice (DM)

The best of the Willamette Valley

ARCHERY SUMMIT ● **Pinot Noir** Arcus Estate
BEAUX FRÈRES ● **Pinot Noir** Beaux Frères Vineyard
CHEHALEM ● **Pinot Noir** Rion Reserve
CRISTOM ● **Pinot Noir** Louise Vineyard
DOMAINE DROUHIN ○ **Chardonnay**
PATRICIA GREEN CELLARS ● **Pinot Noir** Estate
PENNER ASH ● **Pinot Noir** Willamette Valley
PONZI ○ **Pinot Gris** Willamette Valley
DOMAINE SERENE ○ **Chardonnay** Clos du Soleil
KEN WRIGHT CELLARS ● **Pinot Noir** Shea Vineyard

A selection of new classics from Washington State

ANDREW WILL ● **Merlot** Klipsun Vineyard
CHATEAU STE MICHELLE ○ **Col Solare** Columbia Valley
COLUMBIA WINERY ● **Syrah** Red Willow Vineyard
DELILLE CELLARS ● **Chaleur Estate**
DUNHAM CELLARS ● **Cabernet Sauvignon** Columbia Valley
L'ECOLE NO 41 ○ **Semillon** Seven Hills
LEONETTI CELLAR ● **Reserve** Walla Walla Valley
PEPPER BRIDGE WINERY ● **Merlot** Walla Walla Valley
QUILCEDA CREEK VINEYARDS ● **Cabernet Sauvignon** Columbia Valley
WOODWARD CANYON ○ **Chardonnay** Celilo Vineyard

Rest of North America

Besides California, Oregon and Washington State, quality wine production is limited to just a handful of states. However grapes other than vinifera varieties are grown throughout the country. In New York State, for example, hybrid varieties are popular in the production of kosher wines and grape juice. Wines from these tend to have what is quaintly referred to as a 'foxy' character. A very damp pet dog smells not dissimilar. The best developments have been on New York's Long Island, in Maryland, in Virginia and to the far south in Arizona. The odd reasonable bottle has also emerged from Texas and the state may have real potential. Canadian quality wine has traditionally been Niagara icewine, but the developing region of the Okanagan Valley in British Columbia is also providing an increasing number of stylish dry whites and reds.

USA

New York State remains the best bet for quality wines outside the big sources on the western coast. In the north-west of the state the **Finger Lakes** region, just to the south of Lake Ontario, has a protected, very localised climate moderated by the lakes themselves. Both Chardonnay and Riesling are successful here along with a few sparkling wines. Among the best wineries, Fox Run, Dr Konstantin Frank, Lamoreaux Landing and Hermann J Wiemer stand out.

Directly north of New Jersey is the small **Hudson River** AVA where some decent Chardonnay is produced. Perhaps of most significance from a quality point of view are the wineries of **Long Island** and particularly **The North Fork of Long Island**. The climate is strongly maritime and both regions have proved to be impressive sources in recent years of Cabernet Sauvignon, Merlot and Cabernet Franc, along with the occasional striking Chardonnay. Bedell, Corey Creek, Gallucio, Jamesport, Palmer, Paumanok and Pellegrini are all worth a look.

To the south of New York, a few good wines are being produced in **Maryland** which, with its warm maritime climate, has real potential despite the odd wet harvest. Better mesoclimates are being established and one winery in particular, Basignano, stands out for the impressive quality of its Cabernet Sauvignon and meritage wines. There have been attempts to grow vines in **Virginia** since Thomas Jefferson's days, but only recently have these proved to be successful. A string of new wineries have now been established around Charlottesville on the eastern side of the Appalachian Mountains. Piedmont Vineyards is making some impressive **Chardonnay** and others have proved successful with a range of varieties, including those of Rhône and Bordeaux origin. Horton, Prince Michel and Barboursville are also worth looking at.

There is just one winery that stands out in **Arizona**: Callaghan Vineyards, based in the **Sonoita** AVA. The region is cooled by its elevation and the winery has some impressive, well-drained, gravel-dominated vineyards. An extensive range of varieties is planted and the Buena Suerte Cuvée is a notable Bordeaux-style red. From a volume rather than a quality point of view, **Idaho** is significant and home to the giant Ste Chapelle Winery. Quality so far has been sound but uninspirational with simple, straightforward red and white varietals.

Canada

The country has one sizeable wine region at **Niagara** in Ontario and more recently one in the far west in British Columbia. Wine production is now controlled by the VQA (Vintners Quality Alliance) and under these regulations the **Ontario** and generic **British Columbia** appellations were established. As well as in **Niagara Peninsula** good whites and icewine are also produced in Ontario from **Pelee Island** and **Lake Eyrie North Shore**. The vast majority of the country's vineyard area and wine production is still focused on Ontario. It is the icewines that make give Canada its unique stamp. Yet in British Columbia and in particular in the **Okanagan Valley**, although those same magnificent icewines are crafted, there are an increasing number of dry table wines of note as well. Pinot Gris, Chardonnay, Merlot and Syrah have all shown potential in this dry, sparse inland region to the immediate north of the international border with Washington State.

Mexico

To date no wine in significant quantities of any substantial quality has been forthcoming here. This is largely down to a scarcity of local consumers to support a small wine industry. However, the potential of the area is there and in particular in the Baja Peninsula. The only wines to have had any worthwhile distribution so far are those of the LA Cetto company.

WINES OF NOTE

Rest of the USA
BASIGNANI ● **Lorenzino Reserve Red** Maryland £C
BEDELL ● **Cupola** Long Island £D   ● **Merlot Reserve** Long Island £D
CALLAGHAN VINEYARDS ● **Buena Suerte Cuvée** Arizona £D   ● **Matthews Cuvée** Arizona £C
COREY CREEK ○ **Chardonnay** Reserve Long Island £C
FALL CREEK ● **Meritus** Texas Hill Country £C
FOX RUN ○ **Chardonnay** Reserve Finger Lakes £B
DR. KONSTANTIN FRANK ○ **Johannisberg Riesling** Finger Lakes £B
GALLUCCIO ● **Merlot** Andys Field Long Island £D
JAMESPORT ● **Merlot** Long Island £C
LAMOREAUX LANDING ○ **Chardonnay** Reserve Finger Lakes £C
MILLBROOK ○ **Chardonnay** Proprietor's Special Reserve Hudson River £C
PALMER ○ **Chardonnay** Reserve Long Island £C
PAUMANOK ○ **Chardonnay** Barrel Fermented Long Island £C   ○ **Sauvignon Blanc** Late Harvest £E
PELLEGRINI ● **Cabernet Sauvignon** Long Island £C   ● **Merlot** Long Island £C
PIEDMONT ○ **Chardonnay** Special Reserve Virginia £C   Native Yeast Virginia £D
HERMANN J WIEMAR ○ **Johannisberg Riesling** Finger Lakes £B

Canada
BLUE MOUNTAIN   **Pinot Gris Okanagan** Valley £C
BURROWING OWL   **Chardonnay** Okanagan Valley £C
CAVE SPRING CELLARS ○ **Chardonnay** Niagara Peninsula £B
CEDARCREEK ○ **Riesling** Icewine Okanagan Valley £F
CHATEAU DES CHARMES ○ **Chardonnay** Niagara Peninsula £C
GEHRINGER BROTHERS ○ **Riesling** Icewine Okanagan Valley £F   ○ **Pinot Gris** Private Reserve £B
GRAY MONK ○ **Chardonnay** Okanagan Valley £B
HAWTHORNE MOUNTAIN ○ **Gewurztraminer** British Columbia £B
HENRY OF PELHAM ○ **Riesling** Icewine Niagara Peninsula £F
HILLEBRAND ○ **Vidal** Icewine Trius Niagara Peninsula £E
INNISKILLIN ○ **Ice Wine** Niagara Peninsula £F   ○ **Vidal** Icewine Niagara Peninsula £F
INNISKILLIN OKANAGAN ● **Merlot** Okanagan Valley £D
JACKSON-TRIGGS ○ **Riesling** Ice Wine Grand Reserve Okanagan Valley £F
KONZELMANN ○ **Riesling** Ice Wine Niagara Peninsula £F
MISSION HILL ○ **Chardonnay** Grand Reserve Okanagan Valley £C   ● **Shiraz** Okanagan Valley £D
PELLER ESTATES ○ **Vidal** Ice Wine Niagara Peninsula £F
PILLITTERI ESTATES ○ **Riesling** Ice Wine Niagara Peninsula £F
QUAILS' GATE ○ **Chardonnay** Family Reserve Okanagan Valley £C   ○ **Riesling** Okanagan Valley £B
REIF ESTATE ○ **Riesling** Icewine Niagara Peninsula £F
STONEY RIDGE ○ **Chardonnay** Reserve Niagara Peninsula £C
SUMAC RIDGE ○ **Sauvignon Blanc** Okanagan Valley £B
VINELAND ○ **Vidal** Icewine Niagara Peninsula £F

Over the last half decade the wines of both Chile and Argentina have become firmly established on the international wine map. This reputation has been built on value and, particularly in the case of Chilean reds, vibrantly fruity styles. More recently some impressive super-premium wines have emerged, suggesting real potential. There is some way to go before either country can compete in absolute quality terms with either Australia or California but new wines and producers are continuing to surface. The only other county that may also have some potential for fine wine is Uruguay. Tannat is widely planted here but as yet there are only a handful of reasonable examples.

Chile

The country is split into five viticultural zones. Running from north to south, they are: **Atacama**, **Coquimbo**, **Aconcagua**, **Valle Central** and the **Región del Sur**. These zones contain a number of sub-regions and these may also be further subdivided. Atacama and Coquimbo are well to the north of the country. These are hot and dry, requiring mass flood irrigation, and generally produce basic table grapes as well as Pisco, the local brandy. There are new vineyard plantings at Coquimbo nearer the coast, where the climate is moderated by sea breezes. Some good rich and full-bodied reds are now being produced both from the Bordeaux varieties and from Syrah. You have to travel further south, though, to find vineyards capable of providing good quality wines in any volume. The region of Aconcagua includes the important sub-region of **Casablanca**, where the vineyards are cool and nearer the coast. This is now a well-established source for some of the best white wines in the country. Chardonnay, Gewürztraminer and Sauvignon Blanc are all successful here. The **Valle del Aconcagua** itself is warmer and and becomes increasingly hot further inland. Eastern Aconcagua is largely red-wine territory. Some of the best sites are on well-drained slopes, rare here, and the super-premium Seña blend is sourced from the area.

The Valle Central is a substantial zone which includes Chile's capital city Santiago to the north. The suburbs encroach into the vineyards of **Maipo**, the northernmost of the zone's sub-regions. The valley runs 400 km north to south, taking in **Rapel**, **Maule** and **Curicó**. The two key elements which influence grape growing here are the coastal fogs, which drift a long way inland and moderate the climate, and the Andes mountains. The latter provide an important water source for irrigation. One of the problems encountered over the past decade has been over-vigorous and over-productive vineyards. Increased use of sophisticated drip irrigation systems is helping to overcome such vineyard problems. More wines are offering ripe and vibrant fruit now as opposed to some of the overtly green flavours that were so widespread just a few years ago. The best reds from Maipo have traditionally been Cabernet-based but increased plantings of Rhône varieties is a continuing trend.

Rapel is very promising for fine wine production with Cabernet Sauvignon, Merlot and particularly Carmenère successful in the warmer south of the region at **Colchagua**, while earlier-ripening varieties including Chardonnay, Sauvignon Blanc and Pinot Noir are more successful in cooler **Cachapoal**. There are both promising reds and whites to be found at Curicó. Growing conditions are aided by large mid-season temperature fluctuations which help in preserving the acidity in the grapes. **Maule** to the south is largely dominated by white varieties but there is some good Merlot too.

To the south is the Región del Sur including the two sub-regions of Itata and, immediately to the south, Bío Bío. Unsurprisingly, this being the most southerly of the grape-growing regions, the climate is cool and rainfall is also high. Sophisticated trellising and the planting of early-ripening Pinot Noir and Chardonnay as well as Alsace varieties has shown some potential. The best results so far have come from Bío Bío.

Argentina

Argentina is as yet less established internationally than Chile and many wineries seem to have some way to go to match the fruit quality achieved at lower levels by her neighbour across the Andes. The country is, however, the fifth-largest wine producer in the world, with a vast bulk-wine industry centred around the main region of Mendoza, which accounts for around nine out of every ten bottles produced. Argentina does appear to have real promise for good and indeed premium wine production and a number of impressive reds and whites are now being made. Outside expertise from the likes of Michel Rolland is increasing as is investment in new vineyards and wineries.

In the north of the country are the hot and dry vineyards of **Salta**. The lower-lying vineyards are too warm for quality wine production and irrigation is vital. Within the region, though, there are a number of better sites with vineyards planted at high altitude, in particular those in the Calchaquies Valley. Some good results are being achieved with both Malbec and Cabernet Sauvignon as well as the aromatic Torrontes, a native of Spain.

Mendoza itself is the main focus for quality wine production. The two sub-regions that are of particular note are **Luján de Cuyo** and **Tupungato**. The vineyard area is planted at altitude and some of the wines, particularly from Luján de Cuyo, are world class. Malbec is very successful here but there are also widespread plantings of Cabernet Sauvignon, Syrah and Sangiovese. Bonarda is important both varietally and as a component in many wine blends and is the most widely planted red variety. Chardonnay inevitably is important and produces really striking wines in cooler sites.

To the south in Patagonia is the **Río Negro**. The climate is cool and early-ripening Sauvignon Blanc, Sémillon and Chardonnay have all been grown with some success here. However, stylish, elegant examples of the red Bordeaux varieties and Syrah are also appearing and there are ongoing efforts to realise the potential complexity of Pinot Noir.

The Rest of South America

The only other country that would appear to have any real potential for quality wine production in South America is Uruguay. Hybrid varieties are still important in terms of the area planted but high-quality vinifera varieties are becoming increasingly significant. Cabernet Sauvignon, Merlot, Chardonnay and Sauvignon Blanc are all cultivated successfully. Most important from a quality wine perpective is the Tannat. It is now more widely planted here than in France and some reasonable examples have been produced. Elsewhere the climate is too hot and humid, although vinifera varieties are also grown in the southern tip of Brazil.

A-Z of producers by region

South America vintages

Any vintage assessment within the wine zones and regions here has to be very general because of both size and the effect of local mesoclimtes. In general almost all whites with the exception of the top barrel-fermented Chardonnays should be drunk on release. Top reds, though, can develop well in bottle. 2004 looks good for reds and whites in Chile, whereas in Argentina reds look to have benfitted from the hot year. 2003 and 2002 were good for Malbec in Argentina. 2003 was good both red and white in Chile. For earlier vintages of note for top reds in Chile look out for 2002, 2001, 2000, 1999, 1996 and 1995; in Argentina 2000, 1999, 1997, 1996 and 1995 were all good.

1	Elqui	9	Maule
2	Limari	10	Itata
3	Choapa	11	Bío Bío
4	Aconcagua	12	Rio Negro
5	Casablanca	13	Valle de
6	Maipo		Uco/Tupungato
7	Rapel	14	Luján de Cuyo
8	Curicó	15	Maipú
		16	Cafayate

Argentina

ACHAVAL-FERRER Mendoza www.achaval-ferrer.com   A: C&B

Owner: Bodega Achaval-Ferrer   Azcuenaga 453, Luján de Cuyo, 5507 Mendoza
Small, newly established but top-quality Mendoza winery. It is an Argentine/Italian partnership of four friends: Santiago Achaval Becu, Manuel Ferrer Minetti, Italian winemaker and roving consultant Roberto Cipresso and former world rally champion Tiziano Siviero. There are three estate-owned vineyards which are planted at altitude (between 730 and 1,100 m) and there are some leasing arrangements with a number of other vineyard owners. Vinification includes both pumping over and punching the cap during maceration and malolactic takes place in barrel. The 100 per cent Malbec comes from the estate-owned Finca Altamira vineyard planted to venerable vines over 80 years old. The Quimera red is a blend of Malbec, Cabernet Sauvignon and Merlot and is the mainstay of the winery with production now around 3,600 cases a year. These are dense and powerful wines which will keep well for a decade or more but can be broached with three or four years' age. (DM)
● **Quimera**★★★★ £E   ● **Malbec** Finca Altamira★★★★ £F

ALTA VISTA Mendoza www.altavistawines.com   A: J&B, L&W

Owner: Patrick d'Aulan   Alzagar 3972, Chacras de Corja, 5505 Luján de Cuyo, Mendoza
This new venture in Argentina's high-quality Luján de Cuyo region was established by the late Jean-Michel Arcaute and Patrick d'Aulan with the objective of producing cool-grown Malbec and Cabernet Sauvignon of real style and quality. Additional input is now provided by Michel Rolland of BON PASTEUR. There are around 61 ha of vineyards and a range of wines is produced. Two basic blends, Cosecha Blanco and Tinto, offer attractive, fruity easy drinking. There is a varietal Torrontés and an oaky Chardonnay. Regular Malbec is chunky and full of forward, easy-going, brambly fruit; more serious is the Malbec Grande Reserve. The Alto is a very powerfully structured blend of Malbec and Cabernet Sauvignon and has an excellent balance of dark, spicy fruit, supple firm tannins and well-judged oak. The wine is neither fined nor filtered. (DM)
● **Alto** Vistalba★★★★ £F   ● **Grande Reserve** Vistalba★★ £B   ● **Malbec** Luján de Cuyo★ £B
○ **Chardonnay** Luján de Cuyo★ £B

ANUBÍS Mendoza sbalbo@impsat1.com.ar   A: Lib

Owner: Susana Balbo/Alberto Antonini   Rioja 371, Dpto 5, 5500 Ciudad, Mendoza
The first vintage for this relatively new operation was only 1999 but the results so far have been promising and the wines offer excellent value for money. It is a partnership between Susana Balbo, who also produces wine under her own label at DOMINIO DEL PLATA, and Alberto Antonini, formerly of ANTINORI. Fruit is sourced from Luján de Cuyo and Tupungato and a range of vibrant varietals is now being produced. Syrah/Bonarda and Malbec stand out. These are modern, stylish, richly extracted reds that are approachable and supple and may be enjoyed young. Antonini is also involved with estate owner Rodolfo Massera producing a further Malbec, LA REMONTA, from cool La Consulta to the south of Mendoza. (DM)
● **Syrah/Bonarda** Mendoza★★ £B   ● **Tempranillo** Mendoza★ £B   ● **Malbec** Mendoza★★ £B

CATENA ZAPATA Mendoza www.nicolascatena.com   A:Bib

Owner: Dr Nicolás Catena   J Cobos s/n, Agrelo, Luján de Cuyo, Mendoza
The Catena operation is considerable with a number of ranges produced at all price levels. Good straightforward varietal styles are produced under the Argento label, while the Alamos range is a step up. Both the Chardonnay and the Malbec are worth considering. Good to very good whites and reds with real depth and style are produced under the Catena label and are very modern approachable wines. The premium bottlings appear under the Catena Alta label and include Chardonnay, Cabernet Sauvignon and Malbec. The top wine is the super-premium Cabernet Sauvignon Zapata. All are sourced from vineyards

at Luján de Cuyo. Daughter Laura produces an impressive range independently under the Luca brand which includes powerfully structured Malbec, Syrah and Cabernet Sauvignon and toasty Chardonnay from Mendoza, while son Ernesto produces three stylish, modern reds: Corazon, a blend of Bonarda and Malbec; Jubilo which is based on Cabernet Sauvignon; and Amoria, based on Malbec. These are all comfortably worth two stars and have rated three stars in the latest releases. The style throughout the premium ranges is modern and approachable and only limited cellaring will be required. Caro, a blend of Malbec and Cabernet Sauvignon, is a new joint venture with Baron de Rothschild of LAFITE-ROTHSCHILD. (DM)

Catena
● **Nicolás Catena Zapata** Luján de Cuyo★★★★ £F
● **Cabernet Sauvignon** Catena Luján de Cuyo★★ £C Alta Luján de Cuyo★★★ £E
● **Malbec** Alamos Mendoza★ £B Catena Luján de Cuyo★★ £C Alta Luján de Cuyo★★★★ £E
○ **Chardonnay** Alamos Mendoza★ £B Catena Luján de Cuyo★★ £C Alta Luján de Cuyo★★★ £E
Luca
● **Syrah** Mendoza★★★ £E ● **Malbec**★★★ £E
○ **Chardonnay** Mendoza★★★ £E
Tikal
● **Corazon** Mendoza★★★ £D ● **Jubilo** Mendoza★★★ £D

CLOS DE LOS SIETE Mendoza   A: Eno

Owner: Clos de los Siete SA Vista Flore s/n, Tunuyan, Mendoza
This is a major new French investment in Argentina which includes international wine consultant Michel Rolland, who has already established his own successful YACOCHUYA label. In total 250 ha have been planted at the Vistaflores estate, 80 km south of Mendoza. The wines are produced at the Bodega Monteviejo, owned by Catherine Péré-Vergé, the owner of Château MONTVIEL in Pomerol. Of several wines now produced, the Clos de Los Siete red, which is a blend of Merlot, Cabernet Sauvignon, Syrah and Malbec, is full of upfront dark, brambly fruit. It is aged one-third in vats and two thirds in new oak. The Val de Flores label is a low-production wine from some of the best-sited Malbec. Rich and spicy it sees 100 per cent new oak. Lindaflor, also Malbec, is a vineyard selection sourced from 52 ha. Yields are very low indeed at 20 hl/ha and winemaking is modern – a cold-soak prior to fermentation, a gravity-fed winery, 100 per cent new French oak and neither fining nor filtration. Production of Lindaflor is currently capped at around 1,000 cases a year. There is real potential here and it will be interesting to see how things develop as the vineyard ages. (DM)
● **Clos de los Siete** Mendoza★★★ £C ● **Val de Flores** Mendoza★★★★ £E
● **Lindaflor** Mendoza★★★★ £E

DOMINIO DEL PLATA Mendoza www.dominiodelplata.com

Owner: Pedro Marchevsky/Susana Balbo Cochabamba 7801, Agrelo, Mendoza
This is the home winery of Pedro Marchevsky and Susana Balbo who are the manager and winemaker at ANUBÍS. The Crios label offers some attractive, fruit-driven wines including a fine floral Torrontes and two reds, a Cabernet Sauvignon and a Syrah/Bonarda blend. The top Dominio del Plata wines are a serious step up in both quality and price. Of the two labels the Susana Balbo wines offer greater depth and power. They are also produced in much smaller volumes of around 400 to 500 cases each, whereas 2,000 cases of the Ben Marco wines are produced each year. VMS is a blend of Malbec from cool La Consulta as well as Cabernet Sauvignon, Bonarda, Tannat and a little Merlot. Each variety is vinified separately and the wine aged for 12 months in 50 per cent new wood. The top label Brioso means strength and the wine is both deep and concentrated with great poise and refinement. It blends Cabernet Sauvignon, Cabernet Franc, Malbec and Petit Verdot and will develop well for up to a decade. (DM)

Crios
○ **Crios Torrontes** Cafayate★ £B

Ben Marco
● **Malbec** Mendoza★★ £D   ● **VMS** Mendoza★★★ £E

Susana Balbo
● **Malbec** Mendoza★★★ £E   ● **Cabernet Sauvignon** Mendoza★★★ £E
● **Brioso** Mendoza★★★★ £F

NIETO SENETINER   Mendoza   www.nietosenetiner.com   A: **Cap**

Owner: Pérez Companc Group/CDPQ   Vieytes no 2275 Carrodilla – CP 5507 Luján de Cuyo
This is a large operation producing an extensive range of both varietal and blended reds and whites under the Finca Las Marius and Santa Isabel labels. These are relatively ordinary with Malbec and Bonarda offering some attractively dark berry fruit character. Better are the Nieto Reservas. These include an extracted, oaky, dark Malbec, good stylish Cabernet-Shiraz and a good but quite austere Cabernet Sauvignon. New is a lightly oaked Malbec Nieto Reserva as well as a premium Bordeaux blend Con Nicanor produced from 30-year-old vines in Luján de Cuyo. Best of all is the splendid premium Malbec, Cadus, made from 80-year-old vines – a rich, long and very characterful wine offering much better value than many of its peers. (DM)
● **Malbec** Cadus Tupungato★★★★ £D   Nieto Reserva Mendoza★★ £B
● **Cabernet-Shiraz** Nieto Reserva Mendoza★★ £B
● **Cabernet Sauvignon** Nieto Reserva Mendoza★ £B

BODEGA NOEMIA PATAGONÍA   Rio Negro   www.bodeganoemia.com   A: **Lib**

Owner: Contessa Cinzano & H. Vinding-Diers   Carlos Pellegrini 961-1 Piso, C1009ABS B. Aires
This partnership between Contessa Noemi Marone Cinzano of Tenuta ARGIANO in Tuscany and Hans Vinding-Diers is responsible for Argentina's most expensive red wine to date. They acquired a vineyard planted to Malbec in the 1930s in the remote Rio Negro region in Patagonia in the south-east of the country. The area benefits from the climatic influence and natural irrigation from the rivers Neuquen and Limay. Growing conditions are ideal for the tiny 1.5-ha vineyard with warm summers, cool nights and temperate autumns during ripening. The wine is destemmed by the individual berry and carefully vinified with indigenous yeasts at a surprisingly low temperature of 26°C with gentle *pigeage* and a maceration of three weeks. It is aged in all new wood, with a third of the wine run back into new oak a second time, and the malolactic fermentation follows naturally in barrel. The wine is neither fined nor filtered and is aged on its gross lees for up to 24 months in oak. It is impressively rich and opulent, loaded with dark spicy berry fruit but firmly structured too, with a great potential to develop with age in bottle. The output is tiny, a rarity in South America, with just 180 cases produced from the inaugural 2001 vintage. (DM)
● **Malbec** Mendoza★★★★★ £G

MICHEL TORINO   Salta   www.micheltorino.com.ar   A:**Hal**

Owner: Bodega La Rosa/Peñflor   Ruta 40 y Ruta 68, Cafayate, Salta, Mendoza
The vineyards here in the hot Cafayate region in the north of Argentina succeed because of their high altitude. There are 360 ha under vine and the quality end of the spectrum is covered by the Colección and Don David labels. There is a good spicy, brambly Colección Malbec and a better, more concentrated Don David. Cabernet Sauvignon under the Don David label has some piercing blackcurrant character with a lightly herbal note creeping in. Don David Torrontés is sound but not at the same level as the reds. A new flagship red, Altimus, combines Malbec, Cabernet Sauvignon and Syrah. (DM)
● **Cabernet Sauvignon** Don David Cafayate★★ £B
● **Malbec** Colección Cafayate★ £B   Don David Cafayate★★ £B

YACOCHUYA Salta www.yacochuya.com A: His

Owner: Etchart Family & Michel Rolland CC No 1 (4427), Cafayate, Salta
This small winery owned by Michel Rolland and the ETCHART family is based in warm Salta, but crucially the Calchaquies Valley vineyards here are planted at high altitude, some 2,000 m above sea level. Of equal importance is the age of the vines, which are now over 80 years old. The wine, a blend of Malbec and Cabernet Sauvignon, is very dense with marvellous depth and a rich sumptuous texture on the palate. Malolactic takes place in barrel and the wine is aged on lees with micro-oxygenation. It is bottled with minimal fining and without filtration and will develop very well over a decade or so. It is undoubtedly one of the very finest reds to have emerged from South America in recent years. A second wine, San Pedro de Yacochuya, is also being made to ensure the integrity of the Grand Vin, and a white Torrontes is also being made. The Etcharts sold their family winery to Pernod Ricard in the mid 1990s while Rolland, the owner of Le BON PASTEUR in Pomerol, is also now involved in the recently established CLOS DE LOS SIETE operation, south of Mendoza. (DM)
● **Yacochuya** Cafayate★★★★★ £F

Chile

ALMAVIVA Maipo www.conchaytoro.com A: CyT,Sel

Owner: Viña Almaviva SA Av Santa Rosa 821, Paradero 45, Puento Alto, Santiago
Recently established joint venture between CONCHA Y TORO and Baroness Philippine de Rothschild (MOUTON-ROTHSCHILD). The ambitious project is aimed at producing one of, possibly *the* finest red wine yet from Chile. Considerable investment has already gone into both vineyards and winery. Almaviva is undoubtedly impressive but as yet falls some way short of its lofty price tag and on a global scale faces formidable opposition. It is to be hoped that the style will surpass that other Mouton-Rothschild investment OPUS ONE. Under the MAPA label the Rothschilds are producing some good results at a lower level along with a further impressive red, Escudo Rojo. (DM)
● **Almaviva Red** Maipo Valley★★★★ £G

CARMEN Maipo www.carmen.com A: SsG

Owner: Claro family Apoquindo, 3669, Piso 6, Santiago
Carmen is owned by the large SANTA RITA operation. Production here itself is not inconsiderable at over 350,000 cases a year and an extensive range is produced, both red and white. The regular whites and particularly the reds are well-crafted and full of vibrant, ripe and crunchy fruit. The best wines, though, are produced under the Reserve and Winemakers Reserve labels along with impressive organic Nativa Chardonnay and the deep, concentrated and minty Nativa Cabernet Sauvignon. The Reserve label also now includes Sauvignon Blanc, Carmenère/Cabernet and Petite Sirah. The flagship red is the impressive Gold Reserve, which is produced from a small 45-year-old parcel of vines in Maipo. Top reds, particularly the Gold Reserve, will improve with cellaring. (DM)
● **Cabernet Sauvignon** Nativa Maipo★★★ £C Reserve Maipo★★ £C Gold Reserve Maipo★★★ £E
● **Pinot Noir** Reserve Maipo★★ £B ● **Merlot** Reserve Rapel★★ £B
● **Cabernet Syrah** Reserve Maipo★★ £C ● **Winemakers** Reserve Red Maipo★★ £C
O **Chardonnay** Nativa Maipo★ £C Winemakers Reserve Maipo/Casablanca★★ £C

CASA LAPOSTOLLE Rapel www.casalapostolle.com A: MMD

Owner: Marnier Lapostolle/Rabat families Benjamin 2935, Of. 801, Las Condes, Santiago
This is now established as one of the best red wine producers in Chile. Winemaking direction has been provided for a number of years by Michel Rolland of BON PASTEUR. The Chardonnay in both regular and

Cuvée Alexandre versions is moderately rich and oaky, the Sauvignon Blanc quite piercingly tropical and grassy. Tanao is a recent label addition: the red is a blend of Cabernet Sauvignon, Merlot and Carmenère and is full of dark, spicy berry fruit, while the white is a fresh, fruit-driven blend of Chardonnay, Semillon and a hint of Sauvignon Blanc. It is the reds, though, that lift the winery onto a separate quality plateau. Cabernet Sauvignon Cuvée Alexandre is well structured but lacks the sheer opulence of the rich, supple, almost exotic Merlot Cuvée Alexandre. Dark smoky Syrah has also now been added. Currently a serious contender for the best red from Chile is the dense, powerful, opulent and richly textured Clos Apalta. The wine is structured and ageworthy but has all the hallmarks of Rolland's great wines from St-Émilion. (DM)

● **Clos Apalta** Rapel★★★★ £E ● **Tanao** Rapel★★ £C
● **Cabernet Sauvignon** Rapel★★ £B Cuvée Alexandre Rapel★★ £C
● **Merlot** Rapel★★ £B Cuvée Alexandre Rapel★★★ £C
○ **Chardonnay** Casablanca★ £B Cuvée Alexandre Casablanca★★ £C
○ **Tanao** Casablanca/Rapel★★ £C ○ **Sauvignon Blanc** Rapel★ £B

CASA SILVA Rapel www.casasilva.cl A: JNV

Owner: Silva family Hijuela Norte, Angostura, Casilla 97, San Fernando
Among the best of Chile's newly established winery operations, Casa Silva was set up in 1997 and winemaking is supervised by the experienced Mario Geisse Garcia. The winery owns three different estates and has a total of some 830 ha of vineyards, so is not a small operation by any means. All of the vineyards are located in the potentially excellent Colchagua Valley. The top wines are the Reserva labels. In particular, the dark, brambly and intensely spicy Carmenère Reserva and Quinta Generación Gran Reserva Tinto, a blend of both Cabernet and Carmenère, are both ageworthy and will improve for three or four years. A number of impressive Single Vineyard Reserve wines have now been released including Merlot and Chardonnay from Angostura and Carmenère from Los Linques. (DM)

● **Cabernet Sauvignon/Sangiovese** Selected Vines Colchagua★ £B
● **Cabernet Sauvignon** Reserva Colchagua★★ £D
● **Carmenère** Reserva Colchagua★★★ £C Single Vineyard Reserve Los Linques★★★★ £D
● **Merlot** Reserva Colchagua★ £B Single Vineyard Reserve Angostura★★★ £D
● **Syrah** Colchagua★★ £B
● **Quinta Generación** Colchagua★★★ £C
○ **Chardonnay** Reserva Colchagua★ £B Single Vineyard Reserve Angostura★★★ £C
○ **Quinta Generación** Colchagua★★ £C

CONCHA Y TORO Maipo www.conchaytoro.com A: CyT

Owner: Viña Concha y Toro Av Nueva Tajamar 481, Torre Norte Piso 15, Las Condes, Santiago
This is a massive operation with a huge range of commercial wines throughout the vinous spectrum at all price points. It is also involved with MOUTON-ROTHSCHILD of Bordeaux in the super-premium ALMAVIVA project. Production is now well over 10 million cases a year and the company possess more than 3,230 ha of vineyards. Ignacio Recabarren has left VIÑA CASABLANCA to provide consultancy input here and the results are beginning to filter through. Both Trio and Casillero del Diablo offer good value in both red and white while the Terrunyo label has been created to emphasise real regional character. Marqués is a recently added mid-range label producing some good reds and whites. Of the top labels Amelia Chardonnay is ripely tropical and toasty but with good depth. The Don Melchor Cabernet Sauvignon is sourced from the Puente Alto vineyard in the Maipo. It is a powerful, dusty red with dark berry fruit and a lightly leafy, minty component. Yet I feel there should be more complexity at the price. (DM)

● **Cabernet Sauvignon** Terrunyo★ £D Don Melchor★★★ £E ● **Carmenère** Terrunyo★ £C
○ **Chardonnay** Trio★ £B Terrunyo ★★ £B Amelia★★ £C
○ **Gewurztraminer** Trio★ £B
○ **Sauvignon Blanc** Trio★ £B Terrunyo★ £B

CONO SUR Rapel www.conosur.com A: WWs

Owner: Concha Y Toro Nueva Tajamar 481, Of. 1602, Torre Sur Las Condes, Santiago
This operation was established in 1993. There are extensive estate-owned vineyards and the company sources fruit from Casablanca, Maipo, Rapel and the Bío Bío Valley. Under the Isla Negra label some attractively fruity reds and whites are produced. Reserve Cabernet Sauvignon, Merlot and Pinot Noir are all decent and well priced, while the Innovative Visión range is a step up. Top wines are the 20 Barrels Pinot Noir, Merlot and Cabernet Sauvignon. Pinot Noir is also produced in a Limited Edition bottling. The Cabernet and Merlot are extracted and forward as is the case with so many premium Chilean reds and characterised by dark berry, fruit. The Pinot Noir shows a decent balance of strawberry, lightly savoury fruit with marked high-toast oak. (DM)

● **Cabernet Sauvignon** Reserve Colchagua★ £B 20 Barrels Colchagua★★ £C
● **Merlot** 20 Barrels Colchagua★★ £C
● **Pinot Noir** 20 Barrels Colchagua★ £C Limited Edition Colchagua★★ £C

EL PRINCIPAL Maipo Valley vinaep@ctcinterneyt.cl A: WEx

Owner: Patrick Valette Casilla 80, Pirque, Santiago
This 53-ha Maipo estate has been developed by Bordelais Patrick Valette, with the vineyard planted to Cabernet Sauvignon, Carmenère and Merlot (85/8/7 per cent). The wine is a modern Bordeaux style and as at many Bordeaux properties a second wine is produced to ensure the integrity of the Grand Vin. Yields are kept low at 30 hl/ha and El Principal is aged in 100 per cent new oak with malolactic in barrel. Memorias is a good, medium-weight style if a little leafy in 2000. El Principal was unusually 100 per cent Cabernet Sauvignon in 2000, providing a good but somewhat austere wine. Normally the Cabernet is blended with Carmenère and the wine offers greater richness and a rounder, suppler texture. (DM)

● **Memorias** Maipo★★ £B ● **El Principal** Maipo★★★★ £E

ERRÁZURIZ Aconcagua www.errazuriz.com A:HMA

Owner: Eduardo Chadwick Nueva Tajamar 481, Of. 503, Torre Sur Las Condes, Santiago
Errázuriz is based in the Panquehue sub-region of Aconcagua and has some 405 ha of vineyards. Fruit is generally sourced from the home vineyards but also from cool Casablanca for whites. The range is comprehensive and there are some well-made, stylish wines at all levels. The regular varietals show well-defined fruit character. Superior selections come under the Max Reserva label and there are two striking Wild Ferment wines: a Chardonnay full of citrus and lightly smoked oak, and a forward, vibrant Pinot Noir marked by sappy cherry and wild strawberry aromas. Sangiovese and Carmenère Single Vineyard labels are both impressively concentrated as the newly added La Cumbre Syrah. The top reds include the Don Maximiano Founders Reserve and the super-premium partnership with ROBERT MONDAVI, SEÑA, which has real potential. The partnership with Mondavi has also now been extended to include a range of premium varietals at the new LA ARBOLEDA ESTATE. 1999 was also the first vintage of VINEDO CHADWICK, a super-premium blend of Cabernet Sauvignon and Carmenère from a 15 ha vineyard in the Maipo Valley. The wine promises much. Also jointly owns CALITERRA. (DM)

● **Merlot/Cabernet Sauvignon** Rapel★ £B ● **Sangiovese** Single Vineyard★★ £C
● **Cabernet Sauvignon** Max Reserva★ £C ● **Carmenère** Single Vineyard★★ £D
● **Merlot** Curico★ £B Max Reserva★★ £C ● **Syrah** Aconcagua★★ £B
● **Pinot Noir** Wild Ferment★★ £C ● **Don Maximiano** Founders Reserve★★★ £E
O **Chardonnay** Max Reserva★ £B Wild Ferment★★ £C

GRACIA Rapel www.graciawinery.cl A: Pat

Owner: Viña Gracia de Chile S.A. Vitacura 4380, Piso 18, Vitacura 667 0169, Santiago
This is one of the more recently established Chilean operations, formed in 1992. Vineyard planting is ongoing and the objective is to establish up to 1,000 ha of estate-owned vineyards in the Aconcagua, Maipo, Rapel and Bío Bío valleys. There are some well-crafted Reserva wines and the style is full-on and opulent: Chardonnay, is ripe, tropical and toasty; Merlot, plummy and smoky; and Carmenère rich, brambly and supple. The top red is the premium Cabernet Sauvignon RR Reserva Caminante – muscular, dense and powerful. (DM)

● **Carmenère** Reserva Especial Callajero Maipo★ £B
● **Cabernet Sauvignon** Reserva Lo Mejor Porquenó★★ £C ● RR Reserva Caminante★★★ £D
● **Merlot** Reserva Lo Mejor Porquenó★★ £B
● **Pinot Noir** Reserva Lo Mejor Sereno★ £B
O **Chardonnay** Reserva Superior Temporal★ £B

MONTES Curicó www.monteswines.com A: HWC

Owner: Montes family Av. Del Valle 945, Of 2611, Ciudad Empresorial, Huechuraba
This is a large but very variable producer. Some wines have been impressive recently, some decidedly less so. Some 300,000 cases of estate-grown and externally sourced wines are produced. There is a good brambly and moderately dense Reserve Malbec but the best wines are produced under the Montes Alpha label. Chardonnay is in a rich tropical style but has a little finesse, while Cabernet Sauvignon is sound if a little light on occasion. However, it is the Montes Alpha Syrah, premium Montes Folly and premium Montes Alpha M that really stand out. The dark, smoky Syrah is one of Chile's best examples. This has now been joined by the special Montes Folly bottling from the firm's Apalta Mountain Estate in Colchagua, a hand-picked 100 per cent Syrah aged in new French oak, of which less than 1,000 cases are produced. The flagship Montes Alpha M, a Bordeaux blend from the single La Finca estate in Colchagua, is reasonably rich, earthy, extracted and concentrated. I feel it should show more, though, at this price. A late-harvest white is also now offered, a blend of 50/50 Gewürztraminer and Riesling. (DM)

● **Montes Alpha M** Colchagua★★ £E
● **Montes Folly** Santa Cruz★★★★ £D **Montes Alpha Syrah** Santa Cruz★★★ £D
● **Alpha Merlot** Colchagua★ £C ● **Malbec** Reserve Curicó★ £B
O **Alpha Chardonnay** Curicó★ £B

ODFJELL VINEYARDS Maipo www.odfjellvineyards.com A: WTs

Owner: Odfjell Family Camino Viejo Valparaiso, No 7000 PO Box 23, Padre Hurtado
Daniel and Laurence Odfjell have established vineyards in Maipo very recently. By Chilean standards this is a small, almost boutique style of operation with a production of fewer than 40,000 cases a year across their range. Winemaking consultancy input is provided by Paul HOBBS as well as French enologist Arnaud Hereu. There is a simple fruit-driven Cabernet, Rojo, and a budget Armador label with a ripe, plummy Merlot standing out. The Orzada wines are a level up and some very characterful Cabernet Franc, Carmenère and unusually a Carignan stand out. The Cabernet Sauvignon is less impressive, with a slightly green note evident in the 2001. Top of the range is a 100 per cent Cabernet Sauvignon Aliara which is full and rich with dark berry fruit and a ripe, chocolaty character. Abundant oak needs a couple of years to integrate. This is a good new source in contrast to many of the increasingly homogenised styles that are emerging from Chile. (DM)

● **Cabernet Franc** Orzada Maule★★ £B ● **Merlot** Armador Maule★ £B
● **Carmenère** Orzada Maule★★★ £B Armaudor Maule★ £B
● **Cabernet Sauvignon** Orzada Maule★★ £B ● **Carignan** Orzada Maule★★ £B
● **Aliara** Maipo★★★ £D

SANTA RITA Maipo www.santarita.com A: **BWC**

Owner: Viña Santa Rita Apoquindo 3669, Of. 601, Santiago
Long-established, traditional old Chilean winery which had a wake-up call in the late 1990s and is beginning to produce an increasingly fine range of mid-market and premium wines. The 120 range offers some reasonable straightforward easy drinking; the reds are a better bet generally than the whites. Reserva whites are sound but no more; the reds again are better as is the case with the Medalla Real wines. Chardonnay, though, is well crafted in a tropical, toasty style. Both the Cabernet Sauvignon and Merlot Reservas display attractive, moderately concentrated, dark, spicy fruit. The Floresta reds have recently been added to the range. The two wines that really stand out are the red Triple C and Casa Real Cabernet Sauvignon. Triple C is a blend of Cabernet Franc, Cabernet Sauvignon and Carmenère. Casa Real Cabernet is quite traditional in style with well-judged oak, both concentrated and reasonably refined. (DM)

● **Cabernet Sauvignon Floresta Apalta** Rapel★★ £B Medalla Real Maipo Valley★★ £B
● **Cabernet Sauvignon** Casa Real Maipo★★ £D
● **Syrah/Cabernet/Carmenère Floresta** Maipo★★ £B ● **Merlot/Cabernet Floresta** Maipo★★ £B
● **Triple C** Maipo★★ £C
○ **Chardonnay** Medalla Real Maipo★ £B

SEÑA Aconcagua www.senawines.com A: **HMA**,Sel

Owner: Eduardo Chadwick/Mondavi family
This wine partnership between Eduardo Chadwick at ERRÁZURIZ and California's ROBERT MONDAVI vies with Clos Apalta from CASA LAPOSTOLLE, ALMAVIVA and now EL PRINCIPAL for the accolade of best super-premium red from Chile. It is currently a blend of Cabernet Sauvignon, Merlot and Carmenère. The wine is sourced from, among other sites, the finest plots of the vineyard that also supplies the Errázuriz Don Maximiano red. Seña itself is impressively dense, structured and concentrated. It is planned that the wine will eventually be sourced entirely from its own single estate. This is a 350-ha property in the western Aconcagua with some ideal north facing slopes and high-density vineyard planting. As yet, while it is both rich and powerful, I feel there should be just a little more depth and complexity. (DM)

● **Seña** Aconcagua Valley★★★★ £F

VALDIVIESO Curicó www.vinavaldivieso.cl A: **Bib**

Owner: Viña Valdivieso S.A. Juan Mitjans 200, Macul, Santiago
Successful marketing-driven operation which produces an extensive range of wines at all levels. Regular red and white varietals are produced under the Valdivieso and Casa de Piedra labels. At best these offer straightforward easy glugging. Barrel Selections are a step up and the Syrah and Carmenère are good examples – ripe and with decent weight and flesh. Some impressive red is produced under the Reserve label, though whites disappoint. Good Single Vineyard Cabernet Franc and Merlot particularly stand out. The top wines are The Don, which is part aged in American and French oak, and the non-vintaged Caballo Loco, a blend that changes by the year. Top reds particularly Caballo Loco will stand a little age. (DM)

● **Cabernet Franc** Single Vineyard Reserve Curicó★★ £B ● **Merlot** Single Vineyard Reserve Curicó★ £B
● **Malbec** Single Vineyard Reserve Curicó★★ £B ● **Caballo Loco** Curicó★★★ £D

VIÑA CASABLANCA Casablanca rbeckdor@santacarolina.cl A: **Mor**

Owner: Viña Santa Carolina Rodrigo de Araya 1431, Macul, Santiago
Established by SANTA CAROLINA over 10 years ago this has been a consistently impressive producer of good, sometimes very good cool-grown whites. Reds are produced as well but these can be disappointing by comparison; the wines show quite marked evidence of their cool-climate origins and can be peppery at best, green at worst. The best are the Santa Isabel Cabernet Sauvignon and the Neblus, a pricey blend of Cabernet Sauvignon, Merlot and Carmenère. Gewürztraminer is good, with some varietally

pungent character; Sauvignon Blanc is equally stylish, with grassy, tropical notes showing through its piercing fruit. Chardonnay is one of the best in the country, particularly the Barrel Fermented label, which is very intense with marked citrus and subtle lees and oak character. It will develop well with limited ageing. (DM)

● **Cabernet Sauvignon** Santa Isabel Estate Casablanca★★ £B   ● **Carmenère** El Bosque★ £B
● **Merlot** Santa Isabel Casablanca★ £B   ● **Neblus** Casablanca★★ £D
O **Chardonnay** Santa Isabel Casablanca★★ £B   Santa Isabel Barrel Fermented Casablanca★★★ £C
O **Gewurztraminer** Santa Isabel Casablanca★ £B   O **Sauvignon Blanc** Santa Isabel Casablanca★★ £B

VINEDO CHADWICK   Maipo   www.vinedoschadwick.com   A: HMA

Owner: Eduardo Chadwick   Avenida Nueva Tajamar 481, Oficina 503, Torre Sur
A recently established premium label owned by ERRAZURIZ, with a vineyard located on the northern bank of the Maipo river into the foothills of the Andes. The 300-ha property has been in the Chadwick family since 1945. The vineyard covers a mere 15 ha of the best stony/clay soils. It is now planted to the best field selections from both Maipo and the Don Maximiano vineyard of Cabernet Sauvignon, Cabernet Franc and Carmenère. The wine is aged in 100 per cent new French oak. It complements the other top Errazuriz/MONDAVI red, SEÑA, and shows some of the character that can be achieved in the Maipo as well as the Panquehue sub-region of Aconcagua where Errazuriz is based. At present it has impressive depth but is leaner and less opulent than Seña. Firmly structured with a cedary edge to its fruit, it needs at least five years to soften. (DM)

● **Vinedo Chadwick** Maipo★★★★ £F

OTHER WINES OF NOTE

Argentina
ALTOS DE MEDRANO ● **Vigna Hormigas Malbec** Mendoza £C
ALTOS LOS HORMIGAS ● **Malbec** Mendoza £C
LEONCIO ARIZU ● **Malbec Luigi Bosca** Mendoza £B   ●**Petit Verdot Viña Alicia** Mendoza £D
VALENTIN BIANCHI ● **Cabernet Sauvignon** Mendoza £C
ETCHART ● **Arnaldo B Reserva** Cafayate £C
FABRE MONTMAYOU ● **Grand Vin** Luján de Cuyo £D
FINCA EL RETIRO ● **Syrah** Mendoza £B   ● **Malbec** Mendoza £B
FINCA FLICHMAN ● **Dedicado** Maipú £C
LA AGRICOLA ● **Malbec** Familia Zuccardi Q £C
BODEGA LURTON ● **Gran Lurton** Mendoza £B
MAPEMA ● **Primera Zona** Mendoza £E
BODEGA NORTON ● **Privada** Luján de Cuyo £C   ● **Malbec** Reserve £C
FELIPE RUTINI ● **Apartado** Tupungato £D
BODEGAS SALENTIEN ● **Malbec** Mendoza £C   ● **Shiraz** Mendoza £C
BODEGA TERRAZAS DE LOS ANDES ● **Gran Malbec** Luján de Cuyo £D
TRAPICHE ● **Iscay** Maipú £E
RAUL DAVALOS ● **Colomé** Mendoza £D   ● **33 de Davalos** Mendoza £D
● **RD de Davalos** Mendoza £D
VINITERRA ● **Cabernet Sauvignon** Luján de Cuyo £B   ● **Malbec** Luján de Cuyo £B
DOMAINE VISTALBA ● **Infinitus Malbec/Syrah** Río Negro £C
WEINERT ● **Malbec** Luján de Cuyo £C   ● **Cavas de Weinert** Luján de Cuyo £C

Chile
AGUIRRE ● **Tempus** Reserva Especial £B
APALTAGUA ● **Carmenère** Colchagua £B   ● **Envero** Colchagua £B   ● **Grial** Colchagua £B
ARESTI ● **Cabernet Sauvignon** Family Collection £C
BISQUERTT ● **Carmenère** Gran Reserva Casa La Joya £B

VIÑEDOS JULIO BOUCHON ● **Carmenère** Reserva Especial Maule £B   ● **Assemblage**Maule £C
CALITERRA ● **Merlot** Reserva Colchagua £B
CANEPA ● **Cabernet Sauvignon** Magnificum Curicó £C   ● **Carmenère** Private Reserve Valle Centrale £B
CASA RIVAS ● **Carmenère** Gran Reserva Maipo £B
COUSIÑO MACUL ● **Finis Terrae** Maipo £C
DOMAINE PAUL BRUNO ● **Cabernet Sauvignon** Maipo £B
ECHEVERRIA ● **Cabernet Sauvignon** Molina Reserva £C
LUIS FELIPE EDWARDS ● **Cabernet** Reserva Colchagua £B   ● **Merlot** Reserva Colchagua £B
LA ARBOLEDA O **Chardonnay** Casablanca £B   ● **Carmenère** Colchagua £B
● **Syrah** Colchagua £B
MICHEL LAROCHE/JORGE CODERCHE ● **Piedra Feliz** Casablanca £B
● **Colina Negra** Casablanca £B   O **Rio Azul** Casablanca £B
LOS VASCOS ● **Le Dix de Los Vascos** Colchagua £D
LA ROSA ● **Merlot** Gran Reserve La Palmeria Rapel £B
MAPA ● **Merlot** Rapel £B   ● **Cabernet Sauvignon** Maipo £B
MONTGRAS ● **Ninquen** Colchagua £C
SANTA CAROLINA O **Chardonnay** Reservado Maipo £B
TARAPACÁ ● **Syrah** Privada Reserva Maipo £B   ● **Milenium** Maipo £C
TERRANOBLE ● **Carmenère Gran Reserva** Maule £C
TORREÓN DE PAREDES ● **Don Amado** Cachapoal £D
MIGUEL TORRES ● **Manso de Velasco** Curicó £D
VERAMONTE ● **Primus** Casablanca £C
VILLARD ESTATE ● **Equis** Maipo £C
VIÑA LEYDA ● **Carmenère** Leyda £B   ● **Vintage Selection** Leyda £B
● **Lot 21 Pinot Noir** Leyda £C
VIÑA PÉREZ CRUZ ● **Cot** Reserva Limited Edition £C   ● **Syrah** Reserva Limited Edition £C
VIÑA QUEBRADA DE MACUL ● **Domus Aurea** Maipo £E
VIÑA SAN PEDRO ● **Cabernet Sauvignon** Reserva Castillo di Molina £B
VIU MANENT ● **Malbec** Reserva Colchagua £B

Work in progress!!

Wines from the following producers under consideration for the next edition
ANTINORI-MATTE (MAIPO, CHILE)
VINA ANTIYAL (MAIPO, CHILE)
VINA AQUITANIA (MAIPO, CHILE)
BODEGAS CARO (MENDOZA, ARGENTINA)
VINA CLOS QUEBRADA DE MACUL (MAIPO, CHILE)
O. FOURNIER (MENDOZA, ARGENTINA)
VINA HARAS DE PIRQUE (MAIPO, CHILE)
POESIA (MENDOZA, ARGENTINA)
CHEVAL DES ANDES (MENDOZA, ARGENTINA)
MATETIC (CASABLANCA, CHILE)

Author's Choice (DM)

A Chilean selection
ALMAVIVA ● **Almaviva Red** Maipo Valley
CASA LAPOSTOLLE ● **Clos Apalta** Rapel
CASA SILVA ● **Quinta Generación** Colchagua
EL PRINCIPAL ● **El Principal** Maipo
ERRÁZURIZ ● **Vinedo Chadwick** Maipo
GRACIA ● **RR Reserva** Caminante
MONTES ● **Montes Folly** Santa Cruz
ODFJELL VINEYARDS ● **Aliara** Maipo
SEÑA ● **Seña** Aconcagua Valley
VIÑA CASABLANCA ● **Chardonnay** Santa Isabel Barrel Fermented Casablanca

An Argentine selection
ACHAVAL-FERRER ● **Malbec** Finca Altamira
ALTA VISTA ● **Alto** Vistalba
SUSANA BALBO ● **Brioso** Mendoza
BEN MARCO ● **VMS** Mendoza
CATENA ZAPATA ● **Nicolás Catena Zapata** Luján de Cuyo
LUCA ○ **Chardonnay** Mendoza
CLOS DE LOS SIETE ● **Lindaflor** Mendoza
NIETO SENETINER ● **Malbec** Cadus Tupungato
DOMAINE VISTALBA ● **Infinitus Malbec/Syrah** Río Negro
YACOCHUYA ● **Yacochuya Red** Cafayate

The extent to which Australia's global success derives from its easy-to-understand appeal - from mostly varietal labelling of wine names to the direct and overt fruitiness that still characterises many of the wines - can not be underestimated. Yet there are also fine wines with great depth and structure and others of real style, elegance and nuance. The first years of the new century haves witnessed a sea change in placing much greater emphasis on diversity and regionality. The correlation between price and quality is also improving but care is needed when purchasing more expensive bottles. In order to give some coherence to Australia's ever burgeoning vineyard area we have made four broad geopolitical divisions: **South Australia, Victoria & Tasmania, New South Wales & Queensland,** *and* **Western Australia.**

Eastern Plains, Inland &	13 North West Victoria
North of Western Australia	14 Western Victoria
Greater Perth	15 Central Victoria
South West Australia	16 Port Phillip
Central Western Australia	17 North East Victoria
Western Australian South	18 Gippsland
East Coastal	19 Western Plains
Far North	20 Big Rivers
The Peninsulas	21 Southern New South Wales
Mount Lofty Ranges	22 South Coast
Barossa	23 Central Ranges
0 Fleurieu	24 Hunter Valley
1 Lower Murray	25 Northern Slopes
2 Limestone Coast	26 Northern Rivers

South Australia

Almost half of all Australian wine comes from South Australia. The bulk of the cheaper wine comes from the Riverland area, on the Murray River close to Victoria, while many premium wines (red, white and fortified) are made from regions that range from baking hot to distinctly cool. Quality in all the established regions is producer-dependent, as many have chosen to maximise profits by concentrating their efforts on marketing and distribution rather than producing ever better wines. From both the latest wave of high-quality small producers and some of the more established names, the wines are increasingly vineyard-specific but great wines also continue to be blended from a range of mesoclimates.

Barossa

This GI zone, incorporating the Barossa Valley and the Eden Valley, witnessed the greatest revival amongst Australia's many historic winemaking areas during the 1990s.

Barossa Valley

Since the 1840s both English and Silesian immigrants have played an important part in establishing what has become the heart of the Australian wine industry. But in the modern revival of Australian table wines Barossa lost ground to newer areas and its rich viticultural resource of often unirrigated, old-vine Shiraz, Grenache and Mourvèdre began to rapidly disappear under Vine Pull schemes of the 1980s. Fortunately Peter Lehmann, Grant Burge, Charlie Melton and others rode to the rescue by producing wines of a quality that the world couldn't ignore and has since not been able to get enough of. Besides rich, lushly textured old-vine Shiraz and Rhône-style blends, Cabernet Sauvignon has an important place for its distinctive dense, black-fruited blockbusters; such Barossa classics often owe their sweet casing to ageing in American oak. Barossa also has a great history of fortified wines and very high-quality examples, often blended from old wines, continue to be made by Seppelt and others. Though full-flavoured, whites are less suited to the conditions. Chardonnay, whose appeal in the 80s soon waned, does less well than Semillon in the heat.

Eden Valley

The most successful of the whites in the Barossa zone is Riesling, but from over the eastern ranges of the Barossa Valley in the significantly cooler, more elevated vineyards of the Eden Valley. Riesling particularly excels in the higher, more southern reaches where the Mount Lofty Ranges run through from the Adelaide Hills to the south. These areas are known as **High Eden** (a recently approved sub-region), home to Mountadam, Heggies and Pewsey Vale (see Yalumba), and **Springton** and are the source of high-quality Chardonnay, Pinot Noir and Merlot. Viognier shows real potential too, though current quality has been a little overhyped. Great reds, particularly Shiraz but also Cabernet, are also produced from lower altitudes, most notably those from Henschke, near Keyneton.

Mount Lofty Ranges

Though geographically disparate, the Clare Valley and Adelaide Hills both form part of the Mount Lofty Ranges, where altitude plays a significant role in the style of the wines.

Clare Valley

Lying to the north-west of Barossa, the Clare Valley might be expected to be even hotter, but altitude changes the equation and is critical to the success of individual varieties. However, it is warm and even with irrigation vines can suffer water stress in particularly hot years. Several sub-regions have already emerged, including **Auburn, Polish Hill River, Sevenhill, Watervale** and around the township of **Clare** itself – though none have yet received official GI sanction. Most Rieslings from the Clare Valley offer less immediate fruit sweetness than those from the Eden Valley but have better structure and greater style. The best examples can be relatively austere in youth but develop an intense limey, mineral toastiness with 10 years' age or more. Shiraz is the most widely planted variety and the higher west-facing vineyards in particular provide some excellent examples with a captivating smoke, earth and mineral character (superbly illustrated by the likes of Kilikanoon). Cabernet Sauvignon is also a leading variety and if generally less compelling than the best

Shiraz it also shows a distinctive regional stamp. Chardonnay, Semillon and Merlot are the most important of the other varieties.

Adelaide Hills

The Adelaide Hills, in the ranges along and beyond the eastern edge of the state capital, form part of the southern extension of the Mount Lofty Ranges. Elevation is again critical and the reputation of this relatively small vineyard area grows apace, now way beyond its size, since being pioneered by Brian Croser (Petaluma) in the 1970s. Chardonnay, especially from the sub-regions of **Lenswood** and **Piccadilly Valley**, rivals, even surpasses the best in the country but there has also been compelling quality from Pinot Noir and Sauvignon Blanc. The patchwork of vineyards, resulting in part from the perils of spring frost, contrasts with the swathe of low-altitude vineyards that carpet the floor of the McLaren Vale a short distance to the south.

Fleurieu

The Fleurieu Peninsula is dominated by production from the historic and important McLaren Vale but in the past decade wines of quality have begun to emerge from lesser-known neighbouring regions.

McLaren Vale

In the McLaren Vale, tucked between the hills and the coast, the heat is relieved by sea breezes and Shiraz, Grenache, Mourvèdre and Cabernet Sauvignon assume ascendancy. However, care must be taken if the wines are to show balance and depth as well as a lush texture. A re-energising of established producers (such as D'Arenberg) together with the emergence of the likes of Clarendon Hills, Fox Creek, or more recently, Mitolo, have, in conjunction with the general revival in the fortunes of Rhône varieties in South Australia, brought about both greater diversity in red wine styles and ever higher quality. Given the region's mix of soil types it is also encouraging to see increasing identification of the various sub-zones and individual vineyards. Soon the likes of Blewitt Springs, Clarendon and Kangarilla should be as well known for their location as for the wineries named after them. Whites are much less exciting. Some producers persist with Sauvignon Blanc and Chardonnay, the best of which come from the cooler northern end (Clarendon, Kangarilla) of the region where the Adelaide Hills begin, but the long-term success of whites in the area may come to depend more on Rhône and other warmer-climate varieties.

Other Fleurieu regions

Flood-irrigated **Langhorne Creek** on the other side of the Fleurieu Peninsula has long provided soft, ripe Shiraz and Cabernet fruit that contributes to many a well-established blended South Australian red. An absence of high-profile producers has contributed to a lack of identity but Bleasdale, Bremerton, Lake Breeze and others will bring greater recognition. Other pockets of vineyard that have recently been given their own official sanction are **Currency Creek** and **Southern Fleurieu** which lie either side of Langhorne Creek. **Kangaroo Island**, a large (4,350 km[2]), sparsely populated island 110 km south-west of Adelaide, has but a few vines yet shows good potential for Bordeaux-style reds.

Limestone Coast

The south-eastern corner of the state is geographically an extension of Victoria. The Limestone Coast zone is essentially flat yet its magic emerges from low limestone ridges topped with the famous terra rossa (or terra rosa) soil. The most established of these is, of course, Coonawarra.

Coonawarra

Coonawarra only emerged as a high-quality region in the latter half of the 20th century. Despite its renown, quality from this elongated, relatively exposed and coolish region with its terra rossa soils and high water table is highly variable. The combination of intermittent summer heat and cold, wet winters is as significant to quality as the fabled free-draining soils. Cooler vintages in particular demand high standards of viticulture yet much of the mechanically harvested fruit that comes from high-yielding Cabernet Sauvignon vines fails to get fully ripe as does that fromless suitable more water-retentive soils at the limits of the region. Many of the high-volume blends that result denigrate the Coonawarra name. Yet the giant Wynns and a growing number of small or medium-sized estates (such as Bowen Estate or Hollick) are showing the sort of quality that is possible, and from Shiraz as well as Cabernet. There has been much fuss over Coonawarra boundaries but wiser producers are investing their energies on developing other similar, and very promising regions.

Padthaway

Northernmost of the Limestone Coast regions, Padthaway has a far less established reputation than Coonawarra. Despite being the warmer of the two, Padthaway already has a considerable reputation for Chardonnay. There are also substantial plantings of Cabernet Sauvignon and Shiraz and significant amounts of Riesling, Merlot and Pinot Noir. As a recognised GI region it at least has the opportunity to develop a stronger regional identity, though it seems likely that the marketing gurus of the big companies which dominate the vineyard holdings may prefer to promote the Limestone Coast. The emergence of the likes of Henry's Drive and Stonehaven might help.

Mount Benson and Robe

Mount Benson and adjoining Robe lie to the west of Coonawarra and Wrattonbully, right on the coast. Vineyards were non-existent here until 1989. Temperatures during the growing season are lower than in Coonawarra and both wind and frost can be a problem. Cabernet Sauvignon and Shiraz lead the plantings; Shiraz in particular, usually from recently established vines, shows real promise. Interest has been heightened by both the development of Kreglinger Estate, the region's largest, and investment from Chapoutier of the Rhône Valley.

Wrattonbully

To the north of Coonawarra, Wrattonbully is now rapidly emerging as an important region for quality wines. Slightly warmer than Coonawarra, it has similar terra rossa soils underneath the gently undulating surface and also slightly less risk of frost. The lion's share of planting has been to Cabernet Sauvignon but there are also substantial amounts of Merlot and Shiraz if relatively few vineyards planted to white varieties. As the region (and its name) still await ratification as part of the GI programme, wines from the region are labelled Limestone Coast and its regional identity remains concealed from many wine drinkers.

The rest of the Limestone Coast

Smaller newer areas that have yet to take on any real significance include Mount Gambier (in the extreme south of the state), Lucindale (on another Limestone ridge between Mount Benson and Wrattonbully), and Bordertown. The last already has significant plantings that disappear into Limestone Coast blends.

A-Z of producers by region

Barossa Valley
BAROSSA VALLEY ESTATE	705
WOLF BLASS	706
GRANT BURGE	707
BURGE FAMILY	707
CHARLES CIMICKY	709
DUTSCHKE	711
ELDERTON	711
GREENOCK CREEK	712
HAMILTON'S EWELL	713
JACOB'S CREEK/ORLANDO	717
TREVOR JONES	717
PETER LEHMANN	720
CHARLES MELTON	722
PENFOLDS	725
ROCKFORD	728
ST HALLETT	728
SALTRAM	729
SEPPELT	729
TORBRECK	731
TURKEY FLAT	732
VERITAS	732
YALUMBA	735

Eden Valley
HENSCHKE	715
MOUNTADAM	724

Adelaide Plains
PRIMO ESTATE	727

Adelaide Hills
ASHTON HILLS	704
BARRATT WINES	705
CHAIN OF PONDS	708
HILLSTOWE	716
KNAPPSTEIN LENSWOOD	720
NEPENTHE	724
PETALUMA	726
SHAW & SMITH	729
THE LANE WINE COMPANY	731
GEOFF WEAVER	733

Clare Valley
TIM ADAMS	704
ANNIE'S LANE	704
JIM BARRY	706
CRABTREE	710
GROSSET	713
KILIKANOON	718
KNAPPSTEIN	718
LEASINGHAM	719
MITCHELL	723
MOUNT HORROCKS	723
PIKES	727
WENDOUREE	733

McLaren Vale
CASCABEL	708
CHAPEL HILL	708
CLARENDON HILLS	709
CORIOLE	710
D'ARENBERG	710
EDWARDS & CHAFFEY	711
FOX CREEK	712
HAMILTON	713
HARDY'S	714
HASELGROVE	714
MAGLIERI	721
MAXWELL	722
GEOFF MERRILL	722
MITOLO	723
REYNELLA/REYNELL	727
ROSEMOUNT (MCLAREN VALE)	728
TATACHILLA	730
WIRRA WIRRA	733
WOODSTOCK	734

Langthorne Creek
BLEASDALE	706
LAKE BREEZE	719

Coonawarra
BALNAVES	705
BOWEN ESTATE	707
HOLLICK	716
JAMIESONS RUN	717
KATNOOK ESTATE	718
LECONFIELD	719
MCWILLIAM'S OF COONAWARRA	721
MAJELLA	721
PARKER COONAWARRA	725
PENLEY ESTATE	726
WYNNS	734
ZEMA ESTATE	736

Mount Benson
RALPH FOWLER	712
M CHAPOUTIER AUSTRALIA	709

Padthaway
HENRYS DRIVE	715
LINDEMANS	720
STONEHAVEN	730

Other
HARDY WINE COMPANY	714
HEWITSON	716
SOUTHCORP	730
TWO HANDS	732

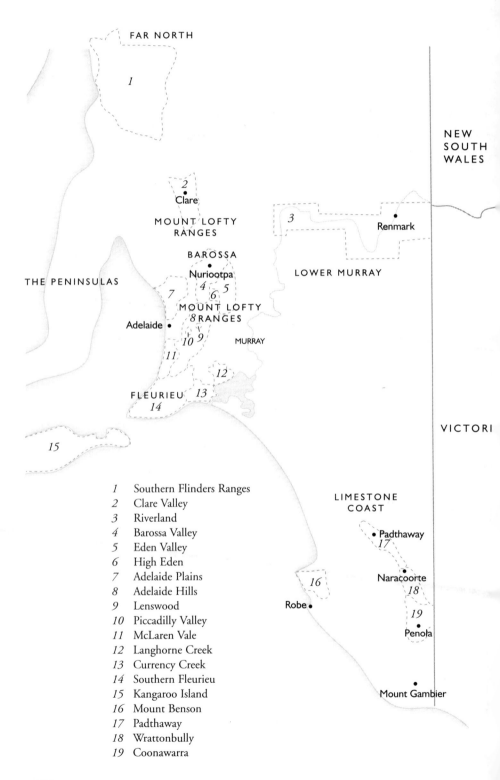

FAR NORTH

NEW
SOUTH
WALES

2
Clare

MOUNT LOFTY
RANGES

3
Renmark

BAROSSA
Nuriootpa

LOWER MURRAY

THE PENINSULAS

7
4
6
5

MOUNT LOFTY
8 RANGES

Adelaide

10 9
MURRAY

11

12

FLEURIEU 13
14

VICTORI

15

1   Southern Flinders Ranges
2   Clare Valley
3   Riverland
4   Barossa Valley
5   Eden Valley
6   High Eden
7   Adelaide Plains
8   Adelaide Hills
9   Lenswood
10   Piccadilly Valley
11   McLaren Vale
12   Langhorne Creek
13   Currency Creek
14   Southern Fleurieu
15   Kangaroo Island
16   Mount Benson
17   Padthaway
18   Wrattonbully
19   Coonawarra

LIMESTONE
COAST

Padthaway
17

16
Naracoorte
18

Robe
19

Penola

Mount Gambier

South Australia vintages

The generalised Vintage charts cover some of the most ageworthy styles and will prove most useful when taken together with comments on style and ageing within individual producer entries. Many wines can be drunk young but an increasing number will not be at their best for at least five years, whether a powerful, full-bodied red or a more structured example of Clare Valley Riesling. Top-quality Chardonnay and Pinot Noir are likely to show at their best only with three to six years' ageing. In terms of longer-term cellaring potential, great Australian Rieslings have been shown to age for a decade or more, while some famous Australian reds have been proven to age for 30 or even 40 years. While it is necessary to be prepared to buy only the best if you want to add breadth to an existing French or European-based cellar, this doesn't always mean purchasing only the most expensive. It should also be noted that those indicated (in producer entries) as needing a minimum amount of ageing should be given it; underestimate their structure at your peril. Both the vintage ratings and when to drink assessments generally only apply to the top rated examples (three star wines or higher).

As in most parts of Australia, 2004 saw a record harvest compensating for the quantity shortfall of the drought-affected 2003 vintage. In terms of quality the picture looks somewhat varied. While Barossa and Clare vineyards were stressed by a February heatwave there was cooler weather closer to harvest. Other parts were more fortunate, including Coonawarra, which looks very promising for reds, and the Adelaide Hills, for Chardonnay.

South Australia vintage chart

	Barossa/Clare Shiraz	Coonawarra Cabernet	Clare/Eden Valley Riesling	Adelaide Hills Chardonnay
2004	★★/★★★★ A	★★★★/★★★★★★ A	★★/★★★ A	★★★★/★★★★★★ A
2003	★★★ A	★★★★ A	★★★★ B	★★★★ B
2002	★★★★/★★★★★★ A	★★★★/★★★★★★ A	★★★★★ B	★★★★★ B
2001	★★★★ A	★★★/★★★★★ A	★★★/★★★★B	★★★ B
2000	★★★ B	★★★★/★★★★★★ A	★★★/★★★★ B	★★★ C
1999	★★★/★★★★ B	★★★★ B	★★★/★★★★ B	★★★/★★★★ C
1998	★★★★★ A	★★★★★ A	★★★★ C	★★★/★★★★★ C
1997	★★★★ B	★★★/★★★★ B	★★★★★ C	★★★★ C
1996	★★★★/★★★★★★ B	★★★★ B	★★★★/★★★★★★ C	★★★★/★★★★★ C
1995	★★★/★★★★ B	★★ C	★★★★ C	★★★★/★★★★★ C
1994	★★★★/★★★★★★ B	★★★★ B	★★★★ C	★★★/★★★★ D
1993	★★★/★★★★ C	★★★/★★★★ C	★★★/★★★★ D	
1992	★★★ C	★★★/★★★★ C	★★★/★★★★ D	
1991	★★★★/★★★★★ C	★★★★/★★★★★ C	★★★★ C	
1990	★★★★/★★★★★★ C	★★★★★ C	★★★★★ C	

TIM ADAMS Clare Valley www.timadamswines.com.au A: **AWA**, ACh, HoM, Por

Owner: Tim & Pam Adams Warenda Road, Clare SA 5453
This is a brilliant Clare Valley producer with marvellously consistent reds and whites of great depth and character. Grapes are sourced both from estate vineyards and local growers and though now up to 30,000 cases annually, production remains modest by Australian standards. Sorby (sold only in the UK) is made in conjunction with Tim's brother, Simon, and combines Barossa and Clare fruit. Aberfeldy, the top red, has a certain elegance as well as masses of fruit and American oak, in which it spends the best part of two years. The Fergus takes its name from a grower who first supplied the Grenache around which a little Shiraz, Cabernet Sauvignon and Cabernet Franc are now woven; at once complex and appealing, it has a deserved following. Riesling and Semillon both have excellent varietal definition and good structure. The prices are exemplary for the quality. (PW)
● Shiraz★★★ £C Sorby★★★ £C Aberfeldy★★★★ £D
● The Fergus★★ £B ● Cabernet★★★ £C
○ Semillon★★★ £C ○ Riesling★★★ £B ○ Botrytis Riesling★★★ £C

ANNIE'S LANE Clare Valley www.annieslane.com.au A: **BBI**, Odd

Owner: Beringer Blass Quelltaler Road, Watervale SA 5452
This Clare Valley range of wines is one of the best of the many in the BERINGER BLASS Australian stable. Named after Annie Wayman, a local personality in the late 19th/early 20th century, the wines were previously made at the historic Quelltaler winery but are now made at the impressive Wolf BLASS facilities in the Barossa. The wines glow with fruit and are full and ripe with good balance and varietal expression. As might be expected for Clare Valley, Riesling and Shiraz particularly shine, as does Shiraz/Grenache/Mourvèdre blend that contains around 50 per cent Shiraz. The premium Copper Trail Shiraz is made in open fermenters from unirrigated vines with part of the wine receiving an extended maceration prior to two years' ageing in mostly French oak barrels. The Riesling, the best value of the lot, harnesses lovely Clare Valley fruit which is checked by good acidity but like all the whites should be drunk young. A Copper Trail version is more structured with better ageing potential. Reds are better with three years' ageing or more but will keep considerably longer. (PW)
○ Riesling★★ £B Copper Trail★★★ £C ○ Chardonnay★ £B ○ Semillon★ £B
● Shiraz★★ £B Copper Trail★★★ £D ● Shiraz/Grenache/Mourvèdre★★★ £C
● Cabernet/Merlot★★ £B

ASHTON HILLS Adelaide Hills A: **Cac**, Rae

Owner: Stephen George Tregarthen Road, Ashton SA 5137
Stephen George is a winemaker of considerable talent, especially given the diverse range of wines he produces to a such high standard. To be equally at home producing fine sparkling wines as cool Adelaide Hills Riesling, Pinot Noir and Chardonnay or rich powerfuls reds from the Clare Valley, as he is in forging the GALAH wines, is remarkable. The small estate-based 3.5-ha Ashton Hills is known first and foremost for two refined yet ripely fruity sparkling wines. The pale pink Salmon Brut is three-quarters Chardonnay yet its strawberry and delicate biscuity flavours owe as much to the balance of Pinot Noir. An intense Riesling has a structure that puts it with the best from Eden Valley, Clare or Adelaide Hills. Pinot Noir (occasionally made as a Reserve) shows great fruit intensity, and increasingly a texture and breadth uncommon to most Australian examples. Chardonnay, too, shows off the potential of the Adelaide Hills. A less successful Obliqua Cabernet/Merlot reflects in part how cool this region can be. Released commercially since 1998, Burra Burra Lone Star Shiraz is made from a vineyard owned and developed by Stephen's father. (PW)
○ Blanc de Blancs★★ £C ◉ Salmon Brut★★★ £C
○ Chardonnay★★★ £C ○ Riesling★★★★ £C
● Pinot Noir★★★ £D

BALNAVES   Coonawarra   www.balnaves.com.au   A: **Lib,** Vne, ACh, But, P&S

Owner: Balnaves family   Main Road, Coonawarra SA 5263
The combination of a new winemaking facility and new winemaker, Peter Bissell (ex WYNNS COONAWARRA), has given this 47-ha estate near the southern end of Coonawarra extra impetus over the past seven or eight years. Even so, The Blend (typically Merlot/Cabernet Franc/Cabernet Sauvignon) and Cabernet Sauvignon/Merlot, while both ripe, round and pleasurable drinking, are a little undistinguished. The Cabernet Sauvignon, by contrast, adds more breadth and style as well as intensity – a really good expression of Coonawarra fruit. A ripe, concentrated Shiraz is also produced in good vintages. The flagship is The Tally Reserve, a big, powerful, oaky Cabernet Sauvignon made in 1998 and 2000 that needs at least five to eight years' ageing. This being Coonawarra there isn't much white but a Chardonnay with delicious fruit and well-worked oak is amongst the better examples from the Limestone Coast. A sweetish Sparkling Cabernet is worth a try if Australian sparkling reds appeal. Doug Balnaves and son Peter also manage vineyards and make wines for others in the district. (PW)
● **The Blend**★★ £C   ● **Cabernet Sauvignon/Merlot**★★ £D
● **Cabernet Sauvignon**★★★ £D   ● **Shiraz**★★★ £D
O **Chardonnay**★★ £C   ● **Sparkling Cabernet**★★ £D

BAROSSA VALLEY ESTATE   Barossa   www.bve.com.au   A: **Cst,** WSc, N&P, Nid, P&S

Owner: BRL Hardy & local growers   Heaslip Road, Angle Vale SA 5117
Established as a co-op (rare in Australia) by around 80 local growers in 1985, BVE is now in partnership with BRL HARDY. The growers have some of the best parcels of very old Shiraz vines in the Barossa. Ebenezer Shiraz is full of berry fruit and American oak and is a good classic expression of the style. Chardonnay and Cabernet have been made in a similarly full-flavoured style but it will be interesting to see what change if any occurs under new winemaker Stuart Bourne. The pricey flagship E & E Black Pepper Shiraz is an explosively rich, powerful but balanced expression of old-vine Barossa fruit, full of preserved black fruits, prunes, licorice and tar and with great length too. Moculta is effectively a second label and includes good Grenache, Shiraz and Chardonnay, while the Spires label is used for competitive, budget-priced red and white. (PW)
● **Shiraz** Ebenezer★★★ £D E & E Black Pepper★★★★ £F
● **Cabernet Sauvignon/Merlot** Ebenezer★★ £C
O **Chardonnay** Ebenezer★ £C

BARRATT WINES   Adelaide Hills   A: **Gun**

Owner: Lindsay & Carolyn Barratt   Collins Road, Summertown SA 5141
One of the Adelaide Hills' small gems directed by Lindsay Barratt. The Barratts now have their own winemaking facility at Lobethal and from just 8.9 ha in two different vineyards (Uley and Bonython) they highlight the region's affinity for Pinot Noir and Chardonnay. Since 2001 Pinot Noir production has been divided between a single-vineyard Bonython version and a superior Reserve. All the grapes are hand-picked and a portion of the fruit is fermented as whole bunches, around 40 per cent in the case of the Reserve. Both the latter and the Chardonnay are made by Jeffrey GROSSET. While the wines are quite powerful, they avoid being heavy – the alcohol being kept in check by the richly textured fruit. Chardonnay will keep for at least five years, Reserve Pinot even longer. A new Merlot (from 2001) is, like the Pinots, fermented in open fermenters and aged in French oak (part of it new). 2002 was the first vintage of an unwooded Sauvignon and the first from which the Pinots have been bottled unfiltered. (PW)
● **Pinot Noir** Bonython★★ £C Reserve★★★ £D
O **Chardonnay**★★★ £D

JIM BARRY Clare Valley www.jimbarry.com   A: **Neg**, Cpp, DWS, Tan, ACh, Hrd, P&S, Sel

Owner: Barry family   Craigs Hill Road, Clare SA 5453

From a large number of some of Clare's best sites Mark Barry continues to build on what his father made famous over four decades, but whether the wines will now show more individuality or refinement remains to be seen. Reds are the mainstay: deep, concentrated if relatively unrefined Shiraz, Cabernet Sauvignon and Cabernet Sauvignon/Malbec under the McRae Wood label. However, it is for The Armagh that Jim Barry is best known. Considered one of the region's super-reds, it is an uncompromisingly big, thick, extracted and oaky Shiraz with a long track record dating back to 1985. It is made from very old, unirrigated vines and nearly always achieves the balance that some mega-Shirazes lack but must be kept for a minimum of a decade. Riesling is sourced from the Florita vineyard (in Watervale), first made famous by Leo Buring. Production is a substantial 60,000 cases, though much of that is accounted for by more ordinary reds and whites. (PW)

- **Shiraz** The Armagh★★★★ £F McCrae Wood★★ £C
- **Cabernet Sauvignon**★ £C McCrae Wood★★★ £C
- **Cabernet/Malbec** McCrae Wood★★ £C **O Riesling**★★ £B

WOLF BLASS Barossa Valley www.wolfblass.com.au   A: **BBI**, AAA

Owner: Beringer Blass   PO Box 396, Nurioopta SA 5355

The Wolf Blass label remains an integral part of the giant BERINGER BLASS wine portfolio but much of the production of one of the great branded successes of Australian wine has for some time seemed to draw little inspiration from the personality and energy of the man himself. Of the more affordable ranges, Shiraz, Cabernet or blends of the two under the various red, yellow and Eaglehawk façades have been pretty uninspiring and, if showing some very recent improvement, they haven't been of the standard they were a decade or more ago. Whites are much improved though there is still better value to be had from elsewhere in Australia or further afield. At a higher price point, Presidents Selection wines offer a lot of upfront fruit and oak and adequate depth and structure. None of these labels however, should be confused with the wines near the top of the hierarchy where quality is much higher and the wines' origins are more discernible. Platinum Label Shiraz and Cabernet are based on single vineyards and aged in French oak, and finally deliver on depth, structure and balance, but platinum is also required to buy them. The wines with perhaps the most convincing price/quality ratio are the newish Gold Label range (an extension from an existing good-quality Gold Label Riesling). All (a vintage-dated sparkling Pinot Noir/Chardonnay excepted) are region-specific and do portray something of their origins. Whether regional sources will change from year to year remains to be seen but currently Pinot Noir, Chardonnay, Cabernet Sauvignon/Cabernet Franc and Shiraz/Viognier all come from the Adelaide Hills, while a straight Barossa Shiraz is also made. Lastly, the richly textured Black Label Cabernet Sauvignon/Shiraz (subjected to a delayed release) is consistently fine, though again at a price. (PW)

- **Cabernet Sauvignon/Shiraz** Black Label★★★★ £F
- **Cabernet Sauvignon/Cabernet Franc** Gold Label Adelaide Hills★★★ £C
- **Cabernet Sauvignon** Presidents Selection★★ £C ● **Shiraz** Presidents Selection★★ £C
- **Shiraz/Viognier** Gold Label Adelaide Hills★★★ £C **O Riesling** Gold Label Eden/Clare Valleys★★ £B
- **O Chardonnay** Presidents Selection★ £B Gold Label Adelaide Hills★★ £C

BLEASDALE Langhorne Creek www.bleasdale.com.au   A: **JEF**, Odd, Nid, FWC

Owner: Potts family   Wellington Road, Langhorne Creek SA 5255

Winemaker Michael Potts is fifth generation, making wines in a National Trust-classified winery and still utilising a lever press constructed in the 19th century. His family's vineyards are flooded annually by the Bremer River. All the wines show an accentuated varietal character and lots of flavour intensity. These include punchy Verdelho with spiced preserved citrus character, an intense peppery Malbec, and a stylish Bremerview Shiraz. While most still want for a little more definition and structure this is not the case with

Frank Potts, a savoury, cedary Cabernet Sauvignon-based blend that includes Malbec and Petit Verdot (78/13/9 in 2002), nor with a profound, complex Generations Shiraz (from a parcel of old vines) that is perhaps the essence of Langhorne Creek with its earth, eucalypt, plum and berry character. Petrel Reserve is another premium Shiraz, first produced in 1999. Sweet, berryish Sparkling Shiraz lacks poise but has smooth tannins. (PW)

● **Shiraz** Bremerview★★★ £B Generations★★★★ £D
● **Frank Potts**★★★ £C ● **Cabernet Sauvignon** Mulberry Tree★★ £B
● **Shiraz/Cabernet**★★ £B ● **Malbec**★★ £B
● **Sparkling Shiraz**★★ £B ○ **Verdelho**★★ £B

BOWEN ESTATE   Coonawarra   A: **AWA**, Tan, NYg, P&S

Owner: Doug & Joy Bowen   Riddoch Highway, Coonawarra SA 5263
Doug Bowen's smallish 33-ha estate continues to maintain a relatively low profile among the Coonawarra giants, though the wines are widely exported. The reds are of consistently high quality: deep, fleshy and textured with very ripe flavours and a certain idiosyncratic style. The grapes are picked very late and a good dose of oak ensures the wines have a sweet succulence particularly in the warmer years. Perhaps surprisingly for Coonawarra, Shiraz is even better than the Cabernet Sauvignon. The Blend is composed of Cabernet Sauvignon, Merlot and Cabernet Franc. A ripe and creamy Chardonnay is also made while Ampelon is a new single-vineyard Shiraz. (PW)

● **Shiraz**★★★★ £C ● **Cabernet Sauvignon**★★★ £C ● The Blend★★★ £C
○ **Chardonnay**★ £B

GRANT BURGE   Barossa Valley   www.grantburgewines.com.au   A: **Ssg**, Vne, ACh, Res, P&S

Owner: Grant Burge   Jacobs Creek, Tanunda SA 5352
Grant Burge has an impressive resource of 200 ha from which to make top Barossa wines. Nearly all the varietals are now prefixed with a vineyard name, though they may sound more like fantasy names. All are made in the recently reacquired old Krondorf winery. Shiraz is naturally the strongest hand, starting with a sweet-fruited Miamba, progressing to a fuller, richer, oaky but characterful Filsell and, from the same vineyard, Meschach, a pricey but powerful, super-stylish classic American-oaked Barossa Shiraz from 80-year-old vines that is more than a cut above the rest. The Cabernet equivalent to Meschach is Shadrach. a deep, rich and intense red, immersed in heather and blackcurrant and aged in French oak. Some early efforts of both wines lacked balance but this is not true of recent releases. Holy Trinity, composed of Grenache, Shiraz and Mourvèdre (40/40/20), mercifully is more modestly priced and is developing into an increasingly complex red; new French oak and an extended maceration on the skins are now employed to good effect. Two whites are oaky and flavoursome, a Summers Chardonnay surpassed by Zerk Semillon. Other good whites include Thorn Riesling, Kraft Sauvignon and late-picked Lily Farm Muscat. Barossa Vines is a decent second label for varietal Shiraz, Semillon and Chardonnay. Sparkling and fortified wines are also made. (PW)

● **Shiraz** Miamba Barossa★★ £B Filsell Barossa★★★ £C Meschach★★★★★ £F
● **Cabernet Sauvignon** Cameron Vale★★ £C Shadrach★★★★ £F
● **Merlot** Hillcot Barossa★ £C ● Holy Trinity★★★ £D
○ **Chardonnay** Summers Eden Valley★ £B ○ **Semillon** Zerk★★ £B ○ **Riesling** Thorn★ £B

BURGE FAMILY   Barossa Valley   www.burgefamily.com.au   A: **NYg**, Fal, UnC

Owner: Rick Burge   Barossa Valley Way, Lyndoch SA 5351
Rick Burge makes classic oak-lined, rich, lush, sweet-fruited Barossa reds. The wines have lots of depth, extract and intensity as well as the varietal expression typical of each grape variety as they perform in the Barossa. The wines have highish alcohol (around 14.5 for most of the reds) but are well balanced, only occasionally showing an excess of oak. Two wines in particular stand out. Olive Hill, roughly equal

proportions of Shiraz, Grenache and Mourvèdre (41/31/28 in 2001), is more complete and characterful than The Renoux, which combines Shiraz with Cabernet Sauvignon and Merlot (45/38/17 in 2001). Better still is Draycott Shiraz, which has lovely depth and style with a lingering, sweet, fruit-intense finish. Rick Burge's Garnacha, mostly old-vine Grenache but also including a little Shiraz and Mourvèdre, has a sweet crushed berry fruit depth but can struggle to balance the high alcohol. Semillon has plenty of rich Barossa citrus and herb character though is not for long keeping. New from the 2002 vintage is G3, a premium blend of Grenache, Shiraz and Mourvèdre. Also made are Olive Hill Riesling and two inexpensive blended reds, Clochemerle and 'A Nice Red'. (PW)

● **Shiraz** Draycott★★★★ £D   ● **Shiraz/Merlot/Cabernet Sauvignon** The Renoux★★ £C
● **Shiraz/Grenache/Mourvèdre** Olive Hill★★★ £D   ● **Grenache** Garnacha★★ £D
O **Semillon** Olive Hill★★ £C

CASCABEL   McLaren Vale   A: **Bib**, HoM, P&S

Owner: Duncan Ferguson & Susana Fernandez,   Rogers Road, Willunga SA 5172
This is still a very young operation, having only made wines since the late 1990s, yet this experienced couple seem to have both the know-how and a clear idea of the sort of wines they wish to fashion. All the wines are characterised by bright, pure fruit and definite restraint in terms of alcohol and oak. Round, soft and agreeable, they are not without substance and are always fruit-rich on the finish. Only relatively small quantities are made of each wine, particularly the lime-streaked Riesling. 'Grenache et al' includes Shiraz and Mourvèdre. These are wines to drink relatively young rather than for long keeping. (PW)

O **Riesling** Eden Valley★★ £B
● **Shiraz** Fleurieu Peninsula★★★ £C   ● **Grenache et al**★★ £C

CHAIN OF PONDS   Adelaide Hills   www.chainofpondswines.com.au   A: **Bib**

Owner: Caj & Genny Amadio   Main Adelaide Road, Gumeracha SA 5233
Established only in 1993 this is a relatively small producer but a sizeable grower (the majority of the grapes are still sold off to PENFOLDS). The family vineyard, Kersbrook, was recently joined by the adjacent Gumeracha plot to give a total of 140 ha. There is an expanding range of now exotically named wines: Zar Brooks, the man behind D'ARENBERG's roll-call of fantasy names, has repeated the trick upon his recent arrival here. Quality has always been high, particularly for Chardonnay and the Amadeus Cabernet; the latter is remarkably profound and tightly furled when young, revealing a deep fruit core with at least five years' ageing. From Kangaroo Island, the Florance Vineyard Cabernets is a blend of the two Cabernets and a little Merlot, while another vineyard has provided Barque Mars Shiraz since 1999. This can be compared with Adelaide Hills Shirazes, Ledge and Graves Gate, the latter sourced from McLaren Vale in 1999 due to frost in Adelaide Hills. The extensive range also includes an unwooded Chardonnay, Nether Hill, and Sauvignon Blanc, Black Thursday. The Novello label includes red, white and rosé, each with an Italian component. Bianco is Semillon/Pinot Grigio, Rosso (the rosé) Sangiovese/Grenache, while Nero is a Barbera/Grenache/Sangiovese blend. (PW)

● **Cabernet Sauvignon** Amadeus★★★ £C
● **Shiraz** Grave's Gate★★ £C Ledge★★ £C
● **Sangiovese** Jupiter's Blood★ £C   ● **Pinot Noir** Jerusalem★ £C
O **Chardonnay** Corkscrew Road★★ £C Morning Star★★★ £D
O **Riesling** Purple Patch★ £B   O **Semillon** Square Cut★★ £B

CHAPEL HILL   McLaren Vale   www.chapelhillwine.com.au   A: **AWA**, ACh, Fsp

Owner: Thomas Schmidheiny (Holcim)   Chapel Hill Road, McLaren Vale SA 5171
Under consultant winemaker Pam Dunsford, Chapel Hill, now Swiss-owned, has built a solid reputation for consistent Cabernet and Shiraz. Quantity (60,000 cases) may be rising but prices are not excessive for wines based on high-quality fruit from 44 ha of McLaren Vale vineyards. The Shiraz is full, concentrated,

and oaky after almost two years in French and American oak (50 per cent of it new). In the same mould and subject to a similar oaking regime is The Vicar, a blend of Cabernet and Shiraz in roughly equal proportions. Some of the Cabernet for both this and a varietal Cabernet Sauvignon comes from Coonawarra, while the Reserve Chardonnay includes a Padthaway component too. An unwooded Chardonnay is simple and less appealing than a tasty Verdelho. (PW)

● Shiraz★★ £C ● The Vicar★★ £D ● Cabernet Sauvignon★★ £B
O Chardonnay Reserve★★ £B O Verdelho★ £B

M CHAPOUTIER AUSTRALIA Mount Benson www.chapoutier.com A: N&P

Owner: Chapoutier Limestone Coast Road, Mount Benson via Robe SA5276
The prestigious Rhône Valley producer CHAPOUTIER has made a sizeable financial commitment to Australia, including developing this 50-ha outpost at Mount Benson. Much of it is being planted to Shiraz as might be expected but there is also a significant percentage of Cabernet Sauvignon and some Marsanne, Viognier and Sauvignon Blanc. Viticultural practices model those in the Rhône and progress has been made towards a fully biodynamic regime. Already the reds show a fine fruit intensity and structure and are improving with each successive vintage, adding more refinement and depth. It is to be expected that Chapoutier will succeed in maximising the potential of its new sites and provide a fascinating contrast to Rhône wines in the future. (PW)

● Shiraz Mount Benson★★★ £C ● Cabernet Sauvignon Mount Benson★★ £C

CHARLES CIMICKY Barossa Valley A: Lwt, CeB, FFW

Owner: Charles Cimicky Gomersal Road, Lyndoch SA 5351
Cimicky is a class act in the Barossa, producing deep, harmonious reds with well-integrated oak from l ow-yielding, dry-farmed vines. Shiraz, Merlot and (under the Daylight Chamber label) Grenache and Grenache/Shiraz all show splendid fruit allied to sleek proportions and a certain refinement. French oak is favoured over the usually more common American oak. Red Blend is Cabernet Sauvignon-based but with a significant percentage of Merlot and Cabernet Franc. Whites, including Sauvignon Blanc and Chardonnay, are less likely to be encountered outside Australia. Prices are still reasonable. (PW)

● Shiraz Signature★★★ £C ● Red Blend★★★ £C ● Grenache Daylight Chamber★★★ £C
● Grenache/Shiraz Daylight Chamber★★★ £C
● Merlot★★★ £C O Sauvignon Blanc★★ £B

CLARENDON HILLS McLaren Vale A: J&B, F&R, N&P, Las, Hrd

Owner: Roman Bratasiuk Brookmans Road, Blewitt Springs SA 5171
If you've drunk Australis then either you or your friends are not short of money. Bratasiuk's unfiltered and unfined, ripe, extracted reds, aged in French oak, are subjected to a long *cuvaison* and exhibit a depth and dimension that most Australian reds don't even approach. Some early vintages had questionable balance and marginal levels of volatility but all is being mastered and refined as the range expands and gains better definition through the use of vineyard or sub-regional names. Bratasiuk, though he's not the first to do so, is providing an alternative to the brand-name-only marketeers who reveal precious little about their sources (likewise yields), even at a premium level. Reds, particularly Shiraz and Grenache are powerful, broadly structured as well as very concentrated, marvellously complex and long in the best bottlings. Intense, muscular and ageworthy Chardonnay and Semillon have also been made (from Hickinbotham Vineyard) but were less successful. Attempting to make Pinot Noir from the same vineyard might seem more extraordinary yet reasonable if brawny examples were produced. All the names refer to a specific vineyard or vineyards. (PW)

● Shiraz Australis✪✪✪✪ £H Piggot Range★★★★★ £G
● Shiraz Brookman★★★★ £F Hickinbotham★★★★ £F Liandra★★★ £F Moritz★★★ £F
● Grenache Romas★★★★★ £F Blewitt Springs★★★★ £E Clarendon★★★★ £E Kangarilla★★★ £E

● **Cabernet Sauvignon** Hickinbotham★★★★ £E Brookman★★★ £E Sandown★★★ £E
● **Merlot** Hickinbotham★★ £E Brookman★★ £E

CORIOLE McLaren Vale   A: **Sec**, Tan, ACh, Res, P&S

Owner: Lloyd family Chaffeys Road, McLaren Vale SA 5171

Coriole has been known for its intense Shiraz almost since its inception in 1967, having inherited some already old vines and planted new ones which now have a few years behind them too. The wine is consistently richly textured with deep, ripe fruit and has been particularly good in recent vintages. Lloyd Reserve Shiraz, made only in very small quantities, is the premium version, with a long-established track record and more structure and oak than the regular version. The powerful, minty Mary Kathleen is an equivalent premium red from Cabernet Sauvignon, Merlot and a little Cabernet Franc, but has a tendency to be excessively structured. Both require much patience. Coriole is also known for its Sangiovese. Lloyd Sangiovese/Cabernet (three-quarters Sangiovese with Cabernet Sauvignon and Merlot) is in the mould of certain Super-Tuscans but also wants for better balance, while a regular version is attractively fruity if lacking the qualities of good Italian examples. Redstone is an appealing blend based on Shiraz but usually including Grenache, Merlot and Cabernet Sauvignon. The rich, concentrated Semillon with both citrus and tropical flavours is easily the best of the whites but a decent fruity Australian Chenin Blanc is also made. (PW)
● **Shiraz**★★★ £C Lloyd Reserve★★★★ £E ● **Sangiovese/Cabernet** Lloyd★★ £C
● **Mary Kathleen**★★★ £D O **Semillon** Lalla Rookh★★ £B

CRABTREE Clare Valley

Owner: Robert & Elizabeth Crabtree North Terrace, Watervale SA 5452

Crabtree of Watervale is a small Clare operation with its own vineyards. The experienced Robert Crabtree produces wines that show good structure and balance without being overdone and give at least a subtle indication of their Watervale origins, though there is a diversity of soils. A tight, minerally but scented Riesling has good potential, while Semillon is full, broad and stylish. Grenache displays an enticing fruit character whether as a red or in an off-dry rosé version and Shiraz has good intensity and complexity. All the wines can be drunk young and the Grenache Rosé certainly needs to be. However, whites will keep and improve and although reds could be drunk from just three to five years' they seem certain to age for twice as long. (PW)
O **Riesling**★★★ £C O **Semillon**★★ £C
● **Shiraz** Picnic Hill★★★ £C ● **Cabernet Sauvignon** Windmill★★ £C ● **Grenache**★★ £C

D'ARENBERG McLaren Vale www.darenberg.com.au   A: **Bib**, Odd, WSc, NYg, Hrd, P&S

Owner: Osborn family Osborn Road, McLaren Vale SA 5171

Jazzed up in recent years, this is a much trumpeted and sizeable producer with a seemingly ever-expanding range totalling 150,000 cases per year. Nearly all the wines are good but only a handful are really exciting; some are a little overhyped. The myriad exotic names don't make this an easy range to negotiate but they surely help with sales. The best reds have exuberant fruit and highish alcohol levels (and plenty of oak to help them on their way), making for enjoyable youthful drinking, but with enough structure to stand a bit of age. The flagship is the Dead Arm Shiraz, with super fruit, excellent concentration and tannins, oak and alcohol all in balance; it needs five years' age or more. Footbolt is very easy to appreciate but faces stiff competition as South Australia has an abundance of fine Shiraz at this level, some with better texture and more depth. The powerful Ironstone Pressings can struggle for balance, while intense sweet-fruited Custodian Grenache often shows some extraordinary flavours if at the cost of elegance and harmony. Varietal Mourvèdre seems more effortless with better depth and structure. Whites, from grapes only planted in 1995, are fruit-driven if sometimes a little coarse and lack the structure for long keeping. Riesling, Semillon and Gewürztraminer have been made in a rich late-harvested style with some success. The Stump Jump red and white are forward, fruity gluggers. New are Lucky Lizard Chardonnay and Feral Fox Pinot

Noir. A sparkling Chambourcin called Peppermint Paddock and a fortified Shiraz are also made. (PW)

O **Sauvignon** Broken Fishplate★ £B O **Riesling** Dry Dam★ £B Noble★★★ £D
O **Chardonnay** Olive Grove★ £B Other Side★★ £C O **Roussanne** Money Spider★★ £B
O **Viognier** Last Ditch★★ £B O **Marsanne/Viognier** Hermit Crab★ £B
● **Mourvèdre** Twenty-Eight Road★★★ £C ● **Grenache** Custodian★★ £B
● **Grenache/Shiraz/Mourvèdre** Ironstone Pressings★★ £D
● **Shiraz/Grenache** D'Arry's Original★★ £B
● **Shiraz** Footbolt★★ £B Dead Arm★★★★ £D ● **Shiraz/Viognier** Laughing Magpie★★ £C
● **Cabernet Sauvignon** High Trellis★ £B Coppermine Road★★★ £D

DUTSCHKE Barossa Valley www.dutschkewines.com A: C&R, UnC

Owner: Dutschke & Semmler Lot 1, God's Hill Road, Lyndoch SA 5351
Shiraz is the thrust of this operation for wines made by Wayne Dutschke from vines belonging to his uncle, Ken Semmler. St Jakobi, with an almost coconutty American-oak influence (60 per cent), displays a deep fruit succulence and plenty of extract. Although oaky it has depth and character and deserves to be judged with five years' bottle age or more. By contrast, Oscar Semmler, the top *cuvée*, is aged in 100 per cent French oak. It is marvellously profound with terrific potential if cellared for at least five to eight years. While not cheap, quality is commensurate with price. Willowbend (a second label) Chardonnay and Shiraz/Merlot/Cabernet are enthusiastically consumed locally. Some fortified wines are also made to a high standard. (PW)

● **Shiraz** St Jakobi★★★ £D Oscar Semmler★★★★ £E

EDWARDS & CHAFFEY McLaren Vale www.edwardsandchaffey.com.au A: ScE

Owner: Southcorp Chaffeys Road, Mclaren Vale SA 5171
One of the many SOUTHCORP brands, this winery, previously known as Seaview, is now named after its original partners. While fizz is very much the order of the day, from inexpensive non-vintage Seaview Brut and Rosé to higher-quality Edwards & Chaffey sparkling wine, between 1992 and 1998 some very good Edwards & Chaffey Section 353 table wines were also made. Chardonnay, Shiraz and Cabernet Sauvignon all showed classic vibrant ripe McLaren Vale fruit (which once set the humbler Seaview varietals apart from competitors) and well-integrated French oak. Production is now limited to sparkling wine only but there is both good quality and value in an attractive, biscuity Seaview Pinot Chardonnay Brut and the Edwards & Chaffey Section 353 Pinot Chardonnay (predominantly Pinot Noir drawn from cool grape-growing regions) which delivers a rich, leesy complexity and ripe powerful fruit. (PW)

O **Pinot Chardonnay** Edwards & Chaffey Section 353★★★ £C Seaview★★ £B
O **Blanc de Blancs** Seaview★ £B

ELDERTON Barossa Valley www.eldertonwines.com.au A: **Fie, BBR**, F&R, Nid, The, P&S

Owner: Lorraine Ashmead 3–5 Tanunda Road, Nuriootpa SA 5355
An unashamedly oaky, full-throttle style has earned this winery a devoted following. The wines are not to everyone's taste but the best examples have a rich fruit core as they are based on old-vine Barossa Valley fruit. The estate is small in Australian terms with less than 30 ha of vineyards. American oak is favoured, the oak once found in nearly all South Australian wineries, which adds intense vanilla, spice, even coconut flavours to the wines. The most successful and sought-after wine is the Command Shiraz which epitomises the high-alcohol, oaky, richly extracted and lusciously fruity style. Late 1990s vintages show better harmony than earlier examples. Positioned at the same level is a single-vineyard Cabernet Sauvignon, Ashmead; here the rich fruit has been meshed with the more amenable French oak. Merlot too is aged in French oak. As well as estate Shiraz and Cabernet Sauvignon, a cheaper Friends version of each is also made from bought-in fruit. CSM is not a Rhône blend but what is now an unusual blend of Cabernet Sauvignon, Shiraz and Merlot. Riesling and Chardonnay are also made and offer plenty of upfront flavour if not much else and are best drunk with just a couple of years' age. An intensely flavoured dessert wine, Botrytis Semillon (or

Golden Semillon), is made from Riverina fruit, while Tantalus Shiraz/Cabernet is a flavoursome budget red from wider origins. (PW)

● **Shiraz★** £C Command★★★ £E ● CSM★★ £D
● **Cabernet Sauvignon★** £C Ashmead Single Vineyard★★ £E ● **Merlot★** £C

RALPH FOWLER Mount Benson   A: **HHB**, P&S, Han

Owner: Ralph & Deborah Fowler   Lot 101, Limestone Coast Road, Mount Benson SA 5275
This is a newish operation based in the up-and-coming coastal area of Mount Benson. The 40 ha of estate vineyards include Cabernet Sauvignon, Shiraz and Viognier. Ralph Fowler (of diverse Australian winemaking experience) currently makes both Shiraz and Cabernet Sauvignon from a blend of Mount Benson and Coonawarra fruit. Both reds show good fleshy texture, depth and definition; the Cabernet had a cooler but not excessive minty, herbal component in 1998 and 99. Fowler has also been recruited to an important new venture undertaken by Kreglinger Australia, the major shareholder in PIPERS BROOK. CHAPOUTIER notwithstanding, this promises to be one of the leading protagonists in Mt Benson over the coming decade. Sauvignon Blanc and Viognier are new. (PW)

● **Shiraz** Limestone Coast★★★ £D
● **Cabernet Sauvignon** Limestone Coast★★★ £D

FOX CREEK McLaren Vale www.foxcreekwines.com.au   A: **NYg**, UnC, F&R, N&P, P&S

Owner: J&H Watts, J&L Roberts, P Watts   Malpas Road, Willunga SA 5172
This young but already much acclaimed McLaren Vale operation is based on vineyards established by the Watt family in 1985. Since 1995 Fox Creek has made rich, ripe and succulent reds with a measure of (mostly) American oak, sometimes lacking finesse and real style. The first wines were made by Sparky Marquis of HENRYS DRIVE but are now made by Dan Hills and Tony Walker. Reserve Shiraz is the leading red and more than any other displays the potency and character of McLaren Vale. Though the varieties are different, there is also classic expression in a more forward but ripe and stylish JSM Shiraz/Cabernet Franc (and a little Cabernet Sauvignon). Reserve Cabernet is rich and earthy with a firm finish. Other reds are less exciting. Merlot and a new Cabernet/Merlot, Duet, show adequate balance and ripeness but lack style and definition. Vixen is a well-balanced if not first-division example of a sparkling Shiraz-based red (but includes both Cabernets). The pick of the whites is a Verdelho with an intense, flavoursome varietal character. Sauvignon Blanc and Semillon/Sauvignon Blanc have delicious ripe tropical fruit and citrus flavours but need to be drunk very young. (PW)

● **Shiraz** Reserve★★★★ £E Short Row★★ £D
● **Shiraz/Cabernet Franc** JSM★★★ £C ● **Sparkling Shiraz/Cabernet Franc** Vixen★★ £C
● **Cabernet Sauvignon** Reserve★★ £D ● **Merlot** Reserve★ £D
○ **Chardonnay★** £B ○ **Verdelho★★** £B ○ **Semillon/Sauvignon Blanc★** £B

GREENOCK CREEK Barossa Valley   A: **THt**, C&B, Bal, NYg, F&M, Hrd, P&S

Owner: Michael & Annabelle Waugh   Radford Road, Seppeltsfield SA 5360
The aim here is for very low yields from unirrigated plots. The grapes are harvested very late, and the wines reveal unusual, almost exotic, ripe flavours and a preserved fruits character. The alcohol levels are high but the wines are balanced. For Shiraz, the Apricot Block is perhaps the most promising vineyard but is quite young; shortcomings in initial releases will be overcome with a little more age. By contrast Creek Block is planted with very old vines, some 80 years old, but the wines are slightly coarse, even jammy, though they don't lack for character. The best wine (at least of those without a completely silly price) is the Seven Acre Shiraz. It has a particularly pronounced preserved fruits profile and reveals real power and intensity on the palate. Cornerstone Grenache (from old vines) and Cabernet Sauvignon usually also show what is possible from the best unirrigated vines. All the wines are expensive due to very low yields, the resultant meagre quantities and their cult status. Also made in tiny quantities but sold for astronomical prices are Roennfeldt

Road Cabernet Sauvignon and Shiraz. New from 2000 is Alice's Block Shiraz. (PW)

● **Shiraz** Seven Acre★★★★ £F Creek Block★★★ £F Apricot Block★★★ £E
● **Grenache** Cornerstone★★★ £E   ● **Cabernet Sauvignon**★★★ £E

GROSSET   Clare Valley   www.grosset.com.au   A: **MSd**, Bal, BBR, Mar, Tur, WSc, P&S

Owner: Jeffrey Grosset   King Street, Auburn SA 5451
Jeffrey Grosset is an Australian superstar and deserves to be as well-known as the country's many sporting greats (in some circles he is). Outstanding Riesling, Chardonnay and Gaia Bordeaux blend all show pristine fruit, wonderful symmetry and excellent concentration and have proven ageability. There are two Rieslings: the fine, intense and limey Polish Hill is made in greater quantity though there is still not much of it; Watervale is fuller and broader. Like the Rieslings and Chardonnay, a delicious Semillon/Sauvignon blend is one of the best Australian examples of its type. The compelling Gaia impresses for its style, complexity and depth; it is no wimp but makes a stark contrast to some of the overoaked, alcoholic monsters made by others. Grosset makes Pinot Noir for the BARRATTs but also produces a little of his own from the same locality in the Adelaide Hills. Given the purity and sheer style of the wines it is perhaps not surprising that Grosset has striven to find the best possible closure for his wines. His choice is Stelvin cap for all but a portion of his production of Gaia. All the wines are made in relatively small quantities and are reasonably priced. (PW)

● **Gaia**★★★★ £E   ● **Pinot Noir**★★★ £E
○ **Riesling** Polish Hill★★★★ £C Watervale★★★★ £C
○ **Chardonnay** Piccadilly★★★★ £D ○ **Semillon/Sauvignon Blanc**★★★ £C

HAMILTON   McLaren Vale   www.hamiltonwines.com   A: **Eno**

Owner: Hamilton Wine Group   Main Road, Willunga SA 5172
Richard Hamilton's McLaren Vale operation shouldn't be confused with Hugh Hamilton or the recently revived HAMILTON'S EWELL in the Barossa, though the extensive family connections run back to one of South Australia's first winemakers. His winemaking team produces some intense, characterful McLaren Vale wines, even if in some years they have lacked balance. Centurion 100-Year-Old Vines Shiraz, Gumpr's Block Shiraz and Burton's Vineyard Old Bush Vine Grenache/Shiraz show good depth and weight, very ripe fruit and often a measure of mint, eucalyptus and gamey notes. Marion's Vineyard Grenache/Shiraz is, like PENFOLDS' Magill, unusual in being a vineyard in the suburbs of Adelaide and shares Magill's flavour intensity. Other wines include Hut Block Cabernets, which has a percentage of Merlot and Cabernet Franc but a tendency to slightly underripe tannins, and Merlot, both a Lot 148 version and the better, French-oaked Reserve Egremont made in part from Coonawarra fruit. Of the whites, the Signature Chardonnay accentuates ripe melony flavours and oak but not at the expense of balance, while Slate Quarry Riesling is also made, somewhat surprisingly, from local McLaren Vale fruit. The Hamilton Wine Group also own LECONFIELD. (PW)

● **Shiraz** Centurion 100 Year Old Vines★★★ £D Gumpr's Block★★ £C
● **Grenache/Shiraz** Burton's Vineyard★★★ £C Marion Vineyard★★ £C
○ **Chardonnay** Signature★★ £B

HAMILTON'S EWELL   Barossa Valley   www.hamiltonewell.com.au   A: **Str**, FWC, Nid, NYg

Owner: Mark & Deborah Hamilton   Siegersdorf Vineyard, Barossa Valley Way, Nuriootpa SA 5352
Richard Hamilton planted South Australia's first commercial vineyard in 1838. Though the original family business was lost in 1979, since 1991 sixth-generation Mark Hamilton has bought back the Hamilton's Ewell name as well as acquiring vineyards, mostly in the Barossa and Eden Valleys, and more recently in Wrattonbully. Only part of the production is retained for an increasingly good range of wines. There is a definite style to the wines and the reds in particular impress for their breadth, depth and character. All show excellent flavour intensity and good ageing potential. As well the bold Limestone Quarry Chardonnay a

Shiraz and Cabernet Sauvignon are also made from Wrattonbully fruit. Other wines include Stonegarden Riesling from Eden Valley fruit and a very small amount of Fuller's Barn Shiraz from the best fruit of this Barossa vineyard. Stuart River wines come from Riverland fruit. (PW)

● **Shiraz** Railway Barossa Valley★★★ £C   ● **Cabernet Sauvignon** Ewell Barossa Valley★★★ £C
● **Grenache/Shiraz** Stonegarden Barossa Valley★★★ £B   O **Chardonnay** Limestone Quarry★★ £C

HARDY WINE COMPANY   www.hardywines.com.au

This is the new name for the BRL Hardy group of mostly Australian wineries and brands which now forms a part of Constellation Wines following the merger with the North American multinational, Constellation Brands. Leading wineries/brands include HARDYS, LEASINGHAM, Renmano, REYNELL, STONEHAVEN and half of BAROSSA VALLEY ESTATE in South Australia; HOUGHTON and Moondah Brook in Western Australia; YARRA BURN in Victoria and Bay of Fires in Tasmania; and Kamberra in the Canberra District (southern New South Wales). Banrock Station, also in South Australia, produces large volumes of decent everyday wines as well as well as developing and maintaining a wetlands site on the Murray River. The Starvedog Lane wines are produced in conjuction with THE LANE. Outside Australia, Domaine de la Baume in Languedoc-Roussillon in France and NOBILO in New Zealand also form part of the group. As well as high-quality wines at mid-level and premium prices, the Hardy group has over recent years had the best record of the big Australians at maintaining quality in its least expensive, most ubiquitous brands. (PW)

HARDYS   McLaren Vale   www.hardys.com.au   A: Cst, Vne, P&S, N&P

Owner: Hardy Wine Company   Reynell Road, Reynella SA 5161

Hardys is one of the great names of Australian wine even if the premium Hardys wines are marginally less well-known than those of some of their rivals. The Eileen Hardy label is reserved for an outstanding Shiraz and a rich, powerful if occasionally slightly over-oaked Chardonnay. Both are sourced from the company's best vineyards, which can extend as far as Tasmania for the Chardonnay and Western Australia for the Shiraz. Brawny, extracted Thomas Hardy Cabernet, made since 1989, is now sourced entirely from Coonawarra. It has terrific depth and can evolve into an equally impressive, if less consistent red. Without the cult status of these flagship wines, the Tintara Limited Release Shiraz and Grenache are full, concentrated and more affordable, if difficult to obtain outside Australia. The Shiraz is open-fermented and basket-pressed like the Eileen Hardy and offers rich succulent fruit. Tintara Cellars Shiraz, Cabernet and Chardonnay are more modest. Hardys sparkling wines, however, show an extra degree of finesse and intensity over most Australian sparklers, as seen in the top two examples, the vintage-dated Sir James Vintage and premium Arras, both Tasmania and Yarra Valley-sourced Pinot Noir/Chardonnay blends. Of the cheaper, everyday brands Nottage Hill varietals are slightly more expensive than the Stamps of Australia dual-variety blends, but offer more than the price differential suggests. The special release of 2001 Oomoo McLaren Vale Shiraz, to celebrate Hardys' 150th anniversary in 2003, revives a 19th-century label. (PW)

● **Shiraz** Eileen Hardy★★★★★ £F   ● **Cabernet Sauvignon** Thomas Hardy★★★★ £F
● **Shiraz** Tintara Limited Release★★★ £C   ● **Grenache** Tintara Limited Release★★★ £C
O **Chardonnay** Eileen Hardy★★★ £C

HASELGROVE   McLaren Vale   www.haselgrove.com.au

Owner: BankWest   Sand Road, McLaren Vale SA 5171

Thus far, recurring changes of ownership haven't prevented this historic McLaren Vale operation from maintaining its reputation for full and powerful reds. Winemaking is now overseen by the very experienced Adrian Lockhart who has the opportunity to use good-quality McLaren Vale fruit (despite the loss of some prime vineyards along the way) to reproduce the quality of the concentrated, chewy, fleshy reds established by Nick Haselgrove (of the original family owners). As the operation rapidly expanded through the late 1990s, Haselgrove produced ever better reds, especially 'H' series Cabernet Sauvignon and Shiraz – both with good ageing potential. Cabernet now comes from Wrattonbully and is distinguished by a pure, intense blackcurrant fruit depth. 'H' series whites, Chardonnay and Viognier, are now sourced from the Adelaide Hills. 2003 'H' Chardonnay is quite oak-influenced but with real zest, fine fruit and definition. Prices are more reasonable than previously. Also made are McLaren Vale-sourced Cabernet, Shiraz and Chardonnay. New and positioned as a flagship red is Limelight Shiraz from McLaren Vale vineyards. Inexpensive Sovereign reds and whites are from more diverse fruit sources. (PW)

● **Cabernet Sauvignon** 'H' Wrattonbully★★★ £C   ● **Shiraz** 'H' McLaren Vale★★★ £C
○ **Chardonnay** 'H' Adelaide Hills★★ £C   ○ **Viognier** 'H' Adelaide Hills★★ £C

HENRY'S DRIVE   www.henrysdrive.com   A: THt, JNi, Bal, F&M, NYg, But, Tur, UnC

Owner: Longbottom family   PO Box 9, Padthaway SA 5271
Sparky and Sarah Marquis (ex FOX CREEK) make the wines at this large Padthaway estate established in 1998. It is planted in the main to Cabernet Sauvignon and Shiraz but also to Chardonnay and Merlot. Given the Marquis's achievements at Fox Creek, it is not surprising that early efforts are promising: Shiraz and Cabernet are both distinctive and intense with good balance and texture. From the 2000 vintage the Shiraz has a gravelly, toasty, spicy, berry fruit in contrast to the cooler more minty, eucalyptus and blackcurrant-leaf character of the Cabernet. The Shiraz is aged in new American oak while the Cabernet receives mostly French oak. Reserve Shiraz was added in 1999 and a Reserve Cabernet has been made since 2000; both are more full-on with more extract and structure. Definitely a producer to watch as this range continues to develop. A Sparkling Shiraz is also made. (PW)

● **Cabernet Sauvignon**★★★ £D Reserve★★★ £D
● **Shiraz**★★★ £D Reserve★★★★ £E

HENSCHKE   Eden Valley   www.henschke.com.au   A: L&W, JNi, NYg, WSc, Hrd, P&S

Owner: Stephen & Prue Henschke   Henschke Road, Keyneton SA 5353
In the mid-to-late 1980s many of these fabulous reds could be bought for a song but eventually the rest of the world got to taste them and this, added to the explosion in wine prices in the 90s, now usually means making do with something cheaper. Since 1979, Stephen Henschke has been fine-tuning these already well-established single-vineyard-based reds while his wife Prue has maintained and gradually renewed the existing vineyard resources. There are now 115 ha of estate vineyards, the largest segment (50 ha) in the Eden Valley. Carefully seasoned American oak is favoured and red wine fermentations are now finished in new oak. Fabulous fruit in a full, supple, lushly textured wine is the classic Henschke style, with additional depth and dimension in the top wines. The most celebrated, and necessarily expensive vineyard, the 8-ha Hill of Grace, includes a parcel of vines (Grandfathers Block) that date in part from the 1860s. From close by, Mount Edelstone (the first to be bottled separately in 1952) is arguably more consistent, with more pepper and spice character, if missing the extra majesty of Hill of Grace. Cyril Henschke Cabernet, previously entirely Cabernet Sauvignon, now includes a little Merlot and Cabernet Franc and shows superb pure blackberry and cassis fruit. The ageing potential of all three top reds is well proven. Abbott's Prayer is based on Merlot but supplemented by both Cabernets and sees only French oak. Like the recently introduced Grenache-dominated blend, Johann's Garden, it is almost immediately drinkable. From a start in the early 1990s whites have steadily improved, particularly the intense, taut and concentrated (and ageworthy) Lenswood Croft Chardonnay and Eden Valley Louis Semillon. There's good varietal intensity in Crane's Chardonnay, Julius Riesling and Joseph's Hill Gewürztraminer, all from Eden Valley fruit. A second Riesling, Green's Hill is sourced from the Adelaide Hills as is Littlehampton Pinot Gris. Tilly's Vineyard is a very gluggable blend of Semillon, Chardonnay and Sauvignon. (PW)

● **Shiraz** Hill of Grace❂❂❂❂❂ £H Mount Edelstone★★★★★ £E
● **Cabernet** Cyril Henschke★★★★ £F   ● **Abbott's Prayer**★★★ £E
● **Shiraz/Cabernet/Merlot** Keyneton Estate★★★ £D
● **Grenache/Mourvèdre/Shiraz** Johann's Garden★★★ £C
○ **Chardonnay** Croft★★★ £D Crane's★★ £C
○ **Semillon** Louis★★★ £C   ○ **Riesling** Julius★★ £C Green's Hill★★ £C
○ **Gewürztraminer** Joseph's Hill★ £C Tilly's Vineyard★ £B

HEWITSON   www.hewitson.com.au   A: **M&V, BBR**, ACh, The, Sel

Owner: Dean Hewitson   66 London Road, Mile End SA 5041

Dean Hewitson secured long-term contracts for fruit from some remarkable old vineyards in the Barossa, Eden Valley and McLaren Vale. As both a Roseworthy and UC Davis graduate, and with extensive winemaking experience both at Petaluma and abroad, he also has the know-how to make an accomplished range of wines. Beyond an intense, powerfully flavoured if broad Riesling are four fine reds. Miss Harry Dry Grown & Ancient is from old-vine Barossa Grenache, Shiraz and Mourvèdre (45/40/15 in the 2003) and is flavoursome, balanced and a very drinkable style. Two Shirazes provide a fascinating contrast: the fig, prune and black plum Barossa character of Ned & Henry's is a foil for the more ambitous and extracted McLaren Vale example with its mint, eucalypt and intense berry fruit depth. Good as these are, they are easily surpassed by a superb Mourvèdre from probably the oldest vineyard (planted 1853) of this variety in the world. There is a marvellous old-viney, pre-*phylloxera* earth, spice and black fruits complexity to this most individual wine. Also made but not tasted is Mermaids Muscadelle, a rare dry varietal version of this grape. (PW)

● **Shiraz** Ned & Henry's Barossa Valley★★★ £C   L'Oizeau McLaren Vale★★★ £D
● **Miss Harry** Dry Grown & Ancient★★ £C   ● **Mourvèdre** Old Garden Barossa Valley★★★★ £D
○ **Riesling** Eden Valley★★ £C

HILLSTOWE   Adelaide Hills   www.hillstowe.com.au   A: **D&D**, Lwt

Owner: Lion Nathan   104 Main Road, Hahndorf SA 5245

In 2001, this estate belonging to the Laurie family, which has deep roots in the area, fell into the clutches of a big Australasian brewer. Recent vintages have been made very competently so it is to be hoped that quality and integrity will be at least maintained – certainly, with the likes of PETALUMA, MITCHELTON and STONIER now under the same ownership, Hillstowe is in good company. Wines labelled Buxton indicate a McLaren Vale origin while Udy's Mill is 17 ha of Lenswood (Adelaide Hills) vineyard. Lenswood Pinot is mostly at the ripe end of the spectrum but is intense and stylish, while the Chardonnay has characteristic Adelaide Hills fruit with a cool, citrusy vigour. A tiny amount of Pinch Row Merlot also comes from Lenswood as does a new Pinot Gris. Mary's Hundred Shiraz – a tribute to the legendary Mary Laurie, a Scottish immigrant and probably Australia's first woman winemaker – is not named for the age of the vines but does include some 100-year-old McLaren Vale fruit. It's not overly refined, but is rich and deeply characterful. The Sauvignon needs to be drunk as young as possible. (PW)

● **Shiraz** Mary's Hundred★★★★ £C   Buxton★★ £B
● **Pinot Noir** Udy's Mill★★★ £C   ○ **Pinot Gris** Scrub Block★ £B
○ **Chardonnay** Udy's Mill★★ £C   Buxton★ £B

HOLLICK   Coonawarra   www.hollick.com   A: **Sec**, JNi, ACh, NYg

Owner: Hollick family   Corner Ravenswood Lane & Riddoch Highway, Coonawarra SA 5263

Now a first-rate producer that shows what Coonwarra is all about across a range of varieties. The Hollicks have 52 ha of vineyards in Coonawarra and another 20 ha in the emerging Wrattonbully region – small amounts by Coonawarra standards. Ian Hollick oversees a diverse range of very well-made wines with good intensity and extra depth in a range of top (Icon) reds that add refinement and complexity with age. All three have a black label; Ravenswood comes from the best parcels of Cabernet Sauvignon, while Wilgha Shiraz and newish Neilson's Block Merlot are site-specific. Ravenswood shows good varietal definition and intelligent use of oak and becomes sleek and stylish with five years' age or more. The range also includes whites: Chardonnay (both Unoaked and an expansive, ageworthy oaked Reserve), toasty, limey, mineral Riesling and a Sauvignon Blanc/Semillon. Other reds include distinctive stylish Pinot Noir, Shiraz/Cabernet Sauvignon (predominantly Shiraz) and Cabernet Sauvignon/Merlot. This last (around 80 per cent Cabernet) shows increased richness in the most recent vintages. Tempranillo is also being developed. As well as an intensely berryish Sparkling Merlot, a Pinot Noir/Chardonnay sparkler is produced. An attractive, light sweet wine, The Nectar, is also produced when conditions allow it. Made in 2003, 01 and 99, it is composed of around 80 per cent Riesling with the balance from Sauvignon Blanc and/or Semillon. (PW)

● **Cabernet Sauvignon** Ravenswood★★★★ £D   ● **Shiraz** Wilgha★★★ £C
● **Merlot** Neilson's Block★★★ £D   ● **Cabernet Sauvignon/Merlot**★★★ £B
● **Pinot Noir**★★★ £B   ● **Sparkling Merlot**★★ £C
○ **Chardonnay** Reserve★★★ £B   ○ **Sauvignon Blanc/Semillon**★★ £B   ○ **Riesling**★★ £B

JACOB'S CREEK/ORLANDO   Barossa Valley   www.jacobscreek.com.au   A: PRc, AAA

Owner: Pernod-Ricard   Barossa Valley Way, Rowland Flat SA 5352
The success of a single brand, namely Jacob's Creek, seems to have swallowed the image of the parent company here. Beyond the mostly meagre, unnatural-tasting offerings of this world-conquering label some serious wines can be found but, internationally at least, once-premium Orlando labels are giving way to the expanding Jacob's Creek range. Riesling has long been a strength here and as well as a good Jacob's Creek Reserve, St Helga and Steingarten versions are still produced. Also still seen is Lawson's Padthaway Shiraz, a wine in the big oaky mould but one that it doesn't lack for fruit or structure either. St Hilary Chardonnay from the same region can be remarkably good value. Jacob's Creek Reserves are generally a big improvement on the basics and a further step up are a Limited Release Chardonnay from Padthway and Limited Release Shiraz/Cabernet (from Barossa and Coonawarra fruit respectively). Relatively inexpensive Jacob's Creek sparkling Chardonnay/Pinot Noir is also made. (PW)

● **Shiraz** Lawson's Padthaway★★★ £D   Jacob's Creek Reserve★ £B
● **Shiraz/Cabernet** Jacob's Creek Limited Release★★★ £E
● **Cabernet Sauvignon** Jacaranda Ridge★★ £E   Jacob's Creek Reserve★★ £B
○ **Chardonnay** St Hilary Padthaway★★ £B   Jacob's Creek Reserve★★ £B
○ **Chardonnay** Jacob's Creek Limited Release★★★ £C
○ **Riesling** Steingarten★★ £C   Jacob's Creek Reserve★★ £B

JAMIESONS RUN   Coonawarra   www.jamiesonsrun.com.au   A: BBI, AAA

Owner: Beringer Blass   Riddoch Highway, Coonawarra SA 5263
As with Jacob's Creek, such has been the commercial success of what began as an inexpensive red blend that it has outgrown the parent label. Here the production of Mildara wines has been subsumed into the Jamieson Run label. The basic red started life with a certain style and complexity (in part from combining Cabernet, Shiraz and Merlot) that similar competitively priced examples lacked, but has, sadly, lost its inspiration. The bright-fruited Chardonnay is rather simple and light but harsh too. Other standard reds are light and simple at best but individual vineyard bottlings are significantly better. French oak is now favoured and McShane's Block Shiraz and Alexander's Block Cabernet show concentrated fruit, evident oak and reasonable depth in top vintages. A third, O'Dea's Cabernet, was first made in 2000. A rich, powerful Jamieson's Run Winemaker's Reserve has been positioned as the flagship wine. Although based on Cabernet Sauvignon it can also include Cabernet Franc, Shiraz, Merlot and Malbec. New are moderately priced Red Terra Reserves of Shiraz and Cabernet Sauvignon. (PW)

● **Winemakers Reserve**★★★ £E
● **Shiraz** McShane's Block★★★ £D   ● **Cabernet** Alexander's Block★★★ £D

TREVOR JONES   Barossa   A: UnC, NYg

Owner: Trevor Jones   Barossa Valley Highway, Lyndoch SA 5351
The grapes for these wines are bought in from diverse sources within South Australia. Experienced Trevor Jones makes very small quantities of varietal wines including a particularly good example of unoaked Chardonnay. This style, though popular, often only makes obvious the lack of really top quality fruit (something that can be partially disguised with sophisticated oak handling); but this example, by contrast, has a tight, pure fruit core and is capable of a little age. Reds tend to be in a big, extracted style but careful

blending from different sites aids balance. Wild Witch Shiraz is sourced from a single vineyard of old-vine Barossa Shiraz. (PW)

● **Shiraz** Dry Grown★★★ £C   Wild Witch★★★ £E   ● **Cabernet/Merlot**★★ £C
O **Chardonnay** Virgin ★★★ £C   O **Riesling** Reserve★★ £B

KATNOOK ESTATE   Coonawarra   www.katnookestate.com.au   A: **Frt, Bib,** Tan, WWs, NYg

Owner: Freixenet   Riddoch Highway, Coonawarra SA 5263
The majority shareholder in this Coonawarra stalwart is the Cava giant FREIXENET but it continues to be directed by Wayne Stehbens, who has made the wine in a 19th-century stone woolshed (used in the region's early vintages) for the past 20-odd years. Much of the grape production has been sold to others but Katnook's reds have been characterised by their intense, concentrated, ripe (often very ripe), sweet fruit and tight structures when young. Whites can show good intensity too but typically lack subtlety and flair. A premium (and pricey) Cabernet (Odyssey) has been complemented by a premium Shiraz (Prodigy) since 1997 and although both show more power and depth than the Katnook Estate versions, they are also markedly oaky – they may be redeemable with moderately long ageing. All the Katnook reds need at least five years' age; Riesling and Chardonnay are usually better with three years. Some very attractive, softly textured fruit-driven wines for early consumption have been made under a second label, Riddoch. (PW)

Katnook Estate:
● **Cabernet Sauvignon**★★ £C   Odyssey★★★ £E   ● **Merlot**★★ £C
● **Shiraz**★★ £C   Prodigy★★★ £E   O **Chardonnay**★★ £C
Riddoch:
● **Shiraz**★ £B   O **Chardonnay**★ £B

KILIKANOON   Clare Valley   www.kilikanoon.com.au   A: **THt,** JNi, Rae, NYg, UnC, P&S

Owner: Kevin Mitchell, Nathan Waks & partners   Penna Lane, Penwortham SA 5453
If you want to know what wines from the Clare taste like you could do a lot worse than to taste Kevin Mitchell's excellent range. Although he lacked his own winemaking facility until 2004, the grapes have always come from estate vineyards. Shiraz in particular is a star, showing off the regional characteristics superbly in both Oracle and Covenant versions. The Oracle has a more berryish accent in contrast to a more classic, mineral- and earth-imbued fruit intensity in the Covenant. An expressive Cabernet Sauvignon shows both its orgins and the style and balance typical of the wines here. Riesling has deep fruit intensity if not always the structure of Clare's finest. Second Fiddle is a well-balanced, fruity Grenache-based rosé. The latest releases are particularly impressive and very good value. New from the 2001 vintage is Medley, a very stylish blend of Grenache, Shiraz and Mourvèdre. (PW)

● **Shiraz** Oracle★★★★ £C   Covenant★★★★ £C   ● **Grenache** Prodigal★★★ £C
● **Cabernet Sauvignon** Blocks Road★★★★ £C   O **Riesling** Morts Block★★ £B

KNAPPSTEIN   Clare Valley   www.knappsteinwines.com.au   A: **LNa,** Odd

Owner: Lion Nathan   2 Pioneer Avenue, Clare SA 5453
Tim Knappstein relinquished his medium-sized winery (to the PETALUMA group) to devote himself full-time to KNAPPSTEIN LENSWOOD VINEYARDS, leaving winemaker Andrew Hardy to draw on the 100 ha of well-established vineyards. The reliable varietals remain moderately priced and widely available but there is now a greater emphasis on Shiraz and a switch to French oak. The premium reds are sold under the Enterprise label, named for the historic former brewery in which the winery is housed. Enterprise Cabernet Sauvignon (which include a very small percentage of Malbec) is made from the best parcels within the 30-year-old Knappstein Vineyard and Enterprise Shiraz is made from a selection of small plots in Clare Valley. Both show classic Clare fruit with good depth and concentration. Of the improving whites, Semillon/Sauvignon is at the rich, ripe end of the spectrum, Riesling is adding more intensity and Gewürztraminer is displaying a truer varietal character than in the past. A sparkling Shiraz, rather

unnervingly called Chainsaw, has also been introduced. (PW)
- **Cabernet Sauvignon** Enterprise★★ £C
- **Shiraz**★ £B Enterprise★★ £C   ● **Cabernet/Merlot**★ £B
- O **Chardonnay**★ £B O **Semillon/Sauvignon Blanc**★★ £B
- O **Gewürztraminer** Dry Style★ £B O **Riesling** Hand Picked★ £B

LAKE BREEZE   www.lakebreeze.com.au   A: **THt**, UnC, F&M, Nid, NYg, Rae, Sel

Owner: Follett family   Step Road, Langhorne Creek SA 5255
One of the emerging quality producers from Langhorne Creek (on the opposite, eastern side of the Fleurieu Peninsula to McLaren Vale). Greg Follett makes the wines from a portion of his family's large holdings, the Folletts having been grape growers since the 1930s. The reds are very competently made; they were even of sound quality in the atypically cool, wet 1999 vintage. Bernoota is from Shiraz and Cabernet Sauvignon (generally equal parts of each) with good complexity and a well-defined palate, Cabernet Sauvignon is of similar quality. Under a Winemaker's Selection label, both varietal Cabernet Sauvignon and Shiraz are made in the best years. If more oaky, they are more concentrated too. (PW)
- **Cabernet Sauvignon**★★★ £C   ● **Cabernet/Shiraz** Bernoota★★★ £C
- **Shiraz** Winemaker's Selection★★★ £D

LEASINGHAM   Clare Valley   www.leasingham-wines.com.au   A: **Cst**, AAA

Owner: Hardy Wine Company   7 Dominic Street, Clare SA 5453
This long-established winery is the HARDY WINE COMPANY's centre for Clare Valley excellence, currently overseen by Kerri Thompson. There are four substantial vineyards (all at least 50 ha) whose fruit is supplemented by bought-in grapes. It is pure speculation, but it might be interesting to see whether any part of any of vineyard is considered to be special enough to be isolated in the future. For the moment the range is simple and consistent. The Classic Clare wines are the most exciting, high in alcohol but packed full of rich, ripe fruit and abundant new oak; the Shiraz comes from the Schobers Vineyard and the Cabernet from Provis Vineyard. The oak theme continues in very good and reasonably priced Bin 61 Shiraz and Bin 56 Cabernet/Malbec. I suspect few of these reds are drunk with much age but all deserve four or five years. Mind you, a rich, untamed infusion of fruit and oak might appeal on some occasions. Prices of these dense, bold Classic Clare reds have risen considerably. Riesling is good with excellent limey, mineral intensity to the Bin 7. Classic Clare Riesling is made in a tighter, more ageworthy style. (PW)
- **Shiraz** Classic Clare★★★ £E Bin 61★★ £B
- **Cabernet Sauvignon** Classic Clare★★★ £E   ● **Cabernet/Malbec** Bin 56
- O **Riesling** Bin 7★★ £B   ● **Sparkling Shiraz** Classic Clare★★ £C

LECONFIELD   Coonawarra   www.leconfield.com.au   A: **Eno**, Nid, Hrd

Owner: Hamilton Wine Group   Riddoch Highway, Coonawarra SA 5263
Leconfield was established by Sydney Hamilton in the early 1970s but sold to his nephew Richard HAMILTON in 1981. The leading wine over more than two decades has been the Cabernet, which made a lasting impact with the 1980 vintage. Yet while some vintages have been very impressive with a deep, rich, assertive berry fruit character, other years have been somewhat leafy and unexpectedly light. Cabernet includes a little Merlot, Cabernet Franc and Petit Verdot but most other wines are 100 per cent varietal. Of these, a more plummy, berryish, at times slightly herbal Merlot has been more consistent than a Shiraz which has occasionally been slightly lean after a much celebrated 1995. However all have refined structures and show archetypal Coonawarra character and fruit intensity when on form. Recent vintages of Chardonnay have shown more elegance, if not the intensity of the more one-dimensional early vintages. A very small amount of flavoursome yet refined Riesling is also made from surviving 1970s vines. The 2002 reds and whites show what is possible here. (PW)
- **Cabernet**★★★★ £D   ● **Merlot**★★★ £D   ● **Shiraz**★★★★ £D
- O **Chardonnay**★★★ £B O **Riesling** Old Vines★★ £B

PETER LEHMANN   Barossa Valley   www.peterlehmannwines.com.au   **A: PLh**, Odd, WSc

Owner: Hess group   Para Road, Tanunda SA 5352
Peter Lehmann is a Barossa institution and a consistently sound bet for accessible but fruit-rich and well-structured Barossa reds. Production is large with much of the fruit bought in under contract. The numerous small parcels and a relatively limited number of wines put the emphasis on blends. The top wine, Stonewell Shiraz is released with five years' age and is based on low-yielding old vines in the Stonewell vineyards but also includes premium fruit from other Barossa districts. Previously aged only in American oak, since 1997 vintage more than two-thirds is French and increasing. It shows terrific concentration, depth and intensity and has majestic proportions, just missing the extra refinement for classic status. Eight Songs, made since 1996 and aged only in French oak, has more recently (1999) shown greater character and complexity if not yet the refinement suggested by the artistic efforts to which its presentation is linked. Mentor, the premium Cabernet-based blend has also seen only French oak since 1998 and usually includes a significant percentage of Merlot, Malbec and Shiraz. Dense and structured, it is best with at least 6 to 10 years' age. New (from 2001) licorice, berry and plum The Futures Shiraz is a significant step up from the regular Barossa Valley Shiraz, which nonetheless remains reasonably priced for an impressive mouthful of fruit. Other Barossa-labelled reds are good too, including GSM, a blend of Grenache, Shiraz and Mourvèdre. Seven Surveys is an improving but relatively light version of the same. A powerful, ageworthy Reserve Riesling from Eden Valley is the best of the whites though a Reserve Semillon is also very good; both are only released with four to five years' bottle-age. Clancy's red is an everday Barossa blend of Shiraz, Cabernet Sauvignon, Merlot and Cabernet Franc, while Weighbridge is a budget label for Shiraz and Chardonnay. (PW)
- **Shiraz** Barossa★★ £B The Futures★★★ £C Eight Songs★★★★ £E Stonewell★★★★★ £E
- **Mentor★★★★** £D ● **Cabernet Sauvignon** Barossa★ £B
- **GSM★★** £B ● **Grenache** Barossa★★ £B ● **Grenache/Shiraz** Barossa★ £B
- **Seven Surveys★** £B ● **Clancy's★** £B
O **Riesling** Barossa★ £B Eden Valley★★ £B Reserve Eden Valley★★★ £C
O **Semillon** Reserve Barossa★★★ £C

LENSWOOD VINEYARDS   www.knappsteinlenswood.com.au   **A: McK**, UnC, Hrd

Owner: Tim & Annie Knappstein   Croft Road, Lenswood SA5240
Having gradually abandoned the Clare Valley for the heart of the Adelaide Hills, Tim Knappstein seems to have found a higher love. From 54 ha of two almost equal parts come consistently fine Sauvignon Blanc – one of Australia's best – and taut, attractively herbal, subtly oaked Semillon. The range also includes powerful, oaky, citrus and melon Chardonnay – not as nuanced as some Adelaide Hills examples but with excellent concentration and flavour and providing excellent value for money. A complex, richly textured Pinot Noir is ripe and intense and has been particularly impressive since the 1997 vintage. Palatine is a blend of Cabernet Sauvignon Merlot and Malbec varying according to the vintage but increasingly based on a nearby vineyard of the same name. The wine has a cool fruit complexity but ripe tannins and good ageing potential. A little Gewürztraminer from a single Adelaide Hills vineyard was first made in 1999 and again since 2001 and has both good fruit expression and structure. (PW)
- **Pinot Noir★★★** £D ● **Palatine★★★** £D O **Chardonnay★★★** £C
O **Semillon★★★** £B O **Sauvignon Blanc★★★** £B O **Gewürztraminer★★** £C

LINDEMANS   Coonawarra & Padthaway   www.southcorp.com.au   **A: ScE**, AAA

Owner: Southcorp   Coonawarra SA 5263 & Naracoorte Road, Padthaway SA 5271
In Coonawarra, Lindemans (also see Victoria) makes a trio of top reds which can be traced back to the mid-1980s, in the case of Pyrus (a Bordeaux blend), and even longer for St George Cabernet and Limestone Ridge Shiraz/Cabernet. But despite some impressive past vintages these wines don't now stack up against the best from Coonawarra (which includes the premium WYNNS wines from the same stable). An initial fullness and fleshy texture and a pleasing complexity are let down by a lack of fruit intensity on the finish

and a stalky, sappy quality that is often apparent. This seems to suggest a mix of good quality fruit and that of more mediocre origins. All three wines are significantly cheaper than the Wynns flagship wines but there are many better Coonawarra wines in their price range. By contrast generally good value is to be had in the Padthaway wines, particularly the Reserve Chardonnay with its pronounced barrel-fermentation character and rich fruit. (PW)

● **Pyrus** Coonawarra★★★ £D ● **Cabernet Sauvignon** St George★★ £D
● **Shiraz/Cabernet** Limestone Ridge★★ £D
● **Shiraz** Padthaway★ £B Padthaway Reserve★★ £C
O **Chardonnay** Limestone Coast★ £B Padthaway Reserve★★ £C

MCWILLIAM'S OF COONAWARRA Coonawarra www.mcwilliams.com.au

Owner: McWilliam's Riddoch Highway, Coonawarra SA 5263
The winery was established by the Brand family but has now become taken over by McWILLIAM'S. As well as taking full control of Brands, McWilliam's is in the process of developing an additional 100 ha of vineyards in Coonawarra (giving a total of 300 ha) and production is set to expand as the new vineyards come on stream. The performance of the Brands reds has been reasonably consistent, with soft fruit and gentle structures, though some have lacked a little ripeness and concentration in weaker vintages. Riesling is the strongest white with intense limey, tropical fruit and a mineral streak, and will sometimes improve with additional bottle age. The top wine, Stentifords Reserve Old Vine Shiraz (known until 1995 as Original Vineyard Shiraz as it is based on a vineyard established in 1896), has been particularly impressive in recent vintages such as 1996 and 98. Patrons Reserve is intended to complement it and is based on Cabernet Sauvignon with lesser amounts of Shiraz, Merlot and Cabernet Franc. Older vintages of all the wines are labelled Brands Laira, as the company used to be known. (PW)

● **Shiraz**★★ £B Stentiford's Reserve Old Vine★★★ £F
● **Cabernet Sauvignon**★★ £B ● **Cabernet/Merlot**★ £B
O **Riesling**★ £B

MAGLIERI McLaren Vale www.maglieri.com.au   A: BBI

Owner: Beringer Blass Douglas Gully Road, McLaren Flat SA 5171
Captured in 1999 by Mildara Blass (now BERINGER BLASS), this relatively small McLaren Vale winery had already made a name for itself with premium reds under the direction of Steve Maglieri as for its locally popular 'Lambrusco'. The reds, currently made by Trevor Tucker, generally show intense ripe fruit and well-integrated oak. Shiraz displays classic McLaren Vale character with slightly smoky, eucalyptus, very ripe dark berry/cherry/plum fruit and a hint of earth, building up dark-chocolate flavours with age. The Steve Maglieri version is more structured, extracted and oaky and needs the best part of a decade's ageing. Merlot is soundly made but, like many South Australian examples, is hardly a classic expression of the grape. The Cabernet is more convincing. Semillon and Chardonnay are both well crafted and better than is typical for McLaren Vale. Quality across the range dipped a little in the 1999 vintage (which was poor in McLaren Vale) but premium reds should continue to be a good bet if the fruit sources are retained. (PW)

● **Shiraz**★★★ £C Steve Maglieri★★★ £E
● **Cabernet Sauvignon**★★ £B ● **Merlot**★ £B
O **Chardonnay**★ £B O **Semillon**★ £B

MAJELLA Coonawarra www.majellawines.com.au   A: All, Odd, Fsp, FFW

Owner: Lynn families Lynn Road, Coonawarra SA 5263
A label gaining in recognition and importance as more and more of the Cabernet and Shiraz grapes from prime Coonawarra land that were previously sold under contract (the Lynns have been an important supplier to WYNNS since 1980) are now being used for Majella wines. From the late 1960s vines began to compete with sheep for space and the first wines were produced in the early 90s. With a new winery and now a full-time winemaker, Bruce Gregory, Majella has increased production to 12,000 cases. The

Cabernet/Shiraz blend once common to many premium South Australian wines but now mostly seen in budget wines has, since 1996, been the basis of a very impressive flagship, Malleea. Very dense, rich and concentrated fruit takes up the French oak treatment and fine tannins promise a long life. Varietal Shiraz and Cabernet are in a similar mould with potent berry fruit and evident oak but are a little more accessible when young. Riesling shows a better, tighter structure than is usual in Coonawarra Riesling. Sparkling Shiraz is also made but you may need to visit the winery to get your hands on it. (PW)

● **Malleea★★★★** £F ● **Cabernet Sauvignon★★★** £D ● **Shiraz★★★★** £D
○ **Riesling★** £B

MAXWELL McLaren Vale www.maxwellwines.com.au   A: **Str**, Nid, FWC

Owner: Maxwell family   Olivers Road, McLaren Vale SA 5171
Still a relatively modest-sized operation, Maxwell is now equipped with a modern winery in order to maximise the potential of its 16-ha vineyard. Though quality has been slightly variable it has always been at least good, sometimes very good and both Ellen Street Shiraz and Lime Cave Cabernet Sauvignon display fine textures, stylish rich ripe fruit and good structure. A little Reserve Shiraz has also been made in a more extracted, blockbuster style. Whites are full of flavour, with good balance and structure too, but a rich, citrusy, herbal Semillon is better and more consistent than the Chardonnay. Grenache and Verdelho are also made. (PW)

● **Shiraz** Four Roads★ £B Ellen Street★★★ £C
● **Cabernet Sauvignon** Lime Cave★★★ £C ● **Cabernet/Merlot★** £B
○ **Chardonnay★** £B ○ **Semillon** Old Vines★★ £B

CHARLES MELTON www.charlesmeltonwines.com.au   A: **Lib**, JNi, Vne, ACh, BBR, Hrd, P&S

Owner: Graeme (Charlie) Melton   Krondorf Road, Tanunda SA 5352
Charlie Melton is one of the saviours of Australian Shiraz along with Rocky O'Callaghan (ROCKFORD), Bob McLean (ST HALLETT) and others. In the late 1980s and early 90s he produced wines of such character and richness from dry-farmed (unirrigated) Barossa old-vine fruit that it rescued the grape from the also-ran category assigned to it in the Cabernet-fixated wine scene that prevailed in Australia at the time. Though Melton is based in the heart of the Barossa, grapes (whether owned, leased or bought-in) are sourced from throughout the area. Both French and American oak are used but the past decade has seen a trend towards the former. Shiraz is arguably the best Melton wine made but a varietal Grenache (from old bush vines) is always very ripe and sweet-fruited. One of Australia's best rosés is also based on Grenache, while Nine Popes is a blend of Shiraz, Grenache and Mourvèdre. Cabernet shows the rich, ripe fruit and oak character typical to all the reds. Made by the traditional method and from Cabernet as well as Shiraz, the Sparkling Red is a very good example of its type; it shows a rich plum, berry and chocolate character with a little age. More exotic again is Sotto di Ferro, made from Pedro Ximenez and Muscadelle grapes (90/10) dried 'under the iron' – beneath a corrugated iron roof. It is well-balanced and complex, including roasted nuts, honey, nougat and dried apricot flavours, with real depth and intensity. Laura Shiraz comes from grapes bought in from vineyards in the Southern Flinders Ranges (north of Clare Valley) near the township of Laura. The last excepted, all the reds benefit from having at least five years' age. Very promising is a new Kirsche Vineyard Shiraz, also from Flinders fruit. (PW)

● **Nine Popes★★★★** £E ● **Grenache★★★** £C
● **Shiraz★★★★** £E Laura★★ £D ● **Cabernet Sauvignon★★★** £E
◉ **Rose of Virginia★★** £C ● **Sparkling Red★★★** £E ● **Sotto di Ferro★★★** £F

GEOFF MERRILL McLaren Vale www.geoffmerrillwines.com   A: **Eve, GWW**, HWC

Owner: Stratmer Vineyards (G Merrill & A Purbrick)   291 Pimpala Road, Woodcroft SA 5162
Geoff Merrill hardly needs any introduction to many wine consumers as he is one of the most instantly recognisable great characters of the Australian wine scene. The wines, made at the renovated Mount Hurtle

winery since 1988, can seem a bit anonymous and simple, apparently at odds with the exuberant personality of their maker. At their best they do achieve a certain elegance and subtlety but more often there isn't the necessary fruit quality there to deliver the regional and varietal expression that is sought. Even the red Reserves, though showing greater intensity and complexity, can taste overly leafy and slightly tired and woody from long oak-ageing. Nevertheless, they are refreshing after some of the more hollow, superficial, high-alcohol efforts that are common in the region. The new Henley Shiraz is being sold at a stratospheric price but does have remarkable depth and complexity within a relatively unobtrusive frame. This, like the Reserves (including Chardonnay), is only released with extended bottle-age. Regular varietals, at their best (when fully ripe), are generally soft, supple and attractive, even if they don't have the greatest weight or intensity. Wines under the Mount Hurtle label can have upfront if simple fruit character. (PW)

● **Shiraz** Reserve★★ £D ● **Cabernet Sauvignon** Reserve★★ £D
O **Chardonnay**★ £B Reserve★★ £C

MITCHELL Clare Valley   A: **MVs**, Tan, ACh, Adm, Por
Owner: Andrew & Jane Mitchell Hughes Park Road, Sevenhill via Clare SA 5453
The Mitchell winery was established in 1975 and is now a medium-sized Clare producer with a strong track record for consistent, well-structured reds and whites. The whites are made without any oak as is a high-alcohol Grenache from old unirrigated bush vines, while the Shiraz and Cabernet (which includes a little Cabernet Franc and Merlot) show a relatively subdued oak influence. Though the wines sometimes lack a little extra flair or personality they nonetheless show typical Clare characteristics and Cabernet, Shiraz and Riesling are capable of long ageing. After some weaker efforts in the late 90s the Riesling is once again intense and concentrated – an all-too-rare inexpensive wine worth cellaring. (PW)

● **Cabernet Sauvignon** Sevenhill Vineyard★★ £B
● **Shiraz** Peppertree Vineyard★★ £B ● **Grenache** Growers★ £B
O **Riesling** Watervale★★ £B O **Semillon** Growers★ £B

MITOLO McLaren Vale www.mitolowines.com.au   A: **GWW**, L&W, Lay, NYg
Owner: Frank Mitolo cnr Angle Vale & John Road, Virginia SA 5120
Mitolo Wines was formed in 2000 after Frank Mitolo decided to expand on early efforts and commercialise his production. Through the winemaking services of Ben Glaetzer a remarkably high standard has been achieved from the outset. Fermentation is completed in primarily French oak (new) in which the wines are subsequently aged for up to 16 months. Three differing Shirazes are notable for their depth, extract and detailed, complex fruit expressions. The fullest demonstration of fruit and *terroir* is revealed in the potentially outstanding McLaren Vale Savitar Shiraz. All must be given at least five years' age. Jester is a second-label Shiraz with good berryish McLaren Vale character. It is attractive but of some substance too. First produced in 2002 is Serpico, a Cabernet Sauvignon made from grapes dried on racks. It is very concentrated and powerful but balanced with black plum and black cherry fruit and avoids any overt raisiny character. 2003 is if anything more structured and intense and will require extra patience. All the wines come complete with a Latin inscription which sheds some light on their names. (PW)

● **Shiraz** Reiver Barossa Valley★★★ £D G.A.M McLaren Vale★★★★ £E Savitar McLaren Vale★★★★ £E
● **Shiraz** Jester McLaren Vale★★ £C ● **Cabernet Sauvignon** Serpico McLaren Vale★★★★ £E

MOUNT HORROCKS Clare Valley www.mounthorrocks.com   A: **Lib**, ACh, WSc, Hrd
Owner: Stephanie Toole Curling Street, Auburn SA 5451
This is a regular but increasingly classy range of wines which all have good structure and ripeness. In recent years Stephanie Toole has been able to centre her production of just 5,000 cases per year around one Watervale source. Great care is taken in producing the best possible fruit from unirrigated vines and also in their vinification (carried out at Jeffrey GROSSET's winery). Riesling is getting better and better, taut with vibrant fruit (lime and grapefruit with floral notes) and great length. Both Semillon and Chardonnay are

from single plots and show good breadth and weight as well as the firm acidity that gives all the whites a certain austerity when young. Though it is barrel-fermented, the citrus and mineral notes in the Semillon are not in the least overwhelmed. Cabernet/Merlot is what others would call simply Cabernet Sauvignon, as it only contains 5 per cent Merlot, but lately it has been ripely berryish with fine tannins. Shiraz has excellent definition with a hint of the Clare mineral, earth character. A sweet version of Riesling, Cordon Cut, is made by allowing the grapes to dehydrate on the vine by severing the cane from the trunk (the French term is *passerillage*; there is no botrytis but a *passerillé* or dried-grape character is achieved). The wine shows an intense, pure, limey, honeyed character checked by good acidity. All the wines deserve an extra couple of years' bottle-age. (PW)

○ **Riesling** Watervale★★★ £C Cordon Cut★★★ £D
○ **Semillon** Watervale★★★ £C ○ **Chardonnay**★★ £C
● **Cabernet/Merlot**★★ £D ● **Shiraz**★★★ £D

MOUNTADAM Eden Valley www.mountadam.com   A: **VCq, Par,** JNi, N&P, Amp, Cam, Hrd

Owner: LVMH High Eden Road, Eden Valley SA 5235
A high-profile and often overhyped winery, Mountadam has had some successes but has never been totally convincing as one of South Australia's leading small producers. Established by the late David Wynn on the elevated High Eden Ridge, it continues to be run by his son Adam despite being purchased by CAPE MENTELLE (part of LVMH) in 2000. At times many of the wines have lacked real depth and complexity, if managing to wow some wine drinkers with their oak and at times beguiling fruit veneer. The Chardonnay has some style and structure and has been the most consistent wine but doesn't match the very top Adelaide Hills examples. Eden Valley Riesling can show exquisite fruit flavours and has had better structure of late than previously. The Red is a blend of primarily Cabernet Sauvignon and Merlot and if it sometimes exhibits rather leafy, underripe characters, it can also develop a cedary, plummy complexity with age. Eden Valley Pinot Noir combines foresty aspects with ripe strawberry and cherry fruit and can also age well. David Wynn Patriarch Shiraz, now labelled simply DW, is rich, composed and seductive. New are a Barossa range of unwooded Chardonnay, Cabernet/Merlot and Shiraz. While of only modest depth and concentration, Shiraz in particular shows good expression. Moderately priced, they will be rated after further releases. (PW)

● **Shiraz** DW Eden Valley★★★★ £D
● **Pinot Noir** Eden Valley★★★ £C ● **The Red** Eden Valley★★★ £D
○ **Chardonnay** Eden Valley★★★ £C ○ **Riesling** Eden Valley★★ £B

NEPENTHE Adelaide Hills www.nepenthe.com.au   A: **Str, GWW,** Odd, WSc, WTs

Owner: Tweddell family Jones Road, Balhannah SA 5242
A very switched-on Adelaide Hills producer excelling with almost everything it touches. The widely travelled owners only established this now medium-sized operation in the mid-1990s yet made an immediate impact both locally and abroad. Winemaker Peter Leske works with owner Ed Tweddell's son James to maximise the potential of the ripe yet cool Lenswood fruit. Predominantly French oak is used, usually a mix of new and used. All the wines have excellent fruit but good texture and balance too. Pinot Noir is particularly impressive with great breadth and intensity on the palate. Good brambly peppery Zinfandel is also made including an expansive Charleston version in 2001. Pinot Noir are also appeared in Charleston designation in 2002 when sourced exclusively from a second, larger vineyard site. Newish Tempranillo shows good varietal character with a spicy blueberry component but wants for a little more depth and structure. As well as the pristine varietal reds, a stylish Cabernet/Merlot blend (with Cabernet Franc from 1999), The Fugue, has been joined by The Rogue, a curious Merlot, Cabernet Sauvignon and Shiraz blend (that included a little Pinot in 2001 and 00). Intense, expressive whites include both oaked and unwooded Chardonnay which are nicely composed with good fruit richness. A Pinot Gris is fruity and floral while Semillon is quite a serious barrel-fermented style. Very lightly oaked Sauvignon is a classic example of the herbal and ripe gooseberry, tropical Adelaide Hills character and Riesling is increasingly fine.

Most affordable are unusual Tryst red (Cabernet, Zinfandel and Tempranillo), with berry fruit and a leafy component, and white (Sauvignon Blanc/Semillon). (PW)

● **Pinot Noir**★★★ £C ● **Zinfandel**★★★ £D ● **Tempranillo**★★ £C
● **The Fugue**★★★ £C ● **The Rogue**★★ £B ● **Tryst**★ £B
O **Chardonnay**★★★ £B Unwooded★★ £B O **Pinot Gris**★★ £B
O **Riesling**★★★ £B O **Semillon**★★★ £B O **Sauvignon Blanc**★★ £B O **Tryst**★ £B

PARKER COONAWARRA ESTATE   www.parkercoonawaraestate.com.au   A: **C&B,** Sel

*Owner: **Rathbone family group** Riddoch Highway, Coonawarra SA 5263*
This singular Coonawarra estate established by John Parker in 1985 produced some great wines during the 1990s, but only very recently added its own winemaking facility. The focus of production is a single premium wine, a Bordeaux-like approach that is also reflected in the provocative name, Terra Rossa First Growth. It was first made in 1988 but not in 92, 95 or 97. In those years (unlike Médoc classed growths) only the second wine, Terra Rossa Cabernet Sauvignon, was released as it was felt the requisite quality hadn't been reached. First Growth is based on Cabernet Sauvignon but also includes Merlot and Cabernet Franc and is aged in 100 per cent new French oak. It is fully ripe and concentrated, if at times a little oaky, with an intense pure fruit core that takes the best part of a decade to unfurl. The second wine, which sees some American as well as French oak, has recently been only a shade behind. A Merlot is also made but is only available in very small quantities direct from the winery. (PW)

● **Terra Rossa First Growth**★★★★ £F
● **Cabernet Sauvignon** Terra Rossa★★★ £D

PENFOLDS   Barossa Valley   www.penfolds.com.au   A: **ScE,**AAA

*Owner: **Southcorp** Tanunda Road, Nurioopta SA 5355*
The leading Australian brand since the renaissance of Australian wine in the early 1950s, Penfolds continues to be number one in the mammoth SOUTHCORP. Grange, Australia's most consistently great wine over five decades, is the pinnacle of production. Like all established investment wines, Grange has a crazy price tag but prices of all the top wines here reflect demand as much as production costs or intrinsic quality. Some top Penfolds reds are produced from a wide range of vineyard sources, which can certainly optimise complexity and aid consistency, although on the downside it might be argued there is less individuality. Importantly, there does seem to be a welcome trend to giving more information about the main components. Further details (i.e regional percentages and specific vineyards used) would offer the drinker (OK, anorak, some might say) more academic pleasure when comparing the top reds or tasting vertically (different years of the same wine). Grange is primarily Barossa and McLaren Vale Shiraz aged in American oak but typically contains around 5 per cent Cabernet (10 per cent from 1992 to 94); while not the most refined expression of Shiraz, it is very powerful and complete, and fabulously complex with age. The RWT is 100 per cent Barossa Shiraz aged in French oak; it has good drive and intensity but is oaky too. Intense Magill Estate is vineyard-specific but can be almost overripe and slightly coarse. St Henri, which includes around 5 per cent Cabernet, is aged in large used oak barrels. The top Cabernet is Bin 707, which includes Coonawarra, Padthaway and Barossa fruit and, like Grange, is aged in American oak; there's terrific flesh and blackberry fruit depth in an uncompromising structure. Bin 407 is based primarily on Coonawarra and Padthaway fruit and aged in both French and American oak. Of the other Bin-labelled reds, the Barossa-sourced Bin 138 Old Vine Shiraz/Grenache/Mourvèdre and long-established Bin 389 stands out. White wines have only taken on real significance here in the last decade. Yattarna, the top Chardonnay, is a classic Australian expression of the grape but while rich and concentrated with lovely fruit and excellent structure it lacks real flair or individuality. A series of Bin-numbered Chardonnays has also been very impressive. For more affordable reds and whites, there are the Koonunga Hill and the slightly cheaper Rawson's Retreat brands which cover some of the same varietals and dual-variety blends. It must take considerable skill to maintain these two ranges, but only occasionally does either brand provide anything particularly interesting or good value. (PW)

● **Grange**✪✪✪✪✪ £H
● **Shiraz** RWT★★★★ £F Magill Estate★★★ £E
● **Shiraz** St Henri★★★ £E Bin 28★★ £B Bin 128★ £B
● **Cabernet Sauvignon** Bin 407★★★ £C Bin 707★★★★ £F
● **Shiraz/Grenache/Mourvèdre** Bin 138 Old Vine★★ £C
● **Cabernet Shiraz** Bin 389★★ £C
● **Shiraz/Mourvèdre** Bin 2★ £B   ● **Old Vine Red**★★ £C
○ **Chardonnay** Adelaide Hills★★ £C Bin 98A★★★ £E Yattarna★★★★ £G

PENLEY ESTATE   Coonwarra   www.penley.com.au   A: **L&W**, NYg, N&P

Owner: Kym Tolley   McLeans Road, Coonawarra SA 5263

Kym Tolley's ancestry and past link him to PENFOLDS but since 1991 he has produced a small but consistently high-quality range of wines under his own label. There are more than 90 ha of estate plantings including nearly 40 ha of Coonawarra Cabernet. The style is for rich, ripe, smooth wines with lush fruit and unobtrusive tannins but with good ageing potential. American oak is favoured for Shiraz, French for Merlot, with a mix of the two for Cabernet. Cabernet Sauvignon Reserve (the same wine was known simply as Cabernet Sauvignon before 1998) has been consistently impressive while Ausvetia is a pricey flagship Shiraz, mostly from McLaren Vale fruit, but including 10 per cent Cabernet Sauvignon. Phoenix and Hyland are lighter, more forward versions of Cabernet and Shiraz respectively. Chardonnay lacks a little elegance but is not short of richness or flavour. (PW)

● **Cabernet Sauvignon** Reserve★★★ £D Phoenix★★ £C   ● **Merlot**★★ £C
● **Shiraz** Ausvetia★★★ £E Hyland★★ £B   ● **Shiraz/Cabernet**★★ £C
○ **Chardonnay**★★ £B

PETALUMA   Adelaide Hills   www.petaluma.com.au   A: **LNa**, Tan, Odd, Vne, F&M, Sel, FFW

Owner: Lion Nathan   Spring Gully Road, Piccadilly SA 5151

As long as Brian Croser remains involved here, it seems certain that Petaluma will always provide ageworthy wines of subtlety and intensity. The formation of the Petaluma group (also KNAPPSTEIN, MITCHELTON, SMITHBROOK and STONIER) seemed to benefit all participants, at least quality- wise. The Petaluma range has always been small and total production is relatively modest. All the wines are site-specific. Riesling is long-established – an excellent, tightly structured, minerally example (now labelled Hanlin Hill for its Clare Valley origins) which needs a minimum of two to three years' age but is capable of much more. The most exceptional white is the brilliant, individual Tiers Chardonnay from the first vineyard planted in the Piccadilly Valley. With great depth, power and a mineral, citrus intensity, its structure and relative austerity when young demand patience. Regular Piccadilly Valley Chardonnay, from other vineyards as well as Tiers also shows a minerally aspect as well as finesse and class that others lack. Complex berry-fruited Coonawarra (equal parts Cabernet and Merlot in a very good 2001) could use a little more weight in cooler years but always reveals greater concentration with age. Croser is an elegant traditional-method sparkling wine, generally around half Chardonnay and half Pinot Noir, that has been consistently fine for more than a decade. A Late Disgorged version has also been produced. All wines have a structure not seen in many of the more immediate premium Australian sparkling wines and must be drunk with some bottle-age. Relatively recent additions are a promising Shiraz (since 2001) and Viognier (since 2002). Both come from the B&V Vineyard on the eastern edge of the Adelaide Hills. Sharefarmers wines including a red (Cabernet/Malbec-based) are sourced from one of two Coonawarra vineyards. Bridgewater Mill 3 Districts wines are blended from sites in Clare, Adelaide Hills and Coonawarra and include Sauvignon Blanc, Chardonnay and Shiraz. (PW)

● **Coonawarra**★★★ £D   ● **Merlot**★★★
○ **Chardonnay** Piccadilly Valley★★★★ £C Tiers★★★★★ £F
○ **Riesling** Hanlin Hill★★★★ £B   ○ **Croser**★★★ £C

PIKES Clare Valley www.pikeswines.com.au A: **L&S**, NYg

Owner: Neil & Andrew Pike Polish Hill River Road, Sevenhill via Clare SA 5453

Pikes is a medium-sized producer with 38 ha of estate vineyards at Polish Hill River and without doubt one of the most reliable names from Clare Valley. The wines are full and flavoursome with weight and intensity across the range. Both Shiraz and Cabernet (which includes 5 per cent Cabernet Franc) show good Clare character with a mineral, earth influence in the rich berry fruit aromas and are ripe, plush and well balanced with restrained oak character. Shiraz/Grenache/Mourvèdre (more than half Shiraz) is a fragrant, nicely textured example of this now-common Australian threesome. Whites include a Chardonnay which shows rich, ripe fruit but includes a mineral, citrus peel component and is capable of a little age. Riesling typically shows a floral, toasty and minerally intensity if not the purity and structure of the best Clare examples. Sauvignon Blanc lacks a real varietal stamp. The wines are decent value although occasional very good Reserves including Riesling, Cabernet, Shiraz and a Merlot are twice the price. Sauvignon Blanc/Semillon is also made, along with Sangiovese (Premio) and, from 2001, a little Viognier. Luccio (Italian for pike) red and white are inexpensive blends; the red adds Sangiovese to Cabernet Sauvignon and Merlot. Pike & Joyce is a partnership with the Joyce family in Lenswood (Adelaide Hills) yielding Pinot Noir, Chardonnay, Sauvignon Blanc as well as a little Pinot Gris. (PW)

O Riesling★★ £B O Chardonnay★★★ £B
● Shiraz★★★ £B ● Shiraz/Grenache/Mourvèdre★★ £B
● Cabernet Sauvignon★★★ £B

PRIMO ESTATE Adelaide www.primoestate.com.au A: **AWA**, NYg, ACh, N&P

Owner: Joe Grilli Old Port Wakefield Road, Virginia SA 5120

From an unpromising location, the hot Adelaide Plains, comes a quite exceptional range of wines, the result of innovation and talent that any wine-producing country would be proud of and which cautious winemakers can only dream of. Joe Grilli was clearly no ordinary Roseworthy graduate and he had both the confidence and ability to go where others are still frightened to follow. He took on the running of his father's vineyard in 1979 and hasn't stopped experimenting since. Estate plantings are now supplemented from vineyards just south of Adelaide and in McLaren Vale proper as well as by bought-in grapes. His Cabernet/Merlot (90 per cent Cabernet) uses partially dried grapes mostly from McLaren Vale. Dubbed Moda Amarone by Grilli, this is a richly textured, exuberant wine full of ripest cassis, blackberry and black plum fruit with plenty of oak, at its best with 5 to 10 years' age. La Magia is a late-harvested Riesling with a long history of experimentation; currently it is composed primarily of botrytised Eden Valley fruit (2001 also includes 25 per cent Traminer). A vibrant fleshy Sparkling Red is produced every two years based on Adelaide Plains Shiraz. New since the 2001 vintage is Pinot Grigio d'Elena. All premium wines are labelled Joseph. Packaging is pretty smart and the prices on the high side yet fair for the quality. Il Briccone, a Shiraz/Sangiovese blend (but including a little Cabernet, Nebbiolo and Barbera), and a zesty tropical and citrus-fruited Colombard white, La Biondina, both under the Primo label are more modestly priced. A tiny amount of fortified Frontignan (Muscat), currently called Fronti IV, is also made, as are vintage-dated olive oils and vinegars. (PW)

● Cabernet Sauvignon/Merlot Joseph★★★ £D
● Shiraz/Sangiovese Il Briccone★ £B ● Sparkling Red★★★ £E
O Riesling La Magia Joseph★★★ £C O Colombard La Biondina★ £B

REYNELLA/REYNELL McLaren Vale www.brlhardy.com.au A: **Cst**, TPg, C&B, N&P

Owner: Hardy Wine Company Reynell Road, Reynella SA 5161

Reynella or Chateau Reynella is a historic property with its origins dating from 1838 when the nation was still in its infancy (and its story is told in any decent book on Australian wine). Bought by the Thomas Hardy company in 1982, it now serves as the corporate headquarters for the much expanded HARDY WINE COMPANY group. Seemingly forever there has been a wealth of old-vine McLaren Vale material and in the 1990s deep, intense, muscular wines were fashioned. Open fermenters and old basket presses are utilised – Basket Pressed is the name that now adorns the reds. These are now wines of great depth, complexity and structure yet with ripe, smooth tannins. Chardonnay is bold and brash with lots of oak – but a good example if you like this style. The wines are sold in Australia as Reynell. (PW)

● **Cabernet Sauvignon** Basket Pressed★★★ £D
● **Cabernet Sauvignon/Merlot** Basket Pressed★★★ £D
● **Shiraz** Basket Pressed★★★ £D   O **Chardonnay**★★ £C

ROCKFORD   Barossa Valley   www.rockfordwines.com.au   A: **AHW**, P&S, HoM

Owner: Robert O'Callaghan   Krondorf Road, Tanunda SA 5352
Rockford wines still taste like true classics. Having been in the vanguard of the Barossa revival, Rocky O'Callaghan seems to have stayed true to the cause better than most. Commercial expansion to fund a fleet of Ferraris has never been the end goal. As a result the wines can be hard to find but they've not been compromised either. Basket Press Shiraz shows the depth and richness that the best old-vine Barossa fruit delivers with ease. An Eden Valley Riesling is picked late with plenty of skin contact giving a very full-flavoured example, but the wine lacks the finesse and other qualities this grape can deliver. Moppa Springs is a Grenache-based blend with Shiraz and Mourvèdre. The Sparkling Shiraz is one of the most famous examples of all but the difficulty in getting hold of it and its cult status-fuelled price mean there's pain before pleasure. (PW)

● **Shiraz** Basket Press★★★★ £D   ● **Cabernet Sauvignon**★★ £C   ● **Moppa Springs**★★ £C
O **Semillon** Local Growers★★ £C   O **Riesling** Eden Valley★★★ £B
● **Sparkling Shiraz** Black Shiraz★★★★ £F

ROSEMOUNT (MCLAREN VALE)   www.rosemountestates.com   A: **ScE**, AAA

Owner: Southcorp   Ingoldby Road, McLaren Flat SA 5171
Rosemount makes several of its best red wines at the McLaren Vale winery. Most famous of these is the McLaren Vale Shiraz sold as Balmoral Syrah, a wine with a real harmony of oak, fruit richness and weight as well as an extra dimension most other Australian examples miss. The Show Reserve Cabernet is sourced from Coonawarra and both French and American oak are utilised in its ageing. Show Reserve Shiraz, by contrast, comes from McLaren Vale and Langhorne Creek and like the Balmoral is aged only in American oak. Traditional is a Bordeaux blend of Cabernet Sauvignon, with 20 per cent Merlot and a smaller amount of Petit Verdot, but the oak used is American not French. GSM stands for Grenache/Shiraz/Mourvèdre (typical percentages 50/40/10), and is one of the most high-profile of these now popular blends. Again, in the classic Australian mould, the oak is American. All the wines show lush fruit and oak, good depth and fine tannins, and if there is less refinement in the GSM there is also more character. Any of these reds will keep for up to 10 years but are most rewarding with just five or six years' age. Also see ROSEMOUNT (under New South Wales & Queensland). (PW)

● **Syrah** Balmoral★★★★★ £F   ● **Shiraz** Show Reserve★★★ £C
● **Cabernet Sauvignon** Show Reserve★★★ £C
● **Traditional**★★★ £C   ● **GSM**★★★ £C

ST HALLETT   Barossa Valley   www.sthallett.com.au   A: **LNa**, AWA, Por, HoM, WSc

Owner: Lion Nathan   St Hallett's Road, Tanunda SA 5352
A decade ago, powered by Bob McLean, St Hallett was one of the bright new stars of Barossa. Now a successful medium-sized operation, it is perhaps the best-known but compared to Charles MELTON, ROCKFORD and others it has now lost some of its lustre. Sound, with good fruit and supple structures, the wines lack flair and individuality. Old Block Shiraz appears to have permanently lost its previous concentration. It would seem that fruit from the many small plots of very old vines is not of an equal standard. An intense, rich, weighty, if slightly coarse and irregular Eden Valley Riesling can be impressive.

Other whites include Semillon/Sauvignon Blanc and from the 2001 vintage, a *barrique*-fermented Blackwell Semillon that is aged on its lees. Biggest volumes come from the blended red and white, called Gamekeeper's Reserve and Poacher's Blend respectively. On a more positive note the wines are widely available and reasonably priced. New from 2002 vintage is GST, unusual in adding Touriga (Nacional) to Grenache and Shiraz. (PW)

● **Shiraz** Faith★ £B Blackwell★★ £C Old Block★★★ £D
○ **Riesling** Eden Valley★★ £B

SALTRAM Barossa Valley www.beringerblass.com.au A: BBI, NYg

Owner: Beringer Blass Nurioopta Road, Angaston SA 5353
Saltram was once one of the most respected names in Australian wine but commercial growth and a lack of focus on the leading reds meant it wasn't the first name on the lips of the many new foreign converts to high-quality Australian wine in the last decade or so. Since 1992 Nigel Dolan has been the man taking responsibility for restoring some pride to these historic wines. Occasional great bottles from the late 50s, 60s and 70s can still be unearthed from Australian cellars (many made by Nigel's father Brian). BERINGER BLASS took control in 1996, the same year Barossa once again became the sole grape source. The wines, particularly the top two reds, now show great richness and depth; Metala Original Plantings comes from 100-year-old vines. From a top vintage like 1998 they should keep for at least a decade. Mamre Brook now offers good value, at least if the prices hold. Pepperjack is a second label seen in Australia and New Zealand. (PW)

● **Shiraz** No. 1 Reserve★★★ £D Metala Original Plantings (Black Label)★★★ £D
● **Shiraz** Mamre Brook★★ £B ● **Shiraz/Cabernet** Metala (White Label)★ £B
● **Cabernet Sauvignon** Mamre Brook★★ £B ○ **Chardonnay** Mamre Brook★ £B

SEPPELT Barossa Valley www.seppelt.com.au A: ScE

Owner: Southcorp PMB 1 Seppeltsfield, via Nurioopta SA 5355
Seppelt's historic Seppeltsfield winery is the centre of production for some marvellous Australian fortified wines but they can be difficult to obtain outside Australia. All are very individual but common to each is a marvellous complexity derived from *rancio* flavours and tertiary bottle-aged characters. The intensity and power of the wines (almost all non-vintage) is not for the faint of heart. While some approximate to a Spanish or Portuguese equivalent, flavours and structures are quite different. Outstanding examples include 'sherries' Amontillado DP 116, Show Fino DP 117 and Show Oloroso DP 38; and Show 'port' Tawny DP 90. Para Liqueur Port is produced in two versions, non-vintage and a 100-year-old version (1897 is the most recent release). From Rutherglen come outstanding Muscat (Show Reserve DP 63) and Tokay (Show Reserve DP 57). Also see SEPPELT GREAT WESTERN (Victoria & Tasmania). (PW)

SHAW & SMITH Adelaide Hills www.shawandsmith.com A: Lib, Tan, Vne, ACh, FFW, Hrd

Owner: Matthew & Michael Hill Smith, Martin Shaw Lot 4, Jones Road, Balhannah SA 5242
The warehouse winemaking operation begun by Martin Shaw and Michael Hill Smith in 1989 has evolved into an estate-based (Balhannah and Woodside), small to medium-sized operation with a stunning new winery. Early success was fuelled by a Sauvignon that proved it was possible to make a distinctive and attractive early-drinking example in the Adelaide Hills. The most impressive wine was a deep, complex and ageworthy Reserve Chardonnay, replaced from the 2000 vintage by a single-vineyard example. The M3 vineyard at Woodside is named not for an often frustratingly slow motorway escape from London but for Martin, Matthew and Michael. The wine is crafted around a core of pristine Adelaide Hills fruit and has excellent texture but is likely to show the greatest expression with around five years' age. Unoaked Chardonnay typically shows nicely concentrated fruit but there are better examples. Merlot has been released under the Shaw & Smith label since 1999 (previously it had been made only under a second label, Incognito). It moves up a notch in 2001 with ripe, small berry fruit and a floral, herbal influence and is

now distinctly varietal. New are Riesling and a superb new Shiraz: the 2002 shows mineral, white pepper, concentrated plum and blackberry fruit, excellent structure, flesh and real class. (PW)

Shaw & Smith:
O **Chardonnay** M3 Vineyard★★★★ £D Unoaked★★ £B
O **Sauvignon Blanc**★★ £B ● **Merlot**★★★ £D

Incognito:
O **Riesling**★ £B O **Chardonnay**★★ £B ● **Merlot**★ £B

SOUTHCORP www.southcorp.com.au
Mammoth Australian company that includes some of Australia's biggest wine names. A merger with ROSEMOUNT (see New South Wales & Queensland) in 2001 has further broadened and enhanced the company's position. Leading brands and wineries in South Australia include, PENFOLDS, ROSEMOUNT (MCLAREN VALE), WYNNS, SEPPELT (SEPPELTSFIELD), LINDEMANS, EDWARDS & CHAFFEY, Leo Buring and Tollana. Victoria provides SEPPELT GREAT WESTERN, LINDEMANS and COLDSTREAM HILLS; Western Australia, DEVIL'S LAIR. Outside Australia, Southcorp owns the James Herrick brand in Languedoc-Roussillon and Seven Peaks in California Central Coast. (PW)

STONEHAVEN Padthaway www.stonehavenvineyards.com.au   **A: Cst**

Owner: Hardy Wine Company Stonehaven Vineyards, Riddoch Highway, Padthaway SA 5271
This state-of-the-art winery processes fruit for what is now the Constellation group from throughout the Limestone Coast. Half of almost 900 ha of vineyard is in Padthaway itself. The wines made by Tom Newton and Sue Bell fall into three ranges. The premium label is called Limited Vineyard Release. Chardonnay is powerful, oak-influenced and rich with lots of intensity and depth but already has proven ageing ability, in fact needing five years. The two reds are powerful, concentrated and extracted, the Shiraz from Padthaway fruit being slightly more convincing than Cabernet Sauvignon which is partly Coonawarra-sourced. Both need a little more refinement but at any rate need eight to ten years' to harmonise fully. A second range of varietals includes Cabernet Sauvignon, Shiraz, Chardonnay and Viognier. The Chardonnay is excellent; tight and poised with real distinction and definition, not unlike a top example of a lesser village white Burgundy. Least expensive are the Stepping Stone wines of which Coonawarra Cabernet Sauvignon and Padthaway Chardonnay stand out. (PW)
O **Chardonnay** Stepping Stone★★ £B Limestone Coast★★★ £B Limited Vineyard Release★★★ £C
● **Cabernet Sauvignon** Stepping Stone★★ £B Limestone Coast★★ £C Limited Vineyard Release★★★ £D
● **Shiraz** Limestone Coast★★ £C Limited Vineyard Release★★★ £D

TATACHILLA McLaren Vale www.tatachillawinery.com.au   **A: LNa,** Maj, Lwt, Nid

Owner: Lion Nathan 151 Main Road, McLaren Vale SA 5171
Part of the Lion Nathan-owned Banksia wine group, the relaunched Tatachilla produces a very extensive range of wines totalling over a quarter of a million cases per year. The top two reds don't lack for structure, extract, fruit or oak, though the Foundation Shiraz is more complete and convincing than the somewhat showy Clarendon Merlot. Most of the wines show good fruit and balance but the emphasis is on upfront fruit and pleasing textures and often the wines fall away a little on the palate and at times lack for real concentration. Keystone is a characterful blend of Grenache and a little Shiraz, with rich fruit and balanced oak. Both Chardonnay and Cabernet Sauvignon are sourced from Padthaway and show distinctive fruit. The Cabernet makes an interesting contrast with the richer, deeper, more black-fruited McLaren Vale example. A premium 1901 Cabernet Sauvignon is a blend of both sources. The inexpensive Breakneck Creek label includes varietal Cabernet, Merlot, Shiraz and Chardonnay. Those listed below are a selection of the wines made. (PW)
● **Merlot** McLaren Vale★ £B Clarendon★★ £D
● **Shiraz** McLaren Vale★★ £C Foundation★★★ £D

● **Grenache/Shiraz** Keystone★★ £B
● **Cabernet Sauvignon** McLaren Vale★★★ £C Padthaway★★ £B
○ **Chardonnay** McLaren Vale★ £B Padthaway★ £B

THE LANE WINE COMPANY Adelaide Hills www.thelane.com.au A: **Cap**, Amp

Owner: John Edwards Ravenswood Lane, Hahndorf SA 5245
John Edwards' estate wines (previously known as Ravenswood Lane) come from 28 ha near Hahndorf in the central part of the Adelaide Hills. Much effort has gone into the packaging and image, and fortunately into the wines too. An exciting lush, peppery, fleshy Shiraz has real potential and does reflect something of the South Australia/Rhône hybrid style claimed for these wines. There is potential too in an intense, lemony Chardonnay that reveals the depth and dimension of a serious Côte de Beaune example. In collaboration with HARDYS winemakers, John Edwards makes the Starvedog Lane wines at Hardys' Tintara winery from a mix of vineyard resources. Unlike the Starvedog Lane version, The Lane Sauvignon (which includes Semillon) is barrel-fermented and adds more breadth, but at the cost of some of the vibrant nettly intensity of the unoaked wine. Perhaps the best Starvedog Lane wine is the Cabernet: cool, complex, but ripe too, with blackberry, blackcurrant, mint and chocolate flavours and an attractive cedary complexity. Shiraz can be good too while Merlot, an unwooded 'No Oak' Chardonnay and a traditional-method sparkling Chardonnay/Pinot Noir/Pinot Meunier are also made. There are no bargains here but nicely textured interesting wines at prices commensurate to quality. (PW)

The Lane:
● **Shiraz** Reunion★★★ £E ● **Cabernet Sauvignon** 19th Meeting★★★ £E
○ **Sauvignon Blanc** Gathering★★ £C ○ **Chardonnay** Beginning★★★ £C
Starvedog Lane:
● **Cabernet Sauvignon**★★★ £C ● **Shiraz**★★ £C
○ **Chardonnay**★★ £C ○ **Sauvignon Blanc**★★ £B

TORBRECK Barossa Valley www.torbreck.com A: **HBJ**, Bal, NYg, Rae, BBR, UnC, Hrd, P&S

Owner: David Powell Lot 51, Roennfeldt Road, Marananga SA 5360
Established in the mid-1990s, Torbreck became one of the most raved-about Barossa wineries by the turn of the century and is one of the few which produces genuinely outstanding wines that match some of the hype. David Powell manages to buy small parcels of fruit from very old unirrigated, low-yielding vineyards and turns into them wine with great aroma, deep fruit, structure and balance. All the reds have highish but balanced alcohol levels and a breadth and extract many other Barossa/Clare/McLaren Vale blockbusters lack. Runrig, the top wine first made in 1995, is Shiraz with a little Viognier (3 per cent); the fruit here is sensational. As well as great depth and class, this wine has the sort of dimension and structure only encountered in the very best Côte-Rôties and needs 8 to 10 years' ageing. Descendant (a vineyard established from Runrig cuttings) includes 7 or 8 per cent Viognier, which contributes to its more open, perfumed character, but it has good extract and intensity too. The Factor, made since 1998 from 100 per cent Shiraz from old unirrigated vines, is tighter, more compact and less expressive yet promises to have the greater ageing potential. The Struie, new from 2001, is a super, stylish blend of equal parts Barossa and Eden Valley fruit, while Juveniles and The Steading are southern Rhône-style blends of Grenache, Shiraz and Mourvèdre (60/20/20 in recent vintages). Both of the latter pair are perfumed with lovely fruit and are supple and long; The Steading, aged in used and large oak, shows the better structure, but not the vibrancy or purity of Juveniles. A new white, VMR (Viognier/Marsanne/Roussanne; 60/20/20 in 2002) keeps to the Rhône theme. Woodcutters red (Shiraz) and white (Semillon) are the more affordable basics and offer good fruit. (PW)

● **Runrig**✪✪✪✪✪ £H ● **The Factor**★★★★★ £G ● **Descendant**★★★★ £G
● **The Struie**★★★ £D ● **The Steading**★★★ £D ● **Juveniles**★★★ £D
● **Woodcutter's Red**★★ £C ○ **Woodcutter's White**★ £C

TURKEY FLAT Barossa www.turkeyflat.com.au   A: **Bal**, NYg, Tan, P&S, The, Nid, But, Hrd

Owner: Peter & Christie Schulz Bethany Road, Tanunda SA 5352

Turkey Flat has a priceless resource of old-vine Barossa fruit. The Schulzes have had the good fortune to have the vines in the family since 1865 (some planted in the 1840s!) though have only been making their own wines since 1990. A decade later they added their own winery but in the interim established their credentials particularly with Shiraz but also Grenache, Semillon and Cabernet. Shiraz is easily the best wine – succulent and full of old-viney fruit without being overwhelmed by oak. Grenache is even more approachable but lacks a little richness and depth by comparison. Butcher's Block is named for a vineyard planted to Mourvèdre, Shiraz and Grenache and although an attractive, perfumed wine it misses the interest and intensity of better examples. Cabernet is powerful but accessible and fleshy with good intensity to its earthy, slightly coarse berry fruit character. Semillon is unoaked but has good ripe fruit, coming as it does from old vines. An unusual Marsanne/Semillon blend is a new departure as is The Turk, a supple juicy blend in which a small amount of Cabernet and Mourvèdre are added to Shiraz and Grenache. Few rosés are worth seeking out but Turkey Flat's fragrant cherry and berry-fruited off-dry example (from Grenache, Cabernet, Shiraz and Dolcetto) is delicious, fresh and balanced if drunk very young. (PW)

● **Shiraz★★★** £D   ● **Cabernet Sauvignon★★** £D
● **Grenache★★** £C   ● **Butchers Block★★** £C   ◉ **Rosé★★** £B

TWO HANDS www.twohandswines.com   A: **All**, P&S, Nid

Owner: Michael Twelftree & Richard Mintz Neldner Road, Marananga SA 5355

There have been a lot of changes here since the initial (and justified) hype quickly turned this into a sought-after label. Grape sources, winemaker and production levels have all changed – the latter significantly with a profusion of limited-production labels – since the first vintage in 2000. The winemaker is Matt Wenk with consultancy from Rolf Binder of VERITAS, where the wines are made. The standard of the reds is generally very high, most with both style and a sense of place allied to an intense fruit expression. Balance and use of oak are also good but there is a lack of dimension and structure in most. Lily's Garden McLaren Vale Shiraz is arguably the most consistently fine of the reds. A very intensely flavoured Riesling, The Wolf, like the reds wants for better definition and structure. As well as the wines rated below, also made are Deer in the Headlights Shiraz from the Barossa and Samantha's Garden Clare Valley Shiraz, while new from 2003 are Brilliant Disguise Moscato (in the style of Moscato d'Asti) and Yesterday's Hero from predominantly old vine Barossa Grenache. A very small amount of a flagship Shiraz, Ares, has been made since 2001. (PW)

● **Shiraz** Lily's Garden McLaren Vale★★★★ £E Angel's Share McLaren Vale★★★ £C
● **Shiraz** Bad Impersonator Single Vineyard Barossa Valley★★★ £E
● **Shiraz/Grenache** Brave Faces Barossa Valley★★★ £D
● **Shiraz/Cabernet Sauvignon** The Bull and the Bear Barossa Valley★★★ £E
○ **Riesling** Clare Valley★★ £C

VERITAS Barossa Valley www.veritaswinery.com   A: **Sec**, L&W, NYg, Hrd

Owner: Rolf Binder & Christa Deans Seppeltsfield Road, Dorrien SA 5355

Veritas is one of the much-lauded new stars of the Barossa. Rolf Binder and his sister Christa Deans draw upon mostly estate vineyards for an annual production of around 35,000 cases. The reds have lost some of their oomph and richness of late but are still deep, powerful, extracted wines, primarily from Rhône varieties. The most acclaimed wines to date are the Heysen Vineyard and Hanisch Shirazes, the former combining an intense, preserved black fruits, earth and licorice character with a powerful structure and requiring at least 8 to 10 years' age to show its full potential. A Shiraz/Mourvèdre Pressings (subtitled Binder's Bull's Blood) has rich black plum and berry fruit, while Heinrich is a more backward, extracted Shiraz/Mourvèdre/Grenache blend. A Cabernet Sauvignon/Merlot (predominantly Cabernet) has intense brambly, cassis fruit and ripe tannins to match. One that doesn't need cellaring is a more forward, supple, raspberryish Shiraz/Grenache under the Christa-Rolf label. An attractive Semillon is also made under the same label. The wines remain well priced despite the early hype but a note of caution regarding recent releases: one or two reds seem to be marred by odd musty and/or menthol-like characters. New are well-made inexpensive Retro 55 red and white. Also new is Cuvée Stephanie, a blend of Shiraz, Mourvèdre and Viognier. (PW)

● **Shiraz** Heysen Vineyard★★★★ £C   ● **Shiraz/Mourvèdre** Pressings★★★ £C
● **Shiraz/Mourvèdre/Grenache** Heinrich★★★ £C   ● **Cabernet Sauvignon/Merlot**★★★ £B
● **Shiraz/Grenache** Christa-Rolf★★ £B   O **Semillon** Christa-Rolf★★ £B

GEOFF WEAVER   Adelaide Hills   www.geoffweaver.com.au   A: **Bal**, Res, Nid

Owner: Geoff Weaver 2 Gilpin Lane, Mitcham SA 5062
From 11 ha of Lenswood vineyards established in the mid-1980s and at over 500m elevation, Geoff Weaver (ex HARDYS) makes a modest amount of increasingly good wine. Whites are best although, while flavoursome and well made, they can lack the extra breadth and subtlety of the finest from the Adelaide Hills. An intensely flavoured and ageworthy Chardonnay vies with an intense toasty, limey and even more cellarworthy Riesling as the best of these. A stylish Sauvignon with ripe gooseberry fruit and a hint of smoke and blackcurrant leaf is also good if drunk with no more than a year's age. Cabernet/Merlot (typically more than 80 per cent Cabernet) needs a warm year like 1998 really to succeed; otherwise cooler leafy, sappy characters become too dominant and the texture too lean. Also made is an improving Pinot Noir with good texture, depth and better structure than previously. (PW)

O **Chardonnay**★★★ £C   O **Riesling**★★★ £B   O **Sauvignon Blanc**★★ £C
● **Cabernet/Merlot**★★ £C   ● **Pinot Noir**★★ £D

WENDOUREE   Clare Valley   A: NYg

Owner: Tony & Lita Brady Wendouree Road, Clare SA 5453
This Clare Valley producer maintains a cult following by sticking rigidly to a formula of maximising the extraordinary fruit produced from 12 ha of vines. The winery dates from 1895 and little seems to have changed in the 100 years or so since. The reds are massive and uncompromising, extracted and tannic yet with dense, earthy impenetrable fruit when young. Balance and ripeness are nearly always there, ensuring these wines will, after 20 years or more, be complex and compelling. Shiraz/ Mataro (Mourvèdre) and Shiraz/Malbec are predominantly Shiraz-based and, together with the varietal Shiraz, are perhaps more consistent than the Cabernet-based reds. None of the wines are made in much more than 500-case lots, so total production remains tiny. The prices are reasonable for the quality, given the considerable demand. Above all they are a cellaring investment for wine drinkers with patience. (PW)

● **Shiraz**★★★★ £F   ● **Shiraz/Mataro**★★★★ £F   ● **Shiraz/Malbec**★★★★ £F
● **Cabernet/Malbec**★★★ £F   ● **Cabernet Sauvignon**★★★★ £F

WIRRA WIRRA   McLaren Vale   www.wirra.com.au   A: **HBJ**, Res, WSc, P&S

Owner: R G & R T Trott Pty McMurtrie Road, McLaren Vale SA 5171
This medium-sized operation (70,000 cases) has a reputation way beyond its size. In recent years it has recruited expert help from the likes of Dr Tony Jordan and, more recently, Tim James (from HARDYS). The wines are technically very sound with all the components to be really fine, yet they miss a certain flair and a natural expression. That said, quality is uniformly high and the top reds will repay keeping for five to eight years. Flagship Cabernet Sauvignon, The Angelus, and Shiraz, RSW, have been complemented by the introduction of a further super-premium range of reds made in exceptional vintages and in very small quantities. The Vineyard Series includes a particularly impressive Cabernet (Penley) and Shiraz (Chook Block) of more specific origins as well as a straight Grenache (Allawah). At a more affordable level, Church Block is a long-standing blend of Cabernet, Shiraz and Merlot (approximately 50/30/20) but it no longer has the vibrant fruit or style of earlier vintages. Original Blend, alluding to the first wine made by the Trott

cousins, contains around two-thirds Grenache and has an accentuated berry fruit character. Wirra Wirra whites are flavoursome but do not match the reds for quality. Adelaide Hills Sauvignon Blanc and Chardonnay are relatively fast-evolving and don't compare with the region's best. Also made are a floral, ripely fruity Riesling and unwooded Sextons Acre Chardonnay. Some fortifieds are made including VP Vintage Fortified Shiraz and Fine Old Tawny. A sparkling wine, The Cousins, is a flavoursome if not particularly refined blend of Pinot Noir and Chardonnay. The Scrubby Rise brand includes both a red and a white blend as well as Shiraz and Chardonnay. (PW)

- ● **Cabernet Sauvignon** The Angelus★★★ £D
- ● **Shiraz** McLaren Vale★★ £C RSW★★★ £D ● **Grenache** McLaren Vale★★ £C
- ● **Grenache/Shiraz** Original Blend★★ £B ● **Cabernet/Shiraz/Merlot** Church Block★ £B
- ○ **Chardonnay** Adelaide Hills★★ £C ○ **Riesling** Hand Picked★ £B

WOODSTOCK McLaren Vale www.woodstockwine.com.au   A: **Ver,** Nid

Owner: Scott & Anne Collett   Douglas Gully Road, McLaren Flat SA 5171
Woodstock is one of McLaren Vale's well-established wineries able to draw on its own vineyards for a solid, reasonably priced range of wines. As well as 22 ha in McLaren Flat, 33 ha of vineyards are located in Langhorne Creek (Angas Vineyard) and a further 27 ha in Limestone Coast (Wirrega Vineyard). The leading variety unsurprisingly is Shiraz, particularly The Stocks, the flagship wine made since 1991. The fruit from very old vines stands up very well to the new American oak in which it is aged. Regular Shiraz and a Cabernet Sauvignon are both rich, ripe and concentrated if lacking a little flair. More straightforward are a berryish Grenache and Five Feet, an improving blend of Cabernet, Petit Verdot, Merlot and Shiraz. Whites include Semillon/Sauvignon Blanc, Riesling, Verdelho, and Chardonnay. All show attractive, ripe, generous flavours but only the latter two can stand a bit of age. Botrytis Sweet White is a blend of Chenin Blanc, Riesling and Semillon and is ripe and intense if not that refined. A small amout of fortified wine is also made. (PW)

- ● **Shiraz**★★ £C The Stocks★★★ £D
- ● **Cabernet Sauvignon**★★ £C ● **Five Feet**★ £B
- ○ **Chardonnay**★ £B ○ **Semillon**★ £B ○ **Verdelho**★ £B ○ **Botrytis Sweet White**★ £C

WYNNS Coonawarra www.wynns.com.au   A: **ScE,** Maj, Odd, Nid, BBR, Sel, WSc

Owner: Southcorp   Memorial Drive, Coonawarra SA 5263
The most famous producer name in Coonawarra is a veritable colossus with 900 ha, around a third of the terra rossa soils. Wynns' great red is the John Riddoch Cabernet, based on unirrigated vines in the heart of the region. Made since 1982 but not in every vintage (there's no 95 or 99), it is a magnificent rich, powerful rendition of Cabernet that makes no apology to any other great Cabernet region and needs to be drunk with 10 years' age or more. Michael Shiraz, made since 1990, is the Shiraz equivalent of John Riddoch. Equally rich and powerful, it is always steeped in oak, which adds to its appeal for some. The fruit is very good indeed and does take up some of the oak with age but not all, leaving a coarse, oaky feel to the finish (in the 94 for instance). The 98 is more promising though still not one for the oak-shy. Both Michael and John Riddoch wines now use only a fraction of the very best fruit available. The famous estate-based Black Label Cabernet is now a big-volume wine but is still relatively inexpensive with the same intense blackcurrant/blackberry fruit, oak and tannin balance it has always had. Shiraz is often at least as good and from a top vintage can add the little extra richness that makes it an excellent buy. Cabernet/Shiraz/Merlot includes only a little Merlot and the Cabernet and Shiraz components invariably merge for a ripe, supple, fruity red. Chardonnay delivers fine fruit and real complexity, a far cry from some of the overoaked efforts of years past. Riesling is often one of Australia's best bargain whites, consistently delivering a floral, limey, fruit-driven intensity. Despite its size, Wynns stands out because of its remarkable viticultural resources. (PW)

- ● **Cabernet Sauvignon** Black Label★★★ £C John Riddoch★★★★★ £F
- ● **Shiraz**★★ £B Michael★★★★ £F
- ● **Cabernet/Shiraz/Merlot**★ £B
- ○ **Chardonnay**★★ £B ○ **Riesling**★ £B

YALUMBA Barossa Valley www.yalumba.com A: **Neg**, BBR, Res, WSc, F&M, Hrd, P&S, Sel

Owner: Hill Smith family Eden Valley Road, Angaston SA 5353
Yalumba is the only big Australian wine company still to be family-owned. Winemaking has been led by Brian Walsh since the late 1980s, when the company's growth was fuelled by the huge success of the inexpensive sparkling wine, Angas Brut. With more than 650 ha of vines from diverse sources, the range is necessarily large and continually evolving, though some wines have a long history. Whites in particular have improved under Louisa Rose. Premium wines begin with The Reserve, a very limited-production Cabernet Sauvignon/Shiraz blend made in 1990, 92 and 96. Others produced on a more regular basis include Octavius, an expensive, richly oaky old-vine Barossa Shiraz, and The Signature (two-thirds Coonawarra Cabernet, one-third Barossa Shiraz), a suave, flattering blend streaked with vanilla from two years in American oak but not always as composed or convincing as it might be. An entirely Coonawarra-sourced Cabernet, The Menzies, is characterised by open, generous fruit in good vintages, while newer and also Coonawarra-derived is Mawson's, which adds Shiraz and a little Merlot to Cabernet. New MGS (Mourvèdre/Grenache/Shiraz) is a ripe, spicy berry-fruited example of this style of Barossa red. There is also Adelaide Hills Pinot Noir and Chardonnay, the latter showing some of the stylish complexity and subtlety typical of the best examples. Much has been made of Yalumba's efforts with Viognier (it pioneered plantings of the variety in South Australia) yet even at the premium level (Virgilius) there is some way to go before it can compete with the best Condrieu producers. Late-harvested/botrytis styles now include Riesling, Semillon and Viognier under a Noble Pick label. Dolcetto, Nebbiolo and other varieties have also been released locally under the Vinnovation Collection label. Y is a series of relatively inexpensive varietals including an unwooded Chardonnay, Riesling, Viognier, Merlot and Shiraz. Even cheaper are the simple, innocuous wines of budget brand, Oxford Landing, produced from Riverlands fruit. Other wineries owned by the family include the Eden Valley estates of Pewsey Vale and Heggies as well as Jansz from the Pipers River area of northern Tasmania. Pewsey Vale's Riesling has been revived with greater intensity and definition in the most recent vintages; a Contours version released with bottle age is impressive too. A very impressive new Mesh Riesling, made in collaboration with Jeffrey GROSSET, is much more European (almost Pfalz-like) in style. The Heggies wines are made by Peter Gambetta and include Riesling (occasionally also made in a botrytised version) with a pure citrus and mineral character, improving Viognier and elegant, complex Chardonnay. The only red is a variable yet sometimes stylish Merlot. Janz sparkling wines easily surpass the Yalumba sparklers, with cooler, better-defined fruit as well as better length and complexity. Smith & Hooper wines come from Wrattonbully fruit and include an ambitious Limited Edition Merlot. (PW)

Yalumba:
● **Shiraz** Barossa★ £B The Octavius★★★ £F ● **Shiraz/Viognier** Handpicked★★★ £C
● **Cabernet Sauvignon** Clare Valley Reserve★ £D Coonawarra The Menzies★★★ £D
● **Cabernet/Shiraz** Barossa★ £B The Signature★★★ £D ● **Cabernet/Shiraz/Merlot** Mawson's★★ £B
● **Grenache** Barossa Bush Vine★ £B Handpicked Tri-centenary Vines★★ £D
O **Chardonnay** Barossa★ £B Adelaide Hills★★★ £C
O **Viognier** Y★ £B Eden Valley★★ £C Virgilius★★★ £D
O **Semillon** Noble Pick★ £D O **Muscat** Museum Release★★★★ £E
● **Sparkling Cabernet/Shiraz** 'D' Black★ £C O **Jansz** Non-Vintage★★ £B Vintage★★★ £C
Heggies:
O **Chardonnay**★★ £B O **Riesling**★★ £B O **Viognier**★★ £C ● **Merlot**★★ £C
Pewsey Vale:
O **Riesling**★★ £B The Contours★★★ £C
Grosset - Hill-Smith:
O **Riesling** Mesh★★★ £C
Smith & Hooper:
● **Cabernet Sauvignon/Merlot**★★ £B ● **Merlot** Limited Edition★★★ £D

ZEMA ESTATE Coonawarra www.zema.com.au   A: **MSd**, Lwt

Owner: Zema family   Riddoch Highway, Coonarra SA 5263
Nearly 50 ha of estate vineyards were built up in Coonawarra by this family during the 1980s and early 90s, the core being in the very heart of the region. The wines express much of the best of Coonawarra with dense, powerful fruit lent a little more structure from oak-ageing. However, the oak is restrained, making for less obvious, slightly firmer wines that really benefit from at least three to five years' bottle-age. The oak is more in evidence, but not overdone, in the lusher Family Selection Cabernet Sauvignon. Harvesting is mechanical as in most vineyards in Coonwarra but the vines are still hand-pruned, which arguably makes a positive impact on quality. If slightly less good in cooler years like 1997, the wines really shine from good to great years such as 2000, 99 and 98. Cluny, a somewhat lighter, softer Bordeaux blend (adding Merlot, Cabernet Franc and Malbec to Cabernet Sauvignon) is the most accessible. A Family Selection Shiraz was also made in the 2000 vintage. (PW)
- **Cabernet Sauvignon**★★★ £C Family Selection★★★ £D
- **Shiraz**★★★ £C ● **Cluny**★★ £C

OTHER WINES OF NOTE

AUSTRALIAN DOMAINE WINES (McLaren Vale) ● **The Hattrick** (Shiraz/Grenache/Cabernet) £E
BARLETTA BROS (McLaren Vale) ● **Grenache/Shiraz** £C ● **Shiraz** Clare Valley £C
● **Sheeraz** (Limestone Coast Shiraz) £B
BASEDOW (Barossa Valley) ● **Shiraz** Johannes £E
BATTLE OF BOSWORTH (McLaren Vale) ● **Cabernet Sauvignon** £C ● **Shiraz** £C
BRIAN BARRY O **Riesling Jud's** Hill Clare Valley £B ● **Cabernet Sauvignon Jud's** Hill Clare Valley £C
BIRCHWOOD ESTATE ● **Shiraz** Decades McLaren Vale £C
● **Cabernet Sauvignon** Twin Rivers Langhorne Creek £C
BETHANY (Barossa Valley) ● **Shiraz** £C ● **Cabernet/Merlot** £C O **Semillon** £B
BLEWITT SPRINGS O **Chardonnay** Coonawarra £B ● **Shiraz** Adelaide £B
● **Cabernet Sauvignon** Langhorne Creek £B ● **Malbec** Langhorne Creek £B
BREMERTON (Langhorne Creek) ● **Shiraz** Old Adam £C ● **Cabernet Sauvignon** Walter's £C
LEO BURING O **Riesling** Leonay Eden Valley £D Leonay Watervale £D
CERAVOLO (Adelaide Plains) ● **Shiraz** £C ● **Petit Verdot** £C
CLASSIC MCLAREN (McLaren Vale) ● **La Testa** (Shiraz/Grenache/Cabernet) £D ● **Shiraz** La Testa £F
CLEGGETT (Langhorne Creek) ● **Cabernet Sauvignon** Legend Series £B
COLONIAL WINE COMPANY (Barossa Valley) ● **Exile** (Shiraz/Mourvèdre) £H
● **Émigré** (Shiraz/Grenache/Mourvèdre/Cabernet Sauvignon) £F
CRANEFORD ● **Cabernet Sauvignon** Coonawarra £C ● **Shiraz** Barossa Valley £C
O **Riesling** Eden Valley £B
GALAH ● **Cabernet/Malbec/Shiraz** Clare Valley £C ● **Shiraz** Clare Valley £C
● **Cabernet Sauvignon** Clare Valley £C
GLAETZER (Barossa Valley) ● **Shiraz** £C Bishop £C O **Semillon** Bush Vine £B
GLENARA (Adelaide Hills) O **Riesling** £B
TIM GRAMP (Clare Valley) O **Riesling** Watervale £B ● **Cabernet Sauvignon** Watervale £B
HAAN WINES (Barossa Valley) O **Viognier** £C ● **Merlot** Prestige £D
● **Wilhelmus** (Cabernet Sauvignon/Merlot/Cabernet Franc/Malbec/Petit Verdot) £E
HEARTLAND (Limestone Coast) ● **Shiraz** £B Directors' Cut £C ● **Petit Verdot** £B
● **Cabernet Sauvignon** £B
HERITAGE WINES/STEPHEN HOFF ● **Shiraz** Barossa £B ● **Cabernet/Malbec** £B
INGOLDBY (McLaren Vale) ● **Shiraz** Reserve £C
IRVINE (Eden Valley) ● **Merlot Grand** James Irvine £F
JEANNERET (Clare Valley) ● **Shiraz** £B ● **Cabernet Sauvignon** £C
JENKE ● **Shiraz** Barossa £C
STEPHEN JOHN (Clare Valley) O **Riesling** Watervale £B

KAESLER ● **Shiraz** Stonehorse £D Old Vine £E ● **Avignon** (Grenache/Shiraz/Mourvèdre) £C O **Semillon** Old Vine £C

KANGARILLA ROAD ● **Shiraz** McLaren Vale £B ● **Cabernet Sauvignon** McLaren Vale £B

KAY BROTHERS/AMERY VINEYARD (McLaren Vale) ● **Shiraz** Hillside £E Block 6 £F

KIES ● **Shiraz** Dedication Barossa Valley £D ● **Cabernet Sauvignon** Chaff Mill Barossa Valley £D

LEABROOK ESTATE (Adelaide Hills) ● **Pinot Noir** Reserve £C

LENGS & COOTER ● **Shiraz** Old Vines Clare Valley £C

LONGVIEW (Adelaide Hills) O **Viognier** Beau Sea £B O **Chardonnay** Blue Cow Unwooded £B ● **Shiraz** Yakka £C

McLEAN'S FARM (Barossa Valley) ● **Barossa Reserve** (Shiraz/Cabernet Sauvignon) £C ● **Shiraz** Barossa Valley £C

MAGPIE ESTATE (Barossa Valley) ● **Shiraz** The Sack £B The Election £E

NOON (McLaren Vale) ● **Shiraz/Grenache** Eclipse £E

PARACOMBE (Adelaide Hills) ● **Cabernet Franc** £C ● **Shiraz** £C

PAULETT (Clare Valley) O **Riesling** Polish Hill River £B O **Chardonnay** Polish Hill River £B ● **Cabernet/Merlot** Polish Hill River £B ● **Shiraz** Polish Hill River £B

PERTARINGA/GEOFF HARDY (Adelaide Hills) ● **Shiraz** Kuitpo £D ● **Cabernet** Kuitpo £D

PIRRAMIMMA (McLaren Vale) ● **Petit Verdot** Reserve £C ● **Shiraz** Stocks Hill £B

PUNTERS CORNER (Coonawarra) ● **Cabernet Sauvignon** £C ● **Shiraz** £C

PYCNANTHA HILL (Clare Valley) ● **Shiraz** £C

RBJ VINTNERS ● **Theologicum** (Mourvèdre/Grenache) £C

RICHMOND GROVE O **Riesling** Watervale £B ● **Shiraz** Barossa £C

RYMILL (Coonawarra) ● **Cabernet Sauvignon** £C ● **Shiraz** £B MC2 (Merlot/Cabernet Sauvignon/Cabernet Franc) £B

SEVENHILL CELLARS O **Riesling** Clare Valley £B ● **Shiraz** Clare Valley £C

SKILLOGALEE O **Riesling** Clare Valley £C ● **The Cabernets** £C ● **Shiraz** Clare Valley £C

STEP ROAD ● **Shiraz** McLaren Vale £B ● **Sangiovese** Langhorne Creek £B

STRINGY BRAE ● **Riesling** Clare Valley £C ● **Shiraz** Clare Valley £C

TAYLORS/WAKEFIELD CELLARS (Clare Valley) O **Riesling** Clare £B St Andrews £C ● **Shiraz** £B St Andrews £D

TEMPLE BRUER (Langhorne Creek) ● **Grenache/Shiraz/Viognier** £B ● **Cabernet/Petit Verdot** Reserve £C

VIKING (Barossa Valley) ● **Grand Shiraz** £E

WANINGA (Clare Valley) ● **Shiraz** £C

THE WILLOWS VINEYARD (Barossa Valley) ● **Cabernet Sauvignon** Barossa £B ● **Shiraz** Barossa £C O **Semillon** Barossa £B

WILSON VINEYARD (Clare Valley) O **Riesling** Gallery Series £B

Author's choice (PW)

12 powerful Barossa/Eden Valley Shiraz

BAROSSA VALLEY ESTATE ● **Shiraz** E&E Black Pepper

GRANT BURGE ● **Shiraz** Meschach

BURGE FAMILY ● **Shiraz** Draycott

CHARLES CIMICKY ● **Shiraz** Signature

DUTSCHKE ● **Shiraz** Oscar Semmler

GREENOCK CREEK ● **Shiraz** Seven Acre

HENSCHKE ● **Shiraz** Mount Edelstone

PETER LEHMANN ● **Shiraz** Stonewell

CHARLES MELTON ● **Shiraz**

ROCKFORD ● **Shiraz** Basket Press

TORBRECK ● **Shiraz** The Factor

VERITAS ● **Shiraz** Heysen Vineyard

12 other top Shiraz

TIM ADAMS ● Shiraz Clare Valley Aberfeldy
JIM BARRY ● Shiraz Clare Valley The Armagh
BOWEN ESTATE ● Shiraz Coonawarra
CORIOLE ● Shiraz McLaren Vale Lloyd Reserve
D'ARENBERG ● Shiraz McLaren Vale Dead Arm
FOX CREEK ● Shiraz McLaren Vale Reserve
HARDYS ● Shiraz Eileen Hardy
HENRY'S DRIVE ● Shiraz Padthaway Reserve
KILIKANOON ● Shiraz Clare Valley Covenant
REYNELLA ● Shiraz McLaren Vale Basket Pressed
ROSEMOUNT ● Syrah McLaren Vale Balmoral
WENDOUREE ● Shiraz Clare Valley

12 leading Cabernet-based reds

D'ARENBERG ● Cabernet Sauvignon Coppermine Road
GROSSET ● Gaia
HENSCHKE ● Cabernet Sauvignon Cyril Henschke
HOLLICK ● Cabernet Sauvignon Ravenswood
LECONFIELD ● Cabernet Coonawarra
MAXWELL ● Cabernet Sauvignon Lime Cave
PARKER COONAWARRA ● Terra Rossa First Growth
PENFOLDS ● Cabernet Sauvignon Bin 707
PENLEY ESTATE ● Cabernet Sauvignon Reserve
PRIMO ESTATE ● Cabernet Sauvignon/Merlot Joseph
WYNNS ● Cabernet Sauvignon John Riddoch
ZEMA ESTATE ● Cabernet Sauvignon Coonawarra

10 ageworthy whites

TIM ADAMS O Semillon Clare Valley
BARRATT O Chardonnay Adelaide Hills
GROSSET O Chardonnay Piccadilly
GROSSET O Riesling Polish Hill
HARDYS O Chardonnay Eileen Hardy
KNAPPSTEIN LENSWOOD O Chardonnay Lenswood
MOUNT HORROCKS O Riesling Watervale
PETALUMA O Chardonnay Tiers
PEWSEY VALE O Riesling The Contours
SHAW & SMITH O Chardonnay M3 Vineyard

10 best buys

ANNIE'S LANE O Riesling Clare Valley
CASCABEL O Riesling Eden Valley
D'ARENBERG O Roussanne Money Spider
TIM GRAMP O Riesling Watervale
KILIKANOON O Riesling Clare Valley Morts Block
PETER LEHMANN ● Shiraz Barossa Valley
TAYLORS/WAKEFIELD CELLARS ● Shiraz Clare Valley
TORBRECK ● Woodcutters Red
WYNNS ● Shiraz Coonawarra
YALUMBA O Viognier Y

Viticulture was more important in Victoria than in either South Australia or New South Wales in the 19th century but the arrival of phylloxera triggered a decline for much of the state. In the late 1960s the first steps were taken towards a revival that has rapidly gained pace since the early 1980s. Victoria offers a diversity of site and climate permutations arguably unequalled in Australia, while much more is being made of Tasmania's cool climatic conditions. As an example of an increasing regionality, Heathcote Shiraz and Tasmanian Pinot Noir – which previously only boasted isolated successes – are now emerging as two potentially outstanding regional styles following a mini-explosion in quality. Other regions such as Henty, Gippsland or Macedon Ranges also seem set to gain wider recognition amongst consumers of quality wines.

North-West Victoria

The most productive area of Victoria, its regions of **Murray Darling** and **Swan Hill** are shared with the Big Rivers zone of New South Wales. It makes a significant contribution to Australia's big volume brand production from highly mechanized viticulture and winemaking. While the grapes from these high-yielding irrigated vineyards are never going to produce wines of real quality, they can be sound as well as inexpensive and are usually much better than the equivalent from most other bulk wine producing areas around the world.

North-East Victoria

Around the towns of **Rutherglen** and **Glenrowan** is the most significant area of Victoria viticulture to have survived its fall. Unique, intensely sweet fortified wines made from raisined Muscat and Muscadelle (sold as Tokay) grapes are often subject to long ageing in hot conditions. A classification of the Rutherglen wines has recently been introduced. Beyond a basic Rutherglen category, in ascending order, are the Classic, Grand and Rare quality levels. Robust, earthy reds are also made from Shiraz, Durif and Cabernet Sauvignon. The heat of Rutherglen is in contrast to the cooler areas to the south-east. Fine Chardonnay and Pinot Noir are made at **Beechworth**. Meanwhile, in the **Alpine Valleys** (including Ovens Valley) and **King Valley**, vineyards extend from the heat of Milawa into the lower reaches of the Australian Alps, part of the Great Dividing Range, where altitude is critical to cooler-climate viticulture in New South Wales. A wide range of grapes is grown but an unusual development is the propagation of Italian varieties.

Western Victoria

One of the strengths of Victoria is the great diversity of Shiraz styles, with top-class examples from Henty, Grampians, Pyrenees and Bendigo, the latter in Central Victoria. **Grampians** (or Great Western as it used to be known), another survivor of Victoria's 19th-century viticulture, has long been famous for its Shiraz including one of Australia's very best from Mount Langhi Ghiran. Elevation makes it cooler than might otherwise be expected, as is the case with the rolling hills of **Pyrenees** where both Shiraz and Cabernet Sauvignon are made, to very high standards in the case of Dalwhinnie. Chardonnay can also be impressive. The **Henty** region is still little known but encompasses a large area in the south-west corner of Victoria. There are climatic and soil similarities with the Limestone Coast (in South Australia) which lies but a short distance to the west. As Drumborg, it is more familiar as the source of the fine sparkling wines produced by the region's pioneer, Seppelt. Riesling and Pinot Noir also show much promise.

Central Victoria

Bendigo is now synonymous with great Shiraz, particularly the examples from the now separate region of Heathcote. In fact, Bendigo achieved fame for its Shiraz in the 19th century and this is once again a very exciting area with a recent surge of new wines set to challenge the leading estate of Jasper Hill. In **Goulburn Valley** another pocket of Victoria's wine production has been maintained. The region is vast, but the best producers are concentrated in the south, in the subregion of **Nagambie Lakes**, an area not a great distance east of Heathcote. Shiraz is brilliant from its leading producers, Tahbilk and Mitchelton, but Cabernet

Sauvignon and Riesling as well as Marsanne and other white and red Rhône varieties are beginning to excel. Vineyards in the **Central Victorian High (or Mountain) Country** and Strathbogie Ranges are most suited to aromatic white varieties.

Port Phillip

The leading region among those lying close to the state capital of Melbourne is the **Yarra Valley**. First developed in the 19th century, its modern revival dates from the 1960s. Within its substantial confines there exist any number of mesoclimates but it is generally cool and damp by Australian standards. The Yarra Valley provides great examples of Pinot Noir and Chardonnay but also fine Bordeaux blends, though there can be a struggle for ripeness in cooler vintages. Shiraz is less important but of high quality from the likes of Yarra Yering. The best wines are fruit-rich but softly textured and stylishly complex. There is also fine fizz although most examples include grapes sourced from outside the region. The Port Phillip zone also includes Geelong, Sunbury and the Mornington Peninsula. **Geelong**, thanks mostly to Gary Farr of Bannockburn, has a reputation for intense, powerful Shiraz, Pinot Noir and Chardonnay. The same theme is echoed in the cool **Mornington Peninsula** whose many small producers, though focusing on Pinot Noir and Chardonnay, can produce elegant, stylish Shiraz too. In **Sunbury,** especially the higher-altitude **Macedon Ranges**, the best reds are at the margins for achieving full ripeness but in the best years the quality is super in wines such as Craiglee's Shiraz or the Virgin Hills Cabernet Sauvignon-based blend.

Gippsland

Gippsland is a vast, cool zone in the south-east of Victoria with some exceptional isolated pockets of vineyards, but its marginal climate is always likely to deter all but a mad few. Yet quality can be very high even if quantities are scarce. Try to find the Pinot Noirs of Bass Phillip or the Chardonnays and Pinots of Nicholson River and Paradise Enough.

Tasmania

Across Bass Strait in Tasmania, the cooler, wetter climate has deterred the industry giants from invasion and its modern development has only really taken off in the past decade. As well as the dominant Pipers Brook group there are now dozens of tiny holdings from which tiny quantities of increasingly fine Pinot Noir are produced by a just a few talented winemakers. Riesling and Chardonnay are also successful, the latter important (with Pinot Noir) in the island's flourishing premium sparkling wine production.

A-Z of producers by region

1 Murray Darling
2 Swan Hill
3 Rutherglen
4 Glenrowan
5 Beechworth
6 Alpine Valleys
7 King Valley
8 Henty
9 Grampians
10 Pyrenees
11 Bendigo
12 Heathcote

13 Goulburn Valley
14 Nagambie Lakes
15 Strathbogie Ranges
16 Upper Goulburn
17 Yarra Valley
18 Mornington Peninsula
19 Geelong
20 Sunbury
21 Macedon Ranges

Victoria & Tasmania vintages

The generalised Vintage charts below cover some of the most ageworthy styles and will prove most useful when taken together with comments on style and ageing within individual producer entries. Many powerful, full-bodied red can be drunk young but an increasing number will not be at their best for at least five years. Top-quality Chardonnay and Pinot Noir are likely to show at their best only with three to six years' ageing. In terms of longer-term cellaring potential, great premium Victorian Shiraz or Cabernet-based reds can improve for at least a decade. Both the vintage ratings and when to drink assessments generally only apply to the top rated examples (three star wines or higher).

In 2004 in Victoria, as with the other eastern states, quantity bounced back after the small, drought-affected early harvest of 2003. Quality-wise it was very good in the Yarra Valley where heat early in the growing season helped facilitate full ripening in the Bordeaux varieties though Pinot Noir is less promising. Shiraz from Central and Western Victoria also looks very promising with concentrated ripe fruit from those vineyards that avoided excessive heat stress. In Tasmania in 2004, cool weather meant a much prolonged season (into June) for many producers with a struggle for ripeness and healthy fruit. Yet despite it being a difficult vintage, wines from producers who achieved full ripening could be very good – with good acidities and flavour complexity.

Victoria & Tasmania vintage chart

	Bendigo/Heathcote Shiraz	Grampians/Pyrenees Shiraz	Yarra Valley Pinot Noir	Tasmanian Pinot Noir
2004	★★★★ A	★★★★ A	★★★ A	★★/★★★★ A
2003	★★★★/★★★★★ A	★★★★ A	★★★★/★★★★★ A	★★★★ A
2002	★★★★★ A	★★★★/★★★★★ A	★★★★★ B	★★★★/★★★★★ B
2001	★★★★/★★★★★ A	★★★★/★★★★★ A	★★★★ B	★★★/★★★★ B
2000	★★★★ B	★★★/★★★★ B	★★★★/★★★★★ B	★★★★ B
1999	★★★★ B	★★★★ B	★★★/★★★★ C	★★★/★★★★ C
1998	★★★★/★★★★★ B	★★★★/★★★★★ B	★★★★/★★★★★ C	★★★★/★★★★★ C
1997	★★★★/★★★★★ B	★★★★ B	★★★★/★★★★★ C	★★★★ C
1996	★★★★ B	★★★★/★★★★★ B	★★★/★★★★ D	
1995	★★★ C	★★★/★★★★ C	★★★ D	
1994	★★★★ C	★★★★ C		
1993	★★★ D	★★/★★★ D		
1992	★★★/★★★★ C	★★★/★★★★ C		
1991	★★★★/★★★★★ C	★★★★/★★★★★ C		
1990	★★★★★ C	★★★★/★★★★★ C		

ALL SAINTS Rutherglen & Glenrowan www.allsaintswine.com.au

Owner: Peter Brown   All Saints Road, Wahgunyah VIC 3687
Peter Brown bought this high-quality producer of Rutherglen Muscat and Tokay from his family (BROWN BROTHERS) in 1999. The fortifieds already have quite a reputation while the table wines are rapidly improving. The Classic-level versions are relatively youthful and raisiny, the Grand add more richness and complexity, but Rare examples are that much more refined with terrific length of flavour. As overwhelming as these wines can be, Rare is a good place to start. Otherwise there's rich, characterful Shiraz and Durif if you're looking for something muscular and meaty. The Shiraz needs at least five years' ageing, the Durif needs 10 or more. (PW)

● **Shiraz** Carlyle★★ £D   ● **Durif** Carlyle★★ £C
O **Rutherglen Muscat** Classic★★ £C   Grand★★★ £D   Rare★★★★ £F
O **Rutherglen Tokay** Classic★★ £C   Grand★★★ £D   Rare★★★★★ £F

BAILEYS OF GLENROWAN Glenrowan www.beringerblass.com.au   A: **BBI**, FFW

Owner: Beringer Blass   Taminick Gap Road, Glenrowan VIC 3675
In acquiring Baileys in 1996, Mildara Blass (now BERINGER BLASS) added some rich, original fortified Australian Muscat and Tokay to its portfolio. Apart from these sometimes outstanding fortified wines, Baileys was known for one of Victoria's most robust and gutsy Shirazes. However, in the most recent vintages the Shiraz has taken on more refinement with finer structure, yet retaining good fruit intensity. 1904 Block and 1920 Block Shiraz are named for when the vineyards on which they are based were planted. The fortifieds are particularly rich, sweet examples, lacking the elegance or refinement of others but with plenty of power and flavour. The finest versions are Winemaker's Selection but these are made only in tiny quantities and are difficult to obtain. (PW)

● **Shiraz** 1920 Block★★ £C   1904 Block★★★ £D
● **Cabernet Sauvignon★** £B
O **Liqueur Tokay** Founder★★★ £B   O **Liqueur Muscat** Founder★★ £B

BALGOWNIE Bendigo www.balgownie.com   A: **Cap**, WRk, GGg

Owner: Forrester family   Hermitage Road, Maiden Gully VIC 3551
After a long period of ownership by Mildara Blass (now BERINGER BLASS) Balgownie is finally returning to the form it originally showed under its founder Stuart Anderson. Major vineyard expansion has extended plantings to 35 ha and the quality of recent releases of Shiraz and Cabernet Sauvignon in particular has been generally very good. Maiden Gully is the new second label, producing fresh, fruit-driven Cabernet/Shiraz and Chardonnay. (PW)

● **Shiraz★★★** £C   ● **Cabernet Sauvignon★★★** £C
● **Pinot Noir★** £C   O **Chardonnay★★** £D

BANNOCKBURN Geelong   A: **L&S**, ACh, Res, NYg

Owner: Philip Harrison   Midland Highway, Bannockburn VIC 3331
Winemaker Gary Farr's achievement is all the more remarkable given the relatively low profile of Geelong as a wine-producing region. Having established a considerable reputation by the mid-1980s he has managed to keep the quality and the profile of Bannockburn among the country's leaders. Cabernet was the fashionable variety and Pinot Noir almost unheard of in Australia when a deep, rich extracted example was first produced by Farr. Many of his practices for handling Pinot Noir, both in terms of viticulture (including high-density planting) and winemaking (part whole-bunch pressing), were modelled on Domaine DUJAC in Burgundy. The wine's deep spice, plum and savoury, undergrowth (at times, stemmy) character has always been individual; never noted for finesse, it is complex, ageworthy and impressively structured. Serré is a version based on particularly close-planted vines. Shiraz also has superb texture and

complexity and the concentrated Chardonnay can be very impressive. Less good is Cabernet/Merlot which can show a leafy, slightly unripe aspect. Sauvignon Blanc and Riesling are also made. The new wines from Gary Farr's own vineyards (BY FARR) or indeed those of his son Nicholas (FARR RISING) make for an interesting comparison. (PW)

● Shiraz★★★★ £D   ● Cabernet/Merlot★★ £C
● Pinot Noir★★★★ £D   O Chardonnay★★★ £D

BASS PHILLIP   Gippsland   A: Box, NYg
Owner: Phillip Jones   Hunts Road, Leongatha South, VIC 3953
Phillip Jones has gone out on a limb, opting for the vast, cool expanse of Gippsland for his winemaking venture. There are other notable wine producers here but they are as remote from each other as from other regions. Leongatha is further south and east than Mornington Peninsula and not far from Wilson's promontory, the mainland's most southerly point. The downside is variable vintage conditions, producing very ripe fruit on occasions, but just as often the vines can struggle for ripeness. From very closely spaced vineyards (at least in Australian terms) he has produced Pinot Noir of a quality that puts it among the very best in Australia. Early vintages, in the mid- to late 1980s, were made in minuscule quantities but the vineyard area has been gradually increased. The quality of the wines shows in the structure and length on the palate and the purity of the fruit. Only grapes of the requisite standard make the successive levels, from the most forward yet still serious regular Pinot through more intense, complex Premium to a deep, structured Reserve that needs at least five years' age. A tiny amount of Chardonnay and Gamay are also made. The wines are very expensive, in part due to their cult status. Two slightly less expensive versions of Pinot Noir, the Crown Prince and the Village, have also recently been produced. (PW)

● Pinot Noir★★★ £F   Premium★★★★ £G   Reserve★★★★ £H

BEST'S   Grampians   www.bestswines.com   A: Cac, JNi, WIE, Fsp, FWC, Ceb, Hrd
Owner: Thomson family   111 Best's Road, Great Western VIC 3377
Best's had its beginnings in 1866 under Henry Best and a family tradition of grape growing and winemaking has been continued by the Thomson family since 1920. Viv Thomson is the current incumbent with eldest son Ben in charge of the vineyards. The Concongella vineyards particularly favour Shiraz, which can be very good indeed, whether the consistently deep and peppery Bin O or a very limited-release Thomson Family version. A varietal Pinot Meunier comes from vines descended from original 1860s vineyard cuttings and is savoury and complex. Recent Riesling and Chardonnay show nicely defined varietal character. Merlot, Cabernet Franc, Pinot Noir and a Late Harvest Muscat are also made. Best's budget Victoria range comes from a separate estate, St Andrews, at Lake Boga (Swan Hill), and includes a decent Shiraz. (PW)

● Shiraz Great Western★★★ £C
● Cabernet Sauvignon Great Western★★ £C
● Pinot Meunier Great Western★★ £C
O Chardonnay Great Western★★ £C   O Riesling Great Western★ £B

R L BULLER & SON   Rutherglen   www.buller.com.au   A: PWt, OWL
Owner: Buller family   Calliope, Three Chain Road, Rutherglen VIC 3685
The Buller family operations include both fortifieds and table wines from wineries in Rutherglen (Calliope) and Beverford in the Swan Hill region. Most exceptional are the outstanding (Rare) Tokay and Muscat from unirrigated Rutherglen vineyards. Made only in very small quantities, there is splendid complexity and superb flavour length as well as sheer age in both. The Premium Fine Old (or Premium Fine) examples are also made in a solera system and have great intensity, complexity and length as well as surprising elegance for the style. Another premium fortified, Premium Fine Old Tawny, more in the style of an aged Tawny Port, has not been tasted. Powerful, robust Calliope Shiraz is also made and other Limited Release reds

include Durif and blends styled on the Rhône and Bordeaux. Prices for the fortifieds are keener than for most Rutherglen examples and represent exceptional value. (PW)

O **Rutherglen Tokay** Premium Fine Old★★★★ £C Calliope Rare★★★★★ £F
O **Rutherglen Muscat** Premium Fine Old★★★★ £C Calliope Rare★★★★★ £F

CAMPBELLS   Rutherglen & Glenrowan   www.campbellswines.com.au   A: **WSS**, ACh

Owner: Campbell family   Murray Valley Highway, Rutherglen VIC 3685
As always in Rutherglen the reputation of this producer depends on the quality of the fortified wines, and here they are consistently good. Impressively flavoursome in the cheaper examples, there is marvellous complexity, intensity and refinement in the Rare-level Isabella Tokay and Merchant Prince Muscat. Campbells reds, in particular The Barkly Durif, can show real intensity but are high in alcohol and, although they are sometimes good examples of a robust, gutsy style, they can also be too coarse, lacking definition and even the balance to repay cellaring. While the potential seems to exist for something better, a Limited Release Malbec needs to be more soundly made. Some white wine is also made. (PW)

O **Rutherglen Tokay** Classic★★★ £C Grand★★★★ £E Rare Isabella★★★★★ £G
O **Rutherglen Muscat** Classic★★ £C Grand★★★★ £E Rare Merchant Prince★★★★★ £G
● **Shiraz** Bobbie Burns★ £C ● **Durif** The Barkly★★ £C

CHAMBERS ROSEWOOD   Rutherglen & Glenrowan   A: **L&W**

Owner: Chambers family   Barkley Street, Rutherglen VIC 3685
Many of the great fortified-wine producers of North-West Victoria have their beginnings in late-Victorian times; Chambers goes as far back as 1858. It is the stocks of extremely old wines that contribute not only to the incredible concentration and intensity of the Rare versions of Rutherglen Muscat and Tokay (previously sold simply as Old Liqueur Tokay and Old Liqueur Muscat) but also their remarkable texture and extraordinary flavour complexity. The tea-leaf elegance of the Tokay contrasts with the more dried-fruits, raisiny character of the Muscat. The Special bottlings, now classified Grand, are also very fine, although at the regular, if relatively inexpensive level, there is good richness but the balance and flavours are much less inspiring. Table wines are also made. Prices below are based on a 75cl bottle, though they are sold in halves. (PW)

O **Rutherglen Muscat**★★ £D Grand★★★★ £F Rare❂❂❂❂❂ £G
O **Rutherglen Tokay**★★★ £D Grand★★★★★ £F Rare❂❂❂❂❂ £G

COLDSTREAM HILLS   Yarra Valley   www.coldstreamhills.com.au   A: **ScE**, PFx

Owner: Southcorp   31 Maddens Lane, Coldstream VIC 3770
This high-profile Yarra Valley winery, founded in 1985 by wine critic James Halliday, is now part of the SOUTHCORP portfolio of small to medium-sized wineries. Production has risen from a little under 500 cases in the first vintage to over 50,000 cases while vineyard holdings exceed 100 ha and further expansion is planned. The wines are made by Andrew Fleming with consultancy from Halliday. Reserves are made from the best fruit and see a greater percentage of new French oak. Burgundy is the inspiration for both Pinot Noir and Chardonnay that are ageworthy but nevertheless emphasise attractive youthful fruit. Whole bunches are used in vinifying the Pinot Noir while Chardonnay undergoes a cool fermentation (and only a small amount of malolactic fermentation) as well as extensive lees contact. Reserves of Cabernet Sauvignon and Merlot show good texture and intensity. Briarston is an oak-aged blend of mostly Cabernet Sauvignon and Merlot. Sauvignon Blanc and Pinot Gris are also made. (PW)

● **Cabernet Sauvignon** Reserve★★★ £E ● **Briarston**★★★ £C
● **Merlot**★★ £C Reserve★★★ £E ● **Pinot Noir**★★ £C Reserve★★★ £E
O **Chardonnay**★★ £C Reserve★★★ £D

CRAIGLEE Sunbury www.craiglee.com.au   A: **M&V**, The, NYg, P&S, FFW

Owner: Carmody family Sunbury Road, Sunbury VIC 3429

Craiglee is a tiny cool-climate winery and vineyard an hour or so north of Melbourne. In 1976 Pat Carmody replanted vines on the site of 19th-century vineyards. He and his family continue to make small quantities of wines in the original winery building. The emphasis here is on structured, elegant, well-crafted wines with a real capacity to age. Chardonnay is marked by a restrained melon character, with well-judged, subtle use of oak. Like nearby VIRGIN HILLS with its Cabernet Sauvignon, the Shiraz here is at the extreme margin for achieving full ripeness. Certainly in the warmer years, it is one of the best in the state. In cooler or more variable vintages the classic pepper and spice character can be slightly overwhelmed by an intense minty/spearmint influence. Very small amounts of Cabernet Sauvignon, Pinot Noir and Sauvignon Blanc are also made. (PW)

● **Shiraz**★★★ £D   O **Chardonnay**★★★ £C

DALWHINNIE Pyrenees www.dalwhinnie.com.au   A: **J&B**, P&S, NYg, FFW

Owner: David & Jenny Jones Forest Hut Rd, Moonambel VIC 3478

This is the best winery in the Pyrenees region and one of the best both in the state and Australia. The 18 ha of organically tended vineyards are planted in granite soils at a higher altitude than many of the neighbouring estates and produce wines of real structure and finesse. With an established reputation for outstanding Shiraz and Chardonnay, the Jones have enlisted outside consultancy and the quality of the wines continues to improve, including an increasingly impressive Pinot Noir. A small amount of Eagle Series Shiraz is made from a tiny 1.2-ha vineyard. Chardonnay is deep yet restrained with real intensity and structured for medium-term cellaring. Both the Cabernet and Shiraz will improve in bottle for five, often 10 years. (PW)

● **Cabernet Sauvignon** Moonambel★★★ £D   ● **Shiraz** Moonambel★★★★ £E
● **Pinot Noir**★★★ £D   O **Chardonnay** Moonambel★★★★ £D

DE BORTOLI (VICTORIA) Yarra Valley www.debortoli.com.au   A: **Deb**, Cam, SFW, WIE

Owner: De Bortoli family Pinnacle Lane, Dixon's Creek VIC 3775

De Bortoli is well-known for its big-volume inexpensive blends and varietals from Riverina but the better wines (the sweet Noble One excepted – see De Bortoli, New South Wales) are made in and, for the most part, sourced from the Yarra Valley. The winemaking is headed by Stephen Webber whose wife Leanne De Bortoli directs operations. Stylish Chardonnay, intense, dark cherry and plum Pinot Noir, and attractive, spicy Shiraz (including very limited quantities of a denser, more complex GS Reserve) appear under the Yarra Valley label, but the wines lack the depth and expression of better examples and can also suffer from a lack of complete ripeness. The flagship Melba Barrel Select is made in small quantities and is predominantly Cabernet Sauvignon with only a little Shiraz, Merlot or Cabernet Franc included. Gulf Station wines are less expensive but also sourced from the Yarra Valley. The Shiraz and Chardonnay stand out and provide good value, though other Gulf Station varietals can sometimes be surpassed by the cheaper Windy Peak wines, which include fruit from wider sources. (PW)

De Bortoli Yarra Valley:
O **Chardonnay**★★ £C   ● **Pinot Noir**★★ £C
● **Shiraz**★★ £C   ● **Melba Barrel Select**★★★ £E

Gulf Station:
O **Chardonnay**★ £B   ● **Shiraz**★ £B

DELATITE Upper Goulburn www.delatitewinery.com.au   A: **JEF**, ACh, Por

Owner: Ritchie family Stoneys Road, Mansfield VIC 3722

Mansfield in the Central High Country of Victoria is one of the state's many cool outposts to be exploited.

Wines have been made from these steep slopes with views across to the alpine retreat of Mount Buller since 1982. The wines are lighter and exhibit cooler, more delicate flavours than the majority of Australian wines. So much so that a lack of ripeness can be a problem and the most successful varieties are those most suited to more marginal climates. There's an interesting aromatic, floral Riesling and a spicy Gewürztraminer, both of which, though light and crisp, are intense and ageworthy. Chardonnay shows some style too, though it lacks a little depth. Reds are markedly cool and minty in style and only occasionally achieve ripe tannins in the Cabernet or Cabernet-based Devil's River, a blend of Cabernet Sauvignon, Malbec and Shiraz. A number of other varietals are made including Sauvignon Blanc, Pinot Gris, Pinot Noir, Merlot and Shiraz. Some sparkling wine, Delmelza Pinot/Chardonnay, is also made. (PW)

O **Riesling**★★ £B   O **Gewürztraminer** Dead Mans Hill★★ £B
O **Chardonnay**★ £C

DIAMOND VALLEY   Yarra Valley   www.diamondvalley.com.au   A: **Cac**, T&W

Owner: David Lance   2130 Kinglake Road, St Andrews VIC 3761
Small winery established in 1982 producing around 7,000 cases a year. While the Yarra Valley range is well crafted with good varietal fruit, it is the Estate wines, in particular the superb Pinot Noir, which stand out. The Chardonnay is rich and lightly tropical with well-judged oak, while the Estate Pinot is marked by concentrated – almost gamey – forward plum and black fruit, all underpinned by a not inconsiderable oak influence. Showy in its youth but with real structure too, it will be all the better for five years' ageing. (DM)

● **Cabernet Merlot**★★ £C   Estate★★★ £D
● **Pinot Noir**★★ £C   Estate★★★★ £D
O **Chardonnay**★★ £C   Estate★★★ £D

DOMAINE A   Tasmania   www.domaine-a.com.au   A: **All**, BFs

Owner: Peter & Ruth Althaus   Teatree Road, PO Box 137, Campania TAS 7026
Peter and Ruth Althaus' Stoney Vineyard is but a short distance from Tasmania's capital Hobart in the Coal River Valley. Something of the viticultural and winemaking philosophy echoes that of many small producers in similarly marginal vine-growing regions in Europe. 11 ha of a 20 ha estate are planted at relatively high densities and both pruning and harvesting are carried out by hand. Domaine A is the top selection, Stoney Vineyard effectively a second label. Cabernet Sauvignon is a particularly good example of cool-grown elegance and much better than many underperforming classed growth Médocs. Domaine A Pinot Noir shows rich plum and cherry fruit and has length and style if missing a little extra depth or dimension to fully justify the price tag. The structure of Lady A, a barrel-fermented and aged Sauvignon is impressive too if the oak influence can teeter on being overdone. The Stoney Vineyard varietals are cool and elegant, generally with sufficient ripeness in fruit and tannins in the Cabernet. All in all an estate deserving of attention. (PW)

Domaine A:
O **Fumé Blanc** Lady A★★★ £E   ● **Pinot Noir**★★★ £E
● **Cabernet Sauvignon**★★★ £E

Stoney Vineyard:
O **Sauvignon Blanc**★★ £C
● **Cabernet Sauvignon**★★ £C

DROMANA ESTATE   Mornington Peninsula   www.dromanaestate.com.au   A: **Cac**, CeB, Hrd

Owner: Dromana Estate Ltd   Old Moorooduc Road, Tuerong VIC 3915
Rollo Crittenden is the winemaker at this Mornington Peninsula-based estate established by his father, Garry. The premium label is Dromana Estate for wines from estate-grown fruit. The focus is on Pinot Noir and Chardonnay but also includes a somewhat leafy but increasingly ripe, spicy berry-fruited Cabernet/Merlot and a stylish, cool but ripe Shiraz. Both Chardonnay and Pinot Noir are good examples

but the relatively restrained, complex Reserves offer much more. Mornington Estate wines come from a separate 20 ha vineyard on the peninsula but much of the interest in Dromana comes from the production of Italian varietals based on King Valley fruit. Sold under the 'i' Garry Crittenden label, all are recently much improved (particularly since 2000) and are generally attractive and well made though only Arneis, Barbera and Dolcetto really come close to the intensity and character of good Italian examples; Nebbiolo and Sangiovese still want for finesse in both fruit and tannins. Schinus is a second label for Sauvignon Blanc, Chardonnay and Merlot of variable quality from diverse sources. The group has also expanded into the Yarra Valley with wines from Yarra fruit labelled as Yarra Valley Hills. Also under the same ownership is David Traeger of Nagambie Lakes. (PW)

Dromana Estate:
● **Pinot Noir★** £B Reserve★★★ £D ● **Cabernet/Merlot★** £B ● **Shiraz★★** £B
○ **Chardonnay★** £B Reserve★★★ £D
i Garry Crittenden:
● **Barbera★** £B ● **Dolcetto★** £B ○ **Arneis★★** £B

BY FARR Geelong   A: Tan, NYg
Owner: Gary Farr c/o Bannockburn, Midland Highway, Bannockburn VIC 3331
In 1999 Gary Farr released four new varietals from 4.8 ha of his own vineyards adjacent to BANNOCKBURN. Initially the wines were known as Bannockburn by Farr but are now simply By Farr. The wines are made at the Bannockburn winery but, coming from new clones on differing soil types and aspects, the wines are distinctly different. Shiraz, Chardonnay and Pinot Noir all show a little more elegance and refined varietal character, if not quite the weight and richness, at least not yet. Viognier is the major point of difference and seems set to show the hallmark Bannockburn weight and structure and therefore eclipse the high-alcohol but structure-deficient character of many Australian examples of this variety. (PW)
● **Pinot Noir★★★★** £D ● **Shiraz★★★** £D
○ **Chardonnay★★★** £D ○ **Viognier★★★** £D

GIACONDA Beechworth www.giaconda.com.au   A: **M&V**, Res, NYg, P&S, Sel
Owner: Rick Kinzbrunner McClay Rd, Beechworth VIC 3747
Production here is remains small at around 2,500 cases per year, although the 3 ha vineyards planted in the 1980s have now doubled in size thanks to more recent plantings. A small amount of wine is exported but most of it is accounted for by a dedicated mailing list. Rick Kinzbrunner's Pinot Noir and Chardonnay are Australian cool-climate classics, almost Burgundian in style with an approach to vinification that mirrors the best of the Côte d'Or. The Pinot Noir is astonishingly rich and opulent, the Chardonnay structured and immensely refined: it requires a minimum of five years' ageing to fully unfurl but is nearly always amongst Australia's finest examples. Cabernet is a classic Bordeaux blend of Cabernet Sauvignon, Merlot and Cabernet Franc. More recently the range has been extended to include: Nantua Les Deux, a full-on blend of Chardonnay with a small amount of Roussanne; Aeolia, a rich powerful and exotic varietal Roussanne; and a richly textured, stylish Shiraz from a neighbouring vineyard. All the wines age very well. Prices reflect both quality and demand. (PW)
● **Cabernet★★★** £F ● **Pinot Noir★★★★** £F
● **Shiraz** Warner Vineyard★★★★ £F
○ **Chardonnay★★★★** £F ○ **Aeolia★★★★** £F ○ **Nantua Les Deux★★★** £E

GREEN POINT VINEYARDS/DOM. CHANDON Yarra Valley   A: **MHn**, Vne, Amp, IVi
Owner: LVMH Maroondah Highway, Coldstream VIC 3770
The prestigious Yarra Valley operation is one of the most important of the Moët-Hennessey foreign investments. It could probably survive on the tourists alone but, with renewed consultancy from Dr Tony Jordan (CEO CAPE MENTELLE, CLOUDY BAY), an increasing number of still and sparkling wines are

made to a high standard. Still and sparkling Pinot Noir and Chardonnay are characterised by clarity, intensity and good breadth. Reserve Chardonnay adds a little depth and more lavish if sophisticated oak treatment; a Reserve Pinot Noir shows concentrated plummy fruit and a powerful structure. Of the sparkling wines the Vintage Brut is the mainstay but a little Blanc de Blancs, Blanc de Noirs and Brut Rosé are also made. All show fine texture, ripe fruit and good richness and improve with a little age. A non-vintage blend is not of the same order. Recently released is a new premium bottling Cuvée Prestige in a richer, late-disgorged (with six years on its lees) style – its first vintage is 1995. The still wines are marketed as Green Point Vineyards, the sparkling wines as part of the worldwide Chandon Estates entity (Green Point by Chandon). (PW)

O **Vintage Brut★★★** £C   O **Vintage Blanc de Blancs★★★** £C   O **Vintage Blanc de Noirs★★** £C
O **Chardonnay★★** £C   Reserve★★★ £D
● **Pinot Noir★** £C   Reserve★★★ £D

HANGING ROCK   Macedon Ranges   www.hangingrock.com.au   A: TWS, AWA, IWD

Owner: John and Ann Ellis   88 Jim Road, Newham VIC 3422
Both John and Ann (née Tyrrell, daughter of the late Murray TYRRELL) are steeped in winemaking experience, having been involved with some of the country's leading producers before securing their own property in 1985. Their vineyards on the Jim Jim, an extinct volcano, are as cool as any in Australia and are planted predominantly to Pinot Noir and Chardonnay for one of Australia's top sparkling wines, Macedon Cuvée. A blend of vintages, the current release (VIII) is 60 per cent Pinot to 40 Chardonnay. Consistency and richness are maintained by drawing from a substantial resource of reserve wines for each successive release. A rich, intense Shiraz is from the warmer Heathcote region, famed for Shiraz of the quality of JASPER HILL. Production resumed in 1997, after a break of five years, from new vineyards (chiefly Athol's Paddock and Colbinabbin Estate) and has been a powerful expression of fruit and oak in every vintage since. Other wines include a cool, crisp Sauvignon Blanc from the Jim Jim vineyards and some late-harvested styles. Victoria-labelled wines come from diverse sources while Rock is an inexpensive second label. (PW)

● **Shiraz** Heathcote★★★ £C
O **Macedon Cuvée★★★** £C
O **Sauvignon Blanc** Jim Jim★ £B

HEATHCOTE WINERY   Heathcote   www.heathcotewinery.com.au   A: WRk

Owner: Stephen Wilkins   183-185 High Street, Heathcote VIC 3523
An improving Central Victoria winery with an intriguing assortment of grape varieties. Vineyards total 25 ha either owned or under contract in a warm elevated area at 200 to 250 m that escapes some of the cloud cover more typical in southern Victoria but is cooler than Bendigo. The Newlan's Lane vineyard provides a Chardonnay with a mix of citrus and ripe peach fruit that is balanced and attractive with just a couple of years' age. The same vineyard also provides an attractive, gently varietal example of Viognier (Curagee), though, as with many Australian examples, it lacks real Viognier weight and definition in the mouth. Curagee Shiraz is bigger and more muscular than the Mail Coach version which is relatively lightly oaked with lovely texture, weight and balance. (PW)

● **Shiraz** Mail Coach★★ £B   Curagee★★ £D
O **Chardonnay★** £B

HOOD WINES/WELLINGTON   Tasmania

Owner: Andrew & Jenny Hood   Cnr Richmond & Denholms Roads, Cambridge TAS 7170
It's surprising that Andrew Hood has time to make a little wine for himself given the number of other small wineries that benefit from his expertise. Numerous tiny estates (including Elsewhere Vineyard and Meadowbank) can boast really good Pinot Noir as well as other varieties that producers from warmer parts of the mainland can only envy. His signature style is full ripeness, good texture, delicate extraction and

restrained oak in both Chardonnay and Pinot Noir. All of his own wines are sold under the Wellington label. A cool, slightly minerally Riesling is also made in an Iced version where the unfermented juice is frozen to remove some water and increase concentration. It is difficult to find these wines, but if you're in Tasmania… (PW)

● **Pinot Noir**★★★ £C
○ **Chardonnay**★★★ £C ○ **Riesling**★★ £C

JASPER HILL Heathcote   A: **Yap**, P&S, NYg, N&P

Owner: Ron Laughton Drummonds Lane, Heathcote VIC 3523
The production here is small at around 3,500 cases per year and the wines can be very difficult to track down but it is worth the effort. As with the finest producers in the northern Rhône, the approach is one of minimal intervention: no irrigation, minimal vineyard treatments and virtually sulphur-free reds. Yields are tiny from the sparse, granite-based soils, between one and two tons to the acre. The two Shirazes are remarkable: both rich, concentrated and full of exotic dark berry fruit and spice, with a marvellous supple texture underpinning them. The Georgia's Paddock is slightly more opulent. They are amongst Australia's very finest. While they will easily age for 20 years or more they can be broached with just a few years in the cellar. For long just one white was also produced, a powerful stuctured Riesling, full of subtle citrus but minerally and toasty with three or four years' ageing. Very small quantities of Nebbiolo and Semillon have been made since 2001. (PW)

● **Shiraz** Georgia's Paddock★★★★★ £F ● **Shiraz/Cabernet Franc** Emily's Paddock★★★★★ £F
○ **Riesling** Georgia's Paddock★★★ £D

STEFANO LUBIANA Tasmania www.stefanolubiana.com   A: NYg, UnC

Owner: Steve & Monique Lubiana 60 Rowbottoms Road, Granton TAS 7030
This small Tasmanian operation is a veritable giant compared to some of the micro-boutique operations that make just a few hundred cases. The 5.6 ha of vineyard at Granton, lying above the Derwent River, form part of a much larger property but produce Pinot Noir and Chardonnay of a persuasive style and refinement. The fruit in each is very pure and intense, the wines elegant and vibrant and capable of at least three or four years' age. As well as second versions of Chardonnay (Sur Lie) and Pinot Noir (Primavera), Sauvignon Blanc and Pinot Grigio are made. A non-vintage Brut sparkling wine is based on Pinot Noir with a little Chardonnay. (PW)

● **Pinot Noir**★★★ £D
○ **Chardonnay**★★★ £D ○ **Riesling**★★ £C

MAIN RIDGE Mornington Peninsula www.mre.com.au   A: **Cac**, NYg

Owner: Nat & Rosalie White 80 William Road, Red Hill VIC 3937
Tiny Mornington Peninsula estate dedicated to Chardonnay and Pinot Noir established back in 1975. In contrast to other pioneering operations such as STONIER and DROMANA ESTATE, Main Ridge has chosen to remain small and artisanal in its production. Nat White, who owns the property with his wife Rosalie, continues to make the wines. Although they can show some vintage variation, at best they are elegant and classy yet with plenty of drive and personality. Prices are high but not dissimilar to those of their neighbours. Pinot Noir comes in two versions, a regular example (labelled The Acre in 2001)and a Reserve, Half Acre, made from a vineyard with shallow topsoil. (PW)

● **Pinot Noir**★★★ £D Half Acre★★★ £E
○ **Chardonnay**★★★ £D

MÉTIER WINES Yarra Valley www.metierwines.com.au   A: **HHB**

Owner: Martin Williams Healesville Road, Yarra Glen VIC 3775
Métier is a small but gradually expanding premium wine operation. Martin Williams also makes the wine

at TALLAROOK and is a partner in Master Winemakers, which provides contract winemaking facilities. Métier's Tarraford Vineyard Chardonnay (from a 2-ha Yarra Valley site) is extremely well crafted with subtle use of oak and lees. Pinot Noir from the same vineyard has a fine texture but is more variable in its fruit quality and ageing potential. Yarra Valley Pinot Noir and Chardonnay have also been made from the 1.4-ha Schoolhouse Vineyard. A tiny amount of Viognier is produced from the high-altitude Kanumbra Vineyard in the Upper Goulburn. Also sourced from this region (since the 2000 vintage) is new and promising Manytrees Shiraz/Viognier. A second range, Milkwood, includes Sauvignon Blanc, Chardonnay, Pinot Noir and Shiraz. (PW)

● **Pinot Noir** Schoolhouse Vineyard★★ £E Tarraford Vineyard★★ £D
○ **Chardonnay** Schoolhouse Vineyard★★★★ £C Tarraford Vineyard★★★★ £D

MITCHELTON www.mitchelton.com.au A: LNa, WSc, FWC, Hrd, F&M, Sel

Owner: Lion Nathan Mitchellstown Road, Nagambie VIC 3608
Located on the banks of the Goulburn River in the Nagambie Lakes region, Mitchelton is part of a prestigious grouping that includes PETALUMA, KNAPPSTEIN and STONIER. A well-established portfolio of wines has been developed and maintained over nearly three decades by the highly respected winemaker Don Lewis. The intense floral and lime-scented Blackwood Park Riesling is also made in Late Harvested and Botrytis versions. Many of the whites combine citrusy flavours with more exotic, tropical notes, together with both vigour and good acidity. The top red, Print Shiraz, can exude a class and finesse not seen in the Barossa blockbuster styles. French oak is favoured for reds and a concerted move to lower yields since the mid-90s has brought increased concentration to many of the wines. A new Vineyard Series label includes varietal Chardonnay, Viognier, Shiraz and Cabernet. Mitchelton was also one of the first to develop red and white Rhône blends, once known as Mitchelton III but now as Airstrip white, comprising Marsanne, Roussanne and Viognier, and Crescent red from Shiraz, Mourvèdre and Grenache. Varietal Marsanne is a speciality with intense honeysuckle aromas and flavours and has even been made in a *vin de paille* version. Victoria Series or Preece-labelled varietals can sometimes prove very good value for money. Least expensive are the Thomas Mitchell wines. (PW)

● **Shiraz** Victoria Series★ £B Vineyard Series★★ £C Print★★★★ £E
● **Shiraz/Mourvèdre/Grenache** Crescent★★ £C
○ **Chardonnay** Victoria Series★ £B Vineyard Series★★ £C
○ **Viognier** Vineyard Series★ £C ○ **Marsanne/Roussanne/Viognier** Airstrip★★ £C
○ **Riesling** Blackwood Park★★★ £C

MOORILLA ESTATE Tasmania www.moorilla.com.au

Owner: Moorilla Estate Trust 655 Main Road, Berriedale TAS 7011
The impressive new Moorilla museum of antiquities appears likely to become more of a magnet for visitors than the wines. Yet this long-surviving Tasmania winery, though no longer family-owned, has been resurgent under Alain Rousseau (although he has now left). Good cool, citrusy whites include a tight, minerally, appley Riesling, sometimes also made in a rare botrytised version. A Reserve Pinot Noir of increasing ripeness and richness, but with impressive texture and complexity too, is one of a growing number of fine Tasmanian Pinots – difficult as they are to acquire. Sourced from the warmer Tamar Valley, Reserve Cabernet and Reserve Cabernet/Merlot might once have tasted rather tough and unripe but in recent good vintages the wines have been ripe and concentrated. Dense, powerful Syrah also shows much promise. (PW)

● **Pinot Noir** White Label★ £B Reserve★★★ £C
● **Cabernet/Merlot** Reserve★★ £C ● **Cabernet Sauvignon** Reserve★★★ £C
○ **Riesling**★★ £B ○ **Chardonnay** White Label★★ £C
○ **Estate Brut**★★ £C

MORRIS   Rutherglen & Glenrowan

*Owner: **Orlando Wyndham group (Pernod Ricard)**   Mia Mia Road, Rutherglen VIC 3685*
Although owned by Orlando since 1970, the tradition of family winemaking, producing some of Australia's excellent fortified wines, continues here – David Morris having taken over from his famous father Mick Morris in 1993. There is great age in these intelligently blended wines, particularly in the Old Premium versions of fortified Muscat and Tokay (Muscadelle). The regular Liqueur Muscat, tasting of intense, rich, slightly toffeed sweet raisins, is very typical of the style, even if it doesn't have the elegance to tempt some palates to come back for more. The Old Premium version of Muscat offers similar intensity but more complexity, while in Old Premium Tokay there is excellent richness but arguably less elegance and less of the classic Tokay flavours of other examples. Nonetheless the quality, richness and complexity in all the Liqueur Muscat and Liqueur Tokay wines can't be disputed. Old Premium 'Amontillado' and 'Tawny Port' are also made. Red wines including Shiraz and Durif can be sound but lack refinement. (PW)

O **Liqueur Muscat★★** £B Old Premium★★★★ £E
O **Liqueur Tokay★★★** £B Old Premium★★★★ £E

MOUNT LANGI GHIRAN   Grampians   www.langi.com.au   A: **Lib**, ACh, Res, Vne, Hrd, P&S

*Owner: **Rathbone family group**   Warrak Road, Buangor, VIC 3375*
This dynamic, go-ahead organic vineyard (now totalling 90 ha) and winery operation owes its reputation to winemaker Trevor Mast. It has recently come under the same ownership as top Yarra Valley producer YERING STATION. Mast's masterpiece is a remarkable and stylish Shiraz, among Australia's top half-dozen examples of the variety. Made from 44-year-old vines, the 2002 includes 2 per cent Viognier. A richly textured Cabernet/Merlot (one third Merlot) from estate vineyards contrasts with the cool, minty Joanna Cabernet which comes from Wrattonbully fruit. Sangiovese looks set to improve as fruit from clones from ISOLE E OLENA starts to come on stream. A second Shiraz, Cliff Edge, first made in 1999, shows promise too while the reasonably priced Billi Billi Creek (mostly Shiraz with around 30 per cent Grenache and a little Cabernet) has plenty of style if not the greatest depth. Whites are well fashioned including a popular, fruit-driven Pinot Gris. The Four Sisters wines (produced in collaboration with Alister Purbrick of TAHBILK) are vinified to emphasise their fruit. (PW)

Mount Langhi Ghiran:
● **Shiraz★★★★★** £E Cliff Edge★★★ £C ● **Cabernet/Merlot★★★★** £D
● **Cabernet Sauvignon** Limestone Coast Joanna★★★ £C
● **Sangiovese** Nut Block★★ £C ● **Shiraz/Grenache/Cabernet** Billy Billy Creek★★ £B
O **Riesling★★** £B O **Pinot Gris★★** £B

Four Sisters:
● **Grenache/Shiraz** McLaren Vale★ £B O **Sauvignon/Semillon** McLaren Vale★ £B

MOUNT MARY   Yarra Valley   A: **Bal, VdV**, JAr, BBR, F&R

Owner: John Middleton   22–24 Coldstream West Road, Lilydale VIC 3140
John Middleton's Mount Mary is one of Victoria's holiest of holies, where the quality is whispered about by devotees, in complete contrast to the ballyhoo that emanates from South Australia's big guns. Quantities are small and grapes come from the estate's unirrigated vineyards. Quintet (Cabernet Sauvignon, Merlot, Cabernet Franc, Malbec and Petit Verdot) is graceful and refined with intense berry and cassis flavours, a wine that will easily keep for 20 years from a good vintage. The Pinot Noir can age for about half as long, starting out deceptively light but building on its pure fruit core with age. Two whites, a Chardonnay and Triolet (a blend of Sauvignon, Semillon and Muscadelle) show restrained fruit and oak but can age well too. (PW)

● **Quintet★★★★** £G ● **Pinot Noir★★★** £G
O **Triolet★★★** £F O **Chardonnay★★★** £F

PARINGA ESTATE Mornington Peninsula www.paringaestate.com.au — A: **Adm,** NYg

Owner: Lindsay & Margaret McCall 44 Paringa Rd, Red Hill South, VIC 3937
Top-notch small estate producing around 6,500 cases annually. What is most remarkable about Paringa is not only the quality of the Chardonnay and Pinot Noir but also its Shiraz. Certainly this tends to work best in warmer years but when vintage conditions are benign the wine benefits from an unusually long ripening period. The Peninsula label is from a combination of bought-in fruit and younger Paringa vines. An unoaked Pinot Gris is also made. (PW)

● **Pinot Noir★★★** £E Peninsula★★ £C   ● **Shiraz★★★★** £D
○ **Chardonnay★★★** £D Peninsula★★ £C

PIPERS BROOK Tasmania www.pbv.com.au — A: **Cap,** ACh, FWC

Owner: Pipers Brook Vineyard Limited 1216 Pipers Brook Road, Pipers Brook TAS 7254
Dr Andrew Pirie founded the winery back in 1974 and it has since risen to become the dominant force in the tiny Tasmanian wine industry with more than 200 ha of vineyards. The majority of shares is now held by Kreglinger Australia, part of the Belgian de Moor family's Kreglinger group, which has also established a new venture in South Australia's Mount Benson region. Early 2003 saw the sudden departure of Andrew Pirie (to PARKER Coonawarra Estate) but the focus has always rightly been on cool-climate varieties, in particular Pinot Noir, Chardonnay and Riesling. The wines generally show lovely varietal fruit character with extra nuance and richness as well as oak in the Reserve wines. Sparkling wine has also been a strength since the much-heralded launch of Pirie, which is arguably the best Australian sparkling wine yet made. The wines don't offer exceptional value but are fairly priced for the quality compared to other Australian examples or equivalent Burgundian quality in Pinot or Chardonnay. With the 1999 vintage a small amount of single-site Pinot Noir (The Blackwood and The Lyre from sections of the Heemskerk Vineyard) joined a Chardonnay (The Summit) made since 1997 from 2 ha. All are priced £E. Ninth Island is a separate entity drawing largely from the former Rochecombe vineyards; as well as very creditable Chardonnay and Pinot Noir the range includes several other varietals and a non-vintage Brut. (PW)

Pipers Brook:
● **Pinot Noir** Estate★★ £C Reserve★★★ £D
○ **Chardonnay** Estate★★ £C Reserve★★★ £D
○ **Riesling** Estate★★ £C **Gewürztraminer** Estate★★ £C
○ **Pirie Vintage★★★★** £D

Ninth Island:
● **Pinot Noir★** £B   ○ **Chardonnay★** £B

SCOTCHMANS HILL Geelong www.scotchmanshill.com.au — A: **Orb,** Odd, Bal, WSc

Owner: Browne family 190 Scotchmans Road, Drysdale VIC 3222
Situated on the Bellarine Peninsula just south-east of Geelong the vineyards enjoy a cool maritime climate. Production is sizeable for the region at more than 60,000 cases but quality remains admirable, particularly considering the prices. The Pinot Noir is a strength, with ripe plum fruits, nicely handled oak and a seductive texture, while Shiraz and Cabernet/Merlot can be individual and appealing, if sometimes struggling for ripeness. The Chardonnay is restrained with just a hint of oak showing through in the background. The Sauvignon is grassy and nettly, and marked by lightly tropical cool-fermentation aromas. It is best drunk as young as possible. New and very pricey are premium Pinot Noir (Norfolk Vineyard) and Chardonnay (Sutton Vineyard). Swan Bay is the second label mainly produced from a second property, Spray Farm, while a separate range of wines is labelled The Hill. (PW)

● **Pinot Noir★★★** £C Swan Bay★ £B   ● **Cabernet/Merlot★★★** £C   ● **Shiraz★★★** £C
○ **Chardonnay★★** £C   ○ **Sauvignon Blanc★★** £B

SEPPELT GREAT WESTERN Grampians www.seppelt.com.au   A: ScE

Owner: Southcorp Moyston Road, Great Western VIC 3377

This is Seppelt's renowned sparkling-wine operation, which also includes quite a number of very good table wines, many of which are sourced from cool-climate areas where the company has significant plantings. The Drumborg varietals, which come from the cool south-west corner of Victoria now called Henty, are some of the best wines in the range. Riesling and Pinot Noir highlight the potential but even Cabernet Sauvignon, which can show a cool, leafy influence, can also be cedary and berryish in the best years. Pinot Grigio and a new Chardonnay are sourced from the same area as is much of the fruit for ripely plummy Sunday Creek Pinot Noir. Dorrien Cabernet Sauvignon, based on an old-vine parcel of a vineyard of the same name in the Barossa, is a richly textured, earthy, cedary and black-fruited wine aged in (mostly) French oak. Partalunga Chardonnay comes from vineyard holdings in the Adelaide Hills; it is only made in the best years but can show some of the distinctive regional character. Harpers Range Cabernet and Chalambar Shiraz are blended across a number of cooler regions but increasingly show good fruit and balanced tannins. The range of sparkling wines has been consolidated but is led by a distinctive creamy, citrusy Salinger (Chardonnay, Pinot Noir and Pinot Meunier), for long one of the most consistent premium Australian sparkling wines, and Drumborg Show Sparkling Reserve, which has six years on its lees. Vintage Brut Fleur de Lys is less expensive and more overtly fruity but with some leesy influence. However, most exceptional of the traditional-method sparkling wines made here is the red Great Western Show Sparkling Shiraz (which spends six years on its lees and is only available around 10 years after the vintage), arguably the most intriguing and complex example of its type. The cheaper Original version comes from South Australian fruit. Inexpensive varietals and blends are sold under the Moyston label. The best wines unfortunately are not always easy to find outside of Australia. (PW)

● **Cabernet Sauvignon** Dorrien★★★ £C Harpers Range★ £B
● **Shiraz** Great Western★★★ £C Chalambar★ £B
● **Pinot Noir** Drumborg★★ £D Sunday Creek★ £C
O **Chardonnay** Partalunga★★★ £C O **Riesling** Drumborg★★ £C
O **Salinger Vintage★★** £C ● **Sparkling Shiraz Vintage Show★★★** £D

SEVILLE ESTATE Yarra Valley www.sevilleestate.com.au   A: Lib, Vne, NYg, ACh

Owner: Brokenwood & others Linwood Road, Seville VIC 3139

Seville Estate, founded by Dr Peter McMahon, was one of the Yarra Valley's pioneers (of the modern era) and has produced small volumes of fine varietals, particularly Shiraz, during the past 30 years. Top New South Wales producer BROKENWOOD has had a major stake since 1997 and the wines are now made by its widely respected winemaker, Iain Riggs. The vineyards are on the cooler side of the valley and accordingly suffer a little in cooler vintages. At their best however they are powerful and fruit-accented with well-integrated oak and good definition both in terms of structure and flavour. Chardonnay can improve for up to five years; reds need as long or more. Small amounts of Reserve Cabernet and Shiraz have recently been produced from vines more than 30 years old. (PW)

● **Shiraz★★★** £C ● **Cabernet Sauvignon★★** £C
● **Pinot Noir★★★** £C O **Chardonnay★★** £C

SHADOWFAX Geelong www.shadowfax.com.au   A: M&V, The, Res, NYg, RGr, P&S

Owner: Mansion group K Road, Werribee VIC 3030

Shadowfax (a name taken from Tolkien's *Lord of the Rings*) is a very new, exciting operation based in Werribee Park between Melbourne and Geelong. Sourcing small parcels of the best grapes from a number of districts, young Matt Harrop has the responsibility of producing wines to match the high standards set by the acclaimed Mansion Hotel, but has a stunning new winery in which to do so. Besides a Sauvignon Blanc/Semillon of good weight and interest, there is full but tightly structured Chardonnay, characterful, textured Pinot Noir (both made from Geelong and Yarra Ranges fruit), and vibrant, spicy, fruit-driven

Shiraz from McLaren Vale. Premium wines in heavy black-labelled bottles promise still more. A 2001 Geelong Pinot Noir is bold and full-flavoured with lots of breadth and extract (if deficient in charm for the present). Two single-vineyard Shirazes from low-yielding Heathcote fruit were also made in 2001: both Pink Cliffs and One Eye are concentrated, meaty, intense examples with obvious potential but requiring 10 years' cellaring. Viognier, Pinot Gris and unusual K Road Sangiovese/Merlot/Shiraz have also been produced. (PW)

O **Sauvignon Blanc/Semillon**★★ £B   O **Chardonnay**★★★ £C
● **Pinot Noir**★★ £C   ● **Shiraz** McLaren Vale★★★ £C

STONIER   Mornington Peninsula   www.stoniers.com.au   A: **LNa**, Bib, DWS, Vne, NYg, Vts

Owner: Lion Nathan   2 Thompsons Lane, Merricks VIC 3916
Established in 1978 by Brian Stonier, this operation was one of the first premium wineries to emerge from the Mornington Peninsula. The potential first highlighted by Stephen Hickinbotham was cemented under his successor Tod Dexter and since the mid-1990s the winemaking mantle has gradually been assumed by Geraldine McFaul. Stonier came under the same ownership as PETALUMA (South Australia) in 1998 and this has only served to highlight the quality here. As well as more than 20 ha of estate vineyards, grapes are sourced from elsewhere on the peninsula. Recent releases of regular Chardonnay and Pinot Noir show lovely fruit and balance, though want for depth and structure; the Reserves however offer much more – more, indeed, than the price differential suggests. The Reserve Chardonnay is splendidly distinctive with a gently spicy, oak-influenced lemon zest, lemon peel and nectarine character and good breadth and intensity. The Reserve Pinot Noir shows balanced oak together with good depth and ripeness. Stonier have also produced small quantities of single-vineyard Pinot Noir and Chardonnay from the KBS Vineyard. (PW)

● **Pinot Noir**★★ £C Reserve★★★ £D
O **Chardonnay**★★ £B Reserve★★★ £C

SUMMERFIELD   Pyrenees   www.summerfieldwines.com   A: **BBR**, NYg

Owner: Summerfield family   Main Road, Moonambel, VIC 3478
This predominantly red-wine producer has been making wines since 1979, having first established vineyards in 1970. The first real leap in quality came with consultancy from Drew NOON (South Australia), the then state oenologist, in the late 1980s. Mark Summerfield is now responsible for the winemaking but retains a measure of input from Noon. He has set about reducing yields and the powerful reds are richer, riper, deeper and more consistent than previously but always with a noticeable dash of oak. Shiraz is the real star, particularly the Reserve (Estate in older vintages). The muscular, minty Reserve Cabernet is now beginning to benefit from the use of some French oak. Both Reserves will keep for a decade or more (PW)

● **Shiraz**★★ £C   ● Reserve★★★ £E
● **Cabernet Sauvignon**★★ £C Reserve★★★ £D
● **Cabernet/Merlot**★★ £C

TAHBILK   Nagambie Lakes   www.tahbilk.com.au   A: **PLh**, Fsp, The

Owner: Purbrick family   Tabilk, VIC 3608
Historic winery which along with HENSCHKE has some of the oldest plantings of Shiraz anywhere in the world. One plot dates back to 1860. Production is not inconsiderable at close to 100,000 cases a year and an extensive range of wines is available at the cellar door. Vinification of the reds is very traditional and open-top wooden fermenters are used. In no small part the considerable age of the vines contributes to the structured, tannic style of the wines when young. They are very ageworthy but demand patience, up to 10 years for the Reserves and 1860 Vines. Of good fruit-driven whites, the Marsanne is a regional benchmark and the largest single planting, it is claimed, anywhere in the world. Some of the vines were planted in 1927. New and promising too are varietal Roussanne and Viognier. (PW)

● **Cabernet Sauvignon**★★ £B Reserve★★★ £D
● **Shiraz**★★ £B Reserve★★★ £D 1860 Vines★★★★ £F
○ **Marsanne**★★ £B ○ **Chardonnay**★ £B
○ **Riesling**★★ £B ○ **Semillon**★★ £B

TALLAROOK Upper Goulburn www.tallarook.com A: **HHB,** F&M

Owner: Luis Riebl Dabyminga, Ennis Road, Tallarook VIC 3659
Tallarook was purchased by Luis Riebl in 1992 and looks an interesting bet for the future thanks to winemaking from Martin Williams MW of MÉTIER. Tallarook's elevated, cool vineyards are located in a part of Victoria with both strong Aboriginal and early colonial links. There are plantings in the Brown Ranges and in an area between the Brown Ranges and the Tallarook Ranges known as the Hornfels Ridge. This provides interesting possibilities both in terms of soil types and microclimate. The 16-ha estate vineyard (now being supplemented by more recent plantings) includes a little Viognier, Marsanne, Roussanne as well as more substantial amounts of Chardonnay, Pinot Noir and Shiraz. The existing range of four well-made varietals includes a toasty Chardonnay of good weight, gently creamy Marsanne and cool, peppery medium-bodied Shiraz. Pinot Noir is bright and supple but is the least convincing thus far. (PW)
○ **Chardonnay**★★ £C ○ **Marsanne**★ £C ● **Shiraz**★★ £C

TALTARNI Pyrenees www.taltarni.com.au A: **Lay, FSt, May,** WRk, T&W

Owner: Red Earth Nominees RMB 4369, Taltarni Road, Moonambel VIC 3478
With 132 ha, this is the Pyrenees' biggest producer. Taltarni, like CLOS DU VAL in the Napa Valley, was established in 1972 by John Goelet. For a long time Dominique Portet crafted the wines here – and his brother Bernard continues to oversee the Clos du Val wines. By the mid-1980s Taltarni was widely admired for its gutsy, structured varietals that highlighted the potential of the Pyrenees. Some wines have been too tough and extracted, others have lacked balance but the best bottles have aged superbly. Dominique Portet departed to make his own wines and under Peter Steer and the wines are now richer, oakier and more modern. The change is perhaps encapsulated in Cephas, a new flagship red that seemlessly combines Shiraz and Cabernet Sauvignon. The other great facet to Taltarni is the sparkling-wine production which reaches its zenith in the classy Clover Hill. This taut, ripe and structured sparkler comes from a dedicated Tasmanian estate with 21 ha planted to Chardonnay, Pinot Noir and Pinot Meunier. A second, smaller Pipers River vineyard, Lalla Gully, is the source of a Sauvignon Blanc that shows good purity, if for early drinking. The Taltarni-labelled Sauvignon, which previously could be a little flat in warmer vintages, now includes a Tasmanian component (from 2003). New Lalla Gully Riesling (from 2003) has promising structure and intensity. Both red and white Fiddleback are newish, fruit-accented second-label blends made from both estate and bought-in grapes. (PW)

Taltarni:
● **Cephas**★★★ £C ● **Shiraz**★★★ £C ● **Merlot**★★ £C ● **Cabernet Sauvignon**★★ £C
○ **Sauvignon Blanc**★★ £C ○ **Brut**★★ £B ○ **Brut Taché**★★ £B
Clover Hill:
○ **Clover Hill**★★★ £C
Lalla Gully:
○ **Sauvignon Blanc**★★ £C

TAMAR RIDGE Tasmania www.tamarridgewines.com.au A: VsV, L&W

Owner: Gunns Limited Auburn Road, Kayena TAS 7270
Tamar Ridge was established by Joe Chromy in 1994 from vineyards retained in the Tamar Valley following the sale of other vineyards in northern Tasmania to Pipers Brook. He sold the company in 2003 to Gunns Limited, Tasmania's largest timber company. There are currently over 60 ha of estate vineyards producing clear-fruited if sometimes slightly austere whites led by an intense, well-structured Riesling. Almost all are

usually better with at least two years' age. A barrel-fermented Chardonnay and Pinot Noir almost succeed in being very Burgundian in their complex, cool fruit expressions. Though the Pinot Noir has been slightly over-extracted with incomplete ripeness in its tannic structure, there is however real potential and it will be interesting to see the impact of the new investment. In addition, Cabernet Sauvignon and Josef Chromy Selection bottlings, including a late-harvest Riesling and sparkling Blanc de Noirs, have also been made. The inexpensive Devil's Corner label includes a simple Pinot Noir and light unwooded Chardonnay. (PW)

O Riesling★★ £C   O Sauvignon Blanc★ £B   O Pinot Gris★★ £B
O Chardonnay★★ £C   O Gewürztraminer★★ £B
● Pinot Noir★★ £C

TARRAWARRA   Yarra Valley   www.tarrawarra.com.au   A: **CRs**, May, WSc, Vts

Owner: Besen family   311 Healesville Road, Yarra Glen VIC 3775
Tarrawarra has been single-minded in its aim of producing top-quality Chardonnay and Pinot Noir modelled on white and red Burgundy. Its success in turning out rich, structured, concentrated and complex examples of both owes much to the dedication and skill of winemaker Clare Halloran. Increasing vine age and growing skill in producing high-quality fruit are also driving quality. Chardonnay is 100 per cent barrel-fermented with some use of *bâttonage*. The Pinot Noir receives a cold pre-fermentation maceration, open fermenters are used and around 25 per cent of the oak is new. Both wines benefit from age and are best at least three to five years after the vintage. Less expensive Yarra Valley Pinot Noir and Chardonnay are made under the Tin Cows label which also includes a Merlot and a Shiraz (the latter in part from Heathcote fruit). Kosher Chardonnay and Shiraz are made under the Kidron label. Owner Marc Besen is also the wealthy benefactor behind the Tarrawarra Art Museum. (PW)

Tarrawarra:
● Pinot Noir★★★ £D   O Chardonnay★★★ £D
Tin Cows:
O Chardonnay★★ £C

VIRGIN HILLS   Macedon Ranges   www.virginhills.com.au   A: **Str**, Vne

Owner: Michael Hope   17 Piper Street, Kyneton VIC 3444
Just one wine is made here, a blend of Cabernet Sauvignon, Shiraz and Merlot. The winery and vineyard are now owned by Michael Hope of HOPE ESTATE in the Hunter Valley after several recent changes in ownership. While there is some vintage variation, the wine is usually amongst the best Cabernet-based reds in Victoria. Vineyard practice is organic, minimal intervention is employed during vinification and the wine is virtually sulphur-free. As the location is at the limit of ripening for these varieties the wine is not produced every year. At its best (as with the 1998) it is a magnificent, elegant, cedary red; in cooler years there can be a marked green undercurrent. (PW)

● Virgin Hills★★★★ £E

YARRA BURN   Yarra Valley   www.brlhardy.com.au   A: **Cst**, Sav

Owner: Hardy Wine Company   Settlement Road, Yarra Junction VIC 3797
Yarra Burn is the headquarters of BRL HARDY'S substantial Yarra Valley operations, though quantities are small. The group only took control of the winery (established in 1975) in 1995 but the wines increasingly bear the hallmarks of premium BRL Hardy examples, with a rich fruit core, balance, complexity and well-integrated oak, though a bold premium Bastard Hill bottling of the Pinot Noir is a bit overdone. The Yarra Burn sparkling wine, which includes all three Champagne grapes, is yet another fine example from the Yarra Valley, with a cool, crisp elegance missing from so many Australian sparkling wines in the past. (PW)

O Chardonnay★★ £B   Bastard Hill★★★ £D
O Yarra Burn★★ £C
● Pinot Noir★★ £C   ● Shiraz★★★ £C

YARRA YARRA   Yarra Valley   A: JAr, Rae

Owner: Maclean family   239 Hunts Lane, Steels Creek, VIC 3775
This small estate is yet another that adds to the prestige and reputation of the Yarra Valley. An original 2 ha
was increased to 7 ha in 1996 but still further plantings are unlikely to satisfy demand for the wines. Syrah
shows plenty of style with pepper, spice, smoke and black fruits – ripe but with some cool-grown elegance.
The 2001 includes 2 per cent Viognier. Cabernets is based on Cabernet Sauvignon with both Cabernet
Franc and Merlot adding to the texture and style. There is usually a cool, leafy Yarra Valley trait but with
its fine, ripe tannins this deserves at least five or six years' ageing. The classy, sophisticated Yarra Yarra
(known as Reserve Cabernet Sauvignon prior to 2000) is a similar blend but riper and more concentrated
with very good texture and savoury complexity with age. A little Semillon/Sauvignon Blanc is also made. (PW)
● **The Yarra Yarra★★★★** £E   ● **Cabernets★★★** £E   ● **Syrah★★★** £D

YARRA YERING   Yarra Valley   A: Adm, JNi, ACh, BBR, NYg, P&S

Owner: Dr Bailey Carrodus   Briarty Rd, Gruyere, VIC 3770
At times considered eccentric by some of his neighbours, Bailey Carrodus produces a remarkable array of
very good to exceptional wines even if on occasion the results have been variable. Many of the vines are
relatively venerable, particularly for the Yarra, with some plantings now over 30 years old. Dry White No.1
is a Sauvignon Blanc/Semillon blend but it is the reds, vinified in small open fermenters, that have long
attracted a cult following. Dry Red No.1 is a blend of mainly Cabernet Sauvignon with Merlot, Cabernet
Franc and Malbec. With Dry Red No.2 he takes up the Shiraz baton, arguably with even more success.
Mainly Shiraz with a little Viognier, this is a wine of terrific fruit richness and depth. Also extremely
impressive is the Underhill Shiraz but all of the reds are very fine, concentrated and show real finesse. The
Pinot Noir is made in a rich, powerful, extracted style, while the few bottles of Merlot made caused a
sensation with an audacious cellar-door price tag from the very first vintage. New and more reasonably
priced are Dry Red No.3, based on Sangiovese, and a Young Vines Cabernet Sauvignon. Also made is a
small amount of an impressive fortified port-style wine, Potsorts. (PW)
● **Dry Red No.1★★★★** £E   ● **Dry Red No.2★★★★★** £E
● **Shiraz** Underhill★★★★ £E
● **Pinot Noir★★★★** £F   ● **Merlot★★★★** £H
O **Dry White No.1★★★** £E   O **Chardonnay★★★** £E

YERING STATION/YARRABANK   Yarra Valley   www.yering.com   A: Eno, ACh, P&S, Res

Owner: Rathbone family group/Champagne Devaux   38 Melba Highway, Yarra Glen VIC 3775
Yering Station was the name of a historic property in the Yarra Valley established in the first half
of the 19th century. Today part of the original estate has been revived complete with a major new
winemaking complex. The winemaking team is led by Tom Carson, furnished by investment and direction
from the Rathbone family (also owners of MOUNT LANGI GHIRAN and PARKER COONAWARRA
ESTATE). There is real style and intensity to the well-structured wines (Merlot is an uncharacteristically
good Australian example) with added class, depth and expression in the Reserves, made only in the best
years. The Reserve Cabernet Sauvignon in particular needs time, as much as 8 to 10 years. New MVR is a
Marsanne, Viognier, Roussanne blend with excellent fruit if more modest depth. Barak's Bridge is a second
label from generally more widely sourced fruit. Yarrabank is Yering Station's joint venture with Champagne
house Devaux. The vintage-dated Yarrabank Brut Cuvée, which spends three years on its lees, is arguably
Australia's finest sparkling wine. Made from 50 percent each of Pinot Noir and Chardonnay, it is intense,
rich and ripe with excellent mid-palate breadth and shows considerable complexity with age. Yarra Edge is
a label used for wines made from a separate (leased) property. (PW)
Yarrabank:
O **Yarrabank Brut Cuvée★★★★** £C

759

Yering Station:
O **Chardonnay★★★** £C Reserve★★★★ £E O **Pinot Gris** Late Harvest★★ £C
● **Pinot Noir★★** £C Reserve★★★ £E
● **Shiraz★★** £C ● **Shiraz/Viognier** Reserve★★★★ £E
● **Cabernet Sauvignon★★** £C Reserve★★★★ £E ● **Merlot★★★** £C
Barak's Bridge:
O **Chardonnay★** £B ● **Pinot Noir★** £B ● **Shiraz★★** £B

YERINGBERG Yarra Valley   A: JAr

Owner: Guill de Pury Maroondah Highway, Coldstream, VIC 3770
Guill de Pury replanted just 2 ha of the slopes made famous by his grandfather in the late 19th century. The original Yeringberg vineyard was just one of many to go in to terminal decline due a combination of *phylloxera* and the economic consequences of the First World War. The wines are gentle and pure but with an underlying strength and intensity that comes from an artisanal approach to winemaking. Modern technological adjustments may be common elsewhere in Australia but here you are more likely to see the true character of the vintage. Yet only occasionally do the reds want for more body or ripeness. Both the whites are subtle and restrained but possess real elegance and flair. The Dry Red is a blend of Cabernet Sauvignon, Merlot, Cabernet Franc and Malbec. Developing richness and a savoury complexity with age, it also acquires a level of elegance and finesse seen in few other Australian reds. (PW)
● **Pinot Noir★★** £E ● **Yeringberg Dry Red★★★★** £E
O **Marsanne/Roussanne★★★** £C O **Chardonnay★★★** £D

OTHER WINES OF NOTE

APSLEY GORGE (Tasmania) ● **Pinot Noir** £C O **Chardonnay** £C
ARTHURS CREEK ● **Cabernet Sauvignon** Yarra Valley £D O **Chardonnay** Yarra Valley £C
BERRYS BRIDGE (Pyrenees) ● **Shiraz** £C ● **Cabernet Sauvignon** £C
BINDI (Macedon Ranges) ● **Pinot Noir** Original Vineyard £E O **Chardonnay** Quartz £E
BROWN BROTHERS (King Valley) ● **Shiraz/Mondeuse/Cabernet** £C O Noble **Riesling** £C
O **Liqueur Muscat** £C O **Very Old Tokay** £C
BULONG ESTATE (Yarra Valley) O **Sauvignon Blanc** £C O **Pinot Gris** £C O **Chardonnay** £C
CHATEAU LEAMON (Bendigo) ● **Shiraz** Reserve £D O **Riesling** £B
CURLY FLAT (Macedon Ranges) ● **Pinot Noir** £E O **Chardonnay** £D
FARR RISING (Geelong) ● **Pinot Noir** Geelong £D O **Chardonnay** £D
FREYCINET (Tasmania) ● **Pinot Noir** £D O **Chardonnay** £C O **Riesling** £C
KARINA VINEYARD (Mornington Peninsula) O **Chardonnay** £C O **Riesling** £B
KNIGHT GRANITE HILLS (Macedon Ranges) ● **Shiraz** £C
KOOYONG (Mornington Peninsula) ● **Pinot Noir** £D
MOOROODUC ESTATE (Mornington Peninsula) O **Chardonnay** Estate £C
● **Pinot Noir** Wild Yeast £D
MOUNT IDA (Bendigo) ● **Shiraz** £C
NICHOLSON RIVER WINERY (Gippsland) O **Chardonnay** £E ● **Pinot Noir** £E
OAKRIDGE ESTATE (Yarra Valley) ● **Merlot** £C ● **Shiraz** £C O **Chardonnay** Reserve £C
OSBORNS (Mornington Peninsula) ● **Pinot Noir** £C O **Chardonnay** £C
PAUL OSICKA ● **Shiraz** Heathcote £B
PARADISE ENOUGH (Gippsland) O **Chardonnay** £C Reserve £C ● **Pinot Noir** £C
PASSING CLOUDS (Bendigo) ● **Angel Blend** (Cabernet Sauvignon) £C
● **Shiraz/Cabernet** Graeme's Blend £C

PLUNKETT ● Shiraz Strathbogie Ranges Reserve £C
DOMINIQUE PORTET ● Shiraz Heathcote £C ● Cabernet Sauvignon Yarra Valley £C
REDBANK (Pyrenees) ● Sally's Paddock (Cabernet Sauvignon/Shiraz/Malbec) £D
RED EDGE (Heathcote) ● Shiraz £E ● Cabernet Sauvignon £E
RED HILL ESTATE (Mornington Peninsula) ○ Chardonnay £C ● Pinot Noir £C
ROCHFORD (Macedon Ranges) ○ Chardonnay £C ● Pinot Noir £D ● Cabernet/Merlot £C
SANGUINE ESTATE (Heathcote) ● Shiraz £D
SORRENBERG (Beechworth) ○ Chardonnay £D ● Shiraz Havelock Hill £C
SPRINGVALE (Tasmania) ○ Chardonnay £C ● Pinot Noir £D
TURRAMURRA ESTATE (Mornington Peninsula) ○ Chardonnay £C ● Pinot Noir £C ● Shiraz £C
WANTIRNA ESTATE (Yarra Valley) ● Cabernet Sauvignon/Merlot Amelia £D ● Pinot Noir Lily £D
WARRENMANG (Pyrenees) ● Shiraz Estate £D ● Grand Pyrenees (Cabernet blend) £D
WILD DUCK CREEK (Heathcote) ● Shiraz Springflat £E Reserve £F

Author's Choice (PW)

10 diverse first-rate Victorian Shiraz
CRAIGLEE ● Shiraz
DALWHINNIE ● Shiraz Moonambel
JASPER HILL ● Shiraz Georgia's Paddock
MITCHELTON ● Shiraz Print
MOUNT LANGHI GHIRAN ● Shiraz
PARINGA ESTATE ● Shiraz
SEPPELT GREAT WESTERN ● Show Sparkling Shiraz
SUMMERFIELD ● Shiraz Reserve
TAHBILK ● Shiraz 1860 Vines
YARRA YERING ● Shiraz Underhill

6 cellarworthy classic red blends
MOUNT LANGHI GHIRAN ● Cabernet/Merlot
MOUNT MARY ● Quintet
REDBANK ● Sally's Paddock
VIRGIN HILLS ● Virgin Hills
YARRA YERING ● Dry Red No. 1
YERINGBERG ● Dry Red

6 exemplary Victorian/Tasmanian Pinot Noir
BANNOCKBURN ● Pinot Noir Geelong
BASS PHILLIP ● Pinot Noir Reserve
DIAMOND VALLEY ● Pinot Noir Estate
GIACONDA ● Pinot Noir
STEFANO LUBIANA ● Pinot Noir Tasmania
PIPERS BROOK ● Pinot Noir Reserve Tasmania

10 top whites with personality
BY FARR O Viognier Geelong
COLDSTREAM HILLS O Chardonnay Yarra Valley Reserve
DALWHINNIE O Chardonnay Moonambel
GIACONDA O Nantua Les Deux
JASPER HILL O Riesling Georgia's Paddock
MÉTIER O Chardonnay Schoolhouse Vineyard
MITCHELTON O Marsanne/Roussanne/Viognier Airstrip
PIPERS BROOK O Riesling Estate
TALTARNI O Clover Hill (sparkling)
YERINGBERG O Marsanne/Roussanne

10 undervalued wines
BALGOWNIE ● Shiraz Bendigo
BEST'S ● Shiraz Great Western
R L BULLER & SON O Rutherglen Tokay Premium Fine Old
DELATITE O Riesling
DROMANA ESTATE O Arneis i Garry Crittenden
DROMANA ESTATE ● Shiraz
HEATHCOTE WINERY ● Shiraz Mail Coach
MITCHELTON O Riesling Blackwood Park
MOUNT LANGHI GHIRAN ● Shiraz/Grenache/Cabernet Billi Billi Creek
TAHBILK O Marsanne

Australia/New South Wales & Queensland

New South Wales not only makes a sizeable contribution to Australia's production of bulk wine but 160 km north-west of its largest city, Sydney, has a wine region of magnetic tourist attraction in the Hunter Valley. Thanks to the Great Dividing Range much potential remains and new regions will continue to make an impact if developed with quality as the foremost consideration.

Hunter Valley

New South Wales' most traditional region is not, regrettably, the state's most suited region to viticulture. The Lower **Hunter Valley** is peppered with estates lying just west of the Brokenback Range but, despite regular cloud cover, conditions are very hot and the greatest part of its rainfall usually comes as the growing season reaches its climax. Great vintages are the exception rather than the norm yet some marvellous ageworthy Shiraz and Semillon are produced, though few of the latter examples are still made in the famed long-lived, minerally, toasty-but-unoaked Semillon style of old. Many Hunter-based producers now source fruit from Mudgee, Cowra or further south in the Central Ranges as well as producing wines from South Australia yet several of the greatest wines are purely Hunter in origin. Other than the big names of Brokenwood and Rosemount new operations are emerging, not least the very small production of Keith Tulloch.

Central Ranges & Southern New South Wales

Mudgee and the other regions which run down the western side of the Great Dividing Range are better protected from cyclonic deluges, making them both cooler and drier. Much of the grape production from Mudgee and **Cowra** has been dominated by the big producers and the harvest has been Hunter-bound. Mudgee produces intensely flavoured Cabernet Sauvignon, Shiraz, Chardonnay and Semillon, though few producers other than Huntington Estate and Rosemount give the region the recognition it deserves. Cowra Chardonnay has a well-established distinctive, lush, full style of its own. Gaining increasing significance are **Orange**, **Hilltops** and, from close to the border with Victoria, the chilly, elevated **Tumbarumba** region. Similarly cool and elevated, with the associated risk of frost damage, are the vineyards of the **Canberra District** lying to the north of the country's capital (but still in New South Wales itself). Despite the difficult, marginal conditions, the best reds are Cabernet/Merlot blends and Shiraz; the latter can show a wonderful cool-climate expression. The best whites are produced from Riesling, Chardonnay and Viognier.

Big Rivers

Big Rivers suggests a lot of water and the vast vineyards of this zone are dependent on irrigation. The zone incorporates the commercially important bulk-producing regions of **Riverina** and, shared with Victoria on the Murray River, **Murray Darling** and **Swan Hill**. Not generally associated with fine quality, Riverina is the source of De Bortoli's Noble One from botrytis-enriched Semillon grapes.

Queensland

Producing wine in sub-tropical Queensland is fraught with difficulties. Nonetheless wine is produced from **South Burnett**, around Kingaroy, and in the **Granite Belt** around Stanthorpe, in the Great Dividing Range, where it is cooler and elevated. Despite sometimes difficult vintage conditions Shiraz can be good

A-Z of producers by region

Hunter Valley

Mudgee

Canberra District

Riverina

1   South Burnett
2   Granite Belt
3   Hastings River
4   Hunter
5   Broke Fordwich
6   Mudgee
7   Orange
8   Cowra
9   Hilltops
10 Gundagai
11 Tumbarumba
12 Canberra District
13 Southern Highlands
14 Shoalhaven Coast

New South Wales vintages

The generalised Vintage charts cover some of the most ageworthy styles and will prove most useful when taken together with comments on style and ageing within individual producer entries. Many wines can be drunk young but an increasing number will not be at their best for at least five years. Hunter Valley Semillon can take two decades in its stride while top Hunter or Mudgee Shiraz and Cabernet have similar ageing potential. Both the vintage ratings and when to drink assessments generally only apply to the top rated examples (three star wines or higher).

Following on from the record early, drought-affected and high quality harvest of 2003, 2004 was a difficult vintage in the Hunter Valley. Two summer heatwaves were followed by two torrential downpours, which for many came before the grapes were picked. The chances of classic long-lived Hunter Shiraz and Semillon from 2004 look slight.

New South Wales vintage chart

	Hunter Valley Shiraz	Central Ranges Shiraz	Hunter Valley Semillon
2004	★★/★★★★ A	★★★/★★★★ A	★★★ A
2003	★★★★/★★★★★★ A	★★★★ A	★★★★/★★★★★★ A
2002	★★★/★★★★ A	★★★★/★★★★★★ A	★★★★ A
2001	★★★/★★★★ B	★★/★★★ B	★★★/★★★★ B
2000	★★★★/★★★★★★ B	★★/★★★ B	★★★★/★★★★★★ B
1999	★★★★ B	★★★/★★★★ B	★★★★ B
1998	★★★★★ B	★★★★ B	★★★★★ B
1997	★★★ C	★★/★★★ C	★★★/★★★★ C
1996	★★★★/★★★★★★ B	★★★★ B	★★★★/★★★★★★ B
1995	★★★/★★★★★ C	★★★★/★★★★★★ C	★★★/★★★★ C
1994	★★★/★★★★ C	★★★★ C	★★★★ C
1993	★★★/★★★★ C	★★/★★★ C	★★★/★★★★ C
1992	★★★ D	★★/★★★ C	★★★/★★★★ C
1991	★★★★★ C	★★★/★★★★ C	★★★★/★★★★★ C

New South Wales & Queensland/A-Z of producers

ALLANDALE   Hunter Valley   www.allandalewinery.com.au   **A: AWA**, HoM

Owner: Wally & Judith Atallah   Lovedale Road, Lovedale NSW 2321
Established in 1978, this is still a relatively small Hunter Valley operation with a reputation for consistently full-flavoured, complex Chardonnay. Archetypal very ripe, oak-influenced Shiraz and classic Hunter-grown Verdelho and Semillon are also produced. Bill Sneddon's winemaking has given the wines their individual stamp and impressive flavour intensity: traditional in the best sense, without compromise to the particular winemaking trend of the day. In addition to the fruit from 7 ha of Allandale vineyards, grapes are bought in from other Hunter growers and increasingly diverse sources including Mudgee, Hilltops and McLaren Vale. Both Orange and Mudgee Cabernet Sauvignon were produced in 2001. New Allandale Reserve red is based on Mudgee Shiraz. (PW)

● **Shiraz** Matthew★★★ £C   ● **Cabernet Sauvignon** Hilltops★★ £C
○ **Chardonnnay**★★★ £B   ○ **Semillon**★★ £B   ○ **Verdelho**★★ £B

BROKENWOOD   Hunter Valley   www.brokenwood.com.au   **A: Lib**, ACh, Ben, P&S, Vne, Odd

Owner: Brokenwood Wines   McDonalds Road, Pokolbin NSW 2320
A benchmark Lower Hunter winery, Brokenwood was established in 1970 by a number of partners including former lawyer and wine writer James Halliday. Production has grown to a not inconsiderable 70,000 cases a year but the quality remains uniformly high. Winemaker Iain Riggs is responsible for the direction of both the widely sourced Brokenwood wines and those of Yarra Valley winery SEVILLE ESTATE, acquired in the late 1990s. While there is good Cabernet Sauvignon it is the Shiraz that has earned the greatest renown. Both the Rayner (McLaren Vale) and Graveyard (Hunter) wines are immensely rich and impressive. The latter has remarkable depth, intensity and length, becoming very complex with the seven or eight years' age it needs to show at its best. It is among Australia's elite in stunning years like 1998 and 2000. Another Hunter example, the Mistress Block, has real panache. The Semillon whites are classic expressions of the grape: low in alcohol, slow to develop, becoming immensely honeyed and very intense as they peak with 8 to 10 years. The ILR version, with classic length, depth and structure, is only released after five years' ageing. There's also aromatic, lightly honeyed Verdelho from Cowra and rich and lightly tropical Chardonnay. The premium Graveyard Chardonnay is fermented with wild yeasts and shows considerable new oak but has real depth and intensity and adds weight and dimension with three or four years. New is a very promising Forest Edge Vineyard Chardonnay from Orange. Relatively inexpensive Harlequin and Cricket Pitch reds and whites are crafted to be immediately appealing and drinkable. In the Cricket Pitch red, Cabernet Sauvignon and Merlot are the major varieties but there is better expression in the Shiraz/Cabernet Franc-dominated Harlequin red. Cricket Pitch white is a grassy, citrusy Sauvignon Blanc/Semillon blend with a hint of barrel-fermentation, while the Harlequin is an unoaked blend of Chardonnay and Verdelho. The range is completed by a fine late-harvest Riesling from the Jelka Vineyard (McLaren Vale), but you'll have to go to the cellar door to get this one. (PW)

● **Shiraz**★★ £C   Mistress Block★★★ £C   Rayner Vineyard★★★★ £D   Graveyard Vineyard★★★★★ £F
● **Cabernet Sauvignon**★★★ £C   ● **Harlequin Red**★★ £B   ● **Cricket Pitch Red**★★ £B
○ **Chardonnay**★★ £C   Forest Edge★★ £C   Graveyard Vineyard★★★★ £D
○ **Semillon**★★★ £B   ILR Reserve★★★★ £C
○ **Harlequin White**★ £B   ○ **Cricket Pitch White**★★ £B   ○ **Verdelho**★★ £B

CAPERCAILLIE   Hunter Valley   www.capercailliewine.com.au   **A: WIE**, Fin, Luv

Owner: Alasdair Sutherland   Londons Road, Lovedale NSW 2325
Scottish wine, well at least the closest thing to it. Scot Alasdair Sutherland has long experience in the Hunter Valley and this is his own small winery. Fruit is bought in from both from the Hunter Valley and further afield for a diverse range of wines of good flavour intensity. The whites, at least the Hunter Valley Chardonnay and Semillon, are if anything more impressive than the reds, with classic Hunter flavours as well as structure and depth. Intense, very berryish Ceilidh Shiraz is the best of the reds, combining Hunter

Valley and McLaren Vale fruit. The Clan (Cabernet Sauvignon with Merlot and Petit Verdot from Coonawarra, Barossa and Orange) is characterful yet a slightly perplexing concoction of cool and ripe fruit. The Ghillie Shiraz is made from a special parcel of Hunter Valley fruit in the best vintages. Gewürztraminer (including a dessert style), red Chambourcin and a sparkling red are also made. (PW)

○ Chardonnay★★★ £C   ○ Semillon★★★ £C
● Shiraz Ceilidh★★★ £C   ● Merlot Orange Highlands★ £C   ● The Clan★★ £C

CLONAKILLA   Canberra District   www.clonakilla.com.au   A: Lib, ACh, P&S, FFW

Owner: Kirk family   Crisps Lane, Murrumbateman NSW 2582
Tim Kirk is realising the potential first developed by his father Dr John Kirk, an Australian research scientist of Irish descent. The vineyard is gradually being expanded from the current 6 ha. Clonakilla's top red, Canberra District Shiraz Viognier, includes around 7 per cent Viognier and is now one of the best in the country, distinguished particularly by its individual expression of an Australian Shiraz-based blend. The pepper, spice, floral and berry amalgam is distinctive, elegant and supported by a depth, weight and structure that deserves at least five years' ageing. Viognier is very good too, with delightful mayblossom and ripe peach aromas - it is tighter, with better structure than most Australian examples, avoiding the excessive ripeness or alcohol of some. Made as they are on a similarly small scale, these really are wines to contrast with examples from good growers of Côte-Rôtie or Condrieu. A Hilltops Shiraz, while much cheaper than the Canberra District version, is quite different: more one-dimensional without the same depth, expression or sheer style. Chardonnay, Riesling, Semillon/Sauvignon Blanc and Cabernet/Merlot are also produced. (PW)

● Shiraz★★★★ £E   Hilltops★★ £C   ○ Viognier★★★ £D

DE BORTOLI   Riverina   www.debortoli.com.au   A: DeB, BBR, FWC, ARe, Cam, SFW, F&M

Owner: De Bortoli family   De Bortoli Road, Bilbul NSW 2680
De Bortoli's Riverina operation is a vast winery based in the Riverina near Griffith. Output is around 4.5 million cases a year and almost all is accounted for by bulk-market labels. The majority of the fine-wine output is accounted for at the Yarra Valley winery (see DE BORTOLI Victoria). Riverina budget labels include Deen De Bortoli (Vat numbered) wines, the Willowglen and Sacred Hill ranges as well as others only likely to be encountered locally. The real interest from a quality point of view is in the botrytis-influenced Semillons and the fortified Black Noble. The latter is produced in a similar fashion to the liqueur Tokays of Rutherglen from a *solera* which is based on Semillon. Its rich, raisiny character is finely balanced with fresh tangy acidity. Noble One is a long-established great Australian sweet wine only surpassed by the best fortified wines. It has the weight, depth and concentration, if not the class, of top Sauternes. It can similarly benefit from long cellaring, needing at least five years to fully reveal its remarkable complex, honeyed character. (PW)

○ Noble One★★★★ £F   ○ Black Noble★★★★ £E

HUNTINGTON ESTATE   Mudgee   www.huntingtonestate.com.au   A: JIC

Owner: Roberts family   Cassilis Road, Mudgee NSW 2850
A consistently excellent winery, now emplying the winemaking skills of Susie Roberts and still the best in Mudgee despite the emergence of ROSEMOUNT labels from the area. Production remains relatively small at around 20,000 cases a year and is spread across a wide range of wines, some of which are only available through mail order and at the cellar door. Cabernet Sauvignon, Shiraz and Cabernet Shiraz are now identified with FB or MB Bin numbers. Special Reserves of Cabernet Sauvignon and Shiraz are quite marked by their full, American-oak component but the quality of the fruit can easily absorb the wood, something many Australian wines fail to achieve. The top white is Semillon which, like many Hunter examples, sees no wood and similarly requires considerable patience – drinking this style too young can prove a disappointment. There is also a rich, barrel-fermented Chardonnay and a fruit-filled, early-drinking Semillon/Chardonnay. The wines represent particularly good value for money and are difficult to find

outside of Australia. (PW)

● **Cabernet Sauvignon**★★★ £B Special Reserve★★★ £C
● **Shiraz**★★★ £B Special Reserve★★★★ £C
○ **Semillon**★★★ £B ○ **Chardonnay** Barrel Fermented★★ £B ○ **Semillon/Chardonnay**★★ £B

LAKE'S FOLLY Hunter Valley www.lakesfolly.com.au A: **Lay**, NYg, P&S, FFW

Owner: Peter Fogarty Broke Road, Pokolbin NSW 2320
This top-quality Lower Hunter producer, originally established in 1963 by Sydney surgeon Max Lake was sold to Peter Fogarty in 2000. Rodney Kempe has taken on the winemaking reins, continuing to make just two wines from 12 ha of mature vineyards which translates to around 4,500 cases per year. The Chardonnay in particular was an early benchmark among Australian whites. During the early to mid-1990s the wines were still good but didn't reach the levels of old. However, aided by excellent vintages in 1996 and 1998 they now seem to be back on top form. The red Cabernet blend (older vintages are labelled Cabernets or simply Cabernet) is mostly Cabernet Sauvignon with some Shiraz, Merlot and Petit Verdot. It is restrained and well-structured with blackcurrant and blackberry fruit but none of the overripeness seen in some Hunter reds. The Chardonnay is rich, opulent and buttery with very well-judged oak adding a subtle, spicy, nutty character. Both are ageworthy: the Chardonnay will keep for up to a decade from a top year, the Cabernet blend often longer. (PW)

● **Cabernet blend**★★★ £E
○ **Chardonnay**★★★★ £E

MCWILLIAM'S MOUNT PLEASANT Hunter Valley www.mcwilliams.com.au

Owner: McWilliam's Marrowbone Road, Pokolbin NSW2320
This is the good stuff, make no mistake. There are other good wines from this large company's other operations including increasingly good wines from Barwang in southern New South Wales but these are the gems. The Semillons, only released with four to five years' bottle-age start out slowly but have marvellous toasty, citrus and herb intensity that continues to build in the bottle over many years. The characteristic intense toastiness is not due to oak but the inherent character that develops when these Hunter Semillons are built to last. Shiraz too is deep and individual. The particular fusion of oak, savoury characters, earth, leather, black cherry and licorice give an indication of the complexity but there are other nuances too here that you just won't get anywhere else. Old Paddock & Old Hill comes from two very old estate vineyards and is particularly long-lived. Intensely flavoured Chardonnay owes some of its complexity to oak but is not overwhelmed by it. Getting hold of these wines can be a problem unless you happen to live in Australia yet perhaps the most remarkable thing is the very reasonable pricing. If you buy the Semillon relatively young, put it away somewhere out of reach for a decade or more. (PW)

● **Shiraz** Rosehill★★ £C Maurice O'Shea★★★ £C Old Paddock & Old Hill★★★★ £D
○ **Semillon** Elizabeth★★★ £B Lovedale★★★★ £D ○ **Chardonnay** Maurice O'Shea★★★ £C

MEEREA PARK Hunter Valley www.meereapark.com.au **Lib**, ACh, Ben,V&C, FFW, Hrd

Owner: Rhys & Garth Eather Lot 3, Palmers Lane, Pokolbin NSW2320
Rhys Eather, one of two brothers who own this Pokolbin-based winery, makes around 10,000 cases per year. The first vintage was 1991 and the wines are all made from bought-in fruit. Ripe, complex Chardonnay is barrel-fermented with natural yeasts and sourced from old Pokolbin vines while both an intensely honeysuckle Viognier and fresh Verdelho with preserved citrus fruit are good examples of these varieties in the Hunter. Semillon, like the Verdelho, is unoaked in the classic Hunter Valley style and will benefit from four or five years' cellaring. Of the reds the Cabernet/Merlot is aged in French oak and is in a leaner style, almost leafy. The Aunts Shiraz is characterful and intense but Alexander Munro has greater depth and style with powerful spice, pepper and smoky black fruit. Made since 2001 is an aromatic Shiraz Viognier (containing around 8 per cent of the latter). Also tasted, and of good fruit and style, are Orchard Road Pinot

Gris and Barbera made from Orange fruit. (PW)

● **Shiraz** The Aunts★★ £C Alexander Munro★★★ £D
● **Shiraz Viognier**★★ £C ● **Cabernet Merlot**★★ £C
○ **Chardonnay** Alexander Munro★★ £D ○ **Semillon** Epoch★★ £B
○ **Viognier** Lindsay Hill★★ £C ○ **Verdelho** Lindsay Hill★★ £B

ROSEMOUNT ESTATE Hunter Valley www.rosemountestates.com A: ScE, AAA

Owner: Southcorp Rosemount Road, Denmman NSW 2064

The already substantial Rosemount enterprises (also see ROSEMOUNT MCLAREN VALE) merged with the huge SOUTHCORP operation in 2001. By mid-2003 there had been a significant fall-out which included the departure of veteran winemaker Philip Shaw who for so long maintained generally high standards throughout the extensive portfolio. The premium red Mountain Blue Shiraz/Cabernet Sauvignon (typically 85/15) from Mudgee is dense, concentrated and aged in American oak. The white equivalent is the intense, complex Roxburgh Chardonnay, a distinctive full-bodied Australian example of the variety, if the most Burgundian in style of the Rosemount Chardonnays. In contrast, but also aged and fermented in *barriques*, is the spicy citrus, ripe peach and melon Orange Vineyard version while the Giants Creek Chardonnay (Hunter) is aged in older oak to preserve its fruit character. Least of the premium Chardonnays, the Show Reserve falls a long way short of its form of a decade or more ago. Usually much better is the Show Reserve Semillon with more classic Hunter expression but requiring at least three or four years' ageing. Reds from the Orange Vineyard, planted at an altitude of almost 900 metres, include well-crafted Cabernet Sauvignon, Shiraz and Merlot that show their cooler climate origins. The Shiraz, aged in French rather than American oak, is particularly classy and restrained with a touch of white pepper and spice. Hill of Gold varietals from Mudgee show good fruit intensity and texture, particularly in good Chardonnay and ripe, black-fruited Shiraz. Lower-priced Diamond varietal and dual varietal labels can offer decent everyday drinking if not a great deal of excitement. The whites in particular, with simple, ripe fruit often outperform many of their competitors at this level.(PW)

● **Shiraz/Cabernet Sauvignon** Blue Mountain★★★★ £F
● **Shiraz** Hill of Gold★★ £B Orange Vineyard★★★ £D ● **Merlot** Orange Vineyard★★ £D
● **Cabernet Sauvignon** Hill of Gold★★ £B Orange Vineyard★★★ £D
○ **Chardonnay** Hill of Gold★★ £B Show Reserve★★ £C Giants Creek★★ £C
○ **Chardonnay** Orange Vineyard★★★ £D Roxburgh★★★★ £F
○ **Semillon** Show Reserve★★ £C ○ **Kirri Billi** Vintage Brut★★ £D

KEITH TULLOCH Hunter Valley A: Gun, Bal, Res, WSc

Owner: Keith Tulloch Lilywood Farm, O'Connors Road, Pokolbin NSW 2325

An experienced Hunter Valley winemaker with stints at Lindemans and Rothbury Estate under his belt, Keith Tulloch has recently also made some wine under his own name. Production is very small with only a few hundred cases of each wine in the first vintages but the wines are undoubtedly a fine distillation of Tulloch's experience. They seem handmade in the best sense, very Hunter Valley with super Hunter fruit and intensity, excellent weight, texture and length of flavour. Above all, they are classy and complex. Unquestionably they will age impressively too (Semillon must be given time); certainly they get better every time you taste them. The stylish fruit in the Forres Blend is predominantly Cabernet Sauvignon but also from Merlot and Petit Verdot. The excellent Shiraz is up another notch in the 2001. While not cheap the wines are very well-priced; the splendid Chardonnay and Semillon are great value for money. Merlot is also made but has only been tasted once. (PW)

○ **Semillon**★★★★ £C ○ **Chardonnay**★★★★ £C
● **Shiraz** Kester★★★★ £D ● **Forres Blend**★★★★ £D

TYRRELL'S Hunter Valley www.tyrrells.com.au A: **Par**, CPp WSc, Hrd, Sel

Owner: Tyrrell family Ashmans, Broke Road, Pokolbin NSW 2320
This family-owned and run winery dates back to 1858 and makes an extensive range of wines, around half a million cases even after the recent sale of the Long Flat brand. The top wines are the Winemakers Selection (Vat numbered) series. The bold, powerful and complex Vat 47 has been one of Australia's great Chardonnays for three decades. Rich and very concentrated, it has always shown refinement and balance. Vat 1 Semillon of great breadth and nuance and only released with several years' age (currently 1997) is one of the finest examples in the region. Of the premium reds, the Vat 9 Shiraz adds an extra dimension and deep earthiness over other good Shiraz but the blended Vat 8 Shiraz/Cabernet (from Hunter and Coonawarra components) and Vat 6 Pinot Noir work less well. Reserves of Semillon and Shiraz are also made to a high standard and released with age. Rufus Stone reds (not tasted) come from vineyards in Heathcote, McLaren Vale and the Limestone Coast. At the level of Brokenback Shiraz, Moon Mountain Chardonnay and Shee-Oak Chardonnay (all Hunter sourced) the wines can be full-flavoured though on occasion want for better balance (and less oak). The unwooded Lost Block Semillon by contrast is more classic. Of the relatively inexpensive Old Winery wines, which are sourced from both from the Hunter and southern states, the Shiraz has decent, smoky, dark berry fruit, while the Semillon has good intensity and length and is better with a little age. Moore's Creek is a new label for basic Shiraz, Cabernet, Chardonnay and Semillon/Sauvignon Blanc. (PW)

● **Shiraz** Old Winery★ £B Brokenback★★ £C Vat 9★★★ £E
O **Chardonnay** Shee-Oak★ £C Moon Mountain★★ £C Vat 47★★★★ £E
O **Semillon** Old Winery★ £B Lost Block★★ £C Vat 1★★★★ £E

OTHER WINES OF NOTE

ABERCORN (Mudgee) ● Shiraz £C
ALLANMERE (Hunter) O **Chardonnay** Durham £C O **Verdelho** £B
● **Shiraz** £C ● **Cabernet Sauvignon** £C
ARROWFIELD (Hunter) ● **Shiraz** Show Reserve £C O **Chardonnay** Show Reserve £C
BIMBADGEN (Hunter) O **Chardonnay** £B ● **Shiraz** £B Signature £C
BOTOBOLAR (Mudgee) ● **Shiraz** £C O **Marsanne** £B
BRINDABELLA HILLS (Canberra District) O **Riesling** £B O **Sauvignon/Semillon** £B
DRAYTONS (Hunter) ● **Shiraz** Bin 5555 £B O **Verdelho** £B
EVANS FAMILY (Hunter) O **Chardonnay** Pinchem £C
GLENGUIN (Hunter) ● **Shiraz** £C Pokolbin Vineyard £C
HOPE ESTATE (Hunter) O **Verdelho** £B O **Chardonnay** £B O **Semillon** £B
● **Merlot** £B ● **Shiraz** £B
LINDEMANS O **Semillon** Hunter River Reserve £D
LARK HILL (Canberra District) ● **Pinot Noir** £D O **Chardonnay** £C O **Riesling** £B
MARGAN FAMILY (Hunter) O **Verdelho** £B O **Semillon** £B ● **Shiraz** £C ● **Cabernet Sauvignon** £C
MIRAMAR (Mudgee) ● **Cabernet Sauvignon** £C O **Chardonnay** £B
POOLE'S ROCK (Hunter) O **Chardonnay** £C
REYNOLDS (Orange) O **Chardonnay** Orange Reserve £B ● **Merlot** Orange Marble Man £C
● **Cabernet Sauvignon** Orange The Jezebal £C
ROTHBURY ESTATE (Hunter) ● **Shiraz** Brokenback £D O **Chardonnay** Brokenback £C
O **Semillon** Hunter Valley £B Brokenback £C
SIRROMET (Queensland) ● **Shiraz** Vineyard Selection £B O **Chardonnay** Seven Scenes £C
TEMPUS TWO (Hunter) O **Semillon** Reserve £B O **Chardonnay** Cowra £B
THISTLE HILL (Mudgee) ● **Cabernet Sauvignon** £B O **Chardonnay** £B
WINDOWRIE (Cowra) ● **Shiraz** Estate £C O **Chardonnay** Estate £C
YARRAMAN ESTATE (Hunter) ● **Chambourcin** Black Cypress £B

Author's choice (PW)

10 classic Hunter/Mudgee reds
ALLANDALE ● Shiraz Matthew
BROKENWOOD ● Shiraz Graveyard Vineyard
BROKENWOOD ● Shiraz Rayner Vineyard
HUNTINGTON ESTATE ● Cabernet Sauvignon
HUNTINGTON ESTATE ● Shiraz
LAKE'S FOLLY ● Lake's Folly red
MCWILLIAM'S MOUNT PLEASANT ● Shiraz Maurice O'Shea
MCWILLIAM'S MOUNT PLEASANT ● Shiraz Old Hill & Old Paddock
ROSEMOUNT ● Shiraz/Cabernet Mountain Blue
TYRRELL'S ● Shiraz Vat 9

10 definitive Hunter/Mudgee whites
ALLANDALE ○ Chardonnay
BROKENWOOD ○ Chardonnay Graveyard Vineyard
BROKENWOOD ○ Semillon ILR Reserve
HUNTINGTON ESTATE ○ Semillon
LAKE'S FOLLY ○ Chardonnay
MCWILLIAM'S MOUNT PLEASANT ○ Chardonnay Maurice O'Shea
MCWILLIAM'S MOUNT PLEASANT ○ Semillon Lovedale
ROSEMOUNT ○ Chardonnay Roxburgh
TYRRELL'S ○ Chardonnay Vat 47
TYRRELL'S ○ Semillon Vat 1

10 new stars
CLONAKILLA ● Shiraz Canberra District
CLONAKILLA ○ Viognier
HOPE ESTATE ○ Verdelho Hunter Valley
LARK HILL ○ Riesling Canberra District
MEEREA PARK ○ Semillon Hunter Valley Epoch
MEEREA PARK ● Shiraz Alexander Munro
ROSEMOUNT ○ Chardonnay Orange Vineyard
ROSEMOUNT ● Shiraz Orange Vineyard
KEITH TULLOCH ○ Semillon Hunter Valley
KEITH TULLOCH ● Shiraz Hunter Valley Kester

Western Australia

Australia's biggest state is virtually all desert but it does have a cool coastal skirt that runs south from the state capital, Perth, and around the south-western corner to parts kept cool and damp under the influence of the Southern Ocean. WA contributes only a tiny amount to Australia's total wine production (3 per cent) but by our reckoning accounts for an unequal share of its premium wine. That said some have dropped the quality baton in the race for bigger volumes and healthier profits so care is needed among some of the better known names.

Greater Perth

The **Swan District** (Swan Valley) is the historic heart of Western Australian viticulture. It is extremely hot and dry but with varieties such as Verdelho, Chenin Blanc, Chardonnay and Semillon some surprisingly good whites have been produced. Houghton dominates production and its ageworthy, big-volume 'White Burgundy' (now HWB) is the most famous and remarkable wine of the region. Reds, including Shiraz and Cabernet Sauvignon, can be characterful and well-made even if the best wines are likely to include a component from Great Southern.

South-West Australia

Nearly all of Western Australia's premium wines come from this zone and its two most important regions, Margaret River and Great Southern.

Margaret River

The **Margaret River** juts into the Indian Ocean but despite problems of wind and the ravenous local wildlife, especially the birds, its 'founding doctors' (establishing Vasse Felix, Moss Wood and Cullen in the late 60s and early 70s) were soon followed by Leeuwin Estate and others. Wines of remarkably rich, pure, deeply textured fruit from Cabernet Sauvignon and Chardonnay have been produced in the decades since and the region continues to grow apace. At its heart, the Willyabrup Valley is the most densely planted, but high quality is also achieved to the north and south. Sauvignon Blanc and Semillon (both individually and combined) and Shiraz are made to a high standard too. To the north and east of Margaret River, **Geographe** incorporates a large swathe of countryside, stretching from the coast inland. Capel Vale, located on the coastal strip, is the leading winery but inland valleys are also being developed.

Great Southern

Great Southern, as its name suggests, is an especially large region. **Frankland River** is currently the most planted of five sub-regions, and often excels with Riesling, Chardonnay, Shiraz, Cabernet Sauvignon and Cabernet Franc. Producers include the likes of Alkoomi and Frankland Estate but grapes are also sourced from here by those based outside the region such as Houghton. **Mount Barker's** potential has long been highlighted by Plantagenet, but others too make particularly fine Shiraz as well as excellent Riesling and Chardonnay. **Porongurup** lies east of Mount Barker while **Albany** and **Denmark**, which can be wetter, reach down to the coast and again scattered vineyards can provide marvellous fruit.

Other regions of the SW Australia zone

Between Great Southern and Margaret River even more far-flung vineyards are appearing in the gaps between extensive tracts of forest in three emerging areas, **Blackwood Valley**, **Manjimup** and **Pemberton**. The latter, the most exposed to the Southern Ocean, has already achieved wider recognition thanks to Picardy and Salitage. Smokier Pinot Noir it is surely not possible to find, the distinctive wines being influenced by the effects of the controlled burning of forest fires. Chardonnay, Shiraz and the Bordeaux varieties are also successful.

A-Z of producers by region

1 Swan District
2 Perth Hills
3 Peel
4 Geographe
5 Margaret River
6 Blackwood Valley
7 Manjimup
8 Pemberton
9 Great Southern
10 Frankland River
11 Mount Barker
12 Porongurup
13 Denmark
14 Albany

Western Australia vintages

These generalised Vintage charts cover some of the most ageworthy styles and will prove most useful when taken together with comments on style and ageing within individual producer entries. While many wines can be drunk young, top full-bodied Margaret River Cabernet demands at least five years' cellaring. Great Southern Shiraz is usually a little more approachable but can also be long-lived. Top-quality Chardonnay and Pinot Noir only show their full potential with three to five years' ageing, while exceptions like Leeuwin Estate Art Series Chardonnay can age for more than 10 years. The best Great Southern Riesling is up there with the best from the eastern states and will keep for at least five to six years. Both the vintage ratings and when to drink assessments generally only apply to the top rated examples (three star wines or higher).

In 2003 Western Australia largely escaped the draught conditions that ravaged the eastern states but intermittent rain, and a mix of humid and drier conditions in the late summer took the edge off the vintage in both Great Southern and Margaret River. In 2004 in the Margaret River the season finished with a heatwave but this followed predominantly cool dry growing conditions (for good whites). The healthiest, more established vineyards of Cabernet Sauvignon are thought to have withstood the stress well. But while vintage prospects are generally excellent some reds may lack full physiological ripeness.

Western Australia vintage chart

	Margaret River Cabernet	Great Southern Shiraz	Margaret River Chardonnay
2004	★★★/★★★★★ A	★★★★/★★★★★ A	★★★★/★★★★★ A
2003	★★★/★★★★ A	★★★ A	★★★/★★★★ B
2002	★★★★ A	★★★★ A	★★★★ B
2001	★★★★/★★★★★ A	★★★★/★★★★★ B	★★★★/★★★★★ C
2000	★★★/★★★★ B	★★★ B	★★★/★★★★ C
1999	★★★★/★★★★★ B	★★★ B	★★★★ C
1998	★★★ C	★★★ C	★★★ C
1997	★★★★ B	★★★★ B	★★★★/★★★★★ C
1996	★★★★/★★★★★ B	★★★★/★★★★★ C	★★★★ C
1995	★★★★/★★★★★ C	★★★★/★★★★★ C	★★★★★ C
1994	★★★★★ C	★★★★/★★★★★ C	★★★★/★★★★★ D
1993	★★★★ C	★★/★★★ D	
1992	★★★/★★★★ C	★★★★ C	
1991	★★★★/★★★★★ C	★★★/★★★★ C	

ALKOOMI Frankland River www.alkoomiwines.com.au A: Lay

Owner: Merv and Judy Lange RMB 234, Wingebellup Road, Frankland WA 6396
This winery in remote Frankland River has now grown to a substantial size (around 80,000 cases) but fruit comes entirely from 82 ha of estate vineyards. Reds include varietal Cabernet Sauvignon, in a refined rather than weighty style, and a Shiraz (including a small amount of Viognier since 2002) full of spicy berry fruit. Jarrah, a premium version of Shiraz from the oldest vines, has real weight and depth. Equally impressive is another premium red, Blackbutt, a blend of Cabernet Sauvignon, Cabernet Franc, Malbec and Merlot which is structured and needs four or five years' ageing. The top white ,Wandoo, is unusual in being 100 per cent Semillon and is partially oak-fermented. Others include a fresh and zesty Sauvignon Blanc, tight and well-structured Chardonnay and a characteristically fine and complex Great Southern Riesling that becomes toasty with age. Fruit-driven basics appear under the Southlands label: Shiraz, Cabernet/Merlot, Semillon/Sauvignon Blanc and unwooded Chardonnay. (PW)
● Cabernet Sauvignon★★ £C ● Blackbutt★★★ £D
● Shiraz★★★£C Jarrah★★★ £D O Wandoo★★★ £E
O Chardonnay★★ £C O Riesling★★★ £B O Sauvignon Blanc★ £B

CAPE MENTELLE www.capementelle.com.au A: VCq, Par, JNi, ACh, Maj, P&S, F&M, Sel

Owner: LVMH Wallcliffe Road, Margaret River, WA 6285
Cape Mentelle has a lower profile than sister winery CLOUDY BAY in New Zealand but has a similar reputation for quality thanks to the efforts of founder David Hohnen, who ran operations until 2003. Direction for both now comes from the widely respected Dr Tony Jordan. Partially oaked, the Semillon/Sauvignon Blanc is ripe, spicy, even smoky, with real class if sometimes wanting for a little more definition and structure. A single-vineyard selection, Wallcliffe, is from the same grapes (but with more Sauvignon) and vinified in American and French oak. It was rather oaky in 2000 but much more restrained in 2001. Chardonnay is rich, powerful and complex, just needing a little class for really fine. Among the reds Cabernet/Merlot from Trinders Vineyard has good depth, breadth and intensity allied to a very ripe dark berry fruit character in warm vintages. Better still is a Cabernet Sauvignon deserving of at least six to seven years' age. Bold and concentrated with well-judged oak, the wine shows impressive dark berry fruit complexity and length of flavour. Dark fruits and black pepper characterise the Shiraz, which gets limited new oak, both American and French. A rare Australia example of Zinfandel is a classic of the variety: full, brambly and with not inconsiderable alcohol. Available locally are Georgiana, a unoaked blend from a mix of Chardonnay, Sauvignon Blanc, Chenin and Semillon, and Marmaduke, from mostly Shiraz, Mourvèdre and Grenache. Both are intended for fruity, early drinking. A sound, small range of reds and whites under the Ironstone label is released in the UK. The wines of FONTY'S POOL are also made by Cape Mentelle. (PW)
● Cabernet Sauvignon★★★★ £D ● Cabernet/Merlot Trinders★★★ £C
● Shiraz★★★ £C ● Zinfandel★★★ £C
O Chardonnay★★★ £C O Semillon/Sauvignon Blanc★★★ £C O Wallcliffe★★★ £D

CAPEL VALE Geographe www.capelvale.com A: MMD, Por

Owner: Dr Peter Pratten Lot 5, Stirling Estate, Mallokup Road, Capel WA 6271
An extensive range of reds and whites is produced at this winery to the north of the Margaret River at Geographe. Production is now around 150,000 cases a year, making it one of a growing number of large producers. The top black label wines can be very good and for the most part not excessively priced for the quality. Particularly good are the two whites, Whispering Hill Riesling (from Mount Barker) and Frederick Chardonnay (Geographe). The Riesling is intense, deep and very well structured, not overly subtle or refined but with super toast, smoke and lime flavour and character. The Chardonnay is rich, opulent and in a sense somewhat old fashioned but can age superbly, as will the Riesling. Of the regular Capel Vale wines, both Verdelho and Riesling are well crafted and Sauvignon Blanc/Semillon can be impressively pungent. Chardonnay is subtly oaked and with real intensity. The top reds combine elegance and expression

with good concentration and plenty of oak. The Kinnaird Shiraz (from the Whispering Hill vineyard in Mount Barker) now usually outshines a more variable premium Merlot, Howecroft (from Geographe). The CV range offers good everyday drinking in both red and white. (PW)

Capel Vale
● **Merlot★★** £C Howecroft★★★ £D ● **Shiraz★★** £C Kinnaird★★★★ £E
O **Chardonnay★★** £C Frederick Reserve★★★★ £D O **Sauvignon Blanc/Semillon★★** £B
O **Riesling★★** £B Whispering Hill★★★ £C O **Verdelho★★** £B

CHATSFIELD Mount Barker www.chatsfield.com.au   A: **Cac, DWS**

Owner: Dr Ken & Joyce Lynch O'Neill Road, Mount Barker WA 6324
An impressive family operation with 16 ha, producing around 10,000 cases per year of well-crafted and very well-priced wines. All are produced at the Porongorup winery, a partnership between Chatsfield and other local wineries. Consultant winemaking comes from JOHN WADE, responsible for the early quality of both PLANTAGENET and HOWARD PARK. Both Gewürztraminer and Riesling are produced in a dry, structured and ageworthy style. The latter is tight, minerally when young and will age superbly. Cabernet Franc is full of bramble and leafy character but fully ripe in an elegant, medium-weight style closer to the Loire Valley than St-Émilion. The Shiraz is great value – chock full of dark fruit, liquorice and black pepper. Refined, supple and long it will benefit from three or four years' ageing but could be drunk sooner. Also made is a sweet white, Indulge. (PW)
● **Cabernet Franc★★** £B ● **Shiraz★★★** £C
O **Riesling★★** £B O **Chardonnay★★** £C O **Gewürztraminer★★** £B

CULLEN Margaret River www.cullenwines.com.au   A: **Lib, ACh, Vne, P&S, F&M, Hrd**

Owner: Cullen family Caves Road, Cowaramup WA 6284
The Cullen's Margaret River winery has a long tradition of excellence and now produces close to 20,000 cases per year from 28 ha of well-established estate vineyards. Made by Vanya Cullen, the wines are marked by their finesse, superior structure and complexity, putting Cullen in a different class to many of its neighbours. The Cabernet Sauvignon/Merlot, usually around two-thirds Cabernet Sauvignon with up to 10 per cent of Cabernet Franc, is now named in honour of Di Cullen who did so much to establish the Cullen reputation. Of top Bordeaux classed growth quality it sets the standard for the Margaret River. Its superb fruit is highlighted by outstanding breadth, depth and structure. The 1999 perhaps just edges the 2000 and there is real promise in 2001 but it always deserves at least five years' ageing. Almost at the same level, Cullen Chardonnay, utilising natural yeasts and whole-bunch pressing, is a magnificently crafted white full of intense, pure citrus fruit and has unmistakable class and great length. The Sauvignon Blanc/Semillon (or sometimes Semillon/Sauvignon Blanc) is part barrel-fermented and shows lovely texture and balance. A powerful, somewhat backward new red blend, Mangan, is named for a vineyard owned by Vanya's brother Rick and his wife and is very good in both 2001 and 2002. Unusually it comes from Malbec, Petit Verdot and Merlot. Also new are Ellen Bussell red (Cabernet/Merlot) and white (Semillon/Sauvignon/Verdelho), from the first vintage (2002) the red is cool and expressive while the white (2003) has good texture. (PW)
● **Cabernet Sauvignon/Merlot** Diana Madeline★★★★★ £E ● **Mangan★★★** £D ● **Pinot Noir★★** £D
O **Chardonnay★★★★** £E O **Sauvignon Blanc/Semillon★★★** £C

EVANS & TATE Margaret River www.evansandtate.com.au   A: **AWs, IRW**, P&S

Owner: Evans & Tate Ltd Lionel's Vineyard, RSM 482 Payne Road, Jindong WA6280
This is now a very substantial operation with most of its development in the Margaret River, though it was the original producer of quality Shiraz in the very hot Swan Valley. Nowadays Gnangara Shiraz is sadly no more than a simple, fruit-driven wine, one of several under the Gnangara label. Of an extensive Margaret River collection, Chardonnay is a ripe, fruit-driven style lacking weight, structure and ageing potential.

Sauvignon Blanc/Semillon has both grassy and riper notes but can be a bit lean, while Cabernet/Merlot (labelled Barrique 61 prior to the 2001 vintage) is very flavoursome with very ripe berryish fruit and Shiraz is similarly very ripe with a spicy intensity. The best wines come from the 26-ha Redbrook vineyard in the Wilyabrup Valley sub-region. Chardonnay is crafted using an array of Burgundian techniques but is surprisingly restrained, recalling the quality of mid-90s Margaret River efforts. Shiraz is spicy and intense, one of the best examples of this variety in the region. Redbrook Cabernet Sauvignon is also quite impressive and ageworthy. (PW)

● **Shiraz** Margaret River★★ £B Redbrook★★★ £D ● **Cabernet/Merlot** Margaret River★★ £B
● **Cabernet Sauvignon** Redbrook★★★ £E ○ **Sauvignon Blanc/Semillon** Margaret River★★ £B
○ **Chardonnay** Margaret River★ £B Redbrook★★★ £D

FERNGROVE VINEYARDS Frankland River www.ferngrove.com.au　A: GWW, Odd, NYg

Owner: Ferngrove Ferngrove Road, Frankland WA 6396
Murray Burton relinquished his family's beef and dairy farming heritage to switch to grape growing and wine production. This is now a thriving, expanding operation with extensive vineyards. If there's good value for money in the regular varietals and dual-variety blends, the superior Orchid bottlings combine concentration and style. Particularly good are the reds from the low-yielding 2001 vintage – attractive and fruit-driven but elegant and expressive too. Quite striking is a Special Late Harvested King Malbec with blackberry and raisin aromas as well as peppery black plum flavours. The Stirlings, a Merlot/Cabernet Sauvignon/Malbec made in 2001, is deep and structured and very promising. There's a wait yet before the next offering, the 2003. The premium whites, Cossack Riesling and Butterfly Chardonnay, haven't been tasted but will be exciting if they show a similar step up in quality to the reds. Other interests include the Karri Oak vineyard at Mount Barker and the Margaret River label, Leaping Lizard, the latter including a sound Semillon/Sauvignon Blanc and Cabernet/Merlot. (PW)

Ferngrove Vineyards
● **Shiraz**★★ £B Dragon★★★ £C ● **Cabernet/Shiraz**★ £B
● **Malbec** King★★★ £C ● **Cabernet Sauvignon** Majestic★★★ £C
○ **Semillon/Sauvignon Blanc**★★ £B ○ **Riesling**★★ £B ○ **Chardonnay**★★ £B

Leaping Lizard
○ **Semillon/Sauvignon Blanc**★★ £B ○ **Chardonnay** Unwooded★ £B ● **Cabernet/Merlot**★★ £B

FONTY'S POOL Pemberton www.fontyspoolwines.com.au　A: Cap, Vnf

Owner: Wemyss family Seven Day Road, PO Box 1709, Manjimup WA 6258
Fonty's Pool wines are made by the CAPE MENTELLE team in the Margaret River. The reds are particularly impressive and offer good value against some of WA's more established labels. Despite the Manjimup location all the wines are labelled as Pemberton in origin. There are cool aspects to a Shiraz of real depth and character which is stylish and long with licorice and plum fruit. A smoky, plummy Pinot Noir has lots of flavour and good breadth within a refined structure. Chardonnay doesn't quite fulfill the potential the fruit suggests, while Sauvignon Blanc/Semillon is a fruit-driven quaffer. Viognier and a Cabernet/Merlot are also made. The Wemyss family (from Fife in Scotland) also owne the Provençale domaine, RIMAURESQ. (PW)

● **Shiraz**★★★ £B ● **Pinot Noir**★★ £C
○ **Chardonnay**★★ £C ○ **Semillon/Sauvignon Blanc**★ £B

FRANKLAND ESTATE Frankland River www.franklandestate.com.au　A: M&V, P&S

Owner: Judi Callam & Barrie Smith Frankland Road, Frankland WA 6396
The vineyards of Frankland Estate, established in 1988, are but a small part of a large Merino sheep farming property located in Frankland River sub-region on the western side of Great Southern. Production has increased to 15,000 cases a year and quality is very good. Great store is placed on managing the vineyards,

including consultancy from expert Richard Smart. The flagship red is Olmo's Reward, a blend of mostly Merlot and Cabernet Franc (but also a little Malbec, Cabernet Sauvignon and Petit Verdot). It is sleek and stylish with ripe, dark, spicy fruit, supple and velvety tannin and good length. The estate-sourced Isolation Ridge wines, comprising Chardonnay, Riesling, Cabernet Sauvignon and Shiraz, are also impressive. The Riesling stands out with its tight, apple and mineral fruit and has the structure for real ageing. Shiraz is full of black pepper and attractive, brambly fruit, the Cabernet marked by an intense, small berry fruit character. There are now two single-vineyard Rieslings, Cooladerah and Poison Hill. The Rocky Gully label includes Riesling, Shiraz and Cabernets, all made from contract-grown fruit. (PW)

● **Olmo's Reward**★★★ £D
● **Cabernet Sauvignon** Isolation Ridge★★ £C   ● **Shiraz** Isolation Ridge★★★ £C
O **Chardonnay** Isolation Ridge★★ £C   O **Riesling** Isolation Ridge★★★ £B

GOUNDREY   Mount Barker   www.goundreywines.com.au

Owner: Vincor   Langton, Muir Highway, Mount Barker WA 6324
In just a few years businessman Jack Bendat built Goundrey into a substantial and high-profile operation before selling it in 2002 to Vincor (owner of AMBERLEY ESTATE as well as Canadian wineries CHATEAU DES CHARMES, MISSION HILL and SUMAC RIDGE amongst others). From an expanse of estate vineyards, production now exceeds a quarter of a million cases per year. Three main ranges are made. The Goundrey Reserves are the most exciting. The Reserve Merlot is full, plummy and approachable, while the Reserve Cabernet Sauvignon is denser and more structured. Reserve Shiraz is medium-weight with some depth, though it does lack the concentration of the top examples from the region. Of the white Reserves, Riesling is well-crafted and full of green apple and and mineral notes, while the Chardonnay is sound but often marked by coarse oak. The Goundrey and Fox River ranges offer an array of simple, attractive, fruit-driven styles. However, the overriding impression is that volume rather than character is the driving force here. (PW)

● **Merlot** Reserve★ £C   ● **Cabernet Sauvignon** Reserve★★ £C   ● **Shiraz** Reserve★ £C
O **Chardonnay** Reserve★ £C   O **Riesling** Reserve★★ £B

HIGHER PLANE   Margaret River   www.higherplanewines.com.au

Owner: Dr Craig & Cathie Smith   PO Box 4123, Mosman Park, WA 6012
A small (7 ha), very promising new vineyard established in 1997 by a husband-and-wife team in the southern Margaret River following a scrupulous search for the best site. Planting is relatively dense by Australian standards and the low yields are reflected in the wines. Consultancy comes from Keith Mugford of MOSS WOOD and early releases (2001 and 2002) are very good, particularly the classic Margaret River styles. Chardonnay has excellent fruit and real verve, while the Cabernet Sauvignon/Merlot blend is intense and concentrated with a Bordeaux-like complexity. Other reds include a varietal Merlot which is a touch more herbaceous yet with ripe tannins and a Pinot Noir. This is well made with ripe strawberryish fruit if not the structure or definition for more; certainly good in the context of Margaret River Pinot. Prices are estimated. (PW)

● **Cabernet/Merlot**★★★ £C   ● **Merlot**★★ £C   ● **Pinot Noir**★★ £C
O **Chardonnay** Reserve★★★ £C

HOUGHTON   Swan District   www.houghton-wines.com.au   A: Cst, WSc, P&S, Maj

Owner: Hardy Wine Company   Dale Road, Middle Swan WA 6056
The biggest operation in Western Australia but being caught up in volume terms by both EVANS & TATE and GOUNDREY. The range is considerable, with fruit sourced throughout the vinegrowing areas of the state. The flapship is the remarkable Jack Mann red, a dense, powerful and sometimes oaky blend of Cabernet Sauvignon, Shiraz and Malbec sourced from Frankland River and Mount Barker. It demands five or six years' ageing to even hint of its best. Regional wines from Frankland River, Pemberton and Margaret

River are also impressive. A premium Gladstones version of Frankland River Shiraz is also produced but difficult to find outside of Australia. There is fine fruit in both Frankland River Riesling and Pemberton Sauvignon Blanc, though the latter in particular wants for more structure. Below the regional range come a mid-price Crofters range (sold only in Australia) then the more basic Line range which includes HWB, known locally in Australia as Show Reserve White Burgundy. This is one of the most successful and impressive of Australia's many volume brands. Of variable composition but generally including Chenin Blanc, Muscadelle and Verdelho, it is almost unique among such wines in that it will age well. In addition to a persistent and intense, ripe fruit character it has depth and structure. (PW)

● **Jack Mann**★★★★ £F   ● **Shiraz** Frankland River★★★ £C
● **Merlot** Pemberton★★★ £C   ● **Cabernet Sauvignon** Margaret River★★ £C
○ **Riesling** Frankland River★★★ £B   ○ **Sauvignon Blanc** Pemberton★★ £B   ○ **HWB**★★ £B

HOWARD PARK   Denmark   www.howardparkwines.com.au   A: **Bib**, L&W, JNi, P&S, NYg

Owner: Jeff & Amy Burch   Scotsdale Road, Denmark WA 6333
Barely a decade ago, this substantial operation with wineries in Denmark in the Great Southern and at Margaret River was a small, high-quality label with just a Riesling and Cabernet-based red produced in small quantities by JOHN WADE while he was winemaker at PLANTAGENET. There are now well over 200 ha of estate vineyards and new planting is going on all the time. The two labels are Howard Park and Madfish. The three top wines are labelled simply Howard Park. Riesling is a superb, complex, structured and very ageworthy example of the variety, arguably the best produced in Western Australia. The Cabernet Sauvignon/Merlot, sometimes labelled Cabernet Sauvignon, is variable both in composition (if usually including around a quarter Merlot) and source, with fruit from Margaret River, Pemberton and Denmark. Dense, powerful and profound it remains one of Australia's great reds although vintages in the late 1990s are not quite as impressive as earlier ones. Chardonnay is in a restrained, tight and very structured style. Backward when young it will evolve well with age. Also under the Howard Park range are impressive region-specific Shiraz and Cabernet Sauvignon. The Scotsdale pair are produced from Great Southern while the Leston wines are from Margaret River. The Madfish label offers wines with immediate fruit character and appeal from widely sourced grapes. The Premium Red and White have been consistent blends of variable composition while a forward, spicy, black pepper and dark-fruited Shiraz and a tropical, smoky Chardonnay have also impressed across a number of vintages. Other wines include Unwooded Chardonnay, Semillon Sauvignon Blanc and Cabernet/Merlot/Cabernet Franc. They are generally well-priced and drink well on release. (PW)

Howard Park
● **Cabernet Sauvignon/Merlot**★★★ £E
● **Cabernet Sauvignon** Scotsdale★★★ £C   Leston★★★ £C
● **Shiraz** Scotsdale★★★ £C   Leston★★★ £C
○ **Riesling**★★★★ £C   ○ **Chardonnay**★★★★ £C
Madfish
● **Premium Red**★ £B   ● **Shiraz**★★ £B   ● **Pinot Noir**★★ £B
○ **Chardonnay**★★ £B   ○ **Premium White**★ £B

LEEUWIN ESTATE   www.leeuwinestate.com.au   A: **DDr**, BBR, P&S, F&M, Hrd, Sel

Owner: Horgan family   Stevens Road, Margaret River WA 6285
One of the very best properties in the Margaret River, Leeuwin Estate has been producing excellent Chardonnay and Riesling under the Art Series label for two decades now. Production is sizeable at more than 60,000 cases a year but still small by comparison to some Margaret River operations. The Art Series wines are the pinnacle. The Sauvignon Blanc is a very stylish example with an impressive mineral structure. Riesling is very intense with mineral, lime and a marvellous toasty persistence with four or five years' age. Chardonnay is extraordinarily rich and and powerful, yet balanced, intense and complex; a long-lived Australian classic. The fruit and texture are such that the oak is seamlessly integrated with three or four years'

cellaring. Art Series reds include Pinot Noir and a fine Cabernet Sauvignon which shows a complex fusion of cooler and riper fruit with excellent structure and length. A second tier of wines, the Prelude Vineyards label, includes a Classic Dry White, based on Sauvignon Blanc, and a Chardonnay with good richness and structure but which evolves much faster than the Art Series wine. Prelude Cabernet/Merlot has good weight and texture. Siblings, a third label, is for everyday Sauvignon/Semillon and Shiraz. Sparkling wine from Great Southern Pinot Noir and Chardonnay was first produced from the 1998 vintage. (PW)

● **Cabernet Sauvignon** Art Series★★★★ £E   ● **Cabernet/Merlot** Prelude Vineyards★★ £C
● **Pinot Noir** Art Series★★ £D
O **Chardonnay** Art Series★★★★★ £E Prelude Vineyards★★ £C   O **Riesling** Art Series★★★ £C
O **Sauvignon Blanc** Art Series★★★ £C   O **Sauvignon Blanc/Semillon** Siblings★ £B

MOSS WOOD   Margaret River   www.mosswood.com.au   A: **Lay**, NYg, P&S

Owner: Keith & Clare Mugford   Metricup Road, Willyabrup WA 6280
The Mugfords have owned this very fine, small 12-ha Margaret River estate (founded by Bill Pannell of PICARDY in 1969) since 1984. Semillon has always been remarkable here and a benchmark for the region. The wine is unwooded and shows restrained fruit in its youth. It will be all the better for five years' ageing. Chardonnay is in a full, opulent style with smoky, spicy new oak evident in its youth. The Cabernet Sauvignon is one of the very finest in the region – complex, powerful and structured, even dense and extracted, in contrast to other more fruit-driven examples from the region. Rich blackberry and cassis emerge as the wine becomes increasingly harmonious with age. In order to expand their business but retain the core quality of the Moss Wood wines, the Mugfords purchased the 6-ha Ribbon Vale vineyard and winery in 2000, adding a further 5,000 cases to production. Vinification takes place at Moss Wood. The range has been reduced to just three wines; while Merlot stands out, a very good Semillon has now been incorporated into the Semillon/Sauvignon Blanc blend. The wines thus far are reasonably concentrated and are produced from fairly low-yielding vines but can be expected to show greater refinement and complexity in the future following changes to their vinification. Moss Wood also produce wines from growers' vineyards: Cabernet Sauvignon from Amy's Vineyard (previously Glenmore) in Yallingup (northern Margaret River), a tiny amount of Green Valley Chardonnay (southern Margaret River), and Chardonnay and Pinot Noir from the Lefroy Brook Vineyard in Pemberton. (PW)

● **Cabernet Sauvignon**★★★★ £F Amy's Vineyard★★★ £C
● **Cabernet Sauvignon/Merlot** Ribbon Vale Vineyard★★★ £D   ● **Merlot** Ribbon Vale Vineyard★★★ £C
O **Chardonnay**★★★★ £E Lefroy Brook Vineyard★★★ £D   O **Semillon**★★★★ £C
O **Semillon/Sauvignon Blanc** Ribbon Vale Vineyard★★ £B

PICARDY   Pemberton   www.picardy.com.au   A: **Lay**, CPp

Owner: Pannell family   Cnr Eastbrook Road & Vasse Highway, Pemberton WA 6260
Picardy is arguably Pemberton's top producer, if less well-known than the pioneering SALITAGE. It is a measure of its success that several top Western Australian wines made by producers based in other regions are sourced partly or wholly from Pemberton fruit. Bill Pannell established MOSS WOOD but diverted his attention to PICARDY in 1993. The Burgundy varieties and Shiraz are all successful. Cabernet Sauvignon, Merlot and Cabernet Franc are also planted although the results are not quite as good. Merlot/Cabernet is a roughly equal blend of the three varieties. Chardonnay has excellent structure and texture revealing fine fruit and complexity with a little age. Pinot Noir is full of dark, berry-fruit aromas which support the judicious oak treatment. In Tête de Cuvée (not tasted) a portion of the Pinot Noir vineyard is treated differently in and attempt to produce a more structured and ageworthy, more Burgundian Pinot Noir. Shiraz shows a real intensity of spice, pepper and berry fruits. (PW)

● **Merlot/Cabernet**★★ £C   ● **Shiraz**★★★ £C
● **Pinot Noir**★★★ £C   O **Chardonnay**★★★ £C

PIERRO   Margaret River

A: **MSd**, BBR, P&S

Owner: Dr Mike Peterkin   PO Box 522, Brusselton WA 6280

Pierro produces one of the finest, most complex Chardonnays in Western Australia. The wine possesses excellent fruit as well as a remarkable array of secondary flavours. Citrus, mineral, grilled nuts and oatmeal predominate and there is great breadth and intensity on the palate. LTC is a fine, youthfully grassy, melony Semillon/Sauvignon Blanc with real intensity and weight and a much better structure than many examples of this blend. Of two reds, a berryish, slightly earthy Cabernet Sauvignon/Merlot has good style and breadth but lacks the concentration of the best Margaret River examples. Pinot Noir has good flavour intensity if at the ripe end of the spectrum. Mike Peterkin also makes the wines of the 9-ha Fire Gully vineyard. Whites, including Semillon/Sauvignon and Semillon, are fresh and fruity and have the edge over the reds, a Cabernet/Merlot and a Shiraz, which want for depth and richness. (PW)

Pierro:
O **Chardonnay★★★★** £E   O **Semillon/Sauvignon Blanc** LTC★★★ £C
● **Cabernet Sauvignon/Merlot★★★** £E   ● **Pinot Noir★★** £D
Fire Gully:
● **Cabernet/Merlot★** £C   O **Semillon/Sauvignon Blanc★★** £B

PLANTAGENET   www.plantagenetwines.com

A: **Lib**, ACh, Ben, Luv, V&C, Vne, P&S

*Owner: **Lionel Sampson & Son**   Albany Highway, Mount Barker WA 6324*

Plantagenet is the top winery at Mount Barker and among the very best in the Great Southern region. Production has risen to over 50,000 cases a year yet a high standard and remarkable consistency have been maintained by winemaker Gavin Berry. The winery is also an important source of contract winemaking facilities for many small estates in the region. Wines under the Plantagenet label (sourced only from estate vineyards) include a ripe, smoky Pinot Noir from Great Southern and Pemberton fruit and splendid expressive and undervalued Chardonnay. Great value too is the perfumed, toasty, limey and well-structured Riesling, among the finest in the region, particularly with five years' age. A distinctive Cabernet Sauvignon shows good richness and a certain elegance but without the extra depth or power found in the best from the Margaret River. Shiraz, on the other hand, is mightily impressive, with smoky, minerally, white pepper and dark fruits character – as much Northern Rhône as Western Australia. Also made from the estate Rocky Horror Vineyard in 2001 were Merlot and an excellent varietal Cabernet Franc. 'Off the Rack' Chenin Blanc is made from partially dried grapes. Omrah is the second label and there is excellent intensity to an impressive Unoaked Chardonnay and good fruit in a Sauvignon Blanc which should be drunk young. Omrah reds include Shiraz, Cabernet/Merlot and Pinot Noir. Hazard Hill red and white are sold locally while fruit is widely sourced for similarly good value exported Hellfire Bay Chardonnay and Shiraz/Grenache. (PW)

Plantagenet:
● **Shiraz** Mount Barker★★★★ £D   ● **Cabernet Sauvignon** Mount Barker★★★ £C
● **Pinot Noir** Great Southern★★★ £C
O **Chardonnay** Mount Barker★★★ £C   O **Riesling** Mount Barker★★★ £B
Omrah:
● **Shiraz★★** £B   ● **Cabernet/Merlot★** £B
O **Chardonnay** Unoaked★★ £B   O **Sauvignon Blanc★** £B

SUCKFIZZLE/STELLA BELLA   Margaret River

A: **All**, Odd, P&S, Sel

Owner: Stuart Pym & Janice McDonald   PO Box 403, Nedlands, WA 6909

Margaret River Wines is the umbrella for three labels: the single-vineyard Suckfizzle wines, Stella Bella and a third label, Skuttlebutt. Winemakers Stuart Pym (Devil's Lair) and Janice McDonald are responsible for all three. The attractive Stella Bella whites have intense, ripe fruit flavours and reasonable structure. The more interesting reds have good potential. There is good style to Shiraz with a definite Margaret River accent, proper regional panache to the Cabernet Sauvignon/Merlot and plenty of character in a Sangiovese/Cabernet Sauvignon blend that successfully marries riper notes with a more leafy aspect. Tempranillo is promising too. Suckfizzle Sauvignon Blanc/Semillon has a barrel-fermented and lees-stirred component in contrast with the herbal, fruit-accented Stella Bella version but is a good example. The cool, cedary Suckfizzle Cabernet Sauvignon is a notch or two up from the Stella Bella reds. It has intense savoury fruit and excellent dimension and depth with ripe tannins, deserving of 5 to 10 years' age. (PW)

Suckfizzle Augusta:
O Sauvignon Blanc/Semillon★★★ £D   ● Cabernet Sauvignon★★★ £D

Stella Bella:
O Sauvignon Blanc★★ £B   O Semillon/Sauvignon Blanc★★ £B   O Chardonnay★★ £B
● Cabernet Sauvignon/Merlot★★★ £C   ● Sangiovese/Cabernet Sauvignon★★★ £C
● Tempranillo★★ £C

VASSE FELIX   www.vassefelix.com.au   A: **Neg**, L&W, Tan, CPp, P&S, Han, Hrd, Sel

Owner: Holmes à Court family   Cnr Caves Road & Harmans South Road, Cowaramup WA 6284
Vasse Felix is now a sizeable Margaret River operation, producing some 125,000 cases a year. There is a large range but its reputation has been maintained over a long period by the top reds. The Cabernet/Merlot shows good plum and berry fruit while the Cabernet Sauvignon is denser and better structured. Shiraz is more subtle than many but has good intensity in the best years. The Heytesbury red is a blend of Cabernet Sauvignon, Shiraz, Merlot and Malbec. Rich and concentrated, it has an additional dimension over the other reds. Fine oak is very well integrated, with the cassis and dark chocolate fruit emerging after four or five years' ageing. Chardonnay is the leading white, with ripe, full fruit and restrained oak in the regular example but more oak, power and complexity in the Heytesbury version, though this wine can sometimes lack balance. Semillon is given a short period of oak treatment in American and French barrels. It takes on a marked toasty character and when successful this meshes well with a good fruit core, though it sometimes tends to excess. There is also a sparkling Brut *méthode champenoise* which is produced from all three Champagne varieties although the Pinot Meunier component is negligible. The Noble Riesling is restricted to vintages when botrytis occurs naturally and is rich and concentrated, with an intense peach and citrus character. Theatre Red and White are early-drinking red and white styles while Classic Dry White and Classic Dry Red offer a touch more depth – all are sourced throughout Western Australia. (PW)

● Heytesbury★★★★ £E   ● Cabernet Sauvignon★★★ £D   ● Cabernet/Merlot★★★ £C
● Shiraz★★★ £D   O Semillon★★ £B   O Semillon/Sauvignon Blanc★★ £B
O Chardonnay★★ £B   Heytesbury★★★ £C   O Noble Riesling★★★ £E

VOYAGER ESTATE   Margaret River   www.voyagerestate.com.au   A: **J&B**, Odd

Owner: Michael Wright   Stevens Road, Margaret River WA 6285
A medium-sized Margaret River producer that has become something of a tourist magnet. The ability to select from an extensive vineyard resource places the winery in an enviable position. The wines are rich and powerful but at times disjointed and overly made. While generally very sound and full of flavour, secondary flavours derived from oak and winemaking can dominate. As a result the wines can sometimes have a strange amalgam of flavours and lack purity or any sense of origin. Given their success, however, clearly these are wines that appeal more to some palates than others. The premium Tom Price red and white, from single vineyard sources, have not been tasted. (PW)

O Sauvignon Blanc/Semillon★ £B   O Semillon★★ £B   O Chardonnay★★ £C
● Cabernet Sauvignon/Merlot★★ £C   ● Shiraz★★ £C

WOODSIDE VALLEY ESTATE Margaret River www.woodsidevalleyestate.com.au **A: May**

Owner: Peter Woods & group of investors   Abbeys Farm Road, Yallingup WA 6282
The Gunyulgup Valley near Yallingup is at the northern end of the Margaret River region. Here an exceptional new project is unfolding. Contrary to the accepted wisdom, the vines have been planted on south-facing slopes rather than the usual north-facing slopes. Production is currently around 1,000 cases, with 5,000 the eventual aim. Four varietals are made by Kevin McKay, each named for members of a French expedition that mapped Western Australia in 1801–03: Le Bas Chardonnay, Bissy Merlot, Bonnefoy Shiraz and Baudin Cabernet Sauvignon. The wines are distinguished by their elegance and purity and a beautifully delineated fruit expression, though Merlot and Chardonnay want for more depth (perhaps due to the relatively young vine age). However all the wines are potentially four star and will be rated after further tastings. As good as they are, prices are high (E/F). (PW)

OTHER WINES OF NOTE

AMBERLEY ESTATE (Margaret River) O Semillon £C   ● Shiraz £D
ASHBROOK ESTATE (Margaret River) O Semillon £C   ● Cabernet/Merlot £C
BOOARA (Perth Hills) O Chenin Blanc £B
BROOKLAND VALLEY (Margaret River) O Semillon/Sauvignon Blanc £B
O Sauvignon Blanc Estate £C   ● Cabernet Sauvignon/Merlot Estate £C
CHESTNUT GROVE (Manjimup) O Verdelho £B   ● Merlot £C
CLAIRAULT (Margaret River) O Semillon/Sauvignon Blanc £B   O Riesling Estate £B
● Cabernet Sauvignon Estate £C   ● Claddagh Reserve (Cabernet Sauvignon/Cabernet Franc/Merlot) £E
PAUL CONTI (Swan District) O Chardonnay Tuarts £B   ● Shiraz Mariginiup £C   Medici Ridge £C
DEVIL'S LAIR (Margaret River) O Chardonnay £D
DRIFTWOOD ESTATE (Margaret River) O Chardonnay £C   ● Shiraz £C
FERMOY ESTATE (Margaret River) O Sauvignon Blanc £B   O Chardonnay £C
O Semillon £B   Reserve £C
GILBERTS (Great Southern) O Riesling £B
HAYSHED HILL (Margaret River) ● Cabernet Sauvignon £C
INDIS (Denmark) ● Shiraz Frankland River £B
KARRIVALE (Great Southern) O Riesling Gibraltar Rock £B   ● Shiraz Gibraltar Rock £C
KARRIVIEW (Great Southern) O Chardonnay £C   ● Pinot Noir £C
KILLERBY (Geographe) O Semillon £B   ● Cabernet Sauvignon £C   ● Shiraz £C
LOST LAKE (Pemberton) O Chardonnay £C   ● Pinot Noir £C   ● Shiraz £C
MOSS BROTHERS (Margaret River) ● Shiraz £C
MOUNT TRIO (Great Southern) O Sauvignon Blanc £B   ● Cabernet/Merlot £B
OLD KENT RIVER (Great Southern) ● Pinot Noir £B   ● Shiraz £C
PALANDRI (Margaret River) ● Cabernet/Merlot £B   ● Shiraz £B
● Cabernet Sauvignon £B   Reserve £C
PALMER WINES (Margaret River) ● Cabernet/Merlot £C   ● Merlot £C
REDGATE (Margaret River) O Chardonnay £C
SALITAGE (Pemberton) O Chardonnay £C   ● Pinot Noir £D
SINCLAIR (Manjimup) ● Cabernet/Merlot Jezebel £B   ● Shiraz Margaret River £B
SMITHBROOK (Manjimup) O Chardonnay £C   ● Cabernet Sauvignon £C
TINGLE-WOOD (Great Southern) O Riesling Yellow Tingle £B

JOHN WADE WINES (Great Southern) O Riesling £B O Merlot/Cabernet Franc £C
WATERSHED (Margaret River) O Sauvignon Blanc £B ● Cabernet/Merlot £B ● Shiraz £B
WEST CAPE HOWE (Denmark) O Chardonnay £C ● Cabernet Sauvignon/Merlot £B ● Shiraz £C
WESTFIELD (Swan District) O Chardonnay £B O Liqueur Muscat £C
WIGNALLS (Great Southern) O Chardonnay £C ● Cabernet Sauvignon £C ● Pinot Noir £C
WILLESPIE (Margaret River) O Semillon/Sauvignon Blanc £B ● Cabernet Sauvignon £C
WILLOW BRIDGE (Geographe) O Semillon/Sauvignon Blanc Winemakers Reserve £B
● Shiraz Winemakers Reserve £C
WOODY NOOK (Margaret River) ● Cabernet Sauvignon £C
XANADU (Margaret River) O Semillon £C O Semillon/Sauvignon Blanc £B O Chardonnay £C
● Lagan Estate Reserve (Cabernet Sauvignon/Cabernet Franc/Merlot) £D ● Shiraz Frankland River £C

Author's choice (PW)

10 top Margaret River reds
CAPE MENTELLE ● Cabernet Sauvignon
CULLEN ● Cabernet Sauvignon/Merlot Diana Madeline
CULLEN ● Mangan
HOWARD PARK ● Cabernet Sauvignon Leston
LEEUWIN ESTATE ● Cabernet Sauvignon Art Series
MOSS WOOD ● Cabernet Sauvignon
PIERRO ● Cabernet Sauvignon/Merlot
XANADU ● Lagan Estate Reserve
VASSE FELIX ● Cabernet Sauvignon
VASSE FELIX ● Heytesbury

10 distinguished WA whites
CAPE MENTELLE O Semillon/Sauvignon Blanc Margaret River
CAPEL VALE O Riesling Whispering Hill
CULLEN O Chardonnay Margaret River
CULLEN O Sauvignon Blanc/Semillon Margaret River
HOWARD PARK O Chardonnay
HOWARD PARK O Riesling
LEEUWIN ESTATE O Chardonnay Arts Series
LEEUWIN ESTATE O Riesling Arts Series
MOSS WOOD O Chardonnay Margaret River
PIERRO O Chardonnay Margaret River

10 Great Southern red stars
ALKOOMI ● Shiraz Frankland River Jarrah
CHATSFIELD ● Shiraz Mount Barker
FRANKLAND ESTATE ● Olmo's Reward
HOUGHTON ● Jack Mann
HOUGHTON ● Shiraz Frankland River
HOWARD PARK ● Cabernet Sauvignon/Merlot
PICARDY ● Pinot Noir Pemberton
PICARDY ● Shiraz Pemberton
PLANTAGENET ● Shiraz Mount Barker
SALITAGE ● Pinot Noir Pemberton

10 excellent value for money wines

ALKOOMI ○ **Riesling** Frankland River
CAPE MENTELLE ● **Cabernet/Merlot** Trinders
CAPEL VALE ○ **Verdelho**
CULLEN ● **Ellen Bussell Red** Margaret River
HOUGHTON'S ○ **HWB**
PALANDRI ● **Cabernet/Merlot** Margaret River
PLANTAGENET OMRAH ○ **Riesling**
PLANTAGENET OMRAH ● **Shiraz**
STELLA BELLA ○ **Sauvignon Blanc** Margaret River
WATERSHED ● **Shiraz** Margaret River

New Zealand

New Zealand's wine profile, with an image first centred on intense, vibrant, fruit-driven whites for immediate consumption is now in a state of perpetual evolution.. It's true many winemakers have fashioned wines based on a dogma of technological expertise but the influence of the European quality revival, that is, one underpinned by better health in the vineyard, is also apparent. Slowly too, the best sites are being unearthed even if more time is still needed to emulate many of the premium old world areas where they've had centuries to define and redefine the grape and site match. The direction for New Zealand provided by well-educated, widely travelled, outward-looking winemakers such as John Buck (Te Mata), Michael Brajkovich (Kumeu River) or more recently Steve Smith (Craggy Range) is now being given increased focus as new talent, be it home-grown or imported, is attracted to what is seen as an increasingly glamourous vocation in a beautiful setting. The result is not only wines of better structure and increased longevity but also of greater individuality and flair.

Changing colours

Despite rapid expansion in the 1990s, first the record harvest of 2002 and now unprecedented production of 2004 (166,000 tonnes), New Zealand's output (three-quarters white) is still small in the global context. With a generally cool climate the question of which grape varieties to plant and where became more important than in warmer, easier climes. Twenty years ago Müller-Thurgau dominated the vineyard area; 10 years later Sauvignon Blanc took on a significance way beyond the area planted to it; and in the last decade Chardonnay has been the vine planted in greatest numbers (if still some way behind Sauvignon in overall production), with Pinot Noir coming up on the rails. Along the way Cabernet Sauvignon has found its place (in Hawkes Bay and on Waiheke Island) and Merlot has been more than a mere flirtation. Gradually the industry has moved southwards through Gisborne and Hawkes Bay before confirming Marlborough as its leading region. There is increasing regional or even site-specific identification for many quality wines with less cross-regional blending than previously. However at the other end of the scale a significant component of some basic New Zealand brands is now sourced from bigger-volume wine producing countries.

The regions

Auckland

New Zealand's first vineyard was planted in the far north of New Zealand in the the Bay of Islands but its early history was centred around Auckland, the country's largest city. Despite the city's often warm, humid conditions, some favourable mesoclimates are to be found in **Kumeu** and **Huapai** (to the west), where producers have been successful with Chardonnay as well as Merlot and Cabernet Sauvignon. Other vineyard pockets on the fringes of a sea of suburbia include **Matakana**, Cleveden and Mangere but it is offshore in the Hauraki Gulf on **Waiheke Island**, where conditions are generally warmer and drier, that Merlot and Cabernet have been most successful, a fact highlighted and confirmed in many vintages since Stonyridge's first in 1987. There are now more than 30 wineries on the island.

Gisborne

In the eastern central part of the North Island are its two most productive regions. Gisborne often struggles with rain and humidity during the growing season yet with the right dedication can also show that good quality fruit is not the sole preserve of the more illustrious Hawkes Bay.

Hawkes Bay

Here it is drier in what has become the country's leading area for blends based on the classic Bordeaux varieties. Malbec, Merlot and Cabernet Franc as well as Cabernet Sauvignon make an important contribution to the region's reds. 1998 saw an unprecedented number of fine, fully ripe examples and the number of premium reds continues to increase. The best reds have an intense berryish fruit, balanced oak, good acidity and ripe tannins. The **Gimblett Gravels**, free-draining gravels centred on an old river bed, are being promoted by a consortium of producers as a geographically-defined 'appellation'. Many leading producers now also make some stylish but ripe Syrah, while Zinfandel is also gaining a foothold. Whites are led by Chardonnay but there's also good Gewürztraminer.

Martinborough/Wairarapa

A long way south of Hawkes Bay is the **Wairarapa** region, lying within the political region anchored by the country's capital, Wellington. The most prized viticultural land, the terraces around the small town of **Martinborough**, is extremely limited, but other favoured pockets of viticulture could yet emerge from a region that benefits, like other protected eastern regions, from a relatively low autumnal rainfall. The best early examples of New Zealand Pinot Noir came from here though they remain relatively few in number. Some potential has also been realised for Chardonnay, Riesling and, lately, Pinot Gris.

Marlborough & Nelson

Marlborough at the north-eastern tip of the South Island is New Zealand's most important viticultural area. Like Hawkes Bay it is favoured both climatically, often with fine weather late into the growing season, and geologically, thanks to mostly free-draining soils. Yet most of the major decisions about where and what to plant were made on a purely commercial basis. That is, where the land was cheapest and the grape most prolific. Montana's development of Marlborough in the 1970s was intended as a cheap source of Müller-Thurgau but some Sauvignon was planted as well and it has never looked back. The vineyard area continues to swallow up increasing amounts of its two main valleys, the Wairau and the Awatere, and even some hillside slopes. The most important grapes are Sauvignon Blanc, source of many of the country's top examples, Chardonnay and Pinot Noir. The range and intensity of flavour can be most impressive where yields are restricted, while the best producers also draw out increased depth and structure. Of growing importance is Pinot Gris, while Riesling, both in dry and sweeter styles, has been successful. **Nelson**, slightly cooler and wetter than Marlborough, perseveres with a similar grape mix but site selection is more critical as is the dedication required from top producers such as Neudorf.

Waipara/Canterbury

The vineyards of **Canterbury** lie to the west of Christchurch, the South Island's largest city, and are well-protected from the worst weather from the west by the Southern Alps. The most promising sub-region, **Waipara**, though usually afforded long fine autumns, requires further protection from north-westerly winds in the form of windbreaks. Although the soils are calcareous and well drained, there seems only just sufficient heat to fully ripen Pinot Noir, Chardonnay and Riesling – the most successful varieties in the region as a whole. Pegasus Bay is Waipara's leading wine producer. In the very south of Canterbury is emerging the country's newest wine region, the **Waitaki Valley**. From the 2004 vintage look out for the new Pinot Noirs sourced from limestone slopes south of the Waitaki River.

Central Otago

In **Central Otago** conditions are like nowhere else in the country. There is even a continental-type climate influence with long hot days and cool nights during the growing season. Interestingly the rock types are much older geologically and hillsides are favoured in order to limit frost damage. Pinot Noir is emerging as the most important variety, though the potential for fine Riesling, Chardonnay, Pinot Gris and Gewürztraminer is already proven too. After a slow start new vineyards and wineries have taken root at an ever increasing pace since the mid-90s. Foreign investment, celebrity ownership (such as actor Sam Neill's Two Paddocks) and high prices for Pinot are all part of the mix but the hype is already backed by some serious quality. How much more is to come with still greater identification of the top sites and from more mature vineyards?

A- Z of producers by region

1   South Burnett
2   Granite Belt
3   Hastings River
4   Hunter
5   Broke Fordwich
6   Mudgee
7   Orange
8   Cowra
9   Hilltops
10 Gundagai
11 Tumbarumba
12 Canberra District
13 Southern Highlands
14 Shoalhaven Coast

NORTHLAND
Whangarei
AUCKLAND
Auckland
Hamilton
WAIKATO
WAIKATO
Rotorua
BAY OF PLENTY
GISBORNE
Gisborne
Taupo
HAWKE'S BAY
New Plymouth
TARANAKI
Napier
Hastings
MANAWATU-
WANGANUI
TASMAN
Nelson
Martinborough
Wellington
WELLINGTON
Westport
WAIRAU
Blenheim
MARLBOROUGH
WEST COAST
Greymouth
CANTERBURY
Waipara
WAIMAKARIRI
Christchurch
Tekapo
RANGITATA
Timaru
Wanaka
WAITAKI
Wakatipu
Te Anau
Queenstown
Alexandra
OTAGO
CLUTHA
UTHLAND
Dunedin
Invercargill

New Zealand vintages

With a few exceptions, New Zealand whites haven't enjoyed a good reputation for ageing and many Chardonnays that were attractive with one or two years' age were falling apart with three or more. However this is changing even if only rare examples of Marlborough Sauvignon can improve in the way a top Sancerre or Pouilly-Fumé can. In fact the majority still need to be consumed within the first year after the vintage. The few exceptions have been noted in the producer entries. Riesling and sweet wines will generally keep a little longer.

Reds do have a growing reputation for keeping thanks to improved viticultural and winemaking practices. While many don't seem to develop and mature in the same way European wines do they do keep and the fruit holds up well. Those based on Cabernet Sauvignon, Merlot or Shiraz, as might be expected, show the greatest longevity and come, in the main, from Waiheke or Hawkes Bay. Top examples now usually need five years' ageing but can keep for 10 from an excellent vintage. In addition to those styles rated in the chart below, the best Waiheke vintages (no recent top vintages) include 2000, 99, 98, 94, 93, 91 and 90, while 97 and 96 aren't bad. Of the mushrooming number of fine Pinot Noirs, three to six years' age is likely to be the window of optimum drinking but some of the newer or more extracted styles might need five years or more. Central Otago has at least as much ageing potential with Pinot Noir but few really good examples were made before 1998. The 2004 vintage in New Zealand was a record harvest, more than twice the frost-decimated 2003 (worst felt in Hawkes Bay) with most producers happy with quality despite significant late summer rain. In a reversal of fortunes, signally the end of a favourable six-year run, Central Otago suffered frost and looks to be significantly down in both quality and quantity on its very successful 2003 vintage crop.

New Zealand vintage chart

	Hawkes Bay reds	Martinborough Pinot Noir	Central Otago Pinot Noir
2004	★★★★/★★★★★★ A	★★★★ A	★★/★★★ A
2003	★★★ A	★★★ B	★★★★/★★★★★ B
2002	★★★★/★★★★★★ A	★★★★/★★★★★ B	★★★★★ B
2001	★★★ B	★★★/★★★★ C	★★★★/★★★★★ B
2000	★★★★/★★★★★★ B	★★★★ C	★★★★/★★★★★ C
1999	★★★/★★★★ C	★★★★ C	★★★★ C
1998	★★★★★ C	★★★★★ C	★★★★/★★★★★ C
1997	★★★★ C	★★★★/★★★★★ D	
1996	★★/★★★ C	★★★★/★★★★★ D	
1995	★★★ D		
1994	★★★★ C		
1991	★★★★/★★★★★ D		

ALPHA DOMUS   Hawkes Bay   www.alphadomus.co.nz   A: **McK**, NYg, Has, Hrd

Owner: Ham family   1829 Maraekakaho Road, RD 1, Hastings
Alpha Domus was established in 1991 and has only been making wines since 1995, yet it has produced some of the best reds from Hawkes Bay in recent top vintages. Grapes are sourced exclusively from 20 ha of vineyard planted to Sauvignon Blanc, Semillon and Chardonnay, plus Merlot, Cabernet Sauvignon, Cabernet Franc and some Malbec. The Navigator, based on Merlot (around 60 per cent) but complemented by the Cabernets and 5 per cent Malbec, is ripe and composed with good concentration – as, too, is a regular Merlot/Cabernet Sauvignon. AD is the premium label. The Aviator (Cabernet Sauvignon with some Merlot, Malbec and Cabernet Franc) is very impressive in its ripeness, intensity and concentration and better balanced than previously. AD Chardonnay is slightly over-worked but richly textured, while an unoaked Chardonnay is tangy and peachy if wanting for more expression. Semillon appears in a regular, very ripe style as well as a rich botrytised version, AD Noble Selection. Newer to the range is a ripe and berryish Pinot Noir. (PW)
● **The Navigator★★★** £D   ● **AD The Aviator★★★** £E
● **Merlot/Cabernet Sauvignon★★** £C   ● **Pinot Noir★★** £C
○ **Chardonnay** Unoaked★★ £B AD★★★ £C   ○ Semillon★★ £B

ATA RANGI   Martinborough   www.atarangi.co.nz   A: **Lib, MHv**, WSc, Kwi, Hrd
Owner: C Paton & P Pattie, O Masters & A Paton   Puruatanga Road, PO Box 43, Martinborough
From an original 5-ha site, brother and sister Clive and Alison Paton and their partners have built an enviable reputation. Their 34.5 ha of vineyards are sited mostly on the Martinborough Terrace, either owned (this includes the recent acquisition of the 2.2-ha Walnut Ridge vineyard) or subject to long-term contracts with neighbouring families. Yields are low, the vine age now averages over 20 years and the quality of the fruit shows in the wines. Clive Paton and Oliver Masters have forged New Zealand's most consistently fine Pinot Noir over the past decade. The wine has a depth and structure that requires a little patience but brings a richness and complexity with three to five years' age. The quality of the spicy, cedary, berryish Célèbre (Syrah/Merlot/Cabernets) is more vintage-dependent but usually offers good depth and richness in a cool style. Craighall, the premium Chardonnay, is produced from a 2.8-ha vineyard adjacent to the winery; a second, Petrie, comes from a 4.5-ha vineyard at East Taratahi to the north of Martinborough. Pinot Gris with intense quince-like fruit is one of the most promising Antipodean examples. Some Sauvignon is made along with a botrytised Riesling, Kahu (when conditions permit), while a varietal Syrah is a new addition from 2001. The complex Walnut Ridge Pinot Noir will keep its own identity and should assume greater consistency from 2002; the rating applies to top years such as 2000. (PW)
Ata Rangi:
● **Pinot Noir★★★★** £E   ● **Célèbre★★★** £C
○ **Chardonnay** Craighall★★★ £C Petrie★★ £B   ○ **Pinot Gris** Lismore★★ £C
Walnut Ridge:
● **Pinot Noir★★★** £D

BLACK RIDGE   Central Otago   www.blackridge.co.nz   A: **BFs**, Kwi
Owner: Verdun Burgess & Sue Edwards   Conroy's Road, R D 1, Alexandra, Central Otago
Black Ridge was a pioneer in Central Otago; holes were first blasted into the barren schist as long ago as 1981. Riesling and Gewürztraminer in particular benefit as the fruit now comes from vines over 20 years old. Both show good depth and varietal intensity (with the cool expressive profiles typical of Central Otago) as well as sufficient structure to ensure that they benefit from at least two or three years' age. A ripe and concentrated, mineral-tinged Chardonnay will also keep. If the Pinot Noir is not quite at the level of the very best from the region, it nonetheless shows good smoky fruit and not inconsiderable density and grip, and requires a little patience. (PW)

● Pinot Noir★★ £D   O Chardonnay★★ £C
O Gewürztraminer★★ £C   O Riesling★★ £C

BORTHWICK   Wairarapa   www.borthwick.co.nz

A: JAr

Owner: Borthwick family   Dakins Road, R D 7, Wairarapa

Widely experienced Roseworthy graduate Paddy Borthwick has pioneered viticulture in the Dakins Road area since the company was established in 1996. His 27 ha of vineyards are planted on free-draining river terraces, like those to the south in Martinborough, and he has similarly placed his faith in Pinot Noir. Though the vines are still very young, the wine already shows impressive ripeness, breadth and complexity. Riesling is promising too: intense and pungent if not yet with the structure to stand long ageing. Sauvignon Blanc, with more than a hint of the tropical fruits trait the region can provide, is similarly intense but should be drunk young. Other wines, all estate-sourced, include varietal Chardonnay and reds from Merlot, Cabernet/Merlot and Sangiovese. More wines will be rated with further tastings. (PW)

O Riesling★★ £B   O Sauvignon Blanc★★ £C   ● Pinot Noir★★★ £C

CHURCH ROAD   Hawkes Bay   www.churchroad.co.nz

A: ADo, Odd

Owner: Montana Wines (Allied Domecq)   150 Church Road, PO Box 7095, Taradale, Hawkes Bay

Compared with MONTANA's vast Marlborough vineyard estates, the Church Road winery in Hawkes Bay is a (relatively) small separate entity. Red wines have been developed under guidance from Bordeaux *négociant* Cordier. A regular Cabernet Sauvignon/Merlot is soundly made but usually wants for a little more richness and ripeness, while a Reserve Cabernet Sauvignon shows good extract and becomes increasingly Bordeaux-like with five years' age. In addition the small-volume, experimental Cuve Series wines can be bought locally. Church Road's winemaker, Tony Prichard, also fashions Montana's flagship red, Tom, named after Tom McDonald, the pioneer of Cabernet in Hawkes Bay. Made from Merlot, Cabernet Sauvignon and Cabernet Franc, this complex, cedary red is more Bordeaux than Hawkes Bay and has excellent dimension and depth but requires patience. Less than 10,000 bottles were produced in the first three vintages (1995, 96 and 98).(PW)

O Chardonnay★ £B   Reserve★★ £C
● Cabernet/Merlot Reserve★★ £C   ● Tom★★★ £F

CLOUDY BAY   Marlborough   www.cloudybay.co.nz

A: VCq, Par, JNi, NYg, Rae, UnC

Owner: LVMH   PO Box 376, Jacksons Road, Blenheim

Established in 1985 by David Hohnen of CAPE MENTELLE (Western Australia), Cloudy Bay is probably New Zealand's best-known winery internationally and produces its most famous Sauvignon Blanc. Both Cape Mentelle and Cloudy Bay are now under the umbrella of French luxury goods giant LVMH. Yet despite ever bigger volumes and changing vineyard sources – there are now 140 ha of vineyards supplemented by bought-in grapes – the Sauvignon remains one of Marlborough's best, thanks in part to continued direction from Cloudy Bay's original winemaker Kevin Judd. The stylish aromas and range of fruit flavours (nettles, blackcurrant leaf and tropical notes) are complemented by a structure that provides an uncharacteristic ability (in the region) to age for at least a year or two – but there's not quite the concentration or intensity of one or two others. Te Koko is a barrel-fermented and aged version; the oak gives complexity yet the nettly fruit is not overwhelmed and it shows considerable style and finesse. It's very good with two or three years' age and promises to keep for longer. Chardonnay has long been made to a high standard though can be a bit overdone in flavour and structure, lacking expression and finesse, while Pinot Noir shows increasing character and intensity if not yet the texture or dimension of the best New Zealand examples. Another highly acclaimed wine is Pelorus, both a creamy, soft fruit-centred and bread dough example with lots of immediate appeal (if no more), and the vintage-dated version, tighter and more intense with better structure and further ageing potential after its release. Late Harvest Riesling and Gewürztraminer are also made. (PW)

O **Sauvignon Blanc**★★★ £C Te Koko★★★ £D O **Chardonnay**★★ £C
O **Pelorus** Non-Vintage★★ £C Vintage★★★ £D ● **Pinot Noir**★★ £D

CRAGGY RANGE Hawkes Bay www.craggyrange.com A: Cap, ACh, NYg

Owner: Peabody family & Steve Smith 253 Waimarama Road, Havelock North, Hawkes Bay
New Zealand's most dynamic winery early in the new century. Named for the Craggy Range in Hawkes
Bay's Tukituki Valley, a stunning new winery complex has been built to process grapes from a patchwork of
outstanding vineyard sites split between Hawkes Bay, Martinborough and Marlborough. Direction comes
from viticultural expert Steve Smith, who established a reputation while providing high-quality fruit for
VILLA MARIA. From the outset all varietals were concentrated and well-structured with an extra intensity
and definition not seen in most New Zealand wines. These include two Marlborough Sauvignon Blancs: a
nettly Avery Vineyard example and a slightly minerally, smoky, classy Old Renwick. Also sourced from
Marlborough is an excellent intense and vibrant Riesling from 25-year-old vines in the Rapaura Vineyard
(and made in a rich botrytised style in 2000). Ripe berryish Merlot and intense nectarine and citrus
Chardonnay have been sourced from the Seven Poplars vineyard in Hawkes Bay. Gimblett Gravels versions
of each were made in 2002, a stylish Chardonnay considerably more successful than an over-extracted
Merlot. An expanding range of Martinborough varietals include Te Muna Sauvignon Blanc, with an
infusion of tropical fruits, and Pinot Noir from young vines which shows good potential. A series of
'Prestige' wines includes: Les Beaux Cailloux, a Gimblett Gravels Chardonnay; The Quarry, also from
Gimblett Gravels, mostly Cabernet Sauvignon with some Merlot and a little Cabernet Franc; Sophia,
Merlot-based but complemented by Cabernet Franc and Malbec; and Syrah, Le Sol. Those tasted over two
vintages have been rated below. While all show great promise, the future reputation of Hawkes Bay for
Syrah seems doubly assured if a very classy, black-fruited Block 14 version ages well. (PW)

O **Sauvignon Blanc** Te Muna★★★ £B Avery Vineyard★★★ £B Old Renwick★★★★ £C
O **Chardonnay** Seven Poplars★★★ £C O **Riesling** Rapaura Road Vineyard★★★ £C
● **Merlot** Seven Poplars★★ £C ● **Syrah** Block 14★★★ £D
● **Sophia**★★★ £E ● **The Quarry**★★★★ £E

DRY RIVER Martinborough A: J&B, NYg, Rae

Owner: Julian Robertson & Oliver family trust Puruatanga Road, Martinborough
This small estate acquired an enviable cult following due to the unstinting devotion of Dr Neil McCallum
to producing the highest quality fruit from around 10 ha of prime Martinborough vineyards. Dry River
has arguably the best record in the country of producing high-quality ageworthy reds and whites. yet despite
its wide acclaim and the evident complexity, depth and richness of texture in the wines – including the best
Gewürztraminer and Riesling in the country – relatively few other producers seem to have been inspired to
reach the same levels. Though under new (American) ownership from 2003 (the same as for TE AWA
FARM), the same direction is being maintained. To date the wines have been mostly sold in New Zealand
through an exclusive mailing list but a little is exported. Don't hesitate to try the wines if the opportunity
arises. (PW)

● **Pinot Noir**★★★★ £E ● **Syrah**★★★ £E O **Pinot Gris**★★★ £D
O **Riesling** Craighall★★★★ £D O **Gewürztraminer**★★★★ £D O **Chardonnay**★★★ £D

ESK VALLEY Hawkes Bay www.eskvalley.co.nz A: HMA, Odd, WSc

Owner: Villa Maria group Main Road, Bay View, P O Box 111, Bay View, Napier, Hawkes Bay
Esk Valley wines are made by Gordon Russell and are deserving of a separate entry (also see VILLA MARIA).
The outstanding wine is The Terraces, a blend of Malbec, Merlot and Cabernet Franc. Made only in top
vintages, it is a rich, intense and powerful Hawkes Bay red and the group's finest wine (recent vintages are
2000, 98 and 95; next will be 2002). Esk Valley Reserve Merlot/Cabernet Sauvignon/Malbec can also be
very good if slightly more variable in quality, while a regular version is increasingly composed and

characterful if not at the same level. Whites are good too, particularly the somewhat Meursault-like Reserve Chardonnay. Other varietals have modest structures but are attractive, ripe and fruit-accented. The Terraces will cost an arm and a leg due to high demand but otherwise these wines are reasonable value for money. (PW)

● **The Terraces**★★★★ £G
● **Merlot/Cabernet Sauvignon /Malbec**★★ £B Gimblett Gravels Reserve★★★ £D
O **Chardonnay**★★ £B Reserve★★★ £C O **Chenin Blanc**★ £B O **Pinot Gris**★ £B

FELTON ROAD www.feltonroad.com   A: **CPW**, BBR, ACh, Rae, P&S, Res, Hrd, Kwi

Owner: Nigel Greening Bannockburn, RD 2, Central Otago
Every now and then a very talented winemaker comes to the fore with unprecedented results in a given region, such as the likes of Didier DAGUENEAU in Pouilly Fumé, Alvaro PALACIOS in Priorat or Helen Turley (MARCASSIN) in Sonoma. Blair Walter is one such. Yet with Pinot-mad Englishman Nigel Greening taking over Stewart Elm's inspired creation in 2000 and Gareth King in the vineyard, this is very much a team effort. The estate comprises 14 ha (The Elms) with an additional 8 ha at Cornish Point as well as leased vineyards (The Sluicings and Calvert). Pinot Noir shows a richness and complexity that most other New Zealand examples have only hinted at – a quality of fruit effortlessly expressed. While there are a number of other promising efforts in Central Otago, the single-vineyard Block 3 and Block 5 in particular set the standard for the region. Chardonnay and Riesling too are very good including a rare and excellent unoaked Chardonnay. Pinot Gris is produced from Cornish Point alongside another fine Pinot Noir with excellent structure. Demand has pushed prices up, particularly for the Pinots, but whites remain affordable. Single-vineyard Block 1 Riesling (made in a rich medium-dry Spätlese style) was produced from 2001 and Block 2 Chardonnay from 2002. (PW)

● **Pinot Noir** Block 3★★★★ £E Block 5★★★★ £E
● **Pinot Noir**★★ £C Cornish Point Drystone★★★★ £E
O **Chardonnay**★★ £C Barrel Fermented★★★ £C O **Riesling**★★ £C Dry★★★ £C

FORREST ESTATE Marlborough www.forrest.co.nz   A: **Adm**, JNi, ACh

Owner: John & Brigid Forrest Blicks Road, Renwick, Marlborough
Forrest Estate is relatively small Marlborough winery achieving good consistency. The wines may not be stunning but they have intense fruit with good varietal character and decent structure. They are not heavy or over-manipulated but show classic Marlborough fruit and vigour. There is an encouraging correlation between price and quality and these wines make a good solid bet especially if drunk young. Vineyard Selection bottlings, available locally, add a small premium. Newton Forrest Estate is a collaboration with Bob Newton producing Hawkes Bay reds from a vineyard in Gimblett Gravels. A Cabernet/Merlot/Malbec is something of a fruit bomb but has good ripeness and fine tannins. New Syrah (from 2001) shows more promise with similar fruit richness but more personality. (PW)

Forrest Estate
O **Sauvignon Blanc**★★ £B O **Riesling** Dry★★ £B O **Gewürztraminer**★★ £C
● **Pinot Noir**★★ £C

Newton Forrest Estate
● **Cabernet/Merlot/Malbec** Cornerstone★★ £C

FROMM Marlborough www.frommwineries.com   A: **L&W**, NYg, Hrd

Owner: George & Ruth Fromm Godfrey Road, RD 2, Blenheim
Fromm is not one winery but two. One is in Malans in Switzerland, the other in Marlborough. Marlborough's Fromm Vineyard is planted almost exclusively to red grapes with a strong leaning towards Pinot Noir (as are the Swiss vineyards). Grapes are also sourced from the William Hoare Vineyard and the Bamfield Vineyard (both in the Brancott Valley), which provide more Pinot Noir as well as other grapes

including Chardonnay and Riesling for the white wines. A separate bottling of Pinot Noir is produced from the gently undulating 15-ha Clayvin Vineyard, owned jointly with UK wine merchant Lay & Wheeler. It has been produced again since 2000 after a break of four years due to replanting. The wines are made by George (Georg) Fromm and Hätsch Kalberer and the philosophy is one of low yields, fully ripe grapes and minimal intervention in the winemaking to give as natural an expression of the wines as possible. All show good character, flavour intensity and structure but the range of wines produced from year to year varies. Only those recently tasted have been rated but a Reserve Syrah is also impressive. Reserve Merlot includes a little Cabernet Franc and Malbec, small quantities of Gewürztraminer and Sauvignon Blanc are produced, and since 1999, a Malbec/Merlot blend. (PW)

La Strada
● **Pinot Noir★** £C Fromm Vineyard★★★ £E Clayvin Vineyard★★★ £D
O **Chardonnay★★** £C O **Riesling★★** £C

GOLDWATER ESTATE Waiheke Island www.goldwaterwine.com A: **Hal,** ACh, Hrd
Owner: Kim & Jeanette Goldwater 18 Causeway Road, Putiki Bay, Waiheke Island
Kim Goldwater pioneered quality wine production on Waiheke Island in Auckland's Hauraki Gulf in 1978 and has long produced a powerful, structured Cabernet Sauvignon/Merlot with good balance, ripeness and concentration in the best years. The wine keeps well and with age impresses more for its elegance and complexity than for concentration but has very good depth and dimension. It deserves to be drunk with a minimum of five years' age. At least as impressive is the pricier Waiheke Island Merlot from the Esslin Vineyard, with rich plum and berry fruit and spicy oak. A little of a premium Chardonnay is also produced from the Zell Vineyard. As well as the 14 ha of vineyards on Waiheke, a further 35 ha in Marlborough are contracted under a long-term lease. New Dog Sauvignon Blanc shows good aromatic Marlborough Sauvignon character (DOG POINT, as it was previously known, now refers to the exciting new estate of Ivan Sutherland and James Healy). Goldwater's Roseland Chardonnay shows good structure and some restraint with attractive citrus flavours and well-integrated oak. A new 8-ha site has recently been planted in the Gimblett Gravels district of Hawkes Bay. Wood's Hill Cabernet/Merlot is produced from younger vines on Waiheke. (PW)
● **Cabernet Sauvigon/Merlot★★★** £E ● **Merlot** Esslin★★★ £F
O **Chardonnay** Roseland★★ £B Zell★★★ £D O **Sauvignon Blanc** New Dog★★ £B

GRAVITAS Marlborough www.new-zealand-wines.com A: **OWL,** JNi, UnC, Sel
Owner: Martyn Nicholls 45 Lanark Lane, RD1, Renwick, Marlborough
Gravitas is a new and exciting young Marlborough operation formed by businessman Martyn Nicholls and his wife Pam. There are some 30 ha of estate vineyards in Wairau Valley (known as Saint Arnaud's Vineyard) including some steep slopes from which a Pinot Noir was first produced in 2004. A deserved early reputation has been based on Sauvignon Blanc and Chardonnay that show a vibrancy, purity and concentration that more should emulate but too few do. Quality raw materials are the secret, resulting from a fastidious approach to viticulture that gives atypically low yields, at least in the context of Marlborough. Rigorous selection then gives winemaker Brian Bicknell (from SERESIN) the kind of fruit others presumably only dream about. It is to be hoped that production is kept to a level where quality can be at least maintained. Also made or in the process of being made are a Vin de Paille, a sparkling wine and from 2005, a Pinot Gris. (PW)
⊃ **Sauvignon Blanc★★★** £B O **Chardonnay★★★** £B

GROVE MILL Marlborough www.grovemill.co.nz A: **CRs,** Odd, Kwi
Owner: The New Zealand Wine Company Ltd Waihopai Valley Road, Marlborough
Grove Mill has grown rapidly since being established in 1988. While many of the grapes are supplied under contract, a series of vineyards have been either leased or bought outright to increase the amount under the

winery's direct control. Since the first vintage the wines made by David Pearce have delivered consistently ripe fruit and are characterised by their almost overwhelming fruit intensity and concentration. In the Sauvignon this is slightly at the expense of greater expression and complexity. A partially *barrique*-fermented and oak-aged Chardonnay, like several of the better examples in the region, can be a touch overdone, not lacking for weight or structure but somewhat dominated by secondary, winemaking-given characters (including the oak) at the expense of a clearer expression of the fruit. A Pinot Gris displays less varietal expression than some but nonetheless shows good richness and balanced acidity, while Pinot Noir can show an overripe character. Sanctuary, named for a wetland project that has been developed at the Waihopai Valley vineyard, is a second label that includes Chardonnay, Riesling and Sauvignon Blanc. A second Pinot Gris is made under the Frog Haven label. (PW)

Grove Mill
O Sauvignon Blanc★★★ £B   O Riesling★★ £B
O Chardonnay★★ £B   O Pinot Gris★★ £B   ● Pinot Noir★ £C

HERZOG Marlborough www.herzog.co.nz   A: NYg
Owner: Hans & Therese Herzog   81 Jeffries Road, R D 3, Blenheim, Marlborough
As immigrants from Switzerland Hans and Therese Herzog are new on the Marlborough scene but have already made considerable impact with tiny quantities of handmade reds. With considerable winemaking experience to draw upon, the philosophy is for unfined, unfiltered wines from low-yielding, hand-picked grapes coming entirely from their own modest 11-ha vineyard. Spirit of Marlborough is a Bordeaux-style red from Merlot, Cabernet Sauvignon, Cabernet Franc and Malbec (65/20/10/5 in the 1999). There is a cool component to the fruit and tannins but this contributes to a stylish, nuanced flavour complexity. As much fuss has been made about an unusual Montepulciano (which includes 15 per cent Cabernet Franc). Ripe and characterful, this shows plenty of Montepulciano flesh and depth as well as good intensity, concentration and length given the relative immaturity of the vines. The 2001 still deserves another three or four years' ageing. Young vines also limit the potential of a Pinot Noir yet it already shows a seductive immediacy on the palate. Small amounts of Chardonnay, Pinot Gris and even Viognier, with something of a cult following, are also made. The winery restaurant is establishing a similarly enviable reputation. (PW)
● Montepulciano★★★ £D   ● Spirit of Marlborough★★★ £D
● Pinot Noir★★ £D

HUNTER'S Marlborough www.hunters.co.nz   A: Lay, WIE, WSc, NYg, Kwi, P&S
Owner: Jane Hunter   Rapaura Road, PO Box 839, Blenheim
Jane Hunter remains one of the best-known personalities in the New Zealand wine industry, having produced some of Marlborough's best wines for a decade and a half. The wines, made by Gary Duke, show a harmony, a charm and a gentler character when compared with some of Marlborough's brasher efforts. Sauvignon Blanc in two versions has always been the focus of production. If the regular unoaked version doesn't show quite the structure or intensity of some of the newer top examples, there is a very fine ripe fruit depth, good concentration and the wine is consistently long and stylish. The Winemakers Selection (previously 'Oak-aged') version has always shown a rare deft touch when integrating a gentle oak structure and creaminess with a ripe tropical fruit intensity. The perfumed raspberry and cherry Pinot Noir is also a good expression of its fruit if missing the intensity or concentration of others. The sparkling wine is also most attractive: well-structured, not hugely complex but with a fresh ripe fruit intensity to it. A little Merlot is also made. (PW)
O Sauvignon Blanc★★★ £B Winemakers Selection★★★ £C
O Riesling★★ £B   O Gewürztraminer★ £C   O Chardonnay★★ £C
O Miru Miru Brut Vintage★★ £C   ● Pinot Noir★★ £C

ISABEL ESTATE www.isabelestate.com A: **M&V**, NYg, Kwi, UnC, P&S, SVS, Hrd, Sel

Owner: Michael & Robyn Tiller 72 Hawkesbury Road, Renwick, Marlborough
The finest privately owned estate in Marlborough produces five outstanding varietals from more than 50 ha of its own well-established vineyards. For many years the grapes had been sold to others and production under the Isabel label only commenced in 1994; almost immediately it became the source of, arguably, New Zealand's finest (certainly one of the top three or four) Sauvignon Blancs. If less established than CLOUDY BAY it has been more consistent over recent vintages. Early vintages showed unprecendented structure and concentration but since 1999 there has been greater expression and refinement including a hint of mineral and smokiness. It can be drunk young or with a little age. The wines, currently made by Anthony Moore, come only from estate vineyards planted at around twice the average density, accounting at least in part for the extra intensity and concentration. Pinot Noir usually impresses with vivid plum, cherry and raspberry flavours and a savoury complexity, with a promising texture and breadth. Chardonnay has been exciting but not consistently so: at its best it is intense without becoming syrupy and has good dimension and depth. A bright, crunchy Riesling shows typical Isabel fruit intensity including limey, citrus and stone fruit flavours. The Pinot Gris, with an attractive pear and quince fruit, is one of the better New Zealand examples. Noble Sauvage, a botrytised Sauvignon Blanc, is made when conditions allow (recently 2000 and 02). (PW)
O **Sauvignon Blanc**★★★★ £C   O **Pinot Gris**★★ £C
O **Chardonnay**★★ £C   O **Riesling** Dry★★★ £C   ● **Pinot Noir**★★★ £D

KUMEU RIVER Kumeu, Auckland www.kumeuriver.co.nz A: **Box, Far**, Ben, WSc, Hrd

Owner: Brajkovich family 550 Highway 16, Kumeu, Auckland
Michael Brajkovich is one of New Zealand's most important winemakers. Although the family vineyards are in the now less than fashionable Kumeu district, west of Auckland, his intelligent, non-conformist approach showed it was possible to make better wines by rejecting some of the rigid, purely technical doctrines of winemaking that dominated styles in the late 1980s. Instead he adapted to a New Zealand context the best from established wine cultures and has made arguably the country's best Chardonnay for more than a decade. The use of indigenous yeasts, hand-picking of the grapes and whole-bunch pressing have now been adopted by others. Both the Kumeu River Chardonnay and Maté's Vineyard (an original vineyard replanted in 1990) are barrel-fermented and aged, and put through a full malolactic fermentation. The resulting wines are richly textured and complex with well-integrated oak characters and are also atypically ageworthy for New Zealand Chardonnay; they are usually best with three to five years' age but often keep for longer. Of the two, the Maté's version can show just a little more refinement and persistence. Melba is a ripe, characterful blend of Merlot, Malbec and Cabernet Franc. In recent vintages both a promising Pinot Noir and a rich yet floral Pinot Gris have been made. Exceptional vintage conditions made it possible for a varietal Merlot to be produced in 2000. The inexpensive second label is now known as Kumeu River Village. All the wines are now bottled under Stelvin caps. (PW)
O **Chardonnay**★★★★ £D Maté's Vineyard★★★★ £D
O **Pinot Gris**★★ £C   ● **Melba**★★ £C

MARTINBOROUGH VINEYARD www.martinborough-vineyard.co.nz A: **Adm**, NYg, ACh

Owner: Duncan Milne & partners Princess Street, Martinborough
Martinborough Vineyard built an international reputation following the recruitment of Larry McKenna as full-time winemaker. From his first vintage in 1986 he set about making Pinot Noir and Chardonnay from fully ripe grapes of the highest possible quality. His success brought acclaim for the region as a whole; its free-draining soil and particularly dry mesoclimate had been recommended in a scientific study and this originally led to the company's establishment by Duncan Milne. Despite a tendency to over-extraction in the Reserve in the mid-1990s, the underlying fruit quality of the Pinot Noir has generally been very good, developing impressive texture and a stylish complexity with three to four years' age or more. Larry McKenna left to develop his own project in 1999 (ESCARPMENT VINEYARD) and current releases from winemaker

Claire Mulholland show a gentler touch but the usual flavour complexity. A bold, oaky and structured Chardonnay now shows a little more refinement but is still rich with intense, ripe peachy/melony fruit and depth and will usually improve for at least three or four years. Riesling is full and intensely flavoured but better structured than many New Zealand examples. In 2003 some of the Riesling was late-picked and partially botrytised for a richer, off-dry style called Manu. Pinot Gris, unusual in being partly barrel-fermented, and Sauvignon Blanc (Pirinoa Block) are also made. New is a second Pinot Noir, Te Tera. (PW)

● **Pinot Noir★★★** £D Reserve★★★ £E
○ **Chardonnay** Martinborough Terrace★★★ £C ○ **Riesling** Jackson Block★★ £C

MATAKANA ESTATE   Matakana, Auckland   A: BWC, Vts

Owner: Vegar family 568 Matakana Road, PO Box 24, Matakana
Conditions on the Matakana peninsula can be similar to those on Waiheke Island. On the 34 ha of granulated clays of Matakana Estate, a classy, individual premium red, Moko, is fashioned from varying percentages of Merlot, Cabernet Franc, Cabernet Sauvignon and Malbec. In 1999 and 2002 Merlot was very successful whilst in 2000 it played almost no part in a blend dominated by Cabernet Franc. Malbec usually contributes around 20 per cent but whatever the blend, the wine is only made when the fruit is of a sufficient standard and no Moko was produced in 2003 or 01. Other recent vintages are excellent. Also very good is a ripe pear- and quince-laden Pinot Gris of good purity and intensity. Goldridge Estate wines are sourced both from estate vineyards in Marlborough and contract growers in Hawkes Bay. (PW)

Matakana Estate
○ **Pinot Gris★★** £C ● **Moko★★★** £D

MATUA VALLEY   www.matua.co.nz   A: BBI, WIE

Owner: Beringer Blass Waikoukou Valley Road, Waimauku, Auckland
From their base at Waimauku, west of Auckland, Ross and Bill Spence were quality pioneers in the 1980s and despite some ups and downs have maintained high quality in both Chardonnays and a Bordeaux-style red from Hawkes Bay for nearly two decades. Matua has been under corporate ownership since 2001 but the brothers continue to oversee what is a very extensive range of wines and the highlights are unchanged. There is a tendency for the winemaking to be a bit heavy-handed, with sometimes an excessive lees enrichment in the Ararimu Chardonnay or too much oak or extraction in the reds but when the fruit character is given full expression the wines can be really fine. This is probably best encapsulated in the Judd Estate Chardonnay which can show just how good Gisborne (Patutahi Hills) fruit can be. Matheson denotes a range of Hawkes Bay varietals including Syrah, while Shingle Peak is the label for the Marlborough varietals. (PW)

○ **Chardonnay** Judd Estate Gisborne★★★ £C Ararimu Hawkes Bay★★ £D
○ **Sauvignon Blanc** Shingle Peak Marlborough★★ £B
● **Merlot/Cabernet Sauvignon** Ararimu Hawkes Bay★★★ £D
● **Merlot** Bullrush Vineyard Hawkes Bay★★★ £D

MILLTON   Gisborne   www.millton.co.nz   A: Vcs, AR●

Owner: James & Annie Millton Papatu Road, Manutuke, Gisborne
New Zealand's leading proponents of biodynamics run the leading winery in the Gisborne region, where most of the vineyards are in the hands of the big producers. Endeavouring to produce 'natural' wines, the Milltons have succeeded admirably in making whites of good fruit richness and intensity. The warm but humid Gisborne autumns favour the development of botrytis and the wines are often characterised by the extra intensity and flavours this brings. From 20 ha (across the Riverpoint, Opou, Te Arai and Naboths vineyard sites) there has been real success with three varieties in particular: Chenin Blanc, Riesling and Chardonnay. Chenin Blanc has been the country's best since the late 80s and the Riesling has rarely been surpassed, but there is a purity and intensity to the fruit in all three wines. More recently, under

a Growers Series label, Viognier from the Tietjen Vineyard and a Gewürztraminer have been made. Late-harvested 'Special Bunch Selection' versions of Riesling and Gewürztraminer are also produced as is some red, including a Merlot/Cabernet. (PW)

O **Riesling** Opou Vineyard★★★ £B   O **Chardonnay** Opou Vineyard★★ £B
O **Chenin Blanc** Te Arai Vineyard★★★ £B

MONTANA   Gisborne, Marlborough & Auckland   www.montanawines.com   A: ADo, AAA

*Owner: **Allied-Domecq** 171 Pilkington Road, Auckland 1130*
Montana is far and away New Zealand's largest producer, responsible for well over half of the country's total output. Its acquisition of Corbans in 2000 further enlarged an already extensive vineyard holding across the three largest wine-producing regions: Gisborne, Hawkes Bay (CHURCH ROAD) and Marlborough. The expansion of a small Corbans vineyard in Waipara (which provided fine Amberley Riesling) to Pinot Noir and more Riesling is a new departure. The Montana volume comes from brands like Timara, Azure Bay and the regular Montana varietals, which include consistently drinkable Chardonnay and Sauvignon Blanc with good varietal character. There are no silly prices here and the Reserves and, more especially, the Estate-labelled wines can add more sophistication, structure and concentration. Newest is 'T' Terraces Estate Pinot Noir (from 2002) which shows promise but doesn't yet rival Marlborough's best. The impressive Brancott Winery is the command centre for more than 1,400 ha of Marlborough vineyards including the Brancott Estate, in a side valley on the south-eastern side of the Wairau Valley, and 300 ha of new plantings in the Awatere Valley. In collaboration with DEUTZ (Champagne house), some of New Zealand's best sparkling wines have also been made in Marlborough. Two other premium wines are Virtu, a *barrique*-fermented and aged botrytised sweet wine from Semillon, and a new non-vintage deluxe *cuvée* of Lindauer called Grandeur. Leading Corbans wines that continue to be produced include the well-established Stoneleigh varietals and premium Cottage Block Marlborough Sauvignon Blanc and Chardonnay. (PW)

Gisborne
O **Chardonnay** Gisborne Reserve★ £B Ormond Estate★★ 'O' £C
O **Gewürztraminer** Gisborne Reserve★ £B Patuthai Estate 'P'★ £C

Montana Brancott Winery
O **Riesling** Reserve★★ £B   O **Sauvignon Blanc** Reserve★ £B Brancott Estate 'B'★★ £C
O **Chardonnay** Reserve★ £B Renwick Estate 'R'★★ £C
● **Pinot Noir** Reserve★ £B   ● **Cabernet Sauvignon** Fairhall Estate 'F'★★ £C
O **Lindauer** Special Reserve★ £B Grandeur★★ £C
O **Deutz** Marlborough Cuvée Non-Vintage★★★ £C
O **Deutz** Marlborough Blanc de Blancs Vintage★★★ £C

Corbans (Marlborough)
O **Sauvignon Blanc** Cottage Block★★ £C
O **Chardonnay** Private Bin★ £B Cottage Block★★ £C

MT DIFFICULTY   Central Otago   www.mtdiffculty.co.nz   A: BFs, Vne, JNi, NYg, Kwi, P&S

Owner: Mt Difficulty partnership   Felton Road, Bannockburn, Cromwell, Central Otago
One of the most promising of a new wave of wineries in Central Otago, established as recently as 1998. The wines are now made in its own modern winemaking facility by Matt Dicey. The four partners, including Matt's father, Robin Dicey, own some 40 ha of vineyard, giving scope for small amounts of single-vineyard interpretations as well as blended examples. Pinot Noir is the star wine, with 2002 and 01 adding more weight and density than previously seen. Chardonnay and Sauvignon Blanc show attractive fruit if less convincing structure and depth. Pinot Gris is a lively, fruit-driven example; a Mansons Farm version is late-harvested. Riesling is made in different versions, varying both in origin and the degree of sweetness. (PW)

Pinot Noir★★★ £D   O **Pinot Gris**★★ £C

MOUNT EDWARD   Central Otago   A: **BFs, BBR**,Vne, JNi,WSc, Kwi, P&S

Owner: Alan Brady   34 Coalpit Road, Gibbston, Queenstown, Central Otago
This very small Central Otago winery is a virtual one-man operation. Having founded the nearby Gibbston
Valley Alan Brady has considerable experience of the particular pecularities of this part of the region. As well
as an increasingly good Pinot Noir there is a small quantity of Riesling planted. Sourced from quite well-
established vines the Pinot has a very attractive ripe yet sappy quality that adds richness with a little age.
Successive vintages show increasing weight and depth. Quantities are likely to remain small but this is one
of the classier examples of Central Otago Pinot Noir. (PW)
● **Pinot Noir**★★★ £E

MOUNTFORD   Waipara, Canterbury   www.mountfordvineyard.co.nz   A: **M&V**, Han, The, NYg

Owner: Michael & Buffy Eaton   434 Omini Road, Waipara, North Canterbury
Mountford's owners are among those who have put their faith in Waipara's limestone-rich soils. They are
aided in their quest to make one of New Zealand's best Pinot Noirs by employing specialist vineyard and
winemaking expertise. Viticultural improvements to 5 ha of vineyards have come from Gerald Atkinson,
enabling blind winemaker C P Lin increasingly to realise an extra class and complexity in the Pinot Noir.
Chardonnay is also made in a full-bodied, concentrated, oak-influenced style. Both wines suggest that the
Eatons have got it right although many others in Waipara are still struggling for both ripeness and
structure. (PW)
● **Pinot Noir**★★★ £E   O **Chardonnay**★★ £D

MUD HOUSE/LE GRYS   www.mudhouse.co.nz   A: **Goe, MMD**, L&W, SVS, Hrd, Kwi, Sel

Owner: Mudhouse Wine Company Ltd   16 Liverpool Street, Riverlands Estate, Marlborough
John Joslin, together with his wife Jennifer, is another immigrant made good in Marlborough. If not one
of the out and out stars of the region, Mudhouse has established a consistent and reasonably priced range
of varietals since the first vintage in 1996. Grapes are sourced both from estate vineyards and local growers.
Winemaking consultancy comes from roving winemaker Matt Thomson and a brand new winery is in
operation from 2004. Whites are attractive with reasonable structure and good depth and intensity,
particularly in the Chardonnay. However Pinot Noir comes across as the real focal point, with a lovely black
cherry and savoury intensity in the Black Swan Reserve. A late harvest Riesling was first made in 2003. Le
Grys is another label for wines of similar quality. (PW)

Mud House
O **Sauvignon Blanc**★★ £B   O **Riesling**★★ £C   O **Chardonnay**★★ £C
● **Pinot Noir** Vineyard Selection★★ £C   Black Swan Reserve★★★ £D   ● **Merlot**★ £C

MURDOCH JAMES ESTATE   www.murdochjames.co.nz   A: **CdP**, Odd, P&S

Owner: Jill & Roger Fraser   PO Box 37, Dry River Road, Martinborough
Pinot Noir and Syrah are the main thrust of production at this expanding organic estate (currently 32 ha)
in Martinborough. Pinot, especially in the top Fraser and Blue Rock bottlings, is ripe, rich and fleshy with
something of a Pommard-like strength. A tendency to slightly overripe fruit and the use of 100 per cen
French oak give the wines a distinctive stamp but they are nonetheless very good. Syrah is in the same moule
with lots of extract; it needs a little more refinement but is promising too. A varietal Cabernet Franc ha
nice texture and flesh with cool, minty, blackcurrant fruit. Sauvignon Blanc is a good Martinborough
example and Riesling, Chardonnay and Pinot Gris are also made. (PW)
● **Pinot Noir** Waiata★ £C   Blue Rock★★★ £D   Fraser★★★ £D
● **Syrah**★★ £C   ● **Cabernet Franc**★★ £C   O **Sauvignon Blanc**★★ £C

NEUDORF Nelson www.neudorf.co.nz A: **RsW**, Cam, UnC, P&S, Kwi, WSc, Sel

Owner: Tim & Judy Finn Neudorf Road, RD 2, Upper Moutere, Nelson
Neudorf stood for fine quality in the Nelson region when neighbouring Marlborough was a fraction of the size it is now. Yet while Marlborough has expanded rapidly, quality in Nelson has been advanced by Neudorf and just a few others dedicated to maximising the quality of the fruit in their vineyards. Moderately high densities and relatively low yields play a part in producing wines with good concentration but which aren't overworked in the winery. Nonetheless even the Finns have resorted to producing a Sauvignon Blanc from Marlborough as well as one from local Moutere fruit. A rich, complex Moutere Chardonnay has been successful too and is a good deal better than most Marlborough examples. Sometimes showing a botrytis influence, it is deep, powerful and if not subtle can be impressively complex with a little age. A second Chardonnay is more widely sourced, while a perfumed Moutere Riesling with floral and mineral aromas has been consistently good. Pure, silky Pinot Noir has become a Neudorf speciality, the fine Moutere example surpassed by a Moutere Home Vineyard version. Wine also comes from younger vineyards at Brightwater. A little Pinot Gris has been made in both Marlborough and Nelson versions. (PW)
O **Chardonnay** Moutere★★★ £E   O **Chardonnay** Nelson★★ £C   O **Riesling** Moutere★★ £B
O **Sauvignon Blanc** Marlborough★★ £C   O **Sauvignon Blanc** Nelson★★ £C
● **Pinot Noir** Moutere★★★ £E

OLSSENS OF BANNOCKBURN Central Otago A: **BFs**, Vne, Han, Swg

Owner: John Olssen & Heather McPherson 306 Felton Road, Bannockburn, RD 2, Cromwell
Like Mt Difficulty and Felton Road, Olssens is located in the superior Bannockburn sub-region of Central Otago, which found itself at the heart of a gold rush in the 19th century. Complete with its own winery since 2001, this husband-and-wife partnership is emerging as one of the region's stars. All fruit is estate-grown and more than half of around 10 ha is planted to Pinot Noir. This is subject to a lengthy cold pre-fermentation maceration which no doubt contributes to the depth and expansive quality of the wines, particularly in the fine Jackson Barry example. A Reserve Slapjack Creek version is also made in the best years. The lime, citrus and floral aromas of the Riesling show something of a regional style if missing the extra definition to be really fine. Other whites include Sauvignon Blanc, Gewürztraminer and Chardonnay, the latter in unoaked, barrel-fermented and Reserve versions. A small amount of late-harvest Riesling, Desert Gold, is also made. Only two wines have been tasted in successive vintages but on the basis of these this is a producer to search out with confidence. More wines will be rated after further tastings. (PW)
● **Pinot Noir**★★ £D Jackson Barry★★★ £E   O **Riesling**★★ £B

PEGASUS BAY Waipara, Canterbury www.pegasusbay.com A: **MHv**, WSc, BBR, Kwi

Owner: Donaldson family Stockgrove Road, Amberley, RD 2, North Canterbury
Pegasus Bay is Waipara's and Canterbury's leading winery. This is very much a family operation and one of Ivan Donaldson's sons, Matthew, has established a very successful winemaking duo with his partner Lynette Hudson, who he recently married. Both are trained winemakers. Matthew's reds include an increasingly good plummy, fleshy Pinot Noir capable of a little age. Prima Donna is a superior selection made only in the best vintages. A Cabernet/Merlot is also produced though this is more variable in quality. Maestro is another special selection. The whites, made by Lynette, are arguably more consistent and include good richly textured examples of Chardonnay and Sauvignon/Semillon as well as a fruit-rich Riesling, especially good in a late-harvested, botrytis-affected version, Aria. When possible a botrytised version of Chardonnay, Finale is also made. (PW)
O **Riesling**★★ £B Aria★★★ £B   O **Sauvignon Blanc/Semillon**★★ £C
O **Chardonnay**★★ £B   ● **Pinot Noir**★★ £C

REDMETAL VINEYARDS   www.redmetalvineyards.co.nz   A: **MHv**, NYg, Kwi

Owner: Grant Edmonds   2006 Maraekakaho Road, RD 1, Hastings

This small 7-ha estate is property of Grant Edmonds, a winemaker at SILENI and once head winemaker for the VILLA MARIA group. Redmetal refers to the local name for the often reddish coloured river gravels on which many of the region's leading vineyards lie. Two-thirds of the vineyard is planted to Merlot, the rest mostly to Cabernet Franc with only a little Cabernet Sauvignon. The main focus is the Basket Press Merlot/Cabernet Franc red, a ripe and structured wine usually better with three to five years' age. Quality is maintained by the production of a more accessible Merlot/Cabernet Franc/Cabernet Sauvignon blend. Also made but only in exceptional vintages (recent vintages are 2000 and 1998), is The Merlot. A selection of the very best fruit, it is intense and richly berryish and the classic scent of very fine Merlot as well as a slightly overripe plum/prune component as well as an impressive structure and good ageing potential. No reds were made at all in 2001. Some rosé is also made. (PW)

● **Merlot/Cabernet Franc** Basket Press★★★ £D   ● **The Merlot**★★★ £F
● **Merlot/Cabernet Franc/Cabernet Sauvignon**★ £C

SERESIN   Marlborough   www.seresin.co.nz   A: **JAr**, P&S, Sel

Owner: Michael Seresin   Bedford Road, Blenheim

Unquestionably style and image play a bigger part than usual in the projection of this rather sophisticated Marlborough winery established by film producer Michael Seresin in 1992. But despite the winemaking expertise of Brian Bicknell, who previous to 1996 did much to establish quality at ERRÁZURIZ, quality has never reached the heights first hinted at. Certainly there are no bad wines and all are both consistent and fruit-intense, yet most of the regular varietals want for better structure, being too reliant on an upfront fruit appeal. There is more depth and complexity in Reserve Chardonnay and both breadth and intensity in the Pinot Noir, though both lack a little flair. Newish vineyards (Tatou Block and Raupo Creek) add substantially to the existing Seresin Estate block of 44.5 ha now certified organic. Small amounts of a Malbec and 'Cabernets' (Cabernet Sauvignon/Cabernet Franc) have also been made. Marama Sauvignon is a new *barrique*-fermented and aged Sauvignon. Olive oil production is taken seriously too. Prices match the presentation. (PW)

○ **Chardonnay**★ £C   Reserve★★★ £C   ○ **Riesling**★ £C   ○ **Pinot Gris**★★ £C
○ **Sauvignon Blanc**★ £C   ● **Pinot Noir**★★ £D

STAETE LANDT   Marlborough   www.staetelandt.co.nz   A: **L&W**

Owner: Ruud Maasdam & Dorien Vermaas   PO Box 258, Blenheim 7315, Marlborough

Staete Landt was the first European name given to New Zealand by passing explorer Abel Tasman (in 1642). 354 years later two more Dutch travellers chose it for their 21 ha of Marlborough vineyard. An emphasis on vineyard health and the highest quality fruit is already apparent in the wines, all of which show an intensity and breadth which set them apart from standard Marlborough examples. The whites are well-structured and concentrated. A small portion of the Sauvignon is barrel-fermented and aged but this is not in the least intrusive, while a complex Chardonnay shows a hint of minerality. Pinot Gris is ripe and powerful but wasn't produced in 2003. The Pinot Noir with mostly ripe berry and floral characters, at once distinctive yet also typical of Marlborough, will develop a fine silky texture with a little age. (PW)

○ **Chardonnay** Marlborough★★ £C   ○ **Sauvignon Blanc** Marlborough★★ £C
○ **Pinot Gris** Marlborough★★ £C   ● **Pinot Noir** Marlborough★★★ £D

STONECROFT   Hawkes Bay   www.stonecroft.co.nz   A: **L&S**, NYg, Rae

Owner: Alan Limmer   Mere Road, RD 5, Hastings

Stonecroft, the project of soil scientist Dr Alan Limmer, earned a reputation for rich, characterful example of Syrah and Gewürztraminer that helped to broaden interest among New Zealand producers in varietie other than the mainstream Chardonnay, Sauvignon Blanc, etc. All the Stonecroft wines, from 10 ha of sheltered and particularly warm vineyards, are bold and richly textured, with concentrated fruit. Syrah, Gewürztraminer and Chardonnay are now the focus of production. The latter is bold and powerful, with a depth and substance missing from most New Zealand Chardonnay if not yet showing the refinement or elegance that should be possible here. Syrah, with a refined mineral, blackcurrant, plum character and a hint of white pepper, is the real star. Structured but with the rich fruit on the finish that is common to all these wines, it is best drunk with five years' age or more. Ruhanui is a blend of Cabernet Sauvignon, Merlot and Syrah (roughly 40 per cent each of Cabernet and Merlot in 2002 and 01 but dominated by Cabernet in 00 and 98). It shows ripe, stylish fruit and ages impressively. From the same varieties a cheaper blend, Crofters, is also made. Zinfandel was added in 1999 (no 2001). Stonecroft's good if unusual spicy, tropical-fruited Sauvignon was made again in 2003 (overturning a decision to finish production with the 2001). (PW)

● Syrah★★★★ £D   ● Ruhanui★★ £B
○ Chardonnay★★★ £C   ○ Gewürztraminer★★★ £C   ○ Sauvignon Blanc★★ £C

STONYRIDGE Waiheke Island www.stonyridge.co.nz   A: MHv, Kwi, NYg, Hfx

Owner: Stephen White 80 Onetangi Road, Waiheke Island

Stephen White's small north-facing vineyard is managed along organic lines and produces what is deservedly the most famous wine from Waiheke Island. The stated aim is to produce the best Bordeaux-style red in the world. Nonetheless it is very much a lifestyle-oriented project with the pleasures of sun and sea woven into its otherwise serious pursuit. Made since 1987, Larose Cabernets is a blend of predominantly Cabernet Sauvignon with lesser amounts of Merlot, Cabernet Franc, Malbec and Petit Verdot. Aided by naturally low fertility, the fruit quality owes much to meticulous vineyard care, resulting in yields typically around 25 hl/ha. The grapes are then transformed into a rich but harmonious blend of new oak and intense berry fruit with impressive ripeness, depth and balance. The fruit intensity holds up well with age though there is perhaps not quite the mellowed evolution in the structure that would be seen in a northern hemisphere red of similar quality. Optimum drinking therefore is probably between three and six years of age, though they will keep for much longer. As well as developing a Grenache/Syrah/Mourvèdre blend, a second wine, Airfields, and a little varietal Merlot and Chardonnay (Row 10) have also been produced. (PW)

● Larose Cabernets★★★★ £F

TE MATA Hawkes Bay www.temata.co.nz   A: JEF, NYg, Kwi, Hrd

Owner: Buck & Morris families Te Mata Road, Havelock North

John Buck revived Te Mata in late 1978 (vines were first planted here in 1892) and almost immediately established it as, arguably, New Zealand's finest. Despite greatly increased competition Te Mata is still a leading light. There has always been a coherence to the estate's direction that has proved an inspiration to other would-be New Zealand winemakers. Production has reached 25,000 cases but the range has not expanded greatly and the quality and image of the wines has been at least maintained. The wines, made by Peter Cowley since 1994, impress for their style, harmony and elegance yet rarely lack for fruit or intensity. One wine, Coleraine, symbolises the estate; its ability to age with some grace and an appreciable mellowing of its structure is almost unique in the country. There can be a trace of greenness in cooler years but with five years' age or more it is usually distinguished by soft, caressing blackcurrant, cherry and berry fruit and a long richly textured finish. Both Coleraine and the more variable Awatea are labelled as Cabernet/Merlot but include Cabernet Franc as well as Cabernet Sauvignon in the blend. Syrah with a stylish, cool pepper, raspberry and black fruit intensity is another star as is the *barrique*-fermented and aged Elston Chardonnay, long one of New Zealand's best. Barrel-fermented Cape Crest Sauvignon Blanc, quite Bordeaux-like in style, is a rare fine Hawkes Bay example. Woodthorpe-labelled wines, from an estate of the same name, are more affordable but less exciting. The Cabernet/Merlot needs a bit more oomph and ripeness, though new Syrah/Viognier is promising. (PW)

Te Mata
● **Cabernet/Merlot** Awatea★★ £C Coleraine★★★★ £D
● **Syrah** Bullnose★★★ £C
○ **Chardonnay** Elston★★★ £C ○ **Sauvignon Blanc** Cape Crest★★ £C

Woodthorpe
● **Cabernet/Merlot**★ £B
○ **Chardonnay**★★ £B ○ **Sauvignon Blanc**★ £B

UNISON Hawkes Bay www.unisonvineyard.co.nz A: **SFW**, N&P

Owner: Bruce & Anna-Barbara Helliwell 2163 Highway 50, RD 5, Hastings
Unison has been dedicated to the production of a top-quality blended red in the Gimblett Gravels of Hawkes Bay since 1993. Two versions are produced, Unison and Unison Selection, based on a 6-ha high-density, low-yielding vineyard planted to Merlot, Syrah and Cabernet Sauvignon. The composition of the wines varies according to the success of each variety in a given year. Unison has a moderately long maceration time (typically 16 to 18 days) and spends a year in oak but only a third of it in *barriques*. Though there is not always a significant step up in quality, the Selection is based on the very best fruit and undergoes a longer maceration (three weeks) and spends 12 months exclusively in *barriques* (new and second use) before further ageing in large oak. Though occasionally struggling for ripeness, both add more breadth, depth and complexity over some of the more overtly fruit-driven Hawkes Bay reds. Both wines typically need at least five years' age to show at their best. (PW)
● **Unison** Gimblett Gravels★★★ £C ● **Unison Selection** Gimblett Gravels★★★ £D

VAVASOUR Marlborough www.vavasour.com A: **C&B**, SVS, Kwi

Owner: Vavasour family Redwood Pass Road, Lower Dashwood, Marlborough
Vavasour's vineyards are a little south and east in the Awatere Valley, where there has recently been extensive planting by other producers and where it is claimed to be drier without the high water table common to much of the plantings in the Wairau Valley. Vavasour's Glenn Thomas makes two ranges of wines from 30 ha of estate vineyards as well as grapes bought in under contract. Two two excellent Vavasour-labelled Sauvignons both show a minerally, ripe fruit intensity and structure and depth matched by few other Marlborough examples. Single Vineyard Sauvignon from a plot on the 'home' Awatere vineyards is fermented and aged in used French *barriques* and shows a restrained oak influence but needs at least two or three years' ageing to reach its best. The regular Vavasour example shows its Awatere origins with good vigour and distinctive mineral, slightly smoky aromas. Tight but creamy Vavasour Chardonnay and a relatively light but fresh, aromatic Riesling are also impressive. Pinot Noir, sourced from still relatively young Awatere vines and Wairau fruit has made real progress with added depth and weight in 2002. Dashwood varietals are by no means a poor second (as is too often the case with a second label) and include an excellent zingy, nettly Sauvignon Blanc and an attractive gently oaked Chardonnay as well as a Cabernet Sauvignon and a Pinot Noir. (PW)

Vavasour
○ **Sauvignon Blanc**★★★ £B Single Vineyard★★★ £C
○ **Chardonnay**★★★ £B ○ **Riesling**★★★ £B
● **Pinot Noir**★★ £C

Dashwood
○ **Sauvignon Blanc**★★ £B ○ **Chardonnay**★★ £B

VILLA MARIA Auckland & Marlborough www.villamaria.co.nz A: **HMA**, Odd, WS

Owner: George Fistonich Mangere, Auckland / Cnr Paynters & New Renwick Road, Blenheim
The formidable Villa Maria group, with impressive wineries in both Auckland and Marlborough, also includes the independently run Hawkes Bay estates of ESK VALLEY and Vidal Estate. Most enviable is th

company's record of combining quality, quantity and consistency. Most impressive are the Reserve-level and new single-vineyard wines. Reserve Chardonnay can impress for its fruit intensity and improves with a little age but often superior are the Reserve Sauvignon Blancs – among Marlborough's best in a succession of good vintages since 1999. New single-vineyard Taylor's Pass Sauvignon promises even more, despite coming from young vines, while a richly textured Fletcher Vineyard Chardonnay (one of five made in 2002) shows similar potential. A single-vineyard Pinot Gris was first made in 2003. There is considerable ambition too with Pinot Noir, as seen in the Reserve and new Seddon Vineyard releases. Both are deeply coloured, intense and concentrated but the latter is at once more individual, expansive and Burgundian. Fine Reserve reds (based on Merlot and Cabernet Sauvignon) from Hawkes Bay have been made for more than a decade both from Villa Maria and Vidal Estate and show lots of ripe plum, berry and blackcurrant fruit intensity, if not quite the depth to match. The premium Vidal red is Joseph Soler Cabernet Sauvignon. The third tier to the Villa Maria range, the Cellar Selection varietals and dual-variety reds and whites, can provide good varietal fruit but the whites need to be drunk young. Even the least expensive Private Bin whites can be very drinkable and despite a sometimes monotone Sauvignon Blanc, there's an adequate citrusy, peachy Chardonnay and a relatively simple but intense Riesling. New Pinots are relatively expensive but prices are otherwise reasonable. New single-vineyard wines will be rated with further tastings. From 2004 all the wines are bottled under Stelvin caps. Also see ESK VALLEY. (PW)

Villa Maria
● **Merlot/Cabernet Sauvignon** Cellar Selection★★ £C Gimblett Gravels Reserve★★★ £D
● **Pinot Noir** Cellar Selection★ £B Reserve★★★ £C
○ **Sauvignon Blanc** Cellar Selection★★ £B Reserve Wairau River★★★ £C Reserve Clifford Bay★★★ £C
○ **Chardonnay** Cellar Selection★★ £B Reserve★★★ £B ○ **Riesling** Cellar Selection★★ £B

Vidal Estate
● **Merlot/Cabernet Sauvignon** Gimblett Gravels Reserve★★ £C ● **Syrah**★★ £C
○ **Chardonnay** Reserve★★ £C

WITHER HILLS Marlborough www.witherhills.co.nz **A: CHk, Odd, WSc, Kwi**

Owner: Lion Nathan 114 New Renwick Road, RD 2, Blenheim
Brent Marris, the experienced winemaker who set up the Wither Hills operation, and his father John, viticulturalist and grape grower, combined their vineyard resources and expertise prior to being bought out in 2002. Holdings run to 300 ha but for the moment just three wines are made: Sauvignon Blanc, Chardonnay and Pinot Noir. To date there has been an admirable combination of quality and quantity and this seems likely to continue as long as the Marris family remains involved. The Sauvignon shows plenty of ripe gooseberry fruit if not quite the structure of the top examples, while Chardonnay displays nicely integrated oak and a lovely ripe peach and melon intensity within a tight structure which promises to develop well, just missing an extra dimension for a higher rating. The Pinot Noir, with full, spicy, ripe cherry and berry fruit flavours and depth, shows good expression that puts it among the better Marlborough examples. Like the Sauvignon Blanc, the Chardonnay and Pinot Noir can be drunk soon after they are released but both should also improve for three or four years. (PW)
○ **Sauvignon Blanc**★★ £B ○ **Chardonnay**★★ £B
● **Pinot Noir**★★ £C

OTHER WINES OF NOTE

Please note that 'Cabernets' indicates that both Cabernet Sauvignon and Cabernet Franc are included in a blend.

AKARUA (Central Otago) ● **Pinot Noir** £D ○ **Pinot Gris** £C
ALANA ESTATE ● **Pinot Noir** Martinborough £C

BABICH ● **Syrah** Winemaker's Reserve Gimblett Road Vineyard £C
● **Pinotage** Winemaker's Reserve Gimblett Road Vineyard £C
● **Pinot Noir** Winemaker's Reserve Marlborough £C
● **Cabernet Sauvignon** The Patriarch £D ● **Cabernet Merlot** Gimblett Gravels £B
O **Chardonnay** Irongate £C Gimblett Gravels £B
BENFIELD & DELAMERE (Martinborough) ● **Merlot/Cabernet** £D
CABLE BAY VINEYARDS (Waiheke Island/Marlborough) O **Sauvignon Blanc** Marlborough £B
O **Chardonnay** Waiheke £C Culley Marlborough £B O **Riesling** Culley Marlborough £B
● **Pinot Noir** Marlborough £D ● **Five Hills** Waiheke (Merlot/Malbec/Cabernet Sauvignon) £D
CAIRNBRAE (Marlborough) O **Sauvignon Blanc** The Stones £C
CARRICK (Central Otago) ● **Pinot Noir** £D O **Sauvignon Blanc** £C
CELLIER LE BRUN O **Marlborough Brut Non-Vintage** £C O **Marlborough Blanc de Blancs** £D
CHARD FARM (Central Otago) O **Riesling** £B O **Chardonnay** Judge & Jury £C
● **Pinot Noir** Finla Mor £C
CLIFFORD BAY ESTATE O **Sauvignon Blanc** Marlborough £B
COLLARDS O **Chenin Blanc** Hawkes Bay £B O **Sauvignon Blanc** Rothesay £C
O **Riesling** Queen Charlotte Marlborough £B O **Chardonnay** Rothesay £C
KIM CRAWFORD O **Sauvignon Blanc** Marlborough £B O **Riesling** Marlborough Dry £B
O **Pinot Gris** Marlborough £B O **Chardonnay** Tietjen Gisborne £C Pia £E O **Rory Brut** Vintage £C
● **Merlot** Te Awanga Hawkes Bay £C ● **Tane** (Merlot/Cabernet Franc) £E
● **Pinot Noir** Anderson Vineyard Marlborough £D
DELEGAT'S O **Chardonnay** Reserve Hawkes Bay £B
DOG POINT VINEYARD (Marlborough) O **Section 94** (Sauvignon Blanc) £D O **Chardonnay** £D
ESCARPMENT VINEYARD (Martinborough) ● **Pinot Noir** £D
FAIRHALL DOWNS O **Sauvignon Blanc** £B
FRAMINGHAM (Marlborough) O **Sauvignon Blanc** £B O **Riesling** Classic £B O **Gewürztraminer** £B
● **Pinot Noir** £C ● **Montepulciano** £C
GIBBSTON VALLEY (Central Otago) O **Chardonnay** Reserve £C ● **Pinot Noir** Reserve £D
GIESEN O **Sauvignon Blanc** Marlborough £B O **Chardonnay** Reserve Canterbury £C
● **Pinot Noir** Reserve £C
GLADSTONE (Wairarapa) O **Sauvignon Blanc** £B O **Riesling** £B O **Pinot Gris** £C ● **Pinot Noir** £C
GREENHOUGH (Nelson) O **Riesling** £B O **Sauvignon Blanc** £B
O **Chardonnay** Hope Vineyard £C ● **Pinot Noir** Hope Vineyard £D
HATTON ESTATE (Hawkes Bay) ● **Tahi** Gimblett Gravels (Cabernets/Merlot) £E
JACKSON ESTATE O **Sauvignon Blanc** Marlborough £B
KARAKA POINT (South Auckland) ● **Syrah** £C
KOURA BAY (Marlborough) O **Chardonnay** Mount Fyffe £B
LAWSON'S DRY HILLS (Marlborough) O **Sauvignon Blanc** £B O **Gewürztraminer** £B
O **Riesling** £B O **Chardonnay** £B
MATARIKI (Hawkes Bay) ● **Quintology** Gimblett Gravels (Cabernets/Merlot/Syrah/Malbec) £D
● **Syrah** Gimblett Gravels Reserve £D O **Sauvignon Blanc** Reserve £B
MILLS REEF (Hawkes Bay) O **Sauvignon Blanc** Reserve £B ● **Cabernet/Merlot** Elspeth £C
MORTON ESTATE (Hawkes Bay) O **Chardonnay** Black Label £C ● **Pinot Noir** Black Label £C
● **Merlot/Cabernet** Black Label £D O **Sauvignon Blanc** Stone Creek Marlborough £B
NAUTILUS O **Sauvignon Blanc** Marlborough £B
NGATARAWA (Hawkes Bay) ● **Merlot/Cabernet Sauvignon** Alwyn Reserve £D
O **Chardonnay** Alwyn Reserve £D O **Riesling** Noble Harvest Alwyn Reserve £E
NGA WAKA (Martinborough) O **Chardonnay** £C Home Block £D ● **Pinot Noir** £D
NOBILO O **Sauvignon Blanc** Marlborough £B Icon Series £B
PALLISER ESTATE (Martinborough) O **Sauvignon Blanc** £B
C J PASK (Hawkes Bay) ● **Cabernet/Merlot** £B ● **Merlot** Reserve £C ● **Syrah** Reserve £C
● **Cabernet Sauvignon** Reserve £C
PROVIDENCE (Matakana) ● **Cabernet/Merlot** £F
RIPPON VINEYARD (Central Otago) ● **Pinot Noir** £D O **Riesling** £C O **Chardonnay** £C
ROCKBURN (Central Otago) ● **Pinot Noir** £D O **Pinot Gris** £C O **Sauvignon Blanc** £C

SAINT CLAIR (Marlborough) O Sauvignon Blanc £B O Chardonnay Omaka Reserve £C
● Merlot Rapaura Reserve £C
ALLAN SCOTT (Marlborough) O Chardonnay £B O Riesling £B O Sauvignon Blanc £B
O Methode Traditionelle Blanc de Blancs Brut Non-Vintage £C
SEIFRIED ESTATE (Nelson) O Riesling £B Dry £B Winemaker's Collection £C
O Sauvignon Blanc £B O Gewürztraminer £B Dry Winemaker's Collection £C
● Pinot Noir Winemaker's Collection £C
SHERWOOD ESTATE (Waipara) O Sauvignon Blanc Marlborough £B Clearwater Vineyards £C
O Riesling Waipara £B ● Pinot Noir Marlborough £B Clearwater Vineyards £C
SILENI (Hawkes Bay) O Semillon Estate Selection £C O Chardonnay Estate Selection £C
● Merlot/Cabernets Estate Selection £C
SQUAWKING MAGPIE (Hawkes Bay) ● Cabernet/Merlot Gimblett Gravels £D
TE AWA FARM (Hawkes Bay) ● Boundary Gimblett Gravels (Merlot/Cabernets) £D
TE MOTU VINEYARD (Waiheke Island) ● Cabernet Sauvignon/Merlot £E
TORLESSE (Waipara) ● Pinot Noir Torlesse Selection £C
TRINITY HILL (Hawkes Bay) ● Cabernet/Merlot Gimblett Road £D ● Syrah Gimblett Road £E
VALLI (Central Otago) ● Pinot Noir Bald Hills £D Colleen's Vineyard £D
VOSS ESTATE (Martinborough) O Riesling £B O Chardonnay Reserve £C ● Pinot Noir £D
WAIPARA WEST ● Pinot Noir Waipara £C O Sauvignon Blanc Waipara £C O Riesling Waipara £C
WHITEHAVEN/MANSION HOUSE BAY (Marlborough) O Sauvignon Blanc £B ● Pinot Noir £C

Author's choice (PW)

10 arresting Sauvignon Blanc
CLOUDY BAY O Sauvignon Blanc Marlborough
CRAGGY RANGE O Sauvignon Blanc Marlborough Old Renwick
GRAVITAS O Sauvignon Blanc Marlborough
HUNTER'S O Sauvignon Blanc Marlborough
ISABEL ESTATE O Sauvignon Blanc Marlborough
NEUDORF O Sauvignon Blanc Marlborough
PALLISER ESTATE O Sauvignon Blanc Martinborough
STAETE LANDT O Sauvignon Blanc Marlborough
VAVASOUR O Sauvignon Blanc Marlborough Single Vineyard
VILLA MARIA O Sauvignon Blanc Marlborough Reserve Clifford Bay

10 convincing Chardonnay
ATA RANGI O Chardonnay Martinborough Craighall
CRAGGY RANGE O Les Beaux Cailloux Chardonnay Gimblett Gravels
ESK VALLEY O Chardonnay Hawkes Bay Reserve
FELTON ROAD O Chardonnay Central Otago Barrel-Fermented
KUMEU RIVER O Chardonnay Kumeu
MATUA VALLEY O Chardonnay Gisborne Judd Estate
PEGASUS BAY O Chardonnay Waipara
TE MATA O Chardonnay Hawkes Bay Elston
VAVASOUR O Chardonnay Marlborough Awatere Valley
VILLA MARIA O Chardonnay Marlborough Fletcher Vineyard

8 diverse high quality whites
ATA RANGI O Pinot Gris Martinborough Lismore
CLOUDY BAY O Pelorus Vintage
DRY RIVER O Pinot Gris Martinborough
FELTON ROAD O Riesling Central Otago Dry

MILLTON O **Chenin Blanc** Gisborne Te Arai Vineyard
MONTANA O **Deutz Marlborough Cuvée** Non-Vintage
SEIFRIED O **Gewürztraminer** Nelson Winemakers Collection Dry
STONECROFT O **Gewürztraminer** Hawkes Bay

10 top Cabernet or Merlot based reds
ALPHA DOMUS ● **AD The Aviator** Hawkes Bay
CRAGGY RANGE ● **The Quarry** Gimblett Gravels
ESK VALLEY ● **The Terraces** Hawkes Bay
MATAKANA ESTATE ● **Moko** Matakana
MATARIKI ● **Quintology** Gimblett Gravels
RED METAL ● **The Merlot** Hawkes Bay
STONYRIDGE ● **Larose Cabernets** Waiheke Island
TE MATA ● **Coleraine** Hawkes Bay
TE MOTU VINEYARD ● **Cabernet Sauvignon/Merlot** Waiheke Island
UNISON ● **Selection** Gimblett Gravels

10 leading Pinot Noir
ATA RANGI ● **Pinot Noir** Martinborough
FELTON ROAD ● **Pinot Noir** Central Otago Block 3
FROMM ● **La Strada Pinot Noir** Marlborough Fromm Vineyard
MARTINBOROUGH VINEYARD ● **Pinot Noir** Martinborough
MOUNT DIFFICULTY ● **Pinot Noir** Central Otago
MOUNTFORD ● **Pinot Noir** Waipara
MURDOCH JAMES ESTATE ● **Pinot Noir** Martinborough Fraser
NEUDORF ● **Pinot Noir** Moutere
OLSSENS OF BANNOCKBURN ● **Pinot Noir** Central Otago Jackson Barry
VILLA MARIA ● **Pinot Noir** Marlborough Seddon Vineyard

8 promising Syrah
BABICH ● **Syrah** Hawkes Bay Winemakers Reserve
CRAGGY RANGE ● **Syrah** Gimblett Gravels Block 14
DRY RIVER ● **Syrah** Martinborough
MURDOCH JAMES ESTATE ● **Syrah** Martinborough
NEWTON FORREST ESTATE ● **Syrah** Cornerstone
STONECROFT ● **Syrah** Hawkes Bay
TE MATA ● **Syrah** Hawkes Bay Bullnose
VIDAL ● **Syrah** Hawkes Bay

South Africa

Dramatic and positive change in South Africa has seen increased involvement in the wine industry by all ethnic groups and much work and research have gone into improving the quality of the nation's vineyards. There is no doubting that wine quality at the upper end of the market here is good and improving. Although still relatively rare, dynamic and truly exciting new producers are continuing to emerge. An increasing number of reds approaching world class are now being made, however South Africa still wants for more wines of indisputable world-class and complexity. There has been a recent trend towards micro-production garage-style wines but it remains to be seen how many of these will stand the test of time.

The Regions

Quality wine production in South Africa is centred around **Stellenbosch** WO. The region is one of the most attractive to visit anywhere in the world, with towering mountains rising seemingly out of the ocean. Stellenbosch itself is not only home to some of the largest wine companies in the country but also to some of its most impressive. There is a wide variation of mesoclimates within the WO with maritime breezes and the Simonsberg and Helderberg mountains playing a role in tempering conditions. In the coolest areas Sauvignon Blanc and Chardonnay (including some impressive barrel-fermented examples) are both successful, as is the occasional Riesling. Chenin Blanc tends to be much in the local style with some residual sugar. Stellenbosch reds are among the best in the country. Pinotage can be particularly striking in the warm vineyards to the north-east of Stellenbosch. Decent Bordeaux-style reds abound and a number of wineries are producing excellent results with Shiraz. Merlot can be good but also a touch vegetal. Although the wines are less rustic than of old and with much of the virus infection once prevalent now removed, a marked minty note found in a number of reds can be overpowering.

To the north of Stellenbosch is the second-largest region, **Paarl**. The area is warm and reds including some very successful Shiraz and Merlot are produced. There are also a number of cooler mesoclimates where the odd decent Sauvignon Blanc and Semillon are made, as well as Chardonnay and some fine Pinot Noir. White Rhône varieties are also increasingly widely planted. To the immediate east is **Franschhoek**. The valley here gets cooler as you move east and up to higher altitudes. Again, very good Shiraz and Cabernet Sauvignon are produced as well as earlier-ripening whites and Pinot Noir. To the east of Stellenbosch is the cool **Durbanville** region and then south of Cape Town **Constantia** is home to a small number of good producers. The climate is cool and moderated by both Indian and Atlantic Ocean breezes and whites are more successful than the reds. Some way to the east of Stellenbosch are the regions of **Worcester** and **Robertson**. The latter has some potential for good whites grown in limestone soils.

The vast, semi-desert and arid expanse of the **Klein Karoo**, several hundred kilometres inland, sees the production of some reasonable fortified styles but is too hot to produce fine table wines. **Swartland** just to the north-west of Paarl appears to have real potential. Hillside vineyards planted on well-drained granite soils are the source of good Pinotage, Shiraz and Merlot.

South African vintages

The top Cape reds will develop and keep well, the best for up to a decade. The majority should be approached sooner. Whites generally need drinking as soon after release as possible although the odd barrel-fermented Chardonnay will develop in the short term. 2004 is potentially good for reds but there has been uneven ripening. 2003 looks to be a very good year for the Cape and earlier years to consider for premium reds are 2002, 2001, 2000, 1998, 1997, 1995 and 1994.

1   Swartland
2   Darling/Groenekloof
3   Tulbagh
4   Paarl
5   Durbanville
6   Constantia
7   Stellenbosch
8   Franschhoek
9   Elgin
10   Walker Bay
11   Elim
12   Overberg
13   Worcester
14   Robertson

BEYERSKLOOF Stellenbosch heidi@beyerskloof.co.za **A: RSo**

Owner: Beyers Truter/Krige family PO Box 107, Koelenhof 7605

Beyers Truter owns this property in partnership with the Krige family, who own KANONKOP (where Truter is also the winemaker with Simon Halliday). Here he makes a stylish and vibrant Pinotage in a lighter style than that at Kanonkop and a dense and burly Cabernet Sauvignon. This is in a rich chocolatey style with abundant evidence of new oak. It will be better with five years' cellaring. Newly added are a fruity rosé and a well-priced red blend, Synergy. This comprises Merlot, Pinotage and Cabernet Sauvignon and is sourced from a number of sites around Stellenbosch. It is ripe, plummy and forward with a spicy hint of oak and can be enjoyed with a couple of years' ageing. (DM)

● **Pinotage** Stellenbosch★ £B ● **Synergy** Stellenbosch★★ £B
● **Cabernet Sauvignon** Stellenbosch★★★★ £D

BON CAP Robertson www.boncaporganic.co.za **A:RsW,SVS**

Owner: Michelle & Roelf du Preeze PO Box 356, Eilandia, Robertson 6705

Michelle and Rolf du Preeze make a well-crafted range of organic reds at their small Robertson farm and have recently added Viognier. The family has in fact been farming in the Robertson region for seven generations but winemaking is much more recent. Production is by no means small – the output of both the fruit-driven Ruins Pinotage and the Bon Cap labels is 15,000 cases a year, with a similar volume sold off in bulk. The vineyards are farmed organically because Roelf du Preeze believes this provides him with a better balance. The minimalist approach is carried over to the vinification and ageing, with no fining and absolute minimal sulphur additions. The resulting wines have good depth and real varietal purity. The Ruins Pinotage is aged in tank, while the Bon Cap reds all see some oak for up to 10 months. Mainly French barrels are used with a fifth being American oak. The Bon Cap-labelled reds will develop well in the short term. (DM)

● **Pinotage** The Ruins★ £B Eilandia★★ £B ● **Syrah** Eilandia★★ £C
● **Cabernet Sauvignon** Eilandia★★ £C

BOEKENHOUTSKLOOF Franschhoek boeken@mweb.co.za **A: Orb,F&M**

Owner: Boekenhoutskloof Investments (Pty) Ltd PO Box 433, Franschoek 7690

This farm is located on the higher and cooler slopes of Franschhoek and is producing some of the most stylish wines in the Cape. Syrah from bought-in fruit is intense, refined and full of black, spicy fruit. It displays the weight and texture of good Hermitage. The Cabernet Sauvignon is in a dense and cedary style with supple, velvety tannin. It will benefit from at least four or five years' ageing. The premium range is completed by a pure and subtly oaked Semillon. Structured and worth cellaring this is of a different order to most South African examples. A full, brambly and spicy Rhône-style blend, the Chocolate Block, is sourced from Franschoek fruit and comprises Syrah, Grenache and some very old-vine Cinsault. It is only available in the UK. There is also a range of attractively fruity and characterful varietal wines under the Porcupine Ridge label, which are sourced from Coastal Region fruit. Most recently added was simple but attractive, fruit-driven Wolftrap, a blend comprising Pinotage, Cabernet Sauvignon, Mourvèdre and Cinsault. (DM)

Boekenhoutskloof
● **Cabernet Sauvignon** Estate Franschhoek★★★★★ £E
● **Shiraz** Estate Franschhoek★★★★ £E
O Semillon Estate Franschhoek★★★ £C

Porcupine Ridge
● **Cabernet Sauvignon**Porcupine Ridge★★ £B ● **Syrah** Porcupine Ridge★★ £B
O Sauvignon Blanc Porcupine Ridge★ £B

BOUCHARD FINLAYSON   Walker Bay   bf.overstrand.co.za   **A: Bib**

Owner: Peter Finlayson/Paul Bouchard   Kleine Hemel en Aarde, PO Box 303, Hermanus 7200
Peter Finlayson was originally the winemaker at neighbouring HAMILTON RUSSELL before establishing his own operation in partnership with Paul Bouchard of the Bouchard family, former owners of BOUCHARD PÈRE ET FILS. There are close to 16 ha of vineyard, dominated by Pinot Noir. The style differs from Hamilton Russell: the wine is more extracted thanks to a period of post-fermentation maceration that makes it denser, but it could do with just a touch more elegance. It will develop nicely with two or three years. A barrel selection Tête de Cuvée is also produced. There are two Chardonnays, Kaaimansgat from the Overberg WO and the opulent, homegrown Missionvale bottling. There is also a clean, zesty Sauvignon Blanc as well as a simple clean-fruited blend of Kerner, Gewürztraminer, Riesling, Sauvignon Blanc and Chardonnay labelled Blanc de Mer. Chardonnay will stand a little ageing; Sauvignon should be drunk young. The most recent addition is Hannibal, an unusual red blend of Sangiovese, Nebbiolo and Pinot Noir. It will be interesting to see how the Italian varieties compare with examples from California and Australia. (DM)
● **Pinot Noir** Galpin Peak Walker Bay★★★ £D
O **Chardonnay** Kaaimansgat Overberg★★ £C   Missionvale Walker Bay★★ £C
O **Sauvignon Blanc** Walker Bay★ £B

DE TOREN   Stellenbosch   www.de-toren.com   **A:WSS**,BBr, Rae,ACh

Owner: Edenhall Trust   PO Box 48, Vlottenburg 7604
Located in the Polkadraai Hills sub-region of Stellenbosch, De Toren makes just 3,000 cases of one of the more striking Bordeaux red blends in the region. The Five is named for the grape varieties which make up the blend: Cabernet Sauvignon, Malbec, Merlot, Cabernet Franc and Petit Verdot. It is a finely structured, dense and concentrated wine with just a slight minty undertone to its plummy, cedary fruit character. Aged in a combination of new and one-year-old oak, both French and American, the wine is comfortably capable of developing well in bottle for 10 years or more. Both the 2001 and 02 are right on the edge of four stars. A well-priced second label, Diversity, is a blend of whichever grapes are not felt to be suitable for the Grand Vin and aged in older oak. It is soft, ripe and forward, with just a touch of dry cedary complexity; drink it soon after release. (DM)
● **Fusion V** Coastal Region★★★ £D   ● **Diversity** Coastal Region★★ £C

FAIRVIEW ESTATE   Paarl   www.fairview.co.za   **A: CHk**,WSc

Owner: Charles Back   PO Box 583, Suider Paarl 7624
Charles Back makes an extensive range at his Paarl farm, with much of the focus centred on Rhône styles. The humorously-named red and white Goats do Roam are well-crafted if very simple Rhône blends. These have been supplemented by Goat Roti, which despite its name actually blends Shiraz with Grenache, Carignan and Viognier. Of more significance are the Red Seal Range Cyril Back Shiraz and Primo Pinotage. The latter is produced from low-yielding old bush vines and avoids some of the more excessive bubble-gum, acetate aromas that the variety can display. A Beacon Block Shiraz is also now produced from younger vines, as is a Solitude Shiraz, aged in a combination of French and American oak. A new label Jakkalsfontein from old bush vines has also now been added. Among the regular Fairview labels is a honeyed, peachy Viognier and a good, unusual, weighty blend of Zinfandel and Cinsault. Chardonnay shows marked oak and is in a very ripe tropical style. Drink the whites young; the reds are very approachable early but will stand limited ageing. Charles Back also owns the SPICE ROUTE COMPANY at Swartland. (DM)
● **Shiraz** Cyril Back Paarl★★ £C   Beacon Paarl★★★ £C   Solitude Paarl★★★ £C
● **Zinfandel/Cinsault** Paarl★ £B   ● **SMV** Paarl★★ £B
O **Chardonnay** Coastal Region★ £B   O **Viognier** Paarl★★ £B

GLEN CARLOU Paarl glencarl@mweb.co.za   A: AWs, NYg

Owner: Finlayson family/Donald Hess PO Box 23, Klapmuts 7625
The Finlaysons produce particularly impressive Chardonnay, quite different from and more stylish than most examples from the Cape. They have some 107 ha of vineyards in the foothills of the Simonsberg Mountains, which they own in partnership with Donald Hess of the HESS COLLECTION in California. There are no overtly rich or tropical notes in either of the two Chardonnays. The regular bottling is tight, minerally and restrained, the Reserve is concentrated, with citrus, cheesy lees notes and toasty oak all entering the equation. Both are structured and capable of three or four years' bottle-development. The Pinot Noir and Grand Classique Bordeaux blend are good and ripe but lack the flair of the Chardonnays. Shiraz and Zinfandel are also now produced. (DM)

● **Grand Classique** Paarl★★ £C   ● **Pinot Noir** Paarl★ £C
O **Chardonnay** Paarl★★ £B Reserve Paarl★★★ £C

GRANGEHURST Stellenbosch www.grangehurst.co.za   A: Bib

Owner: Jeremy Walker PO Box 206, Stellenbosch 7599
Jeremy Walker produces a small handcrafted range of red wines from his 15 ha of vineyards. They are stylish, concentrated and among the better examples produced in the Cape. The Pinotage is impressively ripe and full-bodied with plenty of spicy, dark berry fruit. Nikela is an unusual blend which, as well as those usual suspects Cabernet Sauvignon and Merlot, contains a sizeable dollop of Pinotage. Good and reasonably concentrated it has a vibrant dark berry fruit character with a hint of menthol in the background. The top wine is the Cabernet Sauvignon/Merlot which is structured and in need of three or four years' cellaring. Future plans include a move towards Rhône varieties. (DM)

● **Cabernet Sauvignon/Merlot** Stellenbosch★★★ £C   ● **Nikela** Stellenbosch★★ £B
● **Pinotage** Stellenbosch★★ £B

HAMILTON RUSSELL VINEYARDS Walker Bay   A: Hal, WSc, F&M

Owner: Hamilton Russell family Hemel-en-Arde Valley, PO Box 158, 7200 Hermanus
The original and most impressive producer of both Pinot Noir and Chardonnay in the cool and visually stunning Walker Bay. The wines have much improved over the last decade, with better clones planted and a concerted effort to isolate the very best aspects of the vineyards for each variety. No artificial fertilisers are used in the stony, clay soils and cover crops are planted to optimise fruit ripening. Chardonnay is refined but has attractive, lightly tropical notes and real intensity with a pure, almost European mineral undercurrent. Pinot Noir is rich and full of dark berry fruit, with just a hint of hung meat emerging. Chardonnay as well as Pinot Noir is consistently on the cusp of four stars. A second label, Southern Right, is for Sauvignon Blanc and Pinotage sourced from the Western Cape. (DM)

● **Pinot Noir** Walker Bay★★★★ £D
O **Chardonnay** Walker Bay★★★ £D

KAAPZICHT Stellenbosch www.kaapzicht-wines.com   A: Sec

Owner: Steytler family PO Box 35, Koelenhof 7605
The magnificently sited vineyards here look west towards Table Mountain. Most of the 135 ha of vines are planted on north-facing slopes and Chenin Blanc is gradually being replanted and replaced with top red varieties. In addition, much care is lavished on some old bush vine plantings of Pinotage. A comprehensive range is currently offerred including Chenin Blanc, Sauvignon Blanc and the Combination which blends the two. The most important wines are the reds. As well as the richly textured Vision and Cabernet Sauvignon Steytler some excellent Pinotage is produced, the Steytler among the best in the region. Of the lighter reds are a fruit driven Classic red and a more serious Estate red which blends Cabernet Sauvignon, Cinsault and Shiraz. There are also good estate bottlings of Merlot and Shiraz and the forward Bin 3 which

blends Merlot with Cabernet and Pinotage. (DM)

● **Vision** Steytler Stellenbosch★★★ £D   ● **Cabernet Sauvignon** Stellenbosch★★ £B
● **Pinotage** Steytler Stellenbosch★★★ £D   Stellenbosch★★★ £C

KANONKOP   Stellenbosch   www.kanonkop.co.za   A: RSo

Owner: Krige family   PO Box 19, Elsenburg 7607
This is arguably the best Pinotage producer in South Africa. An extensive holding of old bush vines is a
major contributing factor and winemaker Beyers Truter has a formidable track record with the variety. His
wines are always powerful and chunky with firm but not aggressive tannins. The regular bottling and the
Bouwland Reserve are both impressive, the Auction Reserve even more so. Very good Cabernet Sauvignon
is also produced here; the Paul Sauer label is blended with Cabernet Franc and Merlot and has an extra
dimension. Both wines are rich, cedary and ageworthy with a refinement of fruit rarely encountered in the
Cape. Kadette is a cheerful soft and plummy blend of Pinotage, Cabernet Sauvignon and Merlot. (DM)
● **Cabernet Sauvignon** Stellenbosch★★★ £D   ● **Paul Sauer** Stellenbosch★★★★ £D
● **Pinotage** Stellenbosch★★★ £C

MEERLUST   Stellenbosch   www.meerlust.co.za   A: MMD, Tan, F&M

Owner: Hannes Myburgh   PO Box 15, Faure 7131
Historic old wine farm first established in 1693 and located just to the south of Stellenbosch in a
relatively cool mesoclimate. Reds, produced from the Bordeaux varieties, and rich and toasty Chardonnay
are among the very best of their kind in the Cape. Vineyard holdings are not small: there is a total of nearly
400 ha under vine and Viognier has also been planted in cool False Bay. Merlot is very good and the
Cabernet/Merlot/Cabernet Franc Rubicon blend is rich, concentrated and marked by cedar and exotic dark
fruits, with not a hint of the baked and jammy flavours often found among its peers. Pinot Noir is
good – ripe enough and oaky but it fails to reach the same heights. (DM)
● **Merlot** Stellenbosch★★ £C   ● **Pinot Noir** Reserve Stellenbosch★★ £C
● **Rubicon** Stellenbosch★★★ £D
O **Chardonnay** Stellenbosch★★★ £C

MEINERT   Stellenbosch   meinert@netactive.co.za   A: TWS

Owner: Martin Meinert   PO Box 7221, Stellenbosch 7599
Martin Meinert was the winemaker at VERGELEGEN before André van Rensburg. He established his own
label in 1997 in the Devon Valley and produces around 4,000 cases a year solely from the Bordeaux
varieties. The Merlot is reasonably rich, concentrated and plummy with firm tannins providing the
structure for ageing over the next five years or so. The Cabernet/Merlot is tight and backward in its youth,
quite a lean style that needs cellaring to put on weight but should become more refined and harmonious
with time. Meinert is now focusing fully on Cabernet Sauvignon from the Devon Valley area, which
replaces the Cabernet/Merlot blend. (DM)
● **Cabernet Sauvignon/Merlot** Stellenbosch★★ £C   ● **Merlot** Stellenbosch★★ £C

NICO VAN DER MERWE   Stellenbosch   wilhelmshof@xsinet.co.za

Owner: Nico van der Merwe/Robert Alexander   PO Box 12200, Stellenbosch 7613
Nico van der Merwe is the winemaker at SAXENBERG and CHÂTEAU CAPION in France's Languedoc
region. Under his own label he produces a very fine blend of Shiraz and Cabernet Sauvignon. Production
is small at around 500 cases a year. The Shiraz component is sourced from 27-year-old vines grown in
granite soils, the Cabernet from 11-year-old vines. The vineyards are carefully managed with summer
pruning to keep yields low and irrigation is avoided. Nico plans to source fruit in the future from his own
vineyards towards Walker Bay. Vinification is modern with both hand-plunging and pumping over the cap
during fermentation and the wine is kept on its skins for a further two weeks. Malolactic is in barrel and

50 per cent new oak used for ageing. The result is a dense, classically minty style of Cape red but with real depth and concentration. The wine will drink well young but evolve over a decade or more. (DM)

● **Mas Nicolas** Stellenbosch★★★★ £D

MORGENHOF Stellenbosch www.morgenhof.com   A: McK

Owner: Anne Cointreau-Huchon   PO Box 365, Stellenbosch 7599

Medium-sized, French-owned estate with a production of around 25,000 cases a year. An extensive range includes sparkling and fortified wines. Chardonnay is in an oaky style with marked buttery malolactic character, Sauvignon Blanc is typically zesty and fresh, and there is a barrel-fermented Chenin Blanc with that characteristic hint of residual sugar so typically employed in the vinification of the variety here. Reds include Merlot, Malbec/Merlot and Pinotage but most impressive are the Cabernet Sauvignon and Première Selection. This latter wine is a blend of Cabernet Sauvignon, Merlot and Cabernet Franc. It is sweet and moderately rich while the Cabernet is firm and structured with a characteristic Cape mintiness. Both will stand a little age. Merlot and Cabernet Sauvignon Reserve labels have both been introduced with the 1998 vintage and look promising. (DM)

● **Cabernet Sauvignon** Stellenbosch★★ £C ● **Première Selection** Stellenbosch★ £C
● **Pinotage** Stellenbosch★ £C
O **Chardonnay** Stellenbosch★★ £B

MULDERBOSCH Stellenbosch www.mulderbosch.co.za   A: JAr

Owner: Hydro Holdings   PO Box 548, Stellenbosch 7599

Producer of one of the best piercing varietal Sauvignon Blancs. This is surprising because the mesoclimate of the vineyard here is reasonably hot. The key is tightly controlled yields and harvesting ripe but not over ripe grapes. Subtly oaked Chardonnay, now in Barrel Fermented and regular bottlings, and a Barrel Fermented Sauvignon Blanc are also good but without the intensity of the regular Sauvignon, which is cool-fermented in tank. A Chenin Blanc, Steen-op-Hout, sees a touch of oak and there is a red blend, Faithful Hound, comprising the Bordeaux varieties Merlot, Cabernets Sauvignon and Franc and a touch of Malbec. The latter will improve with three or four years' cellaring but can show a slightly green, angular character. (DM)

● **Faithful Hound** Stellenbosch★★ £C
O **Chardonnay** Barrel Fermented Stellenbosch★★★ £C
O **Sauvignon Blanc** Stellenbosch★★ £B Barrel Fermented Stellenbosch★★ £C

THE OBSERVATORY Cape Town   A: BBR,Odd

Owner: Tom & Catherine Lubbe   21 Bridge Street, Rosebank, Cape Town 7770

Two strikingly original Rhône-style reds are produced here from old Swartland bush vines. Brother and sister Tom and Catherine Lubbe have a small warehouse winery in Cape Town from which just 600 cases are currently produced of both wines. Fruit comes from 5 ha of granite-based soils at Swartland, 2 ha of which are under contract. The Lubbe siblings believe this soil helps accentuate the mineral core they are looking for in their wines. This they certainly achieve: both wines possess a mineral, almost fiery *sauvage* edge to their fruit and are very different from most Cape reds. Everything in the vineyard is handled organically and herbal tisanes are used to help encourage a stable pH and provide good acidity in the wines. The harvest is never picked overripe and vinification includes a long and relatively cool maceration of up to three weeks. The wine is aged in a mix of 225- and 500-litre barrels, just a small percentage new to avoid excessive oakiness, and micro-oyxenation may also be used because they keep the wine on its gross lees during maturation. Both wines will undoubtedly benefit from a few years' ageing and the Syrah needs two or three years to settle down in bottle. Tom Lubbe also has a partnership in Domaine MATASSA in the Côtes du Roussillon. (DM)

● **Syrah** Swartland★★★★ £E ● **Carignan/Syrah** Swartland★★★ £D

QUOIN ROCK Stellenbosch www.quoinrock.com   A: RsW

Owner: Talacar Holdings PO Box 1193, Stellenbosch 7599
This recently established Stellenbosch property is owned by Scotsman Dave King. There are 60 ha of vineyards now planted, including Chardonnay and Sauvignon Blanc at Agulhas the southernmost tip of Africa. Around 5,000 cases are produced a year under the Quoin Rock label, the bulk of the 180 ton annual grape crush is sold off. The cool climate character of the whites clearly comes across, tight and almost minerally. The Sauvignon Blanc possesses none of the overt raw blackcurrant and tropical notes found elsewhere. The Oculus is Sauvignon Blanc barrel-fermented. It is the finest structured of the whites with piercing intensity and should develop well for two or three years. The Merlot while impressively dark, spicy and plummy can show a lot of new oak young, although the 2002 is showing increasing complexity. It will benefit from four or five years. (DM)
● **Merlot** Stellenbosch★★ £C
O **Chardonnay** Stellenbosch★★ £C   O **Oculus** Stellenbosch★★ £C
O **Sauvignon Blanc** Stellenbosch★★ £B

ROZENDAL Stellenbosch www.rozendal.co.za   A: RsW

Owner: Kurt Ammann PO Box 160, Stellenbosch 7599
Small Stellenbosch farm producing around 2,500 cases a year of a top-quality Bordeaux-style blend from the Jonkershoek Valley sub-region in the foothills of the Jonkershoek Mountains. The 25-ha property includes just 6 ha of vines, which since 1994 have been farmed biodynamically and are planted to a Bordeaux Right Bank-style mix of Merlot, Cabernet Sauvignon and Cabernet Franc. The wine is finely structured, elegant and almost European in style with subtle red berry fruit and firm, supple tannins. It is matured in oak, very little of which is new, and bottled without fining or filtration. Give it five years to begin showing its best. (DM)
● **Rozendal Red** Jonkershoek Valley★★★ £D

RUPERT & ROTHSCHILD Franschoek www.rupert-rothschildvignerons.com A:HoK

Owner: Kurt Ammann PO Box 412, Franschoek Valley 7690
This is a partnership between the Rupert family who also own the Cape farms LA MOTTE and L'Ormarins and Baron Benjamin de Rothschild who is one of the family partners in LAFITE-ROTHSCHILD and also owns Château CLARKE in Listrac-Medoc. Consultancy comes from Michel Rolland. The intended style here – successfully achieved – is one of elegance and restraint as opposed to some of the more opulent examples of some of their neighbours. The red Classique is a blend of Cabernet Sauvignon, Merlot and unusually a little Pinotage. It is more obviously fruit-driven than the sturdier and more backward Baron Edmond which blends purely Cabernet Sauvignon and Merlot (the proportion is roughly 2:1). Both wines get just under 20 months maturation in French oak, new in the case of the Baron Edmond. The restrained melon and lightly citrus aromas of the Baroness Nadine Chardonnay are achieved through just 20 per cent new oak and 20 per cent of the wine going through malolactic fermentation. Unlike many South African examples of the grape the Baroness Nadine will benefit from three or four years' age. Both reds will develop well in the medium term, the Baron Edmond for up to a decade. (DM)
● **Classique** Coastal Region★★ £C   ● **Baron Edmond** Coastal Region★★★ £D
O **Chardonnay** Coastal Region★★★ £C

RUSTENBERG Stellenbosch www.rustenberg.co.za   A: Men, L&S,F&M

Owner: Barlow family PO Box 33, Stellenbosch 7599
Considerable investment has been put into this farm in recent years and the winery is now gravity-fed, with some good results. There are three Brampton-label wines sourced from Stellenbosch: a straightforward Sauvignon Blanc with simple gooseberry fruit, a Cabernet/Merlot with soft, forward red berry fruit and an

Old Vines red blend of Merlot and Cabernet. Of greater substance are the Rustenberg wines. Two Chardonnays are produced with intense citrus notes and well-judged oak, as well as the Rustenberg John X Merriman and Peter Barlow reds. The former, a Bordeaux blend with a high proportion of Merlot, shows sweet berry fruit and spicy oak. Peter Barlow is a more structured and ageworthy varietal Cabernet Sauvignon. Shiraz and Viognier are to be added to the range. (DM)

● **Cabernet Sauvignon Peter Barlow** Stellenbosch★★★ £D   ● **John X Merriman** Stellenbosch★★ £C
O **Chardonnay** Stellenbosch★★ £B   Five Soldiers Stellenbosch★★★ £C

SADIE FAMILY WINES   Swartland   sadiefamily@mail.com   A: RsW,NYg,F&M

Owner: Eben Sadie   PO Box 1019, Malmesbury 7299
Eben Sadie, the original winemaker at SPICE ROUTE, formed his own tiny Sadie Family winery in the late 1990s. The very fine red, Columella, is an almost varietal Syrah with just a tiny proportion of Mourvèdre. It is a wine of remarkable dark, spicy complexity; rich, almost exotic, with a supple texture and great intensity. Inevitably it is made from very low yields, from seven leased vineyard parcels around Swartland, half of which are populated with old bush vines. Eben controls all the viticultural aspects. There is no irrigation and he prefers to control vine growth through crop thinning. The must gets a cold soak prior to fermentation and maceration often lasts longer than five weeks. The wine is basket-pressed and aged in oak for close to two years and fining and filtration are avoided. A tiny amount (just over 100 cases) of Palladius, a white blend of Viognier, Chardonnay, Chenin Blanc and Grenache Blanc was first made with the 2002 vintage. Eben is also involved in a new project in Priorat in Spain, producing barely 150 cases of a Carignan and Grenache blend called Dits del Terra. Immediately approachable, Columella will develop very well for a decade or more. (DM)

● **Columella** Swartland★★★★★ £E

SAXENBURG   Stellenbosch   www.saxenburg.co.za   A: Fie

Owner: Buhrer family   PO Box 171, Kulls River 7580
The Swiss owners of this farm also own Domaine CAPION in France's Languedoc region. There are over 90 ha of vineyards here supplemented by bought-in fruit. The Standard, Reserve and Estate ranges provide decent fruit-driven reds and whites but it is the Private Collection Label that particularly stands out. A Cap Classique sparkler, a Chardonnay and a Sauvignon Blanc can be impressive, with good varietal fruit and stylishly handled oak in the Chardonnay. The Private Collection reds comprise a warm and plummy Merlot with rich vanilla oak; a tightly structured Cabernet Sauvignon marked by notes of cassis and cedar; and impressive Shiraz full of dark black fruit and Rhône-like licorice and black pepper. Shiraz Select is richer and fuller with very fine, ripe and supple tannins, long and harmonious. Both Shirazes stand out among South African reds. (DM)

● **Cabernet Sauvignon** Private Collection Stellenbosch★★★ £C
● **Merlot** Private Collection Stellenbosch★★ £C
● **Shiraz** Private Collection Stellenbosch★★★ £C   Select Stellenbosch★★★★ £D
● **Pinotage** Private Collection Stellenbosch★★ £C
O **Chardonnay** Private Collection Stellenbosch★★ £C
O **Sauvignon Blanc** Private Collection Stellenbosch★★ £B

SPICE ROUTE COMPANY   Swartland   A: Eno

Owner: Charles Back   PO Box 645, Malmesbury 7300
Now wholly owned by Charles Back of FAIRVIEW, this warm-climate Swartland property has been good to sometimes very good in recent vintages. There is a regular Cabernet/Merlot blend, along with sound fruity Sauvignon Blanc and Chenin Blanc. Shiraz, Pinotage and Viognier have been added more recently. All are released under the standard label. As well as these, a simple fruit-driven Sauvignon Blanc and a Cabernet/Merlot are released under the third-tier Andrew's Hope label. The Flagship range of red varietals,

though, is a real step up. The round and supple Syrah is full of dark blackberry and spice; the Merlot is softer with marked plum and sweet oak. The Pinotage is loaded with dark black, very ripe fruit and is marked by firm tannin, the structure sometimes threatening to overwhelm the wine. All will develop well in the medium term. (DM)

● **Merlot** Swartland★★★ £C   ● **Pinotage** Swartland★★★ £C   ● **Syrah** Swartland★★★ £C

SPRINGFIELD Robertson www.springfieldestate.com   A: **Bib,SVS**

Owner: Bruwer family   PO Box 770, Robertson 6705
The best property in the warm Robertson area is producing decent fresh, grassy Sauvignon Blanc Life from Stone and some good to very good Chardonnay with close-to-organic practices. Cabernet Sauvignon has been less impressive – quite lean with a marked leafy component behind its fruit. A Méthode Ancienne bottling has now been added which is fermented from wild yeasts and aged on lees after malolactic in barrel. It is bottled without filtration. Chardonnay is tight and citrusy with well-judged oak and a rich, buttery component provided by malolactic fermentation. Of additional weight and substance is the very good special bottling of Chardonnay Méthode Ancienne, produced only in the best years. Wild yeasts are again used to vinify both Chardonnays and filtration is avoided. (DM)

O **Chardonnay** Wild Yeast Robertson★★ £B   Méthode Ancienne Robertson★★★ £C
O **Sauvignon Blanc** Life from Stone Robertson★ £B

STARK-CONDÉ Stellenbosch www.stark-conde.co.za   A:**Str**

Owner: Jonkershoek Cellars (Pty) Ltd   PO Box 389, Stellenbosch 7599
Family-run boutique operation with an output of barely 3,000 cases a year. Quality is good and some striking Cabernet Sauvignons are produced here along with a Pinotage and most recently a Pinot Noir (with the 2001 vintage). The top red is the impressive Condé Cabernet, which comes from the best blocks on the property. It is very much in a minty, berry and light cassis style with just the merest hint of cedar. Supple and nicely rounded tannins should ensure further development with three or four years in bottle. The Stark Cabernet is leaner and more angular in style while still emphasising those minty, eucalyptus characters. The Stark bottling is lightly fined and filtered whereas the Condé gets 25 months maturation in oak and is bottled unfined and unfiltered. A Condé Shiraz will be added from the 2002 vintage. (DM)

● **Condé Cabernet Sauvignon** Stellenbosch★★★ £C
● **Stark Cabernet Sauvignon** Stellenbosch★★ £C

STELLENZICHT Stellenbosch www.stellenzicht.co.za   A: **Hal**

Owner: Lusan Holdings (Pty) Ltd   PO Box 104, 7604 Vlottenburg
A quite extensive range is produced at this Stellenbosch farm by winemaker Guy Webber, who took over from André van Rensburg after he moved to VERGELEGEN. A regular range of varietals under the Hill and Dale label offers decent value and both red and white varietals appear under the Golden Triangle label. Sauvignon Blanc is fresh and zesty and there is some nutty, toasty Chardonnay but best of the whites is a restrained, well-crafted Semillon Reserve. Pinotage is ripe and brambly with a hint of that acetate character frequent in the variety. The flagship Syrah is very classy stuff: structured and impressive with well-judged oak, it will develop well with three or four years' ageing. A premium Stellenzicht Bordeaux blend has now been added. (DM)

● **Cabernet Sauvignon** Stellenbosch★ £B   ● **Stellenzicht** Stellenbosch★★ £C
● **Syrah** Stellenbosch★★★ £C   ● **Pinotage** Stellenbosch★★ £B
O **Sauvignon Blanc** Stellenbosch★ £B   O **Chardonnay** Stellenbosch★★ £B
O **Semillon** Reserve Stellenbosch★★★ £C

THELEMA Stellenbosch www.thelema.co.za A: **Eno**, NYg,F&M

Owner: Gyles Webb PO Box 2234, 7599 Stellenbosch
Gyles Webb is generally accepted as one of the best viticulturalists and winemakers in the Cape. The family's vineyard and winery are located at altitude on the slopes of the Simonsberg and this contributes to the quality of the fruit. The vineyards are well managed and controlled yields are nevertheless reasonably productive. There's good Chardonnay and Cabernet Sauvignon as well as steely, minerally Riesling. Merlot can be less impressive but is reasonably concentrated and ripely plummy. Sauvignon is piercing and full of lightly tropical, green fruits. It should be consumed as soon as it is released. Reserves of Merlot and Cabernet Sauvignon are a step up from the regular examples. Shiraz and Pinotage in as yet very small quantities have now been added to the range. (DM)

● **Cabernet Sauvignon** Stellenbosch★★★ £C   Reserve★★★★ £D   ● **Merlot** Stellenbosch★★ £C
O **Chardonnay** Stellenbosch★★ £C   O **Sauvignon Blanc** Stellenbosch★★ £B
O **Riesling** Stellenbosch★★ £B

VEENWOUDEN Paarl A: **Sec**,NYg

Owner: Deon van der Walt PO Box 7086, North Paarl 7623
The reputation of this property is based on three wines, all of which have their roots in Bordeaux. Production is now around 6,000 cases and Merlot in particular has been outstanding among Cape examples: supple and rich with a real mineral hint of its *terroir*. The Classic, a typical Bordeaux blend, is also impressive. Similar in style, the Vivat Bacchus has a touch of Malbec and is more open and approachable. There is minimal interference in the cellar and fine-quality French oak is used throughout, some of it new. The range has now been marginally expanded to include a Shiraz and a tiny amount of Chardonnay Special Reserve. (DM)

● **Merlot** Paarl★★★ £C   ● **Vivat Bacchus** Paarl★★ £C   ● **Classic** Paarl★★★ £C

VERGELEGEN Stellenbosch www.vergelegen.co.za A: NYg,WSc

Owner: Anglo American Farms Ltd PO Box 17, Somerset West
This historic wine farm dates back to 1700 and is located on hillside vineyards south of Stellenbosch. The winery was designed by French architects but it more closely resembles a new-wave Napa Valley operation than anything else. Gravity plays an important role in cellar-handling operations. André van Rensburg took on the winemaking mantle here after Martin MEINERT moved on to produce his own label. There is a straightforward blended white from Chenin Blanc, Muscat, Sauvignon Blanc, Chardonnay and Semillon, finished with a hint of residual sugar. Varietal Sauvignon Blanc and Chardonnay are both impressive, particularly the Reserves, which have real structure and grip. Merlot is ripe and vibrant and contains 8 per cent Cabernet Sauvignon. Cabernet Sauvignon has a hint of Merlot and Cabernet Franc, while the Vergelegen Red is one of the best reds yet from the Cape. Shiraz has now been added to the range and is impressively refined and stylish. A white Bordeaux style blend is new to the range and promises much. (DM)

● **Cabernet Sauvignon** Stellenbosch★★★ £C   ● **Merlot** Stellenbosch★★ £C
● **Shiraz** Stellenbosch★★★ £C   ● **Vergelegen** Stellenbosch★★★★ £D
O **Chardonnay** Stellenbosch★★ £B   Reserve Stellenbosch★★★ £C
O **Sauvignon Blanc** Stellenbosch★★ £B   Reserve Stellenbosch★★ £C

WARWICK ESTATE Stellenbosch www.warwickwine.co.za A:**LLt**,WSc,F&M

Owner: Norma Ratcliffe PO Box 2 Elsenburg 7607
The Bordeaux red varieties are the most significant plantings on this medium-sized farm neighbouring KANONKOP. Like its neighbour it also has old Pinotage bush vines and these produce one of the better examples of the variety, brambly and concentrated . Some of the harvest is regularly sold off and the balance results in some very good Cabernet Sauvignon and Cabernet Franc and the stylish, structured Trilogy blend,

produced from Cabernet Sauvignon, Merlot and Cabernet Franc. A lighter red blend of Cabernet Sauvignon, Merlot and some Pinotage, Three Cape Ladies, can be enjoyed young. The range is completed by a leesy Chardonnay of reasonable depth and a recently added Sauvignon Blanc, Professor Black. (DM)

● **Cabernet Franc** Stellenbosch★★ £C ● **Cabernet Sauvignon** Stellenbosch★★★ £C
● **Merlot** Stellenbosch★★ £C ● **Pinotage** Old Bush Vines Stellenbosch★★ £C
● **Three Cape Ladies** Stellenbosch★★ £C ● **Trilogy** Stellenbosch★★ £C
○ **Chardonnay** Stellenbosch★ £B

WELGEMEEND Paarl   A:RsW

Owner: Hofmeyr family PO Box 1408, Suider-Paarl 7624
This Paarl property is run by mother and daughter Ursula and Louise Hofmeyr. Ursula looks after the vineyards, while Louise makes the wines. The main focus here is a finely crafted and elegant Estate Reserve red made from a Right Bank blend of Merlot, Cabernet Sauvignon and Cabernet Franc. Two further Bordeaux reds are also produced. Soopieshooghte blends the same varieties as the Estate Reserve in a lighter style, while Douelle comprises Cabernet Sauvignon, Malbec, Cabernet Franc and a little Merlot and is leafier in style. Amadé by contrast is a Rhône-dominated blend of Shiraz, Grenache and Pinotage, a mix of of black pepper and tarry, dark berry fruit. The wines will all benefit from three or four years' patience, particularly the Estate Reserve. (DM)

● **Estate Reserve** Paarl★★★ £C ● **Amadé** Paarl★★ £B

WILDEKRANS Walker Bay www.wildekranswines.co.za   A:WhW

Owner: Bruce Elkin PO Box 200, Elgin 7180
This property is located further inland than most of the Walker Bay estates. As a result, striking, elegant Pinotage as well as the Bordeaux varieties are successfully made here. Some refreshing straightforward, fruit-driven whites offer excellent value: Sauvignon Blanc and Chenin Blanc are both sound as is a blend of the two with Chardonnay, Caresse Marine, which offers upfront, lightly tropical, citrusy and herby flavours. Reserve bottlings of Semillon and Chardonnay are both vinified in oak. There is a good minty, lightly cedary Cabernet Franc/Merlot as well as varietal examples of Cabernet Sauvignon and Merlot. The Pinotages are particularly good. Marked by intense berry fruit, they are subtler than most examples of the variety and show less of the aggressive acetone notes found elsewhere. The Barrel Selection will develop well in the short to medium term. (DM)

● **Pinotage** Walker Bay★★ £B Barrel Selection Walker Bay★★★ £C
● **Cabernet Franc/Merlot** Walker Bay★★ £C
○ **Caresse Marine** Walker Bay★ £B ○ **Chenin Blanc** Walker Bay★ £B

OTHER WINES OF NOTE

ASHANTI ● **Cabernet Sauvignon** Paarl £C ● **Pinotage** Paarl £C
BACKSBERG ● **Klein Babylonstoren** Paarl £B
GRAHAM BECK ○ **Blanc de Blancs** Vintage Robertson £C
BELLINGHAM ● **Cabernet Franc** Spitz Coastal Region £C ● **Pinotage** Spitz Coastal Region £C
BERGKELDER ○ **Pongrácz** Non Vintage Stellenbosch £C
BOPLAAS ● **Cape Vintage Reserve Fortified Red** Calitzdorp £C
BOSCHENDAL ● **Shiraz** Paarl £C ○ **Chardonnay** Reserve Paarl £B
BUITENVERWACHTING ● **Christine** Constantia £C ○ **Chardonnay** Constantia £B
BWC WINES ● **Shiraz** Paarl £C
CABRIÈRE ESTATE ○ **Pierre Jourdan Blanc de Blancs** Non-Vintage Franschoek £C
PAUL CLUVER ○ **Weisser Riesling** Elgin £B
CONSTANTIA UITSIG ○ **Chardonnay Reserve** Constantia £C
CORDOBA ● **Cabernet Sauvignon** Stellenbosch £B

DARLING CELLARS ● Cabernet Sauvignon Groenekloof £B
DELHEIM ● Shiraz Vera Cruz Estate Simonsberg-Stellenbosch £C
DE TRAFFORD ● Cabernet Sauvignon Stellenbosch £C   ● Merlot Stellenbosch £C
DIEMERSFONTEINE ● Pinotage Stellenbosch £B   ● Shiraz Stellenbosch £B
EIKENDAL O Chardonnay Stellenbosch £B
NEIL ELLIS ● Shiraz Stellenbosch £B   O Sauvignon Blanc Groenekloof £B
FLAGSTONE ● Cabernet Sauvignon The Music Room £C
GROOT CONSTANTIA O Chardonnay Reserve Constantia £B
GROOTE POST O Chardonnay Swartland £B   ● Merlot Swartland £C
JACK AND KNOX WINECRAFT O Semillon Greenhill Wellington £B
● Cabernet Sauvignon The Estoril £C   ● Shiraz The Outsider Swartland £C
JORDAN ● Cobblers Hill Stellenbosch £C   O Chardonnay Stellenbosch £B
KLEIN CONSTANTIA O Sauvignon Blanc Constantia £B   O Vin de Constance Constantia £E
LA MOTTE ● Shiraz Franschoek £C   ● Millenium Franschoek £C
LAIBACH ● Cabernet/Merlot Stellenbosch £B   O Chardonnay Stellenbosch £B
L'AVENIR ● Pinotage Stellenbosch £B
LE BONHEUR ● Cabernet Sauvignon Stellenbosch £C
LE RICHE ● Cabernet Sauvignon Reserve Stellenbosch £C
LONGRIDGE O Chardonnay Stellenbosch £B
MONT DU TOIT● Mont du Toit Wellington £D   ● Le Sommet Wellington £F
MURATIE ESTATE ● Shiraz £B
NEDERBURG O Edelkeur Noble Late Harvest Auction Reserve Paarl £E
NEETHLINGSHOF O Noble Late Harvest Stellenbosch £C
OVERGAAUW ● Tria Corda Stellenbosch £C
PLAISIR DE MERLE ● Cabernet Sauvignon Paarl £C
RAATS FAMILY WINES O Original Chenin Blanc Stellenbosch £E   ● Cabernet Franc Stellenbosch £C
RIDGEBACK ● Shiraz Paarl £D
ROOIBERG ● Pinotage Robertson £B
RUST EN VREDE ● Estate Red Stellenbosch £C
SIMONSIG ● Tiara Stellenbosch £C   ● Pinotage Redhill Stellenbosch £C
SIYABONGA ● Pinotage Wellington £C
STEENBERG O Sauvignon Blanc Reserve Constantia £C   O Semillon Constantia £C
UITERWYK ● Pinotage Top of the Hill Stellenbosch £B
VILLIERA ● Cru Monro Paarl £B   O Sauvignon Blanc Traditional Bush Vine Paarl £B
WATERFORD ● Cabernet Sauvignon Stellenbosch £C   O Sauvignon Blanc Stellenbosch £B
ZONDERNAAM O Sauvignon Blanc Stellenbosch £B

Work in progress!!

Wines from the following producers under consideration for the next edition

AGUSTA WINES (FRANSCHOEK)
ANTHONY DE JAGER (PAARL)
ANURA VINEYARDS (PAARL)
ASARA ESTATE (STELLENBOSCH)
BEAUMONT (WALKER BAY)
CEDERBERG (OLIFANTS RIVER)
COLERAINE WINES (PAARL)
DORNIER (STELLENBOSCH)
ERNIE ELS WINES (STELLENBOSCH)
KEN FORRESTER (STELLENBOSCH)
THE FOUNDRY (STELLENBOSCH)
KANU (STELLENBOSCH)
LAMMERSHOEK (SWAERLAND)
LANDAU DU VAL (FRANSCHOEK)
MÔRESON (FRANSCHOEK)

REMHOOTGE ESTATE (STELLENBOSCH)
RIDGEBACK (PAARL)
RUDERA WINES (STELLENBOSCH)
SIGNAL HILL (CAPE TOWN)
SIMUNYE (CAPE TOWN)
THE WINERY (SOMERSET WEST)

Author's choice (DM)

A selection of emerging Cape new classics

BEYERSKLOOF ● Cabernet Sauvignon Stellenbosch

BOEKENHOUTSKLOOF ● Cabernet Sauvignon Estate Franschhoek

GLEN CARLOU ● Chardonnay Reserve Paarl

HAMILTON RUSSELL VINEYARDS ● Pinot Noir Walker Bay

KANONKOP ● Paul Sauer Stellenbosch

NICO VAN DER MERWE ● Mas Nicolas Stellenbosch

RUSTENBERG ● Cabernet Sauvignon Peter Barlow Stellenbosch

SADIE FAMILY WINES ● Columella Swartland

SAXENBURG ● Shiraz Select Stellenbosch

SPICE ROUTE COMPANY ● Syrah Swartland

THELEMA ● Cabernet Sauvignon Reserve Stellenbosch

VERGELEGEN ● Vergelegen Stellenbosch

Six benchmark Pinotage

GRANGEHURST ● Pinotage Stellenbosch

KANONKOP ● Pinotage Stellenbosch

SAXENBURG ● Pinotage Private Collection Stellenbosch

SPICE ROUTE COMPANY ● Pinotage Swartland

STELLENZICHT ● Pinotage Stellenbosch

WARWICK ● Pinotage Old Bush Vines Stellenbosch

Agiorgitiko   Greek for St George and a characterful variety widely planted on the Peloponnese. The only grape variety used for Nemea which can be long-lived.

Aglianico   Late ripening, southern Italy red grape of real importance and considerable potential. Ageworthy with a noble structure, its smoky, minerally, berry-fruited character gains greater complexity and refined texture with keeping. The best wines come from Campania (Taurasi and various IGTs) and to some extent Basilicata (Aglianico del Vulture) and Puglia but don't expect greatness from the increasing amounts of inexpensive Aglianico now appearing from the same regions.

Albana   White variety responsible for mostly nondescript Albana di Romagna DOCG. Much better as a sweet wine produced from dried grapes in *passito* versions.

Albariño   Galicia's (north-west Spain) great white hope, Albariño is often compared to Viognier. It not only shares some of Viognier's perfume and succulent peachiness but also the wide disparity in quality levels. Try only a top rated example from a good producer where yields low and the winemaking expert. As Alvarinho, Portugal's best examples (sold as varietal Vinho Verdes) don't yet match the best from its northern neighbour.

Aleatico   Italian variety found in Puglia, Lazio and southern Tuscany usually vinified as a perfumed sweet red.

Alfrocheiro Preto   Portuguese variety most likely to be encountered in Dão but planted in Bairrada and further south. Best used to add colour and complexity to a blend but has also recently been produced varietally.

Alicante Bouschet   Characterful red-fleshed crossing (that claims Grenache as a parent) once heavily planted in southern France. Though more often used as a blending grape decent varietal examples are made in Portugal's Alentejo, Central Italy (especially Tuscany or Emilia) and California.

Aligoté   Decent examples of Aligoté can be found the length and breadth of Burgundy but relatively few have the verve and subtle spice (without green or hard edges) that make it interesting.

Alvarinho   see Albariño

Ansonica   see Inzolia

Antão Vaz   White portuguese variety increasingly used in the Alentejo, both varietally and in blends.

Arinto   One of Portugal's few native white grapes of substantially proven quality. Its good acidity and citrusy fruit form the basis of many of the better whites in southern Portugal.

Arneis   Piedmont's leading white grape for dry whites is starting to make an impression in California and Australia. Light, dry but rather enticing perfumed examples generally need to be drunk very young; lightly oaked versions will keep a little longer but aren't necessarily superior.

Assyrtiko   Greek white grape of good acidity and fruit with the potential for wines of good structure. Of Santorini orgins but increasingly widely planted.

Bacchus   Not a noble variety as perhaps the name deserves but a German crossing bred for high sugar levels. Some of the best examples of herbal and exotic whites are produced by English wine growers but only when the grapes are fully ripe.

Baga   The grape of Portugal's Bairrada region. Potentially a bruiser but when fully ripe from modest yielding vines it produces wines of great character if not seductive charm. Its distinctive earth, coffee, plum and berry fruit character is allied to depth and richness with age. In decline in the neighbouring Dão region where it is less suited.

Barbera   Marvellous Piedmont grape which comes in any number of styles and quality levels. The greatest acclaim comes for rich, modern oaked-aged versions but some unoaked versions can also be stunning. There are many good examples as both Barbera d'Alba and Barbera d'Asti and occasionally convincing versions from Emilia. Simple, supple, fruity, quaffing Barbera can be good too. Once important in California, this is where the next best examples can be found; Australia also makes adequate versions while potential also exists in Argentina.

Bastardo   A name that can rarely be used to describe the contents of a bottle if speaking varietally as this Portuguese grape is usually found only as minor component in a blend in Dão or for Port. One and the same as Trousseau in France's Jura.

Bical   One of the best native Portuguese varieties for dry whites though that's not saying much. Good body, aroma and acidity are possible if rarely achieved. Luis Pato's single vineyard Vinha Formal seems likely to realise the limits of what is possible. Also made sparkling.

Blaufränkisch   Important red variety in Austria's Burgenland where it is often blended with other varieties to moderate its relatively high acidity and tannin. Of minor importance in Washington State and Germany where it is known as Lemberger. One and the same as Hungary's Kékfrankos.

Boal   Madeira's Boal or Bual is one of the noble varieties giving dark coloured wines of spicy dried fruits intensity. The resulting style is typically sweeter than Verdelho but less rich if more refined than Malvasia.

Bobal   Widely planted red variety in central Spain capable, it would seem, of producing concentrated smoky, black-fruited reds. It is early days but some powerful reds, rich in fruit and extract, from unirrigated, low-yielding old vine fruit are starting to emerge (see Mustiguillo).

Bonarda   In Italy what is called Bonarda is most important in Oltrepò Pavese and Colli Piacentini (as Croatina). In the latter, it can be blend with Barbera for a characterful red, Gutturnio. Argentina's Bonarda is not related but from old vines complex, aromatic, supple reds can be produced.

Brachetto   Unusual Piedmontese variety that has obtained DOCG status in Brachetto d'Acqui. Often it is medium-dry and either *frizzante* or fully sparkling but with a wonderful, grapey perfume and flavour if drunk young and fresh from a producer like Braida.

Cabernet Franc   Parent variety of the more famous Cabernet Sauvignon it is more successful in cooler soils. Only in the Anjou and Touraine in the Loire Valley does it thrive as a varietal as despite its importance on Bordeaux's Right Bank it is almost invariably blended with Merlot and some Cabernet Sauvignon. Its importance as a component in Bordeaux style blends both at home and around the world is undeniable. Though it can emulate the flavours of its off-spring, it can miss its extra richness and depth and also show more of a raspberry-like fruit and a more leafy, herbal or even floral, component.

Cabernet Sauvignon   Grown almost everywhere, a grape of forceful and easily recognisable personality, it is much more fussy in showing at its best. Though capable of great richness, depth and structure, a lack of full ripeness in both fruit and tannin tends to detract from so many examples. A long growing season and well-drained soils are two prerequisites to producing the greatest elegance and classic telltale blackcurrant but also black cherry or blackberry flavours that mesh so well with new French oak. Though Cabernet Sauvignon dominates blends, the majority of top examples many do include a percentage of complementary varietals such as Merlot or Cabernet Franc which complement it in both flavour and structure. Many countries have identified at least one region where it really excels with the greatest riches from the Médoc, Napa Valley, Tuscany, Coonawarra and Margaret River. A significant number of world class examples have also come from Washington State, New Zealand, Chile, Argentina as well as a few from Spain and South Africa.

Canaiolo   Chiefly Tuscan variety and used to complement Sangiovese but discarded by many in favour of Merlot or Cabernet Sauvignon for their Chianti Classico. A mini revival is underway as some producers seek to produce reds of more individual character.

Cannonau   Sardinian version of Grenache, for long produced as an inexpensive quaffing red Cannonau di Sardegna. One of two committed growers are beginning to realize its true potential Rare good fortified versions are also made from late-harvested or dried grapes.

Carignan   Infamous red grape of the Languedoc-Roussillon still widely planted and often very high- yielding resulting in dilute, astringent wine. However from low yields and fully ripe fruit its different beast. Deeply coloured, robust but characterful reds are possible not only in the Midi but also occasionally in Spain (as Cariñena), Sardinia (as Carignano) and California (as Carignane).

Carmenère Old Bordeaux variety of increasing importance in Chile where much of it continues to be sold as Merlot. As they are often planted in a field blend together the disparity in ripening times further compromises the quality of fruit from high-yielding vines. Once isolated and made from well-established low-yielding vines it has excellent potential with a characterful wild berry and spice character. Also thought to be confused with other grapes in regions where plantings were established from Bordeaux cuttings in the 19th century.

Castelão Portuguese grape also still widely known as Periquita, extensively grown in the southern regions but most successful in the Palmela DOC in the Terras do Sado region.

Chardonnay Ironically the only significant wine regions where this grape is not grown are found in France. The great white grape of Burgundy has a great affinity for oak and can produce whites of marvellous texture, depth and richness but will also render a wonderful expression of its origins where yields are low. High quality grapes allied to winemaking sophistication is essential – too many examples, wherever they are made, show a clumsy winemaking fingerprint (excessive leesy, skin contact or oak flavours) or inferior fruit (under-ripe, over-ripe) or are simply unclean, acidified or lacking balance. Chardonnay forms a part of almost all top quality sparkling wines, especially Champagne. When varietal and sparkling it is known as Blanc de Blancs. Rich botrytised versions are unusual but have been made to a high standard in the Mâconnais, Austria and New Zealand.

Chasselas Relatively neutral white grape also known as Fendant in Switzerland where it assumes greater importance and produces whites of higher quality than anywhere else in the world. The best examples reflect something of the specific *terroirs* with good structure and minerality in Dézaley and Calamin. From the opposite, southern shore of Lac Léman in Savoie come the best French examples (including Crépy). Rare decent examples are also made in the Loire (Pouilly-sur-Loire) and Alsace.

Chenin Blanc High quality white grape of Touraine and Anjou in the Loire Valley. Outstanding long-lived wines ranging from dry to sweet are made and owe much to the grape's high acidity. Apple and citrus flavours within a firm, demanding texture are usually complemented by floral, honey and mineral characters with quince, peach even apricot in sweeter styles. Despite there being more extensive plantings in California and South Africa, good examples from outside the Loire remain few. Washington State and New Zealand also provide one or two. Also an important base for some good quality sparkling wines.

Ciliegiolo Difficult central Italian variety, not least, to pronounce. One of several natives (also see Colorino, Canaiolo) being revived by committed growers seeking more authentic Tuscan reds than those that rely in part or whole on foreign varieties. One or two varietal examples from old vine fruit show a captivating wild cherry character.

Cinsaut/Cinsault Characterful Rhône variety where taken seriously. Can add perfume and complexity both to southern Rhône blends and wines from the Languedoc and Corsica, especially when yields are low.

Colorino Deep coloured red grape of Central Italy and Tuscany, once used to beef up Chianti made by the *governo* technique. Mostly used along with Canaiolo to complement Sangiovese but very occasionally contributes significantly to reds of tremendous character, depth and richness, from isolated locations where the vines are of high quality.

Cortese Piedmont grape of moderate quality best known for the mostly undistinguished Gavi. A handful of producers have improved both concentration and character of their wines through lower yields; the subtle use of oak can also help. Other examples such as those from the Monferrato hills can be attractively fruity if rarely showing much depth or refinement.

Corvina Leading red variety in Italy's Veneto for Valpolicella, Amarone and Recioto della Valpolicella. Though only giving moderate colour and tannin its thickish skins help it to resist rot during the drying process or *appassimento*. The related Corvinone can bring more colour, concentration and structure to a blend.

Dolcetto   Piedmont grape capable of wonderful fruit intensity yet lively acidity and moderate tannin. Most of the best examples with a mineral or herbal streak to black cherry or black plum fruit, are unoaked and mean't to be drunk with between one and three years' age but there are ageworthy exceptions, especially those from old low-yielding vines whether in the Dogliani or Alba zones. Known as Ormeasco in Liguria.

Encruzado   Portuguese variety starting to show considerable quality in the Dão region. Subtly oaked it can show good depth, a gentle texture and a refined, perfumed, slightly exotic fruit character.

Erbaluce   Little seen Piedmont white of pronounced acidity but with attractive fruit when fully ripe and dry as Erbaluce di Caluso. Caluso Passito, from dried grapes is potentially better quality while a little sparkling wine is also made.

Falanghina   Another potential star grape from southern Italy set to rival Fiano and Greco. Though still not widely seen the number of good examples, showing impressive texture and flavour with a couple of years' age, is on the increase.

Fiano   Perfumed and flavoursome white grape from Campania from which increasing amounts of spicy, dry whites with fullish peachy, slightly nutty fruit are made. Late-harvested versions and those from botrytis affected grapes have also been successfully made.

Frappato   Fragrant red Sicilian variety that character to Cerasuolo di Vittoria reds.

Freisa   Characterful, perfumed Piedmont grape often made *frizzante* (lightly sparkling), sometimes with a little residual sugar. A handful of dry versions are excellent where its predisposition to astringency on the finish has been mastered.

Furmint   Top quality Hungarian grape giving its greatest expression as the basis of the sweet wines of the Tokaj region thanks to its high acidity, susceptibility to noble rot and refined flavours. Also occasionally made in good dry versions and used by some producers in Austria's Burgenland for sweet Ausbruch wines.

Gaglioppo   Late-ripening southern Italian red variety of chief importance in Calabria. The colour can develop quite quickly and the tannin and alcohol levels can be high. From moderate yields, wines can show impressive depth and develop a rich, chocolaty, savoury complexity.

Gamay   The grape of the Beaujolais region and well-suited to its granitic soils. Examples range from the dilute and insipid to the impressively deep and fruity. Most but not all of it is produced by semi-carbonic maceration producing a supple texture but partly compromising its cherry fruit perfume and flavour. Plantings extend into the Mâconnais to the north where it performs poorly; mercifully, some at least, is being replaced by Chardonnay. The only really significant other area where the true Gamay grape is planted is in Touraine in the Loire Valley.

Garganega   The 'good' grape of Soave capable of producing intense, sleek whites when yields are low. Even more impressive when made from late-harvested or dried grapes (for Recioto di Soave).

Garnacha   see Grenache

Gewürztraminer / Traminer   Both of these names are used to describe a remarkably aromatic distinctive grape variety that has produced good examples from around the world. This versatile grapy white is redolent in scents from the floral and musky to rose petal, lychee and spices. Styles range from the light and fresh to rich, oily textured wines and from dry to off-dry through late-harvested to sweet, botrytised wines. Weaker efforts lack definition and a certain coarseness, particularly on the finish, is only avoided in top quality examples. The greatest range of styles and highest quality come from Alsace which is followed by Italy's Alto Adige and Germany. Though fewer in number the best new world examples arguably come from New Zealand but there is good quality too in Australia, California, Oregon and Canada and in Chile's Casablanca Valley.

Grauburgunder see Pinot Gris

Graciano Mostly a minor component in Rioja this is a variety of limited planting that nonetheless adds character and complexity to Tempranillo dominated blends. Rare varietal examples highlight its intriguing perfume and suggest it has further potential.

Grechetto White variety of greatest significance in Umbria where it is used as a component in Orvieto and Colli Martani but also leading whites such as Cervaro della Sala.

Greco Or more specifically Greco di Tufo (to distinguish it from other similar names) does come originally from Greece and does well on the volcanic soils in Campania's Avellino hills in southern Italy. At its best it is attractively scented with citrus, peachy fruit and a firm texture and slightly nutty finish.

Grenache Leading grape variety in the southern Rhône where it forms the backbone wines from the leading appellations, including Châteauneuf-du-Pape and Gigondas. Quality and style vary enormously but is capable of great longevity when produced from low-yielding fruit. Grenache also forms a component of many of Languedoc-Roussillon's reds including Banyuls and Collioure near the border with Spain. As Garnacha it is the base for some of Spain's top reds in the small but dynamic region of Priorat but is also the leading variety in several other appellations in the north-east of the country. It is also a significant component in many reds from Navarra and Rioja. In Sardinia, it goes under the name of Cannonau. In Australia some of the best vines were uprooted before its quality potential was reassessed. It is now part of, often high quality, fashionable blends that usually include Shiraz and Mourvèdre.

Grenache Blanc Previously undistinguished grape particularly important in southern Rhône and Languedoc whites. Low yields and better winemaking have given it much more personality and it is sometimes made varietally.

Gros Manseng Important grape of South-West France, particularly for the production of the dry wines of Jurançon with an exotic fruit character. Also used for the sweet wines, often together with the related but finer Petit Manseng.

Grüner Veltliner From terraces above the Danube in the Wachau region in Lower Austria, this relatively unknown grape can produce remarkably good full-bodied whites. Neighbouring regions of Kremstal, Kamptal and Traisental can also produce peppery, citrus, yellow plum flavoured wines that become gently honeyed and increasingly complex with age. Its tendency to high alcohol needs to be balanced by good acidity and fruit richness. More everyday examples can be dilute and lack charm.

Hárslevelü Complementary variety to Furmint in the production of Tokaji when it adds aroma. Also makes spicy, perfumed dry whites in other parts of Hungary.

Inzolia Increasingly important white variety in Sicily for fresh dry whites with good perfume and flavour; also a component of some of the best Marsala. As a minor variety in Tuscany it is known as Ansonica.

Jaen Important component in red Dão blends and capable of good fruit intensity if relatively modest structure. Its smoky, spicy, berryish fruit has occasionally been fully expressed in one or two varietal examples. Probably the same grape as the Spain's Mencía.

Kékfrankos see Blaufränkisch

Kerner K is also for Kerner, a productive German crossing (Trollinger x Riesling) of potentially good quality. Though in decline it is still Germany's fourth most planted white variety. Mostly confined to Rheinhessen and Pfalz but also Württemberg and Mosel, often used in large volume, branded whites. Occasionally made varietally - unusually good expressions of the variety come from the Abbazia di Novacella in the south Tyrol (see North-East Italy).

Lagrein Grape found in Trentino-Alto Adige (North-East Italy) and fast becoming the most important red variety in the region. Both supple, fruity everyday reds and deep coloured, concentrated, often oak-aged, reds full of bramble, dark plum and cherry fruit, are being made in increasing numbers. It has the fruit intensity of other native North-East reds but more moderate tannin and acidity levels that suggest it has potential elsewhere too.

Lambrusco The grape behind one of Italy's most discredited wine styles. Real Lambrusco, red and sparkling but dry, refreshing and a good food match too will usually come from one of the best, localised sub-varieties such as Grasparossa, Salamino or Sorbara.

Loureiro Along with Alvarinho and Trajadura one of the principal grapes of Vinho Verde. Like Alvarinho of sufficient quality to be produced varietally for fine, scented dry whites.

Macabeo/Viura Widely used if relatively unexciting variety of greatest importance in northern Spain. Its chief manifestations are white Rioja and Cava (usually with Parellada and Xarel-lo). Also widely planted in Roussillon as Maccabéo or Maccabeu.

Malbec Essentially another of Bordeaux's rejects, the peppery, black-fruited Malbec has found favour as the major constituent of Cahors in South-West France but has become even more strongly associated with Argentina. The latter examples tend to be softer and more approachable but can want for structure but there is high quality from both sources. Good quality is also obtained from a limited amount of old vine plantings in South Australia while it is on the increase in Chile and performs well in New Zealand. It is of minor importance in the Loire Valley where it is known as Cot.

Malvasia This name covers a great many closely related varieties from Italy, Spain and Portugal. In North-East Italy Malvasia Istriana can be a characterful dry white. In Tuscany dried Malvasia grapes bring more quality when added to Trebbiano for Vin Santo while in Lazio Malvasia can rescue the whites of the Colli Albani, such as Frascati, from blandness. In the south it turns sweet when made from *passito* grapes on the volcanic island of Lipari. In Spain it can add substance to some white Rioja while in Portugal's Douro Malvasia grapes could end up in White Port or as a dry white. As Malvasia Fina one or two good varietal white Dão are made while on Madeira it is the grape responsible for the richest, sweetish style of Madeira, Malmsey.

Malvasia Nera A black version of Malvasia of considerable importance in Puglia but also found elsewhere in Italy, mostly in the south but also in Tuscany. Aromatic, its distinctive black plum fruit adds character to reds usually based on either Negroamaro, Primitivo or Sangiovese.

Marsanne At its best this is an intensely flavoured white with succulent peach and apricot fruit and often a tell-tale honeysuckle character. It is particularly important in northern Rhône whites, sometimes in partnership with Roussanne. It is also produced in Hermitage as *Vin de Paille*. It crops up again in blends in Côtes du Rhône whites (but not white Châteauneuf-du-Pape), Languedoc-Roussillon and even in Provence. It is grown too in Switzerland's Valais (as Ermitage) and makes a rare appearance (or two) in Italy. Its use in California is likely to increase while the best examples in Australia come from the Goulburn Valley in Victoria.

Mataro see Mourvèdre

Mavrodaphne Greek grape responsible for the bold, sweet reds of Pátras but also used as a blending component in dry reds.

Melon de Bourgogne The grape responsible for the many bland dry whites of Muscadet. The best examples however can be both refreshing and flavoursome, usually owed, at least in part, to ageing *sur lie*.

Mencía Likely to be a component if you're drinking a red of good fruit concentration and acidity from North-West Spain. Said to be the same as Portugal's Jaen.

Merlot There are very few significant wine producing countries where there isn't at least some Merlot, even Switzerland and Canada have plenty of it. Its home though is in Bordeaux and it can range from a few per cent to almost varietal (as in Château Pétrus). Much Merlot is lean, weedy and under-ripe. In fact few Merlot-dominated wines in fact come close to those of Bordeaux's Right Bank. Although good ripe, lush reds have been produced from Australia, New Zealand, Chile, Argentina, South Africa, California, Washington State and Italy, very few of these combine that richness with the classic berry plumminess and fruitcake, spice, fig or clove character that make it so enticing. Tuscany and California do it most often but in Chile (where it is mixed up with Carmenère) and elsewhere, great examples are the exception.

Mondeuse   Characterful French grape from Savoie. High in acidity but capable of intense beetroot, plum and cherry flavours and an attractive floral scent. Though a localised variety, one producer (Cottanera) has planted it at altitude in Sicily. It may be one and the same as Fruili's Refosco.

Monastrell   see Mourvèdre

Monica   Sardinian variety that has been in decline - mostly transformed into simple fruity everyday reds.

Montepulciano   Gutsy peppery red variety that dominates the adriatic seaboard in central Italy. Most examples are fruity with good extract and colour; a mere handful develop the breadth, refinement and complexity of which it is also capable.

Moscatel   Muscat from Spain or Portugal. Mostly of the Muscat of Alexandria form, styles range from dry and aromatic to sweet, often fortified (as with Moscatel de Setúbal). Moscatel de Grano Menudo is the superior Muscat Blanc à Petit Grains form. Also see Muscat

Moscato   see Muscat

Moschofilero   Decent Greek pink-hued grape variety used increasingly in dry white blends. Muscat like it adds spice and aroma.

Mourvèdre   High quality grape found in southern France at the very limits of ripening. It is most important incarnation is as powerful, tannic and ageworthy Bandol but some in Châteauneuf-du-Pape use it for blending as do producers in the Languedoc-Roussillon. In Spain (as Monastrell) it has been rather neglected in terms of producing high quality but a handful of producers in Jumilla and elsewhere are starting to realize its potential there. In Australia and California it is sometimes called Mataro but in both places it can also excel both varietally and in blends.

Müller Thurgau   Although it once formed the major part of white wine production in New Zealand and still yields generously for basic plonk in Germany, this German crossing has few admirers. It lacks the structure and class of one of its parents (Riesling) but still makes attractive wine in good hands - selected producers in the Alto Adige (North-East Italy) take it as seriously as any.

Muscadelle   Relatively unsung grape of Bordeaux where it is used sparingly in sweet wines (including Sauternes) and in some of the dry whites. Its true potential however, where it can achieve extraordinary complexity (as Tokay), is seen in Victoria, Australia - mostly in and around Rutherglen in the North-East of the state.

Muscadet   see Melon de Bourgogne

Muscat   There is a whole family of Muscat grapes and it comes in many guises however there three principal grapes: Muscat Blanc à Petits Grains, Muscat of Alexandria and Muscat Ottonel. It can be dry, medium-dry or sweet – whether from dried grapes or fortified or a combination of the two. It is also made sparkling. What all the best examples have in common is the intense, heady grapiness – that taste of the grape itself. Only occasionally is it a wine for ageing. Alsace makes it both dry and intensely sweet, in southern France there are the *Vins Doux Naturel* of Beaumes de Venises and Rivesaltes (amongst others). Spain makes light sweet versions of Moscatel while Portugal has the sweet fortified Moscatel de Setúbal. In Italy there's Asti or the better Moscato d'Asti and there's also yellow and pink forms of it (Moscato Giallo and Moscato Rosa) in the North-East – usually made off-dry or medium-sweet. Off-shore from Sicily the grapes Zibibbo are dried for raisiny, apricotty Passito di Pantelleria. In Germany (called Muskateller) it ranges from dry to sweet and Austria's best examples are also sweet. Gelber Muskateller is for the yellow/gold-skinned variant, Roter Muskateller or the red-skinned version. In Greece, Samos Muscat is produced. In North-East Victoria the intense raisiny Rutherglen Muscat is produced while in the US dry, medium-dry and sweet examples are produced by a few (but including Black Muscat and Orange Muscat). From South Africa comes the famed rich, sweet Vin de Constance. In fact there seemly no end to it.

Muskateller   see Muscat

Nebbiolo   The classic variety of Piedmont that remains almost exclusively the source of high quality examples of the grape. Capable of exquisite aroma and flavour its youthful austerity and tannin, while less formidable than in the past, can still present a challenge to some palates. Its dark raspberry, cherry or blackberry fruit, herb and floral aromas take on increasing complexity with age and the best examples give a wonderful expression of their *terroir*. Oak needs to be used with care in order not to overwhelm its unique perfumes and flavour. Lighter, fragrant but fruity examples of the grape can be a bit hit and miss, often being produced from less good sites. The only source of Nebbiolo-based wines in any significant quantity outside Piedmont is as Valtellina Superiore in Lombardy where it is called Chiavennasca.

Négrette   Grape of South-West France of greatest importance in Côtes du Frontonnais where it forms the major part of the blend. It gives supple, perfumed berryish wines with a slightly wild edge.

Negroamaro   For long the basis of many of the often rustic, raisiny reds from Puglia's Salento peninsula in southern Italy including Salice Salentino. Its dark, bitter flavours are not to everyone's taste but are sometimes toned down by other varieties such as Malvasia Nera. Subject to better winemaking it has recently shown much greater potential including some exciting varietal examples.

Nerello Mascalese   Once seen only as a high-yielding blending variety, it is now emerging as a complementary grape to the increasingly highly-regarded Nero d'Avola. From its origins on volcanic soils around the slopes of Mount Etna, it can show good perfume and texture. It also often blended with the related Nerello Cappuccio.

Nero d'Avola   Widely planted in Sicily and currently seen as the island's best native red variety. It produces rich, intense, deep-coloured reds with a peppery black-fruited character and adding more depth and complexity with age. Is said to be related to Syrah.

Neuburger   Unsung Austrian grape that is a crossing of Weissburgunder (Pinot Blanc) and Silvaner. Can form an important component of both sweet (often high quality) and dry wines in Burgenland.

Nielluccio   Leading black grape on the island of Corsica shown to be identical to Sangiovese though seems a more rugged variety from tasting evidence. Often blended with Sciacarello.

Palamino (Fino)   The humble grape that dominates the chalky soils of Jerez is responsible for the diverse, often extraordinary wines that result from the elaboration of Sherry. When vinified as a dry white it is quite ordinary.

Pedro Ximenez   Better known as simply PX, this grape - used for a dark, sweet, treacly Sherry is grown mostly in Montilla-Moriles and also used for Málaga.

Petit Manseng   Quality grape producing sometimes exquisite dry and sweet wines of Jurançon in South-West France. Increasingly used by growers in the Languedoc for its exotic, floral and spicy character that is supported by good acidity. Also gaining a foothold in California.

Petit Verdot   Sometimes an important minor component in Bordeaux, especially the Médoc but increasingly too in similar blends made in other regions where Cabernet Sauvignon is successful. Late ripening, it can show more than hint of violet in aroma as well as intense blackberry fruit. Varietal examples are rare.

Petite Arvine   Of greatest significance in Switzerland's Valais, fine if demanding minerally whites are produced in a range of styles from dry to sweet. Also produced in Italy's Valle d'Aosta.

Petite Sirah   The name given to Durif in California which produces powerful, robust tannic varietal wines with dense spicy, brambly fruit. Also used to add complexity to some leading examples of Zinfandel.

Picolit   White grape in Friuli (North-East Italy) from which are produced stylish, moderately sweet whites with dried peach, pear and floral characters. Its individuality and elegance are often dismissed by those expecting something richer and more powerful.

Piedirosso   A grape variety probably used by the Romans and undergoing something of a revival in Campania's current rebirth. It has good acidity and a dark wild fruit character but is mostly used in blends, often complementing Aglianico.

Pigato   For wines from Pigato, visit Liguria in North-East Italy. Sold under the Riviera di Ligure di Ponente DOC, the best show a terse minerality and contrast with Vermentino from the region.

Pignolo   Previously obscure Friulian variety capable of showing an impressive black-fruited richness and the vibrant acidity typical of reds from native varieties in North-East Italy.

Pinot Bianco   see Pinot Blanc

Pinot Blanc   Variety most associated with Alsace and Italy's Alto Adige and Friuli. In Alsace old low yielding vines give it good character though is often blended with the delightfully scented Auxerrois which can make the better wine. It is also the basis of most Crémant d'Alsace. The Italians take it as seriously as anyone and produce some fine (both oaked and unoaked) whites with a cream and walnuts character. German examples can show good intensity but can be spoilt by a lack of balance or too much oak. Decent examples have also been produced in California, Oregon and Canada.

Pinot Grigio   see Pinot Gris

Pinot Gris   Excellent white grape most associated with Alsace where it produces distinctively flavoured whites of intense spice, pear and quince flavours. Late-harvested it takes on an almost exotic, honeyed richness and nobly-rotted *Sélection des Grains Nobles* can be superb. In Germany as Grauburgunder or Ruländer good examples are made in warmer regions. Beyond simple Italian Pinot Grigio, there are some fine concentrated, delicately creamy examples from Friuli and Alto Adige. Oregon has made something of a speciality of it to complement its Pinot Noir while despite its proven potential in New Zealand it has only recently captured the imagination of a wider number of wine producers. Good examples are also made in Victoria and Canada.

Pinot Meunier   Very important component in most Champagne blends if rarely used for anything else. Early ripening and as a wine, early developing, it complements both Chardonnay and Pinot Noir. While ignored by many New World producers of premium sparkling wines, some do have significant plantings of the variety.

Pinot Noir   Success with Pinot Noir beyond Burgundy has been slow coming but there are now many regions in the world at least emulating the fabulous flavour complexity if not the structure and supreme texture of the top Burgundies. Flavours include cherry, raspberry, strawberry but can also include sappy, undergrowth characters or become more gamey in response to both origin and wine making. The expressions of *terroir* and differing winemaking interpretations in Burgundy are almost endless. Outside of Burgundy those regions or countries emerging with the greatest potential for Pinot Noir are California, Oregon, New Zealand, Tasmania but also cool parts of Victoria, South Australia and Western Australia. Success in Italy, Germany, Austria, Chile and South Africa is considerably more limited yet further potential exists. Pinot Noir is also very important as a component of most of the world's best sparkling wines.

Pinotage   Characterful yet tainted South African variety due to its tendency to produce unattractive paint-like aromas (isoamyl acetate). A crossing of Cinsaut and Pinot Noir, from old bush vines in particular it can produce deep, concentrated reds with spicy, plum and berry fruit flavours uncompromised by any volatile esters. The occasional adequate example is produced in New Zealand.

Primitivo   DNA fingerprinted as one and the same as Zinfandel, though debate continues about where in Europe they originated from. As Primitivo it is increasingly important in southern Italy, particularly in Puglia where old *alberello*-trained vines produce robust, characterful reds with moderate ageing potential.

Prosecco   The grape with the potential for a delightful undemanding sparkling wine of the same name from Italy's Veneto. Pretention or over-elaboration as well as anything more than a smidgen of residual sugar can distort its exuberant, direct freshness.

Refosco (dal Peduncolo Rosso)   Somewhat derided grape but the 'red-stemmed' version has the potential for quality. Only occasionally encountered outside its native Friuli in North-East Italy, poorer examples are characterised by harsh tannins and high acidity but more care in the vineyard is resulting in high quality fruit with a brambly character. Produced both as part of a blend and varietally, good examples are on the increase. It may be related to Mondeuse.

Ribolla   Ribolla Gialla, as it is often called, produces characterful herb-scented dry whites in its native Friuli in North-East Italy.

Rieslaner   High quality late-ripening crossing of Riesling and Silvaner. Tiny amounts of outstanding sweet wines are produced in Germany's Pfalz and Baden regions when the grapes are fully ripe.

Riesling   This outstanding white grape has an almost infinite number of expressions. Styles vary from bone dry to intensely sweet, from low alcohol to powerful and full-bodied. Its impressive range of flavours including apple, citrus, peach and apricot, are complemented by a minerality that subtle differences of place or *terroir* bring. It is nearly almost made varietally and aged in stainless steel or large old wood. Obtaining full ripeness and the right balance between sugar and acidity is crucial to quality. The most delicate, exquisite Riesling comes from Germany though there are many different expressions there while Alsace provides the fullest, most powerful examples. Austria's Wachau is closer to this style than Germany but with purity and minerality of its own. Australia also produces high quality Riesling, showing different expressions from Western Australia to the Clare, Eden Valley and Tasmania. The considerable potential for Riesling in New Zealand has yet to be fully realised. Good examples also come from the US; as much in Washington State and the Fingers Lakes region of New York State as California or Oregon. Some examples of Canadian Icewine are based on Riesling.

Rossese   Mostly confined to basic rendings of little seen Ligurian DOC Rossese di Dolceaqua (Giuncheo's oak-aged version is good) but can form a part of other decent reds from the region.

Roussette   Fine white grape found in Savoie in eastern France where it is also known as Altesse. The best wines with good structure and weight have a mineral, herb and citrus intensity as well as more exotic nuances when produced from low yielding vines on the best steep slopes.

Roussanne   High quality white grape that is difficult to grow. Roussanne's impressive texture and depth can be seen in wines from both the northern and southern Rhône, sometimes on its own but other times complementing Marsanne. It is also favoured by some of the leading quality producers in Languedoc-Roussillon and Provence, if mostly in blends. Also the grape used for fine perfumed Chignin-Bergeron whites in Savoie. Outside France, California and Australia have a few high quality whites based, at least partly, on Roussanne.

Rülander   see Pinot Gris

Sagrantino   Central Italian variety localized at Montefalco in Umbria. Potentially rich in extract tannin and with high acidity its true potential as an outstanding dry red has been realized by a single producer (Caprai) but others make increasingly good examples. Rarer are good sweet *passito* versions from dried grapes.

Sangiovese   The leading variety in Italy and the grape that dominates production in Tuscany. All the classic Tuscan appellations are based on it and the improvement in quality is on-going as the revolution in winemaking is being followed by one in the vineyard. Styles range from the light and fruity to oaky, powerful and tannic but the best are pure, refined and individual. It is made to a very high standard both varietally and in blends with Cabernet Sauvignon and Merlot yet some of the most distinctive expressions include a small percentage of minor native varieties such as Canaiolo or Colorino. The most important area for its production outside Tuscany is Romagna but it also plays an important role in Umbria. Good if not great examples have been produced in California – both varietally or in blends with Cabernet or other varieties. One or two adequate examples are made i

Australia though most are little more than attractive everyday reds.

St-Laurent Pinot Noir like Austrian grape held in high regard locally. Only the very best examples, however show a texture and complexity that suggests top Pinot Noir or Burgundy.

Sauvignon Blanc Aromatic white grape capable of a wide range of expression and quality. The most structured and ageworthy examples come from France whether the classic mineral-laced wines of Sancerre and Pouilly-Fumé (now richer and riper than previously) or the more oak-influenced, peachy examples from Bordeaux (some blended with Sémillon) that will age for more than a decade. The most overt fruit expression is seen in examples from Marlborough in New Zealand but most of these need to be drunk within a year of the vintage. Bright gooseberryish Sauvignon for immediate drinking is also made in Chile's Casablanca Valley and good vibrant, nettly Sauvignon Blanc from South Africa is on the increase. Some of the best Australian examples of Sauvignon Blanc have very ripe gooseberry fruit with a hint of tropical flavours; it is also sometimes blended with Sémillon. California offers both fresh, more herbaceous examples and riper ,melon and fig versions capable of some age. North-East Italy provides high quality Sauvignon with good structure but more restraint. Reasonable examples come from Spain and Austria too though the latter are usually best when unoaked. Sauvignon Blanc is also important in combination with Sémillon for Bordeaux's sweet wines.

Savagnin A top quality grape used in the production of Vin Jaune, the speciality of the Jura, as well as other dry whites from the region.

Scheurebe German crossing that can produce intensely flavoured whites from Spätlese levels and higher. Balance and ripeness are essential to rich and succulent wines with a piercing blackcurrant, grapefruit or peach character. Known as Samling 88 in Austria.

Schiava One as the same as Vernatsch and Trollinger (in Germany's Württemberg). Good light, attractive reds as Alto Adige DOC varietals or under the subzone of Santa Maddalena.

Schioppettino Native of Italy's Friuli, this obscure grape with high acidity but a spicy, wild berry fruit intensity, has recently been treated seriously by one or two dedicated producers.

Sémillon Great Sémillon comes from either of two sources: France or Australia. In Bordeaux Sémillon is made both dry, in usually oak-aged blends with Sauvignon Blanc (as it is in Bergerac), or sweet where it is typically the dominant component in all its great sweet wines. Botrytis enrichment is the key to the power, flavour richness and complexity of the best long-lived Sauternes and Barsac. Lesser appellations can also make attractive sweet wines and some good examples come from neighbouring Monbazillac. The classic Australian Sémillon comes from the Hunter Valley. Though increasing rare, unoaked wines become remarkably toasty and honeyed with a decades' age or more. Oaked-aged examples are made to give more immediate pleasure; those from the Margaret River are usually combined with Sauvignon Blanc. Relatively few rich, sweet Australian examples are also made. New Zealand and South Africa have had some success with dry examples of the grape.

Sercial One of Madeira's noble varieties that translates into the driest palest style. Its usually high voltage acidity can prove too much for some palates but the wines can be superb (and very ageworthy) when the balance is right.

Seyval Blanc Decent quality hybrid grape that manages to get ripe in the coolest of winemaking countries. Can show good weight and an attractively herbal, appley, citrusy freshness. The best examples come from England, Canada and the eastern US.

Shiraz Australian name for the French grape Syrah but also favoured by some South African producers. Australia produces a galaxy of styles from the powerful, American-oaked blockbuster to more elegant, more Rhône-like expressions aged in French oak. Every region produces a different camp whether Hunter Valley, Clare, Barossa, Eden Valley, McLaren Vale, Grampians, Heathcote, Great Southern or one of many other exciting areas to which is added the interpretation and quality achieved by individual producers. Sparkling Shiraz is an Australian speciality and not as frightening as it sounds though a tannic finish can mar some flavousome examples. South Africa also has an increasing number of high quality examples. Also see Syrah.

Silvaner/Sylvaner   The majority of good Silvaner comes from Germany's Franken region while that given the French spelling, Sylvaner, comes from Alsace. A relatively neutral grape it can take on real richness and and a smoky, spicy flavour in the latter (especially when produced from old vines) while the German examples can show more of a minerally, nuanced subtlety – an intriguing earthy, appley character. Occasional good examples are produced in most other German regions but also in Italy's Alto Adige and (as Johannisberg) in Switzerland's Valais.

Spätburgunder   see Pinot Noir

Syrah   The home of Syrah is in the northern Rhône where a range of appellations give the most classic expression to one of the most exciting red grapes in the world. Those showing the most aromatic, smoky, white pepper and herbs expression come from Côte Rôtie (where they often include a little Viognier); broader, more powerful, minerally versions come from the hill of Hermitage. Many good examples also come from the surrounding appellations of Crozes-Hermitage, Cornas and Saint-Joseph. Syrah is also made varietally in the southern Rhône but more often is used to complement Grenache. As well as being important in Provence many of the best wines from the Languedoc-Roussillon are either based on it or include a significant percentage. Some very good varietal Syrah also comes from Italy where it is also added in small amounts to an increasing number of reds. Spain and Portugal also have good quality interpretations of the grape but Australia apart (also see Shiraz) the best Syrah outside of France comes from the US, primarily California but also Washington State. A few good examples of Syrah come from Chile and Argentina.

Tannat   Vine from France's basque country, most important in Madiran where its powerful tannins need to be softened. Also an important component in other reds from this south-west corner of France – such as Irouléguy. Widely grown too in Uruguay but its few decent quality examples have yet to show real consistency.

Teroldego   Extremely localised red grape grown on the gravelly soils of the Campo Rotaliano in Italy's Trentino region. From low yields it produces an impressive smoky, minerally black-fruited red capable of long ageing. Seems certain to have potential elsewhere.

Tempranillo   Spain's leading red grape and a first class one though that has not always been apparent going by the quality from the most famous appellation based on it – Rioja. The grapes need to be concentrated and retain acidity, something more often achieved in Ribera del Duero (as Tinto Fino) where the best powerful blackberry and black plum reds are among Spain's very best. Tempranillo is also important in many other appellations including Toro (as Tinta de Toro) and Costers del Segre (as Ull de Llebre) — both varietally or as blends. As Tinta Roriz it is extremely important both in the production of Port but also as a component in Douro where its splendid aromatic complexity is sometimes fully realised. It is also important both varietally and in blends in several other Portuguese regions where there has recently been a massive increase in planting. In Alentejo in southern Portugal (as Aragonês) it is usually combined with Trincadeira and can develop into deep, savoury reds with age. Tempranillo also has potential in Australia and Argentina.

Tinta Amarela   Another of the more significant and interesting varieties of the Douro. Though productive it can be difficult to maximise its quality and is consequently disliked by some growers. Also appears in some blends from the Dão and Alentejo.

Tinta Barroca   Important component of much Port and red Douro blends giving good colour, perfume and a certain earthiness usually from cooler slopes (in order to prevent raisining). Also one of the leading grapes for fortified styles (and some gutsy table wines) in South Africa.

Tinta Negra Mole   All but the best Madeira tends to be based on this one, prolific grape variety. Only those Madeira that state one of the noble varieties on the label now come from them. Good Madeira however can be produced from Tinta Negra Mole if yields are kept down and high standards are maintained.

Tinta Roriz/Aragonês   see Tempranillo

Tinto Cão   Little planted yet one of the important quality grapes of the Douro (one of the five most recommended) undergoing a small revival due to its perceived quality. Low-yielding and difficult to manage successfully it is prized for its ability to age and the greater class that comes with it.

Tocai Friulano   Found in North-East Italy, this grape produces refined dry whites with herb, citrus and nectarine character. It is difficult to believe but it is said to be related to the poor quality Sauvignonasse (Sauvignon Vert) variety still widely grown in Chile and for long passed off as Sauvignon Blanc.

Touriga Franca   The backbone of much Port and usually blended with Tinta Roriz and Touriga Nacional amongst others. Also important in table wines from the Douro. It has even been made varietally but a profusion of such examples seems unlikely as it usually lacks the definition and distinction of Touriga Nacional and the potential stylish complexity of Tinta Roriz. If sourced from old vines, however, it can show great class and complexity. Previously known as Touriga Francesa.

Touriga Nacional   The most fashionable grape in Portugal's Douro. Increasingly made varietally both in the Douro and most other Portuguese regions. An integral part of most Port blends but often in much smaller percentages than is generally perceived. It is characterised by its deep colour, floral even violet aromas and dark damson plum, mulberry or blackberry fruit and a dash of pepper. Though capable of producing deep, fleshy varietal reds it is usually better complemented by Tinta Roriz, Touriga Franca and other grapes (as it is when made as port).

Trincadeira   Important southern Portuguese grape. It doesn't like rain and needs to be fully ripe – its spicy, blackberry character forms a vital part of most Alentejo red blends.

Uva di Troia   Potentially high quality variety of Puglia, particularly around Castel del Monte. Its intriguing complexity and ageing potential together with the current revival in Puglian viticulture should ensure it becomes better known.

Verdejo   Spanish variety of greatest importance in Rueda where attractive herbal scented whites are produced. The best examples have decent structure and some ability to age. More than holds its own against Sauvignon and Viura and also found in Toro and Cigales

Verdelho   Another of the noble varieties of Madeira that arguably produces the best style of all. A lightly honeyed and preserved citrus character togther with its vibrancy, refinement and general versatility secure its appeal. Known in the Douro as Gouveio, a component of Niepoort's fine dry white Redoma. There are significant plantings in Australia for often very attractive relatively inexpensive dry whites.

Verdicchio   Leading variety in Italy's Marche region on the Adriatic coast. Made both oaked and unoaked it can produce moderately ageworthy whites of good texture and depth if only moderate flavour.

Vermentino   Lemony, herb-scented Italian variety that shows at its best on the Tuscan coast and in the north of Sardinia. The best are extremely stylish and a delight to drink young if only rarely showing more depth or weight.

Vernaccia   Refers to any number of different unrelated grapes in Italy. The Vernaccia of San Gimignano is dry, with some character and style in the best examples.

Verduzzo   Verduzzo Friulano, widely grown in North-East Italy, can be made into a refined sweet wine when late-harvested or from dried grapes. One small zone, Ramandolo, has recently been granted DOCG status.

Vespaiolo   Named for the *vespe* (wasps) drawn to its sweet grapes in the autumn, this white grape is responsible for the late-harvested and passito style sweet whites of one famous producer (Maculan) in Italy's Veneto. It also produces attractive dry whites.

Viognier There is no other Viognier quite like the best Condrieu (in the northern Rhône). From this small appellation the wine is opulent, lush and superbly aromatic – rich in apricot and peach with floral, blossom, honeysuckle and spice. Most are dry and best drunk young though a few age quite well, especially when they have acquired an enhanced structure from delicate oak treatment. One or two examples are made from late-harvested grapes. Viognier has become increasingly important in the southern Rhône, Languedoc-Roussillon and Provence, sometimes made varietally but as often injecting some perfume and fruit into a blend. There's a little in Italy, Austria and Greece. In California and Australia there are a fair number of good examples but only handful of these have the concentration and balance to suffice as a substitute for Condrieu.

Viura see Macabeo

Weissburgunder see Pinot Blanc

Welschriesling White grape with a poor reputation due the nasty whites produced from it in central and eastern Europe. However in Austria's Burgenland it is an important component in many of the best sweet whites. Known as Riesling Italico in North-East Italy.

Xynomavro The 'acid black' Greek grape important in the production of Naoussa and Goumenissa and for dark, slightly rasping if soft centred reds in northern Greece generally.

Zibibbo A form of Muscat of Alexandria grown on the windswept volcanic isle of Pantelleria between the coasts of Sicily and Tunisia for the increasingly popular Moscato di Pantelleria and Passito di Pantelleria sweet wines - the best have a rich apricotty succulence. Also see Muscat

Zinfandel The grape California made its own. From a rich resource of old free-standing vines, rich, powerful and concentrated wines are produced – most typically full of peppery, blackberry fruit and sometimes a riper raisiny, pruny character. Great examples come from Dry Creek, Russian River, Sonoma Valley, even Napa but also the Sierra Foothills and the Central Coast. It also grown successfully in Arizona and Washington State and there's also a little Zinfandel in New Zealand, Australia, Chile and South Africa. Also see Primitivo.

Zweigelt Austrian grape produced from a crossing of St. Laurent and Blaufränkisch. Widely planted, most examples are rather ordinary but as well as one or two decent varietal examples, it also contributes to some leading blended Austrian reds.

A

AC Appellation Controlée is the top category of French wine regulations and guarantees origin, grape varieties and style.

Acidification Addition of acid to must or wine if the wine has either naturally low acidity or is from a particularly warm grown climate. Usually in the form of tartaric acid.

Alberello Free standing bush vines, common in southern Italy.

Alleinbesitz German for sole ownership of a vineyard site, equivalent of (Burgundian) monopole.

Assemblage This is the final blend of a wine prior to its bottling. Many fine wines are assembled from different components after ageing. This process will determine the final selection for wines such as those from top Bordeaux Châteaux.

Autolysis Enzymatic process in sparkling wine whereby dead yeast cells add increased flavour to wine. The longer the period the richer and more complex the characteristic becomes. Sparkling wines with less than 18 months on their yeast sediment will have little or no autolysis character.

B

Bâtonnage Stirring of a wines fine lees to provide additional flavour and texture. Commonplace among top white Burgundies and other premium barrel fermented whites and also now lesser whites as well. Lees also need stirring to provide limited aeration and to avoid the development of off smelling sulphides.

Barriques The most well-known barrel type of 225 litre capacity. The Burgundian Pièce is fractionally larger with thicker staves than the classic Bordeaux barrique.

Biodynamic Method of organic farming that seeks to promote the natural balance of the land. This includes both soil and plants. Natural treatments are used to protect the vineyard and applications carried out in line with lunar and planetary activity. Many first class wine producers now farm biodynamically.

Bocksbeutel Squat, flattened flask-shaped bottle used in Germany's Franken region.

Botte/Botti Large wooden vessels used for ageing wines in Italy. There will be no oak influence on flavour and the containers are often of substantial size. Foudres in France provide similar conditions.

Botrytis Botrytis or Botrytis Cinerea is a fungal infection of the vine which is particularly harmful to red grapes. In certain unique conditions though it provides for the development of Noble Rot in areas such as Sauternes, the Mosel and the Loire Valleys Coteaux du Layon. In late warm harvests with early morning humidity and sunny days the grapes will dehydrate concentrating their sugar and flavour. Wines produced from such grapes have a uniquely intense, peachy character.

Botrytised Wine produced from grapes effected by noble rot.

C

Canopy Management Vineyard management techniques designed to improve yield and quality as well as minimizing risk of vine disease. Utilises a number of trellising/training systems to better expose the vines foliage and fruit to sunlight, resulting in improved photosynthesis and grape ripening.

Carbonic maceration Method used prior to conventional fermentation of red wine whereby colour rather than tannin is extracted. This occurs during a limited fermentation which takes place within grapes kept in anaerobic conditions. The berries will gradually split and fermentation will proceed as normal. Red winemaking particularly of Pinot Noir but also other varieties may involve using whole uncrushed grape bunches and partial carbonic maceration will occur. Greater colour and flavour complexity can be achieved. The flavours are forward and vibrant often resembling bubble gum and can have a hint of green pepper from the grape stems.The process has long been used in Beaujolais but increasingly elsewhere.

Canteiro Term that refers to the supports given to casks of Madeira where they are stored to be heated solely by natural means (without recourse to estufagem) -refers to this system of ageing generally.

Cépage French term for grape variety.

Cépage ameliorateurs This means an improving variety. The term has been widely used in Languedoc-Roussillon where there have been increasing amounts of Syrah, Grenache and Mourvedre planted in addition to the widely distributed Carignan.

Champagne method Method for the production of sparkling wine originating in Champagne. A secondary fermentation takes place in bottle and the wine is left on the resulting yeast lees.The finest sparkling wine is all made in this way.

Chaptalisation The addition of sugar to grape must to increase its alcoholic strength. If added during fermentation has the added effect of prolonging the process. Some winemakers feel this can add complexity.

Clonal Selection see Clones

Clones Vines reproduced by taking cuttings of original plants. Vines reproduced by clonal selection Vines reproduced by taking cuttings of original plants. Vines reproduced by clonal selection provide for uniformity of yield and flavour but wines produced from whole vineyards of the same clone can lack complexity. Many fine winegrowers instead use mass selection (see Sélection Massale) establishing vineyards from a range of original vinecuttings.

Cold maceration Period prior to fermentation where crushed red grapes are kept in solution with the juice at a cool temperature to extract both colour and primary fruit flavours.

Cold soaking See Cold maceration

Commerciante Italian Broker or Merchant

Cork taint See TCA

Coulure Incomplete fruit set after flowering caused by cool or wet conditions. Some fruit loss can be positive to quality.

Crossing The result of a cross between two different grape varieties of the same vine species, almost always Vinifera. While some crossings have been commercially and qualitatively successful they rarely approach the best of what nature has produced (i.e all the most highly regarded varieties).

Cru Classé (CC) Classification of Bordeaux wines. Those from the Médoc (from 1er to 5ème Cru Classé/ first to fifth growth) and Barsac/Sauternes (1er or 2ème Cru Classé/ first and second growths) are covered by a famous classification of 1855. Graves (1959) and Saint-Émilion (Grand Cru Classé or Premier Grand Cru Classé) are also classified, the latter is now subject to revision every ten years (the last in 1996).

Cryo-Extraction Process used during sweet wine production where a must is frozen in order to concentrate the wine. Used in particular in Sauternes in poorer vintages with low botrytis levels. (also see Must Concentration).

Cuvaison This is the period during red wine vinification where the grape skins and other solid matter are kept in solution in the grape juice and then finished wine. This may include a period cold maceration to extract more colour, followed by fermentation and in some cases continued contact post-fermentation to round the wines tannins and provide greater harmony.

Cuve French term for a wine vat or tank. Can be used for fermentation or storage/ageing and is made from wood, stainless steel or concrete.

D

Débourbage Period where white grape juice or wine is left in order for solid matter to settle. Lighter aromatic and fruity whites will require all solids settling whereas a top white Burgundy or Chardonnay is more likely to be vinified from only partially settled must. Straightforward commercial whites may also be fined and even filtered as well prior to fermentation.

Demi-muid A wooden barrel of, generally 600 litre capacity. Although sometimes used to refer to smaller sizes they are always considerably larger than a barrique. (also see Tonneaux)

De-stemmed Most wine must is crushed and de-stemmed prior to fermentation. Some whites however, particularly Chardonnay may be whole bunch pressed and reds may include whole bunches added to the fermentation vat. Wine produced by carbonic maceration will also retain its stems. Traditionally made reds may also be vinified with some of their stems in order to add additional tannin and structure. In the case of the latter aggressive green tannins can be extracted if the stems as well as the grapes are not fully ripe.

DO Denominación de Origen is Spain's main regulatory category which defines both origin and methods of production. It is not however it the highest – Priorat and Rioja have DOC status.

DOC The Italian Denominazione di Origine Controllata is the main category for that country's protection of wine names and styles. Regulations cover origin, grape varieties and both the type and length of ageing permitted. Many have been revised or at least modified in response to progress to higher quality but there is much debate as to how best protect tradition while accomodating those committed to higher quality. There are well over 300 and many of these include sub-categories. While some DOCs boast numerous quality wines, others fail to deliver even a single premium wine. Also see DOCG. In Portugal Denominação de Origem Controlada is the highest regulated category recently extended to include broad regional areas (with sub-zones) to make for easier identification as Portuguese wines increase in popularity.

DOCG The top level of Italian wine appellations, Denominazione di Origine Controllata e Garantita includes a guarantee of origin and stipulates grape varieties but like the French AC it does not ensure top quality.

Dosage Sparkling wine produced from the Champagne method will be topped up after disgorging with a mix of wine and sugar and this dosage determines the style and sweetness of the final wine.

E

Einzellage Individual vineyard site usually preceded by a village name on a label. While providing better definition of a wines origins than a grosslage name there is no classification system that differentiates the best sites from inferior ones. However a classification system is currently being promoted (see Grosses Gewächs).

Élevage The handling of wine from fermentation to bottling.

En Primeur Sale of wine while still in barrel. Commonplace now in Bordeaux and becoming so in Burgundy and other regions.

Enology The science of winemaking.

Enologist A winemaker.

Erste Lage The term used in the Mosel for the first-rate vineyard sites that equate to Grosses Gewächs.

Erstes Gewächs The top tier of the VDP sponsored classification system of top vineyard sites as used in the Rheingau (also see Grosses Gewächs)

Estufagem The process of heating wine (in hot stores or estufa) in the production of Madeira, imulating the sea voyages across the tropics that gave rise to the style.

Extraction Process where tannins, colour and other matter is extracted during Maceration. (also see Cuvaison).

F

Field blend Wine produced from vineyards planted to a mix of grape varieties. The practice is increasingly rare.

Filtration The removal of solid particles by means of a filter prior to bottling. While it saves the time required for a natural settling it may also rob a wine of flavour and character. Where the wine is healthy both filtration and fining (see below) have proved to be unnecessary.

Fining Process used to clarify grape juice or wine by removing the smallest (soluble) microscopic particles which attach themselves to the fining agents added. Great care should be used to avoid stripping the must or wine of flavour.

Flor The thin yeast film found on dry Fino and Manzanilla sherries after fermentation. It is unstable and dissolves when exposed to high alcohol. Amontillado sherries will have started life as Finos but will have been unable to sustain their Flor cover. The salty taste it provides is unique.

Foudres French term for large wooden vats used to age wine in.

G

GI Geographical Indications is the slowly evolving Australian delimitation of its wine regions and is split into four levels. The broadest is the political boundary of 'state' (for example, South Australia), followed by 'zones' (Mount Lofty Ranges) which split the state into smaller parts and give some coherency to a group of often already well-established 'regions' (Adelaide Hills, Clare Valley). More definition within both established or new regions is made possible by the granting of subregions (Lenswood and Piccadilly in the Adelaide Hills).

Grand cru French wine classification. In Burgundy and Alsace this refers to specific vineyard sites. In Champagne to villages with vineyards of the best potential. For Bordeaux see Cru Classé.

Grand Vin Refers to a producers top wine. Commonly used in Bordeaux.

Green harvesting Crop thinning by cutting down the number of grape bunches in order to promote ripening and reduce yields. There will be a greater impact on yield and fruit quality if this is done after veraison (when the berries change colour). Popular among some growers, others maintain a well balanced vineyard with sufficient winter pruning produces the best results.

Grosses Gewächs German system of classification being promoted by the VDP, a consortium of leading estates. The term Grosses Gewächs is used in regions other than the Mosel (see Erste Lage) and Rheingau (see Erstes Gewächs).

Grosslage Broad grouping of vineyards in Germany, often permits the inclusion of grapes from inferior plots in a blend.

Guyot Old and very well established French vine training system. One or two fruiting canes are trained along wires with the new seasons shoots trained above on a second wire.

H

Hybrid Vine variety produced by crossing two different vine species. It should not be confused with a Crossing which is produced from two varieties of the same species. Hybrids of Vinifera formed with the more hardy American vine species are generally held in low regard but a few such as Seyval Blanc can yield good quality wine without any trace of a so-called 'foxy' quality.(also see Crossing, Vinifera

I

IGT Indicazione Geografica Tipica is the Italian equivalent of the French Vins de Pays

Inox French for stainless steel. In wine terms generally refers to fermenting and ageing in stainless steel vessels.

Irrigation Only very selectively permitted in the EU, irrigation is widely practiced in much of the new world where there is insufficient rainfall during the vines growing season. If practiced with restraint it can aid ripening and improve both yield and quality. Most effective is drip irrigation which directly feeds the vines roots. Sprinklers and flood irrigation are much less effective.

L

Lees The sediment left after fermentation, including the dead yeast cells. White wine will often be racked off the gross lees but some sediment will remain which is known as the fine lees. This is important in providing additional flavour and texture as well as acting as an anti-oxidant during early barrel maturation. Lees stirring (see Bâtonnage) is regularly practiced at the same time. An increasing number of top quality reds are also now being aged on lees, some with micro-oxygenation.

Lieu-dit A specific vineyard or climat which has no official classification but identified on a label when that site has been bottled separately from other village-level wine. Regularly found on Alsace and Burgundy labels.

M

Maceration The period during which flavour, colour, tannins and other components are leeched from the grape skins before, during and after fermentation. Temperature plays an important role with primary fruit aromas and colour extracted at cooler temperatures whereas more tannin is released with heat. The cap of grape skins formed during fermentation needs to be kept in solution with the fermenting must and various methods are used which also aid extraction (see Pigeage). Pre-fermentation maceration (see Cold maceration) is regularly practiced as well as extended post fermentation maceration which helps to polymerise the wines tannins, making them rounder and softer in texture. Some skin contact prior to fermentation is also practiced by a number of producers of white wines (see Macération Pelliculaire).

Macération carbonique See Carbonic Maceration

Macération pelliculaire French expression meaning skin contact. In effect it refers to the period of just a few hours where white wine must is macerated with its skins prior to fermentation. Semillon and Sauvignon Blanc in Bordeaux and Chenin Blanc in the Loire as well as more aromatic varieties like Muscat have all successfully been vinified using this technique. Excessive skin contact will result in coarseness and very early oxidation.

Malolactic fermentation Chemical process whereby malic acid is transferred into softer lactic acid. All red wine is put through malolactic but for whites it depends on the variety and style. For aromatic varieties such as Sauvignon Blanc and Riesling the process is avoided. For cool climate top quality Chardonnay it will add weight and texture. It may often be blocked with warmer grown Chardonnay to preserve acidity. Top reds including Cabernet Sauvignon and similarly structured and tannic blends are increasingly having the malolactic conducted in new oak. The wines are lusher and more softly textured, particularly in their youth but long term development remains a questionmark.

Mass Selection See Sélection Massale.

Meritage Term used in the United States to describe a Bordeaux style blend either red or white.

Mesoclimate The localised climate found generally within a vineyard or small specific area and responsible for particular characteristics found in the resulting wines. Often incorrectly referred to as a microclimate. The latter is in fact the very specific climate of the vine canopy.

Méthode Traditionelle See Traditional Method

Metodo Classico See Traditional Method

Micro-oxygenation Cellar operation devised by Patrick Ducournau in Madiran to assist in softening the often aggressively tannic wines produced from the local Tannat. Now increasingly practiced around the globe, small quantities of oxygen are regularly pumped into the ageing wine avoiding the need to rack the wine from one container to another, minimising handling and providing better balanced, finer tannins.

Millerandage Irregular fruit development after flowering caused by cool weather. Yield is reduced because some berries are smaller. Quality though is likely to improve. This characteristic of smaller and larger berries in the same grape bunch is often referred to as hen and chickens.

Moelleux French term meaning medium-sweet.

Monopole French for a solely owned vineyard site, particularly relevant in Burgundy.

Mousseux French for sparkling.

Must Can refer to either unfermented grape juice or the mix of grape juice, skins, pulp and seeds prior to or at the onset of fermentation. *Moût* in French.

Must concentration Any of a series of techniques for removing water from grape juice in order to make more concentrated wine. As well as evaporation under vacuum, freeze concentration (see Cyro-Extraction), which simulates eiswein/icewine production, can be used to remove water. Reverse Osmosis is a sophisticated process that allows the water content in finished wine to be reduced.

N

Négociant French term for a wine merchant. They may buy grapes as well as finished wine and also have their own vineyards and properties. While there has been a trend in Burgundy and other areas to more wines being Domaine-bottled an increasing number of small producers are also now acting as négociants as well.

Négociant-manipulant In Champagne, a merchant who also makes wine. Includes all the great Champagne houses.

Noble Rot See Botrytis.

O

Oenologue French term for an enologist.

Organic An increasing number of winegrowers around the world are now producing wines without recourse to chemical treatments in the vineyard and with a minimum of chemical additives during vinification. (also see Biodynamic).

Oxidation Exposure of must or wine to air. Controlled oxidation is important in the maturation of wine before bottling and can add complexity to fortified wines aiding the production of rancio character. Oxidation of grape juice is also popular in producing barrel fermented white wine particularly premium Chardonnay. Reduction is the opposite of oxidation.

P

Passerillage Grapes that are late-harvested and have dried and become partially raisined concentrating their sugar but are not effected by noble rot.

Passito Italian for wine made from dried grapes.

Phenolics Compounds found in grapes and extracted during vinification. These include tannins, flavour compounds and anthocyanins (responsible for the colour in red wines). See also Cuvaison, Extraction and Maceration.

Phylloxera Vine aphid which was the great scourge of the worlds vineyards in the 19th century. It can be resisted by planting vinifera varieties on resistant American species rootstocks.

Pigeage Method of plunging down the cap produced during red wine fermentation. This can be done by hand plunging with a number of devices or even by foot. A number of specialist automatic machine driven methods have also been developed. Particularly common and successful among the latter is the Rotofermenter. Pigeage can be gentler and less aggressively extractive than remontage or pumping the must back over itself.

Propagated Meaning reproduced. In viticultural terms this most commonly refers to vegetative propagation using cuttings taken from other vines.

Q

Quinta Portuguese term which refers to either a wine estate or a single vineyard.

R

Racked Winery procedure where must or wine is pumped or transferred under gravity from one container to another. This is both to remove the wine from solids but also to provide adequate aeration during maturation.

Rancio Maderised character with burnt, toffee like aromas produced in the development of aged fortified wines through a combination of controlled oxidation and exposure to heat. Banyuls, Maury and Rivesaltes in the Roussillon as well as the fortified Muscats and Tokays of Rutherglen all show classic rancio character.

Récemment dégorgé French term meaning recently disgorged. This can either relate specifically to the actual disgorging of a Champagne method sparkling wine from its bottle sediment but also to the style of wine. These tend to have spent an extended period on there yeast lees. The quintessential example of this style is Bollinger RD.

Reduced This is the opposite of oxidised. Excessive reduction can result in the development foul smelling sulphides during cask ageing and so wines need to be exposed to controlled aeration during this phase, this can be achieved by either racking or more recently the use of micro-oxygenation.

Reductive Refers to wines that are in a reduced state.

Ried Term used in Austria to denote a specific vineyard site.

Residual Sugar There is always a small portion of unfermentable sugar in wine even those that are technically classified as dry. It is commonplace in some whites particularly straightforward fruit driven styles to purposely leave a hint of residual sugar. More serious wines from cooler regions like Alsace and the Mosel may well be completed with some sugar left naturally. Late harvested wines are deliberately left on the vine to accumulate sufficient sugar to ensure considerable sweetness after vinification. (also see Botrytis)

Ripasso Term registered by Valpolicella producer Masi. Used to refer to an enrichment of the already the fermented wine by passing it over the skins of Amarone, adding alcohol, texture and character. Variations exist – see Introduction to North-East, Central & Southern Italy.

Rootstock The plant formed from the root system of the vine to which the scion (fruiting part) is grafted. Most vinifera vines (the european species to which most quality grape varieties belong) are grafted on to rootstocks of American vines (or hybrids of them) due to its resistance to phylloxera.

Roseworthy Famous winemaking college in South Australia whose graduates have had an impact both in Australasia and around the globe.

S

Saignée Running off some free run juice prior to fermentation in order to increase the ratio of skins and solids in the must and therefore flavour and tannin. Regularly practiced in the production of top quality Pinot Noir.

Sélection Massale Mass Selection – the propagation of new plants from existing vines rather than the use of a single clone. Typically only the best vines are used in order to enhance the overall quality within a plot.

Solera A system of fractional blending used in Jerez in the production of sherry to provide consistency and enrichment. It is also used to some extent in other fortified production such as Rutherglen or Madeira. The name is derived from the bottom rung of a series of barrels containing the oldest wine. Only a small part of the wine is drawn from this bottom level at one time. Successive levels are then replenished by younger wines from the level above.

Stelvin/Stelvin Cap Closure used instead of cork to avoid any possible contamination of the wine by TCA, oxidation or other potential spoilage from external sources.

Süssreserve German term for unfermented grape juice used to add sweetness to wines as a means of improving the balance between sweetness and acidity. Less satisfactory than balance that is achieved naturally.

T

TCA Chemical compound, its full name is 2,4,6-trichloroanisole, responsible for most of the off flavours in wine caused by contaminated corks. Chlorine reacts with the cork to produce the contamination and the aroma can be picked up in minute quantities. Cork taint remains a major problem in spoilt wine and alternative methods of closure are on the increase. The chemical or variants of it can also be found elsewhere and has been a cause of contamination in some wine cellars.

Terra Rossa Reddish coloured loam over a limestone base, most famously associated with Coonawarra in South Australia but also found in other wine regions.

Terroir French concept which considers the unique physical environment of a site or vineyard. Also refers to the character in a wine that is derived from its origins rather than the grape variety.

Tonneaux A bordeaux barrel size of 900 litres but can often be used to refer to considerably smaller vessels. What is referred to in Italy as tonneaux can vary from double-sized barriques to that of demi-muid.

Traditional method The classic method of Champagne production (see Champagne method) as it is referred to in other regions for sparkling wines made in this way. Known as méthode traditionelle or méthode classique in other parts of France, as metodo classico in Italy.

Triage Selective sorting of grapes prior to fermentation order to remove inferior quality fruit.

Tris Multiple passages through a vineyard to selectively pick late harvested or botrytis effected grapes. In order to produce great wines it may be necessary to make many such passes. In Bordeaux Tri also refers to the sorting of grapes generally after harvest. This selection process is vital in all wineries to ensure top quality wines.

U

Unfiltered See filtration
Unirrigated See Irrigation

V

Vatting Period where wine is macerated and fermented prior to ageing. See also Cuvaison.

VDP Verband Deutsches Prädikatsweinguter - a consortium of Germany's leading estates (currently with 200 members) founded in 1910. To qualify estates must have vineyards of recognised quality and achieve higher standards than that required by German wine law. The VDP is also behind a three tier classification model for German wines (see Grosses Gewächs). Members use the VDP 'eagle' on their capsules or labels.

Vendange vert See Green Harvesting

Versteigerungswein Auction wines, specifically those set aside by German producers for sale at the annual VDP auction.

Vin Doux Naturels French term for fortified wines. These are sweet, achieved by adding fortifying spirit part way through fermentation in much the same way as is practiced in producing Port.

Vin De Paille Rare type of dry white wine produced from dried and concentrated grapes. Traditional laid out on straw mats after harvesting.

Vin de Pays French category of regional identification for wines that fall outside either the boundaries or regulations of an AC.

Vin Jaune Jura wine made from Savagnin grapes aged in old casks under a voile (a film of yeast not unlike Flor that covers Fino sherry) that results in a distinctive oxidised nutty character.

Vinho Regional Portuguese category of wine regulation that offers the most flexibility in terms of origin and grape variety.

Vinifera Vitis Vinifera is the European species of vine to which nearly all the grape varieties used in global wine production belong.

Vignoble A vineyard or close grouping of vineyards.

Vignaiolo Italian term for a vine-grower.

Volatile Acidity The volatile acids in wine are those that are unstable and chief among these is acetic acid. Excessive exposure of a wine with high volatile acidity to air will encourage a bacterial reaction that causes off volatile aromas (similar to nail varnish) and will eventually convert wine to vinegar.

W

Warehouse Winery This refers specifically to non-estate based wine operations - often located outside the region or regions where the grapes are grown. In some instances the wines are made at another winery and the premises are simply used to age or store the wines.

Winzergenossenschaft German for co-operative.

Y

Yield The size of crop yielded from a vineyard. Yield is fundamental to wine quality. In general the smaller the yield the greater the wine quality. There are though many additional influences. If yield is reduced too much then the vines balance and equilibrium will be disturbed and quality will suffer. Increasingly yields are measured per vine rather than per acre or hectare because of the variable conditions within a vineyard and the density of planting. Older vines are naturally less productive and when their crop is reduced the resulting grapes can be of exceptional quality. In all cases the yield of a vine should be sufficiently restricted in order to achieve complete physiological ripeness.

Agent codes

Buying guide

A code is provided in most A-Z producer entries and these can be found listed alphabetically on the pages that follow. In the first instance these are intended to give the most direct link with that producer in the UK. When the first code given appears in bold this indicates the agent or direct importer of the wines. In some instances such an agent sells only to the trade or acts purely a producers representative in the UK but all should still be able to suggest retail stockists of a given wine. Additional codes (not in bold) indicate a retailer (or regional agent) who are regular stockists of these wines. In a few cases where we have found there to be no UK agent or retailer we have suggested a broker who has traded some vintages of the wine. Where there is no code at all we hope that producers inclusion will prompt someone in the UK to sell these wines. We have already been able to fill in some of the gaps since our first two editions. Many of these codes refer to a leading independent merchant/retailer who sell much of the best or most interesting wine in this country – often very competitively priced against the bigger, better known brands. While we haven't profiled individual merchants, a glance through the codes within any regional section is likely to give a good idea as to which ones have a particular strength there.

In Bordeaux most wine from the leading châteaux is sold through a Bordeaux broker (*courtier*) or agent and then to retailers and merchants in different countries. While the system is elaborate it is not so difficult to obtain many of the wines. Both independent UK merchants, such as one of 'The Bunch' (a group of six leading merchants - Adm, Tan, JAr, C&B, L&W, Yap) and leading broker/shippers (such as Farr Vintners - Far) are the best place to start. These contacts also provide the opportunity to buy wine en primeur or ex-cellars. This requires paying for the cost of the wine before it is shipped with the additional costs (freight, VAT and duty) paid on its arrival in the UK. Purchasing wine in this way was once seen as an investment opportunity for would be speculators, but it is now increasingly important as the only means of obtaining the best, not only from Bordeaux but also from Burgundy, the Rhône, or some Vintage Port. It also usually means that the wine hasn't changed hands several times already. Leading merchants will also prove useful when buying older vintages as will auction houses and brokers (additional contacts have been provided at the end of the list of codes). Bordeaux wines stocked by a large number of merchants have been coded AAA.

This same code (AAA) is also used for wines that are that are easily found in supermarkets or on the high street. Supermarkets account for the bulk of wine sold in the UK. To an extent their ranges tend to be dominated by the ubiquitous big volume brands – much of it outside of the scope of this book. The small production of many high quality estates remains outside their reach whether as part of a deliberate decision on the part of the producer or due to logistical reasons. Nonetheless the best supermarkets include those producers who combine quality and quantity. In addition there is an increasing trend toward the inclusion of a selection of fine wines of more limited availability in their flagship stores or through an on-line facility. Though supermarkets have not been included as agents or leading stockists, a search on their internet site can be used as a quick check for availability. There are also an increasing number of Internet-only retailer whose search engines provide a further aid to tracking down a hard to find wine, the best known being www.everywine.co.uk.

It is also worth noting that a growing number of producers now sell their wine direct via a mailing list or over the internet. Such is the demand for their wines there is no need for them to use an agent and the cost saving is effectively passed on to the wine drinker. This applies particularly to leading new world producer who often have oversubscribed lists composed entirely of consumers in their local market – yet some choose to retain a small percentage of their production for export via a foreign merchant. Individual producer websites are worth checking for information about buying their wines.

Agent codes/A-Z

AAA
Widely available
In supermarkets or the high street
OR
in the case of Bordeaux or Port available
through any number of wine merchants.
also see Buying Guide

A&B – A & B Vintners
Little Tawsden, Spout Lane,
Brenchley, Kent TN12 7AS
Tel 01892 724977
Fax 01892 722673
info@abvintners.co.uk
www.abvintners.co.uk

ABy – Anthony Byrne
Ramsey Business Park, Stocking Fen Road,
Ramsey, Cambridgeshire PE26 2UR
Tel 01487 814555
Fax 01487 814962
admin@abfw.co.Uk
www.abfw.co.uk

ACh – Andrew Chapman Fine Wines
14 Haywards Road, Abingdon,
Oxfordshire OX14 4LB
Tel 01235 550707
Fax 0870 136 6335
info@surf4wine.co.uk
www.surf4wine.co.uk

Add – Addison Wines
165 Battersea Rise, London SW11 1HP
Tel 020 7924 2416
Fax 020 7924 2417
sales@addisonwines.co.uk
www.addisonwines.co.uk

Adm – Adnams
Sole Bay Brewery, Southwold, Suffolk IP18 6JW
Tel 01502 727222
Fax 01502 727223
wines@adnams.co.uk
www.adnams.co.uk

ADo – Allied Domecq Wine UK
Argentum, 2 Queen Caroline Street,
London W6 9DX
Tel 020 8323 8196
Fax 020 8323 8313
www.allieddomecqplc.com

AHW – AH Wines
Back Street, West Camel, Yeovil,
Somerset BA22 7QB
Tel 01935 850166
Fax 01935 851264

Ala – La Alacena
Tel 01604 784159
Fax 01604 784159
info@alacena.co.uk
www.alacena.co.uk

AlF – Alfie Fiandaca
Unit 4, Westpoint Trading Estate,
Alliance Road, London W3 0RA
Tel 01935 850166
Fax 01935 851264

All – Alliance Wine Co
7 Beechfield Road, Willowyard Estate,
Beith, Ayrshire KA15 1LN
Tel 01505 506060
Fax 01505 506066
sales@alliancewine.co.uk
www.alliancewine.co.uk

Alo – Alouette Wines
Prenton Way, North Cheshire Trading Estate,
Prenton, Wirral CH43 3DU
Tel 0151 6089900
Fax 0151 608 8844
info@alouettewines.co.uk
www.alouettewines.co.uk

Alv – Alivini
Units 2 & 3, 199 Eade Road, London N4 1DN
Tel 020 8880 2526
Fax 020 8880 2708
enquiries@alivini.com

Amp – Amps Fine Wines
6 Market Place, Oundle, Peterborough PE8 4BQ
Tel 01832 273502
Fax 01832 273611
info@ampsfinewines.co.uk
www.ampsfinewines.co.uk

AMW - American Wine Merchants
PO Box 34882, London W8 7WD
Tel 07793 816672
sales@americanwinemerchants.co.uk
www.americanwinemerchants.co.uk

Agent codes

Anl – Anglo International Wine Shippers
Chantarella House, 25 New Road,
Esher, Surrey KT10 9PG
Tel 01372 469841
Fax 01372 469816

AoW – Architects of Wine
Grange Park Unit 1, Cheaney Drive,
Northampton NN4 5FB
Tel 0870 121 3610
Fax 0870 121 3655
sales@aow-uk.com
www.aow-uk.com

ARe – Arthur Rackham Emporia
216 London Road, Burpham, Guildford GU4 7JS
Tel 0870 870 1110
Fax 0870 870 1120
cellars@ar-emporia.com
www.ar-emporia.com

Ast – Astrum Wine Cellars
6 Thornsett Road, Earlsfield, London SW18 4EN
Tel 020 8870 5252
Fax 020 8870 2244
sales@astrumwinecellars.com
www.astrumwinecellars.com

AVn – Allez Vins!
PO Box 1019, Long Itchington, Southam,
Warwickshire CV47 9ZU
Tel 01926 811969
Fax 01926 811969
www.allezvins.co.uk

AWA – Australian Wine Agencies
21 Southlea Road, Datchet, Slough,
Berkshire SL3 9BY
Tel 01753 544546
Fax 01753 591369
info@australian–wine.co.uk
www.austwineagencies.com

AWs – Australian Wineries
28 Recreation Ground Road, Stamford,
Lincolnshire PE91EW
Tel 01780 755810
Fax 01780 766063
admin@australianwineries.co.uk
www.australianwineries.co.uk

AWW – Andrew Wilson Wines
Little Acre, Hall Lane, Cotes Heath,
Staffordshire ST21 6RT
Tel 01782 791798
Fax 01782 791787
andrew@awwines.co.uk
www.awwines.co.uk

B&B – Barrels & Bottles
3 Oak Street, Sheffield S8 9UB
Tel 0114 255 6611
Fax 0114 255 1010
sales@barrelsandbottles.co.uk
www.barrelsandbottles.co.uk

B&T – C G Bull & Taylor
6G Hewlett House, Havelock Terrace,
London SW8 4AS
Tel 020 7498 8022
Fax 020 7498 7851
info@cgbull.co.uk
www.cgbull.co.uk

Bal – Ballantynes of Cowbridge
3 Westgate, Cowbridge, Glamorgan CF71 7AQ
Tel 01446 774840
Fax 01446 775253
ballantynes@btinternet.co.uk
www.ballantynes.co.uk

Bac – Bacchus Fine Wines
Warrington House Farm Barn,
Buckinghamshire MK46 4HN
Tel 01234 711140
Fax 01234 711199
wine@bacchus.co.uk
www.bacchus.co.uk

Bat – Bat & Bottles
9 Ashwell Road, Oakham, Rutland LE15 6QG
Tel 0845 108 4407
Fax 0870 458 2505
post@batwine.co.uk
www.batwine.co.uk

BBE – Brown Brothers Europe
River View Lodge, Ray Mead Road,
Maidenhead, Berkshire SL6 8NJ
Tel 01628 776446
Fax 01628 776136
info@brownbrotherswines.co.uk
www.brown–brothers.co.au

BBl – Beringer Blass UK
Regal House, 70 London Road,
Twickenham TW1 3QS
Tel 020 8843 8411
Fax 020 8843 8422
info@beringerblass.co.uk
www.beringerblass.com

BBR – Berry Bros & Rudd
3 St James Street, London SW1A 1EG
Tel 020 7396 9600
Fax 020 7396 9611
orders@bbr.com
www.bbr.com

Bel – Bella Wines Limited
Beaufort House, 28 Lisburn Road,
Newmarket, Suffolk CB8 8HS
Tel 01638 604899
Fax 01638 604901
sales@bellawines.co.uk
www.bellawines.co.uk

Ben – Bennetts
High Street, Chipping Campden,
Gloucestershire GL55 6AG
Tel 01386 840392
Fax 01386 840974
enquiries@bennettsfinewines.com
www.bennettsfinewines.com

BFs – Bonhote Foster
The Mews, Broadagte House, Steeple,
Bumpstead, Suffolk CB9 7DG
Tel 01440 730779
Fax 01440 730789
acf@bonhotefoster.co.uk
www.pinotpeople.co.uk

BFW – Brown-Forman Wines
6th Floor, Regent Arcade House,
19-25 Argyll Street, London W1F 7TS
Tel 020 7478 1300
Fax 020 7287 4661

BGL – Bottle Green Ltd
19 New Street, Horsforth, Leeds LS18 4BH
Tel 0113 2054500
Fax 0113 2054501
nfo@bottlegreen.com
www.bottlegreen.com

Bib – Bibendum
113 Regents Park Road, London NW1 8UR
Tel 020 7449 4100
Fax 020 7722 7354
sales@bibendum-wine.co.uk
www.bibendum-wine.co.uk

Bir – Birchwood Agencies
Birchwood House, Victoria Road,
Dartford DA1 5AJ
Tel 01322 627500
Fax 01322 627488
info@birchwoodagencies.co.uk

Blx – Bordeaux Index
6th Floor, 159 - 173 St John's Street,
London, EC1V 4QJ
Tel 020 7253 2110
Fax 020 7490 1955
sales@bordeauxindex.com
www.bordeauxindex.com

Box – Boxford Wine Co
Spring Cottage, Butchers Lane, Boxford,
Sudbury, Suffolk, CO10 5EA
Tel 01787 210187
Fax 01787 211391
boxfordwine@cs.com

BRW – Big Red Wine Company
41 Dartmouth Road, London, NW2 4ET
Tel 020 8208 0192
Fax 020 8208 0192
sales@bigredwine.co,uk
www.bigredwine.co.uk

B-S – Billecart-Salmon UK
Thornton House, Thornton Road,
London, SW19 4NG
Tel 020 8405 6345
Fax 020 8405 6346
info@billecart-salmon.co.uk
www.billecart-salmon.co.uk

BSh – Burgundy Shuttle
168 Ifield Road, London, SW10 9AF
Tel 020 7341 4053
Fax 020 7244 0618
mail@burgundyshuttle.ltd.uk
www.burgundyshuttle.co.uk

Bur – Burridges of Arlington St
Burridge House, Priestley Way, Crawley,
West Sussex RH10 9NT
Tel 01293 530151
Fax 01293 530104
sales@burridgewine.com
www.burridgewine.com

But – Butler's Wine Cellar
247 Queen's Park Road, Brighton,
East Sussex BN2 2XJ
Tel 01273 698724
Fax 01273 622761
henry@butlers-winecellar.co.uk
www.butlers-winecellar.co.uk

BWC – Berkmann Wine Cellars
10/12 Brewery Road, London, N7 9NH
Tel 020 7609 4711
Fax 020 7607 0018
info@berkmann.co.uk
www.berkmann.co.uk

C&B – Corney & Barrow
No.1 Thomas More Street, London E1W 1YZ
Tel 020 7265 2400
Fax 020 7265 2539
wine@corbar.co.uk
www.corneyandbarrow.com

C&C – Champagnes & Châteaux
21 Abbeville Mews, 88 Clapham Park Road,
London, SW4 7BX
Tel 020 7498 4488
Fax 020 7498 4499
info@champagnesandchateaux.co.uk
www.champagnesandchateaux.co.uk

C&D – C & D Wines
Amapola House, 25 Metro Business Centre,
Kangley Bridge Road, London SE26 5BW
Tel 020 8778 1711
Fax 020 8778 1710
info@canddwines.co.uk
www.canddwines.co.uk

C&O – C & O Wines
14 Roscoe Park Estate, Park Road,
Timperley, WA14 5QH
Tel 0161 976 3696
Fax 0161 962 4542

C&R – Classic & Rare
The Famous Old Brewery, Springfield Road,
Crawley, West Sussex RH10 6AL
Tel 01293 525111
sales@classicrarewines.com
www.classicrarewines.com

Cac – Cachet Wine
Red Duster House, 101 York Street, Hull,
East Yorkshire, HU2 0QX
Tel 01482 581792
Fax 01482 587042
sales@cachetwines.co.uk

Cam – Cambridge Wine Merchants
2 Mill Road, Cambridge CB1 2AD
Tel 01223 568991
Fax 01223 568992
info@cambridgewine.com
www.cambridgewine.com

Cap – Capricorn
Brook House, 4 Northenden Road, Gately,
Cheshire, SK8 4DN
Tel 0161 908 1360
Fax 0161 908 1365
sales@capricornwines.co.uk
www.capricornwines.co.uk

Car – Carringtons
Angel House, Angel Street,
Manchester, M4 1BQ
Tel 0161 832 5646
Fax 0161 832 5626
carringtons@winebeerandspirits.co.uk

Cas – Castang Wine Shippers
8 Cardwen Farm Estate, Pelyent,
Cornwall, PL13 2LH
Tel 01503 220359
Fax 01503 220650
sales@castang-wines.co.uk
www.castang-wines.co.uk

Cav – Cavavin/Le Bon Vin
340 Brightside Lane, Sheffield S9 2SP
Tel 0114 256 0090
Fax 0114 256 0092
cavavin@lebonvin.co.uk
www.lebonvin.co.uk

CBg – Charles Blagden
135 Avenue Joseph Lioter,
84740 Velleron, France
Tel 0033 4 90 20 07 07
Fax 0033 4 90 20 05 77
blagwin@aol.com

CCC – Cave Cru Classé
Unit 13 Leathermarket, Weston Street,
London, SE1 3ER
Tel 020 7378 8579
Fax 020 7378 8544
enquiries@ccc.co.uk
www.cave-cru-classe.com

Cco – Champagne Company
26 Astwood Mews, London, SW7 4DE
Tel 020 7373 5578
Fax 020 7373 4777
ukchampagne@aol.com
www.champagnecompany.co.uk

CdP –Les Caves de Pyrene
Pew Corner, Old Portsmouth Road, Arlington,
Guildford, Surrey, GU3 1LP
Tel 01483 538820
Fax 01483 455068
orders@lescaves.co.uk
www.lescaves.co.uk

CeB –Croque-en-Bouche
221 Wells Road, Malvern Wells,
Worcester WR14 4HF
Tel 0845 658 4323
Fax 0870 706 6282
mail@croque.co.uk
www.croque-en-bouche.co.uk

Che – Cheviot UK / WM Morton
137 Shawbridge Street, Glasgow G43 1QQ
Tel 0141 649 9881
Fax 0141 649 7074

CHk – Charles Hawkins
Hall Gardens, 56 High Street East,
Uppingham, Rutland, LE15 9HG
Tel 01572 823030
Fax 01572 823040
www.charleshawkins-wines.com

Cht– Charterhouse Wine Co Ltd
82 Goding Street, London, SE11 5AW
Tel 020 7587 1302
Fax 020 7587 0982

ChV – Château Vintners
121 Beaufort Street, London, SW3 6BS
Tel 020 7376 8828
Fax 020 7376 8818
chateauvintners@yahoo.co.uk

Cib – Ciborio
Ciborio House, 74 Long Drive, Greenford,
Middlesex, UB6 8XH
Tel 020 8578 4388
Fax 020 8575 2758
www.ciborio.com

CKr – Christopher Keiller Fine Wine
Tel 01209 215706
Fax 01209 215706
ghost@gladys.demon.co.uk
www.gladys.demon.co.uk/finewineservices.html

Coe – Coe Vintners
53 Redbridge Lane East, Ilford, Essex IG4 5EY
Tel 020 8551 4966
Fax 020 8550 6312
enquiries@coevintners.com
www.coevintners.com

Col - Colombier Vins Fins
Colombier House, Ryder Close,
Cadley Hill Industrial Estate,
Swadlincote, Derbyshire, DE11 9EU
Tel 01283 552552
Fax 01283 550675

Con – Connolly's Wine Merchants
Arch 13, 220 Livery Street, Birmingham, B3 1EU
Tel 0121 236 9269
Fax 0121 233 2339
sales@connollyswine.co.uk
www.connollyswine.co.uk

CPp – Christopher Piper Wines
1 Silver Street, Ottery St Mary,
Devon, EX11 1DB
Tel 01404 814139
Fax 01404 812100
sales@christopherpiperwines.co.uk

CPW – Cornish Point Wines
Smallbrook Barn, Thursley, Surrey GU8 6QN
Tel 01252 705102
Fax 01252 705101
nigel@cornishpoint.com

Agent codes

CRs – Chalié Richards
2 Grove House, Foundry Lane, Horsham,
West Sussex, RH13 5PL
Tel 01403 250500
Fax 01403 250123
admin@chalie-richards.co.uk

Cst – Constellation Wines
Hardy House, 140 High Street, Esher,
Surrey, KT10 9QJ
Tel 01372 473000
Fax 01372 473100

CTy – Charles Taylor / Montrachet Fine Wine
59 Kennington Road, London, SE1 7PZ
Tel 020 7928 1990
Fax 020 7928 3415
www.montrachetwine.com

CWF – CWF Ltd (Continental Wine & Food)
Trafalgar Mills, Leeds Road, Huddersfield HD2 1YY
Tel 01484 538333
Fax 01484 544734

CyT – Concha y Toro UK
MWB Business Exchange, John Eccles House,
Robert Robinson Avenue, Oxford OX4 4GP
Tel 01865 338013
Fax 01865 338100
enquiries@conchaytoro.cl
www.conchaytoro.com

D&D – D & D Wines
Adams Court, Adams Hill, Knutsford,
Cheshire, WA16 6BA
Tel 01565 650952
Fax 01565 755295
ddwi@ddwinesint.com

D&F – D & F Wines
Centre House, St Leonards Road,
London, NW10 6ST
Tel 020 8838 4399
Fax 020 8838 4500
inquiry@dandfwines.fsnet.co.uk
www.interreach.com/d&f

Dan – Danmar International
Unit 4, Beta Way, Thorpe Industrial Park,
Egham, Surrey TW20 8RS
Tel 01784 477812
Fax 01784 477813
sales@danmarinternational.co.uk
www.danmarinternational.co.uk

DAy – Dreyfus Ashby & Co
143a High Street, Tonbridge, Kent, TN9 1DH
Tel 01732 361639
Fax 01732 367834
office@dreyfusashby.co.uk

DDr – Domaine Direct
6-9 Cynthia Street, London, N1 9JF
Tel 020 7837 1142
Fax 020 7837 8605
mail@domainedirect.co.uk
www.domainedirect.co.uk

DeB – De Bortoli Wines UK
Minchington Farm, Farnham,
Blandford Forum, DT11 8DE
Tel 01725 516467
Fax 01725 516403
debortoli@talk21.com
www.debortoli.com.au

Dec – Decorum Vintners
Unit 12, Grand Union Centre,
West Row, London W10 5AS
Tel 020 8969 6581
Fax 020 8960 7693
admin@decvin.com
www.decvin.com

Dis – Discover Wine
PO Box 104, Stevenage,
Hertfordshire SG1 3EG
Tel 0870 3300267
Fax 0870 3307910
www.discover-wine.co.uk

DLW – Daniel Lambert Wine Agencies
8 Rhodfas Ceirios, Pen-y-Fai, Bridgend CF31 4GG
Tel 01656 661010
Fax 01656 668088
dwlawine@aol.com
www.dwla.co.uk

Dou – Dourthe UK
The Old Imperial Laundry, 71 Warriner Gardens,
London SW11 4XW
Tel 020 7720 6611
Fax 020 7720 2670
uk@cvbg.com
www.cvbg.com

DWS – Direct Wine Shipments (NI)
5/7 Corporation Square, Belfast, BT1 3AJ
Tel 028 9050 8000
Fax 028 9050 8002
enquiry@directwine.co.uk
www.directwine.co.uk

E&T – Elliot & Tatham
The Wheatsheaf Inn, West End, Northleach,
Gloucestershire, GL54 3EZ
Tel 01451 861688
Fax 01451 861037

Ear – Earle Wines
Applegarth, Wormald Green, Harrogate,
North Yorkshire, HG3 3PS
Tel 01765 677296
Fax 01765 677839
www.earlewines.com

Ecl – Eclectic Wines
47 Linver Road, London SW6 3RA
Tel 020 7736 3733
mary@eclecticwines.com
www.eclecticwines.com

EdV – Eaux de Vie
3 Harcourt Street, London W1H 4EY
Tel 020 7724 5009
Fax 020 7723 7053
info@eauxdevie.co.uk

EGe – Ernst Gorge
73 High Street, Dorchester-on-Thames,
Oxon OX14 3LF
Tel 01865 341817
Fax 01865 343184

Ehr – Ehrmanns
29 Corsica Street, London, N5 1JT
Tel 020 7418 1800
Fax 020 7359 7788
ehrmanns@ehrmanns.co.uk
www.ehrmanns.com

EJG – E & J Gallo
Swan House, Cowley Business Park,
Uxbridge UB8 2AD
Tel 01895 818003
Fax 01895 818043

Eno – Enotria
4-8 Chandos Park Estate, Chandos Road,
London, NW10 6NF
Tel 020 8961 4411
Fax 020 8961 8773
marketing@enotria.co.uk

EoR – Ellis of Richmond
Unit 1, Richmond House, The Links,
Popham Close, Hanworth, Middlesex, TW13 6JE
Tel 020 8744 5550
Fax 020 8744 5581
www.ellisofrichmond.co.uk

Eur – Eurowines
93 Bollo Lane, Chiswick, London, W4 5LU
Tel 020 8747 2100
Fax 020 8994 8054
enquiries@eurowines.co.uk
www.eurowines.co.uk

Eve – Evertons
Main Road, Ombersley, Droitwich, WR9 0EU
Tel 01905 620144
Fax 01905 621073
sales@evertons.com

Evg – Evington's Wines
120 Evington Road, Leicester LE2 1HH
Tel 0116 254 2702
Fax 0116 254 2702
info@evingtons-wines.com
www.evingtons-wines.com

EWG – EWGA
(European Wine Growers Associates)
Challan Hall, Silverdale, Lancashire LA5 0UH
Tel 01524 701723
Fax 01524 701189

ExC – Ex Cellar
20 Craddocks Parade, Ashtead KT21 1QJ
Tel 01372 813937
Fax 01372 813937
simon@excellar.co.uk

F&R – Fine & Rare Wines Ltd
Pall Mall Deposit, 124-128 Barlby Road,
North Kensington, London W10 6BL
Tel 020 8960 1995
Fax 020 8960 1911
wine@frw.co.uk
www.frw.co.uk

F&M – Fortnum & Mason
181 Piccadilly, London W1A 1ER
Tel 020 7734 8040
Fax 020 7437 3278
info@fortnumandmason.co.uk
www.fortnumandmason.com

Fal – Falcon Vintners
74 Warren Street, London W1T 5PF
Tel 020 7388 7055
Fax 020 7388 9546
info@falconvintners.co.uk

Far – Farr Vintners
19 Sussex Street, Pimlico, London, SW1V 4RR
Tel 020 7821 2000
Fax 020 7821 2020
sales@farr-vintners.com
www.farr-vintners.com

FCA – Fraser Crameri Associates
The Stable, Cottenden View, Stonegate,
Wadhurst, East Sussex TN5 7DX
Tel 01580 200304
Fax 01580 200308
fraser@frasercrameri.com
www.frasercrameri.com

FDB – First Drinks Brands
Imperial House, Imperial Way,
Southampton SO15 0RB
Tel 023 8031 2000
Fax 023 8031 1111
contact@first-drinks-brands.co.uk

FEM – F & E May Ltd
Viaduct House, 16 Warner Street,
London EC1R 5HA
Tel 020 7843 1600
Fax 020 7843 1601
sales@fandemay.com
www.fandemay.com

FFW – Food & Fine Wine
760 Eccleshall Road, Sheffield S11 8TB
Tel 01142 668747
Fax 0870 8912376
www.foodandfinewine.com

Fie – Fields Wine Merchants
3 Pickering Place, London SW1A 1EA
Tel 020 7589 5753
Fax 020 759 6179
fields@bbr.com
www.fieldswine.com

Fin – The Fine Wine Company Ltd
145 North High Street, Musselburgh EH21 6AN
Tel 0870 7606205
Fax 0870 7606215
mail@thefinewinecompany.co.uk
www.thefinewinecompany.co.uk

Fol – Folio Wines
The Silver Cellars, Weymouth Avenue,
Dorchester DT1 1QD
Tel 01305 751300
Fax 01305 751302
www.foliowines.com

For – Forth Wines
Crawford Place, Milnathort,
Kinross-Shire KY13 9XF
Tel 01577 866001
Fax 01577 866020
enquiries@forthwines.com
www.forthwines.com

Frt – Freixenet UK
Freixenet House, 23 Wellington Business Park,
Dukes Ride, Crowthorne, Berkshire RG45 6LS
Tel 01344 758500
Fax 01344 758510
enquiries@freixenet.co.uk
www.freixenet.co.uk

Frw – Friarwood
26 New Kings Road, Fulham,
London SW6 4ST
Tel 020 7736 2628
Fax 020 7731 0411
sales@friarwood.com
www.friarwood.com

FSA – see SsG

Fsp – Flagship Wines Ltd
39 Rowan Close, St Albans AL4 0ST
Tel 01727 841968
Fax 01727 841968
info@flagshipwines.co.uk
www.flagshipwines.co.uk

FSt – Frank Stainton Wines
3 Berry's Yard, Finkle Street, Kendal,
Cumbria LA9 4AB
Tel 01539 731886
Fax 01539 730396
admin@stainton-wines.co.uk
www.stainton-wines.co.uk

FWC – Fareham Wine Cellar
55 High Street, Fareham, Hampshire PO16 7BG
Tel 01329 822733
Fax 01329 282355
dominic@farehamwinecellar.co.uk
www.farehamwinecellar.co.uk

FWW – FWW Wines UK Ltd
15 South Ealing Road, London W5 4QT
Tel 020 8567 1589
Fax 020 8567 1594
sales@fww.demon.co.uk

G&C – Growers & Château
Oak House, 271 Kingston Road,
Leatherhead, Surrey KT22 7PJ
Tel 01372 374239
Fax 01372 377610
info@winesite.net
www.winesite.net

Gar – Garrigue Wines
8 Castle Court, Bankside, Falkirk FK2 7UU
Tel 0845 8886677
Fax 01324 670610
themacaloneys@garriguewines.com
www.garriguewines.com

Gau – Gauntleys
4 High Street, Exchange Arcade,
Nottingham NG1 2ET
Tel 0115 911 0555
Fax 0115 911 0557
rhone@gauntleywine.com
www.gauntleywine.com

GBa – Georges Barbier
267 Lee High Road, London SE12 8RU
Tel 020 8852 5801
Fax 020 8463 0398
georgesbarbier@f2s.com

GBr – G Bravo & Son Ltd
28 Shaftesbury Ave, London WC2H 8EG
Tel 020 7836 4693
Fax 020 7836 5657

GCW – Grand Cru Wines
Mas de Moussier, 1100-5 Avenue des Alpilles,
13310 Saint-Martin de Crau, France
Tel 0033 490 47 29 06
gcw@wanadoo.fr

Gel – Gelston Castle Fine Wines
5 Courtyard Cott, Castle Douglas,
Kirkcudbrightshire DG7 1QE
Tel 01556 503012

GFy – Folly Wines
Chestnut Road, London Road, Chalford,
Gloucestershire GL6 8NR
Tel 01453 731509
Fax 01453 731134
info@follywines.co.uk
www.follywines.co.uk

GGg – Great Grog
33-41 Ratcliffe Terrace, Edinburgh EH9 1SU
Tel 01453 731509
Fax 01453 731134
info@follywines.co.uk
www.follywines.co.uk

GID – GIDA (Gruppo Italiano Distribuzione Alimentari Ltd)
1 Hinde Street, London W1U 2AY
Tel 020 7224 0060
Fax 020 7224 0010
info@gida.co.uk

Goe – Goedhuis & Co
6 Rudolf Place, Miles Street,
London SW8 1RP
Tel 020 7793 7900
Fax 020 7793 7170
enquiries@goedhuis.com
www.goedhuis.com

GrD – Growers Direct
2 Station Road, Swavesey,
Cambridge CB4 5QJ
Tel 01954 230176
Fax 01954 231822

Gun – Gunson Fine Wines
Haysbridge Farm, Brickhouse Lane,
South Godstone RH9 8JW
Tel 01342 843974
Fax 01342 843955
gunsonfinewines@aol.com

GVF – Grand Vins de France
Carrayol Arch, 8 Church Crescent,
London, N10 3ND
Tel 020 8442 1088
Fax 020 8444 4288
www.grandvins.co.uk

GWW – Great Western Wine
The Wine Warehouse, Wells Road,
Bath, Somerset BA2 3AP
Tel 01225 322800
Fax 01225 442139
post@greatwesternwine.co.uk
www.greatwesternwine.co.uk

H&B – Hall Batson
28 Whiffler Road, Norwich NR3 2AZ
Tel 01603 415115
Fax 01603 484096
info@hallbatson.co.uk
www.hallbatson.co.uk

Hal – Hallgarten
Dallow Road, Luton, Bedfordshire LU11UR
Tel 01582 722538
Fax 01582 723240
sales@hallgarten.co,uk
www.hallgarten.co.uk

Han – Handford Fine Wine
12 Portland Road, Holland Park,
London W11 4LE
Tel 020 7221 9614
Fax 020 7221 9613
www.handford.net

Har – Harris Fine Wine
4 Albion Way, Kelvin Industrial Estate,
East Kilbride G75 0YN
Tel 01355 571157
Fax 01355 571158

Has – Haslemere Cellar
16 West Street, Haslemere,
Surrey GU27 2AB
Tel 01428 645081
Fax 01428 645108
info@haslemerecellar.co.uk
www.haslemerecellar.co.uk

Hay – Hayward Bros Ltd
44 Willow Walk, London SE1 5SF
Tel 020 7237 0576
Fax 020 7237 6212
wine@haybrowine.co.uk
www.haybrowine.co.uk

HBJ – Hayman Barwell Jones Ltd
24 Fore Street, Ipswich, Suffolk IP4 1JU
Tel 01473 232322
Fax 01473 280381
www.hbjwines.co.uk

Hfx – Halifax Wine Company
18 Prescott Street, Halifax, West Yorkshire HX1 2LG
Tel 01422 256333
andy@halifaxwinecompany.com
www.halifaxwinecompany.com

HHB – H & H Bancroft
1 China Wharf, Mill Street, London, SE1 2BQ
Tel 020 7232 5450
Fax 020 7232 5451
orders@wine-selections.com
www.wine-selections.com

HHC – Haynes, Hanson & Clark
25 Eccleston Street, London, SW1W 9NP
Tel 020 7259 0102
Fax 020 7259 0103
london@hhandc.co.uk

Hil – Hill International Wines (UK)
Stonehouse Farm, Ashby Road, Woodville,
Swadlincote, Derbys DE11 7BP
Tel 01283 217703
Fax 01283 550309

His – Hispa Merchants Ltd
Warwick House Business Centre,
181-183 Warwick Road, London, W14 8PU
Tel 020 7370 4449
Fax 020 7370 5086
sales@hispamerchants.com
www.hispamerchants.com

HMA – Hatch Mansfield Agencies
New Bank House, 1 Brockenhurst Road,
Ascot, Berks, SL5 9DJ
Tel 01344 871800
Fax 01344 871871
sales@hatch.co.uk
www.hatchmansfield.co.uk

HMW – Harvey-Miller Wine Agencies
Craigton House, Fintry, Stirlingshire G63 0XQ
Tel 01360 860012
Fax 01360 860148
www.h-mwa.com

HoK – Hammonds of Knutsford
Warford Grange Farm, Pedley House Lane,
Great Warford, Knutsford, Cheshire WA16 7SP
Tel 01565 872872
Fax 01565 872900
wine@hammondsofknutsford.co.uk

HoM – House of Menzies
Castle Menzies Farm, Aberfeldy,
Perthshire PH15 2JD
Tel 01887 829666
Fax 01887 829666
info@houseofmenzies.com
www.houseofmenzies.com

Hrd – Harrods
Knightsbridge, London SW1X 7XL
Tel 020 7730 1234
Fax 020 7225 5872
www.harrods.com

HRp – Howard Ripley
25 Dingwall Crescent, London, SW18 3AZ
Tel 020 8877 3065
Fax 020 8877 0029
info@howardripley.com
www.howardripley.com

HSA – HS Wine Agencies
76 Impington Lane, Impington,
Cambridge CB4 9NJ
Tel 01223 234604
Fax 01223 234604
hswineagencies@ntlworld.com

HWC – HWCG
Threm Hall, Start Hill,
Bishop's Stortford, Hertfordshire, CM22 7TD
Tel 01279 873500
Fax 01279 873501
wine@hwcg.co.uk
www.hwcg.co.uk

Idg – Indigo Wine
7 Beverstone Road, London SW2 5AL
Tel 020 7733 8391
Fax 020 7733 8391
info@indigowine.com
www.indigowine.com

IGH – Ian G Howe
35 Appletongate, Newark,
Nottinghamshire, NG24 1JR
Tel 01636 704366
Fax 01636 610502
howe@chablis-burgundy.co.uk
www.chablis-burgundy.co.uk

IRW – Irvine Robertson Wines
10-11 North Leith Sands, Edinburgh EH6 4ER
Tel 0131 553 3521
Fax 0131 553 5465
irviner@nildram.co.uk
www.irwines.co.uk

Itv / IWS – Italvini / International Wine Services
Punch Bowl Park, Cherry Tree Lane,
Hemel Hempstead, HP2 7EU
Tel 01442 206800
Fax 01442 206888
iws@intwine.co.uk
www.wine-info.co.uk

IVi – I Vini
No. 6 Hayes House, 6-8 Dyer Street,
Cirencester, Gloucestershire GL7 2PF
Tel 01285 655595
Fax 01285 650684
enquiries@ivini.co.uk
www.ivini.co.uk

IVV – In Vino Veritas
3 Wessex Court, Main Road,
Shuttington, Staffs, B79 0DS
Tel 01827 899449
Fax 01827 899936
webmaster@ivvltd.com
www.ivvltd.com

IWD – Interwine Ltd
The Office Suite, Inn on the Green,
The Old Cricket Common, Cookham Dean, SL6 9NZ
Tel 01628 473920
Fax 01628 478660
info@interwinedirect.com
www.interwinedirect.com

J&B – Justerini & Brooks
61 St James Street, London, SW1A 1LZ
Tel 020 7484 6400
Fax 020 7484 6499

JAr – John Armit
5 Royalty Studios, 105 Lancaster Road,
London, W11 1QF
Tel 020 7908 0600
Fax 020 7908 0601
info@armit.co.uk
www.armit.co.uk

Jas – Jascots Wine Merchants Ltd
The Observatory, Pinnacle House,
260 Old Oak Common Lane, London NW10 6DX
Tel 020 8965 2000
Fax 020 8965 9500
ben@jascots.co.uk
www.jascots.co.uk

JBa – Julian Baker
Pound House, Bures Road, Wissington,
Nayland, Colchester, CO6 4LU
Tel 01206 262538
Fax 01206 263574

Agent codes

JEF – John E Fells
Fells House, Prince Edwards Street,
Berkhamstead, HP4 3EZ
Tel 01442 870900
Fax 01442 878555
info@fells.co.uk
www.fells.co.uk

JFW – James Fearon Wines
Centenary Buildings, Cleveland Avenue,
Holyhead LL65 2LB
Tel 01407 765200
Fax 01407 765620
enquiries@jamesfearonwines.co.uk
www.jamesfearonwines.co.uk

JIC – Just In Case
Symes Corner, Bank Street, Bishops Waltham,
Hampshire SO32 1AN
Tel 01489 892969
Fax 01489 892969

JNi – James Nicholson
27a Killyleagh Street, Crossgar,
County Down, BT30 9DQ
Tel 028 4483 0091
Fax 028 4483 0028
info@jnwine.com
www.jnwine.com

JNV – Jackson Nugent Vintners
30 Homefields Road,
London, SW19 4QF
Tel 020 8947 9722
Fax 020 8944 1048
www.jnv.co.uk

JTD – J T Davies & Son
7 Aberdeen Road, Croydon, CR0 1EQ
Tel 020 8681 3222
Fax 020 8681 5931
postbox@jtdavies.co.uk
www.jtdavies.co.uk

KJn – Kendall Jackson UK
Lamb House, Church Street,
Chiswick, London, W4 2PD
Tel 020 8747 2840
Fax 020 8987 6160
kjsales@kjmail.com

Kwi – Kiwi Wine / The Brilliants Wine Merchants Ltd
62c Salcott Road, London SW11 6DE
Tel 0870 0433944
Fax 0870 0433945
nicholas@kiwiwines.net
www.kiwiwines.net

L&S – Lea & Sandeman
170 Fulham Road, Chelsea,
London, SW10 9PR
Tel 020 7244 0522
Fax 020 7244 0533
info@leaandsandeman.co.uk
www.londonfinewine.co.uk

L&T – Lane & Tatham
12 Market Place, Devizes SN10 1HT
Tel 01380 720123
Fax 01380 720111
wines@lanetat.demon.co.uk

L&W – Lay & Wheeler
Gosbecks Park, 117 Gosbecks Road,
Colchester, Essex CO2 9JT
Tel 0845 330 1855
Fax 01206 560002
sales@laywheeler.com
www.laywheeler.com

LaC – La Caneva
Business Design Centre,
52 Upper Street, London N1 0QH
Tel 020 7354 3738
Fax 020 7354 1015
mail@lacaneva.com
www.lacaneva.com

Las – L'Assemblage
Pallant Court, West Pallant, Chichester,
West Sussex PO19 1TG
Tel 01243 537775
Fax 01243 538644
sales@lassemblage.co.uk
www.lassemblage.co.uk

Lay – Jeroboams / Laytons
8-12 Brook Street, London W1Y 2BH
Tel 020 7259 6716
Fax 020 7495 3314
sales@jeroboams.co.uk
www.jeroboams.co.uk

Lib – Liberty Wines
Unit A53, The Food Market,
New Covent Garden, London SW8 5EE
Tel 020 7720 5350
Fax 020 7720 6158
info@libertywine.co.uk
www.libertywine.co.uk

LLt –Louis Latour UK
7a Grafton Street, London W1S 4EH
Tel 020 7409 7276
Fax 020 7409 7092
enquiries@louislatour.co.uk
www.louislatour.com

LNa –Lion Nathan UK
113 Regents Park Road, London NW1 8UR
Tel 020 7449 4100
Fax 020 7722 7354
www.lionnathangroup.com

LoW – For the Love of Wine
4 Beaver Close, Buckingham,
Buckinghamshire MK18 7EA
Tel 01280 822500
Fax 01280 823833
www.i-love-wine.co.uk

L-P – Laurent Perrier UK
66-68 Chapel Street, Marlow,
Buckinghamshire SL7 1DE
Tel 01628 475404
Fax 01628 471891
enquiries@laurent-perrier.co.uk
www.laurent-perrier.co.uk

Luv – Luvians Bottleshop
93 Bonnygate, Cupar, Fife SL7 1DE
Tel 01334 654820
Fax 01334 654820
info@luvians.com
www.luvians.com

Lwt – Laithwaites / Direct Wines Ltd
New Aquitaine House, Exeter Way,
Theale, Reading, Berkshire RG7 4PL
Tel 0870 444 8383
Fax 0870 444 8182
www.laithwaites.co.uk

LyS – Laymont & Shaw
The Old Chapel, Millpool, Truro,
Cornwall TR1 1EX
Tel 01872 270545
Fax 01872 223005
info@laymont-shaw.co.uk
www.laymont-shaw.co.uk

M&V – Morris & Verdin
Unit 2, Bankside Industrial Estate,
Sumner Street, London SE1 9JZ
Tel 020 7921 5300
Fax 020 7921 5333
info@m-v.co.uk
www.morris-verdin.co.uk

Maj – Majestic Wine Warehouses
Majestic House, Otterspool Way,
Watford WD25 8WW
Tel 01923 298226
Fax 01923 819105
info@majestic.co.uk
www.majestic.co.uk

Mar – Martinez Wines
35 The Grove, Ilkley,
West Yorkshire LS29 9NJ
Tel 01943 603241
Fax 01274 742439
editor@martinez.co.uk
www.martinez.co.uk

Max – Maxxium
Maxxium House, Castle Business Park,
Stirling FK9 4RT
Tel 01786 430500
Fax 01786 430600

May – Mayfair Cellars
203 Seagrove Road, Fulham,
London SW6 1ST
Tel 020 7386 7999
Fax 020 7386 0202
sales@mayfaircellars.co.uk
www.mayfaircellars.co.uk

MCD – Marne & Champagne Diffusion
18 Bolton Street, London W1J 8BJ
Tel 020 7499 0070
Fax 020 7408 0841
sales@mcduk.com

McK – McKinley Vintners
14 Kennington Road, London SE1 7BL
Tel 020 7928 7300
Fax 020 7928 4447
info@mckinleyvintners.co.uk

MCl – Matthew Clark
Whitchurch Lane, Whitchurch,
Bristol BS14 0JZ
Tel 01275 836100
Fax 01275 836726
www.mclark.co.uk

MCW – Morgan Classic Wines
Crown House, 4 Market Lane, Lewes,
East Sussex 7BN 2NT
Tel 01273 487000
Fax 01273 487700
sales@morganclassics.com
www.morganclassicwines.com

Mdl – Mondial Wine Ltd
Mondial House, 190 Garth Road, Morden,
Surrey SM4 4LU
Tel 020 8335 3455
Fax 020 8335 3587
info@mondialwine.co.uk
www.mondialwine.co.uk

Men – Mentzendorff
8th Floor, Prince Consort House,
27-29 Albert Embankment, London SE1 7TJ
Tel 020 7840 3600
Fax 020 7840 3601
www.mentzendorff.co.uk

Mer – Meridian
Brook House, 4 Northenden Road,
Gatley, Cheshire SK8 4DN
Tel 0161 908 1350
Fax 0161 908 1355
www.meridianwines.co.uk

Mgi – Mille Gusti
17 Roseberry Gardens, London W13 0HD
Tel 020 8997 3932
Fax 020 8566 8480
millegusti@hotmail.com

MHn – Moët Hennessey UK
13 Grosvenor Crescent, London SW1X 7EE
Tel 020 7235 9411
Fax 020 7235 6937

**MHv – Margaret Harvey /
Fine Wines of New Zealand**
PO Box 476, London NW5 2NZ
Tel 020 7482 0093
Fax 020 7267 8400
margaret.harvey@btinternet.com
www.fwnz.co.uk

Mis – Mistral Wines
5 Junction Mews, Sale Place, London W2 1PN
Tel 020 7262 5437
Fax 020 7402 7957
info@mistralwines.co.uk

MMD – Maison Marques & Domaines
4 College Mews, St Ann's Hill, London SW18 2SJ
Tel 020 8812 3380
Fax 020 8812 3390
maison@mmdltd.co.uk

Mor – Moreno Wines
26 Macroom Road, Maida Vale, London W9 3HY
Tel 020 8960 7161
Fax 020 8960 7165
sales@moreno-wines.co.uk

MPe – Michael Peace MW
24 Drayson Mews, London W8 4LY
Tel 020 7937 9345
Fax 020 7937 7884
michaelpeace@btinternet.com

MSd – Milton Sandford
The Old Chalk Mine, Warren Row Road,
Knowl Hill, Berskhire, RG10 8QS
Tel 01628 829449
Fax 01628 829424
sales@milton-sandford.demon.co.uk

Msp – Masterpiece Wines
Unit 3.04, Medway Enterprise Centre,
Enterprise Close, Rochester ME2 4SY
Tel 01634 293141
Fax 01634 719109
Harold@masterpiecewines.com
www.masterpiecewines.com

MtC – Morgenrot-Chevaliers
Olde Forge, Bent Street Estate, Kearsley,
Bolton, BL4 9DH
Tel 01204 573093
Fax 01204 861609
sales@morgenrot.co.uk
www.morgenrot-chevaliers.co.uk

MVs – Merchant Vintners
Red Duster House, York Street, Hull,
East Yorkshire, HU2 0QX
Tel 01482 329443
Fax 01482 213616

N&P – Nickolls & Perks
37 High Street, Stourbridge,
West Midlands, DY8 1TA
Tel 01384 394518
Fax 01384 440786
sales@nickollsandperks.co.uk
www.nickollsandperks.co.uk

NDb – Nick Dobson Wines
38 Crail Close, Wokingham, Berkshire RG41 2PZ
Tel 0800 8493078
Fax: 0870 4602358
sales@nickdobsonwines.co.uk
www.nickdobsonwines.co.uk

Neg – Negociants UK
Davenport House, Bowers Way,
Harpenden, Herts, AL5 4EW
Tel 01582 462859
Fax 01582 462867
neguk@negociants.com

Nid – Nidderdale Fine Wines
2a High Street, Pateley Bridge,
North Yorkshire HG3 5AW
Tel 01423 711703
info@southaustralianwines.com
www.southaustralianwines.com

NoG – Noble Grape
21-27 Brandon Terrace, Edinburgh, EH3 5DZ
Tel 0131 556 3133
Fax 0131 556 8766
info@thenoble-grape.co.uk
www.thenoble-grape.co.uk

NWW – New World Wines
519 Old York Road, Wandsworth,
London, SW18 1TF
Tel 020 8877 3555
Fax 020 8877 1476
info@newworldwines.co.uk
www.newworldwines.co.uk

NYg – Noel Young Wines
56 High Street, Trumpington,
Cambridgeshire, CB2 2LS
Tel 01223 844744
Fax 01223 844736
admin@nywines.co.uk
www.nywines.co.uk

Oak – Oakley Wine Agencies
PO Box 3234, Earls Colne,
Colchester, CO6 2SU
Tel 01787 220070
Fax 01787 224734
oakleywine@btconnect.com

Oas – Oastwell
Beechurst, Lingfield, Surrey, RH7 6NZ
Tel 01342 832069
Fax 01342 832385

Ock – Ockse Wines
67 Ashburnham Grove, London SE10 8UJ
Tel 020 8691 2846
Fax 020 8691 2841
office@ocksewines.net
www.ocksewines.net

Odd – Oddbins
31-33 Weir Road, London, SW19 8UG
Tel 0800 328 2323
Fax 0800 328 3848
customer.services@oddbinsmail.com
www.oddbins.com

O-F – Oldacre-Field
York House, 6 Hazel Road, Altrincham,
Cheshire, WA14 1HL
Tel 0161 928 4898
Fax 0161 929 7064

Orb – Orbital Wines
Elkington Lodge, Welford,
Northants, NN6 6HA
Tel 01858 570600
Fax 01858 570601
www.orbitalwines.co.uk

OWL – O W Loeb
3 Archie Street, London SE1 3JT
Tel 020 7234 0385
Fax 020 7357 0440
finewine@owloeb.com
www.owloeb.com

OxW – Oxford Wine Company
The Wine Warehouse, Witney Road, Standlake,
Oxfordshire OX29 7PR
Tel 01865 301144
Fax 01865 301155
info@oxfordwine.co.uk
www.oxfordwine.co.uk

P&S – Philglas & Swiggot
21 Northcote Road, London SW11 1NG
Tel 020 7924 4494
Fax 020 7924 4736
contact@philglas-swiggot.co.uk
www.philglas-swiggot.co.uk

Par – Paragon Vintners
Regent Gate, 21 Dartmouth Street,
London, SW1H 9BP
Tel 020 7887 1800
Fax 020 7887 1810
welcome@paragonvintners.co.uk

Agent codes

Pat – Patriarche Wine Agencies
7 Rickett Street, Fulham, London, SW6 1RU
Tel 020 7381 4016
Fax 020 7381 2023
sales@patriarchewines.com

PaV – Passione Vino
15 Derinton Road, London SW17 8JA
Tel 020 8672 1941
Fax 020 8672 7132
info@passionevino.co.uk
www.passionevino.co.uk

PBW – Paul Boutinot Wines
Brook House, 4 Northenden Road,
Gatley, Cheshire, SK8 4DN
Tel 0161 908 1370
Fax 0161 908 1375
www.paul-boutinot.co.uk

PDn – Pimlico Dozen / Vintage Cellars
33 Churton Street, London, SW1V 2LT
Tel 020 7630 6254
Fax 020 7233 7536
vintagecellars@winecellarsales.co.uk
www.winecellarsales.co.uk

PFx – Percy Fox & Co
Templefields House, River Way,
Harlow, Essex, CM20 2EA
Tel 01279 633542
Fax 01279 633780
percyfoxmarketing@guinnessudv.com

PLB – Private Liquor Brands
Dorset House, 64 High Street,
East Grinstead, RH19 3DE
Tel 01342 318282
Fax 01342 314023
general@plb.co.uk
www.plb.co.uk

PLh – Peter Lehmann Wines UK
Godmersham Park, Godmersham,
Canterbury, Kent, CT4 7DT
Tel 01227 731353
Fax 01227 738538
admin@lehmannwines.com
www.peterlehmannwines.com.au

Pic – Pic Wines
3, rue Basse, 34380 Viols le Fort, France
Tel 0033 499 62 09 27
Fax 0033 467 55 81 28
contact@picwines.co.uk
www.picwines.co.uk

Pol – Pol Roger Ltd
Shelton House, 4 Conningsby Street,
Hereford, HR1 2DY
Tel 01432 262800
Fax 01432 262806
wineshops@polroger.co.uk
www.polroger.co.uk

Por – Portland Wine
152a Ashley Road, Hale, Altrincham, Cheshire
Tel 0161 928 0357
Fax 0161 905 1291
portwineco@aol.com
www.portlandwine.co.uk

POs – Peter Osborne & Co
Watcombe Manor Farm, Ingham Lane,
Watlington, Oxfordshire OX9 5EJ
Tel 01491 612311
Fax 01491 613322
info@peterosbornewine.co.uk
www.peterosbornewine.co.uk

PRc – Pernod Ricard UK
Central House, 3 Lampton Road, Hounslow,
Middlesex TW3 1HY
Tel 020 8538 4484
Fax 020 8538 4488
general@pernodricard-uk.com

Pre – Premier Vintners
Tel 020 7978 4047
Fax 020 7978 4053
info@premiervintners.co.uk
www.premiervintners.co.uk

PVF – Producteurs et Vignerons de France
Toad Hall, Wilbury Road, Hove,
East Sussex BN3 3JJ
Tel 01273 730277
Fax 01273 328691
vdf@pavilion.co.uk
www.pavilion.co.uk

PWa – Peter Watkins Wine
2 Manor Road, Pitsford, Northampton NN2 9AR
Tel 01604 882370
Fax 01604 889465
sales@peterwatkinswine.co.uk
www.peterwatkinswine.co.uk

PWt – Peter Watts Wines
Wisdom's Barn, Colne Road,
Coggeshall, Essex CO6 1TD
Tel 01376 561130
Fax 01376 562925
sales@peterwattswines.co.uk
www.peterwattswines.co.uk

PWy – Peter Wylie Fine Wines
Plymtree Manor, Plymtree,
Cullompton, Devon EX15 2LE
Tel 01884 277555
Fax 01884 277557
peter@wylie-fine-wines.demon.co.uk
www.wyliefinewines.co.uk

Rae – Raeburn Fine Wines
The Vaults, 4 Giles Street, Leith,
Edinburgh EH6 6DJ
Tel 0131 343 1159
Fax 0131 332 5166
sales@raeburnfinewines.com
www.raeburnfinewines.com

Rec – Recount Wines
44 Lower Sloane Street,
London SW1W 8BP
Tel 020 7730 6377
Fax 020 7730 6377

Ren – Renvic Wines
2 School Cottages, Abington Pigotts,
Nr Royston, Herts SG8 0SQ
Tel 01763 852470
Fax 01763 852470

Res – La Réserve / Mark Reynier Fine Wines
56 Walton Street, Knightsbridge,
London SW3 1RB
Tel 020 7589 2020
Fax 020 7581 0250
realwine@la-reserve.co.uk
www.la-reserve.co.uk

Rev – Revelstoke Wine Co
13 Putney Bridge Road, London SW15 2NY
Tel 020 8875 0077
Fax 020 8875 0477
info@revelstoke.co.uk
www.revelstoke.co.uk

RGr – Richard Granger Fine Wine
West Jesmond Station, Lyndhurst Avenue,
Newcastle NE2 3HH
Tel 0191 281 5000
Fax 0191 281 8141
sales@richardgrangerwines.co.uk
www.richardgrangerwines.co.uk

RHW – Roger Harris Wines
Loke Farm, Weston Longville,
Norfolk NR9 5LG
Tel 01603 880171
Fax 01603 880291
sales@rogerharriswines.co.uk
www.beaujolaisonline.co.uk

RMi – R M Wines London
18 Rosebery Avenue, London EC1R 4TD
Tel 0870 350 3520
Fax 0870 350 3521

RRl – Robert Rolls
36-37 Charterhouse Square,
London EC1M 6EA
Tel 020 7606 1166
Fax 020 7606 1144
mail@rollswine.com
www.rollswine.com

RSJ – RSJ Wine
115 Wootton Street, London SE1 8LY
Tel 020 7633 0881
Fax 020 7401 2455
www.rsj.uk.com

RSo – Raisin Social
Tripod House, 105-107 Lansdowne Road,
Croydon CR0 2BN
Tel 020 8686 8500
Fax 020 8681 7939
info@raisin-social.com
www.raisin-social.com

RsW – Richards Walford
Hales Lodge, Pickworth,
Nr Stamford, Lincolnshire PE9 4DJ
Tel 01780 460451
Fax 01780 460276

RTo – Royal Tokay UK
41 St James's Place, London SW1A 1NS
Tel 020 7495 3010
Fax 020 7493 3973
sales@royal-tokaji.com

Agent codes

Rui – Ruinart UK
13 Grovesnor Crescent,
London SW1X 7EE
Tel 020 7416 0592
Fax 020 7416 0593
www.ruinart.com

RWs – Reid Wines
The Mill, Marsh Lane, Hallatrow,
Bristol BS39 6EB
Tel 01761 452645
Fax 01761 452642

RyR – Raymond Reynolds
Station Road, Furness Vale,
High Peak, SK23 7SW
Tel 01663 742230
Fax 01663 742233
info@raymondreynolds.co.uk
www.winesfromportugal.com

Sav – Savage Selection
The Ox House, Market Place, Northleach,
Gloucestershire GL54 3EG
Tel 01451 860896
Fax 01451 860996
wine@savageselection.co.uk
www.savageselection.co.uk

ScE – Southcorp Europe
Grange House, 15 Church Street,
Twickenham TW1 3NL
Tel 020 8917 4600
Fax 020 8917 4646

SCh – Sommeliers Choice
9 Dagnall Park, South Norwood,
London SE25 5PW
Tel 020 8689 9643
Fax 020 8689 9643
sommelierschoice@aol.com

Sec – Seckford Wine Agencies
Dock Lane, Melton, Ipswich, Suffolk IP12 1PE
Tel 01394 446622
Fax 01394 446633
sales@seckfordwines.co.uk
www.seckfordwines.co.uk

Sel – Selfridges & Co
400 Oxford Street, London W1A 1AB
Tel 020 7318 3730
Fax 020 7491 1880
www.selfridges.co.uk

SFW – Stokes Fine Wines
41 Trewint Street, London SW18 4HB
Tel 020 8944 5979
Fax 020 8944 5935
sales@stokesfinewines.com

SsG – Stevens Garnier
47 West Way, Botley, Oxford OX2 0JF
Tel 01865 263300
Fax 01865 791594
info@stevensgarnier.co.uk
www.stevensgarnier.co.uk

Str – Stratford's Wine Agencies
High Street, Cookham on Thames,
Berkshire SL6 9SQ
Tel 01628 810606
Fax 01628 810605
sales@stratfordwine.co.uk
www.stratfordwine.co.uk

SVS – Stone, Vine & Sun
No.13 Humphrey Farms, Hazeley Road,
Twyford, Winchester SO21 1QA
Tel 0845 061 4604
Fax 01962 717545
sales@stonevine.co.uk
www.stonevine.co.uk

SWB – Southern Vintners
The Yarn Store, Dogley Mills, Penistone Road,
Fenay Bridge, Huddersfield HD8 0LE
Tel 01484 608898
Fax 01484 609495
info@southernvintners.com

Swg – Swig
188 Sutton Court Road, London W4 3HR
Tel 08000 272 272
Fax 020 8995 7069
imbibe@swig.co.uk
www.swig.co.uk

T&W – T & W Wines
51 Kings Street, Thetford, Norfolk, IP24 2AU
Tel 01842 765646
Fax 01842 766407
contact@tw-wines.co.uk
www.tw-wines.co.uk

Tan – Tanners Wine Merchants
26 Wyle Cop, Shrewsbury, Shropshire, SY11XD
Tel 01743 234500
Fax 01743 234501
sales@tanners-wines.co.uk
www.tanners-wines.co.uk

Ter – Terroir Limited
Treetops, Grassington Road, Skipton,
North Yorkshire BD23 1LL
Tel 01756 700512
Fax 01756 797856
enquiries@terroirlanguedoc.co.uk
www.terroirlanguedoc.co.uk

The – Theatre of Wine
75 Trafalgar Road, Greenwich, London SE10 9TS
Tel 020 8858 6363
Fax 020 8305 1936
daniel@theatreofwine.com
www.theatreofwine.com

ThP – Thomas Panton
The Wine Warehouse, Hampton Street, Tetbury,
Gloucestershire GL8 8JN
Tel 01666 503088
Fax 01666 503113
sales@wineimporter.co.uk
www.wineimporter.co.uk

THt – Thorman Hunt
4 Pratt Walk, Lambeth, London, SE11 6AR
Tel 020 7735 6511
Fax 020 7735 9779
info@thormanhunt.co.uk

TPg – Thos Peatling
Westgate House, Westgate Street,
Bury St Edmunds, Suffolk IP33 1QS
Tel 01284 755948
Fax 01284 714483
sales@thospeatling.co.uk
www.thospeatling.co.uk

TPt – Terry Platt
Council Street West, Llandudno, LL30 1ED
Tel 01492 874099
Fax 01492 874722
plattwines@clara.co.uk

Tra – Transatlantic Wines
The Magpies, Eye Kettleby Drive, Eye Kettleby,
Melton Mowbray LE14 2TD
Tel 01664 565013
Fax 01664 564938
patrick@transatlantic-wines.co.uk

Tri – Tria Wines Limited
Vine Road, London SW13 0NE
Tel 020 8878 1236
Fax 020 8878 1151
sales@triawines.co.uk
www.triawines.co.uk

Tur – Turville Valley Wines
The Firs, Potter Row, Great Missenden,
Buckinghamshire, HP16 9LT
Tel 01494 868818
Fax 01494 868832
info@turville-valley-wines.com
www.turville-valley-wines.com

TWS – Thierry's Wine Services
Horsefair House, The Horsefair, Romsey,
Hampshire, SO51 8EZ
Tel 01794 507100
Fax 01794 516856
info@thierrys.co.uk
www.thierrys.co.uk

UnC – Uncorked
Exchange Arcade, Broadgate, London EC2M 3WA
Tel 020 7638 5998
Fax 020 7638 6028
drink@uncorked.co.uk
www.uncorked.co.uk

V&C – Valvona & Crolla
19 Elm Road, Edinburgh EH7 4AA
Tel 0131 556 6066
Fax 0131 556 1668
wine@valvonacrolla.co.uk
www.valvonacrolla.co.uk

VCq – Veuve Clicquot
Third Floor, 15 St George's Street,
London, W1S 1FH
Tel 020 7408 7430
Fax 020 7408 7457
yellow@veuve-clicquot.co.uk
www.veuveclicquot.fr

Vcs – Vinceremos Organic Wines
74 Kirkgate, Leeds LS2 7DJ
Tel 0113 244 0002
Fax 0113 288 4566
webinfo@vinceremos.co.uk
www.vinceremos.co.uk

VDu – Van Duuren Wines Ltd
3 Framfield Road, Hanwell, London W7 1NG
Tel 020 8567 4428
Fax 020 8567 4428
svanduuren@aol.com

VdV – Vin du Van
Colthups, The Street, Appledore, Kent TN26 2BX
Tel 01233 758727
Fax 01233 758389

Agent codes

Ver - Veritaus & Co
Unit 7, Caker Stream Road, Alton,
Hampshire GU34 2QA
Tel 0870 7704112
Fax 0870 7704113
info@veritaus.com
www.veritaus.com

Vex - Vinexcel Ltd
29 Rowan Drive, Cheadle Hulme SK8 7DU
Tel 0161 485 4592
Fax 0161 485 1791

Vic - Vickery Wines
Unit 2 Home Farm, Luton Hoo Estate, Luton,
Bedfordshire, LU1 3TD
Tel 01582 456180
Fax 01582 456716
islay@vickerywines.co.uk
www.vickerywines.co.uk

Vim – Vinum
1 Barrow Walk, Brentford, Middlesex TW8 0RA
Tel 020 8847 4699
Fax 020 8847 4771
vinum@vinum.co.uk
www.vinum.co.uk

Vin – Vineyard Cellars
Denford Manor Farm, Lower Denford,
Hungerford, Berkshire, RG17 0UN
Tel 01488 681313
Fax 01488 681411
jameshocking@vineyardcellars.com
www.vineyardcellars.com

Vir – Virgin Wines Online Ltd
St James' Mill, Whitefriars, Norwich NR3 1TN
Tel 0870 164 9593
help@virginwines.com
www.virginwines.com

ViV – Vitis Vinifera
33 Godfrey Way, Great Dunmow, Essex, CM6 2AY
Tel 01371 873383
Fax 01371 873383

VKg - The Vine King
Tel 020 8879 3030
erik@thevineking.com
www.thevineking.com

Vne - Villeneuve Wines Ltd
1 Venlaw Court, Peebles EH45 8AE
Tel 01721 722500
Fax 01721 729922
wines@villeneuvewines.com
www.villeneuvewines.com

Vnf - Vin Neuf
Stratford upon Avon, Warwickshire
Tel 01789 261747
Fax 01789 261749
info@vinneuf.co.uk
www.vinneuf.co.uk

Vni – Vinites UK
37 Montholme Road, London SW11 6HX
Tel 020 7924 4974
Fax 020 7228 6109

Vns – Vinoceros
Stanley Way, Cardrew, Redruth,
Cornwall, TR15 1SP
Tel 01209 314711
Fax 01209 314712
enquiries@vinoceros.com
www.vinoceros.com

VOC – Val d'Orbieu-Cordier Group
73 Moore Park Road, London, SW6 2HH
Tel 020 7736 3350
Fax 020 7731 3695

VRt – Vintage Roots
Farley Farms, Bridge Farm, Reading Road,
Arborfield, Berkshire RG2 9HT
Tel 0118 976 1999
Fax 0118 976 1998
info@vintageroots.co.uk
www.vintageroots.co.uk

VsV – Vinus Vita
The Wine Warehouse, Wells Road, Bath BA2 3AP
Tel 01225 322815
Fax 01225 743077
courtney-clack@vinusvita.com
www.vinusvita.com

VTr – Vine Trail
266 Hotwell Road, Hotwells, Bristol BS8 4NG
Tel 0117 921 1770
Fax 0117 921 1772
enquiries@vinetrail.co.uk
www.vinetrail.co.uk

Vts – Veritas Wines
103 Cherry Hinton Road, Cambridge CB1 7BS
Tel 01223 212500
info@veritaswines.co.uk
www.veritaswines.co.uk

VWs – Vinifera Wines
Units 2&3, 199 Eade Road, London N4 1DN
Tel 020 8880 2526
Fax 020 8442 8215
vinifera@alvini.com
www.alivini.com

WAe – WineAlive.com
18 The Tything, Worcester WR1 1HD
Tel 0800 015 5960
Fax 0800 015 5961
info@winealive.com
www.winealive.com

Wat – Waterloo Wine Co.
6 Vine Yard, London, SE1 1QL
Tel 020 7403 7967
Fax 020 7357 6976
sales@waterloowine.co.uk
www.waterloowine.co.uk

Wav – Waverley Vintners
PO Box 22, Crieff Road, Perth, PH1 2SL
Tel 01738 472000
Fax 01738 630338
contactus@waverley-group.co.uk
www.waverley-group.co.uk

WBn – Wine Barn
2 Stable Cottages, Church Barns, East Stratton,
Winchester, Hampshire SO21 3XA
Tel 01962 774102
Fax 01962 774102
info@thewinebarn.co.uk
www.thewinebarn.co.uk

WEx – Winexcel
Avebury Close, Horsham,
West Sussex RH12 5JY

Wgg – Wigglesworth Wine
Pipe House, Vines Cross, East Sussex, TN21 9EH
Tel 01435 813740
Fax 01435 813866
william@wigglesworth.co.uk
www.wigglesworth.co.uk

WGW - WG White
Caspian House, 650 River Gardens,
Feltham TW14 0RB
Tel 020 8831 1400
Fax 020 8893 2535
sales@wgwhite.co.uk
www.wgwhite.co.uk

WhW – Whittaker Wines
35 Chatsworth Road, High Lane, Bredbury
Cheshire, SK6 8DA
Tel 020 8878 2302
Fax 020 8876 5580
sales@whittakerwines.com
www.whittakerwines.com

WIE – Wine Importers Edinburgh
Unit 7, Beaverhall House, 27 Beaverhall Road,
Edinburgh EH7 4JE
Tel 0131 556 3601
Fax 0131 557 8493
www.wine-importers.net

Win – The Winery
4 Clifton Road, Maida Vale, London, W9 1SS
Tel 020 7286 6475
Fax 020 7286 2733

Wit – Withers Agencies
1 South Street, Lewes, East Sussex, BN7 2BT
Tel 01273 477132
Fax 01273 476612

WRk – Wine Raks
21 Springfield Road, Aberdeen AB15 7RJ
Tel 01224 311460
Fax 01224 312186
enq@wineraks.com
www.wineraks.com

WsB – Wills-Burgundy
Lower Wield, Alresford, Hampshire SO24 9RX
Tel 0845 057 3218
Fax 01256 389173
will@wills-burgundy.com
www.wills-burgundy.com

WSc – The Wine Society
Gunnels Wood Road, Stevenage, SG1 2BG
Tel 01483 741177
Fax 01483 741392
memberservices@thewinesociety.com
www.thewinesociety.com

Agent codes

WSe – Wineservice
Semper Fidelis Mews, Wire Mill Lane,
Lingfield, Surrey RH7 6HJ
Tel 01342 837333
Fax 01342 837444
sales@wineservice.co.uk

WSo – Winesource
393 Ham Green , Holt, Trowbridge,
Wiltshire, BA14 6PX
Tel 01225 783007
Fax 01225 783152
winesource@saqnet.co.uk

WSS – Siegel Wine Agencies
Regent House, 123 High Street, Odiham,
Hampshire, RG29 1LA
Tel 01256 701101
Fax 01256 701518
wine@walter-siegel.co.uk
www.walter-siegel.co.uk

Wtr – Winetraders
3 TBAC Business Centre, Avenue Four,
Station Lane, Witney, Oxfordshire OX28 4BN
Tel 01993 848777
Fax 01993 848778
winetraders@winetraders.org.uk
www.winetraders.org.uk

WTs – The Wine Treasury
69 - 71 Broadway, London, SW8 1SQ
Tel 020 7793 9999
Fax 020 7796 8080
quality@winetreasury.com
www.winetreasury.com

Wvr – Weavers of Nottingham
Vintners House, 1 Castle Gate,
Nottingham NG1 7AQ
Tel 0115 958 0922
Fax 0115 950 8076
weavers@weaverswines.com
www.weaverswines.com

WWs – Western Wines
1 Hawksworth Road, Central Park, Telford,
Shropshire, TF2 9TU
Tel 01952 235700
Fax 01952 235711
manager@western-wines.com
www.western-wines.com

Yap – Yapp Brothers
The Old Brewery, Mere, Wiltshire, BA12 6DY
Tel 01747 860423
Fax 01747 860929
sales@yapp.co.uk
www.yapp.co.uk

Yng – Young and Company
The Ram Brewery, Wandsworth, London,
SW18 4JD
Tel 020 8875 7000
Fax 020 8875 7197
winedirect@youngs.co.uk
www.youngswinedirect.co.uk

3DW – 3D Wines Ltd
1-2 North End, Swineshead, Lincolnshire PE20 3LR
Tel 01205 820745
Fax 01205 821042
info@3dwines.com
www.3dwines.com

Other wine traders of note

Bonhams
65-69 Lots Road, London SW10 0RN
Tel 020 7393 3900
Fax 020 7393 3906
wine@bonhams.com
www.bonhams.com

Christie's
8 King Street, St James's, London SW1Y 6QT
Tel 020 7839 9060
Fax 020 7839 1611
thudson@christies.com
www.christies.com

Sotheby's
34/35 New Bond Street, London W1A 2AA
Tel 020 7293 6423
Fax 020 7293 5961
wine.london@sothebys.com
www.sothebys.com

Uvine (Universal Wine Exchange)
Swan Court, 9 Tanner Street, London SE1 3LE
Tel 020 7089 2200
Fax 020 7089 2211
enquiries@uvine.com
www.uvine.com

Wilkinson Vintners
Unit 1 Bickerton House, Bickerton Road,
London N19 5JT
Tel 020 7272 1982
Fax 020 7263 2643
wilkinson@finewine.co.uk

Index

This producer index is ordered according to the name by which an estate is most commonly referred. There is priority to surnames but otherwise they appear as they are written. 'Domaine' is ignored but 'Château', 'Castello', 'Quinta' etc are respected as is the definite article when implicitly part of the name (eg Il Poggione appears under 'I'). The only exception is in Bordeaux where 'Château' is also ignored and the name of the château or estate takes precedent.

The End.

Not quite.
If you've got this far then you should know about:

Williamson & Moore's 2005 Pocket Wine Annual
RRP £10.00
ISBN – 0-9544097-5-2

Available through all good bookshops and
www.winebehindthelabel.com

and from BACCHUS+,
Wine behind the label
on CD ROM

The full 2005 edition of the acclaimed Wine behind the label *on a fully searchable database allowing you seek out great producers, great wines and where you can buy them from, with consummate ease.*
RRP £22.95 plus p&p

This CD is available as a special offer at: **£15.00 ($27) plus p&p**
to anyone who has bought a copy of WBTL.
Full details on the Williamson Moore Publishing website: www.winebehindthelabel.com

In conjunction with ordering through the site, it will be necessary to send us the coupon below to qualify for the special offer – just cut across the dotted line!
The Bacchus + Cellar Management Suite is also available on the CD, accessed via a password//subscription. Full details on the CD.

Name...

Address...

....

County...Postcode....................................

Complete the above and send to Williamson Moore, 34 Ivy Close Winchester Hants SO22 4QR
This information will not be divulged to any third parties